CONTEMPORARY AMERICAN AUTHORS

CONTEMPORARY
American Authors

A Critical Survey and 219 Bio-Bibliographies

FRED B. MILLETT

New York

HARCOURT, BRACE AND COMPANY

1944

[d·10·44]

A WARTIME BOOK

This complete edition is produced in full compliance with the government's regulations for conserving paper and other essential materials.

PRINTED IN THE UNITED STATES OF AMERICA

CONTENTS

FOREWORD

This book has a dual purpose: to give a fairly full and systematic account of American literature since 1900, and to furnish biographical and bibliographical information concerning 219 contemporary American authors. Both parts of the book should prove useful to a variety of persons: to the reader and student desirous of orienting himself in contemporary literature; to librarians, collectors, and booksellers who desire convenient checklists of a large number of contemporary authors; to reviewers and reference workers in this difficult field, and to teachers whose pleasant opportunity it is to discuss contemporary literature.

The Critical Survey which precedes the Bio-bibliographies treats the major literary types and the major and some of the minor authors who have expressed themselves in these types. It differs from other attempts to survey this rich and bewildering field in the fullness with which it considers, not merely such conspicuous forms as the novel, drama, and poetry, but such neglected forms as biography, criticism, and literary journalism generally. The Critical Survey incorporates about half the material contained in my Introduction to the 1929 edition of Manly and Rickert's *Contemporary American Literature.*

The Survey offers one man's view of the complex literary phenomena of two generations. In the nature of the case, the critical evaluations must be taken as tentative, since the historian of contemporary literature works without the guidance of authority and the winnowing power of taste and time. But the personal judgments set down here, however faulty they may prove to be, are supported in many instances by contemporary critical opinion.

The basic problems in writing the history of contemporary literature involve both facts and values. The basic facts concerning contemporary literature are not only innumerable but relatively inaccessible. It is one of the major functions of this book to assemble in convenient form a very large number of facts about the authors treated. Once the facts have been assembled, the problem of systematizing and organizing them is overpowering. The quantitative difficulty is, however, far inferior to the qualitative one, since it is possible for historians to ignore facts concerning authors or movements of which they are uninformed or in which they are uninterested. But the qualitative problem is raised by every author on whom judgment is passed. In the case of authors belonging to earlier literary periods, the phenomena have been classified and organized, numberless earlier historians have furnished conventional critical judgments, and fundamental revaluations take place so slowly that it is not difficult to assimilate them. But the historian of contemporary literature must depend on his own taste and that of other contemporary readers and critics to assist him in selecting and classifying authors, and in estimating the significance of the men and movements with which he deals. He writes, moreover, with the certainty that in a few years, some of his critical judgments may seem unintelligent, irrational, or absurd. But a contemporary historical-critical account of our literature ought to be of some use, not only to current, but to future readers. What would we not give for a contemporary survey of Elizabethan literature from the pen of even a minor critic? Since the writing of contemporary literary history is one of the most important services a critic can render not only his own age, but posterity, it is not incumbent on anyone to judge too harshly the forays into contemporary literary history which a few bold spirits have made at the expense sometimes of their academic and critical reputations.

In the Bio-bibliographies, authors' names are given in the fullest form possible. The portion of the name appearing outside the parentheses is that which appears on the author's title-page or, in some instances, the name the author has used on his more recent publications.

The biographical sketches which precede the Bibliographies vary in length with the significance of the writer and the amount of available material. In every case, I have appealed to the living authors treated for material to supplement that contained in the obvious biographical reference works, and, in almost two-thirds of the cases, I have received generous amounts of information and have incorporated it in the sketches. In such instances, the printing, as a whole or in part, of the letters received constitutes the first edition of these letters.

The Bibliographies in this book have been constructed with the aid of the most reliable tools: the *United States Catalog* and its supplements, the *English Catalogue*, *Whitaker's Cumulative Book List*, the *Vertical File Service Catalog*, the catalogue of the Library of Congress, the Union catalogue at the Library of Congress, the catalogue of the New York Public Library, the catalogue of the Harvard College Library, the catalogue of the Yale University Library, special collections of first editions in other academic and public libraries, and innumerable booksellers' catalogues. As a result, a large majority of writers are represented by fuller bibliographies than are in existence elsewhere. When bibliographies were already in existence, I have made critical use of them, but such bibliographies have never been accepted as authoritative.

In the Bibliographies, I have attempted to give the full title and date of appearance of the first edition of all books, pamphlets, broadsides, and leaflets published in the form of separates up to January 1, 1939. Works edited, compiled, translated, or illustrated by the author, as well as poems set to music, are included. An author's contribution to a symposium or to a collection is not included, unless it received separate publication later.

Certain features of the Bibliographical style require comment. I have attempted to give the full title of the first edition of all works. An author's name appears in the Bibliographies in title-page form, only when such a form is required for clarification. Otherwise, the name is omitted, as are academic titles following his name, books by him, the expressions "illustrated" and "with illustrations," and other purely descriptive statements if they do not form part of the title proper. Material not part of a title but added to assist clarity is enclosed in brackets [ ]; brackets in the original are shown as ⟨ ⟩. The capitalization is the system common to current American library practice. The punctuation between title and subtitle has been normalized by the use of commas. The date of publication given is the date of the first appearance of the book, whether the book was published in America or elsewhere. If the book appeared under a different title abroad after its appearance in the United States, the American title is given first, and the foreign title and date are added in parentheses. When the foreign title differs from the American title but agrees with it in date, the foreign title is cited in the parentheses following the American title. When a bracketed date follows a date without brackets, the date without brackets is incorrect although it may appear in first editions of the book, and the bracketed date is correct. When the title or classification suggests the format or size of the publication, no further description is given. Full length plays and books in wrappers are not distinguished from those in boards. When, however, the format is not boards, it is generally described, as an aid in locating fugitive publications.

The following abbreviations are used throughout the Bibliographies:

Am. ed.—American edition; comp.—compiled; c.—copyright; ed.—editor, edited, edition; enl.—enlarged; illus.—illustrated, illustrations; intro.—introduction; n.d.—no date of publication; no(s).—number(s); pref.—preface; pseud.—pseudonym; pt.—part; pub.—published; repr.—reprinted; rev.—revised; supp.—supplement; trans.—translator, translation; vol(s).—volume(s).

For the assistance of readers and students, I have attempted to give a classification of titles. Frequently, classification has been extremely difficult and that finally decided upon must be regarded as merely tentative. As rarely as possible, however, have I taken refuge in anomalous classifications. As a further aid to selection, I have placed an asterisk (*) before titles that seem most worthy of the reader's immediate attention.

The Studies listed furnish a valuable index to the amount of critical attention an author has received, not only in the United States and the British Isles, but also on the Continent. In many instances, the Studies constitute a larger bibliography of critical material than is available elsewhere. A dagger (†) has been placed before each of the critical Studies which contain useful bibliographical information. Very few Studies have been listed that run to less than two full pages.

The lists of Articles which appear after many of the bibliographies are frankly selective. It has seemed better to give detailed information about a small number of important articles rather than to give a great many blind references to articles and reviews. To take the place of such lists, I have in every instance directed the reader to the specific volumes in the *Book Review Digest* where such references may be found in large numbers. The reader or student who wishes to trace in detail the critical reception accorded a contemporary author is referred to the following standard indexes of articles and reviews: the *Book Review Digest, Readers' Guide to Periodical Literature, International Index to Periodicals, Annual Bibliography of English Language and Literature*, published by the Modern Humanities Research Association, the annual bibliographies in the *Publications of the Modern Language Association*, and the frequent excellent bibliographies published in the scholarly journal, *American Literature.*

Three types of references will assist a reader in finding relevant material in both parts of the book. (1) The symbol (*q.v.*) following an author's name in the Critical Survey indicates that the author is to be found in the proper alphabetical position among the Bio-bibliographies. (2) At the end of most of the biographical sketches, reference is made to the pages in the Critical Survey where the author is discussed. (3) In the Index of Authors, which appears on pages 711–15, page-references to both the Survey and the Bio-bibliographies follow the names of all the authors treated in this volume.

The plan for the book out of which this book has grown sprang from the fertile mind of Professor Edith Rickert. In teaching contemporary literature at the University of Chicago, Professor Rickert became aware of the very serious need of a book containing essential biographical and bibliographical information concerning the authors whom she was discussing. Such information was first gathered in the form of work-sheets prepared by undergraduate and graduate students. Out of these work-sheets evolved the first slim edition of *Contemporary American Literature*, which she published in 1922 in collaboration with Professor John Matthews Manly. This edition contained no critical survey, but it gave very brief biographies and selected bibliographies of 246 contemporary authors. The second edition of *Contemporary American Literature* which I published in 1929 was on a somewhat more comprehensive scale. It ran to 378 pages, contained a critical Introduction of thirty thousand words, and gave somewhat fuller biographical and bibliographical information. One hundred sixty-six authors were retained from the first edition, eighty authors were dropped, and fifty-three new authors were added.

In the preparation of *Contemporary American Authors*, the biographical and bibliographical work has been done completely afresh. The Critical Survey runs to over a hundred thousand words. The biographies have quadrupled in length, and the bibliographies have become checklists of all the first editions of the authors' books and pamphlets. One hundred seven authors have been dropped from the second edition; six authors who were dropped in the second edition have been restored; thirty authors who appeared for the first time in the second edition have been retained, and 101 new authors have been added.

In a work of this type, the problem of the selection of authors is very acute. The procedure of selection used here was the most satisfactory I could devise. The list of authors treated in my edition of Manly and Rickert's *Contemporary American Literature* (1929) was checked against a large number of guides: lists of prize-winners; lists of best-sellers; lists of authors reviewed in *Time*, the *New Yorker*, and *Poetry;* and lists of authors treated in other manuals of contemporary literature. The resulting list was then submitted to about thirty teachers and critics of contemporary literature, and in those cases where four of these critics agreed in recommending an addition to the list, such an addition was made. The resulting list will satisfy no one, since no two authorities would agree on exactly which two hundred American authors deserve treatment in a book of this type. But it is the best list that I could devise, and I offer it for what it is worth. There are not more than three or four names here whose presence causes me any great critical embarrassment.

The preparation of this book would have been impossible without the unfailing kindness with which officials of the following libraries have put their resources at my disposal: the Library of Congress, the New York Public Library, the Harvard College Library, the Boston Public Library, the Newberry Library, the University of Chicago Libraries, and the Olin Library, Wesleyan University. I should also like to express my appreciation to the reference librarians of Harvard, Yale, Princeton, Dartmouth, the Jones Library at Amherst, and the Chapin Library at Williams, who have assisted me in the locating of first editions in their special collections.

The Harvard College Library is rich in manuscript material as well as in first editions. It has a sizable collection of letters in manuscript or typescript of the following authors: Akins, Allen, Austin, William Rose Benét, Bynner, Canby, Cullen, Heyward, Hillyer, James Weldon Johnson, Kreymborg, Lindsay, MacKaye, Masters, Morley, Robinson, Sandburg, Sarett, Sinclair, Taggard, Teasdale, Carl Van Doren, and Wheelock. It has a large number of letters along with some manuscript poetry, or else a very large collection of manuscript poetry, by "H. D.," Fletcher, Merrill Moore, Santayana, and Untermeyer. Further, it has first editions of the works of Norman Foerster, Frost, Hillyer, Lindsay, Lowell, Marquis, Merrill Moore, Robinson, Sandburg, Santayana, and Stevens, and most of those of John Dewey and Paul Engle.

Equally rich in manuscript material is the Harriet Monroe Poetry

Room of the University of Chicago Libraries. It houses a large collection of letters in manuscript or typescript, and, occasionally, some manuscript poetry, by these authors: Allen, William Rose Benét, "H. D.," Fletcher, Frost, Gregory, Heyward, Kreymborg, Masters, Mencken, Neihardt, Ridge, Riding, Sarett, Schneider, Scott, Stevens, Taggard, Teasdale, Untermeyer, Wheelock, Williams, and Winters. The Poetry Room has a very large collection of first editions of these authors: Bynner, Lindsay, Lowell, and Pound.

The Collection of American Literature at the Yale University Library contains first editions by Allen, Stephen Vincent Benét, Cabell, Churchill, Coffin, "H. D.," Garland, Glasgow, Millay, Morley, Repplier, Robinson, Teasdale, and Wister. It is also fortunate in owning manuscripts by Day, Lewis (nine novels and plays), MacLeish (poetry), Stein (several books), Tarkington (one novel), Wharton (all the manuscripts and papers), and Wilder (the novels).

The Lockwood Memorial Library of the University of Buffalo has manuscript poems contributed by these authors: Bishop, Bogan, Boyle, Burt, Bynner, Cowley, Cullen, Engle, Fletcher, Frost, Hillyer, Hughes, Josephine W. Johnson, Masters, Millay, Marianne Moore, Morley, Nathan, Prokosch, Santayana, Stevens, Taggard, Mark Van Doren, Winifred Welles, Wheelock, and William Carlos Williams.

Partial lists of first editions may be consulted at the Abernethy Library of American Literature, Middlebury, New York University, Princeton, Wellesley, Wesleyan, and the Chapin Library, Williams College. Special collections may be found at the Jones Library, Amherst (Frost and Taggard); Boston University (Leonard); Princeton (Frost and MacLeish); and Wellesley (Frost, Lindsay, Lowell, Masters, Millay, Robinson, Teasdale, and Wylie).

To list the authors who have replied generously to my request for autobiographical information would be to list two-thirds of the authors treated in this book. In most instances, a quotation in the biographies represents a passage from a personal letter of the author's. American publishers, likewise, have been extremely courteous in furnishing me material concerning the authors on their lists.

Such a project as this is bound to be co-operative, and I should have been utterly unable to carry it through if I had not had the constant assistance of professional bibliographers and of undergraduate and graduate students in various academic institutions. Of the latter, I mention the following gratefully: R. R. Hawkins of the Reference Department of the New York Public Library, Sophie Udin (Columbia University School of Library Service), Ernest H. Halstedt (Wesleyan), Arthur R. Youtz (Harvard), Leon Cooper (Illinois), J. Robert Collins (Catholic University), and William J. Shorrock, Thomas Howells, and Robert W. Wadsworth (Chicago). For three years, Mr. Wadsworth has devoted a great deal of time to the collection and organization of the biographical material. I am also deeply indebted to Katharine Krusé for her intensive reading of the Critical Survey. Her highly developed sense of logic and coherence and her acute ear for verbal infelicities have saved me from many a blunder.

I should like to express my appreciation to Wesleyan University for its grant to help defray the very heavy expense of completing this work.

But the book would never have been finished if I had not had the constant advice and encouragement of John Fall of the Reference Department of the New York Public Library. Not only is he primarily responsible for the Bibliographies, but he has given me constant professional counsel and unending encouragement. At every stage of the preparation and publication of the book, his bibliographical skill and expert knowledge have been indispensable; the generosity of his contributions—in thought, energy, and administrative direction—can never be repaid.

Although I cannot undertake to discuss at length my reasons for excluding any reader's favorite authors, I shall appreciate it very much if readers will send me notes of omissions or corrections in title, dates, or classification.

FRED B. MILLETT.

Honors College,
Wesleyan University.

CONTEMPORARY AMERICAN AUTHORS

A CRITICAL SURVEY

THE BACKGROUND

The relationship between American life and American literature is by no means easy to define, but some comprehension of the first of these entities is necessary if one is to evaluate American literature in any except the purest of aesthetic terms. During a period in our literary history when social forces have been extremely influential, it is especially desirable to make some description and analysis of the environment in which American authors have lived and worked with varying degrees of comfort or discomfort, adaptation or maladjustment. Certain elements in American life have been constant: the physical immensity of our country, the tendency of our culture to develop along regional lines, the comparative brevity of our history, and the consciousness—with or without a feeling of inferiority or superiority—of our dependence on older Continental cultures. Other elements have been influential almost from the beginning: the hybrid nature of our racial stock and the consequent assimilation or failure of assimilation of more or less alien strains, and the antithesis between the rural and the urban ways of life, an antithesis steadily being made less conspicuous by such powerful standardizing agencies as transcontinental highways, the automobile, radio, and moving picture, nationally syndicated newspaper features, and national advertising on streets and billboards, in railroad trains and magazines. Intellectually and politically, American life illustrates the interplay on and under its surface of a number of antithetical forces—ruralism vs. urbanism, conservatism vs. liberalism vs. radicalism, regionalism vs. nationalism vs. internationalism. Although America is still fundamentally democratic and nationalistic, the operations of these antithetical forces must be taken into account in any consideration of American political, intellectual, and aesthetic life, and of American literature since 1900.

BEFORE THE WAR

The history of America between the end of the Spanish-American War (1898) and the beginning of the World War (1914) can be described in terms of three important movements. The first of these movements was the tendency on the part of big business to form larger and larger combines, to extend its control, not merely horizontally but vertically, and to maintain its favored economic position by a more or less corrupt and invisible control of political power. The second but opposed tendency was the attempt to control and regulate the mercantile and political activities of big business. The third movement was the process of restoring to the common man a measure of the control over the political machinery of democracy denied him by the alliance between big business and politics.

The movement toward the formation of great trusts was illustrated dramatically at the turn of the century by a rapid multiplication of huge industrial combines.[1] The growth of these organizations was viewed with apprehension by socially-minded thinkers and politicians, and the "trust-busting" campaign launched by President Theodore Roosevelt was indicative of the alarm aroused in the public mind.

But equally significant for the period was the attack on various grounds on that system of *laissez faire* which had made possible the amassing of tremendous fortunes, the control of politics by big business, and the formation of large numbers of great trusts. The ideas that furnished the ammunition for this reform movement had diverse origins. Certain of them were first broached by the Populists, who reached the peak of their power in the early nineties. Those ideas that pertained particularly to the restoration of political power to the common man, originated in reform movements in Oregon and Wisconsin. Still other sources of liberal ideas were socialism and the social service movement associated for many years with the names of Jane Addams in Chicago and Lillian Wald in New York. But whatever the sources of the ideas, the carrying out of them depended on their adoption by the leaders of liberal political groups, first in the Republican party under Theodore Roosevelt and later in the Democratic party under Woodrow Wilson. As one or the other major party assimilated liberal ideas, the earlier leaders and movements were superseded and their functions ceased. The Populist party died because the Democratic party had taken over its program under the influence of William Jennings Bryan. The insurgent movement led by Senator Robert M. LaFollette received a body-blow when Theodore Roosevelt appropriated its ideas, founded the Progressive or Bull Moose party, and was, in turn, defeated by the leader of the reform wing of the Democratic party, Woodrow Wilson.

One of the most striking evidences of the growing hostility to big business and to its control over politics was the rise of the muckraker, the journalist bent on exposing the shortcomings and the vices of the trust and the corruption of politics by business interests. Toward the end of 1902, two series of articles which began to appear in *McClure's Magazine* announced a new variety of political journalism. The first series was Lincoln Steffens' exposures of corruption in municipal politics,

[1] Among these were the Amalgamated Copper Company (1899), The American Smelting and Refining Company (1899), The Standard Oil Company (1899), The Consolidated Tobacco Company (1901), The United States Steel Corporation (1901), and The International Mercantile Company (1902). The total capitalization of these companies was said to reach over two and a half billion dollars. Harold U. Faulkner, *The Quest for Social Justice, 1898–1914*, Macmillan, 1931, pp. 28–29.

a series afterwards collected in *The Shame of the Cities* (1904). The second series was Ida M. Tarbell's carefully documented and relentless history of the Standard Oil Company. *McClure's* circulation increased at so spectacular a rate that soon such magazines as *Everybody's*, *Munsey's*, and the *Cosmopolitan* joined the campaign, and in 1904, Steffens, Miss Tarbell, and Ray Stannard Baker took over the *American Magazine*, and made it a medium of the new political and economic criticism.

Another field ready for the muckraker was the insanitary and unscrupulous methods of manufacturing and distributing foods and useless or dangerous drugs. Patent medicine was attacked in a series of articles in the *Ladies Home Journal* in 1904–05, and in the latter year *Collier's* featured a similar series. In 1906, Upton Sinclair's (*q.v.*) novel, *The Jungle*, horrified the nation by its exposé of insanitary conditions in the packing industry. These revelations led to a modest amount of legislation for pure foods and drugs under the animated leadership of Dr. Harvey Wiley. But the interests involved continued to make it impossible to pass laws adequately protecting the public from impure foods and valueless patent medicines.

The church responded promptly to this stirring of the national social conscience, reconsidered the whole problem of its social responsibilities, and gradually developed liberal inter-church organizations which were to play a very considerable part in reform programs during the war and the post-war period.

Throughout the pre-war period there is abundant evidence of a new social spirit, motivating, in Professor Faulkner's phrase, the quest for social justice. On the economic side, the movement for the state provision of adequate workingmen's compensation laws, which had been frustrated in Massachusetts in 1909, and again in New York by conservative courts in 1910, gained ground. Eleven states passed employers' liability acts in 1911, and by 1921 all but six of the states and the District of Columbia had adopted similar laws. The movement to abolish child labor developed at an accelerated pace. Between 1905 and 1907, two-thirds of the states passed such legislation or strengthened the laws they had already passed. In 1912, the Children's Bureau was established as a part of the Department of Commerce. Attempts to wipe out by federal legislation the hideous blot child labor has made on our economic history have, however, continued to be blocked by a reactionary judiciary or by the pressures of conservative economic or religious groups.

The movement to restore some measure of true democracy to the operation of America's political machinery took the form of the widespread adoption by the states of such measures as the initiative, referendum and recall, the system of direct primaries, woman suffrage, and the popular election of United States Senators. Attempts to introduce a juster system of taxation also made headway. A federal income tax law, passed in 1894, had been rejected as unconstitutional, but by 1909 a constitutional amendment made legal the federal taxation of income, and by 1913 this amendment had received the consent of the requisite number of states. Within five years, this tax was beginning to yield the major portion of the federal government's revenue.

While these important legal changes were taking place, striking social processes were also in progress. The immigration of the foreign-born proceeded with great rapidity. In each of six of the years between 1905 and 1914, over a million immigrants came to America. By 1910, there were more than thirteen million foreign-born in the United States and an equal number of white children born of foreign parents. The high-school population doubled between 1898 and 1914. The number of telephones rose from over a half million in 1900 to three millions and a half in 1910 and nearly six millions in 1915. But more striking in the effects on national habits and psychology was the advent of the automobile and the moving picture. The four automobiles registered in 1895 had grown to eight thousand in 1900, and two and a half millions in 1915. The spread of the moving picture was almost equally sensational. Although programs confined to motion pictures were not shown until the middle of the first decade of the century, there were five thousand theaters devoted to the exhibition of pictures by 1907, and by 1915 the number had grown to eighteen or nineteen thousand.[1]

The most conspicuous figure in American life in the first decade of the twentieth century was Theodore Roosevelt. His services as Police Commissioner of New York in 1895 attracted considerable attention, but his brief and well-publicized experience as a Rough Rider in the Spanish-American War increased his personal popularity tremendously, led to the governorship of New York in 1898, and made it impossible for the Republican party to refuse to nominate him for the vice-presidency, despite President William McKinley's personal antipathy to him, when the latter sought the presidency for the second time in 1900. The innocuous desuetude of the vice-presidency promised the vital Roosevelt a kind of living death, but chance in the form of an assassin's bullet brought him to the presidency for a period of six and a half years beginning on September 14, 1901.

Theodore Roosevelt was the apotheosis of the American ideal of the period. His vitality and aggressiveness, his capacity for racy phrasing and pungent commentary on his opponents, his flair for publicizing his pet notions and nostrums, the ease with which he lent himself to lively and diverting caricature, his high spirits and good humor, his democratic

[1] Since 1915, the number of motion-picture theaters has remained relatively stable. In 1929, the figure was said to be 20,250. (*Motion Pictures*. Reprinted from *A Century of Industrial Progress*, Doubleday, Doran, 1929.) In 1938, the figure was said to be 17,500. (New York *Times*, Oct. 9, 1938, p. X5.)

manners, his avocational interest in big-game hunting and exploration, his skill and reputation as historian and letter-writer, the attractiveness of his energetic and growing family—all these traits and assets made him one of the best-known, best-liked, and best-hated personalities of his time.[1]

The years from 1901 to 1909 which Theodore Roosevelt spent in the White House saw marked changes in the relations between the government and big business. During the earlier part of his administration, the formation of great trusts and the attacks of the muckrakers upon them speeded up the long process of attempting to control and regulate the tendency of big business toward consolidation and monopolization. This attempt at control had had one of its earlier expressions in the Sherman Anti-trust Act of 1890. Roosevelt's "trust-busting" campaign put new teeth in this obsolescent act by further legislation in 1903. He also showed a vigorous interest in the conservation of natural resources, and stretched to the utmost his legal powers to remove valuable lands from the public domain. As a personal administrator he ranged freely over the "twilight zone" of the executive power. Roosevelt was also instrumental in building up the navy and using it in demonstrations of American power in oriental and European waters in the aid of international peace. In the latter connection, one of his major services was bringing about the end of the Russo-Japanese War by the signing of the Treaty of Portsmouth on September 5, 1905. But probably the most spectacular and the most questionable of his acts was the instigation of the revolution in Panama which made it possible for the United States to acquire rights to the land on which the canal was to be built.

Theodore Roosevelt had hoped and expected that his chosen successor, William Howard Taft, would carry on the program of political and economic reform in which he increasingly believed, and on Taft's accession to the presidency, Roosevelt adopted a policy of the maximum self-effacement possible to a personality born for the center of the stage. But temperament, experience, and political philosophy brought it about that Taft became more and more clearly identified with the conservative forces in the Republican party. His pledge to reform the tariff eventuated in the Payne-Aldrich Bill of 1909, but this bill seemed to liberal elements in both parties to demonstrate Taft's sympathies with the interests of big business. The President further alienated liberal opinion by his opposition to the provision for the recall of judges in the proposed constitution for the nascent state of Arizona. His estrangement from the insurgent elements in his own party had a number of causes: his political ineptitude,

[1] Such phrases as "race suicide," "the big stick," the "Ananias Club," "trust-busting," "muckraking," the "Bull Moose party," and the "New Nationalism" illustrate his advertiser's flair for making effective slogans. His "New Nationalism" was the ancestor of Woodrow Wilson's "New Freedom," which in turn fathered the "New Deal" of Franklin D. Roosevelt.

his sincerely conservative convictions, and the fact that Theodore Roosevelt returned from a triumphal ex-regal tour of Europe, irritated by the conservatism of his successor, stirred by renewed political ambitions, and moved by a genuine desire to see to it that his program of reform should not end in ignominious defeat.

The Republican convention of 1912 brought a dramatic quietus to Roosevelt's hopes to become a candidate for president under regular Republican auspices, and precipitated the headlong formation of the Progressive or Bull Moose party. Roosevelt's personality and the moral fervor which the principles of his New Nationalism aroused in liberals of all political faiths won him more votes than any third-party leader had ever polled, but that number proved insufficient to prevent the election of the leader of reform in the Democratic party, Woodrow Wilson, former president of Princeton University and governor of the State of New Jersey.

Woodrow Wilson's personality furnished the sharpest of contrasts to those of his unsuccessful rivals for the presidency. A scholar and historian, an excellent stylist, and a phrase-maker only slightly less telling than Theodore Roosevelt himself, a cool, aloof, and obstinate temperament, a mind accustomed to move in the atmosphere of abstract and somewhat bloodless concepts, Wilson had had sufficient experience of practical politics to realize that, as a minority president, he must organize the reforming element in both parties and work through them to carry out the program to which he had pledged himself. The ideas which Theodore Roosevelt stood for in his final bid for the presidency were not very remote from those of Wilson himself, and the program to which Wilson bent his tenacious will was one which commanded a good deal of enthusiasm among liberals in every camp.

Wilson's program, then, was in almost every essential respect the program in which the reform elements in both parties believed. It is natural, therefore, that in the early days of his administration he should have attempted to further those reforms of which the beginnings had been made during the three preceding Republican administrations. The problem of the revision of the tariff, which Taft had not succeeded in solving to the satisfaction of the liberals, was worked out with considerable success in the Underwood Tariff Act of 1913. Those deficiencies in the banking system which became most conspicuous during periodic financial depressions were remedied in considerable measure by the Federal Reserve Act of 1913, an act which at first aroused the opposition of private bankers but ended by earning their approbation. For the somewhat irrational and impulsive "trust-busting" policy of Theodore Roosevelt, Wilson substituted a careful study of the distinction between corporations which were inimical and corporations which were favorable to the public interest. The creation of the Federal Trade Commission and the passage of the Clayton Anti-trust Act in 1914 provided agencies for the control of the activities, legitimate and illegitimate, of big business.

In foreign affairs, President Wilson pursued a policy of "watchful waiting" which frequently exasperated hotter spirits bent on direct action. During Wilson's first administration, his policy of fair play and patience was sorely tested in America's relations with Mexico. The Huerta regime provoked the Vera Cruz incident, which led to its occupation in 1914, and in 1916, the activities of the bandit-rebel, Francisco Villa, brought the invasion of Mexico by American forces. Controversies with Japan over restrictions on immigration and with Russia over the emigration of Jews also required careful handling. One cause of irritation between America and Great Britain was the toll system in vogue in the Panama Canal which had been completed in April, 1914. In June of that year the Tolls Repeal Act became a law, and alleviated this irritation. In the meantime, Secretary of State William Jennings Bryan was negotiating a series of arbitration treaties with European nations in the hope of preventing recourse to war as a means of settling international disputes.

Despite a series of exposures of the blind and diseased spots in American political and economic life, the pre-war decade and a half was one of great hopefulness and optimism. To many generous spirits the millennium seemed not too far distant, and, although the program of the reformers was growing constantly more ambitious, in many circles there was little doubt that the carrying out of such a program would bring an end to most of our political and economic ills. But the assassination of the heir to the throne of Austria-Hungary at Sarajevo on June 28, 1914, was the first act of a tragedy which was to complicate tremendously the problems that Wilson faced, to involve the United States for the first time in its history in a great European war, to end with the rise of Wilson to a position of power and prestige which made him appear a savior in the eyes of oppressed peoples everywhere, and finally to bring about the defeat, by reactionary forces at home, of Wilson's great dream of a world at peace, his physical collapse, and piteous death.

The outbreak of the World War came as the rudest of shocks to liberal and hopeful America. It necessitated a gradual readjustment to the realities of a world which it had been America's good fortune to be able, in large measure, to ignore.

THE WAR AND AFTER

In the history of America since the beginning of the World War, several distinct periods can be distinguished, each of which has had a more or less direct influence on the kind of literature produced and consumed in America. The more important of these periods may be designated the war period (1914–18), the period of reconstruction (1918–29), and the period of depression and recovery since 1929. Even within these periods, certain phases must be differentiated. The period of the war can be divided historically and psychologically into the years 1914–17, during which America remained technically neutral but was being drawn nearer and nearer to participation in the conflict, and the years 1917–18 of actual participation. So, too, the longer period of reconstruction and of economic expansion had an early phase of difficult and sinister readjustment, from the close of the war to the death of President Harding (August 2, 1923), and the period from the frantic speculation and financial debauchery of the Coolidge era to the crash of the stock market on October 29, 1929. The depression likewise had its recognizable phases; the first, the period of deepening hopelessness and despair from 1929 to the "Banking Holiday" of 1933, and the second, the period of recovery that began with the first administration of President Franklin D. Roosevelt.

The years of American neutrality were years of stress and strain, not only for hyphenate Americans but for those of native stock. The outbreak and continuance of the European war brought far-reaching economic and psychological changes to America. As the most productive of the neutral nations, America became an all-important purveyor of foodstuffs, munitions, and money to the Allies, and the inevitable speeding-up of production meant for the moneyed class and for stock-and-bond-holders generally a period of war prosperity which, though narrow in its economic incidence, had not a little to do with predisposing Americans of the upper economic brackets to favor the cause of the Allies and with ultimately bringing America into the war on the side of the Allies. But more important to the white-collar and the blue-collar workers was the necessity of America's making up its mind about the war. This process was a long and painful one. First of all, it involved a considerable extension of information as to European history and the causes—real or alleged—of the world-embracing conflict. To the dissemination of such information a great many American scholars and publicists devoted the highest intelligence they possessed. But the process of "enlightening" America was inextricably complicated (as it was not easy to see at the time) by the flocking to America of propagandists of every degree of crassness and subtlety, in the pay of either the Entente or the Allies. Upon Americans of foreign birth, especially upon the plentiful stock of German-Americans, the pressure was painful and often tragic. At times, it seemed as though America's melting pot would crack with the violent explosions of contradictory native and alien loyalties. For many intellectuals with liberal or radical sympathies, the pressure of events and ideas brought a movement of the mind and heart that paralleled the changes in attitude of President Woodrow Wilson, who, reelected in 1916 on the ground that "he kept us out of war," was slowly driven from the sound but difficult position that there was a defense for being "too proud to fight" to the intelligible expedient of entry into the

World War "to save the world for democracy." Once the fatal decision had been reached, the melting pot boiled less violently. The clamping down of the draft laws was sufficiently prompt to still the protests and the misgivings of all save a few religious or political intransigents.

It is only by a very considerable effort of the memory that one can recreate the atmosphere surrounding America's participation in the World War. Even in the period of spiritual deflation after the war, it was difficult to remember that the war years saw an outburst of patriotic idealism such as America had never known and will probably never know again. To almost every American, adolescent, adult, or senescent, there came a sense of being caught up in a tremendous international cause in which the individual and his fate were of little or no consequence in comparison with what he might contribute by food- or fuel-saving, by physical or financial gifts, or by the sacrifice of health or life itself, to the "great crusade," the war to end war. What one ate, what one wore, what one read and thought, were all conditioned, were all made transcendently significant by the conviction that both combatant and noncombatant must serve the common cause. The term "slacker" was one of the gravest opprobrium. For Americans, too, the sense of elevation and of ecstatic devotion of self and kin to a great purpose was the deeper since America was in the war too brief a time to experience the searching of heart and the trial of spirit known to those nations already at the point of exhaustion when America entered the conflict.

To the noncombatant, the war made itself felt, especially, in terms of food-rationing, subscribing to Liberty Loans, knitting, sewing, Red Cross and Y.M.C.A. work, and in the pleasant sense that the job he was doing was not only paying well but was regarded as patriotically essential. For the combatant, the war meant, in a relatively small number of cases, not only the exaltation of physical and moral courage and sacrifice, but the horror and agony of modern trench-warfare. For those of whom the last sacrifice was not demanded, it meant an experience of a way of life completely alien to anything they had known before. Whether in training camp or in foreign service, the American youth of those days found himself submitting to a simplification of existence, a reduction to the primitive, a submission to discipline to which he was not by nature too amenable. It also meant, despite the inevitable restrictions of military life, a considerable extension of his geographical and cultural experience. The resultant leveling of class and regional distinctions has not been the least of the influences making for a standardization of American culture. The American soldier's reaction to his overseas experience was necessarily diverse. The untutored and inexperienced found little to like or to admire in his contacts with Allied soldiers or civilians. To the militarized intellectual, contacts with alien cultures proved frequently stimulating and energizing, and the international experience of the war years contributed definitely to the initiation and development of the expatriate literary movement of the post-war period. The nostalgia of certain American veterans for the war years seems intelligible only on the ground that for combatant and noncombatant alike these years were the most exciting and eventful they had ever experienced or were to experience.

Out of the inflated idealism of the war years, with which the liberalism of the pre-war period had ultimately and imperceptibly been blended, two movements, long slowly preparing themselves for acceptance by the American mind, achieved recognition and legalization. These oddly paired movements were prohibition and woman suffrage. The latter achieved legality with the passing of the Nineteenth Amendment by Congress in June, 1919, and its adoption as a part of the Constitution in August, 1920. The process by which woman suffrage became a part of our political machinery was less spectacular than that which brought about prohibition, and the consequences were less immediate and sensational. But woman suffrage was bound to have a permanent effect on American economic and political life, although the widespread discrediting of the processes of political democracy in the post-war period has tended to diminish the radiance of this victory of the feminists.

America's "novel experiment" with prohibition was destined to be shorter-lived. The Eighteenth Amendment became a part of the United States Constitution as a result of the interaction of a number of contradictory causes: the wave of moral idealism generated in the first decade of the century, the prolonged and sinister political activities of the Anti-Saloon League, the recognition during the World War of the economic wastefulness of the consumption of liquor, and the desire to protect soldiers, away from home, from the influences associated with the saloon. As a result of these combined forces, the amount of foodstuffs to be used in the production of liquor was restricted, and the Eighteenth Amendment was passed by Congress in 1917. In 1918, the wartime manufacture and sale of intoxicants were prohibited, and the Eighteenth Amendment became a part of the Constitution of the United States in January, 1919. The complex social and economic consequences of prohibition were unpredictable, and it is not easy to strike a balance between the good and evil results. At first, the evil consequences were far more conspicuous than the good: the rise of the illegal industry of "bootlegging," the growth of "home-brewing," the vogue, among adolescents no less than among adults, of the hip flask, the mushroom development of more or less reputable speakeasies, the spread of drinking among women and young girls, and the shady relationships between nightclubs and corrupt police and politicians—all phases of our social behavior that received perhaps more than their share of attention from journalism and literature. Less noticed by the press and by literature were less questionable results: the decline in public drunkenness, the decline in working-class poverty and degradation due directly to intemperance, the apparently permanent changes in American eating habits that came about with the banning of liquor in hotels and the development of lunch counters, sandwich shops, and coffee shops in hotels.

The period from the end of the war to the beginning of the depression was characterized by an appalling outburst of nationalistic patriotism. This mass-phenomenon had its origin unquestionably in the whipping up of patriotic emotion during the war, but the after-effects were even more hideous than the beginnings. The evilest of its products was the emergence of the Ku Klux Klan, which, from modest beginnings in 1915, arose to menacing proportions in the late twenties. Finding its soil in anti-Semitic, anti-Catholic, anti-radical antipathies, it capitalized the fears and prejudices of the most narrow-minded and ignorant of Americans. On an equally low intellectual plane were the activities of various politicians and journalists who engineered a crusade against allegedly pro-British, anti-American textbooks in the social sciences. Perhaps the grossest form of this nationalistic mania was the crusade against bolshevism, a crusade which appealed to the economic terrors of the moneyed and semi-moneyed classes. Of more serious import were the discussion of the problem of America's capacity to assimilate large numbers of immigrants and the passage of increasingly stringent immigration laws intended to limit immigrants to persons from the more easily assimilable races and cultures. This legal scrutinizing of the hitherto welcome foreign laborer was only one phase of the reaction from the emotional and idealized relationship between America and her Allies during the war. The problem of war debts, the ancient American fear of entangling alliances, the sense of American inferiority to "wily" European diplomats, all helped bring to an early end the cordial relations between America and Great Britain and France, and led to the rejection by the American Congress of the treaty President Wilson had negotiated at Versailles.

Economically the period between the close of the war and the depression was one of overexpansion and frantic speculation. The end of the war meant a sharp and difficult readjustment to the narrower demands of the post-war world, but, once the minor depression of 1920–21 had passed, the time was ripe for a boom period such as America had never known. For the first time large numbers of the petty bourgeoisie learned to their ultimate discomfiture the excitements of dabbling in stocks. Land values soared, and spending in every field increased at an unparalleled speed. For a time it seemed as though the Gilded Age of the later nineteenth century had come again.

But the unhealthy overgrowth of paper fortunes held warnings for the observant. The alliance between unscrupulous financiers and politicians in high places brought to light a series of scandals in the later years of President Harding's regime that amazed our short-memoried public.

With Calvin Coolidge in the presidential chair and Andrew Mellon as Secretary of the Treasury, decency and thrift seemed likely to return, and the boom continued at an accelerated pace. The campaign promises of Herbert Hoover implied a diffusion of prosperity of which Americans of the working class had wistfully dreamed. Of perfect personal integrity and of great administrative ability, President Hoover seemed likely to prove a new type of president, an efficiency expert with incomparable power. But with little or no personal charm, and with political and economic ideas of the most static and conservative variety, he was utterly unsuited to grapple with the tremendous problems created by the depression, and his modest impulses toward social improvement and efficient administration time and the depression treated in the spirit of the bitterest irony. President Hoover's administration saw a slow paralysis of the spirit of the American people under the burden of the depression. Uncertainty and fear gripped them, and inhibited their normal spontaneity, credulity, and aggressiveness. The shrinkage of tremendous fortunes, the collapse of the Insull utilities empire, the mounting problems of local, state, and federal relief, drove the American people to seek for a scapegoat and a redeemer, neither of which was at all easy to find. The psychological depths of the depression coincided with the end of Hoover's regime and the beginning of President Franklin D. Roosevelt's first administration in the euphemistically entitled Banking Holiday of March, 1933.

President Roosevelt was admirably suited by temperament, political experience, and political faith to deal with the overpowering problems that he inherited. His great personal charm was never more potent than on the occasion of his first radio address to a frightened people in the midst of the Banking Holiday. Where Hoover's views of the social and economic process had been static, Roosevelt's were dynamic and creative. With a passion for social justice reminiscent of his predecessor Theodore Roosevelt, an endless ingenuity in the devising of projects to end the depression, and extraordinary courage in the putting of his schemes into action, he attracted in the early years of his first administration a degree of loyalty and enthusiasm rarely lavished on the nation's chief executive. His courage and self-confidence did more to restore the collapsed morale of the American people than any of the projects on which he encouraged the government to embark. For a short time he profited by the extraordinary state of mind into which the American people had fallen in the worst days of the depression.

Thus, with the beginning of Roosevelt's first administration, a new phase of the depression psychology appeared. For a brief time, the American people as a whole seemed to feel that it had found its savior. During that interval, political and economic animosities were forgotten, and the whole nation bent its energies to carrying out the President's program. With the gradual improvement of economic and industrial conditions, this period of psychological unanimity (curiously similar to the unanimity of the war period) came to an end. At both ends of the economic scale, Americans began to feel free to scrutinize the federal program to which they had submitted willingly in their eagerness to end the depression. The Brain Trust and the New Deal, at first regarded with hope and faith, came to be looked on in conservative circles as devices to bring socialism to America, and an irrational wave of anti-radicalism flaunted its absurdities. Politicians insisted on the investigation of the past and present political creeds of the President's advisers, and wealthy businessmen and newspaper proprietors provoked investigations of radicalism in colleges and universities and threatened the existence of academic freedom. With improving economic conditions, radicalism unquestionably became more vocal. Radicalism of the pre-depression period had been an almost exclusively intellectual and urban movement, with little or no support from the real working class, but the conversion of large numbers of American writers to communistic principles early in the depression gave radicalism a voice more potent than it had ever found before, and brought, as we shall see, a sharp change in the atmosphere that invested the production and criticism of American literature.

The middle class, unallured by either the conservative or the radical position, was stirred by the appearance of a number of more or less unintelligent, more or less well-meaning messiahs who promised to lead the American people out of the wilderness of the depression. Such "leaders" as Father Charles Coughlin and Huey Long, and the founder of the Townsend Plan, although they won the unqualified contempt of the intelligentsia, commanded a semi-intelligent following and occasionally attained sufficient influence to make themselves worthy of consideration by the professional politician.

Roosevelt's first administration, also, saw the end of the unfortunate experiment with prohibition. The motives that led to the official rejection of prohibition are less apparent than those that led to its establishment. Possibly the major motive was the slowly growing conviction that it was impossible, even with tremendous expenditures of money and men, to enforce a law which large sections of the population were bent on circumventing. Certainly the rapid growth of the movement for repeal was due, at least in part, to a profound desire to escape, even momentarily, through the consumption of hard liquor, from the psychological pressures of a long period of economic insecurity and deprivation. The reckless spirit manifest in the enthusiastic rejection of the restrictions of prohibition expressed itself in other ways as well: the popularity of various gambling devices, from horse-racing and dog-racing to the multiplication of slot machines in drug stores and bowling alleys, the development of bank nights in moving-picture houses, and the promotion of various forms of "Beano" for the alleged benefit of religious and patriotic organizations.

The emergence from the depression was by no means due solely to the efforts of the President and his advisers. Recovery came about as the result of a number of forces of which the President's program was only one. His opponents indeed pointed with glee to the finding of a commission of the Brookings Institution (1935) that the NRA program had impeded rather than assisted recovery. But if one experiment had failed, others had succeeded, and the psychological turn that came with the election of Roosevelt and the slow processes of recovery at home and abroad gradually made their effects felt throughout the United States and in every class.

With the emergence into recovery, politico-economic cleavages of a traditional sort began to reappear. The central cause of cleavage appeared under a number of guises. Essentially it was a cleavage between a conservative and a liberal attitude toward the Constitution and its sanctity. This cleavage, which has come to the surface again and again in times of political stress and strain, separates those who regard the Constitution as a sacrosanct instrument incapable of radical modification and those who regard the Constitution as an instrument for the bringing about of the general good, a human means that must be modified under the pressure of events. It is a cleavage, as Parrington pointed out in his *Main Currents in American Thought*, between those whose major fidelity is to the Constitution and those whose major fidelity is to the Declaration of Independence. Superficially, the cleavage, in journalistic and rhetorical terms, seemed to be one between Americanism and radicalism, patriotism and socialism, democracy and communism. But these sensational terms served merely to conceal the real conflict and to arouse bad feeling, fear, and prejudice among the unthinking and the uninformed. At root, the opposition was one always close to the surface of American political life, namely, the opposition between those who believe in a static and stand-pat social order and those who believe in one that is dynamic and creative.

THE SOCIAL SETTING

In the decades since the outbreak of the World War, the effect of certain forces on the social habits of Americans has been considerably accelerated. No single force has brought about such radical alterations in American mores as the application of science to the creation of mechanisms calculated to save labor or to heighten profits. The rapid spread of such domestic mechanisms and their characteristically national ubiquity were due primarily to the development in America, on a scale unparalleled elsewhere, of the science or art of advertising and its inseparable companion, high-powered salesmanship.

During this period, the American home was transformed, internally if not externally. Increasing millions of Americans signalized their severance from the soil by moving to rented apartments soaring higher and higher in huge "Babbitt-warrens." Within the apartment or the single dwelling, science altered domestic arrangements profoundly. The onerous duties of the nineteenth-century housewife were steadily being eliminated or lightened by mechanisms or gadgets or by new sources of power, and the home-dwelling wife, not less than the apartment-house wife, found her leisure increasing and, with her children launched in kindergartens on their long educational careers, directed her energies into other channels—business, politics, club work, social work, and more or less innocent country-club intrigues. On the rare occasions when all the members of the family were at home, the peace and quiet that had characterized the nineteenth-century home were dispelled by the ringing of the telephone, interminable conversations with the neighbors, and tuning in for the family's favorite radio programs.

But the family group was increasingly submitted to forces that threatened to disrupt it. Instead of staying at home and reading quietly around the living-room table, members of the family were likely to be attracted to the moving-picture "palace," of which every city neighborhood and every small town boasted at least one, offering two or three changes of program each week. Or, if the movie were uninviting, some or all the members of the family were likely to devote the early evening or the whole of Sunday to an automobile ride. The automobile and later the trailer were increasing tremendously the motility of American life, and large numbers of Americans of modest means were becoming aware of the physical immensity of their country, its striking regional differences, and its standardized comforts and utilities.

The changing domestic habits of the American middle class created a series of problems hotly debated in the press, the magazines, and the novels of the period. Prohibition, for example, forced upon every family the not too simple problem of the exact degree to which it should obey or break an unpopular law. Prohibition brought the pocket flask, the widespread custom of drinking at dances, and an increased recklessness on the highroad. The war had induced not only a spirit of self-sacrifice but a feeling of recklessness in men and women whose lives and happiness might be suddenly and shockingly terminated. With Armistice Day, the self-sacrifice ended; the spirit of recklessness continued, however, and was indeed intensified, paradoxically, by prohibition itself and by the economic boom of the twenties. The short stories and novels of F. Scott Fitzgerald (*q.v.*) popularized the idea of the "jazz age," and its problems complicated the always difficult relations between the older and the younger generations. If Gertrude Stein (*q.v.*) was right in designating the young men who survived the war the "lost generation," there were plenty of the middle-aged who agreed that the younger generation was well on the way to the devil.

With the coming of the depression, there was a sharp change in the social atmosphere. On every economic level, family expenditures had to be sharply curtailed, and the major problem for the younger generation was no longer moral but economic. The centrifugal forces operating on domestic life were temporarily lightened, and there was a marked drawing together of family- and clan-groups in the interest of self-preservation. The profound disturbances of the economic system produced a new seriousness which made the repeal of prohibition (when it came) less of a moral calamity than its defenders had believed it would bring. This mood of seriousness, like every other national American mood, was, however, transitory, and, as a reaction to the self-denials of the depression, or perhaps in imitation of the government's program of free-handed spending, there was a sharp increase in the popularity of all sorts of devices for getting something for nothing, from the Townsend Plan and the chain-letter to dog-racing and petty drug store gambling. The way seemed prepared for another era of reckless expenditure and speculation.

THE ARTISTIC ATMOSPHERE

For the whole period with which we are concerned, a general rise in taste in the field of the pictorial arts, at least, may be posited. The most concrete evidence of this general improvement is the quality of the pictures on the walls of the American home. The disappearance, or virtual disappearance, of the appallingly sentimental chromos of the eighties and nineties resulted from the response of the American housewife to the reading of books and articles in such magazines as the *Ladies Home Journal*, the *Woman's Home Companion*, and *Good Housekeeping*, the hearing of lectures, and the taking of courses given by wily interior decorators. Domestic examples of the pictorial arts improved also with the advances in color-printing, carried further, to be sure, in Germany, but applied profitably and effectively in the United States. Outside the home, interest in the pictorial arts and appreciation of them was apparent in the increased attendance at museums, in the establishment in New York of such collections as the Museum of Modern Art and the Whitney Museum of American Art, and the inclusion in more conservative museums of a good deal of contemporary work. The opening to the public of the Frick Collection and the Bache Collection and the presentation to the nation of the superb art treasures gathered by Andrew Mellon, the magnificent exhibitions of European and American art from private and public American collections at the Chicago Century of Progress Exposition in 1933—all these events received a great deal of publicity, and had their direct and indirect stimulating effect. Throughout the period, regionalism in art, as in literature, strengthened its forces, and under the influence of such artists as Grant Wood and Thomas Benton pointed the way to an indigenous American art. The creation of the WPA Artists Project during the depression made America mural-conscious, and, while many of the murals are likely to prove only temporarily interesting and effective, their appearance in public places gave the art a functional and not a merely decorative value.

In the field of classical music, relatively little advance was made by American composers, though symphony orchestras attempted to elevate a number of composers to the classical Parnassus, and such events as Deems Taylor's *The King's Henchman* (1927), with a libretto by Edna St. Vincent Millay (*q.v.*), Taylor's *Peter Ibbetson* (1931), Louis Gruenberg's *The Emperor Jones* (1933), based on the play by Eugene O'Neill (*q.v.*), and Virgil Thompson's *Four Saints in Three Acts* (1934), with a libretto by Gertrude Stein (*q.v.*), were widely publicized, if rapidly forgotten. The main stream of American musical creative energy flowed, not into classical composition, but into the devising of jazz- and swing-music and into the sophisticated orchestration of folk- or Negro-melodies. On a somewhat higher plane, the collecting and editing of American folk-songs by such scholars as Cecil Sharp and John A. Lomax prepared the way for the popular appreciation of Carl Sandburg's (*q.v.*) *American Songbag* (1927) and the popularity on the radio of mountain and cowboy music by real or pseudo hill-billies or cowboys.

For most Americans classical music had been synonymous with the concert stage or the opera house or the agonies of unmusical children struggling at the pianoforte, but, with the coming of radio, the audience for music broadened, and students were forced to study attentively the radio programs of the era after 1920 for data on the pathology of American taste. From the universal racket of the radio, the only relief was the appearance before the microphone of the greatest musical artists of the period and the broadcasting of operas and symphonies to a circle of listeners hitherto cut off from such experiences. Daily broadcasting was begun by Westinghouse Station KDKA in Pittsburgh on November 2, 1920. By 1926, the chain system of broadcasting had developed, and from that date sustained conversation in the American home practically ceased. The radio joined the movie and advertising in standardizing public taste on a relatively low level. To its credit, however, it did not a little to widen the intellectual and aesthetic horizons of millions of Americans remote from urban cultural centers, and to make respectable an acknowledged interest in prize fighting and politics. In consequence, the chilly radio manner of President Hoover, the warm and friendly tones of President Roosevelt, the hearty vulgarities of Governor Al Smith weighed heavily in the shaping of their political destinies.

But the most powerful influence on American taste during this period was not the radio but the movie, and its successors, the talkie and the color film. Under the dictatorship of shamelessly ignorant and unscrupulous movie magnates, the industry revolutionized American taste in interior decoration, female pulchritude, sexual morality, manners, diction, and pronunciation. The movies dealt the final blow to the touring company and the road show, and the fabulous financial rewards offered authors who were lured to Hollywood to write scenarios, or whose works, bought for incredible sums, emerged on the screen, with or without their original titles or stories, and in more or less bowdlerized versions, had the most serious effects in diverting the talent of myriads of promising writers to the creation of good, bad, and indifferent movie scripts.

If the moving picture dealt a deathblow to the road traveled for generations by touring theatrical companies, it likewise had its effects on the drama and theater in the great urban centers. For millions of Americans, the movie took the place of the drama as a form of entertainment. For other millions, it became a serious rival to the drama on economic and aesthetic grounds. At the beginning of the century, the theater was as commercialized as the movie is now. In the second decade of the century, a revolt against the commercial theater began in the universities, the little theaters, and the community theaters. The revolt, well under way at the incidence of the depression, suffered a severe check during its first years. The drama is the most costly of the arts, and, inevitably, the depression brought an almost complete cessation of theatrical activity in even important theatrical centers, and a sharp decline in the number of theaters occupied, the number of plays produced, and even the size of the audience in New York, America's dramatic capital. But the American appetite for drama is a permanent one, and the persistence through the depression of the best of the little and community theaters, the tremendous increase in semiprofessional theatrical ventures, and the astonishing phenomenon of the summer theater, are indices not merely of a reviving but an undying interest.

Though no very comprehensive studies of the reading habits of the American people have been made, certain tendencies in the consumption of literature are observable. For most Americans, reading is practically limited to the newspaper and an occasional magazine. During this period, marked changes have taken place in the newspapers available to American readers. Since the war, there has been a decided falling-off in the number of newspapers published, a tendency to build up newspaper chains which take their impress from the personality of the single owner, the development of the newspaper from a medium for the dissemination of news, editorial opinion, and advertising, to a magazine-like publication in which the body of syndicated features frequently outshines in attractiveness the regular news stories and editorials. Even newspapers catering to the taste of readers in moderate-sized cities have found it necessary to include among their features several strips of comics (certainly the most widely read of all publications in the United States, and an almost completely neglected source of social history), a metropolitan columnist, advice about health, a woman's page, a column on etiquette, several sporting pages, and radio- and moving-picture publicity. Certain metropolitan newspapers, especially in their Saturday night and Sunday editions, attain such a size that the consumer might very well be pardoned if he found time to read almost nothing else.

If time for less casual reading were found, America offered a variety of magazines unparalleled in the history of publishing. As magazines increased in numbers, they became differentiated in fairly distinct classes: the pulps, the slicks, and the quality magazines. The pulp magazines (so named from the cheap wood-pulp paper on which they were printed) also fell into distinct sub-classifications. There were groups specializing in western stories, detective stories, adventure, aviation, scientific fiction, and sex fiction of the *True Confession* type and lower. These magazines, vended chiefly by drug stores, station stalls, and small-town paper stores, furnished a large section of the reading public all they required in the way of literary wish-fulfillment. Slicks such as the *Saturday Evening Post*, the *American Magazine*, the *Ladies Home Journal*, and the *Woman's Home Companion*, specialized in articles and short stories and serialized novels adroitly aimed at a predominantly feminine audience. The fiction that reached these pages was manufactured wholesale to meet very restricted systems of reader-appetencies and revulsions, and writers like Kathleen Norris, Faith Baldwin, and Temple Bailey showed extraordinary ingenuity in meeting the demands of such audiences and thus reaped their rewards in the form of huge annual incomes and wide subliterary reputations. The "quality" magazines did not suffer directly from the competition of the energetic pulps, but they lost considerable ground in their attempt to keep the attention of the middle-class audience. On the whole, magazines like the *Atlantic*, *Harper's*, and *Scribner's*, despite repeated efforts on the part of young editors to galvanize them into life, declined in prestige, since as a group they failed to adapt themselves to changing currents in contemporary culture, the shifting of the center of culture away from the Atlantic seaboard, and the hybridization of American literature through the admixture of alien stocks and traditions. The quality magazines also struggled to maintain their prestige and popularity in the face of the very stiff competition offered by such lively publications as *Time* and *Newsweek*, the de luxe magazine *Fortune*, and the brilliantly edited and illustrated *Life* and its numerous and sensational imitators. Similarly, ancient and honorable fun-makers like *Judge* and the old *Life* lost either their existence or their popularity in competition with such a magazine as the *New Yorker*, the editor of which gathered about him a staff as brilliant as any other popular magazine possessed, and which, although it appealed definitely to the upper classes and the academic intelligentsia, maintained a genuinely liberal attitude under the guise of a tolerant lightheartedness.

Over the ultimate consumer of literature, the reader of books, played the same forces that conditioned not merely the production of American literature but the development of American culture generally. Temperament, training, economic status, and cultural naïveté or sophistication—all these interwoven elements had their parts in determining the habits and the tastes of American readers. But more clearly upon him than upon the American writer operate the pressures of literary publicity and salesmanship, of social example and prestige. Only the staunch individualist among readers can withstand the force of the tidal waves of popularity on which certain publishers contrive to launch their books. And those readers who allow such standardizing agencies as the Book-of-the-Month Club and the Literary Guild to suggest or dictate their reading habits are unconscious accomplices in the process of popularization. But, whether the reader's taste be high or low, whether he submits to the popular evaluation of current books or revolts against it, whether he is enslaved or emancipated from moral and aesthetic taboos, he plays a usually inglorious part in the making of American literature, though his judgment helps ultimately to create that atmosphere of critical and uncritical opinion that makes an author conspicuous or neglected.

THE NOVEL

Of all the forms of imaginative literature practiced in America during the last generation, the novel has proved the most popular. Despite the birth of the new drama, despite the revival of poetry in the years just preceding the World War, the novel is still the literary form to which most readers turn first for amusement or enlightenment. Over and beyond the elementary appeal of a story vividly and emotionally told, the contemporary novel offers a variety of forms for the most inexacting or fastidious of readers.

On the popular plane, two types of novels have defined and differentiated themselves during the period and achieved enormous popularity. These forms—detective and western fiction—approach literature with the greatest infrequency, though, under the influence of tremendous competition and of the developing discrimination of their readers, they have shown some increase in dexterity, ingenuity, and the exploitation of extraneous allurements. Thus it is that no account of the American novel of our generation is complete without at least the mention of such popular practitioners of the detective story as Dashiell Hammett, S. S. Van Dine, Ellery Queen, and Agatha Christie, or such professional purveyors of westerns as Max Brand, Jackson Gregory, Clarence Mulford, and Charles A. Seltzer. Nor is it possible to omit from a complete picture the wholesale manufacture and distribution of the sentimental novel. Many serious American novelists have their sentimental moments, since sentimentalism is part and parcel of the Anglo-Saxon temper, but it is in the novel dedicated to sentimentalism that diligent authors have reaped their largest rewards in numbers of readers and royalties. A roll call of the sentimental novelists of the last forty years would include the most popular, if not the most praised, novelists of these years, from John Fox, James Lane Allen, Kate Douglas Wiggin, and Alice Hegan Rice, to Harold Bell Wright, Gene Stratton Porter, Joseph C. Lincoln, Temple Bailey, and Faith Baldwin.

Fortunately, the varieties of the contemporary American novel are not limited to the western, the detective story, and the sentimental novel. The fictive impulse has expressed itself seriously in the realistic or naturalistic novel, the social novel, the regional or exotic novel, and the novel conventionally constructed or frankly and violently experimental. Of these major types, the realistic novel demands attention first, since realism, whether infused with sentiment, tempered by regionalism, or pursued into naturalism, has constituted the major mode of fiction cultivated by serious novelists during the last forty years.[1]

GENTEEL REALISM

At the head of the realistic novelists of the older generation stood the *grande dame* of American letters, Edith Wharton (*q.v.*). Both theory and practice linked her with Henry James, whom, indeed, she regarded as the first really artistic English novelist. Her long friendship with him, his constant critical interest in her work and approbation of her methods, confirmed in her an attitude toward life and art closely allied to his. With James, Mrs. Wharton shared the conviction that the novel should have a carefully constructed pattern, presenting a moral problem involving personalities, subtle and unsubtle, in a highly civilized setting. With James, she shared a distaste for the shambling methods of the great English novelists from Fielding to Thackeray, and an almost romantic devotion to old civilizations and to their rich traditions in manners and conduct. They were alike, too, in their somewhat chilly aloofness, in their preoccupation with moral problems of such rarity as to lay them both open to charges of casuistry and unreality. They were alike, finally, in their distaste for the banal in life and art, for the vulgar and crude and morally shabby. Both had the loftiest conception of the functions of the artist and of art in a civilized community, and pursued their own creative activity with immense conscientiousness.

Though Mrs. Wharton's work in the novel was fundamentally realistic, it showed considerable variety within the limits of that mode. Indeed, her early novel, *The Valley of Decision* (1902), was an elaborate and industrious attempt at an historical novel in an eighteenth-century Italian setting. This serious though somewhat frigid treatment of a novelistic type immensely popular just at the turn of the century was not, however, prophetic of her characteristic work. Nor were her short novels of rural New England life, *Ethan Frome* (1911) and *Summer* (1917), entirely typical, though they demonstrated persuasively her ability to create characters outside the narrow limits of her own class, and though the first of these novels, a brilliant picture of fire burning through the gnarled oak of New England character, is as surely a classic as any of her fiction. She was least happy in her ephemeral fiction inspired by the World War; *The Marne* (1918) and *A Son at the Front* (1923) are now interesting chiefly as illustrations of the deceptive illusions of the war psychosis. Mrs. Wharton's most distinctive work concerned the upper reaches of American so-

[1] Lest logicians charge me with violating the principle of division in the organization of this chapter, I hasten to say that I am quite aware of the fact that Realism, Regionalism, Exoticism, and the Historical Novel do not belong to the same logical categories. Though it would have been possible to organize all the material here under the heads of Realism, Romanticism, and combinations of the two, I have sought illumination at the expense of logic.

ciety in a native rather than a Continental setting. In this vein, for instance, were *The House of Mirth* (1905), which laid the foundation of her deserved popularity and esteem; *The Custom of the Country* (1913), a venomous portrait of a beautiful but unscrupulous social climber, Undine Spragg; *The Age of Innocence* (1920), a subtle reconstruction of the New York of Mrs. Wharton's socially cloistered girlhood; and *Hudson River Bracketed* (1929), perhaps the most successful of her later studies of an evanescent period in the social history of New York.

Mrs. Wharton's reputation as a novelist has suffered considerably from the facts that it was already well established by 1914, and that, after that time, her artistry showed little or no advance. Moreover, the technique and tone of her work found serious rivals in the vigorous developments in the novel of the twenties and thirties. But the evidences that her work furnished of both the strength and the weakness of the genteel tradition, should not blind us to her essential and enduring powers: the virtues of design and composition, of clarity and dignity, of good manners and elegance. Time made clear the limitations of her art, which were no other than the limitations of her personality and her experience. Only rarely was she able to depict with sympathy experience beyond her own; vulgar persons who attempted to scale the serene heights on which she dwelt were overwhelmed with merciless satire. Her later works also suffered from her deliberate alienation from her native soil; her negligible contact with contemporary American life forced her to rely on recollection and reminiscence: in consequence, her re-creations of things past, remote from the calculated brutalities of post-war fiction, seemed a little faded and slight. Inflexibility and fastidiousness have their penalties no less than their legitimate rewards.

Echoes of the Jamesian tradition may be heard in the novels of Anne Douglas Sedgwick (*q.v.*). Like James, she was inclined to restrict her characters to the higher economic levels of international society. Her most widely read novels—*Tante* (1911) and *The Little French Girl* (1924)—revealed an enviable power to infuse emotion into essentially well-bred fiction, and to exploit with insight and conviction the vagaries of artistic or alien temperaments.

With the genteel realism of the older generation, it is not inappropriate perhaps to associate the distinguished novels of Willa Cather (*q.v.*). Like Mrs. Wharton and Miss Sedgwick, Miss Cather is steadily on the side of beauty and integrity and against shoddiness, duplicity, and vulgarity in high or low circles. Like them and their master, she regards her art with complete seriousness, and considers each successive novel a challenge to a fresh experiment in subject matter or technique, an obligation not to repeat with increased ease the pattern and manner of an earlier success. Consequently, her work displays a refreshing variety within the field of her particular interests. But the spiritual conservatism of her later work tends to ally her with the older rather than with the younger generation of realistic novelists.

In her most satisfying novels, Miss Cather finds her material in the life of the pioneer, the valiant spirit who adventures dangerously in life or in art. During her early life in Nebraska, she was moved by curiosity and sympathy to study lovingly those Teutonic and Slavic stocks that were carving livelihoods for themselves out of the endless prairies. In more recent works, such as *Death Comes for the Archbishop* (1927) and *Shadows on the Rock* (1931), she has demonstrated the continuation of her interest in the lives and fates of the pioneers, whether they met their fates in the Southwest or in seventeenth-century Quebec. The pioneering spirit in homesteader or artist has always seemed to her more admirable than the spirit of the compact citizen or the vulgarized peasant on Main Street. Her admiration goes out eagerly to those women whose serene and enduring stability have served them well on the frontiers of physical or artistic life, and her Ântonia Shimerda and Thea Kronberg are moving embodiments of the spirits of such women. To her favorite subjects, Miss Cather has always responded appreciatively, and her peasants and artists, her pioneers and churchmen, are singularly alive and unliterary.

In the treatment of her material, Miss Cather has shown unwearied conscientiousness as to form and finish. Her style is perpetually chaste and refreshing. It is permeated with poetic sensibility. It has the simplicity of first-rate work, but it is the simplicity of art, not of nature. She has sought steadily a form of the novel adequate to her purpose. Only in *The Song of the Lark* (1915) has she been entirely contented with the solid superstructure of the realistic novel of the old style. In general, she has preferred to dispense largely with plot, to avoid the big scene, and to build her fiction out of only such material as seems relevant to the creation and evaluation of significant characters. Her art has aimed constantly at the progressive elimination of nonessentials.

If Miss Cather's later novels have not quite fulfilled the promise of such robust creations as *O Pioneers!* (1913) and *My Ântonia* (1918), if such novels of sensibility as *Shadows on the Rock* (1931) and *Lucy Gayheart* (1935) seem somehow unsubstantial and sentimental, one is forced to inquire why Miss Cather seems, not a less distinguished but a less vital novelist than she seemed fifteen or more years ago. The suspicion grows that Miss Cather has never possessed any large measure of the creative imagination, that she has always had to rely on observation and reading for her materials. In the more successful of her later novels, she has inclined more and more to turn to history for her subjects and to present that history in decorous pastel colors. The sparseness of such a tale as *My Mortal Enemy* (1926) or the sentimental fragility of *Lucy Gayheart* (1935) implies a profound movement of her spirit away from coarse vitality toward what is merely soft and pleasant. The exquisite style and finish persist, but the spirit within becomes or threatens to become sentimental and flaccid.

SENTIMENTAL REALISM

In a period in which the dominant literary mode in the novel is realism, it is inevitable that a goodly number of writers should assume its manner without honestly possessing its spirit. It is inevitable, too, that the dominant literary coin should suffer the admixture of alloys which debase it and render it suspect, if not actually illegal tender. The alloy most frequently found in American realism is that of sentiment or sentimentality. The element of sentimentality in the American character is fundamental; it is the slightly morbid by-product of the courage and optimism that have subdued a continent and mechanized a civilization. There is no doubting the existence of sentimentality; the function of the critic is to describe it and detect it when it attempts to pass itself off as something other than it actually is.

Sentimental realism assumes the appearance of realism in its style, its appetite for descriptive detail, and its utilization of colloquial or semi-colloquial discourse. It pretends to offer a picture and an interpretation of the life that is being lived in America today. It is to be distinguished from true realism, not merely by its infatuation with such wishful-thinking as the "happy ending" but by the view of life that lurks behind the pseudo-realistic façade. That view of life, when closely inspected, is a travesty of the vigorous optimism characteristic of the American spirit. The admixture of sentimentalism in realism betrays itself by its decorously veiled eroticism, its well-bred shuddering back from the shadows and complexities of the psychological and economic picture, its over-simplification of human nature as black or white or easily dry-cleaned grays, its reliance upon feeling rather than intelligence to carry characters through a problematical existence, and its hopeful insistence that everything will turn out all right in the end. Though sentimental realism has many followers among fairly reputable American authors, though it has won millions of American and alien readers, it is essentially a bastard literary mode. Only rarely can it produce masterpieces within its own limits: its softness and prettiness restrict it to the middle ranges of novelistic achievement.

Sentimental realism should be distinguished from both pure realism and pure sentimentalism. The differences, to be sure, are differences of degree and not of kind. At the one extreme is realism, with its avowed devotion to the faithful representation of human experience, not in the world of the imagination, but in the world of bread and butter, of grubs and daisies. At the other is sentimentalism, with its exploitation of the tenderer emotions and its fundamental falsification of human values in the interest of a pleasant titillation of the more respectable emotions.

Sentimental realism attempts a compromise between realism and sentimentalism, and, like most compromises, it does justice to neither party. Its hands are the hands of the realist, but its heart is the heart of the sentimentalist.

Since current sentimental realism is more persuasively realistic in its surface manifestations than the sentimental realism of an earlier generation, it is infinitely easier to descry the sentimental element in fiction of the earlier type. Frances Hodgson Burnett (1849–1924) may serve as a convenient norm for the more reputable sentimental realism of the pre-war period. She settled down to the prettification of childhood in *Editha's Burglar* (1886) and *Sara Crewe* (1888), better known under the title of *The Little Princess*, but *Little Lord Fauntleroy* (1886), successfully dramatized (1888) and effectively treated on the screen (1936), seems likely to stand as an exemplar of an expert but fundamentally saccharine study of childhood. In her later work, to be sure, sentimentalism took on a more subtle form, and such novels as *The Secret Garden* (1911) and *T. Tembarom* (1913) are creditable contributions to the sentimental realism of that decade.

In the relaxed atmosphere of pre-war America, the easy optimism of sentimental realism frequently allied itself with humor. Some of the most cherished examples in this genre are not undistinguished creations of American domestic humor. Here belong, for instance, such triumphant fusions of humor and pathos as Kate Douglas Wiggin's *The Birds' Christmas Carol* (1887) and *Rebecca of Sunnybrook Farm* (1903), the latter a best-seller of its day and notably successful as a moving picture later. To this category, too, belong such household favorites as Irving Bacheller's *Eben Holden* (1900), E. N. Westcott's *David Harum* (1900), and Alice Hegan Rice's *Mrs. Wiggs of the Cabbage Patch* (1901). The latter two novels received successful screen presentation as late as 1934.

The most distinguished of the sentimental realists of the early contemporary period is Booth Tarkington (*q.v.*). His prolific activity has not, to be sure, been restricted to realism of this variety. He had his share in the vogue of the pseudo-historical romance at the turn of the century, and in its first decade, deeply conscious of its moral purpose, he contributed to the emergent social novel such familiar titles as *The Gentleman from Indiana* (1899) and *The Conquest of Canaan* (1905). He likewise wrote for the stage a long series of comedies, fundamentally sentimental in nature. But his most popular work in the novel is the genial treatment of adolescent and adult life in the Middle West. In *Penrod* (1914) and *Seventeen* (1916), for example, he delighted a vast audience by superficially faithful but essentially prudish studies of boyhood and adolescence. His more important novels of adult life, *The Turmoil* (1915) and *The Magnificent Ambersons* (1918), are skilled creations of the surfaces of reality, though they descend to flattering the popular American faith in the all-conquering power of integrity and the inevitability of the happy ending. The best work Tarkington has done is in the vein of honest realism which reflects lower-middle-class life in small middle western cities, without an incursion of inappropriate humor or sentimentality. *Alice Adams* (1921) is perhaps the most honest piece of work that has come from his pen. On the whole, his technical expertness has been negated by his ostrich-like sentimentalism.

A goodly company of women novelists of a later generation, wholesale manufacturers of fiction for the not too critical, may legitimately be classified as sentimental realists. Of these the most prolific and conspicuous is Kathleen Norris, whose formula for fiction for the women's magazines has brought her larger financial than artistic returns. Mrs. Norris is skilled in combining the emotionally problematical with a fundamental ethical conservatism that makes her novels morally undisturbing to hundreds of thousands of readers. Among her more than forty novels it is not easy to distinguish the more skillful, but *Mother* (1911), *The Story of Julia Page* (1915), *Certain People of Importance* (1922), *Foolish Virgin* (1928), and *Heartbroken Melody* (1938) have been most enthusiastically welcomed by her immense public. On a slightly more elevated plane of novelistic accomplishment is the work of Fannie Hurst (*q.v.*), a less prolific and more honest manufacturer. Miss Hurst is more adventurous than Mrs. Norris in her quest for material. She is expert in the ways of metropolitan New York, and some of her most effective fictions have drawn on the picturesque careers of characters of Hebraic-American stock. Miss Hurst's crowded canvases are too highly colored, the paint is laid on with strokes too broad to permit of much aesthetic subtlety. But such novels as *Stardust* (1919) and *Mannequin* (1926) render the more flashy aspects of New York existence graphically, and her use of racial material in *Humoresque* (1918) is lively and well informed.

Of the sentimental realists of her particular generation, Edna Ferber (*q.v.*) is probably the most deserving of critical consideration. Her range is wide; her intentions are ambitious. Her first successes—*Emma McChesney and Co.* (1915) and *The Girls* (1921)—concerned the intrusion of women into business and the professions and are now badly dated, but they have some significance as reflecting a particular moment in our economic life. But Miss Ferber has been well advised to diversify her program of production. In *So Big* (1924), *Show Boat* (1926), *Cimarron* (1930), and *Come and Get It* (1935), she has turned to the exploitation of the rich material to be found in middle western economic and social life of the late nineteenth and early twentieth centuries, and the results, although chromolithographic, have proved exceedingly popular contributions to regional-historical fiction.

TOWARD NATURALISM

The genteel tradition of William Dean Howells and Henry James, and of their feminine admirers and emulators, has had a vigorous rival in a less inhibited realism that has gradually merged into naturalism. The naturalists aimed to treat freely all aspects of human experience, to record what they saw without moral or ethical bias, and to set down all the facts they could collect, with as little artistic selection and arrangement as possible. In point of practice, however, most of the naturalists tended to see human life as a relatively undifferentiated form of animal life. At least, they made their horrified readers intensely aware of the animal elements in human behavior.

Such doctrines made their way with difficulty in the face of the ingrained prudery and sentimentality of American publishers and readers, but one can trace their beginnings fairly clearly in the last decade of the nineteenth century in the brilliant innovations of Stephen Crane (1871–1900), their development before the World War in such writers as Frank Norris (1870–1902) and Jack London (1876–1916), and their fruition in Theodore Dreiser (*q.v.*) and the naturalists of the twenties and thirties. Of the work of the pioneers in naturalism that of Stephen Crane seems likely to be of the greatest historical and aesthetic interest. His audacious stylistic experimentation is a continuing influence on the contemporary literary impressionists. Crane's combination of poetically sensitive observation and unqualified realism makes him seem a creature born before his time. In his novel *Maggie, A Girl of the Streets* (1893), he essayed a subject and method which his American contemporaries left cautiously alone. Probably no war novel written in English before 1914 equals *The Red Badge of Courage* (1895) in unflinching fidelity to fact, impressionistic brilliance, and psychological verisimilitude. The interest in his work manifested by writers as diverse as Henry James and Joseph Conrad only strengthens one's sense of the loss American letters suffered in Crane's untimely death. Somewhat more self-consciously masculine than Crane's was the work of Frank Norris, whose life span coincided almost exactly with Crane's and whose work is only slightly less promising. Such a venture into naturalism as *McTeague* (1899) now seems unbearably crude and bathetic, but, at the time, it was a valuable protest against the namby-pamby quality of much American fiction. The grandiose conceptions that underlie such novels as *The Octopus* (1901) and *The Pit* (1903) stir one's admiration for his courage in treating American economic material in an epic vein. The best work of Jack London belongs with the romance of primitive adventure, rather than with naturalism, but his thinly disguised autobiographical fictions, *Martin Eden* (1909) and *John Barleycorn* (1913), as well as his social novels, suggest his courage in breaking with a timorous genteel tradition, while they reveal his exaggerated virility and almost pathological brutality.

But it is in the novels of Theodore Dreiser that naturalism of the traditional Continental variety is most perfectly illustrated. Dreiser, like the great French naturalist, Emile Zola, appreciates the terrible complexity of modern industrial society. In the intense economic struggle, he sees strong-willed financiers or "geniuses" forcing their ways to positions of transient eminence. But he has also seen hundreds of men fail, through inner weakness or outer circumstance, to exact what they desire from the indifferent or hostile social organism. He is moved imaginatively by the misery and poverty in which thousands of people are condemned to live under the competitive capitalistic system. The struggle between impotent individuals and powerful social forces fills Dreiser, not with admiration or triumphant joy, but with a despair that is untempered by the quiet consolation of beauty. To beauty in nature he seems curiously unresponsive, and such luxury and elegance as he sometimes attempts to depict is tasteless and ugly. The world through which Dreiser's characters move is drab and grim and threatening. In his view of life, there is no place for prettiness or sentiment. Since he sees in human character little that is beautiful or admirable except its power to endure mistreatment at the hands of an indifferent society, his interpretation of human experience is, in the main, dispiriting. But the worst that can be said of it is that his interpretation lacks the equable balance of the artist of the first rank, that it is willfully tentative, unsystematic, and agnostic.

Dreiser's often clumsy and imperfect artistry fails to transmit satisfactorily his somber broodings over hapless mankind. His style is sometimes unbearably conventional and commonplace. His control of grammar is intermittent, and his feeling for the fresh or the delightful word seems negligible. A more serious weakness perhaps is his inability to distinguish between the significant and the insignificant detail. He adheres too closely to the naturalistic tenet of inselectivity; he seems to collect facts for the facts' sake, and, though the total effect is undeniably massive, the weight of inconsequential details impedes the movement of the narrative and tends to obscure really crucial events.

But the peculiar virtues of Dreiser go a considerable distance in offsetting his obvious weaknesses. He has a dogged devotion to the collection of material, an unwavering honesty in the contemplation of human motives, and a penetration into the subterfuges and sufferings of hapless mortals which make him perhaps the most skilled of contemporary American novelists in evoking pity and terror from naturalistic tragedy. *An American Tragedy* (1925) is not merely a loving representation of the lives of the obscure, but an oppressively powerful study of a youth who at first seems despicably weak but who through the intensity of his suffering in the grip of the law becomes a heartbreaking symbol of crucified humanity. If the tragedy is not merely American but universal, it is because Dreiser's apprehension of life is perhaps as large and generous as that of any American novelist of our time.

BEYOND NATURALISM

The spirit of naturalism regnant in Dreiser has been conspicuously influential in the American fiction of the post-war years, though it has taken on an astonishing variety of forms and manners. The heavily circumstantial and infinitely detailed naturalism characteristic of Dreiser and his French and German prototypes has not been able to retain the interest or challenge the imitation of the younger and more impatient writers of the jazz age and the depression. The most important ally of realism and naturalism in the fiction of the last generation has been the urge for social reform, the desire to depict the horrors of contemporary society in order to arouse indignation or to suggest a scheme or design for abolishing the evils and for remaking the social system. This alliance between realism and reform has borne such ample fruits that they call for separate and distinct discussion, but it should not be forgotten that this union is perhaps the most important permutation of the spirit of realism.

But naturalism has assumed other guises than that of the novel of social reform. In the main, the naturalistic novel has tended to develop in the direction of deeper and deeper subjectivity or more and more austere objectivity. These two fairly distinct trends become apparent, once one attempts to classify naturalistic phenomena in recent American fiction.

Among the older naturalists, the trend toward the subjective can be illustrated clearly in the work of Sherwood Anderson (*q.v.*). Anderson has concerned himself in the main with the lives and emotions of the folk. On the surface, the life of the folk seems drab and insignificant, but Anderson's intuition and imagination break through the surface dullness, and reveal the intense and complex passion beneath. It is Anderson's mission to give persuasive expression to the inarticulate.

For the furtherance of this purpose, Anderson has had no little difficulty in finding a suitable and significant form. He has little skill in manipulating more than two or three characters, or in working these characters into effective patterns. The secondary characters are often treated very casually and, like the old harnessmaker in *Poor White* (1920), seem to play no integral part in the pattern of the novel. His frequent digressions, his little essays on American ideas and ways, likewise tend to blur the outlines of his creative forms.

Anderson has had greater success in working out a style appropriate to his material, a form of recorded speech far from the conventionality of most novelistic styles. In the brevity of his sentences, the frequency of the *and*-construction, the avoidance of literary diction, his style is closer to the level of American colloquial language than that of any novelist of his generation. But it is lifted above the merely colloquial by his fine sense of rhythm, his sensitive repetitions, and his poetic use of even familiar words and phrases. Not the least striking evidence of Anderson's great influence on younger writers is the intensely colloquial quality of the style of writers as diverse as Ernest Hemingway, James W. Cain, and James T. Farrell.

Anderson's material is somewhat unfortunately limited to his own experience and his own reactions to life. Since the publication of his autobiography, *A Story-Teller's Story* (1924), it has been possible to determine the great frequency with which he has thrown a thin veil of fiction over actual characters and incidents. The judge of the autobiography appears as a minor character in several novels and under several names. Anderson's father, who obviously played a very important part in the boy's psychic development, appears as Windy McPherson's father and in other disguises as well. Anderson's heroes, moreover, seem to be variations on his own introverted personality, most sensitively projected, perhaps, in the hero of *Poor White*. His heroes recapitulate each other's experiences. They tend to run away almost without warning, usually from their wives. Suffering vaguely from a profound dissatisfaction with the universe, they go blundering off in quest of some meaning to life or some solution of their personal problems. Sometimes the hero's quest ends in a woman, as in *Dark Laughter* (1925), and sometimes, as in *Marching Men* (1917), in a vague social idea. But, despite the limitations of Anderson's imagination and his technique, he is as authentically American as a canvas of Grant Wood's, though, of course, more tortuously and deviously introverted.

The trend toward naturalistic subjectivity may be illustrated by the work of a number of younger novelists. The psychological naturalism that is so essential an element in the poetry of Conrad Aiken (*q.v.*) carries over constantly into his fiction, and, although his characters are more subtle, self-conscious, and articulate than those of Anderson, the subjective emphasis is clearly apparent in such novels as *Blue Voyage* (1927), written under the influence of James Joyce's incredibly subjective *Ulysses*, or *Great Circle* (1933). The naturalism of Evelyn Scott (*q.v.*) has an emphatically, not to say a personally subjective quality. Her earlier novels—*The Narrow House* (1921) and *Narcissus* (1922)—specialized in sensitive reactions to the physically unpleasant, and this habit of relentless, almost morbid psychological notation, is not without its influence in her more objective work in the historical novel, *The Wave* (1929), or in her excursion into post-Victorian social life in *Breathe upon These Slain* (1934).

Vardis Fisher (*q.v.*) comes closer to the circumstantial naturalism of Dreiser than any of the other subjective naturalists. Here we have a power similar to Dreiser's in the registering of both objective and subjective details as well as something of the master's gigantesque massiveness. But the impassivity and impartiality of naturalistic objectivism are quite gone. For Fisher's unfatigued but somewhat fatiguing accumulation of external details is nothing in comparison to his avidity in the accumulation of subjective details. His hero's passion for self-analysis is insatiable, and his ill-concealed delight in the exhibition of his interminable agonies runs a very serious risk of alienating even the most patient reader. But in its particular genre, Fisher's tetralogy is as yet unrivaled in American letters.

Vardis Fisher had a serious rival in endurance and prodigious creativeness in Thomas Wolfe (*q.v.*), whose seemingly inexhaustible expressiveness is already legendary. Thomas Wolfe was, of course, a far less subjective writer than Fisher, far less encumbered by the chains of his own personality, but he resembled him in the unending amplitude of his narrative and analysis. In sheer creativeness, he surpassed all the psychological naturalists, and, although his endless flow of observation and incident seemed completely unrestrained and uncritical, the dynamic force of the man overpowered criticism. That force is apparent, not merely in the physical magnitude of such works as *Look Homeward, Angel* (1929) and *Of Time and the River* (1935), but in their imaginative intensity and grandeur. Wolfe had a strong sense of the epic character, an imagination that moved easily on the plane of the grand and the grandiose, and—what is rarer in American fiction—the combination of great vitality and a strong lyrical impulse.

In William Faulkner (*q.v.*), subjective naturalism reaches its climax; it is doubtful whether the method can be carried to any greater depth of psychological experience. For not only does Faulkner restrict himself to a subjective presentation of both mental and physical events, shifting somewhat bewilderingly from mind to mind in successive passages or chapters of his novels, but he frequently deepens the subjectivity by making the experiencing mind intellectually subnormal or emotionally abnormal. The result is that, although in Faulkner's fiction decency and normality are not always brutally victimized, the world in which his characters live is seriously distorted by the nature of the observant narrator. The Deep South, as Faulkner depicts it, is the abode, not of gentility and elegance, but of degeneracy and morbidity. His stress on the more depraved elements in the society of which he writes, ends by giving his fiction, despite the extreme naturalism of his method, a nightmarish quality of diabolism suggestive of Baudelaire and the decadent romanticism of the later nineteenth century. But Faulkner's world is unmistakably his own, and its power over one's imagination and its persuasion of one's emotion are no slight measures of his unquestioned though morbid talent.

Impressive in number and power as are the novels of the subjective naturalists, they cannot be said to be so numerous, popular, or influential as the novels of the objective naturalists. The vogue of naturalism in the decades since the war may be partly a reaction from the orgiastic emotionalism of the war period and partly an evidence of the increasing awareness of the insignificance of the individual experience and the growing importance of the social group. Certainly, both the jazz age and the depression, oddly various as those periods were, contributed toward a hardening of the surface of fiction, a greater frankness and directness in the rendition of characters and their behavior, and the suppression of subtle, psychological analysis as too softheaded and tenderhearted. The sophistication that characterized the jazz age expressed itself in various types of fiction: the excessively imitated depiction of flaming youth in F. Scott Fitzgerald's (*q.v.*) *This Side of Paradise* (1920), the cynical crudities of Ben Hecht's (*q.v.*) *Erik Dorn* (1921), the elegant fantasies of Carl Van Vechten's (*q.v.*) *Peter Whiffle* (1922) and *The Blind Bow-Boy* (1923), and the apish honesties and sardonic humors of Maxwell Bodenheim's *Replenishing Jessica* (1925) and *Georgie May* (1928).

But the form that the spirit of the period assumed most frequently was the objective naturalism illustrated in the novels of Ernest Hemingway (*q.v.*), the founder and master of the "hard-boiled" novel. Upon analysis, the "hard-boiled" elements in Hemingway's fiction turn out to be technical rather than psychological: the reduction of oral discourse to monosyllabic inexpressiveness, the stress on the kaleidoscopic whirl of sensation rather than on freely associated ideas or deeply felt emotions, and the tendency to abandon, or at least to obscure, the more formal elements of plot, and to let the story take form from the whirling sensations and the monosyllabic utterances of the characters. These devices he used with extraordinary effectiveness in both *The Sun Also Rises* (1926) and *A Farewell to Arms* (1929). If the successors to these novels have been written by other authors than Hemingway, it may be because he has come to feel the limited effectiveness of these devices in extended works of fiction; after all, they are more suitable to the smaller canvas of the experimental short story. But on other writers Hemingway's view of life has proved as influential as his technique. The point of view implicit in his novels and short stories is that of a man bent on complete honesty concerning himself and the rest of the world, determined to reject the insidiously soft and sentimental, persuaded of the worth of nothing save the elementary satisfactions of mankind: wine, women, and sport, but ever intent on the preservation of his integrity, on not letting himself or anyone else down despite the threats and menaces of a hostile universe. This determined robustness and grim, not to say taciturn, masculinity—easily and widely imitated as they have been—have turned out to be serious handicaps to Hemingway's development as an artist. His insistence on these qualities has led some critics to suspect in them an excess of protestation, to see them as mechanisms used to defend himself against the demands of a genuinely compassionate and complex personality. Certainly in Hemingway, as in many another "hard-boiled" writer, tenderness, not to mention sentimentality, is not very far beneath the muscular surface.

Many of Hemingway's technical habits can be descried in Erskine Caldwell (*q.v.*): the skilled handling of the colloquial, the vivid objective notation of persons and places, the apparent casualness with which the grotesque and the horrible are accepted. The attitude behind Caldwell's work is less easily distinguishable; the fiction is more purely objective. But something of his attitude may be inferred from his choice of subject and from the emotion that rises out of his presentation of his material. His subject matter is almost steadily coarse and earthy, but the emotions that invest his presentation of brutality and lustfulness are the curiously opposed ones of horror and mirth. The horror, to be sure, is much more easily detected than the mirth, but such novels as *Tobacco Road* (1932) and *God's Little Acre* (1933) are sufficient indications that laughter can arise from an unabashed exhibition of degradation and degeneracy. The peculiar comic quality of these works would seem to depend on the author's success in repressing the normal reactions to physical and moral degeneracy and stressing the exciting vitality which somehow manifests itself in the most grotesque diversions of the will to live. What Caldwell seems to be creating is naturalistic comedy, a genre almost unknown to the American reader; in any case, it is the creation of such comedy rather than the repetitions of the calculated brutalities of naturalistic tragedy that is Caldwell's major innovation.

The gloomy atmosphere of the depression has been an appropriate, if not an inevitable, setting for the vogue of the "hard-boiled" novel. Among the younger contributors to this vogue, John O'Hara (*q.v.*) and James M. Cain deserve brief mention. O'Hara's *Appointment in Samarra* (1934) and *Butterfield 8* (1935), though more subjective than most of Caldwell's fiction, show the same skill in the manipulation of urban and suburban colloquialism, a brilliant rendition of the streams of consciousness of his bourgeois and proletarian characters, and real power in suggesting the empty banality of his characters' outer lives. The tone is only apparently callous; the emotional effect depends on O'Hara's poignant suggestion of his frustrated characters' potentialities for decency and tenderness, not to say happiness. In James M. Cain's *The Postman Always Rings Twice* (1934), the devices characteristic of Hemingway and Caldwell are assiduously and successfully cultivated. Cain's characters are at once inarticulate and uninhibited; for many of his readers, the brutalities of their lives will seem the only and questionable values, but here, as in the novels of Cain's elders, the attentive reader will find, beneath the brutality, a stirring of fine feeling. In consequence, the final effect comes close to that of genuine naturalistic tragedy.[1]

One final instance of objective naturalism may be cited. James T. Farrell (*q.v.*) has made an elaborate and persistent use of the naturalistic

[1] There was no suspicion of tenderness in Jerome Weidman's *I Can Get It for You Wholesale* (1937) and its sequel, *What's in It for Me?* (1938). These accounts of the New York life of Jewish business shysters aroused vigorous protests against the savagery of their naturalism.

technique in his *Studs Lonigan* trilogy (1932–35). It is difficult indeed to see how his chosen material could be presented otherwise. For Farrell's characters inhabit the depressed and decadent areas on Chicago's South Side, and are conditioned early by frequent contacts with street gangs and petty criminals. Most of his characters are casual in their morality; many of them are purely vicious. To the presentation of such unsavory material, Farrell brings stores of information and insight born of experience and observation. He seems blessed with an unlimited interest in the mean creatures of his grimy world, a considerable understanding of them, and sympathy for them. Farrell's naturalism, like most naturalism, is not conspicuous for its restraint, and, though it is not permissible to raise the question of good or bad taste in such determinedly naturalistic fiction, one may be permitted to wonder whether Farrell's wretched hero deserves the hundreds of pages his energetic young author has lavished on him.

The limits of objective naturalism are precise; its potentialities are not unbounded. Moreover, naturalism—both objective and subjective—is relatively new in American literature, and it is certainly alien to the conventional reader. Objective naturalism is too callous, subjective naturalism too morbid, for normal American taste. The tendency of naturalism to take unto itself a moral purpose, a social mission, would seem to be not merely an honorable but an astute step. For naturalism, allied as it frequently was in the period of the depression with a passion for remolding society, is much more likely to gain a respectful hearing from American readers and critics than naturalism intent merely on brutality or self-torture. At any rate, the union of naturalism and social purpose in the proletarian novel makes the latest chapter in the history of the American social novel one of its most exciting.

REGIONALISM

Despite the standardizing influences so conspicuous in American life, despite the fatal lure New York continues to have for the youthful artist and author, despite the concentration of critical and publishing activity in that city, the influence of regionalism is still a pervasive and invigorating element in the American novel of our time. Were it not for its persistence, American fiction would be a vastly less colorful and variegated thing than it is. The influence of regionalism made its appearance in American literature almost as soon as a consciousness arose of differences among the seacoast settlements and between these and the frontier settlements of the interior. But it was only the spread of realism in the nineteenth century that pointed the way of writers to the rich materials various sections of America offered for loving or satirical treatment. The work of writers as different as Harriet Beecher Stowe, Mark Twain, and

Bret Harte takes on a new interest and significance when it is viewed in terms of their regional affiliations and antipathies.[1]

In the earlier phases of the regionalist movement, its association with sentimentalism or romanticism is much more conspicuous than its alliance with realism. The reason for these admixtures is fairly obvious. The cult of the quaint and the picturesque tempted the "local color" writers of the period after the Civil War to a sentimental-humorous exploitation of provincial eccentricities or to a conventionalization of both character and situation that often ended in the sterility of the merely regional. It remained for more robust contemporary novelists to raise regional material to the level of national significance through the facing of the economic and social facts under the picturesque exteriors. Much early—and some recent—regionalism has joined hands easily with the variety of romanticism which relies in large measure for its effectiveness on the exotic elements of its setting. The romantic appeal of the Old South or of the Southwest seems inexhaustible, and its exploitation on both serious or frivolous levels still continues.

But perhaps it has not been sufficiently observed that the concept of regionalism is almost always associated with rural rather than with urban America. There is little logic in this association, though there are some reasons for it. Though certain American cities have individual characters, our cities in general tend, more rapidly than our rural areas, to achieve uniformity and standardization; they become norms for manners and behavior by which regional differences may be measured. The premier position of New York among American cities has tended to obscure in the eyes of writers the interest and the significance of other easily distinguishable cities, and, by and large, a tremendous number of American novels of urban life assume, as a background, not Chicago or New Orleans or San Francisco, but New York. In consequence the American reader is likely to be far better acquainted with Times Square and Park Avenue than he is with Michigan Boulevard or Pennsylvania Avenue.

But, despite the octopus-like grip of New York upon the lives and the imaginations of many American writers, there are signs of interest in the differentia of other urban communities, and, although urban regionalism has not played so conspicuous a part as some might wish in the history of American fiction, the illustrations obtainable are deserving of comment. In fact, the materials offered by both urban and rural regionalism are so abundant and so flavorous that even in a period in which standardization and conventionalization in life and art have made tremendous progress, a large number of contemporary novelists are best understood in terms of the regions of which they write. Such an interpretation is

[1] One man's regionalism is, of course, another man's exoticism: to the northerner the South is exotic; to the westerner, the East. But I have consciously simplified the treatment of regionalism by eliminating a consideration of its exotic appeal to foreigners.

surely legitimate so long as one remembers that regionalism is not a critical category like realism, romanticism, or sentimentalism, and that indeed it allies itself with each of these modes upon occasion.[1]

New England was one of the earliest sections of the country to stimulate the writing of regional fiction, and it is natural that this should be the case. For, as one of the earliest sections of the country to be settled, it has retained its rural character and its fundamental Puritan tradition despite the repeated inroads of immigrants bringing alien cultures, and despite the emergence in the nineteenth century of a Brahmin culture ambitious to escape the bonds of provincialism, and, in such figures as Longfellow, Whittier, and Emerson, able for a time to challenge not only national but international attention. The waning of the influence of the New England sages, the departure from New England of its more robust or more thriftless spirits, the incursion of wave after wave of immigrants—Irish, French-Canadian, Italian, and Slavonic—have served only to make sharper the nature of the purely native tradition, and to encourage its record in the novel and the short story. Its imperiled evanescence at first encouraged the viewing of it as sentimental or humorously quaint. Sarah Orne Jewett (1849–1909), an exquisite idealistic artist, played a very considerable part in directing the attention of novelists and short-story writers to the materials available in quiescent Maine seacoast towns, and Mary E. Wilkins Freeman (1862–1930), in *A Humble Romance* (1887), *A New England Nun* (1891), *Pembroke* (1894), and many succeeding volumes, carried on the Jewett tradition on a somewhat sterner realistic plane. With this older group of regionalists belongs Alice Brown, whose well-established reputation is based on her lifelong intimacy and loving treatment of the New England scene. Her favorite forms have been the novel and the short story, but her play, *Children of Earth* (1915), was deemed worthy of the ten-thousand-dollar prize offered by Winthrop Ames. To the tragic potentialities in the New England character Mrs. Wharton has given classic treatment in *Ethan Frome* (1911), and her novel *Summer* (1917) fluttered Berkshire society by its revelation of decadence among the native stock in the hills.[2]

Little serious use has as yet been made of the slow attrition of the Yankee tradition under the pressure of alien cultures although the Irish influence seems clearly responsible for the union of decadent Brahminism

[1] It has been estimated that two thousand regional novels were published in the two decades since 1918. In *American Regionalism* (1938), Howard W. Odum and Harry E. Moore write, "If we take the years from 1927 through 1936 or in round numbers the last ten years we find the following distribution. The Northeast leads with 449 titles, followed strangely enough by the Northwest with its 'westerns' with 344, the Southeast with 281, the Middle States with 183, the Southwest with 138, and the Far West with 137."

[2] For many years, on a much lower aesthetic plane, Joseph C. Lincoln has been specializing in the salty humors of Cape Cod fisher folk of Yankee stock, but the humorous eccentrics of *Mr. Pratt* (1906) or *Shavings* (1918) are immersed too completely in a stream of sentimentalism to make his work critically considerable.

and religious illiberalism in Boston, the French-Canadian strain is involved in the sorry history of New England mill-towns, and the Slavonic is of the greatest significance for the local revival of New England agriculture. Of the last theme, Edna Ferber's (*q.v.*) novel, *American Beauty* (1931), was a not too well-considered treatment of the theme which was handled on an even more elementary plane in the moving picture, *Wedding Night* (1935).

Boston and its intellectual neighbor Cambridge have provided useful settings for novels in many moods, from Henry James's malicious satire on feminism in *The Bostonians* (1886) and Robert Grant's solemn problem novels, *Unleavened Bread* (1900) and *The Chippendales* (1909), to Upton Sinclair's (*q.v.*) *Boston* (1928), an impassioned denunciation of the city's behavior during the controversy concerning the Sacco-Vanzetti case. Harvard, perhaps more frequently than any other American university, has been subjected to treatment in fiction, from Charles Flandrau's deftly satirical *Harvard Episodes* (1897) and Owen Wister's (*q.v.*) minor academic classic, *Philosophy Four* (1903), to the harsher realism of John Dos Passos' (*q.v.*) *Streets of Night* (1923) and George Weller's *Not to Eat, Not for Love* (1933).

More serious attempts to capture the spirit of New England and explain its mechanisms have been made in George Santayana's (*q.v.*) *The Last Puritan* (1935) and its impish imitation, John P. Marquand's *The Late George Apley* (1937). Santayana's extraordinarily illuminating novel is logical demonstration of the cumulative negation that results from the Puritan's oppressive sense of duty. The sense of responsibility that dominates Oliver Alden makes every promising human relationship not a source of liberating joy but a duty and an obligation. As a result, when circumstances make it possible for the hapless hero to discharge all his obligations, his personal equation is worked out completely. The answer is zero, and Oliver Alden is dead. The operations of this corrosive sense of duty and the pressures of Brahmin conventions are wittily illustrated in Marquand's lighter novel. Written ostensibly by an editor of staid and conventional memoirs, the novel is almost steadily decorous. It is only rarely that the satirist's tongue is seen squarely in the middle of the author's cheek.

Within the last few years, the fictitious potentialities of Maine's great shipbuilding days have been exploited by a number of her native or adopted sons and daughters. Most indefatigable in the genealogical novel of this locality is Mary Ellen Chase (*q.v.*) in such works as *Mary Peters* (1934) and *Silas Crockett* (1936), but Rachel Field (*q.v.*) in *Time out of Mind* (1935) and Robert P. Tristram Coffin (*q.v.*) in *Red Sky in the Morning* (1935), as well as in his biographical and lyrical writing, have continued to treat this somewhat limited and easily exhausted subject matter.

The overwhelming challenge that New York city offers the creative imagination assists perhaps in explaining why neither New York state nor nearby Pennsylvania has been utilized notably in recent years as material for regional fiction. Of the life of upper New York state, Walter D. Edmonds (*q.v.*) is perhaps the most distinguished literary exponent. *Rome Haul*, as a novel (1929), as a play (1935) and moving picture (1935) under the title *The Farmer Takes a Wife*, reached a tremendous audience, and *Drums along the Mohawk* (1936) is one of the finest current examples of regional historical fiction. Though Philadelphia has passed almost unnoticed (in the shadow of New York) as a subject or background for fiction, John T. McIntyre has recently revealed its unexpected potentialities in his well-documented novels of low life there, *Steps Going Down* (1936) and *Ferment* (1937), the former almost pure naturalism, the latter naturalism diluted with social significance. Pennsylvania has had a number of specialists in its strange "Dutch," Mennonite, and Scotch-Irish survivals. Perhaps the most significant part of Margaret Deland's varied literary activity is her treatment of a village long since absorbed in metropolitan Pittsburgh. At least a half-dozen volumes, from *Old Chester Tales* (1899) to *New Friends in Old Chester* (1924), use material somewhat sentimentally recovered from her early life there. Helen R. Martin and Elsie Singmaster have for the most part confined their writing to the presentation in fiction of the Pennsylvania "Dutch." Miss Singmaster's treatment is perhaps the more somberly true to her rather dour puritanical material. Miss Martin's *Tillie, a Mennonite Maid* (1904) provided suitable material for dramatization as sentimental comedy, but her novel *Barnabetta* (1914) degenerated into farce when dramatized as *Erstwhile Susan* (1916) for one of Minnie Maddern Fiske's unhappier excursions in quest of native American plays.

Joseph Hergesheimer (*q.v.*) is, of course, much more than a Pennsylvania regionalist, but his interest in local antiquarianism and in the impedimenta of interior decoration suggests his deep regional roots. He comes closest to realistic regionalism in such novels as *Mountain Blood* (1915) and *Tol'able David* (1923). But the dominant tone of his writing is romantic, and he follows the conventional trails of the escapist, into history in *The Three Black Pennys* (1917), *Java Head* (1919), and *Balisand* (1924), and into exoticism in *The Bright Shawl* (1922), and *Tampico* (1926). In *Linda Condon* (1919) and *Cytherea* (1922), he found in modern life material for the romantically decorative, and in the latter novel added an exotic appeal in the Cuban setting of the vivid death-scene.

Hergesheimer has an unflagging passion for the decorative, and life in his novels is frequently buried under bric-a-brac. In carrying out his admitted purpose, the setting down of "the colors and scents and emotions of existence," he neglects the emotions for the sake of the colors and scents. Thus, *Linda Condon* has an unquestionable but lifeless beauty, and the emotions of *Cytherea* are grotesque and implausible. If Hergesheimer's novels are sometimes as stuffy as an antique shop, or as overdone as a decorator's studio, the reason may be found in his basically rococo taste, his preference for the elaborately decorative.

For a number of reasons, some of which at least it is easy to discover, the South has proved in both this and earlier generations a happy hunting ground for the writer of regional fiction. The only part of the country to create an aristocratic leisure-class culture, it is likewise the only part of the country to be marked by a catastrophe so striking and memorable as the Civil War. In consequence, southern writers have been stirred to recover and record the beauty and decorum of its pre-war civilization, to present their particular view of the war between the states, and to portray the long slow decline of its civilization in the lethargic generations since the war. The sense of its evanescence has been quickened recently by the incursions of the factory system, an invasion that brings not only its own distressing social and economic problems, but makes the contrast between the ugly present and the glamorous past even more painfully striking. Perhaps these considerations suggest why southern regional literature can usually be designated as romantic rather than realistic, sentimental rather than naturalistic. The older writers of this and the last generation have, in the main, been faithful to the moonlight and roses tradition, and the great success of Stark Young's (*q.v.*) *So Red the Rose* (1934) indicates the persistent appeal to the popular reader of the traditional treatment of aristocratic plantation life in the Old South. Some southern writers, however, have moved with the times to a more critical representation of the past and present of the South.

The sentimental and romantic potentialities in southern material were illustrated long ago in the characteristic novels of James Lane Allen (1849–1925) and John Fox (1862–1919). Of the two writers, Allen, best remembered for his *Kentucky Cardinal* (1895) and *The Choir Invisible* (1897), is the more seriously considerable, although his limitations have recently been demonstrated fully in Grant Knight's *James Lane Allen and the Genteel Tradition* (1935). John Fox, a disciple of Allen's, was at one time a genteel competitor with Harold Bell Wright for the suffrages of the sentimentalists. Even in recent years, *The Little Shepherd of Kingdom Come* (1903) and *The Trail of the Lonesome Pine* (1908) have proved rich quarries for the large emotions and the wholesome moralizing of the moving picture. Fortunately, the successors of these early southern regionalists have not remained contented with such an oversimplification.

The work of Ellen Glasgow (*q.v.*), for example, has been sensitively responsive to the barometer of literary taste. She managed to infuse a considerable amount of realism into her semi-historical novels, *The Battle-Ground* (1902) and *The Deliverance* (1904), and to the social novel, much in vogue in the decade before the war, she contributed such novels as *Virginia* (1913) and *Life and Gabriella* (1916), in which she used native material but adapted it to the consideration of ethical problems usually ignored by the self-conscious gentility of her native state. *Barren Ground* (1925) showed her awareness of the somewhat grimmer realism of the post-war period, *The Romantic Comedians* (1926) her keen appreciation of the futilities of a decadent culture, and *Vein of Iron* (1935), though historical in some measure, is a characteristic reflection of the experiences incidental to the depression.

Miss Glasgow is, then, a serious novelist with a considerable range of subject matter and tone. Her essential fastidiousness appears at its most attractive in the fresh and lucid style of which she is past mistress. But the effect of that fastidiousness on the matter of her fiction is less happy. In her reluctance (or her inability) to subject her characters to any thoroughgoing analysis, in her unwillingness to think uncomfortably, she reveals her fundamental allegiance to the inhibitions of gentility. For a Virginia gentlewoman, Ellen Glasgow has gone a long way. She has not, unfortunately, gone far enough to achieve the creatively first-rate.

The aristocratic tradition of the Old South has left unmistakable trace on the work of James Branch Cabell (*q.v.*). His hostility to realism and his belief that literature is primarily escape and compensation rather than confrontation mark him as a complex offspring of an aristocratic culture. But *The Rivet in Grandfather's Neck* (1915) submits the tradition of gentility to ironical scrutiny, and the steady growth of irony in his later work and the rewriting of his purely romantic novels in terms of innuendo and cynicism, suggest the degree of his emancipation from southern conventions. He is, of course, much more than merely a regionalist.[1]

Elizabeth Madox Roberts (*q.v.*) escapes from a decadent gentility through poetry and fantasy. She is, in fact, a poet who, in a prose age, submits her spirit to the more approachable medium. In such escapes into fantasy as *Jingling in the Wind* (1928) and *A Buried Treasure* (1931), she is not particularly happy. She is not gifted with humor, and the combination of the humorous and the fantastic remains unconvincing. She is happiest when her deeply poetic imagination works on the current or the remote history of her native state, Kentucky. She has never, perhaps, quite equaled the extraordinarily touching blend of realism and poetry in her first novel, *The Time of Man* (1926), certainly one of the finest treatments in American fiction of the primitive life of the mountaineers. Her poetic power also stood her in good stead in her historical novel of the great migration, *The Great Meadow* (1930); here and elsewhere, her grasp on life's essentials is unshaken. Of the middle generation, T. S. Stribling (*q.v.*) has overcome most completely the paralysis of southern gentility. Entirely at ease with his material, he grasps and

[1] For a discussion of the exotic elements in Cabell's work, see pp. 73–74.

presents it with sturdy firmness. Though his accustomed literary mode is the solid circumstantial realism of the old school, and though he is not altogether successful in making credible characters of any contradictory subtlety, he was perhaps the first important southern novelist to handle the complex and tragic problems of that life with courage. Marjorie Kinnan Rawlings has been so shrewd as to choose a hitherto unexploited region as the setting for her novels, *South Moon Under* (1935), *Golden Apples* (1935), and *The Yearling* (1937). Her locale is the scrub-wood back country of Florida, a region of swamps and near-jungles, half-tropical and altogether primitive. She has rendered its flora and fauna with affectionate scrupulosity, and re-created the isolated lives of its folk, the language and manners, with almost sociological expertness. She is least happy in her characterizations of persons foreign to this locale, notably successful, though essentially sentimental, in her treatment of the hammock-country children.

The novelists who have concerned themselves primarily with the part and place of the Negro in southern life constitute a fairly distinct group since their aim is the presentation of only one element in that life. The old habit of romanticizing or melodramatizing this fascinatingly alien material has given way to an almost scientific and anthropological interest in it. Its exoticism must always confer upon it an adventitiously romantic tinge, but the tone of contemporary literature is too austere to permit the sentimentalization or vulgarization conspicuous in earlier efforts to treat the Negro in novel, drama, or poetry. Roark Bradford, to be sure, in such books as *Ol' Man Adam an' His Chillun* (1928) and *Ol' King David an' the Philistine Boys* (1930), might at first sight seem to be carrying on the Joel Chandler Harris tradition, but his work, when more closely inspected, turns out to be an almost scientific, although entirely sympathetic, presentation of the Negroid imagination at work on the Hebraic-Christian biblical story. DuBose Heyward (*q.v.*) and Julia Peterkin (*q.v.*) have been equally successful in shedding their Nordic personalities and identifying themselves with the minds and imagination of the race with which they have been chiefly concerned as writers. The effects of such novels as Heyward's *Porgy* (1925) and *Mamba's Daughters* (1929), and Mrs. Peterkin's *Scarlet Sister Mary* (1928), are far more convincing than most earlier efforts at anthropological excavation and reconstruction in fiction. The happy results of this process of identification are apparent by the immense appeal of *Porgy* in both its dramatic (1927) and operatic (1935) forms and by the even more sensational success of *The Green Pastures*, Marc Connelly's (*q.v.*) dramatic presentation (1930) of the material in Bradford's *Ol' Man Adam an' His Chillun.*

In recent years, three of the most striking figures in contemporary fiction have come out of the South: William Faulkner (*q.v.*), Erskine Caldwell (*q.v.*), and Thomas Wolfe (*q.v.*). These novelists are of far more than regional significance, but the regional element in them cannot be overlooked. Whether they can be most illuminatingly interpreted as naturalistic or as perverse neo-romantics, they surely represent a complete overthrow of the genteel tradition. But the violence with which each of these writers has reacted against the code of decorum indicates perhaps both its persistence and its power. At any rate, the violence of the reaction leads one to expect that gentility and the reaction to it will continue to be powerful influences on the prose and poetry of southern regionalism.

Though the Middle West is not so sharply defined geographically and spiritually as New England and the South, it has a consciousness of its identity and a character sufficiently distinct to stimulate the production of a regional literature. In the literature of the Middle West, rather more easily than in the literature of the East, it is possible and desirable to make a distinction between rural and urban regionalism. Chicago, the great nerve-center of the Mississippi valley, has not only drawn to itself, at one or another time, most writers of middle western origin, but also stimulated the writing of a great many novels depicting its own crude and raucous life. The line of demarcation between the Chicago novel and the rural middle western novel is not always clear; there are novels like Dreiser's *Sister Carrie* and Anderson's *Marching Men*, in which rural and urban regionalism are combined. But the pure types exist and have their particular characters. Middle western rural regionalism is, on the whole, more somber than urban regionalism; it also shows a more uniform character and a more lucid development than the Chicago novel. Both are needed, however, if a comprehensive picture of the culture of the Middle West is to be drawn.

The reason for the somber tone of middle western rural regionalism is the economic and geographic nature of the environment. The starkness of the life on the monotonous prairies, the limited potentialities of their isolated and unlovely villages were described as early as 1883 in E. W. Howe's *Story of a Country Town*. In the next decade, the harsh tone was re-echoed in Hamlin Garland's (*q.v.*) *Main-Travelled Roads* (1891) and *Prairie Folks* (1893), books in which the young author, after his flight to Boston, exposed relentlessly the hardships and deprivations of pioneer life. Though Garland's later novels were less stark, though he mixed sentiment and realism freely, or ventured into the historical romance or the social novel, his early work stamped upon the American consciousness an impression of middle western rural life that has been modified only slightly with the passage of the literary generations.

There were, of course, middle western writers of Garland's own generation whose happier experiences furnished a more genial representation of their native culture. Meredith Nicholson and Booth Tarkington (*q.v.*) did not a little to lift the gloom that shrouded the fiction of the Middle West. Perhaps Nicholson's cheery view of affairs found clearest expression in his essays, *The Hoosiers* (1900) and *The Valley of Democracy* (1918). Booth Tarkington has been notoriously eclectic in his writing of fiction, but, whatever form his work takes, one feels behind it a fundamentally genial and inspiriting view of life. The more attractive aspects of Middle West social and economic life find expression in such novels of his as *The Gentleman from Indiana* (1899), *The Conquest of Canaan* (1905), and *The Magnificent Ambersons* (1918).

But the middle western writers emergent since Tarkington have been less inclined to take a roseate view of their material. We should hardly expect so grim a writer as Theodore Dreiser (*q.v.*) to glorify the Middle West, although his record of a middle-aged return to it in *A Hoosier Holiday* (1916) is unexpectedly kindly. But the rural and village landscapes in *Sister Carrie* (1900) and *Jennie Gerhardt* (1911) are graceless and depressing, and his aggressive heroines escape as early as possible from the restrictions of their early environments. Sherwood Anderson's (*q.v.*) view of American rural character, likewise, is not the conventional view, for that character, though not so unlovely as Dreiser would have us believe, is represented as thwarted and repressed and ingrown with environmental starvation. Thus, the more energetic heroes of Anderson's novels—*Windy McPherson's Son* (1916) and *Marching Men* (1917)—escape to the city for some more or less mystical compensation for the frustrations of rural life.

The earlier novels of Sinclair Lewis (*q.v.*) illustrate a similar hostility to the ways of life and thought characteristic of the Middle West. In *Main Street* (1920) and *Babbitt* (1922)—Lewis' main contributions to middle western literature—his objects of attack are the shortcomings of the small town and of the smallish city. *Main Street* was notoriously successful in its delineation of the spiritual and intellectual barrenness of the small town; it was not so successful in its delineation of the way in which spiritual and intellectual richness could be achieved. But it added a memorable panel to the lengthening series of murals representing the limitations of American village culture. What *Main Street* did for the small town, *Babbitt* did for the middle class of a typical American small city. The reportorial value of *Babbitt* is amazingly high: the daily habits and thoughts and attitudes of the American businessman have been set down with incredible fullness and accuracy. Indeed, one measure of its accuracy is the readiness with which not only the American public but the world public recognized with malicious delight the truth of the portrait. The malice arose from that audience's awareness that Lewis was completely hostile to the pretense and vulgarity, the insensitiveness and banality of most of Babbitt's activities.

Less critical and more affectionate views of the Middle West have been set forth in the fiction of a number of Lewis' contemporaries and of the younger generation. Zona Gale (*q.v.*), though not uncritical of the material offered her by the Wisconsin scene, treated it essentially in terms of a realism that is not quite free from the sentimental. Edna Ferber's (*q.v.*) literary ambitions have frequently exceeded her performance, but she has been extremely resourceful in bringing to light unusual historical or economic material from the Middle West and near Southwest, and presenting it in her vivacious and highly colored though rather obviously designed canvases, *Show Boat* (1926), *Cimarron* (1930), and *Come and Get It* (1935). Glenway Wescott (*q.v.*) is too cosmopolitan in his literary allegiances and enthusiasms to be a merely regional writer, but his expatriate's view of his native Wisconsin is not the conventionally abusive one illustrated by such a Parisian production as Robert McAlmon's *Village*, but is a subdued and almost nostalgic recovery of things past. His failure to fulfil the promise of his novels, *The Apple of the Eye* (1924) and *The Grandmothers* (1927), points perhaps to the danger of severance from the source of one's creative powers. The purest example of affectionate acceptance of the Middle West ways is furnished by the work of Ruth Suckow (*q.v.*). It is not that Miss Suckow prettifies her material or dilutes it with sentimentality. Miss Suckow's Middle West is drab, but she loves rather than regrets the drabness. Thus, she keeps safely in the middle road of realism, leaving criticism of her native material to the romanticist and the satirist. It is as though she said, "Here are the facts about us; make of them what you will." On the whole, the place and its people turn out to be a decent if rather uninspiring lot. If one has doubts as to the importance of Miss Suckow's work, they do not arise in connection with her veracity and the patience with which she has accumulated her details. For a faithful, detailed, and sympathetic representation of middle western life, Miss Suckow's *The Folks* (1934) may be taken as a model.

Though Chicago has long since recovered from the shock of being hailed by H. L. Mencken (*q.v.*) as the "literary capital of America," it has naturally drawn to it a great deal of the literary talent of the Middle West, and that talent has given the metropolis considerable if not exclusive attention. Two fairly distinct modes appear in novelistic treatments of Chicago life: the realistic and the social-realistic. The strong impulses toward social amelioration that stirred American life and letters in the first decade of the century did not leave the Chicago novel untouched. Frank Norris' *The Pit* (1903) was in part a product of this impulse, and the long series of social novels from the pen of Robert Herrick (*q.v.*) show how an easterner in exile in Chicago was moved by the crude but dynamic phenomena which he was particularly well placed to observe. The most notorious of the social novels was, of course, Upton Sinclair's (*q.v.*) *The Jungle* (1906), which made the conditions of labor and production in the slaughter-houses a national scandal.

There have been numerous realistic and naturalistic treatments of

Chicago life. In the midst of the elegant if somewhat decadent writing of Henry B. Fuller (1857–1929), there appears one of the first attempts to treat contemporary Chicago realistically in fiction. Though the origins of the impulse in Fuller were foreign rather than indigenous, and though his major literary achievements were exotic rather than regional, his achievement in *The Cliff-Dwellers* (1893) indicated the richness of the material Chicago offered. Since his time the realistic mode has attracted the prolific pens of Henry Kitchell Webster, Janet A. Fairbank, and Margaret Ayer Barnes (*q.v.*). The two latter writers have taken their responsibilities as social historians with no little seriousness. Mrs. Fairbank, to be sure, has not confined her attentions to purely Chicagoan phenomena. *The Cortlands of Washington Square* (1922) moves freely in the larger atmosphere of New York and Washington, although its sequel, *The Smiths* (1925), paints a panorama of Chicago life from the time of the great fire to the present day, and *The Bright Land* (1932) explores the history of the Chicago hinterland. Mrs. Barnes has made herself a specialist in the social history of Chicago's last three generations, and *Years of Grace* (1930) and *Within This Present* (1933) are effective treatments of the American genealogical novel.

But it is the naturalists, perhaps, who have profited most from the rich quarry of Chicago life. The huge, sprawling, crude, violent life of the prairie lake-city tempts writers to a naturalistic presentation of it, and thus it is that Chicago appears most frequently as hog-butcher to the world in the American fiction of the last decade or more. We have already observed the tendency on the part of Dreiser and Anderson to send their more aggressive or rebellious heroes and heroines to cope with the monstrous maelstrom of Chicago. The Chicago phases of the careers of Ben Hecht (*q.v.*) and Maxwell Bodenheim coincided with the sophisticated naturalism of the post-war decade. Hecht's *Erik Dorn* (1921) and Bodenheim's *Blackguard* (1923) may serve to illustrate this transient mood. The younger realists of the "hard-boiled" school have found Chicago a peculiarly appropriate subject for sordid and violent fiction. The earlier novels of Mackinlay Kantor (*q.v.*) feature the more seedy and cheaply garish aspects of the city's life, and Meyer Levin's *The Old Bunch* (1937) shows the vitality of this mode. But the purest naturalism to have its genesis in Chicago appears in the novels of James T. Farrell (*q.v.*), who knows from experience the life of its mean streets and with a frankness resembling effrontery recounts the rise and fall of petty gangsters and disoriented proletarians in the decadent areas of Chicago's old South Side. The *Studs Lonigan* trilogy is perhaps the most consistently unlovely presentation of Chicago's social degeneracy to achieve literary currency.[1]

[1] The naturalistic drama has also found in Chicago material suitable for effective if sensational treatment. Maurine Watkins' *Chicago* (1927) and Ben Hecht (*q.v.*) and Charles MacArthur's *The Front Page* (1928) may be instanced in this connection.

The Southwest and the Northwest have not been neglected as subjects for novelistic treatment, but that treatment has all too frequently been so highly colored that the result is tasteless chromo-lithography. We have already noted the existence of that variety of popular fiction known as westerns, which conscientiously melodramatize the threadbare situations and characters associated with the cattle ranges of the great plains. Occasionally this material has received more serious treatment, and the line is not always easy to draw between a skillfully popular and a virtually literary product.

We have already considered Jack London's place among pioneers of naturalism; he is also of some consequence as a regional writer. But the violence and unrestraint of his imagination, the coarseness of his brushwork deprive such novels as *Martin Eden* (1909) and *John Barleycorn* (1913) of much value as reliable fictional documents; instead, they point the way to the predominantly romantic quality of most later uses of western subject matter. It is not very far, for instance, from the high coloring of London's novels to the immensely popular novels of James Oliver Curwood, who may well be considered the top of competence and skill in sub-literary western fiction. With Zane Grey, we move to a somewhat loftier sphere; here are close observation and intimate knowledge, and a rather imaginative response to the history and characters of the changing West, though the tone remains persistently romantic. The West has been able steadily to resist realistic scrutiny longer than any other section of the country. Of the western writers of the older generation, Stewart Edward White (*q.v.*) is the most deserving of serious consideration. His novels do not abstain from the appeal of the adventurous, but the fidelity of his observation and the dependability of his imagination combine with his professional expertness to make such novels as *The Blazed Trail* (1902) and *The Silent Places* (1904) memorable in the history of the fiction of the Middle and Northwest.

The growth of realism and naturalism has inevitably modified the tone of recent American fiction dealing with the West, though the view of that civilization that underlies Mary Austin's (*q.v.*) writings about the Southwest and the American Indian remains consistently romantic, not to say mystical. With Willa Cather (*q.v.*), a more realistic note is struck, although her more full-bodied works—*O Pioneers!* (1913) and *My Ântonia* (1918)—do not eliminate or eschew the heroic. The southwestern passages in *The Song of the Lark* (1915) are in the vein of refined realism, but in the Tom Outland narrative that constitutes so curious an excrescence on *The Professor's House* (1925), and in *Death Comes for the Archbishop* (1927), the glamour of the Southwest seized Miss Cather's imagination, and the result is a more glowingly colorful setting than her Nebraska novels permitted. The West and the Middle West have served also as the foundations for the ponderous psychological naturalism of the Vardis

Fisher (*q.v.*) tetralogy beginning with *In Tragic Life* (1932). The sufferings of the hero seem to have a personal rather than an environmental basis, but the pioneering conditions described painfully in *In Tragic Life* unquestionably had not a little to do with the lines along which his unhappy hero developed—or failed to develop.

California, despite its obvious possibilities as a subject for fictional treatment, has not attracted such frequent attention as other parts of the West with almost equally distinctive characteristics. Jack London and Upton Sinclair (*q.v.*) made occasional uses of it as background, and Gertrude Atherton (*q.v.*) has used its history to good advantage. In John Steinbeck (*q.v.*), California would seem to have found its most promising young novelist. Steinbeck's novels are noteworthy for their strong regional flavor, their variety, and the evidence they furnish of his increasing maturity and rich potentialities. With the exception of *Cup of Gold* (1929) and *The Grapes of Wrath* (1939), his novels find their settings in the valleys and mountains that lie north, east, and south of Monterey. In this region, Steinbeck has spent most of his life; this is the world that has contributed the realistic and symbolic elements of his fictional locale. This region and its life he has presented in different moods, from the Anderson-like neuroticism of *The Pastures of Heaven* (1932), the Lawrencian celebration of fertility in *To a God Unknown* (1933), and the folk-epic comedy of *Tortilla Flat* (1935), to the social consciousness of his strike novel, *In Dubious Battle* (1936), the tender study of the psychology of transient ranch workers in *Of Mice and Men* (1937), and the passionate indignation of his account of the dispossessed dust-bowl farmers of *The Grapes of Wrath* (1939). What distinguishes these variations in method and tone from a novelist's experimental quest for the most congenial of molds for his imagination is the successful fruition of almost every one of these ventures. Perhaps the earlier novels in which he was following paths blazed by older writers show some uneasiness and uncertainty. But with *Tortilla Flat*, he achieved individual expression, and the succeeding novels are the work of an unmistakable personality with impressive powers over atmosphere and character, description and dialogue, theme and social implication. Since the death of Thomas Wolfe, Steinbeck is the young American novelist whose future seems most exciting and most assured.

Two other important variations of regional fiction require comment: the regional-historical novel and the regional-racial novel. The historical novel—whether regional or racial—is so conspicuous a genre that it requires separate and fairly full treatment. The regional-racial novel adds to the interest of a particular geographical setting and a particular Nordic culture, the interest of the admixture of a more or less powerful racial element. The inclusion of an alien racial element complicates, of course, the texture of the fundamental American culture. The complication may be superficial where the cultures exist side by side with only casual contacts with each other, as in the case of the Negro in Harlem or the Polish agricultural workers in the Connecticut valley. Or the complication may be fundamental where the prolonged juxtaposition of two or more races has had profound social and economic effects on both cultures. In America, the most conspicuous instance of such a fundamental complication is the juxtaposition of the white and black races in the South, but the heavy admixture of Jewish and Italian elements in New York has given the culture of that city a quality that is hardly American. Chicago, likewise, is not so much an American city as a congeries of racial settlements almost mutually exclusive in their racial existence. Simpler illustrations of racial juxtapositions are numerous in America: the Irish in Boston, the French-Canadians in New England generally, the Mexicans and Indians in the Southwest, the Scandinavians in the Middle West, and the Orientals on the West Coast. These alien elements everywhere contribute a new richness to the regional pattern, since the eternally exotic element in the alien gives color and animation to the regional nature of the language, clothes, customs, religion, and physical and psychological physiognomies. Such alien material may be treated in one of two fairly distinct ways. The alien race itself may be the sole subject of treatment, as in the novels of such white writers as DuBose Heyward (*q.v.*) and Julia Peterkin (*q.v.*), and such Negro writers as Claude McKay (*q.v.*) and Langston Hughes (*q.v.*). Or the contact between the native and the alien may itself be the subject of interest, as in Edna Ferber's (*q.v.*) *American Beauty* or Oliver LaFarge's (*q.v.*) *Laughing Boy.*

This sketch of the regional fiction of the last generation will demonstrate, I believe, the importance and the persistence of this type of American novel. A less impressive result would be obtained if we were to study the regional element in the drama of the period, although here, too, the influence has not been insignificant. But the drama—in modern times at least—is primarily an urban form, and urbanization, in literature as well as in life, tends to standardization of manners and customs. To the novel, however, may well be entrusted the not unimportant task of recording and interpreting the elements that continue to lend variety and color to the fabric of American life. Fortunately, the regional novel has sloughed off the superficial quaintness of local-color fiction. The fact that the most conspicuous novelists in contemporary America show distinguishable regional elements seems a certain indication of the novel's healthy future. The American novel is more firmly rooted than ever in the rich American soil.

THE HISTORICAL NOVEL

In the twentieth century, the historical novel has won more popular approval than critical esteem. The reluctance of critics to face the aesthetic problems raised by the historical novel may be due to their suspicion that the historical novel is an illegitimate form, all too frequently the offspring of bad history and worse fiction. But its persistence and popularity force the literary historian to acknowledge that it has elements of wide, if not usually very persistent, appeal. One of its appeals is the romantic glamour that gathers around the great and near-great events and persons in our national history. No matter how scrupulous or unscrupulous a novelist may be in his handling of the events and persons of history, he can count on his audience's emotional associations with his material, associations that it is not necessary for him to build up. He can, moreover, count on his readers' avid curiosity concerning the setting and historical personages of his novel, a curiosity which he cannot be sure of finding when he utilizes merely contemporary material. Furthermore, no matter how great his scrupulousness, he can furnish a means of that escape from the pressures of contemporary life which many readers expect to get through reading.

The historical novel lags, willingly or unwillingly, far behind the discoverable truths and interpretations of the best and most recent historians. Its influence is probably the more potent in that it usually appeals unashamedly, not to the reader's sense of fact but to his patriotic emotions. At its best, the historical novel furnishes its readers not merely excitement and thrills, but the vivid sense of being present on momentous occasions, the spectacle of the frills and furbelows of more picturesque periods, and moving, memorable images of their country's heroes and heroines. In addition, the reader may expect at least a modest adherence to historical fact, as strong as possible an effect of verisimilitude in details of setting and costume, speech and manners, and a convincing, if not an entirely conventional, representation of such historical characters as occupy the spotlight, the middle distance, or the background. The sophisticated reader is furthermore inclined to question the ascription of too great an influence on the turn of events to some unhistorical creation of the author's imagination.

Since 1900, the American historical novel has been written with remarkable frequency, and read with great enthusiasm, first by an audience of adults and later by generation after generation of schoolboys. It has been given very little serious attention by either critics or historians. All that can be done here, however, is to call attention to the richness of the type and to relate it to the successive periods in our history. Almost at once, it becomes clear that serious novelists have given this type at least as much attention as it deserves, and that the historical novel itself has experienced marked ebbs and flows in production and consumption during the period.

Just after 1900, there was an extraordinary outburst of historical-novel writing, an outburst that can be attributed in part to the influence of

Robert Louis Stevenson's attempt to restore the alliance between the novel and the spirit of romance, and in part, perhaps, to the somewhat heady reaction to America's victory over a decadent Spain in the Spanish-American War. By the end of the first decade of the century, this particular peak in the popularity of the historical novel had passed, and in the second decade its appearance was sporadic. Through the middle of that decade, America's preoccupation with the World War and her participation in it left little time for excursions into her past. Indeed, the absence of any general interest in historical fiction persisted until the middle twenties; it is very difficult to think of any historical novel of much importance published between 1914 and 1925. In the latter year, however, James Boyd's (*q.v.*) *Drums* appeared, and after that date and at an accelerated pace, the historical novel increased in numbers, distinction, and popularity, until in the middle thirties, it was favored by a larger number of readers than any other type except such sub-literary species as detective stories, westerns, and sentimental feminine fiction.

Between the historical fiction of the first decade of the century and that of the decade beginning with 1926—the two peaks of its popularity—certain broad distinctions can be made which would not be invalidated by the qualifications a more detailed study would necessitate. In the main, historical fiction of the first period is inclined to be more sentimental, more romantic in tone, more melodramatically plotted, and less carefully documented than that of the second period. By contrast, the fiction of the second period is better informed on the social and economic sides, less prudish, and more scrupulous in its handling of historical persons and settings, manners and customs. It tends to meet more successfully the test of history. There has been a marked cross-fertilization between the regional novel and the historical novel during the latter period. To a certain extent, the earlier historical novels tended to stress the national rather than the regional element in their material. Regionalism has without doubt deepened the circumstantiality of the contemporary historical novel, and sharpened the critical perceptions of readers aware of the economic and psychological significance of regional influences on thought and feeling.

Of the periods into which American history is conventionally and conveniently divided, the Colonial is the one that has been least frequently treated by American writers interested persistently or casually in the writing of historical fiction. For one or another reason, the utilization of Colonial material has been left to the hands of the writers of juveniles, some of whom have won and kept large audiences by their generally innocuous representations of Colonial life. Instances are not lacking, however, of the treatment of Colonial subject matter by serious novelists. Just before the turn of the century, for example, Mary Johnston (1870–1936), the most indefatigable of the historical novelists in the early contemporary group, treated Colonial life of mid-seventeenth-century Virginia under the governorship of Sir William Berkeley in *Prisoners of Hope* (1898), a novel which she followed with *To Have and To Hold* (1900), perhaps her best-known book, a story of colonization in Virginia under the London Trading Company. In the same year, Mary E. Wilkins Freeman turned aside from her regional treatment of New England life to write *The Heart's Highway*, with its scene, the Old Dominion, and its background, the tobacco riots after Bacon's rebellion. These novels constitute the more important of the earlier treatments of Colonial material, and it was not until the revival of interest in historical fiction in the twenties that this particular period received further attention from novelists. Then, the veteran Mary Johnston returned to this subject matter in *Croatan* (1923), a story of Sir Walter Raleigh's first settlement in Virginia, with a rather more careful treatment of background material than her earlier novels had shown. Esther Forbes's *Mirror for Witches* (1928) told the tale of an unhappy child's misadventures during the witch-hunting craze in her native Brittany and later in Salem at the height of that outburst of morbid mass-psychopathology. In the thirties, Colonial life has furnished the setting of a number of popular novels. In 1932, Helen Grace Carlisle (*q.v.*), in *We Begin*, wrote a vivid tale of the adventures of the Pilgrims and their lives in Scrooby and Holland, and during the first twenty years of their experiences at Plymouth. Miss Forbes's *Paradise* (1937) told the happier story of the settlement in the mid-seventeenth century of Canaan, some twenty miles west of Boston, of the history of Jude Parre's estate, Paradise, of the fates of his five children in their relations to the other colonists and to the Indians just before King Philip's War. In the same year, Frances Winwar's *Gallows Hill* found its setting in Salem and its theme the witch-hunting mania. Fresher material engaged the attention of Kathleen Pawle in *Mural for a Later Day* (1938), a story of the settlement of New Sweden by the Swedes and Finns. Rupert Hughes's *Stately Timber* (1939) proved an encyclopedic fiction of seventeenth-century New England life.

Eighteenth-century American history offered historical novelists two great subjects—the American Revolution, and the beginning of the spectacular western movement that was to consume so much pioneering energy for almost two centuries. As early as 1899, Paul Leicester Ford had published the tremendously popular *Janice Meredith*, a novel which suffers somewhat from the excessive romanticism of his heroine but which is memorable for the rather careful portraits of Washington and Hamilton and for its realistic treatment of the social life of the time. The same year brought Winston Churchill's (*q.v.*) *Richard Carvel*, another book that achieved enormous popularity in its day. This novel carried its gallant hero through events in Maryland, Ireland, and London, preliminary to the Revolution, showed him in the service of John Paul Jones, and gave the reader studious glimpses of Horace Walpole, David Garrick, and Charles J. Fox. In the first year of the century, Maurice Thompson's *Alice of Old Vincennes* drew the attention of readers to French Indiana, the George Rogers Clark expedition of 1799, and the fate of Fort Vincennes. In 1901 another regionalist, Sarah Orne Jewett, tried her hand at the historical novel in *The Tory Lover*, with certain scenes in her native Maine as well as in France and England, and with John Paul Jones as a major character, and Benjamin Franklin in a minor role. The following year saw the publication of Mary Johnston's *Audrey*, a tragic romance of a fashionable Virginia landed proprietor and the daughter of a backwoodsman against the background of Virginia in 1727, Emerson Hough's *The Mississippi Bubble*, an account of the adventures of John Law in England, France, and New France, and the success and failure of the great speculative scheme he fathered, and Gertrude Atherton's (*q.v.*) *The Conqueror*, a fictionized biography of Alexander Hamilton, carefully documented from a study of family papers and the public records of the West Indies. Winston Churchill followed up his earlier success, *Richard Carvel*, with *The Crossing* (1904), one of the first of the novels to narrate the beginnings of the western migration into Kentucky and Tennessee. Its hero, David Ritchie, serves as a drummer boy in George Rogers Clark's expedition against the British. This period of interest in eighteenth-century American history terminated with Zane Grey's first and almost unknown book, *Betty Zane* (1903), a tale of the siege of Fort Henry in 1782.

No important historical novel on eighteenth-century American history was published for nearly twenty years. But in 1922, Irving Bacheller, who had reached a popular audience with his stories of Abraham Lincoln, showed in *In the Days of Poor Richard* the part Franklin played at home and abroad during the Revolution. In 1924, Joseph Hergesheimer (*q.v.*) in *Balisand* made a foray into the period of Washington's second administration for his study of the political democracy of the period, though he was rather more concerned with the general atmosphere than with historical events and persons. The Revolution itself, which in the early contemporary period made astonishingly little appeal to the imaginations of our novelists, received vigorous and circumstantial presentation in James Boyd's (*q.v.*) *Drums* in 1925, and the following year brought Mary Johnston's *The Great Valley*, a tale of the Shenandoah in the mid-century and of the events incidental to the immigration of a Scotch minister and his family. Here are introduced the youthful George Washington and the stirring tale of Braddock's defeat. In the same year Stephen Vincent Benét's (*q.v.*) *Spanish Bayonet* presented events preliminary to the Revolution in Minorca in 1769, and in the Floridas a decade later. The potentialities of the Revolution as a subject for novelistic treatment were exploited by Kenneth Roberts (*q.v.*) in a striking series of novels that appeared in the thirties, novels remarkable for their extremely careful documentation, their sternly realistic treatment of historical characters and military events, and a strict attention to atmosphere and setting. The decade opened with *Arundel*, the name of a garrison in southern Maine from which the hero, Steven Nason, departs to accompany his friend Benedict Arnold on his expedition to Quebec, and to experience with him not only the heroic deeds but the dangers, difficulties, and the ultimate failure of the expedition. To the sympathetic delineation of Arnold's character, Roberts returned in *Rabble in Arms* (1933), the sequel to *Arundel*. In this book, events are narrated by the mariner, Peter Merrill, and Arnold's character is contrasted favorably with the undignified squabblings, not to say villainies, of the American Congress. Here a group of men from Arundel is associated with Arnold in the campaign that ends with the Battle of Saratoga. But Roberts' most ambitious fiction and his greatest popular success was *Northwest Passage* (1937), which reverts to the events of 1759, and recounts the adventures of the artist, Langdon Towne, in the company of an American ranger commander, Major Robert Rogers, in his expedition against the Indian town, St. Francis, his efforts to gain London support for his further ventures, and his subsequent career as governor of Michilimackinas (Roberts' passion for documentation led him to publish, in a limited edition, the sources on which the novel was based). A year earlier, another phase of the Revolution had been treated by the skilled hand of Walter D. Edmonds (*q.v.*), in *Drums along the Mohawk*, an ambitious effort to show the effects of the war on the farming population of the New York frontier. As early as 1890, Harold Frederic had made a serious attempt, in *In the Valley*, to show the effects of the war on the New York frontier, but *Drums along the Mohawk* showed a wider range in characters and incident and a more scrupulous realism, and its total effect was to give a far less romantic version of this aspect of the war than that of official historians and imaginative novelists. The Northwest Territory furnished the scene, and the post-revolutionary period the setting of Meade Minnegerode's *Black Forest* (1937), and Neil H. Swanson's *The Forbidden Ground* (1938). Cyril Harris' *Trumpets at Dawn* (1938) found its theme in the conflicting loyalties of a New York family during the Revolution; Esther Forbes's *The General's Lady* (1938) treated with ingenuity the marriage of convenience of a Boston Tory heroine and a general in the Continental army; Van Wyck Mason's *Three Harbours* (1938) introduced a refreshing innovation by stressing the important parts played by seacoast merchants at the beginnings of the Revolution, and Elizabeth Page's *The Tree of Liberty* (1939) painted a huge canvas that showed the histories of three families between 1754 and 1806, introduced a large number of historical characters, and found its central theme in the development of a unified nation out of the scattered colonies.

For American novelists as for American historians, the major event of the nineteenth century was the Civil War, and novels on this subject have proved so numerous as to demand separate treatment. But the century offered other events of almost equal importance, in particular the heroic story of the western sweep of American life and the growing pains of a nation in the process of a tremendous material and political expansion. As early as 1895, Gertrude Atherton (*q.v.*) had begun her fictional explorations of early Californian material. Irving Bacheller contributed, during the first decade of the twentieth century, *D'Ri and I* (1901), a tale of the western frontier between 1810 and 1812, with the War of 1812 as its crucial historical focus. In 1906, Mrs. Atherton produced *Rezânov*, an account of the visit of a Russian plenipotentiary to San Francisco in 1806, on a trading and political mission. Two years later came Mary Johnston's *Lewis Rand*, with a Virginian setting, Jefferson and Burr as the most important historical characters, and the rise of Federalism and the conspiracy and trial of Aaron Burr as the chief historical events. For the first decade of the twentieth century these are the more important novels. Since that date, American life between 1800 and 1835 has received little attention from novelists, although Emerson Hough's *The Magnificent Adventure* (1916) found its inspiration in Lewis and Clark's expedition and in the lives of Aaron and Theodosia Burr at the time of the Louisiana Purchase. But no very popular or very significant novel on this period was published until Kenneth Roberts' (*q.v.*) *The Lively Lady* (1931) and *Captain Caution* (1934). In both cases, the heroes are men from Arundel, Maine, the first the son of the narrator of *Arundel;* in both cases the action concerns, in large part, the struggle between American and British shipping during the War of 1812. The love stories are interjected with considerable ingenuity into accounts of the heroes' adventures on the high seas and of their captivity at the hands of the British. To the theme and period of Mrs. Atherton's *Rezânov* (1906), Hector Chevigny returned in *Lost Empire* (1937); George Dixon Snell's *Root, Hog, and Die* (1937) retold the early history of Mormonism and the trek to Salt Lake in 1847; and Elizabeth Coatsworth's *Here I Stay* (1938) combined the regional and the historical appeals in its account of a young woman who insisted on remaining in Maine when most of her friends had migrated to Ohio in 1817.

The history of America during the second generation of the nineteenth century is richly represented in historical fiction, even when one excludes novels concerned specifically with the Civil War. As early as *The Doomswoman* (1893) and *The Californians* (1898), Gertrude Atherton (*q.v.*) had depicted the life of exotic California in the middle and latter part of the century, respectively, and in 1908, in *The Gorgeous Isle*, she attempted a re-creation of the mid-century society of Nevis in the Leeward group of the West Indies. The first year of the twentieth century saw the publication of Irving Bacheller's first important historical novel, *Eben Holden*, with its setting the St. Lawrence valley, and with sketches of Lincoln, Horace Greeley, and a nineteen-year-old Prince of Wales who was later to be known as Edward VII. Winston Churchill (*q.v.*) continued his work in this fertile and popular vein with *Coniston* (1906), a novel of social and political life from the time of Andrew Jackson to the end of Grant's administration. The end of this decade (1909) brought Emerson Hough's *54–40 or Fight*, with its focal theme the dispute between England and America over Oregon, its scene, Washington and Montreal in the mid-century, and its historical figures, Tyler and Clay, Edward Everett and Sam Houston.

Interest in this period continued fitfully in the second and third decades of the twentieth century. The second decade opened with Emerson Hough's *The Purchase Price*, a political novel with the scene Washington, and the beginnings of the anti-slavery movement as a secondary interest. Stewart Edward White (*q.v.*) continued his explorations in the life and history of the Far West in *Gold* (1913), a picturesque account of the conditions among the forty-niners in Panama and California, and its sequel, *The Gray Dawn* (1915), a tale of the Vigilante period in Californian history. Irving Bacheller published *The Light in the Clearing* (1917), a novel of political and religious life in the North and in Washington in the thirties and forties, with a high-minded statesman, Senator Silas Wright, as hero. But Bacheller's most popular success proved to be *A Man for the Ages* (1919), an account of Lincoln's early life in New Salem and Springfield, Illinois. Of all the historical novels produced in this decade, Bacheller's book is probably the one that continues to be read by a large number of adolescent readers. Three years later, Gertrude Atherton's (*q.v.*) *Sleeping Fires*, treating California's social life in the sixties and seventies, was outdone in popularity by Emerson Hough's less subtle and more heroic tale, *The Covered Wagon*, an account of the adventures of the great wagon trains on their perilous westward trek, which was to provide material for one of the best of the moving pictures (1923) based on American history. Two novels by Stark Young (*q.v.*)—*Heaven Trees* (1926) and *So Red the Rose* (1934), sophisticated reversions to the glamorous mode of portraying plantation life in the South before and during the war—were to serve as curtain raisers to the Civil War novels so conspicuous in the middle-thirties. Contemporary with *Heaven Trees* was Esther Forbes's *O Genteel Lady* (1926), a tale of the heroine's love-adventures amid the cultural distractions of Boston, Concord, and London in the mid-century.

The Civil War has proved the event in our national history most attractive to the imaginations and emotions of novelists in every generation since its conclusion. The interpretation of that conflict in the novel follows roughly the path traced by historians in their accounts of the conflict. Most of the late nineteenth-century treatments of the Civil War erred in the direction of sentimentality or of romantic melodrama, but in 1895 Stephen Crane's *The Red Badge of Courage* introduced a new method into historical fiction. This brilliantly impressionistic novel made no pretense of giving a panoramic view of the political or military events of the conflict. Instead, Crane focused sharply on the consciousness of his pitiful hero, and communicated through his sensitive and apprehensive observations an individual impression of battle. Here there are no large issues, no sectional significances, but one isolated soul immersed unwillingly in conflict. Crane's novel is still memorable for the imaginative skill with which it communicates to the reader the immediate experience of a timid soldier on the battlefield. The lesson Crane had to teach was not one that his immediate successors were quite ready to learn, but, in the long run, Crane's personalization of the historical novel was to bear heavy fruit.

In the meantime, however, the Civil War was to be fought over and over again by one novelist after another. The historical novel of the first busy decade of the century took in the Civil War as it strode through American history. In this field, Winston Churchill (*q.v.*) won a success rivaling the earlier *Richard Carvel* and almost equaling that of his later social novel, *The Inside of the Cup*. *The Crisis* (1901) covers the period from 1857 to 1865, and, perhaps because of Churchill's middle western background, maintains a somewhat steadier balance of sympathies than the Civil War novel usually shows. Through its hero, who displays a slightly excessive ability to be on hand when anything important is taking place, we are given effective portraits of Lincoln, Grant, and Sherman, and catch a glimpse of the Prince of Wales at the St. Louis Agricultural Fair in 1860. In 1902, Ellen Glasgow (*q.v.*) turned her distinguished novelistic powers on this subject and period in *The Battle-Ground*, a careful study of noncombatant life in Virginia before and during the war. The first two books of the novel give us the traditional pre-war plantation life; the latter two carry us through the war years to the fall of Richmond. The tone is remarkably impartial. But in John Fox's *The Little Shepherd of Kingdom Come* (1903), one of the best-sellers of the period, there was a reversion to the sentimental in the account of events in Kentucky during the war.

In the second decade of the century, the conflict between the romantic and the modestly realistic presentation of the Civil War persisted. Of the latter variety were Mary Johnston's *The Long Roll* (1911) and its sequel, *Cease Firing* (1912). In these novels, Miss Johnston left far behind the trappings and suits of banal historical romantic adventure. As a Virginian, the daughter of the Confederate General Joseph E. Johnston, and a novelist of great experience, she was well fitted to give a mature treatment of the Civil War from the aristocratic southern point of view. These novels represent her most serious contributions to historical fiction. The first, *The Long Roll*, traces the opening phases of the war and the Shenandoah valley campaign, and ends with the death of Stonewall Jackson in 1863. Her point of view, though southern, is moderate. She attains clarity here by focusing on the experience, in and out of battle, of a particular regiment, and draws skillful portraits of Jackson and his staff of officers. The second novel, *Cease Firing*, covers the latter years of the conflict, recounts the major battles of the period, ranges widely over the near and far South, and continues the series of portraits initiated in the earlier novel. Her story ends with the march to Appomattox. The more romantic southern treatment of the war was renewed in James Lane Allen's *The Sword of Youth* (1915), a more personalized, less panoramic novel that followed the young hero's adventures in Kentucky and Virginia in 1865, and included an interview with Lee and the inevitable glimpse of Abraham Lincoln.

But the great vogue of the Civil War novel did not begin until more than a decade later, when James Boyd's (*q.v.*) *Marching On* was published in 1927. This novel proved to be the forerunner of an astonishing number of Civil War novels of every degree of popularity and distinction. There were a number of reasons why the historical novel of the decade beginning in 1927 should differ in quality from those of any preceding period in American history. By this time, America's participation in the World War was over but not forgotten. Experience, immediate or vicarious, of that war made it impossible for writers to treat military life and warfare glamorously. The degradation and suffering, the filth and the misery of warfare, were too close to the surface of contemporary consciousness to make a thinly romantic presentation of it endurable. Moreover, the increasing self-consciousness of the South, and the rest of the nation, as to the economic implications of the slavery and plantation system and of the rivalry between northern industry and southern agriculture gave a new emphasis to the treatment of the conflict. Furthermore, the realism and impressionism of the nonhistorical contemporary novel were finally carried over to a type of novel that had tended to be romantic in tone and traditional in technique.

Against this background, the distinction of Boyd's *Marching On* becomes more intelligible. The point of view is that of a sophisticated Southerner. The interest is adroitly focused on the hero and the squad or company to which he belongs; the most powerful impressions left are those of the wastefulness of the struggle and the fundamental inhumanity of war itself. *Marching On* attracted too slight an amount of attention to transform the Civil War novel, but it was a symbol of the evolution that was taking place. Some of the results were more obvious in Evelyn Scott's (*q.v.*) *The Wave* (1929). Though southern in origin, Miss Scott was thoroughly emancipated from nostalgia for the Lost Cause and from the genteel spirit in literature. Thus, *The Wave* is a complete reaction from the gallant Union general and southern belle type of novel. *The*

Wave is a novel without a hero, unless the people submerged and drowned or swimming free of the flood of war can be called the hero. With great imaginative force, she shows the effect of the war, not on the aristocracy alone but on the rank and file of persons touched by the conflict. It is a fictional history of the people in wartime, and as such it is unrivaled by its earlier or later competitors.

But it remained for the mid-thirties to witness an outburst of Civil War novels unequaled in quantity and possibly in quality in our earlier history. The first of this group was Mackinlay Kantor's (*q.v.*) *Long Remember* (1934), a careful reconstruction of the Battle of Gettysburg, not in terms of the participants in the engagement but of the lives of noncombatants on the skirts of the action. By this shift of interest, Kantor was able to refract the historical events through normal human beings, not made self-conscious by their roles in important historical tableaux. Kantor succeeded, as few historical novelists have succeeded, in communicating a vivid sense of history as seen dimly and not too concernedly from the sidelines. Kantor returned to the Civil War for the setting of *Arouse and Beware* (1936), but here the interest is less in the external adventures of two soldiers who have escaped from the Confederate prison at Belle Isle and who are attempting to reach the Union lines on the Rapidan, than in the psychological study of their relations with a woman who is fleeing from Richmond and who shares their desperate plight. But the sensation of 1936 and of several years to come was the publication of Miss Margaret Mitchell's *Gone with the Wind* and its almost immediate leap to a popularity outdoing even that of *Anthony Adverse*. Miss Mitchell's novel combined very skillfully a large number of elements of reader-appeal: a vigorous, impetuous, and ultimately triumphant heroine, a secondary heroine of the clinging variety, a demimondaine, a hero-villain of the dashing devil-may-care erotic type, a crowded action, rapidly shifting scenes, a dash of obstetrics, and not too much tedious history or unpleasant bloodshed. But what gave *Gone with the Wind* its surest appeal was that the history of the period was presented for almost the first time as seen by women; Miss Mitchell's most skillful effect was not her characters, who were the creatures of southern melodrama, but quiet scenes of daily life on the plantations and in Atlanta as the Union armies swept nearer and nearer. By giving a feminine version of the Civil War, the novel attained a freshness and an emotional intensity rare in novels on this topic. Either by chance or by calculation, the following year (1937) added three more novels to this category: Royce Brier's *Boy in Blue*, Clifford Dowdey's *Bugles Blow No More*, and Caroline Gordon's *None Shall Look Back*. Taking his cue, perhaps, from *The Red Badge of Courage*, Brier focuses his attention on a private in the Union ranks and his experiences during the campaign in the Cumberland valley and in the Battle of Chickamauga. Like Crane's earlier novel, this one shows skill in avoiding staff-officer heroics and in revealing what war was like for a rather undistinguished soldier. Clifford Dowdey's *Bugles Blow No More* illustrates another device of integration, in this case the focus on Richmond during the war years. This makes it possible to keep the guns of battle at a distance and to show the changes wrought by war in the social life of a great southern city during the years of conflict. Here we read the social history of the center of southern civilization during the most dramatic period in its history. Miss Caroline Gordon has not yet equaled her early novel, *Penhally* (1931); yet she is the most philosophical of these novelists. A member of the southern agrarian group, dedicated to the belief that the destruction of the plantation society of the Old South meant the triumph of the monster of modern industrialism, Miss Gordon is less concerned with events than with their significance in the tragic pattern of southern history. Though a writer of great intelligence, she is not too adept in the handling of the fundamental elements of fiction—plot and character, and her novel is more important for its overtones than for its essentially fictional elements. Far less ambitious than the sprawling panorama of *Anthony Adverse*, and less serious than the treatments of the Civil War just mentioned, Hervey Allen's *Action at Aquila* (1938) offered his admirers a series of brilliant battle scenes in the deliberately limited range of his drama.

The Civil War novels of the thirties differ from the earlier novels on this subject in their realistic detail, in their less frantic patriotism, and—more significantly—in their stress on noncombatant life beyond the battle, and—most significantly—in their awareness of the economic and philosophical significance of the most tragic event in our history. The contemporary invasion of southern cities by northern industry and of the southern plantations by northern millionaires has intensified regional self-consciousness and turned the thought and imagination of some of the best southern writers to a reconsideration of the significance of the war and of the events which led to the slow destruction of a patrician order with its roots in the slavery of the Negro and the repression of the poor white. A fresh treatment of the Civil War must await a new orientation in our economic and political history.

In the history of America since the Civil War, novelists have found two subjects to challenge their imaginations: the reconstruction of the South, and the development of American civilization in the Middle and Far West. The economic and political life of the Gilded Age was, on the whole, neglected for more spectacular and romantic events. If this period has been more neglected than any other period except the Colonial, the reasons are perhaps its seeming nearness to us, its superficial dullness, and the absorption of the rising group of realistic novelists in current events, an absorption which prevented their utilizing the equally significant events of the period that produced our own. The Spanish-American

War, furthermore, was too close and too brief an experience to produce significant treatments, though it stirred the nation to an excess of hysterical patriotism, and though the subject was attempted by Kirk Munroe in *Forward March* (1899), and in *Crittendon* (1900) by John Fox, Jr., who drew on his own experiences as a war correspondent and as a Rough Rider in Cuba. It remained for social critics like Van Wyck Brooks (*q.v.*) and Lewis Mumford (*q.v.*) to initiate studies necessary for the orientation of serious imaginative writers toward this period.

Two novels appearing in 1898 illustrate the two lines which most novels on post-Civil War American history were to follow. Thomas Nelson Page's *Red Rock* was the first of a large number of novels devoted to Reconstruction, and Gertrude Atherton's (*q.v.*) *The Californians* was a pioneer in its treatment of West Coast life during the second half of the nineteenth century. This novel she followed by *Senator North* (1900), with its scene, Washington in the late nineties, and its theme, American politics against the background of affairs in Cuba and the Spanish-American War. The same year brought *The Voice of the People*, a serious study by Ellen Glasgow (*q.v.*) of life in Virginia during the period of Reconstruction. Two years later came Stewart Edward White's (*q.v.*) best-known work, *The Blazed Trail*, a circumstantial account of the development of the logging and lumber industries in Michigan in the late nineteenth century, a subject which he continued to treat in *The Riverman* (1908). But the most famous novel on this period was Owen Wister's (*q.v.*) *The Virginian* (1902), the humorous adventures of an eastern tenderfoot in Wyoming in the last quarter of the century, based on Wister's own experiences in that country. In 1904, Thomas Dixon began his novelistic career with *The Leopard's Spots*, a history of the Ku Klux Klan, which proved so popular that he gave it even more elaborate treatment in *The Clansman* (1905) and *The Traitor* (1907). Dixon, as an unreconstructed rebel, was perhaps the last of the bitterly controversial defenders of the Old South. His violently prejudiced melodramatic novels attracted a sensational publicity far beyond their deserts. With more recent and less debatable events, Hamlin Garland (*q.v.*) dealt in *The Long Trail* (1907), a tale of the finding of gold in the Klondike and of the sequent gold rush of 1898–99.

The second decade of the century saw the publication of no novels of great importance on the post-Civil War period, although Grace King's *The Pleasant Ways of St. Medard* (1916) portrayed with nostalgic sympathy the life in New Orleans during and just after the Civil War, and Mary Johnston's far-wandering pen took in the reconstructed South in *Michael Forth* (1919). The rich resources of western expansion, however, continued to attract the attention of novelists, great and small. The best of Willa Cather's novels, *O Pioneers!* (1913) and *My Ántonia* (1918), dealt with the hard courageous lives of European immigrants on the plains of Nebraska and the Dakotas. On a lower plane, Zane Grey's *The U. P. Trail* (1918) recounted the stirring history of the building of the Union Pacific and the consequent doom of the rebellious Sioux. In 1920, Stewart Edward White (*q.v.*) completed the Californian trilogy, begun with *Gold* and *The Gray Dawn*, with *The Rose Dawn*, which carried his narrative through the decline of the great cattle ranches into the period of land booms and the development of small-scale intensive farming.

Despite the tremendous vogue of Civil War novels in the twenties and thirties, or perhaps because of it, relatively few novels of the last fifteen years have found their subject matter in American history since the Civil War. A year after the great success of *The Covered Wagon* (1922), Emerson Hough's *North of 36* dealt with a Texas impoverished by the Civil War, and found its foci of interest in trail-making, cattle grazing and thieving, and encounters with the Comanches. In 1926, John M. Oskison's *Black Jack Davy* described early life among the Indian Territory pioneers and the dramatic thrust into Oklahoma in 1889, an episode Edna Ferber (*q.v.*) was to present more popularly in *Cimarron* (1930). The pioneering theme, so beautifully set forth by Willa Cather (*q.v.*) a decade earlier, was resumed with powerful realism in Ole Rölvaag's (*q.v.*) *Giants in the Earth* (1927), the most distinguished and popular of his numerous studies of Norwegian-American life on the great plains. Two years later, Walter D. Edmonds (*q.v.*) was to strike a new vein of historical ore in *Rome Haul*, a careful reconstruction of barge life on the Erie Canal in the fifties. The early and middle thirties were too preoccupied with the Civil War or with the novel of contemporary regional life to pay very much attention to other phases of our history. Conrad Richter's *The Sea of Grass* (1937), however, retold with poetic sweep and vigor the tale of the great days of the cattle kingdoms in Texas; Laura Krey's *And Tell of Time* (1938) recounted events in Texas during Reconstruction from a point of view profoundly sympathetic to the South; and LeGrand Cannon's *The Kents* (1938) traced a family's history from the end of the Civil War through the political revolt led by William Jennings Bryan.

This brief sketch of the contemporary American historical novel will suffice to indicate, on the one hand, the richness of American historical material, and, on the other, the recurrent appeal of that history to novelists of many moods and talents. Though the mortality among historical novels is probably no greater than that among nonhistorical novels, most of the historical novels of the early twentieth century survive, if at all, on reading lists for students in high schools. The destiny of most of the popular historical novels of the later contemporary period would seem to be the even more transient form of the moving picture. But what at least one can be sure of, is that in every period in which America's attention is focused on affairs at home rather than affairs abroad, in which a new temper and a new attitude toward our national history develop, novelists will profit by this turn of fortune to utilize, in one or another spirit—realistic or romantic, historical or imaginative, sentimental or cynical—the immense resources of our political, military, social, and cultural past.

EXOTICISM

The unbroken thread of exoticism in contemporary American fiction furnishes more than adequate evidence of the novelist's yearning for an object of imaginative stimulus more exciting than the flora and fauna of his native heath. Nothing human may be alien to the comprehensive soul of the uninhibited artist, but the alien—because it is alien—summons the creative imagination to the greenest of far-off hills.

The reasons for the appeal of the exotic are by no means simple. Most fundamental of all perhaps is curiosity, which operates without intermission and almost without restraint over the realms of the more or less unfamiliar. How the rest of the world eats and sleeps, works and loves, we never tire of inquiring. Our monkey-like curiosity is aided and abetted by the operation of that psychological mechanism by which the remote is endowed with varying intensities of glamour. The humblest of the stage properties of alien existence take on an aura of that strangeness mingled with beauty which is perhaps the essence of romanticism. The most dynamic process involved in literary exoticism is the mechanism of escape, by means of which artist and audience flee together to a realm of fact or imagination where the exactions of reality are minimized.

Practically, the American attitude toward the exotic moves easily from interest and amusement to suspicion and hostility. This mutability springs perhaps from a fundamental uncertainty as to whether America is actually inferior or superior culturally or morally to older and more sophisticated realms. Even in the lofty art of Henry James there was an uneasy suspicion of the high correlation between cultural sophistication and immorality, though there was never any doubt as to the unfailing lure of the life of sophistication.

Henry James indeed was past master of a decorous variety of exoticism. His own flight from his native land, his long residence in England, and his ultimate identification with it were personal testimony to the dismay and distaste evoked in him by the unlovelier aspects of American life. The life of the English gentry and of cosmopolitan European society seemed to him infinitely more comely and gracious than anything Boston or New York could offer. Thus, novel after novel became an exquisitely modulated tribute to the charm of Paris or London or Rome. But, in his flight from America, James carried in his psychological baggage a vigilant Puritan conscience, and he was never able to prevent its passing judgment—crudely in *The American* (1877) and *Roderick Hudson* (1876), and more subtly in *The Ambassadors* (1903) and *The Golden Bowl* (1904)—on the spiritual corruption underlying graceful bearings and elegant manners. His earlier novels concern themselves with the impact of Europe upon American characters of a sensitive or insensitive sort. Later, he found himself absorbed by the consideration of the character of the artist and of his plight in a civilized but Philistine society. Finally, as the glamour of Europe slowly faded under his relentless scrutiny, he devoted himself to the endless conflict between integrity and depravity. But to the end, his beloved England was invested with a glow of beauty which for him the American scene never possessed. Less subtle, certainly, but still fine perceptions, if inferior artistry, mark the works of such devout Jacobites as Anne Douglas Sedgwick (*q.v.*) and Edith Wharton (*q.v.*), who implied their opinion of America by prolonged absences from it. Miss Sedgwick, in fact, may be taken as an example of an identification with an alien culture so complete that she might well be considered an English rather than an American novelist. Mrs. Wharton, on the other hand, made her contribution to American rural regionalism in *Ethan Frome* (1911) and *Summer* (1917), and to urban regionalism in *The House of Mirth* (1905) and *Hudson River Bracketed* (1929), but in both her way of life and the nature of her art, she withdrew increasingly from the form and spirit of the American life of our time.

The decade following the close of the World War saw exoticism develop into a mass movement and an irrational cult. Its headquarters was Paris, its economic foundation, the devalued franc, and its high priestess, Gertrude Stein (*q.v.*); its media of publications were *transition*, *Broom*, *This Quarter*, and other journalistic ephemora. What the cult had in common was a series of rationalizations: that bourgeois America was hostile to the creative artist, that only when immersed in French culture could the artist function fruitfully, that art must be, not national, but European, and that a revolution in language was as desirable and inevitable as a revolution in spirit. The results of the expatriation of the "lost generation" may be measured by a scrutiny of the contents of *transition* or of Peter Neagoe's anthology, *Americans Abroad* (1932). The "lost generation" was obviously a legion of the maladjusted, ranging from the merely sensitive to the psychotic, with a preponderance of neurotics. In this aesthetic demimonde, the complex personality of Gertrude Stein played no inconsiderable part. Her financial security, knowledge of modern art and artists, masculine vigor, passion for disciples, and unceasing flow of shrewd judgments delivered with the authority of Sinai, made her an unfailing catalyst in this physico-chemical chaos. And, though she has written nothing since *Three Lives* (1909) of any significance as literary art, her experiments with language have had important effects on authors like Anderson and Hemingway, modest experimenters on the eternal renewal of language.

Ernest Hemingway (*q.v.*) was the first novelist of importance to rise from the ranks of the post-war expatriates. Though the code of hyper-masculinity implicit in his fiction is slightly tinged with neuroticism, his artistry seemed incomparable until his imitators had furnished materials for comparison. His variety of objective realism and his hostility to obvious form and structure made his short stories more completely satisfying than his novels, but *The Sun Also Rises* (1926) is not only a literary-historical landmark but a masterpiece in its kind, and *A Farewell to Arms* (1929) seems only less admirable because his cultivation of the unaffected has now become an affectation. His more recent works of nonfiction—*Death in the Afternoon* (1932) and *Green Hills of Africa* (1935)—continue to give evidence of his response to the lure of exoticism, although he occasionally tends to take on the slightly ridiculous aspect of a suburbanite imperfectly disguised by the lion-skin of a Tarzan of neoprimitivism.

In Julian Green and his sister Anne (*q.v.*), exoticism offers perhaps its most and least extreme illustrations. Julian Green has gone as far as it is possible to go in obedience to its urges. Not only the language but the psychology of his fiction is French, and its psychology, moreover, is of so specialized a variety as to seem slightly exotic to the French themselves. Green's relationship to contemporary American literature is merely biological. His sister Anne, a far less serious artist, finds her value, however, in rendering with extraordinary deftness and wit the lighter social aspects of Franco-American contacts. In other contemporary American novelists, exoticism plays its incidental or central part—in the Roman setting and personnel of Thornton Wilder's (*q.v.*) *The Cabala* (1926), the Parisian and Russian background of Vincent Sheean's (*q.v.*) *Gog and Magog* (1930), and the Anglo-French passages in Thomas Wolfe's (*q.v.*) epic of the artist's *wanderjahre*, *Of Time and the River* (1935).

The most distinguished recent invader of the field of European exoticism is Kay Boyle (*q.v.*). Her settings have a pleasing variety: provincial France in *Plagued by the Nightingale* (1931) and *Gentlemen, I Address You Privately* (1933), Paris in *My Next Bride* (1934) and *Monday Night* (1939), the Riviera in *Year before Last* (1932), and the Austrian Tyrol in *Death of a Man* (1936). There is a similar range in her themes: an American girl's adjustment to her marriage into a French provincial family, the struggle between an older and a younger woman for a dying artist, the devastation wrought by a sexual derelict, the tragi-comic life of a primitivistic art-colony, the conflict between love and devotion to a political cause. But though her knowledge of Europe has the assurance of experience, and though her skill in discovering compelling themes is enviable, her distinction lies in profounder powers. Of these, not the least is her style. Her revolt against a conventional literary style is apparent in her "metaphysical" quest for novel and striking metaphors. Frequently the quest fails and the effect is merely extravagant and grotesque. But at her best, Kay Boyle's style renders her painfully acute vision with a freshness and suggestibility unexceled by the best contemporary poetry. Her style, however, is of interest not only of itself, but as a medium precisely contrived for the expression of her shrewd and startling perceptions. She is expert in the ways of human bodies and human souls. Both she strips disconcertingly bare, for, though her values are conscientiously implicit, she is wedded to honesty, and is as avid of ugliness as of beauty. It is her greatest distinction that the world she creates is unique and incomparable. It has sardonic humor and a beautiful cruelty, inhuman amorality, and a secret wisdom wrought out of the ceaseless conflict of living and dying cells, of sentient flesh and supersentient heart.

But the contemporary American novelist has not restricted his quest for exotic material to even the remoter cultures of western Europe. The Near East, it must be admitted, has tempted few American authors of our generation to its imaginative exploitation, although H. G. Dwight's *Stamboul Nights* (1916) pointed out the potentialities of this milieu and by its delicacy of touch and its skillful evocation of atmosphere won the position of a minor contemporary classic.

The Far East, on the other hand, has proved a more energizing stimulus to the imagination of American writers of the last forty years or more. The modern cult of the primitive, for example, found a perfect setting in the island life of the South Seas. More than a generation ago, Robert Louis Stevenson in glowing words and Paul Gauguin in even more glowing colors publicized the physical and sensory allurements of the far-flung islands of the Pacific, and in the early decades of the twentieth century Joseph Conrad made himself the brooding sovereign of many a dank jungle and sun-smitten promontory. No American artists of similar stature have utilized this material with equal effectiveness, but to a brood of lesser talents, the South Seas have become as reliable a waterway to romance as any navigable. Thus, primitive man and nature struggle through the fictive chromo-lithographs of that naïve romantic, Jack London. Such highly colored travel books as Frederick O'Brien's *White Shadows of the South Seas* (1919) and *Atolls of the Sun* (1922) furnished settings and motifs that became the stock in trade of the romance mongers of the stage and screen.[1] Two young American veterans of the World War, James Norman Hall and Charles Nordhoff, moved by a common revulsion from the complexities and frustrations of Western civilization, went into voluntary exile on an island in the South Seas. At first reluctant to

[1] Thus, for a less sophisticated public, R. W. Tully's volcanic drama, *The Bird of Paradise* (1916), furnished its stage-carpenter's thrills, and *Rain* (1923), dramatized by John Colton and Clemence Randolph from Somerset Maugham's short story, "Miss Thompson," made the unfailing appeal of a blend of religiosity and eroticism. To the illiterate song-writer, the South Seas have proved an unfailing boon. That an elementary sort of exoticism is a part of the stock in trade of Tin Pan Alley's lyric writers is suggested by such modestly evocative titles as "Let Me Dream of Hawaii," "South Sea Island Magic," "On a Coconut Island," "Moonlight and Palm Trees," and "Blue Hawaii."

draw the public's attention to their earthly paradise, they ultimately joined the chorus of praise in *Faery Lands of the South Seas* (1921), and in recent years have not only exploited the history of the "Bounty" in a semifictitious trilogy, *Mutiny on the Bounty* (1932), *Men against the Sea* (1934), and *Pitcairn's Island* (1934), but turned their remote and fascinating life to melodramatic account in their popular novels, *Hurricane* (1936) and *The Dark River* (1938).

The rather tawdry uses to which South Sea settings have been put by novel, drama, and moving picture, may be contrasted happily with the more discriminating treatments of Japanese and Chinese culture by American writers. The Oriental has long been a favorite stimulus of those ambivalent emotions which anything alien is likely to arouse in us. Uncertain of the actuality of the alien, aroused imaginatively by its unknown powers, we are now victimized by our terror and again protected by our assumed and amused superiority. Thus, the Oriental has been treated, now, as the most cruelly sinister of human beings, and again as the quaintest and most comical of racial oddities.

The treatment of oriental material in American literature reveals clearly the successive stages in this emotional process; the terrifyingly sinister and the humorously quaint are gradually giving way to sympathetic comprehension. Illustrations of the earlier modes are conveniently at hand in such effective pastiches as David Belasco and John Luther Long's *Madame Butterfly* (1900) and *The Daughter of the Gods* (1902). The quaintly humorous oddities of oriental life and art were popularized by such a forgotten sentimental favorite as Frances Little's *The Lady of the Decoration* (1906) and George Hazelton and J. H. Benrimo's perennially revived drama, *The Yellow Jacket* (1913).[1]

The way for a more serious treatment of oriental material had been prepared for American writers and readers by the activities of that talented international waif, Lafcadio Hearn (1850–1904). The offspring of a Hiberno-Grecian marriage, Hearn seemed destined to be the high priest of exoticism. Thus, during his American period, he was drawn magnetically to the ultra-exotic racial and cultural elements in the far South and in Central America. But a more extravagant exoticism lured him to Japan, and he acknowledged its sway by marrying a Japanese wife and becoming a Japanese subject. For Hearn, the glamour of the Orient slowly faded, but, despite the disillusionment of his later years, he succeeded in a remarkably complete identification with this fantastically alien culture. Twenty or more years ago, Hearn was the center of an enthusiastic if acrimonious cult. His vogue has passed, but at least he

[1] The immature attitudes implicit in such works survive in art-forms like the popular song and the moving picture, directed at relatively uncritical publics. Thus, as sophisticated a writer as Clifford Odets fell back on the sinister-cruel conception of the Oriental in his script for the moving picture, *The General Died at Dawn* (1936).

pointed the way for later if less gifted writers who were to exploit oriental material intelligently on more and more popular levels.

Of such writers, the most strikingly successful has been Pearl S. Buck (*q.v.*). Mrs. Buck's birth and upbringing in China, her devoted study of the Chinese classics, and her incomparably intimate knowledge of Chinese life and character have been inestimable advantages in her successive attempts to make this ancient civilization comprehensible and significant to Western readers. The publication of *East Wind: West Wind* (1930) attracted little attention, but the appearance of *The Good Earth* (1931) was a major event in the history of American exoticism, the most satisfactory endeavor yet made to utilize effectively in fiction the strange and highly stylized lives of Chinese peasants. The successors to this book—*Sons* (1932) and *A House Divided* (1935)—did not suffer the usual fate of sequels, although their style, with the rhythms but without the imaginative vitality of biblical poetry, became increasingly inappropriate to the representation of the Chinese life of our day. In the later novels, Mrs. Buck showed the clash between oriental and occidental ways in modern China with extraordinary insight, but failed to give her characters the stability and vitality of the primitive tradition-bound farmer Wang Lung and his slave-wife O-lan. The oriental novels of Alice Tisdale Hobart are on a considerably lower plane of insight and achievement. Mrs. Hobart's use of this material began with her Manchurian travel book, *Pioneering Where the World Is Old* (1917), and went on with her novel *River Supreme*, first published as *Pidgin Cargo* in 1929. In her first popular success, *Oil for the Lamps of China* (1933), she dramatized the operations of a great Western industrial organization in this exotic setting, and in *Yang and Yin* (1936) she showed the conflicts, disasters, and triumphs that follow the intrusion of Western medical science into an unscientific culture. A far different intention animates Frederic Prokosch's (*q.v.*) *The Asiatics* (1935) and *The Seven Who Fled* (1937), where the young author utilizes oriental themes as the bases for brilliant, if decadently romantic, fantasias.

The combination of the historical and the exotic adds another value to the appeal of the remote. The lure of the temporally remote when superimposed on the geographically distant creates a kind of fourth dimension in exotic fiction. It is not surprising, then, that contemporary writers should have shown a recurrent interest in the revival of the exotic-historical novel. Such recurrences, with inevitable variations, have been fairly conspicuous in American literature of the last forty years, despite the fact that throughout most of this period the flood-tide of fiction has swept most suggestible novelists over the broad plains of the realistic or the social novel.

The end of the nineteenth century saw an attempt on the part of both English and American novelists to recapture some of the romantic appeal of the spacious historical canvases of Sir Walter Scott and his innumerable imitators. Perhaps no writer of the period save Robert Louis Stevenson was endowed with a talent and temperament quite equal to the demands of this revival, but such lesser lights as Sir Rider Haggard in *King Solomon's Mines* (1885) and *She* (1897), and Sir Anthony Hope in *The Prisoner of Zenda* (1894) and *Rupert of Hentzau* (1898), furnished less discouraging objects of imitation. In America, such popular productions as Charles Major's *When Knighthood Was in Flower* (1898) and George Barr McCutcheon's *Graustark* (1901) precipitated what seemed likely to be a romantic revival in American fiction. Of the lighter fiction in this genre, Booth Tarkington's (*q.v.*) *Monsieur Beaucaire* (1900) is still readable and has had a long after-life on stage and screen. More talented novelists joined, at least for a moment, the swelling chorus. Thus, Henry Harland produced an elegant and witty historical diversion in *The Cardinal's Snuff Box* (1900), and the youthful Edith Wharton (*q.v.*) in *The Valley of Decision* (1902) showed what a serious novelist could do toward the re-creation in fiction of eighteenth-century Italy. Two years later (1903) saw one of the first of Mary Johnston's many novels utilizing exotic-historical material. In *Sir Mortimer*, Miss Johnston novelized England's struggle with Spain for naval supremacy at the latter end of the sixteenth century, with stress, of course, on the daring of Sir Francis Drake and with the almost obligatory introduction of Queen Elizabeth, the Countess of Pembroke, Sir Philip Sidney, and others. Despite her absorbed interest in the utilization of American historical material, Miss Johnston persisted during the next twenty years, despite the sharp decline in the production and consumption of the exotic-historical novel, in writing an impressive number of novels in this genre, of which may be mentioned *The Witch* (1914), a tale of the witchcraft mania under James I, *The Fortunes of Garin* (1915), with its setting, France at the time of the Troubadours, *Foes* (1918), a novel of Jacobite adventure in the mid-eighteenth century, *Silver Cross* (1922), a tale of religious life in the reign of Henry VII, *1492* (1923), with the inevitable subject of Columbus and his voyages, and *The Slave Ship* (1924), a reversion to the period of *Foes*, but with scenes that included Edinburgh, Virginia, Africa, and Jamaica.

But the increasing seriousness with which American novelists in the period before the war were facing the tasks imposed by the creed of realism and by America's rediscovery of its social conscience produced a temper unfavorable to either the trivial or the serious utilization of exotic-historical material, and although McCutcheon in *Castle Craneycrow* (1902) and *Beverly of Graustark* (1904) and their successors was furnishing his sentimental public a long series of imitations of his early success, the exotic-historical novel sank rapidly to the level of the sub-literate. Nor were the war years favorable to any attempt to revive this genre. Thought and emotion were too intensely concentrated on the world-crisis to permit an indulgence of the impulse to escape into the unexacting past. An interest in the official history of our allies and enemies supplanted an enthusiasm for unofficial historical romances.

But the boom years of the post-war period, the years in which the expatriates were indulging in their most severe strictures on our native culture, saw here and there, among writers of sophistication, an interest in the manipulation of exotic-historical material. If no popular successes like those enjoyed by the *Graustark* romances were produced, the reason is perhaps that these post-war romancers were too fastidious to play with the easy counters of the sword and buckler melodrama or to dally with the gallant vicissitudes of princes of imaginary kingdoms. Thus Elinor Wylie (*q.v.*), in *Jennifer Lorn* (1923) and *The Venetian Glass Nephew* (1925), re-created in exquisitely decorative prose her vision of a fragile rococo world, and Hilda Doolittle (*q.v.*), the imagist poet, in such recondite fictions as *Palimpsest* (1926) and *Hedylus* (1928), attempting to apply to narrative the inorganic technique of imagistic poetry, produced results that were curious and beautiful rather than satisfying as imaginative narrative. A less esoteric variety of exotic-historical fiction was exemplified in the mid-decade by Isabel Paterson's *The Singing Season* (1924), with its unusual setting, Spain in the late fourteenth century, and *The Fourth Queen* (1926), a tale of England in the period of the Armada, with the Earl of Essex as its hero. In the following year, Mrs. Atherton, in *The Immortal Marriage*, attempted the reconstruction of the Golden Age of Athens with such notables as Socrates and Alcibiades among those present. It was in the twenties, too, that Thornton Wilder (*q.v.*) conducted his first excursion into the field of the exotic-historical. If *The Bridge of San Luis Rey* (1927) was the only book of its kind to reach the great public, the reasons were not so much the originality of the design and the refinement of the style as the variety of its themes and its sincerely felt though conventional message. As *The Woman of Andros* (1930) showed, Wilder is a writer of apologues rather than a novelist. He is primarily intent on communicating his own sense of life's values through the complex disguise of fiction; to him, the allurements of plot and character are decidedly secondary to the ethical import of his tales. To undertake to estimate him as a novelist, much less as a social novelist, is to approach him along the most unprofitable of critical avenues. Wilder's values are to be sought in the sincerity of his Christian convictions, his uncanny feeling for ancient scenes and literatures, and closely studied and impeccable style.

The years of the depression would, at first thought, seem the least favorable of climates for the production and consumption of exotic-historical fiction, and yet the most sensationally successful of these novels, Hervey Allen's (*q.v.*) *Anthony Adverse* (1933), flourished in this hostile air. For hundreds of thousands of depression-weary readers, this mastodon of historical fiction, this cento of all the historical novels ever written, furnished the perfect mechanism of escape. Furthermore, by combining adventures in America and adventures in Europe, it appealed to the reader's interest in the American regional-historical as well as the alluringly exotic. The reading public, unable to endure the pressures of contemporary reality, was easily and completely bewitched by the multitude of characters, amplitude of plot, and variety of picturesque settings offered by *Anthony Adverse*.

Despite such a phenomenon, it seems clear that, if the exotic-historical novel is to be created on a serious aesthetic plane, it must be modernized. That modernization is possible, such novels as Helen C. White's (*q.v.*) *A Watch in the Night* (1933) and *Not Built with Hands* (1935), and Vincent Sheean's (*q.v.*) *Sanfelice* (1936) and *A Day of Battle* (1938) furnish eloquent evidence. Miss White's study of the thirteenth century in her earlier novel and of eleventh-century Italy in its successor are marked not only by a scholarly intimacy with these periods but by an even rarer appreciation of their religious psychology. Sheean approaches the historical novel as a contemporary liberal, and above the brilliant historical recreations rise overtones of current social and political significance. This process of modernization demands not only a close study of historical material but the creation of historical character in terms of contemporary psychology, or an interpretation of social forces in the light of our best knowledge of their complex operation. Such an equipment is bound to be rare; in the meantime, the stage properties of the costume drama and the sawdust puppets of historical romance are available for use by all save the most modestly endowed or the most enthusiastically proletarian.

We have seen how American novelists have used contemporary or historical exotic material realistically or romantically. One American novelist of distinction has used exotic material as a point of departure for fantasias of the imagination. James Branch Cabell's (*q.v.*) Poictesme has some modest relations with medieval France, but it is virtually a land of Cabell's own creation under the stimulus of medieval romance and his own erotic and philosophical fantasies. The atmosphere is dreamlike; the characters and their actions are shadowy; the memorable values of his fiction are the stirring of the imagination and the cynical allegory. Cabell is a romanticist with a difference. Though he extols the glamorous and colorful past, the flowing gesture, and the idolatry of woman, his devotions are qualified by his awareness that none of these objects of admiration is quite worth the emotion it arouses. The illusions of art and love and religion that make life endurable are bound in subtle natures to end in disillusionment, and in simple natures like Jurgen's in a welcome return to unimaginative domesticity. So all Cabell's heroes of whatever kingdom go a-questing, and, though they meet with challenging or exhausting adventures, they oppose the memory of their potency and prowess to the more or less bitter awakening in the light of common day or the approach of senility or death.

Cabell's distinction is not that of the great novelists, the creation of character and the designing of plot, but of a special sort deriving from this complex character as a disillusioned romanticist. The disillusionment is heard in the overtones of humor and satire. His comic range is wide, from the subtler humors of sarcasm and irony to the cruder humors of farce and burlesque. His favorite humorous device is innuendo, the leer of the satyr in poet's clothing. His satire is directed, not at the paraphernalia of the modern world but at its ideals of religion and morality, of patriotism and above all romantic love. Irony is the worm at the root of Cabell's romanticism. His style is what we should expect from a romantic ironist—elaborate, rhythmical, and sophisticated. He has read in strange books, and from them he brings esoteric learning and the vocabulary of ancient romance. He delights in odd flowers and jewels and metals; exotic names that stir his imagination he scatters generously across his pages.

If Cabell seems a less important figure than he seemed a decade or more ago, the reasons for his decline are not difficult to discover. Cabell is an excessively repetitious writer. His views of life and art, expressed most directly in his series of essays, *Beyond Life* (1919) and in the more cynical *Straws and Prayerbooks* (1924), are implicit in everything that he has written since his earliest period of pure and popular romanticism. Moreover, his conviction that art is primarily a mechanism of escape, his hostility to realism and to didactic art, and his characteristic defeatism have come to seem more and more outmoded in the serious depression years. His style, once rapturously admired, is now seen to be the result of artifice rather than of genuine art. Cabell is in danger of being left alone to sardonic contemplation in the ivory tower built by his art. The life-giving currents are flooding far different shores.

THE SOCIAL NOVEL

The social novel, the novel of purpose, or the thesis novel, is related at once to realism and naturalism, and is at times almost indistinguishable from one or the other of these literary modes. The social novel, therefore, is not easy of definition, but it is differentiated from the purely realistic or naturalistic novel by its emphasis on some problem of social, economic, political, or religious significance, a problem which the specific persons and plot-devices may be taken to illustrate and illuminate. Fiction (or drama) of this sort has a twofold interest: concern with the particular characters and their interwoven fates, and the significance these characters and incidents have as illustrative of admirable or contemptible social habits, attitudes, practices, and values. The social novelist's difficulty lies in preserving the balance between the interest of the particular and the significance of the abstract. If the claims of the particular are ignored, the novelist may find that he has written, not a work of genuine creation, but a thin and bloodless moral tract. If the claims of the abstract are ignored, the novel will have lost its intended social meaning and value. The literary critic faces a similar dilemma. He cannot ignore so conspicuous a phenomenon as the social novel, but, if he attempts to cope with it, he finds he must solve an aesthetico-ethical problem of no little complexity. He is not, of course, in a position to insist that the social doctrine presented shall be identical with his own, since the critic who bans from literature all social views save his own is not a critic, but an inquisitor. What he can insist on is that the doctrine shall be presented with admirable artistry and convincing emotion. His judgments may take a number of forms; he may find the doctrine excellent and the artistry bad; the doctrine unsound and the artistry good; or both the doctrine and the artistry bad or good. The rarity of the final combination throws some doubt on the essential legitimacy of this genre.

The social novel seems to flourish in those periods when novelists and readers are in the mood for self-scrutiny and self-criticism, in periods when the tone of public life is serious, not to say censorious. Its popularity has coincided with the less prosperous and ebullient passages in our social and economic life. Obviously, neither the intensely emotional and uncritical period of the World War nor the boom period that succeeded it furnished a congenial atmosphere for good didactic fiction. But during the generations with which we are concerned, there have been two intervals when the social novel has flourished: the period from the end of the Spanish-American War to our entrance into the World War, and the period of the depression.

Most of the social novels of the earlier period, the first decade and a half of the twentieth century, seem at this distance incredibly naïve and oversimplified. Such novels as *The Jungle* (1906) or *The Inside of the Cup* (1913) are now of historical rather than of literary interest. But the tremendous discussion novels of this type occasioned suggests their importance as indices of the moral fervor of the moment. If any unity of theme exists in the novels produced during this period of social reform, that unity lies in the criticism of the inroads into the national integrity made by the unrestrained economic enterprise of big business in the Gilded Age and after. The nineteenth century had not been without its novelistic attacks, but these were merely premonitions of something like a national awakening of a people's conscience. For, by the end of the century, big business was seen as the major source of corruption in American political and professional life, and it was assailed vigorously by novelist after novelist.

Winston Churchill (*q.v.*) was the most popular novelist of the period to turn his attention to the social novel. He had already made a reputation as a historical romancer in the late nineties, but with the turn of the century, he responded to the spirit of the moment, and thereafter staked his literary reputation on the social novel. He did not, however, confine his activities in behalf of the purification of our economic and political life to literature. He was a member of the state legislature of New Hampshire in 1903 and 1905, was active in his attacks on political bosses and the political activities of industrial corporations, and was barely defeated in the contest for the governorship of the state in 1908. At the same time, he was devoting his literary powers to fiction embodying his social ideas. In *Coniston* (1906), he presented a conflict between the political boss, Jethro Bass, and Isaac Worthington, the representative of a railroad corporation with political affiliations. His interest here is in individuals rather than in what they represent, and, in consequence, the novel is aesthetically as satisfying, though by no means so popular, as Churchill's other social novels. *Mr. Crewe's Career* (1908) is drawn directly from its author's experiences in New Hampshire politics. The theme is the manipulation of the state legislature by a monopolistic railroad corporation. The hope he expressed through his reforming hero, Austen Vane, that this domination was ended belongs perhaps to the realm of romance rather than of history. His later novels tend to deal with more definitely personal and moral problems. *A Modern Chronicle* (1910) concerns divorce; *The Inside of the Cup* (1913), one of the most preached-about novels of the period, investigates modernism in theology and the social responsibility of the urban church; *A Far Country* (1915) shows the corruption of a young lawyer through the rewards offered by big business, and *The Dwelling Place of Light* (1917) grapples unsuccessfully with the social implications of the modern factory system. Feeble as it is, this last novel is prophetic of the proletarian novel which the depression was to cause to proliferate fifteen or twenty years later. Morally sound and politically well-intentioned as Churchill's novels are, they are not of very great aesthetic interest or power in themselves. Ironically, his earlier undidactic and colorful historical fiction is superior in vitality and has outlasted in popularity his work in the genre of the social novel.

Robert Herrick's (*q.v.*) important social novels coincide in date almost precisely with those of Winston Churchill. Herrick was admirably situated for a critical presentation of the evils of a highly acquisitive society. A New Englander by birth and education, Herrick spent thirty years of his life in exile in Chicago, a city which furnished him a perfect illustration of the results of uncontrolled economic competition and its social and economic reverberations. Sensitive though austere, avid of integrity, Herrick found at hand ample material for indignant and satirical treatment. He was chiefly interested in studying the struggle of decent human beings with the forces of a materialistic society. In such novels as *The Man Who Wins* (1897), *The Web of Life* (1900), *The Common Lot* (1904), *The Healer* (1911), and *One Woman's Life* (1913), his hero is a professional man whose happiness and integrity are threatened or destroyed by the insidious influences of business associations or by women corrupted by a purely acquisitive social order. Herrick could not but be intensely aware of changing sexual mores, and such novels as *The Gospel of Freedom* (1898) and *Together* (1908) represented marital relations with a frankness that seemed sensational in a period still puritanical. The best of Herrick's novels are those in which the thesis remains implicit. Such a novel as *The Memoirs of an American Citizen* (1905), the autobiography of a ruthless financial buccaneer, reveals its social significance by indirection, and in *Clark's Field* (1914) the influence of property on character and destiny is set forth with a certain imaginative largeness. But the seriousness of Herrick's intention and the purity of his moral purpose were unfortunately unmatched by genuinely creative powers. Though his novels are not overridden with doctrine, they are seriously lacking in warmth and vitality. Herrick was possessed of a higher critical than creative faculty. Furthermore, as the years of creative activity passed, Herrick's view of American life became more and more despairing, and the acerbity of his spirit drove him into querulous and sterile fault-finding. Such a novel as *Waste* (1924) gives an impression of little in American life save the mean and futile.

The critical problem raised in didactic political fiction is illustrated nowhere more clearly than in a consideration of the works of Upton Sinclair (*q.v.*). Sinclair has devoted his life and means to the dissemination of his economic and political views in both imaginative and expository literary forms. In a long series of highly moralistic tracts, he has exposed the villainous criminalities of the capitalistic system. His attack on the meat-packing industry in *The Jungle* (1906) was a national sensation, and led to President Theodore Roosevelt's encouragement of pure food legislation. Sinclair went on to attack Wall Street in *The Money Changers* (1908), the militarists in *Jimmie Higgins* (1919), the post-war red-hunters in *100%, The Story of a Patriot* (1920), the economic struggle for the California oil fields in *Oil!* (1927), and the hounding to death of the radicals Sacco and Vanzetti by Boston's conservatives in *Boston* (1928).

Scrutiny of Sinclair's output as products of the creative imagination makes clear the reasons for his popularity in Soviet Russia and his modest reputation at home. Not only are his economic and political views distasteful to most American readers and critics, but his artistry is almost completely negligible. His heart may be in the right place, but his novelistic powers are obscured by his zeal for denunciation and preachment and his flair for campaign oratory. In contrast to the best proletarian novels of the depression, Sinclair's fiction offers paste-board characters in melodramatic postures and mechanical activities.

Ernest Poole (*q.v.*) and Dorothy Canfield (*q.v.*) may be taken as representative of the optimistic liberalism of the years immediately preceding the World War, a liberalism that, in the light of recent history, seems curiously roseate and uncritical, an emotional liberalism that looked forward to a very early remodeling of the social and economic structure and the dawning of a new and better age. Politically, the spirit of the period is suggested by the reforming insurgency of Theodore Roosevelt and the popularity of a kind of parlor socialism in the academic class. It was further revealed in the influence and prestige of Herbert D. Croly's *The Promise of American Life* (1909), the founding of *The New Republic* as an organ of liberal opinion (1914), the rehabilitation of the *Nation* as a radical journal by Oswald Garrison Villard, and the emergence of Walter Lippmann (*q.v.*) as a hopeful liberal in *A Preface to Politics* (1914). Liberalism of this doctrinaire variety was soon to yield to the pressure and violence of the hysterical war period, but it left its stamp on a whole generation of writers whose youth coincided with these cheerful, hopeful years.

In that literary generation, such writers as Ernest Poole (*q.v.*) and Dorothy Canfield (*q.v.*) were conspicuous. Unfortunately for Poole's reputation, his first novel, the Pulitzer Prize winner, *The Harbor* (1915), is generally regarded as his best. This novel is not only a distinguished example of urban regionalism, a skillful expression of a feeling for New York as the nation's seaport, but, in its dramatic treatment of a dock strike that fails, a revelation of Poole's generous sympathies and his passion for a better world. *Blind* (1920) marks clearly the fate of liberalism during the period of the war and just after. In this novel, the hero moves out of New York's theatrical world into the revolutionary atmosphere of Germany and Russia after the war. The persistently liberal tone sounds strangely mild in comparison with the dissonancies of Russian radicalism and the cacophonies of the jazz age in which Americans were struggling wildly to forget the war and its consequences. Poole's other noteworthy novels are social in the narrower sense. His early novel, *His Family* (1917), depicted shrewdly the varied temperaments of three sisters and their shaping of lives for themselves in the environment of New York. In *The Avalanche* (1924), he recurred to the conflict between science and success so often treated by Robert Herrick (*q.v.*) and soon to be treated even more brilliantly by Sinclair Lewis (*q.v.*) in *Arrowsmith* (1925).

The novels of Dorothy Canfield (*q.v.*) began to appear in the years just preceding America's entry into the World War. Though her first novel, *Gunhild* (1907), showed a group of Americans in an unfamiliar Norwegian setting, her characteristic work belongs to the social novel in its narrower sense, since it is devoted to the exploration of the problems of married life, a presentation that goes beyond mere realism because of the implication of significances larger than the merely personal. Miss

Canfield's insight into the characters and problems of middle-class Americans has unquestionably been deepened by her broad social experience in the Middle West, New England, Norway, and, particularly, France. Her writing is, in the best sense, feminine, since she is especially concerned with the problems of her women characters in their premarital and marital experiences. Her honest treatment of American domestic relations preserves a decorum gratifying to the mass of her readers. *The Squirrel Cage* (1912), the first of her full-length studies of married life, was less rich and sympathetic than either *The Brimming Cup* (1921) or *The Deepening Stream* (1930), both sound, if not brilliant, representations of bourgeois life in the America of the war and post-war periods. The latter novel has the broadest canvas that she has used, since it carries her married hero and heroine through their services in France and the disillusionment of the years after the war. Her novels are the work of an enlightened *bourgeoise*.

Another variety of liberalism is illustrated by the fiction of Ludwig Lewisohn (*q.v.*), whose point of view was formulated in the pre-war and war periods, though it did not find expression in fiction until the twenties. Lewisohn's liberalism is Continental rather than American in origin, and is nurtured on a literature frankly in rebellion against the decorum and repression of nineteenth-century bourgeois society. Over against this system is set up the rather indistinct ideal of individual freedom and self-expression, of the creative life of the spirit in contrast to the mechanical life of the unspiritual. Lewisohn was well fitted by race and culture to play an important part in the liberation of the American spirit from its inhibitions and its provincialities. But the tone of his creative work proved to be much less generous and civilized than his critical work had been. The painful severing of his academic connections during the World War and his deepening sense of racial loyalties alienated him almost completely from any profound understanding of the nature and operation of the American spirit. This physical and spiritual exile from his adopted land brought about in him a sort of exacerbated masochism which make such novels as *Don Juan* (1923) and *The Island Within* (1928) seem self-pitying and peevish. His case against bourgeois America and American women has been tiresomely and monotonously repeated.

Sinclair Lewis (*q.v.*), on the other hand, is as authentically American as the Model T Ford. The union in him of crude vigor and moral earnestness, of tireless activity and comic verve, have won him international favor as realist and satirist. His realistic powers are unquestioned: he has a phenomenal memory or an equally phenomenal industry in amassing details that build up as plausible a picture of American village and city life as the realistic movement has produced. The first hundred pages of *Babbitt* (1922), which render unsparingly the minutest details of a realtor's day, are a masterpiece of malicious reporting. His early satires showed in subject and tone the anti-bourgeois animus of Mencken, the peak of whose influence coincided with the appearance of Lewis' first important novels. In *Main Street* (1920), Lewis recorded once and for all the pettiness and spiritual lassitude of the American village; in *Babbitt*, he exposed to the world the empty pretentiousness of the small American businessman. In *Elmer Gantry* (1927), he drew an extravagantly satirical portrait, in the Mencken manner, of religious hypocrisy. By 1934, however, Lewis was ripe for recantation, and *Work of Art* reversed the verdict on American business enterprise rendered in *Babbitt;* here aesthetic pretentiousness is the main object of his satirical scorn. His essential liberalism proclaimed itself most definitely in the violent anti-Fascist *It Can't Happen Here* (1935). Probably the most satisfying of Lewis' novels are those in which the realist gets the upper hand of the satirist. *Arrowsmith* (1925) is perhaps the best of the American novels dealing with the theme of the scientist and the threat that commercialism and professional jealousy offer to his integrity, and *Dodsworth* (1929), a novel almost devoid of satire, but an extraordinarily fine study of human relations for their own sake, is perhaps the most completely successful, if not the most ambitious, of his novels.

Lewis' powers of observation, ear for authentic speech, comic verve, energy, and moral fervor are remarkable. But his limitations become increasingly apparent. His unlimited familiarity with the clothes, houses, habits, and ideas of his characters results in masses of details that are more impressive as reporting than as creation. His comic verve and his moral fervor are sometimes so unrestrained that in *Elmer Gantry* and *It Can't Happen Here* he defeats his own ends. His passion for reform makes him impatient of the necessity of creating permanently interesting works of art. But he has played a large part in arousing the American public to self-scrutiny and self-criticism. He will probably be remembered, not by his best novels, but by his satirical representation of easily recognizable American types.

During the depression, the social novel assumed so distinct a form that many of its critics and practitioners were inclined to maintain that it constituted a distinct genre, the proletarian novel, not to be confused with other novels devoted to social issues. Theory and practice combined to make this type of novel one of the most conspicuous in the decade of the thirties. The theory, though not unanimously accepted, arose out of the necessity most of the leftist writers and critics felt of relating their activity in the novel with the body of Marxian doctrine to which many of them were converts.

If we compare this latest form of the social novel with earlier forms, perhaps the divergences will tend to clarify themselves. Most of these proletarian novels are naturalistic in subject matter and method. Among these naturalistic novels, one type presents proletarian material with little or no social doctrine. A second type combines naturalistic subject matter and treatment with an implicit or explicit doctrine of revolutionary social change. A third type is that which combines an implicit or explicit revolutionary doctrine with a more or less experimental novelistic technique.

The period in which the proletarian novel appeared was one in which it was peculiarly likely to flourish. The tragic consequences of the depression for worker and artist alike, the universal fear and insecurity, the sudden revelation of the quicksand foundations of our economic life drew the attention of young novelists, in particular, to subjects and problems that had been obscured during the war and the post-war periods. The depression forced serious writers of all varieties to consider the acute problem of finding a way out of this world-crisis and of preventing the recurrence of such crises. To an astonishing number of young American writers, the most appealing way out of the dilemma seemed to be the application of the doctrines associated loosely with the name of Karl Marx. The theories of the class struggle and of the dictatorship of the proletariat, and the world-shaking attempt to apply these theories in contemporary Russia, won the allegiance of a very large number of American intellectuals, an allegiance made public by the admission of many of them into the Communist party, and made systematic by the activities connected with the American Writers' Congresses of 1935 and 1937, the purpose of which was to discuss ways and means by which American writers might throw in their lot with the radical wing of the American working class, and devote their creative powers to furthering the common cause.

The depression, too, furnished not merely ideas but ample material for representation and interpretation. The appalling increase in the number of the unemployed, the attempts on the part of local and national authorities to cope with the problem of relief brought to the attention of sensitive observers the very large number of Americans who in normal times live lives not merely economically insecure but physically and socially debased. The sudden discovery of the importance of the economic motive and its influence on thought and art brought writers to an appreciation of the attempts of the underprivileged to improve their status, attempts that, under the competitive capitalistic system, were bound to end in violence and brutal repressive activities. For the first time, the roseate veil that novelists had drawn over American life was rudely rent, and the horrid actualities underneath were revealed.

The novels of Albert Halper (*q.v.*) will serve to illustrate the type of proletarian novel in which naturalism is combined with a minimum of propaganda. Halper's appetite for life is so insatiable that in such novels as *Union Square* (1933) and *The Foundry* (1934) he seems completely absorbed in extraordinarily vivid and pure representation. In both novels, the unifying principle is, not the fate of a hero, but the life of some larger unit, a city square or a factory in operation. But Halper's sympathies, it is very clear, go out to the persons of his chosen worlds, and those sympathies, no less than his material, justify our including him among the proletarian novelists. In the novels of Josephine Herbst (*q.v.*), the message is equally implicit. Miss Herbst indeed may be considered a proletarian writer, not by reason of her treatment of the lives of the workers, but of the fact that she traces the history of a middle-class American family from the Civil War to the present time, from the point of view of a convert to Marxianism. Her trilogy, *Pity Is Not Enough* (1933), *The Executioner Waits* (1934), and *Rope of Gold* (1939), is, however, so circumspectly circumstantial that it is only on close inspection that the economic significance of her action becomes manifest. She has found perhaps the most satisfactory solution of the problem of blending art and propaganda. In most of the proletarian novels of the thirties, the propaganda is much more overt. Jack Conroy's *The Disinherited* (1933) and *A World to Win* (1935), for instance, are more interesting as the products of a genuine proletarian than as works of art, since they are not merely extremely weak in organization but are melodramatic in action and unrealistic in style.

Certain themes recur in the fiction of proletarian novelists. One of the most popular is the account of the genesis, development, progress, and defeat of a strike, material obviously tempting for its violence of action and its class significance. Superior treatments of this characteristic theme are to be found in William Rollins' *The Shadow Before* (1934) and Robert Cantwell's (*q.v.*) *The Land of Plenty* (1934), the first drawing its material from the ghastly history of a New England textile town, and the latter from the events connected with a strike in a lumber mill in the Northwest. Cantwell's novel is of especial interest, because of his utilization of a number of experimental devices for the intensification of his effects. Less expert, especially in its attempt at an experimental technique, is Clara Weatherwax's *Marching! Marching!* (1935), another novel revolving around a strike in a West Coast lumber mill. Another favorite theme is that of the incursion of the factory system into the South and the social and economic problems that have resulted from this movement. Of a number of novels devoted to this theme, Clement Wood's *Mountain* (1920), Edith Summers Kelley's *Weeds* (1920), Mary Heaton Vorse's *Strike!* (1930), Fielding Burke's *Call Home the Heart* (1932), Myra Page's *Gathering Storm* (1932), and Grace Lumpkin's (*q.v.*) *To Make My Bread* (1932), later dramatized as *Let Freedom Ring*, are perhaps the most noteworthy. Another popular theme was the plight of the agricultural laborer, smitten fore and aft by drought and depression. The harsh lot of the sharecropper and tenant farmer in the South was treated by Miss Lumpkin in *A Sign for Cain* (1935), and more sardonically by Erskine Caldwell (*q.v.*) in *Tobacco Road* (1932). Caldwell's sociological sketches depicted with painful explicitness the lives of the economically underprivileged throughout the United States. The drought-smitten farmers of the West served as grim material for Wellington Roe's *The Tree Falls South* (1937) and Arnold B. Armstrong's *Parched Earth* (1934). A final theme, the demoralizing plight of the unemployed, was one that naturally appealed to the sensitive young novelists of the period. The hopelessness and ignominy of unemployment in a land of plenty, the tragic contrast between the privileged and the underprivileged, the heartbreaking attempts to find a foothold on the economic ladder—all these experiences common to millions of American citizens in the early thirties were set forth with terrifying vividness in such novels as Edward Dahlberg's *Bottom Dogs* (1930) and *Those Who Perish* (1934), Catherine Brody's *Nobody Starves* (1932), Edward Newhouse's *You Can't Sleep Here* (1934), and Nelson Algren's *Somebody in Boots* (1935).

The union of radical sympathies and technical experimentation was first shown conspicuously in the novels of John Dos Passos (*q.v.*). *Three Soldiers* (1921), one of the first of the American novels written to debunk the war, did not, to be sure, show any evidence of the technical audacity of his later novels. *Manhattan Transfer* (1925), however, was a valiant attempt to capture the raucous confusion of the lives of a large number of characters in contemporary New York. Individual lives might touch and cross, but no single life was important enough to represent the many-faceted life of the metropolis. The method of *Manhattan Transfer* was almost purely naturalistic, but in the later novels, two changes are noteworthy: the fusing of the naturalistic technique with certain extra-naturalistic devices and the intensification of the author's social vision. Of the expressionistic devices, three are particularly important: the abbreviated biographical sketch, sometimes extraordinarily shrewd and implicatory, of real or fictitious contemporaries; the newsreel, a blend of newspaper headline, popular song, news story, and current slangy dialogue; and the camera-eye, a poetic presentation of the author's stream of consciousness contemporary with the events narrated. These and other devices create a type of fiction which projects powerfully Dos Passos' view of the nature and meaning of American life. That view shows urban America at its most violent and repellent, as a harsh, cynical, brutal composite of individuals aggressively on the make, corruption in private and public life, raucous speech, and animalistic behavior. Of this view, limited by the omission of common decency, honesty, integrity, and simple and uncorrupted pleasures, Dos Passos' power of presentation is unquestioned. But the limitations of both view and manner threaten his place in the first rank of contemporary American novelists. For extravagance and distortion communicate themselves to his technique and style. One looks in vain for any subtlety or delicacy less violent than the action of steam hammers or steel riveters.

To other than radical readers, the vices of proletarian fiction are more conspicuous than its virtues. What is most likely to distress the only moderately emancipated reader is the unrelieved gloom of most of this fiction. In the novels of so shrewd a writer as Dos Passos, not even his most wanton characters ever enjoy their immorality. In less skilled writers, the misery is unrelieved. One is further distressed by the tendency of the characterization to take on, not the black and white of the old melodrama, but, in Clifton Fadiman's terms, the black and red of radical propaganda. A sharp line is drawn between the virtuous proletarian and the vicious capitalist, and very few characters succeed in crossing that line. In consequence, partly, of this characterization, and partly of the nature of the material, the action is likely to show the excessive violence of melodrama, and to conclude too frequently, even in the midst of unmistakable economic defeat, with a personal conversion to the cause or a mystical vision of the promised land of communism.

But these vices are the vices of a youthful and relatively unsophisticated treatment of a new ideology. On every hand, there are signs that sophistication and subtlety are coming into the treatment of proletarian material, and whatever one may think of the validity of the implicit or explicit propaganda, the proletarian novel is the focus of more creative energy than any other form of contemporary fiction. It has already extended the subject matter and the intellectual content of fiction; it is the most potent of the forms that the social novel has assumed.

THE SHORT STORY

No one can make even a casual survey of contemporary American literature without becoming aware of the ubiquity of the short story, its general excellence, and its occasional distinction. Its ubiquity probably finds its cause in the conditions surrounding magazine publication in America rather than in any essential compulsion of the American creative spirit to express itself in this particular literary form, although some critics have maintained that the concentration, intensity, and "punch" of the short story make the form an especially suitable mode of expression for the American temperament. At any rate, the tremendous production and consumption of short stories in this country have been made possible by the omnipresent if protean magazine. Given magazines with endless pages of advertising to be deftly severed by columns of text, editors were bound to seek for, and readers learned to look for, fiction more manageable and satisfying than the long story continued from issue to issue or the novel printed in installments. No less apparent than the ubiquity of the short story is its general excellence. The standardized American short story is the very creditable and dependable product of a highly organized industry. Nothing demonstrates more clearly the fact that the writing of short stories is an industry and not an art than the numerous manuals of short story courses in colleges and universities, and the teaching of the fundamentals of the craft in correspondence courses. From such circumstances, standardization was bound to come; thus, the most conspicuous weakness of the American short story has been its conformity to a conventionalized notion of exactly what a short story should be. Such a process, however profitable it might prove financially, was bound to make for aesthetic sterility.

The aim of the short story writer has been to achieve distinction either within the limits of the established form or outside the oppressive conventions of subject matter and technique. Vitality is more likely to be encountered in those writers who have striven to present fresh material or to devise new forms for the presentation of conventional material. But over and above thousands of marketable machine-made products, a great deal of excellent work in both the conventional and the unconventional short story form can be discovered among the productions of the last forty or fifty years.

Though short stories in great numbers had been written throughout the nineteenth century, it was only at the end of the eighties that critics became conscious that the short story was a distinct literary form with "laws" and principles of its own. Hitherto, despite the growing influence of Poe's theory and practice, and despite a dim consciousness of what de Maupassant was doing for the short story in France, the short story had been regarded in America as a fragment of a novel and viewed with condescension as something a writer might try his hand at before he set about the serious business of writing novels. The credit for defining the short story belongs probably to Brander Matthews, who signalized his "discovery" by hyphenating the term and laying down its laws.

Matthews' conscious experimentation with H. C. Bunner in their joint volume, *In Partnership* (1884), illustrated the increasing seriousness with which the short story was beginning to be taken. Bunner went on in *Made in France* (1893) to adapt French material and technique to American ways of thought and life, although the most characteristic form developed by Bunner was the brief, swift, pointed sketches of *Short Sixes* (1890) and *More Short Sixes* (1894). To the nineties also belongs the work, if not the later fame, of those two striking talents, Ambrose Bierce and Stephen Crane. The mordant bitterness and *diablerie* of Bierce took the form not only of epigrams but of the stark horrors of *In the Midst of Life* (1891) and *Can Such Things Be?* (1893). But Bierce's reputation did not come into its own until a quarter of a century later, when his influence may have counted for something in encouraging short story writers to attack the genteel conventions cramping the life of the form. Stephen Crane met with a wider recognition among the craftsmen and readers of his own day, but, as with Bierce, time only emphasized the original distinction, not only of his steadily unromantic war novel, *The Red Badge of Courage* (1895), but of his studious avoidance of the sentimental and the lucid precision of his observation and imagination in *The Open Boat* (1898) and *Whilomville Stories* (1900).

In the nineties, which saw the rise of Stephen Crane, Henry James published five volumes of short stories, conventional in form but subtle in execution. In these, he worked out a formula even more fastidious and exacting than Poe's. A scrupulously maintained unity, a concentration on a moral dilemma, the deliberate and severe exclusion of nonessentials, a cautious and calculated building up of emotion and action to the crucial situation—such were the technical precepts James illustrated and transmitted to his admirers. While his interest in the short story and the tale lasted, James treated these forms with the same seriousness and respect that he showed the novel, and his attitude and practice were contagious. Many of the better stories in the quality magazines today reveal the remote influence of James's exquisite technique. But the lofty Jamesian tradition was carried on by two avowed disciples in particular, Edith Wharton (*q.v.*) and Katharine Fullerton Gerould (*q.v.*). In point of view, in temperament, and in artistry, they demonstrated their allegiance and their discipleship. Mrs. Wharton's contribution to the novel has already been considered, and little more need be said as to the major characteristics of her work. In the short story and the tale (for which she shared with James an evident predilection), she manifested her temperamental aloofness and irony, her rich cosmopolitan experience and culture, and the unfailing seriousness of her craftsmanship. The less extensive work of Mrs. Gerould reveals a similar devotion to the traditional technique, and if it is, on the whole, less satisfying than Mrs. Wharton's, the reasons may be the rigidity of her ethical conceptions and the element of Pharisaism in her temperament. Like the master, both Mrs. Wharton and Mrs. Gerould occasionally chose for treatment bizarre moral dilemmas that are rather remote from ordinary experience.

The nineties saw the beginnings but by no means the conclusions of the long literary careers of Hamlin Garland (*q.v.*), Mary E. Wilkins Freeman, and Alice Brown. The earliest work of Hamlin Garland was well attuned to the growing realism of the decade. Brought up in the harsh conditions of prairie life in the Dakotas, but in complete revolt against a sentimental presentation of that life, Garland set out deliberately to reveal the hardships and the spiritual limitations of pioneering existence, in such deservedly famous collections as *Main-Travelled Roads* (1891) and *Prairie Folks* (1893). In the meantime, Mary E. Wilkins Freeman and Alice Brown, inheritors of the strong "local color" tradition, were beginning their extensive explorations of the rich deposits of custom and tradition in New England. Mrs. Freeman's work began virtually with *A Humble Romance* (1887) and *A New England Nun* (1891), and, though the bulk of her memorable writing was to come within the first decade of the new century, its character was pretty well defined by 1900. Less intent on the picturesque aspects of New England life than Sarah Orne Jewett, Mrs. Freeman exploited with honesty and tenderness the involutions of the provincial temperament. Always a meticulous craftsman, she produced volume after volume of fictional studies of the victims of the decline of Puritanism. In the new and invigorating elements of New England life she showed little or no interest. Although Alice Brown has not been so singularly devoted to the short story as Mrs. Freeman, she, too, has remained faithful to the subjects and attitudes apparent in *Meadow-Grass* (1895) and *Tiverton* (1899). She, too, has expended upon her material that painstaking observation and feminine clarity of vision to which New England regional literature owes a large debt. The work of both these women attains a distinction far beyond that of the popular exploitation of New England oddities so dear to the host of uncritical readers of Joseph C. Lincoln's Cape Cod tales.

Such legendary figures as Richard Harding Davis, Jack London, and O. Henry remind one of the close relationship between the short story and journalism. Richard Harding Davis (1864–1916) devoted almost thirty years to incessant journalistic and literary activity, but in this connection he is significant for his share in annexing the short story to the domain of journalism in the first decade of the century. Here, he followed the lead of Kipling, whose astonishing youthful reputation was built on fresh sources of material, vigor and terseness of style, and journalistic economy. Kipling had demonstrated the maximum effect that could be attained within the limits of space allotted by a newspaper editor. Davis' short stories, however, suffer considerably from the haste enforced upon him by his multifarious journalistic activities. They have a superficial glibness and effectiveness, and something of the self-confidence and assertiveness of Davis himself. They lack depth and insight, however, and they are as distinctly dated as the pompadoured Gibson girl or the broad-shouldered and somewhat vacuous Gibson man (of whom Davis is said to have furnished the model). If the Davis tradition persists anywhere, it is probably in the standardized *Saturday Evening Post* narrative of the upstanding young American, cheeky and irrepressible, who overcomes almost automatically all the obstacles that lie between himself and fortune and matrimony.

Equally astounding in quantity, but somewhat less conventional in quality, was the output of Jack London (1876–1916), whose reputation in America reached its peak about 1910. London's contribution consisted, not in making any innovation in the technique of the short story, but in conquering for it new domains of action and emotion. London was a specialist in the brutal and primitive, in the lives of animals and men under harsh conditions on the edges of civilization. On occasion, his use of this material combined extremely vivid sensory impressions and an eloquent appeal to the eternal delight in elemental conflict. His later work, done under the stimulus of huge rewards from editors and publishers, suffered greatly from exaggerated violence and sensationalism. His reputation lives on in Germany, Russia, and France, where the falsity of the high coloring is not checked by any precise information about "primitive" America. His influence survives, not in any writer of much literary importance but in those tales of the struggles of excessively stalwart heroes and incredibly chaste heroines in tropical or frigid climates, tales which continue to furnish vicarious thrills to the unadventurous.

The sensational success of O. Henry (William Sydney Porter, 1862–1910) coincided almost exactly with the first decade of the twentieth century. His amazing vogue in the ten years before and after his death tempts the critic to exaggerate the value of his work. Done, for the most part, in circumstances that gave no opportunity for revision, the mass of his writing shows a rare skill in catching and recording the sharp outlines and lively coloring of the New York of his time, and an almost unfailing facility in the use of a formula that ended with a short sharp shock. Like the other journalistic writers of short stories, O. Henry lacks richness and intensity, and his much admired and imitated surprise-denouements are naturally more effective on the first than on the fifth reading. O. Henry had, however, a remarkable understanding of the types of the metropolitan half-world in which he lived, and that world comes to life in him as it does in no other American short story writer. But the pressure of meeting a deadline and the absence of opportunity for revision left on his pages gross errors in taste, frequent cheapnesses of effect, and too ready a recourse to the devices of the journalistic vaudevillean. Through his insistence on a formula, a hard glittering finish, and technical efficiency, O. Henry has proved to be one of the strongest standardizing influences in the American short story.

On short story writing since the war, a number of causes have operated to increase the aesthetic distance between the conventional and the experimental short stories. The most powerful influence making for conservatism in subject matter, point of view, technique, ethical atmosphere, and moral tone is the rise to circulations of a million or more of such magazines as the *Saturday Evening Post*, *Collier's*, the *Ladies Home Journal*, and the *Woman's Home Companion*, potent media of national advertising. Editors aiming to please vast bodies of readers must walk very warily among the prejudices and preoccupations of their enormous audiences. Prohibitions with regard to subject matter have perhaps been as potent as prohibitions with regard to technique. Certain of these prohibitions, pointed out by William L. Chennery, editor of *Collier's*, in the *Saturday Review of Literature* for June 18, 1938, include preferences for a happy ending and for American rather than European or oriental characters, a limitation on the amount of dialect, and an insistence on the absence of propaganda. Chennery might very well have added the requirement, especially operative in the women's magazines, of an insistence on only a modest amount of realism in the treatment of sex and racial relations and a strict observance of the bourgeois domestic code. A specific illustration of the conservative influence of the great popular magazine is the prestige of the *Saturday Evening Post*. To the commercial writers of short stories, publication in this omnipresent journal is equivalent to admission to the most exclusive of literary Valhallas. Consequently, authors bent on receiving the ultimate accolade are bound to attempt to approximate the standard for fiction set by the editor. While it would be untrue to say that all *Post* stories are written to formula, and while a great many writers of considerable literary reputation have found it possible to adapt themselves to *Post* standards, an inspection of such anthologies as *Post Stories of 1935*, *1936*, or *1937* illustrates the operation on numerous writers of the process of standardization and the consequent sterility of the product. A further influence making for conservatism was the establishment of the O. Henry Memorial Award in 1919, and the annual publication since that date of the *O. Henry Prize Stories*, edited by Blanche Colton Williams from 1919 to 1932, and by Harry Hansen since the latter date. While Hansen's view of the short story is, in some respects, more liberal than that of Miss Williams, the O. Henry influence is still persistent enough to make for a selectivity favoring the well-made and well-tailored short story.

But not all the forces operative on the short story since the war have been conservative in tendency. Perhaps the most important alien influence has been the short stories of the Russian, Anton Chekhov, which Constance Garnett began to translate in 1916, and which were eagerly read in America as illustrations of perfect freedom from the restrictions of the traditional technique. Chekhov's stories show a wide range in length and complexity of structure, but perhaps the most influential stories were those in which an apparent absence of structure was more than compensated for by a superb naturalness of movement and language, an incomparable skill in conveying character and suggesting tone by the smallest number of telling strokes, and the creation by these means of living characters and the reflecting of life through their temperaments.

A more immediate influence has been that of the editor and anthologist, Edward J. O'Brien, whose collections of *Best Short Stories* published since 1916 show the editor fighting and winning the battle for experimentation in fiction. O'Brien's activities as editor have been on a much higher plane than his activities as critic. The biographical and bibliographical material in the appendices, entitled "A Yearbook of the American Short Story," furnish the material necessary for a thoroughgoing history of the form in America since the initiation of his admirable project. Critically, O'Brien suffers from a muddy and turgid style and the temptation natural to the editor of an annual to discover aesthetic mountains that turn out to be molehills and to perceive trends, climaxes, and crises where there are only incidents. But despite one's reservations as to O'Brien's generalizations, no other person has made American writers and critics so conscious of the eternal conflict between tradition and experiment in the American short story, or has set his face so sternly against the merely competent machine-made successes of the big magazines. O'Brien has always ranged widely and curiously for good stories in obscure and struggling experimental journals. He has looked hopefully for new names and new forms in such courageous editorial ventures as the *Midland*, edited by John T. Frederick at Iowa City from 1915 to 1931, the *Frontier*, edited by H. G. Merriam at Helena, Montana, since 1920, the *Prairie Schooner*, edited by Lowry C. Wimberley at Lincoln, Nebraska, since 1927, and *American Prefaces*, edited by Wilbur L. Schramm at Iowa City since 1935. But no experimental periodical has come so close to O'Brien's ideal of such a medium of distribution as *Story*. This extraordinary magazine was first published in mimeographed form in Vienna in 1931 by the American journalists, Whit Burnett and his wife,

Martha Foley; in the following year it was transferred by them to Majorca, where it continued publication until its transfer to New York. From the very beginning, O'Brien was able to find in *Story* the kinds of fiction he most admired, and he borrowed from it more freely than from any other magazine he had anthologized. From its first experimental volume, O'Brien selected four stories, and from the second, eight. The editors were astonishingly astute in their discovery of fresh talent: thus, they have to their credit the first publications of stories by such now well-known writers as Erskine Caldwell (*q.v.*), William Saroyan (*q.v.*), Tess Slesinger (*q.v.*), Peter Neagoe, Dorothy McCleary, Allan Seeger, and Alan Marshall.

In addition to the forces operating specifically on the short story, this genre was also influenced by those aesthetic forces that were at the time potent in the novel. Thus, in the short story as in the novel, three lines of development may be distinguished: the adaptation of the traditional well-made story on the de Maupassant-Jamesian model, experimentation in the direction of naturalistic objectivity, and experimentation in the direction of a deeper and deeper naturalistic subjectivity. These novelistic trends were almost certain to appear in the short story, since most short story writers of distinction were also novelists.

Writers of short stories of the traditional type tended, of course, to submit more or less willingly to the influence of the machine-made short story, but, by the superiority of their artistry or the sensitivity of their perceptions, they were able to turn out hand-made articles of very high value. Thus, Willa Cather's (*q.v.*) transient interest in the short story, as illustrated by *Youth and the Bright Medusa* (1920), produced finely wrought examples of the traditional sort, touched unmistakably by her fineness of feeling for character, her passionate concern for the integrity of the artist in the modern world, and her lucid and slightly poeticized prose. A more consistent devotion to the traditional short story has had notable results in the hands of Wilbur Daniel Steele (*q.v.*). He has taken the conventional form and treated it with such pains and ingenuity as to make it seem fresh and vigorous. His bent is in the direction of the horrifying and the terrible, and, within the strict limits of his form and his interests, his work is distinguished. Steele is one of the few contemporary writers whose fame depends primarily on his short stories.

Nearer to the standards of the "slick" magazines, and more significant for their social than for their aesthetic values, are the short stories of F. Scott Fitzgerald (*q.v.*), whose slightly lurid tales of the post-war jazz age did a good deal to define, if not to create, the atmosphere of that period. Fitzgerald was of precisely the right age and experience to describe the behavior and indicate the tone of the bright young creatures, consciously adrift from the ancestral ethical moorings, compact of disillusionment and cleverness, and passionately intent on escaping from boredom through inebriation and preoccupation with love affairs initiated with a complete conviction of their transitoriness.

American folkloristic material has furnished the stimulus for a recent phase in the varied literary activities of Stephen Vincent Benét (*q.v.*). First concerned seriously with such material in his epical *John Brown's Body* (1928), Benét has shown an astonishing flair for the fantastic-humorous treatment of folk themes in such tales as *The Devil and Daniel Webster* (1937) and *Johnny Pie and the Fool-Killer* (1938). These tales achieve their distinction from Benét's adroit combination of the elements of fantasy and humor, his persuasive evocation of the operations of the folk-mind, and the investiture of his material with an atmosphere of the grotesque and slightly macabre, an atmosphere commoner in American folklore than in American literature.

The strong infusion of naturalism in modern fiction has had important consequences in encouraging experimentation with the potential effects of a strictly objective treatment of the short story. Naturalism in the short story as in the novel has made for an elimination of formal or complex plot, an abstention from auctorial comment, an accumulation of objective details, and a tendency toward the utilization of unlovely or unpleasant material. In every one of these respects naturalism has meant a violation of one or more of the aesthetic or ethical taboos which have made the fiction characteristic of the "slick" magazines and less conspicuous in the "quality" magazines seem adroit but meaningless feats of prestidigitation.

Less naturalistic than realistic, perhaps, were the early stories of middle western life produced by Ruth Suckow (*q.v.*). In her, something of the spirit of the early Hamlin Garland (*q.v.*) persisted, for like him she sees contemporary middle western domestic life not, perhaps, as primitive and brutalizing, but as aesthetically harsh and spiritually mean. Such a collection as *Iowa Interiors* (1926), for instance, represents the peak of Miss Suckow's naturalism. In her novel, *The Folks* (1934), although the method is realistic, the effect of objectivity is considerably modified by an infusion of kindly sentiment.

The high priest of naturalism in the short story is, of course, Ernest Hemingway (*q.v.*), whose *In Our Time* (1925) and *Men without Women* (1927) initiated the vogue of hard-boiled fiction. No follower of Hemingway has equaled him in the incomparable economy of the means by which he attains powerful effects. Indebted originally to Gertrude Stein (*q.v.*) and Sherwood Anderson (*q.v.*) for sensitizing him to the necessity of re-creating the style of prose narrative, Hemingway from the outset of his career showed a facility in the manipulation of the colloquial that is one of the secrets of his extraordinary effectiveness. But Hemingway's colloquial diction and sentence structure are no phonographic recording of actual oral discourse. His use of the colloquial is highly selective. While the diction, sentence structure, and speech rhythm are conscientiously colloquial, there is none of the sprawling diffuseness of oral tale-telling. Only such dialogue and only such descriptive and narrative details have been retained as are absolutely necessary to the communication of a mood or the rendition of an incident. The method is implicatory rather than explicatory, and implication is one of Hemingway's major powers. His deliberately laconic characters merely furnish readers the material for an imaginative construction of their personalities, motives, and values. These values—not only the characters' but Hemingway's likewise—are by now almost too familiar. Hemingway's experiences during the war and the post-war period induced in him, as in countless less articulate souls, a revulsion from idealism, a cynicism as to civilized values, the flagellation of the flesh by an evil spirit for which expression became a kind of exorcism. Out of the moil of embittered epicureanism, Hemingway seized on certain simple values on which he has never tired of insisting—the values of an elementary stoicism, of physical courage and endurance, of basic physical satisfactions, and of an aggressive honesty and hostility toward all kinds of sham. As the limitations of these values have become increasingly conspicuous, they have brought a reaction from the critical enthusiasm which greeted Hemingway in the twenties, but, despite his air of a primitive adolescent keeping a stiff upper lip under tribal torture, Hemingway's effectiveness in his particular variety of naturalistic short story remains unchallenged.

Hemingway's influence in the creation of a hard-boiled school of fiction is perhaps more apparent in the novel than in the short story, but naturalism, with or without the special Hemingway devices, has had its followers. Of these, perhaps the most conspicuous is Erskine Caldwell (*q.v.*), who utilizes a steadily naturalistic technique—minimizing plot, confining himself to the colloquial in dialogue and narration, and favoring as material the grotesque and the physically unpleasant. Caldwell's naturalism appears in its most traditional guise in the brutality and horror at which he aims so frequently in the short stories included in *Kneel to the Rising Sun* (1935). Sometimes the horror seems merely gratuitous, self-conscious, and calculated. Such familiar shock situations as rape, lynching, and murder, having no larger significance than that of the intended neural assault, diminish in effectiveness with repetition. But on those more recent occasions when Caldwell has invested his narrative with an aura of social significance, when the almost unbearably disgusting is made symptomatic of the decay of decency and morality among the economically oppressed poor whites of Georgia, then the naturalism attains a higher justification than that of mere accuracy. Furthermore, Caldwell, although less frequently perhaps in his short stories than in his novels, uses naturalism with the unfamiliar intention of humor. Thus, the effect of disgust is qualified successfully by gusto, lustiness, and the comic vigor which rise out of the miasma of degradation and depravity. In this particular effect of naturalistic comedy, Caldwell is almost alone. More familiar naturalistic effects are illustrated by the short stories of James T. Farrell (*q.v.*) and William March (*q.v.*). Despite the difference in their subject matter—Farrell specializing in urban decline and disorganization, and March in the inhumanity of military life—the methods are those which naturalism has made familiar, and the ethical significance remains on the plane of implication. Farrell stresses the economic and March the more personal causes of oppression, suffering, and demoralization.

The social implications of most contemporary naturalism—implications which impair considerably its strictly and theoretically scientific character—have been deepened by the tremendous concern, during the depression, with the problems of the underprivileged, and with the growth of political radicalism. It is not surprising, therefore, that the short story should have proved attractive to a considerable number of promising writers of proletarian sympathies and radical political allegiance. So popular has the proletarian short story become in the radical journals that it has evolved its own formulas—the progressive decline, economically and morally, of the protagonist, with the crisis centering in the hero's sudden and dramatic conversion to the radical cause, or the account of the progress of a strike through the initial stages of discouragement and apparent failure to a spectacular if momentary triumph of the workers. In proletarian stories of the more naïve sort, the characterization, though economic rather than ethical in its differentiations, does not rise very far above the black and white abstractions of the old melodrama. But there is plenty of proletarian writing which succeeds in avoiding the more tempting clichés, and such young radicals as Ben Field, Albert Maltz, and Alan Calmer vindicate its more impressive potentialities.

Experimentation in subjective naturalism has, on the whole, been more bold and more varied than experimentation in objective naturalism. The full weight of Gertrude Stein's (*q.v.*) extraordinary influence has for years been thrown on the side of experimentation with narrative style, and her *Three Lives* (1909), for the very reason that it was not so idiosyncratic as her later work, pointed the way to a revitalizing of style through the substitution of the rhythm and diction of speech for the rhythm and structure of literary prose, and the apparent repetitiousness and unselectivity of oral colloquial discourse for the rational selectivity of formal prose. These early experiments with style were to prove immensely suggestive to writers bent on saving literature from being too studiously literary. In these stories, moreover, Miss Stein showed a sensitivity to the inner lives of her characters that was to prove stimulating to writers dissatisfied with the effects of superficial realism or the conscientious objectivity of naturalism. Varied as the methods and the effects of the subjectivists were, they shared the common purpose of bringing to light depths of psychological experience which neither realism nor naturalism had been capable of reaching.

Miss Stein's influence has not, of course, been confined to predominantly subjective writers; Hemingway, Wescott, and many other younger objective writers owe a great deal to the stimulus of her self-confident and assertive personality. But it is in the realm of subjectivism that her influence has been most potent. One of the clearest examples of her influence is Sherwood Anderson (*q.v.*), whose short stories and novels all bear the stamp of subjective experimentation. Anderson deliberately rejected the substance, form, and style of the traditional short story. Instead of using a form that states a problem, develops it, and solves it objectively, Anderson cultivates the fluidity of ordinary oral narrative, and such extremely effective stories as "I'm a Fool" and "I Want to Know Why" gain tremendously by being first-person narratives of the hero himself, in each of these cases a not too articulate adolescent male. Anderson's style is consciously shaped out of the speech of the folk he knows best, and it reproduces the diction, grammar, and rhythm of that speech, not merely with perfect fidelity but with a poetic suggestiveness that is Anderson's personal touch upon it. Anderson's constant control over the seemingly uncontrolled flow of the narrative eliminates the pointlessness and circuitousness of most oral tale-telling. Most of his material is drawn from the inner lives of the inexpressive and ineffective old American stock in little towns of the Middle West or near South. Such lives, Anderson's insight and sympathy illuminate and make significant. By these means, *Winesburg, Ohio* (1919) becomes one of the most searchingly American creations of its time.

Another variety of subjectivism appears in the short stories and novels of Conrad Aiken (*q.v.*), who in these genres, as in his poetry, shows the profound influence of psychoanalysis upon him. In such collections as *Bring! Bring!* (1925) and *Costumes by Eros* (1928), Aiken utilized the resources of psychoanalytical theory as foundations for extremely subtle revelations of character in action. The form here approaches the traditional, but the material is freshened by the particular emphasis, and the style is poet's prose, evocative, sensitive, and deeply rhythmical.[1]

It is not surprising that experimentation with subjectivity in fiction should have appealed particularly to women whose consciousness of the richness and complexity of the inner life is perhaps more acute than that of most male writers. The stream of consciousness technique has proved

[1] This vein of subjectivism is illustrated more fully in such novels as *Blue Voyage* (1927) and *Great Circle* (1933), in the first of which the influence of Joyce's *Ulysses* is distinctly perceptible, not merely in structure but in content.

attractive, for example, to Tess Slesinger (*q.v.*), who uses it with somewhat less than aesthetic economy in her rather acrid studies of urban intellectual types. More subtle subjective values arise out of the stories and tales of Katherine Anne Porter (*q.v.*). Although she errs in the direction of super-subtlety, her writing has a very rare poetic power, and her suggestiveness, in this form, is almost incomparable. The subjectivism of Kay Boyle (*q.v.*) is less intensive; indeed, some of her stories are almost completely objective in method. But in such collections as *The First Lover* (1933) and *The White Horses of Vienna* (1936) one is always conscious of the refraction of her characters' experience through a personality of great distinction and definiteness. In these fictions, one is as frequently interested in the author as in the characters and actions she has created. Although she is in no easy superficial sense an autobiographical writer, although her heart is on no one's sleeve, the acute sensory perception, the relentless emotional probing, the flashing swordlike style, reveal the impingement of her personality on whatever material, slight or robust, decadent or tragic, she has chosen to treat.

William Faulkner's (*q.v.*) subjectivity furnishes an interesting contrast to Erskine Caldwell's (*q.v.*) accustomed objectivity. Both are concerned with decadence, but Caldwell's is proletarian while Faulkner's is aristocratic. But the element of robust and earthy humor is completely absent from Faulkner's Dostoevski-like psychological nightmares. In Faulkner, as in Kay Boyle, one is constantly aware of the particular temperament through which life is being refracted. That temperament is unique; it is morbid, saturnine, ridden by nightmares, preoccupied with psychological degeneration, tortured by the decadent and evil creatures of its own imagination, terrified by the fates of decency and gentleness in a world of beasts and ogres. The world of Faulkner's tales is the nightmare-tormented world of a horribly wise and fearfully imaginative child. Its brutalities are more frightful than those of Caldwell, because they are overladen with sinister emotions; they are never simple acts of unconscious evil. Faulkner writes like a man possessed of devils.

Whatever autobiographical reticences other subjectivists may show is more than offset by the excessively revelatory short stories of William Saroyan (*q.v.*). Technically, Saroyan's short stories illustrate the extremity of disintegration. Many of them are hardly more than passages from the author's diary, with little or no attempt at focus or climax, cultivating the technique of free association for rather more than it is worth, and intruding extraneous critical comments on his literary elders and the world of publishing. Stylistically, Saroyan's ideal and frequent achievement is the complete avoidance of formal literary language. The potentialities of that process of colloquializing literature initiated by Gertrude Stein would seem to be completely exhausted by Saroyan's efforts. Despite a great deal of almost entirely ineffective and pointless scribbling, Saroyan's work has a refreshing and individual note. If the ultimate interest in a work of art is the personality that creates it, Saroyan ranks fairly high among contemporary writers, not merely in his arrogance and conscious posturing, but in his disarmingly honest presentation of himself, richness of feeling, sympathy for the despised and rejected, concern for the universally human, and hostility to the essentially inhuman.

Whether the short story is treated adroitly by Wilbur Daniel Steele, subtly by Katherine Anne Porter, brilliantly by Kay Boyle, or cavalierly by William Saroyan, its popularity seems likely to continue. Its vogue among the myriads who confine their reading to magazines is undiminished. It has attracted, and will go on attracting, almost as many varied and distinguished talents as the novel or poetry.

DRAMA AND THEATER

American drama of the pre-war period shared with the drama of most of the nineteenth century the unhappy distinction of being almost negligible as literature. The low level of theatrical taste, the unconditioned control of the theater by avowedly commercial producers, and the persistent and sycophantic dependence—even after the passage of the International Copyright Act in 1893—of American producers on the sensationally successful dramas of England, France, and Germany, go some distance in explaining this deplorable condition. This state of affairs either stimulated native playwrights like Clyde Fitch to imitate foreign models, or failed to supply a "serious" dramatist like Augustus Thomas with an adequately critical audience for his dramas of ideas.

If these conditions have been modified, the change is, in the main, a reflection of the change that came over the European drama in the latter half of the nineteenth century. It has become customary to date the beginning of the modern European drama from the establishment of "free" theaters in Paris and Berlin in 1887 and 1889 respectively. The hearing for serious drama which these and similar enterprises afforded went far to stimulate a wide dramatic activity on the part of some of the best minds of the Continent and Great Britain. The influences of Ibsen, Tolstoy, Hauptmann, and Shaw were potent in America no less than in Europe. The infiltration of such influences on the drama and the theater constitutes no small part of the story of American drama in our time.

The pride of the American drama for a period of twenty years beginning with 1890 was without question the prolific Clyde Fitch. He busied himself with the adaptation of some thirty-six French and German comedies and farces, and with the composition of twenty-one original plays. He achieved both at home and abroad a not inconsiderable reputation. That he had valuable gifts to devote to the drama is obvious: keen observation of manners, language, costume, and setting, a feeling for startling scenic effects, a sensitive insight into feminine psychology, and a flair for dramatic construction. If his work now seems artificial and outmoded, the reasons are not only the limitations of the theater for which he was working but more especially the limitations of his own personality. Fitch's personality was a superficial one: it lacked depth and seriousness. As a result, his characterizations, especially of men, are usually incredible, and his careful attention to superficial detail, though it gives his works some value as documents in our social history, likewise dates them badly. Only one play of his, *The Truth* (1906),[1] goes far enough beneath

[1] Throughout this section, dates that follow the titles of plays are those of first pro-

the surface to give it more than a historical interest. When, in *The City* (1909), he strove to create masculine characters and the gripping scenes of strong drama, he lapsed into implausible melodrama. On the whole, however, Fitch's record is perhaps as commendable as that of any of the commercial dramatists of the period.

Augustus Thomas, when he was content to combine the elements of reliable melodrama and a somewhat superficial study of local color, wrought in such pieces as *Alabama* (1891), *In Mizzoura* (1893), and *Arizona* (1899) picturesque and effective but utterly specious creations. When, with the growing seriousness of the first decade of the twentieth century, he assumed the role of thesis-dramatist, he revealed his incapacity for lucid or distinguished thought and his infirm handling of character in such plays as *The Witching Hour* (1907) and *As a Man Thinks* (1911). Only once, in *The Copperhead* (1918), did he produce a play that is memorable for its searching psychological revelation and its impressive situation.

Similarly, the service of David Belasco to the American drama was not commensurate with the high standards he set himself and other producers in realism of settings, costume, and stage-business. Aside from his innumerable adaptations of shrewdly selected successful foreign plays, his own contribution to the drama took the form of romantic plays in settings that offered lavish opportunities for the expression of his own somewhat baroque taste. Thus, with John Luther Long, he exploited oriental material in *Madame Butterfly* (1900) and *The Darling of the Gods* (1902); alone, or in collaboration, he turned to the picturesque West for highly colored material and characters in *The Girl of the Golden West* (1905) and *The Rose of the Rancho* (1906). Once, in *The Return of Peter Grimm* (1911), he wrote tenderly and skillfully of the theme of communication with the dead, and his artistry and that of the actor David Warfield made this play perhaps his most memorable contribution to the American drama.

In the midst of the prolific but intrinsically unimportant dramatic activities of Fitch, Thomas, and Belasco, sporadic attempts were being made to unite drama and literature again. Most of these attempts were only tentative, but they pointed the way to the lively revival the drama was presently to undergo. One of these efforts rose out of William Vaughn Moody's desire to treat American material with some attention to psychological plausibility. The results were the highly successful *The Great Divide* (1906) and the more distinguished but commercially unsuccessful *The Faith Healer* (1909). Both these plays are notable for their devoted attention to characterization, the fidelity with which scene and business are imagined, and the credible language that is spoken. If the effectiveness

duction and not of first publication. In the bibliographies, the dates are, of course, those of first publication.

of the earlier play has dimmed with time, the incessant use of its theme—the cultured heroine and the primitive male—in trashy melodrama and repetitious moving pictures is a flattering tribute to its dramatic possibilities if not to its psychological honesty. *The Faith Healer*, a study in the religious psychology of humble people, remains an important contribution to authentic American folk drama.

Among the enthusiasts for a revival of the American drama, none was more ambitious and active than Percy MacKaye (*q.v.*), whose father, Steele MacKaye, had been a courageous visionary in the nineteenth-century theater. Percy MacKaye's work is the product of a highly conscious determination to raise the standard of American dramatic fare, and it has suffered not a little from this "uplift" element. Aside from the early poetic dramas on such romantic themes as *Jeanne d'Arc* (1906) and *Sappho and Phaon* (1907), the major part of his drama has utilized historical and contemporary American material in the form of pageants and plays. The Puritan play, *The Scarecrow* (1910), is perhaps the most important of his historical plays, *Caliban* (1916) his most elaborate pageant-masque, and *This Fine-Pretty World* (1923) his most noteworthy, if somewhat too dialectal, contribution to the drama of regionalism.

The plays of Edward Sheldon (*q.v.*) are characteristic of the uncertainty with which dramatic writing in the pre-war period vacillated between the rival claims of the commercial theater and the literary drama. His early plays, *Salvation Nell* (1908) and *The Nigger* (1909), show some evidence of the moral earnestness popular at the moment, but most of his later plays have been purely if effectively theatrical. Of these, the most memorable is *Romance* (1913), an adroit handling of the conflicting claims of flesh and spirit in the relationship between a clergyman and an opera-singer against the pleasantly sketched background of New York during the age of innocence. Over a period of ten years, it served Doris Keane as her most effective vehicle, and it has been revived again and again with considerable success. *Dishonoured Lady* (1930) is nimble erotic melodrama, made momentarily distinguished by the acting of Katharine Cornell.

Zoë Akins (*q.v.*) also moves uneasily between the glamour of the playhouse and the austerities of genuine drama. The root of the difficulty seems to be the fact that she has never recovered from her adolescent infatuation with footlights and greasepaint. Thus, *The Texas Nightingale* (1922) and *O Evening Star* (1935), inspired by Marie Dressler's comeback in the movies, are evidences of the glamour with which she invests the artistic temperament. She has not, moreover, been too fortunate in the dramatic models she has chosen for emulation. Her most serious plays, *Declassée* (1919) and *The Varying Shore* (1921), follow a little haltingly in the footsteps of the problem plays of the nineties.

DECLINE AND REVIVAL IN THE THEATER

From the beginning of the war to the beginning of the depression, one strong current was making for decline and another for revival in the American theater. On the whole, the period was one in which the commercial theater outside New York experienced a marked decline and the art theater a lively growth.

Many reasons underlay the decline of the complex organization of the commercial theater outside New York. The late nineteenth and early twentieth centuries had seen the disappearance of the local stock companies which had made glorious contributions to the history of the American theater. The same period had seen the star-system rise to its most dizzy heights, and the theater as a whole pass into the control of a few groups of men, for whom the theater's chief fascination was its money-making powers. Minnie Maddern Fiske's courageous struggle with the "theatrical trust" measured strikingly the extent to which the theater had come to be dominated by frankly commercial forces. In the period after the war, theater magnates were encountering tremendous economic obstacles: the rise of theater rents in New York and elsewhere, and huge increases in actors' salaries, in the wages of such supernumeraries of the theater as musicians, scene-shifters, and electricians, and in railroad fares and costs of transporting scenery and stage properties. Even more serious rivals of the touring companies and road shows were the movies (after 1905) and the talkies (after 1927). The theatrical trusts were thus caught between the upper millstone of this increased economic pressure and the lower millstone of economic and aesthetic competition with the moving pictures. It is no wonder that striking changes took place in the commercial theater in these years.

If one limits one's attention to New York, the theatrical capital of America, the state of the theater had a deceptive appearance of health. In the first decade after the war, theaters were built on a more and more lavish scale and in larger numbers than ever before, and, despite the tremendous increase in the costs of production and management, the number of plays in New York mounted steadily. The most reliable figures available—those in Burns Mantle's yearbooks of the theater, *The Best Plays*—reveal a significant curve in the number of dramatic productions: 1919–20, 150 productions; 1920–21, 157 productions; 1921–22, 190 productions, with fifty-five playhouses in operation; 1922–23, 190 productions and revivals; 1923–24, 196 productions, of which less than forty were musical; 1924–25, 230 productions, of which twenty-nine were revivals; 1925–26, 263 productions, of which forty-three were revivals, and of which thirty-three dramas ran for more than a hundred performances; 1926–27, 264 productions and revivals; 1927–28, 270 productions, of which forty were revivals (an all-time "high" in number of productions), and 1928–29, 224 productions.

Kenneth Macgowan's *Footlights across America* (1929) furnishes an illuminating view of the growth of the theater in New York and the accompanying decline outside New York. Between 1900 and 1914, the number of plays produced in New York per year rose from 72 to 130. In the same period, the average number of plays on tour fell from 308 to 198. From 1914 to 1927, the number of plays produced in New York per year rose from 130 to 208. In the same period, the number of plays on tour fell from 198 to 68. Macgowan cites from the *Billboard* the statement that in 1910, 1,520 legitimate theaters in America were open and doing fairly regular business, and in 1925, 634 theaters were open. These figures show startlingly the tremendous changes that were taking place in the commercial theater in New York and outside New York.

But if the commercial theater was undergoing opposed processes of expansion and contraction, the noncommercial theater of the period was showing indications of healthy life. Whatever form the noncommercial theater took (and its forms were various), the impulses behind it were the production of plays of distinction in competition with the commercial theater and the furnishing of drama to the increasingly extensive area outside the major cities which the commercial theater had ceased to serve. The remote stimulus of this activity was the dramatic revival on the Continent and in England, a revival that owed a great deal to the energizing example of Henrik Ibsen, and that ultimately engaged the attention and talents of some of the best contemporary creative minds. For the more daring works of these writers, "free theaters" were established in Paris, Berlin, and London, and theaters and workers' theaters, particularly in Germany, fostered the new drama. The sad state of the American provincial theater and the inspiriting example of Europe encouraged the initiation of the art theater movement in America, a movement at first viewed with contempt by such a perfect exemplar of commercialism as David Belasco, who said in 1917, "This so-called new art of the theatre is but a flash in the pan of inexperience. It is the cubism of the theatre, the wail of the incompetent and the degenerate. . . . The whole thing merely shows an ignorance and a diseased and depraved understanding and appreciation of any art at all."

The art theater in America has taken on a number of fairly distinct forms. The least startling is such an organization as the Theatre Guild, an outgrowth of the Washington Square Players (1915–19), a semiprofessional group devoted to the production of one-act plays. The Theatre Guild, which is viewed by such an acidulous critic as George Jean Nathan (*q.v.*) as merely a shrewd business organization, has probably done more than any other organization to raise the standard of plays produced and of ensemble acting and direction. The charge that the Theatre Guild has favored foreign dramatists at the expense of American playwrights is not entirely unfounded, although its services to such playwrights as Eugene O'Neill (*q.v.*), Sidney Howard (*q.v.*), Maxwell Anderson (*q.v.*), and S. N. Behrman (*q.v.*) have been conspicuous, and although it has generously invested a great deal of money in American plays of promise that would not otherwise have had a hearing. Probably the Theatre Guild has rendered its greatest service as an example of what intelligence combined with shrewd commercial sense can achieve; it has also served as a symbol of what the community theater might aspire to become. The services of the Guild to the art of acting in America are overwhelming. One need only mention such names as Alfred Lunt, Lynn Fontanne, Helen Westley, Earle Larimore, Eva Le Gallienne, Pauline Lord, and Judith Anderson to make it clear that the roster of its players is the roll of the most distinguished actors of the post-war period.

An early venture in the art theater movement in New York was the Provincetown Players, whose humble beginnings on Cape Cod gave Eugene O'Neill (*q.v.*) his first opportunity to see his one-act plays staged, and whose activities in Greenwich Village in 1915–22 and 1923–29 gave him and less conspicuous playwrights their first metropolitan hearings. An allied venture was the Neighborhood Playhouse in Grand Street (1915–27). The initial impulse behind this theater was the desire of two philanthropic women, Irene and Alice Lewisohn, to make the best of the drama available to the denizens of the East Side. Though there was little or no interest in the production of new American plays, the high standards of production and the courageous experimentation served as a further stimulus to the creation of art theaters outside New York. A more important project was Eva Le Gallienne's Civic Repertory Theater (1926–31). Operating on a modest subsidy in the drab little Fourteenth Street Theater, Miss Le Gallienne built up a repertory of plays, for the most part foreign in origin, very few of which would ever have reached commercial production in America. Her tasteful and intelligent direction encouraged many a little theater whose budgets had to be stretched to the breaking point.

Outside New York, the art theater has also taken on a variety of forms. Possibly its most characteristic form is the little theater, intent on establishing itself as an independent artistic organism, serving a community more or less abandoned by the commercial theater. Many of these enterprises were transitory ventures; most of them led existences dependent on the enthusiasm and the sacrifices of a few devoted spirits. All of them aspired to become community or civic theaters, and the best of them achieved that status. The most important of the community theaters are the Cleveland Playhouse under the direction of Frederic McConnell, and the Pasadena Community Playhouse under the direction of Gilmor Brown. Of these, and such others as the Dallas Little Theater, the Berkeley Playhouse, and the Petit Théâtre du Vieux Carré at New Orleans, the high standards of repertory and production make it possible to consider them as local Theater Guilds of a stable and enduring character.

A less characteristic but important form of the art theater in America is the academic theater, the group functioning within an academic community, and dependent upon college or university for money, actors, directors, and audience. The academic theater in America may be said to have had its origin in "English 47," a course in playwriting initiated by Professor George Pierce Baker at Harvard University in 1905. Out of this course grew in 1912 the 47 Workshop, which has trained more members of the staffs of little theaters than any other academic organization. Professor Baker's departure from Harvard in 1925 to found the School of the Drama and the University Theater at Yale meant not merely the transference of his activities but their establishment on a firm financial footing. In the meantime, other pedagogues were initiating similar enterprises in other academic strongholds. Thomas H. Dickinson began his dramatic activities in Wisconsin in 1911. At about the same time, Arvid Arnold was making the North Dakota Agricultural College at Fargo the center of state-wide activities in drama and pageant. Thomas Wood Stevens founded the Department of the Drama at the Carnegie Institute of Technology in Pittsburgh in 1913, and Frederick Koch, at North Dakota (1914–18) and (since 1918) at the University of North Carolina has given enthusiastic encouragement to the writing and production of American folk plays. Other colleges and universities, stirred by these examples, elevated haphazard undergraduate activities to a semi-professional level. At the moment, Northwestern University, the University of Michigan, Cornell University, and the University of Iowa are important centers of creative dramatic activity and production.

Harold A. Ehrensberger, former editor of *The Little Theater Monthly*, once estimated that there were 1,050 community and little theaters operating in the United States. A somewhat more precise estimate, that of Kenneth Macgowan, in *Footlights across America* (1929), indicated that about a hundred nonacademic art theaters were making from four to twenty-five productions each annually, and that about a hundred academic theaters were making the same number of productions. About a thousand groups were making one or two serious productions each season. Where the commercial theater had withdrawn, the art theater had stepped in.

THE LEADING DRAMATISTS

The one figure of national and international importance that has appeared in the American drama of the contemporary period is, of course, Eugene O'Neill (*q.v.*). O'Neill was brought up in the atmosphere of the theater, for his father was James O'Neill, the fine romantic actor identified in the American mind with the role of the Count of Monte Cristo. Up to the age of twenty-four, when young O'Neill turned to the writing of plays, he lived a life richer in elemental experience than that of any other dramatist of our time. An engineering expedition to Central America and four voyages as a sailor to South America, South Africa, and England furnished him with the strong colorful material of some of his early one-act plays. But he was not immune to purely literary influences, although he has been somewhat inclined to make light of them. O'Neill assimilated some of the views of American life promulgated by his early admirers and sponsors, Mencken and Nathan. His conception of character has been shaped by a study of the dynamic psychology of Sigmund Freud. There are also traces in his work of such diverse forces as Strindberg, Wedekind, and contemporary German expressionism.

In consequence of the range of his actual and literary experience, the work of O'Neill is so varied that it is not easy to assign his plays to the conventional critical categories. He has occasionally written in the vein of pure realism or pure romance, but his most characteristic and successful pieces are those in which realism and romance are blended, and his most interesting plays are those which are experimental in material or technique. The poet in O'Neill seems to prevent his remaining absolutely faithful to the demands of pure realism. Even in the early sea plays, which are in some respects brutally realistic, there is exoticism of setting and atmosphere and the romantic appeal of violent and sometimes melodramatic action. On the other hand, in such harshly realistic plays as *Diff'rent* (1920) and *The Straw* (1921), in the Strindbergian war of love and hate in *Welded* (1924), one feels that a vital part of the playwright's personality has been repressed, and the result is a lack of poise, an excessive emphasis on warped characters. In so romantic a play as *The Fountain* (1925), where he relinquishes his strong grasp on reality, the result is enfeebled drama, and the poetic flights of *Marco Millions* (1928) do not redeem, but rather suffer from, the banality of its Menckenite satire.

Thus, the most satisfying of O'Neill's plays are those in which the realistic and the romantic elements combine and re-enforce each other. Even *Beyond the Horizon* (1920), his first success in the commercial theater, is written on two distinct levels—the sharply realistic life of the decaying New England farm, and the imaginative life of the brother whom chance condemns to inhabit it and to die on it. The transition from one level to the other is not easy; the slow deterioration of character is portrayed jerkily in a play singularly devoid of action. *Anna Christie* (1921) showed an increase in artistry. The development of something like romance out of a basically sordid situation is managed with considerable adroitness, and though the redemption of the heroine narrowly escapes sentimentality, the ending is only superficially "happy" and is truer to life than to fiction. *Desire under the Elms* (1924) is an expert and subtle blend of the realistic and the poetic. The coarse ugly stuff of the plot is transmuted by O'Neill's imaginative insight into great and powerful beauty, and what might have had its origin in a brutal newspaper story is converted into high tragedy. Here O'Neill has created vital distinct individuals, and conveyed their relationships with truth and subtlety. In the style, too, O'Neill has achieved a prose which, while faithfully colloquial, responds rhythmically to the waves of emotions that flow through this drama.

But the spirit of O'Neill is an uneasy one. He cannot remain satisfied with the form or the content of the conventional drama of this or any other period. His most fascinating work is that in which he attempts one or another technical innovation. Thus, *The Emperor Jones* (1920) and *The Hairy Ape* (1922) are practically monodramas, broken into short scenes without grouping into acts. The first represents the breakdown of a Negroid mentality under the stress of fear and fatigue. The collapse is indicated not only by the monologues of the central figure, but by the hallucinations represented in the form of *tableaux vivants*. *The Hairy Ape* shows the influence of German expressionism in the articulateness arbitrarily conferred on the normally inarticulate hero, and in the representation by masked figures of the degree to which the hero's view of the world is distorted. The influence is seen further in *All God's Chillun Got Wings* (1924), where, although the dialogue and action are attuned to the highest standards of realistic psychological drama, the increasing distortion of the scenery parallels the distortion of the characters' minds.

Up to the present, O'Neill's most elaborate experiments are *The Great God Brown* (1926), *Strange Interlude* (1928), and *Mourning Becomes Electra* (1931). In the first, the complicated use made of masks to distinguish the real self from the assumed self is effective up to the point where the assumption of one personality by another character makes the rest of the drama almost incomprehensible. In *Strange Interlude*, the major innovations are the extension of the drama to nine acts and the revival and development of the aside. Both these devices are daring, and can be justified only if O'Neill creates effects that could be secured by no less ambitious means. *Strange Interlude* is an extraordinary psychological history of its four leading characters; its cumulative power is very great. One has a suspicion that an equally powerful effect could have been secured if a large number of the asides had been omitted, and the action of certain scenes had been foreshortened. *Mourning Becomes Electra* is O'Neill's most ambitious work to date, and it is unquestionably his most powerful reading of life and its meaning. The framework of the play, as the title suggests, is the Orestes-Electra saga, one of the greatest of dramatic stories, already treated, at least in part, by the three great Greek tragic writers. O'Neill has challenged comparison with the greatest of ancient playwrights, and on the whole one feels that he has not suffered by it. What he has done is to re-interpret the ancient legend in terms of puritanism and psychoanalysis. The characters thus become in a sense illustrations of the major neuroses from which modern man suffers. But they remain characters and achieve tragic grandeur. That grandeur is of a strictly modern kind; it is the grandeur of psychological determinism, the new fatalism, for if there is no escape from the tragic web, the surviving heroine can at least accept without flinching the burden of her psychological destiny. The magnitude of her courage is a measure of the trilogy's tragic power.

The Electra trilogy represents perhaps O'Neill's completest tribute to the tragic implications of modern science. But it is clear that he is not completely satisfied with such a desperate faith. In *Dynamo* (1929) and *Days without End* (1934), we see him none too successfully coping with the problem of faith for the modern world. These experiments are perhaps purely tentative. From so prolific, restless, and provocative a playwright, there is much yet to be expected.

In Eugene O'Neill, the elements of weakness and strength are curiously interwoven. His most striking weaknesses are a lack of self-criticism that does not warn him of the extravagances of either realism or romanticism, an absence of clarity in the line of his own philosophical development, and an almost too high scorn for the limitations of the drama as a form and of the theater as a medium. His very great powers are certainly his style, which is in turn rich and earthy, intuitive and illuminating, his deep probing into the motivations of dynamic character, his power in evoking psychic conflicts, and the glamour with which his reading and projection of life are invested.

At the moment, O'Neill's leading rival among our serious dramatists is Maxwell Anderson. In Anderson, as in O'Neill, we find two natures struggling for mastery, the realistic and the poetic, and Anderson's case is complicated by a social passion that takes the place of the philosophic passion in O'Neill. Similarly, Anderson's most successful plays would seem to be those in which the elements in his personality somehow find harmonious expression. In the earlier stages of Anderson's career, the realist and the romancer were kept severely apart. But even in his collaborations with Laurence Stallings (*q.v.*), the dichotomy is clear. *What Price Glory?* (1924) was the first naturalistic war play to reach the American stage. It amazed and horrified audiences by the vigor of its language, the realism of its portraiture, and the disillusioned view taken of life at the front. In the succeeding plays written with Stallings—*First Flight* (1925) and *The Buccaneer* (1925)—Anderson's romantic interest in historical drama expressed itself none too effectively. The poet in him was again repressed in his severely naturalistic *Outside Looking In* (1925), a drama of hobo life in the western environment Anderson had known as a young man. His experiment in pure realism, *Saturday's Children* (1927), demonstrated his complete control over the genre of domestic comedy. But so restricted and colloquial a mode could not satisfy either the poet or the social reformer in Anderson. Henceforth, neither realism nor naturalism was to suffice to express his complicated personality.

Instead, we find plays primarily social, plays primarily romantic, and—the most interesting of the kinds—plays in which social feeling blends with romantic treatment. The purely social plays—*Gods of the Lightning* (1928) and *Both Your Houses* (1933)—right as they are in feeling, are either overviolent in tone or oversimplified in character and action. A happier vein for Anderson has been the poeticized historical drama, where he has been assisted in the creation of atmosphere by reliance on richly connotative characters and settings and where he has felt free to experiment with a loose form of blank verse in which he sometimes gets excellent but more frequently rather flabby poetic effects. *Elizabeth the Queen* (1930) was an effective if not too fresh treatment of the legendary romance of Elizabeth and Essex. Like the story of Joan of Arc, this story is surefire theater, and Anderson's major contribution to it was his complex rendition of the many-faceted character of the Queen. In *Night over Taos* (1932), Anderson made use of material unfamiliar to most of his audience, namely, the last stand of Spanish feudalism against American democracy in New Mexico in 1847, but he failed to interest his audience in material much nearer their lives than the fate of England's subtle queen. With *Mary of Scotland* (1933), he again turned to one of the most reliable of all historical themes, and while the play won a great success, the reading of the character of Mary is oversimplified and sentimentalized, and the rest of the characterization is superficially effective rather than genuinely searching. The reversion to American material in *Valley Forge* (1934) and *The Wingless Victory* (1936) had less happy results. The best intentions in the world failed to make George Washington more than the lay-figure of a historical panorama, and the memories of Euripides' *Medea* and Joseph Hergesheimer's (*q.v.*) *Java Head*, stirred by the latter play, confused the course and significance of its tragedy.

Anderson's most admirable plays are those in which the various elements in his personality achieve fusion. Here, the best examples are *Winterset* (1935), *The Masque of Kings* (1937), and *High Tor* (1937). Of these, *Winterset* is the most ambitious and the most subtle in its effect. A kind of sequel to *Gods of the Lightning*, it is the rare instance of a sequel excelling the original. Here all Anderson's powers are blended—the realistic, the romantic, and the social. The fusion of these difficult elements is extraordinarily perfect; the total effect is massive and moving. *The Masque of Kings* is made of simpler elements, and though its study of the problems of leadership is suggestive, the fusion between history and interpretation is not quite perfect. In *High Tor*, Anderson has achieved his most remarkable harmonization of opposed elements. The thesis of *High Tor* may be banal, but the medium of its communication is an astonishingly perfect blend of the fantastic, satirical, realistic, and social. *High Tor* is certainly as fine a poetic comedy as our time has produced.

Sidney Howard (*q.v.*) had a high respect for the dignity of the drama and had developed a technique applicable to a variety of dramatic materials. He had an absorbed interest in character and a deep concern for the preservation of its integrity. He steadily rejected the temptation to sacrifice truth to life or character for the sake of a surprising theatrical effect. After the respectful reception of his poetic drama *Swords* (1921), and a period of adaptation of plays chiefly from the French, Howard attained creative maturity with *They Knew What They Wanted* (1924), a play that employs a California setting skillfully, and that involves three full-bodied characters whom Howard allows to work out their own destinies in terms of their own temperaments and not in terms of conventional morality. In *Lucky Sam McCarver* (1925) he relinquished the interest of plot to study successive states in the relationship of two diverse characters involved in a marriage of convenience. The man is rough and ready and self-made; the woman, a somewhat tarnished remnant of the aristocratic tradition. Although their relationship ends disastrously and the piece is somewhat undramatic, Howard regarded with complete respect the integrity of his characters. His successful potboiler, *Ned McCobb's Daughter* (1926), proved less significant than the serious drama, *The Silver Cord* (1926), where he dramatized with poignance and malice the plight of two sons dominated by an unscrupulous mother. Though he drove home his point too violently in the scientific tirade that states the thesis of the play, it remains his most powerful independent production. After 1926, his more important plays were adaptations from the French or dramatizations of American novels. Of the former, the most noteworthy was *The Late Christopher Bean* (1932), which he derived from Réné Fauchois' *Prenez Garde à la Peinture*. Of the latter, his dramatization in 1934 of Sinclair Lewis' *Dodsworth* exemplified his technical resourcefulness and his profound respect for the spirit of the original from which he worked.

VARIETIES OF COMEDY

In his normal mood, the American theater-goer prefers to be diverted rather than puzzled or pained by the entertainment he seeks, and it is therefore not surprising that most contemporary American playwrights of the second class should have been touched most frequently by some manifestation of the comic spirit. Though the contemporary period has been, on the whole, hostile to the cultivation of sentimental comedy by more serious playwrights, the element of sentiment has frequently been close to the surface of many an American play. The successful excursion of so serious a playwright as O'Neill into sentimental comedy in *Ah Wilderness* (1933), indicates its power over both playwright and audience. But the major types of comedy cultivated in this period have been the comedy of manners and satirical comedy. A minor vein of realism has done little more than illustrate the difficulty of combining comedy and the realistic method. In the earlier part of the period, farce of the Parisian variety flourished in the hands of such a playwright as Avery Hopwood, but with the coming of the moving picture, farce was relinquished to the screen and to directors intent on violent movement rather than shrewd characterization or significant action.

The tradition of the comedy of manners is strong in the English drama, and while no American play of the period equals the brilliance of Wycherley's *The Country Wife*, Congreve's *The Way of the World*, or Sheridan's *The School for Scandal*, the revival of these plays during the period suggests a public appreciation of sophisticated comedy and furnishes a challenging standard of comparison. But the immediate sources of the contemporary comedy of manners are less remote. The comedies of Oscar Wilde and Clyde Fitch and the dramatized debates of George Bernard Shaw were sufficiently near to stimulate frequent exemplification and imitation. Thus Langdon Mitchell in *The New York Idea* (1906) attempted to apply the manner of social comedy to urban American material, and Jesse Lynch Williams in *Why Marry?* (1917) and *Why Not?* (1922) carried on the tradition in slightly heavy-handed comedies of discussion.

Among the older playwrights, two women—Rachel Crothers (*q.v.*) and Clare Kummer (*q.v.*)—are skilled in the production of comedies of this type. Miss Crothers, to be sure, served her turn in the writing of melodrama in *The Three of Us* (1906), and produced sentimental comedies such as *Old Lady 31* (1916), *A Little Journey* (1918), and *39 East* (1919), but her most memorable writing has the tone of the comedy of manners. She is concerned only vaguely with ideas, or at least with only the more readily accessible ideas of our time, but her wit is ready, her hand is deft in the creation of women characters particularly, and she has the knack of using the intellectual fads and fancies of the period as targets for her not too deadly sharpshooting. Thus she exploited the lighter domestic problems of the jazz age in *Nice People* (1920), the vagaries of the younger generation in *Mary the Third* (1923), psychoanalysis in *Expressing Willie* (1924), the comic contrast between domestic and Continental mores in *As Husbands Go* (1931), and Buchmanism in *Susan and God* (1937), which is typical of her ability to satirize the superficial manifestations of a movement and of her willingness to sacrifice psychological integrity to theatrical effectiveness. Miss Crothers is an accomplished and experienced playwright. But her excessive facility, her somewhat superficial analysis of character and idea, and her habit of offering what is topical rather than permanent in interest make it impossible to take her very seriously.

Clare Kummer's touch is lighter, and the comic effect is less tangible. At her best, one is inclined to think of her as a feminine Barrie. Like Barrie, she is somewhat indifferent to the material which she chooses for treatment. Like him, too, what matters is not the action but the tender-humorous, whimsical-fantastic manner in which the action is rendered. Perhaps no one in our time has written comic dramatic dialogue of quite so effervescent and shimmering a quality as Miss Kummer, although Philip Barry (*q.v.*) came near it in certain passages in *Holiday*. The peril of the tender-witty type of comedy is its fragility and its tendency to lapse into sentimentality as Miss Kummer did in an unhappy venture called *Amourette* (1933). Even *A Successful Calamity* (1917) is fundamentally sentimental in its assumptions, though its lightness of touch helps conceal its shaky foundation. In *Pomeroy's Past* (1926), she attempted to apply her style to the material of farce. But she has been happiest when there was a slightly fantastic element in her material; thus, her most memorable efforts have been *Good Gracious, Annabelle* (1916), a diverting bit of fooling with the alleged distinction between eastern and western culture, *Rollo's Wild Oat* (1920), which romped with the idea that every sensitive young man wants to play Hamlet, and *Her Master's Voice* (1933), which showed just such a young man in the toils of the racket of radio-broadcasting. Miss Kummer's gift is so rare in any period of the drama that it is regrettable that she utilizes it less and less frequently.

Philip Barry (*q.v.*), like other writers of the comedy of manners, has not been content to restrict himself to this somewhat limited mode, but he made his reputation in this genre. His prize play, *You and I* (1923), revealed his gift for witty dialogue and his fine feeling for comic contrasts in character and points of view. It also announced a theme to which he has returned again and again, the far-reaching antithesis between the values of the commercial- and the noncommercial-minded. This was to be treated somewhat more explicitly in *The Youngest* (1924), and it underlies the action in his finest comedy, *Holiday* (1928), where his skill in fantastic verbal foolery reached perfection. The seriousness that underlies Barry's excursions into comedy had already made itself felt in certain plays that bewildered his lighter-minded followers. The poet and the idealist were more conspicuous than the sophisticate in *In a Garden* (1925) and *White Wings* (1926). With *Hotel Universe* (1930), Barry challenged comparison with the soul-searching of Shaw's *Heartbreak House*. In *The Animal Kingdom* (1932), he relied rather too heavily on the idealogy he had already treated more lightly in *Holiday* and *Paris Bound*, and the play suffers from understatement and a refusal to point its meaning. With *Tomorrow and Tomorrow* (1931), he renewed his strength, and this is as solid and as subtle a study of well-meaning adultery as our stage has produced. With *The Joyous Season* (1934), a kind of softness became apparent in Barry's writing and apprehension of life, and *Bright Star* (1935) and *Spring Dance* (1936) marked, for the moment, a pause in his already impressive development. With *Here Come the Clowns* (1938) and *The Philadelphia Story* (1939), Barry reappeared at the height of his powers. The former play, though none too successful on Broadway, was his most satisfying attempt to give his religious apprehension of life dramatically poignant form, and the latter play combined the shimmering wit and beauty of *Holiday* with a more searching and important psychological study.

Less ambitious and less intellectually challenging than Barry's comedies are those of S. N. Behrman (*q.v.*). Barry's tenderness, wistfulness, and flair for slightly mad dialogue are absent from Behrman's witty, worldly comedies. *The Second Man* (1927) showed him already accomplished in dialogue, and shrewd in his penetration of the psychology of a second-rate man of letters and of the women who fluttered about him. In *Meteor* (1929), he attempted a more serious task, the study of the psychology of a crude, unscrupulous, and arrogant representative of big business. He succeeded in dramatizing a portrait rather than in creating a play. With *Brief Moment* (1931), he challenged comparison none too successfully with the vogue of such plays as *Holiday* and *Paris Bound*. He was happier in the lighter mode of *Biography* (1932), where he made excellent comic play between a worldly wise and witty heroine and the stupid or brilliant men who had touched her life at various points. With *Rain from Heaven* (1934) and *End of Summer* (1936), he turned most definitely to the comedy of manners. Here, while his wit and verve are unfailing, one feels the lack of any core of intellectual or spiritual conviction such as one is always aware of in the most discursive of Bernard Shaw's dramatic discussions. The absence of deep concern with life's meaning seems likely to keep Behrman among the lighter and less consequential comic playwrights of the period.

The vein of realistic comedy in the contemporary period is not extremely rich; the effectiveness of realism depends largely on the pleasure of recognition, and the pleasure of recognition is so undependable a reaction on which to build an entire play that there is a great temptation to augment the effect by an excursion into sentiment, sentimentality, or even farce. But a number of playwrights have ventured into this difficult field with success. Such plays as Frank Craven's *Too Many Cooks* (1914) and *That's Gratitude* (1930), for instance, are closer to farce than to true comedy, but *The First Year* (1920), like Maxwell Anderson's more serious *Saturday's Children* (1927), handled with persuasive verisimilitude the tragi-comic adjustments of early married life. J. P. McEvoy combined touches of satire and photographic realism to present the manners and the minds of the petty businessman and his family in *The Potters* (1923).

More serious extensions of the subject matter of domestic comedy were Gilbert Emery's deflation of the pretenses of a returned veteran in *The Hero* (1921), and his honest and ironical treatment of the amatory adventures of the bourgeois male in *Tarnish* (1923).

The most serious devotee of American domestic comedy has been George Kelly (*q.v.*), who at one time seemed the most promising of the realistic playwrights of the period. His considerable experience with the writing and acting of vaudeville sketches encouraged him to write *The Torch-Bearers* (1922), a travesty of the little-theater movement in terms of extravagance and farce. And even *The Show-Off* (1924), a comic characterization of an irrepressibly blatant blow-hard, bristled with wisecracks entirely out of keeping with comedy that would approximate realism. But the unfortunate tendency to overemphasis and the willingness to get a laugh at any cost disappear in his later work, and such plays as *Craig's Wife* (1925) and *Daisy Mayme* (1926) are as faithfully realistic and honest in characterization as any American domestic comedies. Kelly does not boggle at the realist's obligation to make both his heroes and heroines out of the stuff of common life, half-precious and half-repellent. His work since *Daisy Mayme* has seemed less sure and has been less successful. *Maggie the Magnificent* (1929), though astute in its depiction of a wrangling and vulgar family, suffered the penalty of representing a dullness that is as dull as reality itself. *Behold the Bridegroom* (1927) was a none too successful attempt at psychological tragedy, and in *Reflected Glory* (1936) Kelly succumbed completely to the theatrical in his dramatic characterization of an actress of temperament. At the moment, the line of Kelly's development remains obscure.

If the comedy of manners has attracted some of the finer talents at work in the American theater today, satirical comedy has also had lively and at times brilliant exemplification. The chief representative of satirical comedy in the period since the war is George S. Kaufman (*q.v.*), who with a series of collaborators has contributed an extraordinary number of sharp and telling satires of American mores. Their special objective seems the exposure of the conventionalization of American businessmen and their domestic appendages. In *Dulcy* (1921), on a suggestion from the columnist, "F. P. A." (*q.v.*), Kaufman and Marc Connelly (*q.v.*) created a diverting portrait of a moronic wife, who, with the best intention in the world to be her husband's helpmeet, almost succeeds in wrecking his professional chances. In *To the Ladies* (1922), a young husband is saved from his native stupidity by his clever wife, and the formalities of a businessmen's banquet are brilliantly parodied. Above all, in *Beggar on Horseback* (1924), an expressionistic comedy freely adapted from the German, they created a thoroughgoing satire of the excessive systematization of business, and of the aesthetic and domestic standards of entirely commercialized *nouveaux riches*. To the composition of these plays, Kaufman and Connelly brought diverse talents, as is apparent when one considers the nature of the plays Connelly has created alone. Connelly would seem to be the one who furnishes the more delicate touches, the finer feelings, the touches of wistfulness and sentiment; Kaufman, the hard-hitting, wisecracking, satirical vigor. Their dramatization of Harry Leon Wilson's *Merton of the Movies* (1922) was a blend of almost equal parts of sensitivity and rather brash satire on the incredible absurdities of Hollywood. In Connelly's *The Wisdom Tooth* (1926), the deadening effect of business on the sensitive individual is again shown, but what one remembers is the Barriesque juxtaposition of the corrupted adult and the fine boy he used to be. In Connelly's dramatizations of the Roark Bradford stories in *The Green Pastures* (1930) and of Walter D. Edmonds' (*q.v.*) *Rome Haul* under the title *The Farmer Takes a Wife* (1934), the elements of tenderness and poetic feeling are also conspicuous.

Kaufman would seem to work less happily alone than with one or another collaborator, though he was the sole author of the satire on theatrical life, *The Butter and Egg Man* (1925) and of the librettos of *The Cocoanuts* (1925) and *Strike Up the Band* (1927). His plays written in collaboration have tended to take on something of the quality of the personality of his working partner. Thus, *June Moon* (1929) retained something of the Ring Lardner (*q.v.*) masterly control of American speech and his hard-hitting satirically realistic representation of urban vulgarities. And Kaufman's collaborations with Edna Ferber (*q.v.*)—*Minick* (1924), *The Royal Family* (1927), and *Dinner at Eight* (1932)—owe not a little to Miss Ferber's heartiness and inventiveness. Alexander Woollcott's (*q.v.*) enthusiasm for the exotic in life and letters gave a tone rare in Kaufman's work to their dramatization of Guy de Maupassant's *Boule de Suif* under the title of *The Channel Road* (1929) and their macabre mystery play, *The Dark Tower* (1933). In recent years, Kaufman's favorite collaborator has been Moss Hart, and in him he has found encouragement for his own flair for rather broad satire and somewhat extravagant comedy. Thus, *Once in a Lifetime* (1930) finished the easy task of pulverizing Hollywood, begun in *June Moon* and *Merton of the Movies*. *Merrily We Roll Along* (1934), their most serious play, attempted not too successfully to exhibit the corruption of a genuine artist by commercial and social forces, and *You Can't Take It with You* (1936) was a hilarious farce-comedy of a family of eccentrics and their equally eccentric lodgers.

Despite Kaufman's prominence in the contemporary theater, it seems exceedingly doubtful whether more than one or two of his plays will continue to interest audiences in or out of the theater. Kaufman is too topical a writer to deserve prolonged attention. He is also a fundamentally practical playwright. Everything he has done has an immediate and shrewdly calculated effectiveness. But his satire is not very penetrating, his strokes are excessively broad, and his wit has the explosive finality of the wisecrack. Kaufman's view of the world is negligible, and his artistry is too often stage carpentry and not dramatic architecture. He has earned the rewards, and he will pay the penalty, of being a man of the theater rather than a real dramatist.

The satirical element in Robert Sherwood (*q.v.*) is slight but constant. On the whole, Sherwood uses a much finer brush than Kaufman, and there is a freer play of tender feeling and of slightly whimsical humor. Sherwood is usually too alert to descend to farce. His first play, *The Road to Rome* (1927), is in the vein of modernized pseudo-history popularized by John Erskine (*q.v.*). It is harsher and coarser in its devices than his later plays. *The Queen's Husband* (1928) is more characteristic, for it combines deft satire with whimsical humor, and illustrates nonchalantly the formula of incompetence turning masterly. In *Waterloo Bridge* (1930), the comic element in Sherwood is severely repressed for the sake of the sentimental, and the result is only moderately interesting. Sherwood's period of experimentation seems definitely ended with *Reunion in Vienna* (1931), a perfect infusion of Viennese sentiment and pathos, cynicism, worldliness, and sophistication. *The Petrified Forest* (1935), though successful, is less complex in its effects, more studied and implausible in its devices. With *Idiot's Delight* (1936), Sherwood's rare comic powers were again in full flower. Here he is at his most serious in his indictment of the forces making for war in the modern world. The play's thesis is the more telling since it reaches one only through a rich surface of wit and sophistication, vaudeville humors, and adroit satires on national and international types. With *Abe Lincoln in Illinois* (1938), Sherwood revealed new and surprising powers. Moved by contemporary threats to the democratic principle, Sherwood fused his impassioned faith in the American way with a penetrating re-creation of the evolution of the youthful Lincoln. This play demonstrated finally that Sherwood is not only an adroit writer of sophisticated comedies but a serious and thoughtful dramatist.

The presence among current writers of comedy of talents as diverse as those of Barry and Behrman, Kaufman, Connelly, and Sherwood promises well for the future of American social comedy.

REGIONALISM IN THE DRAMA

The regional drama utilizes for dramatic purposes the life and customs of communities more or less untouched by the influences of the machine age and of a fundamentally scientific culture. Regional drama is essentially the drama of local color. Inevitably, perhaps, it stresses, not the essential elements of plot and characterization, but the elements associated with setting: local manners and customs, dialectal speech and imagery, idiosyncracies of acting and of thinking. On the whole, regional dramas have with difficulty made their way into a commercial theater which is admittedly national and not local in its appeal, but a few have achieved extraordinary success there through their impressiveness as dramatic performances, their vogue as curiosities, or their ability to satisfy a growing curiosity concerning American mores, even on the part of the urban bourgeoisie.

Contemporary regional drama had forerunners of a sort in such popular nineteenth-century comedy-dramas as *The Old Homestead*, *Rip Van Winkle*, *Shore Acres*, and *Way Down East*. But the sentimental and melodramatic elements in these plays, however conducive to their popularity, did not carry over to the more literate regional drama of the twentieth century. Even before the war, a number of American writers were making sporadic or persistent attempts to utilize the rich materials of American provincial life. Thus, Mary Austin (*q.v.*) attempted the use of Indian material in *The Arrow Maker* (1911), and Alice Brown achieved a genuinely literary use of rural New England material in *Children of Earth* (1915). A frequent practitioner of regional drama is Percy Mackaye (*q.v.*), in whose lifelong devotion to the creation of a genuinely American drama and pageantry such folk plays as *The Scarecrow* (1910), *Yankee Fantasies* (1912), *This Fine-Pretty World* (1923), and *Kentucky Mountain Fantasies* are important episodes.

But the regional drama was not to attain fame and fortune through the attempts of individual authors to find a place for their strange wares in a conventional commercial theater. The contemporary regional drama owes its initiation and its vogue, not so much to its nineteenth-century forerunners or the examples set by elder playwrights, as to the existence, as a part of the little theater movement, of dramatic organizations bent on the development, not merely of acting talents but the creative abilities of regional dramatists. Of these centers, the most important have been the University of Wisconsin under the influence of Thomas H. Dickinson, and the University of North Carolina under the stimulus of Frederick Koch. To these and other academic leaders belongs the credit for stimulating the regional drama by giving the plays of local authors a sympathetic production and audience. The most important regional playwright to develop under such circumstances is Paul Green (*q.v.*), much of whose early work was produced by Koch and reached the stage through the activities of the Carolina Playmakers. Paul Green finds the subject matter for most of his plays in the lives of whites and Negroes in his native North Carolina. His sympathy with Negroes is so profound that he is able to depict their psychology in ways satisfactory even to the subjects themselves. Such plays as *The Field God* (1927) and *In Abraham's Bosom* (1926) concern Negro life, but *The House of Connelly* (1931) is evidence of his appreciation of the new and old cultural values in the lives of whites in the New South. Of the younger playwrights who owe most to the little theater, Lynn Riggs (*q.v.*) may serve as an example. He handles the folk life of his native Oklahoma with poetic freshness, though not always with dramatic effectiveness. His most successful play, *Green Grow the Lilacs* (1930) blends effectively the methods of folk drama and folk music.

Certain playwrights whose work has reached the public through the medium of the commercial theater have regularly or upon occasion turned to regional material for dramatic treatment; two plays of this sort—*The Green Pastures* and *Tobacco Road*—have been sensational successes in the post-war theater. The poor whites of the South have challenged treatment through their independence and clannishness, their ancient traditional speech and superstitions, and their freedom from the influence of the modern world. Lulu Vollmer's *Sun-Up* (1923), first acted memorably by Lucille LaVerne, has had a long life on the urban and regional stage. Her other plays have followed this vein less profitably. Professor Hatcher Hughes, after toying with drama of a more conventional variety, achieved his greatest success with *Hell-Bent fer Heaven* (1924), which, despite the uncertain imposition of form upon primitive material, was honored by the Pulitzer Prize in 1924. Its successor, *Ruint* (1925), in much the same vein, was less impressive. A more naturalistic treatment of the life of the poor whites reached the stage in Jack Kirkland's dramatization of Erskine Caldwell's *Tobacco Road*, which ran for more than six years in New York after its first production on December 4, 1933, and which toured a great many major and minor cities, despite frequent encounters with censors. No other play of our time is likely to present with such gusto the physical and moral degeneracy of these unhappy people.

The rich instinctive and imaginative life of the southern Negro has long been a potent influence upon music and drama in America no less than upon the novel and poetry. The nineteenth-century minstrel show disseminated a conception of the Negro distorted by the white imagination. But the passing out of favor of this particular form of racial betrayal, the emergence into literature of a considerable number of excellent Negro writers, and the revival of regionalism, have prepared the way for a more authentic representation of the Negro on the American stage. Eugene O'Neill's *Emperor Jones* (1920) synthesized dramatically the history of the Negro and his imagination. Interesting interpretations of the Negro have been given the stage by southern writers. DuBose Heyward's (*q.v.*) *Porgy* (1927) utilized the mass psychology of the urban Negro for dramatic purposes and supplied the libretto for George Gershwin's ambitious and moving folk opera, *Porgy and Bess* (1935). The short-lived dramatization of Julia Peterkin's (*q.v.*) *Scarlet Sister Mary* (1930) proved one of the least happy of Ethel Barrymore's later ventures. The most sensationally successful contemporary dramatic use of Negroid material is, of course, *The Green Pastures* (1930), Marc Connelly's (*q.v.*) sympathetic re-creation of Roark Bradford's accounts of the changes wrought by the picturesque and humorous imagination of the Negro upon the greatest of Old Testament narratives. Solemnly played by a large cast of Negro actors, this fantastic religious drama earned deservedly the immense audiences it reached in both its stage and screen versions.

DRAMA AND THEATER IN THE DEPRESSION

It was inevitable that the theater, and consequently the drama, should suffer deeply during the depression. The drama is the most costly of all the arts; it requires for its full existence a theater, actors, directors, technicians, a box-office and advertising staff. The cost of all these commodities had soared during the boom period after the war. With the coming of the depression, the economic pressure on the theater became tremendous. Large portions of the theater-going audiences in America were driven to seek less expensive or free forms of entertainment. In New York, there was a sensational slump in theatrical enterprises, and in cities like Chicago and San Francisco, the theatrical fare became so scarce as almost to threaten the drama with extinction.

The number of theatrical productions made annually in New York has already served us as an index of theatrical prosperity and dramatic activity. The season of 1927–28 had seen 270 productions in New York, and the following season, 224. The figures for the depression years suggest poignantly the rapid withdrawal of investments from theatrical enterprises. In the first year of the depression (1929–30), its full effects were not yet felt; in fact, the number of productions in this year numbered over 240, of which 134 were dramatic in nature. The next four years, however, show a sharp decline: 1930–31, 190; 1931–32, 195; 1932–33, 180, of which 110 were dramatic; 1933–34, less than 130, a number smaller than that produced in any year in the preceding fifteen. The falling off in the number of productions, however, does not tell the whole story. In the period of Coolidge prosperity, theaters had been shockingly overbuilt in New York and Chicago. During the depression, a very considerable number of these were transformed into moving-picture houses, others were razed to give way to parking areas or apartment houses, and many stood idle for most of the dramatic season. Furthermore, the scaling down of theater rents tempted playwrights whose works had not yet reached the stage to round up an "angel" or two, gather a nondescript company, and try their fortune on Broadway. In consequence, these years saw more plays of little or no merit reach production than any years in the history of the post-war theater. The number of productions was swelled further by the backing of plays by moving-picture companies. The drama still had sufficient prestige to make it worth while to produce plays which might have luck on the screen even if they achieved only a sort of galvanized existence on the stage.

Outside New York, the theatrical situation was desperate. In Chicago, the number of productions per year had risen from 80 in the season of

1921–22, to an average of 100 or slightly more than 100 in the period of 1926–30. Thereafter, the decline was very marked: 1930–31, 84; 1931–32, 74; 1932–33, 50; and 1933–34, 43, of which only 20 deserved serious critical consideration. In other cities than the two major theatrical centers, the slump in the professional drama was even more amazing. To the coast cities, San Francisco and Los Angeles, relatively few touring companies penetrated, and, despite the activity encouraged by the presence in Hollywood of most of the actors and actresses who had had stage careers and more who had not, there were weeks in the season of 1932–33 when no legitimate theater in San Francisco was open.

A further evidence of the inroads the depression was making on the theater was the gradual collapse of the organizations the Theatre Guild had built up in a chain of cities on the Atlantic seaboard and in the Middle West. Its tremendous success in New York and the eagerness of the rest of the country to see its productions had encouraged the Guild to organize local Guilds to sponsor a season of visiting productions. It is doubtful whether under the most favorable circumstances this one group of directors could have met satisfactorily the demands of the huge audience it organized. Their New York troupe had taken on the nature of a stock company, and its members could hardly be on view at the same time in a half-dozen cities. But in the collapse of the local Theatre Guild audiences the depression played its part, and in consequence, the latter years of the depression saw the curtailing of the Guild's activities outside New York and, in some cities, its fusion with its late rival, the American Theater Society, originally a Shubert imitation of the Guild's technique for building up an organized audience outside New York.

In the generally gloomy atmosphere of the depression years, there were a few persistent indications of vitality in the theater and of an unsatisfied appetite for the drama. On occasions, when courageous actress-managers like Katharine Cornell and Eva Le Gallienne planned country-wide tours, they met with an exceedingly enthusiastic response. Another encouraging development, parallel to the depression but only in part caused by it, was the appearance of the summer theater, the semiprofessional or professional dramatic enterprise located in seacoast or mountain resorts and finding its clientele among the summer residents of the neighborhood. The summer theater had its origin in the summer schools of the theater which usually grew out of some academic or near-academic pedagogical organization. At first, they were frankly training schools for actors, scene designers, and costumers. But their increasing popularity and success, and the easy availability of even distinguished actors and actresses who had had lean seasons on the legitimate stage, permitted a mushroom-like growth of organizations of the summer-theater type. The repertory of these theaters usually consisted of the available successes of the previous season. But the more courageous of these groups, like the little theaters throughout the country, frequently conferred a considerable longevity on worthy plays that had reached only a limited Broadway audience. The summer theater was also a relatively inexpensive proving-ground for new plays, and it therefore became a substitute for such tryout towns as New Haven and Stamford. A large proportion of the new plays thus given a hearing were destined, of course, never to reach New York; yet the summer theater offered a new foothold for some of the untried playwrights whose access to the theater the depression had barred.[1]

Two significant noncommercial producing organizations—the Group Theatre and the Theatre Union—began their activities in the depths of the depression. Of these, the Group Theatre has proved the more persistent and successful. Formed around a nucleus of actors belonging to the Theatre Guild company, it began its activities in 1931 under the auspices of the older organization with a production of Paul Green's *The House of Connelly*. Although this memorable performance was followed by several failures and *succès d'estime*, the Group Theatre held on until its great success with Sidney Kingsley's *Men in White* (1933) made clear that it was a producing unit with stability and character. Its assets are an intense loyalty on the part of its acting company, infinitely painstaking production, and a flexibility that permits it to do justice to naturalistic, expressionistic, and fantastic drama. One of its major sources of strength has been its alliance with Clifford Odets, most of whose plays it has produced. Its most noteworthy artistic successes have been Odets' *Waiting for Lefty* (1935) and *Awake and Sing*, first produced in 1935 and effectively revived in 1939, Paul Green's *Johnny Johnson* (1936), Odets' *Golden Boy* (1937), and Irwin Shaw's *The Gentle People* (1938). The Theatre Union was an organization of radical playwrights and actors that specialized in violent social dramas. Its more memorable productions were George Sklar and Albert Maltz's *Peace on Earth* (1933) and George Sklar and Paul Peters' *Stevedore* (1934). Though it failed to find a sufficiently large urban audience to sustain its activities, its repertory of propagandistic plays achieved a wide vogue with amateur radical producing groups. The very successful production of *Pins and Needles* (1937) by the International Ladies' Garment Workers Union marked the incursion into the theater of a highly intelligent, socially conscious workers' group, and brought to light a number of skit- and song-writers of radical sympathies.

But the most important effect of the depression on the drama and theater was the creation and activities of the Federal Theatre Project of the Works Progress Administration. The primary motive behind the launching of the Project in 1935 under the national directorship of Mrs. Hallie Flanagan was the provision of immediate relief for thousands of actors,

[1] The number of summer theaters on or near the Atlantic seaboard rose from 12 in 1932 to 30 in 1933 and 42 in 1934. Since that date, the figures are as follows: 32 (1935), 40 (1936), 37 (1937), 44 (1938).

young and old, who were finding it impossible to support themselves in their chosen profession in the face of an acute shrinkage in the theatrical market. A secondary motive behind the Project was the provision of inexpensive or free entertainment for persons who had modest or no means to secure decent entertainment and who had an unwelcome amount of leisure on their hands. A further, and perhaps a less defensible, motive was that of restoring the drama to great regional areas where the theater had been killed by the moving picture and of building up an audience for the drama in urban centers out of strata of the population unfamiliar with acted plays. Finally, the more optimistic of the persons concerned with the Federal Theatre Project hoped that out of their work would come a national art theater subsidized by federal resources and operating in all the major cities.

But the primary necessity of providing relief to those persons connected with the theater who were in straitened or desperate circumstances meant the sponsoring by the Project of all sorts of theatrical and pseudo-theatrical entertainments, from productions of new plays, revivals of old plays, and the writing and production of musical shows, to traveling repertory companies, vaudeville shows, puppet-shows, circuses, and dialectal and racial productions suitable to the region being served and the talent at hand.

Despite the immensity of the problems involved, difficulties with personnel and supply, and the hostility of most commercial producers and many professional critics—not to mention reactionary and censorious persons of every stripe—the Federal Theatre Project accomplished amazing results. It employed thousands of actors and actresses of all degrees of talent and ineptitude; it provided wholesome and occasionally distinguished entertainment for millions of people, most of whom had never seen anything more dramatic than a moving picture.

But we are chiefly concerned with the contribution of the Federal Theatre Project to the drama. There were, of course, a number of important revivals of classical plays of which perhaps the most successful were those of Marlowe's *Dr. Faustus* and Orson Welles' Negroid *Macbeth*, which was seen, not only in New York, but as far afield as Dallas. But the services of the Project to living dramatists were even more pertinent to the vitality of the theater. In this connection, the most spectacular service rendered a living playwright was the almost simultaneous production of Sinclair Lewis' (*q.v.*) dramatization of his anti-Fascist novel, *It Can't Happen Here*, in nineteen theaters and in a number of dialectal and racial versions. Nothing like this had ever happened in the American theater. But this was only the most striking instance of what the Project could accomplish. John J. Coman's adaptation of Paul Vulpius' *Help Yourself* attained thirteen different productions, Orrie Lashin and Milo Hasting's *Class of '29*, twelve, and Harald Clarke and Maxwell Nurnberg's *Chalk Dust*, eleven.[1]

[1] The project also came to the assistance of more prominent living playwrights. The

But the most considerable achievement of the Federal Theatre Project was the creation of a new dramatic form, the Living Newspaper, which combined elements of the expressionistic drama, the moving picture, and the sideshow to present as forcefully as possible problems of current national and international importance. The most successful examples of this form were *Triple-A Plowed Under*, *Power*, and *One-Third of a Nation.* Each of these editions of the Living Newspaper has presented some acute economic problem so tellingly that congressmen and other busybodies have been deeply concerned with the nature of the propaganda fostered. One ground for criticism was the utilization of this subsidized drama for the dissemination of political and economic views favored by the administration; another, the utilization of this form for the dissemination of political and economic views considered, in some circles, to be "un-American."

Whether or not the political ethics that underlay the government subsidization of the Federal Theatre Project were sound, whether or not the government sponsorship of controversial material was defensible, the Federal Theatre Project not only has done a great deal for established playwrights but also has brought to the attention of theatrical producers and the theater-going public a considerable number of new names and talents. The Living Newspaper, moreover, will probably continue to be used for the visual and dramatic presentation of important social issues, since its technique is easily adaptable to the comment of any organized group on current issues of importance.

A further effect of the depression on the drama was the emergence of a radical or proletarian drama, and this movement in its own right, and in its relation to such drama in the past, deserves treatment in some detail. For the writing of such plays, the European drama had been offering dur-

most successful American production of T. S. Eliot's *Murder in the Cathedral* was that of Orson Welles in New York in 1936. Other first productions or revivals of plays by well-known writers include: Maxwell Anderson, *Both Your Houses* (Oakland, California); *idem, Saturday's Children* (Jacksonville, San Bernardino); Philip Barry, *You and I* (Miami); Zoë Akins, *The Old Maid* (Indianapolis); David Belasco, *The Girl of the Golden West* (San Diego); *idem, The Return of Peter Grimm* (Jacksonville); E. P. Conkle, *200 Were Chosen* (Detroit, Peoria); Marc Connelly, *The Wisdom Tooth* (Los Angeles); Rachel Crothers, *As Husbands Go* (Tampa); *idem, Nice People* (San Bernardino); Virgil Geddes, *Native Ground* (New York); Zona Gale, *Faint Perfume* (Atlanta); Susan Glaspell, *The Inheritors* (Jacksonville); Paul Green, *In Abraham's Bosom* (Seattle); *idem, The House of Connelly* (Indianapolis, Los Angeles, Miami); Sidney Howards, *The Silver Cord* (San Diego); *idem, They Knew What They Wanted* (Indianapolis); George S. Kaufman and Marc Connelly, *Dulcy* (Indianapolis); George S. Kaufman and Edna Ferber, *The Royal Family* (Indianapolis, Waterloo, Iowa); George Kelly, *The Show-Off* (Miami); Oliver LaFarge, *Laughing Boy* (Indianapolis); Clifford Odets, *Awake and Sing* (Los Angeles, in Yiddish); Eugene O'Neill, *The Emperor Jones* (San Francisco, with marionettes); Paul Peters and George Sklar, *Stevedore* (Seattle); Elmer Rice, *On Trial* (Chicago); Lynn Riggs, *Cherokee Night* (New York); *idem, Green Grow the Lilacs* (Los Angeles); Conrad Seiler, *Censored* (Denver); *idem, Sweet Land* (New York); Robert E. Sherwood, *The Road to Rome* (Detroit); Booth Tarkington, *Clarence* (Indianapolis); Dan Totheroh, *Wild Birds* (Los Angeles).

ing the last two generations a series of distinguished models. Henrik Ibsen's *An Enemy of the People* (1883) was a dramatic demonstration of the power of the economic motive in society rather than a drama of the class struggle, but Ibsen's exposure of the economic foundations of bourgeois morality prepared the way for the production of sharply class-conscious dramas. Thus, Gerhart Hauptmann's *The Weavers* (1893), a bitter tragedy of the revolt of the victims of domestic industry against their economic oppressors, became a rallying point, wherever the spirit of the new drama asserted itself. Certain plays by gentlemanly John Galsworthy, more particularly *The Silver Box* (1906) and *Strife* (1909), showed what effective dramatic use could be made of the influence of economic forces on the individual or collective struggle.

The first attempts in America to create a drama of social conflicts were timid and sporadic. The wave of social reform that passed over America in the first decade and a half of the twentieth century produced a number of problem plays inspired by the economic stresses and strains of the period. Charles Klein, after reading Ida M. Tarbell's critical history of the Standard Oil Company, wrote for the commercial theater his tremendously successful drama of big business, *The Lion and the Mouse* (1905). But the theater was too completely under the control of the theatrical trust to encourage noncommercial and possibly subversive dramas, and, between the fall of the trust in 1910 and the coming of the World War, the time was too short for more than an occasional experiment with the drama of social import. But to this period belong Charles Rann Kennedy's *Servant in the House* (1907), an attack on the sterile ethics of official Christianity, Edward Sheldon's (*q.v.*) *The Boss* (1911), dealing with the struggle between capital and labor, and Charles Kenyon's *Kindling* (1911), an exposé of life in the slums of a great American city.

The years between the end of the war and the beginning of the depression saw more frequent reflections of economic problems on the stage, though the mood and tone of the period were hardly propitious for serious work in this mode. In 1921, the conflict between conservatism and liberalism in American academic life was treated idealistically in Susan Glaspell's (*q.v.*) *Inheritors*. In 1922, Eugene O'Neill's (*q.v.*) *Hairy Ape* represented expressionistically the psychological deterioration and defeat of an uncouth proletarian struggling to adjust himself to a complex economic order which he could not understand. Maxwell Anderson also produced during the depression a series of social dramas of considerable importance. His first success, *What Price Glory?* (1924), written with Laurence Stallings (*q.v.*), had shown his firm grasp on the realities that lie behind the official distortions of the experiences of men at war. *Outside Looking In* (1925), a dramatization of Jim Tully's hobo novel, was a more serious indication of his interest in the economically underprivileged, although the method was pure rather than social-critical naturalism. But the clearest evidences of his emancipation from the romantic American legend of the land of opportunity and the full dinner pail are to be found in *Gods of the Lightning* (1928), a hotly sympathetic defense of Sacco and Vanzetti, *Both Your Houses* (1933), a more conventional treatment of the conflict between idealism and corruption in American politics, and *Winterset* (1935), his poetic reworking of the tragic implications of *Gods of the Lightning*.

A not unimportant preparation for an atmosphere favorable to a vigorous social drama is the spirit of a satire that recurs in the dramatic works of George S. Kaufman (*q.v.*) and his numerous collaborators. Such a play as *Beggar on Horseback* (1924) was a Menckenesque satire on the crass materialism, absurd overorganization, and spiritual vacuity of big business. The depression seemed to have redirected Kaufman's attention to some of the more preposterous manifestations of American social and political life, and *Strike Up the Band* (1930), *Of Thee I Sing* (1931), and *Let 'em Eat Cake* (1933) showed how so sportive a form as musical comedy responded to the astringent atmosphere of the bitter years.

The social drama of the last decade or more has been influenced profoundly by German expressionism, a movement inspired by the sense of the desuetude of realism and romanticism insistent on the free utilization of any stylistic or formal method for the presentation of the author's message. Elmer Rice (*q.v.*), an occasional practitioner of expert melodrama in *On Trial* (1914) and *Counselor at Law* (1931), was stirred by the expressionistic movement to the writing of *The Adding Machine* (1923), with its underscored implications of the deadening effects of industrialism on the petty bourgeoisie. More comprehensive criticism of contemporary economic and political behavior appeared in the plays produced under his own management—*We, the People* (1933), and *Judgment Day* (1934), a violent anti-Nazi melodrama. Expressionism also won the adherence of such radicals as John Howard Lawson (*q.v.*) and John Dos Passos (*q.v.*). Lawson's *Roger Bloomer* (1923) is individual rather than social in its implications, but *Processional*, produced by the Theatre Guild in 1925, and revived by the Federal Theatre in 1937, was a far-ranging criticism of economic life in brilliantly expressionistic guise. The novelist, Dos Passos, has also used experimental dramatic forms for the statement of his radical views of American life. But neither *The Moon Is a Gong* (1925), alias *The Garbage Man*, nor *Fortune Heights* (1934) caused more than a passing ripple on the surface of the American drama.

The series of terrible social disasters that followed the onset of the depression impressed on the younger playwrights the need for expressing dramatically the more violent phases of the class struggle. Transitory on the stage but not unimportant in contemporary dramatic history were Claire and Paul Sifton's *Midnight* (1930) and *1931* (1932), the latter an attempt to depict the effects of the depression on its helpless and inoffensive victims. John Wexley's (*q.v.*) powerful projection of death-house psychology in *The Last Mile* (1930) lacked the wide social significance of *They Shall Not Die* (1934), a direct dramatization of the sensational Scottsboro case. A number of young playwrights associated with the radical Theatre Union produced a series of plays that came as close to veritable proletarian drama as America has yet seen. Of this group of playwrights, George Sklar would seem to be a focal figure. With Albert Maltz, who alone was responsible for the coal-mining drama, *Black Pit* (1935), he collaborated in *Merry-Go-Round* (1932), a drama of innocence entrapped by the alliance between corrupt police and the underworld, and *Peace on Earth* (1933), a pacifistic drama with a radical overtone. With Paul Peters, whose *Dirt Farmer* had already been produced by the New Theatre of the Tri-Cities and whose *The Third Parade*, a dramatization of the bonus army episode, was staged by the New York Artef, he collaborated in *Stevedore* (1934), in which the economic and social plight of the American Negro was poignantly illustrated. In *Life and Death of an American*, which the Federal Theatre produced in 1939, he used a combination of naturalism and expressionism to dramatize the tragedy of typical victims of a capitalism running amuck.

The most distinct personality to emerge among the radical playwrights is that of Clifford Odets (*q.v.*), whose *Waiting for Lefty*, a drama of trade unionism, and *Till the Day I Die*, an anti-Nazi horror play, found eager audiences in New York, and, after a series of conflicts with political and economic censors elsewhere, in other American cities in 1935. The shrill tone of these plays was somewhat muffled in such studies of middle-class futility as *Awake and Sing* (1935) and *Paradise Lost* (1935). Here, Odets drew heavily on his intimate knowledge of the lives of middle-class Jewish-Americans caught between the millstones of capitalism in a period of depression. Here, he demonstrated clearly his extraordinary powers over dialect and racial characterization. *Paradise Lost* grappled less successfully than *Awake and Sing* with the problem of establishing a consciously inharmonious tone and with the suspense and continuity expected of even plotless drama. The dominant tone was acrid; the criticism of the foundations of the capitalistic order was explicit. With *Golden Boy* (1937) and *Rocket to the Moon* (1938) Odets abandoned—perhaps temporarily—his concern with economic issues. These naturalistic plays have no radical implications or overtones. Purely as drama, *Golden Boy* is the most completely satisfying play Odets has yet written. The variety of his work and his resourcefulness, his honesty and seriousness justify the judgment that he is the most talented American playwright of his generation.

Of most of the proletarian dramas of the depression years, the defects are more conspicuous than the virtues. The defects are in the main excessive violence and the tendency to represent the class struggle in the elementary terms of traditional melodrama. Their virtues are those of vitality and impassioned conviction, of acute social consciousness, and of the determination that the drama shall not continue to be merely an expensive form of diversion for the bourgeoisie and a profitable form of economic exploitation for the commercial producer. At their least, these plays picture, for after times, the darker aspects of the worst years of the depression. But the possibility that they will aid in bringing about a revolution in America is negligible, since their appeal is primarily to the submerged radicals of a half-dozen American cities and to the small fragment of the bourgeoisie suffering from a stirring of the social conscience.

POETRY

American poetry for generations has lived in the shadow of English precept and example, and no years illustrate more perfectly the habitual dependence of American poetasters on their English models than the closing years of the nineteenth century and the first decade of the twentieth. The major English influence of this time was the tradition of diluted romanticism; the chief medium of this influence was Tennyson in his role as the laureate of sentiment and polite morality and not as the poet of fastidious and distinguished artistry. Under this influence American poetry, growing steadily sweeter and sweeter, became little more than anemic and flaccid poetizing that deserved no more than the attention it got at the tail-ends of the pages of elegant magazines. Such names as Thomas Bailey Aldrich (1837–1907), Edward Rowland Sill (1841–87), and Richard Watson Gilder (1844–1909) recall the perfect gentility of American verse at the cheery conclusion of the nineteenth century.

There were, to be sure, exceptions to the dead level of smooth and insipid performance. Something of the atmosphere and the pleasanter emotions of rural life in Indiana were caught by James Whitcomb Riley (1849–1916) in numerous volumes. By his judicious admixture of humor and sentiment with a not offensively poetic diction he won an intensely enthusiastic local following and a genuinely national audience. But Riley was essentially a versifier whose sense of humor, taste for local color, and agreeable sentimentality preserve him from the Limbo where the hordes of people's poets go. More real poetry came from the brief activity of Richard Hovey (1864–1900) and the more sustained career of William Vaughn Moody (1869–1910). Richard Hovey lives in a few spirited songs that ring with a masculine vigor unwonted in the period that produced them. Moody's slightly longer poetic life is more impressive in both aim and accomplishment. His was a substantial talent aroused to fiery use by his quick sense of social injustice and his anger at national shortsightedness. His conception of the poet's function was nobly Miltonic, and in such splendid poems as "Gloucester Moors" and "An Ode in Time of Hesitation," in his largely conceived if imperfectly executed poetic dramas, he belongs with the soothsayers among the poets. His is the most distinguished poetic figure at the beginning of the contemporary period.

But under the untroubled surfaces of the polite versifying of the period, a number of influences were preparing for a poetic renaissance: the renewal of interest abroad and at home in Walt Whitman's unique personal and poetic character and in his success in presenting his view and vision of

America with epic imagination; the study of the experimental poetic activities of the Symbolist poets of France, and the contagious examples of a few enthusiasts who thought it quite time to take American poetry seriously and to emancipate it from its English leading strings. The most enthusiastic student of modern French poetry was Amy Lowell (*q.v.*), whose *Six French Poets* (1915) was one of the most stimulating influences in the early phase of the revival. Within a short time, she was able to announce self-confidently in *Tendencies in Modern American Poetry* (1917) that there were real poets in America as well as in France. But the person most responsible for the epidemic of writing, publishing, and reading poetry in the years immediately before America entered the war was Harriet Monroe (1860–1936), who founded *Poetry, a Magazine of Verse* in Chicago in 1912, introduced Lindsay, Sandburg, and a host of other poets to an astonished audience, and was promptly imitated by the establishing of numerous magazines devoted exclusively to poetry, its discussion, and criticism. Of these, the most important have proved to be *Contemporary Verse* (1916–29), the *Double Dealer* (1921–26), the *Fugitive* (1922–25), and *Palms* (1923–). The poetic revival was also stimulated by the attention magazines and newspapers gave the critical disputes that arose rapidly as poetry came to receive for a brief time as much critical attention as the novel. If the result of all this publicity was a tremendous overproduction of poetry, yet, out of the fury of creation and discussion, a considerable number of poets emerged, and—what is more important—poetry assumed an assured position in contemporary American letters. Moreover, the critical discussions that rent the literary heavens in the exciting years just before America entered the war have had an invigorating influence that American poetry still feels. For the discussions were focused sharply on the basic problems of the material and the form most suitable for poetry.

By way of subject matter, the poetry of the past offered the emotions conventionally associated with the experiences of love, death, and nature, and the great classical romantic stories. But the modern poet was living in the "blooming, buzzing confusion" of a society transformed from a predominantly agricultural to an industrial order by the direct and indirect results of the Industrial Revolution, and stirred intellectually by the incursions of science into every field of human thought. On the question of the poet's responsibility for the use of such material as the modern world offered him, the widest divergence of views and practices existed. Some poets continued to cling to traditionally poetic material, and demonstrated occasionally that a fresh talent could illuminate a fresh facet of it or impose a novel interpretation upon it. Others felt that the old material might be viewed in a new way, the way of contemporary mankind; thus, Edwin Arlington Robinson (*q.v.*) re-interpreted the Arthurian material in his own terms, and Robert Frost (*q.v.*) and Amy Lowell (*q.v.*)

wrought pathos and tragedy out of the matter of New England life. Others eschewed entirely the ancient and honorable subjects, and strove to lift all the manifestations of contemporary American life to the level of poetry. Many of the early experiments had grotesque results, but, by the time the new movement was well under way, the gonfalon of poetry had been planted on many new continents, and new and glorious kingdoms were rising.

A far bitterer conflict was waged over the form appropriate to modern poetry, a conflict that renews itself under a fresh guise with every poetic generation. In its pre-war stage, the conflict seemed to center in the problem of free verse, but what it really amounted to was a reconsideration of the problem of the borderline between verse and prose. The problem was not whether poetry should dispense with rhyme, although rhyme came in for its share of hearty abuse, but just how much rhythm or how regular a rhythm was needed to differentiate verse from prose. The defenders of free verse maintained that it was quite timely and proper to throw over the regular rhythms of traditional verse, and to substitute for them the more subtle rhythms of a form that should be more rhythmically regular than prose but less mechanically regular than the older verse. There was also animated discussion of the problem of poetic diction and figures. The rebels were all for rejecting the shopworn diction and figures of the poetic past, and building up a new vocabulary and set of figures for modern poetry. The conservatives threw up their critical hands or burst into impolite laughter over the conscious colloquialism, the esoteric diction, the homely or sordid figures of the new poetry, and pointed out that, since the poetic word or phrase is the one that evokes the largest number of pleasurable or painful images or associations, it is impossible to create a quite new poetic style overnight. But that so many unpoetic people should have been stirred by a purely technical discussion suggests the amazingly wide interest aroused by the initiation of the poetic revolt.

Although the later discussions of the matter and form of poetry have assumed forms slightly different from those of the earlier period, at bottom the questions at issue have not altered. Free verse had hardly won its place in the aesthetic scheme of things when poets like Pound and Eliot, steeped in Continental poetic culture, introduced further startling innovations in theory and practice. Such poetry as theirs raised questions of unity and coherence of structure, and, more pressingly, unity and coherence of mood and emotion. The defensibility of substituting an emotional principle of structure for a logical or organic principle of structure was debated. Again, the innovators won over the critics and the younger poets, and another aesthetic battle was ended. The latest poetic controversy has raged over the problem of poetry and propaganda. The poetry of social revolt appeared alongside the proletarian novel and drama, and, at the moment, poets are challenging sharply, not only one another's political faiths, but their opposed conceptions of the function of poetry in the modern world. Whatever one may think of the achievement of particular contemporary poets, he cannot but admit that this long series of critical discussions has played a very important part in the reanimation of modern poetry. By reason thereof, American poetry of the last generation is richer in variety and higher in quality than that of any previous generation in America.

As one surveys the achievements of American poets during the last thirty years, one is not unduly surprised to discover that many of the distinguished poets of the period have worked comfortably within the framework of one or another of the great traditions in English poetry. Of these, the traditions most potent in contemporary American poetry are the romantic and the realistic. The romantic tradition is, of course, the more familiar and perhaps the more immediately ingratiating. It stems from the classico-romantic synthesis attempted during the English Renaissance, ignored by the neoclassicism of the seventeenth and eighteenth centuries, and brought to perfection by English poets during the nineteenth century. Its subject matter tends to be traditional; its technique, somewhat conventional; its aim, the creation of a beauty attained by idealization and by the suppression of the incommodious or inharmonious detail. The second tradition of importance for an understanding of the poetry of our period is the realistic, a relatively minor tradition in the history of English poetry, though it has been exemplified recurrently by such writers as Chaucer, Crabbe, Burns, and Cowper, and the young Wordsworth. Its aim is the presentation of material conventionally regarded as unpoetic with only so much poetic ornament and form as are necessary to raise the subject to the plane of poetry. In their various ways, Frost and Lindsay, Masters and Sandburg are adherents to the realistic tradition. But what is most striking about contemporary American poetry is not its adherence to either the great romantic or the minor realistic tradition, but the amount and variety of technical experimentation, an amount so imposing that one is tempted to regard it as indicating the existence of a tradition that one might call eccentric, in the root meaning of that term. But, since originators of a really new poetic technique are extremely rare, we are not unprepared for the discovery that much of the seemingly novel technique of the period derives from an important though infrequently exemplified English tradition, the metaphysical. The revived interest in John Donne, the father of metaphysical poetry, a revival initiated by scholars here and abroad, has spread to the poets, and some of the best of them show the impress of his influence. Similarly, many other apparently original effects of structure or technique turn out, on inspection, to be the result of the direct or indirect influence of the technique of oriental poetry or of technical experimentation by French Symbolists or Impressionists.

TRADITIONALISM

Despite the complex influences that have played over contemporary American poetry, poetry in some variety of the romantic mode has been conspicuous in quantity and quality. Such achievements demonstrate again and again that a poet of talent can accomplish noteworthy results within the framework of a tradition of almost academic rigidity. Naturally, such poetic effects lack the interest of more spectacular experimentation, but what they lose in strangeness they gain perhaps in communicativeness. Thus, such poets as Lizette Woodworth Reese (*q.v.*), George Santayana (*q.v.*), and William Ellery Leonard (*q.v.*) have shown that complex modern personalities can find moving expression in so traditional a form as the sonnet. Santayana's rich mentality and his uninhibited sensory nature give his sonnets a warm, if not a sumptuous coloring. Leonard has come closer to the matter of contemporary existence in his remarkable sonnet sequence, *Two Lives* (1923), in which a painful personal experience is given dignified and movingly tragic treatment. Elsewhere, Leonard's verse, though obviously sincere, is overburdened with the rhetorical devices of the more expansive Tennysonian tradition.

The most distinguished practitioner of the traditional forms among poets of the older generation was Edwin Arlington Robinson (*q.v.*). Fifteen years before the outburst of the new poetry, Robinson was perfecting his adroit though unobtrusive craftsmanship. Working almost steadily within the old metrical forms, he gradually achieved a style distinctly his own. From the beginning, he tactfully and tastefully avoided the clichés of the Victorian tradition. In the main, he came to utilize the colloquial language of a cultivated and complex personality. Yet, with this familiar vocabulary and this narrow range of figures, he contrived to get that maximum of pleasurable suggestiveness with the minimum of means that characterizes poetry of very high quality. His relatively familiar instruments did not prevent his getting genuinely romantic effects. If his style was upon occasion excessively obscure, it was because his oversubtle mind, impatient of the obvious and the direct, pursued indirection until some of his poems became mazes of the incomprehensible rather than masterpieces of suggestion. From this fastidious circumlocution, he did and will suffer, since the poetry that prides itself upon its difficulty may lose a reader that it aims to win. But Robinson's verse is not barren of sensuous or emotional delights. Almost any page of *Merlin* or *Lancelot* or *Tristram* reveals passages in which he invested the eternally fascinating Arthurian material with sensory richness, emotional suggestiveness, and the somber implications of brooding tragedy.

But whether Robinson's material was the backwater of New England life or the romantic epic of Arthur's fall, the point of view and the implicit values remained the same. For Robinson was a thoughtful, inactive man, brooding over the plight of human beings with inextricably mingled vices and virtues living in a contrary universe. He was utterly scrupulous in noting the shadows that encompass the life of man, and profoundly intent upon what men make of their petty or valiant lives in an indifferent, if not actually hostile world. This unweariedly absorbing spectacle did not move him to bitterness, for he was stirred to both pity and admiration for struggling mankind. Though to Robinson many men seem doomed, their tragic ends may be not ignominious but actually glorious.

In his lifetime, Robinson was given the highest possible place among the thousand and one poets of the period. That he attained this distinction is the more remarkable since his view of life and its values was somber, and his technique remained conventional, in the midst of the whirlwinds of technical experimentation. If he deserved the high place given him, he deserved it not merely for the distinction with which he utilized a traditional technique but for his singularly consistent and magnanimous view of life and a tremendous seriousness that was not unrelieved by sardonic humor. Probably no American poet of our time has produced so much distinguished poetry.

Certain poets, born in the eighties, persisted in their fidelity to traditionalism in the face of the storms of experimentation. Of these, the most loyal to the great romantic tradition are such poets as Sara Teasdale (*q.v.*), John Hall Wheelock (*q.v.*), and Witter Bynner (*q.v.*). Miss Teasdale was well settled in a traditional technique before the storm of experimentation broke, and she was never lured from the safety of her harbor. Though, in her early volumes, she experimented with such sanctified forms as the sonnet and the dramatic monologue, her favorite form was the brief lyric of personal emotional experience. Successive volumes followed the curve of her actual or imaginary emotional life. That experience was a deeply feminine one, and her direct though decorous expression of it won her a wide audience. As the years passed, the emotional content of her poetry became more complex. The note of self-pity, so shrill in the early verses, gave way to a more balanced emotion, a more courageous acceptance of infinite human emotion and its finite satisfactions. Thus, her dexterous and sensitive verse won its not inconspicuous place in the record of modern woman's emancipation from the reticence of silence.

John Hall Wheelock had likewise settled into his technical habits before the rise of the new poetry, and he has remained faithful to his first poetic allegiances. His early poetry shows evidence of his having been moved to that attempt to revitalize late nineteenth-century poetry with which we associate such Americans as Hovey and Moody, and such English poets as Stevenson and Henley. The mood is one of rather overself-conscious affirmation of the worth of life and work, an overdetermined eagerness to play a manly if not a heroic part. This somewhat exuberant romanticism is less extreme in so mature a volume as *The Black Panther*

(1922), but all too often the poetic medium is academic and devitalized. A closer contact with the new poetry or a greater sympathy for it might have made Wheelock's position in the current poetic scene a more prominent one.

Witter Bynner (*q.v.*), on the other hand, illustrates the dangers of a too uncontrolled eclecticism. Facile in expression, plastic in temperament, he has played the sedulous ape to a variety of poetic masters, without, perhaps, ever emerging into genuinely individual maturity and independence. His facility in imitation and his fundamental conservatism were consciously illustrated in *Spectra* (1916), the volume in which, writing with Arthur Davison Ficke under the pseudonym "Anne Knish," he produced a series of experimental poems so superior to the manner parodied that they were received seriously by critics sympathetic with the new poetry. He comes closest to truly individual expression in so late a volume as *Eden Tree* (1931). His major services to American poetry appear in his encouragement of numerous poets younger than himself, in his own experimentation with the treatment of the life of the Southwest where he has long lived, and in his long devotion to the tremendous task of translating Chinese poetry in forms communicable to American readers.

Three poets, born in New England in the nineties—Robert Hillyer (*q.v.*), Winifred Welles (*q.v.*), and Edna St. Vincent Millay (*q.v.*)—likewise write in the tradition of English romanticism. Of the three, Hillyer is the most conservative in temperament and technique. Hillyer is essentially the academic poet, saturated in the best traditions of English literature. These qualities make for respectable if not exciting poetry. Hillyer rarely elevates, and as rarely does he depress the not too expectant reader. He is a not unworthy example of the virtues no less than the vices of academic art. The poetic technique of Winifred Welles is, likewise, essentially traditional, but her feminine refinement, wit, and fancy for the bizarre communicate a sense of personality rarely felt in the somewhat depersonalized utterance of Hillyer. Her narrative poems in *A Spectacle for Scholars* (1935) draw upon her intimate knowledge of that New England material which other regional poets, as we shall see, have found attractive.

To include Edna St. Vincent Millay among poets writing in the romantic tradition may seem at first an unwarranted extension of the term *romantic* or a distortion of the values of her poetry. But that term is so notoriously elastic that it may include even the most diverse of Miss Millay's moods. At least, she is a poet in whom emotion, whatever its guise, is the dominant faculty. Her emotional tone has grown, to be sure, from the adolescent ecstacies of "Renascence" through the willful Bohemianism of *A Few Figs from Thistles* (1920) and the social passions expressed in *A Buck in the Snow* (1928) to the romantic pessimism of *Fatal Interview* (1931), and the tragic desperation of "Epitaph for the Race of Man."

But, despite this range of emotion, her tone, whether cynical or sentimental, homely or tragic, is constantly romantic. And her technique as well, though frequently expert, is essentially traditional and therefore, for her thousands of readers, easily intelligible and ingratiating. At her best, she builds a personal melody on the overfamiliar scale. At her soundest, she draws realistic details from her life on the Maine coast and in the Berkshires into the shining net of her romanticism. At her worst, she relies too heavily upon the tone and phrasing of the earlier romantics; certain of the sonnets in *Fatal Interview* are reminiscent of Shakespeare in his less inspired moments. If there are touches of belated adolescence in much of Miss Millay's writing, if there are many moments of self-dramatization and self-pity, she has likewise her moments of maturity and impersonality. Though her too intensely personal poems are those which have won her as large an audience as any American poet of our time has had, it is to be desired, though it cannot be hoped, that she will be remembered by the products of her more disciplined art and thought.

The power of the great romantic tradition is manifest in the work of even so young a poet as George Dillon (*q.v.*). Here there is no troubling of the waters of technical experimentation; here the ancient virtues of clarity and flexibility, freshness and sensitivity are still honored. *Boy in the Wind* (1927) had, inevitably, its moods of adolescent self-absorption, but *The Flowering Stone* (1931) had moved in the direction of the impersonal and the philosophical, without losing the crystalline purity of the earlier volume. Dillon's poetry is another illustration of the fact that, within the confines of the classico-romantic mode, excellent if not challenging poetry may yet be written.

REALISM AND REGIONALISM

The second poetic mode to demand critical consideration touches realism on the one hand and regionalism on the other. The realistic tradition in poetry is not a major one, but it has its particular utility in the treatment of American life, which, devoid of the traditional allurements of nightingales and mysterious ruins, of the romantic associations of the heroes and heroines of history and literature, seems somewhat too prosaic for elevated poetic presentation. The more realistic of the regional poets have been stirred by the ideal of treating American life in terms as colloquial and undecorated as possible. A medium appropriate to such material has been sought, and, on a number of occasions, found. The relationship between realism and regionalism is not, of course, an inevitable one. Not all realistic poets are regionalists, and not all regional poets are realists. Some of the most "metaphysical" poetry of the period by the members of the *Fugitive* group has its regional associations and inspirations. But there *is* a high correlation between realism and regionalism, and whether the poetry be realistic or experimental, the category of regionalism, in poetry as in the novel and the drama, has its power of critical illumination.

Such New England poets as Edwin Arlington Robinson (*q.v.*), Robert Frost (*q.v.*), and Amy Lowell (*q.v.*), Wilbert Snow (*q.v.*), Robert Hillyer (*q.v.*), and Robert Coffin (*q.v.*), Edna St. Vincent Millay (*q.v.*) and Winifred Welles (*q.v.*), illustrate both the pertinence and the impertinence of the regional classification. Diverse in manner and temperament as these poets are, they draw sustenance in varying degrees from New England's thin-soiled, rock-strewn hills, its clear cold waters.

Though much more than a regional poet, Robinson represented, in a measure, the withering of New England's flowering. The view he took of life was neither that of the hopeful sturdy pioneer nor of the Brahmin satisfied with himself and intent on preserving his stable world, but that of the melancholy spectator and interpreter of the decline of a great American province. If he was preoccupied with eccentrics and failures, if many of his characters' destinies ended in futility, the reason was not merely Robinson's own brooding and foreboding temperament, but the influence upon him of the fading glories and backwater neuroses of New England in decline. In Robinson, modern Puritanism had its solitary sympathetic spokesman among the poets.

Though Robert Frost's (*q.v.*) New England is actually the New England of Robinson, the divergences in their account of it illustrate the disparity in their temperaments. Frost, no less than Robinson, is aware of the waning energies of contemporary New England and is concerned with those eccentricities of humor and madness that the isolated and ingrowing life of the back-country encourages. But on humble natural objects and activities, Frost sets a somewhat higher value than Robinson did, and a quiet sense of humor, that takes the place of Robinson's circuitous wit, protects him from the deepening gloom of the latter's world. If he has drawn, with exquisite sensibility, the shadows in the New England scene, he has also written of its natural and human excellences with contagious delight and with an exalted sense of human integrity and courage.

Robinson and Frost are alike in their avoidance of conventional poetic diction. But Frost's diction comes closer than Robinson's to the language of common speech, closer to Wordsworth's ideal of a natural poetic diction. Nor is his diction alone colloquial; the intrinsic rhythm of his verse is the rhythm of slow cautious New England speech. Even more severely than Robinson has he eliminated poetic ornament, and, if his blank verse is singularly alive, it is because his distinguished capacity for self-criticism requires the utmost sincerity and artistry in any work that is to meet the public eye. As generation after generation of New England farmers has wrung its livelihood from a meager rock-strewn soil, so Robert Frost, out of deliberately prosaic materials and in a scrupulously unpoetic idiom, creates through the intense suggestibility of his vision as authentic poetry as any written in our time.

Of the older New England poets, Amy Lowell (*q.v.*) is the only one who demands notice in this particular category of poetic activity. Amy Lowell's New England was that of the Brahmin, not the Puritan; her cultural contacts were European rather than native; her ambitions, therefore, were national rather than regional. But New England's history and legends, its characters and natural beauties, were very close to her, and, in the midst of her varied poetic activities, her poems, personal and impersonal, of New England life and scenes are not the most transient in interest.

In the current generation, New England can boast of an impressive variety of poetic achievements. Thus, Wilbert Snow's (*q.v.*) poems of Maine coast village life are characterized by scrupulously honest observation, a deep passion for human decency, an enviable gusto and zest, a sturdy faith in the poetic potentialities of the language of common men, and an unusual gift for putting that faith into arresting poetic practice. His folk ballads ring more authentically than Robert P. Tristram Coffin's (*q.v.*) rather willfully masculine and downright tales of Maine life and characters. A sensitive eye and a felicitous hand appear in the poetry of Elizabeth Coatsworth and Winifred Welles (*q.v.*). Miss Coatsworth, to be sure, has ranged far beyond New England for her poetic subjects. In 1923, she contributed *Fox Footprints* to the transient poetic vogue of oriental exoticism, and in *Atlas and Beyond* (1924) she continued to draw on her European experience for poetic material, but in her more recent poems the native element is stronger, and she brings a welcome humor to her gay and ironical treatment of regional life. To specifically New England material, Winifred Welles has dedicated perhaps her most ambitious volume, *A Spectacle for Scholars* (1935), sinister though witty accounts of the lives of four characteristic eccentrics.

More alien currents run through the poems of such young writers as H. Phelps Putnam (*q.v.*) and R. P. Blackmur. The anti-aestheticism of the post-war period and the vogue of the hard-boiled account for some of the aggressive masculinity of Putnam's poems. Here is also that deliberate juxtaposition of the ideal and the sordidly actual which T. S. Eliot has taught his disciples. Putnam has attempted to transmute regional material into the terms of his own sophisticated personal idiom. A similar complexity is to be expected of R. P. Blackmur's *From Jordan's Delight* (1937), for Blackmur's criticism makes as apparent as his poetry does, the subtlety of his intelligence. But what is noteworthy in this particular production is the extraordinary freshness Blackmur achieves through a depersonalized saturation in the harsh realistic language of his island characters. Here a distilled colloquialism communicates satisfactorily the most complex emotions. While such poetry is being written, New England's power over the poetic imagination is still unbroken.

The regional influence of the South is apparent chiefly in the work of the poets once associated with the magazine, *The Fugitive*, but their dominant stylistic character makes more logical their consideration in the category of poetic experimentation. We may, however, consider at this point the poetry produced under the most potent of the racial-regional influences, that of the American Negro. This influence has been felt in all the arts—in the novel and drama, in music and the plastic arts—but the expression of this influence in poetry is of particular interest, on the ground of both material and language. In this poetry, the feelings shared by members of an underprivileged racial minority are of rather less interest than the individual feelings and treatments particular poets have given more or less common experience. Of most of these poets, it is noteworthy that, whatever their geographical or cultural origin, each and every one of them has finally made his way to New York where he could be fairly sure of finding a sympathetic audience from tolerant urban whites and the better-educated Negroes of Harlem. Thus, Florida contributed James Weldon Johnson (*q.v.*), Jamaica, Claude McKay (*q.v.*), Missouri, Langston Hughes (*q.v.*), to the New York literary scene. That Countee Cullen (*q.v.*) is an indigenous New Yorker explains in part the nature of his poetic product. Of the four, Johnson was not only the oldest but the closest to the psychology of the rural Negro. He specialized in the expression of the brilliantly imaginative and emotional experience of the Negro stirred by religion. Johnson's poetry, therefore, is the richest in traditional folk qualities. In Claude McKay, there is more self-possession and sophistication. He is more at ease in the Caucasian world as he finds it. There is less sentimental self-pity in his verse than in much Negro poetry. Langston Hughes draws from yet another vein of racial experience, the nonreligious lyrical "blues" tradition. His language is almost purely colloquial, and his rhythms are as definitely those of the urbanized Negro as any that have been put into print. The race's grim experience of economic competition speaks from his verse. Of these four poets, Countee Cullen is the least Negroid in psychology and style. His medium is hardly affected by his racial origin or racial speech. With him, race has become almost an affectation. But these are only the best known of the Negro poets of our time. Many others of almost equal interest appear in such anthologies as James Weldon Johnson's *Book of American Negro Poetry* (1922) and Countee Cullen's *Caroling Dusk* (1927).

The most noteworthy of the middle western poets of the older generation—Masters, Lindsay, and Sandburg—illustrate more violently than most of the New England or the Negro poets the violent break between the old poetry and the new. These poets found the subject matter for their poetry in phases of the modern world neglected or avoided by poets in the romantic tradition. Upon occasion, they have achieved distinct success in the handling of novel poetic techniques. But, though alike in the boldness with which they have ventured on new poetic conquests and in their inability to discriminate between the good and bad in their own writing, each poet emerges as a distinct and considerable poetic individual.

Edgar Lee Masters (*q.v.*) achieved with a single volume, *Spoon River Anthology* (1915), a reputation which he has found it impossible to sustain. Before the appearance of this notorious volume, he had already published a number of obscure and undistinguished conventional poems and poetic dramas. But, stirred by the influence of the new poets whom Harriet Monroe was introducing in *Poetry* and urged by William Marion Reedy to turn away from his conventional style, he produced a work that is a landmark in the history of contemporary poetry. Here, the life of a small Illinois village was turned inside out for the disapprobation of a horrified world. The device of having the dead in the village graveyard speak out their honest epitaphs made possible a grim exposure of hidden sores and psychological ailments which the conventional tributes of the stonemason had concealed. Masters' temperament or his disillusioning experience as a lawyer emphasized the seamier side of village life at the expense of the smooth, and the boldness of his revelations as much as his innovations in poetic technique won the book a scandalous as well as a poetic triumph. It remains an unforgettable panorama of American village life. The value of its poetic form is less certain. Its form is unrhymed but more or less cadenced prose; the diction is perhaps a little below the level of decorous colloquial language. But, with this fluid and restless medium, Masters showed himself capable, upon occasion, as in "Ann Rutledge," of really moving poetry. All too frequently, however, the poems have the effect of prose broken up into natural and sometimes unnatural phrasal units. In his work since the *Anthology*, there has been an increase of prosiness and a decrease in the amount of poetry. In *Domesday Book* (1920) he attempted a Browningesque subject and technique, but did not show a tithe of Browning's power in transmuting obstinate material into something resembling poetry. *The New Spoon River Anthology* (1924) met with the fate usual to sequels, and of late Masters has turned away from poetry to the novel and biography as media for his memories and visions of American life.

Vachel Lindsay (*q.v.*) was, on the whole, a more attractive and impressive figure than Masters. He attempted deliberately to bring poetry back to the people, first, by writing on subjects and in a style that might attract the unlettered, and, second, by tramping in person over highways and byways as a vendor of his poetry and an apostle of beauty and idealism. Later, he made a considerable reputation for himself as a reader of his own poetry, and, though his methods smacked somewhat of the higher vaudeville, he was as stirring a communicator of primitive rhythm and mass feeling as the reciters of poetry have produced. Like many another American, Lindsay fell a prey to the Messianic delusion, and his work suffers from his inability to criticize either the ideals he espoused or the medium in which he depicted them. He is at his weakest in his political proclamations extolling any idol that happened to attract his naïve idealism, and in his adolescent responses to the suspect charms of popular figures of the moving-picture and sporting worlds. But, despite Lindsay's inability to distinguish between worthy and unworthy objects of admiration, between good and bathetic work, upon occasion he wrote beautifully and stirringly. No poet of our time has come so near as Lindsay to being an authentic folk poet, a vehicle of the imagination of a people. Lindsay's finest achievements are such poems as "The Congo," "The Booker T. Washington Trilogy," and "King Solomon and the Queen of Sheba," poems in which he projects with great power and beauty what he conceived the Negroid imagination to be. In "The Congo," perhaps his most impressive work, he has created a racial vision that is broad and deep and powerful. In poems as dissimilar as "General Booth" and "The Chinese Nightingale," he showed his control over strong but supple rhythms and an insight into personalities dramatically alien to his own. If the weaknesses of his doggerel and if his easy though sincere enthusiasms are only too conspicuous, his command in verse and voice of a wide range of movements and rhythms, his stimulus to a revival of the art of speaking poetry, make him a particularly beguiling figure in American folk culture, if not too permanent a figure in the history of American poetry.

Carl Sandburg (*q.v.*) is a more conscious and critical craftsman than either of his Illinois confreres. His varied experience in manual labor and his more sustained contacts with the more violent aspects of Chicago life motivated his devotion to untraditional and unacademic verse. He is a more discriminating personality than either Masters or Lindsay, and the brutality and crudeness which were at first paramount in his work were the deliberate gestures of a fine and feeling nature. The authentically colloquial language in which he writes is a very different colloquialism from that of Robert Frost (*q.v.*). Here is not distillation of a traditional rural Puritan speech, nor the language of a literate Middle West, but the monosyllables of truck-drivers and stevedores. Harsh and ugly words convey sharply the hard and cruel aspects of urban life, but under the cruelty is a feeling that is natural and strong. The cruder poems have the effectiveness of immediate shock, but their poetic value is sometimes questionable. It is in the exquisitely modulated repetitions of his colloquial cadences, in his feeling for the wide prairies and for inviolate natural loveliness that his best notes are heard. In *The People, Yes* (1936), he has attempted his largest subject, a re-creation in popular language of the mind and heart of the American people. The material is various and fascinating; proverbs, folk similes, riddles, wisecracks, catalogues *à la* Whitman, and other devices precipitate views and ideas common to Americans. But this book is more than a cento of folk wisdom. The poet himself speaks out in defense of a democratic idealism threatened in our time by foes without and foes within. Though less poetically concentrated than the earlier lyrics, this book seems likely to prove Sandburg's noblest expression in verse of the American spirit.

To certain other poets of the generation of Sandburg or younger, the Middle and Far West have furnished inspiration and material. Though John G. Neihardt (*q.v.*), like Sandburg, was born in Illinois, most of his life has been spent in Nebraska, where he lived for some years among the Omaha Indians, and studied their history and lore. Neihardt's special subject is the pioneering days in the West, and he has devoted a series of long poems to the epic of American pioneer life. Here, he faces the peculiarly modern difficulty of sustaining a poetic tone through prolonged narratives on subjects usually regarded as alien to poetry. In poetry written on so grand a scale, there are bound to be passages as flat as the prairies, and the medium becomes incongruously conventional, but, on the whole, Neihardt's attempt to meet the poetic challenge of American aboriginal material must be regarded with admiration if not with intense enthusiasm. Lew Sarett (*q.v.*) is less intent than Neihardt on the utilization of American and Indian historical material, but, in his earlier volumes at any rate, he has drawn on his intimate knowledge of Indian lore and of wilderness ways in the creation of the primitive natural atmosphere of forest and woodland life. A pantheistic feeling for all forms of natural life permeates his poetry. In his later work, much of the earlier material and feeling reappear, though there is somewhat less stress on backwoods material and more of an apprehension and interpretation of the realities of the modern world. Among the younger American poets from the Middle West, Paul Engle (*q.v.*) would seem to be the only one deeply affected by his regional experience. In *American Song* (1934), the rather grandiose idealism of an earlier American epoch was rather rhetorically conveyed. The tone of his second volume, *Break the Heart's Anger* (1936), is somewhat more restrained. The youthful exuberance has abated, a critical sense has appeared, and Engle seems less the flag-waver and more the bewildered and defensive liberal. But there is a chance that he may become the spokesman of a mid-western culture that is peculiarly American.

For two decades or more, the Southwest has been, for artists and poets, a refuge from the intellectual and climatic rigors of less amiable and melodramatic regions. This aesthetic migration has had innumerable consequences, but certainly those in the field of letters have been much less impressive than those in the field of art. The curious amalgam of cultures in the Southwest—Spanish, Mexican, Indian, and American—have been expressed more successfully in paint on canvas than in words on the page. But poets like Witter Bynner (*q.v.*), Haniel Long, and Alice Corbin Henderson, novelists like Oliver LaFarge (*q.v.*) and Paul Horgan, patrons of the arts and enthusiasts of Indian culture like Mary Austin (*q.v.*) and

Mabel Dodge Luhan (*q.v.*), have caught in one or another form the strange spirit of this exotic region. The West Coast, too, has its local and coterie poets, but almost none of them show much evidence of any intimate conditioning of their writing by the physical or spiritual milieu. The sole exception, of course, is Robinson Jeffers (*q.v.*), who is, however, too portentous a figure to be considered merely as a regional poet.

Regionalism has played a very considerable part in conditioning the poetic products of a great variety of personalities. If its influence is less conspicuous in poetry than in the novel, the diverse natures of the media go some distance in explaining the lighter impingement of regional circumstance upon contemporary American poetry.

POETIC EXPERIMENTATION

Every renaissance in the arts depends ultimately on the crossing of two aesthetic strains, one of which is usually native and the other alien. Thus, the fusion of the classical tradition and the medieval tradition produced in the European Renaissance a variety of art and thought hitherto unknown, and the complex phenomena subsumed under the term Romanticism resulted, in large part, from the transmission of the influence of Rousseau and the pre-revolutionary thinkers to a variety of national cultures. With such major movements of the creative spirit, it may seem incongruous to compare so limited a movement as the renaissance in contemporary American poetry, but the analogy is at least suggestive, since it encourages one to look for the alien strains that have operated upon the native American poetic stock. The genetic history of contemporary experimental poetry is by no means simple, but it may not be too inaccurate to suggest that the major influences upon the experimental poetry of this period have been primarily French and secondarily oriental. Though less potent, the oriental influence appeared earliest. For Imagism, the first major contemporary manifestation of poetic experimentation, had its roots in the oriental habit of condensation, of implication rather than explication, of emphasis on the image rather than the idea, and of dependence for effect on the pattern of rhythm rather than on the pattern of rhythm and rhyme.

Whatever its origins, the initiation of the Imagist movement was one of the most exciting moments in the history of contemporary American poetry. This moment was the publication of the Imagist manifesto in *Some Imagist Poets*, edited by Amy Lowell (*q.v.*) in 1915, and followed by others of the same type in 1916 and 1917. The credit for inspiring the movement belongs, however, to Ezra Pound (*q.v.*), who persuaded kindred spirits to join in the anthology, *Des Imagistes*, published in England in 1914. The major principles of the Imagist creed may be stated thus: to use the language of common speech but to employ the exact word; to create new rhythms as the expression of new moods; to allow absolute freedom in the choice of subject; to present an image, not vague generalities; to produce poetry that is hard and clear; to aim at concentration, since concentration is the very essence of poetry.

In the forefront of the Imagist crusade was Amy Lowell, and no better leader could have been selected for so stormy an expedition. With great energy, intelligence, and enthusiasm, she engaged in one critical combat after another, wrote poems to illustrate her theories, made her American companions aware of French experimentation in her *Six French Poets* (1915), honored with an accolade those colleagues deserving of praise in *Tendencies in Modern American Poetry* (1917), and discussed and read the new poetry before astonished and sometimes amused audiences. Her critical work was invigorating rather than discriminating; like most propagandists, she emitted judgments which time has rudely ignored. But it is of greater importance to estimate her creative performance. Miss Lowell herself was not long content to comply with the restrictions of the Imagist creed. She adapted from the French "polyphonic prose," which uses at will regular meter, free verse, assonance, alliteration, and repetition, and with it she created some of her most powerful effects. She also used regular verse forms as eagerly and lightly as she employed the much-discussed medium of free verse.

If the final impression left by Miss Lowell's work is somewhat less deep than that made by the energy and intelligence that created it, its limitations are at any rate those of her temperament: excess of cerebration, a defective emotional apparatus, and a hypersensitiveness to sensory experience. Much of her work is deficient in feeling; more of it dazzles by its incessant visual imagery, and deafens by equally incessant auditory images. Her best work is in those polyphonic passages where action controls the storm of images, and in such historical panoramas as "Guns as Keys," "The Bronze Horses," and "The Hammers," the vitality and imaginative sweep of which have been somewhat obscured by quantities of strained and mediocre work. Despite the obvious weaknesses of much of her poetic output, her vitality, industry, and sheer intelligence are still a little overpowering.

The early work of John Gould Fletcher (*q.v.*) illustrates the weaknesses intrinsic in a strict application of the Imagist creed. The most memorable parts of his early poetry are the eleven color-symphonies in *Goblins and Pagodas* (1916). These remarkable sequences of beautiful images are a practical demonstration of the inability of the human mind to live by images alone. It is not enough to string bright images on the thread of a single color; the reader demands the dynamic allurements of emotion or thought or action. But Imagism was merely a stage in Fletcher's complex development; in succeeding volumes, emotion and thought were not absent, and, while upon occasion the movement of his mind seemed controlled by unconscious rather than by conscious powers, his later elegiac and subdued poetry has turned for its inspiration away from alien to native themes and stimuli.

Of the American members of the original Imagist group, only one has kept the faith, only one has demonstrated the possibilities of a method none too accurately described in the Imagist manifesto. "H. D's" (*q.v.*) early *Sea Garden* (1916) shows the odd and strained conceits of unsure experimentation, but in *Hymen* (1921), she makes pure imagery carry the burden of precipitating intense emotion. In the main, the images are derived from the sensory aspects of the classical world as seen by a fresh modern eye; out of these alien elements "H. D." has devised a rich sensuous concentrated medium in which her characters speak their dramatic monologues. The figures from Greek legend start her imagination working most brilliantly. Her earlier lyrical interpretations of the Hippolytus story led her to the writing of an Imagistic drama, *Hippolytus Temporizes* (1927). Like most of her contemporaries, "H. D." has reverted upon occasion, as in the masque, *Hymen*, to a traditional poetic form, but her favorite vehicle is unrhymed lines patterned by subtle rhythms and repetitions. Though too concentrated for most readers, her poetry has probably revealed the ultimate in the potentialities of Imagism.

It has long been obvious that something new in poetry could be achieved by the Imagistic method, but that to confine poetry to images is to circumscribe it unduly. Although the Imagist manifesto created tremendous excitement, not merely among the poetic but the unpoetic, and stimulated violent critical and aesthetic discussions, the Imagists, as we have seen, soon broke away from their arbitrary creed and their illogical association, and went their various artistic ways. But the Imagist proclamation opened the free-verse controversy which was to have such widespread if harmless results during the next half-dozen years. It also prepared the public for poetic experiments of a boldness of which the Imagists never dreamed.

The break-up of the Imagist group and the dispersal of its heterogeneous associates is symbolic of the centrifugal nature of much early and late experimentation during this period. Among the older poets, Alfred Kreymborg (*q.v.*) may be taken as illustrating a variety of experimentation distinct from Imagism. The anthology, entitled *Others*, which he edited in 1916, 1917, and 1920, lacked the rigid and doctrinaire character of Imagism and offered a haven for a wider variety of poetic experimenters. Kreymborg's own poetic progress shows an oscillating movement between the experimental and the traditional rather than the conventional movement from the traditional to the individual in technique and style. His most characteristic poetry has the form of free verse, with playful and sometimes extravagant repetitions. In tone, he is neither realistic nor romantic, unless the fantastic be considered a variation on the romantic. His world, as the title *Puppet Plays* (1923) suggests, is that of the dehumanized figurine, wry of aspect, and mechanical and galvanized in gesture. The effect is of the wittily rather than the sinisterly grotesque. But in the semicynical operations of poetic puppets lies his distinction, and not in his latter somewhat surprising but none too happy reversion to the sonnet form. Kreymborg has not, in recent years, remained entirely untouched by political radicalism, though his chosen medium is curiously inappropriate for the serious expression of political and social doctrines.

Conrad Aiken's (*q.v.*) early association with the Imagists obscures rather than clarifies the basic movement of his spirit. He was never in any real sense an Imagist, although certain early poems have a harsh reality that made them seem fresh and novel. But he turned quickly away from such external realism to a solitary devotion to the creation of poetry that should come as close as possible to the art of music. To this end, he cultivated the flowing repetitious movement of symphonic music, the emphasis on emotion and feeling at the expense of thought, and the substitution of an emotional coherence for the logical coherence conventional in poetry. He was encouraged in this direction by his enthusiastic conversion to the doctrines of psychoanalysis, and his poetry is most illuminatingly regarded as the poetizing of the stream of consciousness of Aiken himself or of a character assumed by him. In the main, the tone of his poetry is misty and mournful, dreamlike and insubstantial, suggestive and not indicative. Aiken's poetry often has the effect of not too controlled or too clearly-constructed romantic music. His poetry has no cutting edges, and the eternal monologues of a depressed and frustrate unconscious become repetitious and ultimately wearisome.

A more difficult problem is raised by the poetry of Marianne Moore (*q.v.*). At first, the reader is likely to be put off by the peculiar nature of Miss Moore's free verse. For it is obvious that her conception of the poetic line is not that of the fundamental rhythmic unit which the writers of free verse aimed to substitute for the succession of regular accents. Miss Moore's lines frequently consist of single unemphatic monosyllables or a single syllable of longer words. Sometimes, the line-ending assists in bringing a stress upon an important word; more often, the line-ending seems to have little or no rhythmic significance. In terms of form alone, one is perhaps justified in regarding her writing as rhythmic prose that has been submitted to a rather freakish system of lineation. The content, too, offers a critical challenge. Miss Moore's similes and metaphors are extravagant or grotesque; her expertness at keeping out of the grooves of the traditional poetic imagination is superbly admirable. What is more important, however, is that her metaphors, however seemingly outrageous, give one an entirely fresh if slightly distorted vision of the world that outdoes the idiosyncratic imaginings of Edith Sitwell. Here are dissonance and willful cacophony, puzzling abstraction and equally astounding concreteness. Behind it all is a mind stored with rare learning and sharpened by extraordinary wit. For many readers, Miss Moore will seem to have exceeded the limits of the legitimately poetic; to a few readers, she will seem one of the keenest if not the least eccentric of contemporary poetic intelligences.

Experimentation of a more purely external sort is conspicuous in the poetry of E. E. Cummings (*q.v.*). What is first noticeable in his poems is the typographical oddity: the absence of capitalization, the haphazard punctuation, the splitting up of words into ordinary or extraordinary syllables. These devices, borrowed in part or adapted from Guillaume Apollinaire, while they strike the reader's attention, tend to distract it from Cummings' genuine, though perversely exhibited, gifts. These are a genuinely fresh response to a rather idyllic beauty and a boldness and variety of metaphor which would link him with the metaphysical poets, if his metaphors were more intellectual and less emotionalized. Cummings' passion for freakishness seems insatiable; it is to be regretted that his willfulness seems likely to continue to estrange many potential readers.

There is little or nothing in the metric pattern of Laura Riding's (*q.v.*) verse to dismay the hardened reader, but its diction and its tone are likely to repel many lovers of romantic or sentimental poetry. For Miss Riding's tone is aloof and secretive; contemptuous of easy emotion or superficial feeling. Moreover, such hard honest feeling as she admits is rendered in a language so abstract and indirect as to challenge or defy interpretation and thus to make perhaps excessive demands even upon sympathetic readers. Miss Riding is one of the most devout practitioners of "private" poetry.

A more sustained line of poetic experimentation stems from the metaphysical tradition in English poetry, and, like that poetry, finds its motivation in the conviction of a number of contemporary poets that poetry must be rescued from the aesthetically flaccid and intellectually relaxed adherence to the romantic tradition. In the main, contemporary metaphysical poetry, like that of the seventeenth century, shows a strong infusion of thought into whatever emotion it presents. In consequence, metaphysical poetry often seems a little chilly, not to say frigid. It lacks the warm intimacy of romantic poetry, and, upon occasions, it is so completely de-personalized that it takes us out of the world of living beings into a museum of lovely forms. Metrically, most of the metaphysical verse of our time is unproblematically regular. Its diction, imagery, and figures, however, tend to the beautifully exotic rather than the familiarly beautiful. The difficulty of metaphysical poetry is its intellectual involution and its tendency toward dehumanization. At its best, this poetic vein has produced some of the most fastidious and technically scrupulous verse of our time.

Two of the older poets—William Carlos Williams (*q.v.*) and Wallace Stevens (*q.v.*)—show signs of the metaphysical influence although they also offer evidence of contact with the free-verse movement. In both these poets, the vision is fresh if disquieting, since it involves more contradictory elements than the poets in the Romantic tradition attempted to synthesize. But the touches of the anti-poetic and the sordid are not to be taken too seriously or too ethically. They serve merely as the darker colors on palettes predominantly brilliant. In both poets, there is a rare if hardly human music, strange beauty, and genuine poetic wit. In Stevens, perhaps, there is a greater willfulness in mystification, a more marked flair for the exotic.

Elinor Wylie's (*q.v.*) poetry is much more clearly in the metaphysical tradition. Despite her passion for Shelley, the ruling spirit here, as elsewhere in contemporary poetry of the metaphysical type, is that of John Donne. Miss Wylie's poetic skill was extraordinary. Metrically conventional, her poetry, in diction, imagery, and figure, achieved a perfect fusion of beauty and strangeness. A reticent jewel-like nature, Miss Wylie reflected the world coolly and glitteringly. While her deeply introverted personality rejected affection and overt enthusiasm, her artistry was like a sword, intricately carved, magnificently polished, and terribly effective. The world she lived in was not the familiar world of domestic poetry; it was the black and white world of snow and ice, metallic and gleaming. But, within the sheath of ice, there was a core of strange fire, and passion, emotion, and intelligence were fused in highly concentrated and exquisitely finished poetry. Though at times she was a little prettily rococo, at her best she was a distinguished exemplar of the modern poetic baroque.

In two other younger women poets, the metaphysical vein runs strong. In Louise Bogan's (*q.v.*) first slight volume, *Body of This Death* (1923), some of the critics heard echoes of the spirit of Elinor Wylie, but in her later poems, the utterance became individual, within the framework of the metaphysical tradition in which she is working. Here, there is a little less of the self-consciousness and the tendency toward self-dramatization encountered occasionally in Elinor Wylie. The gaze at life is no less searching but it is steadier. Léonie Adams (*q.v.*) is a sort of Vaughan to the Donne of Wylie. Here, spirituality infused with intellectuality dominates the poetic utterance. The world is entirely put away, or, at most, it becomes a taking-off place for the flights of an intense though controlled spirit. Such poetry as these women write makes as many demands on the reader as it makes on the poet; what is of importance is that in each case the demands are amply repaid.

A further modification of the metaphysical tradition appears in the work of those southern writers commonly called the *Fugitive* group, from the title of their important but short-lived periodical. The modification, in this case, is a regional one, since all these poets are southerners, draw on a common cultural inheritance, and share the same neo-agrarian sympathies. Common to this group, then, is an easy allusiveness to a culture with which most of their readers are unfamiliar. Common, too, are their preoccupation with decadence and death, and their cultivation of indirection and involution to the point sometimes of unintelligibility. Their modest fame, except among the poetically aristocratic, is the penalty of their somewhat self-conscious regional and stylistic privacy.

The leader of the group and the determiner of the group's style is John Crowe Ransom (*q.v.*). Ransom's poetic output has been as choice as it has been small. In him, as perhaps in no other contemporary writing in the Donne tradition, the blend of the acrid and the glamorous, the intellectual and the brutal, the macabre and the elegant is perfected. The regional elements—of ancestor worship, vanished elegance, remembered heroism, and slow decay—are transmuted into a highly personal communication. What is most striking and most admirable is the complete honesty which prevents the poet's lowering an eyelid before the uncomfortable or the disconcerting. In no poet of the group is the achievement so uniformly excellent. Of the followers of Ransom, Donald Davidson (*q.v.*) is perhaps the most independent. His sources are not simple but multiple. Eliot and even Masters as well as Ransom have had their part in his development. In him, the hostility the agrarians feel toward the incursion of northern industry into the South finds a vigorous spokesman. Thus, in *The Tall Men* (1927), he sets the heroic pioneer tradition over against the small meannesses of the newly industrialized South. More energetic than Ransom and less fastidious, Davidson is perhaps the most socially aggressive of the *Fugitive* associates. Allen Tate (*q.v.*) is more impressive perhaps as critic and as biographer of southern heroes than as poet, although his poetry is distinguished in its kind. But in Tate, the critical powers clearly exceed the creative; his constant revision of his major poems is a measure of his fastidiousness rather than of his lack of self-assurance. In Tate, moreover, the complexity of Ransom has given way to an obscurity which has a questionable justification. But his range of literary activity and his critical plasticity argue well for his distinction as a man of letters, if not primarily as a poet. Robert Penn Warren (*q.v.*), though the youngest of the *Fugitive* group, is none the less an arresting figure. Warren avoids the obscurity of Tate and the more icy indirection of Ransom. Though his is not the simple Frostian poetry of rural regionalism, his verse transmits with ingratiating directness the rich warm southern earth and its regional characters. Complexity and indirection are present, but they are kept vital by Warren's unbroken contact with the fecund earth.[1]

[1] Merrill Moore (*q.v.*), though originally a member of the *Fugitive* group, shows little or no evidence of its influence upon him. Moore's distinction rests on his individualization of the sonnet form and his incessant use of it for the communication of his wide

A still more complex vein of experimentation is apparent in the works of such influential poets as Ezra Pound (*q.v.*), T. S. Eliot, and Archibald MacLeish (*q.v.*). Of them all, Pound is the most volatile and the most eclectic. The most widely influential American poet of the period, Pound is also the most difficult to define and evaluate. The critical difficulty arises not so much from the nature of his practice in one poetic kind as in the number of poetic kinds that he has practiced. There is almost no twentieth-century poetic pie in which Pound has not had a finger. He launched the Imagist movement in England and America; he was early on the scene with an enthusiasm for oriental poetry; his translations and adaptations from Provençal and Italian poetry widened the cultural horizons of his admirers; his assimilations of the techniques of the French Symbolists revolutionized poetic experimentation in at least one direction. He has been a doughty if often wrong-headed fighter, though much of his critical work is vitiated by his intellectual perversity and his facile devotions at the feet of strange gods.

The most readable of the poems of Pound are the early, willful, witty lyrics, but these were merely finger exercises in preparation for the major works. The translations are too idiosyncratic, too carelessly inaccurate to be more than signposts to Pound's literary enthusiasms. Pound's major work lies in a series of such poems as *Hugh Selwyn Mauberly* (1920), and the *Cantos* which began appearing in 1925. In the Mauberly series, Pound reveals those characteristic devices which have been most widely imitated. Here he sets himself the task of turning into poetry the modern personality and its situation in the contemporary world. Here there is no easy exoticism, no romantic suppression of elements that complicate or denigrate the mood of poetic elevation. Here he adopts the relaxed conversational manner, the tendency toward free association, the rich literary and cultural allusiveness, the conscious utilization of dissonance as an aesthetic principle—devices which were to have a tremendous influence on T. S. Eliot and his followers. These devices are carried much further in the *Cantos*, a formidable series of poetic fragments which constitute as amazing a poetic autobiography as any ever written. For the central figure in the *Cantos* is Pound himself or an approximation to Pound, and the essential willfulness of the poems is the fundamental willfulness of the man. The movement of the poem is as freakish and haphazard as the movements of Pound's literary and cultural enthusiasms. Here, incoherence has become the central principle of the structure of the poems. But the heterogeneous and esoteric cultural elements are only imperfectly assimilated and but dimly illuminative of the history of the spirit of the

experience. His treatment of the sonnet falls little short of the high-handed. His sonnets are as free and bizarre in form and structure as though E. E. Cummings had written them. Moore's fecundity is as astounding as its results are unpredictable. But in the midst of much that is trivial and insignificant, there is much that conveys a sense of the vitality and vision of a modern man.

poet. Brilliant though many passages are, saturated as the poems are in stratum after stratum of western European culture, the poems probably represent as monumental an illustration of misapplied talent as any major poetic project in our time.

Pound's most brilliant disciple, T. S. Eliot, can no longer be considered an American poet, since his persistent residence in England, his identification with English culture, and his becoming a British subject have marked his conscious rejection of his American heritage. Yet no account of American poetry, however brief, can fail to mention his still potent influence. The lessons Eliot learned from Pound and such French masters as Laforgue, Rimbaud, and St. John Perse, he has turned to tremendous profit. For he has avoided Pound's excessive freakishness and, except in *The Waste Land*, the master's oppressive allusiveness. What Eliot's followers have learned from him in particular, are the value of the juxtaposition of the grand manner and the banally colloquial, the substitution for the logic of events of a logic of mood (even when the mood is itself discordant), the cultivation of sensibility, the sense of the disintegration of faiths, and the necessity for some integration of belief. No American poet of importance under Eliot's influence has taken the precise road that he has taken in search of integration, but he has made them terribly conscious, at any rate, of its need.

Of the major followers of Eliot, his influence is clearest upon Archibald MacLeish (*q.v.*). In the earlier poems, the accents of Eliot are clear, and in *The Hamlet of A. MacLeish* (1928), the sense of spiritual disintegration is acute. Two divergences from Eliot have helped establish MacLeish's poetic individuality. In *Conquistador* (1932), the free association, the rich allusiveness, and the colloquial tone are still present, but the material is epic and the tone, though still minor, is that of a nostalgic if disillusioned romanticism. In the poems since *Conquistador*, MacLeish has been led by his experiences during the depression to introduce the social note into his poetry. Unjustified charges of Fascist sympathies compelled him to investigate his political position, and to discover and reveal himself as liberal rather than conservative in his allegiances. Though his social preoccupations have introduced a note of bewilderment into his poetry, they have assisted in controlling MacLeish's somewhat excessive subjectivity and relating him to an important and vital current in post-war American poetry.

Eliot's quest for spiritual integrity has had its influence on poets who have not followed his technical tutelage. In Robinson Jeffers (*q.v.*), the reaction from the modern world is even more violent than in Eliot, and the solution he proposes is even more drastic. To Jeffers, modern man and his works are without equivocation abominable, and the thing most worthy of admiration is the unconsciousness of nature. Such views underlie most of the narrative and lyrical writing of Jeffers.

Jeffers' narrative poems illustrate powerfully the abominations of which man is capable; the lyrics express more directly Jeffers' disgust with modern man and with the modern social order. The manner of Jeffers' narratives is the extravagant exotic manner of the baroque epic. The setting is grandiose, nature appears in only its colossal aspects, and the passions that animate his characters are those terrible forces which only an unflinching scrutiny can discover. Jeffers' reading of man's nature has been profoundly influenced by psychoanalysis, and his most important characters belong to the realm of psychopathology. By stressing man's most antisocial drives Jeffers has been able to build up a shocking contrast between man's evil consciousness and the magnificent unconsciousness of nature.

Jeffers' technical powers are impressive. No other American poet of our time is his equal in imaginative magnitude or emotional violence. But most of the time Jeffers' poetry is overviolent; the coloring is barbaric, and figures that would share the giantism of Michelangelo's are discovered to be façades of hollow plaster and not of perdurable marble. Nor can Jeffers' reading of life go unchallenged. Courageous as his scrutiny is, the solution he proposes is as neurotic as the characters that deserve it. Man's way of salvation can hardly be the unconsciousness from which he emerged. Vile as he may be, he cannot escape from vileness into the womb-like darkness of the unconscious.

An equally tortuous quest for integration appears in the dazzling experimentation of Hart Crane (*q.v.*). For him the adequate symbols for modern man's spiritual pilgrimage were, not men enchained by the giants of the unconscious, but American phenomena such as rivers and forest, bridges and skyscrapers, Edgar Allan Poe and Walt Whitman, Pocahontas and Rip Van Winkle. Crane's vision never attained the deceptive simplicity of Jeffers', but out of his divided soul, he was attempting to precipitate in poetry his vision of an ideal America. The medium in which Crane rendered this view of America's history and its fate is as singular as any that American poetry has created. Crane's attitude toward language was as highhanded as though he were its primal creator. The plasticity of his treatment of language is apparent in the freedom with which he transferred word functions, the recklessness of his compounding of verbal elements, and the reliance on association rather than logic in his treatment of grammatical structure. Noteworthy, too, is his incorporation in his poetic vocabulary of much of the language of modern science and of a machine-dominated society. The boldness of Crane's linguistic experimentation is not unqualifiedly successful. To most readers of poetry Crane's technique presents almost insuperable obstacles. It only imperfectly bore the burden of his tremendous intention.

The appearance of the social note in Archibald MacLeish (*q.v.*), to which we have already referred, is symptomatic of the rise of the poetry of class conflict in the depression and post-depression years. The social note, to be sure, has been heard again and again in the history of English and American poetry, from *Piers Plowman* down to Thomas Hood's "The Song of the Shirt" and Elizabeth Barrett Browning's "The Song of the Children." But the appearance of poets whose major activity is the voicing of social protest or revolutionary idealism is a recent phenomenon in American poetry.

Such poetry has its nearest prototype in the poetry of Lola Ridge (*q.v.*), who sounded the social note long before the depression had turned the younger poets to the critical examination of the social order in which their spirits were frustrated or imprisoned. In her first volume, *The Ghetto* (1918), Miss Ridge represented the more sordid aspects of urban life with courage and beauty, but the revolutionary note grew louder in such volumes as *Sun-Up* (1920), and *Red Flag* (1927). Miss Ridge's work is less interesting for its illustration of the influence of the agitation over the technique of free verse than it is for the marked realism of her diction and figures and the intensity of her social passions. But Miss Ridge's enthusiasm is of a different order from that of the poets who first raised their voices during the depression. Her revolutionary enthusiasm is emotional rather than intellectual. Unlike Miss Ridge, Genevieve Taggard (*q.v.*) is a somewhat belated convert to radicalism. Her earliest work, *For Eager Lovers* (1922), was in the mode of the deeply personal and unaffectedly simple feminine lyric. Her next phase revealed her submission to the vogue of metaphysical poetry launched by Elinor Wylie. This enthusiasm appeared not only in the poems in *Travelling Standing Still* (1928) but also in her anthology of the "varieties of metaphysical verse," *Circumference* (1930). *Calling Western Union* (1936) showed a somewhat self-conscious assumption of an interest in social issues and emotions. Her radicalism is the latest but perhaps not the last phase of her chameleon-like poetic career.

The depression poets have a much clearer idea of revolutionary ideology and are much more self-consciously related to the radical movements stimulated at home and abroad by the Russian Revolution. They are, however, more nearly in agreement in their ideas than in their techniques. A number of them utilize incongruously the most sophisticated experimental devices for the expression of their devotion to the cause of the proletariat. Among them, Horace Gregory (*q.v.*) is perhaps the most established and the most representative. His poetic technique branches directly from the metaphysical stream of Eliot and MacLeish. But his subject matter and his attitudes are much more directly social. The grimness of urban life, the sordidness of the economic struggle, the hopelessness of many modern lives speak out most clearly in such a volume as *Chelsea Rooming House* (1930). In *Chorus for Survival* (1935), a more aggressive and hopeful note is sounded. In any case, despite his principled incoherence and his occasional obscurity, Gregory is the most markedly individual of the younger revolutionary poets. Closest to him in technique is Muriel Rukeyser. More nearly in the mode of Marianne Moore is Kenneth Fearing (*q.v.*), who has adapted this medium to the uses of social criticism and satire. What the passing of the depression will do to these ardent spirits is cynically unpredictable. At the moment, they represent the latest devotees to the creation of a poetry genuinely contemporary in content and manner.

The amount of poetic experimentation in American poetry of the past two decades is impressive in quantity, quality, and variety. A type of poetry that embraces writers as various as Pound, Eliot, Ransom, and Jeffers comes very close to being the most distinguished wing of American poetry of the period. But, aside from their individual achievements, the experimental poets have done incalculable service to both the spirit and the form of American poetry. They have raised it to a respectable mental plane by making it intellectually vigorous and aesthetically exacting. They have increased its complexity by their intricate syntheses of emotion and thought, of the grand manner and the colloquial, of the lofty and the sordid. They have enlarged the vocabulary of poetry by the inclusion of both learned and popular words, and widened the range of metaphorical language by judicious and injudicious selections from strictly contemporary phenomena. If they are less widely read, less popularly heralded than poets in the romantic or realist modes, the best of them have reached eager audiences of young and malleable readers. The more abstruse occupy a prominent place in the most exciting chapter in the history of modern American poetry.

LITERARY JOURNALISM

Since 1900, the informal or personal essay has not been very popular with American writers or readers. The distinguished position it occupied in the dignified magazines of the nineteenth century has been usurped by essays of a more formal and expository nature, devoted to those controversial social or political problems raised by the liberal decade before the war, the profound intellectual and emotional disturbances of the war period, and the shocking events of the depression. In the popular and literary weeklies that proliferated during the war and after, space was too precious to afford the leisurely familiar essay a frequent refuge. Moreover, the material which in the eighteenth or nineteenth centuries would have been pressed into the only superficially rigid mold of the informal essay, now tended to be utilized in the columns and syndicated features of the great city newspapers or in abbreviated sketches suitable for publication in weekly magazines. The names of a number of American authors, however, are closely associated with the informal essay, and an even larger number of extremely well-known names are connected with the presentation of essayistic material in columns, syndicated features, or such sketches as lighten the pages of the *New Yorker*.

With the flora and fauna of half a continent to observe, study, and admire, it is rather astonishing that the nature essay has not been more frequently cultivated by American writers. To be sure, carefully rendered studies of the American scene have furnished settings for novels and short stories of the local-color or regional variety. Stewart Edward White (*q.v.*) has made distinguished use of such material in his novels and tales of the Middle West and Northwest, and popular novelists like Zane Grey and Harold Bell Wright and the nameless authors of thousands of westerns find a not inconsiderable part of their stock in trade in the beauties of the wide open spaces.

In the nature essay, John Burroughs (1837–1921) found the form most suitable for the expression of his devoted studies of nature in America. Beginning with *Wake Robin* (1871), he produced, with exemplary regularity, volume after volume of sensitive and precise nature studies. Slowly, he evolved his own optimistic interpretation of the philosophical significance of natural history, and achieved a broadly grounded and capacious idealism welcome to his public. Distinctly less professional in their concern with nature were such early twentieth-century apostles of gentility as Henry Van Dyke (1852–1933) and Dallas Lore Sharp (1870–1929). Of the various literary enterprises of Van Dyke, the most memorable is his oft-reprinted Christmas story, *The Story of the Other Wise Man* (1896), but this somewhat saccharine performance is probably less satisfactory than his informal sketches of American and Canadian scenes in *Little Rivers* (1895) and *The Blue Flower* (1902). Modestly observant, urbane, gently humorous, they evoke winsome glimpses of wood and stream seen through the lens of a gracious cultivated personality. Professor Sharp's essays grew out of his prolonged and intensive study of the New England world in which he spent most of his life rather than from a delight in rural or woodland holidays as delicate as the urban Van Dyke's. With characteristic Yankee economy, Sharp put to constant and effective use the natural phenomena humorously and accurately observable from his own doorstep in Hingham, Massachusetts. He gave his subject the devotion of a lover and the scrupulous honesty of a scholar; he attained gentility without sentimentality, and shrewdness and humor without meanness or ill nature. To the professional traditions of Burroughs rather than to the amateur tradition of Van Dyke and Sharp belong such contemporary nature writers as William Beebe (*q.v.*) and Donald Culross Peattie (*q.v.*). Beebe combines the utmost scientific accuracy with a style that is extremely rich in sensory values and an enthusiasm that makes his study of even forbidding subjects fascinating. In *Jungle Peace* (1918) and *Edge of the Jungle* (1921) he established himself as one of the best scientific stylists of our time, and exhibited artistic powers in the presentation of scientific observations equaled by few professional men of letters. Peattie, likewise a professional naturalist, approaches his subject matter in a mood more lyrically poetic than Beebe's; he is more concerned than the latter with the influence of the natural environment on human beings. Although his *Almanac for Moderns* (1935) and *A Book of Hours* (1937) are written in prose occasionally a little too lush and purple, they are memorable contributions to a fine though little cultivated American literary genre.

The roll call of those who have used the familiar essay to express their personalities and their individual points of view is so brief as to suggest a certain meagerness in the American temperament or a poverty in our cultural soil. Whatever the reason, not more than a half-dozen contemporary writers are known primarily for their cultivation of the decorous graces of the personal essay. Closest perhaps to the shrewd and salty humors of Oliver Wendell Holmes was the systematic output of Samuel McChord Crothers (1857–1928). He had studied the great familiar essayists, and did not think it ignoble to repay them in the flattering coin of imitation. His point of view in such volumes as *The Gentle Reader* (1903), *The Pardoner's Wallet* (1905), and *Humanly Speaking* (1912), was that of an amiable conservative whose sense of humor and tolerance of characteristically human foibles prevented that automatic rejection of the strange and unaccustomed to which Brahmin gentility is prone. Crothers was one of the last of the gentlemen who wrote with ease of the doings of the well-bred or almost well-bred. Almost the only surviving gentleman-author is Logan Pearsall Smith (*q.v.*), who writes with a maximum of fastidiousness only when he has something he wishes to say. In *Trivia* (1917) and *More Trivia* (1921), he has cultivated single-handed the forms dear to French writers of the eighteenth century—the epigram and the *pensée*. In these and in his few extended pieces, his style is chiseled and polished to the utmost; his condensation and concentration of much meaning into few words are talents as rare as they are enviable.

Less flexible and more shrill than Crothers and Smith are the voices of Agnes Repplier (*q.v.*) and Katharine Fullerton Gerould (*q.v.*). Both stubborn fundamentalists, they defend the traditional in manners and morals with intelligence, and assail the unseemly and the unconventional with acerbity. Miss Repplier's work in the essay is more ample in volume and more attractive in manner than that of Mrs. Gerould. The former has a sharp tongue, a nimble pen, and an unequaled facility in neatly apt quotation. Her taste is more impeccable than Mrs. Gerould's, and the purely literary attractions of her work are more conspicuous. Mrs. Gerould is the least ingratiating of the Brahmins. Her somewhat heavier hand and the arrogance and complacency of her tone make her defense of the old order much less persuasive than that of Miss Repplier.

The more formal noncritical or nonliterary essay which flourished in the era of the great English quarterlies of the nineteenth century has given way in our period to the less formal expository essay whose habitat is the serious monthlies and whose most fortunate destiny is to be collected in volumes by a single author or to be anthologized by canny editors for academic purposes. The subject matter of such essays is much less likely to be archaeology or the habits of primitive people than some current social or political problem. In technique, these essays are less formally constructed and less portentously written than the ponderous essays characteristic of the *Edinburgh Review* or the *Nineteenth Century*. Their tone and style are adroitly designed so that he who runs may read. Countless journalists have developed to a very high degree the technique of making readable their treatment of difficult or specialized economic or political themes. Among the most widely known writers of essays in this category are James Truslow Adams (*q.v.*), Walter Lippmann (*q.v.*), and Stuart Chase (*q.v.*). Adams' specialty is American history, and the most substantial part of his work is the animated and popular treatment of the epic of American history. But for him American history does not come to a conclusion with the Spanish-American war. He is as profoundly concerned with history in the process of making as with history entombed in books. His long residence abroad has given him not only an unusual perspective on American history and culture but strong Anglo-American sympathies. His background and breeding have made him conservative in creed and judgment, but his experience as a historian has developed in him a quality of intelligence infrequently associated with conservatism. If he tends to view current social and governmental processes with alarm, he at least has historical analogies with which to buttress his distress. Less conservative in his origins than Adams, Walter Lippmann has found his most absorbing task in commenting on current social and political events and phenomena. In his early years, he voiced the idealism and the aggressive liberalism of the pre-war period; during the war, he set great store by the generous idealism of President Woodrow Wilson, and had no small share in clarifying Wilson's thought on the progress and issues of the war. In more recent years, his admirers have been struck with dismay by his increasing conservatism. But the movement of his thought has been normal for one whose views have acquired a flattering prestige. Fundamentally individualistic in temperament and faith, Lippmann manifests, not only the liberal's passion for liberty but his dangerous facility for living and playing with abstractions. In consequence, his writing has a deceptive lucidity, smoothness, and unreality; it is curiously lacking in concreteness and fails to give any very vivid sense of the inextricable confusion of human circumstance. A deeper passion for betterment burns hotly in Stuart Chase (*q.v.*). Chase's highly intuitive personality has led him through a series of intellectual liaisons, each of which has produced a numerous progeny. He has rushed headlong from an enthusiasm for the glories of the primitive life in Mexico through a horror at our wasteful exploitation of natural resources into the intricacies of semantics. His technique for getting up one subject after another is that of the publicist rather than the scholar; he turns to the liveliest journalistic use his magpie-like gleanings from serious sociologists, anthropologists, and psychologists. He has the journalist's flair for striking devices of presentation; his most telling quality is the single-minded gusto with which he embraces each successive object of his intellectual devotion.

Not unallied to such social commentators as Adams, Lippmann, and Chase is that super-journalist, Upton Sinclair (*q.v.*), the last of the pamphleteers. His productivity is colossal; his faith in his power to reshape the world closer to his heart's desire does not, like Lippmann's, languish with the years. No subject that has absorbed him—education, politics, journalism, war, peace, the depression—has failed to stimulate the production of tract after tract. Years before the simple-hearted liberalism of the pre-war period had faded, Sinclair was busily at work exposing the sinister influences of capitalism on one after another field of American experience. It is difficult to evaluate Sinclair's pamphleteering, because he is *sui generis* in America. But without attempting to pass judgment on the validity of his theories or his findings, one can admire his indefatigable idealism, his indomitable vitality, and his selfless devotion to what he believes to be, in the realm of economics and politics, the good and the true. His service in the process of sophisticating America's view of herself and of her place in the world will certainly prove no ignoble one.

American literary journalism is, on the whole, richer and more varied on its lighter than on its serious side. Its characteristic form is the syndicated or nonsyndicated daily or weekly feature. The newspaper column now equals in ubiquity the comic strip. On its more serious side, literary journalism may take the form of a weekly commentary on literature or politics like Clifton Fadiman's "Books" in the *New Yorker* or Heywood Broun's (*q.v.*) "Shoot the Works" in the *New Republic*. On its lighter side, it is a miscellaneously constituted column of the sort that appears as a feature in almost every vital or popular newspaper in the United States. It may be made up almost entirely of contributions made by admirers and friends of the columnist or it may be devoted entirely to the sub-acid comments on human folly of a Westbrook Pegler, the metropolitan fantasies of an O. O. McIntyre, or the night-club gossip of a Walter Winchell. But whatever its form, the column flourishes because it is a reflection of the personality of its writer or editor, a personality sometimes so valuable in terms of reader-interest that some columnists have been left free to express views and opinions quite at variance with the editorial policy of their paper. Others, less fortunate, have felt the heavy hand of the editor descending, and, if not "fired," have transferred their activities to a more congenial journalistic atmosphere. But whatever the circumstances of its production, the column, whether daily or weekly in its appearance, is the most popular journalistic medium (if not the only one) for the exploitation of personality, the root motif and attraction of familiar writing. Contemporary columnists are legion, and the history of their progress from one to another journalistic habitat is complex, if not obscure. But though the material and the form of most columns are as ephemeral as the popular songs that rise from Tin Pan Alley, a considerable number of columnists have left strong and fairly persistent impressions of their personalities.

One of the earliest of the newspaper columnists of our period was Ed Howe (1853–1937), whose salty utterances in his "Globe Sights" in the Atchison *Globe* attracted wide journalistic attention and imitation. In the nineties, Eugene Field, now known chiefly as a sentimental lyricist, made his column in the Chicago *Daily News*, and later the *Record*, a vehicle for his slightly sardonic wit and his brilliant light verse. To the nineties, too, we owe the syndicated newspaper feature. It was during that decade that S. S. McClure, attracted by the popularity of George Ade's "Fables in Slang," which appeared in the Chicago *Record* from 1890–1900, and Finley Peter Dunne's Mr. Dooley series, which appeared in the Chicago *Evening Post* from 1892–97 and in the *Journal* from 1897–1900, arranged for their syndication and paved the way for their becoming national figures of fun. The slang in which Ade's fables of contemporary life were told was a language of his own deliberate construction, and its success depended on his skill in creating a racy language of the extravagantly metaphorical sort for which American humor has long been famous. It made little or no pretense to being American slang, although at its best it had the fortune or the misfortune to gain wide currency. The first decade of the century saw the collection of Ade's most telling features, from *Fables in Slang* (1900) to *Breaking into Society* (1904), but this vein of ore was very rapidly exhausted, and Ade devoted his humorous powers more effectively to the writing of such comedies as *The County Chairman* (1903) and *The College Widow* (1904). Basically, the comic form utilized by Finley Peter Dunne (1867–1937) as "Mr. Dooley" was the tried and true device of the encounter of wits of those immortal figures of smoking-room humor, Pat and Mike. But to the elementary humor of dialect, Dunne added the racy imagination, the flair for invective, and the earthy realism of the Irish, and Mr. Dooley's comments on matters of passing political or social moment, collected in such volumes as *Mr. Dooley in Peace and War* (1898) and *Observations by Mr. Dooley* (1902), have a deflationary acuteness that is of not merely temporary interest. Another humorist of the first decade of the century, "O. Henry" (1862–1910), was induced to contribute a weekly story to the New York *Sunday World*, a feature which, when syndicated, brought its author a tremendous audience. Though not carried on as a serial, the terse urban fictions of "O. Henry" did much to popularize the weekly feature with editors and to encourage the development of the daily or weekly columnist. For much of "O. Henry's" vogue was due to the personal stamp upon his contributions, a stamp that myriads were tempted to imitate but that none could quite equal.

The activities of the writers just mentioned prepared the way for the tremendous increase in the number of columnists during the post-war period. For reasons none too easy to come upon, some of the best-known columnists of the second and third decades of the century were men connected with Chicago newspapers. Of these, "B. L. T." (Bert Leston Taylor, 1866–1921) achieved more than a local following with his "Line o'Type or Two" in the Chicago *Tribune*. Taylor had a fine gift for the writing of light verse, a slightly acrid view of current events, and excellent taste in the editing of the innumerable contributions his column attracted. It is no mean tribute to "R. H. L." (Richard Henry Little) that, at least in Chicago, he is regarded as a not unworthy successor to the chair left vacant by Taylor's death. For a brief period, Keith Preston (1884–1927) emerged from the academic world to give a larger public the benefit of his nimble wit and flair for satire. Ben Hecht (*q.v.*), another Chicago product, contributed a daily feature to the Chicago *Daily News* for several years; selections from these were reprinted under the titles, *A Thousand and One Afternoons in Chicago* (1922) and *Tales of Chicago Streets* (1924).

Among practicing columnists, "F. P. A." (Franklin P. Adams) (*q.v.*) now occupies the precarious position of dean. On both "The Conning Tower," which combines the editor's own contributions with those of his gifted metropolitan following, and on "The Diary of Our Own Samuel Pepys," Adams has set the stamp of his personal taste, interests, and opinions. He is perhaps the most literate of the daily columnists; his passion for the preservation of pure English is excelled only by his ingenuity in translations and parodies of the more urbane Latin lyricists. Though his literary taste is frankly middle-brow, his critical dicta carry a good deal of weight. His is not humor of the extravagantly metaphorical variety; his wit is shrewd and cutting, urban and mildly sardonic. Among the older columnists, Don Marquis (*q.v.*) (1878–1937) was perhaps the best beloved. He was not only a nimble epigrammatist and a genial satirist of passing literary fads and fashions, but the admired creator of comic characters whose lives his readers insisted on his prolonging. Of these, the most famous are Hermione, the ardent but essentially unintelligent pursuer of the latest in cultural modes; the Old Soak, the quintessence of inebriated masculine geniality, the eternal protestant against the inhibitions of puritanism, the gusty consumer of cakes and ale; and the inimitable archy the cockroach, and mehitabel the alley cat who has never been able to forget the better days she has once experienced. For Marquis, archy became the medium for the expression of his suspicions that, in contrast to the insect world, the human world was a folly-ridden madhouse. Marquis' major representative of an amoral *joie de vivre* is mehitabel. Undaunted and disreputable, she defiantly embraces sin, knowing full well its inevitable wages.

An uneasy migrant from the newspapers to the weekly magazines, and back again, Heywood Broun (*q.v.*) illustrates the familiar career-pattern of many columnists in post-war America. The successive stages of his journalistic activity as newspaper reporter, sports writer, dramatic critic, daily columnist, and weekly columnist have been paralleled, as a whole or in part, by numerous literary journalists. What distinguishes Broun from most of his fellows is the development of his political ideas from a state of quiescence through a period of lively liberalism to the present state of aggressive radicalism. This progression has involved him in numerous skirmishes with conservative and liberal editors, but Broun's radicalism is so militant and his courage is so unquestioned that he has emerged from the struggle bloody perhaps but unbowed. On whatever he has done, one senses the impress of his slightly blundering but honest and courageous personality.

A number of other columnists have attracted more than local interest. Of the provincial writers, Ted Robinson's column in the Cleveland *Plain Dealer* is perhaps the best known and most frequently quoted, especially for its agile light verse. The variety of metropolitan syndicated columnists ranges from the specious sophistication of the late O. O. McIntyre's daily rambles in New York and the hard-boiled realism of Westbrook Pegler to the news commentaries of the melodramatic Boake Carter and the emotional political prophecies of that goodhearted Cassandra, Dorothy Thompson. The prestige and vogue of the two latter have been enhanced by their weekly radio performances, for the radio has proved an even more potent medium than the newspaper or the weekly magazine in the creation of a genuinely national following. It lends itself, likewise, to a close imitation of the weekly syndicated feature, to a regular commentary on books or persons, on national and international crises and disasters.

Dorothy Thompson is not, of course, the only woman columnist to achieve a wide audience. Once the American newspaper set out to make specific appeals to its women readers, careers were open to a variety of feminine talents to furnish household hints and recipes, beauty-parlor techniques, and advice to the lovelorn. Beatrice Fairfax and Dorothy Dix rapidly became household words, and their progeny are everywhere. With the emergence of American women into political life, a more serious period in feminine journalism began. Miss Thompson, perhaps, has offered the liveliest competition to political commentators like Walter Lippmann and Jay Franklin, but a less emotional and more critical audience has been built up by such an enlightened foreign correspondent as Anne O'Hare McCormick. The most distinguished of women columnists is, of course, Mrs. Franklin D. Roosevelt. Though her conceptions of style are elementary and her critical observations frequently naïve, even her most hostile critics have been forced to bow before her warm humanity, fine social feeling, indefatigable energy, and dauntless magnanimity.

A marked increase in the number of literary journalists followed the establishment in the twenties of such literary, critical, or sophisticated journals as the *Saturday Review of Literature* and the *New Yorker*. With the former journal, both during and since its association with the New York *Evening Post*, one inevitably associates the prolific pen of Christopher Morley (*q.v.*), whose productivity, among American authors, is exceeded only by that of Percy MacKaye (*q.v.*). Of the currently popular columnists, Morley has the widest range of gifts and accomplishments. He has tried his hand at poetry and plays, but his most successful experiments have taken the form of the fantastic narrative and the personal essay. Of the former, *Where the Blue Begins* (1922) and *Thunder on the Left* (1925) have been deservedly the most popular. In both these novels, Morley works in a vein of slightly grotesque or macabre fantasy that is rare in American letters. In the personal essay, he has found perhaps his most completely congenial medium. For this type of writing, Morley has unusual gifts: great energy, a lively enthusiasm for literature and a rich saturation in it, a warm outgoing temperament, strong personal loyalties, a passion for every aspect of book-production and distribution, and an intense delight in oddities of literary and biographical information. In such incessant and excessive literary activity, there is bound to be much chaff, but Morley's wheat is fine, if not of the finest quality. He is happiest in the vein of personal and literary reminiscence, and in his enthusiasm for out-of-the-way and slightly eccentric books and personalities.

The founding of the *New Yorker* in 1925 began a new phase of the popularity of the column in American literary journalism. For its almost immediate success drew to it, and continues to draw to it, perhaps the best writing being done in America in the vein of civilized but good-natured sophistication. From the beginning its tone has been one of worldliness without cynicism, tenderness with urbanity. Characteristic of the *New Yorker* is its deflationary humor. Firm in its hold on simple human values, its lightly satirical spirit plays freely over pomposity and affectation, over excess in zeal or extravagance or narrowness of conviction, in whatever august or solemn spokesman they may appear. Here the Comic Spirit operates steadily in the direction of the sane ideal of Nothing in Excess. It has shown itself skilled in dealing an even-handed justice to the follies of both reactionary and radical. Concerned though it is with the interests of the higher-income class, it manages to escape partisanship by its intelligence, its hostility to stupidity in any quarter, and its almost lyrical apprehension of the eternal verities among the skyscrapers. Its sophistication is as remote as can be imagined from the Europeanized cynicism of Mencken and Nathan in their *Smart Set* days or the booboisie-baiting of their *American Mercury*.

The tone of the *New Yorker* was set by the impeccable taste of E. B. White, in his own right a versifier and essayist of the finest quality but of disappointingly slight quantity. It was White who made its editorial notes, "The Talk of the Town," a unique combination of tenderness and wisdom. The weekly has been extraordinarily successful in attracting to it not merely some of the best nonpolitical cartoonists of the day—Peter Arno, Shermund, Helen Hokinson, and William Steig—but also almost the majority of the nimbler-witted manipulators of light-fingered prose. Of these, perhaps Alexander Woollcott (*q.v.*) is the most widely known. His particular fortes are the sentimental and the macabre. His slightly lush, self-indulgent prose is admirably suited to the vein of sentimental reminiscence, and his extraordinary skill as a raconteur shows best in his versions of those anonymous folk tales of humor or horror for which he has an acute ear. Fundamentally sentimental and intellectually parasitical, he has developed to a very high point the ability to wring the last drop of feeling from himself and his audience.

Narrower in range but more hilarious in spirit is Robert Benchley (*q.v.*), for some time dramatic critic on the *New Yorker*. Unlike Woollcott,

Benchley is the professional humorist, less distinct in the outline of his personality but more adept at exploiting the complexities and absurdities of common experience. He is at his best, perhaps, in his depictions of the struggles of the human animal in the minor crises of normal experience. A sturdier spirit and a quieter humor were the gifts of the late Clarence Day (*q.v.*), who reached a large public only after his writing began to appear in the *New Yorker*. Condemned by years of illness to the most sedentary of lives, Day was forced to draw for material on his earlier and more active experience, and in such series of sketches as *Life with Father* (1935) and *Life with Mother* (1937) he painted only slightly satirical portraits of a late nineteenth-century home dominated by an explosive but gentlemanly paterfamilias and a warm-spirited and beautifully Victorian mother. Day had the born essayist's facility for making a little material go a long way. The accuracy and the friendliness of his essays make them not only good-natured sketches but documents of some social-historical significance.

A madder and more desperate type of humor appears in the writings and drawings of James Thurber (*q.v.*). His view of human nature emerges most clearly in his crude but immensely effective line-drawings of depressed, ineffectual males and moronic, determined females posed in immemorial situations. The same vein of self-deprecatory ineffectualness runs through his reminiscent essays and sketches. The vein is the more ingratiating because the humor is more frequently directed against himself than against the stupid or competent world. Something of the quality of the column or the syndicated feature, strong in personal tone and treating the same or allied characters consecutively, inheres in such *New Yorker* contributions as Art Kober's painfully realistic though warm-spirited dialectal sketches of Jewish-American life in the Bronx, Leonard Q. Ross's equally realistic but more linguistically fantastic accounts of the futile though heroic attempt to Americanize the speech of that superpatriot, Hyman Kaplan, the slightly disoriented *nonsequiturs* of S. J. Perelman, James Reid Parker's knowing exploitation of the quiet humors of life in the academic fold, Richard Lockridge's sensitive revelations of Mr. and Mrs. North's difficulties in communicating to each other the nuances of their rarer moods, and Ruth McKenney's hilarious tales of the misadventures of her sister Eileen.

The *New Yorker* and similar publications and newspaper columns everywhere have done a great deal to develop a skill and taste for a type of verse that is not quite *vers de société* but that might be called *vers de journalisme*. Such older writers as Arthur Guiterman and Franklin P. Adams (*q.v.*) pride themselves on their strict use of the more difficult forms of *vers de société*, but the younger writers prefer in the main the less exacting or more experimental techniques. Of these, Dorothy Parker (*q.v.*) is perhaps the best known of the group that includes Margaret Fishback,

Phyllis McGinley, and Hortense Flexner. Miss Parker, famous as an epigrammatist in private life, represents to perfection the deflationary mood of much post-war humor. She deals lavishly and skillfully in anti-climax. Her romantic attack leads inevitably to the shock of an anti-romantic conclusion. Her tone is that of an embittered and journalistic Millay. In the verse of Ogden Nash (*q.v.*), a more genial spirit expresses itself. He reduces to delightful absurdity the "sprung rhythm" of Gerald Manley Hopkins and shows a Browningesque flair for comically imperfect but difficult rhymes. Less acrid than Miss Parker, more self-deprecatory, Nash views the conventional solemnities and vagaries of the human animal with disarming skepticism, but if he is satirical of the less consequential human follies, his grasp on fundamental human satisfactions is sure, and he keeps constantly in view the distinction between conventionally affected and real personal values. He may feel trapped in the net of circumstance, but he is not deceived into regarding his life in prison as the life of freedom.

BIOGRAPHY AND AUTOBIOGRAPHY

The equivocal nature of biography arises from the fact that it is, at its best, both science and art. The science, of course, is the science of history, and Dryden's definition of biography—"the history of particular men's lives"—is still sound. As a branch of history, then, biography at its most serious relies constantly on the methods of historical research—the application of the scientific method to the study of human as distinct from subhuman or nonhuman phenomena. The scrupulous critic may, thus, demand of biography that it shall show the ingenuity and persistence in discovering source materials, the honesty and exactitude in the documentation of statements, the impartiality in the evaluation of men and movements that one expects in the best historical writing. But the biographer, no less than the historian, is a human being as well as the manipulator of a scientific instrument. Neither the biographer nor the historian can achieve the complete objectivity of the physical or biological scientist. Since he is a man, writing of men and their acts, he cannot avoid, in the last analysis, interpreting their characters with whatever powers of penetration and insight he may possess and measuring them on the scale of his own moral and political values. He cannot escape, moreover, being influenced by the spirit and temper of the age of which he himself is an integral part. For these reasons, neither historical writing nor biographical writing can ever achieve scientific objectivity or finality. The lives of national and racial heroes will, therefore, continue to be written again and again, not only because historians and biographers are fallible human beings but because they, along with their readers, see the figures of the past from either a slightly or a widely different angle from every earlier generation.

But good biography, like good history, is not only a science but an art. Under the influence of the creative impulse, the biographer is moved by the desire to build on the basis of his study of a character and his history a work of art that shall have some of the qualities of the best "biographical" novels: design, climax, philosophical or moral point, credible characterization, and style. Those conceptions of style, structure, tone, and taste that alter from one period to another will likewise have their influence on the aesthetic ideal of both historical and biographical writing. Finally, as in the case of other works of art, the excellence of the biography as a work of art will ultimately depend on the personality behind it; his qualities of magnanimity or pusillanimity, cynicism or sentimentalism, will condition profoundly the nature and the value of his product.

Of any biography, then, two questions may be asked: Is it scientifically sound? Is it aesthetically effective? Biographies that meet the demands of science but not of art have, of course, their particular utility. Still others that are bad science but admirable art belong only by sufferance to the category of biographies. To call them fictionized biography is to flatter them; it would be more honest to call them biographical-historical novels. The best biographies will combine the characteristics of sound science and good art.

Some light on the varieties of good and bad biography is thrown by a consideration of the motives that lie behind biography. The basic motive underlying it is that of all serious historical writing, the discovery of the truth. This goal is peculiarly significant when the truth concerns some national hero whom the love and admiration of his people have invested with an aura of heroism and legend. Another motive, less vigorous in the twentieth than in the nineteenth century, is the desire to do honor to the great or the near-great. This impulse is admirable so long as it is checked by a sharp sense of fact; it is treacherous when it encourages the biographer's suppression of disquieting and unpleasant facts and turning his subject into a striking but hollow idol. Most official biographies of the twentieth century, no less than those of the nineteenth, are vitiated by the operation of the commemorative impulse and the influences of decorum and respectability. A sharpened awareness of the insidious effects of this impulse has led to a violent reaction from it, a reaction which in its most winning guise takes the form of telling the truth about a biographical subject at all costs, and in its least seductive form is little better than commercialized "mud-slinging." A potent urge behind biography writing is the artistic one, the desire to tell the tale of the subject's life with maximum aesthetic effectiveness. The biographer, no less than the historical novelist or playwright, is a creator. But his activity, like theirs, is retrained by the immovable weight of historical events. Within the limits of factual or spiritual fidelity, however, he is concerned as they are with the creation of a work that shall have an independent and admirable existence. Thus, the motives that underlie biographical writing are not merely complex but contradictory; in almost no instance is a single motive operative; in the best examples, contradictory impulses are miraculously resolved and reconciled.

Certain forces conspicuous in the twentieth century have tended to encourage one of the motives significant for biography at the expense of others—the desire to tell the truth even if the truth involves the sacrifice of commemorative decorum. The most conspicuous of the forces is the reaction against those nineteenth-century ideas, attitudes, and values which even in America we are accustomed to call Victorian. This reaction has taken on a number of forms. The most reputable perhaps arises from the conviction that, especially since the World War, we are in a better position than were the denizens of the nineteenth century to judge its heroes and heroines, by reason of the availability of documentary materials and of the perspective that time has given us. A less reputable form, perhaps, is the emotional reaction against Victorian standards of decorum, prudishness, good taste, and all the manifestations of the genteel tradition. This assault on decorum and prudishness has been assisted by the development and vogue of psychoanalysis. Psychoanalysis furnished the biographer a new method for comprehending and interpreting character. It distinguished and defined hitherto unrecognized or unacknowledged mechanisms that control the dynamics of human behavior. In bringing to light the riches and the primal potency of the unconscious mind, it revealed immense new areas of psychological experience. The Freudian system of psychoanalysis, in particular, emphasized the significance of the sexual motivation and behavior of the subject. It trained men and women to confront with equanimity in themselves and in others the most extravagant and anti-social impulses, and speeded up tremendously the movement toward honesty and frankness that the more general reaction against nineteenth-century decorum had initiated.

More specifically, twentieth-century biographical writing in America has been influenced in method and tone by the enormously successful examples of three European biographers—Lytton Strachey, André Maurois, and Emil Ludwig. To the process of fictionizing biography, each of these practitioners has made an important contribution.

Strachey's *Eminent Victorians* (1918) introduced to a large public a distinctive personality and a new model for biographical writing. The personality was cool, ironic, classical, disillusioned. The new biographical model, of the modernity of which Strachey was completely aware, resulted from his conscious attempt to introduce into biographical writing a method and a tone conspicuously absent from the official lives-and-letters with which the later nineteenth century teemed. Strachey's major aim was to fuse the raw material of biography into an artistic creation which should have the economy, elegance, and lucidity of a classical work of art. The method was that of exclusion rather than of inclusion; the style was modeled on the rhetorical style of classical French and English prose of the eighteenth century, when it was not a tongue-in-the-cheek parody of it. Strachey protested, of course, as every biographer is eager to do, that he was bent on telling the truth and nothing but the truth about his victims. But, as a matter of fact, *Eminent Victorians* was written with a violent anti-Victorian bias, and the results, while brilliant, sometimes approach unsympathetic caricatures. But in *Queen Victoria* (1921), the tone was modified. This masterpiece of aesthetic compression shows a marked softening of Strachey's feelings towards his subject, and the tone is amiable, not to say affectionate. In *Elizabeth and Essex* (1928), a tale of an epoch alien to Strachey's experience and sympathies, we are in the realm of fictionized biography. It is the least successful and the most dangerous of Strachey's works. The widespread and not altogether happy imitation of this and earlier works by Strachey caught not his rare spirit, but his mannerisms: the balanced and epigrammatic style, the temperamental coolness and irony, the careful building-up to dramatic scenes, and—what was most dangerous—his indulgence in the re-creation of his subjects' streams of consciousness. Although Strachey was *sui generis*, his imitators in the field of fictionized biography have been legion, and to him rather than to any other single influence perhaps is due the tremendous increase in the number of new-model biographies.

But the Continental writers, Maurois and Ludwig, also contributed to the vogue, and stimulated imitation. Maurois' *Ariel*, based on his unsuccessful novel, *Ni Ange Ni Bête* (1919), was translated in 1924, and became the most popular, as it was the most highly fictionized, of his biographies. It is a charming and graceful fantasia on Shelley's human relations rather than a virtual biographical document. Maurois' later works, *Disraeli* (1927) and *Byron* (1930), came closer to the realm of conventional biography, but *Ariel* had already thrown Maurois' influence definitely on the side of fictionization. Though Ludwig's influence in America is less obvious than that of Strachey and Maurois, the popularity of his work has further encouraged the production of biographies. Ludwig specializes in elaborate psychological portraiture, and, although he is not averse to relying on sources, he succumbs easily to the temptation to use the technique of fiction—dialogue, setting, and action, and to indulge in psychological improvisations for which documents yield little authority. Fortunately, Ludwig's Germanic tendency to somewhat inflated and grandiose philosophizing has not been widely imitated in America.

As a result of these impersonal and personal influences, biographical writing in America in the last two decades has shown a great variety of methods and an equally wide range of types. From a welter of hybrid types, a number of fairly easily distinguishable types stand out. First, there is the scholarly biography, the major aims of which are scientific accuracy and historical soundness. Then, there is the psychoanalytical biography, which attempts to bring to light the secret patterns and mechanisms that underlie human characters and behavior. Allied to the psychoanalytical type is the debunking or journalistic biography, the aim of which is the correction of the angle of vision of less enlightened writers or periods. Remotest from the scientific biography is the fictionized biography, which even at its best utilizes freely some of the creative devices available to the omniscient auctorial observer. Examples of all these types are at hand among the productions of contemporary American biographers.

Scholarly biography represents the genre in its scientific rather than its artistic aspect. Carefully documented, heavy with footnotes, and buttressed with bibliographies, such biographies aim at being definitive, and at their best attain their goal. They command the respect and admiration of scholars; they usually reach the limited audience of the serious-minded. They represent biography in its historical rather than in its artistic aspect. Of such works, recent years have produced such distinguished examples as Jacob Zeitlin and Homer E. Woodbridge's *The Life and Letters of Stuart P. Sherman* (1929); William T. Hutchinson's *Cyrus Hall McCormick: Seed-Time, 1809–1856* (1931), and its sequel, *Cyrus H. McCormick: Harvest, 1856–1884* (1936); Allan Nevins' *Grover Cleveland* (1932); Douglas Southall Freeman's *R. E. Lee, a Biography* (1935); Marquis James's *Andrew Jackson: the Border Captain* (1933), and its sequel, *Andrew Jackson: Portrait of a President* (1937); Odell Shepard's *Pedlar's Progress: the Life of Bronson Alcott* (1937); Harry Barnard's *Eagle Forgotten: the Life of John Peter Altgeld* (1938); and Carl Van Doren's (*q.v.*) *Benjamin Franklin* (1938).

A number of writers whose preoccupations have been creative have also contributed to the scholarly biography. Of these, one of the most notable was Amy Lowell's (*q.v.*) *John Keats* (1925), an elaborate work based on her own collection of Keatsiana and substantially documented. The somewhat unenthusiastic reception of this major enterprise was due in part to her rather excessive claims as to its finality and to her characteristic violation of the dictates of decorum in the presentation of the seamier side of her subject's life. Another poet—Heinrich Heine—has also received full-length and reasonably scientific treatment from Louis Untermeyer (*q.v.*), who, like Miss Lowell, applies a poet's insight to a fellow craftsman's spiritual and physical career. Agnes Repplier's (*q.v.*) biographical studies, though in the traditional vein, come close to hagiography, since the subjects she prefers are figures from the saintly lives of Catholics in Canada and America.

Gamaliel Bradford (*q.v.*) was at once the major American practitioner of the type of biographical criticism perfected by Sainte-Beuve and the precursor of psychoanalytical biography. For his type of study, Bradford invented the rather unlovely term, "psychography"; by it, he wished to indicate his purpose in synthesizing out of all the material available a psychological portrait which should re-create the character he was presenting. Most of Bradford's studies, therefore, are portraits of his subjects rather than cycloramas of their careers. In this type of synthesis, Bradford was singularly happy, and his insight, aesthetic economy, and incessant practice in the form resulted in portraits of very considerable vividness and penetration. Their vitality, however, is impaired not only by the limitations of experience imposed by Bradford's lifelong invalidism but by his submission to the spirit of gentility. But a sight-seeing tour of Bradford's portrait galleries moves one to admiration for his persistence in the face of great physical obstacles and for the delicacy and sureness of his hand in the deliberately limited medium of the biographical miniature.

The psychoanalytical biographies popular in the twenties resembled Bradford's psychographs in aim but not in method or tone. Their aim, like Bradford's, was the discovery of the psychological pattern that underlay the life activity of their subjects. Their method, however, was borrowed from the recently popularized theories of the psychoanalysts, Freud, Jung, and Adler. It involved the discovery, through a study of dreams, symbolic actions, emotional attitudes and relationships, of the unconscious elements which psychoanalysis regarded as more important motivations than the elements passed into consciousness by an ever alert and fairly prudish censor. The danger in the method lay in the fact that while the psychoanalyst's subject is a living human being, the biographer's subject is dead. The subconscious mind of the analyst's subject becomes accessible to him through the use of various techniques. Since the subconscious mind of the biographer's subject is accessible to him only by processes of dubious inference, the results are of doubtful validity. It is not surprising, therefore, that the conclusions arrived at by some of the psychoanalytical biographers throw more light on the biographer than on his subject, and in some cases are obvious unconscious projections of the biographer upon his subject. Two early psychological biographies—Van Wyck Brooks's (*q.v.*) *The Ordeal of Mark Twain* (1920) and his *Pilgrimage of Henry James* (1925)—illustrate both the defects and the virtues of this method. Both these works were written at a time when Brooks was convinced that American civilization was not merely unfavorable but actually hostile to the development of literary genius. The men about whom he wrote were chosen to illustrate these deleterious effects. In other words, these biographical studies belong to the genre of argument rather than the genre of history. The argument of the first is less sound than the argument of the second. The attempt to demonstrate that Mark Twain was potentially a great tragic satirist, but that he was caught and crushed between the barbarity of the frontier and the repressive gentility of the family into which he married, necessitated a weighting of the evidence that comes close to special pleading. The argument concerning Henry James is less spectacular and more convincing. The new insight afforded Brooks by psychoanalysis made it possible for him to bring into the light the psychological pattern of James's life, and to show him escaping further and further from the demands that life might make on him. James, too, was a convenient and an impressive symbol of the reaction of a subtle and complex mind from the crudenesses and banalities of the America from which he fled. Brooks's *Henry James* is still the most satisfactory illustration of the application of the psychoanalytical technique to biographical writing.[1]

[1] Fortunately for American historical criticism, these works of Brooks's—products

There were, of course, other less skilled practitioners of the psychoanalytical method. Joseph Wood Krutch's (*q.v.*) *Edgar Allan Poe* (1926) illustrates the extremity to which the method may be pushed in its application to so complexly neurotic a figure as Poe. But Krutch's psychoanalytical biography represented a passing interest in the new method, and was merely incidental to his larger critical activity. The most persistent devotee of the psychoanalytical biography has been Katherine Anthony, who has been busy since 1933 applying the method to women characters. Of her works in this genre, perhaps the earliest, *Margaret Fuller* (1920), is the most successful, since here the subject lent herself easily to psychoanalytical treatment, and there was a profusion of autobiographical material on which to draw. Of Miss Anthony's studies of popular historical heroines—*Catherine the Great* (1925), *Queen Elizabeth* (1929), and *Marie Antoinette* (1933)—perhaps the first is the most successful from the particular point of view from which Miss Anthony writes. The mystery of Queen Elizabeth resists final analysis, and Marie Antoinette aroused her biographer to partisan sympathy. But *Catherine the Great* is an interesting, if speculative, analysis of an astonishing woman whose sexual life demands psychoanalytical investigation. With *Louisa May Alcott* (1937), Miss Anthony was on less happy ground. The temptation to stress the neurotic elements in her subject has resulted, in this instance, in throwing very considerably out of balance her psychological portrait.

One of the attractions of the psychoanalytical method was, of course, its utility in laying bare those hidden springs of emotion and action which convention and the dictates of decorum had concealed from the subject's contemporaries. This utility was legitimate only so long as its motivation was the discovery of truth; it became illegitimate when the motive was to smear with mud the pompous frock-coated statues of the great and near-great. The impulse to debunk was aroused particularly by the opportunity offered by the overidealization to which the nineteenth century had submitted its heroes and heroines. Here, the impulse was strengthened by the inevitable reaction of one age from that immediately preceding it. It was intensified by the wave of disillusionment and cynicism that swept over urban America in the post-war period. It is not always easy to distinguish between these motives, and biographers have not always been perfectly conscious of the nature of their own motivation. Some of these debunking biographies are still worthy of serious consideration. During the twenties, M. R. Werner (*q.v.*) was most active in biographical writing. Werner never descended to the more suspect methods of the debunkers, but his attitude was modern and sophisticated, and he delighted in presenting from such a point of view the somewhat baroque

of his middle period—were only preliminary to such a mature venture as *The Flowering of New England* (1936).

pomposities of such mighty folk figures as *Barnum* (1923), *Brigham Young* (1925), and *Bryan* (1929). The less exuberant atmosphere of the thirties was uncongenial to the debunking biography, although examples of the type continued to be published. Upton Sinclair's (*q.v.*) *The Flivver King* (1937) continued the anti-capitalistic tone of his earlier muckraking volumes.

There are some slight traces of the debunking spirit in the biographical studies of Herbert J. Gorman and Matthew Josephson (*q.v.*). Gorman's biographies, indeed, may be taken as representing both the vices and the virtues of contemporary journalistic biography. The earlier biographies, *A Victorian American, Henry Wadsworth Longfellow* (1926), and *Hawthorne, a Study of Solitude* (1927), grew out of the impulse, strong at the time, to reconsider the great figures in nineteenth-century America. Both subjects, particularly the first, tempted the biographer to a Stracheyesque and ironical treatment, and the studies are not unmarred by some rather patronizing condescension. More characteristic works of Gorman's are such highly colored fictionized biographies as *The Incredible Marquis, Alexandre Dumas* (1929) and *Scottish Queen* (1932). Here the method is almost that of the historical novel, and the virtues are those of fiction rather than of fact. A more serious biographer than Gorman is Matthew Josephson (*q.v.*), whose critical appreciation of American life has been sharpened by his European interests and his connection with the postwar expatriate movement. His *Portrait of the Artist as American* (1930) reveals most clearly his expatriate sympathies, and aligns him most definitely with the school of social criticism represented by the earlier works of Van Wyck Brooks. Josephson's *Zola and His Time* (1928) is probably the most elaborate biography of Zola yet produced in English. The author maintains his equilibrium in the face of the temptation to sneer at the nineteenth century, and as a result he has painted a memorable panorama of an important cultural movement. His *Jean-Jacques Rousseau* (1931) was a less fresh subject and a less significant treatment of it, but when he turned his attention to American subjects, new facets of his talent were revealed. Josephson's works in the thirties—*The Robber Barons* (1934) and *The Politicos* (1938)—were written in a period sharply critical of the economic morality of the Gilded Age, and provide fresh illuminations and evaluations of some of the neglected but immensely powerful financial forces behind the superficial political phenomena of the period after the Civil War.

Edgar Lee Masters' (*q.v.*) ventures into biographical writing arise, in part, from the impulse to debunk history of its conventional lies, and in part, also, from his strong personal conviction as to the necessity of re-interpreting American history from the point of view of the Middle West. In the face of a strongly entrenched cult devoted to what Masters regards as the "Lincoln myth," he sets himself in *Lincoln the Man* (1931) to correct the habit of apotheosizing the martyred president. Both as man and as leader, Lincoln received rough treatment at Masters' irreverent hands. But the limitations in Masters' scholarship reduce the value of the book as history, and, as interpretation, the work is idiosyncratic and crotchety. Even less successful was Masters' *Whitman* (1937). For the subject itself he seems to have felt considerable distaste, and he was none too successful in assimilating the vast amount of material that has accumulated around America's one poet of epic proportions. The best of Masters' biographies to date is *Vachel Lindsay, a Poet in America* (1935). Writing out of a close personal knowledge of Lindsay and affection for him, Masters was able to tell the tragic tale of Lindsay's life with a sympathy that none of Masters' other biographies show. Here, as elsewhere, the writing is marred by ill-natured or ill-advised commentary, but the book is the most considerable of Masters' biographical achievements and one of the best biographies of a contemporary poet of importance.[1]

A reaction to the debunking biography so popular in the twenties was inevitable. This revulsion from the skepticism and cynicism characteristic of the debunking spirit naturally took the form of a revival of a glowing enthusiasm for America and its past, a reaffirmation of the splendor of the American ideal based on a devoted restudying of the pertinent facts. A curious illustration of the reaction to the debunking school was Bernard DeVoto's (*q.v.*) *Mark Twain's America* (1932), which set out to explode the myth of the cultural barrenness of the frontier and to defend Mark Twain from the charges of suppression which Van Wyck Brooks had leveled at him. The polemics inevitable in DeVoto's writings should not distract the reader from the solidity of his re-creation of frontier life and from his profound understanding of a society remote in place and alien in spirit to most eastern-born literary historians.

But such writers as Constance Mayfield Rourke (*q.v.*), Donald Culross Peattie (*q.v.*), and Carl Sandburg (*q.v.*) are more truly representative of the revulsion from biographical muckraking. Their love of American folkways is as strong as their knowledge of them is deep. Although they are not all professional poets, they are poets in feeling and, in consequence, their description of American character and life has a native idyllic quality rare in American biography. Constance Mayfield Rourke has devoted herself to exploring the byways of nineteenth-century American life, and to bringing some of its most picturesque characters to vital expression. The biographical essays in her first volume, *Trumpets of Jubilee* (1927), show some touches of the debunking spirit popular at the period, and the life of Lotta Crabtree, concealed under the title *Troupers of the Gold Coast* (1928), is somewhat excessively intent on the colorful

[1] Comparable with it, and in most respects superior to it, is Philip Horton's *Hart Crane* (1937), a tactful and courageous handling of a subject of the greatest difficulty.

and ribald life of the days of the gold rush. But in *Davy Crockett* (1934) and *Audubon* (1936) the tone is less consciously picturesque, more quietly poetic, and the latter book, in particular, has high aesthetic qualities of compression and finish. Audubon has also served as the subject of a biography by Donald Culross Peattie, whose scientific experience stood him in good stead in estimating the value of Audubon's painting of American birds as contributions to ornithology. Here, as in his *Green Laurels* (1936), Peattie yields occasionally to the temptation to write a prose lushly and softly romantic rather than at once poetic and hard. Carl Sandburg's magnificent series of biographical volumes on Lincoln are artistically the most important work done on that great subject in our time. For this exacting task Sandburg is suited by temperament, experience, and talent. The scale of his monument to Lincoln is heroic, and it is still too early to see the outlines of the whole design, but enough is visible to warrant one's conclusion that no more sympathetic or deeply American biography of Lincoln has ever been written.

When one turns from contemporary biographical writing to contemporary autobiographical writing, one faces a sharply altered situation. Contemporary American autobiographies have fallen far short of biographies in number, but what they have lacked in numbers they have made up for in quality. It would be interesting to speculate as to the reasons why America has produced relatively few distinguished or memorable autobiographies. It is easy to suggest reasons, and reasons have been suggested: the speed of American life, the preoccupations of Americans with externals, the absence from America of any very rich social or religious life, the limitations of our experience with older and contrasting cultures. Whatever the reasons may be, the American temperament shows a marked disinclination to direct its attention to itself with sufficient steadiness and honesty of scrutiny to bring forth autobiographical material in large quantity. If the modern American temperament is as purely extroverted as it seems, it has come a long way from the soul-searchings of its Puritan and Protestant origins but not far enough to develop the skeptical and untiring self-absorption of a Samuel Pepys or a Michel de Montaigne.

In modern times, *The Education of Henry Adams* (1907) stands almost alone in America as a completely skeptical, not to say sardonic, examination of its author's and the American conscience. Such another book John Jay Chapman might have written, as his brilliant letters have shown, but he was less completely weaned from the life of action than Adams, and the book he might have composed was never written. Almost the only journal of importance produced by a contemporary man of letters was that of Gamaliel Bradford (*q.v.*), edited after the writer's death by Van Wyck Brooks. The special circumstances of Bradford's life encouraged the keeping of elaborate personal records, but those conditions likewise give the journal an introverted invalidic quality that is almost unique among American diarists.

But if the psychological material for American autobiographical writing seems curiously limited, there is no lack of exciting and spectacular external experience and action available to Americans, and probably the best of contemporary autobiographies have been written by men who, like Odysseus, have visited many men and cities and have brought back strange tales of their adventures. Americans' avidity for strange sights, constantly increasing motility, extraordinary amiability, adaptability, and practicality make them easy travelers and welcome sojourners in exotic places. The American's depths may not be profound, but his surface is bright and shining. Contemporary autobiography has further been stimulated by those omnipresent and almost omnipotent agencies, advertising and journalism. Through advertising primarily, publishers have stimulated a general interest not merely in the public lives but in the private affairs of the authors on their lists. The fearless light of journalism beating upon the names that make literary news has habituated writers, like moving-picture stars, to the public's curiosity concerning their amours and their household pets. Finally, the personalizing of syndicated journalism through signed features and the daily column has brought to public attention a very considerable number of personalities who, in earlier days, would have been unknown to a large public.

Since the ultimate source of autobiography is that passion for oneself which, as Oscar Wilde said, is a lifelong romance, its quality depends finally on the nature of the expressive personality. Its interest includes, however, not only the personality itself but the kind and variety of subjective or objective experience the writer has set forth. Autobiographies may be classified most revealingly, therefore, not in terms of varying conceptions of the genre but in terms of types of autobiographers. These may be differentiated by the fundamental bias of their personalities and by the special fields of their interests and activities. On the scale of temperamental bias, we may distinguish personalities that are fundamentally extroverted from those that are basically introverted in their orientation. (Though no absolutely pure types exist, any personality will manifest one dominant manner of adaptation.) The most characteristic modern American personality is extroverted—active and energetic, outgoing and sociable, superficial and external. This type occurs frequently among the journalists whose autobiographies have been especially conspicuous in the thirties, and among those autobiographical writers whose chief concern has been with social and political forces. A type less frequently encountered among autobiographers is the introvert, who is somewhat ill at ease in the world and society, and who, if he is a creative artist, finds a higher value in the world of the imagination than in that of external reality. Poets and novelists, critics and plastic artists, almost without exception, reveal a large if not dominant element of introversion.

Perhaps the most sensationally successful of contemporary autobiographies have been produced by a number of journalists whose business took them to the scene of important and dramatic political events. Contemporary journalists were not, of course, the first to concoct books out of their professional experience, but in the thirties of the twentieth century they have produced an unparalleled number of biographies of considerable attractiveness. The most popular and almost certainly the best is Vincent Sheean's (*q.v.*) *Personal History* (1935). *Personal History* is distinguished from its imitators and successors, not so much by the vividness of the writing or the journalistic knack of being on the spot at the psychological moment, as by the author's view of his experiences among the Riffi, in London's Bloomsbury group, or among the Communists in China as merely milestones in his own spiritual pilgrimage. The conversion of a cynical journalist to a belief, whether profound or superficial, in the cause of the common man everywhere, is narrated with modesty and conviction. The intellectual distinction of this work is echoed only intermittently by the journalistic autobiographies which followed hard on the heels of this justifiably successful book. Walter Duranty's *I Write as I Please* (1935) bears the stamp of his honest and incorruptible personality, John Gunther's *Inside Europe* (1936) finds its distinction in shrewd psychological analyses of those leaders who seem bent on leading Europe into another cataclysm, and Webb Miller's *I Found No Peace* (1936) is a convincing demonstration of contemporary democratic pessimism. In Negley Farson's *The Way of a Transgressor* (1936) we recognize the bustling nonchalant manner of a latter-day Richard Harding Davis.

Walter Duranty's *I Write as I Please* was the first of the journalistic autobiographies to deal at length with the equivocal subject of Russian communism. It is Duranty's distinction that he was able to remain on good terms with the Stalinite regime and at the same time discuss Russian affairs in a way palatable to American bourgeois and radical readers. Duranty's book prepared the way for less judicious and less even-spirited accounts of the Russian experiment. Eugene Lyons' *Assignment in Utopia* (1937) and Fred E. Beal's *Proletarian Journey* (1937) are overridden with disillusionment, in the one case, that of a radical journalist, and in the other, of a radical American worker who did not find Russia what the theorists had promised it would be.

Autobiographers whose preoccupations are, in one or another sense of the word, social range from Mabel Dodge Luhan and Mary Antin to Edward Bok and Joseph Freeman.

Mrs. Luhan's interest and activities are social, in the most inclusive sense of that term. Her massive series of autobiographical volumes, from

Intimate Memories (1933) and *European Experiences* (1935) to *Movers and Shakers* (1936) and *Edge of Taos Desert* (1937), are chapters in one of the most amazing autobiographies written by an American woman. Mrs. Luhan has the fascinated self-absorption of the born diarist and autobiographer. She is probably as honest a person as one of her essentially romantic nature can be. Unmatched, at least among contemporary autobiographers, as a collector of literary and artistic personalities, Mrs. Luhan, after her escape from the convention-ridden life of bourgeois Buffalo, gathered around her in New York, Italy, and New Mexico, an amazing number of the names that make literary news. Exacting and willful, mystical and ruthless, she has made her way through the lives of countless admirers and hangers-on. Of herself and her associates, she writes with impressive if embarrassing frankness. Over a number of important characters—John Reed, Walter Lippmann (*q.v.*), Gertrude Stein (*q.v.*), and D. H. Lawrence—she has been able to cast a somewhat theatrical glamour, and yet she keeps herself high-lighted in the foreground in the role of one of the most striking if preposterous figures on the contemporary literary stage.

The autobiographical literature produced by American immigrants is more conspicuous in quantity than in quality. An early classic of this type was Mary Antin's *The Promised Land* (1912), written and published when America was glad to be called a "melting pot" and before we had developed any economic or cultural scruples about the hordes of foreign-born who were flocking to our shores. Mrs. Antin's book is an important if somewhat romanticized contribution to American social history. *The Americanization of Edward Bok* (1920) illustrates interestingly that excessive adaptation to American ways of life and thought to which the immigrant is sorely tempted. Bok emerges from his autobiography as almost oppressively American; neither his ideals nor his good works distinguish him from a dozen other extremely successful American businessmen. The immigrant's problem of fusing his racial and national tradition with that of the country of his adoption seems to have been solved most successfully by Louis Adamic (*q.v.*), whose *Native's Return* (1934) is an astonishingly vivid rediscovery of the Bohemian culture to which after years in America he returned. Of the American side of the story he tells movingly in *Laughing in the Jungle* (1932) and *My America, 1928–38* (1938). Adamic's life has been too hard and his mind too sharp to allow himself the over-adaptation characteristic of a Bok, though the last volume displays a quality of observant but hopeful Americanism of which the native-born frequently display very little.

It is rather remarkable that a period fraught with social significance should have produced few notable autobiographies reflecting the economic and political storm and stress, the current stages in the struggle between the privileged classes and the common man. Of such autobiographies, certainly the best is *The Autobiography of Lincoln Steffens* (1931). Steffens made his reputation in the muckraking days at the beginning of the century, and his *Shame of the Cities* (1904) is a permanent record of the heroic efforts made by a few reformers to awaken public opinion and to excise the cancerous sources of civic corruption. Steffens lived long after the period of his early fame, but he continued to be a good if less conspicuous assailant of evil in power. The *Autobiography* records one of the most stirring chapters in the history of America's attempt to make herself a democratic and decent social order. A later stage in the eternal struggle is reflected more emotionally and less critically in Mary Heaton Vorse's *A Footnote to Folly* (1935), where the enemy is capitalism in relation to labor rather than capitalism behind the throne of government. Still a third stage in the history of American radicalism, the emergence of a group bent on replacing the capitalistic system by a classless economic order, is set forth somewhat verbosely and tumultuously in *An American Testament* (1936) by Joseph Freeman, a not too generous spirited account of his relations with post-war radicals in America.

Autobiographies richer in introspection and self-analysis, and more sensitive to the life of the mind and of the heart have come, in considerable numbers, from the pens of creative writers and artists like William Ellery Leonard and Edith Wharton, Ludwig Lewisohn and Rockwell Kent.

Perhaps the most distinguished group of contemporary American autobiographies has been produced by the poets. The poet, traditionally, is a man unusually sensitized to experience, and therefore deeply conscious of his immediate experience and its remoter significance. Whatever the reason, a number of American poets have been moved to reveal their life-experience, not only in the mirror-like medium of their verse, but in the guise of formal autobiography. In all these instances, the poet's account of his own experience and its significance to him has marked historical value, and, in most instances, high aesthetic value as well. Of the older poets, perhaps the most interesting autobiographers are Lizette Woodworth Reese (*q.v.*) and William Ellery Leonard (*q.v.*). Miss Reese's slight account of her earlier years in *A Victorian Village* (1929) has the quiet charm and fineness of feeling that one associates with her verse. Leonard's *The Locomotive God* (1927), on the other hand, reveals facets of his personality which the autobiographical sonnet-sequence, *Two Lives* (1923), had not brought into view. This autobiography is an extraordinarily frank account of the paralyzing effect on the poet's life of phobias and compulsions of which he courageously searches out the origins. From the middle generation come the autobiographies of John Gould Fletcher (*q.v.*) and Edgar Lee Masters (*q.v.*). Of the two, Fletcher's *Life Is My Song* (1937) is the less intimate, and perhaps, therefore, the more generally attractive. For Fletcher's account of his life in Arkansas, France, and England, his long sojourn abroad, his version of the rise and decline of the Imagist movement, and his lively portraits of such poets as Amy Lowell, Ezra Pound, and T. S. Eliot have a historical value beyond the limits of the merely personal. Masters' *Across Spoon River* (1936), though sometimes graceless in expression and somewhat embittered in tone, is a remarkable self-portrait. The total effect is that of a repressed and tormented Sherwood Anderson character suddenly become extraordinarily vocal. His personal emotional difficulties occupy rather too large a share of his attention, perhaps. But this autobiography and Masters' biography of his friend Vachel Lindsay constitute a powerful indictment of Philistinism in middle western life at the turn of the century. Less jaundiced accounts of the creative life in the Middle West are drawn by Harriet Monroe in *A Poet's Life* (1938) and Eunice Tietjens in *The World at My Shoulder* (1938). Though both books find their focus in the poetic renaissance heralded by *Poetry, a Magazine of Verse*, Mrs. Tietjens' ranges more widely geographically and culturally in its account of her oriental and dramatic adventures. But Miss Monroe's gives the fuller history of her primal share in launching *Poetry*, and of her tempestuous relations with all the contemporary poets of any importance. If the story is colored by Miss Monroe's seemingly fragile but really indomitable personality, this is just what we should wish. She was hardly in a position to write an unbiased history of the poetic renaissance which she had been largely responsible for creating.

Novelists, likewise, have been moved to recount their life-experience, not merely in the sometimes recognizable disguises of their fiction, but in the unmasked form of autobiography. Of the novelists, Hamlin Garland perhaps has found the autobiographical form most congenial. Garland has lived a long full life. He has seen the Middle West develop, out of the stresses and strains of its pioneering period, a solid and pre-eminently American agricultural culture. He camc early into New England literary circles, and he has continued to move in the orbits of the great and near-great. His feelings toward the harsh conditions against which he rebelled in early years have softened with the passage of time, and his earlier biographies—*A Son of the Middle Border* (1917) and *A Daughter of the Middle Border* (1921)—are not untouched by a nostalgic admiration for the brave spirits that broke the plains. The later volumes do not quite equal the earlier in freshness, and in *Afternoon Neighbors* (1934) one is forced to condone an old man's fondness for not too important literary recollections. With Edith Wharton's (*q.v.*) *A Backward Glance* (1934), we move in a vastly different world from Garland's. Here the atmosphere is Jamesian, critical, subtle, elegant, reticent. Mrs. Wharton's skill in fine brush-work does not desert her here and, of its urbane kind, this autobiography is one of the most attractive and rewarding. Other novelists slightly younger than Mrs. Wharton have also used the autobiographical form successfully. A sensation-stirring publication was Ludwig Lewisohn's (*q.v.*) *Up Stream* (1922). This book was written in a mood of exacerbated exasperation at the mistreatment Lewisohn conceived he had had in American academic circles during the war. Its tone was harsh and bitter; its criticism of the shortcomings of American culture, severe. On the personality revealed here and in the sequel, *Mid-Channel* (1929), must lie some of the onus for the alleged treatment, for the temperament exhibited is egocentric, supersensitive, and arrogant. But this picture of a foreign-born Jew of wide and liberal culture, failing to adapt himself to American academic life, is a memorable contribution to the problem of assimilation. Of the younger novelists, Evelyn Scott (*q.v.*) has turned to autobiography in the early episode, *Escapade* (1923), and in the more elaborate and less strident *Background in Tennessee* (1937). In the first of these, particularly, all the armor of reticence has been stripped off, and we get the painfully naked and quivering experience of an overwrought and self-lacerating personality. But this intense fragment hardly prepares one for the scope and quality of *Background in Tennessee*. Here, the old southern civilization is refracted through a relentlessly honest and adversity-sharpened temperament, and the result is the casting of a harsh white light on a mode of life usually suffused with deceptive stage moonlight.

With Malcolm Cowley's (*q.v.*) *Exile's Return* (1934) we move into an alien if not a larger atmosphere. Cowley's account of his share in the post-war expatriate movement is one of the fullest and shrewdest we have. It escapes the narrow cultishness of most such narratives, for it was written long enough after the decline of the movement to give Cowley some critical perspective, and it is the work of one of the keener and more gifted persons connected with it. Parallel to Cowley's book in period and personalities is Gertrude Stein's (*q.v.*) tour de force, *The Autobiography of Alice B. Toklas* (1933), certainly the most widely read and probably the best of her books. By the device of pretending to focus her attention on her friend and companion, Miss Stein is able to give a picture of her own vigorous personality that has an effect of solidity and objectivity rare in autobiography. The style is a simplification of her later creative manner, and the book is filled with telling caricatures of her friends, enemies, and protégés among artists and writers. The sequel, *Everybody's Autobiography* (1937), is her version of "exile's return." Less studded with important personalities than the earlier book, it is an extremely refreshing account of the impact of American life upon a singularly alert and self-confident mentality. The revolt against American gentility in which Miss Stein has played so distinguished a role was also reflected in Margaret Anderson's *My Thirty Years' War* (1930), a stirring tale of her attempt, in the face of numerous discomfitures, to print in the *Little Review* the best of the new literature. Her success in waging guerrilla warfare can be measured only by the extraordinary distinction of the contributions to this historic journal.

Literary critics, alert to the tides of time and taste, have also found autobiography attractive. Two in particular, Henry Seidel Canby (*q.v.*) and Carl Van Doren (*q.v.*), have attempted to project the pattern of their lives against the stage settings of contemporary life. Canby's experiences have not been spectacular, but he has brought to them a very considerable sensitivity, and, although he realizes that gentility and decorum are no longer in vogue, his autobiographical works—*The Age of Confidence* (1934) and *Alma Mater* (1936)—make no pretense of a factitious robustness and are consciously dated, not only in period but in temper. Van Doren's *Three Worlds* (1936) has a wider geographical and cultural range, and his middle western beginnings gave him a useful perspective on his later life in metropolitan academic and literary circles. Van Doren's spiritual experiences have not been remarkable, but he has moved steadily with the literary current, and from that advantageous position he has been able to re-create New York literary and artistic society with a firm if not too delicate hand.

Literary artists take to autobiography with an ease and grace usually denied artists whose medium is nonverbal. But, occasionally, in the present as in the past, an artist appears who is almost as skillful with the pen as with the brush or chisel. Such an artist is Rockwell Kent (*q.v.*), whose prose matches the sturdy masculinity of his drawings and paintings. Kent has not ventured as yet on a full-length autobiography, but such passages in his life as furnished the material for *N by E* (1930) or *Salamina* (1935) are rendered with the primitive force and simplicity with which his imagination has endowed the human form. A subtler play of light and shadow flashes over the life-history of the American sculptress, Malvina Hoffman, in *Heads and Tales* (1936). Though modest to a degree unusual in artists, Miss Hoffman has ventured into such strange and fascinating places that her story equals Kent's in exoticism, as it differs from it in feminine subtlety and humor.

There seems no reason to believe that American biography is likely to decrease in quantity or that American autobiography will fall off in quality. More frequently than in the past—as it becomes increasingly conscious of its nature, limitations, and potentialities—biography may achieve that fusion of sound science and effective art which is its ideal. The excitement and variety of American life can always be counted on to furnish material for excellent autobiographies of the extrōverted type, and an enhanced social and political consciousness should encourage the production of more books like *The Autobiography of Lincoln Steffens* (1931) and Oswald Garrison Villard's *Fighting Years* (1939). What American autobiography needs is deeper introversion and profounder self-analysis. But for the development of such psychological habits, a turbulent political and economic future will hardly provide a favorable milieu.

CRITICISM

No development in contemporary American letters is more striking or more gratifying than the rise of criticism to a position of hitherto unrivaled distinction. American criticism of the eighteenth and nineteenth centuries had been meagerly productive of significant theories and frequently inconsistent in their application, although such genial cultivated essays as those of James Russell Lowell are still readable and often surprisingly sound in judgment. By the end of the century, however, criticism, like poetry, had become anemic with gentility; except in a few hands, it hardly rose above the level of gossip about books. The eminent position occupied by such commentators as Richard Watson Gilder and Hamilton Wright Mabie—a position curiously prophetic of that of William Lyon Phelps today—is indicative of the discreet though really unprincipled impressionism that passed for criticism in polite circles.

The causes for the revival of interest in criticism are not far to seek, although different forces operated upon its major varieties—aesthetic, sociological, and historical. The study of ancient and modern Continental literatures by Irving Babbitt (*q.v.*) and Paul Elmer More (*q.v.*), and the gradual clarification of their critical positions, underlay the rise and fall of the New Humanism. American interest in Benedetto Croce—as publicized by Joel E. Spingarn—called for a redefinition and realignment of basic aesthetic principles. On the moral-political side, pre-war liberalism and post-war radicalism stimulated an animated controversy as to the proper relations between life and letters in America and the critical implications of such relations. The enormous vogue of the *American Mercury* under the editorship of H. L. Mencken (*q.v.*) and George Jean Nathan (*q.v.*) made thousands of readers conscious of the limitations of a genteel bourgeois culture, and, while the criticism of these writers was destructive rather than constructive, and while their own literary ideals remained carefully undefined, they prepared the way for the systematic exposure of currently popular vital lies about American life and literature. On the historical side, the opening of a new century, the realization that the nineteenth century was over and done with and that the twentieth century gave its inhabitants a vantage point from which to view America's past, and the intellectual and philosophical orientation forced upon Americans by the experience of the World War, stimulated the reinterpretation of American literature. The production of a very considerable number of full-length histories of that literature, based upon the lively researches of countless graduate students and scholars, brought fresh evaluations of the clay-footed giants of America's Victorian era, and replaced such elementary and jejune histories as Reuben P. Halleck's, Charles F. Johnson's, and John S. Hart's. The increase in the number and size of graduate schools in American universities, particularly in the Middle West where the dead hand of New England Brahminism was not felt, meant the application to the study of American literature of those methods of scientific investigation hitherto reserved for the tenth-rate poets of the Middle Ages or the minor dramatists of the Renaissance. American literature might be an ill-favored thing, but it was our own, and the twentieth century has seen an almost excessive amount of energy and intelligence devoted to major and minor figures in our literary past. The weapons handed the biographical critics by the new psychology encouraged the tearing of the veils of decorum from such indecorous men of letters as Edgar Allan Poe, Mark Twain, Ambrose Bierce, and Herman Melville, and tempted the application of the methods of psychoanalysis to biographical criticism. Finally, the emergence in the second decade of the century of the New Poetry and the appearance of numerous gifted or talented novelists, the revolt against the commercial theater and the attempt to restore the alliance between literature and the drama, furnished stimulating contemporary material with which critics must deal and forced upon historians and critics alike the orderly consideration and evaluation of current literary phenomena, and the relating of them, not only to America's literary past, but to contemporary life.

As interest increased in the clarification of critical theories and the systematic application of them, editors, journalists, and critics felt the urge to develop media appropriate to the presentation of their ideas. Newspapers and magazines had always given a modest amount of space to literary publicity in the form of publishers' advertisements, book reviews, and gossip about authors, even when, as in the *Critic* and the early *Bookman*, such journalism was not on a very elevated intellectual plane. But the rising interest in contemporary criticism not only led to an increase in the amount of space assigned to book reviews in such newspapers as the New York *Times*, the Chicago *Daily News*, *Evening Post*, and *Tribune*, and the Boston *Evening Transcript*, but encouraged the development of weekly literary supplements like the New York *Times Book Review* and the New York *Evening Post's Literary Review*. The founding of such weekly journals of opinion as the *New Republic*, the *Nation*, the *Freeman*, the *Masses*, the *Liberator*, the *Commonweal*, and the *New Masses*, the establishment of the *Saturday Review of Literature*, and the launching of the *New Yorker*, gave an outlet to a number of promising older and younger critics, and, by the gradual discrimination of their aesthetic and social views, drew fairly sharp lines between opposing political and critical camps. Moreover, these weeklies gave both time and space to a more leisurely and extensive consideration of books than newspaper reviewing afforded, and, since the audience reached was socially conscious and intellectually acute, the tone, style, and manners of criticism achieved upon occasion a distinction that warranted its collection in the permanent form of anthologies or of collections of essays by single critics.

Thus, study and clarification of contemporary American criticism was made possible by such anthologies as Ludwig Lewisohn's *A Modern Book of Criticism* (1919), the *New Republic's* pamphlet, *On American Books*, which Francis Hackett edited in 1920, Harold E. Stearns's *Civilization in the United States* (1922), the *Dial* pamphlet, *Criticism in America*, by Irving Babbitt (*q.v.*) and others (1924), James C. Bowman's *Contemporary American Criticism* (1926), William A. Drake's *American Criticism, 1926* (1926), *Humanism and America*, edited by Norman Foerster (*q.v.*) in 1930, C. Hartley Grattan's *The Critique of Humanism* (1930), Norman Foerster's *American Critical Essays* (1930), and Morton Dauwen Zabel's *Literary Opinion in America* (1937).

The development of contemporary literary criticism was further fostered by the founding of a number of monthlies and quarterlies devoted primarily to the serious discussion of social and literary problems. Of the earlier monthlies of this type, the *Seven Arts* was easily the most distinguished. Though it survived for only a single year (1916–17), it attracted some of the major literary talents on both sides of the Atlantic. In 1920, the *Dial*, which had had an earlier career in Chicago as a conservative critical weekly, was refounded as a monthly. It was edited by Schofield Thayer from 1920 to 1925, and by Marianne Moore (*q.v.*) from 1925 to 1929, when it was discontinued. The *Bookman*, which since 1895 had been a polite purveyor of literary gossip, was taken over by Seward Collins in 1929, and edited with growing conservatism until 1933, when he discontinued it in order to found the *American Review* for the more effective expression of the Tory views on politics, economics, and religion of himself and his wife, Dorothea Brande.

There has likewise been a remarkable revival of the quarterly magazine, especially under the auspices of a number of southern universities. Of the critical quarterlies, the oldest is the *Sewanee Review*, which was founded in 1893, is sponsored by the University of the South, and has been edited energetically by William S. Knickerbocker since 1926. In 1911, Wilbur L. Cross rehabilitated the *Yale Review*, and made it a critical journal marked particularly for long and authoritative reviews. Since 1925, the *Virginia Quarterly Review* has built up an excellent critical reputation. In Cambridge in 1927 appeared the *Hound and Horn*, a critical journal of great intellectual distinction. It was edited in Cambridge and later in New York by Lincoln Kirstein and others, until it was discontinued in 1935. A journal of similar critical acumen was the short-lived *Symposium*, edited by James Burnham and Philip E. Wheelwright from 1930 to 1934. A recent addition to American critical quarterlies is the

Southern Review (1935), sponsored by Senator Huey Long's reanimated University of Louisiana, and edited by Cleanth Brooks and Robert Penn Warren (*q.v.*). This quarterly is perhaps most notable for its severely critical syntheses of contemporary literary movements. The latest (1938) important addition to the roster of critical journals is the *Kenyon Review*, edited by John Crowe Ransom (*q.v.*).

Despite these guides, any attempt to plot the maze of American theory and practice since the war is fraught with dangers, since no animals are more touchy than critics. But the attempt must be made in the hope of discovering some principles for the differentiation and evaluation of critical activities. Some light may be thrown on the chaos by recalling the fact that critical activities may be distinguished as aesthetic, sociological, or historical in accordance with the aspect of the work of art customarily emphasized by the critic. We must, however, remember that no critic is likely to restrict himself constantly to any one type of criticism; further, that in each of these types of criticism ethical or philosophical implications play a more or less weighty part in the process of illumination and evaluation, and, finally, that a considerable hostility is likely to manifest itself, not merely between aesthetic and sociological critics, but between aesthetic critics of conservative or radical sympathies.

In theory, the aesthetic critic is concerned primarily with the work of art as a work of art and not as a sociological, historical, or psychological document. His purpose is appreciation, on the one hand, and evaluation or appraisal on the other. The brand of criticism first advertised by Joel E. Spingarn under the provocative title, *Creative Criticism*, comes closest in theory to the essential ideal of the aesthetic critic. In his slashing lecture on "The New Criticism," first delivered in 1910 and first printed in 1913, Spingarn attempted to dispose of all the older methods of criticism and to substitute his own system based upon the aesthetic of Benedetto Croce. This lively attack on historical, classical, and romantic criticism may very well be regarded as the beginning of the contemporary revival of interest in the discussion of critical theory. The Spingarnian adaptation of the Crocean system involved the critic's prolonged concentration upon the isolated work of art, a contemplation which has its finest results only when the identification of the critic and the work of art is as complete as possible. Whatever may be the validity of the underlying aesthetic principles, the critical procedure recommended is actually a refurbishing of the method of abstracting the work from its historical setting and relationships and regarding it as absolutely as possible. This method was later described by T. S. Eliot in *The Sacred Wood* (1920), a volume of essays written while Eliot's critical position was still purely aesthetic: It is part of the critic's "business to see literature steadily and see it whole; and this is eminently to see it not as consecrated by time but to see it beyond time; to see the best work of our time and the best work of twenty-five hundred years ago with the same eyes." The emphasis of critics of this type, then, is upon purely aesthetic values.

But even aesthetic critics require standards, and, in the main, types of aesthetic critics may be distinguished according to the particular sets of standards by which they measure the works under consideration. Three fairly distinct sets of standards, American critics have taken over from the great European critical tradition—the classical, the romantic, and the realistic. To one or the other of these three classes, American critics of the aesthetic type may be fairly easily assigned. But, because of the deeply moralistic strain in the American character, there is little pure aestheticism in American criticism. In almost every instance, the aesthetic standard adopted has a fairly close correlation with a definite ethical standard, the classical with traditional Christian ethics, the romantic or impressionistic with liberal ethics, and the realistic with a naturalistic system of ethics. American aesthetic criticism would be unintelligible if its definite ethical and moral preoccupation were not kept constantly in mind.

The classical aesthetic critic must, as Irving Babbitt (*q.v.*) wrote, "rate creation with reference to some standard set above his own temperament and that of the creator. . . . He will begin to have taste only when he refers the creative expression and his impression of it to some standard that is set above both." That standard the classical aesthetic critic finds in the great works of the past, preferably in the Greek and Latin classics, but also in admittedly great works in the English or Continental traditions. The strength of the classical position is the refuge it offers from the aesthetic solipsism of individual impressionism and from the vagaries of the purely and merely personal evaluation. Its weaknesses are its tendency to reduce art to a static and ultimately sterile imitation of ancient masterpieces and its failure to provide for the essentially dynamic and protean character of the creative impulse.

W. C. Brownell's (1851–1928) exegesis of the classical critical procedure was made most systematically and philosophically in his *Criticism* (1914) and *Standards* (1924). It is regrettable that Brownell's critical practice was limited to the consideration of such relatively established figures as the nineteenth-century American classics and the Victorian prose writers. A slightly more liberal expression of the classical and other critical procedures was worked out by George E. Woodberry (1855–1930) in *The Appreciation of Literature* (1907) and *Two Phases of Criticism* (1914). It remained, however, for Irving Babbitt (*q.v.*) (1865–1933) to become the doughty and influential defendant of classicism and a lifelong assailant of what he regarded as romanticism and its hideous progeny. But the effects of his immense learning and his brilliance as a controversialist were negated to some degree by his monomaniacal hatred of romanticism, which he identified with all that in his eyes was aesthetically and ethically evil. In the end, his work betrayed a disconcerting absence of that classical balance and restraint for which he professed admiration, and the violence of his anti-romanticism suggests a less than complete success in exorcising the evil spirit from himself. Paul Elmer More (*q.v.*) was a somewhat less spectacular exponent of classicism in criticism. Perhaps no other critic of our time has applied aesthetic and ethical principles so uniformly and steadily to a variety of literary phenomena. He was least happy in his treatment of contemporary literature on such occasions, for instance, as his chastisement of Dos Passos and Proust with the rigid rod of his Puritan ethics. The limitations of his critical achievement were those of his own temperament and theory—an almost Puritanical conception of life, a touch of aesthetic Pharisaism, and a style that imitated but did not equal that of his master, Matthew Arnold.

Irving Babbitt and Paul Elmer More were the inspirers of the New Humanism, a movement which attracted a good deal of attention in the second decade of the century and which collapsed with dramatic suddenness with the onset of the depression. Babbitt attempted to fuse into a harmony the classical procedure for the creation and criticism of literature, a sort of deodorized Unitarianism, and the tag-ends of oriental mysticism left over from the Emersonian tradition. Paul Elmer More worked as diligently to combine classicism with a rationalistic Episcopalianism, to reconcile Platonism with Christianity, an attempt more successfully if less rationally carried out by his disciple, T. S. Eliot. Humanism, too, owed something to that blend of Hebraism and Hellenism recommended by Matthew Arnold. But Humanism was more remarkable in its negative than in its positive aspects. It was a matter of protest rather than of program. Its face was set sternly against the most characteristic movements of the modern spirit. It was consciously anti-naturalistic, anti-democratic, anti-humanitarian, anti-radical.

The foundations of Humanist doctrine had been laid by Babbitt in *The New Laokoon* (1910), *Rousseau and Romanticism* (1919), and *Democracy and Leadership* (1924), and by Paul Elmer More in *The Drift of Romanticism* (1913) and *Aristocracy and Justice* (1915). But it remained for their disciples, Stuart P. Sherman (*q.v.*), Norman Foerster (*q.v.*), and others to publicize the movement. As early as 1917, Stuart Sherman's *On Contemporary Literature* had been the first and not the most happy attempt to evaluate contemporary letters in Humanistic terms. But Sherman's departure from the academic world into that of metropolitan literary journalism in 1924 led to a liberalizing of his critical principles dismaying to his elder mentors, and his death in 1927 ended his contribution to the movement. The mantle of Elijah fell, therefore, on the willing shoulders of Norman Foerster, and it is to him and his associates that we owe the formalization of the program of Humanism, which received its fullest statement in the anthology of critical essays, *Humanism and America*, which Foerster edited in 1930. Humanism commended itself to the academic and bourgeois mind by its safety, if not by its sanity, and by its condemnation of the disturbing and bewildering elements in American life and literature, and it is not to be wondered at that the disciples of Humanism mounted rapidly the ladder of academic preferment.

But the Humanistic movement was of the nature of a dying gasp rather than of a first breath. Its position and program had no vital relation to the contemporary mind, and after it had been attacked, not merely by left-wing journalists and critics in *The Critique of Humanism*, edited by C. Hartley Grattan in 1930, but by the ultraconservative T. S. Eliot, it passed rapidly into a deserved obscurity. Humanism could do little to make intelligible or meaningful the complex anti-Humanistic development of American literature. It survives in only a few academic critics such as G. R. Elliott, Harry Hayden Clarke, and Harry Hartwick, and in the nonacademic world in such writers as Seward Collins and Dorothea Brande, whose identification with authoritarian religion and with Fascist politics reveals the intellectual connections logical to Humanism.

At present, Yvor Winters (*q.v.*) is the most legitimate descendant of the Babbitt-More dynasty. But he is too subtle an analyst to accept without qualification the code from the Cantabrigian Sinai. Fundamentally, however, as his *Primitivism and Decadence* (1937) shows, he is a defender of the true faith of classicism against the eccentricities of the metaphysicals and the idiosyncracies of the excessively personalized experimenters. Now that Eliot has rejected the Babbitt creed on the grounds of the shocking inadequacy of its theology, and now that More's efforts to reconcile Platonic aesthetics and Anglican theology have ceased, Winters is almost alone in his devotion to the quest for aesthetic finalities.

Contemporary romantic criticism of the aesthetic variety, in most instances, takes the form of impressionism, the enfeebled descendant of the great romantic tradition. Primarily concerned, like the classicist, with the aesthetic aspect of the work of art, the impressionist finds the standard of judgment within himself—in the region of his own refined taste or among his neural sensations. "To have sensations in the presence of a work of art and to express them, that is the function of Criticism for the impressionistic critic"—such is Spingarn's statement of the creed. At its worst, impressionistic criticism becomes, as Professor Lewis E. Gates wrote in the *Atlantic Monthly* for July, 1900, "the record of a momentary shudder across a single set of possibly degenerate nerves." At its best, he said, the impressionistic critic may "realize the manifold charm the work of art gathers into itself from all sources . . . and . . . interpret this *charm* imaginatively to the men of his own day and generation." Another version of this theory appears in one of H. L. Mencken's (*q.v.*) statements of his critical creed. The critic "is trying to arrest and challenge a sufficient body of readers, to impress them with the charm and novelty of his ideas, to provoke in them an agreeable (or shocked) awareness of him."

Since impressionistic criticism is the easiest as well as the most irresponsible type of criticism, it is the kind we may detect most often in the critical remarks embedded in most book reviews; it is the type practiced by the layman who admits that he knows nothing about art but knows what he likes. Very little distinguished impressionistic criticism has been produced in America—none that will compare favorably with that of such Continental impressionists as Anatole France, Walter Pater, and Arthur Symons—and very few contemporary American critics since Mencken would willingly admit their adherence to the impressionists' creed.

Of early practitioners of impressionistic criticism, James Huneker (1860–1921) was the most notable. Equipped with a fairly sensitive apparatus of response, and widely but superficially informed of current European aesthetic phenomena, Huneker became a critical press agent for new and striking figures and movements here and abroad. His weaknesses as a critic were the fundamentally emotional and uncritical nature of his facile ecstasies and enthusiasms, the journalistic superficiality of his information, and his windy bombastic style. Rhetoric at its worst inflates Huneker's turgid pages. But such empurpled volumes as *Melomaniacs* (1902) and *Promenades of an Impressionist* (1910) played no small part in widening the horizon of American culture, in bringing it into the fresh current of European art, and in popularizing an enthusiasm for some of its more garish figures. By the end of the second decade of the century, however, Huneker's point of view and his uncritical exuberance had already begun to seem anachronistic.

In so far as writing about the drama is criticism and not merely publicity, reviewing, or mere vacuity, it usually betrays its alliance with critical impressionism. George Jean Nathan (*q.v.*)—perhaps the most widely-known critic of the current drama since the death of Brander Matthews—is fundamentally impressionistic in his critical procedure. His concern is so steadily with such eminently nonaesthetic intentions as outraging the bourgeoisie, exhibiting his knowledge of the European commercial theater, and snubbing all his reviewing colleagues, that the amount of pure critical activity in Nathan's writing is astonishingly slight. But, on those occasions when he devotes himself to criticism rather than vituperation, his approach to the drama is aesthetic rather than sociological or historical, and the standard by which he measures it is the highly individual and arbitrary one of his own taste, abetted by his persuasion that any American drama (except Eugene O'Neill's) is bound to be a pallid imitation of a third-rate European product, and that only drama that is critical of American civilization is worth considering. The most distressing aspect of his critical technique is his atrocious style, modeled apparently on Huneker's exuberance but considerably distended by journalese.

Ezra Pound (*q.v.*) illustrates the unusual combination of the romantically impressionistic critic and the political conservative. Pound is a highly literate George Jean Nathan. He shares Nathan's arrogance towards other critics; he is as persuaded as Nathan of the fundamental stupidity and barrenness of American culture. Like Nathan and Huneker, not to mention Prometheus, he regards it as his mission to bring the light of his Europeanized culture to his benighted fellow countrymen. The most grossly egocentric of contemporary American critics, Pound can be counted on to put any literary personage or movement in its place. Pugnacious, dogmatic, vituperative, he is the most lively and irritating of literary commentators. His criticism has followed fairly closely the line of his multifarious literary and poetic enthusiasms. His chief service, aside from that of his Huneker-like mission of keeping America informed of his adventures among European masterpieces, is as a counter-irritant to provincialism and to cultural and intellectual complacency. His colossal self-assurance and his conviction of his eternal rightness remain unshaken.

A more decorous adherent to critical impressionism is Louis Untermeyer (*q.v.*). Untermeyer's forte is the making of anthologies of contemporary poetry. This task demands catholicity of taste and a capacity for discrimination between the immediately impressive and the permanently significant, qualities that, on the whole, Untermeyer is well endowed with. His sensitivity to poetic styles has been shown, not only in his adroit parodies of well-known classical and contemporary poets, but also in his brief characterizations of those poets and poetasters who appear and disappear from his recurrent anthologies. In this chameleon-like responsiveness lie Untermeyer's critical service and also his danger. The necessity to be responsive to every variety of serious contemporary poetic endeavor has left him little or no opportunity to define his own critical principles or to adhere to them in his haste to mount every new poetic band wagon.

Pure aesthetic criticism of the realistic or naturalistic type has not had a systematic development in America. The strong infusion of politico-ethical feeling and thinking in American criticism has prevented any critic's very abiding allegiance to the impersonal, scientific, and objective ideal of realistic or naturalistic criticism. The purpose of William Dean Howells' *Criticism and Fiction* (1891) was the introduction of realistic standards into American criticism, but Howells' view of what American life and morals really were was so roseate, his judgments on the improprieties of Continental naturalism were so severe, that he was a halfhearted standard-bearer of the new realism in criticism. The distinguished naturalistic practice of a number of American novelists and playwrights has not stimulated the development of a correspondingly pure naturalistic criticism. Instead, naturalistic aesthetic standards have been borne by critics as conservative politically as H. L. Mencken or as radical as Granville Hicks.

By far the commonest approach to criticism in America is the one that may be designated as sociological. The strong infusion of Puritanism in the American spirit has encouraged the ethical rather than the aesthetic approach to literature, the measurement of literature in terms of its ethical soundness rather than in terms of its aesthetic distinction. Hence have arisen, also, those sporadic efforts of individuals or organizations—self-constituted guardians of public morals—to discourage or suppress works of arts judged subversive of public decency or disturbing to those survivals of Victorian prudishness that have managed to live through the ethical laxity of the war and post-war periods. Though the views of the sociological critics are sharply antagonistic, and though this group is the most contentious and mutually abusive, there is a common factor in their attitudes—the conviction that literature is to be judged in terms of the fidelity of its representation of life. But the group embraces both realists and idealists, and the common purpose of their criticism is to interpret and estimate specific works as more or less imperfect representations, not merely of what the critic believes life and literature in America are, but what they should be. The primary concern, then, is not with literature as art but with literature as mirrored experience. For critics of this variety, therefore, the most significant element is the particular conception each holds of the actuality or the ideality of American life. It is on the basis of these extremely varied conceptions that critics of this type must be distinguished and evaluated.

Of those critics whose aesthetic sympathies were classical and whose ethical convictions were profoundly conservative, the most typical perhaps was Stuart P. Sherman. Of American life, Sherman held a singularly rigid view; Americanism, to him, meant the illusory Puritan tradition, almost unmodified by an awareness of the contemporary degradation of that noble dogma. At least, in the academic phase of his career, he refused to acknowledge as American the "vulgar and selfish and good-humored and sensual and impudent" life of these times, and to him literature that represented that life with fidelity was literature not merely inferior but ethically dangerous. His infatuation with a static conception of Puritanism and his intellectual blind spots led him to insist that literature in America should express its "preponderant moral idealism," even when that idealism had been seriously conditioned by numerous materialistic elements. Sherman's critical propaganda for fidelity to his ideal of American life was strengthened by his wide scholarly acquaintance with the Anglo-Saxon literary past and by his adroit and good-tempered controversial tactics. But the effectiveness of his criticism was seriously impaired by the dry rot at the heart of his life-faith, the narrowly moralistic bias of his judgment. The inadequacy of such a critical position was illustrated again and again in his attempt in *On Contemporary Literature* (1917) to apply his critical principles to modern works to which they were almost completely inapplicable. But under the influence of the freer air of the New York literary coteries, Sherman's ethical and critical judgments showed so many signs of growing more liberal that his recusancy gave his mentor, Paul Elmer More, occasion for grave alarm. Henry Seidel Canby (*q.v.*) is another illustration of the academician turned critic. In so far as his critical practice suggests any definite standard, he would seem to belong to the genteel wing of the conservative sociological group. No ardent propagandist for his critical faith, he made the *Saturday Review of Literature*, during his editorship (1924–36), an organ for criticism which, vague as to principles and tepid as to judgments, usually supported the genteel and academic.

The controversial and stylistic manners of H. L. Mencken (*q.v.*) concealed for a considerable period the temperamental conservatism of that doughty journalist, and his ire would have been stirred by the suggestion that he and Sherman belonged, logically, in the camp of the conservative critics of American life. Mencken's conservatism, to be sure, has an utterly different source than Sherman's. His criticism of the bourgeois way of life and of the enfeebled gentility of academic criticism springs from his adherence to an essentially aristocratic ideal, an ideal, moreover, European rather than American in its character. Mencken's mission, then, was to introduce into American life and literature something of the sophisticated anti-Puritanical Epicureanism of the European aristocracy. Thence sprang his distaste for democracy and his unending warfare against the gentility of the bourgeois ideal and the barbarity of America's social frontiers. He paraded his lively antipathy for democracy, although a democratic order gave him a convenient opportunity to contemplate his own superiority to it. His attitude toward women was also European rather than American; it combined a distaste for essentially feminine characteristics and an admiration for the American woman's ingenuity in getting what she wants from a man-made world. His special object of scorn was the American *booboisie*—its elementary notions of comfort and culture, its standardized language and manners, and its delight in sustaining its ego by joining supposedly exclusive organizations distinguished by esoteric titles and costumes. His distaste for the most characteristic features of American life resulted in his admiring and encouraging those literary works that represent American life as mean or unlovely, or works that expose satirically those aspects of life in America especially distressing to him.

During Mencken's editorship of the *American Mercury*, his influence on younger readers was tremendous. That the influence was not an unmixed good is apparent to any unprejudiced observer. The admirable part of his influence was his sponsoring such important writers as Sinclair Lewis (*q.v.*), Sherwood Anderson (*q.v.*), Willa Cather (*q.v.*), Ruth Suckow (*q.v.*), and Theodore Dreiser (*q.v.*) (whose early fame was due largely to Mencken's steadfast and courageous critical publicity). On this side of the account also belongs his editorial exploitation of unfamiliar but significant aspects of American life, folkways as they expressed themselves in white or Negro folk song, and the picturesque jargons and experiences of tramps, circus-followers, and petty criminals. On the other side of the Mencken ledger are his bumptious and raucous style and his preoccupation with the seamy side of American life. His drum-thumping stylistic effects proved all too easy of imitation. What was more serious was that his turning up for inspection the unlovely sides of American life encouraged younger writers and readers in the belief that decency, graciousness, and idealism were no longer existent in life or desirable in letters. The writers of hard-boiled fiction are among Mencken's less legitimate progeny. But before the *American Mercury* passed from his hands in 1930, Mencken's criticism of bourgeois habits and ways of thought had become a national commonplace; his essential conservatism was widening the gap between himself and the liberal developments of the post-war period. During the depression, his political and economic conservatism grew steadily in opposition to the radical currents of the period, and, at present, his influence is negligible. Mencken's services as a social critic ended almost a decade ago. Except in Tory journals, Mencken is almost a forgotten man.

Among younger conservatives, Bernard DeVoto (*q.v.*), who edited the *Saturday Review of Literature* from 1936 to 1938, has contributed more heat than light to critical controversy. DeVoto is one of the most pugnacious of critical commentators, but he and his readers both suffer from the fact that he is not at all clear just what he is fighting for or against. Like Mencken, he is more easily defined in terms of his antipathies than his sympathies. He is intermittently hostile to psychoanalytical criticism and to radical criticism; at the same time, he is too vigorous to be content with the conscientious tepidity of most academic criticism. He is impatient with the heavy-handed minutiae of literary-historical scholarship. The exasperations and exacerbations that betray his fundamental confusion savor of the frustrations of the creative artist *manqué*. DeVoto's most valuable contribution to criticism arises from his conviction that American literature must be seen in relation to its total rural-urban, eastern-western environment, and not merely as a function of un-American New York literary coteries. But he frequently writes as though he were the only critic who had ever journeyed imaginatively west of the Hudson River, an arrogant assumption belied by the strong regional movements that have absorbed his interests recently.

In contradistinction to the conservative conception of life, the liberal conception is dynamic rather than static. It is inclined to stress the deficiencies and weaknesses of the current economic and ethical order, and to look forward with enthusiasm to a world made better by numerous and diverse reforms. American liberalism stems directly from the deep springs of religious and social idealism from which America's finest characters have drawn their moral strength. Though at times that spirit has been overshadowed by materialism, economic blindness, or callousness, it is, if not a dominant, a constantly operative principle in American society. Liberalism is the attitude of the socially conscious, the politically nonconformist, the ethically unconventional. It may involve allegiance to a specific program of social and economic reform or to a vaguely conceived free and creative existence beyond the stifling pressures of bourgeois respectability. The critic of this type is prone to applaud literature that celebrates unconventional ways of living and thinking, literature that furnishes channels for his idealism, or, perhaps, for his own unrestrained daydreaming of life in a less inhibited society. The major temptation of the liberal critic is to discover excellence in only those works that express the sociological ideas and attitudes dearest to him. His major service lies in stressing the inextricable connection between life and literature and in pointing out influences and values not apparent to the blind spots of conservatism.

As there are conservatives as various as Sherman and Mencken, so there are many degrees and varieties of liberals. Ludwig Lewisohn (*q.v.*), for example, found his critical mission in introducing a Europeanized variety of liberalism into American criticism and in evaluating American literature from the point of view of a man never fettered by Puritanism and uninhibited by bourgeois morality. His miscellaneous criticism in the *Nation* was only preliminary to the systematic application of his standards to classical and modern American literature in *Expression in America* (1932). This book is an eloquent plea for a liberalism fed from Continental rather than American sources; it is bitterly hostile to the root element in American culture, the spirit, pure or perverted, of Puritanism. Lewisohn's ideal is that of the good European, and though he falls far short of that ideal in his intolerance and his arrogance, his book furnishes a valuable European view of American letters. As it is, Lewisohn suffers constantly as a critic from his utter failure to comprehend, much less sympathize with, the strongest strain in our culture, and, even more seriously, from his naïve late-nineteenth-century notion as to what constitutes a creative life emancipated from conventional American social and sexual mores.

Probably the most generally satisfactory and systematic attempt to interpret American literature in liberal terms was that of Vernon L. Parrington (1871–1929) in his *Main Currents in American Thought* (1927–30). This series of studies is written in terms of a liberalism more indigenous, genial, and palatable than Lewisohn's. Parrington wrote out of an impassioned faith in the liberal-humanitarian doctrine which, since the American Revolution, has been in his view one of the major contending forces in American culture. The thesis of this major work is that "at the beginning of our national existence two rival philosophies contended for supremacy in America: the humanitarian philosophy of the French Enlightenment, based on the conception of human perfectibility and postulating as its objective an equalitarian democracy in which the political state should function as the servant of the common well-being; and the English philosophy of *laissez faire*, based on the universality of the acquisitive instinct and postulating a social order answering to the need of an abstract 'economic man' in which the state should function in the interests of trade." Parrington himself would have admitted that this thesis, if rigidly applied, would result in an oversimplification of our cultural history; his studies indeed were devoted to working out the complications and qualifications inherent in this thesis. But, despite the fact that Parrington did not live to carry the great work to completion, his book remains the most stirring and illuminating re-interpretation of our literary culture that our time has produced.

Critics of liberal tendencies gravitated toward the new journals of opinion which came into existence at about the time of the outbreak of the World War. The first of these, the *New Republic*, established in 1914, maintained a consistently liberal position in the face of considerable abuse from right-wing and left-wing critics.[1] Of *New Republic* critics of distinction, Robert Morss Lovett is perhaps the oldest in years of devoted service. In his almost weekly critiques of nineteenth- and twentieth-century social literature in its columns, Lovett has been able to draw on the rich stores of his long experience in teaching the liberal thought of the nineteenth century and on his close contacts with liberal movements of the pre-war and post-war periods. These generous-handed contributions constitute a rich and humane survey of modern literature from an indomitably liberal point of view. Sustained by an unshaken faith in that point of view, Lovett was able to keep his head in the whirling tempests of the war period and through the interminable controversies between liberals and radicals in the post-war period. But Lov-

[1] Under the editorship of Oswald Garrison Villard, the *Nation* was reconstructed in 1918 and assumed a political position somewhat more extreme than that of the *New Republic*. But with few exceptions, the *Nation's* critics did not exhibit any particular political bias, and some of them were as innocuous as the group that gathered under the standard of the *Saturday Review of Literature* or the New York *Times Book Review*. For a brief space, the *Freeman* offered a refuge for critics of no special political bias. To controvert the disturbing "un-Americanism" of such liberal-radical magazines as the *New Republic* and the *Nation*, the *Review* was founded in 1919, but only a few intellectuals of the old guard could be depended on to support the cause of conservatism, and, after passing through various editorial hands, the *Review* merged with the *Independent* in 1920, and it in turn disappeared into the maw of the *Outlook* in 1928. Frequent attempts have likewise been made to build up a radical clientele among readers and writers. The *Masses*, edited by Max Eastman (*q.v.*), managed to survive from 1911 to 1917. The spirit of the *Masses* was revived in the *Liberator* (1918), but its hostility to American participation in the war won it the displeasure of the authorities, and it was suppressed. A third attempt at a proletarian journal took the form of the *New Masses*, which was founded in 1926, and which gained numerous adherents when a wave of radicalism swept over the intelligentsia during the depression.

ett has not been alone in fighting the unending battle of liberalism against insidious forces within and without the movement.

Of Lovett's younger colleagues on the *New Republic*, Randolph Bourne (1886–1919) was emerging at the time of his early death as a brilliantly ironical commentator on political and literary movements. He had a pen as sharp and a mind as cutting as those of any of the liberal critics who survived him into the post-war and depression periods. Van Wyck Brooks (*q.v.*), in the early stage of his career, was a spiritual worker with Randolph Bourne in his attempt to bring a critical spirit to bear upon American culture and its relationship to literature. With a great deal of the manner, and more of the tone, of that great critic of nineteenth-century British culture, Matthew Arnold, Brooks, in his early volumes, *The Wine of the Puritans* (1908), *America's Coming-of-Age* (1915), and *Letters and Leadership* (1918), submitted American culture to an analysis, denounced its commercialism and its Philistinism, and decried its discouragement and crippling of both the creative and the critical spirits. Like his master, Arnold, Brooks called for the creation of a genuine social criticism which should supply an atmosphere conducive to great creation. His share in bringing America to an unaccustomed self-scrutiny and self-consciousness was one of the greatest importance.[1]

The radical critic approaches literature with an apparatus of more or less sharply defined economic and political doctrines, among which literary and critical values must find their place. The earlier radical critics found their political faith in socialism; during the depression, however, socialism yielded in attractiveness to a communism more or less completely in conformity with simon-pure Marxian doctrine. The Marxian doctrine furnished radical critics a sharper weapon than those used by Bourne and Brooks in their attack on bourgeois civilization in America. The liberal's attack had been made on spiritual, anti-commercial, anti-materialistic grounds. The Marxian attack was directed from a naturalistic position, a position which involved the stressing of the commercial and materialistic influences on our culture and the products of that culture, and which looked towards an equalization of creature comforts and opportunities rather than towards the spiritual freedom of the individual artist. The liberal cult of the individual, indeed, was viewed by the Marxians with great suspicion, for they felt that only by the submergence of the artist's personality in proletarian life and thought could vital art be produced for a classless society.

The Marxian critic faced in the acutest form the dilemma of the relative importance of the aesthetic and the social values in a work of art. His reading of Marx had developed in him an awareness of the conditioning of

[1] Brooks's role has not been limited to that of an American Matthew Arnold. His work as an historical critic is considered later in this chapter; his biographical activity, in the chapter on Biography.

artists by the economic society in which they lived and produced. As critic, then, in his historical and interpretative roles, he was furnished with a new tool for the analysis of the genesis and development of works of art. But in his evaluative role, the Marxian critic must find some means of resolving the contradiction between the aesthetic values of a bourgeois work of art and its reprehensible economic implications, and of reconciling the aesthetic values of proletarian art with the soundness or unsoundness of its economic dogma and doctrine.

Though radical sociological criticism has played an especially conspicuous part in both theoretical discussion and practical criticism since the onset of the depression, there had been important pioneers of this particular point of view before the depression. To the post-war Marxians, of course, such a figure as Upton Sinclair (*q.v.*) seemed a naïve and primitive prophet of their own economic and class-conscious sophistication. It was Sinclair who almost singlehanded had familiarized American readers with the radical view in criticism. To Sinclair, as to the cruder Marxian critics, the best writing was naturally the literature of violent social protest, with little or no consideration of its literary merit. If the devil in Irving Babbitt's universe was Romanticism, the devil in Sinclair's universe was Capitalism. In both cases, the identification became an obsession that went far to destroy the validity of these critics' specific judgments. Sinclair believes, as *Mammonart* (1925) showed, that capitalism exerts its influence with incredible subtlety and adroitness, and that it ultimately subjugates most writers in America, however free they may think themselves to be. There is no doubt that the enormous prices that are the rewards for giving the editor and the public what they want have influenced many authors' careers and outputs.[1] But Sinclair's interpretation of the struggle between the capitalistic devil and the angelic artist is as unsound as it is melodramatic; his monster is too insidious and resourceful. He has swathed Sinclair in veils of illusion, until the critic is no longer sure that he has seen what he thinks he has seen.

The simplification to which Sinclair submitted radical theory and practice gave way to a slightly greater sophistication in the theories of V. F. Calverton. In *The Newer Spirit* (1925) and *The Liberation of American Literature* (1932), Calverton expounded his version of radical criticism. He maintained not only that literature represents life but that it is a function of the social order, and can be understood only as a product of economic forces. Like every theorist, Calverton regarded himself as a critical Messiah. Despite an infusion of tepid Marxianism, his theory is actually little more than a restatement of Hippolyte Taine's theory of

[1] A new threat to creative independence appears in the fantastic salaries paid by Hollywood to any writer who makes a favorable impression by work in one or another creative literary form. The most serious effect of commercialism on literature during the last decade has been the buying up of authors by Hollywood and the consequent cessation of their serious creative activities.

the influences on literature of *race*, *milieu*, and *temps*. It remained for younger and more completely indoctrinated critics to present to American readers the complete Marxian doctrine and to illustrate its application to literature and criticism.

Of the early stages of radical criticism in America, Max Eastman (*q.v.*) is another survivor. He was a valiant expositor of the radical point of view in the *Masses* and the *Liberator* during the war. With the passage of years, his radicalism persisted, but, while it did not interrupt his allegiance to what he regards as the pure Lenin-Trotsky variety of communism, it brought his sharp and complete rejection of the theory and practice of the regime of Stalin. His revulsion against its aesthetic regimentation was voiced most clearly in *Artists in Uniform* (1934). As a literary critic, however, Eastman has never taken his radicalism too seriously. For, though he has played a very lively part in factional controversies among the Communists, his own criticism is as incongruously conservative as his poetry. His not too intelligent attack on the "cult of unintelligibility" might have been made by any genteel academic critic aghast at the vagaries of poetic experimenters.

The purest Marxian criticism comes from the pen of Granville Hicks (*q.v.*). Although by no means naïve, Hicks has accepted the Marxian critical doctrine with comparatively few reservations, and, in his practice, has applied that doctrine with commendable consistency. Thus, in *The Great Tradition* (1933), Hicks seeks out in nineteenth-century American literature those writers who showed some awareness of the economic implications of their fiction, then passes current authors through the barrage of his dogmas, and concludes with a clarion call for the creation of a proletarian literature in America. The rigidity of Hicks's doctrines and the consistent application of them have not, however, gone unchallenged, even in radical circles. James T. Farrell (*q.v.*), in *A Note on Literary Criticism* (1936), pointed out the absurdities of too narrow and merely sociological an application of Marxian doctrines, and stated convincingly the case for moderation in the emphasis on economic values. Edmund Wilson (*q.v.*) as well, in his essay "Marxianism and Literature" in *The Triple Thinkers* (1938), urged the desirability of considering both aesthetic and social values in the critical process. The pioneering days for Marxian critics are plainly ended. What we may expect from them in the future is a more subtle and sophisticated application of radical doctrines in the interpretation of literature.

The problems of the relationship between the aesthetic and the sociological approaches to literature, though difficult, are by no means insoluble. Serious attempts to reconcile these approaches have been made by three critics whose careers have been closely associated with the *New Republic*—Kenneth Burke (*q.v.*), Malcolm Cowley (*q.v.*), and Edmund Wilson (*q.v.*). These three contemporaries have been swayed and sometimes bent by the winds of radical doctrine that have swept the American intelligentsia since the Russian Revolution. But the allurements of radicalism have been merely intermittent; fundamentally, they are liberal in spirit. They have not fallen a prey to the ogre of Marxian criticism; they maintain with varying degrees of success a balance between the aesthetic and the social approaches to contemporary literature.

Of the three, Kenneth Burke has been the one most concerned with the theory of criticism. His earlier approach to aesthetic problems was psychological. His objective was the analysis of the conditions governing the creation of works of art and the possible responses to them. Later political interests have served only to broaden the range of his investigations of the complex relations between literature and life. Malcolm Cowley was the most deeply influenced by the expatriate movement of the twenties. Like Brooks, he was concerned with pointing out the inadequacies and provincialities of American culture and with urging a less biased, more international attitude toward American letters. The writings of Edmund Wilson constitute perhaps the most impressive body of criticism to come from any American critic since Paul Elmer More. Wilson has been especially successful in keeping his critical head in the face of the allurements of Communist and Marxian dogma. The approach to literature most congenial to him is subtle and liberally aesthetic, but no one so sensitive as Wilson to the sociological atmosphere of the time could ignore the significance of social values in literature. A stylist of distinction, a technical analyst of great resourcefulness, Wilson is at his best in correcting the overemphasis on either the aesthetic or the social values which critics are prone to emphasize. *Axel's Castle* (1931) and *The Triple Thinkers* (1938) challenge comparison successfully with any other critical productions of the thirties.

Probably no period in the history of American criticism has been richer in theory and practice than that of the decade since the war. One need look no further than Morton Dauwen Zabel's anthology of *Literary Opinion in America* (1937) for evidence of the richness of our criticism on both the theoretical and the practical sides. Though the Humanistic controversy amounted to little more than the flinging about of dead cats, it had its value in marking the cleavage between academic and liberal-radical criticism, and the lively outburst of radical criticism during the depression did a great work of revitalization. What American criticism needs is the development of a serious and closely studied aesthetic criticism, uninhibited by the repressions of conservatism and unbiased by radical preoccupations. Ethically and politically, such aesthetic criticism seems more likely to be allied with the liberal tradition than with conservatism or radicalism. Aesthetically, it will preserve the sensitivity of impressionism, while it insists on a closer scrutiny and analysis of works of art, a sharper definition in its terminology, and a wider frame of reference in its final valuations. That such criticism is being written in America is made obvious by such volumes as Edmund Wilson's (*q.v.*) *Axel's Castle* (1931), Richard P. Blackmur's *The Double Agent* (1935), Allen Tate's (*q.v.*) *Reactionary Essays* (1936), and John Crowe Ransom's (*q.v.*) *The World's Body* (1938).

To contemporary historical criticism of American literature in general, no more than passing consideration can be given here, although within the last decade the story of American literature has been completely rewritten by a number of distinguished academic historians. The appearance during the last decade of a half-dozen full-length histories of our literature indicates the historians' conviction, not merely that our literature deserves careful scholarly treatment, but that the time has arrived to view the whole process of our literary development with a fresh eye. A number of forces have contributed to furnish a new perspective on our literature. In the first place the American national spirit has matured sufficiently to eliminate that sense of subservience to English literature which produced in so many nineteenth-century historians that feeling of mingled humility and arrogance which originates in an irrational sense of inferiority. Furthermore, the attempt to depict the whole pageant of our literary progress in *The Cambridge History of American Literature* (1917–21) threw a light upon many limitations in our knowledge and inadequacies in our historical equipment. Finally, a number of energizing ideas in other than literary fields suggested the reconsideration of our literary history from a number of new angles. One of the most potent of these ideas was that developed by James Harvey Robinson in *The New History* (1912), a call for the writing of history, not merely on political or military lines, but in terms of broad cultural elements—the arts and sciences, and intellectual life generally. The interest aroused by Robinson's theory and practice encouraged the discontinuance of the study of literature in an aesthetic vacuum, and the relation of it to the culture out of which it grew. A by-product of this interest in the cultural background of American literature was the stimulus to the study of folk literature such as the Paul Bunyan stories and the tall tales generally, and of the folk song to which the American Negro had made brilliant contributions. The study of our cultural background also brought to light, as nineteenth-century studies had not done, the influence of regional backgrounds and cultures on literature. Altogether too many nineteenth-century histories of American literature had been written in terms of New England and New York, with some grudging attention to middle western and western phenomena like Mark Twain and Bret Harte, and with a certain condescension to southern writers. The new American literary histories were to be at once regional and national rather than narrowly provincial. Another idea which was to stimulate the rewriting of American literary history was that brilliant intellectual dichotomy which was the heart of Parrington's *Main Currents in American Thought* (1927–30). Parrington's stirring book directed the attention of students to the study of the history of ideas in literature, their definition, influence, and operation. Few were ready to follow the difficult road to the writing of a history of ideas in American literature, but the book was an energizing influence. Finally, the attempt of V. F. Calverton to make an economic interpretation of American literary phenomena sensitized the consciousness of literary historians to the importance of the economic foundations of our literature. An indication of this ferment of ideas is the appearance of *The Reinterpretation of American Literature* (1928), a series of essays edited by Norman Foerster (*q.v.*), laying down a program for the rewriting of the history of our letters.

This ferment of ideas and this call to a re-interpretation of American literature have brought numerous and important results. To point out the number and the solidity of recent literary histories, and to indicate the intellectual position from which they are written, is all that is possible in this place. One of the earliest of the new literary histories was Ernest E. Leisy's *American Literature, an Interpretative Survey* (1929), a book which shows some of the influences which we have just outlined. This work was followed in 1931 by Russell Blankenship's *American Literature as an Expression of National Mind*, an attempt to apply systematically the method sketched in Parrington's unfinished work. The next year brought Grant C. Knight's *American Literature and Culture*, which shows the impress of James Harvey Robinson's influence, and also Ludwig Lewisohn's (*q.v.*) *Expression in America*, which is less a literary history perhaps than a re-interpretation of men and movements in the past and present in terms of its author's Continental liberalism and his temperamental hostility to Puritanism. But these were not the final attempts to achieve a satisfactory history of American letters. Percy Holmes Boynton drew on the experiences of a long life devoted to teaching and studying our literature, in his *Literature and American Life* (1936), a title which suggests a cohesion not always evident in the book itself. The book is rather a series of gracefully turned and shrewdly critical essays on men and movements than an organic history of our literature. Walter F. Taylor's *A History of American Letters* (1936) is more valuable for the comprehensive bibliographies which Harry Hartwick contributed to it than for any novelty of judgment or ingenuity of interpretation.[1]

Of histories of contemporary American literature, the number is small and the quality is undistinguished. One of the earlier attempts to write the general history of contemporary literature was Carl and Mark Van

[1] The most ambitious plan for rewriting the history of American literature is that of Van Wyck Brooks. His subtly evocative *Flowering of New England* (1936) is the first of a series of five volumes which will re-create in detail our literary-cultural past.

Doren's *American and British Literature since 1890* (1925). Though this pioneer work is admirable for its enterprise and its scope, its aim was overambitious. It was obviously impossible to deal adequately with two great contemporary literatures in one slight volume, and even though the authors have limited their comments to the major imaginative forms—novel, drama, and poetry—the result was bound to be superficial and, at this distance, merely suggestive. The most comprehensive history of contemporary American literature that has as yet appeared is Fred L. Pattee's *The New American Literature 1890–1930* (1930). While Pattee's taste was too conservative to permit him to deal sympathetically with many of the striking literary phenomena of the period, and while his scholarly technique leaves something to be desired, the book is noteworthy for its scope, its inclusiveness, and its success in carrying through a very difficult project. No other work of this magnitude has appeared, although the thirties were rapidly increasing our perspective on the literature of pre-war America, and the depression was forcing many sharp revaluations of writers who made their reputations before the genteel tradition collapsed. But Granville Hicks's (*q.v.*) *The Great Tradition* (1933) was written on too narrow and argumentative an intellectual ground to serve as an unbiased and really judicial account of recent literary events, and Vernon Loggins' *I Hear America* (1937) suffers from its exclusions of such important forms as biography, criticism, and the essay, and from an arbitrary organization which brings the most incongruous writers together in the Procrustean bed of his criticism.

A number of foreign literary critics have attempted to furnish their readers a bird's-eye view of contemporary American literature. Of these, perhaps the best known in America is Régis Michaud, the author of *Panorama de la Littérature Américaine* (1926). He interprets the term *contemporary* widely, since he begins by considering the major figures in nineteenth-century American literature. He is most successful in dealing with the contemporary novel, for he discusses only the leading figures in the poetic revival, and is inadequately informed concerning the drama. He also includes a suggestive sketch of the literary activities of the expatriates in Paris. A Danish critic, Frederik Schyberg, in his *Moderne Amerikansk Litteratur* (1930), has produced serviceable and well-informed surveys of the pre-war and post-war novelists, dramatists, and poets. A. C. Ward's *American Literature, 1880–1930* (1932) covers for English readers the ground sketched out by Michaud. Ward writes for a popular British audience, and his tone is not severely critical. But he has read widely if not very discriminatingly, and the book serves well as an elementary guide to the more conspicuous literary phenomena. A Czech writer, Ottakar Vočadlo, has treated with unusual insight the major figures in American literature from Emily Dickinson and Lizette Woodworth Reese to Ernest Hemingway and John Dos Passos. His sympathy with the more experimental novelists and poets is a striking feature of his *Současna literatura Spojených Států.*

The more important literary forms have received more satisfactory historical-critical treatment than our contemporary literature as a whole. Although the problem of selection in both the novel and the drama is very acute, writers have been assisted by the fact that not more than a dozen important novelists and dramatists have towered above the throng, and they have therefore found it easy to turn out series of essays on leading novelists or dramatists instead of writing a comprehensive history of the novel or the drama to include even the fifth-rate figures. Thus, Carl Van Doren's (*q.v.*) *Contemporary American Novelists, 1900–1920* (1922) is a series of fairly discriminating essays but not a history of the contemporary novel, and Helen and Wilson Follett's *Some Modern Novelists* (1918) belongs to the same category of critical works. Régis Michaud's *The American Novel Today* (1927) attempts to systematize the complex phenomena produced by the novel, and has the added advantage of giving an alien though sympathetic estimation of major and minor novelists. Joseph Warren Beach's *The Twentieth Century Novel* (1932) is perhaps the most intellectually distinguished study that has been made of modern American fiction. But Professor Beach's preoccupations are aesthetic rather than historical, and his consideration of American novelists is only incidental to his analysis of contemporary novelistic techniques. The most ambitious surveys of contemporary American fiction are Harry Hartwick's *The Foreground of American Fiction* (1934) and Harlan Hatcher's *Creating the Modern American Novel* (1935). Hartwick's book casts a wider net than any of the earlier volumes, but the book suffers from the author's inability to assimilate the masses of material he has collected and from his condescension to stylistic wisecracks. Harlan Hatcher's book is more serious in tone, but is overambitious and immature in its pronouncements. The most elaborate history of American fiction is Arthur H. Quinn's *American Fiction, an Historical and Critical Survey* (1936). No one has had the courage to undertake a history of American fiction on such a scale as this, and the book will probably stand for a long time as the most satisfactory available presentation of the history of the novel and short story. But it ends its consideration of contemporary fiction abruptly with 1920, and it is much stronger as history than as criticism. Quinn can be trusted in his estimates of the earlier novelists, but when he approaches the contemporary period the dead hand of the genteel tradition rests heavily upon him, he overestimates the leading lady-novelists of the pre-war period, and shows himself completely unsuited to deal critically with the naturalistic and subjectivistic developments in post-war fiction. Since Blanche Colton Williams' *Our Short-Story Writers* (1920) is a useful if not too discriminating series of essays on writers conspicuous at the moment, and since Edward J. O'Brien's

The Advance of the American Short Story (1931) is distended with this writer's characteristic turgidities and pseudo-profundities, the best available account of the American short story is Fred L. Pattee's *The Development of the American Short Story* (1923). It is to be regretted that Pattee has not seen fit to bring this excellent book up-to-date.

The eternal glamour of the playhouse seems to have an unfortunate effect on most historical criticism of the contemporary drama, for there is more inflated and empty writing about the drama than about any other contemporary literary form. One difficulty facing the historian of the drama is the necessity of deciding whether he will concern himself with the literary drama or the popular drama, with the history of the theater or the history of the drama apart from the theater. Since contemporary drama of significance has been produced by not more than a dozen playwrights, there has been a tendency to exalt these playwrights beyond their deserts or to associate with them writers with little or no claim on our literary-critical attention.

On the whole, the contemporary American theater has fared better than the contemporary American drama at the hands of historians. Among many useful books on the contemporary theater, one may distinguish Hiram K. Moderwell's *The Theater of Today* (1914), Arthur Hornblow's *A History of the Theater in America from Its Beginnings to the Present Time* (1919), Kenneth Macgowan's *The Theater of Tomorrow* (1921), Kenneth Macgowan's *Footlights across America* (1929), a well-documented account of the noncommercial theater, Walter Pritchard Eaton's *The Theatre Guild, the First Ten Years* (1929), Helen Deutsch and Stella Hanan's *The Provincetown* (1931), and Willson Whitman's *Bread and Circuses* (1937), a study of the Federal Theatre Project.

Among histories of the contemporary American drama, a pioneering work of polemical rather than of historical interest is Thomas H. Dickinson's *The Case of American Drama* (1915). Montrose J. Moses' *The American Dramatist* (1925), Thomas H. Dickinson's *Playwrights of the New American Theater* (1925), Burns Mantle's *American Playwrights of Today* (1929) and his later *Contemporary American Playwrights* (1938), are collections of critical essays on important and unimportant playwrights rather than systematic histories of the drama. In the case of the drama, as in the case of the novel, the most satisfactory history is Arthur H. Quinn's *A History of the American Drama from the Civil War to the Present Day*, of which a revised and expanded edition appeared in 1937. Quinn has been a lifelong lover and student of the drama and an indefatigable theater-goer. He has had close contacts with many contemporary playwrights, and is a scholar of experience and skill. He writes of the theater and the drama with unflagging if somewhat uncritical enthusiasm, and, though he is inclined to see dramatic mountains where there are only theatrical molehills, he does not suffer here, as he does in the face of the contemporary novel, from the inhibitions of gentility. Eleanor Flexner's *American Playwrights, 1918–1938* (1938) is the first comprehensive treatment of the post-war drama from a conventional left-wing position.

Despite the flourishing state of contemporary American poetry, it has found few satisfactory historians. Here, as in the drama and the novel, an embarrassment of riches confronts the literary historian. Amy Lowell's (*q.v.*) *Tendencies in Modern American Poetry* (1917) offered a justifiably enthusiastic view of a half-dozen poets whose future she forecast with considerable shrewdness. Louis Untermeyer's (*q.v.*) *The New Era in American Poetry* (1919) lacked the perspective needed in historical treatment, but his *American Poetry since 1900* (1923) furnished an opportunity for more carefully considered verdicts. More successful, though now somewhat outmoded, historical accounts are Bruce Weirick's *From Whitman to Sandburg* (1924) and Alfred Kreymborg's (*q.v.*) *Our Singing Strength, An Outline of American Poetry, 1620–1930* (1929), republished as a *History of American Poetry* (1934). The latter is not only more capacious in its design than Weirick's book but is also more satisfactory in its account of the contemporary movement in which Kreymborg played a conspicuous part as poet and editor. Important footnotes to a history of American poetry exist in the successive, constantly expanding editions of Louis Untermeyer's *Modern American Poetry*, though these anthologies naturally offer only very restricted space for more than a sketch of current movements in poetry.

The history of American criticism, general and contemporary, is yet to be written, and it is a task of such importance that only its difficulty can explain its neglect. Such works as Norman Foerster's (*q.v.*) *American Criticism* (1928) and George E. DeMille's *Literary Criticism in America* (1931) sketch in the nineteenth-century background of contemporary criticism but hardly come to grips with the current problems, although Foerster deals with these from the specifically Humanistic point of view in *Towards Standards* (1930). Percy Holmes Boynton's *The Challenge of Modern Criticism* (1931) suggests a possible systematization of the contemporary situation. The way to the materials for a history of contemporary criticism is pointed out by Foerster's anthology, *American Critical Essays, XIXth and XXth Century* (1930), and Morton Dauwen Zabel's *Literary Opinion in America* (1937). Zabel's introductory essay is a systematic and judicious survey of the history of American criticism during the last generation or more. On the basis of his survey, a series of intensive studies of critical theory and practice needs to be made and woven into a consecutive narrative of the important events in the history of contemporary criticism.

CONTEMPORARY AMERICAN BIO-BIBLIOGRAPHIES

F. P. A. *See* Franklin Pierce Adams

Louis Adamic, 1899–

Born at Blato, in Carniola, a Slovenian duchy in Austria, now a part of Yugoslavia, March 23, 1899. His parents were ambitious and sent him to a city school, hoping that he might become a priest. He proceeded to a Gymnasium but was expelled for participation in a Slovenian youth movement in 1913. Balking at the prospect of entering a Jesuit school, he ran away and at fourteen came to the United States.

He found a job in New York as mailer's assistant on a Slovenian newspaper. Using a Slovenian-English dictionary, he seized opportunities for reading about America, and he wrote sketches that were published in the paper. As his English improved he was elevated to the post of editorial assistant and translator of news material.

The failure of the paper forced him to take various jobs in New York and New Jersey. He joined the army in 1917 and served in the Panama Canal Zone and in France. He was discharged in 1920 and returned to New York, after three years of service.

After a year of drifting about the country and taking such jobs as he could find, he went to sea. Upon his return he took factory and laboring jobs in the East and then went to Los Angeles, where, after other work, he became a reporter. He gave up reporting in 1923 and moved to San Pedro.

His career as a writer began in 1928 when he was a dock worker. H. L. Mencken accepted an article for the *American Mercury.* Soon he had contributed to many other magazines; and in 1931 he published *Dynamite*, a study of the American labor movement.

In the next year he published *Laughing in the Jungle*, and received a Guggenheim fellowship. Intending to go to Italy to write a novel, he visited his native land, in which he found himself regarded as a hero, remained there instead, and wrote *The Native's Return*, which was the Book-of-the-Month Club selection for February, 1934. Like *Dynamite*, it was translated into many European languages.

Since his return he has written several books, and been awarded a grant by the Rockefeller Foundation for the study of immigrants in America. He has settled on a farm in New Jersey.

Throughout his career Adamic has shown acute sensitiveness to social and economic aspects of American civilization. His early bitterness, succeeding the immigrant hopes he had cherished of American opportunities, relaxed and was modified by his observations of pioneer American development, as reproduced in the growth of Los Angeles in the 1920's. The growing awareness of social problems forced upon him in the depression of the 1930's was intensified by his observation of the stability and relative calm of the lives of the peasants in his native Central Europe. Loyally devoted to America, he feels that it, like Russia, offers hope of a new order.

For further comment, see Critical Survey, p. 176.

BIBLIOGRAPHY

Novels

Grandsons, a story of American lives, 1935; Cradle of life, the story of one man's beginnings, 1936.

Autobiography

Laughing in the jungle, the autobiography of an immigrant in America, 1932.

Travel

* The native's return, an American immigrant visits Yugoslavia and discovers his old country, 1934.

Social and Economic Studies

Dynamite, the story of class violence in America, 1931 (rev. ed., 1934); My America, 1928–1938, 1938; America and the refugees, 1939 (caption-title; pamphlet).

Belles Lettres

Robinson Jeffers, a portrait, 1929 (pamphlet); The house in Antigua, a restoration, 1937.

Short Story

Lucas, king of the Balucas, 1935.

"Little Blue Book" Pamphlets

The truth about Los Angeles, 1927; Facts you should know about California [by] Louis Adamic and others, 1928; The word of Satan in the Bible, Christians rightly regard Ecclesiastes suspiciously, 1928 (with others).

Broadside

Plymouth Rock and Ellis Island, 1939? (broadside).

Translations

Yerney's justice by Ivan Cankar translated from the Slovenian (Yugoslav), 1926; Struggle, translated from the Yugoslav by Louis Adamic, with a preface by the translator, 1934.

STUDIES

DeVoto	McWilliams, Carey. Louis Adamic & shadow-America. [c1935]

For references to reviews, see *BRD.*, 1931–32, 1934–38.

Franklin P(ierce) Adams, 1881–

Born in Chicago, November 15, 1881. He attended the Armour Scientific Academy, graduated in 1899, and continued his studies at the University of Michigan.

In 1903 he joined the staff of the Chicago *Journal*, and in the following year he went to New York to begin work on the *Evening Mail*. He remained with this paper until 1913, then left and joined the *Tribune*. From 1922 until 1931 he wrote for the *World;* in 1931 he transferred his column "The Conning Tower" from the *World* to the *Herald Tribune*. Since March, 1937, he has been with the New York *Post*.

In 1909 he collaborated with O. Henry in a musical comedy, *Lo*. It is as a columnist, however, writing miscellaneous verse and humor, and editing contributions from his followers, that he has made his reputation, which has been extended recently by his radio appearances. His Saturday diary column, imitating the language and manner of Pepys, is said to have been a powerful influence in spreading the popularity of *Pepys's Diary* among modern readers. He is said to be the original of the character of Rutherford Hayes Adler in Edna Ferber's *The Girls*.

For further comment, see Critical Survey, pp. 159, 162.

BIBLIOGRAPHY

Poems and Humorous Verses

In cupid's court, 1902; Tobogganing on Parnassus, 1911; In other words, 1912; By and large, 1914; Weights and measures, 1917; Something else again, 1920; So there! 1923; So much velvet, 1924; Christopher Columbus and other patriotic verses, 1931; * The melancholy lute, selected songs of thirty years, 1936.

Humor and Miscellany

Overset, 1922; Women I'm not married to, 1922 (contains also: Men I'm not married to by Dorothy Parker); Half a loaf, 1927; Column book of F. P. A., 1928; The diary of our own Samuel Pepys, 1911–1925, 1935; The diary of our own Samuel Pepys, 1926–1934, 1935.

Verses Set to Music

A musical comedy, book & lyrics by O. Henry and Franklin P. Adams, music by A. Baldwin Sloane, management of the Harry Askin co., inc. Lo. Love is all that matters . . . You may always be my sweetheart . . . Little old Main street . . . In Yucatan . . . It's the little things that count . . . Statue song . . . Snap shots . . . Dear Yankee maid . . . Let us sing . . . Never forget your parents . . . While strolling through the forest . . . Caramba . . . Sailor number . . . Tammany on parade . . . Selection, 1909 (cover-title; sheet music; 14 vols.); If, my dear [words by] Franklin P. Adams [music by] Horace Johnson, 1923 (caption-title; sheet music); When Nancy Greenall was very young, poem . . . set for medium voice with piano accompaniment by Ida Bostelmann, 1927 (cover-title; sheet music).

Editor

The Conning tower book, being a selection of the best verses published in the Conning tower edited by F. P. A., in the New York World, 1926; The second Conning tower book, being a collection, in the main, of the best verses published in the Conning tower, edited by F. P. A. in the New York World, during the year 1926, 1927; Poems by Berenice Dewey, 1933.

Compiler

The book of diversion compiled by Franklin P. Adams, Deems Taylor, Jack Bechdolt, aided and abetted by Helen Rowland and Mabel Claire, 1925; Answer this one, questions for everybody compiled by Franklin P. Adams (F. P. A.) and Harry Hansen, 1927.

Contributor

Among us mortals, pictures and legends by W. E. Hill, text by Franklin P. Adams, 1917; Percy Hammond, a symposium in tribute by Franklin P. Adams, John Anderson, Brooks Atkinson, Whitney Bolton, John Mason Brown, Robert Garland, Richard Lockridge, Burns Mantle, George Jean Nathan, Geoffrey Parsons, Grantland Rice, Gilbert Seldes, Walter Winchell, 1936.

STUDIES AND ARTICLES

† Ford (E)
Markey
Untermeyer (C)

Anonymous. "F. P. A. of the New York Tribune." *Everybody's*, May 1916, pp. 598–99; Fadiman, Clifton. "The education of Franklin P. Adams." *N.Yer.*, Nov. 9, 1935, pp. 81–82; Hughes, Rupert. "F. P. A." *Everybody's*, Apr. 1920, pp. 52–53; Taylor, Bert L. "F. P. A." *A.Mag.*, Apr. 1914, pp. 66–68; Van Doren, Carl. "Day in and day out." *Cent.*, Dec. 1923, pp. 308–15. For references to reviews, see *BRD.*, 1913, 1915, 1917, 1920, 1922–25, 1928, 1931, 1935–36.

James Truslow Adams, 1878–

Born in Brooklyn, October 18, 1878, in a family cosmopolitan in background. His father, whose family came from Virginia, was a native of South America, and his mother's family was from New York; relatives had fought on both sides in the Civil War. Although his earliest memories are those of a visit to France when he was three, Adams has had an American education.

As he wanted to be an engineer, he studied at the Polytechnic Institute of Brooklyn, from which he graduated in 1898. Feeling at this time a desire to study and teach philosophy, he proceeded to Yale, where he took his master's degree in 1900. His graduate work, however, made him dissatisfied with this prospect, and he turned instead to business. In the course of some years in Wall Street he achieved a position that enabled him to retire in 1912 and to devote himself to other interests.

After spending a year studying Persian, he began writing history, at first on local subjects and town records. The war interrupted his work. He served as captain in the Military Intelligence Division in the General Staff of the American army, and he was detailed on special duty at the Peace Conference in Paris. "I have been back and forth almost every year since," he wrote early in 1937, "and believe I have crossed the ocean thirty-six times. For about eight years I made my home in London, visiting America for several months each year, but have now returned and bought an old house in Connecticut and expect to remain here permanently."

After the war he resumed his writing with a volume of New England history. Published in 1921 as *The Founding of New England*, it won the Pulitzer Prize in 1922 and established the author as an important historical writer. He has since become a member of many literary and historical societies, including the American Academy of Arts and Letters, and has received many honorary degrees. He is one of the few Americans to be a Fellow of the Royal Society of Literature. He wrote approximately one hundred of the sketches appearing in the *Dictionary of American Biography*. More recently he was made editor-in-chief of the *Dictionary of American History*. An article on politics won the thousand-dollar award of the *Yale Review* in 1933. In addition to a tremendous sale in this country his books have achieved a reputation in European countries and have been translated into French, German, and Danish. In 1938 he was elected to membership in the American Philosophical Society.

Adams regards history as too uncertain and incapable of exact verification to be called scientific. Although he recognizes the value and fascination of the establishment and presentation of facts, he is more especially absorbed by the need for some progressive philosophy for unifying them. ". . . It seems to me that the ripest fruit of knowledge," he declared in 1934 in the *Saturday Review of Literature*, "is to *interpret* facts, to try to find out how they are related and how they influence one another. This calls for wider background and for more concentration of thought." He considers both individuals and social forces potent influences in history, and he thinks that the contemporary interest in biography is a recognition that the individual is still a power.

The same feeling for individual integrity enters Adams' philosophy concerning the world today. He has protested against standardization and other by-products of the mechanical age; and he has revealed his conviction that a moral or ethical code of restraints, so inherent in the tradition of Western civilization as to defy a legal or rational exposition, is a necessary protection against unbridled self-expression and undisciplined and unsatisfying yielding to impulse, and a safeguard for ordered evolutionary progress.

For further comment, see Critical Survey, pp. 155–56.

BIBLIOGRAPHY

Historical and Biographical Studies

Memorials of old Bridgehampton, 1916 (rewritten and pub. as History of the town of Southampton (east of Canoe place) 1918); Notes on the families of Truslow, Horler, and Horley from English records, 1920; The founding of New England, 1921 (The history of New England, vol. I); Revolutionary New England, 1691–1776, 1923 (The history of New England, vol. II); Rhode Island's part in making America, an address delivered at Rhode Island college of education, 1923; New England in the republic, 1776–1850, 1926 (The history of New England, vol. III); A history of American life, volume III, Provincial society, 1690–1763, 1927; Our business civilization, some aspects of American culture, 1929 (English ed., A searchlight on America . . . introduction by Douglas Woodruff, 1930); The Adams family, 1930; * The epic of America, 1931; The tempo of modern life, 1931; The march of democracy [vol. I] the rise of the

Union, 1932 (English ed., A history of the American people to the Civil war, 1933); Henry Adams, 1933; History of the United States . . . volume I, The rise of the Union, 1933; History of the United States . . . volume II, A half-century of expansion, 1933; History of the United States . . . volume III, Civil war and reconstruction, 1933; History of the United States . . . volume IV, America and world power, 1933; The march of democracy, volume II, from Civil war to world power, 1933 (English ed., A history of the American people from Civil war to world power, 1933); America's tragedy, 1934; History of the United States . . . volume V, first part of annual chronicle which will cover ultimately a period of ten years, 1934–37 (loose-leaf); The record of America by James Truslow Adams . . . and Charles Garrett Vannest, 1935; The living Jefferson, 1936; Building the British empire, To the end of the first empire, 1938.

Pamphlets

Some notes on the currency problem, 1908; Speculation and the reform of the New York stock exchange, 1913; America's opportunity, how we lost it and how we may regain it, 1932 [pub. 1933?].

Edited and Compiled Works

Hamiltonian principles, extracts from the writings of Alexander Hamilton, 1928; Jeffersonian principles, extracts from the writings of Thomas Jefferson, 1928; Bibliography of the writings of Henry Adams, 1930; America and the new frontier [by] George Earl Freeland . . . and contributing editor, James Truslow Adams, 1936; America's progress in civilization [by] George Earl Freeland . . . and contributing editor, James Truslow Adams, 1936; America's world backgrounds [by] George Earl Freeland . . . and contributing editor, James Truslow Adams, 1936.

STUDIES AND ARTICLES

Kunitz
National
Schreiber

Bates, Ernest S. "James Truslow Adams, the magazine philosopher." *Mod.M.*, Dec. 1933, pp. 648–55; Hamilton, J. G. de Roulhac. "The liquidation of an ideal." *VQR.*, Apr. 1932, pp. 299–303; Icilius, Quintus. "Epic of America." *P.Jb.*, July 1933, pp. 1–12; † McCracken, Mary J. "Author biography [!] of James Truslow Adams." *BBDI.*, May 1934, pp. 65–68; McGinley, Phyllis, "Ballad for one born in Missouri." *N.Yer.*, May 12, 1934, p. 29. For references to reviews, see *BRD.*, 1921, 1926, 1928–36, 1938–39.

Léonie (Fuller) Adams, 1899–

Born in Brooklyn, December 9, 1899, the daughter of Charles Frederic and Henrietta (Rozier) Adams. She was educated in New York schools and Barnard College, where she graduated in 1922. While an undergraduate she had secretly written verse, without view to publication, although a poem of hers appeared in the *New Republic*. It was with reluctance that she published her first volume in 1925. After graduation she took up teaching and editorial work in New York, editing the *Measure* in 1924–25. The award of a Guggenheim traveling fellowship for creative writing resulted in her going abroad in 1928 and 1929; she lived for a year in London, Oxford, and Paris. She has read her own work for The Poetry Society of America and the Columbia chapter of Phi Beta Kappa, lectured on Victorian poetry at New York University, and taught verse-writing and contemporary poetry at Bennington College. In 1933 she married William Troy, critic and teacher at Bennington.

"I sometimes feel," she writes, "that poetry at present like other things is about to undergo the kind of variation that amounts to the leap to a new genus. I was first preoccupied with sound patterns—that took me to the seventeenth century—then I recognized the necessity for the more modern preoccupation with images which should not be gathered along the way of discourse or meditation, but assumed before starting out, like apparel, or entered into as a world. I have been silent a long time because I am now grappling with the limitations of the lyric."

For further comment, see Critical Survey, p. 146.

BIBLIOGRAPHY

Poems

Those not elect, 1925; High falcon & other poems, 1929; This measure . . . illustrations by George Plank, 1933.

Translations

The lyrics of François Villon done into English verse by Algernon Charles Swinburne, Dante Gabriel Rossetti, William Ernest Henley, John Payne, and Léonie Adams, with an introduction by Léonie Adams, the wood-blocks cut by Howard Simon, 1933.

STUDIES AND ARTICLES

Deutsch
Kreymborg
Kunitz (L)

Sapir, Edward. "Léonie Adams." *P.*, Feb. 1926, pp. 275–79; Untermeyer, Louis. "Three younger poets." *EJ.*, Dec. 1932, pp. 787–99; Zabel, Morton D. "A harrier of heaven." *P.*, Mar. 1930, pp. 332–36. For references to reviews, see *BRD.*, 1925, 1929.

Conrad (Potter) Aiken, 1889–

Born August 5, 1889, in Savannah. His father, a physician and surgeon, and his mother were both from New England; and, after a childhood spent in Georgia, the boy was taken north and attended schools in New Bedford and Cambridge, Massachusetts. He began writing verse at nine. After preparatory study at the Middlesex School in Concord, Massachusetts, he entered Harvard in 1907. At Harvard he was a contemporary of Robert Benchley, Van Wyck Brooks, Heywood Broun, T. S. Eliot, Robert Edmond Jones, Walter Lippmann, Kenneth Macgowan, John Reed, Alan Seeger, and John Hall Wheelock. He wrote for the *Harvard Monthly* and the *Advocate*, and was president of the latter, as well as class poet. His studies were interrupted by a trip abroad, and he graduated with the class of 1912.

Upon graduation, electing literature as a profession, he began a long career of wandering and travel. After a year in England, France, and Italy he came back to New England. Frequent trips abroad followed, and he lived in both Italy and England. Since 1923, when he settled in Sussex, he has made many trips to this country, and in 1927–28 he was a tutor in English at Harvard. He feels that he writes best in England.

He enjoys sports, and writes: ". . . [I am] passionately fond of music (Bach and Beethoven my chief happiness, Haydn and Mozart almost as good), play tennis when I can, and am an ardent movie fan. I read very little, on the whole, and particularly poetry, which I read almost not at all. [I] have lately become increasingly interested in painting, and in fact most of my friends (when they haven't been doctors or psychoanalysts—the latter very importantly) have been painters."

His volume of *Selected Poems* was awarded the Pulitzer Prize for work published in 1929, and received the Shelley Memorial Award. In 1934 the author was given a Guggenheim fellowship.

A contributing editor to the *Dial* in 1917–19, Aiken has written much for the *New Yorker*, *Esquire*, *Scribner's*, and other magazines. He has, however, consistently maintained his position as an independent man of letters; and he has stated his conviction that literary coteries and propaganda groups, or any other claims upon the public attention in which the writer is made to conform or to appear to conform to the political or ethical standards of others, are harmful to the detachment necessary for fine work. He feels that publishers, the reading public, and woman's clubs and similar organizations, in their desire to convince themselves that the writer is not different from ordinary people, exert a type of pressure comparable to that applied by Communists and Fascists; and he thinks that a writer must, if he wishes to work out his artistic salvation, refuse to truckle to this demand. "Our writers must learn once more in the best sense how to *stand clear*," he declared in 1935 in an article in the *New Republic*, "in order that they may preserve that sort of impersonal anonymity, and that deep and pure provincialism, in which the terms approach universals, and in which alone they will find, perhaps, the freedom for the greatest work."

For further comment, see Critical Survey, pp. 33, 95, 144.

BIBLIOGRAPHY

Poems

Earth triumphant and other tales in verse, 1914; The jig of Forslin, a symphony, 1916; Turns and movies and other tales in verse, 1916; Nocturne of remembered spring and other poems, 1917; The charnel rose, Senlin: a biography, and other poems, 1918; The house of dust, a symphony, 1920; Punch: the immortal liar, documents in his history, 1921; Priapus and the pool, 1922; The pilgrimage of Festus, 1923; Priapus and the pool and other poems, 1925; Senlin: a biography, 1925; Conrad Aiken, The pamphlet poets, price 25 cents, 1927 (cover-title; ed. by Louis Untermeyer); Prelude, 1929; * Selected poems, 1929; John Deth, a metaphysical legend and other poems, 1930; The coming forth by day of Osiris Jones, 1931; Preludes for Memnon, 1931; Prelude, a poem . . .

illustrated by John P. Heins, 1932; And in the hanging gardens . . ., 1933; Landscape west of Eden, 1934; Time in the rock, preludes to definition, 1936.

Novels

Blue voyage, 1927; Great circle, 1933; King Coffin, 1935; A heart for the gods of Mexico, 1939.

Short Stories

Bring! bring! and other stories, 1925; Costumes by Eros, 1928; Among the lost people, 1934.

Belles Lettres

Scepticisms, notes on contemporary poetry, 1919; Gehenna, 1930.

Verses Set to Music

By a silent shore, poem by Conrad Aiken [music by] Bainbridge Crist, 1934 (caption-title); Evening [by] Conrad Aiken [music by] Bainbridge Crist, 1934 (caption-title); Knock on the door [by] Conrad Aiken [music by] Bainbridge Crist, 1934 (caption-title); Noontime [by] Conrad Aiken [music by] Bainbridge Crist, 1934 (caption-title).

Edited and Compiled Works

Modern American poets, 1922; Selected poems of Emily Dickinson, 1924; American poetry, 1671–1928, a comprehensive anthology, 1929.

STUDIES AND ARTICLES

Hatcher
† Herrmann
† Johnson (1929)
† Johnson (1932)
† Johnson (1936)
Kreymborg
Kunitz (L)
Loggins
Lowell
† Manly
Monroe (P)
Peterson, Houston. The melody of chaos. 1931
Untermeyer
Untermeyer (C)
Untermeyer (M)
Untermeyer (N)
Widdemer

Aiken, Conrad. "Counterpoint and implication." *P.*, June 1919, pp. 152–59; Ament, William S. "The coming forth by day of Osiris Jones, preludes for Memnon." *UCC.*, Jan. 1932, pp. 86–90; Anderson, Maxwell. "Conrad Aiken and the minor mode." *Meas.*, May 1921, pp. 25–26; Blackmur, Richard P. "The day before the daybreak." *P.*, Apr. 1932, pp. 39–44; Carnevali, Emanuel. "Caliban's love-making." *P.*, Feb. 1920, pp. 283–87; Cowley, Malcolm. "Two American poets." *D.*, Nov. 1922, pp. 563–67; Dillon, George. "Mr. Aiken's poetry." *P.*, Jan. 1931, pp. 221–25; Fletcher, John G. "Conrad Aiken, metaphysical poet." *D.*, May 31, 1919, pp. 558–59; Fletcher. "The poetry of Conrad Aiken." *D.*, Mar. 28, 1918, pp. 291–92; Geddes, Virgil. "Conrad Aiken's selection." *P.*, Apr. 1923, pp. 53–55; Kunitz, Stanley J. "Learned in violence." *P.*, May 1937, pp. 103–06; Monroe, Harriet. "Its inner meaning." *P.*, Sept. 1915, pp. 302–05; Moore, Marianne. "If a man die." *HH.*, Jan.–Mar. 1932, pp.

313–20; Scott, Evelyn. "A flight for angels." *P.*, June 1935, pp. 162–65. For references to reviews, see *BRD.*, 1914, 1916–23, 1925, 1927–31, 1933–36.

Zoë Akins, 1886–

Born October 30, 1886, in Humansville, Missouri, in the Ozark Mountains. As a little girl she showed a marked interest in the theater. Her Negro nurse took her to dramatic performances, and she played with her dolls as actors. She was educated at home and attended the Monticello Seminary at Godfrey, Illinois, and Hosmer Hall in St. Louis.

She began to contribute poems and criticism to *Reedy's Mirror*, and subsequently her work appeared in national magazines. *Papa*, her first play, attracted attention by its frankness, and *The Magical City* was given in a group of short plays by the Washington Square Players. *Déclassée*, produced in 1919 by Charles Frohman at the Empire Theatre in New York, with Ethel Barrymore, made a notable success.

After writing for the Broadway stage for some ten years, Miss Akins turned to the motion pictures, and since 1930 she has lived in California, where she has written for Metro-Goldwyn-Mayer. *Morning Glory* (1933), one of her pictures, was made especially popular by the acting of Katharine Hepburn.

In 1930, however, Miss Akins made an exceedingly successful return to the stage with the comedy *The Greeks Had a Word for It*, which, produced in New York by William Harris, Jr., ran for 253 performances, made handsome royalties for the author, and was subsequently filmed. A few years later, fascinated by the possibilities in Edith Wharton's story *The Old Maid*, Miss Akins obtained Mrs. Wharton's consent and dramatized the novel. Produced early in 1935, with Helen Menken in the title role and Judith Anderson in that of Delia, *The Old Maid* ran for 305 performances, took the Pulitzer Prize, and in the following season made a highly successful tour.

Miss Akins, who has been the friend of many artists and writers, among them Elinor Wylie, Willa Cather, and Carl Van Vechten, is the widow of Captain Hugo Cecil Levinge Rumbold, an artist, and lives in Pasadena.

For further comment, see Critical Survey, p. 100.

BIBLIOGRAPHY

Plays

Papa, an amorality in three acts, 1913; Portrait of Tiero, 192–?; Such a charming young man, comedy in one act, 192–?; * Déclassée: Daddy's gone a-hunting: and Greatness—a comedy, 1923; The old maid dramatized by Zoë Akins from the novel by Edith Wharton, 1935; The little miracle, 1936.

Poems

Interpretations, a book of first poems, 1912; The hills grow smaller, poems, 1937.

Novels

Cake upon the waters . . . illustrated by Lucius W. Hitchcock, 1919.

Verses Set to Music

Corals, a sea idyll composed for high or medium voice with piano accompaniment by Bryceson Treharne, text by Zoë Akins, 1919 (cover-title).

STUDIES

Brown
Dickinson (P)
Mantle (C)
Nathan, George J. Materia critica. 1924
Nathan (TD)
† Quinn (H)
Woollcott
Woollcott (S)

For references to reviews, see *BRD.*, 1919, 1923, 1935, 1937.

Hilda Doolittle Aldington. *See* Hilda Doolittle

(William) Hervey Allen, 1889–

Born in Pittsburgh, December 8, 1889. He attended public schools, the Shady Side Academy, and the United States Naval Academy, from which he was honorably discharged after injuring himself in athletics. In 1915 he graduated, with honors in economics, from the University of Pittsburgh. Subsequently he studied at Harvard.

After a period of work for the Bell Telephone Company he enlisted in the National Guard and served on the Mexican border in 1916. In the war he served in France, where he was seriously wounded in action in 1918, and taught in a French military mission.

Upon his return he settled in Charleston, South Carolina, and taught English in the Porter Military Academy and later in a high school. In 1924 he joined the English department at Columbia, and later he lectured on American literature at Vassar and on modern poetry at the Bread Loaf School of English.

As a teacher in Charleston he became a friend of DuBose Heyward, with whom he founded the Poetry Society of South Carolina. He was a leader in southern post-war poetry and exerted his influence to encourage the revival of narrative poetry. He was successful almost from the beginning, and his poetry won sales and the praise of Thomas Hardy, Amy Lowell, Edwin Arlington Robinson, and other poets and critics. *Toward the Flame*, a record of war experience, and *Israfel*, a life of Poe, both published in 1926, enjoyed enthusiastic receptions, and the latter, reissued in a cheaper edition, has a steady sale as a standard biography.

From these works he turned his attention to the historical novel and began work upon *Anthony Adverse.* Although he rejected, as unsuitable to a work designed for readers of fiction, such scholarly appurtenances as historical introduction, notes, and bibliography, he based the narrative upon reading and research, including an examination not only of literary and artistic sources and standard historical works but also of the diaries of his grand-uncle with their detailed account of the life of the captain of a river steamboat. In May, 1929, he worked out the outline of the book in three parts, each composed of three books.

In the following August, after recovering from a serious illness, he began the actual writing, which he expected to finish in two years. Working steadily, with little pause for revision, he finished the manuscript in February, 1933. By this time it had grown to almost 1,700 pages, written in pencil, and weighing nineteen pounds. Much of it had been written during the author's stay in Bermuda.

Although the tremendous popular appeal of *Anthony Adverse*, in spite of its unusual length, and its success as a film have tended to obscure Allen's other work, he continues to regard himself as only incidentally a novelist and as interested chiefly in poetry. His position he describes as that of a humanist, and he has little interest in formless, chaotic, or confused artistic productions. He ascribes to Coleridge the greatest critical influence on his writing. In his methods of work he arranges a schedule designed to grant the maximum amount of time (usually at night) when he can be uninterrupted and free for imaginative receptivity and intellectual concentration.

For further comment, see Critical Survey, pp. 62, 72–73.

BIBLIOGRAPHY

Novels

* Anthony Adverse . . . decorations by Allan McNab, 1933 (regular ed. in 1 vol., limited ed. in 3 vols.); Action at Aquila, 1938 (German ed., translated by W. E. Süskind and R. v. Scholtz, has title: Oberst Franklin, roman, 1937).

Poems

Ballads of the border, 1916 (pamphlet); Wampum and old gold, 1921; The bride of Huitzil, an Aztec legend, 1922; Carolina chansons, legends of the low country by DuBose Heyward and Hervey Allen, 1922; The blindman, a ballad of Nogent l'Artaud, 1923 (repr. from Wampum and old gold); Christmas epithalamium, 1923; Earth moods and other poems, 1925; New legends, poems, 1929; Sarah Simon, character Atlantean, 1929; Songs for Annette, 1929.

Biography

* Israfel, the life and times of Edgar Allan Poe, 1926 (2 vols.).

War Experiences

Toward the flame, 1926.

Miscellany

When Shady avenue was Shady lane, 1919 (broadside); The Christmas herald, an intelligencer of good wishes, volume 1, no. 1, Charleston, S.C., December 25, 1921, 1921 (leaflet); Three experimental imprints, 1922; DuBose Heyward, a critical and biographical sketch . . . including contemporary estimates of his work, 1927? (pamphlet); The syllabus of a novel to be called Anthony Adverse by Hervey Allen, 1933 (cover-title; pamphlet); The sources of Anthony Adverse reprinted from the Saturday review of literature, 1934 (cover-title; pamphlet); Middlebury college bulletin. Bread Loaf, 1935 (cover-title; pamphlet).

Editor

Year book of the Poetry society of South Carolina for 1921, 1921 (with others); The year book of the Poetry society of South Carolina, 1922 (ed. by Hervey Allen, DuBose Heyward, John Bennett); The year book of the Poetry society of South Carolina, 1923 (ed. by John Bennett, Hervey Allen, DuBose Heyward, assisted by the Committee on publication: Misses Ellen M. Fitzsimons, Mabel L. Webber, Frances Jervey, and Sidney Rittenberg); Poe's brother, the poems of William Henry Leonard Poe, elder brother of Edgar Allan Poe together with a short account of his tragic life, an early romance of Edgar Allan Poe and some hitherto unknown incidents in the lives of the two Poe brothers. Illustrated. With a preface, introduction, comment, and facsimilies [!] of new Poe documents by Hervey Allen and Thomas Ollive Mabbott, 1926; The works of Edgar Allan Poe . . . poems, tales, essays, criticisms, with new notes, special biographical introduction, 1927; The best known works of Edgar Allan Poe in one volume, poems, tales, essays, criticisms, with new notes, special biographical introduction, 1931; The old house in the country by Lizette Woodworth Reese, introduction by Hervey Allen, 1936.

STUDIES AND ARTICLES

Allen, Hervey, American author (novelist, poet, and biographer). [1938] (broadside)

Gibney, Sheridan. "Anthony Adverse," story by Hervey Allen, screen play by Sheridan Gibney, directed by Mervyn Le Roy. 1935 (mimeographed)

Hervey Allen biographical notes. [1938] (caption-title; 2 leaves; mimeographed)

† Johnson (1936)

Kunitz (L)

National

Smith

Stevens, George. Lincoln's doctor's dog and other famous best sellers. [c1939]

[Sullivan, Edward D.] Romeo Reverse by Hardly Alum [*pseud.*] with illustrations by Adolf Dehn. 1934

† Whitall, William Van R. The notable library of Major W. van R. Whitall of Pelham, New York. First editions, manuscripts, autograph letters, and inscribed copies of nineteenth-century authors sold by direction of the Detroit trust co., Detroit, Michigan, trustee. With facsimile reproductions. [1927]

Allen, Hervey. "The sources of 'Anthony Adverse.'" *SRL.*, Jan. 13, 1934, pp. 401, 408–10; Cobb, Sanford. "Anthony hits a million." *PW.*, Aug. 24, 1935, pp. 500–03; Cox, Sidney. "Israfel, the life and times of Edgar Allan Poe." *SR.*, Apr.-June 1927, pp. 241–43; Daniels, Jonathan. "Escape from a legend, 'Action at Aquila' and its aftermath." *SRL.*, Mar. 5, 1938, pp. 3–4, 16, 18; Laing, Alexander. "Noble tales." *P.*, Mar. 1930, pp. 342–46; Monroe, Harriet. "Epic moods." *P.*, Nov. 1925, pp. 96–98; Prezzolini, Giuseppe. "Un Dumas Americano, 'Anthony Adverse' di Hervey Allen." *PanM.*, Sept. 1934, pp. 127–30; Wilson, James S. "Enter a novelist." *VQR.*, July 1933, pp. 433–35; Wilson. "Poe and the biographers." *VQR.*, Apr. 1927, pp. 313–20. For references to reviews, see *BRD.*, 1921, 1925–27, 1929, 1933, 1938.

Maxwell Anderson, 1888–

Born in Atlantic, Pennsylvania, December 15, 1888. His father was a Baptist minister, and, as he moved from Pennsylvania to Ohio, Iowa, and North

Dakota, the son attended several schools. He graduated in 1911 from the University of North Dakota, where he was an original member of the Sock and Buskin Society, and studied with Professor Frederick H. Koch; he spent the next years teaching in North Dakota and California. Joining the faculty of Stanford University as instructor in English, he took his master's degree in 1914 and taught in Whittier College in southern California.

Desirous of more opportunity for writing, and wishing to earn more money than teaching seemed to afford, he entered newspaper work. He had had experience on the Grand Forks (North Dakota) *Herald*, and he worked on the *Chronicle* and the *Bulletin* in San Francisco until 1918. Going East, he served as editorial writer for the *New Republic*, the *Evening Globe*, and the *Morning World* in New York; in this period, also, he wrote poetry, helped found the *Measure*, a journal of poetry, and began his activities as playwright.

Although *White Desert* ran but a few nights in 1923, it attracted the attention of Laurence Stallings, another member of the staff of the *World;* and in the next year the fruit of their collaboration, *What Price Glory?*, was the most successful play of the season. This encouraging beginning led Anderson to resign his newspaper position and devote himself to an independent career as a writer of plays. At present he lives on a farm near New York.

His success may be gauged by the distinctions he has won. *Both Your Houses* took the Pulitzer Prize for 1932–33; and *Winterset* and *High Tor* won the awards of the Drama Critics' Circle for 1935–36 and 1936–37 respectively. The author is a member of the National Institute of Arts and Letters. Four of his plays were given at the Kirby Memorial Theater at Amherst College in 1938–39, and a cycle of eight of his plays was given at the Pasadena Community Playhouse festival in 1939.

For further comment, see Critical Survey, pp. 107–09, 112, 123–24.

BIBLIOGRAPHY

Plays

"Sea-wife," a play in three acts . . . 1926 (cover-title; mimeographed); Three American plays by Maxwell Anderson and Laurence Stallings, 1926 (* What price glory; First flight; The buccaneer); Saturday's children, a comedy in three acts, 1927; Gods of the lightning by Maxwell Anderson and Harold Hickerson, Outside looking in by Maxwell Anderson, based on "Beggars of life" by Jim Tully, 1928; * Elizabeth the queen, a play in three acts, 1930; Night over Taos, a play in three acts, 1932; Both your houses, a play in three acts, 1933; Mary of Scotland, a play in three acts, 1933; Valley Forge, a play in three acts, 1934; * Winterset, a play in three acts, 1935; The masque of kings, a play in three acts, 1936; The wingless victory, a play in three acts, 1936; * High Tor, a play in three acts, 1937; The star-wagon, a play in three acts, 1937; The feast of ortolans, a play in one act, 1938; Knickerbocker holiday, a musical comedy in two acts, book and lyrics by Maxwell Anderson, as written to be set to music by Kurt Weill, illustrated by Robert H. Mutrux, 1938.

Poems

You who have dreams, 1925.

Verses Set to Music

It never was anywhere you . . . words by Maxwell Anderson, music by Kurt Weill, 1938 (caption-title; sheet-music); September song . . . words by Maxwell Anderson, music by Kurt Weill, 1938 (caption-title; sheet-music); Will you remember me? . . . words by Maxwell Anderson, music by Kurt Weill (caption-title; sheet-music).

Essays

The essence of tragedy and other footnotes and papers, 1939.

Editor

Dacotah, 1912, a chapter in the history of the University of North Dakota, vol. v, 1911.

STUDIES AND ARTICLES

American (M)
Block
Brown
Clark
Clark, Barrett H. Maxwell Anderson, the man and his plays. [c1933]
Flexner
Fort
Herrmann
Holmes, Margaret G. The theatre today. 1937 (The University of North Carolina. Library extension publication. vol. III, no. 6)
Kunitz (L)
Lawson
Littell
Loggins
Mantle
Mantle (C)
Mersand
Moses (A)
Nathan (M)
Nathan (TM)
† Quinn (H)
Quinn (R)
Russell
Shakespeare, William. Julius Cæsar [by] Shakespeare, Elizabeth the queen [by] Maxwell Anderson, edited by H. Harding. [c1932]
Skinner
Waugh
Whitman
Zabel

Carmer, Carl. "Maxwell Anderson, poet and champion." *TAM.*, June 1933, pp. 437–46; Childs, Herbert E. "Playgoer's playwright, Maxwell Anderson." *EJ.*, (Col. Ed.), June 1938, pp. 475–85; Gregory, Horace. "Poets in the theatre." *P.*, July 1936, pp. 221–28; Isaacs, Edith J. R. "Maxwell Anderson." *EJ.*, Dec. 1936, pp. 795–804; Mersand, Joseph. "Speech in the new plays." *CE.*, Mar. 1937, pp. 68–69; Mersand. "Speech in the new plays." *CE.*, Apr. 1937, pp. 94, 117–18; Monroe, Harriet. "Quiet music." *P.*, Mar. 1926, pp. 337–38; Wilson, Edmund. "Prize-winning blank verse." *NR.*, June 23, 1937, pp. 193–94. For references to reviews, see *BRD.*, 1925–30, 1932–35, 1937, 1939.

Sherwood Anderson, 1876–

Born in Camden, Ohio, September 13, 1876. His father, at this time in the saddlery-and-harness business, was a drifter, and moved from town to town in Ohio as his fortunes declined. The mother, a beautiful and energetic girl of Italian extraction, died after bearing seven children. "Jobby" Anderson, as the little boy came to be known, had little time for school although, like his brothers and sisters, he was quick in school work, but sold newspapers and popcorn and peanuts, mowed lawns, acted as stable-boy, worked in cabbage fields and on racecourses, and picked up his knowledge in barrooms, streets, and stores. He took factory jobs and read eagerly in his spare time.

When he was about seventeen, he went to Chicago. He lived in a tenement house and took jobs as a common laborer. His urge to write was so powerful that paper and ink acted as nervous stimulants upon him. In order to escape the factory routine and the life of a workman he enlisted in the Spanish-American War; and, although he had few illusions about the toy war, as he regarded it, he consciously took advantage of the attention it brought him and considerably bettered his condition by it.

After returning to Chicago he entered the advertising business, which he thinks helps the novelist by forcing him to act a role. For a short time he tried running a paint factory in Elyria, Ohio. Although it was successful, he found that his writing at night was beginning to affect his work, and one day, in the midst of a letter he was dictating, he walked out of the factory and never returned.

He went back to advertising, and, in an effort to erase the feeling of failure and the stigma attached to losing his friends' money in the factory, contributed to the *Dial* and the *Little Review*, through which he gained a public, and finished his first novel, *Windy McPherson's Son*, in 1916. Although at first editors and publishers were unreceptive to his work, he was given encouragement by such established writers in Chicago as Theodore Dreiser, Ben Hecht, and Floyd Dell; and *Winesburg, Ohio* (1919) brought him reputation as an author.

Moving to New York, he became a member of a literary world including Van Wyck Brooks, Waldo Frank, Paul Rosenfeld, James Oppenheim, and shared in the literary and artistic movements represented by the *Masses*, the *Little Review*, the *Seven Arts*, the *Nation* and the *New Republic*, and the work of Mencken and Nathan. His work attracted the attention of Alfred Stieglitz, Henry Seidel Canby, the Colums, Lawrence Gilman, and Gertrude Stein whose *Tender Buttons* had awakened in him an interest in words.

In 1921, the year in which he was given the *Dial* award of two thousand dollars, the first annual prize for a contribution to letters by a writer for the *Dial*, he went abroad. When he returned, he spent a year living in New Orleans with William Faulkner. Subsequently, in 1925, he bought a farm near Marion, Virginia, where he is settled and edits two newspapers, one Republican and one Democratic. He has been associated in recent years with the *American Spectator*. In 1934 he dramatized *Winesburg, Ohio* for the Hedgerow Theater Group. He is a member of the National Institute of Arts and Letters.

Although writing has at various times in his life afforded him an escape from the limitations of the tasks and preoccupations with which he was necessarily concerned, Anderson feels that reality is essential to imaginative creation and that without reality the imagination must starve. He does not, however, consider the agitation of reforms to be the function of the realistic writer. "It seems to me that the story-teller is one thing, and the thinker, the political economist, the reformer another," he said in Scribner's *Bookbuyer* in 1936. "The business of the story-teller is with life, in his own time, life as he feels it, smells it, tastes it. Not for him surely the making of the revolution."

For further comment, see Critical Survey, pp. 32–33, 46, 95.

BIBLIOGRAPHY

Novels

Windy McPherson's son, 1916; Marching men, 1917; * Poor white, a novel, 1920; Many marriages, 1923; Dark laughter, 1925; Beyond desire, 1932; Kit Brandon, a portrait, 1936.

Short Stories

* Winesburg, Ohio, a group of tales of Ohio small town life, 1919; The triumph of the egg, a book of impressions from American life in tales and poems by Sherwood Anderson, in clay by Tennessee Mitchell . . . photographs by Eugene Hutchinson, 1921; Horses and men, tales, long and short, from our American life, 1923; Hands and other stories, 1925 (selected from Winesburg, Ohio); Alice, and The lost novel . . . being number ten of the Woburn books, 1929; Death in the woods and other stories, 1933.

Essays and Studies

The modern writer, 1925 [1926]; Sherwood Anderson's notebook, containing articles written during the author's life as a story teller and notes of his impressions from life scattered through the book, 1926; Hello towns! 1929; Nearer the grass roots . . . and by the same author, an account of a journey—Elizabethton, 1929; The American county fair, 1930 (pamphlet); Sherwood Anderson on Margaret Anderson from The New republic of July 11th, 1930, 1930 (caption-title; leaflet); Perhaps women, 1931; No swank, 1934; Puzzled America, 1935.

Autobiography

A story teller's story, the tale of an American writer's journey through his own imaginative world and through the world of facts, with many of his experiences and impressions among other writers—told in many notes—in four books—and an epilogue, 1924; Tar, a midwest childhood, 1926 (autobiographical novel).

Poems and Prose

Mid-American chants, 1918; A new testament, 1927.

Plays

Plays, Winesburg and others, 1937 (Jasper Deeter, a dedication; Winesburg, Ohio, a play in nine scenes; The triumph of the egg, a drama in one act from the story by the same title, dramatized by Raymond O'Neil; Mother, a one act play; They married later, a one act play).

Miscellany

[Alfred H. Maurer], 1924 (broadside; also pub. as leaflet with cover-title: An exhibition of paintings by Alfred H. Maurer, beginning January fifteenth 1924, 1924); Harlan miners speak, report on terrorism in the Kentucky coal fields, prepared by members of the National committee for the defense of political prisoners, Theodore Dreiser, Lester Cohen, Anna Rochester, Melvin P. Levy, Arnold Johnson, Charles R. Walker, John Dos Passos, Adelaide Walker, Bruce Crawford, Jessie Wakefield, Boris Israel, Sherwood Anderson, 1932.

Editor

The American spectator year book edited by George Jean Nathan, Sherwood Anderson, Ernest Boyd, James Branch Cabell, Theodore Dreiser, Eugene O'Neill, 1934.

STUDIES AND ARTICLES

Anderson, Sherwood. L'homme qui devint femme. [c1926] (preface by Bernard Faÿ)
Anderson, Sherwood. Winesburg, Ohio, a group of tales of Ohio small town life . . . introduction by Ernest Boyd. [1921?]
Ashley
Baldwin
Baldwin (M)
Beach
Berg
Blankenship
Boynton (L)
Boynton (M)
Bruns
Calverton
Calverton (N)
Canby (2d ser.)
Chase, Cleveland B. Sherwood Anderson. 1927
Cleaton
Collins
Collins (T)
Cowley
Dell
Dondore
† Edgar
† Fagin, Nathan B. The phenomenon of Sherwood Anderson, a study in American life & letters by Bryllion Fagin. 1927
Farrar
Frank
Frank (O)
Frank (S)
Freeman
Garnett
Green (C)
Hackett
Halleck
Hansen
Hartwick
Hatcher
Hazard
Hemingway, Ernest. The torrents of spring, a novel in honor of the passing of a great race. 1926
Herrmann
Hicks
Hind
Huddleston
† Johnson (1929)
† Johnson (1932)
† Johnson (1936)
Karsner
Kunitz (L)
Levinson
Lewis (P)
Lewisohn (E)
Llona
Loggins
Luccock
Lundkvist
McCole
Maillard
Mais
† Manly
Marble
Markey
Michaud
Michaud (P)
More
O'Brien
O'Neil, Raymond. The triumph of the egg, a drama in one act . . . dramatized from the story by Sherwood Anderson. [c1932]
Parrington
Pattee (N)
Quinn
Rascoe
Roberts
Rosenfeld (P)
Saturday
Schyberg
Sherman (C)
Sinclair
Spratling, William P. Sherwood Anderson & other famous Creoles, a gallery of contemporary New Orleans drawn by Wm. Sprat-

ling & arranged by Wm. Faulkner. 1926
† Taylor
Untermeyer (H)
Van Doren
Van Doren (A)
Van Doren (C)
Vočadlo
Ward
Ward (T)
West (S)
Whipple
Wickham
Zabel

† Aaron, Manley. "American first editions, a series of bibliographic checklists edited by Merle Johnson and Frederick M. Hopkins, number 18, Sherwood Anderson, 1876– ." *PW.*, Jan. 27, 1923, p. 251; Alexander, David C. "Sherwood Anderson, a study of the American realist whose work reflects the mental awakening of the proletariat." *L.*, Feb. 1928, pp. 23–29; Anderson, Sherwood. "On being published." *Col.*, Part 1, Art. 7, pp. 1–4 (1930); Anonymous. "Sherwood Anderson." *AB.*, Apr. 1922, pp. 157–62; Boynton, Percy H. "Sherwood Anderson." *N.Amer.Rev.*, Mar. 1927, pp. 140–50; Buchanan, Annabel M. "Sherwood Anderson, country editor." *WT.*, Feb. 1929, pp. 248–53; Calverton, Victor F. "Sherwood Anderson." *MQ.*, Fall 1924, pp. 82–118; Crawford, Nelson A. "Sherwood Anderson the wistfully faithful." *Mid.*, Nov. 1922, pp. 297–308; Fadiman, Clifton. "Sherwood Anderson, the search for salvation." *Nation*, Nov. 9, 1932, pp. 454–56; Fagin, Nathan B. "Sherwood Anderson and our anthropological age." *DD.*, Jan.–Feb. 1925, pp. 91–99; Fagin. "Sherwood Anderson, the liberator of our short story." *EJ.*, Apr. 1927, pp. 271–79; Faÿ, Bernard. "Portrait de Sherwood Anderson, Américain," *R.d.P.*, Oct. 15, 1934, pp. 886–901; Gilman, Lawrence. "An American masterwork." *N.Amer.Rev.*, Mar. 1922, pp. 412–16; Gregory, Alyse. "Sherwood Anderson." *D.*, Sept. 1923, pp. 243–46; Henderson, Alice C. "Mid-America awake." *P.*, June 1918, pp. 155–58; Huebsch, B. W. "Footnotes to a publisher's life." *Col.*, Summer 1937, pp. 406–26; † Jessup, Mary E. "A checklist of the writings of Sherwood Anderson." *AC.*, Jan. 1928, pp. 157–58; Johnson, A. Theodore. "Realism in contemporary American literature, notes on Dreiser, Anderson, Lewis." *Sw.Bul.*, Sept. 1929, pp. 3–16; Lovett, Robert M. "The promise of Sherwood Anderson." *D.*, Jan. 1922, pp. 79–83; Lovett. "Sherwood Anderson." *EJ.*, Oct. 1924, pp. 531–39; McCole, Camille J. "Sherwood Anderson, congenital Freudian." *CW.*, Nov. 1929, pp. 129–33; Morris, Lawrence S. "Sherwood Anderson, sick of words." *NR.*, Aug. 3, 1927, pp. 277–79; Rosenfeld, Paul. "Sherwood Anderson." *D.*, Jan. 1922, pp. 29–42; Smith, Rachel. "Sherwood Anderson, some entirely arbitrary reactions." *SR.*, Apr.–June 1929, pp. 159–63; Van Doren, Carl. "Sinclair Lewis and Sherwood Anderson, a study of two moralists," *Cent.*, July 1925, pp. 362–69; Whipple, Thomas K. "Sherwood Anderson." *Lit.Rev.*, Mar. 11, 1922, pp. 481–82. For references to reviews, see *BRD.*, 1916–21, 1923–27, 1929, 1931–33, 1935–37.

Laura Adams Armer, 1874–

Born in Sacramento, California, January 12, 1874, the daughter of Charles W. and Maria A. (Henry) Adams. Frail health in childhood prevented her going to high school, but she studied drawing and painting at the California School of Design, and Chinese art at the University of California. She married an art student, Sidney Armer, and, since the marriage of their son, has devoted most of her time to painting.

Fascinated by Indian primitive art, Mrs. Armer went to a Navaho reservation and studied Indian folk art at firsthand, living in a hut built for her by

Indians, and often enduring considerable hardship. She won their confidence, secured the privilege of seeing and copying sacred sand paintings, and even witnessed a healing ceremony to which no woman was ordinarily admitted. She secured an extensive knowledge of myth and folklore, and copied one hundred sand paintings now in the Anthropological Museum in Santa Fe. She made an all-Indian motion picture, *The Mountain Chant*, based on a nine-day Navaho religious ceremony.

Her first book, *Waterless Mountain*, dealing with a Navaho subject, brought her the Newbery Medal for juvenile literature. She is well known as a painter of Indian subjects. Of her attitude toward her studies she says: "External things are of less interest to me than psychological research. Only as externals express the urge of man am I interested in them."

BIBLIOGRAPHY

Juvenile Literature

Waterless mountain by Laura Adams Armer illustrated by Sidney Armer and Laura Adams Armer, 1931; Dark circle of branches . . . illustrated by Sidney Armer, 1933; The trader's children . . . with illustrations from photographs by the author, decorations by Sidney Armer, 1937; The forest pool, story and pictures, 1938; Farthest west . . . illustrated by Sidney Armer, 1939.

Belles Lettres

Southwest . . . illustrated from paintings by the author, 1935.

Art and Nature Studies

Sand-painting of the Navaho Indians, 1931; Cactus . . . with frontispiece in color and fifty illustrations in line by Sidney Armer, 1934.

STUDIES

Kunitz

Kunitz (J)

For references to reviews, see *BRD.*, 1931, 1933-35, 1937-38.

Gertrude (Franklin Horn) Atherton, 1857–

Born Gertrude Franklin Horn, October 30, 1857, in San Francisco. Her grandfather was an important influence in the early development of the city, and Benjamin Franklin was her great-granduncle. She had access to her grandfather's fine private library and was educated in private schools in California and Kentucky. Her marriage in 1876 to George H. Bowen Atherton she described as "one of the most important incidents of my school life." After his death (1887) in Chile she traveled extensively and embarked upon her long literary career by seeking rich and varied experience in various parts of the world. During the war she took part in welfare work.

Her writing career, an outgrowth of her enthusiasm for books and for life, has lasted more than forty years and has produced books with settings in France, Germany, Austria, and the West Indies, as well as most of the periods of recorded history of California. "I'd rather write novels of ancient times, as I enjoy research work and projecting myself into the past," she says, "but the public for such work is very small, and I feel as if I were imposing on good-natured publishers. But there is certainly an immense exhilaration in writing such books as *The Immortal Marriage* and *Golden Peacock*." In preparation for the former she visited Greece and read some two hundred books. She has said that she regards reality and vividness of character as essential to a novel, and that historical novels, the type she most enjoys writing, are exacting because of their requirement of rich imaginative details.

Some of her novels, like *The Conqueror* and *Rezánov*, have enjoyed a steady sale for years. The author has been recognized by honorary degrees from Mills College and the University of California, as well as three French decorations, including that of the Legion of Honor, and the gold medal awarded by the International Academy of Letters and Sciences of Italy. She is an honorary member of the Institut Littéraire et Artistique de France. She has served on the board of trustees of the San Francisco Public Library and on the San Francisco Art Commission, and in 1938 she was made chairman of letters in the National League of American Pen Women.

For further comment, see Critical Survey, pp. 55, 57, 63, 72.

BIBLIOGRAPHY

Novels

What dreams may come, a romance by Frank Lin [*pseud.*], 1888; Hermia Suydam, 1889 (London ed., Hermia, an American woman, 1889); Los cerritos, a romance of the modern time, 1890; A question of time . . . [and Mrs. Pendleton's four-in-hand], 1891; The doomswoman, 1893 (also pub. in Lippincott's monthly magazine, September, 1892, with added title page: The doomswoman); A whirl asunder, 1895; His fortunate grace, 1897; Patience Sparhawk and her times, a novel, 1897; American wives and English husbands, a novel, 1898 (new and rev. ed., Transplanted, a novel, 1919); The Californians, 1898; The valiant runaways . . . with illustrations by Walter C. Greenough, 1898; A daughter of the vine, 1899; Senator North, 1900; The aristocrats, being the impressions of the Lady Helen Pole during her sojourn in the Great north woods as spontaneously recorded in her letters to her friend in North Britain, the Countess of Edge and Ross, 1901 (pub. anonymously); * The conqueror, being the true and romantic story of Alexander Hamilton, 1902; Mrs. Pendleton's four-in-hand, 1903; Rulers of kings, a novel, 1904; The travelling thirds, 1905 (also offprint from The Smart set, July, 1905, with cover-title: The traveling thirds); Rezánov . . . illustrated in water-colors, 1906 (London ed., Rezánov, a novel, 1906); Ancestors, a novel, 1907; The gorgeous isle . . . a romance, scene: Nevis, B. W. I., 1842, illustrated by C. Coles Phillips, 1908; Tower of ivory, a novel, 1910; Julia France and her times, a novel, 1912; Perch of the devil, 1914; Before the gringo came ("Rezánov" and "The doomswoman"), 1915 (reissue of Rezánov and The doomswoman. Not the same as Before the gringo came, 1894); Mrs. Balfame, a novel, 1916; The white morning, a novel of the power of the German women in wartime, 1918; The avalanche, a mystery story, 1919; The sisters-in-law, a novel of our time, 1921 (London ed., Sisters-in-law, 1921); Sleeping fires, a novel, 1922 (London ed., Dormant fires, 1922); * Black oxen, 1923; The crystal cup, 1925; The immortal marriage, 1927; The jealous gods, a processional novel of the fifth century B.C. (concerning one Alcibiades), 1928

(London ed., Vengeful gods, 1928); Dido, queen of hearts, 1929; The sophisticates, 1931; Golden peacock, 1936.

Short Stories

Before the gringo came, 1894 (rev. and enl. ed., The splendid idle forties, stories of old California . . . with illustrations by Harrison Fisher, 1902); The bell in the fog and other stories, 1905; The Spinners' book of fiction by Gertrude Atherton, Mary Austin, Geraldine Bonner, Mary Halleck Foote, Eleanor Gates, James Hopper, Jack London, Bailey Millard, Miriam Michelson, W. C. Morrow, Frank Norris, Henry Milner Rideout, Charles Warren Stoddard, Isobel Strong, Richard Walton Tully, and Herman Whitaker, with a dedicatory poem by George Sterling, collected by the Book committee of the Spinners' club. Illustrated by Lillie V. O'Ryan, Maynard Dixon, Albertine Randall Wheelan, Merle Johnson, E. Almond Withrow, and Gordon Ross. Initials and decorations by Spencer Wright, 1907; The foghorn, stories, 1934; The foghorn . . . with a foreword by the author and an illustration by Dorothy Grover. Number four, Contemporary California short stories, published for its members by the Book club of California, 1937 (pamphlet).

Autobiography

Adventures of a novelist, 1932.

Essays and Studies

California, an intimate history, 1914; Life in the war zone . . . Published for the benefit of Le bienêtre du blessé, société franco-américaine pour nos combattants, 1916 (pamphlet); The living present, 1917; Can women be gentlemen? 1938.

Editor

A few of [Alexander] Hamilton's letters, including his description of the great West Indian hurricane of 1772, 1903.

STUDIES AND ARTICLES

Burgess
Canby (2d ser.)
Cooper (F)
Halsey
Hamilton (C)
Harkins (LP)
† Johnson (1929)
† Johnson (1932)
† Johnson (1936)
Kunitz (L)
Marble
National
Overton (H)
Overton (W)
Overton (WW)
Pattee (N)
Pollard
Sinclair
Underwood
Ward (T)

Clemens, Cyril. "Gertrude Atherton." *Overland M.*, Oct. 1932, pp. 239, 253–54; Cooper, Frederic T. "Gertrude Atherton." *AB.*, Dec. 1909, pp. 356–63; Harris, William E. "Gertrude Atherton." *W.*, Mar. 1929, pp. 62–64; † Johnson, Merle D. and Hopkins, Frederick M., *eds.* "American first editions, a series of bibliographic check-lists . . . number 44, Gertrude (Franklin) Atherton, 1857– ." *PW*., Aug. 25, 1923, p. 612; Maurice, Arthur B. "Gertrude Atherton." *AB*., Sept. 1920, pp. 62–64; Paterson, Isabel, "Gertrude Atherton, a personality." *AB*., Feb. 1924, pp. 632–37; Pendennis, *pseud*. "My types, Gertrude Atherton." *Forum*, Nov. 1917, pp. 585–94; Stevenson, Lionel. "Atherton versus Grundy, the forty years' war." *AB*., July 1929, pp. 464–72; Van Vechten, Carl. "A lady who defies time." *Nation*, Feb. 14, 1923, pp. 194, 196. For references to reviews, see *BRD*., 1906–08, 1910, 1912, 1914–19, 1921–22, 1925, 1927–29, 1931–32, 1934, 1936, 1938.

Atlas, *pseud*. *See* **Carl Van Vechten**

Mary (Hunter) Austin, 1868–1934

Born on September 9, 1868, in Carlinville, Illinois, of pioneer stock. She was a gifted child and wrote poetry at seven. She graduated from Blackburn University in 1888 and went to California for her health.

After living on the eastern slopes of the Sierras and on the border of the Mojave Desert and teaching normal school in Los Angeles, she married Stafford W. Austin, a government official in Owens Valley, California. They lived in the Mojave Desert, and she observed the last stages of the mining life of California, the sheepherding industry, and especially the life and beliefs of the American Indian.

After the death of her one child she began to write. With Jack London and George Sterling she founded the literary colony at Carmel, and she wrote *The Land of Little Rain*. This work of poetical prose brought her recognition at once. She traveled abroad several times, threw herself into political and social causes, including the suffrage movement, and wrote for magazines, gave lectures, acted, and wrote publicity material for the Panama-Pacific International Exposition. She spoke in London before the Fabian Society in 1921, and in the summer of the following year she lectured at the University of California.

In 1918 she built a Spanish colonial house, Casa Querida, in Santa Fe, which she filled with things she had collected in the Southwest. In addition to work for the Indians and the Indian Arts Fund she gave help and encouragement to Pueblo artists. Toward the end of her life her main interest was in the Spanish tradition in the Southwest: she worked to revive the colonial arts and to bring back the custom of the annual Spanish market at Santa Fe. Although she maintained a connection with the literary worlds of New York and Europe, she came to feel more and certainly the powerful Americanism and earthy strength of the tradition of the Spanish Southwest and the Indians. She felt that the next burst of culture in the English-speaking world would appear there. Up to the time of her death she lived quietly in her house, enjoying her garden and her kitchen. She was the friend of two presidents, Theodore Roosevelt and Herbert Hoover, and of many writers and other artistic folk, including May Sinclair, George Bernard Shaw, Amy Lowell, Emma Goldman, Diego Rivera, and Willa Cather.

She died in Santa Fe on August 14, 1934.

For further comment, see Critical Survey, pp. 49, 116, 140.

BIBLIOGRAPHY

Essays and Studies

* The land of little rain, 1903; The flock . . . illustrated by E. Boyd Smith, 1906; Christ in Italy, being the adventures of a maverick among masterpieces, 1912; California, the land of the sun, painted by Sutton Palmer, described by Mary Austin, 1914 (also pub. as The lands of the sun, 1927); Love and the soul maker, 1914; The man Jesus, being a brief account of the life and teaching of the Prophet of Nazareth, 1915 (rev. and enl. ed., A small town man, 1925); What the Mexican conference really means. It represents desires of the people, deprived of human rights, to re-establish themselves in the scheme of social evolution, 1915?; The young woman citizen, 1918; The American rhythm, 1923 (new and enl. ed., The American rhythm, studies and reëxpressions of Amerindian songs, 1930); The land of journeys' ending . . . with illustrations by John Edwin Jackson, 1924; Everyman's genius by Mary Austin, appendix and bibliography, with teaching notes by Maxwell Aley, 1925; Taos pueblo photographed by Ansel Easton Adams and described by Mary Austin, 1930; Experiences facing death, 1931; Indian poetry, 1931 (cover-title; pamphlet); Rural education in New Mexico, 1931; Can prayer be answered? 1934; Indian pottery of the Rio Grande, 1934 (cover-title; pamphlet).

Novels

Isidro . . . illustrated by Eric Pape, 1905; Santa Lucia, a common story, 1908; Outland by Gordon Stairs [*pseud.*], 1910; A woman of genius, 1912; The lovely lady . . . frontispiece by Gordon Grant, 1913; The ford . . . with illustrations by E. Boyd Smith, 1917; No. 26 Jayne street, 1920; Starry adventure, 1931.

Short Stories

The Spinners' book of fiction by Gertrude Atherton, Mary Austin, Geraldine Bonner, Mary Halleck Foote, Eleanor Gates, James Hopper, Jack London, Bailey Millard, Miriam Michelson, W. C. Morrow, Frank Norris, Henry Milner Rideout, Charles Warren Stoddard, Isobel Strong, Richard Walton Tully, and Herman Whitaker, with a dedicatory poem by George Sterling, collected by the Book committee of the Spinners' club. Illustrated by Lillie V. O'Ryan, Maynard Dixon, Albertine Randall Wheelan, Merle Johnson, E. Almond Withrow, and Gordon Ross. Initials and decorations by Spencer Wright, 1907; Lost borders, 1909; The green bough, a tale of the resurrection . . . decorations by Frank Bittner, 1913; One-smoke stories, 1934.

Children's Books

The basket woman, a book of fanciful tales for children, 1904; The trail book . . . with illustrations by Milo Winter, 1918.

Autobiography

* Earth horizon, autobiography, 1932.

Poems

The children sing in the far West . . . with drawings by Gerald Cassidy, 1928; When I am dead, 1935 (pamphlet).

Plays

The arrow maker, a drama in three acts, 1911.

Verses Set to Music

Young man, chieftain! an Indian prayer for medium voice and piano by John Alden Carpenter, 1930 (cover-title).

STUDIES AND ARTICLES

Adamic
Burgess
Cady, Mary L. Young women in the new social order, outline for group discussion or individual study, for use with The young woman citizen by Mary Austin, prepared by Mary L. Cady. 1919
Farrar
† Gaer, Joseph, *ed.* Mary Austin, bibliography and biographical data. [1934]
† Johnson (1936)
Kunitz (L)
† Manly
Marble
Overton (W)
Overton (WW)
Quinn
Raines
Tracy
Van Doren (C)
† Van Doren (M)

Anonymous. "Mary Austin." *AB.*, Sept. 1923, pp. 47–52; Du Bois, Arthur E. "Mary Hunter Austin, 1868–1934." *Sw.R.*, Spring 1935, pp. 231–64; Field, Louise M. "Mary Austin, American." *AB.*, Dec. 1932, pp. 819–21; Knickerbocker, Frances W. "The immanent pattern." *SR.*, Jan.–Mar. 1933, pp. 116–18; Steffens, Lincoln. "Mary Austin and the desert." *A.Mag.*, June 1911, pp. 178–81; Van Doren, Carl. "The American rhythm, Mary Austin, discoverer and prophet." *Cent.*, Nov. 1923, pp. 151–56; Wynn, Dudley. "Mary Austin, woman alone." *VQR.*, Spring 1937, pp. 243–56. For references to reviews, see *BRD.*, 1906–09, 1911, 1913–15, 1917–20, 1923–25, 1927–28, 1930–34.

Irving Babbitt, 1865–1933

Born in Dayton, Ohio, August 2, 1865. He was educated at Harvard, graduating in 1889, and at the Sorbonne (1891–92). After taking the master's degree at Harvard in 1893, he taught Romance languages at Williams in 1893–94. In 1894 he returned to Harvard as an instructor in Romance languages, in 1902 was made an assistant professor, and in 1912 became a professor of French literature. He was a guest lecturer at Kenyon College (1920), Yale (1922), Stanford (1922), Amherst (1930), and the University of Toronto (1930); and in 1923, as exchange professor from Harvard, he delivered at the Sorbonne a series of lectures on the romantic school of French literature. He died in Cambridge, July 15, 1933.

Babbitt was opposed to the romantic spirit in letters and in life, feeling that it was, in the final analysis, injurious to the interests of the individual as well as to those of civilization. He deplored the displacement of the religious and classical ideals by those of humanitarianism and utilitarianism, and, concretely, the more blatant features of democracy: the standardization; the lack of good taste or good manners; in education, the increasing stress upon the vocational; and, in literature, the tendency to exalt the ego at the expense of decorum.

His views on all contemporary literary or social issues took shape from this humanistic ideal. He did not object to a highly individual quality in a man's style, but as he wrote in the *Saturday Review of Literature* not long before his death, "it is at least equally important that it should have about it something structural, and this structural quality can arise only from the subordination of the uniqueness that each one of us receives as a free gift of nature to some larger whole." He deplored also the joint influence of Rousseauist and Baconian in undermining the religious tradition of Judaea and the classical or humanistic ideal of Greece; "poised and proportionate living" is to be accomplished "by observing the law of measure" and the general objective of "decorum." Humanism and religion have worked together to inculcate Burke's two principles, the spirit of a gentleman and the spirit of religion; humanitarianism, or the utilitarian-sentimental movement, has undermined both these principles, without substituting anything of equivalent value. Emotionalists of the type of Rousseau on the one hand, and modern scientists on the other, have failed to recognize the importance of the will, and its transcendence over emotion or nature. Exercise of this will to refrain, pushed to extremes in Buddhism and Christianity, but increasingly difficult for modern men, must be achieved if we are to avoid anarchy. The pure authoritarianism of Catholicism is not the only answer; humanism can be an alternative. "The humanist exercises the will to refrain," he wrote in *Forum* in 1930, "but the end that he has in view is not the renunciation of the expansive desires but the subduing of them to the law of measure."

For further comment, see Critical Survey, pp. 185–86.

BIBLIOGRAPHY

Essays and Studies

Literature and the American college, essays in defense of the humanities, 1908; * The new Laokoon, an essay on the confusion of the arts, 1910; The masters of modern French criticism, 1912; * Rousseau and romanticism, 1919; Criticism in America, its function and status, essays by Irving Babbitt, Van Wyck Brooks, W. C. Brownell, Ernest Boyd, T. S. Eliot, H. L. Mencken, Stuart P. Sherman, J. E. Spingarn, and George E. Woodberry, 1924; Democracy and leadership, 1924; Humanist and specialist, address at the dedication of the Marston hall of languages, Brown university, October 13, 1925, 1926; French literature, 1928; On being creative and other essays, 1932.

Editor

Introduction a l'histoire de la littérature anglaise par H. Taine, edited with an essay on Taine, 1898; Souvenirs d'enfance et de jeunesse par Ernest Renan, edited with an introduction and notes, 1902; Zadig and other stories by Voltaire, chosen and edited with an introduction, notes, and a vocabulary, 1905; Racine's Phèdre edited with introduction and notes, 1910.

Translations

The Dhammapada translated from the Pāli with an essay on Buddha and the Occident, 1936.

STUDIES AND ARTICLES

American
Eliot
Eliot, Thomas S. Essays ancient & modern. [1936]
Eliot, Thomas S. For Lancelot Andrewes, essays on style and order. 1929
Frank (R)
Grattan
Kunitz (L)
Leander, Folke. Humanism and naturalism, a comparative study of Ernest Seillière, Irving Babbitt, and Paul Elmer More. 1937
Lynd, Robert. The art of letters. [1920]
MacLean
McMahon, Francis E. The humanism of Irving Babbitt. 1931
Mercier
Mercier (M)
More (O)
Munson
Munson (D)
National
Richard, Christian. Le mouvement humaniste en Amérique et les courants de pensée similaires en France. Preface par Jean Laporte. 1934
Shafer
Sinclair, Upton B. Mammonart, an essay in economic interpretation. [c1925]
Tate
† Taylor
Ward
West
Zeitlin

Adams, James L. "Humanism and creation." *HH.*, Oct.–Dec. 1932, pp. 173–96; Bandler, Bernard, II. "The individualism of Irving Babbitt." *HH.*, Oct.–Dec. 1929, pp. 57–70; Boas, Ralph P. "The humanism of Irving Babbitt." *AR.*, July 1925, pp. 391–99; Cappon, Alexander P. "Irving Babbitt and his fundamental thinking." *NH.*, Sept.–Oct. 1933, pp. 9–13; Colum, Mary M. "Literature, ethics, and the knights of good sense." *Scrib.*, June 1930, pp. 599–608; Colum. "Self-critical America." *Scrib.*, Feb. 1930, pp. 197–206; DeMille, George E. "On being humanite." *SR.*, Apr.–June 1933, pp. 249–51; Dubbel, S. Earl. "He searched the past." *SAQ.*, Jan. 1936, pp. 50–61; Eden, Helen P. "Hearts and heads." *Dub.Rev.*, July 1920, pp. 68–74; Eliot, Thomas S. "The humanism of Irving Babbitt." *Forum*, July 1928, pp. 37–44; Elliott, George R. "Babbitt and religion." *AR.*, Feb. 1934, pp. 487–91; Elliott. "Irving Babbitt as I knew him." *AR.*, Nov. 1936, pp. 36–60; Elliott. "The religious dissension of Babbitt and More." *AR.*, May 1937, pp. 252–65; Elliott. "T. S. Eliot and Irving Babbitt." *AR.*, Sept. 1936, pp. 442–54; Giese, William F. "Irving Babbitt, undergraduate." *AR.*, Nov. 1935, pp. 65–94; Greever, Garland. "Romanticism as a philosophy of life." *SR.*, Jan.–Mar. 1920, pp. 101–05; Hecht, Hans. "Irving Babbitt, Rousseau and romanticism." *E.Studien*, Oct. 1921, pp. 447–57; Hough, Lynn H. "Dr. Babbitt and vital control." *LQR.*, Jan. 1927, pp. 1–15; Jones, Howard M. "Professor Babbitt cross-examined." *NR.*, Mar. 21, 1928, pp. 158–60; MacCampbell, Donald. "Irving Babbitt, some entirely personal impressions." *SR.*, Apr.–June 1935, pp. 164–74; Maddox, Notley S. "Irving Babbitt and the emperor Shun." *AR.*, Jan. 1926, pp. 74–80; Mather, Frank J., Jr. "Irving Babbitt." *HGM.*, Dec. 1933, pp. 65–84; Mercier, Louis J. A. "The legacy of Irving Babbitt." *HGM.*, June 1934, pp. 327–42; More, Paul E. "Irving Babbitt." *AR.*, Apr. 1934, pp. 23–40; Morell, Ray. "Wordsworth and Professor Babbitt." *Scrut.*, Mar. 1933, pp. 374–83; Munson, Gorham B. "The socratic virtues of Irving Babbitt." *Crit.*, June 1926, pp. 494–503; Nickerson, Hoffman. "Irving Babbitt." *AR.*, Feb. 1934, pp. 385–404; Nickerson. "Irving Babbitt." *Crit.*, Jan. 1934, pp. 179–95; Richard, Christian. "Irving Babbitt, the man and the teacher." *CW.*, Oct. 1938, pp. 44–49; Richards, Philip S. "Irving Babbitt, a new humanism." *N.Cent.*, Apr. 1928, pp. 433–44; Richards. "Irving Babbitt, religion and romanticism." *N.Cent.*, May 1928, pp. 644–55; Russell, Frances T. "The romanticism of Irving Babbitt." *SAQ.*, Oct. 1933, pp. 399–411; Salpeter, Harry. "Irving Babbitt, calvinist." *OI.*, July 16, 1930, pp. 421–23, 439; Thompson, Alan R. "Literature and irresponsibility." *AR.*, May 1936, pp. 192–202; Warren, Austin. "A portrait of Irving Babbitt." *Com.*, June 26, 1936, pp. 234–36; Wilson, Edmund. "Notes on Babbitt and More." *NR.*, Mar. 19, 1930, pp. 115–20. For references to reviews, see *BRD.*, 1908, 1910, 1913, 1919, 1924, 1932, 1936.

Margaret Ayer Barnes, 1886–

Born in Chicago, April 8, 1886, the youngest of five children of Benjamin F. Ayer, a prominent lawyer, and Janet Hopkins Ayer, Janet Ayer Fairbank (Mrs. Kellogg Fairbank) is her sister. She was reared in Chicago and educated at the University School for Girls and then at Bryn Mawr, where she graduated in 1907; from 1920 to 1923 she served as alumnae director. In 1910 she married Cecil Barnes, a Chicago lawyer, and she is the mother of three sons. Until she was forty Mrs. Barnes led a busy domestic life, with no attempts at artistic expression more ambitious than amateur acting.

Her literary career began in 1926, after an automobile accident in France had temporarily incapacitated her for any physical activity. Forced, because of a broken back, to spend most of a year in hospitals, she began writing short stories for her own amusement. One of them, submitted at the suggestion of a friend, was bought by the *Pictorial Review*, and she subsequently sold all the others and wrote more. *Prevailing Winds* is a collection of these early stories. Although she has said that the single responsibility of the novelist makes the writing of fiction more congenial to her than working on plays, Mrs. Barnes has done work for the theater, including a dramatization, played by Katharine Cornell, of Edith Wharton's novel, *The Age of Innocence*. In 1937–38 her own best-selling novel, *Edna His Wife*, was successfully presented as a monodrama by Cornelia Otis Skinner. *Years of Grace*, awarded the Pulitzer Prize in 1931, was the best-selling novel of 1932. The author holds honorary degrees from Tufts College and Oglethorpe University.

Mrs. Barnes, who is an enthusiastic theater-goer, concert attendant, and traveler, and spends much time out of doors, does all her writing in a third-floor bedroom in a city house, much of it late at night. She considers "living in a family—the larger the better" "a great boon to a writer," as keeping him "in touch with reality." She feels that an author can learn much from reading, and she rereads frequently her favorite novels. While she considers an important theme, illuminating human experience, essential in any great book, she does not regard any subject as in itself impossible, and disapproves of the tendency of some modern proletarian writers to subordinate their characters and make tracts of their novels. "I think that the books that live in the hearts and minds of the people," she says, "are those that are written, subtly, perhaps, but sincerely, about some conflict of moral forces. . . . I think a great novel can be written about a strike in a textile mill and a great novel can be written about the thoughts of a lady while walking downstairs. It all depends on *how* it is written." She believes that the purpose of a conscientious novelist should be to reproduce, more vividly and accurately than the biographer or historian (although using the same sources), his own time, thus producing a "period" novel more significant than those usually so called; and she has recently said that, even in the face of the obviously tremendous impact of mass movements today, she considers "a brilliant character study of an individual" to be "the most vital thing in literature."

For further comment, see Critical Survey, p. 48.

BIBLIOGRAPHY

Novels

* Years of grace, 1930; Westward passage, 1931; Within this present, 1933; The alleged great-aunt begun by Henry Kitchell Webster, completed by Janet Ayer Fairbank and Margaret Ayer Barnes, 1935; Edna, his wife, an American idyll, 1935; Wisdom's gate, 1938.

Short Stories

Prevailing winds, 1928.

STUDIES AND ARTICLES

Kunitz
Lawrence (S)
"Sheldon et al. v. Metro-Goldwyn pictures corporation et al. Circuit court of appeals, Second circuit. Jan. 17, 1936." *Federal reporter*, second series, 1936, vol. 81, pp. 49–56

Warren, Dale. "Margaret Ayer Barnes." *W.*, Dec. 1934, pp. 434–36. For references to reviews, see *BRD.*, 1928, 1930, 1931, 1933, 1935, 1938.

Philip Barry, 1896–

Born June 18, 1896, in Rochester, New York. Educated at first by priests and nuns, he was a precocious boy and wrote a short story at nine and a play at thirteen. At Yale, where he was an editor of the *Yale Review*, he did some dramatic writing, and during his senior year a play of his was presented by the Yale Dramatic Club.

His college career was interrupted by the war. As weak eyes made military service impossible, he worked in the State Department in Washington and in the American Embassy in London.

He graduated in 1919; and, definitely desirous of a career as a dramatist, went to Harvard to study with Professor Baker. To earn money he wrote advertising copy. *A Punch for Judy*, produced in New York by Professor Baker's 47 Workshop in 1921, toured as far west as Ohio.

With *You and I*, which in 1922 won the Harvard Prize of five hundred dollars and a New York production (1923), Barry's playwriting career had begun. Since that time he has written frequently and successfully for the Broadway stage, and his work has been presented more often outside New York than that of any other American playwright except Eugene O'Neill. He has written also for Metro-Goldwyn-Mayer. He divides his time between New York and the Riviera.

For further comment, see Critical Survey, pp. 111–12.

BIBLIOGRAPHY

Plays

You and I, a comedy in three acts, 1923; The youngest, a comedy in three acts, 1925; In a garden, a comedy in three acts . . . with an introduction by Arthur Hopkins, 1926; White wings, a play . . . with an introduction by Donald Ogden Stewart, 1927; Cock Robin, a play in three acts by Elmer Rice and Philip Barry, 1929; * Holiday, a comedy in three acts, 1929; John, a play, 1929; Paris bound, a comedy, 1929; * Hotel universe, a play, 1930; Tomorrow and tomorrow, a play, 1931; The animal kingdom, a comedy, 1932; The joyous season, a play, 1934; Spring dance, a comedy in three acts . . . (adapted from an original play by Eleanor Golden and Eloise Barrangon), 1936.

Novels

War in heaven, 1938.

Miscellany

The dramatist and the amateur public, an address . . . delivered before the Yale conference of drama, New Haven, Conn., February 12th, 1927, 1927 (cover-title; pamphlet).

STUDIES AND ARTICLES

Brown
Brown (U)
Clark
Flexner
Fort
Halline
Kunitz (L)
Mantle
Mantle (C)
Moses (A)
Moses (R)
National
† Quinn (H)
Quinn (R)
Skinner
Waugh
Whitman

Cajetan, Brother. "The pendulum starts back." *CW.*, Mar. 1935, pp. 650–56; Carmer, Carl. "Philip Barry." *TAM.*, Nov. 1929, pp. 819–26. For references to reviews, see *BRD.*, 1926–27, 1929–32, 1938–39.

Charles A(ustin) Beard, 1874–

Born near Knightstown, Indiana, November 27, 1874. He was reared in his native state and attended De Pauw University. "I came from a long line of farmers and artisans," he writes. "My father, though president of the local bank, believed that boys should be brought up on a farm, out of doors, at hard work in field and forest. By the time I was fifteen I had had enough exercise to last me a life time. My muscles and body were hard as steel. I could ride wild horses bare back, and split an oak log with a maul and wedge. . . . My father had a large library for the time and place—more than a thousand books in history, science and various branches of knowledge. He was an inveterate reader and taught me to read hard books early in my boyhood days. So I combined much reading with outdoor life. . . . My father was a man of means who gave me money generously for books, education, and travel, and I took full advantage of his generosity."

Graduating in 1898, Beard went to England. After an academic year at Oxford he returned to this country to continue his studies at Cornell (1899–1900) and at Columbia, where he took the master's (1903) and doctor's (1904) degrees. He remained at Columbia as an instructor in politics and taught until 1917, when he resigned his professorship, in protest against what he regarded as violations of academic freedom.

From 1917 to 1922 he directed the Training School for Public Service in New York City and devoted his attention to public problems. In 1922 he served as adviser to the Institute for Municipal Research, in Tokyo. After the earthquake of 1923 he accepted an invitation to serve as adviser to Viscount Goto, Japanese Minister of Home Affairs, in matters of civic reconstruction, and in 1927 he accepted a similar invitation in Yugoslavia.

At first interested in English and Continental history, he made his reputation by writing, with James Harvey Robinson, *The Development of Modern Europe*, published in 1907–08. Subsequently, however, the history of the United States and its government demanded more of his attention. He was a pioneer in the economic interpretation of American history. *The Rise of American Civilization*, in which he collaborated with his wife, Mary R. Beard, not only won him wide attention in scholarly circles but, as a selection of the Book-of-the-Month Club in 1927, made a popular success.

Beard wrote the report (1932) of the American Historical Association's Commission on the Social Studies in the Schools, and in 1933 was made president of the Association. In 1939 he was elected to membership in the National Institute of Arts and Letters. The author lives in Connecticut and amuses himself by dairy farming. He attributes his cosmopolitan point of view to his travels, and says, "I feel as much at home among the headhunters of Formosa and the paving pounders of Berlin as in the villages of the Middle West." Although he has known distinguished people, he declares: "The only man that I ever put myself to any inconvenience to meet was Mark Twain. He was worth the trouble, despite my obscurity. What he said about the human race was a joy forever."

Beard believes that in any writing some attitude is sure to make itself felt. ". . . Every writer does in fact have some conception of the world and humanity in it, even when he professes himself to be an idiot, that is, a 'mere reporter.' Every writer is a selector, organizer, and emphasizer of facts—a few out of billions. He may have a muddled philosophy or a clear-cut one, but he has it."

BIBLIOGRAPHY

Political and Historical Studies

The industrial revolution . . . with a preface by F. York Powell, 1901; The office of justice of the peace in England in its origin and development, 1904; An introduction to the English historians, 1906; The development of modern Europe, an introduction to the study of current history by James Harvey Robinson . . . and Charles A. Beard, 1907–08 (2 vols.); European sobriety in the presence of the Balkan crisis, 1908 (cover-title; pamphlet; International conciliation, December 1908, no. 13); Politics, 1908 (pamphlet); Readings in modern European history, a collection of extracts from the sources chosen with the purpose of illustrating some of the chief phases of the development of Europe during the last two hundred years by James Harvey Robinson . . . and Charles A. Beard . . . volume I, the eighteenth century: the French revolution and the Napoleonic period, 1908; The ballot's burden . . . reprinted for the Short ballot organization, 127 Duane st., New York city from Political science quarterly, vol. XXIV, no. 4, 1909 (pamphlet); Readings in modern European history, a collection of extracts from the sources chosen with the purpose of illustrating some of the chief phases of the development of Europe during the last two hundred years by James Harvey Robinson . . . and Charles A. Beard . . . volume II, Europe since the Congress of Vienna, 1909; American government and politics, 1910; American city government, a survey of newer tendencies, 1912; Outlines of European history, part II, from the opening of the eighteenth century to the present day by James Harvey Robinson . . . and Charles A. Beard, 1912 (revision of The development of modern Europe); The Supreme court and the Constitution, 1912; * An economic interpretation of the Constitution of the United States, 1913; American citizenship by Charles A. Beard . . . and Mary Ritter Beard, 1914; Contemporary American history, 1877–1913, 1914; The budgetary provisions of the New York constitution, 1915 (caption-title; pamphlet); Economic origins of Jeffersonian democracy, 1915; Six years' experience with the direct primary in New Jersey, 1917? (pamphlet); The history of the American people, for grammar grades and junior high schools by Charles A. Beard and William C. Bagley, 1918; Address delivered by Charles Austin Beard, Ph.D., "Public service in America," under the auspices of the Educational dep't of the Municipal court, room 676, City hall, Friday, November 14th, at 4 P. M., 1919? (cover-title; pamphlet); A manual to accompany The history of the American people by Charles A. Beard and William C. Bagley, 1919; National governments and the world war by Frederic A. Ogg . . . and Charles A. Beard, 1919; A first book in American history by Charles A. Beard and William C. Bagley, 1920; History of Europe, our own times, the eighteenth and nineteenth centuries, the opening of the twentieth century and the world war by James Harvey Robinson and Charles A. Beard, 1921; History of the United States by Charles A. Beard and Mary R. Beard, 1921; Cross currents in Europe to-day, 1922; The economic basis of politics, 1922; Our old world background by Charles A. Beard and William C. Bagley, 1922 (also pub. as Elementary world history, a revised and simplified edition of Our old world background, 1932); The administration and politics of Tokyo, a survey and opinions, 1923; Government research, past, present and future, 1926 (cover-title; pamphlet); * The rise of American civilization by Charles A. Beard & Mary R. Beard, decorations by Wilfred Jones, in two volumes, volume I, The agricultural era, 1927; * The rise of American civilization by Charles A. Beard & Mary R. Beard, decorations by Wilfred Jones, in two volumes, volume II, The industrial era, 1927; The American party battle, 1928; The Balkan pivot: Yugoslavia, a study in government and administration by Charles A. Beard . . . and George Radin, 1929; The American leviathan, the republic in the machine age by Charles A. Beard . . . and William Beard, 1930; The myth of rugged American individualism, 1932 (pamphlet); The navy: defense or portent? 1932; The future comes, a study of the new deal by Charles A. Beard and George H. E. Smith, 1933; Hitlerism and our liberties, text of address given by Professor Charles A.

Beard at the New school for social research, Tuesday, April 10, 1934, 1934 (caption-title; leaflet); The idea of national interest, an analytical study in American foreign policy by Charles A. Beard, with the collaboration of G. H. E. Smith, 1934; The open door at home, a trial philosophy of national interest by Charles A. Beard with the collaboration of G. H. E. Smith, 1934; The recovery program (1933–1934) a study of the depression and the fight to overcome it by George H. E. Smith and Charles A. Beard, 1934 (pamphlet); The presidents in American history, 1935; Schools in the story of culture [by] Charles A. Beard and William G. Carr, 1935 (cover-title; pamphlet); Cumulative annual guide to American government and politics (1936), 1936; The devil theory of war, an inquiry into the nature of history and the possibility of keeping out of war, 1936; The discussion of human affairs, an inquiry into the nature of the statements, assertions, allegations, claims, heats, tempers, distempers, dogmas, and contentions which appear when human affairs are discussed and into the possibility of putting some rhyme and reason into processes of discussion, 1936; Jefferson, corporations, and the Constitution, 1936; History of civilization, Our own age by Charles A. Beard, James Harvey Robinson, and Donnal V. Smith, 1937; The making of American civilization by Charles A. Beard and Mary R. Beard, color illustrations by Stanley M. Arthurs, 1937; America today by Roy F. Nichols, William C. Bagley, and Charles A. Beard, with drawings by George M. Richards, 1938; America yesterday by Roy F. Nichols, William C. Bagley, and Charles A. Beard, with drawings by George M. Richards, 1938; America in midpassage by Charles A. Beard & Mary R. Beard, drawings by Wilfred Jones, volume III, The rise of American civilization, 1939; Giddy minds and foreign quarrels, an estimate of American foreign policy, 1939.

Miscellany

Unemployment and adult education, a symposium on certain problems of re-education arising from "permanent lay-off"—the displacement of men and women in industry through the introduction of machinery and other labor-saving devices, sometimes known as technological unemployment by Charles A. Beard, Stuart Chase, Paul H. Douglas, Rexford G. Tugwell, Isador Lubin, Elizabeth F. Baker, Sumner Slichter, Newton D. Baker, Robert I. Rees, Spencer Miller, jr., J. C. Wright, Wesley A. O'Leary, N. C. Miller, A. Caswell Ellis, James E. Russell, and others, Morse A. Cartwright, editor, 1931 (pamphlet); Report of the Commission on the social studies, part VII. The nature of the social sciences in relation to objectives of instruction, 1934; The unique function of education in American democracy, 1937 (First draft of the report contained in this volume prepared by Charles A. Beard for National education association of the United States. Educational policies commission).

Edited and Compiled Works

Readings in American government and politics, 1909; Loose leaf digest of short ballot charters, a documentary history of the commission form of municipal government . . . first edition—five hundred copies, no. , 1911; Documents on the state-wide initiative, referendum and recall by Charles A. Beard . . . and Birl E. Shultz, 1912; The city manager plan of municipal government (Reprinted from Beard's Loose-leaf digest of short ballot charters), 1913 (cover-title; pamphlet); Whither mankind, a panorama of modern civilization, 1928; Toward civilization, 1930; America faces the future, 1932; A century of progress, 1932; Report of the Commission on the social studies, part I. A charter for the social sciences in the schools drafted by Charles A. Beard, 1932 (American historical association); Current problems of public policy, a collection of materials edited by Charles A. Beard with the collaboration of George H. E. Smith, 1936.

STUDIES AND ARTICLES

Ames, Edgar W. New York state government by Edgar W. Ames . . . revised by Charles H. Seaver with a chapter on Comparative government and an outline of federal war organization. 1918 (supplement to Ashley's The new civics and Beard & Beard's American citizenship)

Blinkoff, Maurice. The influence of Charles A. Beard upon American historiography . . . published under the direction of the Committee on publications on the Roswell Park publication fund. [1936]

Chamberlain

Edman

Ely, Lena A. Study guide for problems in American history, a pupil's manual based on Beard and Bagley's History of the American people, by Lena A. Ely and Edith King . . . and Martin J. Stormzand. [c1926]

Ely, Lena A. Teaching American history by the problem method, a teachers' manual to accompany a pupils' manual based on Beard and Bagley's History of the American people, by Lena A. Ely and Edith King . . . and Martin J. Stormzand. [c1926]

Erbe, Carl H. Questions and problems in American government to accompany Beard's American government and politics, fifth edition. 1929

Erbe, Carl H. Questions and problems in American government to accompany Beard's American government and politics, sixth edition, by Carl H. Erbe . . . Revised edition. 1931

Freeman (J)

National

Stormzand, Martin J. American history teaching and testing, supervised study and scientific testing in American history, based on Beard and Bagley's The history of the American people. 1925

Agar, Herbert. "A plea to Mr. Charles A. Beard." *AR.*, Jan. 1935, pp. 297–309; Davis, Elmer. "No comfort for optimists." *SRL.*, May 20, 1939, pp. 3–4; Giddens, Paul H. "The views of George Bancroft and Charles A. Beard on the making of the constitution." *JAH.*, Vol. 27, No. 3, 1933, pp. 129–41; Gideonse, Harry D. "National collectivism and Charles A. Beard." *JPE.*, Dec. 1935, pp. 778–99; Herring, Hubert. "Charles A. Beard, free lance among the historians." *Harper's*, May 1939, pp. 641–52; Lerner, Max. "Beard's 'economic interpretation.'" *NR.*, May 10, 1939, pp. 7–11. For references to reviews, see *BRD.*, 1907, 1909–15, 1918, 1922, 1927–37, 1939.

(Charles) William Beebe, 1877–

Born in Brooklyn, July 29, 1877. He was educated at Columbia and remained after graduation in 1898 for a year of graduate study. In 1899 he was made honorary curator of ornithology in the New York Zoological Society, and in addition to this post he has been for years director of the Department of Tropical Research.

In the course of his work he has been on expeditions to Mexico, Borneo, and Brazil, and directed work at the Society's Tropical Research Station in British Guiana. In 1923 and 1925 he made trips to the Galapagos Islands. Between 1930 and 1934 more than thirty descents were made in the bathysphere, Beebe's device, designed by his associate Otis Barton, for facilitating underwater observation by deep-sea diving.

He has written, in addition to his books, many scientific papers, and he is interested in all kinds of literature. He admires especially the work of Lord Dunsany, Kipling, Buchan, and A. A. Milne. A hard, steady worker, capable of concentration under the most varied circumstances, he takes copious notes on his trips and organizes them carefully and in great detail. His informal nature studies, written without the effort and pains characteristic of his more technical work, have been successful in making science attractive to the untrained reader.

Beebe has been honored by membership in many scientific societies in this country and abroad and with honorary doctor's degrees, and he holds the Elliott and John Burroughs Medals. In 1939 he was elected to membership in the National Institute of Arts and Letters.

For further comment, see Critical Survey, p. 154.

BIBLIOGRAPHY

Nature and Scientific Studies

Two bird-lovers in Mexico . . . illustrated with photographs from life taken by the author, 1905; The bird, its form and function . . . with over three hundred and seventy illustrations chiefly photographed from life by the author, 1906; The log of the sun, a chronicle of nature's year . . . with fifty-two full page illustrations by Walter King Stone and numerous vignettes and photographs from life, 1906; Geographic variation in birds with especial reference to the effects of humidity, 1907 (in *Zoologia* [!] *scientific contributions of the New York zoological society*, vol. 1, no. 1, September 25, 1907); Ecology of the hoatzin, An ornithological reconnaissance of northeastern Venezuela, 1909 (in *Zoologica*, vol. 1, nos. 2, 3, December 28, 1909); New species of insects collected by C. William Beebe in South America. I, Mallophaga from the hoatzin by Vernon L. Kellogg. II, A new mantis from British Guiana by A. N. Caudell. III, New species of Lepidoptera from British Guiana, 1910 (in *Zoologica*, vol. 1, no. 4, January 15, 1910); Our search for a wilderness, an account of two ornithological expeditions to Venezuela and to British Guiana by Mary Blair Beebe and C. William Beebe . . . illustrated with photographs from life taken by the authors, 1910; Racket formation in tail-feathers of the motmots, Three cases of supernumerary toe in the broad-winged hawk, 1910 (in *Zoologica*, vol. 1, nos. 5, 6, January 15, 1910); The undescribed juvenal plumage of the Yucatan jay by C. William Beebe . . . and Lee S. Crandall, 1911 (in *Zoologica*, vol. 1, no. 7, December 5, 1911); New blood pheasants, 1912 (in *Zoologica*, vol. 1, no. 10, August 17, 1912); Notes on No. 12, The ontogeny of the white ibis by C. William Beebe. No. 13, Specialization of tail down in ducks by C. William Beebe and L. S. Crandall. No. 14, Effect of postponed moult in certain passerine birds by C. William Beebe, 1914 (in *Zoologica*, vol. 1, nos. 12, 13, & 14, February 1914); No. 17, Review of the genus Gennaeus by C. William Beebe . . . No. 18,

Notes on Costa Rican birds by Lee S. Crandall, 1914 (in *Zoologica*, vol. I, nos. 17 & 18, September 1914); Preliminary pheasant studies, 1914 (in *Zoologica*, vol. I, no. 15, April 1914); A tetrapteryx stage in the ancestry of birds, 1915 (in *Zoologica*, vol. II, no. 2, November 1915); No. 3, Notes on the birds of Pará, Brazil. No. 4, Fauna of four square feet of jungle debris, 1916 (in *Zoologica*, vol. II, nos. 3 & 4, February 1916); Tropical wild life in British Guiana, zoological contributions from the Tropical research station of the New York zoological society by William Beebe . . . G. Inness Hartley . . . and Paul G. Howes . . . with an introduction by Colonel Theodore Roosevelt, volume I, photographs and other illustrations by the authors, 1917; Jungle night, 1918 (cover-title; pamphlet); * Jungle peace, 1918; A monograph of the pheasants . . . in four volumes . . . Published under the auspices of the New York zoological society . . ., 1918–22 (also pub. in 2 vol. revision: Pheasants, their lives and homes . . . Published under the auspices of the New York zoological society, 1926); The higher vertebrates of British Guiana with special reference to the fauna of Bartica district. No. 7, List of amphibia, reptilia, and mammalia. No. 8, Birds of Bartica district. No. 9, Lizards of the genus Ameiva, 1919 (in *Zoologica*, vol. II, nos. 7, 8, 9, May 1919); Contributions of the Tropical research station, 1916 to 1921, 1921 (in *Zoologica*, vol. III, no. 2, September 1921); * Edge of the jungle, 1921; Notes on Galapagos Lepidoptera, 1923 (in *Zoologica*, vol. V, no. 3, January 11, 1923); Williams Galapagos expedition, 1923 (in *Zoologica*, vol. V, no. 1, December 31, 1923); Galapagos, world's end . . . with 24 coloured illustrations by Isabel Cooper and 83 photographs, mostly by John Tee-Van. Published under the auspices of the New York zoological society, 1924; Jungle days, 1925; Studies of a tropical jungle, one quarter of a square mile of jungle at Kartabo, British Guiana, 1925 (in *Zoologica*, vol. VI, no. 1, March 11, 1925); The variegated tinamou, crypturus variegatus variegatus (Gmelin) . . . contributions to the life history and anatomy of the birds of Kartabo, Bartica district, British Guiana, 1925 (in *Zoologica*, vol. VI, no. 2, March 18, 1925); The Arcturus adventure, an account of the New York zoological society's first oceanographic expedition . . . with 77 illustrations from colored plates, photographs, and maps, published under the auspices of the Zoological society, 1926; The Arcturus oceanographic expedition, 1926 (in *Zoologica*, vol. VIII, no. 1, November 4, 1926); The three-toed sloth, bradypus cuculliger cuculliger Wagler . . . contributions to the life history and anatomy of the mammals of Kartabo, Bartica district, British Guiana, 1926 (in *Zoologica*, vol. VII, no. 1, March 25, 1926); Pheasant jungles . . . with sixty illustrations from photographs by the author, 1927; * Beneath tropic seas, a record of diving among the coral reefs of Haiti . . . with sixty illustrations, 1928; The fishes of Port-au-Prince bay, Haiti, with a summary of the known species of marine fish of the island of Haiti and Santo Domingo by William Beebe . . . and John Tee-Van, 1928 (in *Zoologica*, vol. X, no. 1, December 31, 1928); Deep sea fish of the Hudson gorge, taken at Station 113 of the Arcturus and Station 114 of the eleventh expedition of The department of tropical research . . . volume XII, number 1, April 30, 1929, 1929 (in *Zoologica*); Haplophryne Hudsonius, a new species, description and osteology . . . volume XII, number 2, April 30, 1929, 1929 (in *Zoologica*); Bermuda oceanographic expeditions, 1929–1930. No. 1—Introduction. No. 2—List of nets and data, 1931 (in *Zoologica*, vol. XIII, nos.

1 and 2, April 1, 1931); New species of fish from the West Indies by William Beebe and Gloria Hollister, volume XII, number 9, March 22, 1931, 1931 (in *Zoologica*); Notes on the gill-finned goby, Bathygobius soporator (Cuvier and Valenciennes) . . . volume XII, number 5, July 30, 1931, 1931 (in *Zoologica*); Bermuda oceanographic expeditions, 1931, individual nets and data, 1932 (in *Zoologica*, vol. XIII, no. 3, March 1932); New Bermuda fish, including six new species and forty-three species hitherto unrecorded from Bermuda by William Beebe and John Tee-Van, 1932 (in *Zoologica*, vol. XIII, no. 5, March 23, 1932); Nineteen new species and four post-larval deep-sea fish, 1932 (in *Zoologica*, vol. XIII, no. 4, March 1932); Nonsuch: land of water . . . with 55 illustrations, published under the auspices of the New York zoological society, 1932; Ontological notes on remora remora, 1932 (in *Zoologica*, vol. XIII, no. 6, September 19, 1932); Deep-sea fishes of the Bermuda oceanographic expeditions, No. 1—Introduction, No. 2—Family Alepocephalidae, No. 3—Family Argentinidae, 1933 (in *Zoologica*, vol. XVI, nos. 1, 2, and 3, August 1933); Deep-sea isospondylous fishes, two new genera and four new species, 1933 (in *Zoologica*, vol. XIII, no. 8, July 25, 1933); Field book of the shore fishes of Bermuda by William Beebe, SC.D. and John Tee-Van, published under the auspices of the New York zoological society, 343 illustrations, 1933; Nomenclatural notes on the shore fishes of Bermuda by William Beebe and John Tee-Van, 1933 (in *Zoologica*, vol. XIII, no. 7, February 21, 1933); Deep-sea fishes of the Bermuda oceanographic expeditions, family Idiacanthidae, 1934 (in *Zoologica*, vol. XVI, no. 4, March 1934); Half mile down . . . with 123 illustrations and 8 colored plates, published under the auspices of the New York zoological society, 1934; A new genus and species of scaleless blenny, Somersia furcata, from Bermuda, by William Beebe and John Tee-Van, 1934 (caption-title; pamphlet); Deep-sea fishes of the Bermuda oceanographic expeditions. No. 1—Family Derichthyidae. No. 2—Family Nessorhamphidae, 1935 (in *Zoologica*, vol. XX, nos. 1, 2, December 24, 1935); The fishes of Union Island, Grenadines, British West Indies, with the description of a new species of star-gazer [by] William Beebe . . . and Gloria Hollister, 1935 (in *Zoologica*, vol. XIX, no. 6, December 31, 1935); Deep-sea fishes of the Bermuda oceanographic expeditions. No. 3—Family Serrivomeridae [by] William Beebe & Jocelyn Crane, 1936 (in *Zoologica*, vol. XX, no. 3, Nov. 30, 1936); Zaca venture . . . with 24 illustrations, published under the auspices of the New York zoological society, 1938.

Selected Work

Exploring with Beebe, selections for younger readers from the writings of William Beebe . . . illustrated with photographs by the author, 1932.

STUDIES AND ARTICLES

Beebe, Charles W. Jungle peace . . . foreword by Theodore Roosevelt. [1925]
Gillis
† Johnson (1929)
† Johnson (1932)
† Johnson (1936)
Kunitz (L)
† Manly
National
Shaw
Sherman (M)
Tracy
Wilson (D)

Barr, Mark. "Roughing it in the tropics." *A.Mo.*, Nov. 1927, pp. 611–20; Beebe, Charles W. "Contributions of the Tropical research station, 1916 to 1921." *Zoologica, scientific contributions of the New York zoological society*, Sept. 1921, vol. III, no. 2; Grierson, Helen. "A bookful of delight." *CR.*, Jan. 1928, pp. 94–100; Roosevelt, Theodore. "A naturalist's tropical laboratory." *Scrib.*, Jan. 1917, pp. 46–64; Roule, Louis. "L'exploration directe des grandes profondeurs de la mer par la bathysphère, du Dr. William Beebe." *R.Sci.*, May 25, 1935, pp. 323–29; Wilson, Edmund. "A conversation in the Galapagos, Mr. William Beebe and a marine Iguana." *A.Mo.*, Nov. 1925, pp. 577–87. For references to reviews, see *BRD.*, 1906–07, 1918, 1921, 1924–28, 1932–34, 1938.

S(amuel) N(athaniel) Behrman, 1893–

Born June 9, 1893, in Worcester, Massachusetts. After a rather lonely childhood, the stage-struck boy ran away to act; he wrote a vaudeville sketch which was played by the Worcester Stock Company and then given on the Poli circuit; he performed in it in New York. Persuaded by his family to continue his education, he entered Clark University, where he came to know G. Stanley Hall, in 1911; and in 1914 he proceeded to Harvard, where he graduated in 1916. He was in Professor George P. Baker's 47 Workshop course with Sidney Howard. Going to New York and finding himself without employment, he studied for the master's degree in English at Columbia, working with Brander Matthews and John Erskine. Then he held various jobs, reviewing books, reading plays, and acting as a theatrical press agent. Since the production of *The Second Man* by the Theatre Guild in 1927 he has been highly successful as a writer of comedy, and in recent years has done much writing for Hollywood, including the film *Queen Christina*, played by Greta Garbo.

Behrman prefers "legitimate" theatrical writing to working for the screen, and believes that motion-picture producers must pay well to induce even hack writers to work for them, as writing for the films is not only less enjoyable than stage writing, but harder. He feels that, as long as producers of moving pictures are forced to be responsive to a large and undiscriminating public on the one hand, and racketeering artists and writers on the other, no sophistication or profundity can be expected to emerge from Hollywood studios, and that in filming good plays executives have already taken risks dangerous to the point of foolhardiness.

For further comment, see Critical Survey, p. 112.

BIBLIOGRAPHY

Plays

Bedside manners, a comedy of convalescence by Kenyon Nicholson and Samuel Behrman, 1924; A night's work, a comedy in one act by Kenyon Nicholson and Samuel Behrman, 1926; * The second man, a comedy in three acts, 1927; Meteor, 1930; "Brief moment," a comedy in three acts, 1931? (mimeographed; pub. with title Brief moment, a comedy in three acts, 1931); * Biography, a comedy, 1933; Three plays . . . Serena Blandish, Meteor, The second man, 1934; Rain from heaven, a play in three acts, 1935; End of summer, a play in three acts, 1936; Wine of choice, a comedy in three acts . . . with an introduction by John Anderson, 1938; No time for comedy, 1939.

Adaptation

Amphitryon 38, a comedy in a prologue and three acts by Jean Giraudoux, adapted from the French, 1938.

Moving Picture Scripts

"Anna Karenina," dialogue cutting continuity, film editor Robert J. Kern [screen play by Clemence Dane and Salka Viertel, dialogue adaptation by S. N. Behrman], 1935 (cover-title; mimeographed); "A tale of two cities," dialogue cutting continuity . . . [screen play by W. P. Lipscomb and S. N. Behrman adapted from the novel by Charles Dickens], 1935 (cover-title; mimeographed).

STUDIES

Brown
Flexner
Forsythe
Kunitz
Lawson
[Loos, Anita.] "Biography of a bachelor girl," dialogue cutting continuity . . . [screen play by Anita Loos, additional dialogue by Horace Jackson, based on a play by S. N. Behrman]. 1934 (cover-title; mimeographed)
Mantle (C)
Mersand
Moses (A)
Moses (R)
Nathan (TM)
† Quinn (H)
Whitman
Zabel

For references to reviews, see *BRD.*, 1927, 1930–31, 1933–36, 1938.

Robert (Charles) Benchley, 1889–

Born September 15, 1889, in Worcester, Massachusetts. He was educated at Harvard and graduated in 1912, after notable success as a humorous actor, writer, and speaker. He was president of the *Lampoon.*

From college he entered advertising with the Curtis Publishing Company, of Philadelphia, and in 1914–15 he engaged in industrial personnel work in Boston. In 1916 he began his career as a journalist by joining the staff of the New York *Tribune.* After the war, in which he served in Washington as secretary in the Aircraft Board, he became managing editor of *Vanity Fair*, and in 1920–21 conducted a column in the New York *World.* From 1920 to 1929 he was the dramatic editor of *Life*, and in 1929, in a similar capacity, he joined the *New Yorker.* In 1923–24 he appeared with the Music Box Revue, and in recent years he has made numerous "shorts" for motion-picture companies and has been featured on radio broadcasts.

For further comment, see Critical Survey, pp. 161–62.

BIBLIOGRAPHY

Humorous Essays

* Of all things, 1921; Love conquers all . . . illustrated by Gluyas Williams, 1922; Pluck and luck . . . with illustrations by Gluyas Williams, 1925; The early worm . . . with illustrations by Gluyas Williams, 1927; The bridges of binding, containing a brief introductory note which precedes an essay entitled:

The woolen mitten situation, a confidential report by Robert Benchley, 1928 (Issued by Harrison & Smith company, Minneapolis); 20,000 leagues under the sea, or, David Copperfield . . . with illustrations by Gluyas Williams, 1928; * The treasurer's report and other aspects of community singing by Robert Benchley, drawings by Gluyas Williams, 1930; No poems, or, Around the world backwards and sideways, 1932; From bed to worse, or, Comforting thoughts about the bison, 1934; Why does nobody collect me? 1935; My ten years in a quandary and how they grew, 1936; After 1903—what? . . . with drawings by Gluyas Williams, 1938.

STUDIES AND ARTICLES

Markey

Benchley, Robert. "Why does nobody collect me?" *Col.*, Part 18, Art. 5, pp. 1–5 (1934). For references to reviews, see *BRD.*, 1921–22, 1925, 1927–28, 1930, 1932–33, 1936, 1938.

Stephen Vincent Benét, 1898–

Born July 22, 1898, in Bethlehem, Pennsylvania. His family, of Minorcan origin, had come to Florida in the eighteenth century; his father and grandfather were both army men. His father was also a tasteful and discriminating student of literature, and his brother and sister are the poets William Rose Benét and Laura Benét.

Stephen Benét spent his childhood in California and Georgia, where his father was stationed at government arsenals. At a tender age he began writing, and won prizes from *St. Nicholas*. He prepared himself for college at Summerville Academy, and entered Yale in 1915.

By this time he had already published a collection of dramatic monologues, and when he was still in college he issued another volume of poetry. His friends at Yale included Philip Barry, Archibald MacLeish, and Thornton Wilder, and he was chairman of the *Yale Literary Magazine* in 1919, the year in which he took his degree.

After graduation and a venture into advertising he returned for his master's degree (1920), wrote a novel in the following summer, and in the fall went to France on a fellowship to study at the Sorbonne. When he returned to this country, he devoted himself to writing; and by his versatility and resourcefulness he has supported himself by his pen ever since.

He became dissatisfied, however, with his successful short stories; and, in 1926, he seized the possibilities afforded by a Guggenheim fellowship and spent two years in France writing an epic poem on the Civil War. A popular success, *John Brown's Body* took the Pulitzer Prize for 1928. In 1930 Benét moved from Rhode Island, where he had lived since his return from Europe, and settled in New York, where he has continued his literary work. In 1932 he was given the Shelley Memorial Award. The earlier *King David* had taken the *Nation's* poetry prize in 1923. The author was awarded in 1933 the Roosevelt Medal of the Roosevelt Memorial Association for his contribution to American letters. Except for Colonel Lindbergh, he was the youngest of the twenty-nine Americans to have received this medal. In the same year, he unveiled a portrait of his grandfather, General Stephen Benét, at the University of Georgia, and read his poem of presentation: "Poem, delivered on alumni day, May 6, 1933." He was made honorary doctor of letters by Middlebury College in 1936. In 1937 his operetta, *The Headless Horseman*, for which Douglas Moore wrote the music, was performed over the radio. In 1938 Benét read a special ode at the tercentenary celebration of the founding of New Haven, and he was elected to membership in the American Academy of Arts and Letters. The world première of his opera, *The Devil and Daniel Webster*, took place in New York on May 19, 1939. He is a vice-president of the National Institute of Arts and Letters; and is the editor of the "Yale Series of Younger Poets."

He is said to be the original of the character of Ben Vincent in Cyril Hume's *The Wife of the Centaur* (1923).

For further comment, see Critical Survey, pp. 55, 92.

BIBLIOGRAPHY

Poems

Five men and Pompey, a series of dramatic portraits, 1915; Yale university prize poem, 1917, The drug-shop, or, Endymion in Edmonstoun, 1917 (pamphlet); Young adventure, a book of poems, 1918 (foreword by C[hauncey]. B. T[inker]); Heavens and earth, a book of poems, 1920; The ballad of William Sycamore, 1790–1880, 1923; King David . . . "The Nation" prize poem for 1923, 1923; Tiger joy, a book of poems, 1925; * John Brown's body, 1928; Ballads and poems, 1915–1930, 1931; A book of Americans by Rosemary and Stephen Vincent Benét, illustrated by Charles Child, 1933; A poem written and delivered by Stephen Vincent Benét, 1919, at the Society dinner held in New York, January 29th, 1934, 1934; A portrait [by Laurence Vincent Benét] and a poem [by Stephen Vincent Benét], 1934; Burning city, new poems . . . decorations by Charles Child, 1936; The ballad of the Duke's mercy, 1939.

Short Stories

The barefoot saint, 1929; The litter of the rose leaves, 1930 (pamphlet); The devil and Daniel Webster, illustrated by Harold Denison, 1937; * Thirteen o'clock, stories of several worlds, 1937; Johnny Pye & the Fool-killer . . . drawings by Charles Child, 1938.

Novels

The beginning of wisdom, 1921; Young people's pride, a novel . . . illustrations by Henry Raleigh, 1922; Jean Huguenot, 1923; Spanish bayonet, 1926; James Shore's daughter, 1934.

Play

The devil and Daniel Webster, play in one act, 1939.

Radio Play

The headless horseman by Stephen Vincent Benét (based upon "A legend of Sleepy Hollow" by Washington Irving). Music by:—Douglas Moore, 1937 (cover-title; mimeographed).

Libretto

The devil and Daniel Webster, an opera in one act . . . for the opera by Douglas Moore, 1939.

Miscellany

Tamburlaine the Great, who, from the state of a shepherd in Scythia, by his rare and wonderful conquests became a most puissant and mighty monarch [by Christopher Marlowe], 1919 (acting version prepared under direction of Edgar Montillion Woolley & Stephen Vincent Benét); The story of the United press as told . . . in the magazine Fortune, 1933 (cover-title); The magic of poetry and the poet's art, 1936.

Verses Set to Music

Rosemary. I. Chemical analysis. II. A sad song. III. A nonsense song. IV. To Rosemary on the methods by which she might become an angel. Four choruses for women's voices, 3 & 4 part unaccompanied, lyrics from "Tiger joy" by Stephen Vincent Benét, set to music by Randall Thompson, 1930 (cover-title; sheet-music); John Brown's song, a choral poem from "John Brown's body," by Stephen Vincent Benét, set to music for mixed voices and orchestra or piano accompaniment by Robert Delaney. Both poem and music were written by Fellows of the John Simon Guggenheim memorial foundation during their fellowship years, 1932.

Editor

The Yale book of student verse, 1910–1919, edited by John Andrews, Stephen Vincent Benét, John C. Farrar, Pierson Underwood, with an introduction by Charlton M. Lewis . . . & an epilogue by William Rose Benét, 1919.

Translations

Ode aux voiles du nord de J. L. Le Marois. Lettre de Pierre Drieu La Rochelle. Traduction de Stephen Vincent Benét. Dessin gravé par Brodovitch, 1928.

STUDIES AND ARTICLES

Blankenship
Cook
Countryman press. The Countryman press now has the pleasure of announcing Johnny Pye and the Fool-killer by Stephen Vincent Benét with drawings by Charles Child, limited edition, signed by author & artist. [1938] (cover-title; leaflet; prospectus)
† Johnson (1932)
† Johnson (1936)
Kreymborg
Kunitz (L)
† Manly
Markey
Schreiber
Untermeyer
Untermeyer (C)
Wilde, Percival. Blood of the martyrs, a play in one act . . . based on a short story by Stephen Vincent Benét. c1937

Andelson, Pearl. "A prize-winner." *P.*, Mar. 1922, pp. 340–43; Benét, Stephen V., "The sixth man." *Col.*, Part 15, Art 6, pp. 1–4, (1933); Daniels,

Sidney R. "A saga of the American civil war." *CR.*, Oct. 1934, pp. 466–71; Johnson, Merle, *ed.* "American first editions, Stephen Vincent Benét." *PW.*, Jan. 16, 1932, pp. 290–91; Monroe, Harriet, "A cinema epic." *P.*, Nov. 1928; pp. 91–96; North, Jessica N. "A playful tiger." *P.*, Feb. 1926, pp. 279–81; Zabel, Morton D. "American grain." *P.*, Aug. 1936, pp. 276–82. For references to reviews, see *BRD.*, 1919–23, 1925–26, 1928, 1931, 1933–34, 1936–38.

William Rose Benét, 1886–

Born February 2, 1886, at Fort Hamilton, in New York Harbor. Having received his elementary education in different cities, he attended Albany Academy; and, although it had been planned that he should enter West Point and follow the career of his father and grandfather, he proceeded to the Sheffield Scientific School at Yale. He graduated in 1907, after serving as chairman of the *Yale Courant* and editor of the *Yale Record.*

By this time he wished to follow the career of the poet. From his father, an officer in the Ordnance Department of the army, he had inherited a love for such verse forms as the rondo, the triolet, and the ballad; and in a school paper he had printed some of his own work. After a period spent in California with his family he got a job on the *Century Magazine*, first as an office boy addressing envelopes, later (1911–14) as a reader. From 1914 to 1918 he was an assistant editor.

During the war, after some instruction in aviation in fields in Texas and Ohio, he was commissioned second lieutenant in the air service in February, 1918, and was honorably discharged, after ground service, in the same year.

An advertising job and a position as assistant editor of the *Nation's Business* followed; and in 1920 he helped found the *Literary Review* of the New York *Evening Post*, of which he was an associate editor until 1924. In that year he left the *Review*, with Christopher Morley, to begin a new magazine, the *Saturday Review of Literature.* Until 1929 he was an associate editor; since then he has been a contributing editor. In 1929–30 he was an editor in the publishing firm of Brewer and Warren.

A lover not only of poetry but of painting as well, Benét prefers narrative verse to poems of pure intellectuality. ". . . I have recently taken up lecturing or talking, rather," he writes, "on American poetry, throughout the country and reading some of my own work aloud." His *Poems* (1927) he dedicated to his second wife, Elinor Wylie. In 1921 he was awarded an honorary master's degree from Yale, and in 1933 he received an honorary doctorate from Dickinson College. Like his younger brother, Stephen Vincent Benét, he is a member of the National Institute of Arts and Letters.

BIBLIOGRAPHY

Poems

Merchants from Cathay, 1913; The falconer of God and other poems, 1914; The great white wall, a poem . . . illustrated by Douglas Duer, 1916; The burglar of the zodiac and other poems, 1918; Perpetual light, a memorial, 1919; Moons of grandeur, a book of poems, 1920; * Man possessed, being the selected poems of William Rose Benét, 1927; Sagacity, 1929 (pamphlet); Rip tide, a novel in verse, 1932; Starry harness, 1933; A bakers' dozen of emblems, drawings by W. A. Dwiggins and verses by William Rose Benét, collected from various numbers of the Saturday review of literature issued in 1927 and 1928, and Electra, a new linotype face from the hand of the said W. A. D., 1935; Golden fleece, a collection of poems and ballads old and new, 1935; Harlem and other poems, 1935.

Novels

The first person singular, 1922.

Essays and Sketches

Saturday papers, essay on literature from the Literary review, the first volume of selections from the Literary review of the New York evening post by Henry Seidel Canby, William Rose Benét, Amy Loveman, 1921; Wild goslings, a selection of fugitive pieces, 1927; The prose and poetry of Elinor Wylie, 1934.

Children's Book

The flying king of Kurio, a story for children . . . illustrated by Janet Smalley, 1926.

Miscellany

Reviewing ten years, a personal record of the Saturday review of literature, 1933 (comp. by W. R. B.; cover-title; pamphlet).

Translations

The East I know by Paul Claudel . . . translated by Teresa Frances and William Rose Benét, 1914.

Edited and Compiled Works

Poems for youth, an American anthology, 1925; Twentieth-century poetry edited by John Drinkwater, Henry Seidel Canby, and William Rose Benét, 1929; Adventures in English literature edited by H. C. Schweikert . . . Rewey Belle Inglis . . . Alice Cecilia Cooper . . . Marion A. Sturdevant . . . William Rose Benét . . . illustrated by Decie Merwin and George Bell, 1931; Collected poems of Elinor Wylie, 1932; Fifty poets, an American auto-anthology, 1933; The pocket university, Guide to daily reading edited by William Rose Benét . . . in consultation with Henry Seidel Canby . . . and Christopher Morley . . . Volume XIII, 1934; From Robert & Elizabeth Browning, a further selection of the Barrett-Browning family correspondence, introduction and notes by William Rose Benét, 1936; Great poems of the English language, an anthology compiled by Wallace Alvin Briggs with a supplement of recent poetry selected by William Rose Benét, 1936; Mother Goose, a comprehensive collection of the rhymes made by William Rose Benét, arranged and illustrated by Roger Duvoisin, 1936; The Oxford anthology of American literature chosen and edited by William Rose Benét and Norman Holmes Pearson, 1938; Poems for modern youth, edited by Adolph Gillis . . . and William Rose Benét, 1938.

STUDIES AND ARTICLES

Farrar
† Johnson (1936)
Kreymborg
Kunitz (L)
Lowden
† Manly
Markey
Maynard
Schreiber
Untermeyer
Untermeyer (N)

Anonymous. "William Rose Benét." *AB.*, Oct. 1923, pp. 135–39; Humphries, Rolfe. "Journeyman of letters." *P.*, May 1934, pp. 108–11; Monroe, Harriet. "Benét and the zodiac." *P.*, Oct. 1919, pp. 48–51; North, Jessica N. "Mr. Benét's selected poems." *P.*, June 1928, pp. 159–62; Tietjens, Eunice. "Cathay again." *P.*, Mar. 1917, pp. 322–24; Wilkinson, Marguerite. "Mirrors of the renaissance." *AB.*, Apr. 1921, pp. 168–70. For references to reviews, see *BRD.*, 1914, 1917–18, 1920, 1922, 1925–27, 1932–33, 1935, 1938–39.

Alvah C(ecil) Bessie, 1904–

Born in New York, June 4, 1904. He was educated at Columbia University, and graduated in 1924. He worked as naturalist, actor, bookstore clerk, filing clerk, proofreader, and editor, and was rewrite man on the Paris *Times*. He wrote two novels which he later destroyed, and made translations from the French. Recently he has spent five years in Vermont, the last on a Guggenheim fellowship. After the expiration of the fellowship and the publication of *Dwell in the Wilderness* he turned to journalism. For ten months he served as drama editor of the Brooklyn *Daily Eagle* and for three as literary editor.

Early in 1937 he left the paper to work for the Spanish Information Bureau, which he described as "a news agency that disseminates information on behalf of the Madrid Government." "Right now," he wrote in 1937, "it seems to me that Spain and its defeat of Fascism is the most important thing in the world, and I am devoting all my time to this work. We are, I feel, at a definite turning point in human history, and in common with many of the younger writers I am convinced that a left turn is indispensable to the continuance of human dignity and culture." He went to Spain in February, 1938, to serve with the Lincoln Battalion. After five weeks of training he saw his first fighting in the Aragon retreat when Franco drove through to the Mediterranean. He was in the Ebro defensive from July until September, when all international brigades were withdrawn from the Loyalist lines.

BIBLIOGRAPHY

Novels

Dwell in the wilderness, 1935.

Memoirs

Men in battle, a story of Americans in Spain, 1939.

Translations

Pierre Louÿs' The songs of Bilitis translated from the Greek, 1926; Alias Bluebeard, the life and death of Gilles de Raiz by Émile Gabory, English version, 1930; Théophile Gautier. Mademoiselle de Maupin, translation revised and amended . . . with an introduction by Guy Endore, illustrations by Steele Savage, 1930; Torture garden translated from the French of Octave Mirbeau . . . with a foreword by James Huneker, illustrated by Jeanette Seelhoff, 1931; Batouala, a novel by René Maran translated by Alvah C. Bessie and illustrated by Miguel Covarrubias, 1932; Roger Vercel. In sight of Eden translated from the French by Alvah C. Bessie and illustrated by Rockwell Kent, 1934 (English ed., Jealous waters, translated from the French of Roger Vercel, 1934).

STUDIES

Burnett

For reference to reviews, see *BRD.*, 1935.

John Peale Bishop, 1891–

Born in Charles Town, West Virginia (the "Mordington" of his fiction), in the Shenandoah valley, where he lived until he was fifteen, absorbing the antebellum southern traditions and way of living characteristic of the place. He was educated in private and public schools, including the Mercersburg Academy, and graduated from Princeton in 1917. He joined the army, and served as first lieutenant of infantry with the 333rd Infantry and the 309th Headquarters Troop, of the 84th Division. After the Armistice he was placed in charge of a company guarding a large group of German prisoners.

Returning to New York, in 1919, he took a position with *Vanity Fair*, and soon afterwards became managing editor. A co-worker was Edmund Wilson, whom he had previously succeeded as editor of the *Nassau Literary Magazine*. In 1922 he married Margaret Grosvenor Hutchins, and from 1922 to 1924 they lived in Paris and Sorrento. After another period in New York (1924–26), which was occupied partly by work for Paramount Pictures, he returned to France; and until 1933 he divided his time between Paris and an old country house dating from the time of Louis XIII. His three children were born in France.

He returned to this country, and, after traveling in the East and South, he settled on Cape Cod, where he likes the sea, the climate, and the people.

"As to my tastes," he writes, "I like to eat and drink, and above all to talk; I am fond of looking at paintings, sculpture, architecture and formal gardens; in a very modest way, I paint and garden myself. In particular, I like the architecture of humanism and the music of the eighteenth century. I prefer the ballet —at its best—to the theatre. I no longer care very much for reading, except for information. . . ."

Of the relation between literature and life, he says, "Since life proceeds independently of man's consciousness, there is a necessary opposition to literature, where nothing happens, or can happen, which has not passed through the conscious mind. It must conform to the demands, to the inner desires and necessities of that consciousness, as well as make an outward show of conforming to life as the same man observes it. It must, in short, offer both credibility and significance."

He is said to be the original of the character of Tom D'Invilliers in F. Scott Fitzgerald's *This Side of Paradise* (1920).

BIBLIOGRAPHY

Poems

Green fruit, 1917; The undertaker's garland [by] John Peale Bishop [and] Edmund Wilson, jr., decorations by Boris Artzybasheff, 1922; Now with his love, poems, 1933; Minute particulars, 1935.

Novels

Act of darkness, 1935.

Short Stories

Many thousands gone, 1931.

STUDIES AND ARTICLES

Markey Tate

Radford, Manson. "Act of darkness." *So.R.*, July 1935, pp. 205–08; Warren, Robert P. "Working toward freedom." *P.*, Mar. 1934, pp. 342–46. For references to reviews, see *BRD.*, 1931, 1933–36.

Louise Bogan, 1897–

Born at Livermore Falls, Maine, August 11, 1897. Her parents were of Irish extraction, and her grandfather had been a Maine sea captain. She was educated at Mount St. Mary's Academy, Manchester, New Hampshire, the Girls' Latin School in Boston, and Boston University, and for some years she has lived in New York. She traveled abroad on a Guggenheim fellowship in 1933 and 1937, and had previously spent a year in Vienna and one in Santa Fe, New Mexico. Since the first appearance of her work in the *New Republic* in 1923, she has contributed verse, fiction, and criticism to that magazine, the *New Yorker*, and *Poetry*, and since 1931 she has reviewed poetry in the *New Yorker*. In 1930 she was awarded the John Reed Memorial Prize given by *Poetry*, and in 1937 she received the Helen Haire Levinson Prize offered by *Poetry*.

"I am extremely fond of music," she writes, "and I am able to read anything which is well-written, from a travel-folder on. . . . I believe that many modern poets never lift themselves over the threshold between childhood and maturity, and I believe that unless this spiritual growth occurs, one's art comes to nothing. Yeats and Rilke, in our time, are rare examples of this growth." Writing in *Poetry* in April, 1937, on the work of the Austrian poet Rilke, she declared: "In a period when the facing of inner truth is in no way a popular conception—since too many flights away from the task, from war to suicide, are not only accessible but even morally respectable—a dedicated career like Rilke's becomes an heroic career. . . . Rilke was often exhausted, often afraid, often in flight, but he was capable of growth and solitude, a process and a state denied to the coward's or the delinquent's existence. And he stands as an example of integrity held through and beyond change—one of the few examples of such integrity that our times have produced."

For further comment, see Critical Survey, p. 146.

BIBLIOGRAPHY

Poems

Body of this death, poems, 1923; Dark summer, poems, 1929; * The sleeping fury, poems, 1937.

STUDIES AND ARTICLES

Jones
Kreymborg
Kunitz (L)

Ford, Frick M. "The flame in stone." *P.*, June 1937, pp. 158–61; Winters, Yvor. "The poetry of Louise Bogan." *NR.*, Oct. 16, 1929, p. 247; Wolf, Robert L. "Impassioned austerity." *P.*, Mar. 1924, pp. 335–38; Zabel, Morton D. "The flower of the mind." *P.*, Dec. 1929, pp. 158–62. For references to reviews, see *BRD.*, 1923, 1929, 1937.

James Boyd, 1888–

Born July 2, 1888, into a southern family living in Dauphin County, Pennsylvania. When he was thirteen, he moved to North Carolina. He attended Princeton and Trinity College, Cambridge. Although, in deference to the wishes of his father, he studied chemistry, he abandoned any plan for a scientific career and instead entered the publishing business and joined the staff of Doubleday, Page and Company. During the war he was a first lieutenant, A.A.S., and served in the Saint-Mihiel and Meuse-Argonne offensives.

When he returned to this country, he went south for his health. Settling at Southern Pines, North Carolina, where he still lives, he devoted himself to writing. At first he sold short stories to the magazines; then a visit from Galsworthy inspired him to make more ambitious efforts. *Drums*, a popular novel of the American Revolution, and *Marching On*, a Civil War story chosen by the Book-of-the-Month Club as a selection for 1926, brought him wide notice as a writer of historical novels. A successful film, *Our Daily Bread*, was produced by R.K.O.

Despite his northern childhood Boyd has won a solid place in the southern community in which he resides; and his knowledge and experience of a relatively unchanging society have equipped him for reproducing faithfully the speech and manners of people similar to those among whom he has lived. Although riding, fox hunting, and sailing take much of his time and enthusiasm, he reads historical literature, draws well, and writes good comic verse. His social charm not only has made him well liked in the South but resulted in his great popularity with the men serving under him in the war.

Boyd feels that autobiography used as a basis for fiction has a tendency to weaken pattern, and he has said that he cannot write strictly autobiographical novels. He believes, however, that authors' literary generalizations, even about their own work, offer little guidance or illumination to students, critics, or other writers, and thinks that their writings themselves, and not any conscious pronouncements concerning them, must be the most fruitful contribution of literary men to aesthetic theory. ". . . There is everything to be said for method and design," he writes, "but the *essential* value of a man's work will always lie outside it and in an elusive and mysterious field which he can neither control nor explain."

For further comment, see Critical Survey, pp. 53, 55, 60.

BIBLIOGRAPHY

Novels

* Drums, 1925; Marching on, 1927; Long hunt, 1930; Roll river, 1935; Bitter creek, 1939.

STUDIES AND ARTICLES

Kunitz (L)

† Stone, Frank, *comp.;* Blanck, Jacob, *ed.* "American first editions, James Boyd, 1888– ." *PW.*, Apr. 15, 1939, p. 1461. For references to reviews, see *BRD.*, 1925, 1927, 1930, 1939.

Nancy Boyd, *pseud.* *See* Edna St. Vincent Millay

Thomas (Alexander) Boyd, 1898–1935

Born in Defiance, Ohio, July 3, 1898, into a family of Ohio pioneer tradition. He was educated in Ohio, and left high school at eighteen to volunteer in the marines. Upon its formation he joined the second division of the American Expeditionary Force. He served at Verdun, Belleau Wood (*Croix de guerre*), Soissons, and Saint-Mihiel. In October, 1918, he was gassed at Blanc Mont, and he was sent home to the United States.

In 1920 he began writing in St. Paul. In 1922, when he was literary editor of the St. Paul *Daily News*, he published a war novel, *Through the Wheat.* In the ensuing years he wrote novels and biographies. He settled in Vermont.

In 1934, having examined in his mind the American tradition, he decided to ally himself with the Communists. He felt that they were the logical forces to carry on the work of the American revolutionary spirit, and in the fall of 1934, as Communist candidate for governor of Vermont, he received fifteen hundred signatures and the nomination. A member of the League of American Writers, he was an early supporter of the plan for the first American Writers' Congress in 1935.

Early in the year he went to New York on publishing business. A slight stroke was followed two weeks later by a cerebral hemorrhage, and he died suddenly in Ridgefield, Connecticut, at the home of a friend, January 27, 1935. A few days earlier he had finished *Poor John Fitch.*

BIBLIOGRAPHY

Novels

Through the wheat, 1923; The dark cloud, 1924; Samuel Drummond, 1925; Shadow of the Long Knives, a novel, 1928; In time of peace, 1935.

Biography

Simon Girty, the white savage, 1928; Mad Anthony Wayne, 1929; Light-horse Harry Lee, 1931; Poor John Fitch, inventor of the steamboat, 1935.

Short Stories

Points of honor, 1925.

For references to reviews, see *BRD.*, 1923–25, 1928–29, 1931, 1934.

Kay Boyle, 1903–

Born in St. Paul, Minnesota, February 19, 1903. As a child she traveled in Europe and painted, wrote, and studied music. She went to the Shipley School, Bryn Mawr, Pennsylvania, and studied architecture at the Ohio Mechanics Institute in Cincinnati and the violin at the Cincinnati Conservatory of Music. During the war years her family was poor and lived in a garage operated by her father in Cincinnati. Miss Boyle, already writing copiously, worked as a telephone operator and wrote radical verse for her mother's campaign on the Farmer-Labor ticket for a schoolboard office. She married a French student of engineering at the University of Cincinnati, and they both worked in New York, where Miss Boyle wrote book reviews and fashion articles, and attended night classes at Columbia.

Since 1922, when, on borrowed money, Miss Boyle and her husband went to France, she has lived in Europe, where she has done her writing. In 1931 she married the writer Laurence Vail, and has now settled down in a permanent home at Megève, Haute Savoie, France, writing and spending the winters skiing and the summers climbing mountains. She was a warm sympathizer with the defendants in the Scottsboro case and used her influence to assist them. In 1934 she was awarded a Guggenheim fellowship, and her story "The White Horses of Vienna," took the first prize of the O. Henry Memorial Award for 1935.

An admirer of a clear, direct prose style, Miss Boyle does not especially enjoy reading the work of women, which she thinks is disposed to be tame, conventional, and unexciting. She makes an exception, however, of Gertrude Stein. Of her own work she declares: "The longer I live and the more I write, the more completely am I convinced that my interest in people and in writing is of so unnational a character that, for me, the question of 'roots' in any particular soil or tradition is not of any moment."

For further comment, see Critical Survey, pp. 67–68, 96.

BIBLIOGRAPHY

Novels

* Plagued by the nightingale, 1931; Year before last, 1932; Gentlemen, I address you privately, 1933; My next bride, 1934; Death of a man, 1936; Monday night, 1938.

Short Stories

Short stories, 1929; Wedding day and other stories, 1930; * The first lover and other stories, 1933; The white horses of Vienna and other stories, 1936.

Poems

A statement . . . number 3, pamphlet series one, 1932 (pamphlet); A glad day, 1938.

Children's Book

The youngest camel . . . with illustrations by Fritz Kredel, 1939.

Translations

Don Juan by Joseph Delteil, translated from the French by Kay Boyle, illustrated by Charles Sandford, 1931; By R. Radiguet, foreword by Aldous Huxley, translation by Kay Boyle. The devil in the flesh, 1932.

Editor

365 days edited by Kay Boyle, Laurence Vail [and] Nina Conarain, 1936.

STUDIES AND ARTICLES

Hatcher Kunitz

Harter, Evelyn. "Kay Boyle, experimenter." *AB.*, June 1932, pp. 249–53; Hawkins, A. Desmond. "Death of a man." *Crit.*, Apr. 1937, pp. 498–501. For references to reviews, see *BRD.*, 1930–34, 1936, 1938–39.

Gamaliel Bradford, 1863–1932

Born in Boston, October 9, 1863, a direct descendant of Governor William Bradford of Plymouth Colony. He was educated in public schools and by tutors, and prepared for Harvard. He entered the university in 1882, but ill health forced him to withdraw and live quietly in Wellesley Hills, Massachusetts.

His first desire was to be an original and creative writer, and for some thirty years he worked at novels, plays, and poems, few of them published, and none of them successful. In 1912, however, he hit almost accidentally upon the type of biographical writing which was to make him widely read; in that year his biography of Lee was published. This was the beginning of twenty years' devotion to the writing of biography. He died on April 11, 1932.

Lifelong ill health makes his achievement the more remarkable. Although a typical program of his activities in 1897 indicates hard work, wide reading, and recreation, all packed into one short day, he was never able to work for extended periods, and vertigo sometimes made it dangerous for him to leave his bed. In some years he could do no more than fifteen or twenty minutes a day of actual writing. He had no secretary, and worked at a typewriter near the bed, usually typing a first draft and seldom revising or correcting it. He kept a journal and carried on a voluminous correspondence with people most of whom he had never seen. His frequent visitors included Bliss Perry, Edwin Arlington Robinson, and M. A. De Wolfe Howe.

Besides his writing he enjoyed music, watched baseball, and even tried his hand at billiards. Although not widely traveled in America, he visited central and southern Europe. In his reading he avoided searching problems of social development and religious interest, preferring literature less strenuous in its demands upon the moral sense. He found figures like Aaron Burr and Samuel Pepys more attractive than more didactic characters like Harriet Beecher Stowe, Frances Willard, and Louisa May Alcott. In literature he was fond of Shelley, Leopardi, and Sainte-Beuve, and felt the influence of Keats. He was afraid that his own work, which he regarded as very different from Lytton Strachey's, was overelaborate in structure.

He regarded biography, or "psychography," as he termed his own kind of biography, as a soul-exploring, an examination of the elements in an individual common to all humanity. The art of psychography, he wrote, was to disentangle its subject's habits "from the immaterial, inessential matter of biography, to illustrate them by touches of speech and action that are significant and by those only, and thus to burn them into the attention of the reader."

For further comment, see Critical Survey, pp. 168–69, 173–74.

BIBLIOGRAPHY

Biography

Lee the American, 1912; Confederate portraits, 1914; A portrait of General George Gordon Meade, 1915 (cover-title); Portraits of women, 1916; Union portraits, 1916; Portraits of American women, 1919; American portraits, 1875–1900, 1922; * Damaged souls, 1923; Bare souls, 1924; The soul of Samuel Pepys, 1924 (London ed., Samuel Pepys, 1924); Wives, 1925; Darwin, 1926; D. L. Moody, a worker in souls, 1927; The haunted biographer, dialogues of the dead, 1927; As God made them, portraits of some nineteenth-century Americans, 1929; Daughters of Eve, 1930; The quick and the dead, 1931; Biography and the human heart, 1932; Saints and sinners, 1932; * Portraits and personalities . . . edited by Mabel A. Bessey, 1933.

Novels

The private tutor, 1904; Between two masters, 1906; Matthew Porter, a story of to-day by Gamaliel Bradford, jr. . . . with a frontispiece in colour by Griswold Tyng, 1908.

Poems

A pageant of life, 1904; A prophet of joy, 1920; Shadow verses, 1920.

Literary and Historical Studies

A naturalist of souls, studies in psychography, 1917; Early days in Wellesley, being casual recollections of boyhood and later years—1867 to 1881, 1928; Elizabethan women . . . edited by Harold Ogden White, 1936.

Letters and Journals

The journal of Gamaliel Bradford, 1883–1932, edited by Van Wyck Brooks, 1933; The letters of Gamaliel Bradford, 1918–1931, edited by Van Wyck Brooks, 1934.

Plays

Unmade in heaven, a play in four acts, 1917.

Belles Lettres

Types of American character, 1895; Life and I, an autobiography of humanity, 1928.

Translations

The founding of the German empire by William I based chiefly upon Prussian state documents by Heinrich von Sybel, translated by Marshall Livingston Perrin . . . assisted by Gamaliel Bradford, jr., 1890–91 (vols. 1–5).

Editor

Macaulay's life of Samuel Johnson, 1895.

STUDIES AND ARTICLES

Adair, Ward. Vital messages in modern books. [c1926]
American
Balch, Marston, *ed.* Modern short biographies. 1935.
Brewton, William W. The South must publish her own books, an exposé. 1928 (cover-title; pamphlet)
[Houghton Mifflin company, *firm, publishers, Boston.*] Gamaliel Bradford, naturalist of souls. [1932?] (cover-title; leaflet)
† Johnson (1929)
† Johnson (1932)
† Johnson (1936)
Kunitz (L)
Longaker, John M. Contemporary biography. 1934
† Manly
Mencken, Henry L. Spiritual autopsies. [1922] (pamphlet)
National
Pattee (N)
Phillips
Rand, Edward K. Life and I. 1928

Chamberlayne, Lewis P. "Two recent books on Lee." *SR.*, Jan.–Mar. 1913, pp. 108–18; Chew, Samuel C. "O heart, rise not up against me as a witness," *YR.*, Winter 1934, pp. 392–97; Fadiman,. Clifton. "Other people's lives." *N.Yer.*, Sept. 9, 1933, pp. 77–78; Forsythe, Robert S. "The journal of Gamaliel Bradford, 1883–1932." *NEQ.*, Dec. 1933, pp. 830–33; Greever, Garland. "Saul among the poets." *SR.*, Apr. 1921, pp. 222–29; Hicks, Granville. "An insulated littérateur." *Nation*, Sept. 27, 1933, pp. 358–59; Knickerbocker, Frances W. "Gamaliel Bradford looks at his art." *SR.*, Jan.–Mar. 1934, pp. 91–99; Lincoln, Virginia C. "Gamaliel Bradford." *W.*, May 1928, pp. 155–58; Macy, John. "Gamaliel Bradford, portrayer of souls." *AB.*, May 1932, pp. 144–49; Wagenknecht, Edward. "Psychography, the first forty years." *VQR.*, Apr. 1927, pp. 285–91; Ware, Leonard, Jr. "Gamaliel Bradford, a challenge." *W.*, June 1932, pp. 155–58; Warren, Dale. "Gamaliel Bradford, a personal sketch." *SAQ.*, Jan. 1933, pp. 9–18; Woodruff, M. Dorothy. "Gamaliel Bradford, a searcher of souls." *SAQ.*, Oct. 1929, pp. 419–28. For references to reviews, see *BRD.*, 1906, 1908, 1912, 1914, 1916–34, 1936.

Louis Bromfield, 1896–

Born December 27, 1896, in Mansfield, Ohio. His family was of pioneer stock, and his forbears had come west from New England and Maryland at the close of the eighteenth century. The boy attended public schools and proceeded to the College of Agriculture at Cornell. He had planned to be a farmer, and after a year his father removed him from college and allowed him to manage the family farm. At the end of a year, deciding against farming, Bromfield entered the School of Journalism at Columbia.

The war terminated his study. For two years he served as an attaché in the French army, and his duties called him to every sector of the front from Switzerland to the North Sea. He was awarded a *Croix de guerre* and received an honorary war degree in 1920 from Columbia University. In 1939 the French government made him a chevalier of the French Legion of Honor, the highest distinction that the government can confer for civil service, both for his literary work and for his work as chairman of the refugee committee to repatriate foreign volunteers in the Spanish civil war.

After the Armistice he lived for several months in France and came to be thoroughly familiar with the customs of the French people. Upon his return to New York he began working for the New York City News Association and (later) the Associated Press. Somewhat later he spent a year as foreign editor of *Musical America.* Finding journalism uninteresting, however, he served as assistant to a theatrical producer and finally joined the staff of G. P. Putnam's Sons as advertising manager. He has also written criticism for the *Bookman.*

After he had written four novels that he regarded as unworthy of publication, Bromfield issued *The Green Bay Tree*, a story of life in an American steel town and an expression of the author's reaction against the usual drab presentation of middle western subjects. It was dramatized by the author as *The House of Women.* Of the three subsequent novels on similar themes the second, *Early Autumn*, was awarded the Pulitzer Prize for 1926. The collection *Awake and Rehearse*, published in 1929, included three prize stories. His books have been translated into many languages. He is a member of the National Academy of Arts and Letters.

For many years Bromfield has divided his time between France and the United States. ". . . I am a confirmed internationalist," he declares, "and my friends belong to all sorts of race, creed, color and religion. . . . France is my second country. I've lived here half my life and served in the French army during the war. I have never lived in Montparnasse or on the Riviera but in the French countryside in the Oise. India fascinates me politically, economically, culturally and about half my friends are Indian, all sorts—politicians, poets, merchants, Maharajahs. I go there every other year to spend the winter. . . . I have a definite hate on anything nationalistic and provincial and believe with Doctor Johnson that 'patriotism is the last refuge of the scoundrel.' Also I have a hate on all 'expatriate' nonsense which strikes me as one of the greater pests of provinciality."

He prefers the country to the city and takes great satisfaction in the professional quality of his achievements as a gardener. "As for sports," he says, "I have a passion for skiing and am a Class A skier." In political point of view he is sympathetic to the democratic idea and ready to fight for it, and declares himself "convinced that democracy, with all its blunders, is the best system yet evolved by man." "I am always anti-Republican in politics," he writes, "and believe with Jefferson in the need of constant change and revolution as a purge for the national health." In his enthusiasm for the new Democratic administration he spent the winter of 1933–34 in this country, but found himself so pleasantly distracted that he was unable to work and was forced to return to France in the spring.

There he lives in an old *presbytère* in Senlis, to which are attached a thirteenth-century chapel and a medieval cemetery. He feels that, living in Europe, he can get a truer view of the American character than if he lived in the United States. He holds high hopes for his native country and her contributions to literature. "I was born in Ohio," he says, "and still remain a good Ohioan. I think if I chose a place in all the world to be reborn, it would still be the Middle-West with its qualities of vigor, curiosity, energy, ambition, restlessness and friendliness. To the genuine Middle-Westerner the whole world is always an oyster."

BIBLIOGRAPHY

Novels

* The green bay tree, a novel, 1924; Possession, a novel, 1925 (London ed., Lilli Barr, 1926); Early autumn, a story of a lady, 1926; A good woman, 1927; The strange case of Miss Annie Spragg, 1928; Twenty-four hours, 1930; A modern hero, 1932; * The farm, 1933; The man who had everything, 1935; It had to happen, 1936; The Louis Bromfield trilogy, The green bay tree, Possession, Early autumn, 1935; The rains came, a novel of modern India, 1937.

Short Stories

Awake and rehearse, 1929; Tabloid news, 1930; Here today and gone tomorrow, four short novels, 1934.

Omnibus Volume

It takes all kinds, 1939.

Pamphlets

The work of Robert Nathan . . . containing also a bibliography, 1927?; Shattered glass, 1930? (contains opening chapters of Twenty-four hours); England, a dying oligarchy, 1939.

STUDIES AND ARTICLES

Baldwin (M)
Bromfield, Louis. The farm . . . edited by Winfield H. Rogers. [c1935]
Farnol, Lynn. One heavenly night novelized . . . from the screen story by Louis Bromfield, adapted by Sidney Howard, with illustrations from the Samuel Goldwyn production. [c1931]
† Johnson (1932)
† Johnson (1936)
Kildal
Kunitz (L)
Llona
Lundkvist
Marble
Nathan (TM)
National
Redman, Ben R. Louis Bromfield and his books, a sketch. [1928] (cover-title; pamphlet)
Schyberg

Bordeaux, Henry. "Un nouveau romancier Américain, Louis Bromfield." *RH.*, May 16, 1931, pp. 267–74; Field, Louise M. "Louis Bromfield, novelist." *AB.*, Apr. 1932, pp. 43–48; Fuller, Henry B. "The Bromfield saga." *AB.*, Apr. 1927, pp. 200–03; Gillet, Louis. "Terre d'Amérique, Louis Bromfield." *RDM.*, Nov. 1, 1933, pp. 201–13; Lefèvre, Frédéric. "Une heure avec Louis Bromfield, romancier Américain." *NL.*, Nov. 3, 1934, p. 6. For references to reviews, see *BRD.*, 1924–30, 1932–35, 1937–39.

Van Wyck Brooks, 1886–

Born in Plainfield, New Jersey, February 16, 1886. Educated in local schools, he went to Harvard and took his degree in 1907 after three years of study. During the years immediately after graduation he went to England and did editorial work for the *Standard Dictionary*, *World's Work*, and Doubleday, Page and Company. *Wine of the Puritans*, a presentation of American civilization as seen by expatriates, appeared in 1908 and made such an impression that the author was asked to teach English at Stanford in 1911. He remained until 1913.

From 1915 until 1917 he was on the editorial staff of the Century Company; in 1917 and 1918 he was associate editor of the *Seven Arts Magazine*, and, in 1920–24, of the *Freeman*. In 1927 he collaborated with Alfred Kreymborg, Lewis Mumford, and Paul Rosenfeld in editing the first *American Caravan*, but his health forced him to give up this work and confine himself to his own writing.

In 1923 he won the Dial Award of two thousand dollars because of his contributions to the creation of a new point of view in criticism. *The Flowering of New England*, one volume of the literary history of the United States upon which Brooks is working, appeared in 1936 and received the Pulitzer Prize for that year. It was designated by the American Booksellers' Association "the most distinguished non-fiction book of 1936," and was declared by the publisher Dutton to be the most successful book published by the firm in its eighty years of business history. It received the second Gold Medal of the Limited Editions Club.

Brooks is a member of the American Academy of Arts and Letters, and received honorary degrees from Columbia, Tufts, and Bowdoin in 1937. Absorbed in the problem of the conscientious and scrupulous artist, he has devoted much consideration, in his studies in American literature and civilization, to the narrowing effects of American life upon literature.

For further comment, see Critical Survey, pp. 63, 169–70, 195, 200.

BIBLIOGRAPHY

Essays and Studies

The wine of the Puritans, a study of present-day America, 1908; The soul, an essay towards a point of view, 1910 (pamphlet); The malady of the ideal: Obermann, Maurice de Guérin and Amiel, 1913; * America's coming-of-age, 1915; Letters and leadership, 1918; Emerson and others, 1927; Sketches in criticism, 1932; Three essays on America, 1934; * The flowering of New England, 1815–1865, 1936.

Biography

John Addington Symonds, a biographical study, 1914; The world of H. G. Wells, 1915; The ordeal of Mark Twain, 1920; * The pilgrimage of Henry James, 1925; The life of Emerson, 1932.

Poems

Verses by two undergraduates [Van Wyck Brooks and John Hall Wheelock], 1905 (cover-title).

Translations

The flame that is France by Henry Malherbe translated by V. W. B., 1918; The story of Gotton Connixloo followed by Forgotten by Camille Mayran, 1920; Paul Gauguin's Intimate journals . . . preface by Emil Gauguin, 1921; Jean Jacques Rousseau by Henri-Frédéric Amiel, 1922; Some aspects of the life of Jesus from the psychological and psycho-analytic point of view by Georges Berguer . . . translated by Eleanor Stimson Brooks and Van Wyck Brooks, 1923; Henry Thoreau, bachelor of nature by Léon Bazalgette, 1924; Summer, being volume two of The soul enchanted by Romain Rolland translated from the French by Eleanor Stimson & Van Wyck Brooks, 1925; Mother and son . . . by Romain Rolland, translated from the French, 1927; The road by André Chamson, translated by Van Wyck Brooks, with a foreword by Ernest Boyd, 1929; Roux the bandit by André Chamson, 1929; The crime of the just by André Chamson, 1930; Philine, from the unpublished journals of Henri-Frédéric Amiel . . . with an introduction by Edmond Jaloux, 1930; The private journal of Henri Frédéric Amiel, translated by Van Wyck Brooks and Charles Van Wyck Brooks, introduction by Bernard Bouvier. Enlarged and revised edition conforming to the original text, 1935.

Editor

By Randolph Bourne. History of a literary radical and other essays, edited with an introduction, 1920; Journal of first voyage to America by Christopher Columbus, with an introduction, 1924; The American caravan, a yearbook of American literature edited by Van Wyck Brooks, Alfred Kreymborg, Lewis Mumford, Paul Rosenfeld, 1927; The journal of Gamaliel Bradford, 1883–1932, 1933; The letters of Gamaliel Bradford, 1918–1931, 1934.

STUDIES AND ARTICLES

American (C)
Beach
Berg
Cowley
Foerster (T)
Frank (S)
† Herrmann
Johnson, Edgar. One mighty torrent, the drama of biography. [c1937]
Kunitz (L)
Mumford, Lewis. Aesthetics, a dialogue . . . Troutbeck leaflets number three. 1925
National
Rosenfeld (P)
Saturday
Shafer
Stearns
Van Doren (R)
Wilson (D)

Collins, Seward B. "Criticism in America." *AB.*, June 1930, pp. 241–56, 353–64; Colum, Mary M. "An American critic, Van Wyck Brooks." *D.*, Jan. 1924, pp. 33–41; Flint, Frank C. "A cycle of New England." *VQR.*, Jan. 1937, pp. 122–26; Foerster, Norman. "The literary prophets." *AB.*, Sept. 1930, pp. 35–44; Glicksberg, Charles I. "Van Wyck Brooks." *SR.*, Apr.–June 1935, pp. 175–86; Jones, Howard M. "The pilgrimage of Van Wyck Brooks." *VQR.*, July 1932, pp. 439–42; Kenton, Edna. "Henry James and Mr. Van Wyck Brooks." *AB.*, Oct. 1925, pp. 153–57; Maynard, Theodore. "Van Wyck Brooks." *CW.*, Jan. 1935, pp. 412–21; Munson, Gorham B. "Van Wyck, his sphere and his encroachments." *D.*, Jan. 1925, pp. 28–42; Smith, Bernard. "Van Wyck Brooks." *NR.*, Aug. 26, 1936, pp. 69–72; Wade, John D.

"The flowering of New England." *So.R.*, Spring 1937, pp. 807–14; Wilson, Edmund. "Imaginary conversations, Mr. Van Wyck Brooks and Mr. Scott Fitzgerald." *NR.*, Apr. 30, 1924, pp. 249–54. For references to reviews, see *BRD.*, 1910, 1914–15, 1918–19, 1925, 1927, 1932, 1934, 1936.

Heywood (Campbell) Broun, 1888–1939

Born in Brooklyn, the son of the founder and owner of a printing establishment. He was educated at the Horace Mann School in New York, where he edited the school paper and was prominent in basketball and football, and at Harvard University (1906–10).

In intervals of his college career he worked on the New York *Morning Telegraph;* and in 1912 he joined the staff of the *Tribune.* From rewrite man he became baseball reporter and later dramatic critic. In the last-named capacity he served for eight years, first on the *Tribune* and later on the *World.* In 1917 he served as correspondent for the American Expeditionary Forces. This brief experience, terminating in his being sent home after he had commented on the inefficiency of the War Department, resulted in his becoming a pacifist; and in the time of the post-war Red scare he opposed with ridicule the current hysteria.

His column, "It Seems to Me," in the *World*, managed for a time to please almost everybody, despite its candor, its irony, and its opposition to such current phenomena as the Ku Klux Klan. But in 1927, in his desire to fight for the defendants in the Sacco-Vanzetti trial, Broun found himself silenced by his publisher, Ralph Pulitzer, and resigned his position. Won back in 1928, he was discharged when he wrote an article for the *Nation* and referred to the *World* as not a truly liberal paper, even though the most liberal in New York.

He transferred his column to the *World Telegram*, where it has since appeared as a feature of the Scripps-Howard chain. His interest in labor problems and politics now became dominant. In 1930 he ran for Congress on the Socialist ticket and was defeated. Not long afterward, discouraged by internal dissension, he left the party.

With the development of labor organization in the ranks of newspaper writers, however, his opportunity had come; and in 1933 he was active in founding the American Newspaper Guild, "formed to better wages and working conditions of newspaper men and women, and to raise the ethical standards of the craft." Broun was made president. By energetic and militant tactics the Guild succeeded in placing itself in a much stronger position, won its objectives in strikes, and affiliated itself with the American Federation of Labor.

Broun, who has painted for his own amusement, in recent years has written regularly for the *Nation* and the *New Republic*, and he was one of the writers, producers, and performers of *Shoot the Works*, a revue presented in 1931, designed to employ actors and theatrical workers thrown out of work by the depression. From 1938 to 1939, he was an editor of the *Connecticut Nutmeg;* then he became its owner, and continued its publication as *Broun's Nutmeg*. "The snobbishness of the white-collar groups is on the whole exaggerated," he wrote in 1935. "If clerks, newspapermen, accountants, and professional men have been slow in organizing, it has not been altogether because of reluctance. It is rather an inability. We have neither the tradition nor the training."

He died on December 18, 1939.

For further comment, see Critical Survey, p. 159.

BIBLIOGRAPHY

Essays and Sketches

Seeing things at night, 1921; Pieces of hate and other enthusiasms, 1922; Sitting on the World, 1924; If New York were socialist! By Paul Blanshard, Heywood Broun, Nathan Fine, Morris Hillquit, Edward Levinson, Henry J. Rosner, Norman Thomas, 1931 (cover-title; pamphlet); * It seems to me, 1925–1935, 1935.

Novels

The boy grew older, 1922; The sun field, 1923; Gandle follows his nose, 1926.

Short Story

A shepherd, 1926.

Biography

Anthony Comstock, roundsman of the Lord by Heywood Broun & Margaret Leech, 1927.

Social Study

Christians only, a study in prejudice by Heywood Broun & George Britt, 1931.

War Journalism

The A.E.F., with General Pershing and the American forces, 1918; Our army at the front, 1918.

Miscellany

Nonsenseorship by Heywood Broun, George S. Chappell, Ruth Hale, Ben Hecht, Wallace Irwin, Robert Keable, Helen Bullitt Lowry, Frederick O'Brien, Dorothy Parker, Frank Swinnerton, H. M. Tomlinson, Charles Hanson Towne, John V. A. Weaver, Alexander Woollcott, and the author of "The mirrors of Washington," edited by G. P. P., sundry observations concerning prohibitions, inhibitions, and illegalities, illustrated by Ralph Barton, 1922; What is freedom of the press? [By] Heywood Broun, Will Irwin, Julian S. Mason. Broadcast from the Town hall, New York, over Station WJZ and associated stations under the auspices of the League for political education, inc. and the National broadcasting company. Edited by Lyman Bryson, 1936 (pamphlet).

STUDIES AND ARTICLES

Baldwin (M)
Cleaton
Farrar
† Ford (E)
Gillis
The Guild reporter, Nov. 23, 1933–.
Herrmann
Markey
Minton, Bruce and Stuart, John. Men who lead labor . . . with drawings by Scott Johnson. [c1937]
National

A., R. "The rabbit that bit the bulldog." *N.Yer.*, Oct. 1, 1927, pp. 18–22; Adams, Franklin P. "Comrade Broun." *Nation*, Oct. 1, 1930, pp. 341–42;

Anonymous. "Heywood Broun." *AB.*, Nov. 1923, pp. 275–79; Marshall, Margaret. "Columnists on parade, Heywood Broun." *Nation*, May 21, 1938, pp. 580–83; Ross, Virginia P. "Emotional prodder, a portrait of Heywood Broun." *Outl.*, Oct. 30, 1929, pp. 330–32, 357–58; Van Doren, Carl. "Day in and day out." *Cent.*, Dec. 1923, pp. 308–15; Woollcott, Alexander. "Heywood Broun." *AB.*, July 1921, p. 443. For references to reviews, see *BRD.*, 1918, 1921–24, 1926–27, 1931, 1935.

Louis Brucker Brumfield. *See* **Louis Bromfield**

Pearl S(ydenstricker) Buck, 1892–

Born Pearl Sydenstricker in Hillsboro, West Virginia, June 26, 1892. She comes of German, Dutch, and French extraction. Her parents were missionaries, and she passed a lonely childhood in China, living in Chinkiang, on the Yangtse, where she came to know her Chinese neighbors, and listened to the tales of her Chinese nurse. At seven she began to read Dickens, and through him came to love England devotedly. At an early age she contributed frequently to an English-language newspaper in Shanghai. She was prepared for college by her mother, who also stimulated her musical and artistic tastes. After attending boarding school in Shanghai she went to the Randolph-Macon Woman's College, where she felt herself to be a misfit, although she was a leader and became president of her class.

After returning to China she married (1917) John Lossing Buck, an American missionary, with whom she spent five years in North China, undergoing famine and bandit terrorism, and coming to know the Chinese thoroughly and to love them. Mr. Buck then took a position in the University of Nanking, and Mrs. Buck taught English literature at this institution and in the National South-eastern (later the National Central) University, as part of her work as a Presbyterian missionary.

In 1922 Mrs. Buck began to write articles, the first of which appeared in 1923 in the *Atlantic*. On her way back to America she wrote the story that grew into *East Wind: West Wind* and was published in *Asia* in 1924. What was to have been her first novel was destroyed when, in 1927, the Nationalist soldiers entered Nanking, and the Bucks escaped barely with their lives, thanks to the faithful devotion of Chinese servants and friends.

In 1930 *The Good Earth* was finished, and, published in 1931, it was a best-seller for twenty-one months, took the Pulitzer Prize (1932), and was translated into almost twenty languages; there were three Chinese translations. It has since been dramatized and filmed.

In New York in 1932 Mrs. Buck delivered an address criticizing the theory and administration of foreign missions. Attacked by the Fundamentalist party in the Presbyterian church, she resigned her church position, saying that every missionary who had tried to understand or appreciate the culture of the people to whom he had been sent had met similar opposition in the church. In 1935 she divorced Mr. Buck and married Richard J. Walsh, president of the John Day Company, her publishers. They live on a farm in Pennsylvania, and Mrs. Walsh is an editor in the company and directs the book-reviewing in *Asia*.

She received an honorary A.M. from Yale in 1933, and the Howells Medal for fiction in 1935; and in 1936 she was elected to membership in the National

Institute of Arts and Letters. In 1938, the third American to receive the honor, she was awarded the Nobel Prize for Literature "for rich and genuine epic portrayals of Chinese peasant life, and for masterpieces of biography."

In a lecture before the School of Journalism of Columbia University she once said: ". . . I must confess that I happen to be a somewhat peculiar person, . . . because the truth is I cannot be happy without writing novels. . . ." She feels that the novelist is an unhappy medium through which other lives and characters are brought into being, and she is herself interested in writing chiefly as it brings about the revelation of human character and motive.

The manuscripts of Mrs. Buck's novels will be given to the rare book collection of Randolph-Macon Woman's College at Lynchburg, Va.

For further comment, see Critical Survey, p. 70.

BIBLIOGRAPHY

Novels

East wind: west wind, 1930; * The good earth, 1931 (trilogy, I); Sons, 1932 (trilogy, II); The young revolutionist, 1932; The mother, 1934; A house divided, 1935 (trilogy, III); House of earth: The good earth, Sons, A house divided, 1935; This proud heart, 1938; The patriot, 1939.

Short Stories

The first wife and other stories, 1933 (intro. by Richard J. Walsh).

Biography

The exile, 1936; Fighting angel, portrait of a soul, 1936.

Literary Criticism

The Chinese novel, Nobel lecture delivered before the Swedish academy at Stockholm, December 12, 1938, 1939.

Pamphlets

An autobiographical sketch of Pearl S. Buck, author of East wind: west wind, The good earth, The young revolutionist, and Sons, 1932; East and West and the novel. Sources of the early Chinese novel. Addresses before the convocation of the North China union language school, February 1932, 1932; Is there a case for foreign missions? 1932; The Laymen's mission report . . . reprinted by permission from The Christian century issue of November 23, 1932, 1932? (cover-title); A biographical sketch of Lin Yutang, 1937 (pamphlet copyrighted by the John Day co., inc.; contains A profile of Lin Yutang by Pearl S. Buck); Full page to appear in N. Y. times book review—Oct. 17th. A letter from Pearl Buck, 1937 (broadside).

Translations

All men are brothers ⟨Shui hu chuan⟩ translated from the Chinese, 1933 (2 vols.).

STUDIES AND ARTICLES

Fisher, Dorothy C. The fighting angel and The exile by Pearl S. Buck. [1936] (caption-title; leaflet)
† Johnson (1936)
Kildal
Kirkland
Kunitz
Lawrence (S)
Lawrence (W)
National
[Walsh, Richard J.] A biographical sketch of Pearl S. Buck. [c1936]

Bentley, Phyllis. "The art of Pearl S. Buck." *EJ.*, Dec. 1935, pp. 791–800; Bogardus, Emory S. "Culture distance in a house divided." *SSR.*, May 1936, pp. 473–77; Buck, Pearl S. "The writing of East wind, west wind." *Col.*, Part 12, Art. 6, pp. 1–4 (1932); Canby, Henry S. "The good earth, Pearl Buck and the Nobel prize." *SRL.*, Nov. 19, 1938, p. 8; Catel, Jean. "Pearl Buck." *EA.*, Jan.–Feb. 1939, pp. 98–99; Cowley, Malcolm. "Wang Lung's children." *NR.*, May 10, 1939, pp. 24–25. For references to reviews, see *BRD.*, 1930–39.

Kenneth (Duva) Burke, 1897–

Born in Pittsburgh, May 5, 1897. He was educated at Ohio State University and at Columbia. In 1926–27 he acted as research worker for the Laura Spelman Rockefeller Memorial, and in 1928–29 he did editorial work for the Bureau of Social Hygiene in New York City. In 1927 he became music critic on the *Dial.*

He has written, besides musical criticism, literary reviews, stories, and translations. Much of his criticism has appeared in the *Nation,* for which he was music critic from 1933 to 1935; and he has contributed also to the *New Republic,* the *Little Review,* the *Bookman, Broom,* the *Symposium, Vanity Fair,* and the *Hound and Horn.* He was given in 1928 the Dial Award of two thousand dollars for distinguished service to American letters; and in 1935 he was awarded a Guggenheim fellowship. In 1937 he lectured at the New School for Social Research in New York on literary criticism in theory and practice.

In a consideration, in the *Nation* for December 13, 1933, of the relation of art to capitalism, Burke pointed out the dislocation under capitalism of the basic relationship between work-patterns and art and the frequent substitution of competitive for co-operative enterprise, with the resultant danger of the use of war as an outlet for the co-operative energies of mankind, and declared that it is ethically necessary, under such conditions, that art become, to a certain extent, propaganda. "Art cannot safely confine itself to merely using the values which arise out of a given social texture and integrating their conflicts, as the soundest, purest art will do," he said. "It must have a definite hortatory function. . . ." At the same time he admitted the value of pure art in making more tolerable the world as it is, and stated his belief that much proletarian literature, presenting no vision of anything desirable or worth fighting for, and operating only to motivate acquiescence to squalor, lacks value for either purpose.

Of his way of life and work, Burke writes, "Trained under the aegis of the 'Esthetic Opposition,' and have been trying to modify that ever since. Modify it; not abandon it. So now call myself an 'Agro-Bohemian' (i.e., as per Cicero's 'If you have a garden and a library . . .'). Hence, life on a run-down farm between early spring and late fall—and hibernating among the piles of NY (that has its summer of talk and congregation about Jan.–Feb.). Distrust the over-sedentary trend of our culture—and so have dreamed of inventing a typewriter that one could operate with an axe, thus combining physical exercise with verbal expression. Unfortunately, such an ideal would better fit a lumberjack constitution, height six feet four, than my own five feet four. It makes the picture, in my case, a bit sentimental. Nevertheless . . . (which is, incidentally, my device for a 'scutcheon—on the theory that each generation should start the 'scutcheon all over again). When I had the money to put in a bathroom, I allocated it to a dam for a pond instead. Maybe that too indicates a trend. Every time I light the oil lamps, I delight in the thought that I am spurning the light-and-power company whose line now is up to our place. A day can, by coaching, be filled to brimming with such negative accomplishments. Believe that 'Nulla dies sine linea' is a better slogan for fish than writers—and so should like to reduce writing to a minimum, to the saying only of that which simply *had* to be said, but obviously one can't carry that out and continue to be a taxpayer."

For further comment, see Critical Survey, pp. 197–98.

BIBLIOGRAPHY

Philosophical and Historical Studies

Permanence and change, an anatomy of purpose, 1935; Attitudes toward history, 1937 (2 vols.).

Literary Studies

* Counter-statement, 1931.

Novels

Towards a better life, being a series of epistles or declamations, 1932.

Short Stories

The white oxen and other stories, 1924.

Translations

Death in Venice translated from the German of Thomas Mann, 1925; Genius and character by Emil Ludwig, 1927; Saint Paul by Émile Baumann, translated from the French . . . with a frontispiece by Émile Bernard and decorations by René Pottier, 1929.

STUDIES AND ARTICLES

Cowley (E) Winters

Du Bois, Arthur E. "Accepting and rejecting Kenneth Burke." *SR.*, July–Sept. 1937, pp. 343–56; Glicksberg, Charles I. "Kenneth Burke, the critic's critic." *SAQ.*, Jan. 1937, pp. 74–84; Parkes, Henry B. "Attitudes toward history." *So.R.*, Spring 1938, pp. 693–706; Warren, Austin. "Kenneth Burke, his mind and art." *SR.*, July–Sept. 1933, pp. 344–64. For references to reviews, see *BRD.*, 1924, 1931, 1937.

W(illiam) R(iley) Burnett, 1899–

Born November 25, 1899, in Springfield, Ohio. After school in Springfield and Dayton and high school in Columbus, he went to the Miami Military Institute at Germantown, Ohio, and graduated in 1919. When, in 1918, he tried to enter the balloon service, he was refused. He studied for one semester in the College of Journalism at Ohio State University, then dropped out and worked in a factory for a while, sold insurance, and finally got a job as statistician in the Department of Industrial Relations of the State of Ohio.

During the seven or eight years that he held this position he wrote at night; and in 1927 he gave up his job and went to Chicago to take miscellaneous jobs and write *Little Caesar*, a novel of Chicago gangs. Published in 1929, it was a best-seller and a selection of the Literary Guild, and was issued in England and translated into Swedish, Danish, French, Dutch, and Portuguese. "It happened to appear at the right time," says the author, "and was a tremendous success. Far more successful than any of my later books, although it is not my best book by any means. When it appeared, the cry of Hemingway was immediately heard on all sides. As a matter of record I'd like to state that I'd never read a line of Hemingway till after the appearance of *Little Caesar*. The resemblance is accidental or probably *Little Caesar* is a manifestation of a spirit in American writing which appeared also in some of the work of Hemingway. I'm not trying to take anything away from Hemingway. He is without a doubt one of the world's outstanding writers and in *Farewell to Arms* he has written one of the few books of our time which I think has a chance of survival. But I'll admit that I got very tired of Mr. Hemingway when my first three or four books were classed as imitations. After the publication of *Goodbye to the Past* (far and away my best book; so much better than the rest of my work that it sticks out like a sore thumb) I heard no more about it. As a matter of fact, there is but a superficial resemblance between my work and Hemingway's. I'm an objective writer and not in the least autobiographical; Hemingway is subjective and autobiographical. Character creation is my chief virtue; and Hemingway's chief weakness."

Filmed in 1930, *Little Caesar* was triumphant in both this country and England, and established the vogue of the gangster picture (and of the phrase "he can't take it"). *Iron Man* a selection of the Book-of-the-Month Club in 1930, and *Saint Johnson* (1930) were also filmed, the latter as *Law and Order*, and in the same year the short story "Dressing Up" won the O. Henry Memorial Award. *The Giant Swing* and *Dark Hazard*, the latter a Book-of-the-Month Club selection in 1933, were, like most of Burnett's novels, published in England; both were filmed, and the latter was translated into Czech.

The author, who, in addition to his novels, has written serials for magazines, one of which was filmed with Edward G. Robinson as *The Whole Town's Talking*, and original motion pictures as well, enjoys writing so much that he does not consider it labor; but, although he is a fast worker, writing at night and keeping himself alert with black coffee, he says that books develop slowly in his mind. He thought about *Little Caesar* for a year before he wrote a word of it; and, when it finally appeared, he had already written five novels, perhaps a hundred short stories, and a play. *The Giant Swing* required ten years, two rewritings, and the cutting out of some twenty thousand words.

Burnett, who regards as his best books *Goodbye to the Past* and *The Goodhues of Sinking Creek*, both of which were poorly received by professional critics, has a low opinion of reviewers and prefers the judgments of his wife, who is the only critic he respects. "Before writing *Little Caesar*," he says, "I was absorbed in the study of three writers, who really were the deciding factors in the style and approach I finally adopted; these writers were Prosper Mérimée, Pio Baroja, and Giovanni Verga. When I first got to New York, after the Literary Guild had accepted *Little Caesar*, I was talking with a couple of well-known critics about my work and when I told them about these three authors, they were stunned and then they laughed in my face. . . . I found later that one of the critics had never read a line of any of the three authors, and that the other had read *Carmen* by Mérimée and nothing else; and had never heard of Pio Baroja; so much for critics. It may sound far-fetched but I think a reading of such a story as Mérimée's *Mateo Falcone* or the second volume of Pio Baroja's trilogy *The Struggle for Life* or any of the stories in Verga's two translated volumes of short tales will show you what I mean. They all write objectively and with great condensation and they deal as a rule with dramatic subjects and not with the humdrum and the usual, which is the bane of the middle-class novel, now dying; or dead, I hope!" He feels that motion-picture executives have been unduly afraid of their public and too cautious to accept originality in their writers.

Burnett lives in Glendale, California, and amuses himself by reading constantly, occasionally composing music, and indulging his taste for animals, particularly dogs, and sports and games.

BIBLIOGRAPHY

Novels

* Little Caesar, 1929; Iron man, 1930; Saint Johnson, 1930; The silver eagle, 1931; The giant swing, 1932; Dark Hazard, 1933; Goodbye to the past, scenes from the life of William Meadows, 1934; King Cole, a novel, 1936 (English ed., Six days' grace, 1937); The dark command, a Kansas Iliad, 1938.

Novelette

The Goodhues of Sinking creek . . . with woodcuts by J. J. Lankes, 1934.

STUDIES

Chanslor, Roy. Lady luck [i.e. Wine, women, and horses], a screenplay by Roy Chanslor from a novel by W. R. Burnett. [1937] (mimeographed)

Kunitz

Lait, Jack. The beast of the city by Jack Lait, adapted from the original motion picture story of W. R. Burnett, illustrated with scenes from the Metro-Goldwyn-Mayer picture, a Cosmopolitan production. [c1932]

McCall, Mary. "Doctor Socrates" by W. R. Burnett, screen play by Mary McCall, jr. 1935. (mimeographed)

For references to reviews, see *BRD.*, 1929–34, 1936, 1938.

(Maxwell) Struthers Burt, 1882–

Born in Baltimore, October 18, 1882, of a Philadelphia family. He was reared in Philadelphia and educated in private schools. Finishing early, he spent two years, as the youngest reporter in the city, on the Philadelphia *Times*. At eighteen he entered Princeton, the college of his father and grandfather, where he served on the editorial boards of the *Nassau Literary Magazine* and the *Bric-a-brac* and was editor-in-chief of the *Tiger*. He wrote two libretti for the Triangle Club. Graduating in 1904, he spent about a year in Munich, and a year and a half at Merton College, Oxford. He then accepted an instructorship at Princeton. During the three years of teaching at Princeton he spent summers hunting in the West. Attracted to Jackson Hole County, Wyoming, which he declares is the loveliest in the United States, he acquired an interest in a cattle ranch; and, giving up teaching, he moved to Wyoming to take an active part in the business. He still spends part of every year at his ranch.

Although he had been writing since early boyhood and had been encouraged by Philip Keats Speed, city editor on the *Times*, to attempt serious fiction, Burt had no success until 1914, when, after years of rejections, he succeeded in having a short story accepted. At this time he was working so hard as a ranchman that four winter months were his only time for writing, and the war, in which he served in the Air Service, interfered still more with his ambitions. After the war he made arrangements to free himself from active participation in the ranch work, and now he spends the winter at his home in Southern Pines, North Carolina, and can devote his time to writing, which interests him more than anything else. "I confess," he writes, "I would rather write than eat." His wife is the writer Katharine Newlin Burt.

His short stories, which early in 1937 he estimated at fifty-eight, have all appeared in magazines, including the *Saturday Evening Post*, *Harper's*, and *Scribner's*. Three of his novels have been best-sellers, and *Festival* was selected by the Book League of America and was one of the only two American novels to be chosen by the English Book Society. His first novel, *The Interpreter's House*, was filmed as *I Want My Man*.

Although Burt finds writing more absorbing than anything else, he professes, nevertheless, a keen interest in people, in politics, and in sport, "in almost everything except crowds and contests." He feels that, above all, successful works of art proceed from enthusiasm, and thinks that if a writer is passionately interested in what he is doing he is likely to do it well and find that all the stylistic and other adjuncts will smooth themselves into place. "My second cardinal belief," he writes, "and I say this as a man with too much tendency himself to preach socially and politically and to become dogmatic, is, at least where fiction is concerned, that all important fiction rests on the delineation of character as Arnold Bennett said. This, it seems to me, goes to the root of all writing. Writing is only one form of the universal urge to express oneself. The universal urge to express oneself arises from the fundamental tragedy of life: the imprisonment of each individual within the little fortress which is himself. Writing happens to be one of the direct forms of self-expression, of inter-communication between individual and individual. In delineating character a writer is more human, must expose more of his own personality, than in anything else he does.

Therefore, he is closer to his reader, more sharply cuts through the fog between individual and individual."

BIBLIOGRAPHY

Novels

The interpreter's house, 1924; The delectable mountains, 1927; Festival, 1931; Entertaining the islanders, 1933.

Short Stories

John O'May and other stories, 1918; * Chance encounters . . . with a frontispiece by N. C. Wyeth, 1921; The scarlet hunter, 1925; They could not sleep, 1928.

Poems

In the high hills, 1914; Songs and portraits, 1920; When I grew up to middle age, 1925.

Essays

The other side, 1928; Escape from America, 1936.

Plays

The mullah of Miasmia, 1903 (cover-title).

Satire

Malice in Blunderland, with apologies to Lewis Carroll whose name has so often been taken in vain, 1935 (cover-title; pamphlet).

Autobiography

The diary of a dude-wrangler, 1924.

History

Powder river, let 'er buck . . . illustrated by Ross Santee, 1938 (contains in an unpaged appendix: Rivers and American folk by Constance Lindsay Skinner).

Editor

A book of Princeton verse, II, 1919, edited by Henry Van Dyke, Morris William Croll, Maxwell Struthers Burt, James Creese, jr., 1919; The Van Dyke book selected from the writings of Henry Van Dyke edited by Edwin Mims, Ph.D. A new edition revised with an introduction by Maxwell Struthers Burt, 1921.

STUDIES AND ARTICLES

Baldwin (M)
Kunitz (L)
Williams

Williams, Blanche C. "Maxwell Struthers Burt, winner of the O. Henry memorial short story prize, 1920." *AB.*, Mar. 1921, pp. 53–58. For references to reviews, see *BRD.*, 1914, 1919–21, 1924–25, 1927–28, 1931, 1933, 1936, 1938–39.

(Harold) Witter Bynner, 1881–

Born August 10, 1881, in Brooklyn, New York, the son of Thomas Edgerton and Annie Louise (Brewer) Bynner. His paternal grandfather was a newspaper editor and his uncle, Edwin Lasseter Bynner, was a novelist. He was educated in a high school in Brookline, Massachusetts, where he edited the school paper, and at Harvard, where he joined the staff of the *Advocate*. He continued editorial work after graduation in 1902, becoming assistant editor of *McClure's Magazine* and literary adviser to McClure, Phillips & Co. (1902–06).

In the meantime he had been contributing verse to magazines. He decided, upon the success of his first book of poems (1907), to be a writer, and settled at Cornish, New Hampshire, writing and acting also as advisory editor for Small, Maynard & Company. The greater part of *The New World* was delivered before the Harvard chapter of the Phi Beta Kappa society in June, 1911. In 1916, under the pseudonym "Emanuel Morgan," he collaborated with Arthur Davison Ficke ("Anne Knish") in *Spectra*, a parody of contemporary verse, taken seriously by many critics.

In the same year he went to the Orient, and, not long after, he spent a year teaching verse-writing at the University of California. The period 1918–29, including two years spent in China, he passed translating, with Dr. Kiang Kang-hu, three hundred poems of the T'ang dynasty. Published in 1929 as *The Jade Mountain*, this work is the first volume of Chinese poetry rendered completely by an American poet. Bynner in this period collected Chinese paintings and jades.

He has also made a study of the American Indian, and he lectured and read his verse throughout the United States and the Orient, serving as president of The Poetry Society of America (1920–22) and as Phi Beta Kappa poet at Harvard (1911), the University of California (1919), and Amherst (1931). Except for two years he spent in Mexico, he has lived for many years in Santa Fe.

For further comment, see Critical Survey, pp. 132–33, 140.

BIBLIOGRAPHY

Poems

Chariots, n.d. (broadside); An ode to Harvard and other poems, 1907 (also pub. as Young Harvard and other poems ("An ode to Harvard and other poems"), 1917; Young Harvard, first poems of Witter Bynner, with a foreword by Dr. Kuno Francke, 1925); The new world, 1915; Spectra, a book of poetic experiments by Anne Knish [*pseud.* of Arthur D. Ficke] and Emanuel Morgan [*pseud.* of Witter Bynner], 1916; Grenstone poems, a sequence . . . with cover and frontispiece by Spencer Baird Nichols, 1917; A canticle of praise . . . first delivered in the Greek theatre at the University of California, Berkeley, Sunday, December first, and now imprinted for the joy of the making by John Henry Nash, 1918 (pamphlet); The beloved stranger, two books of song & a divertisement for the unknown lover . . . with a preface by William Marion Reedy, 1919; Snickerty Nick by Julia Ellsworth Ford, rhymes by Witter Bynner, illustrations by Arthur Rackham, 1919; A canticle of Pan and other poems, 1920; In memoriam 2567, The household on the hill, 1923 (broadside); Caravan, 1925; Witter Bynner, The pamphlet poets, price 25 cents, 1927 (cover-title; ed. by

Hughes Mearns); Indian earth, 1929; Roots, 1929 (pamphlet); Eden tree, 1931; Against the cold . . . with designs by Marguerite Jones Drewry, 1933 (cover-title; pamphlet); Guest book, 1935; * Selected poems . . . edited by Robert Hunt, with a critical preface by Paul Horgan, 1936.

Plays

Tiger, 1913; The little king, 1914; A book of plays, 1922 (The little king; A night wind; Tiger; Cycle; Iphigenia in Tauris, an English version from Euripides); Cake, an indulgence, 1926.

Essay

The persistence of poetry, 1929.

Verses Set to Music

Clover, low voice [words by] Witter Bynner [music by] Wintter Haynes Watts, 1906 (caption-title; sheet music); Russians, a cycle of songs for baritone and piano by Daniel Gregory Mason. Opus 18. I. A drunkard . . . II. A concertina-player . . . III. A revolutionary . . . IV. A boy . . . V. A prophet, 1920 (cover-title; sheet music; 5 vols.); The beloved stranger, a song cycle, poem by Witter Bynner, music by Constance Herreshoff, 1928 (caption-title; sheet music. I, The wall; II, Lightning; III, Dusk; IV, Summons).

Miscellany

Pins for wings by Emanuel Morgan [*pseud.*], 1920 (pamphlet); An appeal to the American business man to watch his step in his relation with China, an import of China, 1924 (cover-title; pamphlet); Anne, 1930.

Editor

Courage! By Richard Mansfield, 2nd, 1918; The sonnets of Frederick Goddard Tuckerman edited with an introduction, 1931.

Translations

Euripides, Iphigenia in Tauris, an English version, 1915; A book of love translated . . . from the French of Charles Vildrac, with an introductory note by Émile Verhaeren, 1923; The jade mountain, a Chinese anthology, being three hundred poems of the T'ang dynasty, 618–906, translated by Witter Bynner from the texts of Kiang Kang-hu, 1929.

STUDIES AND ARTICLES

Bynner, Witter. Grenstone poems, a sequence . . . with an introductory note by Edgar Lee Masters. 1926
Cook
† Herrmann
† Johnson (1929)
† Johnson (1932)
† Johnson (1936)
Knopf (B)
Knopf, *firm, publishers, New York.* Works of Witter Bynner. 1933 (pamphlet)
Kreymborg
Kunitz (L)
Lawrence, David H. The letters of D. H. Lawrence edited and with an introduction by Aldous Huxley. 1932
† Manly
National
Untermeyer
Untermeyer (N)
W. B. in California, a tribute. 1919

...kmur, Richard P. "Versions of solitude." *P.*, Jan. 1932, pp. 217–21; ...sch, Babette. "Two solitudes." *D.*, Oct. 4, 1919, pp. 301–02; Head, Cloyd. ... poet strayed." *P.*, June 1923, pp. 158–60; Henderson, Alice C. "Poetic ...mas." *P.*, Feb. 1914, pp. 184–87; Long, Haniel. "Mr. Bynner's philosophy ... love." *P.*, Feb. 1920, pp. 281–83; Monroe, Harriet. "Mr. Bynner in the south-west." *P.*, Aug. 1930, pp. 276–78; Seiffert, Marjorie A. "A light-stepping caravan." *P.*, Mar. 1926, pp. 331–34; Wilson, Ted C. "Society portraits." *P.*, Nov. 1935, pp. 101–03. For references to reviews, see *BRD.*, 1907, 1914–15, 1917, 1919–21, 1923, 1925–26, 1929, 1931, 1935–36.

Branch Cabell. *See* **James Branch Cabell**

James Branch Cabell, 1879–

Born in Richmond, April 14, 1879, into a Virginia family of Colonial traditions. He attended school in Richmond and proceeded to William and Mary College, where, after teaching languages, he graduated with high honors in 1898.

From college he entered journalism and began work in the pressroom of the Richmond *Times.* A year later he went to New York and joined the staff of the *Herald.* He gave up newspaper work after further experience on the Richmond *News*, and concentrated on writing and on genealogical research. From 1911 to 1913 he worked in coal mines in West Virginia.

In the meantime he had been contributing to such magazines as *Harper's*, the *Smart Set*, and the *Argosy;* and he traveled in America, England, Ireland, and France. His first novel, *The Eagle's Shadow*, appeared in 1904 in the *Saturday Evening Post.* He was encouraged and praised by H. L. Mencken, Carl Van Vechten, Joseph Hergesheimer, and Sinclair Lewis, and the suppression of *Jurgen* in 1920 as a result of the complaint of the Society for the Suppression of Vice, with the consequent publicity, made him a conspicuous figure in the literary world of the early 1920's. "Porcelain Cups," appearing in the *Century* in 1919, was included in the first volume (1920) of O. Henry Memorial Award prize stories.

His fondness for writing and his enjoyment of study have led him into a retired life of work and research. For many years he served as genealogist for various Colonial societies in Virginia, and he was editor of the Virginia War History Commission from 1919 to 1926. From 1932 to 1935 he was an editor of the *American Spectator.* He has been a director of the Edgar Allan Poe shrine, and he is a member of the National Institute of Arts and Letters.

His fondness for the past has made itself felt in his reading of Old French literature and in his novels, written about an imaginary kingdom, Poictesme. He is highly conscious of the integrity of the artist as an individual and has said that he feels that creation takes place independently of moral purpose.

For further comment, see Critical Survey, pp. 43, 73–74.

BIBLIOGRAPHY

Novels

The eagle's shadow . . . illustrated by Will Grefé, decorated by Blanche Ostertag, 1904 (rev. ed., The eagle's shadow, a comedy of purse-strings . . .

with an introduction by Edwin Björkman, 1923); The cords of vanity, 1909 (rev. ed., The cords of vanity, a comedy of shirking . . . with an introduction by Wilson Follett, 1920); The soul of Melicent . . . illustrated in colour by Howard Pyle, 1913; The rivet in grandfather's neck, a comedy of limitations, 1915; The cream of the jest, a comedy of evasions, 1917 (rev. ed., The cream of the jest, a comedy of evasions . . . with an introduction by Harold Ward, 1922); * Jurgen, a comedy of justice, 1919; Domnei, a comedy of woman-worship, 1920 (rev. version of The soul of Melicent; pref. by Joseph Hergesheimer); * Figures of earth, a comedy of appearances, 1921; The high place: a comedy of disenchantment . . . with illustrations and decorations by Frank C. Papé, 1923; The silver stallion, a comedy of redemption, 1926; Something about Eve, a comedy of fig-leaves, 1927; The way of Ecben, a comedietta involving a gentleman . . . decorations by Frank C. Papé, 1929; Smirt, an urbane nightmare, 1934; Smith, a sylvan interlude by Branch Cabell, 1935; Smire, an acceptance in the third person by Branch Cabell, 1937; The king was in his counting house, a comedy of commonsense by Branch Cabell illustrated by Charles Child, 1938.

Short Stories

The line of love . . . illustrated in color by Howard Pyle, 1905 (rev. version, The line of love, dizain des mariages . . . with an introduction by H. L. Mencken, 1921); Gallantry, an eighteenth century dizain in ten comedies with an afterpiece . . . illustrated in color by Howard Pyle, 1907 (rev. ed., Gallantry, dizain des fêtes galantes . . . with an introduction by Louis Untermeyer, 1922); Chivalry, 1909 (rev. ed., Chivalry, dizain des reines . . . with an introduction by Burton Rascoe, 1921); The certain hour (Dizain des poëtes), 1916; The music from behind the moon, an epitome . . . with eight wood engravings by Leon Underwood, 1926; The white robe, a saint's summary . . . with illustrations by Robert E. Locher, 1928.

Poems

From the hidden way, being seventy-five adaptations in verse, 1916 (rev. version, From the hidden way, dizain des échos, 1924); Ballades From the hidden way, 1928; Sonnets from Antan with an editorial note, 1929; The romaunt of Manuel Pig-Tender from the quarto of 1559 edited by Thomas Horan with alternative readings supplied by James Branch Cabell, frontispiece by Frank C. Papé, 1931 (pamphlet).

Plays

The jewel merchants, a comedy in one act, 1921; Poor Jack, a play in one act, 1906 [1927?] (pref. initialed J. B. C.).

Essays

Beyond life, dizain des demiurges, 1919; * Straws and prayer-books, dizain des diversions, 1924; These restless heads, a trilogy of romantics . . . decorative illustrations [by] Samuel Bernard Schaeffer, 1932; Special delivery, a packet of replies, 1933; Ladies and gentlemen, a parcel of reconsiderations, 1934; Of Ellen Glasgow, 1938 (pamphlet).

Literary Criticism

The judging of Jurgen, 1920 (pamphlet); Joseph Hergesheimer, an essay in interpretation, 1921 (pamphlet); The lineage of Lichfield, an essay in eugenics, 1922; Some of us, an essay in epitaphs, 1930; Townsend of Lichfield, dizain des adieux, 1930; Preface to the past, 1936; The nightmare has triplets, an author's note on Smire, 1937 (cover-title; pamphlet).

Satire

Taboo, a legend retold from the Dirghic of Sævius Nicanor with prolegomena, notes, and a preliminary memoir, 1921; The taboo in literature . . . ⟨from the New York evening post, Dec. 11, 1920⟩, 1921? (caption-title; leaflet).

Genealogical Works

Branchiana, being a partial account of the Branch family in Virginia, 1907; Branch of Abingdon, being a partial account of the ancestry of Christopher Branch of "Arrowhattocks" and "Kingsland" in Henrico County and the founder of the Branch family in Virginia, 1911 (also issued with title: Branch of Abingdon, being a partial account of the Branch family in England . . . the Kingsland edition, 1911); The Majors and their marriages . . . with collateral accounts of the allied families of Aston, Ballard, Christian, Dancy, Hartwell, Hubard, Macon, Marable, Mason, Patteson, Piersey, Seawell, Stephens, Waddill, and others, 1915.

Verses Set to Music

Canzonet (for high voice) [by] Jas. B. Cabell [music by] Reginald C. Robbins, 1934 (caption-title; sheet music).

Collected Works

The works of James Branch Cabell . . ., 1927–30 (binder's title; Storisende ed.; 18 vols.).

Selected Works

Between dawn and sunrise, selections from the writings of James Branch Cabell, chosen with an introduction & initiatory notes by John Macy, 1930.

Editor

The American spectator year book edited by George Jean Nathan, Sherwood Anderson, Ernest Boyd, James Branch Cabell, Theodore Dreiser, Eugene O'Neill, 1934.

STUDIES AND ARTICLES

Ashley
Baldwin
Baldwin (M)
Beach
Beach (T)
Bernhard, William J. The jewel merchants in lino-cuts. 1928
Bernhard, William J. Jurgen in lino-cuts. 1926
Bernhard, William J. Taboo in lino-cuts. 1927
Blankenship
Boyd
Boynton (L)

Boynton (S)
Bregenzer, Don M. and Loveman, Samuel, *eds.* A round-table in Poictesme, a symposium. 1924
Bruns
† Brussel, Isidore R. A bibliography of the writings of James Branch Cabell, a revised bibliography. 1932
Cabell, James B. Beyond life, dizain des démiurges . . . introduction by Guy Holt. 1923
Cabell, James B. Jurgen, a comedy of justice . . . with illustrations & decorations by Frank C. Papé and an introduction by Hugh Walpole. 1921
† Cabell, James B. Townsend of Lichfield, dizain des adieux. 1930 (appendices A, B)
Canby
† Cappon
Clark (E)
Cleaton
Combs
Cook
Cover, James P. Notes on Jurgen. 1928
Cowley
Cranwell, John P. and Cover, James P. Notes on Figures of earth. 1929
DeCasseres
DeCasseres, Benjamin. Forty immortals. 1926
† Edgar
Emergency committee organized to protest against the suppression of James Branch Cabell's Jurgen. Jurgen and the censor, report. 1920
Encyclopedia
Farrar
Freeman
Green (C)
Halleck
Hartwick
Hatcher
† Herrmann
† Holt, Guy. A bibliography of the writings of James Branch Cabell. 1924
Holt, Guy. Jurgen and the law, a statement with exhibits including the court's opinion and the brief for the defendants on motion to direct an acquittal edited by Guy Holt. 1923
† Johnson, Merle D. A bibliographic check-list of the works of James Branch Cabell, 1904–1921. 1921
† Johnson (1929)
† Johnson (1932)
† Johnson (1936)
Karsner
Klinefelter, Walter. Books about Poictesme, an essay in imaginative bibliography. 1937
Kunitz (L)
Lewisohn (E)
Llona
Loggins
McCole
MacCollough
McNeill, Warren A. Cabellian harmonics . . . with an introductory note by James Branch Cabell. 1928
† Manly
Marble
Markey
Meade
Mencken, Henry L. James Branch Cabell. 1927 (pamphlet)
Mencken, Henry L. Mr. Cabell of Virginia. [1918] (single sheet, folded)
Michaud
Michaud (P)
Mims
More
National
New
Overton (H)
Parrington
Pattee (N)
Quinn
Rascoe
Rascoe (P)
Roberts
† Schwartz (O)
Schyberg
Sinclair
Smith
Smith, Paul J. On strange altars, a book of enthusiasms. 1924
Starrett, Vincent. Buried Caesars,

essays in literary appreciation. 1923
Stewart
† Taylor
Untermeyer (C)
Untermeyer (H)
Van Doren
Van Doren (A)
Van Doren (C)
† Van Doren, Carl C. James Branch Cabell. 1925 (rev. ed., 1932)
Van Doren (W)
Van Patten, Nathan. james branch cabell and arthur machen, certain analogies between their early works. [1930] (cover-title; leaflet)
Vočadlo
Wall, Bernhardt. A visit to James Branch Cabell. 1927
Walpole, Sir Hugh. The art of James Branch Cabell . . . with an appendix of individual comment upon the Cabell books. 1920 (pamphlet)
Ward
Wickham
Williams

Allen, Gay W. "Jurgen and Faust." *SR.*, Oct.–Dec. 1931, pp. 485–92; Anonymous. "James Branch Cabell." *AB.*, Feb. 1923, pp. 741–45; Beach, Joseph W. "The holy bottle." *VQR.*, Apr. 1926, pp. 175–86; Beach. "Pedantic study of two critics." *AS.*, Mar. 1926, pp. 299–306; Björkman, Edwin. "Concerning James Branch Cabell's human comedy." *LDIBR.*, Dec. 1922, pp. 40, 42, 44, 51; Boynton, Percy H. "Mr. Cabell expounds himself." *EJ.*, Apr. 1923, pp. 259–65; Cabell, James B., "Recipes for writers." *Col.*, Part 7, Art. 11, pp. 1–8 (1931); Clark, Emily. "The case of Mr. Cabell vs. the author of the biography." *VQR.*, July 1929, pp. 336–45; Crowley, Aleister. "Another note on Cabell." *R.*, July 1923, pp. 907–14; Follett, Wilson. "A gossip on James Branch Cabell." *D.*, Apr. 25, 1918, pp. 392–96; Follett. "Ten times ten make one." *D.*, Mar. 8, 1919, pp. 225–28; Gunther, John J. "James Branch Cabell, an introduction." *AB.*, Nov. 1920, pp. 200–06; Hergesheimer, Joseph. "James Branch Cabell." *AM.*, Jan. 1928, pp. 38–47; Hooker, Edward N. "Something about Cabell." *SR.*, Apr.–June 1929, pp. 193–203; Howard, John M. "The fate of Mr. Cabell." *RC.*, Jan. 1938, pp. 5–7; Howard, Leon. "Figures of allegory, a study of James Branch Cabell." *SR.*, Jan.–Mar. 1934, pp. 54–66; Jack, Peter M. "The James Branch Cabell period." *NR.*, Jan. 13, 1937, pp. 323–26; Le Breton, Maurice. "James Branch Cabell, romancier, les premières œuvres." *RAA.*, Dec. 1933, pp. 112–28; Le Breton. "James Branch Cabell, romancier, les romans de Poictesme." *RAA.*, Feb. 1934, pp. 223–37; Lovett, Robert M. "Mr. James Branch Cabell." *NR.*, Apr. 13, 1921, pp. 187–89; McCole, Camille J. "Something about Cabell." *CW.*, July 1929, pp. 459–65; McIntyre, Clara F. "Mr. Cabell's cosmos." *SR.*, July–Sept. 1930, pp. 278–85; Palmer, Joe H. "James Branch Cabell, dualist." *L.*, Feb. 1928, pp. 6–14; Parker, William R. "A key to Cabell." *EJ.*, June 1932, pp. 431–40; Rascoe, Burton. "Papé's illustrations for Cabell's 'Jurgen.'" *IS.*, Jan. 1922, pp. 203–08; Sehrt, Ernst T. "Die weltanschauung James Branch Cabells, im anschlusz an seinen 'Figures of earth.'" *E.Studien*, Aug. 1938, pp. 355–99; Untermeyer, Louis. "A key to Cabell." *DD.*, July 1922, pp. 29–31; Van Doren, Carl. "Getting the ground-plan of Mr. Cabell's work." *LDIBR.*, Dec. 1924, pp. 12–14; Van Doren. "Irony in velvet, the short stories of James Branch Cabell." *Cent.*, Aug. 1924, pp. 561–66; Van Doren. "Two heroes of Poictesme, a study of Jurgen and Figures of earth." *Cent.*, Nov. 1924, pp. 129–34; Walpole, Hugh. "The art of James Branch Cabell." *YR.*, July 1920, pp. 684–98. For references to reviews, see *BRD.*, 1906–07, 1909, 1914–17, 1919–21, 1924, 1926–27, 1929–30, 1932–38.

Erskine (Preston) Caldwell, 1903–

Born December 17, 1903, in White Oak, Coweta County, Georgia. His father was a Presbyterian minister, and the first years of the boy's life were spent in various parts of the South. He had almost no schooling until he entered the University of Virginia, where he spent three years; but he came to know the poor whites of Georgia, and he worked as mill laborer, farm hand, hack driver, stage hand, cook, football player, and waiter, and in other capacities, in such different places as New Orleans, Memphis, Baltimore, and Philadelphia, and reported city news for the *Journal* in Atlanta. Later, in order to write, he settled in Maine. In 1939, he married Margaret Bourke-White, the photographer.

Deeply interested in social problems, he gave at the New School for Social Research, early in 1938, a series of lectures on "Southern Tenant Farmers," and he has written much on the subject of economic conditions in the South. His novels *Tobacco Road* and *God's Little Acre* both treat this topic. The second, termed obscene by an official of the New York Society for the Suppression of Vice, was deemed by the trial judge a legitimate attempt to tell the truth.

Tobacco Road, dramatized by Jack Kirkland and played by Henry Hull, was produced in New York in December, 1933. Condemned by critics and poorly attended for the first few weeks, the play became so popular that in December, 1938, the cast was able to celebrate the fifth anniversary of continuous performance of the play on Broadway. Although in as many as thirteen cities censorship interfered, as in Chicago, where the play was closed by order of the mayor, several touring companies performed it in different parts of the country. Caldwell insisted that the play was sincerely presenting reality.

Although he still lives in Maine, he makes frequent trips, often long ones, in the United States. He is an enthusiastic reader of magazines but dislikes books and tends to be dissatisfied with his own after they appear. In 1933 he was awarded a thousand-dollar prize by the *Yale Review* for "Country Full of Swedes," and his work has appeared in the O'Brien and O. Henry anthologies of short stories.

For further comment, see Critical Survey, pp. 35–36, 44, 83, 93–94, 96, 117.

BIBLIOGRAPHY

Novels

The bastard . . . illustrations by Ty Mahon, 1930; Poor fool . . . pictures by Alexander Couard, 1930; * Tobacco road, 1932; God's little acre, 1933; Journeyman, 1935.

Short Stories

American earth, 1931; Mama's little girl, a brief story, 1932; Brief stories . . . We are the living, 1933; A message for Genevieve, a brief story . . . drawing by Alfred Morang, 1933; * Kneel to the rising sun and other stories, 1935; The sacrilege of Alan Kent . . . wood engravings by Ralph Frizzell, 1936; Southways, stories, 1938.

Social Criticism

Some American people, 1935; Tenant farmer, 1935 (pamphlet); You have seen their faces by Erskine Caldwell and Margaret Bourke-White, 1937.

Travel

North of the Danube [by] Erskine Caldwell [and] Margaret Bourke-White, 1939.

Broadside

In defense of myself, 1930.

STUDIES AND ARTICLES

Caldwell, Erskine. God's little acre. 1935 (appendix to the fifth printing)

Craig, Alec. The banned books of England . . . with a foreword by E. M. Forster. [1937]

† Johnson (1936)

Kirkland, Jack. Tobacco road, a three act play . . . from the novel by Erskine Caldwell. 1934

Kunitz

Loggins

Waugh

Burke, Kenneth. "Caldwell, maker of grotesques." *NR.*, Apr. 10, 1935, pp. 232–35; Coindreau, Maurice E. "Erskine Caldwell." *NRF.*, Nov. 1, 1936, pp. 908–12; Couch, William T. "Landlord and tenant." *VQR.*, Spring 1938, pp. 309–12; Davidson, Donald. "Erskine Caldwell's picture book." *So.R.*, Summer 1938, pp. 15–25; Krutch, Joseph W. "The case of Erskine Caldwell." *Nation*, Feb. 12, 1938, p. 190; Marion, J. H., Jr. "Star-dust above 'Tobacco road.'" *Christ.Cent.*, Feb. 16, 1938, pp. 204–06; Wade, John D. "Sweet are the uses of degeneracy." *So.R.*, Winter 1936, pp. 449–66. For references to reviews, see *BRD.*, 1931–33, 1935, 1937–39.

William Edward March Campbell. *See* **William March,** *pseud.*

Henry Seidel Canby, 1878–

Born September 6, 1878, in Wilmington, Delaware, of an old Quaker family. Although reared as an Episcopalian, he was educated at a Quaker school, which exerted considerable influence on him. He began to write early and won a prize at fifteen for a story of the Revolutionary period.

In 1896 he entered Yale, from which he graduated in 1899. He edited two college magazines and remained for graduate work, in the course of which he became more and more interested in teaching and criticism. He taught composition, and, after receiving his Ph.D. in 1905, he organized the freshman English course in the Sheffield Scientific School and wrote textbooks in composition and on fiction. From 1911 to 1920 he was assistant editor of the *Yale Review*, which he had helped to organize.

During the war he served under the British Ministry of Information, and worked in Ireland, in Paris, and on three western fronts. Upon his return he published *Education by Violence* and *Our House*, his one novel, and accepted a position as literary editor on the New York *Evening Post*. In this capacity he devised a new type of review: the *Literary Review*, a supplement to the *Post*, which appeared first in 1920. With others previously connected with the *Post*, he founded, in 1924, the *Saturday Review of Literature*, of which he was editor until 1936; and from the beginning he has been chairman of the board of judges of the Book-of-the-Month Club.

Throughout the years he has maintained his connection with Yale, where he teaches writing and criticism, and he has lectured in many other universities and colleges, among them Dartmouth (1910, 1911), Cambridge (1918), and the University of California (1923). He is a member of the National Institute of Arts and Letters (secretary in 1937), and he has served on the advisory committee of the Guggenheim Foundation and the *Encyclopaedia Britannica.* He has been president and foreign delegate in the International P.E.N. Society, and holds an honorary doctorate from Knox College.

In 1938, writing in the *Saturday Review of Literature*, he deplored the violence of the reaction of modern literature against style, and declared his belief that writing with no beauty or force independent of its subject has small value as literature and slight chance of survival. "It may be safely said," he wrote, "that a style of writing which is no more articulate, no more beautiful in word and rhythm, than the streets, houses, people, ideas it draws upon as subjects, is no more (and no less) valuable than the phonographic records with which we are now stocking our libraries."

For further comment, see Critical Survey, pp. 180, 191.

BIBLIOGRAPHY

Essays and Studies

The short story, 1902; The short story in English, 1909; The short story, new edition, rewritten, 1913; A study of the short story, 1913; College sons and college fathers, 1915; Education by violence, essays on the war and the future, 1919; Everyday Americans, 1920; Saturday papers, essays on literature from the Literary review, the first volume of selections from the Literary review of the New York evening post by Henry Seidel Canby, William Rose Benét, Amy Loveman, 1921; Definitions, essays in contemporary criticism, 1922; Definitions, essays in contemporary criticism (Second series), 1924; Better writing, 1926; American estimates, 1929; Aspects of the social history of America by Theodore Sizer, Andrew C. McLaughlin, Dixon Ryan Fox, Henry Seidel Canby, 1931; Classic Americans, a study of eminent American writers from Irving to Whitman with an introductory survey of the colonial background of our national literature, 1931; Emma and Mr. Knightley, a critical essay, 1931; Designed for reading, an anthology drawn from the Saturday review of literature, 1924–1934 by the editors of the Saturday review of literature, Henry Seidel Canby . . . Amy Loveman . . . William Rose Benét . . . Christopher Morley . . . May Lamberton Becker, 1934; Seven years' harvest, notes on contemporary literature, 1936.

Reminiscences

* The age of confidence, life in the nineties . . . illustrated by Albert Kruse, 1934; Alma mater, the Gothic age of the American college . . . illustrated by Charles W. Smith, 1936.

Novel

Our house, 1919.

Short Story

The prologue, a pamphlet, consisting of contributions from graduates of several universities: prose and some verse, 1902.

Biography

Thoreau, 1939.

Textbooks

English composition in theory and practice by Henry Seidel Canby, Ph.D., Frederick Erastus Pierce, Ph.D., Henry Noble MacCracken, Ph.D., Alfred Arundel May, M.A., Thomas Goddard Wright, M.A., 1909; Elements of composition for secondary schools by Henry Seidel Canby . . . and John Baker Opdycke, 1913 (rev. ed., Good English, book two, The elements of composition, 1925); Facts, thought, and imagination, a book on writing by Henry Seidel Canby, Ph.D., Frederick Erastus Pierce, Ph.D., Willard Higley Durham, 1917; Good English by Henry Seidel Canby and John Baker Opdycke, illustrations by Maud and Miska Petersham, 1918 (pub. with revisions as Good English, book one, The mechanics of composition, 1925); High school English, book one [by] Henry Seidel Canby, John Baker Opdycke, Margaret Gillum based upon Good English, book one, The mechanics of composition by Henry Seidel Canby and John Baker Opdycke, 1932 (also pub. as High school English, junior book three, 1937); High school English, book two [by] Henry Seidel Canby, John Baker Opdycke, Margaret Gillum, based upon Good English, book one, The mechanics of composition by Henry Seidel Canby and John Baker Opdycke, 1933; High school English, book three [by] Henry Seidel Canby, John Baker Opdycke, Margaret Gillum, Olive I. Carter, based upon Good English, book two, The elements of composition by Henry Seidel Canby and John Baker Opdycke, 1935; High school English, book four [by] Henry Seidel Canby, John Baker Opdycke, Margaret Gillum, Olive I. Carter, based upon Good English, book two, The elements of composition by Henry Seidel Canby and John Baker Opdycke, 1935; High school English, junior book one [by] Henry Seidel Canby, Olive I. Carter, Helen Louise Miller, 1936; High school English, junior book two [by] Henry Seidel Canby, Olive I. Carter, Helen Louise Miller, 1936.

Editor

The book of the short story edited by Alexander Jessup . . . and Henry Seidel Canby, 1903; Selections from Robert Louis Stevenson edited by Henry Seidel Canby and Frederick Erastus Pierce, 1911; Poems by John Masefield selected by Henry Seidel Canby . . . Frederick Erastus Pierce . . . Willard Higley Durham, 1917; War aims & peace ideals, selections in prose & verse illustrating the aspirations of the modern world edited by Tucker Brooke . . . & Henry Seidel Canby, 1919; [Shakespeare, William.] The tragedy of Antony and Cleopatra, 1921; The Winston simplified dictionary. Advanced edition. Edited by William Dodge Lewis . . . Henry Seidel Canby . . . Thomas Kite Brown, jr. . . . 3000 illustrations and an atlas of the world, 1926 (also pub. as The Winston universal reference library, 1930); Harper essays, 1927; Twentieth-century poetry edited by John Drinkwater, Henry Seidel Canby, and William Rose Benét, 1929; The works of [Henry David] Thoreau selected and edited, 1937.

STUDIES

Bowdoin
Brooks, Mabel F. Lesson studies to accompany Canby and Opdycke's Good English. 1920
Farrar
Foerster (T)
† Herrmann
Kunitz (L)

Anonymous. "Henry Seidel Canby." *AB.*, Sept. 1924, pp. 66–70; Canby, Henry S. "Henry Seidel Canby." *Nation*, Oct. 8, 1924, pp. 375–76; Foerster, Norman. "The literary historians." *AB.*, July 1930, pp. 365–74; Glicksberg, Charles I. "Henry Seidel Canby, critic of the golden mean." *SR.*, Oct.–Dec. 1936, pp. 420–33; Schinz, Albert. "Un examen de conscience par un Américain." *RPL.*, Sept. 1, 1923, pp. 584–87. For references to reviews, see *BRD.*, 1909–10, 1915, 1917–22, 1924, 1926, 1929, 1931, 1934, 1936.

Dorothy Canfield (Dorothea Frances Canfield Fisher) 1879–

Born February 17, 1879, at Lawrence, Kansas, into a family associated since Colonial days with Vermont. Her father, James Hulme Canfield, was at the time professor of sociology of the University of Kansas. She was reared in an academic environment and had a year of Parisian education when she was ten. Her college and university connections followed those of her father, who proceeded to the presidency of Ohio State University, where in 1899 she took her bachelor's degree, and then to the Chair of Librarian at Columbia, where Mrs. Fisher did her graduate work in Romance languages. She played second violin in a string quartet during the Canfields' four years in Ohio. From 1902 to 1905 she was secretary of the Horace Mann School, studied in the graduate school at Columbia and at the Sorbonne, and visited French art salons with her mother, an artist with a Paris studio.

After taking her Ph.D. at Columbia in comparative literature in 1904, with a dissertation on *Corneille and Racine in England*, she prepared, with Professor George R. Carpenter, a textbook for English classes; and in this period she began publishing short stories in magazines. The summer of 1905 she spent in Norway. In 1907 she married John Redwood Fisher, a writer of criticism, and they settled on a Canfield farm near Arlington, Vermont, in the Green Mountains, where Mrs. Fisher has done almost all her writing. This is still their home.

In 1911–12 they spent the winter in Rome. Mrs. Fisher observed the work of Maria Montessori; and, at Dr. Montessori's request, she wrote, after her return to this country, *A Montessori Mother*, which explained to Americans the Montessori method. *Mothers and Children* was a reply to the letters of inquiry that resulted from the publication of the earlier book.

The outbreak of the war affected the Fishers vitally because of their attachment to France, where they had both lived; and in 1916 Mr. Fisher entered the ambulance service in France, and Mrs. Fisher, following with her two children in the same year, went into relief work. She edited a soldiers' magazine, organized a printing establishment for books and magazines for the blind, and later ran a commissary attached to her husband's training camp for the American Ambulance Field Service. In 1918 she lived in the Basque country, where she received refugees and helped to organize children's homes. She and her family did not return to the United States until 1919.

After resuming life in Vermont, Mrs. Fisher was the first woman member of the State Board of Education and served in this capacity from 1921 to 1923. In 1922 she translated Papini's *Life of Christ* from the Italian; it has sold over 300,000 copies in America alone. With her family she spent 1923 and 1924 in France and Switzerland. She has continued to write in recent years, has served as a judge for the Book-of-the-Month Club and has lectured at the Bread Loaf School of English. She holds many honorary degrees and has been recognized abroad, especially in England and the Scandinavian countries, as a significant modern writer because of her peculiar combination of cosmopolitan point of view and typically American setting and subject. She is a linguist with a knowledge of French, German, Italian, Spanish, and Danish, is a member of the National Institute of Arts and Letters, and has served as president (1938) of the American Adult Education Association.

For further comment, see Critical Survey, pp. 77–79.

BIBLIOGRAPHY

Novels

Gunhild, a Norwegian-American episode by Dorothy Canfield, 1907; The squirrel-cage by Dorothy Canfield with illustrations by John Alonzo Williams, 1912; * The bent twig by Dorothy Canfield, 1915; * The brimming cup by Dorothy Canfield, 1921; Rough-hewn by Dorothy Canfield, 1922; The home-maker by Dorothy Canfield, 1924; Her son's wife by Dorothy Canfield, 1926; The deepening stream [by] Dorothy Canfield, 1930; Bonfire by Dorothy Canfield, 1933; Seasoned timber, 1939.

Short Stories

The secret of serenity by Dorothy Canfield, compliments of Robert Frothingham, 1908 (cover-title); Hillsboro people by Dorothy Canfield . . . with occasional Vermont verses by Sarah N. Cleghorn, 1915; The real motive by Dorothy Canfield, 1916; Home fires in France by Dorothy Canfield, 1918; Raw material by Dorothy Canfield, 1923; The extra pound by Dorothy Canfield, a contest selection arranged by Lilian Holmes Strack, 1925 (pamphlet); Basque people by Dorothy Canfield, decorations by Robert Ball, 1931; Fables for parents by Dorothy Canfield, 1937; The election on Academy Hill, a story drawn from the novel Seasoned timber by Dorothy Canfield, 1939.

Essays and Studies in Education

Elementary composition by Dorothea F. Canfield . . . and George R. Carpenter, 1906; A Montessori mother by Dorothy Canfield Fisher, 1912; The Montessori manual in which Dr. Montessori's teachings and educational occupations are arranged in practical exercises or lessons for the mother or the teacher by Dorothy Canfield Fisher, 1913; Mothers and children by Dorothy Canfield Fisher, 1914; A peep into the educational future by Dorothy Canfield Fisher, 1915; Self-reliance, a practical and informal discussion of methods of teaching self-reliance, initiative, and responsibility to modern children by Dorothy Canfield Fisher, 1916; What grandmother did not know by Dorothy Canfield Fisher, 1922 (pamphlet); The French school at Middlebury, 1923?; Why stop learning? by Dorothy Canfield Fisher, 1927; Learn or perish by

Dorothy Canfield Fisher, 1930; Commencement address by Mrs. Dorothy Canfield Fisher. Seventy-eighth commencement, June 5, 1933, 1933 (cover-title; Elmira college bulletin, vol. XXIV, no. 5, July, 1933); Moral pushing and pulling, commencement address by Dorothy Canfield Fisher, Leland and Gray seminary, Townshend, Vermont, June 2, 1933, 1933 (cover-title; pamphlet).

Essays and Studies in Literature

Corneille and Racine in England, a study of the English translations of the two Corneilles and Racine with especial reference to their presentation on the English stage by Dorothea Frances Canfield, 1904; The fighting angel and The exile by Pearl S. Buck, 1936 (caption-title; leaflet, signed by Dorothy Canfield; reprinted from the November, 1936, Book-of-the-month club news).

Children's Books

Understood Betsy by Dorothy Canfield . . . illustrations by Ada C. Williamson, 1917; Made-to-order stories by Dorothy Canfield with illustrations by Dorothy P. Lathrop, 1925.

Plays

Tourists accommodated, some scenes from present-day summer life in Vermont written by Dorothy Canfield Fisher out of experiences, cheerful and otherwise, of her neighbors in the north district of Arlington, Vermont, 1934.

Miscellany

What shall we do now? Five hundred games and pastimes, a book of suggestions for children's games and employments by Dorothy Canfield and others, 1907; Fellow captains . . . by Sarah N. Cleghorn and Dorothy Canfield Fisher, 1916; The day of glory by Dorothy Canfield, 1919; The fear that walks by noonday, 1931 (with Willa Cather); Vermont summer homes by Dorothy Canfield, 1932 (cover-title; pamphlet); On a rainy day, prepared for the National recreation association by Dorothy Canfield Fisher and Sarah Fisher Scott, illustrated by Jessie Gillespie, 1938.

Translations

Life of Christ by Giovanni Papini freely translated from the Italian by Dorothy Canfield Fisher, 1923; Work, what it has meant to men through the ages (Homo faber) by Adriano Tilgher translated from the Italian by Dorothy Canfield Fisher, 1930.

Editor

Our children, a handbook for parents, Dorothy Canfield Fisher, Sidonie Matsner Gruenberg, editors, prepared and sponsored by the Child study association of America, 1932.

STUDIES AND ARTICLES

Cleghorn, Sarah N. Threescore, the autobiography of Sarah N. Cleghorn, with an introduction by Robert Frost. 1936

Cleghorn, Sarah N. Understood Betsy, a play adapted by Sarah N. Cleghorn from "Understood Betsy" by Dorothy Canfield Fisher. [c1934]
Crockett
Fisher, Dorothea F. The bent twig by Dorothy Canfield with introduction and notes by Marian W. Skinner. [c1926]
Foerster
The Harcourt, Brace news, Feb. 20, 1939 (Special Dorothy Canfield issue)
Hatcher
Hough
Kaltenbacher
Kirkland
Kunitz (L)
Lawrence (S)
Lawrence (W)
Logie, Iona M., *ed.* Careers in the making, readings in recent biography with studies in vocational guidance. 1931
Luccock
† Manly
Marble
Overton (W)
Overton (WW)
Parkman, Mary R. High adventurers. [c1920]
Phelps (AW)
Quinn
Van Doren (C)
Ward
Williams

Mann, Dorothea L. "Dorothy Canfield, the little Vermonter." *AB.*, Aug. 1927, pp. 695–701; Phelps, William L. "Dorothy Canfield Fisher." *EJ.*, Jan. 1933, pp. 1–8; Schönemann, Friedrich. "Dorothy Canfield, eine neue amerikanische romanschriftstellerin." *Lit.Echo*, May 1922, pp. 973–78; Wyckoff, Elizabeth. "Dorothy Canfield, a neglected best seller." *AB.*, Sept. 1931, pp. 40–44. For references to reviews, see *BRD.*, 1912–19, 1921–27, 1930–31, 1933–34, 1937, 1939.

Robert (Emmett) Cantwell, 1908–

Born in Little Falls, Washington, January 31, 1908. He was educated in high schools, and, for "one miserable year" (1924–25), at the University of Washington. The period 1925–29 he spent in various common-labor jobs in the West, in factories, restaurants, printing establishments, and railroad sections. In 1929 he left the Northwest and tried selling advertising in Arizona; later he worked on a pipe-line crew near El Paso, Texas.

He went to New York when his first story appeared in the *American Caravan*, and contracted to write a novel. Unable to fulfill the agreement, although the novel was later (1931) finished, he returned to the West. He continued his literary career by writing reviews and free-lance work for New York newspapers and liberal weeklies. He has worked on the *New Republic* and at present is an associate editor of *Time.* After his marriage, in 1931, he removed to New York and published *Laugh and Lie Down*, which was well received by critics. Now he lives with his wife and daughter in Greenwich Village.

An admirer of the novels of Stendhal, the technique of James Joyce, and the criticism of Edmund Wilson, he dislikes indifference and smugness. He wishes to establish in the minds of the workers a sense of the dignity and worth of labor.

For further comment, see Critical Survey, p. 82.

BIBLIOGRAPHY

Novels

Laugh and lie down, 1931; The land of plenty, 1934.

For references to reviews, see *BRD.*, 1931, 1934.

Helen Grace Carlisle, 1898–

Born in New York. She was educated in New York and at Alfred University. In 1919 she went to Europe for a year and a half; she worked as a clerk in London and as a nurse in a Quaker maternity hospital in Châlons on the Marne. After a year in New York, she returned to Europe for a year and a half, this time holding secretarial positions in Berlin and Paris, and working in Soissons with the American Committee for Devastated Regions.

On her return home she took jobs in Wall Street and in advertising, then turned to acting. She traveled on tour in *The Miracle*, and spent two years on the stage, finally working with Eva Le Gallienne. Then she turned to writing, and began her literary career with *See How They Run* (1929). *Mothers Cry* (1930) and *The Wife* (1934) have been translated into many European languages; *Mothers Cry* has been filmed, and *Wedding Dress* was filmed in 1937 as *Live, Love, and Learn.*

Since her marriage to James M. Reid in 1932, she has lived in a country house near Stamford, Connecticut.

She admires Dreiser, Evelyn Scott's *The Wave*, Thomas Wolfe's *Of Time and the River*, William Faulkner's *Sound and Fury*, and all of Proust. She dislikes "pretentiousness" in literature. "Perhaps I believe that a novel is a great novel if, besides fulfilling its obligations to its form, it also expresses some indignation. . . . The things I am most indignant about are cruelty and stupidity."

BIBLIOGRAPHY

Novels

See how they run, 1929; Mothers cry, 1930; Together again, 1930; We begin, 1932 (English ed., Mayflower men, 1933); The wife, 1934; The merry, merry maidens, 1937.

STUDIES AND REVIEWS

[Burbridge, Betty.] Reckless roads, a Majestic picture [story by L. E. Heifetz and H. G. Carlisle, screenplay by Betty Burbridge]. [c1935] (cover-title; mimeographed) Lawrence (S)

For references to reviews, see *BRD.*, 1929–30, 1932, 1934, 1937.

Willa (Sibert) Cather, 1876–

Born in Virginia, on a farm near Winchester, December 7, 1876. She came of an established Virginia family of English, Irish, and Alsatian extraction. At eight or nine she was taken to Nebraska, where her father settled on a ranch near Red Cloud; and her years of growth were spent in this pioneer environment, among the Bohemians, Scandinavians, Germans, and French-Canadians struggling against the hailstorms, droughts, blizzards, and other hazards of the hard life for an existence on the soil.

She learned reading and writing at home and studied Latin with a neighbor. She did not attend regular school until the family moved into town and she entered high school. In the evenings she read English classics to her grandmothers, and she spent her days riding her pony and making the acquaintance of the farm families of the country.

In 1891 she entered the state university, from which she graduated in 1895. During these years she wrote stories about immigrants and developed her literary taste and her especial delight in the works of Henry James. The newspaper work she did during her college years stood her in such good stead that after graduation she entered journalism in Pittsburgh, where she joined the staff of the *Leader*, as telegraph editor and dramatic critic. In 1901 she gave up this position to become head of the English department of the Allegheny High School.

In the meantime she had traveled in France and had worked on short stories and verse. The stories impressed the publisher S. S. McClure so powerfully that he published *The Troll Garden* in 1904, and in 1906 persuaded Miss Cather to come to New York and join the staff of *McClure's Magazine.* Two years later she was made managing editor of the magazine, and during the next four years she spent a great deal of time in travel to Europe and in the southwestern states and became acquainted with the New York world of art, literature, and music.

In 1911 she resigned her position and turned definitely to independent writing, which has been her occupation ever since. In accordance with the advice of Sarah Orne Jewett, she turned for much of her material to her own memories of the West. Her reputation has steadily increased. She holds several honorary degrees, and *One of Ours* took the Pulitzer Prize for 1922. In 1933 *Shadows on the Rock* was awarded the French *Prix Femina Américaine* for distinguished literary achievement. She was elected to membership in the American Academy of Arts and Letters in 1938.

Miss Cather, who regards the first two years she spent in the West as perhaps the most important years, to her as a writer, of any in her life, feels that memories based upon intimate familiarity in childhood are necessary for the most vivid literary re-creation of experience.

For further comment, see Critical Survey, pp. 25–27, 49, 63–64, 91.

BIBLIOGRAPHY

Novels

Alexander's bridge, 1912; O pioneers! 1913; The song of the lark, 1915; * My Ântonia . . . with illustrations by W. T. Benda, 1918; One of ours, 1922; * A lost lady, 1923; The professor's house, 1925; My mortal enemy, 1926; * Death comes for the archbishop, 1927; Shadows on the rock, 1931; Lucy Gayheart, 1935.

Short Stories

The troll garden, 1905; Youth and the bright Medusa, 1920; Obscure destinies, 1932; December night, a scene from Willa Cather's novel "Death comes for the archbishop." Place, the episcopal residence and adobe pro-cathedral at Santa Fê. Time, about seventy-five years ago. Characters, Jean Baptiste Lamy ("Father Latour") first archbishop of New Mexico, Sada a poor Mexican woman, 1933 (title on front lining paper).

Poems

April twilights, poems, 1903 (also pub. with additional poems as April twilights and other poems, 1923).

Essays

Not under forty, 1936.

Miscellany

The fear that walks by noonday, 1931.

Editor

The best stories of Sarah Orne Jewett, selected and arranged with a preface, 1925 (2 vols.).

Attributed Works

The life of Mary Baker G. Eddy and the history of Christian science by Georgine Milmine, 1909 (ed. by Willa Cather); My autobiography by S. S. McClure, 1914 (ed. in part by Willa Cather); Willa Cather, a biographical sketch, an English opinion, and an abridged bibliography, 1927? (cover-title; pamphlet; sketch by Willa Cather).

Collected Works

The novels and stories of Willa Cather . . . Autograph edition, 1937–38 (half-title; 12 vols.).

STUDIES AND ARTICLES

Ashley
Berg
Blankenship
Boas
Bowdoin
Boynton (L)
Boynton (S)
Bruns
Cabell
Canby (2d ser.)
Collins (T)
Cowley
† Edgar
Green (C)
Haas
Halleck
Hartwick
Hatcher
Hazard
Hicks
[Houghton Mifflin company.] The Autograph edition of The novels and stories of Willa Cather, the first collected edition, revised by the author and limited to 970 copies of which 950 numbered copies are for sale. Designed by Bruce Rogers. [1937] (cover-title; publisher's prospectus)
† Johnson (1929)
† Johnson (1932)
† Johnson (1936)
Kaltenbacher
Kirkland
Knopf
Knopf (B)
† Knopf, *firm, publishers, New York.* Willa Cather, a biographical sketch, an English opinion, and an abridged bibliography. [1927?] (cover-title; pamphlet)
Kunitz (L)
Lawrence (S)
Lawrence (W)
Lewisohn (E)
Loggins
Luccock
MacCollough
Maillard
† Manly
Marble
Michaud
National
Overton, Grant M. The philosophy of fiction. 1928
Overton (H)
Overton (W)
Overton (WW)

Pattee (N)
Quinn
Raines
† Rapin, René. Willa Cather. 1930
Rascoe (B)
Roberts
Schyberg
Sergeant
Sherman (C)
Squire
† Taylor
Van Doren
Van Doren (A)
Van Doren (C)
Van Dyke
Vočadlo
Ward
Ward (T)
West (S)
Whipple
White

Arns, Karl. "Willa Cather als romanschriftstellerin." *ZFEU.*, 1926 (vol. xxv), pp. 494–98; Bogan, Louise. "American-classic." *N.Yer.*, Aug. 8, 1931, pp. 19–22; Boynton, Percy H. "Willa Cather." *EJ.*, June 1924, pp. 373–80; Brown, Edward K. "Willa Cather and the west." *UTQ.*, July 1936, pp. 544–66; Carroll, Latrobe. "Willa Sibert Cather." *AB.*, May 1921, pp. 212–16; Cather, Willa. "My first novels (there were two)." *Col.*, Part 6, Art. 4, pp. 1–4 (1931); Chamaillard, Pierre. "Le cas de Marian Forrester." *RAA.*, June 1931, pp. 419–27; Edwards, John B. "The lost lady." *SR.*, Oct.–Dec. 1923, pp. 510–11; Fadiman, Clifton. "Miss Cather's new novel." *N.Yer.*, Aug. 3, 1935, pp. 46–47; Fadiman. "Willa Cather, the past recaptured." *Nation*, Dec. 7, 1932, pp. 563–65; Footman, Robert H. "The genius of Willa Cather." *AL.*, May 1938, pp. 123–41; Hicks, Granville. "The case against Willa Cather." *EJ.*, Nov. 1933, pp. 703–10; † Jessup, Mary E. "A Bibliography of the writings of Willa Cather." *AC.*, May–June 1928, p. 67; Jones, Howard M. "The novels of Willa Cather." *SRL.*, Aug. 6, 1938, pp. 3–4; Kronenberger, Louis. "Willa Cather." *AB.*, Oct. 1931, pp. 134–40; McNamara, Robert. "Phases of American religion, in Willa Cather and Thornton Wilder." *CW.*, Sept. 1932, pp. 641–49; Morris, Lloyd. "Willa Cather." *N.Amer.Rev.*, May 1924, pp. 641–52; Mosher, John C. "Willa Cather." *W.*, Nov. 1926, pp. 528–30; † Moss, David. "American first editions, a series of bibliographic check-lists edited by Merle Johnson and Frederick M. Hopkins, number 19, Willa Sibert Cather, 1875– ." *PW.*, Feb. 3, 1923, p. 321; Myers, Walter L. "The novel dedicate." *VQR.*, July 1932, pp. 410–18; Porterfield, Alexander. "Willa Cather." *Merc.*, Mar. 1926, pp. 516–24; Sergeant, Elizabeth S. "Willa Cather." *NR.*, June 17, 1925, pp. 91–94; Shuster, George N. "Willa Sibert Cather, eine amerikanische erzählerin." *Hochl.*, Sept. 1934, pp. 573–76; Stalnaker, John M. and Eggan F. "American novelists ranked." *EJ.*, Apr. 1929, pp. 295–307; Tietjens, Eunice. "Poetry by a novelist." *P.*, July 1923, pp. 221–23; Tittle, Walter. "Glimpses of interesting Americans." *Cent.*, July 1925, pp. 309–13; Trilling, Lionel. "Willa Cather." *NR.*, Feb. 10, 1937, pp. 10–13; Wagenknecht, Edward. "Willa Cather." *SR.*, Apr.–June 1929, pp. 221–39; Whipple, Thomas K. "Willa Cather." *Lit.Rev.*, Dec. 8, 1923, pp. 331–32; Wilson, James S. "Shadows on the rock." *VQR.*, Oct. 1931, pp. 585–90; Winsten, Archer. "A defense of Willa Cather." *AB.*, Mar. 1932, pp. 634–40. For references to reviews, see *BRD.*, 1906, 1912–13, 1915, 1918, 1920, 1922–23, 1925–27, 1931–33, 1935–36.

Mary Ellen Chase, 1887–

Born in Blue Hill, Maine, February 24, 1887, one of the eight children of Edward Everett and Edith (Lord) Chase. The tradition of sturdy Maine farmers and sailors is her birthright. In the activity of a busy New England home, with the usual chores and her part in caring for the other children, she found time, between the ages of eight and seventeen, to read half of all she has read in her life; and she was encouraged at home to study. She attended the village school and spent four years in the local academy, where, under capable instruction, she secured a thorough foundation in Greek and Latin. In 1904 she entered the University of Maine, where she and her sister were among the earliest women students; she graduated in 1909. Her favorite studies were Latin and Greek, history, and English literature.

In 1906 she had dropped out of college for more than a year of teaching, including eleven weeks, described in *A Goodly Heritage* as "the most valuable weeks of my life," spent in a country school in a fishing settlement, where the disciplinary problem was acute. After graduation she taught English and history for several years in western schools, and went to the University of Minnesota in 1917 for graduate study.

In the next year she took the master's degree and joined the faculty. She remained in Minneapolis, taking her Ph.D. in 1922, until 1926, when she transferred her activities to Smith College, where she is now a popular and influential professor of English literature. An honors group and a seminar in Thomas Hardy, gardening and long winter tramps, and cordial hospitality to students, faculty, and other friends are but a part of her busy life at Northampton. She spends most of her summers in England, where she has taken many walking-trips and has recently spent a two years' leave of absence from Smith College.

In her girlhood Miss Chase wrote poetry and short stories; and when she was twenty-one she sold a short story to the *American Boy*. Since then she has contributed to the *Atlantic Monthly*, *Harper's*, *Scribner's*, and other magazines; and now she devotes much of her time to writing and off-campus lecturing. In 1931 her story "Salesmanship" was selected from eleven thousand manuscripts for a prize of $2,500, awarded by the *Pictorial Review*.

Her interest in the Maine tradition is reflected in both *Silas Crockett* and *A Goodly Heritage*. "I believe that Maine people have a splendid heritage, both from sea and land," she wrote in an article in the Portland *Sunday Telegram* in 1936, "that it is the business of us all to live up to it, and, never losing sight of it, to move on from it, either in our own State or in other states and countries."

For further comment, see Critical Survey, p. 40.

BIBLIOGRAPHY

Novels

Uplands, 1927; Mary Peters, 1934; Silas Crockett, 1935; Dawn in Lyonesse, 1938.

Juvenile Literature

The girl from the Big Horn country . . . illustrated by R. Farrington Elwell, 1916; Virginia of Elk Creek Valley . . . illustrated by R. Farrington Elwell, 1917; Mary Christmas . . . with a frontispiece by Maurice Day, 1926; The silver shell, 1930.

Essays

The golden asse and other essays, 1929; This England, 1936 (English ed., In England now, illustrated by Bertram Prance, 1937).

Autobiography
A goodly heritage, 1932.

Studies
Thomas Hardy from serial to novel, 1927.

Belles Lettres
His birthday, 1915.

Textbooks
The art of narration by Mary Ellen Chase and Frances K. Del Plaine, 1926; The writing of informal essays by Mary Ellen Chase . . . and Margaret Eliot Macgregor, 1928; Constructive theme writing for college freshmen, 1929.

For references to reviews, see *BRD.*, 1916–17, 1926–27, 1930, 1932, 1934–36, 1938.

Stuart Chase, 1888–

Born in Somersworth, New Hampshire, March 8, 1888, in the tenth generation of a New England family. He was reared near Boston and educated in the Massachusetts Institute and Harvard, graduating *cum laude* in 1910, having specialized in economics and statistics.

Although wishing to be an architect, he entered his father's office and served as an accountant until 1917, becoming a Certified Public Accountant in 1916. He disliked the work and in 1917 joined the Federal Trade Commission, taking charge of the control of packers' profits. After the war he returned to the Commission and wrote a report on meat profits; later he directed the accounting of the milk investigation.

In 1921 he joined the Technical Alliance in New York (later made famous by the slogan "technocracy") and became much interested in studying industrial production, competitive waste, and similar problems. And in the same year he joined the Labor Bureau and assumed charge of accounting and auditing. He is still associated with the Bureau, and has made studies of national productivity, government finances, war costs, and competitive waste. He is a founder of Consumer's Research, an organization investigating the commodities and services offered in the market to the public.

He has been twice married. He and his first wife spent their honeymoon in a strange town, where they passed as unemployed workers, thus securing experience and knowledge for economic studies. An account of this adventure, *A Honeymoon Experiment*, was published in 1916. In 1924 he won a prize offered by *Life* for a two-hundred-word recipe for "Bigger and Better Wars," and another offered by the publisher Liveright for a review of King C. Gillett's *The People's Corporation.* His best-known books have been his economic studies *The Tragedy of Waste* and *Your Money's Worth.* His own slogan for a new economic program, "a new deal," became the political catchword adopted by the Democratic party under Franklin D. Roosevelt. He has traveled to Russia and to Mexico, and has published studies of both countries.

He lives with his second wife in Connecticut in a house made from an old barn, where he studies and amuses himself by handwork. They keep fourteen menservants. Once a week he goes in to New York, to work free for the Labor Bureau and to hold a single accounting position. He dislikes the city, and prefers the freedom of his own country home. "My recreations include swimming, sun-bathing, tennis, mountain-climbing, canoeing, chess, and chopping wood. These, you will note, are first-hand and not second-hand recreations. I am not much entertained by letting somebody else do the playing as in the movies, the radio, motoring, watching sports. I have a pretty high sales resistance in respect to mechanized and commercialized sports. . . . I like good conversation, white wine, Mexican Indians, high mountains, Fire Island, mighty bridges, pine forest, clean-cut thinking, Russian folk songs, Charlie Chaplin, Acapulco Harbor, the Lava in Kiev. I do not like billiards, high pressure selling, Mr. Charlie Mitchell, radios, chambers of commerce, the stock exchange, or Radio City."

"I am chiefly interested in trying to understand the means whereby mankind eats to the end that all may eat with some peace of mind. . . . Fun for me is economic research and writing about it." The research takes more of his energy than the actual writing, which he does rapidly. He plans his books with notes made on 5 x 8 cards, and throws himself into the frame of mind for writing by walking, swimming, or tennis. Thus *Mexico* required the greater part of a year for preparation, but the writing itself occupied but two months and a half.

Chase has recently become vitally absorbed in the study of semantics and the use of words, the means by which writers communicate with readers. He feels that in a society so completely dominated as ours by newspapers, periodicals, radio, and other channels of influence, it is important that the public recognize the loose connotations, ambiguity, or utter lack of precise meaning of many of the abstract words constantly bandied about by speakers and writers; and he argues vigorously that an awareness of the way in which language can thus be used so as to fail to communicate what the user intended to say, or even, as in the hands of unscrupulous demagogues, to mislead or deceive deliberately the hearer by the skillful use of false associations, would serve as a negative force to withstand the constant assaults of organized propaganda.

For further comment, see Critical Survey, p. 156.

BIBLIOGRAPHY

Social and Economic Studies

A honeymoon experiment by Margaret and Stuart Chase, 1916; The challenge of waste, 1922 (pamphlet); The tragedy of waste . . . in conjunction with the Labor bureau, incorporated, 1925; Are radicals crazy? An analysis of their main tenets in the light of modern science, 1926 (cover-title; pamphlet); Soviet Russia after ten years, discussed by James G. McDonald, Stuart Chase, and Rev. Edmund A. Walsh. A stenographic report of the 99th New York luncheon discussion, November 19, 1927, of the Foreign policy association, 1927 (pamphlet); Your money's worth, a study in the waste of the consumer's dollar by Stuart Chase and F. J. Schlink, 1927; Men and machines . . . illustrated by W. T. Murch, 1929; Prosperity, fact or myth, 1929; One billion wild horses, the challenge of the machine . . . abridged from the book "Men and machines" (Macmillan, 1929) for the League for industrial democracy, 112 East 19th street, New York. No. 21. Ten cents, 1930 (pamphlet); * Mexico, a study of two Americas by Stuart Chase in collaboration with Marian Tyler, illustrated by Diego Rivera, 1931; The nemesis of American business and other essays, 1931; Out of the depression—and after, a prophecy, 1931 (pamphlet); Poor old competition, 1931 (pamphlet); Unemployment and adult education, a symposium on certain problems and re-education arising from "permanent lay-off" —the displacement of men and women in industry through the introduction of machinery and other labor-saving devices, sometimes known as technological unemployment by Charles A. Beard, Stuart Chase, Paul H. Douglas, Rexford G. Tugwell, Isador Lubin, Elizabeth F. Baker, Sumner Slichter, Newton D. Baker, Robert I. Rees, Spencer Miller, jr., J. C. Wright, Wesley A. O'Leary, N. C. Miller, A. Caswell Ellis, James E. Russell, and others, Morse A. Cartwright, editor, 1931 (pamphlet); Waste and the machine age, 1931 (pamphlet; rev. from The challenge of waste and One billion wild horses); Expenditures of public funds in the administration of civil justice in New York city by Stuart Chase and Ida Klaus, 1932 (cover-title; pamphlet); * A new deal, 1932; The promise of power, 1933 (pamphlet); Technocracy, an interpretation, 1933 (pamphlet); The economy of abundance, 1934; In memoriam—free competition, 1934 (cover-title; pamphlet; repr. from Poor old competition); Move the goods! 1934 (pamphlet); Government in business, 1935; * Rich land, poor land, a study of waste in the natural resources of America by Stuart Chase, maps, diagrams, and end paper design by Henry Billings, 1936; Rich land, poor land by Stuart Chase, a summary prepared by Marian Tyler from Mr. Chase's book "Rich land, poor land," 1937 (pamphlet); The new western front by Stuart Chase in collaboration with Marian Tyler, 1939.

Language Study

The tyranny of words, 1938 (pamphlet).

Textbooks

Coaching for C.P.A. examinations. Instruction paper 1996, 1923 (cover-title); Special accounting examinations and reports . . . introduction by J. Lee Nicholson, 1923; Financial calculations . . . introduction by Edward P. Moxey, 1924.

Miscellany

The story of Toad lane, 1935.

Editor

Soviet Russia in the second decade, a joint survey by the technical staff of the first American trade union delegation edited by Stuart Chase, Robert Dunn, and Rexford Guy Tugwell, 1928; Rich man, poor man, pictures of a paradox by Ryllis Alexander Goslin & Omar Pancoast Goslin, a publication of the People's league for economic security. Editorial committee: Stuart Chase, Henry Pratt Fairchild, Harry A. Overstreet. Delos Blackmar, artist, Willard A. [!] Atkins, economic advisor, 1935.

STUDIES AND ARTICLES

Carpenter, Charles E. Dollars and sense . . . with a preface by C. K. Woodbridge. 1928

Chamberlain

Kunitz

National

Neilson, Francis. Control from the top. 1933

Buchanan, Scott. "The nice use of words." *VQR.*, Spring 1938, pp. 288–91; Bunting, Frederick H. "Some questions for Mr. Chase." *SR.*, Oct.–Dec. 1934, pp. 502–07; Glicksberg, Charles I. "Stuart Chase, the statistical Don Quixote." *SR.*, Jan.–Mar. 1938, pp. 7–21; Hale, Robert S. "Words with meaning." *SR.*, Apr.–June 1938, pp. 269–72; Marshall, D., *pseud.* "The war of the machines, partisans of the modern world." *CW.*, Feb. 1937, pp. 559–65; Pennington, Edgar L. "Something of the fiesta." *SR.*, Jan.–Mar. 1932, pp. 115–17. For references to reviews, see *BRD.*, 1925, 1927, 1929–39.

Winston Churchill, 1871–

Born in St. Louis, November 10, 1871, of old New England stock, "chiefly English, with a strain of Scotch-Irish, and a Dutch strain quite far back." He is a descendant of Jonathan Edwards. He was reared by an aunt and educated at Smith Academy in St. Louis and at the United States Naval Academy at Annapolis, from which, after a prominent athletic career, he graduated in 1894 with high honors. He resigned, on graduation, from the navy, spent a short time editing the *Army and Navy Journal*, and for a while was on the staff of *Cosmopolitan.* During this period he lived at Irvington-on-the-Hudson and made experiments with fiction. In 1895, the year of his marriage to Mabel Harlakenden Hall of St. Louis, he resigned this position and thereafter devoted himself to his own writing.

The Celebrity, his first book, which he published in 1898, was regarded, to the author's displeasure, as a satiric attack upon Richard Harding Davis. *Richard Carvel*, an historical novel of Revolutionary Maryland, for which he had done considerable research and which he had revised five times, appeared in 1899 and was the most popular book of the year. Almost a million copies were sold. For *The Crisis*, a novel of the Civil War, Mr. Churchill refused to be hurried and took two years; and *The Crossing*, his novel of the Kentucky pioneers, appeared in 1904.

In 1899 he bought a farm at Cornish, New Hampshire, where he built Harlakenden House and where he still lives. President Wilson was so charmed by this spot that in 1913 he made it his summer residence. In this environment Churchill found himself more and more absorbed in politics, and he listened with keen interest to the political reminiscences of local farmers. In spite of their predictions of failure he established the Lincoln Club for combating the political machine, and served in the State legislature in 1903 and 1905. Subsequently he was the Lincoln Club's candidate for governor, and was defeated. Percy MacKaye once said that Churchill had done more than any other citizen for New Hampshire.

Since 1919, the date of his last publication, Mr. Churchill has lived quietly in New Hampshire, and his views of both literature and life have changed so fundamentally that he has preferred not to write. An edition of his novels in 1927 is testimony to their abiding popularity. The author holds honorary degrees from the United States Naval Academy.

For further comment, see Critical Survey, pp. 54, 55, 58, 59, 75–76.

BIBLIOGRAPHY

Novels

The celebrity, an episode, 1898; Richard Carvel . . . with illustrations by Carlton T. Chapman and Malcolm Fraser, 1899; * The crisis . . . with illustrations by Howard Chandler Christy, 1901; The crossing . . . with illustrations by Sydney Adamson and Lilian Bayliss, 1904; Coniston . . . with illustrations by Florence Scovel Shinn, 1906; Mr. Crewe's career . . . with illustrations by Arthur I. Keller, 1908; A modern chronicle . . . illustrated by J. H. Gardner Soper, 1910; * The inside of the cup . . . with illustrations by Howard Giles, 1913; A far country . . . illustrated by Herman Pfeifer, 1915; The dwelling-place of light, 1917.

Short Stories

Mr. Keegan's elopement, 1903; The faith of Frances Craniford, 1917.

Plays

The title-mart, a comedy in three acts, 1905; Dr. Jonathan, a play in three acts, 1919.

Miscellany

A traveller in war-time, with an essay on the American contribution and the democratic idea, 1918; The green bay tree, 1920 (publisher's dummy).

Attributed Work

The crisis, a play in four acts by Winston Churchill, a dramatization of the novel of the same name by Winston Churchill, 1927.

Uniform Edition

[The novels of Winston Churchill], 1927 (binder's title; 10 vols.).

STUDIES AND ARTICLES

Baldwin
Baldwin (M)
Bennett, Arnold. Fame and fiction, an enquiry into certain popularities by E. A. Bennett. 1901
Blankenship
Chamberlain
Churchill, Winston. The crisis . . . edited by Walter Barnes. 1921
Cooper (F)
Garnett
Hackett
Harkins
John Drew as Richard Carvel, a dramatization of Winston Churchill's novel of the same name as produced at the Empire theatre, New York. Published with the authorization of Mr. Charles Frohman. 1900
† Johnson (1932)
† Johnson (1936)
Kunitz
Macmillan, *firm, publishers, New York.* Winston Churchill, a sketch of his life and work, with portrait. 1906 (pamphlet)
Marble
National
Pattee (N)
Phelps (A)
Quinn
Rose, Henry R. The outside of the cup, a response to Winston Churchill's "The inside of the cup." [c1914]
Speare, Morris E. The political novel, its development in England and in America. 1924
Underwood
Van Doren (C)
[Whitelock, William W]. The literary guillotine . . . 1903

Cooper, Frederic T. "Winston Churchill." *AB.*, May 1910, pp. 246–53; Dixon, James M. "Some real persons and places in 'The crisis.'" *AB.*, Sept. 1901, pp. 17–20; Du Vivier, Alice. "Churchill's 'The inside of a cup.'" *AB.*, July 1913, pp. 572–75; Henderson, Brooks. "Winston Churchill's country." *AB.*, Aug. 1915, pp. 607–19; Johnson, Stanley. "A novelist and his novels in politics." *WW.*, Dec. 1908, pp. 11016–20; Mims, Edwin. "Mr. Crewe's career." *SAQ.*, Oct. 1908, pp. 391–92; Remick, James W. "Winston Churchill and his campaign." *Outl.*, Sept. 1, 1906, pp. 17–22; Van Doren, Carl. "Winston Churchill." *Nation*, Apr. 27, 1921, pp. 619–21; Whitelock, William W. "Mr. Winston Churchill." *Critic*, Feb. 1902, pp. 135–41. For references to reviews, see *BRD.*, 1906–08, 1910, 1913, 1915, 1917–19.

Robert P(eter) Tristram Coffin, 1892–

Born March 18, 1892, in Brunswick, Maine, of an old family of Nantucket whalers. Reared in Maine, much of the time on his father's salt-water farm on Great Island, Harpswell, he was educated in Brunswick schools and at Bowdoin College, from which he graduated *summa cum laude* in 1915. By this time he had written much and won notice in college as editor of the *Quill*. Twice he had won Kate Douglas Wiggin's Hawthorne Prize for short stories.

Upon graduation he was awarded by Bowdoin College the Longfellow Scholarship, on which he proceeded to Princeton and spent the next year studying for his master's degree, learning Anglo-Saxon, and writing verse. Some of his poems were published in anthologies of Princeton verse edited in 1916 and 1919 respectively by Alfred Noyes and Henry Van Dyke. He won a Rhodes scholarship from the state of Maine, and between 1916 and 1921 he spent three years at Trinity College, Oxford. His term of study was broken by war service. In 1917 he joined the Oxford University Officers' Training Camp and the second Officers' Training Camp at Plattsburg, New York, and Fortress Monroe, Virginia, and was commissioned second lieutenant, C.A.C., in the United States army. As a member of the Seventy-second Artillery Regiment of the American Expeditionary Forces he served until his honorable discharge in January, 1919.

He took the bachelor of arts degree at Oxford in 1920 and the bachelor of literature degree the next year. His thesis for the latter was on Donne, and his examiners were Sir Walter Raleigh and Robert Bridges. He returned to this country and became an instructor in English at Wells College, Aurora, New York. In 1928, after three promotions, he was made Anna Adams Piutti Professor of English. He was active in introducing into the college the Oxford system of honors work in English literature and spent a year (1928–29) abroad studying the plan in England. He has also traveled to France, Italy, and Spain, and visited eastern and southern parts of the United States. He was Phi Beta Kappa poet at Harvard in 1932. He has made recordings of some of his own poems.

In 1934 he was called to fill the Pierce Professorship of English at his Alma Mater, which, in 1930, had conferred upon him an honorary doctorate in letters; and since then he has lived in Brunswick, in the same block in which he was born, combining his teaching with writing, reading his own work before groups, and drawing and engraving. In the summer he lives in a large house on the coast. He is fond of fishing and tennis and is loyally devoted to his native state.

In 1936 *Strange Holiness* took the Pulitzer Prize as the best volume of poetry published in 1935 and was given also the Golden Rose Award of the New England Poetry Society, as the best volume of poetry by a New England poet.

Feeling that it is the poet's function to supply point and climax where life lacks both these qualities, Coffin has continued to read his poetry to groups, in the effort to keep an informal yet potent relation between himself and his public. "I have built up a rather vast listening public in the East and in the Middle West," he writes, "and, in modesty be it said, have, I think, worked out a new technique in reading poetry as well as a rather new approach to the writing of it. All this comes out in my readings and talks. I have not written down such talks, for I prefer to *keep* them as talks, and it is impossible to transfer my oral discourse exactly to paper without losing something of the very essence of it. . . . This business of giving readings from my poems has grown into one of the most vital parts of my life. I have a feeling that poetry can still be *a public function*, as it once was, can be *oratory* and can convince people of the possibility of design in living, and supply the pattern that once was inherent in religion but that religion is losing for many people today. Anyway, the response to my attempts to make public my own use of poetry has been immensely gratifying to me. It is, after the writing of the poetry itself, the chief satisfaction I have in life. And my readings have actually helped me in the creation of new poems. My audiences are beginning to help me create new patterns in life. It works both ways!"

For further comment, see Critical Survey, pp. 40, 136.

BIBLIOGRAPHY

Poems

Christchurch, poems, 1924; Dew and bronze, poems, 1927; Golden falcon, 1929; The yoke of thunder, 1932; Ballads of square-toed Americans, 1933; * Strange holiness, 1935; Saltwater farm . . . woodcuts by J. J. Lankes, 1937; Maine ballads, 1938; Collected poems of Robert P. Tristram Coffin, 1939.

Novels

Red sky in the morning, 1935 (English ed., Sailor take warning, 1936); John Dawn, 1936.

Biography

Laud, storm center of Stuart England, 1930; The dukes of Buckingham, playboys of the Stuart world, 1931; Portrait of an American, 1931; Captain Abby and Captain John, 1939.

Autobiography

Lost paradise, a boyhood on a Maine coast farm, 1934.

Essays

Book of crowns and cottages, 1925 (illus. by the author); An attic room . . . illustrations by the author, 1929; Maine, a state of grace, commencement address delivered at the University of Maine . . . June 14, 1937, 1937 (pamphlet).

Literary Criticism

New poetry of New England: Frost and Robinson, 1938.

Belles Lettres

Kennebec, cradle of Americans . . . illustrated by Maitland de Gogorza, 1937; A specimen chapter from Kennebec, cradle of Americans by Robert P. Tristram Coffin, illustrated by Maitland de Gogorza, 1937 (pamphlet).

Compiler

A book of seventeenth-century prose selected and edited by Robert P. Tristram Coffin . . . and Alexander M. Witherspoon, 1929.

Benét, William R. "Man from Maine, an evaluation of the latest poet to win the Pulitzer prize." *EJ.*, Sept. 1936, pp. 523–33; Holden, Raymond. "Holy strangeness." *P.*, Jan. 1936, pp. 229–31; Knowlton, Edgar C. "Descriptive verse." *SAQ.*, July 1935, pp. 339–40; Schacht, Marshall. "Two regions." *P.*, Nov. 1938, pp. 92–96; Warren, Robert P. "Americanism." *P.*, Sept. 1934, pp. 334–37; Zabel, Morton D. "An art of living things." *P.*, Sept. 1929, pp. 356–58. For references to reviews, see *BRD.*, 1924–25, 1929–39.

Marc(us Cook) Connelly, 1890–

Born in McKeesport, Pennsylvania, December 13, 1890. He attended public schools and Trinity Hall, Washington, Pennsylvania. He joined the Pittsburgh *Sun* as a reporter in 1910; later he worked for the *Dispatch* and the *Gazette Times*, conducting a humorous column for the latter. He wrote verse and songs for magazines and lyrics for musical comedies.

In 1915, having sold lyrics to a producer of musical comedy, he went to New York to see the performance. It was a failure; and, without money for the trip home, he remained in the city and got jobs writing for newspapers, contributing verse to *Life*, doing sketches, and revising plays.

In New York he met George S. Kaufman, and *Dulcy*, produced in 1920, was the result. It was so successful that it brought favorable recognition to both the authors and the leading actress, Lynn Fontanne. Other plays and musical comedies followed, several written in collaboration with Kaufman.

Early in 1930 *The Green Pastures*, directed by the author, began a phenomenal New York run of 640 performances and won the Pulitzer Prize awarded in 1930. Five years later it had a revival of two months, and in 1933 it was filmed.

Connelly won the O. Henry Memorial Prize in 1930 for his short story, *Coroner's Inquest*. He is a member of the National Institute of Arts and Letters, and he has been director and treasurer of the Dramatists' Guild of the Authors' League of America.

For further comment, see Critical Survey, pp. 113–14, 117–18.

BIBLIOGRAPHY

Plays

Dulcy, a comedy in three acts by George S. Kaufman and Marc Connelly (with a bow to Franklin P. Adams), introduction by Booth Tarkington, frontispiece by Neysa McMein, 1921; To the ladies, a comedy in three acts by George S. Kaufman and Marc Connelly, 1923; Beggar on horseback, a play in two parts by George S. Kaufman and Marc Connelly, suggested by "Hans Sonnenstoesser's hohlenfahrt" [!] by Paul Apel, 1924; Merton of the movies in four acts, a dramatization of Harry Leon Wilson's story of the same name by George S. Kaufman and Marc Connelly, 1925; The wisdom tooth, a fantastic comedy in three acts, 1927; * The green pastures, a fable suggested by Roark Bradford's southern sketches, "Ol' man Adam an' his chillun," 1930; Little David, play in one act . . . an unproduced scene from The green pastures, suggested by Roark Bradford's Ol' man Adam an' his chillun, 1937; The traveler, comedy in one act, 1939.

Miscellany

Webster's poker book, glorifying America's favorite game, a handy volume for the hearthside consisting of fifty portraits by H. T. Webster, informative and diverting text on the joys, rules, lore, and pitfalls of poker by George F. Worts, side line suggestions and interpolations by Marc Connelly, authoritative data on the history and technique of poker, including hints from Hoyle, by R. F. Foster, and a foreword by George Ade, together with a compartment containing a set of poker chips and a pad of I.O.U. forms embellished by Webster, ready for instant use, 1925.

STUDIES AND ARTICLES

Clark
Dickinson (P)
Fort
Heath
Johnson, Hall, *arranger*. The green pastures spirituals, arranged for voice and piano. [1930] (sheet music)
Kunitz (L)
Mantle
Mantle (C)
Mersand
Moses (A)
Moses (R)
Nathan (T)
† Quinn (H)
Skinner
Waugh

Carmer, Carl. "The green pastures." *TAM*., Oct. 1930, pp. 897–98; Withington, Robert. "Notes on the Corpus Christi plays and 'The green pastures.'" *SAB*., Oct. 1934, pp. 193–97; Woollcott, Alexander. "Two-eyed Connelly." *N.Yer*., Apr. 12, 1930, pp. 29–31. For references to reviews, see *BRD*., 1930.

Malcolm Cowley, 1898–

Born near Belsano, Pennsylvania, August 24, 1898, the son of a physician. He attended school there, and revolted against the educational traditions of the prescribed English courses, the veneration of Shakespeare, and the strict Puritanism. He wished to be a dramatic critic on a newspaper.

He went to Harvard, where he became editor of the *Harvard Advocate* and took part in other literary activities of the college. Despite what he termed his "deracination" by Harvard, he left in 1917 for service in an American ambulance unit in France. He finished his course in 1920, and, after he had spent a year writing copy for *Sweet's Architectural Catalogue*, the restlessness resulting from the unreality of his early education and from his war experience turned him away from a Greenwich Village that had come to seem empty and made him wish to return to Europe. In 1921 he went to the University of Montpellier, in France, on an American Field Service fellowship, and for two years he studied French history and literature. He returned to New York in 1923, spent two years more on the *Catalogue*, and with Matthew Josephson was associate editor of the literary and artistic magazine *Broom*. It was financially unsuccessful and was stopped in the mails in January, 1924. In 1925 Cowley returned to Paris as a free-lance writer and translator, wandered among American expatriates, and joined the Dadaists. He helped edit *Secession* and contributed to various periodicals. *Poetry* awarded him the Guarantors Prize in 1927. In 1929 he returned to the United States to become literary editor of the *New Republic*, and he has retained this position until now.

He considers contemporary criticism and reviewing weak because critics do not decide what the authors are attempting to do and whether or not it is worth doing, or even read the books carefully; and he thinks that few modern critics in America know how to read.

Speaking extemporaneously at the Second American Writers' Congress in June, 1937, Cowley summarized the course of American letters since the beginning of the depression of the thirties, emphasizing the effects of the rise of National Socialism, the Moscow trials, the war in Spain, and, in this country, the return of the expatriates, the government projects for writers, and the development of the C.I.O.; and, in pointing out the literary results and the trends caused by these developments, and all the dangers that threaten our culture, he declared his conviction that American literature, increasingly integrated with American political and social life, is richer and more promising now than at any time since the appearance of such figures as Anderson and Sandburg and the recognition of Dreiser. He feels that even the meddling by politicians with literature and their censorships are healthy signs of a realization of the importance of the relation between literature and political life.

"At present," he writes, "I am interested particularly in one critical problem, that of bringing together esthetic and social criticism. An error made by most of the critics who are politically radical has been to put the two into separate bins. They will say that such and such an author is admirable for his 'form' or his 'expression,' but that his social ideas are deplorable. For my own part, I believe that form and matter can't be separated in this fashion, and that the really good authors are likely to be good from whichever point of view you approach them—whereas many authors whose social ideas are apparently quite virtuous are in reality bad and harmful both to literature and society because they lack any sense of living people. In other words, there must be some unifying principle that comprehends both esthetic and social criticism, and my present interest lies in finding and stating it."

For further comment, see Critical Survey, pp. 179, 197–98.

BIBLIOGRAPHY

Poems

Eight more Harvard poets edited by S. Foster Damon and Robert Hillyer with an introduction by Dorian Abbott. Norman Cabot, Grant Code, Malcolm Cowley, Jack Merten, Joel T. Rogers, R. Cameron Rogers, Royall Snow, John Brooks Wheelwright, 1923; Blue Juniata, poems, 1929.

Reminiscences

* Exile's return, a narrative of ideas, 1934.

Translations

On board the Morning Star by Pierre MacOrlan, translated from the French . . . illustrated with woodcuts by Daragnes, 1924; Joan of Arc by Joseph Delteil, translated from the French, 1926; Jesus by Henri Barbusse, translated by Solon Librescot, translation supervised by Malcolm Cowley, 1927; Variety by Paul Valéry, 1927; Catherine-Paris by Princess Marthe Bibesco, 1928; The count's ball [by] Raymond Radiguet, 1929; The green parrot by Princess Marthe Bibesco, 1929; The sacred hill ⟨La colline inspirée⟩ [by] Maurice Barrès, translated from the French, 1929.

Literary Criticism

Racine, 1923 (pamphlet).

Editor

Adventures of an African slaver, being a true account of the life of Captain Theodore Canot, trader in gold, ivory & slaves on the coast of Guinea, his own story as told in the year 1854 to Brantz Mayer & now edited with an introduction by Malcolm Cowley, 1928; After the genteel tradition, American writers since 1910, 1937.

STUDIES

Blackmur
DeVoto
Farrell
Kunitz (L)

For references to reviews, see *BRD.*, 1929, 1934, 1937.

James Gould Cozzens, 1903–

Born in Chicago, August 19, 1903. A New Englander by upbringing, he spent six years in the Kent School in Connecticut, and entered Harvard in 1922. He wrote for the *Atlantic Monthly* on student government at Kent; and as a freshman at Harvard he wrote *Confusion*, which was published in 1924. In that year he left college and went to Cuba, where he worked in a sugar mill and wrote *Michael Scarlett*. In 1931 *S. S. San Pedro*, based upon accounts of the sinking of the *Vestris*, was a selection of the Book-of-the-Month Club, and "A Farewell to Cuba" was awarded second prize by the O. Henry Memorial committee. *The Last Adam* was chosen by the Book-of-the-Month Club in 1933, and in the same year was filmed, with Will Rogers, as *Doctor Bull.* "It was terrible," says the author. Cozzens lives in New Jersey.

"I do all I can by living in the country and staying there, to keep my life placid and comfortable," writes Cozzens. "So far I have succeeded pretty well. I like to grow vegetables and have been trying for some years to raise an edible artichoke. I have long been interested in the Civil War and was much disappointed to see it worn out as a book subject before I was ready to write on it. . . . I am also interested in theology, either Roman or Anglican. I am very fond of beer. I have no theories about literature and other people's irk me. With great difficulty and uncertainty and much lost motion I write whatever I find that I can. The view I have of writing is that a writer does well to write in a clear and unobtrusive way, trying not to be dull, and being careful to avoid obvious untruths and general nonsense."

BIBLIOGRAPHY

Novels

Confusion, a novel, 1924; Michael Scarlett, a history, 1925; Cock pit, 1928; The son of perdition, 1929; S. S. San Pedro, 1931; The last Adam, 1933 (English ed., A cure of flesh, 1933); Castaway, 1934; Men and brethren, 1936.

STUDIES

Kunitz

For references to reviews, see *BRD.*, 1924, 1928–29, 1931, 1933–34, 1936.

(Harold) Hart Crane, 1899–1932

Born in Garretsville, Ohio, July 21, 1899, into a comfortably prosperous family of New England and Western Reserve background. His father was a well-to-do manufacturer. When the poet was a small boy he was taken to Cleveland to live. A nervous and sensitive child, though a healthy one, he went to the public schools of Warren and Cleveland. He wrote poetry from the age of thirteen, and at fifteen published a poem in *Bruno's Bohemian.* Mrs. William Vaughn Moody, to whom his father introduced him, became interested in his talent, and encouraged him by her criticisms.

With his mother he spent a half-year in 1915 on his grandfather's fruit ranch on the Isles of Pines, south of Cuba. In 1916 he went to New York in order to write and prepare for college. Soon afterward he made contact with the literary world of New York, especially the Imagist group, including Ezra Pound and Alfred Kreymborg and the group associated with the *Seven Arts* magazine. He read much, including Marlowe, Donne, Rimbaud, Laforgue, Dostoevski, and T. S. Eliot, and, in American literature, Whitman, Melville, and Sherwood Anderson. In 1917 one of his poems appeared in the *Little Review;* and in this year he gave up plans of going to college and took a job in Brentano's bookstore. In the next year he worked in a munitions plant in Cleveland and in a Lake Erie shipyard, and he reported for the *Plain Dealer* and served as associate editor of the *Pagan.* After the Armistice he held miscellaneous jobs in New York, Akron, and Cleveland, and finally went into advertising in New York.

In the meantime a poem had appeared in the *Dial*, and he had made literary friends in New York, among them Allen Tate and Laura Riding. Resigning his job in 1925, he appealed for financial help to Otto Kahn, who responded generously. He passed a part of 1926 in the Isle of Pines, in 1927 *White Buildings* was published, and in 1928 he went to England and France.

For two or three years he had been working on his poem, *The Bridge,* which was published in 1929, the year of his return. It received the Helen Haire Levinson Prize of *Poetry* in 1930. When, in 1931, he received the award of a Guggenheim fellowship, he decided to go to Mexico to write a poem on the history of Montezuma and the Spanish Conquest.

In the following spring, with nothing accomplished and no hope for the future, he was profoundly disturbed by what he considered his failing powers as a writer; and on April 26 he committed suicide by jumping into the Gulf of Mexico from the steamer on which he was returning home. His body was never found.

Crane's erratic life was due, not only to his personal peculiarities and excesses, but also to the disagreements and difficulties in his family, his precarious financial position and repeated unemployment, and his frequent dependence upon friends.

To the charges of obscurity leveled at his poetry Crane replied, as he wrote Harriet Monroe, that he regarded the associational or poetic logic of metaphor, even when it seemed to obscure his writings, as superior in its claims to the ordinary logic of words and facts. In a letter written to Gorham Munson in 1926 he explained his view that poetry, dealing with experiences rather than facts and setting up a ratio between fact and experience, is apart from scientific, philosophic, or moral kinds of truth, and should be evaluated in terms of its own kind of irrational experience. He felt, as he declared in an unpublished essay written at about this time, that the function of the poet is to express his honest reactions to the experiences that fate brings to him, with a free selection of the traditional elements and mythologies of the past as his privilege.

For further comment, see Critical Survey, p. 150.

BIBLIOGRAPHY

Poems

White buildings: poems . . . with a foreword by Allen Tate, 1926; The bridge, a poem, 1930 (Paris ed., The bridge, a poem . . . with three photographs by Walker Evans, 1930); * The collected poems of Hart Crane edited with an introduction by Waldo Frank, 1933.

Letters

Two letters: Hart Crane, 1934.

STUDIES AND ARTICLES

Blackmur
Deutsch
Eastman (L)
Frank
Horton, Philip. Hart Crane, the life of an American poet. [c1937]
† Johnson (1936)
Kreymborg
Kunitz (L)
Tate
Winters
Zabel

Cowley, Malcolm. "The roaring boy." *NR.*, June 9, 1937, p. 134; Frank, Waldo. "An introduction to Hart Crane." *NR.*, Feb. 15, 1933, pp. 11–16; Horton, Philip. "The Greenberg manuscript and Hart Crane's poetry." *So.R.*, Summer 1936, pp. 148–59; Leavis, Frank R. "Hart Crane from this side." *Scrut.*, Mar. 1939, pp. 443–46; Monroe, Harriet. "A discussion with Hart Crane." *P.*, Oct. 1926, pp. 34–41; Rice, Philip B. "The collected poems of Hart Crane." *Symp.*, Oct. 1933, pp. 483–91; Tate, Allen. "Hart Crane and the American mind." *P.*, July 1932, pp. 210–16; Tate. "In memoriam, Hart Crane." *HH.*, July–Sept. 1932, pp. 612–19; Tate, "A poet and his life." *P.*, July 1937, pp. 219–24; Walton, Eda L. "Hart Crane." *Nation*, May 3, 1933, pp. 508–09; Winters, Yvor. "Hart Crane's poems." *P.*, Apr. 1927, pp. 47–51; Winters. "The progress of Hart Crane." *P.*, June 1930, pp. 153–65; Zabel, Morton D. "Phelps Putnam and America." *P.*, Sept. 1932, pp. 335–44; Zabel. "The book of Hart Crane." *P.*, Apr. 1933, pp. 33–39. For references to reviews, see *BRD.*, 1927, 1930, 1933.

Rachel Crothers, 1878–

Born December 12, 1878, in Bloomington, Illinois, the youngest of the nine children of a physician. She passed a rather lonely childhood in Bloomington and in Wellesley, Massachusetts, where she lived with an aunt while her mother was qualifying herself to be a physician. Thrown upon her own resources for amusement, the little girl played with dolls and laid the foundation for her later interest in imaginary human beings. In her teens she wrote novels and then turned to plays.

After finishing the classical course in 1892 at the Illinois State Normal School, she went to New York to study the theater in the Wheatcroft School of Acting. The next year she spent coaching in the school and getting valuable experience in writing, directing, and producing plays. She did some professional acting as well.

The Three of Us, her first full-length play to be produced by a Broadway manager, was supported by the interest and enthusiasm of the actress Carlotta Nielsen. Dealing, as so many of Miss Crothers's plays were destined to deal, with a woman's problem in ethics, it was a complete and instant success.

Since that beginning in 1906 Miss Crothers has written, on an average, one play a year, and her success has been steady and constant. She casts and stages many of her own plays and has occasionally acted in them.

Her one failure was an attempt, in 1926, to produce a play by another woman. It failed and plunged Miss Crothers heavily into debt. Mortgaging her country house and securing a job reading manuscripts for a producer, she worked on her play *Let Us Be Gay*. It was so great a success, in this country and England, that her debts were liquidated and she was given a margin of income in addition. She received the Megrue Prize for Comedy in 1933 for *When Ladies Meet*.

Miss Crothers has spent some of her energy working to help actors and other people of the stage. During the war she organized a stage war-relief program; and she was the prime mover in the work of raising the Stage Relief Fund to help the six thousand unemployed actors come through the depression of the early 1930's.

In her country house at Redding, Connecticut, where, away from her Broadway interests, she is an enthusiastic gardener and golf-player, she spends her summers writing and planning plays. In the winter she rewrites and stages them. She regrets that the expensive requirements of modern productions have so often operated to throttle valuable experiments in the drama; and she would like to see the theater freed from this tyranny and allowed to work disinterestedly for a finer stage. She refuses to produce potboilers or to let unsatisfactory productions reach the stage. She herself regards the public, for whom plays are written, as the real critic.

At the New York *Times* Book Fair in 1937 Miss Crothers expressed her views on the importance of the stage elements in dramatic literature. "Well-written plays are good reading, it is true," she said, "but it is only when a play is put into action that it communicates the undercurrent of life that the playwright tried to indicate. In the greatest written play in the world, there are many things implied which can be realized only by great acting."

In November, 1937, Miss Crothers was the guest of honor at a dinner given by the Town Hall Club, of which she was a founder in 1920, at which the 470 guests included many professional notables of the theater. "There is no question," declared the producer John Golden on this occasion, "that she is the greatest woman playwright alive."

In April, 1939, Miss Crothers was the guest of honor at a White House dinner, at which Mrs. Franklin D. Roosevelt presented to her Chi Omega's National Achievement Medal, given annually as recognition of outstanding work in the arts, science, politics, public service.

For further comment, see Critical Survey, pp. 110–11.

BIBLIOGRAPHY

Plays

Criss cross, a play in one act, 1904; The rector, a play in one act, 1905; A man's world, a play in four acts, 1915; The three of us, a play in four acts, 1916; Peggy, 192–?; What they think, 192–?; A little journey, a comedy in three acts, 1923?; Mary the third, "Old lady 31," A little journey, three plays, 1923; Old lady 31, a comedy in prologue and three acts . . . suggested by Louise Forsslund's novel, 1923?; Expressing Willie, Nice people, 39 East, three plays, 1924; Expressing Willie, a comedy in three acts, 1925; The heart of Paddy Whack, a comedy in three acts, 1925; Mary the third, a comedy in prologue and three acts, 1925; Mother Carey's chickens, a little comedy of home in three acts by Kate Douglas Wiggin and Rachel Crothers from the book of the same title by Kate Douglas Wiggin, 1925; Once upon a time, a comedy in four acts . . . played by Mr. Chauncey Olcott, 1925; Six one-act plays, 1925 (The importance of being clothed; The importance of being nice; The importance of being married; The importance of being a woman; What they think; Peggy); 39 East, a comedy in three acts, 1925; * Let us be gay, a comedy, 1929; "Everyday," a comedy drama in three acts, 1930; "As husbands go," a comedy, 1931; Caught wet, a comedy in three acts, 1932; When ladies meet, a comedy, 1932; He and she, a play in three acts, 1933; "The valiant one," a comedy drama in three acts, 1937; * Susan and God, 1938.

Writings on the Theater

The art of playwriting, lectures delivered at the University of Pennsylvania on the Mask and wig foundation by Jesse Lynch Williams, Langdon Mitchell, Lord Dunsany, Gilbert Emery [*pseud.*], Rachel Crothers, 1928.

STUDIES AND ARTICLES

Dickinson (P)
Eaton
Flexner
Hackett
Kunitz
Mantle
Mantle (C)
Mayorga (S)
Moses (A)
Moses (R)
Nathan (TD)
National
† Quinn (H)
Quinn (R)
Skinner

Anonymous. "Rachel Crothers, pacemaker for American social comedy." *TAM.*, Dec. 1932, pp. 971–72. For references to reviews, see *BRD.*, 1915, 1929, 1931–32, 1938.

Countee Cullen, 1903–

Born May 30, 1903, in New York. His father, the Reverend Frederick Asbury Cullen, was the minister of the Salem Methodist Episcopal Church, which he had founded in 1902. The young boy was educated in the city schools and attended the De Witt Clinton High School. In 1925 he took his bachelor's degree from New York University, and in the following year he earned his master's degree in English literature at Harvard.

In the meantime he had begun writing. In his high-school days a poem he had written at fourteen had been published in the *Modern School Magazine* in 1918, and "I Have a Rendezvous with Life" had taken first prize in a contest conducted by the Federation of Women's Clubs. *The Crisis*, the official organ of the National Association for the Advancement of Colored People, had printed some of his early verse. More appeared, subsequently, in the *Bookman*, *Harper's*, the *American Mercury*, *Century*, *The Nation*, *Poetry*, *Opportunity*, and the *Messenger*, and in "F. P. A."'s column in the New York *World*. In 1924 "The Ballad of the Brown Girl" won second prize in a contest held by the Poetry Society of America, in which there were seven hundred competitors. In 1925 he won four prizes, including the John Reed Memorial Prize offered by *Poetry;* and in 1928 he was awarded a Guggenheim fellowship. He has served as assistant editor of the Negro journal *Opportunity*.

"For the past two years," he wrote early in 1937, "I have been too busy earning my livelihood as a teacher of French in one of the Junior High Schools here in New York City to do any writing. My chief diversions are dancing, bridge, and a trip to Paris every summer."

Cullen has been much influenced by Tennyson and more profoundly by Keats. He admires also the work of A. E. Housman, Edna St. Vincent Millay, and Edwin Arlington Robinson. He feels that poetry should not be judged according to the race of the author, and that Negro poets are accountable to the purely artistic canons applicable to any others.

For further comment, see Critical Survey, p. 137.

BIBLIOGRAPHY

Poems

Color, 1925; The ballad of the brown girl, an old ballad retold by Countee Cullen with illustrations and decorations by Charles Cullen, 1927; Copper sun . . . with decorations by Charles Cullen, 1927; The black Christ & other poems . . . with decorations by Charles Cullen, 1929; The Medea and some poems, 1935.

Novels

One way to heaven, 1932.

Verses Set to Music

Saturday's child, op. 42, an episode in color for mezzo-soprano, tenor, and chamber orchestra by Emerson Whithorne, poems by Countee Cullen, arranged for voices and pianoforte by the composer, 1926 (poems repr. from Color); The grim troubadour, for medium voice and string quartet, by Emerson Whithorne, op. 45, poems by Countee Cullen, arranged for voice and pianoforte by the composer, 1927 (sheet music).

Editor

Caroling dusk, an anthology of verse by Negro poets . . . decorations by Aaron Douglas, 1927.

STUDIES AND ARTICLES

Brawley
Herrmann
Johnson
Kreymborg
Kunitz (L)

Dillon, George. "Mr. Cullen's first book." *P.*, Apr. 1926, pp. 50–53; James, Bertha T. E. "On the danger line." *P.*, Feb. 1930, pp. 286–89; North, Jessica N. "Mr. Cullen's second book." *P.*, Feb. 1928, pp. 284–86; Wood, Clement. "The Negro sings." *YR.*, July 1926, pp. 822–24. For references to reviews, see *BRD.*, 1925–29, 1932, 1935.

E(dward) E(stlin) Cummings, 1894–

Born in Cambridge, Massachusetts, October 14, 1894, the son of Edward Cummings, who had taught English at Harvard, and later became prominent as a public lecturer and minister of Old South Church in Boston.

He was educated at Harvard and took the bachelor's degree in 1915 and the master's in 1916. During the war he served with the Norton Harjes Ambulance Corps. Because of an error of the military censor's he was thrown for three months into a detention camp (described in *The Enormous Room*). For a time he was a private in the American army at Camp Devens, Massachusetts.

After 1920 he lived in poverty in Paris, gradually securing recognition as both a writer and a painter. He has contributed to the *Dial* and *Vanity Fair* and to magazines devoted to advanced movements in the arts and letters, and exhibited paintings with the Society of Independent Artists and the Salons of America. In 1925 he was given the *Dial* Award for distinguished service to American literature. His poetry is noteworthy for its eccentricities in typographical details of presentation. Some of his verse, read by the author, has been recorded on phonograph disks.

His home at present is in New York.

For further comment, see Critical Survey, p. 145.

BIBLIOGRAPHY

Poems

Eight Harvard poets, E. Estlin Cummings, S. Foster Damon, J. R. Dos Passos, Robert Hillyer, R. S. Mitchell, William A. Norris, Dudley Poore, Cuthbert Wright, 1917; Tulips and chimneys, 1923 (enl. ed., 1937); &, 1925; XLI poems, 1925; Is 5, 1926; Christmas Tree, 1928; W, 1931; No thanks, 1935 (cover-title); 1/20, poems, 1937; * Collected poems, 1938.

War Experiences

* The enormous room, 1922.

Satire and Humor

By E. E. Cummings with illustrations by the author, 1930; Eimi, 1933.

Plays

Him, 1927.

Ballet

Tom, 1935.

Drawings and Paintings

CIOPW, 1931.

Translations

Louis Aragon. The red front, 1933.

STUDIES AND ARTICLES

Blackmur
Deutsch
Eastman (L)
† Johnson (1932)
† Johnson (1936)
Kreymborg
Kunitz (L)
Moses (A)
Rascoe (B)
Riding
Rosenfeld (M)
Saturday
Sitwell
Sparrow
Tate
Zabel

Bishop, John P. "The poems and prose of E. E. Cummings." *So.R.*, Summer 1938, pp. 173–86; Blackmur, Richard P. "Notes on E. E. Cummings' language." *HH.*, Jan.–Mar. 1931, pp. 163–92; Blum, W. C. "The perfumed paraphrase of death." *D.*, Jan. 1924, pp. 49–52; Carver, George. "The enormous room." *Mid.*, Nov. 1922, pp. 309–13; Dos Passos, John. "Off the shoals." *D.*, July 1922, pp. 97–102; Hayakawa, Samuel I. "Is indeed 5." *P.*, Aug. 1938, pp. 284–92; Lesemann, Maurice. "The poetry of E. E. Cummings." *P.*, Dec. 1926, pp. 164–69; Monroe, Harriet. "Flare and blare." *P.*, Jan. 1924, pp. 211–15; Moore, Marianne. "A penguin in Moscow." *P.*, Aug. 1933, pp. 277–81; Tate, Allen. "Personal convention." *P.*, Mar. 1932, pp. 332–37. For references to reviews, see *BRD.*, 1922–23, 1925–27, 1931, 1933, 1935, 1938.

H. D. *See* Hilda Doolittle

Donald (Grady) Davidson, 1893–

Born in Campbellsville, Tennessee, August 18, 1893. He came of Tennessee pioneer stock, and both his parents were teachers. He attended a private school for boys and took the bachelor's and master's degrees at Vanderbilt University in 1917 and 1922, respectively. During the war he served in the infantry in the American forces, and became a first lieutenant.

He has taught in state schools, private schools, and Kentucky Wesleyan College, and since 1920 he has been in the English department at Vanderbilt. A member of the *Fugitive* group, he was a founder and an editor of that periodical, and from 1924 to 1930 he was literary editor on the Nashville *Tennessean.*

"Fire on Belmont Street," used as the epilogue to *The Tall Men*, was chosen Southern Prize poem for 1926.

Davidson has played a significant role in the sectional movement developing in the *Fugitive* group and leading to the more recent position favoring the agrarianizing of areas in the South. "For the past few years," he writes, "while all the discussion of agrarianism has been going on hereabouts, I have been engaged principally with a series of essays on sectionalism and regionalism." For the agrarian movement he has directed discussions and prepared symposia, and he contributed material to the agrarian-distributist symposium *Who Owns America?* (1936).

For further comment, see Critical Survey, p. 147.

BIBLIOGRAPHY

Poems

Armageddon by John Crowe Ransom, A fragment by William Alexander Percy, Avalon by Donald Davidson, 1923; An outland piper, 1924; * The tall men, 1927; Lee in the mountains and other poems, including The tall men, 1938.

Essays and Studies

I'll take my stand, the South and the agrarian tradition by twelve southerners, 1930; The attack on leviathan, regionalism and nationalism in the United States, 1938.

Textbook

American composition and rhetoric, 1939.

Editor

British poetry of the eighteen-nineties, 1937.

STUDIES AND ARTICLES

Fletcher

Millspaugh, C. A. "A long perspective." *P.*, May 1939, pp. 108–11; Monroe, Harriet. "Tennesseans." *P.*, Jan. 1928, pp. 222–24; Warren, Robert P. "A note on three southern poets." *P.*, May 1932, pp. 103–13. For references to reviews, see *BRD.*, 1924, 1927, 1932, 1938.

Clarence (Shepard) Day, 1874–1935

Born in New York, November 18, 1874, the son of a Wall Street broker and the grandson of the founder of the New York *Sun*. His family was prosperous, had a town house in a fashionable part of New York, and spent summers in Connecticut. He was educated at St. Paul's School, Concord, New Hampshire, and Yale, where he graduated in 1896.

Entering business, he became a member of the New York Stock Exchange in 1897 and later a partner in his father's firm. In 1898, however, he enlisted in the navy. Although he saw no active service, he fell a victim to arthritis, and for the rest of his life he was an invalid. Relinquishing his seat on the Exchange, he retired from business and spent some time in Arizona and Colorado, then returned to New York, where he lived for the rest of his life.

In 1905, he bought the *Yale Alumni Weekly* and ran it with Edwin Oviatt for four years. He then turned it over to a body of representative alumni.

Not long after retirement he began writing verses for the magazines. They were so successful that he became literary editor of the *Metropolitan Magazine* and a contributor to the *New Republic.* His peculiar gift expressed itself more completely in the illustrated books that began with *This Simian World.* He reached his widest audience, however, with his recollections of his own family life and especially of his father. Published originally in the *New Yorker* and other magazines, they made up the volumes *God and My Father* and *Life with Father*, the latter of which was a Book-of-the-Month and the second on the list of best-sellers of 1935. He was secretary of the Yale Class of 1896 and published its *Half-Way Book* in 1915.

To carry on his work he moved from his father's house to an apartment of his own, where he ran a glove business from his bed and speculated on the market. In 1928 he married Katharine Briggs Dodge.

He slept during the day and worked at night, with his elaborate indexed files close at hand. His nocturnal hours and the lights shifting from window to window of his apartment caused him to be investigated during the war as the possible source of signaled messages to the German fleet. Although his writing and drawing were accomplished in spite of very imperfect control of his hands and fingers, at the time of his sudden death, due to pneumonia, December 28, 1935, he had in his files notes for half a dozen biographies and materials for a series of articles and for two books, one on his father and one on his mother.

For further comment, see Critical Survey, p. 162.

BIBLIOGRAPHY

Essays and Sketches

The story of the Yale university press told by a friend, 1920 (anonymous); This simian world . . . with illustrations by the author, 1920; The crow's nest . . . with illustrations by the author, 1921; In the Green mountain country, 1934; After all, 1936 (rev. enl. ed. of The crow's nest).

Biographical Sketches

God and my father, 1932 (English ed., My father's dark hour, 1932); * Life with father, 1935; Life with mother, 1937.

Drawings and Verses

Thoughts without words, 1928; Scenes from the Mesozoic and other drawings, 1935 (English ed., Yesterday is to-day, drawings and rhymes, 1936).

Class Books

Sexennial record, class of eighteen hundred and ninety-six, Yale college, 1902 (comp. by Clarence Day with the assistance of Henry S. Johnston); Decennial record of the class of 1896, Yale college, compiled by Clarence S. Day, jr., class secretary, 1907; A record of the quindecennial reunion of the class of 1896, Yale college, compiled by Clarence S. Day, jr., class secretary, assisted by the Class secretaries bureau, 1912; The '96 half-way book by Clarence Day, jr., class secretary . . . Printed for the friends and members of the class of 1896, Yale college, 1915 (with illus. by Clarence Day).

Illustrator

At a venture by Charles A. Bennett with twenty full-page drawings by Clarence Day, jr., 1924; The delicatessen husband and other essays by Florence Guy Seabury, illustrated by Clarence Day, jr., 1926.

Editor

The Mikado and other plays by W. S. Gilbert, introduction by Clarence Day, jr., 1917; The Colby essays, volume one. The pursuit of humor and other essays by Frank Moore Colby selected and edited . . . In two volumes, 1926; The Colby essays, volume two. Tailor blood and other notes and comments by Frank Moore Colby selected and edited . . . In two volumes, 1926.

Broadside

The world of books, 1937.

STUDIES AND ARTICLES

Knopf (B)
Van Doren (R)
Woollcott, Alexander, *ed.* Woollcott's second reader. 1937

† Blanck, Jacob, *ed.* "American first editions edited by Jacob Blanck, Clarence (Shepard) Day, 1874–1935, checklist compiled by Robert E. Kingery." *PW.*, June 17, 1939, pp. 2187–88; Canby, Henry S. "Clarence Day, jr." *SRL.*, Aug. 24, 1935, pp. 18–19. For references to reviews, see *BRD.*, 1909, 1920–21, 1928, 1932, 1935–37.

Mrs. Basil de Sélincourt. *See* Anne Douglas Sedgwick

Floyd Dell, 1887–

Born June 28, 1887, in Barry, Illinois. He came of Pennsylvania-German and Irish Protestant stocks. He was educated in Barry and Quincy, Illinois, and in Davenport, Iowa; but, because of poverty, he was compelled to drop out of high school and work in a factory. By this time he had read widely and had written poems that had brought him recognition in school and that had been accepted by magazines; and at early age he was converted to socialism.

In 1905 he became a reporter for the Davenport *Times* and subsequently joined the staff of the *Democrat.* In the meantime he had continued to write and sell poetry, had edited the *Tri-City Workers' Magazine*, and had begun a novel that was never finished. In 1908 he went to Chicago and became a reporter on the *Evening Post.* When, in 1909, the *Friday Literary Review* of the paper was begun, he was assistant literary editor under Francis Hackett, and in another year he was made associate editor. He succeeded Hackett in 1911, and came to know Carl Sandburg, Theodore Dreiser, Sherwood Anderson, and other literary figures of Chicago in the years before the war.

He went to New York in 1913, secured a position as an editor of the *Masses*, made the acquaintance of the Provincetown group, and became a part of the Bohemian artistic world of Greenwich Village. The suppression in 1917 of the *Masses* by the federal government was followed by the arrest of the editors and an inconclusive trial for treason in 1918, after which they were freed. In the meantime they had begun to issue the *Liberator*, of which Dell remained an editor until 1924.

His marriage in 1919, his buying a house in Croton, N.Y., and the success of *Moon-Calf* in 1920 made him independent of the group movements in art with which he had previously been associated; and he has come to represent a liberal, rather than a radical, point of view.

In 1929 the Megrue Prize for Comedy was awarded to *Little Accident*, written by Dell and Thomas Mitchell.

". . . Some years ago," he wrote in 1937, "I got my bellyful of dictatorships, even though proletarian, and now describe myself as a liberal (not in the least 'tired,' though the New Deal does work me overtime on my Washington W.P.A. job . . .). I hope in my old age to find a world sufficiently settled (and settled right) for conversation and literature to return to the theme of sex, since both handle so poorly the themes of politics and human misery. I don't think we really quite finished with Freud before we took up Marx. For a year and a half I have been working here in Washington. . . . Strangely enough the W.P.A. draws a magic circle of its own about one, more like the magic circle of creative art than anyone could possibly imagine. It is a universe of its own, with nothing left out, and it can absorb all one's thoughts and energies. I shall always be glad to have had the opportunity of knowing and working with so many people who are wise, efficient and goodhearted. And never in my life, except for myself, never as a farm hand or factory hand or reporter or anything else, have I worked so hard. An absence of the Wall Street point of view in Washington is in itself a pleasure. It is at once a small village and one of the world's great capitals. . . ."

BIBLIOGRAPHY

Novels

* Moon-calf, a novel, 1920; The briary-bush, a novel, 1921; Janet March, a novel, 1923; Runaway, a novel, 1925; This mad ideal, a novel, 1925; An old man's folly, a novel, 1926; An unmarried father, a novel, 1927 (also pub. as Little accident, 1930); Souvenir, a novel, 1929; Love without money, 1931; Diana Stair, 1932; The golden spike, 1934.

Short Stories

Love in Greenwich Village, 1926.

Plays

The Provincetown plays. First series, 1916 (Bound east for Cardiff by E. G. O'Neill; The game by Louise Bryant; King Arthur's socks by F. Dell); The angel intrudes, a play in one act by Floyd Dell as played by the Provincetown players, 1918; Sweet and twenty, a comedy in one act, 1921; King Arthur's socks and other village plays, 1922.

Essays and Studies

Women as world builders, studies in modern feminism, 1913; Were you ever a child, 1919; Looking at life, 1924; Intellectual vagabondage, an apology for the intelligentsia, 1926; The outline of marriage, 1926; Love in the machine age, a psychological study of the transition from patriarchal society, 1930; Children and the machine age, from the seventh Iowa conference on child development and parent education, 1934.

Autobiography

Homecoming, an autobiography, 1933.

Biography

Upton Sinclair, a study in social protest, 1927.

Edited and Compiled Works

Poems [by] Wilfrid Scawen Blunt, 1923 (selected by Floyd Dell); Poems of Robert Herrick edited with an introduction, 1924; Poems and prose of William Blake edited with introduction and notes, 1925; The anatomy of melancholy by Robert Burton now for the first time with the Latin completely given in translation and embodied in an all-English text, edited by Floyd Dell and Paul Jordan-Smith, 1927 (2 vols.); Daughter of the revolution and other stories by John Reed edited with an introduction, 1927.

STUDIES AND ARTICLES

Anderson
Baldwin (M)
Eastman
Farrar
Freeman (J)
Hansen
Hatcher
Kunitz (L)
Maillard
† Manly
Sherman (C)
Sinclair
Van Doren (C)

Anonymous. "Floyd Dell." *AB.*, Mar. 1923, pp. 65–71; Lewis, Sinclair. "Floyd Dell." *AB.*, May 1921, p. 245. For references to reviews, see *BRD.*, 1913, 1919–22, 1924–27, 1929–34.

Bernard (Augustine) DeVoto, 1897–

Born in Ogden, Utah, January 11, 1897, to an ex-Catholic father of Italian blood and a mother of Mormon family and pioneer background. He led an outdoor life, was educated in a convent school and the public schools, and worked at various odd jobs. By 1914, when he went to the University of Utah, he had already begun writing and reporting for Ogden papers, and he had espoused socialism. Disgusted with the attitude of the university authorities toward free speech, he left for Harvard in 1915, and finished his undergraduate course at Cambridge in 1920 and graduated "as of" 1918. In the meantime he had served as second lieutenant in the army and drilled soldiers in marksmanship in southern cantonments.

Refusing offers of journalistic jobs, he returned to Ogden for two years, and absorbed facts and traditions of the West. He taught in a junior high school in 1921–22, and in 1922 accepted a position as instructor in English at Northwestern University. He taught in Evanston for five years and married a student. During this period he had been writing books on American pioneer life, contributing reviews to newspapers in Chicago and Evanston, and selling articles to such magazines as *Harper's* and the *American Mercury;* and, with hope of literary independence, he refused promotion and left for Cambridge, where he spent the next ten years.

Popular magazines readily accepted his work, and some of the time he taught composition and contemporary American literature at Harvard. From 1930 to 1932 he edited the *Harvard Graduates Magazine*, and used his influence to support freedom of bookselling in Boston and more consideration and aid for the poorer students at the university.

With *Mark Twain's America* (1932) his reputation was made. In November, 1935, he assumed charge of the column "The Easy Chair" in *Harper's*, and in September, 1936, was made editor of the *Saturday Review of Literature*, a position which he resigned in 1937.

DeVoto, who is an enthusiastic mountaineer, a good marksman, and an adept at boxing and tennis, says of his habits of work: "My methods of writing are quite simple: I have written every morning from nine to twelve for the last ten years, at least, and most evenings, with vacations of less than two months all told. I give everything three drafts, at least, and have given many things many more drafts. I have never missed a deadline, nor failed to bring an article, a story, a novel, or anything else out at the end anywhere but at the exact point of space I designed it to go to in advance."

His views on critical theory he has stated with vigor and emphasis. "I believe that criticism is necessarily an imprecise method of studying literature," he declared at a meeting of the Modern Language Association in 1936. "It must never ignore two of the conditions under which it operates, that it cannot phrase its aims unequivocally and cannot apply its methods objectively." He feels that the most fruitful study of literature attempts, as does his *Mark Twain's America*, to relate literary phenomena, not to the personality of the reader, but to the social group to which they can be fairly objectively assigned. Hence social history is of prime importance to the critic. "To determine what a writer 'meant' in his work as a whole is clearly a subjective undertaking. But what a writer meant at any given time to any clearly defined group of people is an objective fact and can be determined with some objectivity. Such an inquiry seems to me not only the most meaningful but also the most important occupation of literary criticism."

DeVoto has long since ceased to hold any authoritarian or absolute scale of values in religion or social theory; and he has been much interested in Pareto's application of the objective methods of natural and physical science to the study of human society in its sentiments and taboos, regarded as nonlogical acts, in place of the metaphysical and philosophical approaches (of which Marxism is one) born of the evolutionary biological theories typical of the nineteenth century.

Similarly he has attacked the application by literary theorists of their normal processes of introspection, intuition, and selection and interpretation, to the historical phenomena of the past, and the presentation of their conclusions as fact; and he insists that such works should be clearly labeled metaphor, autobiography, fiction, or psychological theory, or by any other name than history or biography. He deplores the tendency of literary critics' fitting authors and their works to their own *a priori* theories, their presenting such evidence as supports their views, and conveniently disregarding everything tending to destroy their logical conclusions.

"It seems to me," he writes, "that for some time American literature has been the most interesting in the world and far better on the whole and in individual high spots than English literature."

For further comment, see Critical Survey, pp. 172, 192.

BIBLIOGRAPHY

Novels

The crooked mile, 1924; The chariot of fire, an American novel, 1926; The house of sun-goes-down, 1928; We accept with pleasure, 1934.

Essays and Studies

The taming of the frontier, El Paso: Ogden: Denver: St. Paul, San Francisco: Portland: Kansas City, Cheyenne: San Antonio: Los Angeles, by ten authors, edited by Duncan Aikman, 1925; * Mark Twain's America . . . illustrated by M. J. Gallagher, 1932; Forays and rebuttals, 1936; Approaches to American social history edited by William E. Lingelbach, 1937; Writing for money, 1937 (caption-title; leaflet).

Textbook

The writer's handbook, a manual of English composition by W. F. Bryan, Arthur H. Nethercot, Bernard DeVoto, 1927.

Editor

The life and adventures of James P. Beckwourth edited by T. D. Bonner, 1931.

STUDIES AND ARTICLES

† Forsythe, Robert S. Bernard DeVoto, a new force in American letters. 1928 (pamphlet)

† Mattingly, Garrett. Bernard DeVoto, a preliminary appraisal. 1938

Wilson, Edmund. "Complaints, Bernard DeVoto." *NR.*, Feb. 3, 1937, pp. 405–08. For references to reviews, see *BRD.*, 1924, 1926, 1928, 1932, 1934, 1936.

John Dewey, 1859–

Born in Burlington, Vermont, October 20, 1859. He was educated in the schools of his native town, and graduated in 1879 from the state university. Studying for a time at home, he proceeded to graduate work at Johns Hopkins, taking his Ph.D. in 1884. In the same year he began, at the University of Michigan, his long teaching career.

He remained at Ann Arbor, except for a year at the University of Minnesota, for ten years, and spent the next ten at the University of Chicago, where he became famous as an educational theorist and director of the School of Education, an exponent of the practical values in education, and the view that education is not merely preparation for life, but rather life itself.

After transferring to Columbia in 1904, he broadened this theory to the proportions of a philosophy of experience, and became internationally known as an empiricist. His seventieth birthday was made the occasion of a two-day celebration at Columbia University.

He was an organizer and the first president of the American Association of University Professors, was president in 1905–06 of the American Philosophical Association and in 1899–1900 of the American Psychological Association, and is a member of the National Academy of Sciences and a corresponding member of L'Institut de France. In recent years he has allied himself with Socialists and liberals. He has lectured in Edinburgh, Tokyo, and Peking, and reported to the government of Turkey on the reorganization of the national schools; and he holds honorary degrees from the Peking National University and the University of Paris, as well as American universities. He has studied education in China, Japan, Constantinople, and Russia.

Dewey looks to a philosophy relying upon experience for the solution to modern skepticism and doubt. He regards fixed standards in science, religion, morals, or any other department of human thought as hangovers from religious and intellectual authoritarianism, and of no value in giving meaning to a world which science has shown to be constantly changing, and hence setting up new meanings and new values for every experience. "Such happiness as life is capable of," he has declared, "comes from the full participation of all our powers in the endeavor to wrest from each changing situation of experience its own full and unique meaning." Religion, he feels, adjusts itself to new social and scientific conditions; only as it continues to develop faith in experience will it survive.

Science and technology have opened up new possibilities for experience in our economic life, and the uncultural and inartistic social values of the day, with their effects upon the intellectual life of rich and poor, are capable of great modification. Similarly, international relations, economically and politically, must be improved before the full value of experience for the individual can be realized. In domestic affairs an intelligent appreciation of existing values forces one to the conclusion that our marriage institutions are "romantic in theory and prosaic in operation," and indicative of a masculine idealism, which must be forsaken for more realistic standards.

The breakdown of tradition in all these fields of thought, and the resulting doubt, afford a splendid opportunity for the exploration of the possibilities of an empirical philosophy.

BIBLIOGRAPHY

Education

Applied psychology, an introduction to the principles and practice of education by J. A. McLellan . . . and Prof. John Dewey, 1889?; The psychology of number and its applications to methods of teaching arithmetic by James A.

McLellan . . . and John Dewey, 1895; My pedagogic creed by Prof. John Dewey also The demands of sociology upon pedagogy by Prof. Albion W. Small, 1897 (cover-title; pamphlet); The school and society, being three lectures . . . supplemented by a statement of the University elementary school, 1899; The child and the curriculum, 1902; The educational situation, 1902; Ethical principles underlying education . . . reprinted from the third yearbook of the National Herbart society, 1903 (pamphlet); Education, direct and indirect, 1904 (pamphlet); The third yearbook of the National society for the scientific study of education. Part I, The relation of theory to practice in the education of teachers [by] (1) John Dewey, (2) Sarah C. Brooks, (3) F. M. McMurry, T. D. Wood, D. E. Smith, C. H. Farnsworth, G. R. Richards, edited by Charles A. McMurry . . ., 1904 (pamphlet); The school and the child, being selections from the educational essays of John Dewey . . . edited by J. J. Findlay, 1907; Moral principles in education, 1909; Educational essays by John Dewey . . . edited by J. J. Findlay, 1910; The "Dewey" school, reprinted from the Elementary school record published by the University of Chicago in 1900, 1913? (cover-title; pamphlet); Interest and effort in education, 1913; Some dangers in the present movement for industrial education, 1913? (cover-title; pamphlet); Schools of to-morrow by John Dewey and Evelyn Dewey, 1915; Democracy and education, an introduction to the philosophy of education, 1916; Federal aid to elemetary [!] education [by] John Dewey [and] P. P. Claxton (reprinted from the Child labor bulletin, vol. VI, no. 1, May, 1917), 1917 (cover-title; pamphlet); Vocational education in the light of the world war . . . (Read at the convention of the Vocational education association of the middle west, Chicago, January 25, 1918), 1918 (pamphlet); Tenth series, no. 10, March 1, 1919, Teachers college bulletin. The psychology of drawing, Imagination and expression, Culture and industry in education, reprints of articles, 1919 (cover-title; pamphlet); Address . . . on culture and professionalism in education delivered at the opening exercises of Columbia university, Wednesday, September 26, 1923, 1923 (cover-title; pamphlet); Progressive education and the science of education, 1928 (cover-title; pamphlet); Am I getting an education? By George A. Coe, John Dewey, William Lyon Phelps, Paul Porter, Frank D. Slutz, J. Stitt Wilson, Sherwood Eddy, 1929; Art and education by John Dewey, Albert C. Barnes, Laurence Buermeyer, Thomas Munro, Paul Guillaume, Mary Mullen, Violette De Mazia, 1929; The sources of a science of education . . . the Kappa delta pi lecture series, 1929; American education past and future, 1931 (cover-title; pamphlet); The Inglis lecture, 1931. The way out of educational confusion, 1931; The educational frontier, written in collaboration by William H. Kilpatrick (editor) . . . Boyd H. Bode . . . John Dewey . . . John L. Childs . . . R. B. Raup . . . H. Gordon Hullfish . . . V. T. Thayer, 1933; First yearbook of the John Dewey society. The teacher and society, written in collaboration by William H. Kilpatrick, editor, John Dewey, George D. Stoddard, George H. Hartmann, Hilda Taba, Ernest O. Melby, Goodwin Watson, Jesse H. Newlon, Laura Zirbes, 1937; Experience and education, 1938.

Philosophy

Leibniz's new essays concerning the human understanding, a critical exposition, 1888; The significance of the problem of knowledge, 1897 (pamphlet); Essays, philosophical and psychological, in honor of William James, professor in Harvard university by his colleagues at Columbia university, 1908; The influence of Darwin on philosophy and other essays in contemporary thought, 1910; Creative intelligence, essays in the pragmatic attitude by John Dewey, Addison W. Moore, Harold Chapman Brown, George H. Mead, Boyd H. Bode, Henry Waldgrave Stuart, James Hayden Tufts, Horace M. Kallen, 1917; Reconstruction in philosophy, 1920; Chance, love, and logic, philosophical essays by the late Charles S. Peirce . . . edited with an introduction by Morris R. Cohen, with a supplementary essay on The pragmatism of Peirce by John Dewey, 1923; * Experience and nature . . . lectures upon the Paul Carus foundation, first series, 1925; The philosophy of John Dewey selected and edited by Joseph Ratner, 1928; The quest for certainty: a study of the relation of knowledge and action . . . Gifford lectures, 1929, 1929; Context and thought, 1931 (cover-title; pamphlet); Philosophy and civilization, 1931; A credo, 1932? (cover-title; pamphlet); * Art as experience, 1934; Intelligence in the modern world, John Dewey's philosophy edited and with an introduction by Joseph Ratner, 1939.

Psychology

Psychology, 1887; Second supplement to the Herbart year book for 1895. Interest as related to will by Dr. John Dewey of the Chicago university, edited by Charles A. McMurry, secretary of the society, 1896 (pamphlet); Psychology and philosophic method. The annual public address before the Union, May 15, 1899, 1899 (pamphlet); Psychology and social practice, 1901 (pamphlet); How we think, 1910; * Human nature and conduct, an introduction to social psychology, 1922

Ethics

The ethics of democracy, 1888 (cover-title; pamphlet); Outlines of a critical theory of ethics, 1891; Logical conditions of a scientific treatment of morality, 1903 (pamphlet; repr. from University of Chicago, The Decennial publications, 1st series, vol. III); Ethics, 1908 (pamphlet); Ethics by John Dewey . . . and James H. Tufts, 1908.

Logic

Studies in logical theory . . . with the co-operation of members and fellows of the Department of philosophy. The decennial publications, second series, volume XI, 1903; Essays in experimental logic, 1916; Logic, the theory of inquiry, 1938.

Religion

A common faith, 1934.

Political and Social Sciences

German philosophy and politics, 1915; Internal social reorganization after the war, 1918 (caption-title; pamphlet; repr. from The Journal of race development, April, 1918); China, Japan, and the U.S.A., present-day conditions in the Far East and their bearing on the Washington conference, 1921; Outlawry of war, what it is and is not, a reply to Walter Lippmann, reprinted for the American committee for the outlawry of war from the New republic of October 3d and 24th, 1923, 1923 (pamphlet); The public and its problems, 1927; Characters and events, popular essays in social and political philosophy by John Dewey edited by Joseph Ratner, 1929 (2 vols.); Impressions of soviet Russia and the revolutionary world, Mexico—China—Turkey, 1929; Construction and criticism . . . the first Davies memorial lecture delivered February 25, 1930, for the Institute of arts and sciences, 1930; Individualism, old and new, 1930; Are sanctions necessary to international organization? Yes [by] Raymond Leslie Buell . . . No [by] John Dewey, 1932 (cover-title; pamphlet); The place of minor parties in the American scene, 1932 (pamphlet); Steps to economic recovery. ⟨An address over radio station WEVD⟩, 1933? (cover-title; pamphlet); Education and the social order, 1934 (cover-title; pamphlet); The meaning of Marx, a symposium by Bertrand Russell, John Dewey, Morris Cohen, Sidney Hook, Sherwood Eddy, 1934; Liberalism and social action . . . The Page-Barbour lectures, 1935; Freedom and culture, 1939.

Travel

Letters from China and Japan by John Dewey . . . and Alice Chipman Dewey edited by Evelyn Dewey, 1920.

Miscellany

Enlistment for the farm, 1917 (cover-title; pamphlet); John Dewey on Henry George and what some others say, 1927 (cover-title; pamphlet); Reflections on the Sacco-Vanzetti tragedy. Fear by Edna St. Vincent Millay, Vanzetti's last statement by William G. Thompson, Psychology and justice by John Dewey, The martyrs of Massachusetts by C. I. Claflin, 1927 (pamphlet); The curriculum for the liberal arts college, being the report of the curriculum conference held at Rollins college January 19–24, 1931, John Dewey, chairman, together with the reports of Rollins college committees on curriculum, 1931 (cover-title; pamphlet); The case of Leon Trotsky. Report of hearings on the charges made against him in the Moscow trials, by the Preliminary commission of inquiry, John Dewey, chairman, Carleton Beals (resigned), Otto Ruehle, Benjamin Stolberg, Suzanne La Follette, secretary, 1937; "Truth is on the march" . . . report and remarks on the Trotsky hearings in Mexico, 1937 (pamphlet); Not guilty, report of the Commission of inquiry into the charges made against Leon Trotsky in the Moscow trials, 1938; International encyclopedia of unified science, volume 11, number 4. Theory of valuation, 1939.

Syllabi

Educational ethics, syllabus, n.d.; Educational psychology, syllabus, n.d.; The study of ethics, a syllabus, 1894; The University of Chicago. Pedagogy I B 19, Philosophy of education, 1898–1899 winter quarter, 1898 (pamphlet); The pragmatic movement of contemporary thought, a syllabus, 1909 (pamphlet); Syllabus for philosophy 191–192, Types of philosophic thought, Columbia university, 1922–1923, 1922? (multigraphed); Syllabus for philosophy 131–132, Social institutions and the study of morals, Columbia university, 1923–1924, 1923? (multigraphed).

Edited and Compiled Works

Selections from the writings of George MacDonald, or, Helps for weary souls, 1885; The Alexander-Dewey arithmetic, Elementary book by Georgia Alexander . . . edited by John Dewey, 1914; The Alexander-Dewey arithmetic, Advanced book by Georgia Alexander . . . edited by John Dewey, 1921; The Alexander-Dewey arithmetic, Intermediate book by Georgia Alexander . . . edited by John Dewey, 1921; New York and the Seabury investigation, a digest and interpretation of the reports by Samuel Seabury concerning the government of New York city prepared by a committee of educators and civic workers under the chairmanship of John Dewey, 1933 (pamphlet).

STUDIES AND ARTICLES

Adler, Mortimer J. Art and prudence, a study in practical philosophy. 1937

Allen, Devere, *ed.* Adventurous Americans . . . illustrated with etchings by Bernard Sanders. [c1932]

Arndt, Ruth S. John Dewey's philosophy of education. 1929

Baumgarten, Eduard. Der pragmatismus, R. W. Emerson, W. James, J. Dewey. [1938]

Beach

Boggs, Lucinda P. Über John Dewey's theorie des interesses und seine anwendung in der pädagogik. 1901

Bogoslovsky, Boris B. The technique of controversy, principles of dynamic logic. 1928

Buyse, Omer. Méthodes américaines d'education générale et technique. 1908

Cambridge

Choy, Jyan. Etude comparative sur les doctrines pédagogiques de Durkheim et de Dewey. 1926

Claparède, Édouard. La pedagogía de John Dewey. 1926

[Cooley, Edwin G.] Dr. John Dewey on the Commercial club and their vocational education bill. [n.d.] (pamphlet)

Coons, John W. The idea of control in John Dewey's philosophy. [c1936]

Crockett

Crowell, Nelson J. John Dewey et l'education nouvelle, avec applications. 1928 (pamphlet)

Dewey, John. L'école et l'enfant traduit par L.-S. Pidoux avec une introduction par Ed. Claparède. [1913]

Dewey, John. Intelligence in the modern world, John Dewey's philosophy, edited and with an introduction by Joseph Ratner. [c1939]

Durant

Durant (S)

Eastman

Edman

Edman, Irwin. Adam, the baby, and the man from Mars. 1929

Elliott, William Y. The pragmatic revolt in politics, syndicalism, fascism, and the constitutional state. 1928

Essays in honor of John Dewey on the occasion of his seventieth birthday, October 20, 1929. [c1929]

Feldman, William T. The philosophy of John Dewey, a critical analysis. 1934

Fite, Warner. Moral philosophy, the critical view of life. [c1925]

Forsythe

Frank (R)

Frank (T)

Fuchs, Henry C. Die pädagogik Herbarts und Deweys in vergleichender betrachtung. 1935

† Geyer, Denton L. The pragmatic theory of truth as developed by Peirce, James, and Dewey. [1916]

Gillis

Haldane, Richard B. Haldane *1st viscount.* Human experience, a study of its structure. 1926

Hennig, Paul. Die weltanschaulichen grundlagen von John Deweys erziehungstheorie. 1928

Hook, Sidney. John Dewey, an intellectual portrait. 1939

Horne, Herman H. The democratic philosophy of education, companion to Dewey's Democracy and education, exposition and comment. 1932

Horne, Herman H. The philosophy of education being the foundations of education in the related natural and mental sciences . . . Revised edition with special reference to the educational philosophy of Dr. John Dewey. 1927

Horne, Herman H. This new education. [c1931]

Howard, Delton T. John Dewey's logical theory. 1918

Jacobsson, Malte. Pragmatiska uppfostringsprinciper av Malte Jacobsson jämte Barnet och skolkursen av John Dewey, auktoriserad översättning av Agnes Jacobsson Undén. [1912]

James, William. Pragmatism, a new name for some old ways of thinking, popular lectures on philosophy . . . New impression. 1908

John Dewey society. Yearbook. [c1937–38]

John Dewey, the man and his philosophy, addresses delivered in New York in celebration of his seventieth birthday. 1930

Kandel, Isaac L. *ed.* Twenty-five years of American education, collected essays. 1924

Klyce, Scudder. Dewey's suppressed psychology, a psychological study of John Dewey, as exhibiting professionally the mathematical, exact-scientific, philosophical, theological, autocratic, idealistic, introverted, dogmatic mind—such sorts of minds being shown to be the same at bottom, and to be more or less (but mistakenly) opposed to the commonsense, extroverted or observing, realistic, or soundly scientific and religious, non-dogmatic, democratic mind of the common, genuinely scientific, practical man. Being correspondence between John Dewey . . . and Scudder Klyce . . . but omitting, in conformance with Dewey's explicit prohibition, verbatim reproduction of all but one of his letters. (As one Dewey letter is printed, and as the substance of Dewey's otherwise suppressed views are, with Dewey's permission, clearly given and considered in the reproduced Klyce letters, Klyce does not venture to assert that he alone is the author of this queer book, but leaves that to the reader's pleasure.)—With a few appendixes by Klyce, and title page, contents, introduction, afterword, and index by Klyce. 1928 (mimeographed)

Kunitz

Leander, Folke. The philosophy of John Dewey, a critical study. 1939

Le Boutillier, Cornelia G. Religious values in the philosophy of emergent evolution. 1936 (cover-title)

Leroux, Emmanuel. Le pragmatisme américain & anglais, étude historique et critique suivie d'une bibliographie méthodique. 1923

Lewisohn (E)

McLellan, James A. The public school arithmetic for grammar grades based on McLellan and Dewey's "Psychology of number" by J. A. McLellan . . . and A. F. Ames. 1902

Macy

Mayhew, Katherine C. and Edwards, Anna C. The Dewey school, the laboratory school of the University of Chicago, 1896–1903 . . . introduction by John Dewey. [c1936]

Mencken

Mercier

Meyer, Adolph E. John Dewey and modern education and other essays. 1931

Meyer, Henry H. Psychology, introductory course, guide to How we think by John Dewey. 1912 (pamphlet)
More (O)
Mueller
Mumford
Munson
National
Naumburg, Margaret. The child and the world, dialogues in modern education. [c1928]
O'Hara, James H. The limitations of the educational theory of John Dewey. 1929
Ou Tsuin-Chen. La doctrine pédagogique de John Dewey, avec la traduction du "Credo pédagogique" de John Dewey. 1931
Pell, Orlie A. Value-theory and criticism. 1930
Pratt, James B. What is pragmatism? 1909
Ragusa, Thomas J. The substance theory of mind and contemporary functionalism. 1937
Riley, Isaac W. American thought from Puritanism to pragmatism and beyond by Woodbridge Riley. 1923
Rippe, Fritz. Die pädagogik John Deweys unter besonderer berücksichtigung ihrer erfahrungswissenschaftlichen grundlage. 1934
Roe, Chungil Y. The true function of education in social adjustment, a comparative estimate and criticism of the educational teachings of Confucius and the philosophy of John Dewey with a view to evolving a project for a system of national education which will meet the needs of Korea. 1927
Rogers
Santayana, George. Obiter scripta, lectures, essays, and reviews . . . edited by Justus Buchler and Benjamin Schwartz. 1936
Saturday
Schalkwijk, Louis M. van. De sociale paedagogiek van John Dewey en haar filosofiese grondslag. 1920
Schilpp, Paul A. 1859–1929. Commemorative essays in celebration of the seventieth anniversary of the first publication of Darwin's "Origin of species" and of the seventieth birthday of Henri Bergson, Edmund Husserl, John Dewey. [c1930]
Schinz, Albert. Anti-pragmatism, an examination into the respective rights of intellectual aristocracy and social democracy. [c1909]
Slosson, Edwin E. Six major prophets. 1917
Smith (P)
Teachers college record, Dec. 1929, vol. 31, no. 3 [John Dewey number]
† Thomas, Milton H. and Schneider, Herbert W. A bibliography of John Dewey. 1929
Townsend, Harvey G. Philosophical ideas in the United States. [c1934]
Walker, Leslie J. Theories of knowledge, absolutism, pragmatism, realism. 1910
Wallenrod, Reuben. John Dewey, éducateur. 1932
Ward
Wickham, Harvey. The unrealists, James, Bergson, Santayana, Einstein, Bertrand Russell, John Dewey, Alexander, and Whitehead, 1930

Angier, Roswell P. "The conflict theory of emotion." *Am.J.Psych.*, Dec. 1927, pp. 390–401; Ayres, Clarence E. "Dewey, master of the commonplace." *NR.*, Jan. 18, 1939, pp. 303–06; Ayres. "John Dewey, naturalist, a report of the Carus lectures for 1922." *NR.*, Apr. 4, 1923, pp. 158–60; Barron, Joseph T. "Professor Dewey and truth." *CW.*, Nov. 1922, pp. 212–21; Bates, Ernest S. "John Dewey, America's philosophical engineer." *Mod.M.*, Aug. 1933, pp. 387–96; Bixler, Julius S. "The patriot and the pragmatist." *J.Relig.*, July 1934, pp. 253–64; Bixler. "Professor Dewey discusses religion." *HTR.*, July

1930, pp. 213–33; † "The books of John Dewey." *The Journal of the National Education Association*, Dec. 1929, p. 296; Bourne, Randolph S. "John Dewey's philosophy." *NR.*, Mar. 13, 1915, pp. 154–56; Chassel, Laura M. and Chassel, Clara F. "Restatement of important educational conceptions of Dewey in the terminology of Thorndike." *JEM.*, Mar. 1924, pp. 286–98; Cohen, Morris R. "John Dewey's philosophy." *NR.*, Sept. 2, 1916, pp. 118–19; Cohen. "On American philosophy, John Dewey and the Chicago school." *NR.*, Mar. 17, 1920, pp. 82–86; Crawford, Claude C. "Functional education in the light of Dewey's philosophy." *SS.*, Sept. 24, 1938, pp. 381–85; Crissman, Paul. "Dewey's theory of the moral good." *Monist*, Oct. 1928, pp. 592–619; Frank, Waldo. "Our leaders, the re-discovery of America." *NR.*, June 20, 1928, pp. 114–17; Fries, Horace S. "The method of proving ethical realism." *Phil.Rev.*, Sept. 1937, pp. 485–502; Geyer, Denton L. "The wavering aim of education in Dewey's educational philosophy." *Educ.*, Apr. 1917, pp. 484–91; Hall, Royal G. "The significance of John Dewey for religious interpretation." *OC.*, June 1928, pp. 331–40; Handschy, Harriet W. "The educational theories of Cardinal Newman and John Dewey." *Educ.*, Nov. 1928, pp. 129–37; Haydon, Albert E. "Mr. Dewey on religion and God." *J.Relig.*, Jan. 1935, pp. 22–25; Hook, Sidney. "Our philosophers." *CH.*, Mar. 1935, pp. 698–704; Kandel, Isaac L. "Influence of Dewey abroad." *SS.*, Nov. 23, 1929, pp. 700–04; Knight, Frank H. "Pragmatism and social action." *Int.J.E.*, Jan. 1936, pp. 229–36; Lamont, Corliss. "John Dewey capitulates to 'God.'" *N.Masses*, July 31, 1934, pp. 23–24; Leander, Folke. "John Dewey and the classical tradition." *AR.*, Oct. 1937, pp. 504–27; McDougall, William. "Can sociology and social psychology dispense with instincts?" *Am.J.Soc.*, May 1924, pp. 657–70; McGill, V. J. "Pragmatism reconsidered: an aspect of John Dewey's philosophy." *S.Soc.*, Summer 1939, pp. 289–322; McNutt, Walter S. "Instrumentalism at its best." *Educ.*, Nov. 1925, pp. 149–53; Manny, Frank A. "John Dewey." *Sev.Arts*, June 1917, pp. 214–28; Marvin, Francis S. "Science and society." *Nature*, Mar. 5, 1932, pp. 329–31; Mead, George H. "The philosophies of Royce, James, and Dewey in their American setting." *Int.J.E.*, Jan. 1930, pp. 211–31; Mead. "The philosophy of John Dewey." *Int.J.E.*, Oct. 1935, pp. 64–81; Miller, Clyde R., *comp.* "Some popular appraisals of John Dewey." *TCR.*, Dec. 1929, pp. 207–23; Moore, Ernest C. "John Dewey's contribution to educational theory." *SS.*, Jan. 11, 1930, pp. 37–47; Murphy, Arthur E. "Objective relativism in Dewey and Whitehead." *Phil.Rev.*, Mar. 1927, pp. 121–44; Nash, James V. "The ethics of John Dewey." *OC.*, Sept. 1924, pp. 527–38; Newlon, Jesse H. "John Dewey's influence in the schools." *SS.*, Nov. 23, 1929, pp. 691–700; Parkes, Harry B. "John Dewey." *So.R.*, Autumn 1936, pp. 260–78; Randall, John H., Jr. "Individuality through social unity." *WU.*, Dec. 1930, pp. 193–201; Reid, John R. "The apotheosis of intelligence." *J.Phil.*, July 4, 1935, pp. 375–85; Rothman, Robert. "Value and intelligence." *J.Phil.*, Mar. 26, 1936, pp. 176–86; Sanford, Hugh W. "Experience and nature." *SR.*, Oct.–Dec. 1925, pp. 496–99; Search-light, *pseud.* "The man who made us what we are." *N.Yer.*, May 22, 1926, pp. 15–16; Seth, James. "Pragmatism and idealist ethics." *Phil.Rev.*, Mar. 1923, pp. 182–97; Shearer, Edna A. "Dewey's esthetic theory, the earlier theory." *J.Phil.*, Nov. 7, 1935, pp. 617–27; Shearer. "Dewey's esthetic theory, the present theory." *J.Phil.*, Nov. 21, 1935, pp. 650–64; Sheldon, Wilmon H. "Professor Dewey, the protagonist of democracy." *J.Phil.*, June 9, 1921, pp. 309–20; Slosson, Edwin E. "John Dewey, teacher of teachers." *Ind.*, Mar. 26, 1917, pp. 541–44; Smith, Thomas V. "Dewey's theory of value." *Monist*, July 1922, pp. 339–54; Strong, Edward W. "Metaphors and metaphysics." *Int.J.E.*, July 1937, pp. 461–71; Vivas, Eliseo. "A note on the emotion in Mr. Dewey's theory of art." *Phil.Rev.*, Sept. 1938, pp. 522–31; Wallner, Nico. "John Dewey." *N.Mon.*, July–Aug. 1934, pp. 322–48; Ward, Paul W. "The doctrine of the situation and the method of social science." *JSF.*, Oct. 1930, pp. 49–54; Wieman, Henry N. "Religion in John Dewey's philosophy." *J.Relig.*, Jan. 1931, pp. 1–19; Yarros, Victor S. "Empiricism and philosophic method." *OC.*, Oct. 1925, pp. 586–92; Yarros. "Metaphysics, psychology and philosophy." *OC.*, Nov. 1925, pp. 669–75; Yarros. "The province and issues of philosophy." *OC.*, Dec. 1925, pp. 755–66; Yocum, Albert D. "Dr. Dewey's liberalism in government and in public education." *SS.*, July 4, 1936, pp. 1–5. For references to reviews, see *BRD.*, 1908–10, 1915–17, 1920–22, 1925, 1927–31, 1933–35, 1938.

George Dillon, 1906–

Born in Jacksonville, Florida, November 12, 1906. When he was five years old, his parents removed from Jacksonville, and since that time he has moved about and lived in various places. His early education he received in Louisville and other Kentucky cities, in Cincinnati, and at the School of Fine Arts in St. Louis. In 1923 he entered the University of Chicago, where he joined the Poetry Club, of which he became president, and founded a poetry magazine, the *Forge.* His first book of poems was written during his undergraduate years, and in 1925 his student poetry earned him the John Billings Fiske Prize. In the same year he was awarded the Young Poet's Prize given by *Poetry*, and was made an associate editor of the magazine by its editor, Harriet Monroe. He served in this capacity until 1927, when, after graduation, he took a position as writer of advertising copy. When his employer went out of business in 1930, he turned again to literary work.

Boy in the Wind (1927), his first published volume of verse, was the first selection of the Poetry Book Club, and three years later the author was given a prize by the Friends of American Writers, of Chicago. *The Flowering Stone* brought him not only the Pulitzer Prize for the best volume of verse published in 1931 but a Guggenheim award that made it possible for him to travel abroad and study. For two years he lived in France, becoming interested especially in history and economics, the classics, and English literature; and since his return he has occupied himself mainly with study. At present he is the editor of *Poetry.* He is an admirer of some of the modern British poets, including T. S. Eliot and W. H. Auden, and feels that the best contemporary poetry is that dealing with social themes.

For further comment, see Critical Survey, p. 134.

BIBLIOGRAPHY

Poems

Boy in the wind, 1927; * The flowering stone, 1931.

Translations

Flowers of evil, from the French of Charles Baudelaire by George Dillon [and] Edna St. Vincent Millay, with the original texts and with a preface by Miss Millay, 1936.

STUDIES AND ARTICLES

Kreymborg Kunitz

Freer, Agnes L. "Baudelaire in English." *P.*, June 1936, pp. 158–62; Lovett, Robert M. "George Dillon's second volume." *P.*, Mar. 1932, pp. 328–32; Luhrs, Marie. "Spring snow." *P.*, Mar. 1928, pp. 343–45; Untermeyer, Louis. "Three younger poets." *EJ.*, Dec. 1932, pp. 787–99. For references to reviews, see *BRD.*, 1928, 1931.

Mabel Dodge. *See* Mabel Dodge Luhan

H(ilda) D(oolittle) 1886–

Born September 10, 1886, in Bethlehem, Pennsylvania, where her father, Charles L. Doolittle, was professor of mathematics and astronomy at Lehigh University. When she was still a little girl, he was made director of the Flower Astronomical Observatory at the University of Pennsylvania; so her school education, begun in Bethlehem, was continued at the Gordon School in Philadelphia. In 1902, she went to the Friends' Central School to prepare for Bryn Mawr, and she entered college in 1904.

When her health forced her to leave Bryn Mawr after two years, she turned to writing. She had written ever since childhood and, while in college, had translated Latin lyrics. Some of her children's stories found their way into a Presbyterian paper published in Philadelphia.

In 1911 she went to Europe for a short visit to Italy, France, and England. In London she met Ezra Pound and became interested in the current poetry movement. She was one of the first Imagists and remained one of the most loyal. Pound used his influence to get her work published in *Poetry* in 1913. She was a contributor to *Des imagistes*, 1914, and to *Some imagist poets*, 1915, 1916, and 1917. *Poetry* awarded her the Guarantors Prize in 1915. She married the British Imagist poet, Richard Aldington, and settled in England. With Aldington she made translations from Greek and Latin poets. Her first book, *Sea Garden*, was published in England in 1916; and during her husband's service in the war she took his place as editor of the *Egoist*. She returned to the United States to spend a few months in California in 1920. *Poetry* announced in the November, 1938, issue the award of the Helen Haire Levinson Prize to H. D. for "Two Poems," in recognition of the high merit of her contribution to modern literature.

Writing of her activities since the war, she says: "I . . . have been separated from my husband since the end of the War . . . and have occupied myself with work, with studies in Greek history, art, and translation, and with psychological investigation. I have made a number of visits to Greece, lived for some years in Switzerland, and made frequent visits subsequently, and now am resident in London. I have occupied my time for a number of years upon a study of London during the last war, which may, or may not, be published."

For further comment, see Critical Survey, pp. 72, 143.

BIBLIOGRAPHY

Poems

Sea garden by H. D., 1916; The tribute and Circe, two poems by H. D., 1917; Hymen by H. D., 1921; Heliodora and other poems by H. D., 1924; * Collected poems of H. D., 1925; H. D., 1926 (pamphlet; ed. by Hughes Mearns); Red roses for bronze [by] "H. D.," 1929 (pamphlet); Red roses for bronze by H. D., 1931.

Play in Verse

Hippolytus temporizes, a play in three acts by H. D., 1927.

Stories

Palimpsest:—παλίμψηστος: a palimpsest, i.e., a parchment from which one writing has been erased to make room for another [by] H. D., 1926; Hedylus by H. D., 1928; The hedgehog by H. D., 1936.

Translations

Choruses from Iphigeneia in Aulis translated from the Greek of Euripides by H. D., 1916; Choruses from the Iphigeneia in Aulis and the Hippolytus of Euripides, translated by H. D., 1919; Euripides. Ion translated with notes by H. D., 1937.

STUDIES AND ARTICLES

Bush
Collins, H. P. Modern poetry. 1925
Cook
Deutsch
Fletcher
Hughes
Kreymborg
Kunitz (L)
Lowell
Lowell (T)
Lucas
Monro
Monroe
Taupin
Untermeyer
Untermeyer (C)
Untermeyer (N)
Vočadlo
Whitall

Blackmur, Richard P. "The lesser satisfactions." *P.*, Nov. 1932, pp. 94–100; Bryher, Winifred. "Spear-shaft and cyclamen-flower." *P.*, Mar. 1922, pp. 333–37; Doggett, Frank A. "H.D., a study in sensitivity." *SR.*, Jan.–Mar. 1929, pp. 1–9; Fletcher, John G. "H.D.'s vision." *P.*, Feb. 1917, pp. 266–69; Monroe, Harriet. "H.D." *P.*, Aug. 1925, pp. 268–75; Seiffert, Marjorie A. "Glacial bloom." *P.*, Dec. 1924, pp. 160–64; Sinclair, May. "The poems of H.D." *D.*, Feb. 1922, pp. 203–07; Sinclair. "The poems of H.D." *Fort.Rev.*, Mar. 1927, pp. 329–45. For references to reviews, see *BRD.*, 1932.

John (Roderigo) **Dos Passos,** 1896–

Born in Chicago, January 14, 1896. His mother came from a family from Maryland and Virginia, and his father, a lawyer, was the son of a Portuguese immigrant. Both enjoyed travel, and the little boy's childhood experiences included trips to Mexico and Belgium and a year of school in England. The first school that he attended was in Washington, D.C., and he spent some years on a farm in the tidewater section of Virginia. After preparatory work at the Choate School he proceeded to Harvard in 1912 and graduated *cum laude* in 1916.

In order to study architecture he traveled to Spain. Once in Europe, however, he enlisted in the Norton Harjes Volunteer Ambulance Service in the French army. Subsequently he joined the Red Cross in Italy, and in 1918 he entered the Medical Corps of the American army as a private. *One Man's Initiation*, his first book, was written about his war experiences in these years.

After the war he went to Spain as a correspondent and wrote *Three Soldiers*, a novel of war experience, which aroused heated argument and considerable difference of opinion. One hostile reviewer, however, who had attacked the book as insulting the army, received a letter of protest from Sidney Howard and John Peale Bishop, both war veterans, praising the truth of the book as a picture of war. For a time Dos Passos was one of the Americans in Gertrude Stein's group in Paris.

Returning to the United States, he lived in different sections of the country and developed his acquaintance with different kinds and classes of Americans, becoming increasingly conscious of social groups. In 1926 he went to jail with Michael Gold, editor of the *New Masses*, for taking part in a demonstration sympathetic to Sacco and Vanzetti.

His literary reputation came in 1925 with *Manhattan Transfer*. Although in recent years he has spent most of his time writing, he paints and sketches and has designed stage scenery. He has also translated the poetry of Blaise Cendrars and adapted for the motion pictures a novel by Pierre Louys. He wrote the English titles for the Mexican film *Redes*, and contributed an introductory comment to George Grosz's *Inter-Regnum*. He lives in Provincetown, near an art-colony group, but works regularly and industriously by himself, with swimming and sailing for relaxation. He is a member of the National Institute of Arts and Letters. In 1939 he was awarded a Guggenheim fellowship to write a series of essays on the basis of the present American conceptions of freedom of thought.

In *The 42nd Parallel*, *1919*, and *The Big Money* Dos Passos presents a history of America from 1900 to 1909, built up by the use of biographies of a shifting set of characters, actual life-stories of representative figures of the time, running documentation taking the form of passing allusions to speeches, popular songs, headlines, and news stories, and autobiographical flashes revealing the author's own developing point of view. Dos Passos, feeling that a writer should be an "architect of history," tries to record and arrange his materials, including the autobiographical elements, without any decorative additions detrimental to the truth and justice of the whole representation.

For further comment, see Critical Survey, pp. 40, 83–84, 124.

BIBLIOGRAPHY

Novels

One man's initiation—1917, 1920; Three soldiers, 1921; Streets of night, 1923; * Manhattan transfer, 1925; The 42nd parallel, 1930; 1919, 1932; The big money, 1936; * U. S. A. 1. The 42nd parallel. 2. Nineteen nineteen. 3. The big money, 1937 [1938]; Adventures of a young man, 1939.

Poems

Eight Harvard poets, E. Estlin Cummings, S. Foster Damon, J. R. Dos Passos, Robert Hillyer, R. S. Mitchell, William A. Norris, Dudley Poore, Cuthbert Wright, 1917; A pushcart at the curb, 1922.

Plays

The garbage man, a parade with shouting, 1926; Airways, inc. . . . a New playwrights' theatre production, 1928; Three plays: The garbage man, Airways, inc., Fortune heights, 1934.

Description and Travel

Rosinante to the road again, 1922; Orient express . . . with illustrations in color from paintings by the author, 1927; In all countries, 1934; Journeys between wars, 1938.

Sociological Studies

Facing the chair, story of the Americanization of two foreignborn workmen, 1927; Harlan miners speak, report on terrorism in the Kentucky coal fields, prepared by members of the National committee for the defense of political prisoners, Theodore Dreiser, Lester Cohen, Anna Rochester, Melvin P. Levy, Arnold Johnson, Charles R. Walker, John Dos Passos, Adelaide Walker, Bruce Crawford, Jessie Wakefield, Boris Israel, Sherwood Anderson, 1932.

Translations

Manuel Maples Arce. Metropolis, 1929; Panama, or, The adventures of my seven uncles by Blaise Cendrars translated from the French and illustrated by John Dos Passos, 1931.

STUDIES AND ARTICLES

Baldwin (M)
Beach (T)
Bowdoin
Calverton
Chamberlain, John. John Dos Passos, a biographical and critical essay. [c1939] (pamphlet)
Cowley
† Edgar
Grattan
Hartwick
Hatcher
Henderson
Herrmann
Hicks
Hicks, Granville. John Dos Passos . . . reprinted from "The Bookman." [1938?] (cover-title; pamphlet)
† Johnson (1932)
† Johnson (1936)
Kunitz (L)
Lewis, Sinclair. John Dos Passos' Manhattan transfer. 1926
Llona
Loggins
Luccock
Lundkvist
McCole
Markey
† Neuse, Werner. Die literarische entwicklung von John Dos Passos. 1931
Saturday
Schreiber
Schyberg
Smith
Taylor (W)
Vočadlo
Zabel

Calmar, Alan. "John Dos Passos." *SR.*, July–Sept. 1932, pp. 341–49; Chamberlain, John. "John Dos Passos." *SRL.*, June 3, 1939, pp. 3–4, 14, 15; Cowley, Malcolm. "The poet and the world." *NR.*, Apr. 27, 1932, pp. 303–05; Cowley. "Reviewers on parade." *NR.*, Feb. 2, 1938, pp. 371–72; Cowley. "Reviewers on parade." *NR.*, Feb. 9, 1939, pp. 23–24; Cowley. "Disillusionment." *NR.*, June 14, 1939, p. 163; DeVoto, Bernard. "John Dos Passos, anatomist of our time." *SRL.*, Aug. 8, 1936, pp. 3–4, 12–13; Fadiman, Clifton. "Mr. Dos Passos' newsreel, continued." *N.Yer.*, Aug. 8, 1936, pp. 52–53; † Gibson, William. "A Dos Passos checklist." *Book collector's journal*, Apr. 1936, p. 7, May 1936, pp. 6, 9; Gold, Michael. "The education of John Dos Passos." *EJ.*, Feb. 1933, pp. 87–97; Hicks, Granville. "Dos Passos' gifts." *NR.*, June 24, 1931, pp. 157–58; Hicks. "John Dos Passos." *AB.*, Apr. 1932, pp. 32–42; Leavis, Frank R. "A serious artist." *Scrut.*, Sept. 1932, pp. 173–79; Reid, John T. "Spain as seen by some contemporary writers." *Hisp.*, May 1937, pp. 139–50; Rosati, Salvatore. "John Dos Passos." *Nuova Ant.*, Apr. 16, 1935, pp. 633–35; Schwartz, Delmore. "John Dos Passos and the whole truth." *So.R.*, Autumn 1938, pp. 351–67; Soupault, Philippe. "John Dos Passos." *Europe*, Feb. 1934, pp. 282–86; Wade, Mason. "A novelist of America, John Dos Passos." *N.Amer.Rev.*, Autumn 1937, pp. 349–67; Whipple, Thomas K. "Dos Passos and the U. S. A." *Nation*, Feb. 19, 1938, pp. 210–12. For references to reviews, see *BRD.*, 1921–22, 1925–27, 1930, 1932, 1934, 1936, 1938–39.

Edward Dragonet, *pseud. See* **Thames Williamson**

Dreamer. *See* **Amy Lowell**

Theodore (Herman Albert) Dreiser, 1871–

Born August 27, 1871, in Terre Haute, Indiana. His father was a native of southern Germany and a strict Catholic. His mother came from a prosperous Moravian family in Indiana. Before the birth of Theodore Dreiser, the twelfth of thirteen children, the family fortunes had been wiped out by fire, theft, and other misfortunes.

He attended Catholic schools in Terre Haute, Sullivan, and Evansville, and read novels, poetry, and magazine fiction. In Warsaw, Indiana, where he attended a public school, he read Hawthorne, Irving, and other American authors in the public library, and his father bought him sets of Thackeray, Scott, and Dickens. He became acquainted also with Mark Twain, Emerson, and Thoreau, and with Fielding, Dryden, Pope, and other authors.

After some three years in Warsaw he went to Chicago. He took different laboring jobs and fell under the spell of the city. He was extremely fond of the theater, and some of the men with whom he came in contact introduced him to Whitman and Marlowe and to German and Scandinavian literature. A former teacher, at this time a principal in Chicago, urged him to enter Indiana University at her expense, but after a year, more anxious for life than study, Dreiser returned to Chicago and took another job.

By this time he was submitting contributions for the column run on the *News* by Eugene Field. When he was twenty-one, he secured a position working for the Christmas Fund of the Chicago *Herald*, and not long afterward he began reporting for the *Globe*.

Newspaper work on the *Globe-Democrat* and the *Republic* in St. Louis followed, and he went on to Pittsburgh and New York. In the meantime a few short stories had been accepted, and, at the suggestion of an encouraging friend, he wrote *Sister Carrie*. Thanks to the influence of Frank Norris, then a publisher's reader, the book was published; but the objections of the wife of one of the publishers resulted in the suppression of the issue by the company.

Dreiser continued to write and to do editorial work for magazine publishers, finally becoming editor-in-chief of the Butterick publications. He left this post in 1910 to spend a year with the *Bohemian Magazine*, then accepted the release brought him by the success of *Jennie Gerhardt.* Since 1911 he has held no editorial position except for his connection in 1932–34 with the *American Spectator.* He has lived in different parts of the country, but New York has been his headquarters. In 1927 he made a trip to Russia. In 1931, as chairman of the National Committee for the Defense of Political Prisoners, Dreiser led a group to Harlan County, Kentucky, to investigate atrocities in the coal district.

His work, regarded at first as brutally frank and morally questionable, came to command a considerable audience and enjoyed the enthusiastic support of such critics as H. L. Mencken. *An American Tragedy*, banned in Boston, was a popular success and was dramatized and filmed; and, more than twenty years after the publication of the novel, *Jennie Gerhardt* appeared as a moving picture. The wealth of detail and observation of fact in his writings and the author's profession of indifference toward the ethical problems concerned reflect his agnostic position (a result of his reading of Herbert Spencer), his determinism, and his view that the earth is inhabited by organisms engaged in a disorderly struggle for conquest and survival.

For further comment, see Critical Survey, pp. 30–31, 46.

BIBLIOGRAPHY

Novels

* Sister Carrie, 1900; Jennie Gerhardt, a novel, 1911; The financier, a novel, 1912 (completely rev. ed., 1927); The Titan, 1914; The "genius," 1915; * An American tragedy, 1925 (2 vols.).

Short Stories

Free and other stories, 1918; Twelve men, 1919; Chains, lesser novels and stories, 1927; A gallery of women . . . in two volumes, 1929; Fine furniture, 1930 (pamphlet).

Poems

Moods, cadenced and declaimed, 1926 (enl. eds., Moods, cadenced & declaimed . . . with fifteen symbols by Hugh Gray Lieber, 1928; Moods, philosophic and emotional, cadenced and declaimed [intro. by Sulamith Ish-Kishor], 1935); The aspirant, 1929 (pamphlet); Epitaph, a poem . . . decorations by Robert Fawcett, 1929.

Plays

Plays of the natural and the supernatural, 1916 (The girl in the coffin, The blue sphere, Laughing gas, In the dark, The spring recital, The light in the window, "Old Ragpicker"; English ed., Plays natural and supernatural, 1930, contains also: Phantasmagoria, The court of progress, The dream, The hand of the potter); The hand of the potter . . . a tragedy in four acts, 1918 [1919].

Autobiography

A book about myself, 1922 (also pub. as A history of myself [vol. 2] Newspaper days, 1931); * A history of myself, Dawn, 1931 (vol. 1).

Political and Social Studies

Life, art, and America . . . reprinted from the February, 1917, issue of the Seven arts, 1917 (cover-title; pamphlet); Dreiser looks at Russia, 1928; The Carnegie works at Pittsburgh, 1929? (pamphlet); Tragic America, 1931; Harlan miners speak, report on terrorism in the Kentucky coal fields, prepared by members of the National committee for the defense of political prisoners, Theodore Dreiser, Lester Cohen, Anna Rochester, Melvin P. Levy, Arnold Johnson, Charles R. Walker, John Dos Passos, Adelaide Walker, Bruce Crawford, Jessie Wakefield, Boris Israel, Sherwood Anderson, 1932.

Essays

Hey rub-a-dub-dub, a book of the mystery, and wonder, and terror of life, 1920; Neurotic America and the sex impulse, and Some aspects of our national character . . . (from "Hey rub-a-dub-dub" by Theodore Dreiser, copyright, 1920, by Boni and Liveright, New York), 1924 (pamphlet); Catalogue of an exhibition of paintings by Jerome Blum, with a foreword by Theodore Dreiser, January 28th–February 9th, 1929 (cover-title; leaflet); Divorce as I see it by Bertrand Russell, Fannie Hurst, H. G. Wells, Theodore Dreiser, Warwick Deeping, Rebecca West, André Maurois, and Lion Feuchtwanger, 1930.

Description and Travel

A traveler at forty . . . illustrated by W. Glackens, 1913; A Hoosier holiday . . . with illvstrations by Franklin Booth, 1916; The color of a great city . . . illustrations by C. B. Falls, 1923; My city . . . illustrated with eight etchings in color by Max Pollak, 1929.

Miscellany

The bulwark, 1916 (publisher's dummy); Notice, 1920 (broadside).

Attributed Work

On the banks of the Wabash, far away, song & chorus by Paul Dresser, 1897 (cover-title; sheet music; chorus by Theodore Dreiser); A princess of Arcady by Arthur Henry, 1900 (last chapter attributed to Theodore Dreiser).

Editor

The American spectator year book edited by George Jean Nathan, Sherwood Anderson, Ernest Boyd, James Branch Cabell, Theodore Dreiser, Eugene O'Neill, 1934; The living thoughts of Thoreau presented by Theodore Dreiser. The Living thoughts library edited by Alfred O. Mendel, 1939.

STUDIES AND ARTICLES

Adcock

American (C)

Anderson (S)

Anderson, Sherwood. Horses and men, tales, long and short, from our American life. 1923

Baldwin

Baldwin (M)

Beach

Beach (T)

Berg

Blankenship

Boni & Liveright, *firm, publishers.* Announcing the winner of the essay contest on Theodore Dreiser's An American tragedy. [1926] (broadside)

Boni & Liveright, *firm, publishers.*

A book about Theodore Dreiser and his work. [1926] (cover-title; pamphlet)
Boni & Liveright, *firm, publishers.* Free and other stories. [1920] (pamphlet)
Boni & Liveright, *firm, publishers.* The hand of the potter. [1918] (pamphlet)
Bourne
Boyd
Boynton (L)
Boynton (S)
Bruns
Calverton
Carnegie
Chamberlain
Cleaton
Combs
Cowley
Davis, Hubert. The symbolic drawings of Hubert Davis for An American tragedy. [c1930]
Dreiser, Theodore. Free and other stories . . . introduction by Sherwood Anderson. [c1925]
Dreiser, Theodore. The "genius." [c1923] (foreword by [Merton S. Yewdale])
Dudley, Dorothy. Forgotten frontiers, Dreiser and the land of the free. 1932 (English ed., Dreiser and the land of the free, a novel of facts. 1933)
Eastman (L)
† Edgar
Foerster
Follett
Ford
† Ford (E)
Ford, Ford M. Portraits from life, memories and criticisms of Henry James, Joseph Conrad, Thomas Hardy, H. G. Wells, Stephen Crane, D. H. Lawrence, John Galsworthy, Ivan Turgenev, W. H. Hudson, Theodore Dreiser, Algernon Charles Swinburne. 1937 (English ed., Mightier than the sword. 1938)
Frank (O)
Frank (T)
Gard
Garnett
Grabo, Carl H. The technique of the novel. [c1928]
Green (C)
Halleck
Harris, Frank. Contemporary portraits. Second series [c1919]
Hartwick
Hastings, William T., *ed.* Contemporary essays. [c1928]
Hatcher
Hazard
† Herrmann
Hicks
† Johnson (1929)
† Johnson (1932)
† Johnson (1936)
Karsner
Knight
Kunitz (L)
Lane, John, *firm, publisher.* Theodore Dreiser: America's foremost novelist. [1916?] (pamphlet)
Levinson
Lewisohn
Lewisohn (E)
Llona
Loggins
Luccock
McCole
MacCollough
† McDonald, Edward D. A bibliography of the writings of Theodore Dreiser . . . with a foreword by Theodore Dreiser. 1928
Macy
Maillard
Mallory
† Manly
Marble
Markey
Mencken, Henry L. A book of prefaces . . . ⟨opus 13⟩. 1917
Mencken, Henry L. The creed of a novelist. [1916] (pamphlet)
Mencken, Henry L. Prejudices, forth series. [c1924]
Michaud
Michaud (P)
More
Moses (A)
Muller
Mumford

Munson (D)
Nathan (I)
Nathan (TD)
National
† Orton, Vrest. Dreiserana, a book about his books. 1929
Orton, Vrest. Notes to add to a bibliography of Theodore Dreiser. 1928 (pamphlet)
Overton (H)
Parrington
Pattee (N)
Powys, Llewelyn. The verdict of Bridlegoose. [c1926]
A protest against the suppression of Theodore Dreiser's The "genius." [191–] (caption-title; pamphlet)
Quinn
Rascoe (B)
Rascoe, Burton. Theodore Dreiser. 1925
Rascoe (P)
Richards, Grant. Author hunting by an old literary sportsman, memories of years spent mainly in publishing, 1897–1925 . . . with seventeen illustrations. 1934
Roberts
Rosenthal, Elias. Theodore Dreiser's "Genius" damned. [1916] (cover-title; pamphlet)
Salzman
Schelling
† Schwartz (O)
Schyberg
Sherman (M)
Sherman, Stuart P. On contemporary literature. [1931]
Sinclair
Smith
Squire
† Taylor
Van Doren
Van Doren (A)
Van Doren (B)
Van Doren (C)
Van Doren (W)
Vočadlo
Whipple
Woollcott

Avary, Myrta L. "Success, and Dreiser." *Col.*, Autumn 1938, pp. 598–604; Bercovici, Konrad. "Romantic realist." *Mentor*, May 1930, pp. 38–41; Birss, John H. "Record of Theodore Dreiser, a bibliographical note." *NQ.*, Sept. 30, 1933, p. 226; Bourne, Randolph S. "The art of Theodore Dreiser." *D.*, June 14, 1917, pp. 507–09; Bourne. "Theodore Dreiser." *NR.*, Apr. 7, 1915, Suppl. pp. 7–8; Boynton, Percy H. "Theodore Dreiser." *EJ.*, Mar. 1923, pp. 180–88; Chamberlain, John. "Theodore Dreiser." *NR.*, Dec. 23, 1936, pp. 236–38; Chesterton, Gilbert K. "Skeptic as critic." *Forum*, Feb. 1929, pp. 65–69; Dreiser, Theodore. "The early adventures of 'Sister Carrie.'" *Col.*, Part 5, Art. 4, pp. 1–4 (1931); Duffus, Robert L. "Dreiser." *AM.*, Jan. 1926, pp. 71–76; Fadiman, Clifton. "Dreiser and the American dream." *Nation*, Oct. 19, 1932, pp. 364–65; Ford, Ford M. "Theodore Dreiser." *AM.*, Apr. 1937, pp. 488–96; Freeman, John. "An American tragedy." *Merc.*, Oct. 1927, pp. 607–14; Gilkes, Martin. "Discovering Dreiser." *Adel.*, Dec.–Feb. 1928, pp. 178–81; Gilman, Lawrence. "The biography of an amorist." *N.Amer.Rev.*, Feb. 1916, pp. 290–93; Huth, John F., Jr. "Dreiser and success, an additional note." *Col.*, Summer 1938, pp. 406–10; Huth. "Theodore Dreiser, success monger." *Col.*, Winter 1938, pp. 120–33; Huth. "Theodore Dreiser, 'the prophet.'" *AL.*, May 1937, pp. 208–17; Johnson, A. Theodore. "Realism in contemporary American literature, notes on Dreiser, Anderson, Lewis." *Sw.Bul.*, Sept. 1929, pp. 3–16; † Johnson, Merle D. and Hopkins, Frederick M., *eds.* "American first editions, a series of bibliographic check-lists . . . number 56, Theodore Dreiser, 1871– by W. W. Lange." *PW.*, Dec. 22, 1923, p. 1925; Le Verrier, Charles. "Un grand romancier Américain, Theodore Dreiser." *RH.*, Jan. 21, 1933, pp. 280–94; McCole, Camille J. "The tragedy of Theodore Dreiser." *CW.*, Oct. 1930, pp. 1–7; McDonald, Edward D. "Dreiser before 'Sister Carrie.'" *AB.*, June

1928, pp. 369–74; Mencken, Henry L. "The Dreiser bugaboo." *Sev.Arts*, Aug. 1917, pp. 507–17; Monroe, Harriet. "Dorothy Dudley's frontiers." *P.*, Jan. 1934, pp. 208–15; Powys, John C. "An American tragedy." *D.*, Apr. 1926, pp. 331–38; Powys. "Theodore Dreiser." *Little Rev.*, Nov. 1915, pp. 7–13; Reader, Constant, *pseud.* "Words, words, words." *N.Yer.*, May 30, 1931, pp. 69–72; Rüegg, A. "Theodore Dreisers abkehr vom katholizismus." *S.Rund.*, vol. 31, pp. 915–23, 1084–95; Scavenger, The., *pseud.* "The dionysian Dreiser." *Little Rev.*, Oct. 1915, pp. 10–13; Schneider, Isidor. "Theodore Dreiser." *SRL.*, Mar. 10, 1934, pp. 533–35; Search-light, *pseud.* "Profiles, the colossus of children." *N.Yer.*, Aug. 15, 1925, pp. 6–7; Sebestyén, Karl. "Theodore Dreiser at home." *Liv.Age*, Dec. 1930, pp. 375–78; Sherman, Stuart P. "The naturalism of Mr. Dreiser." *Nation*, Dec. 2, 1915, pp. 648–50; Smith, Edward H. "Dreiser, after twenty years." *AB.*, Mar. 1921, pp. 27–39; Taylor, George R. S. "The United States as seen by an American writer." *N.Cent.*, Dec. 1926, pp. 803–15; Tittle, Walter. "Glimpses of interesting Americans." *Cent.*, Aug. 1925, pp. 441–47; Van Doren, Carl. "Jurgen in limbo." *Nation*, Dec. 6, 1922, pp. 613–14; Van Doren. "Theodore Dreiser." *Nation*, Mar. 16, 1921, pp. 400–01; Vivas, Eliseo. "Dreiser, an inconsistent mechanist." *Int.J.E.*, July 1938, pp. 498–508; Waldman, Milton. "Theodore Dreiser." *Merc.*, July 1926, pp. 283–91; Walker, Charles R. "How big is Dreiser?" *AB.*, Apr. 1926, pp. 146–49. For references to reviews, see *BRD.*, 1907, 1911–12, 1914–16, 1918–20, 1922–23, 1925–32, 1935.

E. P. *See* Ezra Pound

Max (Forrester) Eastman, 1883–

Born January 4, 1883, in Canandaigua, New York. His parents were both Congregational ministers, his mother being the first of her sex in the denomination in New York State. He was educated at Mercersburg Academy and Williams College, and at the latter institution was a friend of Stuart P. Sherman. He graduated in 1905 and began advanced work at Columbia in 1907 while he taught logic and philosophy in the university. He never took his degree, and abandoned teaching for writing and social work.

In the meantime he had become interested in the suffrage movement, and in 1910 he founded the first men's league for woman suffrage. In 1911, with a group of radical writers and artists, he began publishing the *Masses*, of which he was an editor for several years. As a result of its opposition to the Allied cause and the entry of the United States into the World War, it was suppressed by the federal government in 1917, and the editors were arrested and brought to trial in 1918. After two trials, in the second of which Eastman addressed the jury in his own behalf, the case was dismissed because of the inability of the jury to reach a decision.

The editors had already begun to publish the *Liberator*, a similar magazine, and Eastman remained with it as editor until 1922, when he left in order to study Russia under the Soviet regime. He returned much depressed by what he felt to be the perversion, by the governing group, of the original purpose of the Revolution; his sympathies with Trotsky earned him the distrust of the Communist party, and he was expelled.

In recent years he has devoted himself chiefly to lecturing and writing. In 1937 he compiled and edited a film history of the Russian Revolution, *Tsar to*

Lenin. His identification with Trotsky, to whom he paid a visit in 1932, has resulted in increased bitterness of feeling toward him among Communists. In the spring of 1938, declaring that "Every man who believes in . . . democratic civilization as against tyranny and barbarism ought to fight the American Communist Party with every weapon in his grasp . . .," he brought suit for libel against the *Daily Worker*, Clarence A. Hathaway, the editor, and Earl Browder, the general secretary of the Communist party.

For further comment, see Critical Survey, p. 197.

BIBLIOGRAPHY

Poems

Child of the Amazons and other poems, 1913; Colors of life, poems and songs and sonnets, 1918; Kinds of love, poems, 1931.

Novel

Venture, 1927.

Essays and Studies

* Enjoyment of poetry, 1913; Journalism versus art, 1916; Understanding Germany, The only way to end war and other essays, 1916; The sense of humor, 1921; The literary mind, its place in an age of science, 1931; Art and the life of action with other essays, 1934; * Artists in uniform, a study of literature and bureaucratism, 1934; Enjoyment of laughter, 1936.

Political Studies

Since Lenin died, 1925; Marx, Lenin and the science of revolution, 1926; The end of socialism in Russia, 1937.

Biography

Leon Trotsky: the portrait of a youth, 1925.

Pamphlets

Is woman suffrage important? 1912 (cover-title); Values of the vote. Address before the Men's league for woman suffrage of New York, March 21, 1912, 1912 (cover-title); Woman suffrage and sentiment, 1913 (cover-title); Is the truth obscene? 1915; Washington to Petrograd—via Rome, some observations on President Wilson's reply to Pope Benedict XV, 1917? (cover-title; leaflet); Max Eastman's address to the jury in the second Masses trial in defense of the socialist position and the right of free speech, 1918 (cover-title); The trial of Eugene Debs . . . with Debs' address to the court on receiving sentence, 1918? (cover-title); Russia [by] Nicolai Lenin, Tchicherin, John Reed, Max Eastman, 1919 (cover-title); The last stand of dialectic materialism, a study of Sidney Hook's Marxism, 1934.

Editor

Capital, the Communist manifesto and other writings by Karl Marx edited with an introduction by Max Eastman, with an unpublished essay on Marxism by Lenin, 1932.

Translations

Leon Trotsky. The real situation in Russia, 1928; Gabriel, a poem in one song by Alexander Pushkin . . . illustrated by Rockwell Kent, 1929; Leon Trotsky. The history of the Russian revolution, vol. 1, The overthrow of tzarism, translated from the Russian, 1932; Leon Trotsky. The history of the Russian revolution, volume two, The attempted counter-revolution, translated from the Russian, 1932 [1933]; Leon Trotsky. The history of the Russian revolution, volume three, The triumph of the soviets, translated from the Russian, 1932 [1933]; Leon Trotsky. The revolution betrayed. What is the Soviet union and where is it going? 1937.

STUDIES AND ARTICLES

Brooks
Calverton
Hackett
Kallen
Kunitz
McKay
† Manly
Proletarian
Reed, John. To Max Eastman. [1915] (broadside)

Glicksberg, Charles I. "Max Eastman, literary insurgent." *SR.*, July–Sept., 1936, pp. 323–37; Henderson, Alice C. "'Child of the amazons.'" *P.*, Oct. 1913, pp. 31–33; Henderson. "Lazy criticism." *P.*, Dec. 1916, pp. 144–49; Kunitz, Stanley J. "A note on Max Eastman." *N.Masses*, May 8, 1934, pp. 24–25; Mangan, Sherry. "Mush." *P.*, Oct. 1931, pp. 51–54; Monroe, Harriet. "Poetry, a zest for life." *P.*, July 1913, 140–42; Monroe. "A radical-conservative." *P.*, Mar. 1919, pp. 322–26. For references to reviews, see *BRD.*, 1913, 1916–18, 1921, 1925, 1928, 1931, 1934–37.

Walter D(umaux) Edmonds, 1903–

Born July 15, 1903, in Boonville, New York. He came of a New England family and was educated at the Cutler School, St. Paul's School, Concord, New Hampshire (1916–19), the Choate School, Wallingford, Connecticut (1919–21), and Harvard, where he graduated in 1926.

He had earned some notice as a member of the board of the *Choate Literary Magazine;* in his freshman year in college he became an editor of the *Advocate*, and he was later made secretary and president. In 1925 one of his productions, a parody number imitating the *Dial*, was banned by Boston authorities. His writing won the attention of Professor Charles Townsend Copeland; and one of his class stories, sold to *Scribner's* in 1925, appeared in the following year in that magazine.

Other stories were bought by *Scribner's*, the *Atlantic*, the *Dial*, and *McCall's*, and in 1926 he won second prize in the *Harper's* intercollegiate competition. The results as a whole, however, discouraged the author from relying upon writing alone as a source of support, and he applied for editorial work on the *Atlantic* and on other staffs. At the suggestion of Ellery Sedgwick he spent the winter of 1927–28 in Boston, at work on a novel about the Erie Canal; and *Rome Haul*, cut down considerably from the manuscript version, was published in 1929. The novel, which is the basis for the play *The Farmer Takes a Wife* (1934), written by Marc Connelly and Frank B. Elser and played by Henry Fonda and June Walker, established Edmonds as a writer on New York history.

Since then he has written stories for the *Saturday Evening Post* and other magazines, and other novels, based upon reading and study of such material as "travel books, almanacs, newspapers, some letters, and some biographies." In 1936, the year of the publication of *Drums along the Mohawk*, he was given an honorary degree by Union College, Schenectady, as "second builder of our Grand Canal," and in 1937 he was the guest of honor at a meeting held at Fort Herkimer Church in celebration of Oriskany Day, August 6.

"As much as I can I like to be in upstate New York," he says. "So far I have no inclination to write of any other region. One reason is that upstate is still, as it has been, the passageway of America and all America has in one form or another passed through it and left a taste of itself. Another is that I know and love the country." Except for winters passed in New England he lives at Boonville, where he can fish and garden and do work about the farm. He enjoys especially reading history, which he feels should be studied, not through lives of "historical figures," but "through the daily life and opinions of the plain people." "Dates and events," he says, "make less impression on me than weather, and markets, and styles, and food."

His methods of work are regular and methodical, and, although he has sometimes had to rewrite stories two or three times, he has never rewritten a large part of a novel. For *Drums along the Mohawk*, however, the writing of which required less than six months, he threw away a thousand pages of false starts. "I have never found it possible to plan a book entirely in my head," he writes. "I have the instincts of a laborer I think and must work it out with my hands." He is an admirer especially of Swift and Tolstoy and, in American literature, of Mark Twain and Willa Cather. "*Huckleberry Finn*," he says, "seems to me the purest writing turned out by an American." In recent American writing he regards highly the work of Kenneth Roberts in *Arundel* and *Rabble in Arms*, and, in criticism, that of Stephen Vincent Benét, Bernard DeVoto, and Clifton Fadiman.

For further comment, see Critical Survey, pp. 41, 56, 64.

BIBLIOGRAPHY

Novels

Rome haul, 1929; The big barn, 1930; Erie water, 1933; * Drums along the Mohawk, 1936.

Short Stories

Mostly canallers, collected stories, 1934.

STUDIES AND ARTICLES

Kunitz

Kohler, Dayton. "Walter D. Edmonds, regional historian." *EJ.*, Jan. 1938, pp. 1–11; McCord, David. "Edmonds country." *SRL.*, Dec. 11, 1937, pp. 10–11. For references to reviews, see *BRD.*, 1929–30, 1933–34, 1936.

Paul (Hamilton) Engle, 1908–

Born in Cedar Rapids, Iowa, October 12, 1908, the son of Thomas Allen and Evelyn (Reinheimer) Engle. Reared and educated in Cedar Rapids, he worked his way through Coe College by doing various odd jobs, and received his bachelor's degree in 1931. Continuing his study, he took a master's degree at the University of Iowa, studied at Columbia University for a year on the Lydia Roberts Scholarship, and spent three years at Oxford as Rhodes Scholar from Iowa (1933–36), traveling in Europe also during this period. Studying at Merton College, he took work in English literature with Edmund Blunden, and delved into philosophy, politics, history, and economics. He was also active on the college rowing team. Since his return to this country he has given lectures; at present he is resident poet and poetry lecturer at the University of Iowa.

He is much interested in making American history and legend into verse, and tries to put into poetry American speech rhythms and slang. He believes "that poetry should have one ear to the ground and the other to the voices of the people talking around it, that it must be social, in this most social of all centuries."

BIBLIOGRAPHY

Poems

Worn earth, 1932; American song, a book of poems, 1934; Break the heart's anger, 1936; A book of poems, Corn, 1939.

Editor

West of the great water, an Iowa anthology edited by Paul Engle and Harold Cooper with a preface by Norman Foerster, 1931; Ozark anthology by G. F. Newburger, 1938.

ARTICLES

Fletcher, John G. "The American dream." *P.*, Feb. 1935, pp. 285–88; Monroe, Harriet. "Paul Engle's first book." *P.*, July 1933, pp. 220–22; Zabel, Morton D. "Because I love you so." *P.*, July 1936, pp. 228–31. For references to reviews, see *BRD.*, 1932, 1936, 1939.

John Erskine, 1879–

Born in New York, October 5, 1879. Reared in New York City, he was educated at the Columbia Grammar School and Columbia College, and graduated in 1900. He took his master's and doctor's degrees in 1901 and 1903, respectively, at Columbia, and went to Amherst as instructor in English in 1903. He returned to Columbia in 1909, after six years as instructor and associate professor at Amherst, and became adjunct professor of English. Since 1916 he has been full professor, and his lectures, delivered informally without notes, have been extremely popular. He is a member of the Modern Language Association and has been secretary of the executive committee of the American Council of Learned Societies and a trustee of the Protestant Episcopal Public Schools of New York.

During the war Erskine served as chairman of the Army Educational Committee of the American Expeditionary Force (1918–19) and educational director of the A.E.F. University at Beaune (1919); and in 1919 he was made Chevalier de la Legion d'Honneur and honorary citizen of Beaune.

At first a writer of educational and scholarly books, Erskine produced anthologies and collaborated in the editing of *The Cambridge History of American Literature*. His doctoral dissertation, *The Elizabethan Lyric*, enjoyed a fourth printing in 1931. *The Private Life of Helen of Troy*, a sophisticated treatment of old Greek legends, written late at night in the space of six months, was very successful in 1925 and encouraged the author to write *Adam and Eve* and *Penelope's Man*.

In the meanwhile Erskine's early interest in music revived and in 1923 he resumed his work at the piano. During one season he toured as soloist with the New York Symphony Orchestra under Damrosch; and he played with the symphony orchestras of Detroit, Minneapolis, and Chicago. In 1927 he was made a trustee of the Juilliard School of Music in New York and chairman of the committee on administration; and he was president from 1928 until 1936. He remains a director of the school and a trustee of the Juilliard Foundation, and has been chairman of the management committee of the Metropolitan Opera Association. He has stated his opinion that the future of the musician in the society of today lies in his accepting a craftsman's position, much like that of eighteenth-century organists and composers like Bach, and not depending for his career upon concert tours of the type made popular by Liszt and other virtuosi.

A member of the National Institute of Arts and Letters, Erskine was president in 1922 of the Poetry Society of America and has thrice been president of the Authors' Club of New York. "I am deeply interested," he writes, "in those novels which try to give a specific picture of one time and place, or which advocate some contemporary theory or uncover some contemporary problem, but I do not care to write such novels myself, even if I could. The superficial appearance of society changes so fast that a literal picture is soon out of date; yet it is the contemporary scene and contemporary problems which interest me. I try to present them under forms which have been somewhat timeless in the race memory. This is the traditional method of narrative poetry. I like to use it in prose narrative."

BIBLIOGRAPHY

Novels

* The private life of Helen of Troy, 1925; Galahad, enough of his life to explain his reputation, 1926; Adam and Eve, though he knew better, 1927; Penelope's man, the homing instinct . . . end papers by D. Putnam Brinley, 1928; Sincerity, a story of our time, 1929 (English ed., An experiment in sincerity, a story of our time, 1930); Uncle Sam in the eyes of his family . . . a novel, 1930; Unfinished business, 1931; Tristan and Isolde, restoring Palamede, 1932; Bachelor—of arts, 1934; Forget if you can, a novel, 1935; Solomon, my son! 1935; The brief hour of François Villon, 1937; The start of the road, a novel, 1938.

Short Stories

The enchanted garden, 1925; Cinderella's daughter and other sequels and consequences . . . with illustrations by Graham Erskine, 1930; Peter kills the bear, 1930; Young love, variations on a theme, 1936.

Poems

Actæon and other poems, 1907 [1906]; Ash Wednesday, 1914 (pamphlet); The city flag, 1915 (broadside); The shadowed hour, 1917; Collected poems, 1907–1922, 1922; Sonata and other poems, 1925.

Essays and Studies

The Elizabethan lyric, a study, 1903; Leading American novelists . . . with six portraits, 1910; Great American writers by W. P. Trent . . . and John Erskine, 1912 (English ed., Great writers of America by W. P. Trent . . . and John Erskine, 1912); The moral obligation to be intelligent and other essays, 1915; Democracy and idealism, 1917 (pamphlet); Walt Whitman, 1919 (cover-title; pamphlet); Democracy and ideals, a definition, 1920; The kinds of poetry and other essays, 1920; The literary discipline, 1923; English literature, an illustrated record in four volumes, volume IV. From the age of Johnson to the age of Tennyson by Edmund Gosse . . . with a supplementary chapter on the literature from 1892 to 1922 by John Erskine, 1926; American character and other essays selected from the writings of John Erskine, especially for the Chautauqua home reading series, 1927; Prohibition and Christianity and other paradoxes of the American spirit, 1927; The delight of great books, 1928; George Edward Woodberry, 1855–1930, an appreciation . . . A list of writings by and about him compiled by R. R. Hawkins, 1930 (pamphlet); The influence of women and its cure, 1936.

Librettos

Jack and the beanstalk, a fairy opera for the childlike . . . for music by Louis Gruenberg, 1931; Helen retires, an opera in three acts . . . for music by George Antheil, 1934.

Play

Hearts enduring, a play in one scene, 1920.

Pageant

A pageant of the thirteenth century for the seven hundredth anniversary of Roger Bacon given by Columbia university, the plan and the notes by John J. Coss . . . the text by John Erskine . . . the illustrations by Claggett Wilson, 1914.

Textbook

Written English, a guide to the rules of composition by John Erskine . . . and Helen Erskine, 1910.

Miscellany

Educational plans for the American army abroad [by] Anson Phelps Stokes . . . being the reports presented to and approved by General Pershing with supplementary reports showing progress of the work by Professor John Erskine . . . and Professor Reginald Aldworth Daly, 1918; The President's mystery story, propounded by Franklin D. Roosevelt, solved by Rupert Hughes, Samuel Hopkins Adams, Anthony Abbot [*pseud*], Rita Weiman, S. S. Van Dine [*pseud.*], John Erskine, with a preface by Fulton Oursler, 1935.

Music

The governor's vrouw, a comic opera in two acts, dedicated to the class of 1900, Columbia college . . . Book by Henry Sydnor Harrison and Melville Henry Cane: lyrics by Melville Henry Cane: music by John Erskine . . ., 1900; Love immeasurable, song for voice and piano by John Erskine, poem by George S. Hellman, 1934 (cover-title; sheet music).

Editor

Selections from Spenser's The faerie queene edited with notes and an introduction, 1905; The golden treasury selected from the best songs and lyrical poems in the English language and arranged with notes by Francis T. Palgrave . . . edited for the use of schools by W. P. Trent and John Erskine, 1912; Selections from Tennyson's Idylls of the king, 1912; International conciliation, special bulletin. Contemporary war poems with an introduction, 1914 (cover-title; pamphlet); Poems of Wordsworth, Shelley, and Keats selected from "The golden treasury" of Francis Turner Palgrave, edited for the use of schools by W. P. Trent and John Erskine, 1914; Interpretations of literature by Lafcadio Hearn selected and edited with an introduction . . . with frontispiece, 1915 (2 vols.); Appreciations of poetry by Lafcadio Hearn selected and edited with an introduction, 1916; The Cambridge history of American literature edited by William Peterfield Trent . . . John Erskine . . . Stuart P. Sherman . . . Carl Van Doren . . ., 1917–21 (4 vols.; English ed., A history of American literature); Life and literature by Lafcadio Hearn selected and edited with an introduction, 1917; Talks to writers by Lafcadio Hearn selected and edited with an introduction, 1920; Books and habits from the lectures of Lafcadio Hearn selected and edited with an introduction, 1921; Pre-Raphaelite and other poets, lectures by Lafcadio Hearn selected and edited with an introduction, 1922; A short history of American literature based upon the Cambridge history of American literature edited by William Peterfield Trent, John Erskine, Stuart P. Sherman, and Carl Van Doren, 1922; The outline of literature edited by John Drinkwater, 1923 (3 vols.; ed. by John Erskine); A musical companion, a guide to the understanding and enjoyment of music edited with an introductory note, 1935.

STUDIES AND ARTICLES

Bourne
Cohen (M)
† Herrmann
Kilmer
Kunitz (L)
Levinson
† Manly
Marble
National
† Robinson, Henry M. John Erskine, a modern Actæon . . . together with Mr. Erskine's radio speech of September 18, 1927, a short biography and bibliography. [1927] (pamphlet)

Crawford, Nelson A. "The professor as critic." *P.*, Oct. 1921, pp. 54–57; Knickerbocker, William S. "John Erskine, enough of his mind to explain his art." *SR.*, Apr.–June 1927, pp. 154–74; Maurice, Arthur B. "The history of their books, John Erskine." *AB.*, Apr. 1930, pp. 165–66; Robinson, Henry M. "John Erskine, a modern Actæon." *AB.*, Aug. 1927, pp. 613–18; Smith,

Helena H. "Professor's progress." *N.Yer.*, Dec. 10, 1927, pp. 27–29. For references to reviews, see *BRD.*, 1907, 1910, 1915, 1920, 1922–23, 1925–32, 1934–38.

F. P. A. *See* Franklin Pierce Adams

William Falkner. *See* William Faulkner

James T(homas) Farrell, 1904–

Born February 27, 1904, in Chicago. He had no literary or intellectual interests in his boyhood. At the St. Anselm Grammar School he worked hardest at baseball; and at the St. Cyril High School he took letters in football and basketball. He went on, however, to attend classes at De Paul University and the University of Chicago; and at the latter he began writing and made up his mind to be a writer. The *Studs Lonigan* trilogy had its origin in a short story called "Studs" written while Farrell was a student there. His experiences have included work as clerk for an express company and in a cigar store, salesman of advertising, reporter for a Hearst newspaper, and filling-station attendant.

His work was published first in the Haldeman-Julius *Debunker*, but has since appeared in the *Nation*, the *New Republic*, the *New Freeman*, the *American Mercury*, the *Saturday Review of Literature*, the New York *Post*, and many other newspapers and magazines. "As far as my books are concerned," he wrote in 1937, "they are part of an extended series of works, novels, novelettes, plays, sketches, stories, and character sketches which are envisioned as one project, loosely integrated, but withal, integrated and connected. I have listed plays here, but I have, as yet, completed none. I hope, however, to include some plays in the series of works I am writing. This series, when completed, should run to from twenty-five to fifty volumes, of which eight have so far been completed."

Although he has lived in France and his work has been enthusiastically received in Europe as well as in the United States, he does not regard himself as an expatriate.

He is a careful and conscientious workman. Every novel goes through three or four developments, with revisions and condensations and abundant corrections on the proofs. Speaking at the New York *Times* Book Fair (1937) on the responsibilities of American writers, Farrell said: "We are fond of saying here we are the freest people in the world. There is a very simple reason for it. We don't need censorship here. American writers do not try to tell enough of the truth to invite censorship."

For his achievement in *Studs Lonigan* and other works and the evidences of future promise, Farrell was awarded one of the four fellowships established in 1936 by the Book-of-the-Month Club.

For further comment, see Critical Survey, pp. 36–37, 48, 94, 197.

BIBLIOGRAPHY

Novels

Young Lonigan, a boyhood in Chicago streets . . . introduction by Frederic M. Thrasher, 1932; Gas-house McGinty, a novel, 1933; The young manhood of Studs Lonigan, 1934; Judgment day, 1935; * Studs Lonigan, a trilogy . . . Young Lonigan, The young manhood of Studs Lonigan, Judgment day, 1935 (intro. by John Chamberlain); A world I never made, 1936; No star is lost, 1938; Tommy Gallagher's crusade, 1939.

Short Stories

Calico shoes and other stories, 1934; Guillotine party and other stories, 1935; Can all this grandeur perish? and other stories, 1937; Fellow countrymen, collected stories of James T. Farrell, 1937; The short stories of James T. Farrell, 1937 (Calico shoes; Guillotine party; Can all this grandeur perish? intro. by Robert Morss Lovett).

Literary Criticism

A note on literary criticism, 1936.

STUDIES AND ARTICLES

McCole

Birney, Earle. "The fiction of James T. Farrell." *CF.*, Apr. 1939, pp. 21–24; † Blanck, Jacob, *ed.* "American first editions . . . James T⟨homas⟩ Farrell ⟨1904–⟩ compiled by Irvin Haas and Robert Gordon." *PW.*, Mar. 20, 1937, p. 1353; Farrell, James T. "A novelist begins." *A.Mo.*, Sept. 1938, pp. 330–34; Glicksberg, Charles I. "Contemporary criticism." *SAQ.*, Oct. 1936, pp. 455–57; Lovett, Robert M. "James T. Farrell." *EJ.*, May 1937, pp. 347–54. For references to reviews, see *BRD.*, 1932–38.

William Faulkner, 1897–

Born in Mississippi, of a family of governors, statesmen, and other public figures. His great-grandfather, Colonel William Falkner, was the author of a popular novel, *The White Rose of Memphis.* Early in his childhood he went to live in Oxford, Mississippi, and it has been his home almost uninterruptedly ever since. He was educated at the University of Mississippi. When the war came he joined the Canadian Flying Corps and served in the British Royal Air Force in France, where he was wounded in an airplane accident. During his period of training in England he read Elizabethan poetry at Oxford. A lieutenant at the end of the war, he returned to this country, attended college, painted roofs, worked for two years as postmaster at the university, took a job in a bookstore in New York, returned to Mississippi to work as a carpenter, and shared an apartment in New Orleans with Sherwood Anderson and wrote descriptive newspaper articles.

His first poem to be published appeared in the *Double-Dealer* in June, 1922, and a collection of pastoral verses, *The Marble Faun*, was privately issued in 1924. Of this edition most copies were sold to a bookstore at about ten cents each. Other poems and articles came out in the *Double-Dealer*, but his published novels sold poorly. *Sanctuary*, a horror tale written as a money-maker, was rejected; and the author, laying it aside, wrote *As I Lay Dying* while he was supporting himself by shoveling coal in a power plant.

The publication of the rewritten *Sanctuary* in 1931 was the turning point in Faulkner's career, and his novels and stories have since been widely read. Although he has made several visits to Hollywood, where he has written for the films, his home is a large plantation house a century old, in Oxford, Mississippi; and he prefers this quiet environment to the noise and crowds of New York. In January, 1939, he was elected to membership in the National Institute of Arts and Letters.

For further comment, see Critical Survey, pp. 34, 44, 96.

BIBLIOGRAPHY

Novels

Soldiers' pay, 1926; Mosquitoes, 1927; Sartoris, 1929; * The sound and the fury, 1929; As I lay dying, 1930; Sanctuary, 1931; Light in August, 1932; Pylon, 1935; Absalom, Absalom! 1936; The unvanquished, drawings by Edward Shenton, 1938; The wild palms, 1939.

Short Stories

Idyll in the desert, 1931; These 13, stories, 1931; Miss Zilphia Gant, 1932 (pref. by Henry Smith); Doctor Martino and other stories, 1934.

Poems

The marble faun, 1924 (pref. by Phil Stone); This earth, a poem . . . with drawings by Albert Heckman, 1932 (pamphlet); A green bough, 1933.

Miscellany

Sherwood Anderson & other famous Creoles, a gallery of contemporary New Orleans drawn by Wm. Spratling & arranged by Wm. Faulkner, 1926; Complete issue by William Faulkner. Contempo, a review of books and personalities, volume 1, number 17, February 1, 1932, Chapel Hill, N.C., 1932 (caption-title); Salmagundi by William Faulkner and a poem by Ernest M. Hemingway, 1932 (pref. by Paul Romaine).

STUDIES AND ARTICLES

Canby (S)
Cecchi, Emilio. Scrittori inglesi e americani . . . [1935]
† Edgar
Ford
Hartwick
Hatcher
Henderson
Hicks
† Johnson (1932)
† Johnson (1936)
Junius Junior [*pseud.*]. Pseudo-realists . . . printed for a fistful. [1931]
Kildal
Kunitz (L)
Larbaud, Valery. Ce vice impuni, la lecture . . . domaine anglais. [c1936]
Lewis
Linn
Loggins
McCole
Saturday
† Schwartz
Scott, Evelyn. On William Faulkner's "The sound and the fury." [1930?] (pamphlet)
Tendencies
Ward

Birney, Earle. "The two William Faulkners." *CF.*, June 1938, pp. 84–85; Buttitta, Anthony. "William Faulkner, that writin' man of Oxford." *SRL.*,

May 21, 1938, pp. 6–8; Cecchi, Emilio. "William Faulkner." *Pan M.*, May 1934, pp. 64–70; Cochran, Louis. "William Faulkner, literary tyro of Mississippi." *Commercial Appeal* (Memphis, Tenn.), Nov. 6, 1932, Mag. Sec., p. 4; Coindreau, Maurice E. "William Faulkner." *NRF.*, June 1, 1931, pp. 926–30; DeVoto, Bernard. "Witchcraft in Mississippi." *SRL.*, Oct. 31, 1936, pp. 3–4, 14; Fadiman, Clifton. "Faulkner, extra-special, double-distilled." *N.Yer.*, Oct. 31, 1936, pp. 62–64; Green, A. Wigfall. "William Faulkner at home." *SR.*, July–Sept. 1932, pp. 294–306; Harnack-Fish, Mildred. "William Faulkner, eine amerikanischer dichter aus grosser tradition." *Die Lit.*, Nov. 1935, pp. 64–67; Hicks, Granville. "The past and future of William Faulkner." *AB.*, Sept. 1931, pp. 17–24; Le Breton, Maurice. "Technique et psychologie chez William Faulkner." *EA.*, Sept. 1937, pp. 418–38; Lewis, Wyndham. "A moralist with a corn-cob, a study of William Faulkner." *LL.*, June 1934, pp. 312–28; McCole, Camille J. "The nightmare literature of William Faulkner." *CW.*, Aug. 1935, pp. 576–83; Malraux, André. "Préface à 'Sanctuaire' de W. Faulkner." *NRF.*, Nov. 1, 1933, pp. 744–47; Redman, Ben R. "Faulkner's double novel." *SRL.*, Jan. 21, 1939, p. 5; Rosati, Salvatore. "Letteratura Americana, William Faulkner." *Nuova Ant.*, Jan. 16, 1938, pp. 225–30; Sartee, Jean-Paul. "Sartoris." *NRF.*, Feb. 1938, pp. 323–28; Schappes, Morris U. "Faulkner as a poet." *P.*, Oct. 1933, pp. 48–52; Smith, Marshall J. "Faulkner of Mississippi." *AB.*, Dec. 1931, pp. 411–17; † Starke, Aubrey. "An American comedy, an introduction to a bibliography of William Faulkner." *Col.*, Part 19, (1934) 12 pp.; Thompson, Alan R. "The cult of cruelty." *AB.*, Jan. 1932, pp. 477–87. For references to reviews, see *BRD.*, 1926–27, 1929–36, 1938–39.

Kenneth Fearing, 1902–

Born in Oak Park, Illinois. He was educated at the University of Wisconsin. For a time he held a job as mill hand; he also engaged in journalism. Later he became a free-lance writer in New York. In 1927 "Old Men" appeared in *Poetry*, and one of Fearing's stories was published in the annual collection of Edward J. O'Brien for the next year. His first book of poems, *Angel Arms*, appeared in 1929, and there have been two subsequent volumes, the second, *Dead Reckoning*, being a collection of lyrics in free verse. In 1939 he was awarded a Guggenheim fellowship for creative writing.

For further comment, see Critical Survey, p. 152.

BIBLIOGRAPHY

Poems

Angel arms, 1929; Poems . . . introduction by Edward Dahlberg, 1935; Dead reckoning, a book of poetry, 1938.

Novel

The hospital, 1939.

ARTICLES

Gregory, Horace. "A contrast in satires." *P.*, Feb. 1937, pp. 282–85; Wilson, Ted C. "The real thing." *P.*, Apr. 1939, pp. 26–29. For references to reviews, see *BRD.*, 1929, 1935, 1938–39.

Edna Ferber, 1887–

Born in Kalamazoo, Michigan, August 15, 1887. When she was two, her family removed to Wisconsin and settled in Appleton, where her father ran a general store. Here she attended grade and high schools and, upon graduation, began her career as a writer by reporting for the Appleton *Daily Crescent.* In the course of her six years or so of reporting, for this paper and others, including the Milwaukee *Journal* and the Chicago *Tribune*, she had almost every kind of assignment, made many contacts, and developed her style.

Her first novel, *Dawn O'Hara*, she wrote in Milwaukee. Feeling, after she had finished it, that it was worthless, she threw it away; but her mother rescued it from the wastebasket, and it was published successfully when she was twenty-four. Her short story "April 25th, as Usual" was reprinted in the *O. Henry Memorial Award Prize Stories* for 1919; and the novel *So Big* was awarded the Pulitzer Prize for 1924. *The Royal Family*, *Show Boat*, and *Dinner at Eight*, plays in which she collaborated with George Kaufman, were unusually successful on Broadway. Many of her novels and plays have been made into films. The author, who has lived for many years in New York, holds an honorary doctorate in letters from Columbia and is a member of the National Institute of Arts and Letters.

For further comment, see Critical Survey, pp. 29, 40, 47.

BIBLIOGRAPHY

Novels

Dawn O'Hara, the girl who laughed . . . frontispiece in colors by R. Ford Harper, 1911; Fanny herself . . . illustrated by J. Henry, 1917; The girls, 1921; * So Big, 1924; * Show boat, a novel, 1926; Cimarron, 1930; American beauty by Edna Ferber, woodcut decorations by Rudolph Ruzicka, 1931; Come and get it, 1935; Nobody's in town, 1938 (Nobody's in town; Trees die at the top).

Short Stories

Buttered side down, stories . . . with frontispiece in color by R. Ford Harper and other illustrations in black-and-white by Thomas Fogarty and Irma Dérêmeaux, 1912; Roast beef, medium, the business adventures of Emma McChesney . . . with twenty-seven illustrations by James Montgomery Flagg, 1913; Personality plus, some experiences of Emma McChesney and her son, Jock . . . with fifteen illustrations by James Montgomery Flagg, 1914; Emma McChesney & co. . . . with four illustrations by J. Henry, 1915; Cheerful, by request, 1918; Half portions, 1920; Gigolo, 1922 (English ed., Among those present, 1923); My story that I like best by Edna Ferber, Irvin S. Cobb, Peter B. Kyne, James Oliver Curwood, Meredith Nicholson, H. C. Witwer, with an introduction by Ray Long, editor of Cosmopolitan, 1924; The homely heroine . . . a contest selection, 1926 (pamphlet); The man who came back . . . a contest selection, 1926 (pamphlet); Mother knows best, a fiction book, 1927; They brought their women, a book of short stories, 1933.

Plays

$1200 a year, a comedy in three acts by Edna Ferber and Newman Levy, 1920; Old man Minick, a short story by Edna Ferber. Minick, a play based on the short story, by Edna Ferber and George S. Kaufman, also a brief and quite gratuitous explanation by the authors, 1924; The eldest, a drama of American life, 1925; Minick, a comedy in three acts by George S. Kaufman and Edna Ferber, 1925; The royal family, a comedy in three acts by George S. Kaufman and Edna Ferber, 1928 (English ed., Theatre royal, a play in three acts, 1936); * Dinner at eight, a play by George S. Kaufman and Edna Ferber, 1932; Stage door, a play by Edna Ferber and George S. Kaufman, 1936 (also issued in mimeographed form with cover-title: "Stage door," by Edna Ferber and George S. Kaufman, 1936).

Autobiography

A peculiar treasure, 1939.

STUDIES AND ARTICLES

Agate (F)
Agate (M)
† Dickinson, Rogers. Edna Ferber, a biographical sketch with a bibliography, written by Rogers Dickinson, with many quotations from Edna Ferber's autobiographical articles. [1928] (pamphlet)
† Dickinson, Rogers. Edna Ferber, whose novel "So Big" was awarded the Pulitzer prize for the best American novel of 1924, a biographical sketch with a bibliography, written by Rogers Dickinson, with many quotations from Edna Ferber's autobiographical articles. [1925] (pamphlet)
Farrar
Ferber, Edna. Show boat . . . with a foreword by Jerome Kern. 1935
Ford
† Ford (E)
[Furthman, Jules and Murfin, Jane. Come and get it, screen play by Jules Furthman and Jane Murfin from the novel by Edna Ferber.] [1936] (mimeographed)
Giesen, Felicitas. Amerika im werke der Edna Ferber. 1935.
Hammerstein, Oscar. "Show boat," from the novel by Edna Ferber, screenplay by Oscar Hammerstein II. 1935 (cover-title; mimeographed)
† Johnson (1932)
† Johnson (1936)
Kaltenbacher
Kern, Jerome. Show boat, an all American musical comedy adapted from Edna Ferber's novel of the same name, produced by Florenz Ziegfeld, music by Jerome Kern, book and lyrics by Oscar Hammerstein, 2nd . . . vocal score. c1928
Kunitz (L)
Lawrence (S)
Lawrence (W)
Marble
Marion, Frances and Mankiewicz, Herman J. Dinner at eight . . . screen play by Frances Marion and Herman J. Mankiewicz from the Sam H. Harris stage play by George S. Kaufman and Edna Ferber, additional dialogue by Donald Ogden Stewart . . . [1933] (cover-title; mimeographed)
Mersand
National
Pattee (N)
Phelps (AW)
Overton (W)
Overton (WW)
Williams

Allen, Margaret P. "'The odd women' and 'The girls.'" *N.Amer.Rev.*, Nov. 1922, pp. 691–94; Anonymous. "Edna Ferber." *AB.*, Jan. 1922, pp. 434–39; Anonymous. "Imitative school." *AB.*, May 1912, pp. 225–27; Anonymous. "Our 'beautiful young idiots.'" *Lit.Dig.*, Oct. 3, 1931, pp. 18–19; Anonymous. "The way of a novelist." *Lit.Dig.*, Dec. 5, 1931, p. 14; Banning, Margaret C.

"Edna Ferber's America." *SRL.*, Feb. 4, 1939, pp. 5–6; Bromfield, Louis. "Edna Ferber." *SRL.*, June 15, 1935, pp. 10–12; Overton, Grant. "The social critic in Edna Ferber." *AB.*, Oct. 1926, pp. 138–43; Patrick, Arnold. "Getting into six figures." *AB.*, Apr. 1925, pp. 164–68; White, William A. "Edna Ferber." *WW.*, June 1930, pp. 36–38, 90; White. "Edna Ferber in the forefront of the reporters of her age." *World Today*, Aug. 1930, pp. 221–25; White. "A friend's story of Edna Ferber." *EJ.*, Feb. 1930, pp. 101–06. For references to reviews, see *BRD.*, 1911–15, 1917–18, 1920–22, 1924–27, 1930–33, 1935–36, 1938–39.

Rachel (Lyman) Field, 1894–

Born September 19, 1894. She was reared in Massachusetts, attended schools in Stockbridge and Springfield, and went to Radcliffe. There she wrote a one-act play, *Three Pills in a Bottle*, and worked with Professor Baker.

From college she went to New York and took a job as editor in a motion-picture company. After five years, however, she left the position to devote all her time to writing. She has written tales, sketches, and verse, and has illustrated many of her own books. Many of her plays have been performed by little-theater groups. She has been careful to avoid condescension in her books for children, and the result has been that they have proved attractive to adults. *Hitty* (1929) won the Newberry Medal (1930) as "the most distinguished contribution to literature for American children." Miss Field was the first woman to receive this recognition. In addition to her books she has written reviews for the *Saturday Review of Literature* and *Books* (New York *Herald Tribune*).

For further comment, see Critical Survey, p. 40.

BIBLIOGRAPHY

Novels

Time out of mind, 1935; To see ourselves by Rachel Field and Arthur Pederson, 1937; * All this, and heaven too, 1938.

Poems

A circus garland, 1930; Points east, narratives of New England, 1930; Fear is the thorn, 1936.

Biography

God's pocket, the story of Captain Samuel Hadlock, junior, of Cranberry isles, Maine, 1934.

Plays

Plays of the 47 workshop: Three pills in a bottle by Rachel Lyman Field, "The good men do" by Hubert Osborne, Two crooks and a lady by Eugene Pillot, Free speech by William L. Prosser, 1918; Rise up, Jennie Smith: a play in one act: by Rachael L. Field. Prize play, Drama league of America patriotic play competition, 1918; Six plays: Cinderella married, Three pills in a bottle, Columbine in business, The patchwork quilt, Wisdom teeth, Theories and thumbs . . . with foreword by George P. Baker, 1924; The cross-stitch heart and other plays: The cross-stitch heart, "Greasy luck," The nine days' queen,

"The Londonderry air," At the junction, "Bargains in Cathay," 1927; Patchwork plays . . . illustrated by the author, 1930 (Polly Patchwork; "Little Square-toes"; Miss Ant, Miss Grasshopper, and Mr. Cricket; Chimney sweeps' holiday; The sentimental scarecrow); At the junction, a fantasy for railroad-stations in one act, 1931; Bargains in Cathay, a comedy in one act, 1931; The cross-stitch heart, a sampler fantasy in one act, 1931; Greasy luck, a fragment out of the New England whaling days in one act, 1931; The Londonderry air, a play of the day before yesterday in one act, 1931; The nine days' queen, an historical fantasy in one act, 1931; Cinderella married, a comedy in one act, 1934?; Columbine in business, a modern harlequinade in one act, 1934; The patchwork quilt, a fantasy in one act, 1934?; Polly Patchwork, comedy in three scenes, from the story of the same title, 1934?; The sentimental scarecrow, a comedy in one act, 1934?; Theories and thumbs, a fantasy for museums in one act, 1934?; Three pills in a bottle, a fantasy in one act, 1934?; Wisdom teeth, a comedy in one act, 1934?; First class matter, a comedy in one act, 1936; The bad penny, a drama in one act, 1938; The fifteenth candle, drama in one act, 1938.

Children's Books

Eliza and the elves . . . illustrated by Elizabeth MacKinstry, 1926; The magic pawnshop, a New Year's eve fantasy . . . decorated by Elizabeth MacKinstry, 1927; Little dog Toby, pictures & story, 1928; Polly Patchwork, 1928; American folk and fairy tales selected by Rachel Field with drawings by Margaret Freeman, 1929; Hitty, her first hundred years . . . with illustrations by Dorothy P. Lathrop, 1929 (English ed., Hitty, the life and adventures of a wooden doll, 1932); Pocket-handkerchief park, 1929; Calico bush by Rachel Field, engravings on wood by Allen Lewis, 1931; The yellow shop . . . illustrated by the author, 1931; The bird began to sing by Rachel Field, pictures by Ilse Bischoff, 1932; Hepatica Hawks by Rachel Field, engravings on wood by Allen Lewis, 1932; Just across the street by Rachel Field, pictures by the author, 1933.

Children's Verses

The pointed people, verses & silhouettes, 1924; An alphabet for boys and girls, 1926; Taxis and toadstools, verses and decorations, 1926; A little book of days, 1927; Branches green . . . with decorations by Dorothy P. Lathrop, 1934; Susanna B. and William C., 1934.

Verses Set to Music

Gypsies, poem by Rachel Lyman Field [music by] Henry Hadley, 1934 (caption-title; sheet music); Roads, poem by Rachel Lyman Field [music by] Henry Hadley, 1934 (caption-title; sheet music); Thrushes, poem by Rachel Lyman Field [music by] Henry Hadley, 1934 (caption-title; sheet music).

Adaptations and Arrangements

The white cat and other old French fairy tales by Mme. la comtesse d'Aulnoy arranged by Rachel Field and drawn by E. MacKinstry, 1928; Fortune's caravan by Lily Jean-Javal adapted . . . from the translation by Marion Saunders, illustrated by Maggie Salcedo, 1933; People from Dickens, a presentation of leading characters from the books of Charles Dickens, arranged by Rachel Field, with illustrations by Thomas Fogarty, 1935.

Illustrator

Punch & Robinetta by Ethel M. Gate with silhouettes by Rachel Lyman Field, 1923.

STUDIES

Kunitz (J) Kunitz (L)

For references to reviews, see *BRD.*, 1926–39.

Dorothy Canfield Fisher. *See* Dorothy Canfield

Vardis (Alvero) Fisher, 1895–

Born in Annis, Idaho, March 31, 1895, the son of Joseph O. and Temperance (Thornton) Fisher. He began writing in childhood. He was educated at the University of Utah (A.B., 1920) and the University of Chicago (A.M., 1922; Ph.D., 1925). In 1918 he served as corporal in the Coast Artillery Corps, and in the same year he married Leona McMurtrey. He has taught English in the University of Utah (1925–28) and New York University (1928–31), but regards the work as mere pot-boiling. After the death of his first wife he married (1929) Margaret Trusler. He wrote most of *Idaho, A Guide in Word and Picture* and wrote, or rewrote, practically all *The Idaho Encyclopedia.* In 1939 he received the Harper Novel Prize ($7,500) for *Children of God*, a story of the Mormons.

Fisher's attempt in fiction is to achieve realism and honest representation of truth, although he does not regard an honest book as possible today; his writings have no other purpose or aim. He is an admirer of Thomas Wolfe, William Faulkner, and James Branch Cabell.

"I am not sure that the artist can move fully in the current of events, as novelists especially are doing more and more, and escape the superficial," he wrote in 1937. "If there is any general theme running through my novels it must be this, that the human race has been betrayed by an assumption of compensatory virtues which are still indefinitely beyond fulfillment, and in self-defense has fled into countless evasions that have become so inflexibly fixed in patterns that it is very difficult to get out of them or understand what they are doing to us. Though widely dubbed a Freudian, I am not and have never been. Of great assistance in an attempt to understand has been Jung's concept of the mind as a closed energic system; and more recently my brother's (Vivian Ezra Fisher's) new theory of neurosis as outlined in his book, just out, *Auto-correctivism: A New Theory of Nervousness.* He sees, in sum, the conflict in the more intelligent and sensitive human beings today as that between egoistic and racial drives, with a harmony of the two not often achieved. His theory offers the easiest and simplest approach to orientation that I know of, and is to be the chief basis in my novel forthcoming next year. I still stand by a statement in one of the essays in *The Neurotic Nightingale*, that an attempt to believe ourselves virtuous beyond what we are yet capable of, and the evasions which in consequence we have been driven to in an attempt to keep our self-esteem, have made the human race greedy and brutal beyond any reach that its natural endowment could ever have led it to."

For further comment, see Critical Survey, pp. 33–34, 49–50.

BIBLIOGRAPHY

Novels

Toilers of the hills, 1928; Dark Bridwell, 1931; * In tragic life, 1932 (English ed., I see no sin, 1934); Passions spin the plot, 1934; We are betrayed, 1935; No villain need be, 1936; April, a fable of love, 1937; Forgive us our virtues, a comedy of evasions, 1938; Children of God, an American epic, 1939.

Poems

Sonnets to an imaginary madonna, 1927.

Short Story

Odyssey of a hero, 1937.

Essays

The neurotic nightingale, 1935.

Guide Book

Idaho, a guide in word and picture, prepared by the Federal writers' projects of the Works progress administration. The library edition, 1937 (by Vardis Fisher and others).

Editor

The Idaho encyclopedia, compiled by the Federal writers' project of the Works progress administration, Vardis Fisher, state director, 1938.

STUDIES AND ARTICLES

† Johnson (1936)
Kunitz
Rein, David. Vardis Fisher: challenge to evasion . . . preface by Vardis Fisher. 1938

Bishop, John P. "The strange case of Vardis Fisher." *So.R.*, Autumn 1937, pp. 348–59. For references to reviews, see *BRD.*, 1928, 1931–32, 1934–38.

Clarke Fitch, *pseud.* *See* Upton Sinclair

F(rancis) Scott (Key) Fitzgerald, 1896–

Born September 24, 1896, in St. Paul, Minnesota, of Irish and Maryland English stock. Francis Scott Key was a great-granduncle. During his earliest years he traveled around the country with his family, and lived in Syracuse and Buffalo. He read G. A. Henty, Horatio Alger, and Richard Henry Barbour, and, even at this period, wanted to write. As this ambition interfered with his school-work, his parents sent him in 1911 to the Newman School in Hackensack, New Jersey, in the hopes that he might do more studying. Instead, he became interested in musical comedy, and, largely because of the Triangle Club, devoted to such productions, he entered Princeton in 1913.

In college, where he wrote an operetta in his freshman year, he had a hand in three productions of the Triangle Club, once collaborating with Edmund Wilson on a libretto, and acted in one show as a chorus girl. He contributed stories and poems to the *Princeton Tiger* and the *Nassau Literary Magazine*, and was a member of the editorial board of each.

In 1917 he left college to join the army, and served in the infantry as second lieutenant and first lieutenant. For a few months he was aide-de-camp to Brigadier General J. A. Ryan. He was not sent abroad, and he spent his spare time writing a novel, which he finished in his week-ends during three months. As he could not get it published and was unable to find work as a reporter, he took a poorly-paid job as advertising writer in 1919–20 and wrote stories, sketches, poems, lyrics, and other material. Finally, in June, 1920, he sold a story for thirty dollars, left his job, and went home to rewrite his novel. In two months he had finished *This Side of Paradise*, which, highly successful, resulted in his selling stories to magazines; and his days of struggle were over.

He has since been able to travel and live in Europe, swim and fish, and indulge his taste for books and modern music and literature. He has lived on Long Island and in Wilmington, Baltimore, and North Carolina. He feels that he has been influenced by Samuel Butler, H. G. Wells, Compton Mackenzie, H. L. Mencken, and John Peale Bishop.

For further comment, see Critical Survey, pp. 35, 91–92.

BIBLIOGRAPHY

Novels

* This side of paradise, 1920; The beautiful and damned, 1922; The great Gatsby, 1925; Tender is the night, a romance . . . decorations by Edward Shenton, 1934.

Short Stories

Flappers and philosophers, 1920; Tales of the jazz age, 1922; All the sad young men, 1926. John Jackson's Arcady by F. Scott Fitzgerald, a contest selection arranged by Lilian Holmes Strack, 1928 (pamphlet); Taps at reveille, 1935.

Play

The vegetable, or, From president to postman, 1923.

Musical comedies

The evil eye, a musical comedy in two acts, presented by the Princeton university Triangle club, 1915–1916. Book by E. Wilson, jr., '16. Lyrics by F. Scott Fitzgerald, '17, 1915 (cover-title); Safety first, a musical comedy in two acts, presented by the Princeton university Triangle club, 1916–1917. Book by J. F. Bohmfalk, '17, J. Biggs, jr., '18. Lyrics by F. Scott Fitzgerald, '17, 1916.

STUDIES AND ARTICLES

Baldwin (M)
Boyd
Cleaton
Farrar
Hatcher
Kunitz (L)
Linn
Markey
Rosenfeld (M)
Shaw
Stewart
Van Doren (C)
Ward
Ward (T)
Wilson (D)

Anonymous. "F. Scott Fitzgerald." *AB.*, Mar. 1922, pp. 20–25; Bishop, John P. "The missing all." *VQR.*, Jan. 1937, pp. 107–21; Mosher, John C. "That sad young man." *N.Yer.*, Apr. 17, 1926, pp. 20–21; Wilson, Edmund. "Imaginary conversations, Mr. Van Wyck Brooks and Mr. Scott Fitzgerald." *NR.*, Apr. 30, 1924, pp. 249–54. For references to reviews, see *BRD.*, 1920, 1922–23, 1925–26, 1934–35.

Waldo Fleming, *pseud. See* **Thames Williamson**

John Gould Fletcher, 1886–

Born in Little Rock, Arkansas, January 3, 1886. His father, a Confederate veteran, came from a Scotch-Irish pioneer family that had gone to Tennessee before the Revolution, and had moved westward in the early nineteenth century. His mother, an accomplished and gifted woman of German and Danish extraction, gave him his early education.

He was instructed in Latin and German by tutors, and at eleven he entered school. High school in Little Rock (1899–1902) and a year at Phillips (Andover) Academy came next, and in 1903 he entered Harvard. In his senior year his father died, leaving money enough to give him independence; and he left college.

He had been writing since boyhood, and had read widely in English and French literature; and he settled in Boston for a year of writing. After a trip to Puye and Mesa Verde with an expedition from the Peabody Museum, he sailed to Italy in the summer of 1908. He proceeded in the next year to London and in the year following to Paris, where he devoted himself to the study of French literature. Returning to London, he worked on his own poetry and published five volumes in 1913.

Recognition was not immediate, but *Irradiations, Sand and Spray*, was published in America in 1915. He joined the Imagists and became an experimenter, a leading exponent of the "new" poetry and of polyphonic prose. He was a devotee of Whitman and the French Symbolists, and was deeply interested in modern French art and in the music of Debussy.

At the outbreak of the war he returned to the United States. Feeling oppressed, after residence in New York, Arkansas, and Boston, and trips in the West, by what he felt to be a lack of unity in America, he returned to England in 1916. He remained there, making occasional visits to this country for lectures and the gathering of material, until 1933, when he came back to live in Arkansas. He has contributed to the *Yale Review*, the *Dial*, the *North American Review*, the *Nation*, and other magazines. In 1933 the University of Arkansas conferred upon him an honorary doctorate. In 1939 he received the Pulitzer Prize for Poetry.

"I hold the chief function of literature to be the transposition of life into the medium of language, rather than any direct attempt to imitate life," Fletcher writes. "I do not therefore regard very highly literature that aims at realism—I prefer fantasy and imagination to exact documentation. Literature should interpret and order the facts of life; and the interpretation I try to present is always colored by the imagination. In short, I suppose you would call me a romantic, insofar as I rate the sensibility of the author as being of equal importance with the material with which he deals. I also question the social importance of literature—it seems to me a matter of individual taste."

For further comment, see Critical Survey, pp. 142–43, 177–78.

BIBLIOGRAPHY

Poems

The book of nature, 1910–1912, 1913; The dominant city (1911–1912), 1913; Fire and wine, 1913; Fool's gold, 1913; Visions of the evening, 1913; Irradiations, Sand and spray, 1915; Goblins and pagodas, 1916; Japanese prints . . . with illustrations by Dorothy Pulis Lathrop, 1918; The tree of life, 1918; Breakers and granite, 1921; Preludes and symphonies, 1922 (a reissue of Irradiations, sand and spray; Goblins and pagodas); Parables . . . with woodcut frontispiece by John J. A. Murphy, 1925; Branches of Adam, 1926; The black rock, 1928; XXIV elegies, 1935; The epic of Arkansas, 1936; * Selected poems, 1938.

Essays and Studies

La poésie d'André Fontainas, 1919 (cover-title; pamphlet); The Chapbook, a monthly miscellany, no. 11 (vol. II) May 1920. Some contemporary American poets, 1920 (cover-title; pamphlet); The crisis of the film, 1929 (pamphlet); I'll take my stand, the South and the agrarian tradition by twelve southerners, 1930; The two frontiers, a study in historical psychology, 1930 (English ed., Europe's two frontiers . . . a study of the historical forces at work in Russia and America as they will increasingly affect European civilization, 1930).

Biography

Paul Gauguin, his life and art . . . with ten illustrations, 1921; John Smith—also Pocahontas, 1928.

Autobiography

Life is my song, the autobiography of John Gould Fletcher, 1937.

Translations

The dance over fire and water by Elie Faure authorized translation, 1926; The reveries of a solitary by Jean Jacques Rousseau translated with an introduction, 1927.

STUDIES AND ARTICLES

Aiken
Hughes
Kreymborg
Kunitz
Lowell
Lowell (P)
Lowell (T)
† Manly
Monroe
Taupin
Untermeyer
Untermeyer (N)

Blackmur, Richard P. "Versions of Fletcher." *P.*, Mar. 1936, pp. 344–47; Crawford, Nelson A. "Philosophy in verse." *P.*, Jan. 1928, pp. 216–18; Deutsch, Babette. "A lost address." *P.*, Sept. 1938, pp. 347–51; Dudley, Dorothy. "Poet and theorist." *P.*, Oct. 1916, pp. 43–47; Fulkerson, Baucum. "John Gould Fletcher." *SR.*, July–Sept. 1938, pp. 275–87; Grudin, Louis. "A naïve mystic." *P.*, Feb. 1923, pp. 270–75; Henderson, Alice C. "Irradiations, sand and spray." *P.*, Oct. 1915, pp. 44–47; Lowell, Amy. "Mr. Fletcher's verse." *NR.*, May 15, 1915, pp. 48–49; Monroe, Harriet. "John Gould Fletcher." *P.*, Jan. 1926, pp. 206–10; Pound, Ezra. "Peals of iron." *P.*, Dec. 1913, pp. 111–13; Sherry, Laura. "Fletcherian colors." *P.*, Dec. 1921, pp. 155–57; Warren, Robert P. "A note on three southern poets." *P.*, May 1932, pp. 103–13; Zabel, Morton D. "Dust discrowned." *P.*, Jan. 1929, pp. 222–24. For references to reviews, see *BRD.*, 1915–16, 1918–19, 1921–22, 1929–30, 1935, 1937–38.

Norman Foerster, 1887–

Born in Pittsburgh April 14, 1887, the son of a composer, Adolph Foerster, and the grandson of a portrait painter. He attended a public high school in Pittsburgh and Carnegie Institute, where he was president of the Andrew Carnegie Naturalists' Club. In high school he was a pupil of Willa Cather. He wrote articles on ornithology for Pittsburgh newspapers and the Boston *Evening Transcript.* He continued his study at Harvard, where, in his own words, he was "bowled over by Babbitt in one semester," and worked also under Bliss Perry, Kittredge, and Neilson. He was an editor of the *Harvard Monthly* and took the Sohier Prize and the Bowdoin Prize. He graduated in 1910.

The next year he was an instructor at the University of Wisconsin, and he took the master's degree there in 1912. He remained at Wisconsin until 1914, when he accepted an assistant professorship at the University of North Carolina. He held this position until 1919, when he was made a full professor. He remained at North Carolina until 1930. In that year he became the director of the School of Letters at the University of Iowa. He has taught Paul Green, Howard Mumford Jones, Wilbur Lang Schramm, and Paul Engle. In 1920–21 he studied at Oxford, and in 1927–28, he was Kenan Traveling Professor in Paris and Munich. He has lectured in the University of Munich and the University of Berlin.

For further comment, see Critical Survey, pp. 186, 200, 204.

BIBLIOGRAPHY

Criticism

The intellectual heritage of Thoreau, 191–?; Nature in American literature, studies in the modern view of nature, 1923; Ralph Waldo Emerson, his appreciation of nature, 1924; Emerson on the organic principle in art, 1926; American criticism, a study in literary theory from Poe to the present, 1928; The American scholar, a study in litterae inhumaniores, 1929; * Toward standards, a study of the present critical movement in American letters, 1930; The American state university, its relation to democracy, 1937; The future of the liberal college, 1938.

Textbooks

Outlines and summaries, a handbook for the analysis of expository essays, 1915; American ideals, a syllabus for the use of extension centres, 1918; Sentences and thinking, 1918 (with John M. Steadman, jr.; pamphlet); Sentences and thinking, a practice book in sentence making by Norman Foerster . . . and J. M. Steadman, jr., 1919 (2d rev. ed., Writing and thinking, a handbook of composition and revision, 1931).

Edited and Compiled Works

Essays for college men, education, science, and art chosen by Norman Foerster, Frederick A. Manchester, Karl Young, 1913; Selected literary essays from James Russell Lowell with introduction by Will David Howe . . . and Norman Foerster, 1914; Essays for college men, second series, chosen by Norman Foerster, Frederick A. Manchester, Karl Young, 1915; The chief American prose writers, selected prose by Franklin, Irving, Cooper, Poe, Hawthorne, Emerson, Thoreau, Lowell, and Holmes, 1916; American ideals edited by Norman Foerster . . . and W. W. Pierson, jr., 1917; English poetry of the nineteenth century, a connected representation of poetic art and thought from 1798 to 1914 edited by G. R. Elliott . . . and Norman Foerster, 1923; American poetry and prose, a book of readings, 1607–1916, edited by Norman Foerster . . . under the general editorship of Robert Morss Lovett, 1925; Recent American poetry and prose, a book of readings, 1855–1916, Walt Whitman to Carl Sandburg, under the general editorship of R. M. Lovett, 1925 (also pub. as Recent American literature, a book of readings, 1855–1916, Walt Whitman to Carl Sandburg, 1925?; repr. from American poetry and prose); The reinterpretation of American literature, some contributions toward the understanding of its historical development edited by Norman Foerster for the American literature group of the Modern language association, 1928; American critical essays, XIXth and XXth centuries edited with an introduction, 1930; Humanism and America, essays on the outlook of modern civilisation, 1930; Adventures in American literature, revised edition, edited by H. C. Schweikert . . . Rewey Belle Inglis . . . John Gehlmann . . . Norman Foerster . . . illustrated by Charles Perry Weimer and George Bell, 1936.

STUDIES AND ARTICLES

Eliot
Grattan
Kallen
Mercier
Tate

Booker, John M. "Norman Foerster, the American scholar, a study in litterae inhumaniores." *E.Studien*, May 1931, pp. 448–51; Fischer, Walther. "Norman Foerster, American criticism, a study in literary theory from Poe to the present." *E.Studien*, Apr. 1932, pp. 445–50; French, Robert D. "American scholar." *NEQ.*, Jan. 1931, pp. 94–107; Knickerbocker, William S. "A humanist tract for the times." *SR.*, July–Sept. 1929, pp. 366–69; Lüdeke, Heinrich. "Norman Foerster, the American scholar." *E.Studien*, Feb. 1931, pp. 319–22; Pochmann, Henry A. "Norman Foerster, (ed.) Humanism and America, essays on the outlook of modern civilization." *E.Studien*, Aug. 1931, pp. 149–54. For references to reviews, see *BRD.*, 1915–17, 1923, 1925, 1928–31, 1937.

Webster Ford, *pseud. See* Edgar Lee Masters

Waldo (David) Frank, 1889–

Born August 25, 1889, in Long Branch, New Jersey. His father was a New York lawyer interested in political reform.

He was a precocious child and wrote a play before he was five. A novel accepted by a New York publisher when the author was but sixteen was withdrawn by his father. He attended public schools in New York City and spent a year in a school in Switzerland. Although at Yale he rebelled against the usual conventions, he graduated in 1911 with Phi Beta Kappa rank; and in his senior year he ran a column of drama criticism in the New Haven *Courier-Journal.*

After graduation and some time spent ranching in Wyoming, he continued newspaper writing on the New York *Evening Post* and the New York *Times.* In this period also he wrote plays. In 1913 he left for a year abroad; and when he returned, after staying in Paris and Germany and studying the French and German stage, he settled on the East Side as a free-lance writer. In 1916, with James Oppenheim, he founded the *Seven Arts*, which he edited until its demise in 1917. During the war he was a conscientious objector.

Besides his own work and his translations and editions of French authors he has written for *Scribner's*, *Harper's*, the *Adelphi*, and important magazines in Mexico and South America; and he has been American correspondent for *La Nouvelle Revue Française* and *Europe*, as well as corresponding editor for the *New Republic.* He has lectured on modern art and literature at the New School for Social Research in New York.

Often identified with radical groups, he has referred to himself as a "philosophical social revolutionary." Among his friends are Sherwood Anderson, Romain Rolland, Jules Romains, Jacques Copeau, and Leo Ornstein. His first wife, Margaret Naumberg, famous as the founder of the Walden School, was a leader in applying psychoanalysis to education. Although he has been called obscure, he regards himself as perfectly unmistakable to minds less limited than those of most who judge him. In Spain, France, and Russia, and especially in the Latin-American countries, he has been extraordinarily well received. A lecture tour to South America in 1929 met with wide public acclain. He found audiences who had actually read his books, and was given the use of a government airplane for this travel. His lectures were published at once in Spain. Frank attributes the weaker impression he has made in England and America to the ineptitude of most people of those countries at coping with aesthetic and philosophical problems, and deplores the fact that most serious books are likely to be absorbed at second hand and never really read.

BIBLIOGRAPHY

Novels

The unwelcome man, a novel, 1917; The dark mother, a novel, 1920; * City block, 1922; Rahab, 1922; Holiday, 1923; Chalk face, 1924; The death and birth of David Markand, an American story, 1934; The bridegroom cometh, 1938.

Essays and Studies

The art of the Vieux Colombier, a contribution of France to the contemporary stage, 1918; Our America, 1919 (English ed., The new America . . . with an introduction by Hugh Walpole, 1922); The novel of tomorrow and the scope of fiction by twelve American novelists, 1922; Salvos, an informal book about books and plays, 1924; Five arts by Waldo Frank, Mark Turbyfill, Karleton Hackett, C. J. Bulliet, W. Roger Greeley. Man and his world, volume ten, edited by Baker Brownell, 1929; * The re-discovery of America, an introduction to a philosophy of American life, 1929; Primer mensaje a la América hispana, 1930; America hispana, a portrait and a prospect, 1931; In the American jungle ⟨1925–1936⟩ . . . photographic decorations by William H. Field, 1937.

History and Travel

Virgin Spain, scenes from the spiritual drama of a great people, 1926; Dawn in Russia, the record of a journey, 1932.

Plays

New Year's eve, a play, 1929.

Biographical Sketches

Time exposures by Search-light [*pseud.*] being portraits of twenty men and women famous in our day, together with caricatures of the same by divers artists, to which is appended an account of a joint report made to Jehovah on the condition of man in the city of New York ⟨1926⟩ by Julius Caesar, Aristotle, and a third individual of less importance, 1926.

Translations

Deux psaumes pour chant et orchestre (version pour chant et piano par l'auteur), musique de Ernest Bloch, poèmes adaptés de l'hébreu par Edmond Fleg, traductions anglaises de Waldo Frank, psaume 114 . . . psaume 137, 1919 (cover-title; sheet music; 2 vols.); Psaume 22 pour baryton et grand orchestre, réduction pour chant et piano par l'auteur, musique de Ernest Bloch, transcription française d'Edmond Fleg, traduction anglaise de Waldo Frank, 1919 (cover-title); Lucienne by Jules Romains, 1925

Editor

Plays by Molière, introduction by Waldo Frank, 1924; Tales from the Argentine edited with a foreword by Waldo Frank, translated from the Spanish by Anita Brenner, illustrations by Mordecai Gorelik, 1930; The collected poems of Hart Crane edited with an introduction, 1933; America & Alfred Stieglitz, a collective portrait, edited by Waldo Frank, Lewis Mumford, Dorothy Norman, Paul Rosenfeld, & Harold Rugg, with 120 illustrations, 1934.

STUDIES AND ARTICLES

Baldwin (M)
Beach (T)
Hatcher
Herrmann
Horton
Instituto de las Españas en los Estados Unidos. Waldo Frank in America Hispana. 1930
Kunitz (L)
† Munson, Gorham B. Waldo Frank, a study. [c1923]
Munson (S)
O'Brien
Rosenfeld (M)
Schreiber

Cestre, Charles. "Trois romans de Waldo Frank." *RAA.*, Feb. 1925, pp. 232–35; Colum, Mary M. "Rahab." *Freeman*, Apr. 26, 1922, pp. 162–64; Davidson, Donald. "Waldo Frank." *AR.*, Dec. 1934, pp. 233–38; Gilman, Lawrence. "Franko-American." *N.Amer.Rev.*, Jan. 1920, pp. 133–37; Glicksberg, Charles I. "Waldo Frank, critic of America." *SAQ.*, Jan. 1936, pp. 13–26; Hughes, Merritt Y. "The rediscovery of America." *SR.*, July–Sept. 1929, pp. 379–81; Jocelyn, John. "Getting at Waldo Frank." *SR.*, Oct.–Dec. 1932, pp. 405–14; Josephson, Matthew. "Instant note on Waldo Frank." *Broom*, Dec. 1922, pp. 57–60; Rees, Richard. "Waldo Frank's masterpiece." *Adel.*, June 1935, pp. 147–53; Reid, John T. "Spain as seen by some contemporary writers." *Hisp.*, May 1937, pp. 139–50; Rosenfeld, Paul. "The novels of Waldo Frank." *D.*, Jan. 1921, pp. 95–105; Salaberry, Robert C. "North America looks south." *Liv.Age*, June 1, 1930, pp. 424–29; Salaberry. "Waldo Frank et le nouvel idéal américain, à propos de conférences en Argentine." *MF.*, Apr. 15, 1930, pp. 353–62; Valle, Rafael H. "Diálogo con Waldo Frank." *Univ.(Mex.)*, Jan. 1937, pp. 36–44. For references to reviews, see *BRD.*, 1917, 1919–20, 1922–24, 1926–27, 1929–32, 1934–35, 1937, 1939.

Robert (Lee) Frost, 1875–

Born in San Francisco, of New England extraction, March 26, 1875. His father, a southern sympathizer during the Civil War, taught school, worked on a Democratic newspaper, and entered politics. When he died almost penniless, the mother brought the little boy of ten back to New England, and settled in her parents' home in Lawrence, Massachusetts, where she taught school.

When he was but fourteen he sold a poem, and in school he applied himself to such good effect that in 1892 he graduated valedictorian of his class. For a few months he attended college at Dartmouth; but the regular discipline irked him, and he returned to Lawrence to be a bobbin boy in a mill. After other jobs, including the teaching of Latin in his mother's school and reporting and editing on a weekly paper, he married (1895) and in 1897 enrolled at Harvard.

He remained only two years, studying especially the classics, in which he made high marks, and drifted back to teaching, newspaper work, and even shoemaking. In 1900 he moved to a farm near Derry, New Hampshire, and from 1905 to 1911 he taught English at the Pinkerton Academy at Derry. In 1911–12 he taught psychology at the New Hampshire State Normal School.

For years publishers had been unreceptive to his literary work; and, feeling that poetry was better received in England than in the United States, he sold his farm in 1912 and moved to England, settling in Buckinghamshire and later (1914) moving to a farm in Hertfordshire, where he was a neighbor of Wilfrid Gibson and Lascelles Abercrombie.

A Boy's Will and *North of Boston* were published in England and made him well known; then the war brought him, now famous, home to New England. He settled near Franconia, New Hampshire, on a farm; and in 1916 he was made professor of English at Amherst, where he taught until 1938. His career there has been broken by two years (1921–23) spent at the University of Michigan as poet in residence and another (1925–26) passed at the same institution as fellow in letters.

A recipient of honorary degrees from many colleges and universities, Frost has been made an associate fellow of Pierson College at Yale; and he was a founder of the Bread Loaf School of English at Middlebury College in Vermont. He has received the Pulitzer Prize three times: in 1924 for *New Hampshire;* in 1931 for his *Collected Poems;* and in 1937 for *A Further Range.* The *Collected Poems* also took the first poetry award of the Russell Laines Memorial Fund. Twice he has won prizes from *Poetry*, and in 1916 he was Phi Beta Kappa poet at Harvard. In 1939 he received the gold medal of the National Institute of Arts and Letters, and was appointed as first incumbent of the new Ralph Waldo Emerson Fellowship in poetry at Harvard. The February 1939 number of *Touchstone* (Amherst College) was devoted to Frost, and the April 1939 number of *American Prefaces* (Iowa City) was a gesture of homage to him. He is a member of the American Academy of Arts and Letters.

He has made recordings of a number of his poems, including "The Death of the Hired Man."

With the independence that has marked his career, Frost has remained aloof from any literary and political factions and has refused to be hurried into publication.

For further comment, see Critical Survey, pp. 135–36.

BIBLIOGRAPHY

Poems

Twilight, 1894 (cover-title; 2 copies printed); A boy's will, 1913; North of Boston, 1914; Mountain interval, 1916; New Hampshire, a poem with Notes and Grace notes . . . with woodcuts by J. J. Lankes, 1923; Selected poems, 1923 (enl. ed., 1928; 3d ed., 1934); Housewarming at the fireside of The Hampshire bookshop, the fifteenth of February, nineteen hundred and twenty-four, Northampton, Massachusetts, 1924 (folder); Several short poems, 1924 (caption-title; leaflet); Dust in the eyes, 1928 (broadside); West-running Brook, 1928; Birches, 1929 (leaflet); Christmas trees, a poem . . . sent to you with holiday greetings from Ann & Joseph Blumenthal, 1929 (pamphlet; also issued with 3 variant title pages); The cow's in the corn, a one-act Irish play in rhyme, 1929; The lovely shall be choosers, 1929 (pamphlet); Collected poems, 1930; A hillside thaw, 1930? (broadside); My November guest, 1930? (broadside); The runaway, 1930? (broadside); The sound of the trees, 1930? (broadside); The Augustan books of poetry, Robert Frost, 1932 (cover-title); The lone striker, 1933 (cover-title; pamphlet); Two tramps in mud-time, a new poem . . . sent with holiday greetings from Elinor & Robert Frost, Christmas, 1934, 1934 (pamphlet; also issued with 5 variant title pages); The Gold Hesperidee, 1935 (pamphlet); Mending wall, 1935 (broadside); Neither out far nor in deep, a poem . . . woodcut by J. J. Lankes. Sent with holiday greetings at Christmas 1935 from Elinor & Robert Frost, 1935 (pamphlet; also issued with 7 variant title pages); Three poems, 1935 (pamphlet); Book six. A further range, 1936 (also pub. as A further range . . . Book six, 1936); From snow to snow . . . Storm fear, January. A winter Eden, February. To the thawing wind, March. Blue-butterfly day, April. Spring pools, May. The tuft of flowers, June. The mountain, July. The oven bird, August. The cow in apple time, September. The road not taken, October. Good-bye and keep cold, November. Stopping by woods on a snowy evening, December, 1936 (pamphlet); Selected poems . . . chosen by the author, with introductory essays by W. H. Auden, C. Day Lewis, Paul Engle, and Edwin Muir, 1936; To a young wretch, 1937 (pamphlet); * Collected poems, 1939.

Play

A way out, a one act play, 1929.

Essays

Amherst alumni council news. Education by poetry, a meditative monologue . . . Supplement to vol. IV, number 4, March, 1931, reprinted from Amherst graduates' quarterly, Feb., 1931, 1931 (cover-title; pamphlet); King Jasper, a poem by Edwin Arlington Robinson, with an introduction by Robert Frost, 1935.

STUDIES AND ARTICLES

† Allegheny college, Meadville, Pa. Library. An exhibition of the work of Robert Frost in connection with the opening of the John Scott Craig reading room in the Reis library and the delivery of the John C. Sturtevant lecture. 1938 (pamphlet)

Blankenship

Bowdoin

Bowles, Ella S. Let me show you New Hampshire . . . with an introduction by Kenneth Roberts. 1938

Boynton

Boynton (H)

Boynton (L)

Boynton (S)

Braithwaite

Brenner

Bruns

† Clymer, William B. and Green, Charles R. Robert Frost, a bibliography . . . foreword by David Lambuth. 1937

Coffin, Robert P. New poetry of New England: Frost and Robinson. 1938

Cohen (M)

Cook

Cox, Sidney. Robert Frost, original "ordinary man." [c1929]

Crockett

Deutsch

Elliott, George R. The cycle of modern poetry, a series of essays toward clearing our present poetic dilemma. 1929

Erskine

Farrar

† Ford, Caroline. The less traveled road, a study of Robert Frost. 1935 (pamphlet)

Garnett

Gillis

Green (C)

Halleck

Holliday, Robert C. Literary lanes and other byways. [c1925]

Holt, Henry, and co., *firm, pub-*

lishers. Robert Frost, the man and his work. [1923] (cover-title; pamphlet)
Holt, Henry, & company, inc., *firm, publishers*. Robert Frost, the man and his work. [1936] (cover-title; leaflet)
† Howes, Martin K., *bookseller*. Robert Frost, first editions of his books and other Frost material. 1937 (cover-title; mimeographed; stapled)
† Johnson (1929)
† Johnson (1932)
† Johnson (1936)
Jones
Kreymborg
Kunitz (L)
Lewisohn (E)
Loggins
Lowden
Lowell
Lowell (T)
Mallory
† Manly
Maynard
Michaud (P)
Monroe
Munson, Gorham B. Robert Frost, a study in sensibility and good sense. 1927
National
New
New Hampshire federation of women's clubs. An anthology of New Hampshire poetry. [c1938]
Phelps
Recognition of Robert Frost, twenty-fifth anniversary, edited by Richard Thornton. [c1937]
Schreiber
† Schwartz (O)
Sergeant
Sessions
Smith
Squire
† Taylor
Untermeyer
Untermeyer (C)
Untermeyer, Louis. Doorways to poetry by Louis Untermeyer in consultation with Bertha Evans Ward . . . and Ruth M. Stauffer [c1938]
Untermeyer (M)
Untermeyer (N)
Van Doren
Van Doren (A)
† Van Doren (M)
Vočadlo
Ward
Weirick
† Wesleyan university, Middletown, Conn. Library. Robert Frost, a chronological survey compiled in connection with an exhibit of his work at the Olin memorial library, Wesleyan university, April 1936. 1936 (comp. by L. R. Thompson)
Weygandt, Cornelius. The White hills, mountain New Hampshire, Winnepesaukee to Washington. [c1934]
Whipple
Wood

Anonymous. "Robert Frost." *AB.*, May 1923, pp. 304–08; † Anonymous. "Robert Frost, a check-list bibliography." *Reading and Collecting*, Sept. 1937, p. 15; Aykroyd, George O. "The classical in Robert Frost." *P.Lore*, Winter 1929, pp. 610–14; † Boutell, Henry S., *comp.* "A bibliography of Robert Frost." *Col.*, Part 2, Art. 9, pp. 8–10, 1930; Boynton, Percy H. "Robert Frost." *EJ.*, Oct. 1922, pp. 455–62; Cestre, Charles. "Amy Lowell, Robert Frost, and Edwin Arlington Robinson." *JHAM.*, Mar. 1926, pp. 363–88; Collamore, H. Bacon. "Some notes on modern first editions." *Col.*, Summer 1938, pp. 354–56; Cox, Sidney H. "New England and Robert Frost." *NMQ.*, May 1934, pp. 89–94; Cox. "The sincerity of Robert Frost." *NR.*, Aug. 25, 1917, pp. 109–11; Dabbs, James M. "Robert Frost and the dark woods." *YR.*, Spring 1934, pp. 514–20; Dabbs. "Robert Frost, poet of action." *EJ.*, June 1936, pp. 443–51; DeVoto, Bernard. "The critics and Robert Frost." *SRL.*, Jan. 1, 1938, pp. 3–4, 14–15; Dudley, Dorothy. "The acid test." *P.*, Mar. 1924, pp. 328–35; Elliott, George R. "The neighborliness of Robert Frost." *Nation*, Dec. 6, 1919, pp. 713–15; Elliott. "An undiscovered America in Frost's poetry." *VQR.*, July 1925, pp. 205–15; Engle, Paul. "About Robert Frost." *American Prefaces*, April 1939, p. 100; Farrar, John. "Robert Frost and other green mountain writers." *EJ.*, Oct. 1927, pp. 581–87; Feuillerat, Albert. "Poètes américains d'aujourd'hui, M. Robert Frost." *RDM.*, Sept. 1, 1923, pp. 185–210; Fisher, Dorothy C. "Robert Frost's hilltop." *AB.*, Dec. 1926, pp. 403–05; Freeman, John. "Robert Frost." *Merc.*, Dec. 1925, pp. 176–87; Garnett, Edward. "A new American poet." *A.Mo.*, Aug. 1915, pp. 214–21; Hillyer, Robert. "Robert Frost 'lacks power.'" *NEQ.*, Apr. 1932, pp. 402–04; Holden, Raymond. "North of Boston." *N.Yer.*, June 6, 1931, pp. 24–27; † Johnson, Merle D. and Hopkins, Frederick M., *eds.* "American first editions, a series of bibliographic check-lists . . . number 16, Robert (Lee) Frost 1875– by Frederic G. Melcher." *PW.*, Jan. 6, 1923, p. 24; Jones, Llewellyn. "Robert Frost." *AR.*, Mar. 1924, pp. 165–71; Melcher, Frederic G. "Robert Frost & his books." *Col.*, 1930, Part 2, Art. 9, pp. 1–7; Mitchell, Stewart. "Notes on nightingales." *NEQ.*, Apr. 1932, pp. 404–07; Monroe, Harriet. "Frost and Masters." *P.*, Jan. 1917, pp. 202–07; Monroe. "A frugal master." *P.*, Mar. 1929, pp. 333–36; Monroe. "Robert Frost." *P.*, Dec. 1924, pp. 146–53; Moore, Merrill. "Poetic agrarianism, old style." *SR.*, Oct.–Dec. 1937, pp. 507–09; Munson, Gorham B. "Robert Frost." *SRL.*, Mar. 28, 1925, pp. 625–26; Munson. "Robert Frost and the humanistic temper." *AB.*, July 1930, pp. 419–22; Newdick, Robert S. "The early verse of Robert Frost and some of his revisions." *AL.*, May 1935, pp. 181–87; Newdick. "Robert Frost and the American college." *JHE.*, May 1936, pp. 237–43; Newdick. "Robert Frost and the dramatic." *NEQ.*, June 1937, pp. 262–69; Newdick. "Robert Frost and the sound of sense." *AL.*, Nov. 1937, pp. 289–300; Newdick. "Robert Frost as teacher of literature and composition." *EJ.*, Oct. 1936, pp. 632–37; Newdick. "Robert Frost looks at war." *SAQ.*, Jan. 1939, pp. 52–59; Newdick. "Three poems by Robert Frost." *AL.*, Nov. 1935, p. 329; Pound, Ezra. "A boy's will." *P.*, May 1913, pp. 72–74; Pound. "Modern georgics." *P.*, Dec. 1914, pp. 127–30; Schwartz, Karl. "Robert Frost, ein dichter neu englands." *H.Aus.*, Mar. 1935, pp. 46–50; Sergeant, Elizabeth S. "Robert Frost, a good Greek out of New England." *NR.*, Sept. 30, 1925, pp. 144–48; Untermeyer, Louis. "Play in poetry." *SRL.*, Feb. 26, 1938, pp. 3–4, 14, 16; Van Doren, Carl. "The soil of the puritans, Robert Frost, quintessence and subsoil." *Cent.*, Feb. 1923, pp. 629–36; Van Doren, Mark. "The permanence of Robert Frost." *A.Schol.*, Mar. 1936, pp. 190–98; Warren, Clarence H. "An original, ordinary man, Robert Frost and his vision of nature." *Bookm.*, Jan. 1931, pp. 242–44; Warren, Robert P. "Hawthorne, Anderson, and Frost." *NR.*, May 16, 1928, pp. 399–401; Wheelwright, John. "Back to the old farm." *P.*, Oct. 1936, pp. 45–48; Wilson, James S. "Robert Frost, American poet." *VQR.*, Apr. 1931, pp. 316–20. For references to reviews, see *BRD.*, 1915–16, 1923, 1928–31, 1936, 1939.

Zona Gale, 1874–1938

Born August 26, 1874, in Portage, Wisconsin, of New England ancestry. She was precocious and at seven had written and illustrated a book of fiction and verse. When she was twelve she published a poem in a local newspaper; at thirteen she wrote a novel; when in high school she wrote a play; and at sixteen she wrote a story for the Milwaukee *Evening Wisconsin.*

She attended local schools and graduated in 1895 from the University of Wisconsin. She had difficulty with mathematics and languages but took three prizes for fiction and verse. She received her master's degree there in 1899.

After finishing college she joined the staff of the *Evening Wisconsin.* She proceeded to the New York *World* in 1901, and until 1904 wrote continually with no response but rejections.

In that year she returned to Portage, determined to fulfill her promise and devote herself to writing. In the same year a story was accepted, and in 1911 another took a two thousand dollar prize awarded by the *Delineator. The Neighbours*, a one-act play, was performed by the Wisconsin Players in Milwaukee and the Washington Square Players in New York in 1912, and in 1921 *Miss Lulu Bett*, dramatized from her novel, won the Pulitzer Prize.

Miss Gale's reputation as an author was secure, and she subsequently published plays, poems, essays, and stories, and her work appeared in the *Smart Set*, the *Atlantic Monthly*, the *Yale Review*, the *New Republic*, and other magazines. She also lectured at many colleges and universities, and established the Zona Gale Scholarships for the aid of young writers.

She spent the rest of her life in Portage, where her husband, William L. Breese, was in business. In her native town and state she was known for her public-spirited generosity and for her activity in behalf of the La Follettes. She was chairman of the Wisconsin Free Library Commission and a member of the board of regents of the state university (1923–29), and she held honorary degrees from the University of Wisconsin, Rollins College, and Wooster College. On a trip to Chicago, she fell a victim of pneumonia and died December 27, 1938.

Miss Gale was a lover of the small town as an American institution and once described it as "a place where one can find plenty of leisure, where people talk about their gardens, where children have a place in the home, where members of the family come into intimate contact with each other, and where there is not that air of breathlessness that plants one impression on top of another so fast that all are lost."

For further comment, see Critical Survey, pp. 46–47.

BIBLIOGRAPHY

Novels

Romance Island . . . with illustrations by Hermann C. Wall, 1906; Mothers to men, 1911; Christmas, a story . . . with illustrations by Leon V. Solon, 1912; Heart's kindred, 1915; A daughter of the morning . . . illustrated by W. B. King, 1917; Birth, 1918; * Miss Lulu Bett, 1920; Faint perfume, 1923; Preface to a life, 1926; Borgia, 1929; Papa La Fleur, 1933; Light woman, 1937; Magna . . . introduction by Charles Hanson Towne, 1939.

Short Stories

The loves of Pelleas and Etarre, 1907; Friendship Village, 1908; Friendship Village love stories, 1909; Neighborhood stories . . . with frontispiece, 1914; Peace in Friendship Village, 1919; Yellow gentians and blue, 1927; Bridal pond, 1930; Old-fashioned tales, 1933.

Reminiscences and Essays

When I was a little girl . . . with illustrations by Agnes Peeton, 1913; Portage, Wisconsin, and other essays, 1928.

Plays

Wisconsin plays, Thomas H. Dickinson, editor, original one-act plays from the repertory of the Wisconsin dramatic society [by] Zona Gale, Thomas H. Dickinson, William Ellery Leonard, 1914 (The neighbours by Zona Gale); The neighbours, 1920; Miss Lulu Bett, an American comedy of manners, 1921; Uncle Jimmy, 1922; Mister Pitt, 1925; Evening clothes, 1932; Faint perfume, a play with a prologue and three acts, 1934; The clouds, 1936?

Poems

The secret way, 1921.

Biography

Frank Miller of Mission inn, 1938.

Pamphlets

Civic improvement in the little towns, 1913; What women won in Wisconsin by Zona Gale, Wisconsin member of National council woman's party, 1922 (cover-title).

STUDIES AND ARTICLES

The Biographical cyclopaedia of American women, volume III, compiled under the supervision of Erma Conkling Lee [and] Henry C. Wiley. 1928
Follett, Wilson. Zona Gale, an artist in fiction. [1923?] (pamphlet)
Gale, Zona. Birth . . . with a preface by William Lyon Phelps. 1923
Gale, Zona. Miss Lulu Bett, edited by Lella B. Kelsey. [c1928]
Garland
Heath
† Herrmann
† Johnson (1929)
† Johnson (1932)
† Johnson (1936)
Kunitz (L)
Latham, Jean L. The Christmas party dramatized by Jean Lee Latham from the story by Zona Gale. [c1930] (pamphlet)
† Manly
Mantle
Marble
Michaud
National
Overton
Overton (A)
Overton (WW)
Quinn
Salzman
Stedman
Untermeyer (H)
Van Doren (C)

Anonymous. "Zona Gale." *AB.*, Apr. 1923, pp. 168–72; Hurst, Fannie. "Zona Gale." *AB.*, Apr. 1921, p. 123; Smith, Bertha W. "Zona Gale." *W.*, Mar. 1927, pp. 95–96. For references to reviews, see *BRD.*, 1906–09, 1911–15, 1917–23, 1925–30, 1933, 1937–38.

Hamlin Garland, 1860–

Born September 16, 1860, on a farm near West Salem, Wisconsin. When he was still very young, his father, a pioneer from New England, and a soldier in the Civil War, took the family west to Iowa. Hamlin Garland did farm work and went to school. Earning money as a day laborer for his father, he saved enough to enable him to complete the course at the Cedar Valley Seminary at Osage, Iowa, in 1881. He was an industrious reader, and was influenced considerably by Joaquin Miller and William Dean Howells.

Upon finishing school, he traveled in the Middle West and the East, and taught school in Illinois. In 1883, in a landseekers' boom, he staked a claim to a farm in Dakota, but in the next year he mortgaged it and went east to Boston to prepare himself for teaching and writing. He gave lectures on literature and drama, taught private classes, and read diligently at the public library. He studied, and later taught, at Moses True Brown's Boston School of Oratory.

Visits to the Middle West confirmed him in his feeling of the importance of the realistic writing he had been attempting, and, after a year in New York, he settled in Chicago in 1893. For many years he was an important figure in the literary and artistic world of the city. His friends included Lorado Taft, who became his brother-in-law, Henry B. Fuller, and Eugene Field; and he organized the Cliff Dwellers in 1907. In this same period he bought the house in West Salem where he had been born and brought his parents back to it, and in 1898 he made a trip to the Yukon valley.

In 1916, desiring to live in the center of the American literary world, he moved to New York. Literary recognition came in the years ensuing. He was made a member of the American Academy of Arts and Letters in 1918, and in 1922 he was awarded the Pulitzer Prize for biography for *A Daughter of the Middle Border*. Honorary degrees have been conferred upon him by the University of Wisconsin (1926) and Northwestern University (1933), and in 1931 he won the Roosevelt Memorial Association Medal.

In the course of his literary career and his travels in this country and abroad Garland has been personally acquainted with many of the major writers of his time, among them Holmes, Howells, Whitman, Stephen Crane, Mark Twain, Barrie, Conrad, and Kipling, and his volumes of reminiscences treat of such friendships. His interest in spiritualism is reflected in *Forty Years of Psychic Research*. It is the "Middle Border" series, however, treating of the trials and hardships, as well as the pleasures, of pioneer life, for which he is best known. As uncompromising as when, in his early days in Boston, he refused, even though in need of the money, to write romantic love stories and startled conservative people by speaking for the single tax, he has striven to record truth about a significant aspect of American culture; and some of his works, as records of this civilization, have been translated and read abroad.

"In general I have tried to present life as I have seen it and lived it," he writes. "My aim was to present the average men and women in their normal modern relationships. It would have been easier to pick out the occasional murder, seduction, or adulterous episode, but I preferred to write drab or dull books of the ordinary well-meaning folks with whom my life was associated. Even in my stories of the mountains and the plains I kept away from the customary saloon and dance hall characters. The formulated pandering which had become so successful did not interest me. As I hate jazz music—or rather jazz tomtomming—and the obscene whine of the crooner so I avoid the adulterous cabaret play. In short I am an evolutionist and I do not enjoy seeing men and women returning to the morality of monkeys."

For further comment, see Critical Survey, pp. 45, 63, 87, 178.

BIBLIOGRAPHY

Novels

Jason Edwards, an average man, 1892; A little Norsk, or, Ol' pap's Flaxen, 1892; A member of the third house, a dramatic story, 1892; A spoil of office, a story of the modern West, 1892; Rose of Dutcher's Coolly, 1895; The spirit of Sweetwater, 1898 (also pub. as Witch's gold, being a new and enlarged version of "The spirit of Sweetwater," 1906); Boy life on the prairie . . . illustrated by E. W. Deming, 1899; The eagle's heart, 1900; Her mountain lover, 1901; The captain of the Gray-horse troop, a novel, 1902; Hesper, a novel, 1903; The light of the star, a novel, 1904; The tyranny of the dark, 1905; The long trail, a story of the northwest wilderness, 1907; Money magic, a novel . . . illustrated by J. N. Marchand, 1907 (also pub. as Mart Haney's mate, 1922); The Moccasin Ranch, a story of Dakota, 1909; Cavanagh, forest ranger, a romance of the mountain West, 1910; Victor Ollnee's discipline, 1911; The forester's daughter, a romance of the Bear-Tooth Range, 1914.

Short Stories

* Main-travelled roads, six Mississippi Valley stories, 1891; Prairie folks, 1893; Wayside courtships, 1897; Other main-travelled roads, 1910; They of the high trails, 1916; The book of the American Indian written by Hamlin Garland . . . pictured by Frederic Remington, 1923.

Poems

Prairie songs: being chants rhymed and unrhymed of the level lands of the great West . . . with drawings by H. T. Carpenter, 1893; Iowa, O Iowa! . . . with a rubber-cut by Richard Gates, 1935.

Plays

Under the wheel, a modern play in six scenes, 1890.

Family Chronicles

* A son of the middle border . . . with illustrations by Alice Barber Stephens, 1917 (part 2); A daughter of the middle border, 1921 (part 3); Trail-makers of the middle border . . . illustrated by Constance Garland, 1926 (part 1); Back-trailers from the middle border . . . illustrations by Constance Garland, 1928 (part 4).

Reminiscences

Roadside meetings . . . decorations by Constance Garland, 1930 (vol. 1); Companions on the trail, a literary chronicle . . . decorations by Constance Garland, 1931 (vol. 2); My friendly contemporaries, a literary log . . . decorations by Constance Garland, 1932 (vol. 3); Afternoon neighbors, further excerpts from a literary log, 1934 (vol. 4).

Essays

Money, land and transportation. I. "A new declaration of rights," Hamlin Garland. II. "The farmer, investor, and the railway," C. Wood Davis. III. "The Independent party and money at cost," R. B. Hassell, 1892 (pamphlet; cover-title); Crumbling idols, twelve essays on art dealing chiefly with literature, painting, and the drama, 1894; Out-of-door Americans, Mr. John Burroughs, Mr. Ernest Seton-Thompson, Dr. David Starr Jordan, Mr. Ernest Ingersoll, Mr. Hamlin Garland, and others, 1901 (cover-title); Commemorative tribute to James Whitcomb Riley . . . read in the 1920 lecture series of the American academy of arts and letters, 1922 (pamphlet); Commemorative tributes to: Metcalf by Royal Cortissoz, Bartlett by Royal Cortissoz, Sherman by Hamlin Garland. Prepared for the American academy of arts and letters. 1927, 1927 (pamphlet); The westward march of American settlement . . . with illustrations by Constance Hamlin Garland, 1927; Joys of the trail, 1935.

Biography

Ulysses S. Grant, his life and character, 1898; Learn one thing every day. February 2, 1920. Serial no. 196. The Mentor. Theodore Roosevelt by Hamlin Garland. Department of biography, volume 7, number 24, twenty cents a copy, 1920 (cover-title: pamphlet); A pioneer mother, 1922 (pamphlet).

Miscellany

The trail of the goldseekers, a record of travel in prose and verse, 1899.

Psychical Research

The shadow world, 1908; Forty years of psychic research, a plain narrative of fact, 1936; The mystery of the buried crosses, a narrative of psychic exploration . . . illustrated with photographs and endpapers, 1939.

Verses Set to Music

A breezy song, Do you fear the wind? lyric by Hamlin Garland, music by Geoffrey O'Hara, 1935 (cover-title; sheet music).

Selected Works

Prairie song and western story . . . illustrated by Constance Garland, 1928 (comp. by Stella S. Center, with appendix).

Editor

Old favorites from the McGuffey readers edited by Harvey C. Minnich . . . associate editors: Henry Ford, James M. Cox, Hamlin Garland, Mark Sullivan, John H. Finley, William L. Bryan, John W. Studebaker, Hugh S. Fullerton, Simeon D. Fess, William F. Wiley, John F. Carlisle, Walter D. Cocking, Charles B. Glenn. 1836–1936, 1936.

STUDIES AND ARTICLES

Baldwin

The Barnwell bulletin. Printed for students and alumni of the Central high school of Philadelphia by the Mary Gaston Barnwell foundation, the Philadelphia trust company, trustee. Vol. 2, Apr. 1925, no. 12. The Barnwell addresses. 9, Memories of the middle border, Mr. Hamlin Garland. 10, Thirty years among the Labrador fishermen, Dr. Wilfred T. Grenfell. 11, The education of Abraham Lincoln, Dr. Cheesman A. Herrick. 12, The American Rhodes scholar at Oxford,

Dr. Frank Aydelotte. [1925] (cover-title; pamphlet)
[Blanc, Marie T.] Questions américaines . . . 1901
Blankenship
Boynton (L)
Brigham
Chamberlain
Chubb, Edwin W. Stories of authors, British and American. 1926
The Cyclopedia of American biography. Supplementary edition, with an introduction by Rossiter Johnson . . . extending the original work in six volumes issued by the present publishers in 1915. Volume XII, non-alphabetical with index, edited by L. E. Dearborn. 1931
Dickinson
Dondore
Garland, Hamlin. The long trail edited by Barbara Grace Spayd. 1935
Garland, Hamlin. Main-travelled roads, being six stories of the Mississippi Valley . . . with an introduction by W. D. Howells and decorations by H. T. Carpenter. 1893
Haas
Hamlin Garland memorial. 1939 (pamphlet)
Harkins
Harley, Joel A., *ed.* Distinguished Americans for young Americans. [c1935]
Hazard
Hicks
Howells, William D. Life in letters of William Dean Howells edited by Mildred Howells. 1928 (2 vols.)
† Johnson (1932)
† Johnson (1936)
Keiser
Kunitz (L)
Lieberman
[Macmillan, *firm, publishers, New York.*] Hamlin Garland, a son of the middle border. [1926] (pamphlet)
Maillard
† Manly
Marble
Markey
Mencken
National
Parrington
Pattee
Pattee (N)
Pattee, Fred L. Tradition and jazz. [c1925]
Pollard
Quinn
† Taylor
Van Doren (C)
Williams

Anonymous. "Garland in ghostland, a book-study." *Arena*, Aug. 1905, pp. 206–16; Bowen, Edwin W. "Hamlin Garland, the middlewest short-story writer." *SR.*, Oct. 1919, pp. 411–22; Gale, Zona. "National epics of the border." *YR.*, July 1922, pp. 852–56; Howells, William D. "Mr. Garland's books." *N.Amer.Rev.*, Oct. 1912, pp. 523–28; † Johnson, Merle D. and Hopkins, Frederick M., *eds.* "American first editions, a series of bibliographic check-lists . . . number 30, Hamlin Garland, 1860, compiled by E. B. Hill." *PW.*, Apr. 21, 1923, p. 1270; Mott, Frank L. "Exponents of the pioneers." *Pal.*, Feb. 1930, pp. 61–66; Nevins, Allan. "Garland and the prairies." *Lit.Rev.*, Aug. 19, 1922, pp. 881–82; Raw, Ruth M. "Hamlin Garland, the romanticist." *SR.*, Apr.–June 1928, pp. 202–10; Van Doren, Carl. "Hamlin Garland." *Nation*, Nov. 23, 1921, pp. 596–97. For references to reviews, see *BRD.*, 1906–11, 1914, 1916–17, 1921, 1923, 1926, 1928, 1930–32, 1934, 1936.

Frederick Garrison, *pseud. See* **Upton Sinclair**

Katharine Fullerton Gerould, 1879–

Born in Brockton, Massachusetts, February 6, 1879, the daughter of the Reverend Bradford Morton and Julia M. (Ball) Fullerton. She was educated in France, at Miss Folsum's School in Boston, and at Radcliffe College (A.B., 1900; A.M., 1901). When the *Century* magazine instituted a contest for the best short story by a college graduate of 1900, she competed and won the prize.

In 1901 she began teaching English composition at Bryn Mawr, where she inaugurated the narrative-writing course still in the curriculum. She remained "reader in English" until her marriage, taking a leave of absence in 1908–09 for a winter in England and France. In 1910 she married Professor Gordon Hall Gerould of Princeton; and since that time she has led a secluded existence divided between her domestic life with her husband and her two children, and her writing.

"You will see, I know," she wrote, in reply to a critic's request for details, "why I can't be biographically interesting. It is the old case of the happy countries that have no history. They don't make good reading. I don't even attend literary gatherings or keep up relations outside my own circle of friends. My husband is the sole critic before the event, and I suppose the fact is that we take out all these things in talk together rather than with other people or in larger groups. But what is there to be said about any hearthstone?"

For further comment, see Critical Survey, pp. 86–87, 155.

BIBLIOGRAPHY

Novels

A change of air . . . illustrated by H. J. Mowat, 1917; Lost Valley, a novel, 1922; Conquistador, 1923; The light that never was, 1931.

Short Stories

* Vain oblations, 1914; The great tradition and other stories, 1915; Valiant dust, 1922.

Essays

Modes and morals, 1920; Ringside seats, 1937.

Description and Travel

Hawaii, scenes and impressions . . . illustrated from photographs, 1916; The aristocratic West, 1925.

Literary Criticism

Edith Wharton, a critical study, 192–? (cover-title; pamphlet).

STUDIES AND ARTICLES

Burgess
† Manly
Sherman, Stuart P. The genius of America, studies in behalf of the younger generation. 1923

Bennett, Charles A. "Life through fiction, the knight's move." *AB.*, May 1926, pp. 308–12; Brooks, Cleanth, Jr., and Warren, Robert P. "Dixie looks at Mrs. Gerould." *AR.*, Mar. 1936, pp. 585–95; Gerould, Katharine F. "Newest woman." *A.Mo.*, May 1912, pp. 606–11; Gilman, Lawrence. "The strange case of Mrs. Gerould." *N.Amer.Rev.*, Apr. 1920, pp. 564–68. For references to reviews, see *BRD.*, 1914–17, 1920, 1922–23, 1925, 1931, 1937.

Ellen (Anderson Gholson) Glasgow, 1874–

Born April 22, 1874, in Richmond, Virginia. Her father, coming from a family of lawyers and teachers, was the well-to-do manager of an ironworks that had supplied cannon for the Confederate army. A delicate child, she was educated at home by her mother and tutors; and when she was still very young her aunt read to her from the novels of Scott. At thirteen she was reading Browning; and five years later, for all her sheltered southern upbringing, she was making a study of political economy. "At eighteen," she says, "I was the only Socialist, I think, in Richmond." At first she did not use her name in her writing, in order not to hurt the friends she was unavoidably attacking.

She became much absorbed in the problem of freeing women from the traditions that kept them in their "position"; and, when she was gathering material for *The Voice of the People*, she broke precedent by attending, surreptitiously, the state Democratic convention in Virginia. She has lived in New York and traveled far and wide, but she lives and works now in her old home in Richmond, where she can enjoy her flower garden. She is a member of the National Institute of Arts and Letters and holds an honorary degree from the University of North Carolina. In recent years her interest in politics has subsided and yielded place to her major concern with letters.

". . . I was born a novelist," she declares, "and literature has been my long vocation. I have felt for it all my life more a passion than a preference. Though I am interested in every aspect of the profession of letters, naturally my special province is the field of imaginative literature." Heartily in accord with the reaction against old-fashioned sentimental evasions of reality, she feels, nevertheless, that realism, in its excesses of horror, has gone too far and has failed to achieve a just representation of life. ". . . The novel, in my opinion," she writes, "must justify itself by some increased understanding of life. It must illuminate experience." She values finished pattern, as well as material, and thinks that style acts as a preservative in literature. She admires, accordingly, the work of English writers, especially that of Virginia Woolf. In recent literature, however, she has enjoyed many American novels, and she believes that in this country the historical novel has reached a high stage of development. "Our best work lies, I think, in a realistic portrayal of the American scene outside the big cities," she writes. "Our worst work is certainly in the form of the 'tough' mystery story."

For further comment, see Critical Survey, pp. 42–43, 59, 63.

BIBLIOGRAPHY

Novels

The descendant, a novel, 1897 (anonymous); phases of an inferior planet, 1898; The voice of the people, 1900; The battle-ground . . . illustrated by W. F. Baer and W. Granville Smith, 1902; The deliverance . . . a romance of the Virginia tobacco fields with illustrations by Frank E. Schoonover, 1904; The wheel of life, 1906; The ancient law, 1908; The romance of a plain man, 1909; The miller of Old Church, 1911; Virginia, 1913; Life and Gabriella, the story of a woman's courage . . . frontispiece by C. Allan Gilbert, 1916; The builders, 1919; One man in his time, 1922; * Barren ground, 1925; The romantic comedians, 1926; They stooped to folly, a comedy of morals, 1929; The sheltered life, 1932; Vein of iron, 1935.

Short Stories

The shadowy third and other stories . . . frontispiece by Elenore Plaisted Abbott, 1923 (English ed., Dare's gift and other stories, 1924).

Poems

The freeman and other poems, 1902.

Collected Works

The Old Dominion edition of the works of Ellen Glasgow . . . , 1929–33 (8 vols.); Ellen Glasgow . . . Virginia edition, 1938 (12 vols.).

STUDIES AND ARTICLES

Cabell
Cabell, James B. Of Ellen Glasgow. 1938
† Cappon
Clark (E)
Collins (T)
Cooper
Cooper (F)
Field, Louise M. Ellen Glasgow, novelist of the old and the new South. An appreciation . . . together with a critical essay and an index to her works. [c1923] (pamphlet)
Harkins (LP)
Hatcher
† Johnson (1932)
† Johnson (1936)
Kaltenbacher
Kilmer
Kunitz (L)
Lawrence (S)
Library
Loggins
Luccock
† Manly
† Mann, Dorothea L. Ellen Glasgow . . . with critical essays and a bibliography. 1927 (pamphlet)
Marble
Meade
Mims
National
Overton (H)
Overton (W)
Overton (WW)
Pattee (N)
Quinn
[Scribner, *firm, publishers, New York.*] The Virginia edition of the works of Ellen Glasgow ⟨limited⟩ sold only by subscription. [1938] (pamphlet; prospectus)
Sherman (C)
Sherman, Stuart P., Haardt, Sara, and Clark, Emily. Ellen Glasgow, critical essays. 1929 (pamphlet)
Smith
Van Doren (C)
Wellington, Amy. Women have told, studies in the feminist tradition. 1930

Canby, Henry S. "Ellen Glasgow, ironic tragedian." *SRL.*, Sept. 10, 1938, pp. 3–4, 14; Chamberlayne, Lewis P. "Virginia." *SR.*, Oct.–Dec. 1913, pp. 500–03; Clark, Emily. "Ellen Glasgow." *VQR.*, Apr. 1929, pp. 182–91; Cooper, Frederic T. "Ellen Glasgow." *AB.*, Aug. 1909, pp. 613–18; Freeman, Douglas S. "Ellen Glasgow, idealist." *SRL.*, Aug. 31, 1935, pp. 11–12; Haardt, Sara. "Ellen Glasgow and the south." *AB.*, Apr. 1929, pp. 133–39; Mann, Dorothea L. "Ellen Glasgow, citizen of the world." *AB.*, Nov. 1926, pp. 265–71; Marcosson, Isaac F. "The personal Ellen Glasgow." *AB.*, Aug. 1909, pp. 619–21; Meade, Julian R. "Ellen Glasgow, a true genius." *W.*, Oct. 1930, pp. 239–41; Mims, Edwin. "The social philosophy of Ellen Glasgow." *JSF.*, Mar. 1926, pp. 495–503; Overton, Grant. "Ellen Glasgow's arrow." *AB.*, May 1925, pp. 291–96; Parker, William R. "Ellen Glasgow, a gentle rebel." *EJ.*, Mar. 1931, pp. 187–94; Rogers, Cameron. "Realism from the romantic south." *WW.*, May 1925, pp. 99–102; Tyler, Annie M. "Ellen Glasgow." *BNM.*, Aug. 1912, pp. 843–48; Villard, Léonie. "L'oeuvre d'Ellen Glasgow, romancière américaine." *RAA.*, Dec. 1933, pp. 97–111; Wilson, James S. "Ellen Glasgow, ironic idealist." *VQR.*, Winter 1939, pp. 121–26; Wilson. "Ellen Glasgow's novels." *VQR.*, Oct. 1933, pp. 595–600; Wilson. "Two American novels." *VQR.*, Oct. 1935, pp. 620–25. For references to reviews, see *BRD.*, 1906, 1908–09, 1911, 1913, 1919, 1923, 1925–26, 1929, 1932, 1935.

Susan Glaspell, 1882–

Born July 1, 1882, in Davenport, Iowa. She was educated at Drake University in Des Moines. After graduation she served as statehouse and legislative reporter for the Des Moines *Daily News*, and subsequently she reported for the *Capital*. The short story "A Jury of her Peers" is the result of her observation when she was reporting a murder trial. Her work began to appear in the magazines, and *The Glory of the Conquered* was successful enough to make it possible for her to spend a year in the Latin Quarter of Paris.

After her return she lived for a time on a ranch in Idaho, then settled in Provincetown, Massachusetts. In 1913 she married George Cram Cook, with whom she threw herself into the little-theater movement. They organized the Provincetown Players, and presented plays in a theater built on a wharf in Provincetown. Miss Glaspell served as actor, author, and producer. They continued their work in New York in the Playwrights' Theatre, a converted stable in Greenwich Village.

In 1922 they made a trip to Greece, where, in the next year, Mr. Cook died. In 1925 Miss Glaspell married Norman Matson, author and critic, with whom she lives on Cape Cod.

Alison's House, her play based upon the life of Emily Dickinson, was produced by Eva Le Gallienne at the Civic Repertory Theatre in New York, December 1, 1930, and received the Pulitzer Prize for the season 1930–31.

For further comment, see Critical Survey, p. 123.

BIBLIOGRAPHY

Plays

The Provincetown plays. Second series: Freedom: John Reed. Enemies: Neith Boyce and Hutchins Hapgood. Suppressed desires: George Cram Cook and Susan Glaspell, 1916; Trifles, 1916; Suppressed desires, 1917 (with George Cram Cook); The people and Close the book, two one-act plays, 1918; Plays, 1920 (Trifles; The people; Close the book; The outside; Woman's honor; Bernice; Suppressed desires, in collaboration with George Cram Cook; Tickless time, in collaboration with George Cram Cook. English ed., Trifles and six other short plays [two of them written in collaboration with George Cram Cook], 1926; omits Bernice); * Inheritors, a play in three acts, 1921; The verge, a play in three acts, 1922; Bernice, a play in three acts, 1924; Three plays, 1924 (binder's title. The verge; Inheritors; Bernice); Tickless time, a comedy in one act by Susan Glaspell in collaboration with George Cram Cook, 1925; The comic artist, a play in three acts by Susan Glaspell and Norman Matson, 1927; Alison's house, a play in three acts, 1930.

Novels

The glory of the conquered, the story of a great love, 1909; The visioning, a novel, 1911; Fidelity, a novel, 1915; Brook Evans, 1928 (also pub. as The right to love, 1930); Fugitive's return, 1929; Ambrose Holt and family, 1931.

Short Stories

Lifted masks, stories, 1912; Looking after Clara . . . a contest selection arranged by Lilian Holmes Strack, 1926 (pamphlet); Whom mince pie hath joined together . . . a contest selection arranged by Lilian Holmes Strack, 1926 (pamphlet); A jury of her peers, 1927.

Biography

Greek coins, poems by George Cram Cook, with memorabilia by Floyd Dell, Edna Kenton, and Susan Glaspell, 1925; The road to the temple, 1926.

STUDIES AND ARTICLES

Brigham
Clark
Dickinson (P)
Goldberg
Kunitz (L)
Lewisohn (E)
Lewisohn, Ludwig. The drama and the stage. [c1922]
† Manly
Mantle (C)
Mayorga (S)
Moses (A)
Quinn
† Quinn (H)
Sinclair
Skinner
Van Doren
Van Doren (A)
Ward

Crawford, Bartholow V. "Susan Glaspell." *Pal.*, Dec. 1930, pp. 517–21; Lewisohn, Ludwig. "Susan Glaspell." *Nation*, Nov. 3, 1920, pp. 509–10; Lewisohn. "The verge." *Nation*, Dec. 14, 1921, pp. 708–09. For references to reviews, see *BRD.*, 1909, 1911–12, 1915, 1920–21, 1927–31.

Laura Riding Gottchalk. *See* Laura Riding

Laura Riding Gottschalk. *See* Laura Riding

Tom Graham, *pseud.* *See* Sinclair Lewis

Anne Green, 1899–

Born in Savannah, Georgia, November 11, 1899, of a distinguished Southern family of Scotch-Irish descent. Before she was a year old her family moved to France, and her father became established with an American firm as its agent in Paris, where Miss Green has spent most of her life and where she lives now. She was educated at home and in a large French school, the Lycée Molière. Before she was eighteen she entered war service as a nurse. She traveled in both this country and Europe after the war, and began to write articles for newspapers. At the suggestion of the president of E. P. Dutton and Company she tried her hand at novel-writing, and finished *The Selbys* in 1930.

She lives with her brother, Julian Green, the distinguished French novelist, in an apartment in Paris.

For further comment, see Critical Survey, p. 67.

BIBLIOGRAPHY

Novels

The Selbys, 1930; Reader, I married him, 1931; Marietta, 1932; A marriage of convenience, 1933 (English ed., Painter's despair, 1933); Fools rush in, 1934; That fellow Perceval, 1935; Winchester house, 1936; 16 rue Cortambert, a novel, 1937; Paris, a novel, 1938; The silent duchess, 1939.

Translation

A crime by Georges Bernanos, 1936.

STUDIES AND ARTICLES

Kunitz (L)

Steell, Willis. "Anne and Julian Green." *AB.*, Aug. 1932, pp. 349–53. For references to reviews, see *BRD.*, 1925, 1930–38.

Paul (Eliot) Green, 1894–

Born March 17, 1894, on a farm near Lillington, North Carolina. Although he came of a landowning family, he worked in the fields and came to have an intimate knowledge of the Negroes and great affection for them. One year he was champion cotton-picker in his county.

His early education was slight, as he had only a few months each year for school; but he entered Buie's Creek Academy and graduated in 1914. Then he taught school for two years and played semiprofessional baseball in the summers to earn his college expenses.

He entered the University of North Carolina in 1916, and in his freshman year wrote a play that won a class prize. Leaving the university in the next year to go to war, and feeling that he might never live to publish anything more, he issued at his own expense a book of verse. After service in the army as private, corporal, sergeant, sergeant major, and second lieutenant, he returned to the university in 1919, and graduated in 1921.

In his study of drama he had come under the influence of Professor Frederick H. Koch, and he remained for a year of graduate work. After a year of further study at Cornell he came back to teach philosophy at the University of North Carolina in 1923, and he has been there ever since.

He was active in little-theater groups, and most of his early plays were given by the Carolina Playmakers. A short play, *The No 'Count Boy*, produced by the Dallas Little Players, won the Belasco Trophy in the Little Theater Tournament of 1925. *In Abraham's Bosom*, presented in New York in 1926–27 by the Provincetown Players, was forced to close; but it was awarded the Pulitzer

Prize for the season and was revived with success. The author studied abroad in 1928 and 1929 on a Guggenheim fellowship, and has written scenarios in Hollywood. In 1925 he edited a literary quarterly, *The Reviewer*. His historical pageant, *The Lost Colony*, was written for the 350th anniversary of Virginia Dare's birth, August 18, 1937. It was acted on Roanoke Island during the summers of 1937–39.

Green, who has said publicly that he has no dramatic technique, thinks that it is illogical to try to fit a story into a form built upon an artificial arrangement of scenes, climaxes, and dénouement, and says that he tells his stories directly, episode after episode.

For further comment, see Critical Survey, p. 116.

BIBLIOGRAPHY

Plays

Day by day, a comedy of farm life . . . issued by Dept. of rural social organization, N.Y. State college of agriculture, Cornell university, Ithaca, N.Y., 1923 (cover-title; mimeographed); In Aunt Mahaly's cabin, a Negro melodrama in one act, 1925; The Lord's will and other Carolina plays . . . illustrated from the photographs of the original productions of the plays with a foreword by Frederick H. Koch, 1925 (The Lord's will; Blackbeard; Old Wash Lucas: the miser; The no 'count boy; The old man of Edenton; The last of the Lowries); Lonesome road, six plays for the Negro theatre . . . with an introduction by Barrett H. Clark, 1926 (In Abraham's bosom; White dresses; The hot iron; The prayer-meeting; The end of the row; Your fiery furnace); The field god and In Abraham's bosom, 1927; The man who died at twelve o'clock, a Negro comedy in one act, 1927; In the valley and other Carolina plays, 1928 (In the valley; Quare medicine; Supper for the dead; Saturday night; The man who died at twelve o'clock; Unto such glory; The no 'count boy; The man on the house; The picnic; In Aunt Mahaly's cabin; The goodbye); * In Abraham's bosom, 1929; The last of the Lowries, a play of the Croatan outlaws of Robeson county, North Carolina, 193–; The no 'count boy, play in one act, 193–; * The house of Connelly and other plays: The house of Connelly, Potter's field, Tread the green grass, 1931; Fixin's, the tragedy of a tenant farm woman by Erma and Paul Green, 1934; The Lord's will, a tragedy of a country preacher, play in one act, 1934; Roll sweet chariot, a symphonic play of the Negro people, in four scenes, 1935 (rev. ed. of Potter's field); Shroud my body down, a play in four scenes . . . with four rubber-cuts by Richard Gates, 1935; White dresses, drama in one act, 1935; Hymn to the rising sun, a play in one act, 1936; Johnny Johnson, the biography of a common man in three acts . . . music by Kurt Weill, 1937; The lost colony, an outdoor play in two acts (with music, pantomime, and dance), 1937; The southern cross, a play in one act, 1938; Out of the South, the life of a people in dramatic form, 1939 (The house of Connelly; The no 'count boy; Saturday night; The field god; Quare medicine; The hot iron; In Abraham's bosom; Unto such glory; Supper for the dead; Potter's field; The man who died at twelve o'clock; White dresses; Johnny Johnson; Hymn to the rising sun; The lost colony).

Novels

The laughing pioneer, 1932; This body the earth, 1935.

Short Stories

Wide fields, 1928.

Criticism

Modern plays and playwrights [by] Caro Mae Green Russell, with some notes on the theater and the screen by Paul Green, 1936 (pamphlet).

Study Outlines

University extension division. University of North Carolina extension bulletin. Contemporary American literature, a study of fourteen outstanding American writers by Paul Green . . . and Elizabeth Lay Green . . . A program for women's clubs issued by the Bureau of public discussion, 1925.

Compiler

The lost colony song-book, songs, hymns, dances, and other music from the play, The lost colony by Paul Green, with additional lyrics. Special music by Lamar Stringfield, additional settings by Lamar Stringfield and Adeline McCall, 1938.

STUDIES AND ARTICLES

Berkeley, Reginald C. The house of Connelly [i.e. "Carolina"] adapted to the screen . . . from the play by Paul Green . . . [1933] (mimeographed)
Block
Brown (U)
Clark
Clark, Barrett H. Paul Green. 1928 (pamphlet)
Clark (E)
Cohen (M)
Eaton (D)
Green
Green, Paul and Green, Elizabeth A. Twentieth-century American literature by Marjorie N. Bond, a revision of Contemporary American literature by Paul Green and Elizabeth Lay Green. [c1933]
Halline
Hammond
Heath
Kunitz (L)
Loggins
Mantle
Mantle (C)
† Quinn (H)
Roanoke island historical association, inc. The lost colony, souvenir and program, 1587–1937, 350th anniversary celebration of the beginning of Anglo-American civilization with the founding of the Roanoke island colonies, and of the birth of Virginia Dare, first child born of English parents in America, and an historical guide. Published by the Roanoke island historical association, inc. . . . Donoh Hanks, editor. c1937
Russell
Skinner
Whitman

Carmer, Carl. "Paul Green, the making of an American dramatist." *TAM.*, Dec. 1932, pp. 995–1002, 1005–06; Clark, Barrett H. "Notes on Paul Green." *Drama*, Jan. 1926, pp. 137, 155; Clark. "Paul Green." *TAM.*, Oct. 1928, pp. 730–36; Jones, Howard M. "Paul Green." *Sw.R.*, Autumn 1928, pp. 1–8; Malone, Andrew E. "An American folk-dramatist, Paul Green." *Dub.Mag.*, Apr.–June 1929, pp. 31–42; Meade, Julian R. "Paul Green." *AB.*, Jan.–Feb. 1932, pp. 503–07. For references to reviews, see *BRD.*, 1926–28, 1931–32, 1935, 1937, 1939.

Horace (Victor) Gregory, 1898–

Born in Milwaukee, April 10, 1898, of English, Scotch-Irish, and German extraction. He was tutored at home, and enjoyed the use of an uncle's large private library. He studied painting at the Milwaukee Academy of Fine Arts and entered the German-English Academy. When he was still in this preparatory school, he wrote a play, which was produced by a group in Milwaukee. He also wrote verses at this time.

In 1919 he entered the University of Wisconsin. He had been attracted by Byron, then Pope and Dryden, and then Landor, in English poetry; now he felt his single interest to be Latin poetry. He took part in the conduct of a student newspaper and undergraduate magazines. After his graduation in 1923 he moved to New York, living in a poor neighborhood in Chelsea, and earning his way by free-lance writing. His poems appeared in *Vanity Fair*, *Poetry*, and the *Nation*. His experiences in New York, where he was introduced to the writers and artists at work on the *New Masses*, affected him profoundly; and the poverty around him made him despise as shallow the language and imagery of the verse written for established magazines, and the indifference of his own prosperous class to so much suffering. His own poetry was now accepted only by *Poetry* until *transition* began its existence.

To support himself he read for publishers, reviewed books, and wrote film criticism for a radical weekly. In 1925 he married the poet Marya Zaturenska; she received the Pulitzer Prize for Poetry in 1938. He won the Young Poets' Award, in 1928, and the Helen Haire Levinson Prize, in 1934, both from *Poetry*, and in 1933 read the Phi Beta Kappa poem at Columbia. Since 1934 he has taught writing and lectured in poetry and criticism at Sarah Lawrence College.

"My 'new' work since 1924," he writes, "contains, briefly, the following 'influences' which affect its technic as well as its 'content': its imagery [is] derived largely from an urban environment, utilizing in poetry the technics of the radio and film; its language (or diction) is 'conversational,' rather than 'poetic' in the conventional sense; its elliptical quality of sound and image is directed toward a dramatic as well as lyrical conclusion: the poems are never narratives, and if monologues in which different characters speak, the speech is internal as well as external monologue. I believe that the cultural heritage (or mythos) as it is reasserted, transformed or crystallized within the poetic imagination of the individual is the thing we talk about when we speak of poetry: perhaps the most coherent and sophisticated discussion of this point is contained in Thomas Mann's paper which he prepared in homage to Sigmund Freud. I also believe that literature is perhaps the most useful of all the arts and that I am prejudiced in this not very original point of view because I write in English, a language in which the poetic imagination has dominated and has continued to dominate all other kinds of imagination, from Skelton's day to this. And again I believe that literature is discontinuous in its usefulness: that one poet may be of greater value today than yesterday, or that the same poet may be of minimum value tomorrow and of even greater value day after tomorrow. Paul Valéry has said all this far better than I. I believe literature rises out of the environment in which it is written and is subject to all the social, religious and moral forces of its time."

For further comment, see Critical Survey, pp. 151–52.

BIBLIOGRAPHY

Poems

Chelsea rooming house, poems, 1930 (English ed., Rooming house, 1932); No retreat, poems, 1933; A wreath for Margery . . . drawing by Alexander Byer, 1933 (cover-title; pamphlet); * Chorus for survival, 1935.

Critical Study

Pilgrim of the Apocalypse, a critical study of D. H. Lawrence, 1933.

Translations

The poems of Catullus translated by Horace Gregory with drawings by Zhenya Gay, 1931.

Editor

New letters in America, editor Horace Gregory, associate editor Eleanor Clark, 1937.

STUDIES AND ARTICLES

Deutsch Kunitz

Blackmur, Richard P. "The ribbon of craft." *P.*, July 1933, pp. 217–20; Burke, Kenneth. "The hope in tragedy." *P.*, July 1935, pp. 227–30; Humphries, Rolfe. "Catullus resartus." *P.*, Nov. 1931, pp. 93–96; Kunitz, Stanley J. "Horace Gregory's first book." *P.*, Apr. 1931, pp. 41–45. For references to reviews, see *BRD.*, 1930, 1933, 1935, 1937.

H. D. *See* Hilda Doolittle

Albert Halper, 1904–

Born in Chicago, August 3, 1904. He grew up in the slums; his father was a storekeeper and his mother a slave to housework. After graduation from high school he worked for seven years at different jobs, in a mail-order house, a factory, an office, a jeweler's, a tobacco firm, and a foundry. He wrote songs and at night studied accounting and law. After dropping both he spent fourteen months as night clerk in the central post office in Chicago, leaving the job in 1928, on the day of receiving notice of promotion.

"From then on," he wrote of himself in 1933, "I have been drifting about but writing steadily. Sketches, novels, short stories, one-act plays, have flown from my typewriter like leaves before a wind." The first short story to be published appeared in the *Dial* in 1929, and *Harper's*, the *American Mercury*, and the *New Republic* also have accepted his work. *Union Square*, his first published novel, was accepted after three previous manuscripts had been rejected by the publisher. The inspiration came to him when, in 1931, having returned from a summer spent waiting on table in a camp in the Adirondacks, he saw a man rapidly walking backward down the street. He wrote the book in poverty, living in squalor in the midst of the scenes of which he wrote. It was the Literary Guild selection for March, 1933. In 1934 he was awarded a Guggenheim fellowship and spent some months in England and on the Continent.

He works best, however, in retirement and freedom from interruption; he concentrates for days until the inspiration fails. A single experiment with life in an artists' colony showed him the interference caused by social duties and obligations. He has lived in New York and London in small flats or rooms, getting his own meals.

"I feel that any writer who considers himself a serious workman must have a 'message' or he is not worth his salt," he writes. "All the great writers in history, Tolstoi, Turgenev, Dostoevski, Zola, Flaubert, Gogol, to mention only novelists, in mirroring their times, gave impetus to the great 'push.'"

For further comment, see Critical Survey, pp. 81–82.

BIBLIOGRAPHY

Novels

* Union square, 1933; The foundry, 1934; The chute, 1937.

Sketches

Chicago side-show . . . number 6, pamphlet series one, 1932 (pamphlet); On the shore, young writer remembering Chicago, 1934.

STUDIES

Kildal

For references to reviews, see *BRD.*, 1933–34, 1937.

Owen Hatteras, *pseud.* of H. L. Mencken and George Jean Nathan

Ben Hecht, 1894–

Born in New York, February 28, 1894. He moved to the Middle West at an early age and attended high school in Racine, Wisconsin. Feeling that college represented narrowness and dogmatism, he ended his formal education at the high-school level, joined Costello's road show as an acrobat, and toured through towns in Wisconsin.

When he was still in his teens, he went to Chicago to earn money with his violin; instead, however, he became (1910) a reporter on the *Journal.* Later (1914) he joined the staff of the *Daily News*, and after the war he served in the office of the paper in Berlin.

By this time he had become notable as an iconoclastic member of the literary world of Chicago, which included such figures as Llewellyn Jones, Carl Sandburg, and Sherwood Anderson. The publication of *Erik Dorn* provoked considerable discussion, and *Fantazius Mallare* was confiscated as objectionable. Leaving the *News* in 1923, he founded the radical Chicago *Literary Times*, which he edited until 1924.

Although he had written plays for years, many of them one-act productions given by small theaters, it was with *The Front Page* (1928), in which he collaborated with Charles MacArthur, that his status as professional dramatist was established. The play ran for 276 performances in New York. A few years later he began writing for the films, and in 1937 he signed a contract, at a figure said to be the highest paid for scenario work, to write for Samuel Goldwyn. He is the author of the scenarios of *Hallelujah*, *I'm a Bum*, *Turn Back the Clock*, *Design for Living*, *Viva Villa*, *The Upper World*, *Twentieth Century*, *Shoot the Works*, *Scarface*, *Topaze;* and, with Charles MacArthur, *Crime without Passion*, and *The Scoundrel.*

Hecht has been an enthusiastic reader, especially of Arthur Symons, George Moore, Arthur Machen, Anatole France, Theophile Gautier, and the French decadents, and he has been deeply interested in psychiatry. In American literature he has expressed preference for Hawthorne and Poe, and, among more recent writers, H. L. Mencken.

For further comment, see Critical Survey, pp. 35, 48, 158.

BIBLIOGRAPHY

Novels

* Erik Dorn, 1921; Fantazius Mallare, a mysterious oath . . . drawings [by] Wallace Smith, 1922; Gargoyles, 1922; The Florentine dagger, a novel for amateur detectives, 1923; Humpty Dumpty, 1924; The kingdom of evil, a continuation of the journal of Fantazius Mallare . . . twelve full page illustrations by Anthony Angarola, 1924; Count Bruga, 1926; A Jew in love, 1931.

Short Stories and Sketches

A thousand and one afternoons in Chicago . . . design and illustrations by Herman Rosse, 1922; Cutie, a warm mamma by Ben Hecht and Maxwell Bodenheim, 1924; Broken necks, containing more "1001 afternoons," 1926; The champion from far away, 1931; Actor's blood, 1936; A book of miracles, 1939.

Plays

Minna and myself [by] Maxwell Bodenheim, 1918 (contains The master poisoner, a one-act poetic play by Maxwell Bodenheim and Ben Hecht); The hero of Santa Maria, a ridiculous tragedy in one act by Kenneth Sawyer Goodman and Ben Hecht, 1920; The wonder hat, a harlequinade in one act by Kenneth Sawyer Goodman and Ben Hecht, 1920; The hand of Siva, a melodrama by Kenneth Sawyer Goodman and Ben Hecht, 1923; The wonder hat and other one-act plays by Kenneth Sawyer Goodman and Ben Hecht, prefatory note by Thomas Wood Stevens, 1925 (The wonder hat; The two lamps; An idyll of the shops; The hand of Siva; The hero of Santa Maria); Christmas eve, a morality play, 1928; * The front page by Ben Hecht and Charles MacArthur, introduction by Jed Harris, 1928; The great magoo, a love-sick charade in three acts and something like eight scenes recounting the didoes of two young and amorous souls who nigh perished when they weren't in the hay together. This simple and slightly uncouth saga is the work of Messrs. Ben Hecht & Gene Fowler, illustrated by Herman Rosse, 1933; To Quito and back, 1937.

"Little Blue Book" Pamphlets

Broken necks and other stories, 1924; Tales of Chicago streets, 1924; Infatuation and other stories of love's misfits, 1927; Jazz and other stories of young love, 1927; The policewoman's love-hungry daughter and other stories of Chicago life, 1927; The sinister sex and other stories of marriage, 1927; The unlovely sin and other stories of desire's pawns, 1927.

Moving-Picture Scripts

Design for living, release dialogue script . . . [screen play by Ben Hecht adapted from the play by Noel Coward], 1933 (cover-title; mimeographed); Miracle in Forty-ninth street [i.e. The scoundrel] by Ben Hecht and Charles MacArthur, 1935? (caption-title; mimeographed).

Essay

Nonsenseorship by Heywood Broun, George S. Chappell, Ruth Hale, Ben Hecht, Wallace Irwin, Robert Keable, Helen Bullitt Lowry, Frederick O'Brien, Dorothy Parker, Frank Swinnerton, H. M. Tomlinson, Charles Hanson Towne, John V. A. Weaver, Alexander Woollcott, and the author of "The mirrors of Washington," edited by G. P. P. Sundry observations concerning prohibitions, inhibitions, and illegalities, illustrated by Ralph Barton, 1922.

STUDIES

Baldwin (M)
Bodenheim, Maxwell. Duke Herring. [c1931]
Hansen
Hecht, Ben. "Nothing sacred," synopsis of the film by Ben Hecht. [c1937] (pamphlet)
† Johnson (1929)
† Johnson (1932)
† Johnson (1936)
Junius Junior [*pseud.*] Pseudo-realists . . . printed for a fistful. [1931] (pamphlet)
Karsner
Kunitz (L)
† Manly
Markey
Mersand
Michaud
Nathan (P)
Nathan (TM)
Rascoe (B)
Sherman (C)
Smith
[Yessipova, Marie A.] My first husband by his first wife. [c1932]

For references to reviews, see *BRD.*, 1921–23, 1926, 1928, 1931, 1936, 1938, 1939.

Ernest Hemingway, 1898–

Born in Oak Park, Illinois, July 21, 1898, the son of a physician. As a boy he attended public schools, in which he was prominent in football and boxing, and accompanied his father on hunting trips in northern Michigan. He contributed the class prophecy to the 1917 class book of the Oak Park High School. When still in his teens he began to earn his living and took jobs as day laborer, farm hand, dishwasher, sparring partner, and writer on the Kansas City *Star*. In the war he served as volunteer in an American ambulance unit, then joined the Italian Arditi and served on the Italian front, where he was wounded. He was decorated with the Medaglia d'Argento al Valore Militare and the Croce di Guerra.

He returned to newspaper work in the United States and became foreign correspondent in the Near East and Greece for the Toronto *Star*. Proceeding to Paris, he became a correspondent for the Hearst newspapers, a prominent figure among expatriate American writers, and a friend of Ezra Pound and Gertrude Stein.

Hemingway's first signed work appeared in *Poetry*, January, 1923. His first short stories appeared in *transition* and *This Quarter*, and the *Atlantic* and *Scribner's* accepted some of his work. *The Sun Also Rises* was a best-seller. He became well known, both for his writing (he has more imitators than perhaps any other contemporary American writer) and for his passion for outdoor sports, athletics, and bull-fighting. He has contributed specimens of fish to the Academy of Natural Sciences in Philadelphia, has been vice-president of the Salt Water Anglers of America, and has been honored in the name *Neomerinthe hemingwayi*, of a species of rosefish.

After returning from France and living for a time in Florida, Hemingway became absorbed by the problems connected with the civil war in Spain. Giving generously from his own means to help raise money for ambulances, he went to Spain to aid the Loyalists by helping prepare a film, *The Spanish Earth*, showing the course of the war. He helped write the story, translated the Spanish dialogue, and wrote and recited the interlocutory comments. Before the Second National Congress of American Writers (June, 1937) he declared that writers could not avoid the realities of war in Spain and that if truth, projected vividly into the reader's experience, is the writer's objective, fascism, based upon lies backed by force, can never produce good literature. In August, 1937, he returned to Spain to write for the North American Newspaper Alliance.

For further comment, see Critical Survey, pp. 35, 66–67, 92–93.

BIBLIOGRAPHY

Novels

The sun also rises, 1926 (English ed., Fiesta, 1927); The torrents of spring, a romantic novel in honor of the passing of a great race, 1926; * A farewell to arms, 1929; To have and have not, 1937.

Short Stories

In our time, stories, 1925; * Men without women, 1927; Present-day American stories by Ernest Hemingway, Thomas Boyd, Stark Young, Morley Callaghan, Conrad Aiken, Struthers Burt, Ring W. Lardner, F. Scott Fitzgerald, 1929; God rest you merry gentlemen, 1933; Winner take nothing, 1933; The fifth column [a play] and the first forty-nine stories, 1938.

Description and Travel

Green hills of Africa . . . decorations by Edward Shenton, 1935.

Bullfighting

Death in the afternoon, 1932 (English ed., Death in the afternoon . . . with a frontispiece from a painting by Juan Gris: The bullfighter and eighty-one reproductions from photographs, 1932).

Poem

Salmagundi by William Faulkner and a poem by Ernest M. Hemingway, 1932 (pamphlet).

Play

Today is Friday, 1926 (caption-title; pamphlet).

Miscellany

Three stories: Up in Michigan, Out of season, My old man, & ten poems: Mitraigliatrice, Oklahoma, Oily weather, Roosevelt, Captives, Champs d'honneur, Riparto d'assalto, Montparnasse, Along with youth, Chapter heading, 1923 (pamphlet); in our time . . . A girl in Chicago: Tell us about the French women, Hank. What are they like? Bill Smith: How old are the French women, Hank? 1924; Introduction to Kiki of Montparnasse, 1929 (pamphlet); Death in the afternoon, 1932 (publisher's dummy); The Spanish earth . . . with an introduction by Jasper Wood, illustrations by Frederick K. Russell, 1938.

STUDIES AND ARTICLES

Anderson
Ashley
Beach (T)
Burnett
Canby (S)
Charters, James. This must be the place, memoirs of Jimmie, the barman (James Charters) as told to Morrill Cody, with an introduction by Ernest Hemingway. [c1937]
Cleaton
† Cohn, Louis H. A bibliography of the works of Ernest Hemingway. 1931
Cowley
DeVoto
Eastman
† Edgar
† Ford (E)
Forsythe (R)
Hanemann, Henry W. The facts of life, a book of brighter biography executed in the manner of some of our best or best-known writers, scriveners, & scribes . . . & illustrated by that merry wag, Herb Roth. 1930
Hartwick
Hatcher
Hemingway, Ernest. A farewell to arms . . . introduction by Ford Madox Ford. [1932]
Hemingway, Ernest. In our time, stories . . . with an introduction by Edmund Wilson. 1930
Hemingway, Ernest. The sun also rises . . . introduction by Henry Seidel Canby. [1930]
Hicks
† Johnson (1932)
† Johnson (1936)
Kildal
Kunitz (L)
Lewis
Linati
Llona
Loggins
Lundkvist
McCole
McKay
Marsh, W. Ward. One moment, please! . . . reprinted by the J. B. Savage co. without comment [from the] Cleveland plain dealer, July 24, 1938. [1938] (cover-title; leaflet)
Muller
O'Brien
Phillips
Rosenfeld
Russell, Leonard, *ed.* Parody party [by] E. C. Bentley, John Betjeman, Ivor Brown, Cyril Connolly, Francis Iles, D. B. Wyndham Lewis, Rose Macaulay, A. G. Macdonell, J. B. Morton, L. A. Pavey, Edward Shanks, G. B. Stern, Rebecca West, Douglas Woodruff, edited by Leonard Russell. Nicolas Bentley drew the pictures. [1936]
Saturday
Schreiber
† Schwartz
Schyberg
[Stein, Gertrude.] The autobiography of Alice B. Toklas. [c1933]
† Taylor
Vočadlo
Walden book shop, *Chicago*. Bib-

liographical notes on Ernest Hemingway. [1930] (leaflet)
Ward

The Wesleyan cinema club, *Middletown, Conn.* The Wesleyan cinema club, program 2, February 15, 1939. A farewell to arms (1932) adapted from Ernest Hemingway's novel, directed by Frank Borzage for Paramount, starring Helen Hayes and Gary Cooper with Adolphe Menjou. [1939] (broadside by Ralph Pendleton)
Zabel

Adams, James D. "Ernest Hemingway." *EJ.*, Feb. 1939, pp. 87–94; Anonymous. "Tiger, tiger." *SRL.*, Oct. 16, 1937, p. 8; Benchley, Robert. "Why does nobody collect me?" *Col.*, Part 18, Art. 5, pp. 1–2 (1934); Bishop, John P. "Homage to Hemingway." *NR.*, Nov. 11, 1936, pp. 39–42; Bishop. "The missing all." *VQR.*, Jan. 1937, pp. 107–21; Bütow, Hans. "Ernest Hemingway, ein schriftsteller aus U.S.A." *FZ.*, July 5, 1934, pp. 335–36; Campbell, Kenneth. "An appreciation of Hemingway." *AM.*, July 1938, pp. 288–91; Cohn, Louis H. "A note on Ernest Hemingway." *Col.*, Summer 1935, pp. 119–22; Cowley, Malcolm. "A farewell to Spain." *NR.*, Nov. 30, 1932, pp. 76–77; Cowley. "Hemingway in Madrid." *NR.*, Nov. 2, 1938, pp. 367–68; Dewing, Arthur. "The mistake about Hemingway." *N.Amer.Rev.*, Oct. 1931, pp. 364–71; Dietrich, Max. "Ernst Hemingway." *Hochl.*, Apr. 1933, pp. 89–91; Eastman, Max. "Bull in the afternoon." *NR.*, June 7, 1933, pp. 94–97; Eastman. "Red blood and Hemingway." *NR.*, June 28, 1933, p. 184; Fadiman, Clifton. "Ernest Hemingway, an American Byron." *Nation*, Jan. 18, 1933, pp. 63–64; Fadiman. "Hemingway." *N.Yer.*, Oct. 16, 1937, pp. 76–77; Fadiman. "A letter to Mr. Hemingway." *N.Yer.*, Oct. 28, 1933, pp. 58–59; Fallada, Hans. "Ernest Hemingway oder woran liegt es?" *Die Lit.*, Sept. 1931, pp. 672–74; Herrick, Robert. "What is dirt?" *AB.*, Nov. 1929, pp. 258–62; Jameson, Storm. "The craft of the novelist." *Eng.Rev.*, Jan. 1934, pp. 28–43; Johnson, Merle (ed.). "American first editions, Ernest Hemingway." *PW.*, Feb. 20, 1932, p. 870; Kirstein, Lincoln. "The canon of death." *HH.*, Jan.–Mar. 1933, pp. 336–41; Leighton, Lawrence. "An autopsy and a prescription." *HH.*, July–Sept. 1932, pp. 519–39; Lewis, Wyndham. "The dumb ox, a study of Ernest Hemingway." *AR.*, Summer 1934, pp. 289–312; Littell, Robert. "Notes on Hemingway." *NR.*, Aug. 10, 1927, pp. 303–06; Lovett, Robert M. "Ernest Hemingway." *EJ.*, Oct. 1932, pp. 609–17; Mann, Klaus. "Ernest Hemingway." *N.S.Rund.*, vol. 24, 1931, pp. 272–77; Orton, Vrest. "Some notes bibliographical and otherwise on the books of Ernest Hemingway." *PW.*, Feb. 15, 1930, pp. 884–86; Parker, Dorothy. "The artist's reward." *N.Yer.*, Nov. 30, 1929, pp. 28–31; Paul, Elliot. "Hemingway and the critics." *SRL.*, Nov. 6, 1937, pp. 3–4; Reid, John T. "Spain as seen by some contemporary writers." *Hisp.*, May 1937, pp. 139–50; Root, Edward M. "Aesthetic puritans." *Christ.Cent.*, Aug. 25, 1937, pp. 1043–45; Schwartz, Delmore. "Ernest Hemingway's literary situation." *So.R.*, Spring 1938, pp. 769–82; Stein, Gertrude. "Ernest Hemingway and the post-war decade, autobiography of Alice B. Toklas." *A.Mo.*, Aug. 1933, pp. 197–208; Wilson, Edmund. "Ernest Hemingway." *A.Mo.*, July, 1939, pp. 36–46; Wilson. "The sportsman's tragedy." *NR.*, Dec. 14, 1927, pp. 102–03. For references to reviews, see *BRD.*, 1925–27, 1929, 1932–33, 1935, 1937–38.

Josephine (Frey) Herbst, 1897–

Born in Sioux City, Iowa, of Pennsylvania-German extraction. She attended public schools, Morningside College, and the University of Iowa, and taught, did typing, and worked in a printing shop. Later, she worked in Seattle and the Middle West, and studied at the University of Washington and at the University of California, from which she graduated in 1919.

After holding jobs of different kinds in New York and reading for magazines, she went abroad for three years and spent more than a year in Germany. In 1925 she married the writer John Herrmann; and, although their home is Erwinna, Pennsylvania, where they have an old Pennsylvania-German house, she has traveled about the country with him, lived in France, Germany, and Italy, and passed winters in Florida and Mexico. In more recent years she has visited areas of trouble and unrest, including the farming region of the Middle West in 1934. "It was the time of the drought," she writes, "and I stayed for a while with many different farm families in country I had once seen green. In January of 1935 I went to Cuba and was there during the General Strike in March. I made a trip to Oriente, to the Realengo 18 where very few people, even Cubans, had ever gone, to see the association they had formed to fight forcible eviction from the land they had tilled and lived on for many years. When I came back, I left almost at once for Germany and did a series of articles for a chain of newspapers on Germany. In March of 1936 I received a Guggenheim fellowship in the field of the novel. I broke off work in February 1937 to go to Flint at the time of the sitdown strike at General Motors and when I came back I had gone too far to stop, I left for Spain. In Spain I was mostly in Madrid and in little towns along the central front. The peasants were sowing crops and they were not at base much different from the farmers in Iowa or around my home here or from the men who planted coffee and bananas in Realengo."

Miss Herbst is concerned with the breakdown of capitalist society and the shift toward collectivism, and has been interested not only in American history but in the economic struggles in this country and elsewhere today. "I am on a kind of pursuit," she says, "and neither a political slogan nor a statement of faith would give the full answer. I have followed first the kind of haunting history of my family to its natural decay and end, that history only meaningful because of its wider implication. Then I found I had to begin picking up clues of my own life and some of them went back to observations seen early in life and those in turn carried me along to a point where an automobile worker in Flint, a peasant in Cuba, a soldier in Spain had become more real and moving than any memory of my buried family, but not obliterating that family or its meaning either. . . . I have to know things through my own skin and I have found some clues and have to learn them fully as I can. How fully one may learn is something I do not know either but I am on my way. I know that as one world turns black another turns green and the entire future seems so bound up with the future of the worker and the farmer that I cannot even seem to live any more without not only closer touch but closer participation with this vital world. I speak of it here for this relationship it bears to my work, first as a necessity that would exist for me now, even if I could not write a line. I can breathe better among people who struggle and see a purpose to their existence. All my interests and living center around this fact. This country, marvelous and rich for writing, seems all the time to offer more the closer one participates in the life its workers live. Their language and their living are making new creative patterns that are the richest materials for writing and for living. I am speaking of the kind of soil that seems to me best for growth, both for living and for writing and the two are not separate. Writing is not a substitution for life but an extension of it."

For further comment, see Critical Survey, p. 82.

BIBLIOGRAPHY

Novels

Nothing is sacred, 1928; Money for love, 1929; * Pity is not enough, 1933; The executioner waits, 1934; Rope of gold, 1939.

Pamphlet

Behind the swastika, 1936 (cover-title).

STUDIES

Kunitz

For references to reviews, see *BRD.*, 1928–29, 1933–34, 1939.

Joseph Hergesheimer, 1880–

Born in Philadelphia, February 15, 1880, into a family of Pennsylvania-German stock. His father was an officer in the Coast and Geodetic Survey, and the boy was reared in a suburb of Philadelphia in the home of his maternal grandfather, a Scottish-American type-founder and hymn-writer.

Rather delicate in health, the child attended a Quaker school and pored over maps and listened to music. He accomplished little in school and read mediocre books until late in his teens, when he began reading Conrad, Turgenev, Jeremy Taylor, and George Moore. In the same period he entered upon the study of painting at the Pennsylvania Academy of the Fine Arts, and when the deaths of the other members of his family left him independent, he went to Italy for further study.

When his money gave out, he returned to the United States and began to write. Establishing himself in the mountains in Virginia, he worked for some thirteen or fourteen years, writing and rewriting, before he published his first group of magazine articles in 1913 and sold his first novel, *The Lay Anthony. The Three Black Pennys*, *Linda Condon*, and *Java Head* established his reputation. He has been a frequent contributor to the *Saturday Evening Post.*

A loving student of early furniture, old porcelain, and beautiful glass, Hergesheimer remodeled a Pennsylvania-German house on the outskirts of West Chester, Pennsylvania, and lives there with his collection of objects of art. He has done his writing in a downtown office. Although his historical books represent research and familiarity with customs of times past, he writes easily and fluently, with many revisions for polish and perfection.

For further comment, see Critical Survey, pp. 41–42, 55.

BIBLIOGRAPHY

Novels

The lay Anthony, a romance, 1914; Mountain blood, a novel, 1915; The three black Pennys, a novel, 1917; Gold and iron, 1918 (Wild oranges; Tubal Cain;

The dark fleece); * Java Head, 1919; Linda Condon, 1919; Wild oranges, 1919 (repr. from Gold and iron, 1918); The bright shawl, 1922; Cytherea, 1922 (special ed., 1921); The dark fleece, 1922 (repr. from Gold and iron, 1918); Tubal Cain, 1922 (repr. from Gold and iron, 1918); Balisand, 1924; Tampico, a novel, 1926; The party dress, 1930; The limestone tree, 1931; The foolscap rose, 1934.

Short Stories

The happy end, 1919; Tol'able David, 1923; Merry Dale, 1924; Quiet cities, 1928; Triall by armes . . . being number seventeen of the Woburn books, 1929; Love in the United States and The big shot, 1932; Tropical winter, 1933.

Autobiographical Sketches

The Presbyterian child, 1923; From an old house, 1925.

Description and Travel

San Cristóbal de la Habana, 1920; Berlin, 1932.

Biography

Sheridan, a military narrative, 1931.

History

Swords & roses, 1929.

Literary Criticism

Hugh Walpole, an appreciation . . . Together with notes and comments on the novels of Hugh Walpole, 1919; Hugh Walpole, appreciations by Joseph Conrad, Arnold Bennett, Joseph Hergesheimer, together with notes and comments on the novels of Hugh Walpole by Grant Overton, 1923 (pamphlet).

STUDIES AND ARTICLES

Adcock
Baldwin
Baldwin (M)
Beach
Beach (T)
Blankenship
Boyd
Boynton (L)
Boynton (M)
[Brown, Martin and Wellesley, Gordon W.] "Java head." [1935?] (caption-title; mimeographed)
Bruns
Burgess
Cabell
Cabell, James B. Joseph Hergesheimer, an essay in interpretation. 1921 (pamphlet)
Cabell, James B. Straws and prayer-books, dizain des diversions. 1924
Canby (D)
Clark (E)
Farrar
Garnett
Graham
Green (C)
Hartwick
Hatcher
Herrmann
† Johnson (1929)
† Johnson (1932)
† Johnson (1936)
Jones, Llewellyn. Joseph Hergesheimer, the man and his books. 1920 (pamphlet)

Knopf
Knopf (B)
Kunitz (L)
Levinson
Lewisohn (E)
Mais
† Manly
Marble
Markey
Mencken (P)
National
Overton (H)
Pattee (N)
Quinn
Rascoe
Roberts
Roberts, Kenneth L. Antiquamania edited by Kenneth L. Roberts, the collected papers of Professor Milton Kilgallen [*pseud.*] F. R. S. of Ugsworth college, elucidating the difficulties in the path of the antique dealer and collector, and presenting various methods of meeting and overcoming them. With further illustrations, elucidations, and wood-cuts done on feather-edged boards by Booth Tarkington. 1928
† Schwartz (O)
Schyberg
Sinclair
Smith
Squire
† Swire, Herbert L. A bibliography of the works of Joseph Hergesheimer. 1922
† Taylor
Van Doren
Van Doren (C)
Vočadlo
Ward (T)
Williams

Anonymous. "Hergesheimer, literary meteor or newly discovered star?" *Cur.Op.*, Feb. 1920, pp. 229–33; Anonymous. "Joseph Hergesheimer." *AB.*, May 1922, pp. 247–51; Boynton, Percy H. "Joseph Hergesheimer." *EJ.*, May 1927, pp. 335–45; Cabell, James B. "About one and another, a note as to Joseph Hergesheimer." *NYHTB.*, June 15, 1930, pp. 1, 6; Cabell. "In respect to Joseph Hergesheimer." *AB.*, Nov. 1919, pp. 267–73; Fadiman, Clifton. "The best people's best novelist." *Nation*, Feb. 15, 1933, pp. 175–77; Fischer, Walther. "Joseph Hergesheimer, ein beitrag zur neuesten amerikanischen literaturgeschichte." *JP.*, vol. 1, 1925, pp. 393–412; Gagnot, Berthe. "Un romancier américain, Joseph Hergesheimer." *RAA.*, Aug. 1926, pp. 505–10; Gray, Jerome B. "An author and his town, West Chester and Joseph Hergesheimer get used to each other." *AB.*, Apr. 1928, pp. 159–64; Haardt, Sara. "Joseph Hergesheimer's methods." *AB.*, June 1927, pp. 398–403; Hergesheimer, Joseph. "Biography and bibliographies." *Col.*, Part 8, Art. 3, pp. 1–8; (1931); † Johnson, Merle D. and Hopkins, Frederick M., *eds.* "American first editions, a series of bibliographic check-lists . . . November [!] 15, Joseph Hergesheimer, 1880–, compiled by Marston E. Drake." *PW.*, Dec. 30, 1922, p. 2221; Kelley, Leon. "America and Mr. Hergesheimer." *SR.*, Apr.–June 1932, pp. 171–93; Priestley, John B. "Joseph Hergesheimer, an English view." *AB.*, May 1926, pp. 272–80; Shaw, Vivian. "Blood and irony." *D.*, Mar. 1922, pp. 310–13; West, Geoffrey. "Joseph Hergesheimer." *VQR.*, Jan. 1932, pp. 95–108. For references to reviews, see *BRD.*, 1914–15, 1917–22, 1924, 1926, 1928–34.

Robert Herrick, 1868–1938

Born April 26, 1868, in Cambridge, Massachusetts, the son of a Boston lawyer and a descendant, through generations of New England stock, of a nephew of the English poet Herrick. His mother's father and her uncle were Congregational ministers, and another uncle was a professor at Amherst.

His education was in Cambridge, at a small private school, the public schools, and the Cambridge Latin School, where he was prepared for Harvard. He entered Harvard in 1885, but dropped out during the sophomore year for reasons of health, and traveled with a classmate to Nassau, Cuba, Mexico, California, Alaska, Yellowstone Park, Colorado, and other places at that time infrequently visited by travelers.

Returning to Harvard, he became prominent as an editor of and contributor to both the *Advocate* and the *Harvard Monthly*, almost ruining the latter financially because he published in it the first translation of Ibsen's *The Lady from the Sea.* He studied writing under Barrett Wendell and was thrown in contact with William Vaughn Moody, Robert Morss Lovett, George Santayana, and Norman Hapgood, his fellow editor on the *Monthly.* "It was to the associations formed in connection with this literary magazine," he declared later, "that I attribute my training and enthusiasm for the writer's life."

Graduating in 1890, he began teaching at the Massachusetts Institute of Technology in the English department, which was being reorganized by George Rice Carpenter to approximate Harvard practice. He was enthusiastic about writing as a creative exercise, and assumed that any intelligent person had something to say and should be encouraged, by frequent practice and careful supervision, to make it effective. In this period he wrote stories appearing in *Scribner's* and the *Atlantic.*

In 1893 he left the Institute for the new University of Chicago, where he remained for thirty years, resigning in 1923. During this time he divided his energies between writing and teaching, working with mature students of composition, and teaching contemporary literature. During a period of some fifteen years he wrote a novel about every two years, edited manuscripts, and collaborated in a secondary-school textbook. "Whether such divided allegiance to teaching and writing is a good thing for the individual or for the University is not a matter that can be settled generally," he said. "Each case is special. I should not encourage a young writer thus to divide his loyalties, but many have been obliged to do so, and have made a tolerable compromise."

After 1909 he was actually at the university only about half the year, and during the war years he spent very little time in residence. He traveled much in Europe, mainly in France and Italy. Before the outbreak of the war he began a regular Sunday article in the Chicago *Tribune*, and he spent much of 1915, 1916, and 1917 in Europe near the scenes of war, which affected him profoundly. "I realized before I left Europe in May 1917," he said many years later, "that the War meant far more to the world than the fighting, the killing of millions, and that its specious 'causes' were almost all pure fiction. I knew that it was rather a moving of cosmic forces the end of which is not yet, and that some abysmal faults in our social system were being uncovered."

After the war he traveled in California and the Southwest, spent winters in the Caribbean and Florida, and went back for visits to Europe. In 1935 he was appointed government secretary of the Virgin Islands, and his death occurred December 23, 1938, in St. Thomas. His home, "legally and sentimentally," after 1913, was his small house on two acres of land in York Village, Maine.

For further comment, see Critical Survey, pp. 47, 76–77.

BIBLIOGRAPHY

Novels

The man who wins, 1897; The gospel of freedom, 1898; The web of life, 1900; The real world, 1901 (also pub. as Jock O'Dreams, or, The real world, 1908; Jack O'Dreams, or, The real world, 1917); The common lot, 1904; * The memoirs of an American citizen, 1905; Together, 1908; A life for a life, 1910; The healer, 1911; His great adventure, 1913; One woman's life, 1913; * Clark's field, 1914; Homely Lilla, 1923; Waste, 1924; Chimes, 1926; The end of desire, 1932; Sometime, 1933.

Short Stories

Literary love-letters and other stories, 1897; Love's dilemmas, 1898; Their child, 1903; The master of the inn, 1908; The conscript mother, 1916; Wanderings, 1925.

Dog Story

Little black dog, 1931.

War Book

The world decision, 1916.

Miscellany

Methods of teaching rhetoric, 1899 (cover-title; pamphlet); Jungle law, 191–? (broadside).

Textbook

Composition and rhetoric for schools by Robert Herrick . . . and Lindsay Todd Damon, 1899 (also pub. as New composition and rhetoric for schools by Robert Herrick . . . and Lindsay Todd Damon . . . , a revision by Lindsay Todd Damon, 1911).

Editor

George Eliot's Silas Marner edited with notes and an introduction, 1895; The house of the seven gables by Nathaniel Hawthorne edited for school use, 1898; Twice-told tales by Nathaniel Hawthorne edited for school use by Robert Herrick . . . and Robert Walter Bruère, 1903.

STUDIES AND ARTICLES

Baldwin
Baldwin (M)
Björkman
Blankenship
Chamberlain
Cooper (F)
[Goodrich, John F. and Martin, John L.] The healer . . . [scenario by J. F. Goodrich and J. L. Martin adapted from the novel by Robert Herrick]. [1935] (cover-title; mimeographed)
Hansen
Hazard
Hicks
Kilmer
Kunitz
† Manly
Marble
National

New
Pattee (N)
Quinn
Robert Herrick & his work. [1914?] (cover-title; pamphlet)
Simmons, Joseph P. Working plans for New composition and rhetoric by Robert Herrick . . . and Lindsay Todd Damon . . . prepared by J. P. Simmons. [c1923]
Van Doren (C)

Anonymous. "Robert Herrick." *NR.*, Jan. 18, 1939, p. 302; Björkman, Edwin. "The Americanism of Robert Herrick." *RR.*, Mar. 1911, pp. 380–81; Cooper, Frederic T. "A prose epic of marriage." *Forum*, Aug. 1908, pp. 134–38; Cooper. "Robert Herrick." *AB.*, Dec. 1908, pp. 350–57; Hicks, Granville. "Robert Herrick, liberal." *NR.*, June 17, 1931, pp. 129–30; Howells, William D. "The novels of Robert Herrick." *N.Amer.Rev.*, June 1909, pp. 812–20; Lüdeke, Heinrich. "Robert Herrick, novelist of American democracy." *E.Studies*, April 1936, pp. 49–57; Neilson, Harald. "Robert Herrick." *P.Lore*, Sept. 1908, pp. 337–63; Van Doren, Carl. "Robert Herrick." *Nation*, Aug. 31, 1921, pp. 230–31. For references to reviews, see *BRD.*, 1906, 1908, 1910–14, 1916, 1923–26, 1931–33.

DuBose Heyward, 1885–

Born in Charleston, South Carolina, August 31, 1885. The aristocratic southern family to which he belonged suffered from the aftermath of the Civil War. When he was only two he lost his father. At nine he sold papers, and at fourteen he left school to take a job in a hardware store. After a period of illness he secured work on the Charleston waterfront with a steamboat line, and as checker in a big cotton shed. Then, with a friend as partner, he entered the insurance business, in which he was successful enough to secure some time for writing. His material had come to him in the course of his acquaintance with Negroes on the docks of Charleston, and his experience organizing them at the time of the war.

In 1918 he met Hervey Allen, and they began gathering legends of Charleston for *Carolina Chansons*. Two years later they founded the Poetry Society of South Carolina, and the duties of reading and lecturing began to interfere with Heyward's business and to build up a reputation for him as a poet. The Society became a distinctive part of the literary life of the South.

Heyward's marriage in 1923 to Dorothy Hartzell Kuhns, a playwright whom he had met at the MacDowell colony, led to his decision to give up his business; and in 1924, deciding upon authorship as a career, they moved to a farm near the Great Smoky Mountains.

Porgy, his first novel, an interpretation of Negro character, was so successful that Mrs. Heyward began working on a dramatization. Her husband worked with her; and the play was accepted and produced by the Theatre Guild, with sets by Cleon Throckmorton, direction by Rouben Mamoulian, and a Negro cast. Then followed an extended tour, an unusual reception in London, and two successful return engagements in New York. The opera *Porgy and Bess*, with music by George Gershwin and lyrics by Ira Gershwin, was produced in 1935–36 to a libretto by Mrs. Heyward and with direction by Mamoulian. Film rights to the novel *Porgy* were sold before the play was written.

Besides his books Heyward has written for American and English magazines; and he made a screen adaptation of Eugene O'Neill's play *The Emperor Jones*.

His poem "Gamesters All" was the Contemporary Verse Prize Poem for 1921. He is a member of the Poetry Society of America and the National Institute of Arts and Letters, and holds an honorary degree from the University of North Carolina.

For further comment, see Critical Survey, pp. 44, 51, 117.

BIBLIOGRAPHY

Poems

Carolina chansons, legends of the low country by DuBose Heyward and Hervey Allen, 1922; Skylines and horizons, 1924; Jasbo Brown and selected poems, 1931.

Novels

* Porgy . . . decorated by Theodore Nadejen, 1925; Angel, 1926; Mamba's daughters, 1929; Peter Ashley, 1932; Lost morning, 1936; Star spangled Virgin . . . decorations by Theodore Nadejen, 1939.

Short Story

The half pint flask, 1929.

Plays

Porgy, a play in four acts by Dorothy Heyward and DuBose Heyward from the novel by DuBose Heyward. The Theatre guild acting version, 1927; Brass ankle, a play in three acts, 1931; Mamba's daughters, a play by Dorothy and DuBose Heyward, dramatized from the novel Mamba's daughters by DuBose Heyward, 1939.

Opera

The Theatre guild presents Porgy and Bess, music by George Gershwin, libretto by DuBose Heyward, settings by Sergei Soudeikine, lyrics by DuBose Heyward and Ira Gershwin, orchestra conductor Alexander Smallens, production directed by Rouben Mamoulian, 1935 (also pub. as Porgy and Bess, an opera in three acts by George Gershwin, libretto by DuBose Heyward, lyrics by DuBose Heyward and Ira Gershwin, production directed by Rouben Mamoulian, 1935; founded on Porgy, a play in four acts . . ., 1927).

Moving-Picture Script

John Krimsky and Gifford Cochran present Paul Robeson in "The Emperor Jones," from the stage play by Eugene O'Neill, screen version by DuBose Heyward, directed by Dudley Murphy, 1933 (cover-title; hectographed).

Historical Study

Fort Sumter by DuBose Heyward and Herbert Ravenel Sass, 1938.

Children's book

The country bunny and the little gold shoes, as told to Jenifer . . . pictures by Marjorie Flack, 1939.

Verses Set to Music

Bess, you is my woman. The Theatre guild presents Porgy and Bess, music by George Gershwin, libretto by DuBose Heyward, lyrics by DuBose Heyward and Ira Gershwin, production directed by Rouben Mamoulian, 1935 (cover-title; sheet music; lyric by DuBose Heyward and Ira Gershwin); I got plenty o' nuttin'. The Theatre guild presents Porgy and Bess, music by George Gershwin, libretto by DuBose Heyward, lyrics by DuBose Heyward and Ira Gershwin, production directed by Rouben Mamoulian, 1935 (cover-title; sheet music; lyric by Ira Gershwin and DuBose Heyward); My man's gone now. The Theatre guild presents Porgy and Bess, music by George Gershwin, libretto by DuBose Heyward, lyrics by DuBose Heyward and Ira Gershwin, production directed by Rouben Mamoulian, 1935 (cover-title; sheet music); Summertime. The Theatre guild presents Porgy and Bess, music by George Gershwin, libretto by DuBose Heyward, lyrics by DuBose Heyward and Ira Gershwin, production directed by Rouben Mamoulian, 1935 (cover-title; sheet music); A woman is a sometime thing. The Theatre guild presents Porgy and Bess, music by George Gershwin, libretto by DuBose Heyward, lyrics by DuBose Heyward and Ira Gershwin, production directed by Rouben Mamoulian, 1935 (cover-title; sheet music).

Editor

Year book of the Poetry society of South Carolina for 1921, 1921 (with others); The year book of the Poetry society of South Carolina, 1922 (ed. by Hervey Allen, DuBose Heyward, John Bennett); The year book of the Poetry society of South Carolina, 1923 (ed. by John Bennett, Hervey Allen, DuBose Heyward); The year book of the Poetry society of South Carolina, 1924 (ed. by John Bennett, DuBose Heyward, Henrietta Kollock, Josephine Pinckney).

STUDIES AND ARTICLES

Allen, Hervey. DuBose Heyward, a critical and biographical sketch . . . including contemporary estimates of his work. [1927?] (pamphlet)
Clark (E)
† Johnson (1936)
Kunitz (L)
Levinson
Moses (A)
[Shackley, George.] Spiritual songs from the Theatre guild production Porgy [arranged and edited by George Shackley]. 1928 (sheet music)
Skinner

Clark, Emily. "DuBose Heyward." *VQR.*, Oct. 1930, pp. 546–56; Monroe, Harriet. "The old south." *P.*, May 1923, pp. 89–92; Monroe. "A poet of the Carolinas." *P.*, Dec. 1924, pp. 164–67; White, Newman I. "Skylines and horizons." *SAQ.*, Oct. 1924, pp. 377–78; Wilson, James S. "The perennial rooster." *VQR.*, Jan. 1926, pp. 15–55. For references to reviews, see *BRD.*, 1924–26, 1929, 1931–32, 1936, 1938, 1939.

Granville Hicks, 1901–

Born in Exeter, New Hampshire, September 9, 1901, the son of a white-collar worker. He attended public schools and in 1923 graduated with highest honors in English at Harvard.

In 1925, after graduating from the Harvard Divinity School, he went to Smith College and taught biblical literature and English. At this time he began contributing to the *American Mercury*, the *Forum*, the *Nation*, the *New Republic*, and other magazines.

Three years later he returned to Harvard, served as assistant to Bliss Perry, and took his master's degree in 1929. In the same year he was appointed assistant professor of English at the Rensselaer Polytechnic Institute, and taught there for a number of years while he made a reputation as a radical literary critic and historian.

In addition to magazine criticism he wrote poetry reviews for the New York *World*. In 1931 he began to write for the *New Masses* and other radical publications, and in 1932 he helped found the League of Professional Groups. In 1934 and again in 1937 he was made literary editor of the *New Masses*. He has also been a member of the editorial board of the Book Union and of the executive committee of the League of American Writers.

In 1925 he was dismissed from his post at the Rensselaer Institute. Although, in answer to protest from many sources, the administration explained its action by need for retrenchment, an investigating committee of the American Association of University Professors laid it to Hicks's identification with radical movements.

Hicks was awarded a Guggenheim fellowship for 1936–37 for the preparation of a work on English literature since 1890, and from 1938 to 1939 he was a fellow in American history at Harvard.

As a Marxist he is, in his own words, "interested in the labor movement and in literature by and for the working classes."

For further comment, see Critical Survey, pp. 197, 201.

BIBLIOGRAPHY

Literary Criticism

* The great tradition, an interpretation of American literature since the civil war, 1933; Literature and revolution, 1935 (pamphlet); John Dos Passos . . . reprinted from "The Bookman," 1938? (cover-title; pamphlet).

Social Study

I like America . . . decorations by Richard M. Bennett, 1938.

Biography

One of us, the story of John Reed in lithographs by Lynd Ward, narrative by Granville Hicks, 1935; John Reed, the making of a revolutionary by Granville Hicks with the assistance of John Stuart, 1936.

Study of Religion

Eight ways of looking at Christianity, 1926.

Poem

The new light, an Easter cantata, for soli and chorus of mixed voices, with piano, organ or orchestral accompaniment, poem by Granville Hicks, music by Stuart B. Hoppin, 1928.

Pamphlet

Margaret Fuller to Sarah Helen Whitman, an unpublished letter, 1930.

Editor

Proletarian literature in the United States, an anthology edited by Granville Hicks, Joseph North, Michael Gold, Paul Peters, Isidor Schneider, Alan Calmer, with a critical introduction by Joseph Freeman, 1935; The letters of Lincoln Steffens, volume I: 1889–1919, edited with introductory notes by Ella Winter and Granville Hicks with a memorandum by Carl Sandburg, 1938; The letters of Lincoln Steffens, volume II: 1920–1936, edited with introductory notes by Ella Winter and Granville Hicks with a memorandum by Carl Sandburg, 1938.

STUDIES AND ARTICLES

Adamic
Blackmur
Farrell
Strachey

Farrell, James T. "Mr. Hicks, critical vulgarian." *A.Spect.*, Apr. 1936, pp. 21–26; Glicksberg, Charles I. "Granville Hicks and Marxist criticism." *SR.*, Apr.–June 1937, pp. 129–40; Gregory, Horace. "Two critics in search of an absolute." *Nation*, Feb. 14, 1934, pp. 189–91; Matthiessen, Francis O. "The great tradition, a counter-statement." *NEQ.*, June 1934, pp. 223–34. For references to reviews, see *BRD.*, 1933, 1935–36, 1938.

Robert (Silliman) Hillyer, 1895–

Born June 3, 1895, in East Orange, New Jersey. He went to the Kent School and graduated at Harvard in 1917, after winning a poetry prize in 1916. He served during the war with the Norton Harjes Ambulance Service in the French army and as first lieutenant with the American Expeditionary Force. In 1919–20 he acted as courier for the Peace Conference.

Returning to this country in 1919, he became an instructor in English at Harvard. In 1920–21 he held a fellowship awarded by the American-Scandinavian Foundation and studied at the University of Copenhagen; and in 1926–28 he was assistant professor of English at Trinity College in Connecticut, where in 1928 he received an honorary master's degree. He is now Boylston Professor of Rhetoric and Oratory at Harvard.

From 1923 to 1925 he was president of the New England Poetry Club; he has been Phi Beta Kappa poet at Harvard and Columbia, and in 1934 he was given the Pulitzer Prize for his collected verse. He is a fellow of the American Academy of Arts and Sciences.

His home is in Pomfret, Connecticut, and he attributes the lack of violence and confusion in his verse to his delight in the Connecticut countryside. A lover of music, he has composed, and music is nearer to his heart than anything but poetry. Distrusting egocentric literary work that appears to be merely self-expression and usually self-indulgence, he believes in the necessity of standards of artistic restraint. The work of Robert Bridges, which has influenced his own, he admires more than that of any other modern poet.

For further comment, see Critical Survey, p. 133.

BIBLIOGRAPHY

Poems

Eight Harvard poets, E. Estlin Cummings, S. Foster Damon, J. R. Dos Passos, Robert Hillyer, R. S. Mitchell, William A. Norris, Dudley Poore, Cuthbert Wright, 1917; Sonnets and other lyrics, 1917; Alchemy, a symphonic poem . . . with decorations by Beatrice Stevens, 1920; The five books of youth, 1920; The hills give promise, a volume of lyrics together with Carmus, a symphonic poem . . . with five drawings by Beatrice Stevens, 1923; The halt in the garden . . . with an introduction by Arthur Machen, 1925; The happy episode, 1927; The seventh hill, 1928; The gates of the compass, a poem in four parts, together with twenty-two shorter pieces, 1930; * The collected verse of Robert Hillyer, 1933; A letter to Robert Frost and others, 1937; In time of mistrust, 1939.

Novel

Riverhead, 1932.

Plays

The engagement ring, a comedy, 1927; The masquerade, a comedy, 1928.

Essays and Studies

Some roots of English poetry, 1933; First principles of verse, 1938.

Miscellany

The coming forth by day, an anthology of poems from the Egyptian Book of the dead together with an essay on the Egyptian religion, 1923.

Verses Set to Music

For He is risen, an Easter cantata for soli, mixed chorus and antiphonal chorus of treble voices, poem by Robert Hillyer, music by Joseph W. Clokey, 1926.

Editor

Eight more Harvard poets edited by S. Foster Damon and Robert Hillyer with an introduction by Dorian Abbott: Norman Cabot, Grant Code, Malcolm Cowley, Jack Merten, Joel T. Rogers, R. Cameron Rogers, Royall Snow, John Brooks Wheelwright, 1923; Essays of today ⟨1926–1927⟩ selected by Odell Shepard and Robert Hillyer, 1928; Literary fragments by Francis Slocum Parks, 1931; Prose masterpieces of English and American literature edited by Robert Silliman Hillyer . . . Kenneth Ballard Murdock . . . Odell Shepard, 1931.

Translations

A book of Danish verse translated in the original meters by S. Foster Damon and Robert Silliman Hillyer selected and annotated by Oluf Friis, 1922.

STUDIES AND ARTICLES

Kunitz National

Blackmur, Richard P. "In search of the soul." *P.*, Mar. 1932, pp. 340–42; Gregory, Horace. "At the cross-roads." *P.*, June 1928, pp. 165–67; Haraszti, Zoltan. "First novels by two poets, Robert Hillyer's 'River head.'" *NEQ.*, June 1936, pp. 273–80; Hicks, Granville. "A letter to Robert Hillyer." *NR.*, Oct. 20, 1937, p. 308; Holden, Raymond. "The pence of persistence." *P.*, Nov. 1934, pp. 99–103; Knister, Raymond. "Carmus and others." *P.*, Feb. 1925, pp. 281–83; Luhrs, Marie. "Delicate and pure." *P.*, Feb. 1927, pp. 284–86; Millspaugh, C. A. "Harvard has it." *P.*, Feb. 1938, pp. 267–70. For references to reviews, see *BRD.*, 1918, 1920–21, 1923, 1928, 1930–34, 1937–39.

William Hogarth, jr., *pseud.* *See* **Rockwell Kent.**

Sidney (Coe) Howard, 1891–1939

Born in Oakland, California, June 26, 1891, of a family of pioneer traditions on the West Coast. Reared in an atmosphere of books and reading, he attended the University of California, where he graduated in 1915. In college he was active in class plays, pageants, and other undergraduate enterprises, and developed his ability as a reporter; and after graduation and a year spent in Switzerland for the benefit of his health, he continued his study at Harvard, where he worked in Baker's "47 Workshop" course.

Entering the service in the war, he drove an ambulance at Saloniki, and later transferred his activity to the western front, where he was captain in command of a combat squadron in the air force of the American army.

On his return he found the outlook unpromising for a career in the theater, and turned to journalism. An editor of *Life*, and a radical reporter for the *New Republic* and *Hearst's International Magazine*, he investigated labor problems and wrote an exposé of the traffic in narcotics. In the meantime he had been writing plays, and his first to be produced, *Swords*, appeared in 1922, the year of his marriage to his first wife, the actress Clare Jenness Eames. His importance as a dramatist was recognized with the success of *They Knew What They Wanted*, which he wrote in Venice in 1923, and which took the Pulitzer Prize as the best play of 1924–25. Howard wrote many successful plays, and in recent years did a great deal of work for the motion pictures. In 1926–27 the Theatre Guild produced successfully both *Ned McCobb's Daughter* and *The Silver Cord;* and the Guild secured options on all his plays for a subsequent term of years.

Howard, who divided his time between New York and a farm in the Berkshires, was a member of the American Academy of Arts and Letters; and, as president of the Dramatists' Guild of the Authors' League of America, he tried to assist other authors. He is the author of the scenarios of *Bull-Dog Drummond*, *Condemned*, *Raffles*, *A Lady to Love*, *Free Love*, *The Greeks Had a Word for It*, *Arrowsmith*, *The Silver Cord*, *Christopher Bean*, and other moving pictures.

"I suppose that I enjoy travel more than anything else," he wrote, "but I seldom have either the time or money to indulge myself. . . . In the winter I go to hear music with a good deal more pleasure than anything else. It gives me much more pleasure than either theatre or screen, though I have almost never missed a chance to see any production of a play by Shakespeare. I am enormously interested in contemporary American painting, go to most of the picture shows here in New York and occasionally, very occasionally, get my nerve up to buying a picture. Since I gave up being an air pilot I have never done any sport at all seriously. I began writing for the screen in 1928 and have, I suppose, averaged a picture a year since that time, but without any particular satisfaction to myself. Because the screen now means so much more to the general public than the theatre, I recognize it to be the medium about which a dramatist should nowadays be thinking, but the factory pressure of Hollywood has never given me, at least, a chance to find out what I can do with the medium beyond developing a certain technical ingenuity. . . . Every time I write a play I swear that I will never write another, because the whole business of gathering together a cast of actors is at best such a bore and in these days of movies and radio such an appalling discouragement."

He was killed in a tractor-accident on his farm in Tyringham, Massachusetts, on August 23, 1939.

For further comment, see Critical Survey, p. 109.

BIBLIOGRAPHY

Plays

Swords, 1921; "Lexington," a pageant drama of the American freedom founded upon great sayings to be acted in dumb show compiled and in part written by Sidney Howard for the celebration of the one hundred and fiftieth anniversary of the battle of Lexington, April 19th, 1775. Stage manager Waldo F. Glidden, musical director Charles Repper, director of chorus Clarence E. Briggs, 1924 [1925]; * They knew what they wanted, a comedy in three acts . . . the Theatre guild version with two illustrations from photographs of the Theatre guild production, 1925; Lucky Sam McCarver, four episodes in the rise of a New Yorker, 1926; Ned McCobb's daughter, a comedy, 1926; * The silver cord, a comedy in three acts, 1927; Half gods, 1930; Alien corn, 1933; The late Christopher Bean . . . founded upon Prenez garde à la peinture by René Fauchois, 1933; Sinclair Lewis's Dodsworth dramatized by Sidney Howard with comments by Sidney Howard and Sinclair Lewis on the art of dramatization, 1934; Yellow jack, a history by Sidney Howard in collaboration with Paul De Kruif with illustrations by Jo Mielziner, 1934; Paths of glory, a play, adapted by Sidney Howard from the novel by Humphrey Cobb, with a foreword for college theatres by Sidney Howard, 1935; The ghost of Yankee Doodle, a tragedy, 1938.

Short Stories

Three flights up, 1924.

Sociological Studies

The labor spy, a survey of industrial espionage by Sidney Howard with an introduction by Dr. Richard C. Cabot . . . based on a report made for Dr. Cabot under the auspices of the Cabot fund for industrial research by Sidney Howard and Robert Dunn, 1921 (cover-title; pamphlet; enl. ed., The labor spy by Sidney Howard with the collaboration of Robert Dunn, 1924); Professional patriots edited by Norman Hapgood, material assembled by Sidney Howard and John Hearley, an exposure of the personalities, methods, and objectives involved in the organized effort to exploit patriotic impulses in these United States during and after the late war, 1927.

Moving-Picture Script

"Dodsworth" [screen play from the novel by Sinclair Lewis], 1936 (caption-title; mimeographed).

Translations

Casanova, a play in three acts by Lorenzo de Azertis [*pseud.* of Lorand Orbók] translated by Sidney Howard, 1924; Olympia [by] Ferenc Molnar, English text, 1928.

STUDIES AND ARTICLES

Brown (U)
Clark
Farnol, Lynn. One heavenly night novelized . . . from the screen story by Louis Bromfield, adapted by Sidney Howard, with illustrations from the Samuel Goldwyn production. [c1931]
Flexner
Hammond
Heath
† Herrmann
Kunitz (L)
Lawson
Mantle
Moses (A)
Moses (R)
Nathan
National
† Quinn (H)
Quinn (R)
Skinner
Waugh
Whitman
Zabel

Krutch, Joseph W. "The dramatic variety of Sidney Howard." *Nation,* Sept. 13, 1933, pp. 294–95. For references to reviews, see *BRD.*, 1921, 1926–27, 1930, 1933–35, 1938.

(James) Langston Hughes, 1902–

Born in Joplin, Missouri, February 1, 1902, the son of a lawyer and the descendant of Negroes freed before the emancipation. A granduncle had been a Congressman. As a boy he lived in Kansas City, Buffalo, and Colorado Springs, and in Mexico; and he attended high school in Cleveland, where he graduated in 1920.

During the next year he taught English in a business academy in Mexico and worked on his father's ranch; and the year following he spent as a student at Columbia. Then began a period of varied activity, during which he was a farmer on Staten Island, worked in New York, sailed to Europe and the tropics, and was a doorman and cook in Paris and a beachcomber in Italy. From Paris, where he arrived with seven dollars and supported himself for almost a year, he worked his way through Italy and Spain and came back to New York with a quarter.

While he was working as busboy in a hotel in Washington, his gifts were recognized by Vachel Lindsay, who read some of his verse to an audience in the hotel. In 1925 *Opportunity* awarded first prize in a contest for Negro poetry to one of the poems that appeared in *The Weary Blues* in 1926; another early poem was accepted by the *Crisis.* In 1926, as a student at Lincoln University, Hughes won the first prize in the Witter Bynner contest for undergraduates; and, after his graduation in 1929, he won the Harmon Award for distinguished achievement in literature for *Not without Laughter*, 1930.

He made an American tour reading his poetry in the season of 1931–32, and in the next year he made a visit to the Soviet Union. In 1935 he was given a Guggenheim fellowship for creative writing. Hughes is a member of the editorial board of the *New Masses*.

For further comment, see Critical Survey, pp. 51, 137.

BIBLIOGRAPHY

Poems

* The weary blues . . . with an introduction by Carl Van Vechten, 1926; Fine clothes to the Jew, 1927; Dear lovely death, 1931; The Negro mother and other dramatic recitations . . . Titles: The colored soldier, Broke, The black clown, The big-timer and Dark youth, with decorations by Prentiss Taylor, 1931 (cover-title; pamphlet); The dream keeper and other poems . . . with illustrations by Helen Sewell, 1932 (intro. by Effie L. Power); Scottsboro limited, four poems and a play in verse . . . with illustrations by Prentiss Taylor, 1932 (pamphlet); A new song . . . introduction by Michael Gold, frontispiece by Joe Jones, 1938.

Novel

Not without laughter, 1930.

Short Stories

The ways of white folks, 1934.

Children's Book

Popo and Fifina, children of Haiti by Arna Bontemps and Langston Hughes, illustrations by E. Simms Campbell, 1932.

Verses Set to Music

Four Negro songs for medium voice and piano by John Alden Carpenter, I Shake your brown feet, honey! II The cryin' blues, III Jazz-boys, IV That soothin' song, 1927 (sheet music).

STUDIES AND ARTICLES

Brawley
Calverton
Johnson
Kunitz (L)
Lundkvist
Ovington

† Blanck, Jacob, *ed.* "American first editions." *PW.*, Nov. 28, 1936, p. 2135 (comp. by John H. Birss); Peterkin, Julia. "Negro blue and gold." *P.*, Oct. 1927, pp. 44–47. For references to reviews, see *BRD.*, 1926–27, 1930, 1932, 1934.

Fannie Hurst, 1889–

Born in Hamilton, Ohio, October 19, 1889, the only child of a well-to-do Jewish family from St. Louis. She was reared in St. Louis and attended public schools and Washington University, where she took the bachelor's degree in 1909. She was precocious and early showed interest in literature; she was active also in athletics and dramatics. At an early age she had written poetry, and during this time she wrote short stories for *Reedy's Mirror*.

After graduation and a brief attempt to teach school in St. Louis, she began to write constantly, and sent out large numbers of manuscripts, most of them rejected. Her parents, feeling doubtful of her ability to support herself, kept her at home in 1909–10; but in 1910 she went to Columbia for graduate work in Anglo-Saxon. She continued writing, with small success; the Street Publishing Company rejected eleven stories after taking one, and the *Saturday Evening Post* took one after rejecting thirty-five.

To keep herself without assistance from her parents, who wanted her to stay at home, she worked as waitress, salesgirl, nursemaid, and laundry employee, and acted a small part in a Belasco production. These experiences and those incident to crossing the Atlantic in steerage gave her insight into people of a kind she had never known.

Encouraged by the editor of *Munsey's Magazine*, she kept up her writing, although she was to some extent torn between authorship and acting. She published her first book in 1914. In the same year she married a musician, Jacques Danielson. For five years, by living separately and pursuing their different careers, they kept the marriage secret. As early as 1923, when *Lummox* appeared, Miss Hurst had become a nationally-known figure. Besides her novels and stories she has written plays and done work for the screen. She has given lectures, made trips (1924 and 1928) to Russia, and traveled elsewhere. Although her writing is her chief purpose, her broad social and humanitarian interests have made her work intimate with the life about her, especially that in New York City, from which she has never withdrawn herself. Much interested in sociological as well as literary problems, she not only has been president of the Authors' Guild of the Authors' League of America, but has espoused woman's suffrage and the single tax, been active in plans for slum clearance, and been a member of the World's Fair Commission for 1939.

For further comment, see Critical Survey, p. 29.

BIBLIOGRAPHY

Novels

Star-dust, the story of an American girl, 1921; * Lummox, 1923; Appassionata, 1926; Mannequin, 1926; A president is born, 1928; Five and ten, 1929; Back street, 1931; Imitation of life, a novel, 1933; Anitra's dance, 1934; Great laughter, 1936.

Short Stories

Just around the corner, romance en casserole, 1914; Every soul hath its song, 1916; Gaslight sonatas, 1918; Humoresque, a laugh on life with a tear behind it, 1919; Humoresque, a laugh on life with a tear behind it, 1920 (separate); The vertical city, 1922; Song of life, 1927; Procession, 1929; We are ten, 1937.

Miscellany

Divorce as I see it by Bertrand Russell, Fannie Hurst, H. G. Wells, Theodore Dreiser, Warwick Deeping, Rebecca West, André Maurois, and Lion Feuchtwanger, 1930; No food with my meals, 1935; Today is ladies' day, 1939 (pamphlet).

Literary Criticism

America's town meeting of the air, December 26, 1935, number 9. Literature and life [by] Christopher Morely, Fannie Hurst, Audrey Wurdemann, T. S. Stribling, Francis Talbot, S. J., 1935 (cover-title; pamphlet; ed. by Lyman Bryson).

STUDIES AND ARTICLES

Adams, John, *pseud.* Symphony of six million, a novelization by John Adams [*pseud.*] of the Fannie Hurst screen story, an RKO radio picture, 1932 (English ed., Melody of life, 1932)
Burgess
Collins (T)
Farrar
Harper & brothers, *firm, publishers.* Fannie Hurst, a biographical sketch, critical appreciation, & bibliography. 1928 (pamphlet)
Herrmann
Kilmer
Kunitz (L)
Lawrence (S)
Loggins
Mersand
National
Overton (WW)
Sibley, Carroll. Barrie and his contemporaries, cameo portraits of ten living authors . . . with a foreword by Cyril Clemens. 1936
Williams

Anonymous. "Fannie Hurst." *AB.*, Jan. 1924, pp. 552–56; Hurst, Fannie. "Fannie Hurst, by herself." *Mentor*, Apr. 1928, pp. 50–51; Hurston, Zora N. "Fannie Hurst." *SRL.*, Oct. 9, 1937, pp. 15–16; Maurice, Arthur B. "The history of their books, Fannie Hurst." *AB.*, May 1929, pp. 258–60; Roberts, Mary F. "Fannie Hurst, art collector, she roamed through Moscow, Madrid, Florence, London, to find the background for her New York apartment." *Arts & Dec.*, Nov. 1935, pp. 9–11, 51; Salpeter, Harry. "Fannie Hurst, sob-sister of American fiction." *AB.*, Aug. 1931, pp. 612–15. For references to reviews, see *BRD.*, 1914, 1916, 1918–19, 1921–23, 1926–29, 1931, 1933–34, 1936–37.

I. S. *See* Isidor Schneider

(John) Robinson Jeffers, 1887–

Born in Pittsburgh, January 10, 1887. His father, a teacher of theology, trained him thoroughly in the classics and took him on walking trips in Europe, and he attended schools in this country and in Germany and Switzerland. After about three years abroad, he returned to America and entered the University of Western Pennsylvania. In the next year, 1903, he moved to California and entered Occidental College, from which he graduated two years later at the age of eighteen. After further study at the University of Zürich, the University of Southern California (in medicine), and the University of Washington (in forestry), he decided to devote himself to poetry, which had become his all-absorbing interest. In his teens he had been attracted by the poems of Rossetti; in 1903 verse of his own had been published in the undergraduate magazine at Occidental, and more had appeared in the *Youth's Companion* in 1904.

His desire to devote himself to literature was made realizable by a legacy left him in 1912 by a cousin, an amount large enough to insure his independence.

At his own expense he published *Flagons and Apples* in the same year, and in the next he married Una Call Kuster, who became an important influence on his work. They planned to go to England, but upon the outbreak of the war settled down in Carmel, California, still their home. Near his house, which he made of boulders, Jeffers built, for the most part with his own hands, a stone tower on a bluff overlooking Carmel Bay, Tor House, in which he does much of his writing. Except for infrequent travels, including a trip in 1929 to the British Isles and one the next year to New Mexico, Jeffers has lived in virtual seclusion with his wife and his twin sons. Although he has been regarded, since 1925, as one of the most powerful figures in contemporary American verse, he cares little for contact with the literary world, and prefers to remain detached and free to follow his own inclinations.

He was given an honorary doctorate in 1937 by Occidental College, is a member of the National Institute of Arts and Letters, and was awarded in 1937, in recognition of the merits of *Solstice and Other Poems*, a fellowship of $2,500 by the Book-of-the-Month Club. In 1938 a collection of his manuscripts and first editions was presented to Occidental College by Albert M. Bender, of San Francisco.

For further comment, see Critical Survey, pp. 141, 149–50.

BIBLIOGRAPHY

Poems

Flagons and apples, 1912; Californians, 1916; Tamar and other poems, 1924; Roan stallion, Tamar, and other poems, 1925; The women at Point Sur, 1927; An artist, 1928 (pamphlet; contains: Robinson Jeffers, the man by Benjamin DeCasseres; Letter from Havelock Ellis; An artist; A bibliography of the books by Robinson Jeffers compiled by R. H. Griffith); Cawdor and other poems, 1928; Poems . . . introduction by B. H. Lehman, 1928; Dear Judas and other poems, 1929; Apology for bad dreams, 1930 (pamphlet); Stars, 1930; Winter sundown, 1930 (broadside); Descent to the dead, poems written in Ireland and Great Britain, 1931; Thurso's landing and other poems, 1932; Give your heart to the hawks and other poems, 1933; S. S. Alberts. A bibliography of the works of Robinson Jeffers, 1933 (contains poems and autobiographical fragments); Return, an unpublished poem, 1934 (leaflet); Solstice and other poems, 1935; The beaks of eagles, an unpublished poem, 1936 (pamphlet); Four poems and a fragment, 1936 (mimeographed; pamphlet); Hope is not for the wise, an unpublished poem, 1937; Such counsels you gave to me & other poems, 1937; * The selected poetry of Robinson Jeffers, 1938.

Miscellany

George Sterling, with comment by Robinson Jeffers, 1935 (pamphlet).

STUDIES AND ARTICLES

Adamic
Adamic, Louis. Robinson Jeffers, a portrait. 1929 (pamphlet)
† Alberts, Sydney S. A bibliography of the works of Robinson Jeffers. 1933
Bennett, Melba B. Robinson Jeffers and the sea. 1936

Blankenship
Boni & Liveright, *firm, publishers.* Roan stallion, Tamar, and other poems. [1925] (pamphlet; prospectus)
Bush
Canby (S)
Cowley
DeCasseres
DeCasseres, Benjamin. Robinson Jeffers: tragic terror [1928] (pamphlet)
DeCasseres, Benjamin. The superman in America. 1929 (pamphlet)
Deutsch
† Gilbert, Rudolph. Shine, perishing republic, Robinson Jeffers and the tragic sense in modern poetry. [c1936]
Greenan, Edith. Of Una Jeffers, [c1939]
† Jeffers, Robinson. An artist. [c1928] (pamphlet; contains A bibliography of the books by Robinson Jeffers compiled by R. H. Griffith)
† Johnson (1932)
† Johnson (1936)
Kunitz (L)
Loggins
† Los Angeles. Occidental college. Robinson Jeffers, 1905–1935, an exhibition commemorating the thirtieth anniversary of his graduation from Occidental college, at the Occidental student union, Los Angeles, California, April 11 to 18. [1935] (cover-title; pamphlet)
National
Powell, Lawrence C. An introduction to Robinson Jeffers. Thesis for the doctorate of the university, presented at the Faculty of letters of Dijon. 1932
Powell, Lawrence C. Robinson Jeffers, the man & his work . . . a foreword by Robinson Jeffers, decorations by Rockwell Kent. 1934 (rev. ed. of An introduction to Robinson Jeffers. 1932)
Saturday
Schmalhausen, Samuel D. Our changing human nature. 1929
Scripps college, *Claremont, Calif.* Scripps college papers, number two. Lectures on significant tendencies in contemporary letters delivered in Janet Jacks Balch hall in November, 1929. 1930 (pamphlet)
Steffens, Lincoln. Lincoln Steffens speaking. [c1936]
Sterling, George. Robinson Jeffers, the man and the artist. 1926
† Taylor
Untermeyer (M)
Van Wyck, William. Robinson Jeffers. 1938
Winters
Zabel

Anonymous. "Rats, lice and poetry." *SRL.*, Oct. 23, 1937, p. 8; Brown, Edward K. "The coast opposite humanity." *CF.*, Jan. 1939, pp. 309–10; Busch, Niven, Jr. "Duel on a headland." *SRL.*, Mar. 9, 1935, p. 533; Cestre, Charles. "Robinson Jeffers." *RAA.*, Aug. 1927, pp. 489–502; Daly, James. "Roots under the rocks." *P.*, Aug. 1925, pp. 278–85; Davis, Harold L. "Jeffers denies us twice." *P.*, Feb. 1928, pp. 274–79; DeCasseres, Benjamin. "Robinson Jeffers, tragic terror." *AB.*, Nov. 1927, pp. 262–66; Flanner, Hildegarde. "Two poets, Jeffers and Millay." *NR.*, Jan. 27, 1937, pp. 379–82; Fletcher, John G. "The dilemma of Robinson Jeffers." *P.*, Mar. 1934, pp. 338–42; Gierasch, Walter. "Robinson Jeffers." *EJ.*, (Col. Ed.), Apr. 1939, pp. 284–95. Hatcher, Harlan. "The torches of violence." *EJ.*, Feb. 1934, pp. 91–99; Humphries, Rolfe. "Robinson Jeffers." *Mod.M.*, Jan. 1935, pp. 680–89; Humphries. "Robinson Jeffers." *Mod.M.*, Feb. 1935, pp. 748–53; Humphries. "Two books by Jeffers." *P.*, June 1932, pp. 154–58; Jeffers, Robinson. "First book." *Col.*, Part 10, Art. 1, pp. 1–8 (1932); Lehman, Benjamin H. "Robinson Jeffers." *SRL.*, Sept. 5, 1931, pp. 97–99; Lind, Levi R. "The crisis in literature,

literature today." *SR.*, Jan.–Mar. 1939, pp. 47–50; Monroe, Harriet. "Power and pomp." *P.*, June 1926, pp. 160–64; Morris, Lloyd S. "Robinson Jeffers, the tragedy of a modern mystic." *NR.*, May 16, 1928, pp. 386–90; Pinckney, Josephine. "Jeffers and MacLeish." *VQR.*, July 1932, pp. 443–47; Waggoner, Hyatt H. "Science and the poetry of Robinson Jeffers." *AL.*, Nov. 1938, pp. 275–88; Walton, Eda L. "'Beauty of storm disproportionally.'" *P.*, Jan. 1938, pp. 209–13; Wann, Louis. "Robinson Jeffers, counterpart of Walt Whitman." *Pers.*, July 1938, pp. 297–308; Warren, Robert P. "Jeffers on the age." *P.*, Feb. 1937, pp. 279–82; Winters, Yvor. "Robinson Jeffers." *P.*, Feb. 1930, pp. 279–86; Zabel, Morton D. "The problem of tragedy." *P.*, Mar. 1929, pp. 336–40. For references to reviews, see *BRD.*, 1916, 1925, 1927, 1929–30, 1932–33, 1935, 1937–39.

James Weldon Johnson, 1871–1938

Born June 17, 1871, at Jacksonville, Florida, where he received his early education. He attended Atlanta University and graduated in 1894. Ten years later he took the master's degree, and he studied for three years at Columbia.

In the meantime he had been principal of the Stanton Central Grammar School for Negroes in Jacksonville, and had been admitted to the bar in Florida in 1897. Even in his undergraduate days he had attempted to support himself by writing; and finally, in 1901, he moved to New York, where, collaborating with his brother, J. Rosamond Johnson, a singer, he wrote popular songs and librettos, and arranged spirituals. He made an English translation of the libretto of the Spanish opera *Goyescas* (music by Granados), produced at the Metropolitan in 1915.

By this time, however, he was launched upon a career in the diplomatic service. Appointed consul to Puerto Cabello, Venezuela, in 1906, and in 1909 to Corinto, Nicaragua, he served during two revolutionary movements. He returned to this country in 1912, and devoted his energies to literary and academic work and to the Negro problem. From 1916 to 1930 he served as secretary of the National Association for the Advancement of Colored People, and led a vigorous fight against lynching. His own investigation of American misrule in the Black Republic of Haiti led to governmental inquiry and the restoration of Haitian government. His other public services included his work as director of the American Fund for Public Service and as a trustee of Atlanta University. In 1930 he became Spence Professor of Creative Literature at Fisk University in Nashville; he also served as Visiting Professor of Creative Literature at New York University. He held honorary degrees from Talladega College (1917) and Howard University (1923), and was a member of the Academy of Political Science and the Ethical Society.

During a long literary career he contributed to *Century*, *Harper's*, the *American Mercury*, *Crisis*, and other magazines, ran a column for ten years in a Negro newspaper, the New York *Age*, and wrote for the *Encyclopaedia Britannica.* In 1916 he won a prize from the Philadelphia *Public Ledger* for an editorial, and in 1925 he was awarded the Spingarn Medal for services to the Negro. In 1933 he received the W. E. B. Du Bois Prize for Negro Literature. He made recordings of selections from *God's Trombones*.

On June 26, 1938, he was killed in an automobile accident in Maine. Honorary pallbearers at the funeral, held at the largest church in Harlem, included

Colonel Theodore Roosevelt, Deems Taylor, Carl Van Vechten, and the Reverend Stephen S. Wise.

Dr. Johnson was an earnest champion of the Negro's claim to artistic recognition, in this country as well as in Europe, where, he felt, the works of Pushkin, Dumas, and Coleridge-Taylor, all of part-Negro extraction, had secured respect for the race. He thought that in such phenomena as the "Uncle Remus" stories, the spirituals, the cakewalk, and ragtime the Negro had voiced the only truly American artistic expression; and he pointed to the history of Negroes' writings, from colonial times to the twentieth century, as support for his view that Negroes are destined to make significant additions to American literature, even if, because of their peculiar racial situation in this country, they are likely to be slower than Latin-American Negroes to acquire a cosmopolitan point of view.

For further comment, see Critical Survey, p. 137.

BIBLIOGRAPHY

Poems

Fifty years & other poems . . . with an introduction by Brander Matthews, 1917; * God's trombones, seven Negro sermons in verse by James Weldon Johnson, drawings by Aaron Douglas, lettering by C. B. Falls, 1927; Saint Peter relates an incident of the resurrection day, 1930; Saint Peter relates an incident, selected poems, 1935.

Novel

The autobiography of an ex-colored man, 1912 (anonymous).

Autobiography

Along this way, the autobiography of James Weldon Johnson, 1933.

Essays and Studies in Negro Life

Africa in the world democracy, 1919 (with Horace M. Kallen); The larger success, 1923 (cover-title; repr. from the Southern workman, Sept. 1923); Native African races and culture, 1927 (pamphlet); Black Manhattan, 1930; Negro Americans, what now? 1934.

Pamphlets

Self-determining Haiti . . . four articles reprinted from the Nation embodying a report of an investigation made for the National association for the advancement of colored people together with official documents, 1920 (cover-title); The race problem and peace presented to the VI international summer school of the Women's international league for peace and freedom, Chicago, May 1924, 1924.

Verses Set to Music

National hymn for the colored people of America. "Lift every voice and sing," words by J. W. Johnson, music by Rosamond Johnson, 1900 (cover-title; sheet music); Congo love song, words by J. W. Johnson, music by Rosamond Johnson, arr. for guitar by C. de Janon, 1903 (caption-title; sheet music); The glory of the day was in her face, words by James W. Johnson, music by H. T. Burleigh, 1915 (caption-title; sheet music); Her eyes twin pools, words by James W. Johnson, music by H. T. Burleigh, 1915 (caption-title; sheet music); Your eyes so deep, words by James W. Johnson, music by H. T. Burleigh, 1915 (caption-title; sheet music); Your lips are wine, words by James W. Johnson, music by H. T. Burleigh, 1915 (caption-title; sheet music); The creation, a Negro sermon for voice and eight instruments by Louis Gruenberg, op. 23, poem by James Weldon Johnson, 1926 (title-page and text in English and German; sheet music).

Translations

Goyescas, an opera in three tableaux, the book by Fernando Periquet, the music by Enrique Granados, English version by James Weldon Johnson, 1915; (also pub. without the music as Goyescas or, The rival lovers, opera in three tableaux, the book by Fernando Periquet, the music by Enrique Granados, English version by James Weldon Johnson, 1915).

Editor

The book of American Negro poetry chosen and edited with an essay on the Negro's creative genius, 1922; The book of American Negro spirituals edited with an introduction by James Weldon Johnson, musical arrangements by J. Rosamond Johnson, additional numbers by Lawrence Brown, 1925; The second book of Negro spirituals edited with an introduction by James Weldon Johnson, musical arrangements by J. Rosamond Johnson, 1926.

STUDIES AND ARTICLES

Brawley
Dell
Herrmann
Kerlin
Kildal
Kunitz (L)
Ovington

Aery, William A. "James Weldon Johnson, American Negro of distinction." *SS.*, Sept. 3, 1938, pp. 291–94; Gale, Zona. "Autobiography of distinction." *WT.*, Jan. 4, 1934, pp. 20–21; Johnson, Charles S. "Native African races and culture." *Am.Fed.*, Jan. 1928, pp. 49–53; Monroe, Harriet. "Negro sermons." *P.*, Aug. 1927, pp. 291–93; Rosenberg, Harold. "Truth and the academic style." *P.*, Oct. 1936, pp. 49–51; Villard, Oswald G. "Issues and men." *Nation*, July 9, 1938, p. 44; Wohlforth, Robert. "Dark leader." *N.Yer.*, Sept. 30, 1933, pp. 22–26. For references to reviews, see *BRD.*, 1918, 1922, 1925–28, 1930–31, 1933–35.

Josephine (Winslow) Johnson, 1910–

Born June 20, 1910, in Kirkwood, Missouri. She attended local schools and Washington University, where she studied art in the School of Fine Arts. Some of her water colors have been exhibited in St. Louis.

After finishing school she engaged in social-service work and wrote for magazines. One of her stories found its way into the O. Henry Memorial Collection for 1934, the year in which she studied at the Bread Loaf School of Writing in

Middlebury, Vermont. She has since been an instructor in that institution. Her first novel, *Now in November*, took the Pulitzer Prize for 1934.

Miss Johnson, who has lived since 1922 on a farm outside St. Louis, is interested in domestic life as well as reading, writing, and painting; and she is much concerned with "the struggle to bring about some sort of economic justice and sanity." "It seems to me," she writes, "that the author must be participant as well as observer in many things and today writing is so bound up with actual living that it is ridiculous to quibble over the separation line."

"I recognize beauty and strength in writing apart from the particular ideas expressed," she declares, "and for this reason my taste in literature is very catholic. The one unchanging standard is not found in *viewpoint* but in *effect*."

BIBLIOGRAPHY

Novels

Now in November, 1934; Jordanstown, a novel, 1937.

Short Stories

Winter orchard and other stories, 1935.

Poems

Year's end, 1937.

STUDIES

McCole

For references to reviews, see *BRD.*, 1934–35, 1937.

Matthew Josephson, 1899–

Born in Brooklyn, February 15, 1899. He was educated at Columbia University, where he studied French literature, and graduated in 1920. For a time he worked as financial and literary editor on the Newark *Ledger;* then he allied himself with the surrealists and literary exiles of Paris and became associate editor of *Broom.* When the expense connected with the magazine became too great, he left it and entered a broker's office on Wall Street as a "customers' man." Although prosperous for a time, he abandoned business for literature, serving as contributing editor on *transition* and as book editor for the Macaulay Company.

In 1930 he planned to go abroad to write, but the loss of his house and manuscripts in a disastrous fire changed his plans, and he remained in America. A member of the Authors' League of America, he has contributed to the *New Republic*, the *Nation*, the *Outlook*, and other magazines, and held a Guggenheim traveling fellowship for creative literature in 1933–34 which enabled him to write *The Robber Barons.*

As he has shown in *Portrait of the Artist as American*, Josephson has been profoundly concerned with the possibilities afforded by American civilization to creative workers, and he said several years ago that he regarded the struggle between machinery and ideas as so significant that he preferred not to live abroad but to remain here to observe the outcome. He lives in Connecticut and devotes himself entirely to writing and research.

For further comment, see Critical Survey, p. 171.

BIBLIOGRAPHY

Historical and Biographical Studies

Zola and his time, the history of his martial career in letters, with an account of his circle of friends, his remarkable enemies, cyclopean labors, public campaigns, trials, and ultimate glorification, 1928; Jean-Jacques Rousseau, 1931; * The robber barons, the great American capitalists, 1861–1901, 1934; The politicos, 1865–1896, 1938.

Literary Studies

Portrait of the artist as American, 1930.

Poems

Galimathias and other poems, 1923.

Pamphlet

Nazi culture, the brown darkness over Germany, 1933.

Translations

The poet assassinated by Guillaume Apollinaire translated from the French with a biographical notice and notes, 1923; Who will be master, Europe or America? by Lucien Romier translated from the French, 1928; A season in hell, the life of Arthur Rimbaud by Jean-Marie Carre, translated by Hannah and Matthew Josephson, 1931.

STUDIES

Kunitz (L) Wilson (D)
Rascoe (B)

For references to reviews, see *BRD.*, 1928, 1930, 1932–34, 1938.

R. K. *See* Rockwell Kent

MacKinlay Kantor, 1904–

Born in Webster City, Iowa, February 4, 1904. Through his father he was descended from sixteen generations of cantors; from his mother he received the heritage of a family of Iowa pioneers, an enthusiasm for American history and lore, and, probably, some of his literary ability, as she was editor of the local newspaper that her son delivered in town. The boy's education was twice interrupted in the high-school period: once, when, in order to take a job, he left the Chicago school for which he had abandoned Webster City; and again when he left a Des Moines high school to work for the state highway commission.

Back again in high school in Webster City, he wrote for the school paper and helped his mother edit a local daily. He took a leading part in the class play and won a prize from the Des Moines *Register* for a short story. His verse was accepted by magazines, although his stories were rejected; and a ballad on the miner Floyd Collins drew attention to him in the "Line-o'-Type" column of Richard Henry Little in the Chicago *Tribune*.

In the meantime he had written a novel and traveled about the Middle West during the summers. Going to Chicago, he found work in political offices and later in advertising. After his marriage he re-entered newspaper work in Iowa but lost his job when the paper was absorbed by another. Not long after, he induced Coward McCann, then a new publisher, to accept *Diversey*.

In recent years he has contributed considerable material to periodicals. "My short stories," he writes, "have appeared in an appalling number of magazines, sublime and ridiculous and penny-dreadful. I used to write a great deal of stuff for the pulp detective-and-crime story magazines, in the years when I had to make my living that way, and I don't think that my rather complicated talents were harmed in the least. The severe routine of such endeavor stimulated my sense of plot and construction, which needed such stimulation very badly indeed. I was well aware that the stuff I wrote had little value, except that in most cases it made entertaining narrative." His story, *The Voice of Bugle Ann*, which appeared in the *Atlantic* in 1934, was subsequently filmed; and "Silent Grow the Guns," in the *Redbook* in 1935, was published in the O. Henry collection of short stories for the year.

Kantor's success in the past four or five years has enabled him to travel and to establish a winter residence in Florida, although he finds New York more stimulating to actual work.

His characteristic enthusiasm is revealed in what he has termed "a personal fixation on the Civil War," which accounts for his related interest in fife music. These are the natural results of his heritage and a boyhood spent in absorbing the tales of veterans of the war; and they are reflected in *Long Remember*, which was perhaps responsible for the recent succession of Civil War novels, just as *Diversey* set the fashion for novels of Chicago gangsters and *Bugle Ann* was the first of two or three on fox-hunting. Concerning this evidence of his ability to attract the interest of both writers and readers to previously neglected subjects, Kantor says: "The facts . . . prove . . . that I write about any phase of American life, past or present, which appeals to me, and that I have never been guilty of writing a novel merely because the public was in a mood to read something on that subject."

For further comment, see Critical Survey, pp. 48, 61.

BIBLIOGRAPHY

Novels

Diversey, 1928; El goes South, 1930; The Jaybird, 1932; * Long remember . . . decorations by Will Crawford, 1934; Arouse and beware, a novel, 1936; The noise of their wings, 1938.

Stories

The voice of Bugle Ann, 1935; The boy in the dark . . . with a foreword by Cyril Clemens, 1937; The romance of Rosy Ridge . . . with illustrations by Will Crawford, 1937; Valedictory . . . illustrated by Amos Sewell, 1939.

Poems

Turkey in the straw, a book of American ballads and primitive verse, decorations by Will Crawford, 1935.

Kantor, MacKinlay. "First blood." *Col.*, Summer 1937, pp. 317–22; Kantor, MacKinlay. "My memoirs of the civil war." *Col.*, Spring 1936, pp. 541–48. For references to reviews, see *BRD.*, 1928, 1930, 1932, 1934–39.

George S. Kaufman, 1889–

Born in Pittsburgh, November 16, 1889. He went to the public schools, studied law for a few months, and had a playwriting course under Clayton Hamilton and Hatcher Hughes at Columbia. For a while he worked as chainman and then as transit man on a surveying corps; later he held jobs as window clerk, worker in a county tax office, stenographer, and traveling salesman. When he was nineteen, he left for New York, where, with voluntary contributions to Franklin P. Adams' column, then in the *Evening Mail*, he entered newspaper work. Through the influence of "F. P. A." he was given charge of a column on the Washington *Times* in 1912–13, and he enjoyed moderate success in 1914–15 as one of Adams' successors on the *Mail*. Later he joined the dramatic staffs of the *Tribune* and the *Times*, and, in 1918, began his long career of playwriting with *Someone in the House*, which, characteristically, he wrote in collaboration. Since then he has had perhaps the most prosperous career of any American dramatist of his time, with a long record of successful plays, written usually with the assistance of other dramatists. Kaufman has also staged and directed his own work and that of other writers, and acted in *Once in a Lifetime* (1930–31), in which he and Moss Hart satirized Hollywood and the new "talking" pictures. *Once in a Lifetime* received the Megrue Prize for Comedy in 1931. He has twice taken the Pulitzer Prize, in 1932 for the musical play *Of Thee I Sing*, on which he collaborated with Morrie Ryskind and Ira Gershwin, and in 1937 for *You Can't Take It with You*, in which he collaborated with Moss Hart. After professional runs, *Stage Door* and *You Can't Take It with You* averaged four or five hundred non-professional performances a year for a number of years.

Kaufman thinks that freedom from tradition and control has helped the drama prosper, and he has said that he considers the stage more profitable than the screen.

For further comment, see Critical Survey, pp. 113–15, 124.

BIBLIOGRAPHY

Plays

* Dulcy, a comedy in three acts by George S. Kaufman and Marc Connelly (with a bow to Franklin P. Adams) introduction by Booth Tarkington, frontispiece by Neysa McMein, 1921; To the ladies, a comedy in three acts by George S. Kaufman and Marc Connelly, 1923; Beggar on horseback, a play in two parts by George S. Kaufman and Marc Connelly, suggested by "Hans Sonnenstoesser's hohlenfahrt [!]" by Paul Apel, 1924; This volume contains: Old man Minick, a short story by Edna Ferber. Minick, a play based on the short story by Edna Ferber and George S. Kaufman, also a brief and quite gratuitous

explanation by the authors, 1924 (The play also issued separately with title: Minick, a comedy in three acts by George S. Kaufman and Edna Ferber, 1925); Merton of the movies, in four acts, a dramatization of Harry Leon Wilson's story of the same name by George S. Kaufman and Marc Connelly, 1925; The butter and egg man, a comedy in three acts, 1926; If men played cards as women do, a comedy in one act, 1926; * The royal family, a comedy in three acts by George S. Kaufman and Edna Ferber, 1928 (English ed., Theatre Royal, a play in three acts, 1936); June moon, a comedy in a prologue and three acts by Ring Lardner and George S. Kaufman, 1930; Once in a lifetime, a comedy by Moss Hart and George S. Kaufman, 1930; The still alarm, a play in one act, 1930; The good fellow, a play in three acts by George S. Kaufman and Herman J. Mankiewicz, 1931; Dinner at eight, a play by George S. Kaufman and Edna Ferber, 1932; Of thee I sing, a musical play by George S. Kaufman and Morrie Ryskind, lyrics by Ira Gershwin, with a foreword by George Jean Nathan, 1932; Let 'em eat cake, a sequel to "Of thee I sing," a musical play by George S. Kaufman and Morrie Ryskind, lyrics by Ira Gershwin, illustrated by Donald McKay, 1933; The dark tower, a melodrama by Alexander Woollcott and George S. Kaufman, 1934; Merrily we roll along, a play by George S. Kaufman and Moss Hart, 1934; Prom night, a farce in one act by George S. Kaufmann[!], 1934; Cheating the kidnappers, a farce in one act, 1935; First lady, a play in three acts by Katharine Dayton and George S. Kaufman, 1935 (also issued as mimeographed script with title: First lady by Katharine Dayton and George S. Kaufman, 1935); * Stage door, a play by Edna Ferber and George S. Kaufman, 1936 (also issued as mimeographed script with cover-title: "Stage door" by Edna Ferber and George S. Kaufman, 1936); * You can't take it with you by Moss Hart and George S. Kaufman, 1936 (mimeographed; regular ed. has title: You can't take it with you, a play by Moss Hart and George S. Kaufman, 1937); I'd rather be right, a musical revue by George S. Kaufman & Moss Hart, lyrics by Lorenz Hart, 1937; The fabulous invalid, a play in two acts by Moss Hart and George S. Kaufman, 1938; The American way by George S. Kaufman and Moss Hart, 1939.

Moving-Picture Script

"A night at the opera," dialogue cutting continuity . . . [screen play by George S. Kaufman and Morrie Ryskind from a story by James Kevin McGuinness], 1935 (cover-title; mimeographed).

STUDIES AND ARTICLES

Agate (F)
Agate (M)
Brown
Clark
Cohen
Dickinson (P)
Flexner
Gershwin, George. Of thee I sing. Music by George Gershwin, lyrics by Ira Gershwin, book by George S. Kaufman and Morrie Ryskind. c1932
† Herrmann
Kunitz (L)
[Leigh, Rowland.] "First lady." (Dialogue transcript.) c1937 (cover-title; mimeographed)
Mantle
Mantle (C)
Marion, Frances and Mankiewicz, Herman J. Dinner at eight . . . screen play . . . from the Sam H. Harris stage play by George S. Kaufman and Edna Ferber,

additional dialogue by Donald Ogden Stewart . . . [1933?] (cover-title; mimeographed)
Mersand
Moses (A)
Moses (R)
Nathan (P)
Nathan (TM)
† Quinn (H)
Taylor, Deems. A kiss in Xanadu, pantomime in three scenes, scenario by Winthrop Ames . . . as performed in the play "Beggar on horseback" by George S. Kaufman and Marc Connelly. 1924
Wilbur, Crane. "Dance, Charlie, dance," screen play by Crane Wilbur from outline by William Jacobs [based on the play, The butter and egg man by G. S. Kaufman]. [1937] (mimeographed)

Carmer, Carl. "George Kaufman, playmaker to Broadway." *TAM.*, Oct. 1932, pp. 807–15; Chapman, John. "The gloomy dean." *SEP.*, Jan. 1, 1938, pp. 16, 33–34; Moses, Montrose J. "George S. Kaufman, a satirist in the American theatre." *N.Amer.Rev.*, Jan. 1934, pp. 76–83; Woollcott, Alexander. "The deep, tangled Kaufman." *N.Yer.*, May 18, 1929, pp. 26–29. For references to reviews, see *BRD.*, 1921, 1924, 1926, 1928, 1932, 1934–35, 1937, 1939.

George (Edward) Kelly, 1887–

Born in Philadelphia. He attended public schools, began to act in New York in 1912, and toured in juvenile roles for five years. Later he performed in vaudeville acts of his own composition for the Keith and Orpheum circuits. At about thirty-five he took a professional friend's advice and began writing plays instead of sketches for vaudeville. His three-act farce, *The Torchbearers*, a satire on the little-theater movement, was the result of an idea conceived originally for a vaudeville sketch. This was his first full-length play. *Craig's Wife*, produced October 12, 1925, was awarded the Pulitzer Prize for 1925–26. When *Philip Goes Forth* was received coldly in 1931, Kelly, feeling that Broadway had "practically no appeal right now for the writer interested in a serious, analytical study of characters and situations," went to Hollywood. Since then he has lived in California much of the time, and his play *Reflected Glory*, starring Tallulah Bankhead, was presented in 1936, first in San Francisco and later in New Haven and New York. *The Show-Off* (1924) was filmed.

Educated in the exacting school of vaudeville, Kelly learned early the value of making every word count, and the sort of material that audiences will like. He has described himself as being entirely without technical knowledge or method and as governed simply by a desire to show truth in such a way that actors can perform it and audiences will come to see it.

For further comment, see Critical Survey, p. 113.

BIBLIOGRAPHY

Plays

Finders-keepers, a play in one act, 1923; The torch-bearers, a satirical comedy in three acts . . . preface by Kenneth Macgowan, 1923; * The show-off, a transcript of life in three acts . . . preface by Heywood Broun, 1924; The flattering word and other one-act plays, 1925 (The flattering word; Smarty's party; The weak spot; Poor Aubrey); * Craig's wife, a drama, 1926; Daisy

Mayme, a comedy, 1927; Behold, the bridegroom—, 1928; Philip goes forth, a play in three acts, 1931; Reflected glory, a play, 1937.

STUDIES AND ARTICLES

Brown (U)
Clark
Dickinson (P)
Eaton (D)
Flexner
Heath
Kunitz
[McCall, Mary C. Craig's wife, screen play by Mary C. McCall based on the play by George Kelly.] [1936] (mimeographed)
Mantle
Mantle (C)
Moses (A)
Moses (R)
Nathan (M)
† Quinn (H)
Skinner
Skolsky
Wolff, William A. The show-off, a novel . . . from the play by George Kelly. 1924
Zabel

Carmer, Carl. "George Kelly." *TAM.*, Apr. 1931, pp. 322–30; Krutch, Joseph W. "The austerity of George Kelly." *Nation*, Aug. 30, 1933, pp. 240–42; Van Druten, John. "Small souls and great plays." *TAM.*, July 1927, pp. 493–98; White, Kenneth. "George Kelly and dramatic device." *HH.*, Apr.–June 1931, pp. 384–400. For references to reviews, see *BRD.*, 1923–28, 1931, 1937.

Rockwell Kent, 1882–

Born June 21, 1882, in Tarrytown, New York. He was educated carefully and in early childhood showed ability at drawing. He attended the Horace Mann School in New York. Although he never graduated, he took college-entrance examinations successfully and, as a student in the School of Architecture at Columbia, led his class.

In the meantime he had been devoting his vacations and his spare time to the study of art; and, convinced that he could succeed as a painter, he left the university and gave up architecture as a career. Among his art teachers were William M. Chase, Robert Henri, and Abbott H. Thayer. Although when still in his twenties he exhibited paintings at the National Academy of Design and won the critics' praise with a one-man exhibition in New York, he found himself forced to do architectural work and draw for funny papers, as he could not sell his pictures.

When still a very young man, he had felt a growing disapproval of existing class distinctions, and had withdrawn to an island off the Maine seacoast, earned his living at hard jobs, become a fisherman, a handy man, and a skilled carpenter, and had come to know and respect the simple men with whom he was thrown. In 1918, with his youngest boy, he spent a year in Alaska, living in a house he had built himself; and *Wilderness*, his first published book, though not his first literary work, is the record of that experience. *Voyaging Southward from the Strait of Magellan*, and *N by E* are accounts of later trips respectively to Tierra del Fuego and Cape Horn and to Greenland, where he made weather observations for the Pan American Airways. In the second of these trips, undertaken in 1929 in a small boat, the author suffered shipwreck in Greenland. Recently he traveled to Puerto Rico and South America.

In the meantime Kent had become well known as a successful illustrator of books; his improved fortunes have enabled him to settle on a farm in the Adirondacks. In 1937 he completed two murals in the building of the Post Office Department in Washington. He has taken a political stand favoring revolution, and in the presidential campaign of 1936 he was chairman of the Committee of Professional Groups for Browder and Ford.

His position as an artist has been recognized by the exhibition of his paintings in museums, not only in the United States, but also in Europe and South America, and he is a member of the International Society of Sculptors, Painters, and Engravers. In 1927–28 he was the editor of *Creative Art.* The hard, clear smoothness of his work is perhaps an expression of his avowed preference for the bolder and more rugged natural scenes and for mountains, seas, and cold climates.

For further comment, see Critical Survey, p. 180.

BIBLIOGRAPHY

Books

Wilderness, a journal of quiet adventure in Alaska by Rockwell Kent, with drawings by the author and an introduction by Dorothy Canfield, 1920; The golden chain, a fairy story, March 2, 1922, 1922; Voyaging southward from the Strait of Magellan by Rockwell Kent with illustrations by the author, 1924; Down with the gang, a message to republican voters, 1929? (leaflet); Elmer Adler, a sketch written and illustrated by Rockwell Kent, 1929;* N by E, 1930 (illus. by the author); A birthday book, 1931; Rockwellkentiana, few words and many pictures by R. K. and, by Carl Zigrosser, a bibliography and list of prints, 1933; How I make a wood cut, 1934(illus. by the author);* Salamina by Rockwell Kent, illustrated by the author, 1935; What is an American? 1936 (pamphlet).

Portfolios and Collected Illustrations

The seven ages of man illustrated in four drawings, 1918 (cover-title); Drawings by Rockwell Kent, a portfolio of prints, 1924; The bookplates & marks of Rockwell Kent with a preface by the artist, 1929; Forty drawings done by Rockwell Kent to illustrate the works of William Shakespeare, 1936; Later bookplates & marks of Rockwell Kent with a preface by the artist, 1937.

Miscellany

The nineteen hundred & four Columbian. The year book of the junior class, 1902 (art editors: Rockwell Kent, chairman, Frederick Squires, Jaxon Knox); Alaska drawings by Rockwell Kent with a letter from Rockwell Kent to Christian Brinton, 1919 (pamphlet; illus. by Rockwell Kent); American institute of graphic arts. Fifty prints exhibited by the Institute, 1927. An introduction by Rockwell Kent, 1928 (illustration by Rockwell Kent); Breaking into print, being a compilation of papers wherein each of a select group of authors tells of the difficulties of authorship & how such trials are met, together with biographical notes and comment by an editor of the Colophon, Elmer Adler, 1937.

Books Illustrated, or with Decorations, by Rockwell Kent

Architec-tonics, the tales of Tom Thumtack, architect [*pseud.* of Frederick Squires] volume one, 1914; The modern school by Carl Zigrosser, 1917 (pamphlet); The cruise of the Kawa, wanderings in the South Seas by Walter E. Traprock, F. R. S. S. E. U. [*pseud.* of George S. Chappell] with seventeen illustrations and a map, 1921; 1689–1921. First retrospective exhibition of American art under the direction of Mrs. Albert Sterner, inaugurating the Junior art patrons of America, 1921; Rollo in society, a guide for youth by George S. Chappell embellished with cuts by Wm. Hogarth, jr. [*pseud.* of Rockwell Kent] A new edition, revised by the author, 1922; Chronicles of Kennebunk, being scenes and episodes in an old Maine village & vicinity by Wm. E. Barry, with illustrations by the writer, redrawn by Rockwell Kent, 1923; A basket of poses, verses by George S. Chappell, pictures by Hogarth, jr. [*pseud.* of Rockwell Kent], 1924; Catalogue. Twenty-third annual international exhibition of paintings, April twenty-fourth, June fifteenth MCMXXIV. Carnegie institute, Pittsburgh, 1924 (cover design by Rockwell Kent); Victory ball program, American legion, 1924; The memoirs of Jacques Casanova de Seingalt complete in twelve volumes as translated into English by Arthur Machen, with an introduction by Arthur Symons, a new preface by the translator and twelve drawings by Rockwell Kent, volume one [–twelve], 1925; Our enemy the child by Agnes de Lima, 1925 (cover design by Rockwell Kent); By various American authors. Americana esoterica, introduction by Carl Van Doren, decorations by Rockwell Kent, 1927; Dreams & derisions [by John Burke], 1927; The ballad of Yukon Jake by Edward E. Paramore, jr. Black and white illustrations by Hogarth, jr. [*pseud.* of Rockwell Kent], 1928; Louis Untermeyer. Burning bush, 1928; Moses, a novel by Louis Untermeyer, 1928; On the duty of civil disobedience [by] Henry David Thoreau, 1928; La raison suffisante. Candide [by] Jean Francois Marie Arouet de Voltaire illustrated by Rockwell Kent, 1928; Unser Kent by W[aldo] P[ierce], 1928; The Woodcut, an annual edited by Herbert Furst, 1928; The bridge of San Luis Rey by Thornton Wilder, 1929 (Paper books series); The bridge of San Luis Rey by Thornton Wilder, illustrated by Rockwell Kent, 1929; The decorative work of T. M. Cleland, a record and review, with a biographical and critical introduction by Alfred E. Hamill and a portrait lithograph by Rockwell Kent, 1929; Gabriel, a poem in one song by Alexander Pushkin, translated by Max Eastman, illustrated by Rockwell Kent, 1929; The Canterbury tales of Geoffrey Chaucer, together with a version in modern English verse by William Van Wyck, illustrated by Rockwell Kent, 1930 (2 vols.; illustrations also used in: Canterbury tales rendered into modern English by J. U. Nicolson, with illustrations by Rockwell Kent and an introduction by Gordon Hall Gerould, 1934); Commando [by] Deneys Reitz, a Boer journal of the Boer war with a preface by General J. C. Smuts, 1930; The fool of the family, continuing the story of Sanger's circus from "The constant nymph" [by] Margaret Kennedy, 1930; The master of the day of judgment [by] Leo Perutz translated from the German by Hedwig Singer, 1930; Moby Dick, or, The whale by Herman Melville, volume I [II, III] illustrated by Rockwell Kent, 1930 (3 vols.; trade ed. in 1 vol., 1930); My reminiscences as a cowboy [by] Frank Harris, illustrations by William Gropper, 1930; Prize poems, 1913–1929, edited by Charles A. Wagner, with an introduction by Mark Van Doren, 1930; The return of the hero [by] Darrell Figgis, with an introduction by James Stephens, 1930; Seed, a novel of birth control, by Charles G. Norris, 1930; City child, poems by Selma Robinson, decorations by Rockwell Kent,

1931; Eskimo by Peter Freuchen, translated by A. Paul Maerker-Branden and Elsa Branden, 1931; Venus and Adonis by William Shakespeare, illustrated by Rockwell Kent, 1931; A Yankee in Patagonia, Edward Chace, by Robert & Katharine Barrett, with frontispiece and introduction by Rockwell Kent, 1931; Beowulf, 1932 (verse trans. by William Ellery Leonard); Harvest of time, poems, by Harold Trowbridge Pulsifer, 1932; Rockwell Kent by Merle Armitage, 1932; All men are enemies, a romance by Richard Aldington, illustrations by Rockwell Kent, 1933; Zest by Charles G. Norris, 1933; Candy by L. M. Alexander with illustrations by Rockwell Kent, 1934; Erewhon by Samuel Butler now printed from the revised edition of MCMI by the Pynson printers of New York in MCM XXX IV for the members of the Limited editions club, with a special introduction by Aldous Huxley, and the illustrations and a special design for each chapter made by Rockwell Kent, 1934; Fifty years, 1884, A. B. Dick company, 1934, privately printed [written by Glen Buck], 1934; Hans, the Eskimo, his story of Arctic adventure with Kane, Hayes, and Hall, by Edwin Gile Rich, with illustrations by Rockwell Kent, 1934; Robinson Jeffers, the man & his work, by Lawrence Clark Powell, a foreword by Robinson Jeffers, decorations by Rockwell Kent, 1934; Roger Vercel. In sight of Eden, translated from the French by Alvah C. Bessie and illustrated by Rockwell Kent, 1934; The story of the star stones, being the first of a series of little books which will be issued from time to time [by Marcus and company] and which will have to do with the legends, histories, occurrence, and fashion of precious stones, 1935; The complete works of William Shakespeare, the Cambridge edition text, as edited by William Aldis Wright, including the Temple notes, illustrated by Rockwell Kent, with a preface by Christopher Morley, 1936 (2 vols.; also pub. in 1 vol. ed.); Leaves of grass by Walt Whitman illustrated by Rockwell Kent, 1936; Kristmann Gudmundsson. Morning of life translated from the Norwegian by Elizabeth Sprigge and Claude Napier, 1936; The saga of Gisli, son of Sour, translated from the old Icelandic by Ralph B. Allen, illustrated by Rockwell Kent, 1936; The story of the emerald being the third of a series of little books which are issued from time to time [by Marcus and company] and which have to do with the legends, histories, occurrence, and fashion of precious stones, 1936; The story of the pearl. The second of a series of little books which are issued from time to time [by Marcus and company] and which have to do with the legends, histories, occurrence, and fashion of precious stones, 1936; Strike of Vermont marble company workers. Verbatim report of public hearing, Town hall, West Rutland, Vt., Feb. 29, 1936, 1936 (pamphlet); Richard Aldington. Very heaven, 1937 (cover design by Rockwell Kent); The story of the diamond. The fourth of a series of little books which are issued from time to time [by Marcus and company] and which have to do with the legends, histories, occurrence, and fashion of precious stones, 1937; The story of the sapphire and the ruby. The fifth of a series of little books which are issued from time to time [by Marcus and company] and which have to do with the legends, histories, occurrence, and fashion of precious stones, 1938.

STUDIES AND ARTICLES

Allen, Arthur S. Under sail to Greenland, being an account of the voyage of the cutter, "Direction," Arthur S. Allen, jr., captain, to Greenland in the summer of 1929, together with the log, letters, and other memoranda, illustrated with photographs taken on the cruise. 1931

Armitage, Merle. Rockwell Kent. 1932

Birchman

† Bolton, Theodore. American book illustrators, bibliographic check lists of 123 artists. 1938

Demcourier, vol. VI, no. 10, Oct. 1937 (Rockwell Kent issue; illus. by Rockwell Kent)

Ford

† *The Index of twentieth century artists*, vol. I, no. 7, pp. 104–10, April 1934; vol. I, no. 12, pp. xxiii–xxiv, Sept. 1934; vol. II, no. 12, p. xxx, Sept. 1935

† Johnson (1932)

† Johnson (1936)

† Kent, Rockwell. Rockwellkentiana, few words and many pictures by R. K. and, by Carl Zigrosser, a bibliography and list of prints. 1933

Kunitz (L)

National

[Pierce, Waldo.] Unser Kent by W. P. 1928

Beebe, Lucius. "Artist adventurer, the saga of Rockwell Kent." *Forum*, Feb. 1932, pp. 90–96; Hind, Charles I. "Rockwell Kent in Alaska and elsewhere." *IS.*, June 1919, pp. 105–12; Kent, Rockwell. "Alias Kent, by Hogarth, Jr." *Col.*, Part 13, Art. 7, pp. 1–8 (1933); Kent. "On being famous." *Col.*, Spring 1936, pp. 580–84; Price, F. Newlin. "Rockwell Kent, voyager." *IS.*, July 1924, pp. 272–76; Rockwell, Norman. "Rockwell, before or after?" *Col.*, Spring 1936, pp. 584–86; Young, Stark. "The world of Rockwell Kent." *NR.*, May 4, 1927, pp. 302–03. For references to reviews, see *BRD.*, 1920, 1924, 1930–31, 1933, 1935–36.

Milton Kilgallen, *pseud.* *See* Kenneth Roberts

Sidney Kingsley, 1906–

Born in New York, October 18, 1906, son of A. and Sonia (Kirschner) Smoleroff. In high school he was a leader in dramatics; and he wrote, acted in, and directed plays at Cornell, where he was conspicuous in the dramatic club. A Miltonian masque brought him a first prize; and his one-act play *Wonder-Dark Epilogue* took a prize awarded annually by Professor A. M. Drummond. When he graduated in 1928, he had decided to enter upon a career in the theater.

For six months he acted in a stock company at the Tremont Theatre in the Bronx, and he played a small role in the Broadway success *Subway Express*. Turning his attention from acting to writing, he took a job as play reader for Brandt Brothers and wrote scenarios for Columbia Pictures, in Hollywood. For five years he wrote plays that attracted producers but never actually appeared on the boards.

One of them, *Men in White*, after three years of delay, was produced by the Group Theatre in 1933. It brought the author the medal offered by the Theatre Club, took the Pulitzer Prize for the season of 1933–34, and was filmed. Kingsley's merits were further recognized by the enthusiastic reception given *Dead End*, produced in the season of 1936–37 by Norman Bel Geddes. Again the Theatre Club awarded him its medal, and film rights were bought by Samuel Goldwyn for $165,000.

BIBLIOGRAPHY

Plays

Men in white, a play in three acts, 1933; * Dead end, a play in three acts, 1936.

STUDIES

Brown
Mersand
Nathan (TM)

For references to reviews, see *BRD.*, 1934, 1936.

Alfred Kreymborg, 1883–

Born December 10, 1883, in New York; of Danish extraction. He was educated in city schools and left high school after two years. Early in his life he demonstrated a remarkable skill at chess, in which he was expert at the age of ten; and for many years in his youth he supported himself by teaching and playing the game. He took clerical jobs, sold music at Aeolian Hall, and came to know such musicians as Harold Bauer and Josef Hofmann.

His enthusiasm for music and his feeling for rhythm gave him an intense interest in the theater and in poetry. He organized "Others," a group of radical poets, and edited three volumes of their work, and founded and edited the *Glebe*, a poets' magazine; and in 1921 he helped found the international magazine *Broom* in Rome. Later, with Paul Rosenfeld, Lewis Mumford, and Van Wyck Brooks, he edited *The American Caravan*, a collection of new American literature. He has lectured at Oxford on modern poetry and traveled from coast to coast as lecturer before school and college groups, and literary and social organizations. Other activities have included the giving of puppet plays or "poem-mimes" before schools and clubs, and for two years he was connected with the Federal Theatre. He received the Guarantors Prize from *Poetry* in 1922.

Although in his early poetry Kreymborg made conscious experiments with meter and rhythm, his later work has taken such conventional forms as those of the quatrain, the couplet, and the sonnet. In his recitations the author is accompanied by his own music on the mandolute, an instrument of his own invention.

Of his peace-allegory poetic drama for radio, *The Planets*, written originally as a free dramatization of Gustav Holst's orchestral suite of the same name and presented by the National Broadcasting Company in 1938, the author said: "The verse forms vary with the moods and action of the play: balladry, free verse, blank verse and rhythmic prose."

For further comment, see Critical Survey, pp. 143–44, 204.

BIBLIOGRAPHY

Poems

Bruno chap books . . . Mushrooms, 16 rhythms, 1915 (cover-title; pamphlet); Bruno chap books . . . To my mother, 10 rhythms, 1915 (cover-title; pamphlet); Mushrooms, a book of free forms, 1916 (rev. ed., Mushrooms, 1928);

Blood of things, a second book of free forms, 1920; Less lonely, 1923; Scarlet and Mellow, 1926; Alfred Kreymborg, The pamphlet poets, price 25 cents, 1928 (cover-title; ed. by Paul Rosenfeld); The lost sail, a Cape Cod diary, 1928; Manhattan men (poems and epitaphs), 1929; A song cycle, Body and stone, 1929 (pamphlet); Prologue in hell . . . original wood cuts by Walter Cole, 1930; The little world, 1914 and after, 1932; Two New Yorkers, fifteen lithographs, paintings, and etchings by Alexander Kruse, with fourteen lyrics by Alfred Kreymborg, edited by Stanley Burnshaw, 1938.

Plays

The Provincetown plays, third series: The two sons: Neith Boyce, Lima beans: Alfred Kreymborg, Before breakfast: Eugene O'Neill, 1916; Plays for poem-mimes, 1918 (When the willow nods, a dance-play; Jack's house, a cubic-play; Lima beans, a scherzo-play; Blue and green, a shadow-play; Manikin and Minikin, a bisque-play; People who die, a dream-play); Plays for merry Andrews, 1920 (Vote the new moon, a toy play; At the sign of the thumb and nose, an unmorality play; Uneasy street, a folk play; The silent waiter, a tragi-comedy; Monday, a lame minuet); * Puppet plays . . . with a preface by Gordon Craig, 1923 (When the willow nods; Blue and green; Manikin and Minikin; Jack's house; Lima beans; People who die; Pianissimo); Lima beans, a scherzo-play in one act, 1925; Manikin and Minikin, a bisque-play in one act, 1925; Rocking chairs and other comedies, 1925 (Rocking chairs; Helpless Herberts; Adverbs; Trap doors; Not too far from the angels); There's a moon tonight, a romantic comedy in three acts, a prologue and an epilogue, 1926; Jane, Jean, and John, a play in one act, 1929?; How do you do, sir? and other short plays, 1934 (I'm not complaining; How do you do, sir?; Haverstraw hair-cut; America, America!; Limping along; Frank and Mr. Frankenstein; Nothing ever happens; Brother Bill; Good story); America! America! a mass recital, 1936 (pamphlet); I'm not complaining, a kaffeeklatsch, 1936; The planets, a modern allegory, 1938; The four apes, and other fables of our day, 1939.

Novels

Erna Vitek, 1914; I'm no hero, 1933.

Short Story

Bruno chap books . . . Edna, the girl of the street, 1915 (cover-title; pamphlet).

Children's Book

Funnybone Alley . . . illustrated by Boris Artzybasheff, 1927.

Literary Criticism

Our singing strength, an outline of American poetry (1620–1930), 1929 (also pub. as A history of American poetry, Our singing strength, 1934).

Autobiography

* Troubadour, an autobiography, 1925.

Miscellany

Love and life and other studies, 1908; Apostrophes, a book of tributes to masters of music, 1910 (pamphlet).

Editor

Others, an anthology of the new verse, 1916; Others, an anthology of the new verse (1917), 1917; Others for 1919, an anthology of the new verse, 1920; The American caravan, a yearbook of American literature edited by Van Wyck Brooks, Lewis Mumford, Alfred Kreymborg, Paul Rosenfeld, 1927; The second American caravan, a yearbook of American literature edited by Alfred Kreymborg, Lewis Mumford, Paul Rosenfeld, 1928; The new American caravan, a yearbook of American literature edited by Alfred Kreymborg, Lewis Mumford, Paul Rosenfeld, 1929; Lyric America, an anthology of American poetry (1630–1930) 1930 (also pub. as An anthology of American poetry, Lyric America, 1630–1930, 193–); American caravan IV, edited by Alfred Kreymborg, Lewis Mumford, Paul Rosenfeld, 1931; The new caravan edited by Alfred Kreymborg, Lewis Mumford, Paul Rosenfeld, 1936.

STUDIES AND ARTICLES

Aiken
Beach
Collins
† Herrmann
Kunitz (L)
Lowell
† Manly
Monroe
National
Rosenfeld
Rosenfeld (M)
Untermeyer
Untermeyer (N)

Carmer, Carl. "America's poets." *TAM.*, Feb. 1930, pp. 177–78; Crawford, Nelson A. "For assimilators of culture." *P.*, May 1930, pp. 110–12; Crawford. "A poet's progress." *P.*, Aug. 1934, pp. 269–74; Johns, Orrick. "Plays for poet-mimes." *Drama*, Aug. 1918, pp. 414–16; Mansfield, Margery S. "Whimsical wisdom." *P.*, Jan. 1927, pp. 226–28; Michelson, Max. "The radicals." *P.*, June 1916, pp. 151–55; Monroe, Harriet. "A staccato poet." *P.*, Oct. 1916, pp. 51–54; Seiffert, Marjorie A. "Kreymborg's plays for poet-mimes." *P.*, Jan. 1919, pp. 224–27; Sherry, Laura. "Little theatre rhythms." *P.*, July 1921, pp. 218–21; Zabel, Morton D. "Souvenirs." *P.*, Dec. 1929, pp. 168–69. For references to reviews, see *BRD.*, 1914, 1916, 1920, 1923, 1925–27, 1930, 1932–33, 1936, 1938–39.

Joseph Wood Krutch, 1893–

Born November 25, 1893, in Knoxville, Tennessee. He was educated in a secondary school in Knoxville and at the State university, taking his bachelor's degree in 1915. From an early preoccupation with science he was directed toward literature by the plays of George Bernard Shaw; and, entering graduate study in the English Department at Columbia, he took the master's degree in 1916 and achieved the doctorate in 1923. Since this period he has devoted himself to literature as student, teacher, critic, and writer.

During the war he served in the Psychological Corps of the American army, and in 1919–20 he traveled abroad on a Columbia University fellowship. In

1923 he married a Frenchwoman, Marcella Leguia. He has taught English at the Polytechnic Institute of Brooklyn, at Vassar, in the School of Journalism at Columbia, and in the New School for Social Research. In 1924 he became dramatic critic and associate editor, and in 1932 he was made an editor, of the *Nation*. Although in 1937 he resigned his position as editor to accept a professorship in English at Columbia, he continues to write dramatic criticism for the magazine. He was a founder, with Zona Gale, Glenn Frank, and Carl Van Doren, of the Literary Guild in 1926. In 1930 a Guggenheim fellowship enabled him to spend six months abroad writing an essay on aesthetics.

Philosophically he regards human thought as constantly achieving, through exercise of the will and the possibilities afforded by the peculiarly human power of choice, a balance of some kind between the natural or animal and the human, non-natural, or intellectual impulses of the human being, a balance shifting and never in permanent equilibrium, but veering from something like the harmony established by nature for the lower animals to the conscious attempts made by some religions to achieve harmony by overcoming nature. He distrusts the claims of any one system or code of morals as an answer to this fundamental human problem. "Possibly it is significant," he writes, "that my youthful interests were scientific, that I originally intended to be a mathematician, and that I have retained considerable interest in the sciences. Politically I am still an unreconstructed Liberal whose ideas my more radical friends insist belong to the nineteenth century—if not to the eighteenth."

He is a methodical writer, and turns out about a thousand words a day when he is working on a book or a series of articles. As a critic he recognizes value in the suggestions of Marxian critics, but declares unequivocally, ". . . The so-called Marxian theory seems to me absurd as an account of literary value." It is partly from the point of view of a professional journalist (". . . I am more often compelled to write when I haven't ideas than to forgo an opportunity to express those that I have") that Krutch is interested in literary craftsmanship. "To me Shakespeare is incomparably the greatest writer," he declares, "and in general the seventeenth and eighteenth century writers are those I admire most." He admires especially, among contemporary writers, Thomas Mann and Marcel Proust. "Contemporary American literature seems to me to be on a level of considerable competence but I have few heroes. O'Neill at least will be remembered I believe and also—purely as a writer and after people have stopped bothering whether they agree with him or not—Mencken." In American literature as a whole he admires particularly Melville, Thoreau, and Mark Twain.

For further comment, see Critical Survey, p. 170.

BIBLIOGRAPHY

Essays and Studies

Comedy and conscience after the restoration, 1924; Edgar Allan Poe, a study in genius, 1926; * The modern temper, a study and a confession, 1929; Five masters, a study in the mutations of the novel, 1930; Experience and art, some aspects of the esthetics of literature, 1932; Was Europe a success? 1934.

Editor

The comedies of William Congreve edited with an introduction by Joseph Wood Krutch, 1927.

STUDIES AND ARTICLES

Eastman (L)
Frank
Harris, Mark. The case for tragedy, being a challenge to those who deny the possibility of a tragic spirit in the modern world. 1932
Kunitz (L)
Lewisohn (E)
National
Strachey

Baugh, Hansell. "Mutations of the novel." *SR.*, Oct.–Dec. 1931, pp. 507–10; Glicksberg, Charles I. "Joseph Wood Krutch, critic of despair." *SR.*, Jan.–Mar. 1936, pp. 77–93; Hill, Helen. "Pause before resurrection." *VQR.*, Apr. 1933, pp. 313–15; Hoffman, Ross J. S. "Mr. Krutch and Europe." *AR.*, Nov. 1934, pp. 56–66. For references to reviews, see *BRD.*, 1925–26, 1929–32, 1935.

Clare (Rodman Beecher) Kummer

She was born Clare Rodman Beecher of the family to which belonged Harriet Beecher Stowe and Henry Ward Beecher. She began her career as a song writer and came first into public notice with the popularity of her song "Dearie," which was a hit of 1906. Her interest shifted to the theater, and in 1912 she opened her career as a playwright with *The Opera Ball*, in which she collaborated with Sydney Rosenfeld. From her first short plays she progressed to longer works. *Good Gracious Annabelle!* was presented in 1916 with Roland Young and Walter Hampden, and subsequently in musical form as *Annie Dear*, it was produced by Florenz Ziegfeld with Billie Burke. More recently Mrs. Kummer has written dialogue for the motion pictures. In private life she is Mrs. Arthur Henry. Her daughter Marjorie is the wife of Roland Young.

For further comment, see Critical Survey, p. 111.

BIBLIOGRAPHY

Plays

The robbery, a comedy in one act, 1921; "Be calm, Camilla!" A comedy in two acts, 1922; Bridges, 1922; Chinese love, a play in one act, 1922; The choir rehearsal, a play in one act, 1922; "Good gracious, Annabelle," a romantic farce comedy in three acts, 1922; * Rollo's wild oat, a comedy in three acts, 1922; A successful calamity, a comedy in two acts, 1922; The rescuing angel, a comedy in three acts, 1923; Pomeroy's past, a comedy in three acts, 1926; So's your old antique, a comedy in one act, 1928; Papers, comedy in one act, 193–?; Her master's voice, a comedy in two acts, 1934.

Humorous Verses

Bible rimes for the not too young by Clare Beecher-Kummer with drawings by Oliver Herford, 1909 [1910].

Music and Verses

The summerland song, 1901 (cover-title; sheet music); A rich coon's babe . . . sung with great success by Marie Dressler, 1902 (cover-title; sheet music); Egypt, 1903 (caption-title; sheet music); I'm a-goin to change my man, 1903 (caption-title; sheet music); June, 1903 (caption-title; sheet music); Take yo' name off ma door, words and music, 1903 (caption-title; sheet music); Down in Somaliland, words & music, 1904 (caption-title; sheet music); In the dingle-dongle-dell, words and music, 1904 (caption-title; sheet music); Miranda, written & composed, 1904 (cover-title; sheet music); "Sufficiency," 1904 (caption-title; sheet music); On the rialto, words and music, 1905 (caption-title; sheet music); A valentine song, "Dearie," 1905 (cover-title; sheet music); Wilderness, words and music, 1905 (caption-title; sheet music); My very own, 1906 (caption-title; sheet music); "Popular songs," 1906 (caption-title; sheet music); Mary come down, 1907 (caption-title; sheet music).

STUDIES AND ARTICLES

Best
Dickinson (P)
Hackett
† Quinn (H)
[Schary, Dore and Sauber, Harry.] Her master's voice, third draft, October 7, 1935 [scenario by Dore Schary and Harry Sauber, adapted from the play by Clare Kummer]. [1935] (cover-title; mimeographed)

Littell, Philip. "Clare Kummer." *NR.*, Apr. 20, 1921, pp. 233–35.

Oliver (Hazard Perry) La Farge, 1901–

Born December 19, 1901, in New York, the son of a well-known architect. Through his mother, who was a personal friend of Theodore Roosevelt, Henry Adams, and other public figures, he was a descendant of New England sea captains; and among his ancestors were Benjamin Franklin, Commodore Oliver Hazard Perry, and the painter John La Farge, his paternal grandfather. Christopher La Farge, writer, painter, and architect, is his brother.

He passed his childhood in Rhode Island and attended St. Bernard's School and the Groton School, from which he graduated in 1920. Proceeding to Harvard, he became a member of the rowing team, an editor of the *Lampoon*, president of the *Advocate*, and poet of the Class of 1924. He remained for two years after graduation as Hemenway Fellow in Anthropology and took the master's degree in 1929.

In the meantime he had spent two years at Tulane University as assistant in ethnology, and had made three archaeological expeditions for Harvard to Indian regions in the West, and two trips to Mexico and Guatemala for Tulane. His experiences with the Indians, who trusted him and showed him their customs and observances, supplied him with a wealth of material for his books. *Laughing Boy*, a novel of the Navahos, won the Pulitzer Prize for 1929, and the story "Haunted Ground" took the O. Henry Memorial Prize for 1930.

In that year he made an extended trip on horseback through the Indian territory near Santa Fe and the Grand Canyon, and in 1931 he became research associate in ethnology at Columbia. In the next year he directed an expedition to Guatemala. In spite of the breadth of his travels, however, La Farge describes himself as "a practically incurable Yankee."

In recent years he has divided his time between writing and scientific work, and he has been a member of organizations concerned with Indian affairs.

Characterizing his approach to literary creation as instinctive rather than consciously planned, he says: ". . . I was trained as an anthropologist, and . . . out of my scientific work among the Indians arose much of my writing. I would say definitely that my view of human nature and of the world had been coloured by that training, and influenced deeply also by the Indians themselves. . . . I originally wrote in a very florid, periodic style and was cured of it by the influence of the Indian myths which at one time I studied intensively, particularly the really remarkable literature of the Navajos."

For further comment, see Critical Survey, pp. 51, 140.

BIBLIOGRAPHY

Novels

* Laughing boy, 1929; Sparks fly upward, a novel, 1931; Long pennant, a novel, 1933; The enemy gods, 1937.

Short Stories

All the young men, stories, 1935.

Indian Studies

Tribes and temples, a record of the expedition to middle America conducted by the Tulane university of Louisiana in 1925, vol. I, 1926 (by Frans Blom and Oliver La Farge); Tribes and temples, a record of the expedition to middle America conducted by the Tulane university of Louisiana in 1925, vol. II, 1927 (by Frans Blom and Oliver La Farge); The Year Bearer's people by Oliver La Farge II [and] Douglas Byers, 1931 (The Tulane university of Louisiana, Middle American research series, publication no. 3).

Editor

Exposition of Indian tribal arts, inc. Introduction to American Indian art to accompany the first exhibition of American Indian art selected entirely with consideration of esthetic value, 1931 (2 vols.; editorial board: Frederick Webb Hodge, Herbert J. Spinden, Oliver La Farge).

STUDIES AND ARTICLES

Kunitz (L) Raines

Bird, John. "The future of Oliver La Farge." *AB.*, Sept. 1930, pp. 11–14.
For references to reviews, see *BRD.*, 1929, 1931, 1933, 1935, 1937.

Ring(gold) W(ilmer) Lardner, 1885–1933

Born March 6, 1885, in Niles, Michigan. Although his mother wished him to study for the ministry, his father favored engineering; and, after graduating from the local high school in 1901, he went to Chicago to attend the Armour Institute of Technology.

After finishing his studies, however, he became a newspaperman. At first a reporter for two years on a South Bend paper, he later proceeded to Chicago. In 1910–11 he was editor of *Sporting News* (St. Louis), and between 1911 and

1919 he was a sports-writer on the Boston *American*, the Chicago *American*, and other papers. In the latter year he joined the Bell Syndicate, for which he wrote sports articles until his death, September 25, 1933.

Lardner began writing the "You know me Al" sketches when he was conducting a sports column on the Chicago *Tribune*. He denied the existence of any "method" in his work and is said to have remarked: "When I begin a story I have no idea what it is going to be about. I force myself to make a start and then just flounder along."

Although the first story was at once rejected, editors soon recognized the authenticity and force of the "urban-clodhopper" idiom in which they were written, and their popularity grew until the publication in 1924 of *How to Write Short Stories* brought him serious critical recognition. In addition to these sketches and satires Lardner wrote verse and, with George S. Kaufman, a play, *June Moon*, which appeared on Broadway in the season 1929–30 and was filmed in 1931; and he collaborated with George M. Cohan in the motion picture *Fast Company*.

BIBLIOGRAPHY

Short Stories

Gullible's travels, etc. . . . illustrated by May Wilson Preston, 1917; How to write short stories ⟨with samples⟩, 1924; Charles Scribner's sons present Ring W. Lardner in The golden honeymoon and Haircut, American booksellers association, St. Louis, May 13, 1926, 1926; * The love nest and other stories . . . with an introduction by Sarah E. Spooldripper, 1926; Round up, the stories of Ring W. Lardner, 1929; Ring Lardner's best stories including Haircut, Alibi Ike, The golden honeymoon, and all the other brilliant stories originally collected in Round-up—together with his inimitable novel of a not-so-dumb mid-westerner in the wilds of New York, entitled, The big town, with a foreword by William McFee. De luxe edition, 1938.

Wit and Humor

Treat 'em rough, letters from Jack the Kaiser killer . . . illustrated by Frank Crerie, 1918; Own your own home . . . illustrated by Fontaine Fox, 1919; The real dope . . . illustrated by May Wilson Preston and M. L. Blumenthal, 1919; The young immigrunts by Ring W. Lardner, jr. with a preface by the father, portraits by Gaar Williams, 1920; Symptoms of being 35 by Ring W. Lardner, silhouettes by Helen E. Jacoby, 1921; Say it with oil, a few remarks about wives, 1923 (contains also Say it with bricks, a few remarks about husbands by Nina Wilcox Putnam, inverted, with separate title page); What of it? 1925; The story of a wonder man, being the autobiography of Ring Lardner illustrated by Margaret Freeman, 1927; Lose with a smile, 1933; First and last, 1934 (pref. signed: Gilbert Seldes).

Novels

You know me Al, a busher's letters, 1916; The big town, how I and the Mrs. go to New York to see life and get Katie a husband by Ring W. Lardner, illustrations by May Wilson Preston, 1921.

Play

June moon, a comedy in a prologue and three acts by Ring Lardner and George S. Kaufman, 1930.

War Book

My four weeks in France . . . illustrated by Wallace Morgan, 1918.

Rhymes

Bib ballads . . . illustrated by Fontaine Fox, 1915; Regular fellows I have met . . . with illustrations by regular cartoonists, 1919.

Compiler

March 6th, 1914. The home coming of Chas. A. Comiskey, John J. McGraw, James J. Callahan, 1914 (comp. with Edward G. Heeman).

STUDIES AND ARTICLES

American (C)
Anderson (S)
Ashley
† Ford (E)
Haines, William W. "Alibi Ike," original story by Ring Lardner, screen play by William Wister Haines, supervisor Edward Chodorov. 1935 (mimeographed)
† Johnson (1929)
† Johnson (1932)
† Johnson (1936)
Kunitz (L)
Littell
Loggins
† Manly
Masson
Mencken (P)
National
Rascoe (B)
Rourke
Sherman (M)
Skolsky
Stewart
† Van Doren (M)

Anderson, Sherwood. "Four American impressions." *NR.*, Oct. 11, 1922, pp. 171–73; Anonymous. "Ring Lardner, interpreter of life." *Lit.Dig.*, Oct. 14, 1933, p. 19; Bibesco, Elizabeth. "Lament for Lardner." *Liv.Age*, Dec. 1933, pp. 366–68; Fadiman, Clifton. "Ring Lardner and the triangle of hate." *Nation*, Mar. 22, 1933, pp. 315–17; Fitzgerald, Francis S. "Ring." *NR.*, Oct. 11, 1933, pp. 254–55; Littell, Robert. ". . . And other stories." *NR.*, Sept. 29, 1926, pp. 147–49; Nevins, Allan. "The American moron." *SRL.*, June 8, 1929, pp. 89–90; Overton, Grant. "Ring W. Lardner's bell lettres." *AB.*, Sept. 1925, pp. 44–49; R., D. "The reigning jester." *Ind.*, May 23, 1925, p. 590; Tittle, Walter. "Glimpses of interesting Americans." *Cent.*, July 1925, pp. 313–17; Van Doren, Carl. "Beyond grammar, Ring W. Lardner, philologist among the low-brows." *Cent.*, July 1923, pp. 471–75; Wheeler, John N. "Ring Lardner." *Collier's*, Mar. 17, 1928, pp. 16, 44. For references to reviews, see *BRD.*, 1917–18, 1924–27, 1929–30, 1933–34.

John Howard Lawson, 1895–

Born in New York, September 25, 1895. He attended high school in Yonkers, the Cutler School in New York, and Williams College.

In 1914, fresh from college, he entered newspaper work. In 1914–15 he was cable editor on Reuter's Press Cables in New York. Emboldened by his success in 1914 in selling his first play to George M. Cohan and Sam Harris, he gave up his job and wrote plays. He had two failures in 1916–17.

In the war, with which he felt no sympathy, he served with an ambulance corps in France and Italy. After the war he wrote *Roger Bloomer* in Paris. It was produced in New York in 1923, and in 1925 the Theatre Guild presented *Processional.* In recent years he has written for the motion pictures, and he has been associated with the Theatre Union, the left-wing dramatic group in New York.

Lawson favors radical changes in the theater and blames much of the decline of the Broadway stage upon its outmoded ideas; he thinks that the old type of artificial drawing-room comedy must give place to a fresh presentation of the contemporary scene. He regards the films, because of mass-production methods, as at present more barren artistically than the stage, but he hopes that in the future more original work will be done in the moving pictures. He has written dialogue for the films *Dynamite, The Sea Bat, Blushing Brides,* and *Success at Any Price,* the screen version of his *Success Story,* and scenarios for *Blockade* and *Algiers.*

For further comment, see Critical Survey, p. 124.

BIBLIOGRAPHY

Plays

Roger Bloomer, a play in three acts . . . foreword by John Dos Passos, illustrations by Roland Young, 1923; * Processional, a jazz symphony of American life in four acts . . . the Theatre guild version, with eight illustrations from photographs of the Theatre guild production, 1925; Loud speaker, a farce . . . introduction by Joseph Wood Krutch, a New playwrights' theatre production, 1927; The international . . . a New playwrights' theatre production, 1927 [1928]; Success story, a play, 1932; With a reckless preface, two plays . . . with a foreword by Harold Clurman, 1934 (The pure in heart; Gentlewoman); Marching song, a play, 1937 (also issued in mimeographed form with title: Marching song [temporary title], 1937).

Studies

Theory and technique of playwriting, 1936.

Miscellany

A southern welcome (in Georgia and Alabama) a report, 1934 (cover-title; pamphlet).

STUDIES

Dickinson (P)
Kunitz
Moses (A)
Nathan (H)
Nathan (P)
Skinner

For references to reviews, see *BRD.*, 1924–25, 1932, 1934, 1936.

William Ellery (Channing) Leonard, 1876–

Born in Plainfield, New Jersey, January 25, 1876, the son of a clergyman and newspaper writer. The most important incident in his childhood, if not his entire life, was his being seriously frightened by a locomotive in 1878, when he was about two and a half; he imagined it to be God, about to kill him. Later two or three unhappy incidents became associated with the locomotive in such a way as to be recalled by the locomotive terror.

His childhood as a whole, however, was happy, although he was nervous and subject to worry and fright. His mother, who conducted a kindergarten and was interested in scientific methods of education, taught him to read. He was a bright boy, with athletic ability, and was successful in school. When he was in his teens, the family moved to Bolton, Massachusetts, where his father took a Unitarian pulpit; and the youth came to feel thoroughly at home in a New England environment. Because of the inadequacy of the local schools he was thrown upon his own efforts at self-education, and read widely and so well that what he read remained with him for years. The spell of Byron, later his subject for graduate study, was especially powerful at this time.

The poverty of his parents prevented their giving him a college education and he was admitted to Boston University on a scholarship. He earned money partly by writing, and skimped along on small handouts. His interests were in classical and English literature and civilization, and he took part with considerable success in dramatics. At this time also he showed a taste for geology.

He graduated in 1898 and proceeded to Harvard, where he studied Latin, English literature and drama, with Kittredge and Baker, and metaphysics, with William James. Not long after beginning these studies, he began teaching Latin and English in Boston University.

After securing his master's degree in 1899 he accepted a high-school principalship in a New England village, and thereafter spent two years abroad. At this time he developed his powers as a linguist, and was much influenced by the example of German scholarship. He studied at Göttingen and Bonn, and traveled in Germany and Italy. Because of dissatisfaction with his preparation for the task of teaching Latin in Boston, he changed his field of study to English and Germanic philology.

He resumed graduate study at Columbia, where he worked under Trent, and, after a short trip abroad and a period of teaching German and history in a private school, took his doctor's degree. Teaching appeared to be too heavy a strain, and he accepted an editorial position on the staff of a dictionary to be published by Lippincott. The project was abandoned after he had been on it for two years; and, after trying his strength at reporting and serving as tutor, he took an instructorship at the University of Wisconsin in 1906. Three years later he married.

The mental collapse and suicide of his first wife in 1911, and the scandal and unpleasantness following it, as well as an attack of terror in the same year associated definitely with a locomotive, operated to bring on the triumph of the neurotic fears occasioned by the original fright. Physicians, relatives, and friends have been unable to assist him much in overcoming his phobia, which, by its association with trains and in other ways, shows clearly its relation to two or three incidents of his childhood. His teaching has been successful, and he has managed to find time for writing. Except for occasional short trips, and a journey in 1916 to New York, he has been confined to his home and the vicinity. He was unable to go east to say good-bye to his father or to attend his funeral. For a time the pressure was so great as to prevent his leaving the house for classes. A city apartment near the campus, with a half-mile "beat" or safety zone surrounding it, within which he can go about unafraid, was the solution. Although his social life has been restricted to this area, within it he has entertained Sinclair Lewis, Upton Sinclair, Vachel Lindsay, and Eugene Debs.

Leonard has tried to overcome the phobia by reasoning and analysis and such procedures as twilight sleep, crystal-gazing, and the examination of dreams, and careful re-creations, with photographs, of the scenes of the frights of his childhood. He has traced the source of the trouble to three experiences, in 1878, 1885, and 1911, but he has been unable to overcome, in his subconscious mind, the fear and the conviction of the abnormal importance of these frights. He continues to teach at the university, where he has been a full professor since 1926, and conducts a course in philology. He has been married three times.

Poetry he regards as the result of an hereditary inclination, creative energy, and a desire to communicate a vision. The poet, like the child, but with the maturity of the man, is more naïvely sensitive than others to impressions; and, while books and reading contribute to the store of images and ideas, a greater wealth is likely to come from his daily experience. The theme comes of itself, from various sources, and the whole organizes itself while still below the level of conscious activity. This organization is the hallmark of a mature work of art. Details of form and meter come bound up in the organization, sometimes preceding, because more urgent, the desire for the expression of a particular theme. Form and theme act upon each other as stimuli. ". . . A good poem isn't put together," he wrote in the *Bookman* in 1932, "but grows together,—and by subconscious processes as yet unexplained except in a few *aperçus*."

For further comment, see Critical Survey, pp. 131, 177.

BIBLIOGRAPHY

Poems

Sonnets and poems, 1906; Aesop and hyssop, being fables adapted and original with the morals carefully formulated, 1912; The vaunt of man and other poems, 1912; Poems, 1914–16, 1916; The lynching bee and other poems, 1920; * Two lives, a poem, 1922 (anonymous); Tutankhamen and after, new poems, 1924 (contains Two lives, some opinions of critical readers, with diverse intellectual or artistic callings, in several lands); A son of earth, collected poems, 1928; This midland city, etchings of some of its best people, 1930.

Plays

Glory of the morning, a play in one act, 1912; Red Bird, a drama of Wisconsin history in four acts, 1923.

Autobiography

* The locomotive-god, 1927.

Essays and Studies

Byron and Byronism in America . . . submitted in partial fulfilment of the requirements for the degree of doctor of philosophy in the Faculty of philosophy,

Columbia university, 1905; The Poet of Galilee, 1909; Socrates, master of life, 1915; Wisconsin . . . reprinted from the Wisconsin magazine of history, volume VI, number 3, March, 1923, 1923 (cover-title; pamphlet); La mētrica del Cid, 1931.

Verses Set to Music

The city of triumph, a cycle, words by William Ellery Leonard, music by Louis Adolphe Coerne, op. 78. I. Brown angry people, II. Unclouded stars, III. At dawn he rose. (Medium voice), 1915; A cycle of love-lyrics, words by William Ellery Leonard, music by Louis Adolphe Coerne, op. 73 (thematically correlated). I. I need you so, II. You will understand, III. I have your word, IV. Crones of the valley, V. Window and hearth. (The five songs, each of which has its own completeness, form, when combined, a larger unit with implicit narrative: that is, they represent an attempt at a true "lyrical ballad.") (Medium voice), 1915; Flower-lyrics, words by William Ellery Leonard, music by Louis Adolphe Coerne, op. 77. I. Wild violet, II. Garden rose-bud, III. Pond-lily, IV. Wild rose, V. Cardinal flower. (Medium voice), 1915; Incantation, words by William Ellery Leonard, music by Louis Adolphe Coerne, opus 80, 1915 (cover-title); Inland waters, a cycle of five lyrics, words by William Ellery Leonard, music by Louis Adolphe Coerne, op. 76. I. In twilight, II. The bells are ringing far away, III. Drifting at midnight, IV. By land and water, V. Willow walk. (Medium voice), 1915.

Editor

The Oregon trail of Francis Parkman, 1910.

Translations

The fragments of Empedocles translated into English verse, 1908; The inauguration of Professor Eugen Kuehnemann as the first Carl Schurz memorial professor, 1912; The vale of content. Das glück im winkel, a drama in three acts by Hermann Sudermann, 1915 (cover-title); Belgium and Germany, a Dutch view (De belgische neutraliteit geschonden) by Dr. J. H. Labberton, 1916; T. Lucretius Carus. Of the nature of things, a metrical translation, 1916; Beowulf, a new verse translation for fireside and class room . . . with comments and word list, 1923 (also pub. as Beowulf [illus. by Rockwell Kent], 1932; Beowulf translated into verse . . . and illustrated by Lynn Ward, 1939); Gilgamesh, epic of old Babylonia, a rendering in free rhythms, 1934.

STUDIES AND ARTICLES

Bruns
Hughes
Kreymborg
Kunitz (L)
Lewisohn
Lewisohn (E)
National
Taylor, William S. and Culler, Elmer. The problem of The locomotive-god. . . . Reprinted from the Journal of abnormal and social psychology, vol. XXIV, no. 3, October–December, 1929. [1929] (cover-title)
Untermeyer

Boehme, Traugott. "Mr. Leonard's fables." *OC.*, Nov. 1919, pp. 709–12; Cason, Clarence E. "William Ellery Leonard." *VQR.*, July 1928, pp. 359–66; Griswold, Louise. "The poetical work of William Ellery Leonard." *QJUND.*, Jan. 1926, pp. 149–63; Jones, Howard M. "William Ellery Leonard." *DD.*, May 1926, pp. 332–38; Lewisohn, Ludwig. "Poet and scholar." *Nation*, June 6, 1923, pp. 660–61; Lewisohn. "The problem of modern poetry." *AB.*, Jan. 1919, pp. 550–57; Meyer, Ernest L. "William Ellery Leonard." *AM.*, July 1934, pp. 334–40; Monroe, Harriet. "A modern agonist." *P.*, Feb. 1926, pp. 272–75; Taylor, William S. and Culler, Elmer A. K. "The problem of the locomotive-God." *JAR.*, Oct. 1929, pp. 342–99; Taylor and Culler. "The problem of the locomotive-God." *JAP.*, Oct. 1931, pp. 340–41. For references to reviews, see *BRD.*, 1925, 1927–29, 1934.

Sinclair Lewis, 1885–

Born February 7, 1885, at Sauk Center, Minnesota, to a New England father, and a mother of Canadian extraction who died five years later. His father, his maternal grandfather, an uncle, and a brother were all physicians.

Taking a distaste to the curriculum of the local schools, which he attended until 1902, he read widely and erratically, engaged in outdoor sports, and studied Greek with a clergyman. A nonconformist, he decided to go east rather than attend the state university, and, after six months of preparation at Oberlin Academy in Ohio, entered Yale in 1903. In college he became known as a promising but eccentric youth, not interested in athletics or social activities, but a great reader, an editor of the *Yale Literary Magazine*, and a contributor to that magazine and the *Courant.* He earned his way by newspaper work done at night. In two of his summer vacations he made trips to England on cattle-boats, and in 1905, at Sauk Center, he worked at a novel which subsequently was worked over into *Main Street.*

In 1906–07, tired of college, he dropped out to become a member of Upton Sinclair's Socialist community at Helicon Hall in Englewood, New Jersey. After serving as janitor in this group he went to New York to get free-lance jobs. In 1907 he was assistant editor of *Transatlantic Tales*, and made translations from German and French. In the fall he traveled steerage to Panama, but failed to find a job, returned, and resumed his studies at Yale. He finished his course in 1908, and launched upon a career as free-lance writer.

After a period of miscellaneous jobs, rather unsuccessful newspaper work, and spare-time writing, he turned to publishing, and spent two years reading manuscripts for Frederick A. Stokes. He was assistant editor of *Adventure*, an editor and reviewer of the Publishers' Newspaper Syndicate, and editor and advertising manager for George H. Doran. He terminated this connection in 1915, by which time he had sold stories to the *Saturday Evening Post.*

His first wife was Grace Livingston Hegger. Their son Wells published his first novel, *They Still Say No* (1939), while he was a student at Harvard.

During the next five years he traveled about the country and earned his living by magazine stories. With the publication of *Main Street* in 1920 he at once became an important literary figure. In the next year he gave some lectures, but disliked them and stopped. Much of the next few years he spent abroad, and *Arrowsmith*, for which he had gathered material in a tropical trip with Paul de Kruif, was written near Fontainebleau and revised in London. He and

Dorothy Thompson reported the Viennese revolution of 1918 for the New York *Evening Post* and the Philadelphia *Public Ledger*. In 1928 he married Miss Thompson and bought a farm in Vermont.

Often regarded as unsympathetic to American letters and American life, Lewis has attacked the academic and Humanistic traditions in American criticism and deplored the tendency of Americans to fear any national literature that is not a glorification of the national life. ". . . Never have American authors had so tremendous a chance for real supremacy as now . . .," he declared in *News-Week* in 1937. The American writer ought to perceive that he has—not necessarily excepting China and Russia—the most exciting country in the world: the greatest diversity of races, from Icelanders to Japanese and Negroes; the widest sweep of climates.

Offended by the restrictions attaching to the Pulitzer Prize, which he declared to be an effort to make writers "safe, polite, obedient and sterile," Lewis refused the thousand-dollar award when it was offered him in 1926 for *Arrowsmith.* Subsequently (1930) he was the first American to be honored with the Nobel Prize in Literature, which was awarded to him in recognition of his work in *Babbitt;* and in 1935 he was elected to membership in the National Institute of Arts and Letters. In 1936 Yale conferred upon him an honorary doctor's degree. He has given Yale University Library the manuscripts of nearly all his writings, the notebooks used in composing them, foreign translations of his novels, and other material.

For further comment, see Critical Survey, pp. 46, 79–80, 121.

BIBLIOGRAPHY

Novels

Our Mr. Wrenn, the romantic adventures of a gentle man, 1914; The trail of the hawk, a comedy of the seriousness of life, 1915; The innocents, a story for lovers, 1917; The job, an American novel, 1917; Free air, 1919; *Main street, the story of Carol Kennicott, 1920; *Babbitt, 1922 (English ed., 1922, has an intro. by Hugh Walpole and a glossary); *Arrowsmith, 1925 (English ed., Martin Arrowsmith, 1925); Mantrap, 1926; Elmer Gantry, 1927; The man who knew Coolidge, being the soul of Lowell Schmaltz, constructive and Nordic citizen, 1928; Dodsworth, a novel, 1929; Ann Vickers, 1933; Work of art, 1934; It can't happen here, a novel, 1935; The prodigal parents, a novel, 1938.

Short Stories

Selected short stories of Sinclair Lewis, 1935.

Play

Jayhawker, a play in three acts by Sinclair Lewis and Lloyd Lewis, 1935; It can't happen here, a new version by Sinclair Lewis of the play by John C. Moffit and Sinclair Lewis from the Lewis novel, 1938.

Juvenile Literature

Hike and the aeroplane by Tom Graham [*pseud.*] with illustrations in two colors by Arthur Hutchins, 1912.

Literary Criticism

John Ames Mitchell, the man who is responsible for "Life," author of "Pandora's box," "Amos Judd," etc. Articles by Sinclair Lewis, Thomas L. Massón, John Ames Mitchell, James S. Metcalfe, reprinted from The Book news monthly, March, 1912, 1912 (cover-title; pamphlet); John Dos Passos' Manhattan transfer, 1926 (pamphlet); A letter to critics, 1931 (broadside); Les prix Nobel en 1930. The American fear of literature, Nobel address delivered in Stockholm, December 12, 1930, 1931 (pamphlet); Why Sinclair Lewis got the Nobel prize, address by Erik Axel Karlfeldt, permanent secretary of the Swedish academy, at the Nobel festival, December 10, 1930, and Address by Sinclair Lewis before the Swedish academy, December 12, 1930, 1931 (pamphlet); Sinclair Lewis on The valley of the moon, 1932 (cover-title; pamphlet); Sinclair Lewis's Dodsworth dramatized by Sidney Howard with comments by Sidney Howard and Sinclair Lewis on the art of dramatization, 1934.

Sociology

Cheap and contented labor, the picture of a southern mill town in 1929, 1929 (pamphlet).

Miscellany

Launcelot, 1932 (pamphlet); Samples, a book containing many fine pages from the books to be published by the Limited editions club in its seventh series, with A note on book collecting by Sinclair Lewis, 1936.

STUDIES AND ARTICLES

Adamic
American (M)
Anderson
Annand, George. A map of Sinclair Lewis' United States as it appears in his novels with notes by Carl Van Doren. [1934] (broadside)
Baldwin
Baldwin (M)
Berg
Birkhead, L. M. Is Elmer Gantry true? [1928] (pamphlet)
Blankenship
Boas
Boyd
Boynton (L)
Boynton (M)
Brown
Bruns
Cabell
Cabell, James B. Sinclair Lewis: a critical essay. With a foreword by Harvey Taylor. 1932
Calverton
Canby (S)
Carnegie
Cleaton
Combs
Cowley
Dell
DeVoto
Dickinson
Dondore
† Edgar
Farrar
† Ford (E)
Forster, Edward M. Sinclair Lewis interprets America. [1932] (pamphlet)
Forsythe
Frank (S)
Frank (T)
Gillis
Green (C)
Halleck
Hamilton (C)
Harrison, Oliver, *pseud.* Sinclair Lewis. [1925] (pamphlet)
Hartwick
Hatcher

Hazard
Herrmann
Hicks
Hind (M)
[Howard, Sidney C.] "Dodsworth" [screen play from the novel by Sinclair Lewis]. [1936] (caption-title; mimeographed)
Huddleston
† Johnson (1929)
† Johnson (1932)
† Johnson (1936)
Karsner
Kunitz (L)
Levinson
Lewis, Grace H. Half a loaf. [c1931]
Lewis, Sinclair. Elmer Gantry, roman traduit de l'anglais par Régis Michaud. [c1932] (preface by H. L. Mencken)
Lewisohn (E)
Linati
Lippmann
Llona
Loggins
Luccock
McAlpin, Edwin A. Old and new books as life teachers. 1928
MacCallum, Thomas W. and Taylor, Stephen, *eds.* The Nobel prize-winners and the Nobel foundation, 1901–1937 . . . with an introduction by Professor Gilbert Murray. 1938
Mais
† Manly
Marble
Marble, Annie R. The Nobel prize winners in literature, 1901–1931. 1932
Markey
Michaud
Michaud (P)
Morgan, Louise. Writers at work. 1931
Nathan (I)
Nathan (M)
National
Overton (H)
Parrington
Parrington, Vernon L. Sinclair Lewis, our own Diogenes. 1927 (pamphlet)
Pattee (N)
Quinn
Roberts
Robinson, Casey. "I married a doctor," based on a novel by Sinclair Lewis, screen play. [1936] (mimeographed)
Rourke
Russell, Frances T. The young Mr. Lewis [1928] (cover-title; pamphlet)
Salisbury, William. To our Nobel prize winner, an open letter to Mr. Sinclair Lewis. [1931] (cover-title; pamphlet)
Saturday
Schreiber
Schyberg
Shaw
Sherman (P)
Sherman, Stuart P. The significance of Sinclair Lewis. [c1922] (cover-title; pamphlet)
Sinclair
Smith
Smith, Lewis W., *ed.* Ventures in contemporary reading selected by Lewis Worthington Smith . . . Vincent Holland Ogburn . . . and Harold Francis Watson. 1932
Squire
Stewart
Stokes, Sewell. Pilloried! . . . illustrations by Gabriel Atkin. 1929
Taft, Kendall B., *ed.* College readings in contemporary thought selected and edited by Kendall B. Taft, John Francis McDermott, Dana O. Jensen. 1929
† Taylor
Taylor (W)
Tendencies
Thierry, James F. When Roosevelt is dictator—and how! A fascist prophecy . . . A reply to "Red" Lewis's novel "It can't happen here." [c1936] (cover-title; pamphlet)
Untermeyer (H)
Van Doren
Van Doren (A)

Van Doren (B)
Van Doren (C)
† Van Doren, Carl C. Sinclair Lewis, a biographical sketch . . . with a bibliography by Harvey Taylor. 1933
Van Doren (W)
Vočadlo
Ward
Ward (T)
Wells, Carolyn. Ptomaine street, a tale of Warble Petticoat. 1921
West (S)
Whipple
White
Woolf
Zabel

Abbott, Laurence F. "Honoré de Balzac and Sinclair Lewis." *Outl.*, July 6, 1927, pp. 307–09; Anderson, Sherwood. "Four American impressions." *NR.*, Oct. 11, 1922, pp. 171–73; Anonymous. "Sinclair Lewis." *AB.*, Sept. 1922, pp. 54–59; Anonymous. "Sinclair Lewis." *SRL.*, Nov. 22, 1930, p. 357; Baker, Joseph E. "Sinclair Lewis, Plato, and the regional escape." *EJ.*, Coll. Ed., June 1939, pp. 460–68; Baldensperger, Fernand. "Un romancier Américain d'aujourd'hui, M. Sinclair Lewis." *Corres.*, Dec. 25, 1925, pp. 835–54; Bellessort, André. "Littérature étrangère, États Unis, Sinclair Lewis." *Corres.*, July 10, 1931, pp. 119–28; Benét, William R. "The earlier Lewis." *SRL.*, Jan. 20, 1934, pp. 421–22; Binnse, Harry L. and Trounstine, John J. "Europe looks at Sinclair Lewis." *AB.*, Jan. 1931, pp. 453–57; Bogardus, Emory S. "Social distances in fiction, analysis of Main street." *SSR.*, Nov. 1929, pp. 174–80; Boynton, Percy H. "Sinclair Lewis." *EJ.*, Apr. 1927, pp. 251–60; Brunner, Karl. "Amerikas 'mittlerer western,' Sinclair Lewis, 'Main street' und 'Babbitt.'" *NS.*, Oct.–Dec. 1923, pp. 362–66; Cabell, James B. "A note as to Sinclair Lewis." *AM.*, Aug. 1930, pp. 394–97; Calverton, Victor F. "Sinclair Lewis, the last of the literary liberals." *Mod.M.*, Mar. 1934, pp. 77–86; Canby, Henry S. "Sinclair Lewis." *ASR.*, Feb. 1931, pp. 73–76; Canby. "Sinclair Lewis's art of work." *SRL.*, Feb. 10, 1934, pp. 465, 473; Cantwell, Robert. "Sinclair Lewis." *NR.*, Oct. 21, 1936, pp. 298–301; Crocker, Lionel. "Sinclair Lewis on public speaking." *QJS.*, Apr. 1935, pp. 232–37; Davis, Elmer. "Sinclair Lewis's hick of genius." *SRL.*, Jan. 27, 1934, pp. 433, 437; Demmig, Charlotte. "Sinclair Lewis." *Gral.*, Apr. 1931, pp. 637–43; DeVoto, Bernard. "Sinclair Lewis." *SRL.*, Jan. 28, 1933, pp. 397–98; Durtain, Luc. "Un témoin des États-unis, le romancier Sinclair Lewis." *RH.*, Nov. 30, 1929, pp. 554–64; Fadiman, Clifton. "Nobel prizewinner." *N.Yer.*, July 13, 1935, pp. 56–58; Faÿ, Bernard. "Portrait de Sinclair Lewis, l'américain à rebrousse-poil." *R.d.P.*, May 15, 1934, pp. 401–15; Fischer, Walther. "Samuel Dodsworth bereist Europa." *NGH.*, June 1933, pp. 31–42; Fischer. "Sinclair Lewis, der Nobelpreisdichter." *NJWJ.*, Dec. 1931, pp. 700–09; Forster, Edward M. "A camera man." *LL.*, May 1929, pp. 336–43; Forsythe, Robert. "Sinclair Lewis's good intentions." *N.Masses*, Nov. 30, 1937, p. 12; Hicks, Granville. "Sinclair Lewis and the good life." *EJ.*, Apr. 1936, pp. 265–73; Hülsenbeck, Richard. "Sinclair Lewis." *Liv.Age*, Jan. 1931, pp. 479–82; Johnson, A. Theodore. "Realism in contemporary American literature, notes on Dreiser, Anderson, Lewis." *Sw.Bul.*, Sept. 1929, pp. 3–16; Jones, Howard M. "Mr. Lewis's America." *VQR.*, July 1931, pp. 427–32; Karfeldt, Erik A. "Sinclair Lewis and the Nobel prize." *SRL.*, Jan. 10, 1931, p. 524; Krutch, Joseph W. "Dodsworth." *Nation*, Mar. 14, 1934, pp. 311–12, 314; Le Verrier, Charles. "La femme affranchie d'après M. Sinclair Lewis, Ann Vickers." *RH.*, May 13, 1933, pp. 228–37; Lewis, Sinclair. "And that was me." *N.Yer.*, Jan. 2, 1937, pp. 20–21; Lewis. "Breaking into print." *Col.*, Winter 1937, pp. 217–21; Loiseau, Jean. "La croisade de Sinclair Lewis." *EA.*, Apr.–June 1938, pp. 120–

33; McCole, Camille J. "The future significance of Sinclair Lewis." *CW.*, Dec. 1930, pp. 314–22; McNally, William J. "Americans we like, Mr. Babbitt, meet Sinclair Lewis." *Nation*, Sept. 21, 1927, pp. 278–81; Mainsard, Joseph. "Les Américains d'après S. Lewis." *Etudes*, Apr. 1930, pp. 23–47; Marshall, Archibald. "Gopher prairie." *N.Amer.Rev.*, Mar. 1922, pp. 394–402; Morris, Lloyd R. "Sinclair Lewis, his critics and the public." *N.Amer.Rev.*, Summer 1938, pp. 381–90; Mumford, Lewis. "The America of Sinclair Lewis." *CH.*, Jan. 1931, pp. 529–33; Muzzey, David S. "Sinclair Lewis's attack on the clergy." *Stand.*, July 1927, pp. 7–10; Neumann, Henry. "Arrowsmith, a study in vocational ethics." *AR.*, Mar. 1926, pp. 184–92; O'Dell, George E. "The American mind and Main street." *Stand.*, July 1922, pp. 17–20; Overton, Grant. "The salvation of Sinclair Lewis." *AB.*, Apr. 1925, pp. 179–85; Phelps, William L. "As I like it." *Scrib.*, Mar. 1931, pp. 325–28; Roz, Firmin. "M. Sinclair Lewis et le nouveau roman américain." *RPL.*, Jan. 17, 1931, pp. 55–59; Russell, Frances T. "The growing up of Sinclair Lewis." *UCC.*, July 1930, pp. 319–24; Russell. "The young Mr. Lewis." *UCC.*, Oct. 1928, pp. 417–27; Schönemann, Friedrich. "Sinclair Lewis." *Lit.Echo*, Apr. 1923, pp. 683–88; Search-light, *pseud.* "In America's image." *N.Yer.*, July 18, 1925, pp. 10–11; Shillito, Edward. "'Elmer Gantry' and the church in America." *N.Cent.*, May 1927, pp. 739–48; Van Doren, Carl. "Sinclair Lewis and Sherwood Anderson, a study of two moralists." *Cent.*, July 1925, pp. 362–69; Velte, F. Mowbray. "Sinclair Lewis." *Mod.Lib.*, Apr. 1933, pp. 129–34; de Villeneuve, R. "Le nationalisme de Sinclair Lewis." *MF.*, Dec. 1, 1937, pp. 286–307; Von Hibler, Leo. "Sinclair Lewis und die amerikanische wirtschaft, zum 50. geburtstag des autors." *Ang.*, July 1935, pp. 448–60; Waldman, Milton. "Sinclair Lewis." *Merc.*, Jan. 1926, pp. 273–81; Williams, Michael. "The Sinclair Lewis industry." *Com.*, Mar. 30, 1927, pp. 577–79; Woodward, W. E. "The world and Sauk Center." *N.Yer.*, Jan. 27, 1934, pp. 24–27; Woodward. "The world and Sauk Center." *N.Yer.*, Feb. 3, 1934, pp. 24–27; Zweig, Arnold. "Improvisation über Sinclair Lewis." *Die Lit.*, Jan. 1931, pp. 185–86. For references to reviews, see *BRD.*, 1914–15, 1917, 1919–20, 1922, 1925–29, 1933–35, 1938.

Ludwig Lewisohn, 1882–

Born in Berlin, May 30, 1882, the only child of Jews who had thoroughly assimilated German Gentile culture. His childhood in Germany was spent in a comfortable middle-class home, and he was educated carefully in the *Vorschule* of a Gymnasium.

He was brought to the United States in 1890, when the family settled in South Carolina. The boy was sent to local schools and prepared by his mother for high school. When he was ten, he had a sudden creative urge that led him to write German prose and verse. But this was temporary, and constituted almost the last vestige of German feeling; he became thoroughly American and Gentile, and an attendant in the Methodist Church.

After two years they removed to Charleston, where he entered high school in 1893. He received a liberal education, associated with teachers and students whom he liked, and wrote great quantities of verse. He went to the College of Charleston, where he was the most promising student on the campus. He read widely in English and graduated in 1901 with two degrees.

Disappointed in his hopes of securing a teaching position, he spent a year at home, studying and writing, and at twenty went to Columbia. He took the master's degree in 1903, and remained for another year of study. At this time he became a close friend of William Ellery Leonard, and in later years he came to know Theodore Dreiser, Sinclair Lewis, and Sherwood Anderson.

Failing to revise his dissertation, he left the university without a doctor's degree, and began a short career in editorial work and writing for publication. His stories, accepted at first, were too somber for editors, and his early novels were unsuccessful. By reviewing and doing other odd jobs he scraped along until he secured a position teaching German at the University of Wisconsin in 1910.

From 1911 until 1919 he taught German at Ohio State, and, after the war, English and Latin in a private secondary school in New York. He left teaching for editorial work on the staff of the *Nation* in 1919. Since 1924 he has devoted his entire time to writing and lecturing, and he has become increasingly absorbed in the Zionist movement and other Jewish issues. For ten years he lived abroad; he now lives in Vermont with his second wife and their son.

In a life of trying to fit himself to Gentile patterns, only to feel himself an outcast because of his nationality, Lewisohn has had opportunity to observe the intolerance and bigotry of middle-class Christian Americans as revealed by the war and prohibition, and has come to feel the importance of nationality and the futility of attempts at "assimilation" of alien culture. In his studies and travels he has come to think that only as Jews can Jews make significant contributions to civilization; and he has espoused Zionism as a movement to strengthen national solidarity among his people.

Jewish philosophy he regards as more realistic than either pagan or Christian thought, offering hope of something more than mere understanding of the world about us, but avoiding the ascetic ideal of Christianity. The bankruptness of the latter, and the inevitability of its compromising with the world about it, he considers demonstrated by the World War, and by the failure of Christians, whatever their artistic and scientific achievements, to unite satisfactorily Hebraism and Hellenism and to attain moral stability and peace. The failure of Jesus to understand perfectly the Jewish traditions he was teaching, and Paul's spreading the un-Jewish elements in Christ's teachings, he regards as responsible for much of our present-day confusion, and he thinks that the tradition of Hebraism, so similar in many ways to these misinterpreted teachings of Jesus, has possibilities for indicating the way to the application of nationalism to peaceful culture rather than to politics, the understanding of the international community of interests, and peace and moral perfection.

For further comment, see Critical Survey, pp. 79, 178–79, 193, 200.

BIBLIOGRAPHY

Novels

The broken snare, 1908; Don Juan, 1923; The case of Mr. Crump, 1926; The defeated, 1927 (Am. ed., The island within, 1928); Roman summer, 1927; Stephen Escott, 1930 (English ed., The memories of Stephen Escott, 1930); The golden vase, 1931; The last days of Shylock . . . with drawings by Arthur Szyk, 1931; An altar in the fields, a novel, 1934; Trumpet of jubilee, a novel, 1937; For ever wilt thou love, 1939.

Short Stories

The romantic, a contemporary legend, 1931; This people, 1933.

Plays

A night in Alexandria, 1909; Adam, a dramatic history in a prologue, seven scenes and an epilogue, 1929.

Autobiography

* Up stream, an American chronicle, 1922; Mid-channel, an American chronicle, 1929.

Literary Criticism

George Sylvester Viereck: an appreciation by Ludwig Lewissohn [!] . . . reprinted from the Sewanee review, April 1904, 1904 (cover-title; pamphlet); The modern drama, an essay in interpretation, 1915; The spirit of modern German literature, lectures delivered before the University of Wisconsin, 1916; The poets of modern France, 1918 (with translations); The drama and the stage, 1922; The creative life, 1924; Cities and men, 1927; * Expression in America, 1932 (also pub. with title: The story of American literature, 1937).

Philosophical and Social Studies

Israel, 1925; The permanent horizon, a new search for old truths, 1934; The answer, the Jew and the world: past, present, and future, 1939.

Selected Works

Vérité et poésie, traduction de Régis Michaud et Franck L. Schœll, 1929; A Jew speaks, an anthology from Ludwig Lewisohn edited by James Waterman Wise, 1931.

Editor

German style, an introduction to the study of German prose, 1910; A modern book of criticism edited with an introduction, 1919; Creative America, an anthology chosen and edited, 1933; Rebirth, a book of modern Jewish thought selected and edited, 1935.

Editor and Translator

Letters from an American farmer by J. Hector St. John Crèvecoeur, reprinted from the original edition, with a prefatory note by W. P. Trent and an introduction by Ludwig Lewisohn, 1904; Health and suggestion, the dietetics of the mind by Ernst von Feuchtersleben . . . translated and edited, 1910; The dramatic works of Gerhart Hauptmann (Authorized edition) edited by Ludwig Lewisohn . . . volume one: social dramas, 1912; The dramatic works of Gerhart Hauptmann (Authorized edition) edited by Ludwig Lewisohn . . . volume two: social dramas, 1913; The dramatic works of Gerhart Hauptmann (Authorized edition) edited by Ludwig Lewisohn . . . volume three: domestic dramas, 1914; The dramatic works of Gerhart Hauptmann (Authorized edition) edited by Ludwig Lewisohn . . . volume four: symbolic and legendary dramas, 1914; The dramatic works of Gerhart Hauptmann (Authorized edition) edited by Ludwig Lewisohn . . . volume five: symbolic and legendary dramas, 1915; The dramatic works of Gerhart Hauptmann (Authorized edition) edited by Ludwig Lewisohn . . . volume six: later dramas in prose, 1915; The dramatic works of Gerhart Hauptmann (Authorized edition) edited by Ludwig Lewisohn . . . volume seven, miscellaneous dramas, 1917.

Translations

Elisabeth Koett by Rudolf Hans Bartsch, 1910; The Indian lily and other stories by Hermann Sudermann, 1911; The treasure, a drama in four acts by David Pinski, 1915; The mothers by Georg Hirschfeld translated and with an introduction, 1916; The judgment of peace, a novel by Andreas Latzko, 1919; The world's illusion by Jacob Wassermann authorized translation, 1920 (2 vols.); The goose man by Jacob Wassermann . . . authorized translation by Allen W. Porterfield, 1922 (trans. in part by Ludwig Lewisohn); Wedlock by Jacob Wassermann, 1926; The sorcerer's apprentice translated from the German of Hanns Heinz Ewers . . . illustrated by Mahlon Blaine, 1927; Bernhard Guttmann. Ambition, authorized translation, 1930; The eternal road, a drama in four parts by Franz Werfel, English version, 1936 (also issued in mimeographed form with title: The eternal road, a new play. Music by Kurt Weill, direction by Max Reinhardt, scenic and costume designer Norman Bel Geddes, 1935).

STUDIES AND ARTICLES

Beach
Brande
Bridges, Horace J. The God of fundamentalism and other studies. 1925
Collins (T)
Gillis, Adolph. Ludwig Lewisohn, the artist and his message. [c1933]
Kunitz (L)
Levinson
Lewisohn, Ludwig. Der fall Herbert Crump, roman . . . mit einem vorwort von Thomas Mann. [c1928]
Llona
† Manly
Mersand
National
Saturday
Schyberg
Shafer
Sherman
Zeitlin

Adeney, Marcus. "A voice from Israel." *CB.*, Sept. 1930, pp. 179–82; Austin, Mary. "Up stream." *D.*, June 22, 1922, pp. 634–39; Bates, Ernest S. "Lewisohn into Crump." *AM.*, Apr. 1934, pp. 441–50; Brande, Dorothea. "Mr. Lewisohn interprets America." *AR.*, Dec. 1933, pp. 189–98; Bridges, Horace J. "Up stream, Mr. Lewisohn versus America." *Stand.*, July 1923, pp. 14–23; Lewisohn, Ludwig. "Ludwig Lewisohn." *Nation*, Nov. 21, 1923, pp. 583–84; Lowell, Amy. "The case of modern poetry versus Professor Lewisohn." *AB.*, Jan. 1919, pp. 558–66; Moody, Minnie H. "Impressions of expression." *SR.*, Oct.–Dec. 1932, pp. 506–08; Snider, Charles L. "Tolerance, two social studies." *VQR.*, Oct. 1926, pp. 623–30. For references to reviews, see *BRD.*, 1908, 1915–16, 1918, 1920, 1922–34, 1936–37, 1939.

Frank Lin, *pseud.* *See* **Gertrude (Franklin Horn) Atherton**

(Nicholas) Vachel Lindsay, 1879–1931

Born November 10, 1879, in Springfield, Illinois. His father was a physician and his mother a woman of cultivation and energy, and they planned that the book-loving son, who pored over the Doré illustrations of the *Inferno* and *Paradise Lost*, would study medicine. Actually, he was dominated early in life by a threefold attraction to religion, poetry, and art; and, after education in a private school and the local grade and high schools and three not very successful years at Hiram College in Ohio (1897–1900), he decided to study art, and proceeded to get a job in the wholesale department of Marshall Field and Company and take night work at the Art Institute of Chicago.

After three years, although he was already writing poetry, he was still enthusiastic about a career as an artist, and went to New York to study with William M. Chase and Robert Henri at the New York School of Art. He supported himself by giving lectures on art at the West Side Y.M.C.A., making pen-and-ink designs, and working for a time as a guide in a museum. He failed, however, to find work drawing for magazines or even reporting for newspapers, and finally left New York for a long walking-tour in the spring of 1906. He wandered through the South from Florida to Tennessee, distributing a poem, "The Tree of Laughing Bells," and receiving in return food and shelter.

His parents were ill-pleased by this mode of life and in the summer took him to Europe, where he visited English and Continental art galleries. After his return he gave Y.M.C.A. lectures in New York and made a poetic walking-tour in 1908 through New Jersey and Pennsylvania, and, back in Springfield, lectured at the Y.M.C.A. and attempted to organize local literary groups. At this time he considered himself a failure. Always an enthusiastic reformer, he lectured during 1909–10 in central Illinois for the Anti-Saloon League. In the summer of 1912 he tramped through the Middle West and Southwest, distributing *Rhymes to Be Traded for Bread* and attempting to make converts to "the gospel of beauty"; but, when he got as far as New Mexico, he gave up.

His fortunes were changed magically by the success of his poetry. "General William Booth Enters into Heaven," which he sent Harriet Monroe when she asked to see his work, was printed in *Poetry* in January, 1913, and won him an audience, and *The Congo and Other Poems* (1914) enjoyed wide popular acclaim. The author, furthermore, soon became much in demand as a lecturer and a chanter of his own verse. He performed before many American colleges, clubs, and similar institutions; in 1920 he visited England and appeared before groups of people in London, and he was the first American poet to be invited to recite his poems at Oxford University. In 1923–24 he taught literature for three semesters in Gulf Park College, Mississippi. Many of his books of poetry were illustrated by the poet's own drawings.

In 1925 he married Elizabeth Conner and settled for three years in Spokane. In 1929 he returned to Springfield, now a respected citizen and neighbor. His powers, however, were declining; and, depressed by a combination of ill health, poverty, and a feeling of general defeat, he committed suicide on December 5, 1931.

Lindsay was a born crusader, inheriting this impulse from his mother, and much of his verse was written in support of principles of communal recitation and communal enjoyment. He was much interested in poetry as sound, and admired the work of Poe, Lanier, and Swinburne. There are phonograph records of his chanting. "General Booth" was responsible for the institution, by *Poetry*, of the Guarantors Prize. *The Chinese Nightingale* (1917) took the Helen Haire Levinson Prize, and in 1928 *Poetry* gave him the Award of Honor (five hundred dollars) for genius and originality. He was a member of the Poetry Society of America and the National Institute of Arts and Letters.

For further comment, see Critical Survey, pp. 137–39.

BIBLIOGRAPHY

Poems

Under Spokane's brocaded sun, 19— (broadside); The cup of paint, 1905 (card); The tree of laughing bells, 1905 (cover-title; pamphlet; cover design by the author); We who are playing to-night, 1905 (leaflet); I heard Immanuel singing, 1907? (broadside); God help us to be brave, a poem concerning the twenty-six representative citizens of the world from Rameses II to Roosevelt, 1908? (caption-title; pamphlet); The heroes of time, a poem illustrating the position of Abraham Lincoln among the dominating personalities of history, 1908? (caption-title; pamphlet; cover designed by the author); The dance of unskilled labor, 1908 (cover-title; leaflet); The last song of Lucifer, 1908 (contains prose; caption-title; pamphlet); On the building of Springfield, 1908 (caption-title; leaflet); To the sweet singer of Israel, a poem, 1908 (leaflet); Drink for sale, 1909 (leaflet; illus. by the author); The tramp's excuse and other poems, 1909 (cover-title; illus. by the author); The moon worms, 1910 (broadside); To the United States Senate, 1911? (broadside); The gospel of beauty, being the new "Creed of a beggar" by that vain and foolish mendicant Nicholas Vachel Lindsay, 1912 (broadside); Proclamation of the gospel of beauty, 1912 (broadside); Rhymes to be traded for bread, being new verses by Nicholas Vachel Lindsay, Springfield, Illinois, June, 1912. Printed expressly as a substitute for money, 1912 (caption-title; pamphlet); General William Booth enters into Heaven and other poems, 1913; The wedding of the rose and the lotus, 1913 (pamphlet); The Congo and other poems . . . with an introduction by Harriet Monroe, 1914; The Chinese nightingale and other poems, 1917; The golden whales of California, 1919 (broadside); The Daniel jazz and other poems, 1920; The golden whales of California and other rhymes in the American language, 1920; I know all this when gipsy fiddles cry, 1922 (leaflet); So keep going to the sun, 1922? (broadside); Collected poems, 1923 (rev. and illus. ed., 1925; illus. by the author); Going-to-the-sun, 1923; When the stuffed prophets quarrel, 1924 (broadside); The candle in the cabin, a weaving together of script and singing, 1926 (illus. by the author); Going-to-the-stars, 1926; Hamlet in Springfield, 1927 (broadside); Our little cave-man, 1927 (broadside); Johnny Appleseed and other poems . . . illustrated by George Richards, 1928; The Virginians are coming again, 1928 (broadside); Every soul is a circus . . . decorations by the author and George M. Richards, 1929; Rigamarole, rigamarole, 1929 (pamphlet); The Ezekiel's chant, 1930 (broadside); Selected poems of Vachel Lindsay edited with an introduction by Hazelton Spencer, 1931.

Description and Travel

Adventures while preaching the gospel of beauty, 1914; A handy guide for beggars, especially those of the poetic fraternity, being sundry explorations made while afoot and penniless in Florida, Georgia, North Carolina, Tennessee, Kentucky, New Jersey, and Pennsylvania. These adventures convey and illustrate the rules of beggary for poets and some others, 1916.

Studies

The art of the moving picture, 1915 (also pub. as The art of the moving picture intended, first of all, for the new art museums springing up all over the country. But the book is for our universities and institutions of learning. It contains an appeal to our whole critical and literary world and to our creators of sculpture, architecture, painting, and the American cities they are building. Being the 1922 revision of the book first issued in 1915 and beginning with an ample discourse on the great new prospects of 1922, 1922).

Verses Set to Music

A cycle of songs for baritone. The Congo, poem by Vachel Lindsay, music by Arthur Bergh, 1918 (sheet music); Animals and insects, seven songs for a medium voice and piano accompaniment (words by Vachel Lindsay) by Louis Gruenberg, op. 22. 1. The lion, 2. An explanation of the grasshopper, 3. The spider and the ghost of the fly, 4. A dirge for a righteous kitten, 5. The mysterious cat, 6. The mouse that gnawed the oak-tree down, 7. Two old crows, 1925 (title page and text in English and German; sheet music); The Daniel jazz for a voice and eight instruments . . . by Louis Gruenberg, op. 21 [words by] Vachel Lindsay, deutsch von R. St. Hoffmann, 1925 (pamphlet; text in English and German); Vachel Lindsay's poem Daniel with musical score by Harvey Enders, 1925; General William Booth enters into Heaven, a setting for low or medium voice, with piano, of the poem by Vachel Lindsay by Sidney Homer, 1926 (cover-title); Two old crows, an exercise in stuttering for male voices, an original setting by Harvey Enders, poem by Vachel Lindsay, 1932 (caption-title); To a golden haired girl (S.A.T.B. divided) poem by Vachel Lindsay . . . music by George F. McKay, 1936 (caption-title; sheet music).

Miscellany

The village improvement parade, 1908? (pamphlet); Map of the universe, 1909 (broadside); War bulletin number one, 1909 (caption-title; pamphlet); War bulletin number two, 1909 (caption-title; pamphlet); War bulletin number three, 1909 (caption-title; pamphlet); War bulletin number five, 1909 (caption-title; pamphlet); A letter about my four programmes for committees in correspondence, 1910 (pamphlet; illus. by the author); The village magazine, 1910 (cover-title; pamphlet); A letter for your wicked private ear only, 1912? (broadside); The soul of the city receives the gift of the Holy Spirit, 1913 (pamphlet); The kind of visit I like to make, 1919 (broadside); The golden book of Springfield by Vachel Lindsay, a citizen of that town, being the review of a book that will appear in the autumn of the year 2018 and an extended description of Springfield, Illinois, in that year, 1920; The village magazine [2d imprint], 1920 (cover-title); A letter for your wicked private ear only, 1921 (caption-title;

pamphlet); The village magazine, 1925 (cover-title; 3d revision); The village magazine, fourth imprint, written and illustrated, 1925; The litany of Washington street, 1929; The village improvement parade, souvenir programme of recital by Mr. and Mrs. Vachel Lindsay, at the First Christian church, October 13, 1930, 1930? (pamphlet).

STUDIES AND ARTICLES

Aiken
Blankenship
Boynton
Boynton (H)
Bruns
Bryant, Arthur. The American ideal. 1936
Canby (S)
Chesterton
Cook
Davison, Edward L. Some modern poets and other critical essays. 1928
Dell
Deutsch
Dictionary
The Elementary English review, May 1932, vol. 9, no. 5. Memorial number, Vachel Lindsay.
Garland, Hamlin. Companions on the trail, a literary chronicle . . . decorations by Constance Garland. 1931
Gerstmann, Ilse. Die technik des bewegungseindrucks in gedichten Edith Sitwells und Vachel Lindsays. 1936
Graham
Graham, Stephen. Tramping with a poet in the Rockies . . . with thirty-eight emblems by Vernon Hill. 1922
Hackett
Halleck
Hazard
† Herrmann
James, Philip. General William Booth enters into Heaven, a rhapsody for male chorus, poem by Nicholas Vachel Lindsay, music by Philip James. c1933 (caption-title)
† Johnson (1929)
† Johnson (1932)
† Johnson (1936)
Jones
Kreymborg
Kunitz (L)
Lewisohn (E)
Lindsay, Nicholas Vachel. General William Booth enters into Heaven and other poems . . . with an introduction by Robert Nichols. 1919
Loggins
Lowden
Lowell
Lynd, Robert. Books and authors. 1923
† Manly
Masters, Edgar L. Vachel Lindsay, a poet in America. 1935
Maynard
Monroe
Monroe (P)
Morley, Christopher D. Ex libris carissimis. 1932
Munson (D)
National
Pattee (N)
Phelps
Phelps (AW)
Rittenhouse
Saturday
Smith
Squire
Stidger, William L. Giant hours with poet preachers . . . introduction by Edwin Markham. [c1918]
† Taylor
Tietjens
† Trombly, Albert E. Vachel Lindsay, adventurer. 1929
Untermeyer
Untermeyer (C)
Untermeyer (H)
Untermeyer (M)
Untermeyer (N)
Van Doren

Van Doren (A)
† Van Doren (M)
Vočadlo
Ward
Weirick
Whipple
Widdemer
Williams-Ellis
Wood

Aiken, Conrad. "A letter from Vachel Lindsay." *AB.*, Mar. 1932, pp. 598–601; Anonymous. "Mr. Vachel Lindsay." *D.*, Oct. 16, 1914, pp. 281–83; Davies, Charles, and Lucas, Llewellyn. "Two aspects of Vachel Lindsay." *PP.*, Sept. 1927, pp. 294–303; Davison, Edward. "Nicholas Vachel Lindsay." *Merc.*, Apr. 1928, pp. 652–65; Drinkwater, John. "Two American lives." *QR.*, Jan. 1936, pp. 122–35; DuBois, Arthur E. "Lindsay and especially Masters." *SR.*, July–Sept. 1936, pp. 377–82; Gorman, Herbert S. "Vachel Lindsay, evangelist of poetry." *N.Amer.Rev.*, Jan. 1924, pp. 123–28; Henderson, Alice C. "The Congo and other poems." *P.*, Mar. 1915, pp. 296–99; Lesemann, Maurice. "Two trampers, and a poem." *P.*, July 1923, pp. 212–15; Macfarlane, Peter C. "A vagabond poet." *Collier's*, Sept. 6, 1913, pp. 7–8, 32; Masters, Edgar L. "The tragedy of Vachel Lindsay." *AM.*, July 1933, pp. 357–69; Masters. "Vachel Lindsay." *AB.*, Oct. 1926, pp. 156–60; Masters. "Vachel Lindsay and America." *SRL.*, Aug. 10, 1935, pp. 3–4, 15; Monroe, Harriet. "Celestial jazz." *P.*, May 1920, pp. 101–04; Monroe. "The limnal Lindsay." *P.*, Jan. 1927, pp. 217–21; Monroe. "Lindsay." *P.*, Jan. 1932, pp. 206–12; Monroe. "The Lindsay biography." *P.*, Mar. 1936, pp. 337–44; Monroe. "Lindsay's poems." *P.*, Feb. 1914, pp. 182–83; Monroe. "Notes and queries from Mr. Lindsay." *P.*, Feb. 1921, pp. 262–66; Monroe. "Still alive." *P.*, Jan. 1918, pp. 214–17; Monroe. "Vachel Lindsay." *P.*, May 1924, pp. 90–95; Moore, Marianne. "An eagle in the ring." *D.*, Nov. 1923, pp. 498–505; Moses, William R. "Vachel Lindsay, ferment of the poet's mind." *So.R.*, Spring 1936, pp. 828–36; Rittenhouse, Jessie B. "Vachel Lindsay." *SAQ.*, July 1933, pp. 266–82; Robinson, Henry M. "The ordeal of Vachel Lindsay, a critical reconstruction." *AB.*, Apr. 1932, pp. 6–9; Spencer, Hazelton. "The life and death of a bard." *AM.*, Apr. 1932, pp. 455–62; Starke, Aubrey, and others. "They knew Vachel Lindsay, a symposium of personal reminiscences." *Lat.Q.*, Autumn 1934, pp. 128–40; Tietjens, Eunice. "Bids for premature judgment." *P.*, Sept. 1923, pp. 330–33; Trombly, Albert E. "Vachel Lindsay's prose." *Sw.R.*, Summer, 1928, pp. 459–68; Van Doren, Carl. "Salvation with jazz, Vachel Lindsay, evangelist in verse." *Cent.*, Apr. 1923, pp. 951–56; Wimberly, Lowry C. "Vachel Lindsay." *FM.*, Mar. 1934, pp. 212–16. For references to reviews, see *BRD.*, 1914–17, 1920–21, 1923, 1926, 1929.

Walter Lippmann, 1889–

Born September 23, 1889, in New York. In his childhood he attended local private schools and traveled abroad during the summers. In 1906 he entered Harvard, and he became a member of President Eliot's last graduating class (1910), which included John Reed, Alan Seeger, Robert Edmond Jones, Edward Sheldon, Clarence Cook Little, and Heywood Broun. Actually, however, he took his bachelor's degree in 1909, and remained the next year as assistant in philosophy to Professor Santayana. At this time he was in contact with William James and took a course in political theory and psychology given by Graham Wallas. He also served as editor of the *Harvard Monthly*.

After finishing his graduate studies he entered journalism. For a short while he worked as investigator with Lincoln Steffens on *Everybody's Magazine*, but left the magazine to do free-lance writing for the New York *Times* and periodicals.

In 1912 he went to Schenectady as secretary to the new Socialist mayor, George R. Lunn. In the same year he read Freud, and his *A Preface to Politics*, described by Freud as the first political study with a Freudian basis, appeared, as a result, in 1913. Regarded highly by ex-President Theodore Roosevelt, it was a feature of the campaign of the Progressive party; and, when a group of liberal writers bent their energies to found the *New Republic* in 1914, Lippmann was one of them. The increasingly political color of his thinking appeared in *Drift and Mastery* and especially *The Status of Diplomacy*, in which he argued for the internationalizing of backward areas and countries for their benefit and protection.

His interest in international relations and war and peace found a more practical release when, in 1917, he became assistant to Newton D. Baker, Secretary of War; and in the same year he served as secretary of "The Inquiry," a group of research workers collecting information as to the probable requirements for a satisfactory peace. In 1918 he went abroad to confer with those working in a similar capacity for Allied governments, and as captain of the Military Intelligence Division he was expected to advise the army on questions of propaganda. With Frank Cobb, editor of the New York *World*, he assisted Colonel House by preparing an interpretation of President Wilson's Fourteen Points.

Returning to this country before the close of the Peace Conference in 1919, he joined again the staff of the *New Republic*, and continued to publish books. In 1921 he was made an editorial writer on the *World*, and, after a trip abroad, he took responsibility for the editorial page (1923). In 1929 he became editor. When the *World* ceased publication in 1931, he joined the *Herald-Tribune*, in which his column, widely syndicated, has come to have a considerable influence on public opinion. Lippmann, who holds many honorary degrees, is a member of the American Academy of Arts and Letters.

A "connoisseur of public affairs," Lippmann has, in the course of his career as author and thinker, swung from a liberal faith in simple democracy to a position of distrust toward the impulses of the masses, and reliance upon experiment and verifiable fact. In *A Preface to Morals* he substitutes for divine revelation an ethical code based upon prophecies of inspired men, the results of modern science, and the needs of our world. Thus scientific authority is made to corroborate the visions of past thinkers and point out, as the way to human happiness, an objective sort of virtue, which is the only solution that will satisfy the demands of the modern world.

For further comment, see Critical Survey, p. 156.

BIBLIOGRAPHY

Political and Social Studies

* A preface to politics, 1913; Drift and mastery, an attempt to diagnose the current unrest, 1914; The New republic, a journal of opinion. The campaign against sweating . . . reprinted from the issue of March 27, 1915 for the National consumers' league, 1915 (cover-title; pamphlet); The stakes of diplomacy, 1915; The world conflict in its relation to American democracy, 1917 (caption-title; pamphlet); The basic problem of democracy, 1919 (cover-title; pamphlet); L.F.N.A. The fourteen points and the League of nations, an ad-

dress delivered before the League of free nations association on April 5th, 1919 at Hotel Commodore, New York city, 1919 (cover-title; pamphlet); The political scene, an essay on the victory of 1918, 1919; Liberty and the news, 1920; A test of the news by Walter Lippmann and Charles Merz, prepared with the assistance of Faye Lippmann, an examination of the news reports in the New York times on aspects of the Russian revolution of special importance to Americans March 1917–March 1920, 1920 (cover-title; pamphlet); France and the European settlement, an address . . . before the Foreign policy association, Hotel Astor, New York, February, 1922, 1922 (caption-title; pamphlet); Public opinion, 1922; Mr. Kahn would like to know . . . reprinted from the July 4 issue of the New republic by the Foreign policy association, 1923 (caption-title; leaflet); The phantom public, 1925; Men of destiny . . . drawings by Rollin Kirby, 1927; American inquisitors, a commentary on Dayton and Chicago . . . Barbour-Page lectures, University of Virginia, 1928, 1928; Notes on the crisis, 1931; Repeal the Eighteenth amendment. I, The repeal of the Eighteenth amendment, an address delivered at Pasadena, California, March 17, 1931 by Nicholas Murray Butler. II, The great Wickersham mystery, an article printed in Vanity fair for April 1931 by Walter Lippmann. III, Prohibition enforcement—Wickersham report, a speech made in the Senate of the United States, February 17, 1931 by Senator Robert F. Wagner of New York. IV, Resolutions unanimously passed by the Women's organization for national prohibition reform, assembled at their second annual conference, Washington, D.C., April 14 and April 15, 1931, 1931 (pamphlet); Interpretations, 1931–1932 . . . selected and edited by Allan Nevins, 1932; Poverty and plenty, an address delivered before 4,500 delegates to the National conference of social work, Philadelphia, May 20th, 1932, 1932; The scholar in a troubled world, an address delivered as the Phi beta kappa oration at the commencement exercises of Columbia university May 31, 1932, 1932; Shall we deflate some more? . . . Reprinted by the Committee for the consideration of inter-governmental debts . . . New York city from the New York herald tribune, November 23, 1932, 1932 (cover-title; leaflet); The United States in world affairs, an account of American foreign relations, 1931, Walter Lippmann in collaboration with William O. Scroggs, 1932; A new social order, an address delivered on Charter day at the University of California at Berkeley, California, on March 23rd, 1933, 1933; The United States in world affairs, an account of American foreign relations, 1932, prepared by Walter Lippmann with the assistance of the research staff of the Council on foreign relations, 1933; The method of freedom, 1934; Self-sufficiency: some random reflections by Walter Lippmann. Planning international trade by G. D. H. Cole, 1934 (cover-title; pamphlet); The new imperative, 1935; Interpretations, 1933–1935 . . . selected and edited by Allan Nevins, 1936; An inquiry into the principles of the good society, 1937 (English ed., The good society, 1937); The Supreme court, independent or controlled? 1937.

Ethics

* A preface to morals, 1929.

Literary Criticism

H. L. Mencken . . . reprinted from the Saturday review of literature December 11, 1926, 1926 (cover-title; pamphlet).

Editor

The poems of Paul Mariett, 1913; The United States in world affairs, an account of American foreign relations, 1933, prepared by William O. Scroggs, and the research staff of the Council on foreign relations edited and with an introduction by Walter Lippmann, 1934; A modern reader, essays on present-day life and culture selected and edited with the collaboration of Walter Lippmann and Allan Nevins, 1936.

STUDIES AND ARTICLES

Dewey, John. Characters and events, popular essays in social and political philosophy . . . edited by Joseph Ratner. Volume II. [1929]

Dewey, John. Outlawry of war, what it is and is not, a reply to Walter Lippmann, reprinted for the American committee for the outlawry of war from the New republic of October 3d and 24th, 1923. 1923 (pamphlet)

Encyclopedia

Kunitz (L)

Luccock

Macmillan, *firm, publishers, New York.* Walter Lippmann, connoisseur of public affairs. [n.d.]

National

Smith, Beverly. Preface to Walter Lippmann. 1932 (pamphlet)

Baker, Newton D. "The good society of the future." *A.Mo.*, Nov. 1937, pp. 612–16; Collins, Seward B. "Almost a distributist." *AR.*, Sept. 1934, pp. 537–44; Gooch, Robert K. "Government and public opinion." *VQR.*, Jan. 1926, pp. 142–46; Kayden, Eugene M. "An exercise in evasions." *SR.*, July–Sept. 1935, pp. 383–84; Knight, Frank H. "Lippmann's 'The good society.'" *JPE.*, Dec. 1938, pp. 864–72; Laprade, William T. "Public opinion." *SAQ.*, Oct. 1922, pp. 367–68; Lerner, Max. "Do free markets make free men?" *So.R.*, Winter 1938, pp. 626–32; Lien, Arnold J. "The phantom public." *SR.*, Apr.–June 1926, pp. 230–33; Meadows, Harold. "The liberalism of Walter Lippmann." *N.Masses*, May 1933, pp. 6, 8–9; Morrow, Felix. "Preface to morals." *Men.J.*, Feb. 1930, pp. 97–117; Pinchot, Amos. "The liberal position." *N.Amer.Rev.*, Winter 1937–38, pp. 368–88; Pinchot. "Walter Lippmann, the great elucidator." *Nation*, July 5, 1933, pp. 7–10; Pinchot. "Walter Lippmann, the new tammany." *Nation*, July 12, 1933, pp. 36–38; Pinchot. "Walter Lippmann, obfuscator de luxe." *Nation*, July 19, 1933, pp. 67–70; Pinchot. "Walter Lippmann, on democracy." *Nation*, Aug. 2, 1933, pp. 126–31; Rubenstein, Annette T. "Disinterestedness as ideal and as technique." *J.Phil.*, Aug. 13, 1931, pp. 461–66; Stolberg, Benjamin. "Walter Lippmann, connoisseur of public life." *Nation*, Dec. 7, 1927, pp. 639–42; Terman, Lewis M. "The great conspiracy, or, the impulse imperious of intelligence testers, psychoanalyzed and exposed by Mr. Lippmann." *NR.*, Dec. 27, 1922, pp. 116–20; Young, Stark. "Art and the moral life, dedicated to Walter Lippmann." *NR.*, July 1929, pp. 228–30. For references to reviews, see *BRD.*, 1913–15, 1919–20, 1922, 1925–29, 1932–37.

Amy Lowell, 1874–1925

Born February 9, 1874, in Brookline, Massachusetts, of a distinguished New England family. James Russell Lowell was a cousin of her grandfather, and the astronomer Percival Lowell and Abbott Lawrence Lowell, president of Harvard, were her brothers. As a child she was educated by her mother, a student of languages and a musician, and she attended private schools. When she was eight she was taken to Europe for six months in the British Isles and on the Continent, and at nine she made a trip to California; for the most part she spent her time in Brookline and Boston. She inherited a love for gardens, and came to enjoy horseback riding and to love animals. At one time she had seven sheep-dogs.

After the death of her mother in 1895 Miss Lowell went again to Europe, and the winter of 1897–98 she spent on the Nile. These travels, like those of her childhood, brought on a breakdown, and in 1898–99 she spent a winter on a fruit ranch at El Cajon, California. The following summer she passed in Devonshire; and in 1900, the year of her father's death, she bought the family estate, "Sevenels," in Brookline, and settled down as a solid citizen and, more specifically, a leader in the movement to improve libraries in Massachusetts.

Although in her childhood she had written verse and stories, it was not until about 1902 that she made up her mind to study poetry seriously; and her career from this point forward was shaped with this object in mind. She read classical literature, studied poetic techniques, and traveled and met poets and authors. Her first published poem appeared in the *Atlantic Monthly* in 1910, and her first volume, *A Dome of Many-Colored Glass*, in 1912. During these years she had gone to Europe and even reached Greece and Turkey; and in 1913 she made a trip to England. Here she met Ezra Pound, John Gould Fletcher, H. D., and Richard Aldington, and identified herself enthusiastically with the Imagist movement. *Sword Blades and Poppy Seeds*, published in the following year, included her first poems in free verse and "polyphonic prose," and made her the leader of the Imagist group. From this time on she was an ardent critical champion of the "new" poetry, and studied the work of French poets, experimented with verse techniques, and began her lecture career. She was a warm friend and supporter of the new magazine of verse, *Poetry*.

In 1915 she gave lectures in Boston, New York, and Chicago; and in 1917–18 she lectured for the Brooklyn Institute of Arts and Sciences. In 1921 she lectured on the Francis Bergen foundation at Yale, on the occasion of the hundredth anniversary of the death of Keats, and was Marshall Woods lecturer at Brown University. She was Phi Beta Kappa poet at Tufts College (1918) and Columbia (1920), and was awarded the Helen Haire Levinson Prize of *Poetry* in 1924. In 1920 she received an honorary doctor's degree from Baylor University.

Her last years she spent at work on a thorough biographical study of Keats, and the strain from her work and the effects of years of poor health resulted in her death on May 12, 1925, from a paralytic stroke, in the midst of plans for an English lecture tour. *What's O'clock*, which appeared in the same year, was awarded the Pulitzer Prize for Poetry in 1926.

"I made myself a poet," Miss Lowell is said to have remarked of herself, "but the Lord made me a business man." Her driving, organizing genius was as much a part of her contribution to the "new poetry" movement as her fastidiousness and accuracy in details of diction and even punctuation. Her distress over even a misplaced comma in the printed form of her work was matched by her energy and enthusiasm in behalf of writers and poets, and her kindness and aid to Duse in the latter's last American tour; and both traits were brought the more sharply to public attention by such personal eccentricities as her unusual appearance and mode of dress, her nocturnal habits of work, and her habit of smoking cigars. She was conventional in her views on politics and social issues. A fascinating and magnetic conversationalist, she could read her lectures and poems with vigor and great rhythmic effectiveness.

For further comment, see Critical Survey, pp. 128, 136, 141–42, 168, 204.

BIBLIOGRAPHY

Poems

A dome of many-coloured glass, 1912; Sword blades and poppy seed, 1914; Ballads for sale. Fresh new ballads with the ink scarce dried upon them, 1916 (broadside); Men, women, and ghosts, 1916; Can Grande's castle, 1918; Pictures of the floating world, 1919; Fir-flower tablets, poems translated from the Chinese by Florence Ayscough . . . English versions by Amy Lowell, 1921; Legends, 1921; Dear sir (or dear madam) who happen to glance at this title-page printed you'll see to enhance its æsthetic attraction, pray buy, if you're able, this excellent bargain: A critical fable, the book may be read in the light of a sequel to the "Fable for critics" a volume unequal (or hitherto so) for its quips and digressions on the poets of the day, without undue professions, I would say that this treatise is fully as light as the former, its judgments as certainly right as need be. A hodge-podge delivered primarily in the hope of instilling instruction so airily that readers may see, in the persons on view, a peripatetic, poetic Who's who. An account of the times by a poker of fun, WITT D., O.S., A.I., 1922 (pamphlet); What's o'clock, 1925; East wind, 1926; Ballads for sale, 1927; The madonna of Carthagena, 1927; * Selected poems of Amy Lowell edited by John Livingston Lowes, 1928.

Biography

* John Keats, 1925 (2 vols.).

Literary Criticism

Six French poets, studies in contemporary literature, 1915; Tendencies in modern American poetry, 1917; Poetry and poets, essays, 1930.

Stories

Dream drops, or, Stories from fairy land by a dreamer, 1887 (with Katherine Lowell Bowkler and Katherine Bigelow Lowell).

Translation

Weeping Pierrot and laughing Pierrot, Pierrot qui pleure et Pierrot qui rit, a comedy with music in one act, French text by Edmond Rostand, English version by Amy Lowell, music by Jean Hubert, vocal score with dialogue, n. 1.25, 1914.

Verses Set to Music

Carl Engel. Two lyrics by Amy Lowell for a solo voice, with piano accompaniment [by Carl Engel]. 1. The sea-shell. 2. The trout, 1911 (cover-title;

sheet music; 2 vols.); Three poems by Amy Lowell, composed by Carl Engel for medium voice and piano. Opal, A decade, A sprig of rosemary, 1922 (cover-title; sheet music; 3 vols.); Reflections [by] Amy Lowell [music by] Camille W. Zeckwer, 1924 (caption-title; sheet music); The shower [by] Amy Lowell [music by] Camille W. Zeckwer, 1924 (caption-title; sheet music); Song, Sea shell, poem by Amy Lowell, music by Felix White, medium voice, in E♭, low voice in C, 1926 (cover-title; sheet music); Four lacquer prints, words by Amy Lowell, music by Alexander Steinert, 1932 (caption-title; sheet music).

STUDIES AND ARTICLES

Aiken
Anderson
Auslander
Blankenship
Boas
Boynton
Boynton (H)
Boynton (L)
Boynton (S)
Braithwaite
Brenner
Bruns
Bryher, Winifred. Amy Lowell, a critical appreciation. 1918
Canby
Cestre, Charles. Poetry of Amy Lowell translated by Dana Hill from an article in La Revue anglo-americaine with bibliography and critical appreciation. [1927?] (pamphlet)
Collins (T)
Cook
† Damon, Samuel F. Amy Lowell, a chronicle, with extracts from her correspondence. 1935
Dictionary
Erskine
Farrar
Fletcher
Garnett
Hill, Edward B. In memoriam A. L. Lilacs, poem for orchestra . . . op. 33. [Suggested by the poem by Amy Lowell.] [c1931]
Hind (M)
Hoskier, Herman C. "The bronze horses," a comment on the prose-poem of Amy Lowell. 1930
Hughes
Hunt, Richard. Amy Lowell, a sketch of her life and her place in contemporary American literature. [1917] (cover-title; pamphlet)
Hunt, Richard and Snow, Royall H. Amy Lowell, sketches biographical and critical. [1921] (cover-title; pamphlet)
† Johnson (1929)
† Johnson (1932)
† Johnson (1936)
Jones
Kilmer
Kreymborg
Kunitz
Loggins
Lowden
Lowes, John L. Essays in appreciation. 1936
Mallory
† Manly
Maynard
The Mentor. Makers of modern American poetry—women, Amy Lowell, one. c1920 (broadside)
Michaud (P)
Monroe
Monroe (P)
National
Phelps
Rittenhouse
Sargent, George H. Amy Lowell, a mosaic. 1926
Sergeant
Sessions
Sinclair
Taupin
† Taylor
Tietjens
Untermeyer
Untermeyer (C)
Untermeyer (H)

Untermeyer (M)	Ward
Untermeyer (N)	Williams-Ellis
Van Doren	Wood
Van Doren (A)	Wood, Clement. Amy Lowell. 1926
Vočadlo	

Aiken, Conrad. "Miss Lowell abides our question." *D.*, Oct. 18, 1919, pp. 331–33; Allen, Hervey. "Amy Lowell as a poet." *SRL.*, Feb. 5, 1927, pp. 557–58, 568; Allen. "The passing of Amy Lowell." *AB.*, July 1925, pp. 519–23; Anonymous. "Amy Lowell." *AB.*, Dec. 1923, pp. 418–24; Ayscough, Florence. "Amy Lowell and the far east." *AB.*, Mar. 1926, pp. 11–18; Benét, William R. "Amy Lowell and other poets." *YR.*, Oct. 1921, pp. 175–80; Boynton, Percy H. "Amy Lowell." *EJ.*, Nov. 1922, pp. 527–35; Catel, Jean. "Mort d' Amy Lowell." *MF.*, Aug. 1, 1925, pp. 826–31; Cestre, Charles. "Amy Lowell, Robert Frost, and Edwin Arlington Robinson." *JHAM.*, Mar. 1926, pp. 363–88; Cestre. "L'oeuvre poétique d'Amy Lowell." *RAA.*, Aug. 1925, pp. 481–500; Chew, Samuel C. "Miss Lowell's biography of Keats." *N.Amer.Rev.*, Mar. 1925, pp. 545–55; Clarke, George H. "Amy Lowell's life of John Keats." *SR.*, July–Sept. 1925, pp. 335–50; Damon, Samuel F. "East wind, west wind." *YR.*, Apr. 1927, pp. 587–91; Erskine, John. "John Keats and Amy Lowell." *VQR.*, July 1925, pp. 271–75; Fletcher, John G. "Living history." *P.*, June 1917, pp. 149–53; Fletcher. "Miss Lowell's discovery, polyphonic prose." *P.*, Apr. 1915, pp. 32–36; Hammond, Josephine. "Amy Lowell and the pretorian cohorts." *Pers.*, Oct. 1920, pp. 14–36; Isoré, Pierre. "L'originalité d'Amy Lowell." *RAA.*, Apr. 1929, pp. 317–26; † Johnson, Merle D. and Hopkins, Frederick M., *eds.* "American first editions, a series of bibliographic check-lists . . . number 34, Amy Lowell, 1874– compiled by Mildred C. Smith." *PW.*, May 19, 1923, p. 1515; † Kemp, Frances. "Bibliography of Amy Lowell." *BBDI.*, May–Aug. 1933, pp. 8–9; † Kemp. "Bibliography of Amy Lowell." *BBDI.*, Sept.–Dec. 1933, pp. 25–26; † Kemp. "Bibliography of Amy Lowell." *BBDI.*, Jan.–Apr. 1934, pp. 50–53; Kizer, Helen B. "Amy Lowell, a personality." *N.Amer.Rev.*, May 1918, pp. 736–47; Lippmann, Walter. "Miss Lowell and things." *NR.*, Mar. 18, 1916, pp. 178–79; Lovett, Robert M. "Amy Lowell." *NR.*, May 27, 1925, p. 17; Lowes, John L. "The poetry of Amy Lowell." *SRL.*, Oct. 3, 1925, pp. 169–70, 174–75; MacLeish, Archibald. "Amy Lowell and the art of poetry." *N.Amer.Rev.*, Mar. 1925, pp. 508–21; Monroe, Harriet. "Amy Lowell." *P.*, Oct. 1924, pp. 32–38; Monroe. "Amy Lowell on Keats." *P.*, July 1925, pp. 220–26; Monroe. "The Amy Lowell scholarships." *P.*, Aug. 1925, pp. 276–77; Monroe. "A daughter of the Caesars." *P.*, Jan. 1936, pp. 212–19; Monroe. "A decorative colorist." *P.*, Jan. 1917, pp. 207–09; Monroe. "Her books and herself." *P.*, Mar. 1928, pp. 338–43; Monroe. "A keen east wind." *P.*, Dec. 1926, pp. 160–63; Monroe. "Memories of Amy Lowell." *P.*, July 1925, pp. 208–14; Monroe. "Miss Lowell and polyphonic prose." *P.*, Nov. 1918, pp. 97–102; Monroe. "Miss Lowell on tendencies." *P.*, Dec. 1917, pp. 151–56; Monroe. "That bookshelf." *P.*, Oct. 1919, pp. 39–42; Patterson, William M. "New verse and new prose." *N.Amer.Rev.*, Feb. 1918, pp. 257–67; Perkins, Elizabeth W. "Amy Lowell of New England." *Scrib.*, Sept. 1927, pp. 329–35; Schwartz, William L. "A study of Amy Lowell's far eastern verse." *MLN.*, Mar. 1928, pp. 145–52; Scott, Winfield T. "Amy Lowell after ten years." *NEQ.*, Sept. 1935, pp. 320–30; Sergeant, Elizabeth S. "Amy Lowell memory sketch for a biographer." *NR.*, Nov. 18, 1925, pp. 322–26; Tittle, Walter. "Glimpses of interesting Americans." *Cent.*, June 1925, pp. 177–80; Tupper, James W. "The poetry of Amy Lowell." *SR.*, Jan. 1920, pp. 37–53; Yeaman, Virginia. "Amy Lowell at Sevenels." *Forum*, July 1925, pp. 76–79. For references to reviews, see *BRD.*, 1914–19, 1921, 1925–28, 1930.

Mabel (Ganson) Dodge (Sterne) Luhan, 1879–

Born Mabel Ganson, February 26, 1879, in Buffalo, where her well-to-do family was socially important. She traveled abroad and attended St. Margaret's School in Buffalo, Miss Graham's School in New York, and the Chevy Chase School in Washington, D.C. She made her début at a formal ball in Buffalo.

Her marriage to Carl Evans in 1900, the birth of a son, and her husband's death in 1902 caused her to go to Europe to live. She married a wealthy Boston architect, Edwin Dodge, and they established themselves in a fifteenth-century villa in Florence, where they entertained numbers of artists and writers. Eleanora Duse, Gertrude Stein, Alice B. Toklas, and Gordon Craig were among their guests.

To educate her son she returned to this country in 1913 and settled in New York. Amicably divorced from Mr. Dodge, she set up a Fifth Avenue salon on the edge of Greenwich Village. It soon became a rendezvous for artistic, literary, and political radicals of that day. Emma Goldman, Walter Lippmann, John Reed, Edwin Arlington Robinson, Margaret Sanger, Lincoln Steffens, and Carl Van Vechten were in the group. She helped organize a significant post-impressionist art exhibit and the Textile Strike Pageant in Madison Square Garden, and she gave an impetus also to the interest developing in the psychological theories of Freud.

In 1916 she married Maurice Sterne. Two years later she went southwest to join him in Santa Fe, where he was painting. Fascinated by New Mexico and the life of the Pueblo Indians, she settled in an adobe house at Taos and completely abandoned the life she had known. She and Mr. Sterne were divorced, and in 1923 she married Antonio Luhan, a full-blooded Pueblo Indian. With him she lives in Taos, trying to free herself from the artificial conventions in which she was brought up and attempting to get some glimmer of the richness of what she feels is a finer culture than the one in which she was reared. "I believe the race to which I belong is disintegrating with ever increasing momentum," she declares, "and I believe the future of these continents lies in the fate of the Indian Americans."

When she settled in New Mexico, Mrs. Luhan was writing short newspaper sketches. In 1926, however, she began writing her autobiography. "My principal interest in life," she said in 1937, "is in living at each moment but my secondary one is to give a picture of it as I have lived in it for the last 58 years conditioned by heredity and environment, and then released from those by—luck, a 'planned universe,' destiny? This I am attempting to do in the series called 'Intimate Memories.'"

Her connection with literary and artistic men and women of her time has been so intimate that the story serves as a record of many of their activities. At Taos, as in New York and in Europe, she has been hostess to the great and distinguished. "My life seems to seek those who care more for reality than illusion," she says, "and any person with an *excellence* in his or her character, whether it be in the simplest avocations or the most sophisticated, is welcome to me. I hate mediocrity, hypocrisy and cowardice. Because I admire proficiency (for it usually denotes *character*) I am often accused of lion hunting. This is not an accurate judgment for I have as many unknown as known in my environment. I do not like second-rate people or things." Mary Austin, John Dewey, and others of note visited her in New Mexico; *Lorenzo in Taos* relates the story of her friendship with D. H. Lawrence.

"I am interested in human documents," writes Mrs. Luhan. "I don't care for what D. H. L. called 'literary' books. I like honest self-observant autobiography and dislike false, camouflaged ones. I am interested in any attempt to add to consciousness and dislike anything that seems to delay or obstruct that tendency."

She is said to be the original of the character Edith Dale in Carl Van Vechten's *Peter Whiffle* (1922), and to appear as a character in George O'Neill's *American Dream* (1933).

For further comment, see Critical Survey, pp. 141, 175–76.

BIBLIOGRAPHY

Autobiography

Intimate memories, background, 1933; European experiences, volume two of Intimate memories, 1935; Winter in Taos, 1935; * Movers and shakers, volume three of Intimate memories, 1936; Edge of Taos desert, an escape to reality, volume four of Intimate memories, 1937.

Biography

Lorenzo in Taos, 1932.

STUDIES AND ARTICLES

Brett, Dorothy. Lawrence and Brett, a friendship. [c1933]

Hicks, Granville and Stuart, John. John Reed, the making of a revolutionary by Granville Hicks, with the assistance of John Stuart. 1936

Kunitz

Raines

Stein, Gertrude. Portrait of Mabel Dodge at the Villa Curonia. [n.d.] (pamphlet)

Fadiman, Clifton. "The making of a squaw." *N.Yer.*, Sept. 18, 1937, pp. 72–73, Sergeant, Elizabeth S. "Sphinx of Taos desert." *SRL.*, Nov. 26, 1938, pp. 12–14; Skinner, Cornelia O. "Dithers and jitters." *N.Yer*, Apr. 24, 1937, p. 21. For references to reviews, see *BRD.*, 1932–33, 1935–37.

Grace Lumpkin

Born in Georgia, of Colonial (Virginia) stock. She has spent a large part of her life in South Carolina. Her novel *To Make My Bread*, which was given the Maxim Gorky Award, was dramatized by Albert Bein as *Let Freedom Ring* (1935) and ran for more than one hundred performances. Miss Lumpkin has contributed short stories to the *New Masses*, and "A Miserable Offender" appeared in 1935 in the *Virginia Quarterly Review*.

"I have lived most of my life in the South," she wrote in 1937, "though at present my husband and I live in New York in a small house near the East River. . . . I darn my husband's socks, cook and clean house, plant window boxes in the spring, gossip with my neighbors, go to an occasional party, swim whenever I can, take as much active part in unions as possible, read a great deal, and work sometimes twelve to fifteen hours a day at writing. . . .

"I think a writer should continually study, plan and work, like a surgeon who learns all that the past has to give him, but always keeps up with what the present and future suggest. A writer should not be afraid of any idea that may take hold of him or his characters. He should be bold in creation and completely ruthless with his own natural inertia in planning a piece of work, so that every detail is thought out. . . . I know this is the only complete satisfaction a writer gets from his work. There are other satisfactions such as money, appreciation from others, but this is the only lasting satisfaction: persistent creative work, thinking out the relation of the parts to the whole, a strict plan at the basis of every work, true characterization.

"Along with technical and aesthetic considerations I believe a writer must have some idea to present. For myself this idea is the one that humanity is making progress, that it has been making progress. That a new step is to be taken, and that only the working-class and those sympathetic with that class can lead to this new step. That 'in the midst of the madness of hunger-producing plenty, of million-murdering wars, of civilization-strangling Fascism, the struggle of the workers represents the struggle for sanity; for individual sanity maintained by fighting the madness called capitalist civilization, for social sanity gained by the building of a saner world.' In one form or another, without distorting character or truth, I hope to present this idea in whatever I write."

For further comment, see Critical Survey, p. 82.

BIBLIOGRAPHY

Novels

To make my bread, 1932; A sign for Cain, 1935; The wedding, 1939.

STUDIES

Bein, Albert. Let freedom ring, a play in three acts . . . foreword by Don West. 1936 (based on the Grace Lumpkin novel To make my bread)

Zabel

For references to reviews, see *BRD.*, 1932, 1935, 1939.

William (Morley Punshon) McFee, 1881–

Born at sea, June 15, 1881, on a square-rigged three-masted ship designed, built, owned, and commanded by his father. His mother was a Canadian, and his father and grandfather and five uncles were English sea captains. The family settled in New Southgate, near London, where the little boy attended several schools. He was slow at learning to read, but at about eight began reading eagerly and extensively. Interested in mechanics, he did not care much for school, but preferred to read and write and was passionately fond of ships. He was oppressed by what he considered the excessive attention paid to matters of form and to athletics, and found it advisable to pretend interest in these things while he could secretly write.

Leaving the East Anglian School in Bury St. Edmunds, Suffolk, he entered upon an apprenticeship in McMuirland's Engineering Shops at Aldersgate in 1897 and remained until 1900, when he took a job on a waterworks at Tring. Then he entered the service of an engineering firm. As a commercial traveler for five years he read widely on trains, took up socialism, collected books, and became a devotee of Kipling, on whom he even gave lectures. He lived in Chelsea and met some of the literary men of the London of his day.

As the sea appealed to him more than his office job, he resigned and in 1906 became junior engineer on a ship bound for Genoa. In the autumn of the next year he passed a high Board of Trade examination and became third engineer on another ship; he rose to be chief engineer of the Woodfield Steamship Company.

In 1912 he came to the United States and settled in New Jersey, to write and to support himself by writing miscellaneous articles and advertising. His love for the sea, however, was too strong, and in the next year he became a licensed chief in the American Merchant Marine, joined the United Fruit Company's fleet, and worked in New Orleans on the port engineering staff.

In 1914, upon the outbreak of the war, he returned to England to enlist, was refused by the army, and instead entered service as engineer officer on a transport. Later he was a sub-lieutenant in the navy. He served for most of the war in the Mediterranean, and steeped himself thoroughly in the life and traditions of the countries and ports at which he called. He contributed a series of articles to *Land and Water* describing the Mediterranean naval service.

At the end of the war he returned to this country and soon was back with the United Fruit Company, as first assistant engineer, then chief engineer, on a liner carrying cargoes of bananas to New York from the Caribbean. On these trips, as on earlier voyages, he read widely.

In 1922 he came ashore to stay, and settled in the group of authors and artists in Westport, Connecticut. He is much interested in American life, of which he is a keen observer, and has read such American writers as Harry Leon Wilson, Ring Lardner, and H. C. Witwer. He finds time for writing, reading, and the indulgence of his tastes for gardening and sport. In 1936 an honorary master's degree was conferred upon him by Yale.

McFee feels that prose, rather than poetry, is the natural and appropriate medium for our mechanistic age, and regards poetry, especially when long, as being as much out of date as opera, and valuable chiefly as an apprenticeship for a writer mastering his craft. He objects to the obscurity and essential unoriginality of much modern verse and says: " . . . The apparatus of Poesie has been allowed to fall into the hands of a gang of lightfingered gentry who can only avoid a suspicion of petty larceny by printing their effusions privately and for their own delight. They can only avoid open arrest for obtaining money under false pretenses by wearing a disguise. The truth is that in most cases they are congenitally incapable of the inventiveness, the technical skill and the understanding of humanity which are necessary to succeed as writers of prose fiction."

BIBLIOGRAPHY

Novels

Aliens, 1914; * Casuals of the sea, the voyage of a soul, 1916; Captain Macedoine's daughter, 1920; Command, 1922; Race, 1924; Pilgrims of adversity, 1928; North of Suez, 1930; The harbourmaster, a novel, 1931; No castle in Spain, 1933; The beachcomber, a novel, 1935; Derelicts, a novel, 1938.

Short Stories

A Port Said miscellany, 1918 (cover-title; pamphlet); Sailors of fortune, 1929; Sailor's bane, 1936.

Essays and Sketches

Letters from an ocean tramp, 1908 (American ed., An ocean tramp, 1921); A six-hour shift, 1920; An engineer's note book, essays on life and letters, 1921 (pamphlet); Harbours of memory, 1921; Swallowing the anchor, being a revised and enlarged collection of notes made by an engineer in the merchant service who secured leave of absence from his ship to investigate and report upon the alleged superiority of life ashore, 1925; Born to be hanged, 1930; More harbours of memory, 1934; Sailor's wisdom, 1935; Some expert testimony on ships. William McFee says . . ., 1936 (cover-title; leaflet).

Reminiscences and Poems

The reflections of Marsyas, 1933.

Travel

The gates of the Caribbean, the story of a Great white fleet Caribbean cruise, 1922 (pamphlet); Sunlight in New Granada, 1925.

Biography

The life of Sir Martin Frobisher, 1928 (English ed., Sir Martin Frobisher, 1928).

Miscellany

Editorial 11, The Bowling green. (Special edition. For private circulation only.) Captain Macedoine cocktail (extract from a letter from William McFee), 1921 (printer's proofs; also issued as folder, with title: The Captain Macedoine cocktail, 1930).

STUDIES AND ARTICLES

† Babb, James T. A bibliography of the writings of William McFee . . . with an introduction and notes by William McFee. 1931
Baldwin (M)
Cooper
Dell
† Johnson (1929)
† Johnson (1932)
† Johnson (1936)
Kunitz (L)
McFee, William. Casuals of the sea . . . with an introduction by Christopher Morley. [1931]
Mais
Marble
† Maule, Harry E. William McFee,

author-engineer, a note on his life and works containing a complete chronological bibliography. [c1923] (cover-title; pamphlet; repr., 1928)
Morley
[Morley, Christopher D.] Have you read "Casuals of the sea"? [1923] (leaflet)
Morley (P)
Morley (S)
Tomlinson, Henry M. Out of soundings . . . with drawings by H. Charles Tomlinson. 1931

Elder, Arthur J. "William McFee, engineer and author." *AB.*, Sept. 1916, pp. 57–62; † Johnson, Merle D. and Hopkins, Frederick M., *eds.* "American first editions, a series of bibliographic check-lists . . . number 13, William McFee, 1881– compiled by Frank Shay." *PW.*, Dec. 9, 1922, p. 2054; McFee, William. "Getting into print." *Col.*, Part 1, Art. 11, pp. 1–8 (1930); North, Jessica. "The wrong-headed poets." *P.*, June 1929, pp. 156–60. For references to reviews, see *BRD.*, 1908, 1916, 1918, 1920–22, 1924–25, 1928–30, 1932–35, 1938.

Claude McKay, 1890–

Born in Sunny Ville, Jamaica, British West Indies, September 15, 1890. When still a boy he moved to the city of Kingston, enlisted in the constabulary, and began writing poetry in the Jamaican Negro dialect. In 1912 *Songs of Jamaica* was published at Kingston, and *Constabulary Ballads* was issued in London; and the author was virtually poet laureate of Jamaica. He was the first Negro to be awarded (1912) the medal of the Institute of Arts and Sciences.

In the same year, with a scholarship fund, he came to the United States and began to study at Tuskegee Institute, with the intention of returning to Jamaica to help his race. After a few months he entered the State Agricultural College of Kansas. Two years of this training made him certain that neither farming nor teaching agriculture appealed to him, and he left school and went to New York. To support himself he took jobs in hotel and boardinghouse kitchens, and worked as waiter in dining cars. Resuming his writing, he published two sonnets in the *Seven Arts* in 1917 which attracted considerable attention; and soon he was writing for other magazines and acting as associate editor for the *Liberator*. He was encouraged by Frank Harris, Max Eastman, and Floyd Dell.

The period 1919–21 he spent in England, where *Spring in New Hampshire* was published, and 1922–23 he passed in Russia, where he was well received by Trotsky and attended the Fourth Congress of the Communist International. He spent some months in Germany, and then joined American expatriates in Paris. He spent several years in France and traveled to Africa. In 1929 he received the Harmon Foundation Award in Literature, and more recently (1937) he has been honored by the James Weldon Johnson Literary Guild.

For further comment, see Critical Survey, pp. 51, 137.

BIBLIOGRAPHY

Poems

Constab ballads, 1912; Songs from Jamaica, 1912; Songs of Jamaica . . . with an introduction by Walter Jekyll, 1912; Spring in New Hampshire and other poems, 1920; * Harlem shadows, the poems of Claude McKay with an introduction by Max Eastman, 1922.

Novels

Home to Harlem, 1928; Banjo, a story without a plot, 1929; Banana Bottom, 1933.

Short Stories

Gingertown, 1932.

Autobiography

A long way from home, 1937.

STUDIES

† Blanck, Jacob, *ed.* "American first editions." *PW.*, Oct. 30, 1937, pp. 1767–68 (checklist comp. by Andrew M. Burris)

Brawley

Johnson

Kerlin

Kunitz (L)

Levinson

Wickham

For references to reviews, see *BRD.*, 1922, 1928–29, 1932–33, 1937.

Percy (Wallace) MacKaye, 1875–

Born March 16, 1875, in New York. His father, Steele MacKaye, was an actor, dramatist, stage designer, and teacher; and Percy MacKaye, brought up in New York and New England and early introduced to the theatrical life, at seventeen collaborated with his father by writing choral songs for a spectacle to be presented at the Columbian Exposition in Steele MacKaye's Spectatorium. When he was but sixteen, his first performed play was presented in Shirley Center, Massachusetts, in the town hall.

From public and private schools he proceeded to Harvard, from which he graduated in 1897 with the degree A.B. *cum laude.* His first book, a narrative poem of Harvard life, *Johnny Crimson*, appeared in 1895; and at his commencement he delivered the first student address on modern drama ever to be given at Harvard, "The Need of Imagination in the Drama of To-day."

His marriage to Marion Homer Morse took place in 1898, and the next two years he and his wife spent in travel and study in Europe. In 1899–1900 he was a matriculated student at the University of Leipzig. Upon his return to this country in 1900 he accepted a position as teacher in the Craigie School for Boys in New York City, which he held until 1904.

A Garland to Sylvia, which, although he had finished it in Europe by 1899, remained unpublished until 1910, attracted the attention of E. H. Sothern, who gave the author commissions to write *The Canterbury Pilgrims* and *Fenris, the Wolf.* Upon receiving the offer for the second play MacKaye left his school in 1904 and moved to Cornish, New Hampshire, where he and his family settled in the artists' colony. Since then he has devoted most of his time to literary work and the direction of performances of his own productions.

His first play to be produced professionally, *Jeanne d'Arc*, was played successfully by Sothern and Marlowe in the United States and England in 1906–07. During the next few years MacKaye lectured on drama before American university audiences, and in 1909 he read his poem "Ticonderoga" at the tercentenary celebration of the discovery of Lake Champlain. *The Immigrants*, the first American grand opera to be written on professional commission, MacKaye wrote to music by F. S. Converse, for the Boston Opera House. Subsequent operas were produced by the Metropolitan and Chicago companies, with music by Reginald De Koven.

The ideals implicit in his Harvard commencement address, worked out in the American folk plays written as early as 1901, and set forth in his lectures on a democratic theater and communal drama, MacKaye expressed in a group of super-dramas. The first, *Saint Louis, a Civic Masque*, was presented in 1914 at a civic festival in St. Louis, with some eight thousand actors, to the accompaniment of choruses composed by Converse. The use of the character "The Spirit of Saint Louis" and the plan of a great "eagle-airplane" in the final scene resulted, in 1927, in the naming of Colonel Lindbergh's plane "The Spirit of St. Louis." *Caliban*, a similar masque, was presented with 2,500 actors in New York, May 24, 1916, for the Shakespeare tercentenary. On the first night the performance was opened by Isadora Duncan.

In 1913–15 MacKaye supported the woman-suffrage agitation, and his "Hymn for Equal Suffrage," presented at Cooper Union in 1914, was read widely in the course of the movement. Besides occasional poems he wrote the communal masques *The Evergreen Tree* and *The Roll Call*, and the folk play *Washington* as contributions to the American cause in the war. In 1919, at the celebration of the centenary of the birth of James Russell Lowell, he read at Harvard his poem, "The Returning Host," to returned Harvard soldiers. In the same year he read his sonnet "Leaves of Grass" in honor of Walt Whitman at the centenary celebrated on Long Island, and experimentally introduced communal chanting of modern American poetry in Central Park in New York.

The first American fellowship in poetry, established in 1920 by Miami University in Ohio, was awarded to MacKaye, who held it until 1924. As the chair required no active teaching, he was free to write and study. In 1921, with his wife and son, he went into the remoter mountainous regions of Kentucky, in search of the folk elements disappearing from the American tradition because of the machine and the development of improved methods of communication. The result was a considerable collection of drama, poetry, and fiction in which the author tried to reveal the language and the racial traits of the mountaineers.

In 1922 he made a tour of the West and South, reading his works, and in the next year he read a narrative poem, "The Skippers of Nancy Gloucester," at Gloucester, at the tercentenary of the founding of the colony of Massachusetts Bay. The years from 1923 to 1927 MacKaye devoted to the writing of *Epoch*, his biography of his father. As a member of the Dramatists' Guild he was invited by the Norwegian government to represent the United States at the Ibsen Centennial in 1928, but was unable to go. In 1929 he was made advisory editor of *Folk-Say*, a journal of American folklore, and he conducted a poetry and folklore seminar in Rollins College in Florida until 1931.

In the latter year he was asked by the George Washington Bicentennial Commission to write a festival drama, and *Wakefield, a Folk-Masque* was produced in Washington, February 22, 1932. In 1932–33 he was visiting professor at Sweet Briar College, and in 1933 he was director of folk tales at the White Top

Mountain Folk Festival in Virginia; 1933–34 he spent in North Carolina, Florida, and Virginia, collecting folk materials; and, more recently, he has been traveling in Europe and writing.

"Though . . . I have written about fifty published volumes," MacKaye writes, "yet nine-tenths of all I have written has been conceived by me, primarily, not for the printed page but for the utterance of the human voice—in plays, masques, Pindaric poems, operas, etc.; for always that which has concerned me most to express has been the spirit of poetry, in its various forms—a spirit more allied to illiteracy than to literacy."

In addition to this interest in the sound of poetry, which is responsible for his readings and his desire to record primitive folk rhythms, MacKaye has been eager to bring poetry and drama to large groups of people, as in his masques and communal-chanting groups, and to unite, as in his grand operas, the stage arts, music, and poetry. Among his many artistic and literary friends have been E. C. Stedman, Edwin Arlington Robinson, Ridgely Torrence, William Vaughn Moody, Josephine Preston Peabody, and William Dean Howells. MacKaye has been (1930) a member of the MacDowell colony at Peterboro, New Hampshire, and is a member of the National Institute of Arts and Letters. He has read a Phi Beta Kappa poem at Harvard (1908) and many festival odes, and he holds honorary degrees from Dartmouth College (1914) and Miami University (1924).

For further comment, see Critical Survey, pp. 100, 116.

BIBLIOGRAPHY

Poems

Johnny Crimson, a legend of Hollis hall by Percy Wallace MacKaye, '97. Cover design by Eric Pape, 1895 (pamphlet); Ode on the centenary of Abraham Lincoln, 1909; Poems, 1909 (also pub. as The Sistine Eve and other poems, 1915); Uriel and other poems, 1912; The present hour, a book of poems, 1914; Poems and plays . . . in two volumes, volume 1, Poems, 1916; Dogtown common, 1921; The skippers of Nancy Gloucester, 1924; The gobbler of God, a poem of the southern Appalachians . . . illustrations by Arvia MacKaye, 1928; Songs of a day, 1929 (pamphlet); Moments en voyage, nine poems for the Harvard class of 1897, 1932; In another land, poems inter-translated by Percy MacKaye and Albert Steffen, 1937 (English and German title pages); The far familiar, fifty new poems . . . frontispiece by Arthur Rackham, 1938.

Plays

Po' white trash and other one-act dramas by Evelyn Greenleaf Sutherland, certain of the plays being written in collaboration with Emma Sheridan-Fry and Percy Wallace MacKaye, 1900; The Canterbury pilgrims, a comedy, 1903; Fenris, the wolf, a tragedy, 1905; Jeanne d'Arc, 1906; Sappho and Phaon, a tragedy set forth with a prologue, induction, prelude, interludes, and epilogue, 1907; Mater, an American study in comedy, 1908; The scarecrow, or, The glass of truth, a tragedy of the ludicrous, 1908; Anti-matrimony, a satirical comedy, 1910; A garland to Sylvia, a dramatic reverie with a prologue, 1910; To-morrow, a play in three acts, 1912; Yankee fantasies, five one-act plays, 1912 (Chuck: an orchard fantasy; Gettysburg: a woodshed commentary; The antick:

a wayside sketch; The cat-boat: a fantasy for music; Sam Average: a silhouette); A thousand years ago, a romance of the Orient . . . with an introduction by Clayton Hamilton, 1914; Poems and plays . . . in two volumes, volume II, Plays, 1916; Washington, action dramatique . . . traduite de l'anglais par Pierre de Lanux, esquisse scénique par Robert Edmond Jones, frontispiece par Arnold Genthe, 1919; Washington, the man who made us, a ballad play . . . with scene designs by Robert Edmond Jones, 1919; George Washington, a dramatic action with a prologue . . . scene design by Robert Edmond Jones, together with comments and suggestions in regard to its production by the author, the scene designer, and Walter Hampden, first impersonator of the title-role of the three-act play, from which this action is selected, entitled Washington, the man who made us, a ballad play by Percy MacKaye. Published by Alfred A. Knopf, New York, 1920 (also pub. as George Washington at the Delaware, a dramatic action with a prologue . . ., 1920); This fine-pretty world, a comedy of the Kentucky mountains, 1924; Kinfolk of Robin Hood, a play in four acts, 1926; Washington and Betsy Ross, a dramatic action in two scenes . . . an arrangement from the three-act play entitled Washington, the man who made us, a ballad-play by Percy MacKaye, 1927; Young Washington at Mt. Vernon, a dramatic action in three scenes and a prologue . . . selected from the three-act play entitled Washington, the man who made us, a ballad-play by Percy MacKaye, 1927; Kentucky mountain fantasies, three short plays for an Appalachian theatre . . . illustrations by Arvia MacKaye, 1928 (Napoleon crossing the Rockies; The funeralizing of Crickneck; Timber); The sphinx, a comedy in three scenes, 1929; Gettysburg, play in one act, 1934.

Masques

The book of words of the pageant and masque of Saint Louis, the words of the pageant by Thomas Wood Stevens, the words of the masque by Percy MacKaye. Published by authority of the Book committee, Saint Louis pageant drama association, 1914; Saint Louis, a civic masque, 1914; Sanctuary, a bird masque . . . with a prelude by Arvia MacKaye, illustrated with photographs in color and monotone by Arnold Genthe, 1914; The new citizenship, a civic ritual devised for places of public meeting in America, 1915; Caliban by the yellow sands, 1916; The evergreen tree, 1917 (with three monographs on the masque written by the author, the scenic designer [Robert Edmond Jones] and Arthur Farwell, composer of the music); The roll call, a masque of the Red cross, 1918; The will of song, a dramatic service of community singing devised in co-operation with Harry Barnhart by Percy MacKaye. For use as a two days' song festival in two parts, part I: Soul of earth, part II: Soul of light. Cover design by Claude Bragdon, 1919; The Pilgrim and the Book, a dramatic service of the Bible designed to be used in churches, written for the American Bible society . . . cover design from statue by Augustus Saint-Gaudens by special permission, together with comments and suggestions in regard to participation in the service and words and music of the hymns, 1920; Wakefield, a folk-masque of America, being a mid-winter-night's dream of the birth of Washington . . . with illustration designs by Arvia MacKaye, together with three monographs on the masque written by the author, the illustration-designer, and John Tasker Howard, adapter and composer of the music. Designed and written for the United States commission for the celebration of the two-hundredth anniversary of the birth of George Washington, 1732–1932, 1932 (loose-leaf; also pub. in bound form).

Operas

The immigrants, a lyric drama . . . with an introduction by Frederic C. Howe, 1915 (text only); The Canterbury pilgrims, an opera, the text by Percy MacKaye, the music by Reginald De Koven, 1916 (text only); Sinbad, the sailor, his adventvres with Beavty and the Peacock lady in the castle of the forty thieves, a lyric phantasy, 1917 (text only); Rip Van Winkle, folk-opera in three acts . . . for which the music has been composed by Reginald DeKoven, 1919 (text only; also pub. as Rip Van Winkle, folk-opera in three acts, the text by Percy MacKaye, the music by Reginald De Koven, 1919).

Folk Tales

Tall tales of the Kentucky mountains . . . decorations by E. MacKinstry, 1926; Weathergoose—woo! . . . illustrations by Arvia MacKaye, 1929.

Writings on the Theater

The playhouse and the play and other addresses concerning the theatre and democracy in America, 1909; The civic theatre, suggestions regarding its scope and organization, an address delivered at the annual convention of the American federation of arts, Washington, D.C., May 17, 18, 19, 1910, 1910 (caption-title; pamphlet); The civic theatre in relation to the redemption of leisure, a book of suggestions, 1912; Community drama, its motive and method of neighborliness, an interpretation, 1917; Robert Edmond Jones, a comment on his work in the theatre, 1920 (pamphlet).

Essays and Studies

A substitute for war by Percy MacKaye with an introduction by Irving Fisher . . . and with prefatory letters by the Right Hon. Viscount Bryce . . . and Norman Angell, 1915; The faith of poetry, an essay . . . read before the culminating convention of the World fellowship of faiths held during the Century of progress world's fair at Hotel Morrison, Chicago, September 8, 1933. Reprinted from the winter issue of the Oxford criterion, February, 1934, 1934 (pamphlet).

Biography

Epoch, the life of Steele MacKaye, genius of the theatre, in relation to his times & contemporaries, a memoir by his son, Percy MacKaye, profusely illustrated, in two volumes, 1927; Letters to Harriet by William Vaughn Moody edited with introduction and conclusion by Percy MacKaye, 1935.

Autobiographical Sketch

Percy MacKaye, a sketch of his life with bibliography of his works, reprinted from the twenty-fifth anniversary report of the class of 1897, Harvard college, 1922 (pamphlet).

Verses Set to Music

Three songs from Sanctuary—a bird masque, the text by Percy MacKaye, set to music by F. S. Converse. No. I. Veery, veery, viero! No. II. Come here, come here. No. III. Oreo! When shawes ben sheen, 1914 (cover-title; sheet music); Choruses of Caliban, a Shakespeare masque, words by Percy MacKaye, music by Arthur Farwell, 1916 (cover-title; sheet music); The lads of Liege, the words by Percy MacKaye, the music by Carl Paige Wood, 1916 (cover-title; sheet music); Many are the wonders of time, chorus from the "Antigone" of Sophocles, translation by Percy MacKaye, music by Arthur Farwell, 1916 (caption-title; sheet music); The battle-call of alliance, music by Reginald de Koven, poem by Percy MacKaye, 1917 (cover-title; sheet music); Book of music of The evergreen tree, a Christmas community masque of the tree of light for community singing and acting devised and written by Percy MacKaye, the music composed by Arthur Farwell, 1917; American consecration hymn by Percy MacKaye for music by Francis Macmillen, dedicated by the author and the composer to President Woodrow Wilson in response to the great incentive of his own words: "The right is more precious than peace," 1918 (cover-title; sheet music); The ballads from George Washington, a play . . . the illustrations by Arvia MacKaye, 1920 (cover-title; pamphlet); The choruses for Wakefield, a folk-masque by Percy MacKaye, from The music for Wakefield, selected, adapted, and composed by John Tasker Howard, designed and written for the United States George Washington bicentennial commission, 1932 (sheet music).

Translations

The Canterbury tales of Geoffrey Chaucer, a modern rendering into prose of the Prologue and ten tales . . . with pictures in colour by Walter Appleton Clark, 1904; The modern reader's Chaucer. The complete poetical works of Geoffrey Chaucer now first put into modern English by John S. P. Tatlock . . . and Percy MacKaye . . . Illustrations by Warwick Goble, 1912; Chaucer's Canterbury tales, selections from The modern reader's Chaucer by John S. P. Tatlock . . . and Percy MacKaye . . . Chosen and edited by Carl W. Ziegler, 1923.

STUDIES AND ARTICLES

Announcement concerning "The roll call," a masque of the Red cross by Percy MacKaye to be produced during Roll call week, December 16 to 23, 1918, by local chapters, branches, and auxiliaries of the American red cross with the co-operation of young people's societies in the churches, Sunday schools, women's clubs, Boy scouts, Girl scouts, dramatic clubs in schools, colleges and universities, and other groups of young people. [1918] (cover-title; leaflet)

Benchley, Robert C. Of all things . . . with illustrations by Gluyas Williams. [c1921]

Burgess

Burleigh, Louise. The community theatre in theory and practice. 1917.

Burrell, Percy J. A guide to "The evergreen tree," a masque of Christmas time for community singing and acting by Percy MacKaye, with music by Arthur Farwell and scenes and costume designs by Robert Edmond Jones. A series of questions and answers compiled by Percy J. Burrell. [1917] (cover-title; pamphlet)

Burton

Caliban news, [vol. 1, no. 1]–5, July–Oct. 1917

Cheney, Sheldon. The new movement in the theatre. 1914

Clark (B)

Converse, Frederick S. For the piano. Scarecrow sketches, six excerpts from the photo-music-drama, Puritan passions, based upon Percy MacKaye's stage play, The scarecrow. The music composed for the Film guild, inc. by Frederick S. Converse. [c1924]

Cook

De Koven, Reginald. The Canterbury pilgrims, an opera in four acts, the book by Percy Mackaye . . . the music by Reginald de-Koven. [c1916]

De Koven, Reginald. Rip Van Winkle, folk-opera in three acts, the text by Percy MacKaye, the music by Reginald De Koven, opus 414, vocal score. [c1919]

Dickinson (P)

Doggett, Frank A. Dipped in sky, a study of Percy MacKaye's "Kentucky mountain cycle." 1930

[Doubleday, Page and company, *firm, publishers.*] For publication April 1st, Mr. Percy MacKaye's Shakespeare tercentenary masque entitled Caliban by the yellow sands. [1916] (caption-title; leaflet)

Gorges, Raymond. Ernest Harold Baynes, naturalist and crusader. 1928

† Grover, Edwin O., *ed.* Annals of an era, Percy MacKaye and the MacKaye family, 1826–1932, a record of biography and history, in commentaries and bibliography, edited with an introduction . . . Comprising records chiefly included in the MacKaye collection at the Dartmouth college library. Prefatory note by Gamaliel Bradford. Published under the auspices of Dartmouth college. 1932

Grover, Edwin O., *ed.* Illustrations for the limited edition. Annals of an era, Percy MacKaye and the MacKaye family, 1826–1932, a record of biography and history, in commentaries and bibliography, edited with an introduction . . . Comprising records chiefly included in the MacKaye collection at the Dartmouth college library. Prefatory note by Gamaliel Bradford. Published under the auspices of Dartmouth college. 1932

Howard, John T. The music for Wakefield, a folk-masque by Percy MacKaye, selected, adapted, and composed by John Tasker Howard, designed and written for the United States George Washington bicentennial commission. [c1932] (sheet music)

† Johnson (1929)

† Johnson (1932)

† Johnson (1936)

Kilmer

Kunitz (L)

† List B—Percy MacKaye, a chronological list of the dramatic works of Percy MacKaye—(1917). 1917 (broadside)

Macgowan, Kenneth and Jones, Robert E. Continental stagecraft. [c1922]

† MacKaye, Percy. Percy MacKaye, a sketch of his life with bibliography of his works, reprinted from the twenty-fifth anniversary report of the class of 1897, Harvard college. 1922 (pamphlet)

MacKaye, Percy. Wakefield, a folk-masque of America, being a midwinter night's dream of the birth of Washington . . . with music selected, adapted, and composed by John Tasker Howard, directed by Percy Jewett Burrell and Marie Moore Forrest. Presented at Constitution hall, Washington, D.C., February 21, 25, 26, 1932 under the auspices of United States George Washington bicentennial commission and District of Columbia George Washington bicentennial commission. [1932]

Macmillan company, *firm, publishers, New York.* The Kentucky mountains in plays, tales, & poems by Percy MacKaye. This fine-pretty world, a Kentucky mountain comedy, comments by Edwin Arlington Robinson, Glenn Frank, Oliver Herford, Booth Tarkington, Hamlin Garland, Ida M. Tarbell, and others on the notable New York production of this play. [1924] (pamphlet)

† Manly
Mayorga
Mayorga (S)
Moses
Moses (R)
Nathan (TD)
National

The Pageant and masque of Saint Louis bulletin. Feb.–Mar. 1914

The pageant and masque of Saint Louis, what it is and why it is produced. [1914] (cover-title; leaflet)

Percy MacKaye, a symposium on his fiftieth birthday, 1925, foreword by Amy Lowell. 1928

The Pioneer press, *Washington, D.C.* Annals of an era, Percy MacKaye and the MacKaye family, 1826–1932, a record of biography and history in commentaries and bibliography, edited with an introduction by Edwin Osgood Grover . . . Comprising records chiefly included in the MacKaye collection at the Dartmouth college library. Prefatory note by Gamaliel Bradford. 1932 (cover-title; leaflet; prospectus)

The Pioneer press, *Washington, D.C.* Moments en voyage by Percy MacKaye. [1932] (cover-title; folder; publisher's announcement)

† Quinn (H)
Quinn (R)
Russell (J)

Sagamore sociological conference. [Proceedings of] eighth year, Sagamore beach, Massachusetts, U.S.A., June 30 to July 2, 1914. [1914] (pamphlet)

Saint Louis pageant drama association. Official programme, The pageant and masque of Saint Louis, Forest park, Thursday, Friday, Saturday, and Sunday, May 28th, 29th, 30th, and 31st, 1914, each evening from 6:30 to 10:00 oclock (with an intermission). 1914 (pamphlet)

Saint Louis pageant drama association. Pageant and masque of Saint Louis 1914, reports of the chairman of committees. 1916

Saint Louis pageant drama association. Proceedings of the Conference of cities held in connection with The pageant and masque of St. Louis, May 29–31, 1914. 1914 (pamphlet)

Sayler

Shakespeare tercentenary celebration committee, New York. The New York city Shakespeare tercentenary celebration committee presents the community masque of the art of the theatre, Caliban by the yellow sands by Percy MacKaye . . . Produced at the stadium of the College of the City of New York on the evenings of May 23, 24, 25, 26, and 27, 1916. [1916] (pamphlet)

Stanley, Albert A. Greek themes in modern musical settings. 1924

Stedman

Steele, H. V. Wakefield, a folk-masque of America by Percy MacKaye, a review of its production and the published book. [1932?] (caption-title; pamphlet)

Villard

Baker, George P. "The pageant and masque of Saint Louis." *WW.*, Aug. 1914, pp. 389–99; Botkin, Benjamin A. "Folk speech in the Kentucky mountain cycle of Percy Mackaye." *AS.*, Apr. 1931, pp. 267–76; Collier, John. "Caliban by the yellow sands, the Shakespeare pageant and masque reviewed against a background of American pageantry." *Survey*, July 1, 1916, pp. 343–

50; Dickinson, Thomas H. "The epic of the world finder." *VQR.*, Apr. 1928, pp. 275–78; Farwell, Arthur. "The pageant and masque of St. Louis, a people's drama on a national scale." *RR.*, Aug. 1914, pp. 187–93; Knaufft, Ernest. "Two great pageants." *RR.*, May 1916, pp. 593–97; Roberts, Mary F. "The dramatic engineer and the civic theater, a new idea for bringing the stage back to the people." *Craftsm.*, May 1914, pp. 139–47; Roberts. "Rehearsing a community masque." *Craftsm.*, Aug. 1916, pp. 483–88; Sherry, Laura. "Pageantry and rhetoric." *P.*, Oct. 1921, pp. 51–53; Zabel, Morton D. "A mountain folk play." *P.*, Sept. 1928, pp. 352–54. For references to reviews, see *BRD.*, 1906–17, 1919–21, 1923–24, 1926–29.

Archibald MacLeish, 1892–

Born May 7, 1892, in Glencoe, Illinois, to a Scottish-born merchant and a mother of New England inheritance who had taught at Vassar. He attended public schools, and then the Hotchkiss School, Lakeville, Connecticut. At Yale, where he was prominently connected with undergraduate activities, the literary magazine, the football and swimming teams, the senior society, and Phi Beta Kappa, he was a member of a group including Stephen Vincent Benét, H. Phelps Putnam, and Thornton Wilder.

After his graduation in 1915 he entered, "to avoid going to work," the Harvard Law School, where in the second year he led his class. In 1916 he was married. In 1917 he joined a hospital unit and went to France. After being transferred to the field artillery and spending a few weeks at the front in 1918, he was ordered home to train soldiers. At the end of the war he had the rank of captain of field artillery.

Even in his undergraduate days he had been writing, and in 1917 the Yale Press had issued a volume of his poems. After his return from service, and a year of teaching in the Harvard Law School, he entered an office in Boston and practiced law for three years. His work, though successful, interfered with his writing, and he left in 1923, with his wife and two children, for Paris. In the same year he began writing steadily, and he read constantly, mostly French and English poetry, and traveled in southern Europe, on the Mediterranean, and into Persia. He spent a summer in Normandy.

In 1928 he returned to this country and moved to a farm he bought in Massachusetts. In 1929, when he was working on *Conquistador*, he made a trip to Mexico and followed Cortez's route from the coast to the valley of Mexico. In the following winter, the opening of the depression, he began writing for *Fortune*, and began traveling in America, Europe, and Japan as a journalist, while he continued his writing and publishing. *Poetry* awarded him the John Reed Memorial Prize in 1929, and in 1932 he received the Shelley Memorial Award. In 1933 he was awarded the Pulitzer Prize for *Conquistador*, as the best volume of verse published in 1932.

Passionately concerned in the Loyalist cause in Spain, he declared before the Second Congress of American Writers in 1937 that the fight against fascism is the immediate concern of all interested in freedom of publication; and in his poem, "Speech to the Scholars," read before the Columbia chapter of Phi Beta Kappa in June, 1937, he called upon scholars to give their assistance to the cause against barbarism. With Ernest Hemingway, Joris Ivens, and Lillian Hellman he collaborated on the story of the film, *The Spanish Earth*, written to give an account of the Spanish Revolution sympathetic to the Loyalists; and to assist this work he and John Dos Passos formed Contemporary Historians, Inc., and sent experts to Spain to gather materials.

From 1938–39 he was custodian of the Nieman Collection of Journalism at Harvard. In 1939 he received an honorary degree at Yale, and was made Librarian of Congress.

MacLeish has clearly stated his position as to the relation of poetry to social issues in an article in 1934 in the *Saturday Review of Literature.* "There are no *a priori* rules about subject matter in verse, and the man who contends that there are is either an academician or that equally unimportant American phenomenon, the revolutionary pedant." To the theory that poetry must reflect awareness of the contemporary state of social evolution he replies that truth, not to theory and dogma, but to actuality, regarded as artistically significant, has always been the concern of the finest poets, who have always placed their art and its demands before every other loyalty.

For further comment, see Critical Survey, p. 149.

BIBLIOGRAPHY

Poems

Class poem, 1915, 1915 (cover-title; leaflet); Yale university prize poem, 1915. Songs for a summer's day (a sonnet-cycle), 1915 (pamphlet); Tower of ivory . . . with a foreword by Lawrence Mason, 1917; The happy marriage and other poems, 1924; The pot of earth, 1925; Streets in the moon, 1926; The Hamlet of A. MacLeish, 1928; Einstein, 1929; New found land, fourteen poems, 1930; Before March . . . drawings by Leja Gorska, 1932 (cover-title; pamphlet); Conquistador, 1932; Frescoes for Mr. Rockefeller's city, 1933 (pamphlet); * Poems, 1924–1933, 1933; Public speech, poems, 1936; Land of the free, 1938 (English ed., Land of the free—U.S.A., 1938).

Plays in Verse

Nobodaddy, a play, 1926; Panic, a play in verse, 1935; The fall of the city, a verse play for radio, 1937; Air raid, a verse play for radio, 1938.

Sociological and Political Studies

Housing America by the editors of "Fortune," 1932 (reprint of MacLeish's articles on housing in Fortune, 1932); Jews in America by the editors of Fortune, 1936 (repr. from MacLeish's article in Fortune, Feb. 1936); Background of war by the editors of Fortune, 1937 (by MacLeish, except for: We thank our führer).

Verses Set to Music

Merry-go-round, part-song for men's chorus [words by] Archibald MacLeish [music by] Elinor Remick Warren, 1934 (caption-title; sheet music).

Adaptation

The Columbia Shakespearean cycle. "King Lear," radio adaptation . . . as presented over the Columbia broadcasting system on Monday, August 9th, 1937, 1937 (mimeographed).

STUDIES AND ARTICLES

Deutsch
† Johnson (1936)
Kreymborg
Kunitz (L)
Loggins
† Mizener, Arthur. A catalogue of the first editions of Archibald MacLeish . . . prepared for an exhibition of his works held in the Yale university library beginning January 7, 1938. 1938 (pamphlet)
Proletarian
Saturday
Schreiber
Strachey
Tate
Untermeyer (M)
Zabel

Aiken, Wellington E. "Poetic form in conquistador." *MLN.*, Feb. 1936, pp. 107–09; Blackmur, Richard P. "A modern poet in Eden." *P.*, Sept. 1926, pp. 339–42; Blake, Howard. "Thoughts on modern poetry." *SR.*, Apr.–June 1935, pp. 187–96; Chamberlain, John. "Archibald MacLeish." *SRL.*, June 24, 1939, pp. 10–11. Dangerfield, George. "Archibald MacLeish, an appreciation." *AB.*, Jan. 1931, pp. 493–96; Denison, Merrill. "Radio and the writer." *TAM.*, May 1938, pp. 365–70; Deutsch, Babette. "Certain good." *VQR.*, Apr. 1934, pp. 298–302; Eaton, Walter P. "MacLeish, lecturer." *Com.*, Mar. 25, 1938, pp. 602–03; Fitts, Dudley. "To Karthage then I came." *HH.*, July–Sept. 1931, pp. 637–41; Gillmor, Frances. "The curve of a continent." *NMQ.*, May 1934, pp. 114–22; Gregory, Horace. "Poets in the theatre." *P.*, July 1936, pp. 221–28; Humphries, Rolfe. "Archibald MacLeish." *Mod.M.*, June 1934, pp. 264–70, 274; Isaacs, Hermine R. "The fall of another city, air raid." *TAM.*, Feb. 1939, pp. 147–49; Jones, Llewellyn. "Archibald MacLeish, a modern metaphysical." *EJ.*, June 1935, pp. 441–51; Kirstein, Lincoln. "Arms and men." *HH.*, Apr.–June 1932, pp. 484–92; Lind, Levi R . "The crisis in literature, literature today." *SR.*, Jan.–Mar. 1939, pp. 50–54; MacMullan, Hugh M. "Poems, 1924–33." *Sw.R.*, Winter 1934, Book sect., pp. 2, 4–6; Mathiessen, Francis O. "Yeats and four American poets, poems, 1924–33." *YR.*, Spring 1934, pp. 611–17; † Melcher, Frederic G. *comp.* "Check list of Archibald MacLeish." *PW.*, July 15, 1933, p. 180; Mizener, Arthur. "The poetry of Archibald MacLeish." *SR.*, Oct.–Dec. 1938, pp. 501–19; Monroe, Harriet. "Archibald MacLeish." *P.*, June 1931, pp. 150–55; Monroe. "The conqueror." *P.*, July 1932, pp. 216–22; Pinckney, Josephine. "Jeffers and MacLeish." *VQR.*, July 1932, pp. 443–47; Rosenberg, Harold. "The God in the car." *P.*, Sept. 1938, pp. 334–42; Schappes, Morris U. "The direction of A. MacLeish." *Symp.*, Oct. 1932, pp. 476–94; Van Ghent, Dorothy. "The poetry of Archibald MacLeish." *S.Soc.*, Fall 1938, pp. 500–11; Wade, Mason. "The anabasis of A. MacLeish." *N.Amer.Rev.*, Summer 1937, pp. 330–43; Wilson, Edmund. "The omelet of A. MacLeish." *N.Yer.*, Jan. 14, 1939, pp. 23–24; Zabel, Morton D. "Cinema of Hamlet." *P.*, June 1934, pp. 150–59; Zabel. "The compromise of A. MacLeish." *P.*, Aug. 1930, pp. 270–75. For references to reviews, see *BRD.*, 1918, 1924–27, 1929–30, 1932–34, 1936–39.

William March, *pseud.* (William Edward March Campbell) 1893–

Born in Mobile, Alabama, September 18, 1893. His full name is William Edward March Campbell. His father worked in a sawmill, and the family lived in different sawmill towns. He was educated in backwoods schools, at the University of Valparaiso, and at the University of Alabama, where he studied law for one year. As a child he was interested in music and the stage, rather than in writing. He worked in Mobile and for a law firm in New York. In 1917 he enlisted in the marines, was gassed and wounded in the war, and was discharged with honor as a sergeant in 1919, having received a Croix de Guerre. On his return he began work for the Waterman Steamship Corporation, of Mobile. Later he was put in charge of traffic and still later made a vice-president.

About 1928, when he was working in New York for the steamship firm, he began writing short stories, some of which were published. His first book, *Company K*, dealt with war, and was an attempt to show, not war itself, but the reactions of men to war. In *The Tallons*, which he regards as much his best work, he tried to strike some kind of balance between the under-individualized characters of modern novels and the prolixities of the older ones. "The only thing I dislike about the hard, fast-moving modern novel," he writes, "is the fact that the people all seem to be cut out of the same piece of wrapping paper, and that they must be oversimplified. The old-timey, subjective book is too damned long and too omniscient, and too tiresome. So I wanted to solve the problem, if I could, by writing an objective book on the surface and, by projecting the emotions of the people on to animals, scenery, or inanimate objects, give them an added depth of character and subtlety and variation." This method, he felt, made *The Tallons* unusual; and he was disappointed in the unfavorable reception it received, and the charge of superficiality, which he denies. "I know, of course, that many people have identified character with scenery, or a mood of a character with a natural phenomenon, but indicating a deep level of the human mind by what is noticed through the conscious mind I thought fairly good, and fairly fresh. Not one of the critics, in America, at least, had the faintest idea what I was doing."

For further comment, see Critical Survey, p. 94.

BIBLIOGRAPHY

Novels

Come in at the door, 1934; The Tallons, 1936 (English ed., A song for harps, 1936).

Short Stories and Sketches

Company K, 1933; The little wife and other stories, 1935; Some like them short, 1939.

For references to reviews, see *BRD.*, 1933–36, 1939.

Don(ald Robert Perry) Marquis, 1878–1937

Born in Walnut, Illinois, July 29, 1878. After leaving school at fifteen he worked on a railroad, for a sewing-machine company, in a drug store, a bank, and a poultry slaughterhouse, and for a clothing firm. At one period he worked in a newspaper office, at typesetting, and later at editorial work. When he was eighteen, he contributed lampoons to a local paper.

He left to study at the Corcoran Art School in Washington, and began working for the Census Bureau and reporting for the Washington *Times*. For a brief period he acted with a traveling stock company, then returned to newspaper work. After a short career in Philadelphia he went to Atlanta in 1902 to become associate editor of the *News*, and from 1904 to 1907 he wrote editorials for the *Journal.* After two years as assistant editor of the *Uncle Remus Magazine*, he left the South in 1909 and moved to New York. From 1912 to 1920 he conducted his own column, known as "The Sun Dial," in the *Sun*, and for two years ran a similar one ("The Lantern") on the *Tribune.* In 1922 he retired from newspaper work and devoted himself to writing plays and books and contributing to magazines.

Although Marquis aspired to tragedy (*The Dark Hours*, a play of the life of Christ, was produced unsuccessfully in 1932), his one successful play, *The Old Soak* (1922), was a comedy which became a profitable stage hit. He produced quantities of light verse, usually on the inspiration of the moment, and, in his early career, wrote powerful political editorials, sometimes also in verse. In 1923 he was elected to membership in the National Institute of Arts and Letters, and, more recently, he was awarded the Mark Twain Medal for his "outstanding contribution to American humor for a quarter of a century."

In 1936 he suffered a stroke which proved to be the first of a series, and after a long illness he died of a cerebral hemorrhage in his home at Forest Hills, Long Island, December 29, 1937.

For further comment, see Critical Survey, p. 159.

BIBLIOGRAPHY

Poems

Dreams & dust, poems, 1915; Poems and portraits, 1922; The awakening & other poems, 1924.

Plays

The dark hours, five scenes from a history, 1924; Words and thoughts, a play in one act, 1924; The Old Soak, a comedy in three acts, 1926; Out of the sea, a play in four acts, 1927; Master of the revels, a comedy in four acts, 1934.

Novels

Danny s own story . . . illustrated by E. W. Kemble, 1912; The cruise of the Jasper B., 1916; Pandora lifts the lid by Christopher Morley and Don Marquis, 1924; Off the arm, 1930; Sons of the Puritans with a preface by Christopher Morley, 1939.

Short Stories

Carter and other people, 1921 (contains the play Words and thoughts); The revolt of the oyster, 1922; When the turtles sing and other unusual tales, 1928; A variety of people, 1929; Chapters for the orthodox, 1934; Sun dial time, 1936.

Humorous Verse

Noah an' Jonah an' Cap'n John Smith, 1920 (pamphlet); Noah an' Jonah an' Cap'n John Smith, a book of humorous verse, 1921; Sonnets to a red-haired lady (by a gentleman with a blue beard) and famous love affairs . . . drawings by Stuart Hay, 1922; * archy and mehitabel, 1927; Love sonnets of a cave man and other verses . . . drawings by Stuart Hay, 1928; archys life of mehitabel, 1933; archy does his part . . . illustrated by george herriman, 1935.

Wit and Humor

* Hermione and her little group of serious thinkers, 1916; Prefaces . . . decorations by Toni Sarg, 1919; The Old Soak and Hail and farewell . . . line drawings by Sterling Patterson, 1921 (contains verses); The Old Soak's history of the world with occasional glances at Baycliff, L.I. and Paris, France . . . with drawings by Stuart Hay, 1924; The almost perfect state, 1927; Her foot is on the brass rail, 1935; The Old Soak, The Old Soak's history of the world, 1937.

Ephemera

Mr. Hawley breaks into song, 1923; An ode to Hollywood, 1929 (anonymous); A certain club, 1936 (broadside); There is another day, 1936.

Verses Set to Music

The tom-cat. Text by Don Marquis. Music by Mrs. M. H. Gulesian. Low voice, 1928 (cover-title; sheet music).

STUDIES AND ARTICLES

DeCasseres, Benjamin. Don Marquis. [c1938] (pamphlet)
Farrar
† Ford (E)
Freeman
Kunitz (L)
Markey
Masson
Morley
Morley (L)
Morley (S)
Schreiber
Sherman (C)
† Van Doren (M)
Widdemer

Anonymous. "Don Marquis, American minstrel." *Cur.Op.*, Nov. 1922, pp. 662–64; Anonymous. "Don Marquis and his place in the Sun." *Cur.Op.*, Aug. 1919, p. 119; Anonymous. "Don Marquis of the Evening Sun." *Everybody's*, June 1916, pp. 720–21; † Blanck, Jacob, *ed.* "American first editions." *PW.*, July 17, 1937, pp. 209–10 (checklist comp. by Rodman Gilder); Marquis, Don. "Don Marquis." *Everybody's*, Jan. 1920, pp. 29, 85; Morley, Christopher. "O rare Don Marquis." *SRL.*, Jan. 8, 1938, pp. 13–14; Tittle, Walter. "Glimpses of interesting Americans." *Cent.*, Aug. 1925, pp. 437–41; Van Doren, Carl. "Day in and day out." *Cent.*, Dec. 1923, pp. 308–15. For references to reviews, see *BRD.*, 1912, 1915–16, 1919, 1921–22, 1925–26, 1928–30, 1933–36, 1939.

Edgar Lee Masters, 1869–

Born in Garnett, Kansas, August 23, 1869. When he was a year old, the family returned to Illinois, where Masters was to spend most of his life. His father, a lawyer who had failed in Kansas and returned to work on his father's farm, entered politics as state's attorney in Petersburg; the family moved there, and the little boy started school. For a time he attended a German private school, and learned that language. In this part of the country, rich in memories of Lincoln and his vanished New Salem, and the Civil War, the boy absorbed the traditions of the Middle West.

In 1880 his family settled at Lewistown, where he spent the next eleven years, near the Spoon River he was later to make famous. Here he attended school, worked in a printer's office, published verses, and spent his money on books. While he was reading (Bryant, Poe, Burns, and later Shelley), he studied law, as his father, feeling literature to be a slender support, wished him to enter his own profession. He continued to read and write; some of his verses reached the Chicago *Inter-Ocean*, and he contributed to Eugene Field's column "Sharps and Flats" in the Chicago *Daily News*. By the time he was twenty-four he had written about four hundred poems, done local newspaper work, and served as correspondent for Chicago and St. Louis papers.

After high-school and academy training in Lewistown he went to Knox College in Galesburg in 1889; but his father was unwilling to help him, and he was forced to drop out and return to his father's law office. He was admitted to the bar in 1891. By this time, however, thanks to his studies, he had become acquainted with classical authors, Elizabethan dramatists, Goethe, Milton, Addison, Locke, Emerson, Poe, Whitman, Swinburne, and other English writers.

In the next year he went to Chicago and after some delay secured a job with the Edison Company which kept him alive until he entered a law partnership in 1893. He climbed to a secure social, professional, and financial position, married, and continued his writing. He supported Bryan and Altgeld, and was president of the Jefferson Club of Chicago. In 1903 he became the partner to a famous criminal lawyer. He traveled in the West in 1904 and in Europe in 1906. He came to know William Marion Reedy and Theodore Dreiser, and wrote plays with a view to retiring when he should have made enough money. His law partner defaulted, and the business broke up in 1911.

In 1911 he set up his own law business, and continued to write for William Marion Reedy's paper. Chicago was suddenly flowering with literary and artistic movements, and Masters was a member of the *Poetry* group of writers and those associated with the Press Club. He met such people as Masefield, Ridgely Torrence, and Padraic Colum, Harriet Monroe, Eunice Tietjens, and Alice Corbin Henderson, Mrs. William Vaughn Moody, Amy Lowell, Vachel Lindsay, and Carl Sandburg, all temporary or resident elements in the new literary movement in Chicago.

Out of this seething world, at a time when he was conducting an important case for a waitresses' union, came *Spoon River*, the first installment of which appeared in *Reedy's Mirror* May 29, 1914. Although violent attacks were made upon it, the book was very successful, and enjoyed a tremendous sale. In 1916 he received the Helen Haire Levinson Prize given by *Poetry*. The efforts made by the author at this time resulted in illness. The falling to pieces of the Chicago literary world during the war, and the refusal of his wife to free him for marriage with another woman, clouded the next few years, and in 1921 he traveled in the Mediterranean.

When he returned, professional and political enemies combined against him, and his prospects in Chicago became so discouraging that he abandoned his family and removed to New York. In 1925 he made an extensive lecture tour.

In that year he was divorced, and he remarried in 1926. Now he lives alone in an inconspicuous hotel in New York.

Masters regards himself as the victim of a professional career which, however successful, he considers to have been a mistake. To his energetic nature and a driving conscience he gives credit for his keeping at writing and bearing his misfortunes. ". . . I feel that no poet in English or American history," he writes in his autobiography, *Across Spoon River*, "ever had a harder life than mine was in the beginning at Lewistown, or among a people whose flesh and whose vibrations were better calculated to poison, to pervert, and even to kill a sensitive nature." His lifelong love of poetry, however, has kept him from abandoning his writing. *Spoon River* was the result of his reading, the suggestions of William Marion Reedy, and, specifically, the *Greek Anthology*, upon which it was formed.

For further comment, see Critical Survey, pp. 137–38, 171–72, 177–78.

BIBLIOGRAPHY

Poems

A book of verses, 1898; The blood of the prophets by Dexter Wallace [*pseud.*], 1905; Songs & sonnets by Webster Ford [*pseud.*], 1910; * Spoon River anthology, 1915; The great valley, 1916; Songs and satires, 1916; Toward the gulf, 1918; Starved Rock, 1919; Domesday book, 1920; The open sea, 1921; The new Spoon River, 1924; Selected poems, 1925; The fate of the jury, an epilogue to Domesday book, 1929; Lichee nuts, 1930; The serpent in the wilderness, 1933; invisible landscapes, 1935; The golden fleece of California, original wood engravings by Randolph Wardell Johnston, 1936; Poems of people, 1936; The new world, 1937; More people, 1939.

Plays in Verse

Maximilian, a play in five acts, 1902; Lee, a dramatic poem, 1926; Jack Kelso, a dramatic poem, 1928; Gettysburg, Manila, Âcoma, 1930; Godbey, a dramatic poem, 1931; Dramatic duologues, four short plays in verse, 1934 (Henry VIII and Ann Boleyn; Andrew Jackson and Peggy Eaton; Aaron Burr and Madam Jumel; Rabelais and the Queen of Whims); Richmond, a dramatic poem, 1934.

Plays

Althea, a play in four acts, 1907; The trifler, a play, 1908; The leaves of the tree, 1909; Eileen, a play in three acts, 1910; The locket, a play in three acts, 1910; The bread of idleness, a play in four acts, 1911.

Novels

Mitch Miller . . . with illustrations by John Sloan, 1920; Children of the market place, 1922; The nuptial flight, 1923; Skeeters Kirby, a novel, 1923; Mirage, 1924; Kit O'Brien, 1927; The tide of time, 1937.

Biography

Levy Mayer and the new industrial era, a biography, 1927; Lincoln, the man, 1931; * Vachel Lindsay, a poet in America, 1935; Whitman, 1937; Mark Twain, a portrait, 1938.

Autobiography

Across Spoon River, an autobiography, 1936.

Essays

The new star chamber and other essays, 1904; Browning as a philosopher. Paper read . . . before the Chicago literary club, November 18, 1912, 1912 (caption-title; pamphlet).

History

The tale of Chicago, 1933.

STUDIES AND ARTICLES

Aiken
Baldwin (M)
Beach, Joseph W. The concept of nature in nineteenth-century English poetry. 1936
Berg
Blankenship
Boynton
Boynton (H)
Boynton (L)
Boynton (S)
Chandler, Josephine C. The Spoon River country. c1923
Cook
Deutsch
Erskine
Farrar
Ford
Frank (O)
Gard
Green (C)
Hackett
Hansen
† Johnson (1929)
† Johnson (1932)
† Johnson (1936)
Jones
Karsner
Kreymborg
Kunitz (L)
Lewisohn (E)
Littell
Loggins
Lowell
Lowell (T)
† Manly
Markey
Maynard
Mencken (P)
Monroe
Monroe (P)
National
Pattee (N)
Phelps
Savage, Henry. A long spoon and the devil, being fish quaint and queer from the Spoon River, the property of Edgar Lee Masters, poached by Henry Savage and preserved [i.e.: published] by Cecil Palmer. [1922]
Schreiber
Schyberg
Sessions
Sinclair
† Taylor
Tietjens
Untermeyer
Untermeyer (C)
Untermeyer (N)
Van Doren
Van Doren (A)
Van Doren (C)
Vočadlo
Ward
Weirick
Wilkinson
Wood

Anonymous. "Edgar Lee Masters." *AB.*, Aug. 1922, pp. 572–76; Baldensperger, Fernand. "Une confession poétique de l'ouest Américain." *Corres.*, Dec. 25, 1924, pp. 833–47; Boynton, Percy H. "The voice of Chicago, Edgar Lee Masters and Carl Sandburg." *EJ.*, Dec. 1922, pp. 610–20; Childs, Herbert E. "Agrarianism and sex, Edgar Lee Masters and the modern spirit."

SR., July–Sept. 1933, pp. 331–43; Coffin, Robert P. T. "Poets of the people." *VQR.*, Jan. 1937, pp. 126–31; DuBois, Arthur E. "Lindsay and especially Masters." *SR.*, July–Sept. 1936, pp. 377–82; DuBois. "Shelley, Browning, and Masters." *Pers.*, Oct. 1937, pp. 405–16; Dudley, Dorothy. "Large measures." *P.*, June 1918, pp. 150–54; Fletcher, John G. "Masters and men." *P.*, Mar. 1937, pp. 343–47; Freer, Agnes L. "Spoon river to the open sea." *P.*, Dec. 1922, pp. 154–58; Gilman, Lawrence. "Moving picture poetry." *N.Amer. Rev.*, Aug. 1915, pp. 271–76; Henderson, Alice C. "Spoon river anthology." *P.*, June 1915, pp. 145–49; Jones, Llewellyn. "Edgar Lee Masters, critic of life." *AR.*, Sept. 1924, pp. 517–23; Monroe, Harriet. "A census spiritual." *P.*, July 1921, pp. 214–18; Monroe. "Edgar Lee Masters." *P.*, July 1924, pp. 204–10; Monroe. "Frost and Masters." *P.*, Jan. 1917, pp. 202–07; Monroe. "In bardic robes." *P.*, Mar. 1927, pp. 336–42; Monroe. "The Lindsay biography." *P.*, Mar. 1936, pp. 337–44; Monroe. "Spoon river again." *P.*, Feb. 1925, pp. 273–78; Powys, John C. "Edgar Lee Masters." *AB.*, Aug. 1929, pp. 650–56; Pratt, Julius W. "Whitman and Masters, a contrast." *SAQ.*, Apr. 1917, pp. 155–58; Scott, Evelyn. "The test of maturity." *P.*, July 1937, pp. 215–19; Seiffert, Marjorie A. "Starved rock." *P.*, June 1920, pp. 151–56; Van Wyck, William. "Edgar Lee Masters and twentieth century prosody." *Pers.*, Jan. 1937, pp. 75–80; Wilkinson, Marguerite. "Poets of the people." *Touchstone*, May 1918, pp. 172–77; Wisewell, George E. "Marivaux and E. L. Masters." *RLC.*, Apr. 1930, pp. 298–303; Wright, Willard H. "Mr. Masters' Spoon river anthology, a criticism." *Forum*, Jan. 1916, pp. 109–13. For references to reviews, see *BRD.*, 1915–16, 1918–33, 1935–38.

H(enry) L(ouis) Mencken, 1880–

Born September 12, 1880, in Baltimore, into a family of German extraction, and descended from a line of professors of law and history. His father, a business man, was interested in engineering. The boy, who in his teens showed creative literary and musical ability, after early private-school preparation entered the Baltimore Polytechnic Institute at twelve.

He showed no enthusiasm for embarking upon a business career or undertaking engineering, and in 1899 he began reporting for the Baltimore *Morning Herald.* In 1903 he became city editor, and by 1906, the last year of its existence, he had become chief editor of the *Evening Herald*, and he was offered jobs by all the other papers in town when his own ceased.

Joining the *Sun*, he served as Sunday editor, wrote editorials, and in 1910 moved to the editorial page of the *Evening Sun.* Except for a short time during the war he has remained continuously with this publication, which he regards as the finest evening paper in the United States. Until 1916 he ran a department of his own, "The Free Lance," which he gave up in order to go to Germany as correspondent for a group of newspapers including the *Sun.* The entrance of this country into the war and the censorship forced him to give up this job; and in 1918 he returned to the *Evening Sun.* He writes editorials appearing usually in Monday issues.

Although his chief interest is in daily-newspaper journalism, Mencken has had a long and varied association with magazines. In 1908 he became a literary critic for the *Smart Set*, and in 1914 he and George Jean Nathan became joint editors. In this position they were able to influence literary taste and to introduce a number of authors to the public.

In 1923 they left this publication and founded a new one, the *American Mercury*, published by Alfred A. Knopf. When Nathan resigned his editorship a year later, Mencken took complete charge, and left the magazine only in 1933. After twenty years of magazine work, including a contributing-editorship to the *Nation*, and writing for many other periodicals, he decided to withdraw from this type of work. He continues to live in Baltimore, which he prefers to New York, in the house in which he has lived since 1883.

Thanks to his vigorous contributions to magazines and newspapers, his editorial remarks in the *American Mercury*, and his series of *Prejudices*, Mencken's views on almost everything have become well known. With Nathan he ridiculed the current hysterias and popular errors at the time of the war and later; and, more than Nathan, whose devotion to the theater he does not share, he has retained his interest in what goes on in public life. "Bible Belt," "booboisie," "smuthound," and "Boobus americanus" are among his contributions to the American language he has so thoroughly studied. Mencken's thesis is the simple one that in the United States life is made more delightful than anywhere else because Americans have so effectively burlesqued every pretentious appeal to human idealism that religion, politics, and every other organized attack upon the intellect has become absurd and hence harmless and impotent. ". . . Everyone ought to know by this time," he wrote in the *Forum* in 1930, "that a mountebank, thinking only of tomorrow's cakes, is far safer with power in his hands than a prophet and martyr, his eyes fixed frantically upon the rewards beyond the grave." His philosophy, accordingly, is one of skepticism toward anything not established by objective, scientific evidence, and making the most of the enjoyment afforded any reasonable man by the ironies and absurdities of even an imperfect existence. Hence he refuses to support Liberal movements in politics, which he expects to run aground, as they have before, on some mistaken faith in the impossible. "The one article in my political credo," he writes," is a violent belief in liberty. It seems to me that is the most valuable thing ever desired by man. I believe in allowing its exercise up to the last limits of the endurable. I am opposed to politicians of all parties on the ground that all of them seek to diminish it in one way or another. I am convinced with Jefferson that the best government is the weakest, and am hence opposed to all efforts to curb the Supreme Court, for it has served admirably to check the pretensions of both the executive and legislative arms. That it may be wrong now and then is irrelevant. The main thing is that the President and Congress should realize at all times that there is a definite limit to their power. If the Supreme Court reached its decisions by shooting dice I'd still be in favor of it."

As writer, critic, and student of language Mencken has struck at academic tradition, called for an end to our bowing to foreign influence in literature, and stood forth as the champion of post-war realism and naturalism. Thus he has given aid and comfort to Sherwood Anderson, Ben Hecht, Eugene O'Neill, George Ade, James Branch Cabell, Carl Sandburg, and Willa Cather, and crossed critical swords with Stuart P. Sherman. "My belief is that American literature is gradually finding itself," he writes. "It will take us another generation or two to absorb the more recent immigrants, but in the long run we'll produce a genuinely national spirit. I believe that the old subservience to

England is gradually diminishing. Whether, when we have gained our freedom, we'll have anything worth while to say remains to be seen."

He has small respect for the current literary criticism. "Most book reviewing, at least in this country, is done by notably inferior persons. There is a pansy cast to great deal of it. It is largely in the hands of journalists who have turned out to be too stupid to be good police reporters. We have never produced a purely literary critic who was worth a damn." His own writing serves to articulate his own personality and makes no efforts to satisfy critics. "I have no purpose in writing save to express my own ego. Whether or not what I write wins assent from others is to me a complete irrelevance. Some of the things that seem to me to be my best have never got any notice, whereas those that struck me as third-rate have been read rather widely. I never pay any attention to criticism. I read it, of course, but so far as I can recall it has never seriously influenced me.

"My personal preference in all of the arts is for good workmanship. I admire the first movement of Beethoven's third symphony simply because it is the most astonishing piece of technical virtuosity in all music. It seems to me that content is a secondary matter, and so I can't find any sympathy for the Proletarian brethren who argue that every book should support the revolution. Most good authors, in point of fact, are opposed to whatever current of thought prevails in their time. In brief, the artist is not the spokesman of his race and era; he is the critic of them—that is, in so far as he has any ideas at all. Sometimes he has none, and yet remains a great artist."

For further comment, see Critical Survey, pp. 181, 187, 191–92.

BIBLIOGRAPHY

Essays, Studies, and Criticism

George Bernard Shaw, his plays, 1905; The philosophy of Friedrich Nietzsche, 1908; Men versus the man, a correspondence between Robert Rives La Monte, socialist, and H. L. Mencken, individualist, 1910; The creed of a novelist, 1916 (pamphlet); A book of prefaces . . . ⟨opus 13⟩, 1917; Ireland and her books, 1917 (pamphlet); Pistols for two by Owen Hatteras [*pseud.* of H. L. Mencken and George Jean Nathan], 1917 (pamphlet); Damn! a book of calumny, 1918 (also pub. with title: A book of calumny ⟨first printed as "Damn"⟩, 1918); In defense of women, 1918; Mr. Cabell of Virginia, 1918 (single sheet, folded); Prejudices, first series, 1919; The American credo, a contribution toward the interpretation of the national mind by George Jean Nathan and H. L. Mencken, 1920 (pref. by H. L. Mencken); The literary capital of the United States, 1920 (pamphlet); Prejudices, second series, 1920; Prejudices, third series, 1922; Spiritual autopsies . . . an article on Gamaliel Bradford reprinted from the Literary review of the New York evening post, 1922 (cover-title; pamphlet); Criticism in America, its function and status, essays by Irving Babbitt, Van Wyck Brooks, W. C. Brownell, Ernest Boyd, T. S. Eliot, H. L. Mencken, Stuart P. Sherman, J. E. Spingarn, and George E. Woodberry, 1924; Prejudices, fourth series, 1924; Notes on democracy, 1926; Prejudices, fifth series, 1926; James Branch Cabell, 1927 (pamphlet); Prejudices, sixth series, 1927; * Selected prejudices, 1927 (English ed., with variant text, 2 vols.: Selected prejudices, 1926; Selected prejudices, second series, 1927);

Three years, 1924 to 1927, the story of a new idea and its successful adaptation with a postscript by H. L. Mencken, 1927; Treatise on the gods, 1930; Gamaliel Bradford, naturalist of souls, 1932? (cover-title; leaflet); Treatise on right and wrong, 1934; Erez Israel, 1935; 1837–1937; The Sunpapers of Baltimore by Gerald W. Johnson, Frank R. Kent, H. L. Mencken, Hamilton Owens, 1937.

Language Studies

The American language, a preliminary inquiry into the development of English in the United States, 1919; The American language, an inquiry into the development of English in the United States . . . second edition, revised and enlarged, 1921; The American language, an inquiry into the development of English in the United States . . . third edition, revised and enlarged, 1923; Fourth edition corrected, enlarged, and rewritten. The American language, an inquiry into the development of English in the United States, 1936.

Poems

Ventures into verse being various ballads, ballades, rondeaux, triolets, songs, quatrains, odes, and roundels all rescued from the Potters' field of old files and here given decent burial ⟨peace to their ashes⟩ . . . with illustrations & other things by Charles S. Gordon & John Siegel, 1903.

Plays

The artist, a drama without words, 1912 (also pub. with title: The artist, a satire in one act, 1917); Heliogabalus, a buffoonery in three acts by H. L. Mencken and George Jean Nathan, 1920.

Satire

A book of burlesques . . . ⟨opus 12⟩, 1916.

Travel

Europe after 8:15 by H. L. Mencken, George Jean Nathan, Willard Huntington Wright, with decorations by Thomas H. Benton, 1914.

Journalism

Making a president, a footnote to the saga of democracy, 1932.

Miscellany

What you ought to know about your baby by Leonard Keene Hirshberg . . . [and H. L. Mencken] a text book for mothers on the care and feeding of babies with questions and answers especially prepared by the editor, 1910; A little book in C major . . . ⟨Opus 11⟩, 1916; The American credo, 1921 (caption-title; leaflet; an appendix to The American credo); A personal word, 1922 (caption-title; pamphlet); The Smart set, George Jean Nathan, H. L. Mencken, editors. Suggestions to our visitors, 1923 (cover-title; leaflet); To the friends of The American mercury, a statement by the editor, 16 April, 1926, 1926 (cover-title; pamphlet); Lo, the poor bookseller, 1930 (cover-title; pamphlet).

Editor

The players' Ibsen, A doll's house newly translated from the definitive Dano-Norwegian text, edited with introduction and notes, 1909; The players' Ibsen,

Little Eyolf newly translated from the definitive Dano-Norwegian text, edited with introduction and notes, 1909; The gist of Nietzsche arranged by Henry L. Mencken, 1910; The free lance books, II, edited with introductions by H. L. Mencken. Ventures in common sense by E. W. Howe, 1919; The free lance books, I, edited with introductions by H. L. Mencken. Youth and egolatry by Pío Baroja translated from the Spanish by Jacob S. Fassett, jr. and Frances L. Phillips, 1920; The free lance books, III, edited by H. L. Mencken. The antichrist by F. W. Nietzsche translated from the German with an introduction by H. L. Mencken, 1920; The free lance books, IV, edited with introductions by H. L. Mencken. We moderns: enigmas and guesses by Edwin Muir, 1920; The free lance books, V, edited with introductions by H. L. Mencken. Democracy and the will to power by James N. Wood, 1921; Americana 1925, 1925; Americana 1926, 1926; Essays by James Huneker selected with an introduction by H. L. Mencken, 1929; Books-Baltimore. The 10,000 best American books in print, 1930; The American democrat by James Fenimore Cooper edited with an introduction, 1931; Sara Haardt. Southern album edited with a preface by H. L. Mencken, 1936; The charlatanry of the learned (De charlataneria eruditorum, 1715) by Johann Burkhard Mencken (1674–1732) translated from the German by Francis E. Litz, with notes and an introduction by H. L. Mencken, 1937.

STUDIES AND ARTICLES

Babbitt, Irving. On being creative and other essays. 1932

Beach

Benchley

Berg

Bookman

Boyd

† Boyd, Ernest A. H. L. Mencken. 1925

Boynton (C)

Boynton (L)

Braithwaite

Brooks

Cabell

Calverton (N)

Canby

Chesterton, Gilbert K. All is grist, a book of essays. [1931]

Clark (E)

Cleaton

Combs

Cowley

Davis, Elmer H. Show window. 1927

DeCasseres, Benjamin. Mencken and Shaw, the anatomy of America's Voltaire and England's other John Bull. [c1930]

Dudley, Dorothy. Forgotten frontiers, Dreiser and the land of the free. 1932

Egan

Farrar

† Ford (E)

Forsythe

Forsythe (R)

Frank

† Frey, Carroll. A bibliography of the writings of H. L. Mencken . . . with a foreword by H. L. Mencken. 1924

Gillis

Goldberg, Isaac. H. L. Mencken. [c1924] (pamphlet)

Goldberg, Isaac. The man Mencken, a biographical and critical survey. 1925

Goldberg (T)

Graham, John E. The way of the skeptic. [c1931]

Green (C)

† H. L. Mencken. Fanfare by Burton Rascoe, The American critic by Vincent O'Sullivan, Bibliography by F. C. Henderson. 1920 (pamphlet)

Harris, Frank. Contemporary portraits, fourth series. [c1923]

Harrison, Joseph B. A short view of Menckenism in Menckenese. 1927 (pamphlet)
Hatteras, Owen A. [*pseud.*] Pistols for two. 1917
† Herrmann
Huneker, James G. Intimate letters of James Gibbons Huneker collected and edited by Josephine Huneker with a foreword by Benjamin DeCasseres. 1936
Jerome, Helen. The secret of woman. 1923
† Johnson (1929)
† Johnson (1932)
† Johnson (1936)
Knopf
Knopf (B)
Kunitz (L)
Levinson
Lewis (P)
Lewisohn (E)
Lippmann
Lippmann, Walter. H. L. Mencken . . . reprinted from The Saturday review of literature, December 11, 1926. [1926?] (cover-title; pamphlet)
Littell
Logan, John D. A literary chameleon, a new estimate of Mr. H. L. Mencken . . . with a foreword by J. L. O'Sullivan. 1926 (pamphlet)
Loggins
Luccock
MacCollough
MacLean
† Manly
Markey
Menckeniana, a schimpflexikon. 1928
Munro, Charles K. The true woman, a handbook for husbands and others. [c1932]
Nathan (I)
National
Pattee, Fred L. Side-lights on American literature. 1922
Pattee (N)
Rascoe
Rascoe (B)
Roberts
Rogers, Cameron. Oh splendid appetite! . . . with a foreword by William Rose Benét. [c1932]
Saturday
Schmidt, W. E. Mencken, monkeys and men. 1929
Schreiber
† Schwartz (O)
Sergeant
Shafer
Shaw
Sherman
Sherman (C)
Sinclair
Smart
Smith
Smith, Samuel S. The craft of the critic. [c1931]
† Taylor
Three years, 1924 to 1927, the story of a new idea and its successful adaptation with a postscript by H. L. Mencken. 1927
Untermeyer (H)
Van Doren
Van Doren (A)
† Van Doren (M)
Van Doren (W)
Van Roosbroeck, Gustave L. The reincarnation of H. L. Mencken. 1925 (pamphlet)
Wells, Gabriel. Intimations. 1927
Wickham
Zabel

Angoff, Charles. "Mencken twilight, another forgotten man, that enfant terrible of our era of nonsense." *N.Amer.Rev.*, Winter 1938–39, pp. 216–32; Anonymous. "H. L. Mencken." *AB.*, Feb. 1922, pp. 551–54; Anonymous. "Mr. Mencken and the prophets." *Freeman*, Oct. 13, 1920, pp. 103–04; Armstrong, Everhardt. "Mencken and America." *N.Cent.*, Jan. 1927, pp. 117–25; Babbitt, Irving. "The critic and American life." *Forum*, Feb. 1928, pp. 161–76; Beach, Joseph W. "Pedantic study of two critics." *AS.*, Mar. 1926, pp. 299–306; Boyd, Ernest A. "Mencken, or virtue rewarded." *Freeman*, Feb. 2, 1921, pp. 491–92; Bridges, Horace J. "Presenting Mr. H. L. Mencken."

Stand., Apr. 1927, pp. 237–48; Calverton, Victor F. "H. L. Mencken, a devaluation." *Mod.M.*, Dec. 1936, pp. 7–11; Chesterton, Gilbert K. "The skeptic as a critic." *Forum*, Feb. 1929, pp. 65–69; Collins, Seward B. "Criticism in America, the origins of a myth." *AB.*, June 1930, pp. 241–56, 353–64; Collins. "Criticism in America, the revival of the anti-humanist myth." *AB.*, July 1930, pp. 400–15; Espy, Willard R. "The Baltimore 'Sun' goes down." *Nation*, Feb. 4, 1939, pp. 143–46; Fitzgerald, Francis S. "Baltimore anti-Christ." *AB.*, Mar. 1921, pp. 79–81; Gillis, James M. "Mencken, moralist!" *CW.*, June 1934, pp. 257–66; Gilman, Lawrence. "The American language." *N.Amer.Rev.*, May 1919, pp. 697–703; Harrold, Charles F. "Two critics of democracy." *SAQ.*, Apr. 1928, pp. 130–41; Kelley, William V. "At the sign of the basilisk." *Meth.R.*, July 1925, pp. 518–27; Kronenberger, Louis. "H. L. Mencken." *NR.*, Oct. 7, 1936, pp. 243–45; Lippmann, Walter. "H. L. Mencken." *SRL.*, Dec. 11, 1926, pp. 413–14; Lippmann. "The near Machiavelli." *NR.*, May 31, 1922, pp. 12–14; McFee, William. "Mencken and Menken, or the gift of tongues." *AB.*, Dec. 1921, pp. 361–63; Maynard, Theodore. "Mencken leaves the American Mercury." *CW.*, Apr. 1934, pp. 10–20; Melamed, Samuel M. "H. L. Mencken's encyclopaedia of platitudes." *Reflex*, May 1930, pp. 3–17; Mencken, Henry L. "H. L. Mencken." *Nation*, Dec. 5, 1923, pp. 647–48; Mencken. "On breaking into type." *Col.*, Part 1, Art. 3, pp. 1–8, (1930); Mencken. "Testament." *RR.*, Oct. 1927, pp. 413–16; Michaud, Régis. "Henry Mencken ou le collectionneur de préjugés." *NL.*, June 9, 1928, p. 8; Monroe, Harriet. "Mephistopheles and the poet." *P.*, July 1926, pp. 210–15; † Moss, David. "American first editions, a series of bibliographic check-lists edited by Merle Johnson and Frederick M. Hopkins, number 31, H. L. (Henry Lewis) Mencken, 1880–." *PW.*, Apr. 28, 1923, pp. 1327–28; Muret, Maurice. "La philosophie à coups de matraque, Mencken contre l'Amérique." *J.Debats*, Oct. 24, 1930, pp. 681–83; Parshley, Howard M. "H. L. Mencken, an appreciation." *AR.*, Jan. 1925, pp. 72–84; Phelps, William L. "As I like it." *Scrib.*, Aug. 1930, pp. 205–08; Rascoe, Burton. "Those who can, criticize." *AB.*, Feb. 1928, pp. 670–76; Ratcliffe, Samuel K. "Mencken, an English plaint." *NR.*, Apr. 13, 1921, pp. 191–92; Root, Edward M. "Aesthetic puritans." *Christ.Cent.*, Aug. 25, 1937, pp. 1043–45; Salisbury, William. "Mencken, the foe of beauty." *AP.*, July 1926, pp. 34–49; Saroyan, William. "The American clowns of criticism." *Overland M.*, Mar. 1929, pp. 77–78, 92–93; Schneider, Isidor. "Mencken, a portrait in shadows." *N.Masses*, Sept. 29, 1936, pp. 17–18; Semper, Isidore J. "H. L. Mencken and catholicism." *CW.*, Sept. 1930, pp. 641–50; Semper. "H. L. Mencken, doctor rhetoricus." *CW.*, Oct. 1929, pp. 30–41; Sergeant, Elizabeth S. "H. L. Mencken." *Nation*, Feb. 16, 1927, pp. 174–76, 178; Shaw, Albert. "Mencken and his aims." *RR.*, Oct. 1927, p. 412; Sherman, Stuart P. "Mr. Brownell and Mr. Mencken." *AB.*, Jan. 1925, pp. 632–34; Simrell, Earle V. "H. L. Mencken the rhetorician." *QJS.*, Nov. 1927, pp. 399–412; Sinclair, Upton. "Mr. Mencken calls on me." *AB.*, Nov. 1927, pp. 254–56; Swinnerton, Frank. "The great Mencken fight." *AB.*, Dec. 1926, pp. 463–67; Tacke, C. A. "H. L. Mencken." *NWM.*, Feb. 1930, pp. 124–32; Van Doren, Carl. "Smartness and light, H. L. Mencken, a gadfly for democracy." *Cent.*, Mar. 1923, pp. 791–96; Williams, Michael. "Mr. Mencken's bible for boobs." *Com.*, Apr. 2, 1930, pp. 607–10; Wilson, Edmund, Jr. "H. L. Mencken." *NR.*, June 1, 1921, pp. 10–13. For references to reviews, see *BRD.*, 1908, 1914, 1917, 1919–22, 1924–28, 1930, 1932, 1934, 1936–37.

George Milburn, 1906–

Born in Coweta, Indian Territory, April 27, 1906. Educated in local public schools, he began reporting for an Oklahoma daily in 1922; and in 1923–24, the year he spent at the University of Tulsa, he was on the news staff of the Tulsa *Tribune.* Later (1925) he was a student at the Oklahoma A. & M. College, worked in the publicity department, and edited a college comic paper called *Aggievator*. In the same year he left college and "bummed" his way to Chicago, where he spent two years as free-lance writer of joke collections and editor of "classics" for a publisher of paper-bound books. He took to the road again in 1927, and began a walking-trip through the mountains of Arkansas. He stopped for a time to study at Commonwealth College, then proceeded to New Orleans, where he spent a year living and writing in an attic in the French Quarter. In 1928, forced by his father's illness to return to Oklahoma, he entered the state university, in which he remained until 1930 and supported himself by proof-reading and writing jokes for *Judge.*

Since then he has traveled and lived independently. He has contributed to many magazines, and to anthologies of short stories and college textbooks. He spent the summer of 1932 at the artists' colony at Yaddo, Saratoga Springs, and subsequently he did free-lance work at Provincetown, at Lake George, and in Wilton, Connecticut. He was awarded a Guggenheim fellowship in 1934 and spent 1934–35 in England and Spain. Since his return he has lived in Missouri.

BIBLIOGRAPHY

Novel

Catalogue, a novel, 1936.

Short Stories

Oklahoma town, 1931; No more trumpets and other stories, 1933.

"Little Blue Book" Pamphlets

The best Jewish jokes edited by George Milburn, 1926; A book of interesting and amusing puns edited by George Milburn, 1926; A book of popular recitations selected by George Milburn, 1926; Casey at the bat and other humorous favorites edited by George Milburn, 1926; A handbook for amateur magicians, 1926; Lives of the U.S. presidents . . . with portraits by Peter Quinn, 1926; The best hobo jokes edited by George Milburn, 1927; The best jokes about drunks edited by George Milburn, 1927; The best rube jokes edited by George Milburn, 1927; A book of the best Ford jokes edited by George Milburn, 1927; How to become a United States citizen, 1927; How to prepare manuscripts, 1927; How to tie all kinds of knots . . . drawings by Hans Kueffer, 1927; A rapid calculator, how to make rapid arithmetical calculations edited by George Milburn, 1928.

Compiler

The hobo's hornbook, a repertory for a gutter jongleur collected and annotated by George Milburn, decorations by William Siegel, 1930.

For references to reviews, see *BRD.*, 1930–31, 1933, 1936.

Edna St. Vincent Millay, 1892–

Born February 22, 1892, in Rockland, Maine. She spent her childhood in New England and attended school in Rockland and Camden, Maine. She studied music and literature and soon showed promise as a poet. Verses written by her as a child appeared in *St. Nicholas*, and at her high-school graduation she presented a prize-winning essay in verse. A well-to-do friend, impressed with her qualities, assisted her to go to college.

As a student at Vassar, from which she graduated in 1917, she wrote and took part in college plays, and won the Intercollegiate Poetry Contest. "Renascence," submitted for a prize contest, failed to win it, but was published in *The Lyric Year* (1912), an anthology, edited by Ferdinand Earle, of the best poems submitted.

After graduation she moved to New York to take a room in Greenwich Village and work at her writing. She wrote and acted for the Provincetown Players, and took part in productions by the Theatre Guild; and, to support herself, she published short stories over the pseudonym "Nancy Boyd." She wrote and published poetry and made experiments in drama. *The Lamp and the Bell*, one of her poetic plays, was performed at the Vassar commencement exercises in 1921, and the Provincetown Players presented *Aria da Capo*, a one-act satire on war. In 1925 the Metropolitan Opera Association commissioned her to write the book for an opera, the music to be written by Deems Taylor; and *The King's Henchman*, produced in 1927 with Edward Johnson and Lawrence Tibbett, was perhaps the most successful American opera given in New York to that time. In 1920 *Poetry* gave Miss Millay a cash prize, and in 1931 it awarded her the Helen Haire Levinson Prize. She is a member of the National Institute of Arts and Letters, and holds several honorary degrees. She was awarded the Pulitzer Prize in 1923 for *The Harp Weaver and Other Poems.*

In the same year she married Eugen Jan Boissevain, and not long after they moved from Greenwich Village to a country house in the Hudson valley, then to a farm in the Berkshires. Now they live in New York State, and recently they have bought an island off the Maine coast. Since her marriage Miss Millay has traveled and given lectures and readings of her own work. She is especially interested in the sonnet. Among American poets she admires most of all Robinson Jeffers.

For further comment, see Critical Survey, pp. 133–34.

BIBLIOGRAPHY

Poems

Renascence and other poems, 1917; Possession, a sonnet, 1918 (pamphlet); A few figs from thistles, poems and four sonnets, 1920 (pamphlet; new and enl. eds., 1921, 1922); Second April, 1921; The ballad of the harp-weaver, 1922 (pamphlet); * The harp-weaver and other poems, 1923; Poems, 1923; Renascence, a poem . . . Printed for the first time in separate form by Frederick & Bertha Goudy on the handpress on which William Morris printed the Kelmscott Chaucer. At the Anderson galleries, New York: March MCMXXIV, 1924 (pamphlet); Edna St. Vincent Millay, The pamphlet poets, price 25 cents, 1927 (cover-title; ed. by Hughes Mearns); The buck in the snow & other poems, 1928; Edna St. Vincent Millay's poems selected for young people, illustrations and decorations by J. Paget-Fredericks, 1929; * Fatal interview, sonnets, 1931; Twice required, 1931 (publisher's dummy; contains 3 sonnets); Wine from these grapes, 1934 (trade ed. in 1 vol.); Wine from these grapes, 1934 (vol. 1, ltd. ed.); Epitaph for the race of man, 1934 (vol. 2, ltd. ed. of Wine from these grapes); Vacation song [by] E. Vincent Millay, 1936 (pamphlet); Conversation at midnight, 1937; Huntsman, what quarry? Poems, 1939.

Plays

Aria da capo (a play in one act) . . . The Chapbook (a monthly miscellany) no. 14, August 1920, 1920; The lamp and the bell, a drama in five acts, 1921; Two slatterns and a king, a moral interlude . . . First produced at Vassar college, 1921 (pamphlet); The king's henchman, lyric drama in three acts, book by Edna St. Vincent Millay, music by Deems Taylor, opus 19 . . ., 1926 (1st complete ed. without the music, The king's henchman, a play in three acts, 1927); Three plays, 1926 (Two slatterns and a king; Aria da capo; The lamp and the bell); The princess marries the page, a play in one act . . . decorations by J. Paget-Fredericks, 1932.

Humor

Distressing dialogues by Nancy Boyd [*pseud.*] with a preface by Edna St. Vincent Millay, 1924.

Social Study

Fear, 1927? (pamphlet); Reflections on the Sacco-Vanzetti tragedy. Fear by Edna St. Vincent Millay, Vanzetti's last statement by William G. Thompson, Psychology and justice by John Dewey, The martyrs of Massachusetts by C. I. Claflin, 1927 (pamphlet).

Verses Set to Music

Tune:—"St. Vincent." Words and music by Edna St. Vincent Millay, '17, 1917 (broadside); Thursday [words by] Edna St. Vincent Millay [music by] Horace Johnson, 1923 (caption-title; sheet music); Where she lies [by] Edna St. Vincent Millay, Henry Cowell, Curwen edition, 1925 (cover-title; sheet music); From a very little sphinx, seven poems by Edna St. Vincent Millay, set to music for medium voice and piano by Bernard Wagenaar, 1926; My candle (it gives a lovely light) words by Edna St. Vincent Millay, music by Annabel Morris Buchanan, 1928 (cover-title; sheet music); The return from town, poem by Edna St. Vincent Millay, music by Constance Herreshoff, 1928 (caption-title; sheet music); Song, The little tavern, poem by Edna St. Vincent Millay, music by Ruth Wright Vanderlip, high voice in F, medium voice in D♭, 1929 (cover-title; sheet music); Elaine [words by] Edna St. Vincent Millay [music by] Constance Mills Herreshoff, 1931 (caption-title; sheet music); God's world, song, poem by Edna St. Vincent Millay, music by Jacques Wolfe, 1932 (cover-title; sheet music); The harp weaver, a choral ballad for baritone solo, three-part women's chorus, piano, and two harps, the text by Edna St. Vincent Millay, set to music by Elinor Remick Warren, 1932 (cover-title); Charivaria, five poems by Edna St. Vincent Millay, set to music by Maurice Besly. Contents: No. 1, Afternoon on a hill . . . No. 2, The unexplorer . . . No. 3, To the not impossible him . . . No. 4, My candle burns at both ends . . . No. 5, Epitaph . . ., 1933 (pamphlet); Thursday, song, "And if I loved you Wednesday" [words by] Edna St. Vincent Millay, music by Iris Brussels, 1933 (cover-title; sheet music); Afternoon on a hill, words by Edna St. Vincent Millay, music by Grace Becker, 1934 (cover-title; sheet music); A prayer to Persephone, song for voice and piano by Ben Burtt . . . [words by Edna St. Vincent Millay], 1936 (cover-title; sheet music); Vanished summer, poem by Edna St. Vincent Millay, music by Edward Harris, 1936 (cover-title; sheet music).

Translations

Flowers of evil from the French of Charles Baudelaire by George Dillon [and] Edna St. Vincent Millay, with the original texts and with a preface by Miss Millay, 1936.

STUDIES AND ARTICLES

Atkins, Elizabeth. Edna St. Vincent Millay and her times. [c1936]
Blankenship
Bowdoin
Brenner
Bruns
Collins (T)
Combs
Cook
Cowley
Deutsch
Farrar
Green (C)
Halleck
Harmati, Sandor. God's world, words by Edna St. Vincent Millay, music by Sandor Harmati. [c1934] (cover-title; sheet music)
† Johnson (1929)
† Johnson (1932)
† Johnson (1936)
Jones
Kirkland
Kreymborg
Kunitz (L)
Lewisohn (E)
Loggins
Lucas
Madeleva, *sister* Mary. Chaucer's nuns and other essays . . . foreword by B. H. Lehman. [c1925]
† Manly
Maynard
Monroe
National
Quinn (H)
Ransom
Schuman, William H. God's world, song for voice and piano, the poem by Edna St. Vincent Millay, the music by William H. Schuman. [c1933] (cover-title; sheet music)
Simonson, Lee. Minor prophecies. [c1927]
Stidger, William L. Flames of faith . . . introduction by Edwin Markham. [c1922]
Tate
† Taylor
Untermeyer
Untermeyer (M)
Untermeyer (N)
Van Doren
Van Doren (A)
Van Doren, Carl C. Edna St. Vincent Millay. Youth and wings, Edna St. Vincent Millay: singer. [1927?] (pamphlet)
† Van Doren (M)
Vočadlo
Widdemer
Wood
† Yost, Karl. A bibliography of the works of Edna St. Vincent Millay . . . with an essay in appreciation by Harold Lewis Cook, introductions and three poems by Edna St. Vincent Millay. 1937

Anonymous. "Edna St. Vincent Millay." *AB.*, Nov. 1922, pp. 272–78; Barry, Griffin. "Vincent." *N.Yer.*, Feb. 12, 1927, pp. 25–27; Beatty, Jerome; "'Best sellers' in verse, the story of Edna St. Vincent Millay." *A.Mag.*, Jan. 1932, pp. 102–06; Bishop, John P. "A diversity of opinions." *P.*, Nov. 1937, pp. 99–104; Bogan, Louise. "Conversion into self." *P.*, Feb. 1935, pp. 277–79; Burton, Katherine. "Edna St. Vincent Millay." *Com.*, Mar. 11, 1938, pp. 544–45; Bynner, Witter. "Edna St. Vincent Millay." *NR.*, Dec. 10, 1924, Suppl. pp. 14–15; Chubb, Thomas C. "Shelley grown old." *N.Amer.Rev.*, Spring 1938, pp. 170–80; Dabbs, James M. "Edna St. Vincent Millay, not resigned." *SAQ.*, Jan. 1938, pp. 54–66; Davison, Edward. "Edna St. Vincent Millay." *EJ.*, Nov. 1927, pp. 671–82; Du Bois, Arthur E. "Edna St. Vincent Millay." *SR.*, Jan.–Mar. 1935, pp. 80–104; Flanner, Hildegarde. "Two poets, Jeffers and Millay." *NR.*, Jan. 27, 1937, pp. 379–82; Freer, Agnes L. "Baudelaire in English." *P.*, June 1936, pp. 158–62; Hennecke, Hans. "Edna St. Vincent Millay." *N.Rund.*, June 1938, pp. 627–28; Monroe, Harriet. "Advance or retreat?" *P.*, July 1931, pp. 216–21; Monroe. "Edna St. Vincent Millay." *P.*, Aug. 1924, pp. 260–66; Monroe. "First books of verse." *P.*, Dec. 1918, pp. 167–68; Monroe. "Miss Millay in opera." *P.*, Apr. 1927, pp. 42–46; Monroe. "Miss Millay's new book." *P.*, Jan. 1929, pp. 210–14; Nelson, June. "Miss Millay's 'The fatal interview.'" *Stand.*, Jan. 1932, pp. 145–48; Parks, Edd W. "Edna St. Vincent Millay." *SR.*, Jan.–Mar. 1930, pp. 42–49; Preston, John H. "Edna St. Vincent Millay." *VQR.*, July 1927, pp. 342–55; Ransom, John C. "The poet as woman." *So.R.*, Spring 1937, pp. 783–806; Strobel, Marion. "A flourish of trumpets." *P.*, Dec. 1921, pp. 151–54; Van Doren, Carl. "Youth and wings, Edna St. Vincent Millay, singer." *Cent.*, June 1923, pp. 310–16. For references to reviews, see *BRD.*, 1918, 1921, 1923–24, 1927–32, 1934, 1937, 1939.

Marianne (Craig) Moore, 1887–

Born November 15, 1887, in St. Louis. Much of her girlhood was spent in Pennsylvania. She was given preparatory training at the Metzger Institute, Carlisle, Pennsylvania, where she studied from 1896 to 1905; and she took the bachelor's degree at Bryn Mawr in 1909. The next year she spent taking a course at the Carlisle Commercial College; and from 1911 until 1915 she taught stenography in the government Indian school at Carlisle. In 1911 she traveled in England and France.

Not long after, she began to publish verses in the *Egoist*, an English periodical. She was so diffident about her poetry, however, that a collection of it appeared in 1920 only as a result of the action of some friends, one of whom was "H. D." It was issued without the knowledge of the author, who was at this time an assistant in a branch of the New York Public Library. Four years later, however, she published an American volume of verse, *Observations*, and in that year she was given the *Dial* Award of two thousand dollars for poetry, for distinguished service to American letters.

In the following year she left the library to become acting editor of the *Dial*, and she remained with the magazine until it ceased publication in 1929. In 1933 *Poetry* awarded her the Helen Haire Levinson Prize for Poetry.

Miss Moore ascribes much of her urge to do as fine work as possible to the authors she reads and enjoys; the list includes many of the greatest figures in English literature. "I might mention as authors for whom I have an especial liking," she writes, "Chaucer, Robert Henryson, Bunyan (including the poems), Anthony Trollope, Thomas Hardy, W. H. Hudson, Marjory Fleming, W. B. Yeats." Her delight in animals and outdoor life and sports, in music, and in printing and typography has also afforded inspiration, not only in itself, but also in her consequent interest in technical and trade journals, advertisements, reviews, criticisms, and other specialized forms of writing on these subjects.

In her own work Miss Moore is painstaking and careful. At various times she has deliberately striven to record accurately the speech that she has heard. Although she has stated that her guiding principle has been that no trouble is too great, she has confessed that nothing she has written has met her own standards. "Like every other writer," she says, "I am interested in getting the exact equivalent for the thing felt. I value an effect of naturalness, make an effort to avoid the stock phrase, and regard clearness among first requirements. Over accent and over emphasis are to be avoided, it seems, to me; and I feel that mathematics as we have it in music, can be of inestimable help to a poet. Luxury is a theme which revenges itself upon a writer however uncomplimentary to it he may be, and I cannot but feel that a writer must have a sense of responsibility regarding world matters such as the prevalence of crime, the pre-eminent demand for material comfort, the tendency of nations to settle disputes by force."

For further comment, see Critical Survey, pp. 144–45.

BIBLIOGRAPHY

Poems

Poems, 1921 (arranged by H. D. and Mr. and Mrs. Robert McAlmon); Observations, 1924 (reprint, with additions, of English ed., Poems, 1921); * Selected poems . . . with an introduction by T. S. Eliot, 1935; The Pangolin and other verse, five poems . . . with 8 drawings by George Plank, 1936.

STUDIES AND ARTICLES

Blackmur
Kreymborg
Kunitz (L)
Munson (D)
Riding
Rosenfeld (M)
Taupin
Untermeyer
Ward
Zabel

Monroe, Harriet. "Symposium on Marianne Moore." *P.*, Jan. 1922, pp. 208–16; Wescott, Glenway. "Concerning Miss Moore's observations." *D.*, Jan. 1925, pp. 1–4; Williams, William C. "Marianne Moore." *D.*, May 1925, pp. 393–401; Winters, Yvor. "Holiday and day of wrath." *P.*, Apr. 1925, pp. 39–44; Zabel, Morton D. "A literalist of the imagination." *P.*, Mar. 1936, pp. 326–36. For references to reviews, see *BRD.*, 1925, 1935.

Merrill Moore, 1903–

Born September 11, 1903, in Columbia, Tennessee. His father, John Trotwood Moore, was a writer and editor; and his mother, Mary Brown Daniel Moore, State Librarian of Tennessee, had been a music teacher in Nashville. In 1907 the family moved to Nashville, where Mr. Moore had charge of the *Taylor-Trotwood Magazine;* and Merrill Moore went to city and county schools. About six years later they moved out into the country, where the family home has been ever since.

Merrill Moore was prepared for college at the Montgomery Bell Academy, 1916–20, and in the latter year entered the College of Arts and Sciences of Vanderbilt University, from which he graduated in 1924. In college he associated with Donald Davidson and Allen Tate, and was much influenced by John Crowe Ransom, who was one of his teachers. He was prominent in literary and political student activities, and in 1922 joined the *Fugitive* group, which had begun its existence in the previous year. From 1922 to 1926 he assisted in the editing of the *Fugitive* and made contributions of his own. Although he usually spent summer in outdoor work, in 1923 he went abroad and spent several months in Germany.

His father wished him to enter editorial work on a country newspaper, but, although he was interested in writing, he chose medicine for his career and entered the Medical School at Vanderbilt in 1924. ". . . I think that practically everything I am or am doing now," he declares, "represents a split identification with my father in that my interest in writing represents a poetic or literary identification with him while my medical interests represent a negative identification with him or against him as the case may be. . . . I . . . feel a deep interest on the one hand in poetry and writing and on the other hand in medicine and science, to a degree that is rather difficult even for me to explain about myself." He earned money for some of his expenses by working at various jobs and by teaching in night school and in a Negro university. In 1928 he received his M.D. degree, and, after a summer in Europe, he assumed an interneship in Nashville. In 1929 he was made Neurological House Officer at the Boston City Hospital, and since that time he has held various positions in institutions in Boston and has been associated with the Harvard Medical School. Throughout his medical study he has concentrated more and more on nervous and mental diseases. From 1932 to 1935 he held a Commonwealth research fellowship in psychiatry at Harvard and worked at the Boston Psychopathic Hospital on the diseases of the nervous system. At present he serves on the staffs of several hospitals, teaches psychiatry at Harvard, and conducts a private practice in psychiatry in Boston.

". . . I think that I am most interested in human personality, and its problems," writes Dr. Moore, who has twice been psychoanalyzed and feels that the experience is essential to success in psychotherapy, "and it is on that common interest in my own life that medicine and poetry meet. . . . I am very much interested in the development of psychiatry and mental hygiene in medical school and hospitals. . . . I think the education of children is about as important a point as any that can be studied or dealt with, particularly, in regard to the aim of preventing the development of psycho-neurotic and delinquent tendencies in personality."

"I enjoy poetry very much," says Dr. Moore, "and if you ask me to name a favorite, I believe that I would name Thomas Hardy. I think his collected poems are tremendously impressive, and I feel that he is an even greater poet than he is a prose writer." Among the contemporaries he admires Archibald MacLeish, T. S. Eliot, and especially John Crowe Ransom, and he is still interested in the activities of the group formerly associated with the *Fugitive*. "I have never been very active in politics," he writes, "but am what is generally called a Democrat with strong Socialistic leanings (and no hostility to Communism)."

For further comment, see Critical Survey, pp. 147–48.

BIBLIOGRAPHY

Poems

The noise that time makes . . . with a foreword by John Crowe Ransom, 1929; It is a good deal later than you think, 1934; Six sides to a man, new sonnets . . . with an epilogue by Louis Untermeyer, 1935; Poems from the Fugitive . . . ⟨1922–1926⟩, 1936; M: one thousand autobiographical sonnets, 1938; Sonnets from New directions . . . with a preface by William Carlos Williams, 1938 (pamphlet).

STUDIES AND ARTICLES

Untermeyer, Louis. Merrill Moore.
1935 (pamphlet)

Fitts, Dudley. "The sonnets of Merrill Moore." *SR.*, Apr.–June 1939, pp. 268–93; Holden, Raymond. "Activities of an amateur." *P.*, Oct. 1935, pp. 49–52; McCord, David. "M-m-m-m-m." *SRL.*, Jan. 7, 1939, p. 10; Untermeyer, Louis. "Experiment and tradition." *YR.*, Spring 1939, pp. 608–09; Untermeyer. "Merrill Moore, a comment on his 'American' sonnet." *SR.*, Jan.–Mar. 1935, pp. 58–61; Untermeyer. "Three younger poets." *EJ.*, Dec. 1932, pp. 787–99; Winters, Yvor. "Merrill Moore's poems." *P.*, May 1930, pp. 104–06. For references to reviews, see *BRD.*, 1929, 1935, 1938.

Paal Mørck, *pseud. See* **O. E. Rølvaag**

Paul Elmer More, 1864–1937

Born in St. Louis, December 12, 1864. He was educated in that city at Washington University and graduated in 1887. After teaching at Smith Academy in St. Louis he took the master's degree in 1892 and proceeded to Harvard, where he took the master's degree in 1893. His field of interest was the ancient languages and literatures, and he taught Sanskrit at Harvard in 1894–95 and, from 1895 to 1897, Sanskrit and classical literature at Bryn Mawr College.

Resigning this position, he spent some time on a farm near Shelburne, New Hampshire, where he began the *Shelburne Essays.* In 1901 he joined the staff of the New York *Independent* as literary editor, and two years later he accepted a similar position on the *Evening Post*, which he held until, in 1909, he became editor of the *Nation.* In 1914 he resigned and retired to Princeton to study and teach philosophy, and in the next year he was elected to membership in the American Academy of Arts and Letters.

A lecturer on Plato, he was a champion of classical standards in art and philosophy, and with Irving Babbitt he advanced the ideal of humanism as an antidote to the naturalism in vogue during the war period and after. He admired greatly Plato, Socrates, and Athanasius, and was conservative in religion and politics and classical in literary criticism. He held honorary degrees from several American institutions and from the University of Glasgow.

He died March 9, 1937.

For further comment, see Critical Survey, p. 186.

BIBLIOGRAPHY

Critical Essays

Shelburne essays . . . First series, 1904; Shelburne essays . . . Second series, 1905; Shelburne essays . . . Third series, 1905; Shelburne essays . . . Fourth series, 1906; Shelburne essays . . . Fifth series, 1908; Shelburne essays . . . Sixth series ⟨Studies of religious dualism⟩, 1909; Shelburne essays . . . Seventh series, 1910; * The drift of romanticism, Shelburne essays, eighth series, 1913; Aristocracy and justice, Shelburne essays, ninth series, 1915; With the wits, Shelburne essays, tenth series, 1919; A New England group and others, Shelburne essays, eleventh series, 1921; Academy papers, addresses on language problems by members of the American academy of arts and letters: Paul Elmer More, William Milligan Sloane, William Crary Brownell, Brander Matthews, Bliss Perry, Paul Shorey, Henry Van Dyke, Robert Underwood Johnson. The Evangeline Wilbour Blashfield foundation, 1925; The demon of the absolute . . . New Shelburne essays volume I, 1928; * Selected Shelburne essays, 1935; On being human . . . New Shelburne essays volume III, 1936.

Philosophical and Religious Studies

Nietzsche, 1912; The paradox of Oxford . . . from the Proceedings of the Michigan schoolmasters' club and classical conference held at Ann Arbor, Michigan, April 4, 1913. Humanistic papers, second series, III. Reprint from the School review, June 1913, 1913 (pamphlet); Platonism . . . lectures delivered at Princeton university, October 29, 30, 31, November 6, 7, 1917, 1917 [The Greek tradition, Complementary vol.]; The religion of Plato, 1921 (The Greek tradition, vol. I); Christianity and problems of to-day, lectures delivered before Lake Forest college on the foundation of the late William Bross, 1922 (with others); Hellenistic philosophies, 1923 (The Greek tradition, vol. II); The Christ of the New Testament, 1924 (The Greek tradition, vol. III); Christ the Word, 1927 (The Greek tradition, vol. IV); The Catholic faith, 1931 (The Greek tradition, Complementary vol.); The sceptical approach to religion . . . New Shelburne essays volume II, 1934; Christian mysticism, a critique, 1932 (repr. from The Catholic faith).

Poems

Helena and occasional poems, 1890.

Novel

The Jessica letters, an editor's romance, 1904 (pub. anonymously; by Paul Elmer More and Mrs. L. H. Harris).

Autobiography

Pages from an Oxford diary, 1937.

Biography

Benjamin Franklin, 1900; Commemorative tribute to Henry Adams . . . prepared for the American academy of arts and letters, 1920, 1922 (pamphlet).

Textbook

The study of English literature by Samuel Pendleton Cowardin, jr. . . . and Paul Elmer More, 1936.

Editor

The great refusal being letters of a dreamer in Gotham, 1894; The complete poetical works of Lord Byron, Cambridge edition, 1905; Anglicanism, the thought and practice of the Church of England illustrated from the religious literature of the seventeenth century, compiled and edited by Paul Elmer More . . . and Frank Leslie Cross, 1935; Thackeray. Vanity fair, a novel without a hero, 1935 (2 vols.).

Translations

The judgment of Socrates, translation of Apology, Crito, and closing scene of Phaedo, n.d.; A century of Indian epigrams chiefly from the Sanskrit of Bhartrihari, 1898; The Prometheus bound of Æschylus translated with introduction and notes, 1899.

STUDIES AND ARTICLES

Grattan
Hough, Lynn H. Adventures in the minds of men. [c1927]
Jones, Llewellyn. How to read books. [c1930]
Kunitz (L)
Leander, Folke. Humanism and naturalism, a comparative study of Ernest Seillière, Irving Babbitt, and Paul Elmer More. 1937
Lewisohn (E)
† Manly
Mencken, Henry L. Prejudices, third series. [1924]
Mercier
Mercier (M)
Mueller
Munson
Munson (D)
National
Pattee (N)
Ransom, John C. God without thunder, an unorthodox defense of orthodoxy. [c1930]
Schelling
Shafer, Robert. Paul Elmer More and American criticism. 1935
Sherman
Sherman, Stuart P. The emotional discovery of America and other essays. [c1932]
Spingarn, Joel E. A Spingarn enchiridion, being passages from the writings of J. E. Spingarn in reply to Paul Elmer More's charge that he has taught that "criticism is only impression" collected by Alain T. Peters. 1929 (pamphlet)
Tate
Ward
West
Wilson, Edmund. The triple thinkers, ten essays on literature. [c1938]
Zeitlin

Bourne, Randolph S. "Paul Elmer More." *NR.*, Apr. 1, 1916, pp. 245–47; Brett, George S. "Paul Elmer More, a study." *UTQ.*, Apr. 1935, pp. 279–95; Collins, Seward B. "Criticism in America." *AB.*, June 1930, pp. 241–56, 353–64; Cory, Herbert E. "An aristocratic voice in the wilderness." *D.*, June 22, 1916, pp. 16–20; Eliot, Thomas S. "A commentary." *Crit.*, July 1937, pp. 666–70; Elliott, George K. "More's christology." *AR.*, Apr. 1937, pp. 35–46; Elliott. "Mr. More and the gentle reader." *AB.*, Apr. 1929, pp. 143–47; Grattan, Clinton H. "The so-called humanism of Paul Elmer More." *NH.*, Nov.–Dec. 1935, pp. 219–23; Harper, George M. "More's Shelburne essays." *A.Mo.*, Oct. 1906, pp. 561–70; Leander, Folke. "More, 'puritana à *rebours*.'"

A.Schol., Oct. 1938, pp. 438–53; Leo, Brother. "Paul Elmer More." *CW.*, Nov. 1922, pp. 198–211; Mather, Frank J., Jr. "Paul Elmer More, 1864–1937." *PAAAS.*, May 1938, pp. 368–72; Mercier, Louis J. A. "The challenge of Paul Elmer More." *HGM.*, June 1926, pp. 556–69; Moore, Cecil A. "Berkeley's influence on popular literature, a review of a review." *SAQ.*, July 1915, pp. 263–78; Morrow, Felix. "The serpent's enemy, Mr. More as a social thinker." *Symp.*, Apr. 1930, pp. 168–93; Murry, John M. "Puritan or platonist?" *D.*, Aug. 1921, pp. 236–41; Parkes, Henry B. "Paul Elmer More, manichean." *HH.*, Apr.–June 1932, pp. 477–83; Peck, Harvey W. "Some aspects of the criticism of Paul Elmer More." *SR.*, Jan. 1918, pp. 63–84; Richards, Philip S. "An American platonist." *N.Cent.*, Apr. 1929, pp. 479–89; Richards. "The religious philosophy of Paul Elmer More." *Crit.*, Jan. 1937, pp. 205–19; Rinaker, Clarissa. "The dualism of Mr. P. E. More." *Phil.Rev.*, July 1917, pp. 409–20; Seillière, Ernest A. A. L. "La réaction contre le naturisme aux États-Unis, à propos du livre challenge of humanist, de L. Mercier." *J.Débats*, Oct. 13, 1933, pp. 580–82; Stamm, Rudolf. "Paul Elmer More's suche nach einer lebendigen tradition." *E.Studien*, Oct. 1937, pp. 58–72; Warren, Austin. "Mr. More discovers Christianity." *SR.*, Apr.–June 1928, pp. 246–50; Wilson, Edmund. "Mr. More and the mithraic bull." *NR.*, May 26, 1937, pp. 64–68; Wilson. "Notes on Babbitt and More." *NR.*, Mar. 19, 1930, pp. 115–20; Zabel, Morton D. "An American critic." *P.*, Sept. 1937, pp. 330–36; Zeitlin, Jacob, *ed.* "Stuart P. Sherman and Paul Elmer More, correspondence." *AB.*, Sept. 1929, pp. 43–53. For references to reviews, see *BRD.*, 1906–10, 1912–13, 1915, 1918–19, 1921, 1924, 1928–29, 1932, 1935–37.

De Wolfe Morgan, *pseud.* *See* Thames Williamson

Emanuel Morgan, *pseud.* *See* Witter Bynner

Christopher (Darlington) Morley, 1890–

Born in Haverford, Pennsylvania, May 5, 1890. His parents were English-born Quakers, and his father, a distinguished mathematician, was a professor at Haverford College. His mother was a musician and poet. In 1900, when Professor Morley accepted the chair of pure mathematics at Johns Hopkins, the family moved to Baltimore. As a boy Christopher Morley became acquainted with the family library and the Enoch Pratt Free Library and spent summers in England.

He entered Haverford College in 1906 and during his four years, in which he contributed to the college paper, made so brilliant a record that in 1910 he was sent to Oxford as Rhodes Scholar from Maryland. The three years he spent at New College stimulated his interest in poetry; and in 1912 his first book of poems appeared. In the next year he returned to the United States and took a fifteen-dollar-a-week job with Doubleday, Page and Company. Leaving this in 1917, he began his long career in journalism by joining the staff of the *Ladies Home Journal*, and in 1918–20 he worked on the Philadelphia *Evening Ledger*.

"The Bowling Green," the column which he contributes to the *Saturday Review of Literature*, he began on the New York *Evening Post*, for which he wrote from 1920 to 1923; and he says that conducting a signed column taught him the value of anonymity. Upon the expiring of the *Post* in 1924 he took his column to the *Saturday Review*, where it still appears. Morley is a contributing editor of the *Saturday Review*.

About 1921 he made his decision to abandon, partly at least, his bookish essays and verses of home life for more serious work. The reception of *Where the Blue Begins* was encouraging, and with his family he spent a summer in a Norman village writing *Thunder on the Left*. His enthusiasm for the theater led to his joining Gribble, Milliken, and Cleon Throckmorton in 1928 in presenting, in a theater in Hoboken, N.J., old favorites of the type of *After Dark* and *The Black Crook*. This project was given up in 1930.

In his reading, he feels that he collaborates with the author, and he regards such authors as Chaucer and Shakespeare as the greatest influences on his work. Distrustful of doctrinaire thought, he relies instead on his sense of humor and his imagination, and lives in the present or future rather than the past. He considers the subconscious to be of the greatest value in art, and holds that what an author says can mean more than he intended it should.

For further comment, see Critical Survey, pp. 160–61.

BIBLIOGRAPHY

Essays and Sketches

Shandygaff, a number of most agreeable inquirendoes upon life and letters, interspersed with short stories and skitts, the whole most diverting to the reader, accompanied also by some notes for teachers whereby the booke may be made usefull in class-room or for private improvement by Christopher Morley, reputed also to be the authour of "Parnassus on wheels" and "Songs for a little house," 1918; Christopher Morley on The amenities of book collecting. Issued for free distribution to lovers of books, 1919 (pamphlet); Mince pie, adventures on the sunny side of Grub street . . . illustrated by Walter Jack Duncan, 1919; Pipefuls . . . illustrated by Walter Jack Duncan, 1920; Plum pudding of divers ingredients discreetly blended & seasoned by Christopher Morley and merrily embellished by Walter Jack Duncan, 1921; The child and the book, 1922 (caption-title; leaflet); An apology for Boccaccio, 1923; Conrad and the reporters, 1923; Inward ho! 1923; The powder of sympathy . . . illustrated by Walter Jack Duncan, 1923; Outward bound, 1924; Religio journalistici, 1924; Forty-four essays . . . with an introduction by Rollo LaVerne Lyman, 1925 (English ed., Safety pins and other essays, 1925 [intro. by H. M. Tomlinson]); A golden string, 1925 (caption-title; leaflet); Paumanok, 1926; The Romany stain . . . illustrated with pen drawings by Walter Jack Duncan, 1926 (enl. limited ed., 1926); Two prefaces by Walt Whitman, the original preface to Leaves of grass, 1855, and A backward glance o'er travel'd roads, 1888, with an introductory note by Christopher Morley, 1926; The case of Bouck White, 1927 (pamphlet); The Century, reprinted by permission from an article appearing in the Saturday review of literature, April 2, 1927, 1927 (pamphlet); My one contribution to seventeenth century scholarship, 1927 (pamphlet); Essays, 1928; a letter to leonora, 1928 (pamphlet); Off the deep end, 1928; A ride in the cab of the Twentieth century limited, 1928 (pamphlet); An essay on Transylvania . . . decorations by Geri Pine, 1929; The palette knife . . . illustrated by René Gockinga . . ., 1929; Apologia pro sua preoccupatione, 1930; Sun cured, a peccadillo ⟨from the vanished Shoestring revue, by request⟩, 1930 (pamphlet); Don't open until Christmas with decorations by Howard Willard, 1931; On visiting bookshops, 1931; Internal revenue, 1933; Barns . . . woodcut by Asa Cheffitz, the first edition, 1934; "Effendi," Frank Nelson Doubleday, 1862–1934, 1934; BR's secret passion, 1935 (pamphlet); Old Loopy, a love letter for Chicago . . . photographs by Guy Ederheimer, jr., 1935; "Rare" books, an essay, 1935 (pamphlet); Streamlines, 1936; Preface to "Bartlett," 1937; Sir Kenelm reads in bed, 1937 (pamphlet); History of an autumn, 1938; No Crabb, no Christmas, 1938 (pamphlet); Letters of askance, 1939.

Poems

The eighth sin by C. D. Morley, 1912 (pamphlet); Songs for a little house, 1917; The rocking horse, 1919; The Christmas tobacco sent with all honest greetings by the author, 1920, 1920 (cover-title; pamphlet); Hide and seek, 1920; Chimneysmoke . . . illustrated by Thomas Fogarty, 1921; Translations from the Chinese, 1922; Parson's pleasure, 1923; Epigrams in a cellar, 1927 (cover-title; leaflet); Translations from the Chinese . . . illustrated by Gluyas Williams, 1927; Toulemonde, 1928; Poems, 1929; Mandarin in Manhattan, further Translations from the Chinese, 1933; Footnotes for a centennial, 1936; Dedication for a bookseller's window, 1937 (caption-title; leaflet); Blanket to cover a set of sheets, or, Prolegomenon to a pack of sybilline leaves from Argus, 1938 (broadside).

Novels

Parnassus on wheels, 1917; The haunted bookshop, 1919; Kathleen . . . frontispiece by Wallace Morgan, 1920; Where the blue begins, 1922; Pandora lifts the lid by Christopher Morley and Don Marquis, 1924; Thunder on the left, 1925; Pleased to meet you, 1927; Rudolph and Amina, or, The black crook, 1930; Human being, a story, 1932; Swiss family Manhattan, 1932 (presentation ed., 1931); The Trojan horse, 1937; Kitty Foyle, 1939.

Short Stories

Tales from a rolltop desk . . . frontispiece by Walter Jack Duncan, 1921; The arrow, 1927 (English ed., enl., The arrow and two other stories, 1927); The tree that didn't get trimmed, 1927; The worst Christmas story . . . privately uttered at Random house for thirteen gentlemen of the trade, 1928.

Plays

Rehearsal, a comedy in one act, 1922; Thursday evening, 1922; One act plays, 1924 (Thursday evening; Rehearsal; Bedroom suite; On the shelf; Walt; East of Eden); Where the blue begins, a divine comedy by Christopher Morley assisted by E. S. Colling. N.B., This is one of 100 advance copies, printed for production purposes and for private circulation only, 1925; Good theatre, a fancy in one scene, 1926 (also pub. as Good theatre, 1926); Really, my dear . . . a play in one act . . . and with drawings by Johan Bull, 1928; "In modern dress," a one-act play, 1929; The blue and the gray, or, War is hell, revised and edified by Christopher Morley from an old script by Judson Kilpatrick and J. Owen Moore, 1930.

Reminiscences

John Mistletoe, 1931.

Description and Travel

Travels in Philadelphia . . . with drawings by Frank H. Taylor, 1920 (intro. by A. Edward Newton); Blythe mountain, Vermont, 1931; Notes on Bermuda, 1931; Hasta la vista, or, A postcard from Peru, 1935.

Humor

In the sweet dry and dry by Christopher Morley and Bart Haley illustrated by Gluyas Williams, 1919; The story of ginger cubes . . . reprinted from the Bowling green of the New York evening post, 1922 (cover-title; pamphlet).

Children's Books

I know a secret . . . illustrated by Jeanette Warmuth, 1927; The goldfish under the ice . . . being number fourteen of the Woburn books, 1929 [1930].

Lectures

Ex libris carissimis, 1932; Shakespeare and Hawaii, 1933.

Miscellany

The story of a Belgian dog, 1915 (pamphlet); Gentles, attend! March 30, 1920, 11 P.M. This being a passport and handy companion unto the gracious City of Philadelphia, issued unto Sidney Williams, gent., 1920 (broadside); A Christmas card to Woodrow Wilson from the New York evening post, December 3, 1921, 1921 (folder); In re Logan Pearsall Smith, 1921 (folder); The youth of Parnassus, 1921? (pamphlet); A booksellers' author, 1922 (card); Have you read "Casuals of the sea"? 1923 (folder); Ballade of the day's run, 1924 (card); A bookseller's breviary being a few runes and rituals on bibliophagy & cetera, written by Christopher Morley and put together for the health and piety of ambitious booksellers and sundry other paramours of print, 1924 (pamphlet); The Equitable trust company of Atlantic City, 1924? (folder); "In small proportions we just beauties see," 1924 (leaflet); The Concord edition of the works of Joseph Conrad, 1925 (leaflet); Full and by, being a collection of verses by persons of quality in praise of drinking, here illustrated by Edw. A. Wilson and edited by Cameron Rogers, with prefaces by Don Marquis and Christopher Morley, 1925; Hostages to fortune . . . a collection of poems, essays, and short stories written for the Haverfordian by Christopher Morley during his college days, 1925; On minding our manners in speech, a review, 1926? (leaflet); In an auction room, 1927 (card); The writings of A. Edward Newton, a bibliography by George H. Sargent with cogitations by Christopher Morley, 1927; The House of Dooner, the last of the friendly inns by Christopher Morley & T. A. Daly, 1928; The Old Rialto theatre, Hoboken, "New York's last sea-coast of Bohemia." Management of Christopher Morley, Cleon Throckmorton, Conrad Milliken, Harry Wagstaff Gribble, 1928 (pamphlet); Advance comment by Christopher Morley in "The Saturday review of literature" for April 20, 1929. "All quiet on the western front," 1929; Mr. Hutaf sees Hoboken in aquiline perspective, 1929 (leaflet); Passport, Hoboken free state, 1929 (booklet); A prologue for the Old Rialto theatre, Hoboken, written by Christopher Morley in the manner of the famous "Drury Lane prologue," with no end of apologies to Dr. Johnson, and spoken by Mr. Morley at the first performance of "After dark, or, Neither maid, wife, nor widow," at the Old Rialto, December 10, 1928, 1929 (broadside); Seacoast of Bohemia . . . Published for the Old Rialto theatre, 118 Hudson street, Hoboken, New Jersey, 1929; Born in a beer garden, or, She troupes to conquer, sundry ejaculations by Christopher Morley, Cleon Throckmorton, and Ogden Nash, and certain of the Hoboken ads with a commentary on them by Earnest Elmo Calkins. Embellishments by Edward A. Wilson, George Illian, Cleon Throckmorton, August William Hutaf, and Jay, 1930; The Foundry, 1930 (leaflet); On the nose, 1930; Christopher Morley reviews one day's news in . . . the New York times, 1931 (pamphlet); "When we speak of a tenth=," 1931 (pamphlet); Christopher Morley, Rosenbach fellow in bibliography. Ex libris carissimis, 1932 (cover-title; leaflet; prospectus); Bureau of literary control, 1933 (single sheet, unsigned); Christopher Morley again reviews one day's news in . . . the New York times, 1933 (cover-title; pamphlet); Christopher Morley's scrapbook, 1933 (pamphlet); Riesenberg's "The log of the sea," 1933 (broadside); America's town meeting of the air, December 26, 1935, number 9. Literature and life [by] Christopher Morley, Fannie Hurst, Audrey Wurdemann, T. S. Stribling, Francis Talbot, S.J., 1935 (cover-title; pamphlet; ed. by Lyman Bryson); A Christmas salute, 1935 (pamphlet); Morrell household calendar for 1936, 1935 (a calendar; stories selected by Christopher Morley); Christopher Morley's briefcase, 1936 (cover-title; pamphlet); "It's a kind of a memorabilia," a letter about The Trojan horse, written to F. P. Frazier (of J. B. Lippincott company) . . . Printed by permission, 1937 (pamphlet).

Selected Works

Fifth avenue bus, an excursion among the books of Christopher Morley with a note by the conductor, 1933 (also pub. as Omnibus, an excursion among the books of Christopher Morley, 1936); Morley's magnum: Swiss family Manhattan, Rehearsal, Mandarin in Manhattan, The Romany stain, Chimneysmoke, Hasta la vista, 1938; Four favorite books . . . four volumes in one, Parnassus on wheels, The haunted bookshop, Where the blue begins, Thunder on the left, 1939.

Collected Works

The Haverford edition of Christopher Morley, 1927 (half-title; 12 vols.).

Edited and Compiled Works

Record of the Class of nineteen-ten of Haverford college, Haverford, Pa., September 26, 1906 - - June 10, 1910, 1910; American Rhodes scholars, Oxford, 1910 - - 1913, 1913 (ed. by Christopher Morley, assisted by Elmer Davis and John Crowe Ransom); The Bookseller's blue book, February–August, 1914, intended to be of use to those who sell books. This copy belongs to - - -. In case of accident please notify - - -. With the compliments of Doubleday, Page & co., 1914; The Bookseller's blue book, October–February, 1914–15, intended to be of use to those who sell books. This copy belongs to - - -. In case of accident please notify - - -. With the compliments of Doubleday, Page & co., 1914 (ed. by Christopher Morley?); The Kaiser, a book about the most interesting man in Europe edited by Asa Don Dickinson, 1914 (with Christopher Morley); Making books and magazines.

A commentary on the motion picture film taken at the Country life press. Doubleday, Page & company will be glad to loan this film to churches, libraries, schools, clubs, colleges, or any other organizations for educational display. Address: Doubleday, Page & company, editorial department, Garden City, N.Y., 1916 (pamphlet); Modern essays selected, 1921 (abridged ed., Modern essays for schools selected, 1922); The Bowling green, an anthology of verse selected, 1924; Modern essays (second series) selected, 1924; A book of days, being a briefcase packed for his own pleasure by Christopher Morley & made into a calendar for sundry paramours of print. [For] 1931, 1930 (2d. ed., 1931); Ex libris, a small anthology, printed and bound (and sold) at the first national book fair sponsored by the New York times and the National association of book publishers. Compiled at their request by Christopher Morley. New York city: November 1936, 1936; Familiar quotations, a collection of passages, phrases, and proverbs traced to their sources in ancient and modern literature by John Bartlett. Eleventh edition, revised and enlarged. Christopher Morley, editor, Louella D. Everett, associate editor, 1937; The rag-picker of Paris, or, The modest modiste by Edward Stirling, esq., first produced at the Royal Surrey theatre, London, June 23, 1847, now revised and re-edified, 1937.

Translations

Two fables, 1925; Max and Moritz, or, The adventures of two naughty boys by Wilhelm Busch translated with a foreword . . . illustrated by Jay, 1932.

STUDIES AND ARTICLES

Adcock
Ashley
Baldwin (M)
Black, Jean F. Thunder on the left, a play in three acts . . . from the novel of the same name by Christopher Morley. c1934
† Bookshop of Harry Stone, *New York*. Christopher Morley, his books in first edition, with an introduction by Burton Emmett. 1930
Bowdoin
Cain, Mildred P. Mildred Palmer Cain's copy of Christopher Morley's "Parnassus on wheels." 1925
Canby
Cohen (M)
Cook
Daye, Stephen, press, *Brattleboro, Vt.* The Stephen Daye press announces immediate publication of "Blythe Mountain, Vt." by Christopher Morley, with a frontispiece etching by Andrew R. Butler. [1931] (broadside)
† Doubleday, Page & company. Christopher Morley, his history done by divers hands, together with a list of works by this author, thus modestly offered to your attention. 1922 (pamphlet; enl. ed., 1925)
† Duschnes, Philip C., *firm, bookseller, New York*. Catalogue 23. "The eighth sin on Parnassus, or, Where the blues begin." First editions, rare trivia, & pamphlets of Christopher Morley. [1936] (cover-title; pamphlet)
† Ford (E)
Hatcher
† Hughes, Babette. Christopher

Morley, multi ex uno. 1927 (pamphlet)

Hutaf, August W. Bird's-eye view of Hoboken, New Jersey, U.S.A., New York's last seacoast of Bohemia with location of its many theatres, past and present, together with routes for easy access. Executed for Messrs Morley and Throckmorton whose revivals of 'After dark' and 'The black crook' established records. 1929 (map)

† Johnson (1929)

† Johnson (1932)

† Johnson (1936)

Karsner

Kunitz (L)

† Lee, Alfred P. A bibliography of Christopher Morley. 1935

† Manly

Marble

Markey

Masson

Morley, Christopher D. Catalogue of first editions of esteemed authors. Pre-publications of their works in proof and page proof form. Original manuscripts, association books. Inclusive manuscripts of Christopher Morley ⟨some never printed⟩. William McFee. Rare pamphlets mostly inscribed: by Cabell, Chesterton, Conrad, Coolidge, Fitzgerald, O'Henry, Hergesheimer, Huxley, Hudson, Joyce Kilmer, Lawrence, Newton, Tomlinson, Wilder, and others. The property of Christopher Morley, esq., of Roslyn, L.I., sold by his order. Inclusive, additions from the library of a friend (arranged in a separate alphabet) consisting of choice modern press books, first editions, inclusive, the rare William Andrew Clark catalogue series, original drawings by Beardsley, original manuscript of a playlet by G. Bernard Shaw. [1930] (pamphlet)

Overton

Overton (A)

Rascoe (B)

Schreiber

† [Schwartz, Harry W.] Checklists of twentieth century authors. Second series. James Joyce, Aldous Huxley, Martin Armstrong, Richard Aldington, Christopher Morley. 1933 (cover-title; pamphlet)

Schyberg

Thunder on the left, comments and controversies by various critics. [n.d.] (pamphlet)

† Van Doren (M)

Walpole, Sir Hugh S. Thunder on the left, an appreciation of Christopher Morley's new novel. [1926?] (pamphlet)

Ward

Widdemer

† Johnson, Merle D. and Hopkins, Frederick M., *eds.* "American first editions, a series of bibliographic check-lists . . . number 35, Christopher Morley, 1890– compiled by Aaron Mendoza." *PW.*, June 2, 1923, pp. 1705–06; McCord, David. "Christopher Morley." *EJ.*, Jan. 1930, pp. 1–9; Morley, Christopher. "The eighth sin." *Col.*, Part 3, Art. 2, pp. 1–8 (1930); O'Sullivan, Vincent. "America and the English literary tradition." *Liv.Age*, Oct. 18, 1919, pp. 170–76; Van Doren, Carl. "Day in and day out." *Cent.*, Dec. 1923, pp. 308–15. For references to reviews, see *BRD.*, 1917–33, 1935–39.

Lewis Mumford, 1895–

Born in Flushing, Long Island, October 19, 1895, into a home of middle-class comfort. He was educated in the New York schools, and spent his boyhood on the upper West Side. He learned much by taking walks in the city with his grandfather. He made experiments with wireless, and, when in his early teens, wrote articles on radio telegraphy for electrical magazines. Because of these interests he went to the Stuyvesant (technical) High School, where he came under the influence of foreign students, Socialist thought, and occasional hints of such new ideas in science as relativity and the electronic theory of matter.

Dislike of mathematics and a youthful love affair caused him to decide to be a writer, and he chose newspaper work as his means of entering the profession of novelist. At eighteen he published an article and a story in *Forum*. He continued his education at the College of the City of New York and other New York institutions. In night courses in City College, then a small school, he studied under Earle Palmer, J. S. Schapiro, and J. P. Turner. He plunged at once into senior and advanced courses in politics, philosophy, and English, and found his fellow students interesting and mature. His interests shifted from philosophy to sociology, and later he became absorbed in architecture, the subject of much of his later writing. His mechanical bent continued to stand him in good stead, and in the war he served as radio operator in the American navy.

During the same period, however, he was experimenting with the novel, and writing one-act plays, some of which, although they were never produced, attracted the attention of theatrical companies. In 1919 he began contributing reviews to the fortnightly *Dial*, of which he became associate editor, and in the next year he was acting editor of a British publication, the *Sociological Review*. He has written for the *New Republic*, the *Freeman*, the *American Mercury*, *Harper's*, and architectural journals, collaborated on the *American Caravan*, and given lectures on cultural subjects, especially literature and architecture, at the New School for Social Research, the School of International Studies at Geneva, and Dartmouth College. In 1939 he wrote the narrative for *The City*, a documentary film shown at the City Planning Exhibit of the New York World's Fair.

He believes that in the modern world individual opportunities and freedoms depend upon security and guarantees of continuity of life and minimum economic decency, and that communism is a response to this demand. The emphasis upon property values in Western countries (except Russia), excessive specialization, and our neglect of the cultural aspects of human life, as well as the cleavage between the lives and opportunities of the leisure class and those of the working class, he regards as stunting our existences and preventing us from reaching the fullness and completeness of experience represented by such works as *Moby Dick*, *War and Peace*, and *The Magic Mountain*. ". . . We should subject ourselves," he wrote in *Forum* in 1930, "to every activity that is necessary for a full experience and a complete understanding of life—knowing at first hand both manual toil and esthetic ecstasy, periods of hard routine and periods of adventure, intellectual concentration and the animal relaxation, strict discipline and random activity." Mumford is an admirer of Sir Patrick Geddes because he feels that Geddes showed the possibility of uniting broad and diverse special interests in a well-knit, integrated life.

For further comment, see Critical Survey, p. 63.

BIBLIOGRAPHY

Essays and Studies

The story of Utopias . . . with an introduction by Hendrik Willem Van Loon, 1922; Sticks and stones, a study of American architecture and civilization, 1924; Architecture, 1926; The golden day, a study in American experience and culture, 1926; American taste, 1929; The brown decades, a study of the arts in America, 1865–1895, 1931; Modern architects by Alfred H. Barr, jr., Henry-Russell Hitchcock, jr., Philip Johnson, and Lewis Mumford, 1932; * Technics and civilization, 1934; The culture of cities, 1938; Men must act, 1939.

Biography

Herman Melville, 1929.

Dialogues

Aesthetics, a dialogue . . . Troutbeck leaflets number three, 1925.

Editor

The American caravan, a yearbook of American literature edited by Van Wyck Brooks, Alfred Kreymborg, Lewis Mumford, Paul Rosenfeld, 1927; The second American caravan, a yearbook of American literature edited by Alfred Kreymborg, Lewis Mumford, Paul Rosenfeld, 1928; The new American caravan, a yearbook of American literature edited by Alfred Kreymborg, Lewis Mumford, Paul Rosenfeld, 1929; American caravan, IV, edited by Alfred Kreymborg, Lewis Mumford, Paul Rosenfeld, 1931; America & Alfred Stieglitz, a collective portrait edited by Waldo Frank, Lewis Mumford, Dorothy Norman, Paul Rosenfeld, & Harold Rugg, with 120 illustrations, 1934; The new caravan edited by Alfred Kreymborg, Lewis Mumford, Paul Rosenfeld, 1936.

STUDIES AND ARTICLES

Foerster (T)
Frank
Gard
Kunitz (L)
Levinson
National
Schreiber

Ayres, Clarence E. "Talking of cities." *So.R.*, Autumn 1938, pp. 227–34; Buchanan, Scott. "Mumford tilts at windmills." *VQR.*, July 1934, pp. 447–51; Case, Clarence M. "Technics and civilization." *SSR.*, Jan. 1935, pp. 210–17; Foerster, Norman. "The literary prophets." *AB.*, Sept. 1930, pp. 39–44; Forsythe, Robert S. "Mr. Lewis Mumford and Melville's Pierre." *AL.*, Nov. 1930, pp. 286–89; Glicksberg, Charles I. "Lewis Mumford and the organic synthesis." *SR.*, Jan.–Mar. 1937, pp. 55–73; Jones, Howard M. "Metropolis and utopia." *N.Amer.Rev.*, Autumn 1938, pp. 170–78; Rourke, Constance. "In time of hesitation." *Nation*, Feb. 18, 1939, pp. 206–07. For references to reviews, see *BRD.*, 1922, 1924, 1926–27, 1929, 1931, 1934, 1938–39.

Ogden Nash, 1902–

Born August 16, 1902, in Rye, New York. He attended St. George's School, Newport, Rhode Island (1917–20), and Harvard (1920–21). For several years his light verse has been appearing in the *New Yorker*, the *Saturday Evening Post*, and other magazines. In it nonsense, wit, and satire appear in varying degrees, and most of it is notable for eccentricities of meter, including line-lengths ranging from two syllables to sixty-two, and for studied and startling inaccuracies of rhyme. Nash, who married Frances Rider Leonard in 1931, is the father of two children and lives in Baltimore.

BIBLIOGRAPHY

Humorous and Satirical Verse

Free wheeling, illustrated by Soglow, 1931; Hard lines, illustrated by Soglow, 1931; Happy days, illustrated by Soglow, 1933; Four prominent so and so's. Lyrics, Ogden Nash. Music, Robert Armbruster. Illustrations, Otto Soglow, 1934 (pamphlet; also pub. as broadside with title Four prominent bastards are we, 1934); The primrose path, illustrated by Soglow, 1935; The bad parents' garden of verse . . . illustrated by Reginald Birch, 1936; Bon voyage, 1936 (cover-title; folder); * I'm a stranger here myself, 1938.

Children's Book

The cricket of Carador by Joseph Alger & Ogden Nash, illustrations by Christopher Rule, 1925.

Sketches

Born in a beer garden, or, She troupes to conquer: sundry ejaculations by Christopher Morley, Cleon Throckmorton and Ogden Nash, and certain of the Hoboken ads, with a commentary on them by Earnest Elmo Calkins. Embellishments by Edward A. Wilson, George Illian, Cleon Throckmorton, August William Hutaf and Jay, 1930.

Editor

P. G. Wodehouse. Nothing but Wodehouse edited by Ogden Nash, 1932.

ARTICLES

Bacon, Leonard. "Humors and careers." *SRL.*, Apr. 29, 1939, pp. 3–4, 22; McCord, David. "Lightest of the arts." *YR.*, Winter 1939, pp. 392–94; Untermeyer, Louis. "Inventory of Nash, 1938." *SRL.*, June 4, 1938, pp. 6–7. For references to reviews, see *BRD.*, 1931, 1933, 1935–36, 1938.

George Jean Nathan, 1882–

Born February 14, 1882, in Fort Wayne, Indiana. He was educated at Cornell, where he took the bachelor's degree in 1904, and at the University of Bologna, where he spent the year 1904–05.

In 1905 he joined the editorial staff of the New York *Herald*, and since that time he has done editorial work and written dramatic observations and criticism for a number of periodicals, including the *Bohemian Magazine*, *Outing*, *Harper's Weekly*, *Judge*, the *New Freeman*, *Arts and Decoration*, and *Vanity*

Fair, and written for newspapers, American and British, syndicates, and the *Encyclopaedia Britannica*. With Mencken he edited the *Smart Set*, of which he had been dramatic critic since 1908, from 1914 until 1923; and together they founded the *American Mercury* in 1924. Leaving the editorship in 1925, Nathan continued to write for this magazine until 1930. In 1932, with Theodore Dreiser, Eugene O'Neill, James Branch Cabell, and Ernest Boyd, he founded and edited the *American Spectator*. For a time he contributed a dramatic column to *Scribner's*. He has been influential in bringing before the American public Eugene O'Neill, Lord Dunsany, F. Scott Fitzgerald, James Joyce, and Aldous Huxley.

In his personal philosophy Nathan is frankly and unblushingly hedonistic, and confesses readily that his real interest is in matters directly concerning his personal comfort and ease. His program for a life of pleasure is devotion to literature, drama, music, and the arts, with good friends and the comforts of good living. He is opposed on principle to reforms, on the grounds that the world should satisfy anyone but those prevented by their own limitations from enjoying it. Because he prefers candor to hypocrisy he admires J. Pierpont Morgan but despises Rockefeller, and regards Woodrow Wilson as less admirable than Clemenceau. "An infinite belief in the possibilities of oneself," he wrote in *Forum* in 1930, "with a coincidental critical assessment and derogation of one's achievements; self-respect combined with a measure of self-surgery; aristocracy of mind combined with democracy of heart; forthrightness with modesty or at least with good manners; dignity with a quiet laugh; honor and honesty and decency—these are the greatest qualities that man can hope to attain. And as one man, my hope is to attain them."

In literature he considers the contemporary American cynicism toward romantic love as a mere hard-boiled cover concealing the normal American's abundant sentimentality, and believes that romantic love is "the privilege of emperors, kings, soldiers, and artists" and "the butt of democrats, traveling salesmen, magazine poets, and the writers of American novels." He feels that only the superficial artist is capable of fixing on an actual goal and achieving it again and again. "I believe that Richard Strauss is the only substantial living musician; that Sinclair Lewis is the most significant American novelist, though Willa Cather is the best writer; that there is not a living painter worth serious critical consideration; that Stephen Phillips is a much greater poet than many think; that the only young, serious dramatist in Europe worth talking about is Franz Werfel; . . . that Lindbergh, Coste, Byrd, and all that crew are absurd futilitarians; . . . that the only completely original playwright since Ibsen is Pirandello. . . ."

For further comment, see Critical Survey, pp. 181, 188–89.

BIBLIOGRAPHY

Essays and Criticism

Another book on the theatre, 1915; Mr. George Jean Nathan presents, 1917; The popular theatre, 1918; Comedians all, 1919; The theatre, the drama, the girls, 1921; The critic and the drama, 1922; The world in falseface, 1923; Materia critica, 1924; The house of Satan, 1926; Land of the pilgrims' pride, 1927; Art of the night, 1928; Testament of a critic, 1931; The intimate notebooks of

George Jean Nathan, 1932; * Since Ibsen, a statistical historical outline of the popular theatre since 1900, 1933; Passing judgments, 1935; The theatre of the moment, a journalistic commentary, 1936; The morning after the first night, 1938.

Play

Heliogabalus, a buffoonery in three acts by H. L. Mencken and George Jean Nathan, 1920.

Novel

Monks are monks, a diagnostic scherzo, 1929.

Adaptations

The Avon flows, 1937.

Description and Travel

Europe after 8:15 by H. L. Mencken, George Jean Nathan, Willard Huntington Wright, with decorations by Thomas H. Benton, 1914.

Biography

Pistols for two by Owen Hatteras [*pseud.* of H. L. Mencken and George Jean Nathan], 1917 (pamphlet).

Miscellany

Bottoms up, an application of the slapstick to satire, 1917; A book without a title, 1918; The American credo, a contribution toward the interpretation of the national mind by George Jean Nathan and H. L. Mencken, 1920 (rev. and enl. ed., 1921); The American credo, 1921 (caption-title; leaflet; an appendix to The American credo); The Smart set, George Jean Nathan, H. L. Mencken, editors. Suggestions to our visitors, 1923 (cover-title; leaflet); The autobiography of an attitude, 1925; The new American credo, a contribution toward the interpretation of the national mind by George Jean Nathan. Completely revised and enlarged edition, 1927.

Editor

The theatre of today edited by George Jean Nathan. Chicago by Maurine Watkins, 1927; The theatre of today edited by George Jean Nathan. Twelve thousand, a play in three acts by Bruno Frank, translated from the German by William A. Drake, 1928; The theatre of today edited by George Jean Nathan. Lysistrata, a comedy in four acts by Maurice Donnay, translated from the French by William A. Drake, with a foreword by George Jean Nathan, 1929; The theatre of today edited by George Jean Nathan. Of thee I sing, a musical play by George S. Kaufman and Morrie Ryskind, lyrics by Ira Gershwin, with a foreword by George Jean Nathan, 1932; The American spectator year book edited by George Jean Nathan, Sherwood Anderson, Ernest Boyd, James Branch Cabell, Theodore Dreiser, Eugene O'Neill, 1934.

STUDIES AND ARTICLES

Benchley
Boyd
Broun, Heywood C. Pieces of hate and other enthusiasms. 1922
Brown
Brown (U)
† Ford (E)
Forsythe
Goldberg, Isaac. George Jean Nathan, a critical study. [c1925] (pamphlet)
Goldberg, Isaac. The theatre of George Jean Nathan, chapters and documents toward a history of the new American drama. 1926
Hatteras, Owen A. [*pseud.*] Pistols for two. 1917 (pamphlet)
† Johnson (1929)
† Johnson (1932)
† Johnson (1936)
Knopf (B)
Kozlenko, Vladimar. The quintessence of Nathanism. 1930
Kunitz (L)
MacCollough
† Manly
Markey
Mencken
National
Roberts
Shaw
Smart

Anonymous. "George Jean Nathan." *AB.*, Aug. 1924, pp. 695–700; Anonymous. "A slapstick satirist of the broadway drama." *Cur.Op.*, Aug. 1917, p. 95; Boyd, Ernest. "George Jean Nathan." *TAM.*, Jan. 1927, pp. 59–64; Boyd. "Readers and writers." *Ind.*, Oct. 24, 1925, p. 477; Hazlitt, Henry. "George Jean Nathan." *Nation*, Feb. 18, 1931, pp. 186–87; † Johnson, Merle D. and Hopkins, Frederick M., *eds.* "American first editions, a series of bibliographic check-lists . . . number 41, George Jean Nathan, 1882–." *PW.*, July 28, 1923, p. 380; Saroyan, William. "The American clowns of criticism." *Overland M.*, Mar. 1929, pp. 77–78, 92–93; Shaw, Charles G. "Through the magnifying glass." *N.Yer.*, Oct. 15, 1927, pp. 30–31. For references to reviews, see *BRD.*, 1915, 1917–29, 1931–33, 1935–38.

Robert (Gruntal) Nathan, 1894–

Born in New York, January 2, 1894. He is a descendant of Rabbi Gershom Seixas, who came to America in 1710 and helped found Columbia College; and his aunt, Annie Nathan Meyer, was founder of Barnard College. He was educated in private schools in this country and abroad, and attended the Ethical Culture and Dutch Collegiate schools in New York, the Château de Lancy in Geneva, and Phillips Exeter Academy; and he went on to Harvard. In college, where he took part in athletics and wrote for the *Monthly*, he began his writing career; and without taking a degree he dropped out to go to New York to take a job in an advertising agency. He gave it up when it interfered with the writing of verse and short stories. For a time he lived in California, but he returned to New York and for a year (1924–25) lectured at the New York University School of Journalism. In 1930, the year of his second marriage, he went to Paris and spent the winter. He now lives in New York.

As a writer Nathan is a slow, careful worker, and revises diligently. He enjoys particularly writing about children and animals. A man of versatile gifts, he is not only an author but a musician and an illustrator, as well as a fencer, a fine tennis-player, and an expert swimmer. He is a singer, a pianist, and a cellist, and has composed a sonata for violin and piano and many songs. At Exeter he established a music club, and he belongs to several artists' clubs and organizations in New York City. He is a charter member of P.E.N. and The Poets. In 1936 he was elected to membership in the Department of Literature of the National Institute of Arts and Letters.

BIBLIOGRAPHY

Novels

Peter Kindred, 1919; Autumn, 1921; The puppet master, 1923; Jonah, 1925 (English ed., Son of Amittai, 1925); The fiddler in Barly, 1926; The woodcutter's house, 1927; The bishop's wife, 1928; There is another heaven, 1929; The orchid, 1931; One more spring, 1933; Road of ages, 1935; The enchanted voyage, 1936; * The Barly fields, a collection of five novels . . . with an introduction by Stephen Vincent Benét, 1938 (The fiddler in Barly; The woodcutter's house; The bishop's wife; The orchid; There is another heaven); Journey of Tapiola . . . with decorations by Georg Salter, 1938; Winter in April, 1938.

Poems

Youth grows old, 1922; A cedar box . . . with a foreword by Louis Untermeyer, 1929; Selected poems of Robert Nathan, 1935.

Illustrator

Tina Mina by Dorothy Mayer with illustrations by Robert Nathan, 1930.

STUDIES AND ARTICLES

Baldwin (M)
Blankenship
Bromfield, Louis. The work of Robert Nathan . . . containing also a bibliography. [1927?] (pamphlet)
Hatcher
† Johnson (1932)
† Johnson (1936)
Kunitz (L)
Loggins
Marble
Mersand

Dorian, Edith M. "While a little dog dances, Robert Nathan, novelist of simplicity." *SR.*, Apr.–June 1933, pp. 129–40; Tapley, Roberts. "Robert Nathan, poet and ironist." *AB.*, Oct. 1932, pp. 607–14. For references to reviews, see *BRD.*, 1920–23, 1925–29, 1931, 1933, 1935–36, 1938.

John G(neisenau) Neihardt, 1881–

Born near Sharpsburg, Illinois, January 8, 1881. He passed his childhood in northwestern Kansas with his grandparents, in Kansas City, and in Wayne, Nebraska.

Although poverty prevented his having many books, he read eagerly the volumes of Tennyson and Browning that he managed to secure and wrote his own first poem when he was twelve. He worked his way through the scientific course in the Nebraska Normal College in Wayne, and received encouragement and private instruction that enabled him at fifteen to read Vergil at sight. By studying Greek by himself he became familiar with Homer and Aeschylus.

Graduating in 1897, he took various town and country jobs and then, becoming an assistant to the Indian agent at the Omaha Indian Reservation near Bancroft, Nebraska, he spent the years from 1901 to 1907 living with the Indians and becoming familiar with their customs, history, and thought.

In 1908, having won praise with his published lyrics and written successful Indian stories for magazines, he turned his back on a promising career and made up his mind to prepare an epic poem of frontier history; and, to familiarize himself with the scenes and incidents to be included, he descended the Missouri River in an open boat from Fort Benton, Montana. *The River and I* is an account of the trip. He examined records and absorbed legends and traditions relating to the early traders and trappers.

In 1912 he began work on his epic cycle; and *The Song of Hugh Glass*, the first part to be published, although the second in order in the final arrangement of the cycle, appeared in 1915. *The Song of Three Friends*, properly the first section, was the second to appear and won the five-hundred-dollar prize of the Poetry Society for the best volume of verse to be published by an American in 1919.

Other honors followed. In 1921 Neihardt was made poet laureate of the state of Nebraska, and in 1923 was appointed to a chair of poetry with an honorary professorship at the state university. In 1926 he accepted an appointment as literary editor of the St. Louis *Post-Dispatch*. In 1936, in recognition of the merits of *The Song of the Messiah*, he received the poetry award of the Foundation for Literature of the Friends of American Writers, and was given the Gold Scroll Medal of Honor of the National Poetry Center of New York. He holds honorary degrees from the University of Nebraska and Creighton University, and has received tokens of respect and affection from the Indians with whom he has lived; he has lectured at many educational institutions and traveled from coast to coast.

For further comment, see Critical Survey, p. 140.

BIBLIOGRAPHY

Poems

The divine enchantment, a mystical poem, 1900; A bundle of myrrh, 1103 [1903] (5 copies, privately printed); A bundle of myrrh, 1907; Man-song, 1909; The stranger at the gate, 1912; The song of Hugh Glass, 1915; The quest, 1916; The song of three friends, 1919; The song of the Indian wars . . . illustrated by Allen True, 1925; * Collected poems of John G. Neihardt, volume I, 1926; * Collected poems of John G. Neihardt, volume II, 1926; The song of the Messiah, 1935.

Play in Verse

Two mothers, 1921.

Novels

The dawn-builder, 1911; Life's lure, 1914.

Short Stories

The lonesome trail, 1907; Indian tales and others, 1926.

Literary Criticism

Laureate address of John G. Neihardt upon official notification of his choice as poet laureate of Nebraska, 1921; Poetic values, their reality and our need of them, 1925.

History

The splendid wayfaring, the story of the exploits and adventures of Jedediah Smith and his comrades, the Ashley-Henry men, discoverers and explorers of the great central route from the Missouri river to the Pacific ocean, 1822–1831, 1920.

Travel

The river and I . . . with 50 illustrations, 1910.

Miscellany

A man oughtn't to grumble if he don't get a pat hand, as long as the deal's fair, John G. Neihardt, n.d. (broadside); Black Elk speaks, being the life story of a holy man of the Ogalala Sioux as told to John G. Neihardt (Flaming Rainbow) illustrated by Standing Bear, 1932.

Editor

The poet's pack, John G. Neihardt, editor-in-chief, Lily A. Long, Clinton Scollard, Fanny Hodges Newman, associate editors, 1921.

STUDIES AND ARTICLES

Hazard
House, Julius T. John G. Neihardt, man and poet. 1920
† Johnson (1929)
† Johnson (1932)
† Johnson (1936)
Keiser
Kunitz (L)
Macmillan, *firm, publishers, New York.* America's epic poet. [n.d.] (pamphlet)
† Manly
National
Neihardt, John G. The song of Hugh Glass . . . with notes by Julius T. House. 1919
Neihardt, John G. The song of three friends & The song of Hugh Glass . . . with notes by Julius T. House. 1924

Adkins, Nelson F. "A study of John G. Neihardt's 'song of three friends.'" *AS.*, Apr. 1928, pp. 276–90; Beach, Joseph W. "Fourth dimensional." *P.*, Sept. 1926, pp. 350–52; Benét, William R. "Poets in collected editions." *YR.*, Jan. 1928, pp. 367–74; Monroe, Harriet. "A laurelled poem." *P.*, Nov. 1920, pp. 94–98; Monroe. "The Nebraska laureate." *P.*, July 1921, pp. 212–13; Monroe. "What of Mr. Neihardt?" *P.*, May 1927, pp. 99–104; Van Slyke, Berenice. "Neihardt's epic." *P.*, Mar. 1926, pp. 328–31. For references to reviews, see *BRD.*, 1907–09, 1911–12, 1914–16, 1919–21, 1925–27, 1935.

Clifford Odets, 1906–

Born July 18, 1906, in Philadelphia, where his father was a printer. His mother was Rumanian. In 1908 the family moved to New York, and he was reared in the Bronx and educated at the Morris High School, which he left after two years.

He soon began acting with small groups of players, gathered together a troupe that performed on a sustaining radio program in the period 1925–27, and recited poetry over the radio and in vaudeville. He worked also as announcer, gag writer, and producer of sound effects, and acted with a stock company and performed on tour in Pennsylvania. In the season 1928–29 he joined the Theatre Guild.

This connection led to his becoming, in 1930, a member of the Group Theatre. While he was acting in this company, he finished, in 1933, the play produced in 1935 as *Awake and Sing!* It proved to be very successful, and, with the two plays *Waiting for Lefty* and *Till the Day I Die*, it made the author one of the most notable figures of the season 1934–35. *Waiting for Lefty* won the Yale Drama Prize for 1935, and Odets was soon called to Hollywood to write motion-picture scripts.

An avowed revolutionary, he has been a leader in the "proletarian" drama, and values the motion pictures and the Federal Theatre for their ability to reach larger audiences than those of Broadway. "My only interest in the theatre," he says, "is to write plays for a collective like the Group theatre, a collective of writers, directors, actors and other theatre craftsmen who form and work out a collective technique to express a collective ideology. Vachtonov, the Russian director, said it well: 'A theatre is an ideologically cemented collective; otherwise it is a corpse.' The new Federal Theatre may work into such a sense of theatre if given good materials, enough budget money, and good plays. . . . Otherwise I don't care if a play of mine never appears on Broadway." He believes truth, attractively and entertainingly presented, to be the legitimate object of the dramatist in exposing the situation of the unfortunate; as he looks upon every work of art as an advocate for some mode of conduct, he regards works written with this particular end in view, however revolutionary in their faithfulness to fact, as essentially no more "propaganda" than any others. He is a diligent note-taker and keeps files of clippings, pictures, and observations of personal traits, for use in writing. He is also a lover of music, and Beethoven was the subject of one of his early dramatic attempts.

For further comment, see Critical Survey, pp. 69, 120, 125.

BIBLIOGRAPHY

Plays

Awake and sing . . . a play in three acts, 1935; Three plays . . . Awake and sing, Waiting for Lefty, Till the day I die, 1935; Waiting for Lefty and Till the day I die, two plays, 1935; Paradise lost, a play in three acts, 1936; * Golden boy, a play in three acts, 1937; Rocket to the moon, a romance in three acts, 1939; Six plays of Clifford Odets with a preface by the author, 1939 (Waiting for Lefty; Awake and sing!; Till the day I die; Paradise lost; Golden boy; Rocket to the moon; Three introductions by Harold Clurman).

Social Study

Rifle rule in Cuba by Carleton Beals and Clifford Odets, including the Report of the American commission to investigate labor and social conditions in Cuba, 1935 (pamphlet).

STUDIES AND ARTICLES

Block
Brown
Flexner
Lawson
Mantle (C)
Mersand
Nathan (TM)
National
Van Doren (A)

Isaacs, Edith J. R. "Clifford Odets, first chapters." *TAM.*, Apr. 1939, pp. 257–64; McCarten, John. "Revolution's number one boy." *N.Yer.*, Jan. 22, 1938, pp. 21–27; Vernon, Grenville. "Clifford Odets." *Com.*, Dec. 16, 1938, p. 215. For references to reviews, see *BRD.*, 1935–36, 1938–39.

John (**Henry**) **O'Hara,** 1905–

Born in Pottsville, Pennsylvania, January 31, 1905, the eldest of the seven children of a physician. After a random education in the Fordham Preparatory School, the Keystone State Normal School, and the Niagara Preparatory School, from which he graduated in 1924, he worked as engineer, boat steward, secretary in a briquetting plant, a callboy and freight clerk on the Pennsylvania Railroad, a soda clerk, gas-meter reader, amusement-park guard, laborer in a steel mill, motion-picture press agent, and secretary to Heywood Broun, and he wrote criticisms and reported and edited features for various newspapers and magazines, including the New York *Herald Tribune* and the *New Yorker*. For a short time he was editor-in-chief of the Pittsburgh *Bulletin-Index*. He has been a writer for Paramount Pictures, and he played a minor part in the picture *The General Died at Dawn*.

For further comment, see Critical Survey, p. 36.

BIBLIOGRAPHY

Novels

Appointment in Samarra, a novel, 1934; Butterfield 8, a novel, 1935; Hope of heaven, 1938.

Short Stories

The doctor's son and other stories, 1935; Files on parade, 1939.

STUDIES AND ARTICLES

Canby (S)

Fadiman, Clifton. "Disappointment in O'Hara." *N.Yer.*, Oct. 19, 1935, pp. 77–78; Gibbs, Wolcott. "Watch out for Mr. O'Hara." *SRL.*, Feb. 19, 1938, pp. 10–12. For references to reviews, see *BRD.*, 1934–35, 1938.

Eugene (**Gladstone**) **O'Neill,** 1888–

Born in New York City, October 16, 1888. His father, James O'Neill, the actor, toured for years as the star of *The Count of Monte Cristo;* and for his first seven years the little boy moved about with his family as his father traveled on road tours. Then he attended Catholic schools and Betts Academy at Stamford,

Connecticut. After a year at Princeton he dropped out of college (1907) and took jobs where he could find them.

He worked for a mail-order house in New York, then prospected for gold in Honduras. Back in the United States, he was assistant manager of his father's company in its tour playing *The White Sister*. He worked his way to Buenos Aires on a Norwegian bark and found jobs in the drafting department of the Westinghouse Electric Company, a Swift and Company packing plant, and an office of the Singer Sewing Machine Company. After working as mule-tender on a cattleboat trip to South Africa, he returned to New York as seaman on a tramp steamer, and became an able-bodied seaman in the transatlantic service of an American line.

After he had settled down as first an actor in his father's company and later a reporter for the New London, Connecticut, *Telegraph*, it was discovered that he had incipient tuberculosis; and in the winter of 1912–13 he entered a sanitarium.

This enforced illness proved to be a decisive period in his life, as it turned his interests to playwriting. After a complete recovery in 1913 he settled down to writing single-act plays, and he entered Professor Baker's "47 Workshop" course. After a year at Harvard he joined a radical group in Greenwich Village, and in the next summer he went to Provincetown, Massachusetts, where most of his early plays were given by the local group of actors. The Provincetown Players, organized in New York, were instrumental in giving O'Neill an opportunity for production. In 1923, with Robert Edmond Jones and Kenneth Macgowan, he reorganized the Provincetown group of actors and he directed the Provincetown Playhouse and the Greenwich Village Theatre.

He was forced to accept help from his father in publishing his first plays in 1914, but H. L. Mencken and George Jean Nathan encouraged him and published some of his work in the *Smart Set*. In 1920 *Beyond the Horizon*, his first full-length play to be given on Broadway, was so successful as to win the Pulitzer Prize. In the ensuing years, with increasing success, he drifted away from the Provincetown group and became a Broadway playwright. His work was given a powerful impetus by the production by the Theatre Guild in one year of both *Marco Millions* and *Strange Interlude*, and he made an agreement with the Guild giving it right of refusal to all his major plays to be written.

Besides two other Pulitzer Prizes, for *Anna Christie* (1922) and *Strange Interlude* (1928), O'Neill has been the second American dramatist to be given the Gold Medal (1922) of the National Institute of Arts and Letters and the second American to be awarded (1936) the Nobel Prize for literature, an honor indicative of the fact that he is virtually the first American dramatist to be read and studied in Europe. He is an associate member of the Irish Academy of Letters and belongs to the Authors' League of America, the Dramatists' Guild, and the American Academy of Arts and Letters.

His early familiarity with the theater has stood O'Neill in such good stead that he prefers to envision productions as he writes, and usually stays away from actual performances of his plays. His writing has been independent and has reflected his interest in moral problems, or, as he has termed it, the relation not of man to man but of man to God; *Strange Interlude* and *Ah, Wilderness!*, nevertheless, were successful films. He can work almost anywhere and has lived in France, Switzerland, Bermuda, and the Canary Islands, as well as various parts of the United States. In 1937 he sold his house at Sea Island Beach, Georgia, and bought land near San Francisco for a Spanish Mission house.

For further comment, see Critical Survey, pp. 19, 104–07, 117, 123.

BIBLIOGRAPHY

Plays

Thirst and other one act plays, 1914 ("Thirst"; "The web"; "Warnings"; "Fog"; "Recklessness"); Before breakfast, a play in one act, 1916; The Provincetown plays. First series: Bound east for Cardiff [by] Eugene G. O'Neill, The game [by] Louise Bryant, King Arthur's socks [by] Floyd Dell, 1916; The Provincetown plays. Third series: The two sons [by] Neith Boyce, Lima beans [by] Alfred Kreymborg, Before breakfast [by] Eugene O'Neill, 1916; The moon of the Caribbees and six other plays of the sea, 1919 (The moon of the Caribbees; Bound east for Cardiff; The long voyage home; In the zone; Ile; Where the cross is made; The rope); Beyond the horizon, a play in three acts, 1920; Gold, a play in four acts, 1920 [1921]; The Emperor Jones, Diff'rent, The straw, 1921; * The Emperor Jones . . . first performed by the Provincetown players, November, 1920, 1921; The hairy ape, Anna Christie, The first man, 1922; Anna Christie, a play in four acts, 1923; All God's chillun got wings and Welded, 1924; Alle kinder Gottes haben flügel, ein stück in zwei teilen von Eugene O'Neill uebertragen von Alfred Wolfenstein, 1925; * Desire under the elms, 1925; The great god Brown, a play in four acts, 1926; The great god Brown, The fountain, The moon of the Caribbees, and other plays, 1926 (The great god Brown; The fountain; The moon of the Caribbees; Bound east for Cardiff; The long voyage home; In the zone; Ile; Where the cross is made; The rope); Lazarus laughed (1925–26) a play for an imaginative theatre, 1927 (also pub. as Lazarus laughed, 1927); A play, Marco Millions, 1927 (also pub. as Marco Millions, a play, 1927); A play, Strange interlude, 1928 (also pub. as Strange interlude, 1928); Dynamo, 1929; The hairy ape . . . with nine illustrations by Alexander King, 1929; * Mourning becomes Electra, a trilogy, 1931 (Homecoming, a play in four acts, part one of the trilogy; The hunted, a play in five acts, part two of the trilogy; The haunted, a play in four acts, part three of the trilogy); Ah, wilderness! 1933; Days without end, 1934; Ile, 1939; In the zone, 1939; Where the cross is made, 1939.

Poems

A bibliography of the works of Eugene O'Neill by Ralph Sanborn and Barrett H. Clark, 1931 (part 3: Collected poems by O'Neill).

Miscellany

Extracts from "The Strange interlude," 1929 (caption-title; pamphlet).

Editor

The American spectator year book edited by George Jean Nathan, Sherwood Anderson, Ernest Boyd, James Branch Cabell, Theodore Dreiser, Eugene O'Neill, 1934.

Collected Plays

The complete works of Eugene O'Neill, volume one, 1924 [1925] ("Anna Christie," Beyond the horizon, "The first man," Diff'rent, Gold, The moon of the Caribbees, Bound east for Cardiff, The long voyage home, In the zone, Ile); The complete works of Eugene O'Neill, volume two, 1924 [1925] (The Emperor Jones, "The hairy ape," All God's chillun got wings, Desire under the elms, Welded, The straw, The rope, The dreamy kid, Where the cross is made, Before breakfast); Plays: "Anna Christie," All God's chillun got wings, Diff'rent, 1925 (vol. 1); Plays: Beyond the horizon, The straw, Before breakfast, 1925 (vol. 2); Plays: Desire under the elms, "The hairy ape," Welded, 1925 (vol. 3); Plays: The Emperor Jones, Gold, "The first man," The dreamy kid, 1925 (vol. 4); Nine plays . . . selected by the author, introduction by Joseph Wood Krutch, 1932 (The Emperor Jones; "The hairy ape"; All God's chillun got wings; Desire under the elms; "Marco Millions"; The great god Brown; Lazarus laughed; Strange interlude; Mourning becomes Electra: Homecoming, The hunted, The haunted); Representative plays of Eugene O'Neill: Marco Millions, The Emperor Jones, "Anna Christie," Where the cross is made, The moon of the Caribbees, 1932; The plays of Eugene O'Neill . . . Wilderness edition, 1934–1935 (12 vols.).

STUDIES AND ARTICLES

Agate

Agate (F)

Agate, James E. The contemporary theatre, 1923. 1924

Anderson, John. The American theatre by John Anderson and The motion picture in America by Rene Fülöp-Miller. 1938

Blankenship

Block

Boyd

Brie, Friedrich. Eugene O'Neill als nachfolger der griechen (Mourning becomes Electra). [1933] (caption-title; pamphlet)

Brown

Brown (U)

Bruns

Canby (S)

Chisholm, Cecil. Repertory, an outline of the modern theatre movement, production, plays, management. [1934]

Clark

Clark (B)

† Clark, Barrett H. Eugene O'Neill. 1926

† Clark, Barrett H. Eugene O'Neill, the man and his plays. 1929 (rev. eds., 1933, 1936)

Cohen (M)

Combs

Cook, George C. Greek coins, poems . . . with memorabilia by Floyd Dell, Edna Kenton, and Susan Glaspell. [c1925]

Cordell, Kathryn C. and Cordell, William H., *eds.* The Pulitzer prize plays, 1918–1934 . . . introduction by William Lyon Phelps. [c1935]

Cowley

Dickinson (P)

Dukes

Eaton (D)

Eaton, Walter P. The Theatre guild, the first ten years . . . with articles by the directors. 1929

Emmel, Felix. Das ekstatische theater. 1924

Essay annual, a yearly collection of significant essays, personal, critical, controversial, and humorous [edited by] Erich A. Walter. 1933, 1936

Flexner

Foerster

Fort

Geddes, Virgil. The melodramadness of Eugene O'Neill. 1934 (pamphlet)

Gillis

Goldberg

Goldberg (T)

[Goodrich, Frances and Hackett, Albert.] "Ah, wilderness!" dialogue cutting continuity . . . [screen play from the celebrated stage success by Eugene O'Neill]. 1935 (cover-title; mimeographed)

Green

Green (C)

Gruenberg, Louis. The Emperor Jones . . . opera in two acts, a prologue, an interlude and six scenes (after Eugene O'Neill's play) by Louis Gruenberg, op. 36, deutsche übertragung von R. St. Hoffmann, vocal score . . . c1932 (title page and text in English and German)

Gruenberg, Louis. The Emperor Jones, opera in two acts, a prologue, an interlude and six scenes (after Eugene O'Neill's play). Music by Louis Gruenberg. Op. 36. Libretto compiled by Kathleen de Jaffa. 1932 (pamphlet)

Halleck

Halline

Hamilton

Hamilton, Clayton M. Conversations on contemporary drama . . . a series of nine lectures, delivered in Earl hall, at Columbia university, from February 11 to April 7, 1924. 1924

Heath

† Herrmann

Heyward, DuBose. John Krimsky and Gifford Cochran present Paul Robeson in "The Emperor Jones," from the stage play by Eugene O'Neill, screen version by DuBose Heyward, directed by Dudley Murphy. [1933] (caption-title; hectographed)

Hicks

† Johnson (1929)

† Johnson (1932)

† Johnson (1936)

Karsner

Kaucher, Dorothy J. Modern dramatic structure. 1928

† Koischwitz, Otto. O'Neill. 1938

Kunitz (L)

Lawson

Levinson

Lewisohn (E)

Loggins

Luccock

Lundkvist

McCole

Maier, Norman R. and Reninger, Harry W. A psychological approach to literary criticism. [c1933]

Mais

† Manly

Mantle

Mantle (C)

Marion, Frances. Anna Christie, adapted . . . from the play by Eugene O'Neill. [1930]

Mayorga

Mayorga (S)

Michaud (P)

Mickle, Alan D. Six plays of Eugene O'Neill. [1929]

Mirlas, León. "El teatro de O'Neill," estudio de su personalidad y sus obras. [1938]

Moses

Moses (A)

Moses (R)

Nathan

Nathan (H)

Nathan (I)

Nathan (P)

Nathan (T)

Nathan (TD)

Nathan (TM)

National

O'Hara, Frank H. and Bro, Margueritte H. A handbook of drama. 1938

O'Neill, Eugene G. The Emperor Jones, Anna Christie, The hairy ape . . . with an introduction by Lionel Trilling. [c1937]

O'Neill, Eugene G. The Emperor Jones, The straw . . . introduction by Dudley Nichols. [1928]

O'Neill, Eugene G. The moon of

the Caribbees and six other plays of the sea . . . introduction by George Jean Nathan. [c1923]

O'Neill, Eugene G. The moon of the Caribbees and six other plays of the sea . . . with an introduction by St. John Ervine. [1923]

O'Neill, Eugene G. Plays: First series. The straw, The Emperor Jones, and Diff'rent . . . with an introduction by C. E. Bechhofer. [1922]

Pellizzi

Quinn, Arthur H., *ed.* Contemporary American plays edited with an introduction upon recent American drama. [c1923]

† Quinn (H)

Quinn (R)

Roberts

Russell

Salisbury, William. A dress suit becomes Hamlet. Why not, if Mourning becomes Electra? A dissertation upon the comedies of Eugene O'Neill addressed to the author. [1931?] (cover-title; pamphlet)

Salzman

† Sanborn, Ralph and Clark, Barrett H. A bibliography of the works of Eugene O'Neill. 1931

Sayler

Schelling

Schyberg

Scribner, *firm, publishers, New York.* The complete plays of Eugene O'Neill, The Wilderness edition ⟨limited⟩ sold by subscription and in sets only. [1934] (cover-title; pamphlet; prospectus)

Sergeant

Shakespeare, William. Macbeth [by] William Shakespeare, The Emperor Jones [by] Eugene O'Neill, edited by Benjamin A. Heydrick . . . and Alfred A. May. [c1933]

Shipley, Joseph T. The art of Eugene O'Neill. 1928 (pamphlet)

Sinclair

Skinner

Skinner, Richard D. Eugene O'Neill, a poet's quest . . . with a correct chronology of the O'Neill plays as furnished by Eugene O'Neill. 1935

Skolsky

Stewart

Stuart, Donald C. The development of dramatic art. 1928

Sutton, Graham. Some contemporary dramatists. [1924]

† Taylor

Van Doren

Van Doren (A)

Van Doren (B)

Villard

Vočadlo

Ward

Watson, Ernest B. and Pressey, Benfield, *comps.* Contemporary drama, American plays . . . [c1931, c1938] (vols. 1, 2)

Waugh

Whipple

Whithorne, Emerson. At the court of Kublai Kaan, from the incidental music to "Marco Millions" (Eugene O'Neill) by Emerson Whithorne. [1928] (cover-title; sheet music)

Whitman

Whitman, Charles H., *ed.* Seven contemporary plays. [c1931]

Winther, Sophus K. Eugene O'Neill, a critical study. 1934

Woollcott (S)

Woollcott (W)

Wrubel, Allie. Emperor Jones, inspired by the United artists' picture of Eugene O'Neill's famous play by the same name produced by John Krimsky & Gifford Cochran, with Paul Robeson and Dudley Digges, words and music by Allie Wrubel. [c1933] (cover-title; sheet music)

Zabel

Anderson, John. "Eugene O'Neill." *TAM.*, Nov. 1931, pp. 938–42; Anonymous. "Eugene O'Neill." *W.*, Dec. 1926, pp. 585–87; Aronstein, Philipp.

"Eugene O'Neill." *N.Mon.*, June 1930, pp. 311–25; Aronstein. "Eugene O'Neill." *N.Mon.*, July–Aug. 1930, pp. 376–82; Baker, George P. "O'Neill's first decade." *YR.*, July 1926, pp. 789–92; Baldensperger, Fernand. "Eugène O'Neill, prix Nobel de littérature." *RPL.*, Feb. 6, 1937, pp. 73–78; Barron, Samuel. "The dying theater." *Harper's*, Dec. 1935, pp. 108–17; Baughan, Edward A. "The plays of Eugene O'Neill." *Fort.Rev.*, May 1923, pp. 852–60; Bodenheim, Maxwell. "Roughneck and romancer." *N.Yer.*, Feb. 6, 1926, pp. 17–18; Breese, Jessie M. "Home on the dunes." *CL.*, Nov. 1923, pp. 72–76; Brie, Friedrich. "Eugene O'Neill als nachfolger der griechen, Mourning becomes Electra." *GRM.*, Jan.–Feb. 1933, pp. 46–59; Burton, Katherine. "Aldous Huxley and other moderns." *CW.*, Aug. 1934, pp. 552–56; Cajetan, Brother. "The pendulum starts back." *CW.*, Mar. 1935, pp. 650–56; Catel, Jean. "Eugène O'Neill, prix Nobel de littérature 1936." *MF.*, Mar. 1, 1937, pp. 422–26; Cestre, Charles. "La dernière oeuvre d'Eugène O'Neill." *RAA.*, Dec. 1926, pp. 118–21; Cestre. "Eugène O'Neill et les surgissements du tréfond." *RAA.*, Dec. 1928, pp. 131–44; Clark, Barrett H. "Aeschylus and O'Neill." *EJ.*, Nov. 1932, pp. 699–710; Clark. "Eugene O'Neill, a chapter in biography." *TAM.*, May 1926, pp. 325–30, 333–36; Clark. "O'Neill's 'Dynamo' and the village experiments." *Drama*, Apr. 1929, pp. 199–201, 222–23; De Voto, Bernard. "Minority report." *SRL.*, Nov. 21, 1936, pp. 3–4, 16; Dobrée, Bonamy. "The plays of Eugene O'Neill." *So.R.*, Winter 1937, pp. 435–446; Dony, Françoise. "La tragédie d'Eugène O'Neill et l'idée de fatalité." *R.d.UB.*, Dec. 1935, pp. 170–88; Dukes, Ashley. "The English scene, O'Neill succeeds." *TAM.*, Feb. 1938, pp. 101–02, 105–07; Eaton, Walter P. "American drama flowers, Eugene O'Neill as a great playwright." *WW.*, Nov. 1926, pp. 105–08; Eaton. "Eugene O'Neill as a dramatist." *TAM.*, Oct. 1920, pp. 286–89; Eaton. "O'Neill, 'new risen attic stream'?" *A.Schol.*, Summer 1927, pp. 304–12; Fagin, Nathan B. "Eugene O'Neill contemplates mortality." *OC.*, Apr. 1931, pp. 208–19; Fergusson, Francis. "Days without end." *AR.*, Feb. 1934, pp. 491–95; Fergusson. "Eugene O'Neill." *HH.*, Jan.–Mar. 1930, pp. 145–60; Garland, Robert. "Eugene O'Neill and this big business of Broadway." *TAM.*, Jan. 1925, pp. 3–6, 9–12, 15–16; Geddes, Virgil. "Eugene O'Neill." *TAM.*, Nov. 1931, pp. 943–46; Gillet, Louis. "La clef des songes." *RDM.*, Jan. 15, 1929, pp. 453–64; Halman, Doris F. "O'Neill and the untrained playwright." *W.*, July 1928, pp. 215–17; Hayward, Ira N. "Strindberg's influence on Eugene O'Neill." *P.Lore*, Winter 1928, pp. 596–604; Hofmannsthal, Hugo von. "Eugene O'Neill." *Freeman*, Mar. 21, 1923, pp. 39–41; Hohoff, Curt. "Über Eugene O'Neill." *Hochl.*, Oct. 1938, pp. 40–50; † Johnson, Merle D. and Hopkins, Frederick M., *eds.* "American first editions, a series of bibliographic check-lists . . . number 29, Eugene (Gladstone) O'Neill 1888– " by Frank Shay. *PW.*, Apr. 14, 1923, p. 1216; Jones, Carless. "A sailor's O'Neill." *RAA.*, Feb. 1935, pp. 226–29; Katzin, Winifred. "The great god O'Neill." *AB.*, Sept. 1928, pp. 61–66; Kemelman, H. G. "Eugene O'Neill and the highbrow melodrama." *AB.*, Sept. 1932, pp. 482–91; Knickerbocker, Frances W. "A New England house of Atreus." *SR.*, Apr.–June 1932, pp. 249–54; Krutch, Joseph W. "The god of stumps." *Nation*, Nov. 26, 1924, pp. 578–80; Kühnemund, Richard. "Das drama Eugene O'Neills, eine kritische interpretation." *Ang.*, Sept. 1928, pp. 242–87; Loving, Pierre. "Eugene O'Neill." *AB.*, Aug. 1921, pp. 511–20; Lundkvist, Artur. "Eugene O'Neill." *BLM.*, Dec. 1936, pp. 784–86; Macgowan, Kenneth. "Broadway in the spring, New York sees its first expressionist play." *TAM.*, July 1922, pp. 179–82, 187–90; Mackall, Leonard. "Eugene O'Neill's bibliography." *NYHTB.*, Aug. 9, 1931, p. 15; Mainsard, Joseph. "Le théâtre d'Eugène O'Neill." *Etudes*, Oct. 5, 1930, pp. 57–78; Malone, Andrew E. "The plays of Eugene O'Neill." *CR.*,

Mar. 1926, pp. 363–72; Malone, Kemp. "The diction of Strange interlude." *AS.*, Oct. 1930, pp. 19–28; Martinez Hague, Carlos. "Eugenio O'Neill, premio Nobel." *Letras*, Vol. 2 (1936), pp. 427–32; Montgomery, Guy. "Strange interlude." *UCC.*, July 1928, pp. 364–68; Moses, Montrose J. "The 'new' Eugene O'Neill." *N.Amer.Rev.*, Dec. 1933, pp. 543–49; Mullett, Mary B. "The extraordinary story of Eugene O'Neill." *A.Mag.*, Nov. 1922, pp. 34, 112, 114, 116, 118, 120; Nathan, George J. "The case of O'Neill." *AM.*, Apr. 1928, pp. 500–02; Nathan. "O'Neill's finest play." *AM.*, Aug. 1927, pp. 499–506; Nathan. "O'Neill's latest." *AM.*, Feb. 1926, pp. 247–49; Nathan. "O'Neill's new play." *AM.*, Aug. 1926, pp. 499–505; † Nicholls, Norah. "Check list of Eugene O'Neill." *Bookm.*, Sept. 1933, p. 300; Parks, Edd W. "Eugene O'Neill's symbolism, old gods for new." *SR.*, Oct.–Dec. 1935, pp. 436–51; Quinn, Arthur H. "Eugene O'Neill, poet and mystic." *Scrib.*, Oct. 1926, pp. 368–72; Sayler, Oliver M. "The real Eugene O'Neill." *Cent.*, Jan. 1922, pp. 351–59; Sergeant, Elizabeth S. "O'Neill, the man with a mask." *NR.*, Mar. 16, 1927, pp. 91–95; Skinner, Richard D. "O'Neill, and the poet's quest." *N.Amer.Rev.*, June 1935, pp. 54–67; Smith, Joseph. "Mourning becomes Electra, a trilogy." *MT.*, Aug. 1932, pp. 359–63; Soupault, Philippe. "Le théâtre aux États-Unis." *R.dP.*, June 1933, pp. 936–44; Stevens, Thomas W. "How good is Eugene O'Neill?" *EJ.*, Mar. 1937, pp. 179–87; Sullivan, Frank. "Life is a bowl of Eugene O'Neills." *N.Yer.*, Nov. 21, 1931, pp. 17–18; Sutton, Graham. "Eugene O'Neill." *Bookm.*, May 1923, pp. 126–28; Tetauer, F. "Eugene O'Neill, studie o novém dramate." *Apollon*, Vol. 2, 1924–25, pp. 10–13, 30–31, 40–41; Trilling, Lionel. "Eugene O'Neill." *NR.*, Sept. 23, 1936, pp. 176–79; Whipple, Thomas K. "The tragedy of Eugene O'Neill." *NR.*, Jan. 21, 1925, pp. 222–25; White, Arthur F. "The plays of Eugene O'Neill." *WRUB.*, Aug. 1928, pp. 20–36; Woodbridge, Homer E. "Eugene O'Neill." *SAQ.*, Jan. 1938, pp. 22–35; Young, Stark. "Eugene O'Neill's new play." *NR.*, Nov. 11, 1931, pp. 352–55. For references to reviews, see *BRD.*, 1919–22, 1924–29, 1931, 1933–34.

E. P. *See* Ezra Pound

Dorothy (Rothschild) Parker, 1893–

Born in West End, New Jersey, August 22, 1893, as Dorothy Rothschild. Her father was Jewish and her mother Scotch. After education at Miss Dana's School in Morristown, New Jersey, and the Blessed Sacrament Convent in New York, she began writing on the editorial staff of *Vogue* at ten dollars a week in 1916. In 1917, the year of her marriage to Edwin Pond Parker II, she became dramatic critic of *Vanity Fair*, but left in 1920 to do free-lance writing.

Franklin P. Adams had printed some of her verses in the *Daily Mail;* and *Enough Rope*, a book of light verse that appeared in 1927, was a best-seller. In the same year the author became book-reviewer ("The Constant Reader") on the *New Yorker*, and in 1929 she took an O. Henry Memorial Prize with her story "Big Blonde," which was published in 1930 in *Laments for the Living*. By this time Mrs. Parker, whose quips were quoted everywhere, was regarded as one of the most brilliant wits of the literary world of New York.

In 1933, having divorced Mr. Parker in 1928, she married the writer Alan Campbell, with whom she has written for the films. They live on a farm in Pennsylvania. "In theory," she writes, "I love to garden, but I'm awfully lazy about it. . . ." She is devoted to dogs and enjoys walking.

Opposed on principle to such manifestations of the Puritan spirit as censorship and reform movements, she considers herself a satirist. She admires Ernest Hemingway's work, and in her own she whittles and pares to achieve simplicity and strength.

For further comment, see Critical Survey, pp. 162–63.

BIBLIOGRAPHY

Poems

Nonsenseorship by Heywood Broun, George S. Chappell, Ruth Hale, Ben Hecht, Wallace Irwin, Robert Keable, Helen Bullitt Lowry, Frederick O'Brien, Dorothy Parker, Frank Swinnerton, H. M. Tomlinson, Charles Hanson Towne, John V. A. Weaver, Alexander Woollcott, and the author of "The mirrors of Washington," edited by G. P. P. Sundry observations concerning prohibitions, inhibitions, and illegalities, illustrated by Ralph Barton, 1922; Enough rope, poems, 1926; Sunset gun, poems, 1928; Death and taxes, 1931; Collected poems: Not so deep as a well, decorated by Valenti Angelo, 1936 (also issued as Not so deep as a well, 1936).

Short Stories and Sketches

Laments for the living, 1930; After such pleasures, 1933; Here lies. The collected stories of Dorothy Parker, 1939.

Play

Close harmony, or, The lady next door, a play in three acts by Dorothy Parker and Elmer L. Rice, 1929.

Wit and Humor

High society, advice as to social campaigning and hints on the management of dowagers, dinners, debutantes, dances, and the thousand and one diversions of persons of quality, the drawings by Fish, the prose precepts by Dorothy Parker, George S. Chappell, and Frank Crowninshield, 1920; Men I'm not married to, 1922 (contains also, inverted and with separate title-page, Women I'm not married to by Franklin P. Adams).

STUDIES AND ARTICLES

† Johnson (1936)
Kunitz (L)
Lawrence (S)
Loggins
Masson
Woollcott (W)

Luhrs, Marie. "Fashionable poetry." *P.*, Apr. 1927, pp. 52–54; North, Sterling. "More than enough rope." *P.*, Dec. 1928, pp. 156–58; Rosenberg, Harold. "Nor rosemary nor rue." *P.*, Dec. 1931, pp. 159–61; Van Doren, Mark. "Dorothy Parker." *EJ.*, Sept. 1934, pp. 535–43. For references to reviews, see *BRD.*, 1927–28, 1930–31, 1933, 1936, 1939.

Donald Culross Peattie, 1898–

Born in Chicago, June 21, 1898; the son of Robert Burns Peattie, a "journalist and wit," and Elia (Wilkinson) Peattie, novelist, essayist, and critic. Reared in a cultivated home, he was educated at the University of Chicago and Harvard, specialized in natural sciences, and graduated *cum laude* at Harvard in 1922.

The next few years he spent with the Department of Agriculture, working in the Office of Foreign Seed and Plant Introduction, and doing botanical research on frost-resistance in tropical plants. In 1923 he married Louise Redfield, a writer. His own literary ambitions led him to write, during his spare time, a book on plants, *Cargoes and Harvests*, and to give up his work for free-lance writing and the conduct of a nature column in the Washington *Star*.

In 1928 he took his family to France, where they lived for five years, in the hills of Provence and the seaside city of Menton. Returning in 1933 to the United States, he was struck forcibly with the beauty of his own country. He settled in Glenview, Illinois, near Chicago, and revived his column in the Chicago *Daily News*.

In 1935 he was awarded the first annual Gold Medal, given by the Limited Editions Club to the author of the book (*An Almanac for Moderns*) written in the previous three years most likely to become a classic. *Green Laurels* (1936) was a Literary Guild selection.

Writing in the *Saturday Review of Literature* in 1937, Peattie pointed out vigorously the low standard of much contemporary writing about nature, and urged that nature-writers should emancipate themselves from the Thoreau tradition (and all others as well), and give expression to "the deep biological undertow beneath the shining surface of nature," substituting for "the obviously pretty" "the sinews of nature, the big, slow, shouldering of her causative forces." Nature-writing, he thinks, can be improved by higher standards among publishers and their steady refusal to issue rubbish, willingness and ability on the part of good scientists to write interestingly for intelligent laymen, as English scientists are doing now, and the development of the illustrated and digest types of book, like the new pictorial and synopsis types of magazine.

For further comment, see Critical Survey, pp. 154, 173.

BIBLIOGRAPHY

Novels

Up country, a story of the vanguard by Donald Culross Peattie and Louise Redfield Peattie, 1928; Port of call, 1932; Sons of the Martian, 1932 (English ed., Karen's loyalty, 1933); The bright lexicon, 1934.

Nature Studies and Essays

Reprinted from Rhodora, vol. 24, April–May, 1922. The Atlantic coastal plain element in the flora of the great lakes, 1922 (caption-title; pamphlet); Cargoes and harvests . . . maps by Beatrice Siegel, 1926; Trillium in North and South Carolina, a critical systematic reconnaissance . . . reprinted from Journal of the Elisha Mitchell scientific society, vol. 42, nos. 3 and 4, May, 1927, 1927 (cover-title; pamphlet); Reprinted from Journal of the Elisha Mitchell scientific society, vol. 44, no. 1, September, 1928. Flora of the Tryon region of North and South Carolina. An annotated list of the plants growing spontaneously in Polk county, North Carolina, and adjacent parts of South Carolina, in Greenville and Spartanburg counties. Part 1. Introduction: soils, climate, etc., ferns, and conifers (Pteridophyta, Gymnospermae), 1928 (caption-title; pamphlet); Reprinted from the Journal of the Elisha Mitchell scientific society, vol. 44, no. 2, April, 1929. Flora of the Tryon region, an annotated list of the plants growing spontaneously in Polk county, North Carolina, and adjacent parts of South Carolina, in Greenville and Spartanburg counties. Part II. Cat-tail family to orchid family (Typhaceae to Orchidaceae), 1929 (caption-title; pamphlet; contains part III); Flora of the Indiana dunes, a handbook of the flowering plants and ferns of the Lake Michigan coast of Indiana and of the Calumet district, 1930; Reprinted from Journal of the Elisha Mitchell scientific society, vol. 45, no. 1, November, 1929. Flora of the Tryon region. Part IV. Mimosa family to dogwood family (Mimosaceae to Cornaceae), 1929 (caption-title; pamphlet); Reprinted from the Journal of the Elisha Mitchell scientific society, vol. 45, no. 2, May, 1930. Flora of the Tryon region. Part V. Wintergreen family to lobelia family (Pyrolaceae to Lobeliaceae), 1930 (caption-title; pamphlet); Reprinted from Journal of Elisha Mitchell scientific society, vol. 46, no. 2, June, 1931. Flora of the Tryon region. An annotated list of the plants growing spontaneously in Polk county, North Carolina, and adjacent parts of South Carolina, in Greenville and Spartanburg counties. Part VI. Daisy family (Compositae). List of new names published, errata, summary, 1931 (caption-title; pamphlet); A natural history of Pearson's Falls and some of its human associations, 1932 (pamphlet); Trees you want to know . . . illustrations of the eastern trees from the classic "Sylva of North America" by Francois Andre Michaux, illustrations of western trees by Ethel Bonney Taylor, 1934; * An almanac for moderns . . . with drawings by Lynd Ward, 1935; Old-fashioned garden flowers, 1936 (cover-title); Spring song at the grove, 1938 (caption-title; pamphlet); This is living, a view of nature with photographs, text by Donald Culross Peattie, photographs selected and book designed by Gordon Aymar, 1938; Flowering earth, wood engravings by Paul Landacre, 1939.

Biography

Singing in the wilderness, a salute to John James Audubon, 1935; * Green laurels, the lives and achievements of the great naturalists, 1936.

History

Vence, the story of a Provencal town through two thousand years, 1930; A prairie grove, 1938.

Belles Lettres

Blown leaves, written and printed by Donald C. Peattie, fourth year University high school, 1916; Bounty of earth by Donald Culross Peattie and Louise Redfield Peattie, decorations by Margaret Evans Price, 1926; A book of hours . . . decorations by Lynd Ward, 1937.

Animal Stories

Down wind, secrets of the underwoods by Donald Culross and Louise Redfield Peattie, 1929.

Description and Travel

The happy kingdom, a Riviera memoir by L. R. and D. C. Peattie, 1935.

Editor

A gathering of birds, an anthology of the best ornithological prose, edited, with biographical sketches . . . illustrated by Edward Shenton, 1939.

Juvenile Books

A child's story of the world, from the earliest days to our own time . . . illustrations by Naomi Averill, 1937 (pub. also in six separate vols. Contents: The story of the first men, The story of ancient civilization, The story of the middle ages, The story of the new lands, The story of America, The story of the modern world from the French revolution to now); The story of America . . . illustrations by Naomi Averill, 1937; The story of ancient civilization . . . illustrated by Naomi Averill, 1937; The story of the first men . . . illustrations by Naomi Averill, 1937; The story of the middle ages . . . illustrations by Naomi Averill, 1937; The story of the modern age from the French revolution to now . . . illustrations by Naomi Averill, 1937; The story of the new lands . . . illustrations by Naomi Averill, 1937.

Fadiman, Clifton. "Mr. Peattie again." *N.Yer.*, Apr. 17, 1937, pp. 75–77; Van Doren, Mark. "A new naturalist." *N.Amer.Rev.*, Sept. 1937, pp. 162–71; Weeks, Mangum. "Artist and backwoodsman." *VQR.*, Jan. 1937, pp. 140–43. For references to reviews, see *BRD.*, 1926–29, 1932, 1934–39.

Julia (Mood) Peterkin, 1880–

Born Julia Mood, October 31, 1880, in Laurens County, South Carolina. Her father was a physician, and she was reared, with an elder brother who also became a physician, and two elder sisters, by her grandmother. Although she describes her upbringing as one substituting for the "facts of life" the values of the next world and the more superficial cultural phases of this one, she became a freethinker. She graduated in 1896 from Converse College and in the next year, though not yet seventeen, she took her master's degree. She then taught a country school.

In 1903 she married William George Peterkin, a cotton planter, and became the mistress of Lang Syne Plantation, near Fort Motte, South Carolina. In this new life she was cut off from intimate contact with any but a very few white people and was surrounded by hundreds of Negro workers on the plantation. She was obliged to assume the duties of a doctor and a judge, and her isolation led her to develop new outdoor interests that she could cultivate by herself. She enjoys hunting, riding, and swimming, and has indulged in gardening and pigeon-raising.

Feeling the need of a new occupation when her son went away to school, she began, at forty, to study music and made two long trips every week to take lessons in Columbia. Her tales of life on the plantation so impressed her teacher that he urged her to try her hand at writing, and he brought Carl Sandburg to meet her.

With this encouragement, and with a background of years of observation, she began writing stories of the South Carolina Negro as she had known him. Her success was such that *Scarlet Sister Mary* (1928) took the Pulitzer Prize in 1929 and was dramatized and produced with Ethel Barrymore as leading actress. "The Diamond Ring" was one of the O. Henry Memorial Prize Stories of 1930.

Although she has relinquished to her son the work of actual management, Mrs. Peterkin still lives on the plantation among the Negroes who have become a part of her life. She belongs to clubs and societies and enjoys dancing, cards, and tennis, and she has lectured at the Bread Loaf Writers' Conference. Asked, some years ago, to express her views of life, she outlined a deterministic faith in a regular universe governed by laws of heriditary development, emphasized the comfort she found in the evidences of order in the world, and said that she regarded her own part in society to be her duty of realizing as completely as possible her own potentialities.

For further comment, see Critical Survey, pp. 44, 51, 117.

BIBLIOGRAPHY

Novels

Black April, a novel, 1927; * Scarlet sister Mary, 1928; Bright skin, 1932.

Short Stories

Green Thursday, stories, 1924.

Negro Life

Roll, Jordan, roll, the text by Julia Peterkin, the photographic studies by Doris Ulmann, 1933.

Essay

A plantation Christmas by Julia Peterkin, decorations by David Hendrickson, 1934.

STUDIES AND ARTICLES

Clark (E)
Herrmann
Kunitz (L)
Loggins
Overton (WW)

Bennett, Isadora. "Lang syne's miss, the background of Julia Peterkin, novelist of the old south." *AB.*, June 1929, pp. 357–66; Law, Robert A. "Mrs. Peterkin's Negroes." *Sw.R.*, Summer 1929, pp. 455–61. For references to reviews, see *BRD.*, 1924, 1927–29, 1932–33.

A poker of fun. *See* **Amy Lowell**

Ernest Poole, 1880–

Born in Chicago, January 23, 1880. As a boy he played with a gang in the lumber-yards, took part in athletics, attended private school, and studied the violin. Entering Princeton, he tried without much success to secure recognition in extracurricular activities of a journalistic and dramatic nature, but read considerably and graduated with honor standing in 1902.

In the autumn of that year he went to New York to live on the lower East Side, where for months he could observe the life of the poor and wretched in some of its uglier aspects. He wrote articles on Chinatown, the police, tenement life, and similar subjects for *McClure's* and other magazines. In 1904, as the *Outlook's* correspondent in the stockyards strike in Chicago, he sat in on meetings of the strike committee; and in the next year he went to Russia to cover the 1905 revolution, traveled from St. Petersburg to the Caucasus, was arrested and released near Persia, and sent articles and stories from all parts of Europe.

After his return and his marriage he settled down in Greenwich Village near Washington Square and wrote plays and novels. Two of his plays were given New York productions, and a third, *Take Your Medicine*, had a road career. They were not so successful as his novels, which were the result of his direct observation of tenement and harbor life and his personal experiences.

In the fall of 1914 the *Saturday Evening Post* sent Poole to Berlin as war correspondent; and, writing articles for the *Post*, *Everybody's*, and other magazines, he followed the Bavarian army into France. Home again, he finished *His Family*, which took the first Pulitzer Prize as the best novel of 1917, and then returned to Europe, this time to describe for the *Post* village life in Russia during the Revolution. He was a member of the Foreign Press Bureau of the Committee on Public Safety.

Since the war he has lived in New York, with long sojourns in the White Mountains near Franconia, New Hampshire, where he can tramp, ride horseback, and play golf. He continues to read extensively, write stories and articles for periodicals, and work at long novels.

"Characters grow real to me through their voices, not their faces," writes Poole, who works with sketches, outlines, and copious notes, and as many as eight or nine revisions on his novels. He has spent about a year and a half on each one. Many have been internationally successful: *With Eastern Eyes* ran as a serial in France; *Blind* appeared as a book and ran twice as a serial in Germany; and *The Harbor* was published, in serial form, book form, or both, in nine countries, and translated into many European languages.

For further comment, see Critical Survey, pp. 77–78.

BIBLIOGRAPHY

Novels

The voice of the street, 1906; * The harbor, 1915; His family, 1917; His second wife, 1918; Blind, a story of these times, 1920; Beggars' gold, 1921; Millions, 1922; Danger, 1923; The avalanche, 1924; The hunter's moon . . . illustrated by Decie Merwin, cover design by Abram Poole, 1925; With eastern eyes, 1926; Silent storms, 1927; The car of Croesus, 1930; The destroyer, 1931; Great winds, 1933; One of us, 1934.

Short Stories

The little dark man and other Russian sketches, 1925.

Studies and Sketches

Business—a profession by Louis D. Brandeis with a foreword by Ernest Poole, 1914; "The dark people," Russia's crisis, 1918; The village, Russian impressions, 1918; Nurses on horseback, 1932.

Pamphlets

Child labor—The street, 1903 (caption-title); The plague in its stronghold, tuberculosis in the New York tenement, 1903 (cover-title); Katharine Breshkovsky "For Russia's freedom" by Ernest Poole reprinted by permission of the Outlook, 1905.

STUDIES AND ARTICLES

Baldwin (M)
Kunitz
† Manly
Marble
Mencken
Quinn
Van Doren (C)

Holt, Hamilton. "The problem of poverty, by an aristotelian." *Unpop.Rev.*, Oct. 1916, pp. 245–63; More, Paul E. "The problem of poverty, by a platonist." *Unpop.Rev.*, Oct. 1916, pp. 231–45. For references to reviews, see *BRD.*, 1907, 1915, 1917–18, 1920–27, 1930–34.

Katherine Anne Porter, 1894–

Born at Indian Creek, Texas, May 15, 1894, a descendant of Daniel Boone. She attended southern schools for girls and at a tender age showed a pronounced taste for writing.

She is well read in the classics of English and world literature, and has lived in many parts of the world. Somewhat left of center, she has written on political subjects; and she has done reviewing, editing, and hack work, in addition to the short stories she has published in magazines. In 1930 a limited edition of *Flowering Judas*, a volume of short stories, was sold out in a month. In 1931 she received a Guggenheim fellowship for foreign travel and writing, and in 1937 the Book-of-the-Month Club, in consideration of her previous achievement and her promise for the future, awarded her a fellowship of $2,500.

For further comment, see Critical Survey, p. 96.

BIBLIOGRAPHY

Short Stories

* Flowering Judas, 1930 (enl. ed., Flowering Judas and other stories, 1935); Hacienda, 1934; Noon wine, 1937; Pale horse, pale rider, three short novels, 1939 (Old mortality; Noon wine; Pale horse, pale rider).

Study

Outline of Mexican popular arts and crafts by Katherine Anne Porter. Upon the occasion of the Traveling Mexican popular arts exposition in the United States of North America under the auspices of the Ministry of industry, commerce, and labor of Mexico, Don Xavier Guerrero, being the art director, has caused this book to be published. It contains a study by Miss Katherine Anne Porter of the popular arts and crafts of Mexico. Cover design by Xav. Gro. Photographs from the collection of Roberto A. Turnbull, 1922.

Translations

Katherine Anne Porter's French song-book, 1933.

STUDIES AND ARTICLES

Horton Kunitz	† Blanck, Jacob, *ed.* "American first editions." *PW.*, June 18, 1938, p. 2382 (checklist by John H. Birss)

For references to reviews, see *BRD.*, 1930, 1934–35, 1937, 1939.

Ezra (Loomis) Pound, 1885–

Born in Hailey, Idaho, October 30, 1885, of New England stock. His mother was distantly related to Henry Wadsworth Longfellow. Before he was two years old he was taken to Pennsylvania, and was brought up in the East. He spent two years at the University of Pennsylvania, enrolled as a special student so that he could study what he thought important, and in 1903 he entered Hamilton College, in Clinton, New York, from which he graduated in 1905.

As a fellow in Romance languages and literatures, and an "instructor with professorial functions," he returned to the University of Pennsylvania in 1905 and took his master's degree in the following June. The next academic year he spent abroad in search of material for a thesis on Lope de Vega, and he traveled in Spain, Italy, and France. Returning to this country in the fall of 1907, he accepted an instructorship in Wabash College, Crawfordsville, Indiana. After four months he was released from it on the grounds that he was too European and unconventional. He returned to Europe and after a short time in Gibraltar and Italy settled in London.

His first book of verse was published in Venice in 1908, and in London two more appeared in the next year. Mr. Pound became a powerful literary figure, lecturing on art and assisting young writers and artists. When Harriet Monroe asked him in 1912 to help the struggling new *Poetry*, he sent verse of his own and others and acted as foreign correspondent until 1919. He was an early champion of the Imagist group of poets and is said to have invented the name. He helped stimulate in England and the United States the popularity of Chinese and Japanese verse. With Wyndham Lewis he founded *Blast* (1914–15), an organ of the Vorticists, and from 1917 to 1919 he was London editor of the *Little Review*. In 1914 he acted as informal literary executor for Ernest Fenollosa's work on the Japanese No drama and oriental poetry.

In 1920, feeling that England was sterile, he moved to Paris, and four years later he took up residence in Rapallo, in the Italian Riviera. In 1927 he founded and edited the short-lived periodical, the *Exile*, and in the same year he won the *Dial* Award of two thousand dollars for distinguished service to American literature. In 1939, during his first visit to America in eighteen years, Pound received an honorary degree at Hamilton College.

A man of changing and varied interests, Pound has composed an opera (*Le Testament*), made translations and adaptations from medieval Provençal, Chinese and Japanese, Latin, and French, and assisted such persons as James Joyce, Rabindranath Tagore, Georges Antheil, and Gaudier-Brzeska, and he has contributed much to literary periodicals. He vigorously opposes the academic approach to modern literature.

For further comment, see Critical Survey, pp. 141, 148–49, 188–89.

BIBLIOGRAPHY

Poems

A lume spento, 1908 (pamphlet); A quinzaine for this Yule being selected from a Venetian sketch-book, "San Trovaso," 1908 (pamphlet); Exultations of Ezra Pound, 1909; Personae of Ezra Pound, 1909; Provença, poems selected from Personae, Exultations, and Canzoniere of Ezra Pound, 1910; Canzoni of Ezra Pound, 1911; Ripostes of Ezra Pound whereto are appended the complete poetical works of T. E. Hulme, with prefatory note, 1912; Canzoni & Ripostes of Ezra Pound whereto are appended the complete poetical works of T. E. Hulme, 1913; Personae & Exultations of Ezra Pound, 1913; Lustra of Ezra Pound, 1916 (also privately printed with additional poems); Lustra of Ezra Pound with earlier poems, 1917; The fourth canto, 1919 (pamphlet); Quia pauper amavi, 1919; Hugh Selwyn Mauberley by E. P., 1920; Umbra, the early poems of Ezra Pound, all that he now wishes to keep in circulation from "Personae," "Exultations," "Ripostes," etc. With translations from Guido Cavalcanti and Arnaut Daniel and poems by the late T. E. Hulme, 1920; Poems 1918–21, including three portraits and four cantos, 1921; A draft of XVI. cantos of Ezra Pound from the beginning of a poem of some length now first made into a book with initials by Henry Strater, 1925; Personæ, the collected poems of Ezra Pound including Ripostes, Lustra, Homage to Sextus Propertius, H. S. Mauberley, 1926; A draft of the cantos 17–27 of Ezra Pound. Initials by Gladys Hynes, 1928; *Ezra Pound. Selected poems edited with an introduction by T. S. Eliot. This selection includes Personæ of Ezra Pound, Ripostes, Lustra, Cathay, H. S. Mauberley, and some early poems rejected by the author and omitted from his collected edition, 1928; *A draft of XXX cantos, 1930; Eleven new cantos, XXXI–XLI, 1934 (English ed., A draft of cantos XXXI–XLI, 1935); Homage to Sextus Propertius, 1934; The fifth decad of cantos, 1937.

Literary Criticism

The spirit of romance, an attempt to define somewhat the charm of the pre-renaissance literature of Latin Europe, 1910; The Little review [Feb. 1918] a magazine of the arts, making no compromise with the public taste. "A study of French modern poets," by Ezra Pound, 1918 (cover-title); Instigations of Ezra Pound together with an essay on the Chinese written character by Ernest Fenollosa, 1920; How to read, 1931; Prolegomena 1. How to read, followed by The spirit of romance, part I, 1932; A B C of reading, 1934; Make it new, essays, 1934.

Essays and Studies

Pavannes and Divisions, 1918; Antheil and the Treatise on harmony, 1924; Imaginary letters, 1930 (pamphlet); A B C of economics, 1933; Jefferson and/or Mussolini, l'idea statale, fascism as I have seen it, 1935; Social credit: an impact, 1935 (pamphlet); Polite essays, 1937; Culture, 1938 (English ed., Guide to kulchur, 1938).

Biography

Gaudier-Brzeska, a memoir . . . including the published writings of the sculptor, and a selection from his letters with thirty-eight illustrations consisting of photographs of his sculpture, and four portraits by Walter Benington, and numerous reproductions of drawings, 1916.

Social History

Indiscretions, or, Une revue de deux mondes, 1923.

Verses Set to Music

The garret [poem by] Ezra Pound [music by] Josef Holbrooke, Curwen edition, 1922 (cover-title; sheet music); Salutation [poem by] Ezra Pound [music by] Josef Holbrooke, Curwen edition, 1922 (cover-title; sheet music); "Tame cat" . . . song, with clarinet obligato, words by Ezra Pound, music by Joseph Holbrooke, 1913 [1923] (cover-title; sheet music); Two compositions for chorus of women's voices by Aaron Copland, no. 444, an immorality, 3 part with soprano solo & pianoforte accompaniment, words from "Lustra" by Ezra Pound, 1926 (sheet music).

Editor and Translator

Certain noble plays of Japan from the manuscripts of Ernest Fenollosa, chosen and finished by Ezra Pound with an introduction by William Butler Yeats, 1916; 'Noh,' or, Accomplishment, a study of the classical stage of Japan by Ernest Fenollosa and Ezra Pound, 1916.

Editor

The Catholic anthology, 1914–1915, 1915; Poetical works of Lionel Johnson, 1915; Passages from the letters of John Butler Yeats selected by Ezra Pound, 1917; Active anthology, 1933; The Chinese written character as a medium for poetry by Ernest Fenollosa. An ars poetica. With a foreword and notes by Ezra Pound, 1936.

Compiler

Profile, an anthology collected in MCMXXXI, 1932.

Translations

Selections from collection of Yvette Guilbert, English translations by Ezra Pound, harmonized and arranged by Gustave Ferrari, 19 ?; The sonnets and ballate of Guido Cavalcanti with translation and introduction, 1912 (English ed., Sonnets and ballate of Guido Cavalcanti, with translations of them and an introduction, 1912); Walter Morse Rummel (1912). Hesternae rosae, serta II. Neuf chansons de troubadours des XIIième et XIIIième siècles pour une voix avec accompagnement de piano, adaptation française par M. D. Calvocoressi, adaptation anglaise par Ezra Pound, 1913 (sheet music); Cathay, translations by Ezra Pound for the most part from the Chinese of Rihaku from the notes of the late Ernest Fenollosa and the decipherings of the professors Mori and Ariga, 1915 (pamphlet); Dialogues of Fontenelle, 1917 (pamphlet); The natural philosophy of love by Remy de Gourmont translated with a postscript, 1922; Ta hio, the great learning, newly rendered into the American language, 1928 (pamphlet).

STUDIES AND ARTICLES

Aiken
Amdur, Alice S. The poetry of Ezra Pound. 1936 (pamphlet)
Anderson
Blackmur
Bullough, Geoffrey. The trend of modern poetry. 1934
Bush
Cook
Deutsch
Eliot, Thomas S. After strange gods, a primer of modern heresy . . . the Page-Barbour lectures at the University of Virginia, 1933. [c1934]
† [Eliot, Thomas S.] Ezra Pound, his metric and poetry. 1917
Engel, Carl. Discords mingled . . . essays on music. 1931
Fletcher
Gilkes, Martin H. A key to modern English poetry. [1937]
Huddleston
Hughes
Johns, Orrick. Time of our lives, the story of my father and myself. [c1937]
† Johnson (1929)
† Johnson (1932)
† Johnson (1936)
Kreymborg
Kunitz (L)
Leavis, Frank R., *ed.* Determinations, critical essays with an introduction. 1934
Leavis, Frank R. How to teach reading, a primer for Ezra Pound. 1932 (pamphlet)
Leavis, Frank R. New bearings in English poetry, a study of the contemporary situation. 1932
Lewis (T)
Lewisohn (E)
Linati
Loggins
Lowell
† Manly
Monro
Monroe
Monroe (P)
National
Sitwell
Sparrow
Tate
Taupin
Untermeyer
Untermeyer (C)
Untermeyer (M)
Untermeyer (N)
Vines, Sherard. Movements in modern English poetry and prose . . . with an introductory note by G. S. Gordon. [1929]
Vočadlo
Ward
Widdemer
Winters
Yeats, William B. A packet for Ezra Pound. 1929
Zabel

Aiken, Conrad. "Personae." *P.*, Aug. 1934, pp. 276–79; Aldington, Richard. "A book for literary philosophers." *P.*, July 1920, pp. 213–16; Anonymous. "Pound sterling." *LL.*, Aug. 1934, pp. 632–36; Barry, Iris. "The Ezra Pound period." *AB.*, Oct. 1931, pp. 159–71; Benét, William R. "Poets in collected editions." *YR.*, Jan. 1928, pp. 366–74; Blackmur, Richard P. "Masks of Ezra Pound." *HH.*, Jan.–Mar. 1934, pp. 177–212; Bodenheim, Maxwell. "Isolation of carved metal." *D.*, Jan. 1922, pp. 87–91; Bottrall, Ronald. "xxx cantos of Ezra Pound, an incursion into poetics." *Scrut.*, Sept. 1933, pp. 112–22; Bronner, Milton. "A panel of poets." *AB.*, Apr. 1912, pp. 156–58; Carnevali, Emanuel. "Irritation." *P.*, Jan. 1920, pp. 211–21; Delmer S. "Ezra Pound." *ZFEU.*, Vol. XXIX, 1930, pp. 92–110; Eliot, Thomas S. "Isolated superiority." *D.*, Jan. 1928, pp. 4–7; Fitts, Dudley. "Music fit for the odes." *HH.*, Jan.–Mar. 1931, pp. 278–89; Fletcher, John G. "Ezra Pound, collected poems." *Crit.*, Apr. 1929, pp. 513–24; Geddes, Virgil. "Ezra Pound today." *P.*, Nov. 1922, pp. 95–100; Gorman, Herbert S. "Bolingbroke of bards." *N.Amer.Rev.*, June 1924, pp. 855–65; Gregory, Horace. "The a.b.c. of Ezra

Pound." *P.*, Aug. 1935, pp. 279–85; Gregory. "The search for a frontier." *NR.*, July 26, 1933, pp. 292–94; Hale, William G. "Pegasus impounded." *P.*, Apr. 1919, pp. 52–55; Laughlin, James, 4th. "Ezra Pound's Propertius." *SR.*, Oct.–Dec. 1938, pp. 480–91; Lesemann, Maurice. "Mr. Pound and the younger generation." *P.*, July 1927, pp. 216–22; McClure, John. "New poems of Ezra Pound." *DD.*, May 1922, pp. 269–71; Mangan, Sherry. "Poetry for scholars, scholarship for poets." *P.*, Mar. 1933, pp. 336–39; Michelson, Max. "A glass-blower of time." *P.*, Mar. 1918, pp. 330–33; Monroe, Harriet. "Ezra Pound." *P.*, May 1925, pp. 90–97; Moore, Marianne. "The cantos." *P.*, Oct. 1931, pp. 37–50; Moore. "A draft of xxx cantos." *Crit.*, Apr. 1934, pp. 482–85; Pound, Ezra. "D'Artagnan twenty years after." *Crit.*, July 1937, pp. 606–17; Preston, John H. "Three American poets." *VQR.*, July 1927, pp. 450–62; Sandburg, Carl. "The work of Ezra Pound." *P.*, Feb. 1916, pp. 249–57; Schwartz, Delmore. "Ezra Pound's very useful labors." *P.*, Mar. 1938, pp. 324–39; Sinclair, May. "The reputation of Ezra Pound." *N.Amer.Rev.*, May 1920, pp. 658–68; Tate, Allen. "Laundry bills." *P.*, Nov. 1932, pp. 107–12; Taupin, René. "La poésie d'Ezra Pound." *RAA.*, Feb. 1931, pp. 221–36; Untermeyer, Louis. "Ezra Pound, proseur." *NR.*, Aug. 17, 1918, pp. 83–84; Zukovsky, Louis. "The cantos of Ezra Pound, one section of a long essay." *Crit.*, Apr. 1931, pp. 424–40. For references to reviews, see *BRD.*, 1911, 1916–18, 1920, 1922, 1927, 1933–39.

Frederic Prokosch, 1909–

Born in Madison, Wisconsin, May 17, 1909. He is of Austrian descent and is the son of the late Eduard Prokosch, Sterling Professor of Germanic Languages at Yale. He was educated in Germany, France, Austria, and England, as well as in Wisconsin, Texas, Pennsylvania, New York, and Connecticut. He has traveled extensively in Europe and Asia.

At eighteen he graduated from Haverford College at the top of his class, and he took the master's degree at the same institution in 1928. Further study followed at the University of Pennsylvania, where he held a fellowship in 1929–30, and at Oxford; and, after work at Cambridge on pseudo-Chaucerian manuscripts, he took his Ph.D. at Yale in 1932, with a dissertation on "The Chaucerian Apocrypha." From 1931 to 1933 he taught English at Yale, and from 1932 to 1934 he was a research fellow. In 1936–37 he was an instructor in New York University.

By this time he had published *The Asiatics*, so successful a novel that it was translated into five European tongues, and *The Assassins*, a highly-regarded volume of poems. *The Seven Who Fled*, selected by Sinclair Lewis, Thornton Wilder, and Louis Bromfield from more than six hundred manuscripts, was chosen Harper Prize Novel in 1937, and the author was given the award of $7,500. A Guggenheim fellowship enabled Prokosch to travel in 1937–38 in Europe and Asia.

He has won several tennis championships, and has played squash for Cambridge and Yale. He won the squash championship in Connecticut in 1933. His recreations include cricket-playing, marionettes, painting, and music. "At the moment," he wrote from Prague in 1937, "my chief interests are tennis, squash, baroque architecture, the Greek Islands, mediaeval Latin poetry, and trying to avoid the vulgarizations of money and publicity."

Although recognizing the value of contemporary radical literary criticism, he disapproves of dogmatic pronouncements. His preferences run toward modern British rather than modern American literature, and among poets in English he admires especially Yeats and T. S. Eliot. He likes also the novels of E. M. Forster, T. F. Powys, and Julian Green, as well as the work of several foreign novelists.

For further comment, see Critical Survey, p. 70.

BIBLIOGRAPHY

Novels

The Asiatics, 1935; The seven who fled, 1937; Night of the poor, 1939.

Poems

The assassins, poems, 1936; The carnival, poems, 1938.

Bishop, John P. "Final dreading." *P.*, Mar. 1937, pp. 337–39; Morse, Samuel F. "Spectre over Europe." *P.*, Nov. 1938, pp. 89–92; Rubin, Joseph J. "Young man of letters." *SR.*, Jan.–Mar. 1938, pp. 122–24. For references to reviews, see *BRD.*, 1935–38.

(Howard) Phelps Putnam, 1894–

Born in Boston, July 9, 1894, of New England stock. He attended public schools, Phillips Exeter Academy, and Yale, from which he graduated in 1916. In college he was a member of the brilliant group including Archibald MacLeish, Thornton Wilder, and Stephen Vincent Benét.

After graduation, in reaction from the academic world he had known, he went west and took a job in the engineer's office of a copper mine at Bisbee, Arizona. Subsequently he worked in Washington in a government post, in an importing business in New York, in a Connecticut foundry, and in an editorial office in Boston. He left this last job in 1920 to spend a year in Provence.

Since that time he has written independently, traveled about the United States, living in Colorado and New Hampshire, New Mexico and Maryland, and worked as a staff member of the editorial force on the *Atlantic Monthly*. In 1930 he was awarded a Guggenheim fellowship, which enabled him to continue his writing and later to make a trip to Italy.

For further comment, see Critical Survey, p. 136.

BIBLIOGRAPHY

Poems

Trinc, 1927; The five seasons, 1931.

STUDIES AND ARTICLES

Kreymborg Kunitz

Zabel, Morton D. "Phelps Putnam and America." *P.*, Sept. 1932, pp. 335–44. For references to reviews, see *BRD.*, 1927, 1931.

R. K. *See* **Rockwell Kent**

John Crowe Ransom, 1888–

Born in Pulaski, Tennessee, April 30, 1888, of Scotch-Irish descent. His father was a minister, and the family was one of southern traditions—his granduncle had been a founder of the Ku Klux Klan.

He graduated in 1909 from Vanderbilt and spent three years as Rhodes Scholar at Oxford, taking the bachelor's degree in 1913 in Christ Church College in classics and mathematics. From 1914 until 1937, with two interruptions, he taught at Vanderbilt in the English department; he has lectured also at the Colorado State Teachers College, the Peabody College for Teachers, the University of New Mexico, and other institutions. During the war, in which he was a first lieutenant in the field artillery, he taught in an art school at Saumur, in France, and in 1931–32, as Guggenheim Fellow, he was a member of the staff of the University College of the Southwest, at Exeter. Since 1937 he has been Professor of English at Kenyon College. He founded the *Kenyon Review* in 1938, and was Phi Beta Kappa poet at Harvard in 1939.

His poetry became known partly through the interest of Christopher Morley. He was a founder and editor of the *Fugitive* (1922–25), a southern journal devoted to the publication of original verse. In June, 1937, he was honored by a dinner given in Nashville by the *Saturday Review of Literature*, the *Southern Review*, the *Virginia Quarterly Review*, and the *Sewanee Review* to recognize his "long and distinguished service to literature."

For further comment, see Critical Survey, p. 147.

BIBLIOGRAPHY

Poems

Poems about God, 1919; Armageddon by John Crowe Ransom, A fragment by William Alexander Percy, Avalon by Donald Davidson, 1923; * Chills and fever, poems, 1924; Grace after meat . . . with an introduction by Robert Graves, 1924; Two gentlemen in bonds, 1927.

Literary Criticism

The world's body, 1938.

Studies

God without thunder, an unorthodox defense of orthodoxy, 1930; I'll take my stand, the South and the agrarian tradition by twelve southerners, 1930.

Pamphlet

Shall we complete the trade? A proposal for the settlement of foreign debts to the United States . . ., 1933 (cover-title).

Editor

American Rhodes scholars, Oxford, 1910–1913, 1913 (ed. by Christopher Morley assisted by Elmer Davis and John Crowe Ransom); Topics for freshman writing, twenty topics for writing with appropriate materials for study, selected and edited, 1935.

STUDIES AND ARTICLES

Deutsch
Kreymborg
Riding

Henderson, Alice C. "An American georgian." *P.*, Apr. 1930, pp. 51–52; Knickerbocker, William S. "Mr. Ransom and the old south." *SR.*, Apr.–June 1931, pp. 222–39; Knickerbocker. "Theological homebrew." *SR.*, Jan.–Mar. 1931, pp. 103–11; Luhrs, Marie. "A conjurer." *P.*, June 1927, pp. 162–65; Warren, Robert P. "John Crowe Ransom, a study in irony." *VQR.*, Jan. 1935, pp. 93–112; Warren. "A note on three southern poets." *P.*, May 1932, pp. 103–13. For references to reviews, see *BRD.*, 1919, 1924, 1927, 1930–31, 1938.

Lizette Woodworth Reese, 1856–1935

Born in Waverly, Baltimore County, Maryland, January 9, 1856. Her mother was German; her father became a Confederate soldier in the Civil War. Educated in private and public schools, she began teaching, when she was seventeen, at a parish school in Waverly; and at eighteen she published her first poem, "The Deserted House." Subsequently she taught at a German-English school in Baltimore, in a Negro high school, and in the Western High School in Baltimore, from which she retired in 1921, after twenty years of service in the school and forty-eight in the public-school system of the city.

In the meantime she had written poetry, essays, Sunday-school stories, and other work. Although she did little writing during the last decade of her teaching career, the Western High School honored her by the erection, in 1923, of a bronze tablet on which was inscribed the best known of her poems, the sonnet "Tears." In 1931 she was awarded the Mary P. L. Keats Memorial Prize of eight hundred dollars, and an honorary doctorate in letters was conferred upon her by Goucher College. She was elected to membership in Phi Beta Kappa in William and Mary College in 1925. She died December 17, 1935, in Baltimore.

For further comment, see Critical Survey, pp. 131, 177.

BIBLIOGRAPHY

Poems

A branch of May, poems, 1887; A handful of lavender, 1891; A quiet road, 1896; A wayside lute, 1909; Edgar Allan Poe, a centenary tribute by William P. Trent . . . Oliver Huckel . . . John Prentiss Poe . . . Lizette Woodworth Reese and Mrs. John C. Wrenshall edited by Heinrich Ewald Buchholz, 1910; Spicewood, 1920; Wild cherry, 1923; * The selected poems of Lizette Woodworth Reese, 1926; Little Henrietta, 1927; Lizette Woodworth Reese, The pamphlet poets, price 25 cents, 1928 (cover-title; ed. by Hughes Mearns); White April and other poems, 1930; Pastures and other poems, 1933; The old house in the country . . . introduction by Hervey Allen, 1936.

Reminiscences

A Victorian village, reminiscences of other days, 1929.

Miscellany

The York road . . . with decorations by Richard Bennett, 1931.

Unfinished Novel
Worleys . . . introduction by John Farrar, 1936.

Verses Set to Music
A song for Candlemas, words by Lizette Woodworth Reese, music by Margaret Ruthven Lang, 1898 (caption-title).

STUDIES AND ARTICLES

Kreymborg
Kunitz (L)
Library
Rittenhouse (Y)
Smith
Untermeyer
† [Wirth, Alexander C.] Complete bibliography of Lizette Woodworth Reese. 1937

Adams, Leonie. "Winter bloom." *P.*, Apr. 1934, pp. 40–42; Benét, William R. "Poets in collected editions." *YR.*, Jan. 1928, pp. 366–74; Harriss, Robert P. "April weather, the poetry of Lizette Woodworth Reese." *SAQ.*, Apr. 1930, pp. 200–07; Luhrs, Marie. "A child comes and goes." *P.*, Feb. 1928, pp. 283–84; Monroe, Harriet. "Faint perfume." *P.*, Mar. 1924, pp. 341–42; Monroe. "Honor to Lizette Reese." *P.*, Feb. 1936, pp. 277–78. For references to reviews, see *BRD.*, 1910, 1921, 1924, 1926–27, 1929–31, 1933, 1936.

Elmer L. Reizenstein. *See* **Elmer Rice**

Agnes Repplier, 1858–

Born April 1, 1858, in Philadelphia, of French extraction. Although as a little girl she was slow at learning to read, she was precocious in being a writer even in her youth. She went to school at the Convent of the Sacred Heart, Torresdale, Pennsylvania, where she was taught by French nuns.

As a young woman she turned to literature as a career and a means of support, and began writing for the *Catholic World*. The editor urged her to avoid fiction as unsuited to her limited experience and observation, and she has in the main followed the suggestion for the more than fifty years of her literary career. Although she has produced both fiction and biography, the essay has been her typical form of expression, and a large body of her work has appeared in the *Atlantic Monthly*. She is an admirer of Andrew Lang and Augustine Birrell.

She has led a quiet life in Philadelphia, with travels abroad to France and in Canada. For a period she tried giving lectures, but disliked the work and stopped. At the Ibero-American Exposition in Seville in 1928–29 she was one of the American commissioners. Honorary degrees have been conferred upon her by the University of Pennsylvania (1902), Yale (1925), Columbia (1927), and Marquette (1929); and in 1911 the University of Notre Dame awarded her the Laetare Medal. In 1935 she received the Gold Medal of the National Institute of Arts and Letters.

For further comment, see Critical Survey, pp. 155, 168.

BIBLIOGRAPHY

Essays

Books and men, 1888; Points of view, 1891; Essays in miniature, 1892; Essays in idleness, 1893; In the dozy hours and other papers, 1894; Varia, 1897; Compromises, 1904; A happy half-century and other essays, 1908; Americans and others, 1912; Counter-currents, 1916; Points of friction, 1920; The promise of the bell, Christmas in Philadelphia . . . with illustrations by John Wolcott Adams, 1924 (pamphlet); Under dispute, 1924; Times and tendencies, 1931; To think of tea! 1932; In pursuit of laughter, 1936; * Eight decades, essays and episodes, 1937.

Biography

Appreciations of Horace Howard Furness: Our great Shakespere critic by Talcott Williams from the Century magazine, November, 1912, Horace Howard Furness by Agnes Repplier from the Atlantic monthly, November, 1912, 1912 (pamphlet); J. William White, M.D., a biography . . . with portraits, 1919; Père Marquette, priest, pioneer, and adventurer . . . decorations by Harry Cimino, 1929; Mère Marie of the Ursulines, a study in adventure, 1931; Junípero Serra, pioneer colonist of California, 1933; Agnes Irwin, a biography . . . Published under the auspices of the Agnes and Sophy Dallas Irwin memorial fund, frontispiece portrait by Cecilia Beaux, 1934.

Reminiscences

In our convent days, 1905.

History

Philadelphia: the place and the people . . . with illustrations by Ernest C. Peixotto, 1898.

Books on Cats

The fireside sphinx . . . with illustrations by E. Bonsall, 1901; The cat, being a record of the endearments and invectives lavished by many writers upon an animal much loved and much abhorred, collected, translated, and arranged by Agnes Repplier . . . with illustrations by Elisabeth F. Bonsall, 1912.

Literary Criticism

University extension lectures. Syllabus of a course of six lectures on books and reading by H. Morse Stephens . . . Miss Agnes Repplier . . . Arthur T. Hadley . . . Brander Matthews . . . Bliss Perry . . . Hamilton W. Mabie, 1899 (pamphlet); Counsel upon the reading of books by H. Morse Stephens, Agnes Repplier, Arthur T. Hadley, Brander Matthews, Bliss Perry, Hamilton Wright Mabie, with an introduction by Henry Van Dyke, 1900.

Miscellany

What does the victory or defeat of Germany mean to the United States, 191– (broadside); Germany and democracy the real issue, the views of two average Americans, a reply to Doctor Dernburg by Agnes Repplier and J. William White, 1914 (pamphlet); The stranger within our gates, 1916 (pamphlet); Abuse of hospitality, 1919 (broadside); Saints or spirits? 1920 (pamphlet).

Edited and Compiled Works

A book of famous verse selected, 1892; For remembrance, a little record of loyalty and fidelity made with much love by the children of Eden, edited at their request, 1901.

STUDIES AND ARTICLES

Collins (T)
Halsey
† Johnson (1936)
Kunitz (L)
MacDermott, William A. Down at Caxton's by Walter Lecky [*pseud.*] 1895
Matthews, Brander. Americanisms and Briticisms with other essays on other isms. 1892
National
Newton, Alfred E. End papers, literary recreations . . . Dream-children edition, with illustrations. 1933
Pattee
Schelling
Steck, Francis B. Miss Repplier's "Père Marquette," a review and a refutation. 1929 (pamphlet)

Adams, Mildred. "Our Miss Repplier." *AB.*, June 1927, pp. 410–12; Browne, Edythe H. "The abiding art of Agnes Repplier." *Thought*, Dec. 1930, pp. 396–410; Chase, Mary E. "The dean of American essayists." *Com.*, Aug. 18, 1933, pp. 384–86; Reilly, Joseph, jr. "A daughter of Addison." *CW.*, Nov. 1938, pp. 158–66; Repplier, Agnes. "Miss Repplier's reply." *Nation*, Apr. 8, 1915, p. 385; Stratton, George M. "Crooked thinking in regard to war." *Nation*, Apr. 8, 1915, pp. 384–85; Wade, Mason. "Agnes Repplier at eighty." *NR.*, Dec. 8, 1937, p. 140. For references to reviews, see *BRD.*, 1906, 1908–09, 1912–13, 1916, 1919–20, 1924, 1929, 1931–34, 1936–37.

Elmer (L.) Rice, 1892–

Born September 28, 1892, in New York, as Elmer Reizenstein. He was educated in public schools in New York, but dropped out before finishing high school and entered business. After less than a year, dissatisfied with his progress, he began the study of law, going to the New York Law School at night and working in a law office during the day. He graduated *cum laude* in 1912 and passed the bar examinations. Again he felt himself to be a failure, and he gave up the law for authorship.

He mailed the manuscript of *On Trial* to two New York managers, and both accepted it at once. It was successful in both New York and London. Rice's career had begun, and since then he has written and produced plays of his own, collaborated with Hatcher Hughes, Dorothy Parker, and Philip Barry, and written scenarios for the motion pictures he later satirized in a novel. In *On Trial* he employed for the first time on the stage the familiar film device (the "cutback" or "flashback") of reversing chronology in the order of the scenes, showing first the effect and then the cause. *The Adding Machine* was an experiment in expressionism with an American subject. *Street Scene*, despised of producers and finally presented by one considered so old and injudicious that his own son refused to help him, was the Pulitzer Prize play of the season 1928–29.

After this success and a trip to Europe Rice himself produced successfully *The Left Bank* and *Counsellor-at-Law.* He has directed settlement dramatic work, and in 1935 he was regional director of the Federal Theatre Project of the Works Progress Administration. Recently, with Maxwell Anderson, S. N. Behrman, Sidney Howard, and Robert Sherwood, he formed the Playwrights' Producing Company, for the financing and production of plays by the dramatists themselves.

For further comment, see Critical Survey, p. 124.

BIBLIOGRAPHY

Plays

On trial, a dramatic composition in four acts by Elmer L. Reizenstein, 1914; The Morningside plays. Hattie, a drama by Elva De Pue. One a day, a fantasy by Caroline Briggs. Markheim, a dramatization by Zellah Macdonald. The home of the free, a comedy by Elmer L. Reizenstein. With an introduction by Barrett H. Clark, 1917; * The adding machine, a play in seven scenes . . . with a foreword by Philip Moeller, the Theatre guild version with eight illustrations from photographs of the Theatre guild production, 1923; Wake up, Jonathan, a comedy in a prologue and three acts by Hatcher Hughes and Elmer L. Rice, 1928; Close harmony, or, The lady next door, a play in three acts by Dorothy Parker and Elmer L. Rice, 1929; Cock Robin, a play in three acts by Elmer Rice and Philip Barry, 1929; * Street scene, a play in three acts, 1929; The subway, a play in nine scenes, 1929; See Naples and die, a comedy in three acts, 1930; Counsellor-at-law, a play in three acts, 1931; The left bank, a play in three acts, 1931; The house in Blind alley, a comedy in three acts, 1932; Plays of Elmer Rice, containing The adding machine, Street scene, See Naples and die, Counsellor-at-law, 1933; We, the people, a play in twenty scenes, 1933; The home of the free, a comedy in one act by Elmer Rice, 1934; Judgment day, a melodrama in three acts, 1934; The passing of Chow-Chow, comedy in one act, 1934; Three plays without words, 1934 (Landscape with figures; Rus in urbe; Exterior); Other plays and Not for children, being four plays, 1935 (Between two worlds; Judgment day; We, the people; Not for children); Two plays: Not for children and Between two worlds, 1935; Black sheep, a comedy in three acts, 1938; American landscape, a play in three acts, 1939.

Novels

A voyage to Purilia, 1930; Imperial city, a novel, 1937.

STUDIES AND ARTICLES

Agate
Agate (M)
Best
Block
Brown
Clark
Dukes
Eaton (D)
Heath
Kunitz (L)
Lawson
Mantle
Mantle (C)
Mersand
Moses (A)
Moses (R)

Pellizzi
† Quinn (H)
Skinner
Skolsky
Torbett, D., *pseud.* On trial, the story of a woman at bay by Elmer L. Reizenstein, made into a book from the play of the same name. 1915
Ward
Zabel

Levin, Meyer. "Elmer Rice." *TAM.*, Jan. 1932, pp. 54–62; Rice, Elmer. "Things I have never done." *N.Yer.*, Aug. 15, 1931, pp. 24, 26. For references to reviews, see *BRD.*, 1923, 1929–30, 1932–33, 1935, 1937, 1939.

Barbara Rich, *pseud.* *See* Laura Riding

Lola Ridge, 1884–

Born in Dublin. She spent her girlhood in Australia and New Zealand and studied art at the Académie Julienne in Paris. Coming to the United States in 1907, with a collection of verses which she subsequently destroyed, she earned her living by writing fiction for magazines. At the end of three years, she abandoned this type of writing in order to avoid artistic suicide, and took miscellaneous jobs in advertising, factory work, and the organizing of an educational movement. She assisted Alfred Kreymborg in editing *Others*, a magazine for experimental poetry, and later assumed complete editorial responsibility for it.

Her radical poetry published in the *New Republic*, and her first volume in 1918 made her favorably known. She was awarded the Guarantors Prize by *Poetry* in 1923. A sympathizer with labor, she was stirred by the execution of Sacco and Vanzetti to write *Firehead*, lyrics on the Crucifixion, and other poems. She has suffered considerably from poor health and has been unable, ordinarily, to work steadily. An invitation to spend the summer of 1929 at Yaddo, the artists' colony on the Trask estate at Saratoga, New York, made it possible for her to finish *Firehead*. In 1934 and 1935 she received the Shelley Memorial Prize, and in 1935 she was awarded a Guggenheim fellowship.

For further comment, see Critical Survey, p. 151.

BIBLIOGRAPHY

Poems

* The Ghetto and other poems, 1918; Sun-up and other poems, 1920; Red flag, 1927; Firehead, 1929; Dance of fire, 1935.

STUDIES AND ARTICLES

Aiken
Kreymborg
Kunitz (L)
Untermeyer
Untermeyer (N)
Widdemer

Aiken, Conrad. "The literary abbozzo." *D.*, Jan. 25, 1919, pp. 83–84; Carnevali, Emanuel. "Crucible." *P.*, Mar. 1921, pp. 332–34; Flanner, Hildegarde. "Miss Ridge's quest." *P.*, Oct. 1935, pp. 40–42; Hackett, Francis. "Lola Ridge's poetry." *NR.*, Nov. 16, 1918, pp. 76–77; Kreymborg, Alfred. "A poet in arms." *P.*, Mar. 1919, pp. 335–40; Monroe, Harriet. "A banner in the wind." *P.*, June 1927, pp. 154–59; Monroe. "A symphony of the cross." *P.*, Apr. 1930, pp. 36–40. For references to reviews, see *BRD.*, 1918, 1920–21, 1927, 1929–30, 1935.

Laura Riding, 1901–

Born January 16, 1901, in New York City. Despite her American birth and her association with the *Fugitive* group of southern poets, she feels herself an alien in this country and prefers to live elsewhere. "America was living abroad to me," she once declared, and she expressed her feeling that the English people and their language are the only ones to be seriously considered. She lived in Deyá, Majorca, until the Spanish civil war drove her to England and Switzerland in 1936. Avowedly preferring partisanship to neutrality, she has written for *transition*, and she has sympathized with the position of the Negro. She has said that she regards painting as mute writing and music as "a poetic crime," and that she feels poetry to be the only final truth. With the British poet Robert Graves, with whom she has written studies of modern poetry and edited *Epilogue, a Critical Summary*, she established the Seizin Press in 1927.

For further comment, see Critical Survey, p. 145.

BIBLIOGRAPHY

Poems

The close chaplet by Laura Riding Gottschalk, 1926; Voltaire, a biographical fantasy [by] Laura Riding Gottschalk, 1927; Love as love, death as death, 1928; Poems, A joking word, 1930; Twenty poems less, 1930; Laura and Francisca, 1931; The life of the dead . . . with ten illustrations by John Aldridge, engraved on wood by R. J. Beedham, 1933; Poet: a lying word, 1933; Americans, 1934; Collected poems, 1938.

Novels

No decency left by Barbara Rich [*pseud.* of Laura Riding and Robert Graves], 1932; Laura Riding & George Ellidge. 14A, 1934; A Trojan ending, 1937; Lives of wives, 1939.

Short Stories

Progress of stories, 1935.

Essays and Studies

A survey of modernist poetry by Laura Riding and Robert Graves, 1927; Anarchism is not enough, 1928; Contemporaries and snobs, 1928; A pamphlet against anthologies by Laura Riding and Robert Graves, 1928; Experts are puzzled, 1930; The world and ourselves, 1938; The left heresy in literature and life by Harry Kemp; Laura Riding, and others, 1939.

Miscellany

Four unposted letters to Catherine, 1930; Though gently, 1930; Everybody's letters collected and arranged by Laura Riding with an editorial postscript, 1933.

Translations

Anatole France at home by Marcel LeGoff translated by Laura Riding Gottchalk with unpublished photographs and documents, 1926; Almost forgotten Germany by Georg Schwarz translated by Laura Riding and Robert Graves, 1936.

STUDIES AND ARTICLES

Kallen Kunitz

Hays, H. R. "The expatriate consciousness." *P.*, May 1939, pp. 101–04; Wheelwright, John. "Multiplied bewilderment." *P.*, Aug. 1932, pp. 288–90. For references to reviews, see *BRD.*, 1928–29, 1935, 1937–39.

Lynn Riggs, 1899–

Born near Claremore, Oklahoma, then in Indian territory. He attended school, sang at a moving-picture house, and worked as a cowpuncher and farm boy. Jobs in Chicago and New York followed, and for a time he was a motion-picture "extra." Subsequently he returned to Tulsa and joined the staff of the *Oil and Gas Journal.* By this time definitely interested in literature, he was reading and writing poetry.

When he entered the University of Oklahoma, his ability as a playwright came to the fore, and his comedy *Cuckoo* was produced by the dramatic department in 1922. In the same year Riggs made a tour as second tenor in a quartet, and his earnings enabled him to join the artists' colony in Santa Fe.

Knives from Syria, acted by the Santa Fe Players, encouraged him to write *The Primitives*, his first full-length play; and *Sump'n like Wings*, which was performed at the Detroit Playhouse, attracted the attention of eastern theatrical interests. In 1927 *Big Lake*, produced at the American Laboratory Theatre, gave new evidence of the author's interest in Oklahoma folk material. Through the indirect influence of Barrett H. Clark, he was awarded a Guggenheim fellowship in 1928 which enabled him to live in Paris and finish *Green Grow the Lilacs.* It was accepted by the Theatre Guild. It was not produced, however, until early in 1931, after *Roadside*, a play begun in Europe and finished while the author was writing a film, had been given on Broadway in the preceding fall. *Green Grow the Lilacs* was decidedly successful and drew critical attention to the author. His plays have been performed at the Hedgerow Theatre near Philadelphia, and he has directed college performances of them at Northwestern University and the University of Iowa. Riggs, who has written poetry for *Poetry* and the *Nation*, is of the firm opinion that to be a fine playwright one must be a poet, and he feels also that the theater is in a position to benefit from the spiritual and emotional fervor of the day.

For further comment, see Critical Survey, pp. 116–17.

BIBLIOGRAPHY

Plays

Big Lake, a tragedy in two parts as produced by the American laboratory theater, New York city . . . foreword by Barrett H. Clark, 1927; Knives from Syria, a play in one act, 1928; Sump'n like wings and A lantern to see by, two Oklahoma plays, 1928; Roadside, a comedy . . . foreword by Arthur Hopkins, 1930; * Green grow the lilacs, a play, 1931; Russet mantle, and The Cherokee night, two plays, 1936.

Poem

The iron dish, 1930.

Moving-Picture Script

The plainsman . . . [by Waldemar Young, Harold Lamb, and Lynn Riggs], 1936 (mimeographed).

Editor

Cowboy songs, folk songs, and ballads from Green grow the lilacs by Lynn Riggs (as produced by the Theatre guild, inc.), 1932 (cover-title; pamphlet).

STUDIES AND ARTICLES

Brown
Clark
Kunitz
Moses (A)
Skinner

Glover, James W. "Plays from Oklahoma." *TAM.*, Feb. 1929, pp. 154–55; Lowe, Robert L. "The lyrics of Lynn Riggs." *P.*, Mar. 1931, pp. 347–49; Mitchell, Lee. "A designer at work." *TAM.*, Nov. 1934, pp. 874–77; Vestal, Stanley. "Lynn Riggs, poet and dramatist." *Sw.R.*, Autumn 1929, pp. 64–71. For references to reviews, see *BRD.*, 1930–31, 1936.

Elizabeth Madox Roberts, 1886–

Born near Springfield, Kentucky, of a family that had been associated with the State since the days of Boone. She was brought up in this agricultural region and spent several years in the mountains in Colorado. In 1917 she entered the University of Chicago; and, after a brilliant career, in which she was associated with Glenway Wescott and other promising young writers, and took the McLaughlin Prize for essay-writing and the John Billings Fisk Prize for poetry, she graduated in 1921.

She went to New York to write, and published *Under the Tree*, which had taken the Fisk Prize, in 1922. Her first novel, *The Time of Man* (1926), received high praise from British and American critics, including Arnold Bennett, Rebecca West, Hugh Walpole, Sherwood Anderson, and Zona Gale, and was translated into German and Scandinavian.

After spending some time in California, Miss Roberts returned to Kentucky where she now lives. She holds an honorary doctor's degree from Centre College in Danville. She has studied the archaisms in the local speech. In 1928 she was given the John Reed Memorial Prize by *Poetry;* in 1930 "The Sacrament of the Maidens" was awarded the O. Henry Memorial Prize; and in the next year she was given another award by the Poetry Society of South Carolina.

For further comment, see Critical Survey, p. 43.

BIBLIOGRAPHY

Novels

* The time of man, a novel, 1926; My heart and my flesh . . . a novel, 1927; Jingling in the wind, 1928; The great meadow, 1930; A buried treasure, 1931; He sent forth a raven, 1935; Black is my truelove's hair, 1938.

Short Stories

The haunted mirror, stories, 1932.

Poems

In the great steep's garden, poems by Elizabeth Madox Roberts, pictures by Kenneth Hartley, 1915 (cover-title); Under the tree, 1922.

STUDIES AND ARTICLES

Adams, J. D. Elizabeth Madox Roberts, an appraisal by J. Donald Adams, a personal note by Rosamond Milner, with criticisms by Robert Morss Lovett, Edward Garnett, Harry Hansen, Allan Nevins, Carl Van Doren, Harry Emerson Wildes, Mary Ross, Joseph Henry Jackson, Louis Untermeyer. 1938 (pamphlet)
Halleck
† Johnson (1936)
Kunitz (L)
National
Overton (WW)
Roberts, Elizabeth M. The time of man . . . with an introduction by J. Donald Adams. [c1935]
Saturday
Wescott, Glenway. Elizabeth Madox Roberts, a personal note . . . with criticisms by Robert Morss Lovett, Edward Garnett, Mary Ross, Allan Nevins, Carl Van Doren, Louis Untermeyer. 1930 (pamphlet)

Adams, James. "Elizabeth Madox Roberts." *VQR.*, Jan. 1936, pp. 80–90; Hartley, Lodwick C. "A Kentucky idyl." *SR.*, July–Sept. 1930, pp. 381–84; Janney, Francis L. "Elizabeth Madox Roberts." *SR.*, Oct.–Dec. 1937, pp. 388–410; Teasdale, Sara. "A child sings." *P.*, July 1931, pp. 227–29; Van Doren, Mark. "Elizabeth Madox Roberts, her mind and style." *EJ.*, Sept. 1932, pp. 521–29; Winters, Yvor. "Under the tree." *P.*, Apr. 1923, pp. 45–48. For references to reviews, see *BRD.*, 1923, 1926–28, 1930–32, 1935, 1938.

Kenneth (Lewis) Roberts, 1885–

Born at Kennebunk, Maine, December 8, 1885, of Colonial ancestry. He was reared in the Arundel country of which he later wrote, and attended Cornell, where he graduated in 1908.

For two years he had edited the college humor magazine, and in 1909 he began his career as a professional journalist on the Boston *Post*, for which he served as a reporter and conducted a humor column. Subsequently he joined the staffs of *Puck* and *Life;* then he entered the war.

After serving in the intelligence section of the Siberian Expeditionary Force, he spent nine years as traveling correspondent for the *Saturday Evening Post.* In this period he wrote articles on foreign conditions and immigration, and his opinions on the latter problem were credited by a commissioner-general of immigration with the responsibility for the passage of the restrictive immigration law.

Already the author of several books, Roberts withdrew in 1928 to Italy and began work on a series of historical novels of the period of the Revolution and the War of 1812. The first, *Arundel*, appeared in 1930. It won enthusiastic praise, and the later volumes were also acclaimed as among the finest contemporary historical novels. A part of *Northwest Passage* appeared in the *Saturday Evening Post*.

Feeling that fiction, because of its requirement of vividness in the presentation of truth, is more adapted than any other literary medium to the exigencies of historical writing and the exposure of falsehood, Roberts has engaged in painstaking and close research on the period of his books. *Arundel* and *Rabble in Arms* each involved two years of study, and the sources for the latter included some hundred books, including journals and records of travel, as well as government material from England and Canada and manuscripts at the Fort Ticonderoga Museum. In the course of his work he collated sources for accuracy of detail, sifted out errors in such particulars as the accounts of the vessels in the American fleet at the battle of Valcour Island, and compared and corrected information in various biographies of Benedict Arnold. The maps, drawings, tables of chronology, and literary and stylistic annotations are preserved on the yellow sheets of the original manuscript of *Rabble in Arms*, which Roberts presented in 1937, with twenty-two source books and other material, to the Baker Memorial Library at Dartmouth; and alterations and workings-over are continued into the various typewritten and printed stages of the book. He has also completely revised several novels since first publication.

Devotedly loyal to his native state, he has spent most of his time in recent years at Kennebunk, with winter sojourns in Italy. Preferring privacy and independence to the usual forms of conspicuous success, he has refused to give lectures or to speak over the radio. In his relations with the book trade he has used his influence to induce publishers to be more open and generous to authors in their contracts and in their releasing of information concerning sales, and he has taken the position that cheap editions should never be issued without the consent of the writer.

A member of the National Institute of Arts and Letters, he is an honorary member (Dartmouth) of Phi Beta Kappa and holds honorary doctorates from Dartmouth, Colby, and Middlebury colleges.

For further comment, see Critical Survey, pp. 55–56, 57.

BIBLIOGRAPHY

Historical Novels

Arundel, being the recollections of Steven Nason of Arundel, in the province of Maine, attached to the secret expedition led by Colonel Benedict Arnold against Quebec and later a captain in the Continental army serving at Valcour Island, Bemis Heights, and Yorktown, 1930; The Lively Lady, a chronicle of certain men of Arundel in Maine, of privateering during the war of impressments, and of the circular prison on Dartmoor, 1931; Rabble in arms, a chronicle of Arundel and the Burgoyne invasion, 1933; Captain Caution, a chronicle of Arundel, 1934; * Northwest passage, 1937 (also pub., 1937, in limited and signed 2 vol. ed., [vol. 1] Northwest passage, [vol. 2] Northwest passage, appendix containing the courtmartial of Major Robert Rogers, the courtmartial of Lt. Samuel Stephens and other new material with notes).

Essays and Sketches

Concentrated New England, a sketch of Calvin Coolidge, 1924; For authors only and other gloomy essays, 1935; Trending into Maine . . . with illustrations by N. C. Wyeth, 1938.

Journalism and Travel

Europe's morning after, 1921; Sun hunting, adventures and observations among the native and migratory tribes of Florida, including the stoical time-killers of Palm Beach, the gentle and gregarious tin-canners of the remote interior, and the vivacious and semi-violent peoples of Miami and its purlieus, 1922; Why Europe leaves home, a true account of the reasons which cause central Europeans to overrun America, which lead Russians to rush to Constantinople and other fascinating and unpleasant places, which coax Greek royalty and commoners into strange byways and hedges and which induce Englishmen and Scotchmen to go out at night . . . with illustrations from photographs from accurate and de-propagandized information gathered in England, Scotland, France, Belgium, Holland, Germany, Danzig, Poland, Czecho-Slovakia, Italy, Turkey, and Greece in the years 1920 and 1921, 1922; Black magic, an account of its beneficial use in Italy, of its perversion in Bavaria, and of certain tendencies which might necessitate its study in America, 1924; Florida loafing, an investigation into the peculiar state of affairs which leads residents of 47 states to encourage Spanish architecture in the 48th, 1925; Florida, 1926.

Satire and Humor

The collector's whatnot, a compendium, manual, and syllabus of information and advice on all subjects appertaining to the collection of antiques, both ancient and not so ancient. Compiled by Cornelius Obenchain Van Loot [*pseud.* of Booth Tarkington] Milton Kilgallen [*pseud.* of Kenneth Roberts] and Murgatroyd Elphinstone [*pseud.* of Hugh MacNair Kahler], 1923; Antiquamania edited by Kenneth L. Roberts, the collected papers of Professor Milton Kilgallen [*pseud.*], F. R. S., of Ugsworth college, elucidating the difficulties in the path of the antique dealer and collector and presenting various methods of meeting and overcoming them. With further illustrations, elucidations, and wood-cuts done on feather-edged boards by Booth Tarkington, 1928; It must be your tonsils, with pictures by Paul Galdone, 1936.

Play

The brotherhood of man, a drama in one act by Kenneth L. Roberts and Robert Garland, 1934.

Opera

Panatela, a political comic opera in three acts, written for the Cornell Masque. Book and lyrics by Kenneth L. Roberts '08, Romeyn Berry '04. Music by T. J. Lindorff '07, H. C. Schuyler '10, H. E. Childs '09, 1907.

Pamphlet

Watchdogs of crime, 1927.

Editor

Northwest passage, appendix containing the courtmartial of Major Robert Rogers, the courtmartial of Lt. Samuel Stephens and other new material with notes, 1937; March to Quebec, journals of the members of Arnold's expedition, compiled and annotated . . . during the writing of Arundel, 1938.

STUDIES AND ARTICLES

Doubleday, Doran & company, inc. Kenneth Roberts, an American novelist. [c1938]

[Leonard, Chilson H.] Kenneth Roberts, a biographical sketch, an informal study, his books and critical opinions. [c1936]

Wyeth, Newell C. A set of the illustrations painted by N. C. Wyeth for "Trending into Maine" by Kenneth Roberts, reproduced by offset lithography in four printings by The Tudor press, inc., Boston. [1938]

† Blanck, Jacob, *ed.* "American first editions." *PW.*, Oct. 16, 1937, pp. 1595–96, (checklist by Frank Stone); Williams, Ben A. "Kenneth Roberts." *SRL.*, June 25, 1938, pp. 8–10. For references to reviews, see *BRD.*, 1921–22, 1924, 1926, 1929–31, 1933–38.

Edwin Arlington Robinson, 1869–1935

Born December 22, 1869, in Head Tide, Maine. When he was still a baby, his family moved to Gardiner, Maine, and he was reared in this town, which became the "Tilbury" of his poems.

He was a precocious child and read and recited poetry at an early age. His father, a retired shipbuilder and merchant, encouraged this inclination and read poems to him. At seven he was reading Shakespeare, and at eleven he was writing verses of his own. When he was in his teens and a student of blank verse, he made translations of a part of Vergil and all the *Antigone* of Sophocles.

After an education in local schools he entered Harvard in 1891. He remained for two years, but was forced by family illness and poverty to return home. He continued to write verse and enjoyed the friendship and stimulus of a cultivated neighbor, a connoisseur of poetry, with whom he studied metrics. When he had forty poems that he considered worthy of publication, he made them into *The Torrent and the Night Before* and tried to find a publisher. Having no success, he issued the book at his own expense in an edition of three hundred paper-bound copies, and distributed it among literary people and critics. The comments made on the collection varied, but were sufficiently favorable to encourage the poet to continue in his vocation; and, after the death of his parents and the sale of the house in Gardiner, he settled in New York, determined to be a writer.

Before long, however, it became necessary for him to support himself; and, despite the publication of both *Children of the Night* and *Captain Craig*, he took a laboring job on the Interborough subway under construction in Manhattan. When after a year the work gave out, he went to Boston and wrote advertising for a department store.

The change in his fortune came when his work caught the attention of President Theodore Roosevelt in the winter of 1904–05. The President suggested a post in a foreign country in the immigration inspection service, but Robinson preferred to live in New York and accepted a position in the customhouse. A second edition of *Children of the Night* received favorable notice in a review written by the President in *Outlook* in 1905, and he used his influence to find a publisher for *The Town down the River.*

Leaving his government post in 1910, Robinson devoted himself entirely to writing. From 1911 he spent the summer months in the MacDowell colony at Peterboro, New Hampshire, where he enjoyed stimulating society and leisure for work. *The Man against the Sky* (1916) made him a national literary figure, and his fiftieth birthday (1919) was the occasion of public tributes by sixteen American poets. His *Collected Poems* (1921) won the first Pulitzer Prize for Poetry (1922) and recognition by the Authors' Club of New York as the most significant contribution for that year to American literature. *Poetry* awarded him the Helen Haire Levinson Prize in 1923. In two subsequent years, 1925 and 1928, he took the Pulitzer Prize with *The Man Who Died Twice* and *Tristram,* and in 1929 he was awarded the Gold Medal of the National Institute of Arts and Letters. He received, as "the foremost living poet," an honorary degree from Yale in 1922, and he was honored also by Bowdoin College and by membership in the American Academy of Arts and Letters. *Tristram,* the third selection of the Literary Guild, accompanied by an appreciative study of the poet by Mark Van Doren, sold, within a few months, twelve thousand copies in the Guild edition and more than fifty thousand in the trade edition. Upon its publication the author was honored by a reception in New York, preceded by a reading by Mrs. August Belmont from the poem. The private edition of *The Torrent and the Night Before* that once went begging has commanded in recent years as much as five hundred dollars for a single copy. He was awarded posthumously the Medal of the International Mark Twain Society.

The quality of his work, and the singleness of his devotion to it, made Robinson widely regarded, at the time of his death, April 6, 1935, as the greatest poet of his time; and his personal reticence, which expressed itself in his never giving lectures or public readings, seemed to confirm the impression. Described by Mabel Dodge Luhan as "without doubt the most inarticulate man I have ever known," and regarded by his friends as shy and aloof, he made poetry his only life for his last twenty-five years. Never a man to pronounce convictions or opinions, he was a fatalist and an agnostic, and this point of view was represented not only in his own work but in his literary enthusiasms, and especially his admiration and love for the work of Hardy.

For further comment, see Critical Survey, pp. 131–32, 135.

BIBLIOGRAPHY

Poems

The torrent and The night before by Edwin Arlington Robinson, Gardiner, Maine, 1889–1896, 1896 (pamphlet); The children of the night, a book of poems, 1897; Captain Craig, a book of poems, 1902 (rev. ed. with additional poems, 1915); The town down the river, a book of poems, 1910; The man against the sky, a book of poems, 1916; Merlin, a poem, 1917; Lancelot, a poem, 1920 (also pub. as Lancelot, a poem . . . special edition of 450 copies for the Lyric society, New York, 1920); The three taverns, a book of poems, 1920; Avon's harvest, 1921; Roman Bartholow, 1923; The man who died twice, 1924; Dionysus in doubt, a book of poems, 1925; Tristram, 1927; Fortvnatvs, 1928; Sonnets, 1889–1927, 1928; Three poems, 1928; Cavender's house, 1929; Modred, a fragment, 1929; The prodigal son, 1929 (pamphlet); The glory of the Nightingales, 1930; The valley of the shadow, 1930; Edwin Arlington Robinson, Poems selected with a preface by Bliss Perry, 1931 (also pub. as An introduction to Edwin Arlington Robinson by Charles Cestre . . . and Selected poems with a preface by Bliss Perry, 1931); Matthias at the door, 1931; Nicodemus, a book of poems, 1932; Talifer, 1933; Amaranth, 1934; King Jasper, a poem . . . with an introduction by Robert Frost, 1935; Hannibal Brown, posthumous poem . . . with illustrations by M. Klinke, 1936 (pamphlet).

Collected Poems

Collected poems, 1921 (also pub. as The collected poems of Edwin Arlington Robinson in two volumes . . ., 1921); Collected poems, The children of the night, Captain Craig, 1927 (vol. 1); Collected poems, The man against the sky, The town down the river, The man who died twice, 1927 (vol. 2); Collected poems, Merlin, Lancelot, Tristram, 1927 (vol. 3); Collected poems, The three taverns, Dionysus in doubt, 1927 (vol. 4); Collected poems, Roman Bartholow, Avon's harvest, 1927 (vol. 5); Collected poems of Edwin Arlington Robinson, 1929 (New ed. complete in 1 vol.); * Collected poems of Edwin Arlington Robinson, 1937 (Complete ed. with additional poems).

Plays

Van Zorn, a comedy in three acts, 1914; The porcupine, a drama in three acts, 1915.

Miscellany

The Peterborough idea, 1917 (cover-title; pamphlet); Thoreau's last letter, with a note on his correspondent, Myron B. Benton . . . Troutbeck leaflets, number five, 1925 (pamphlet).

Music

Slumber song by Edwin Arlington Robinson. Words by Louis V. Ledoux, piano accompaniment by Lewis M. Isaacs, 1935 (cover-title; sheet music).

Verses Set to Music

John Evereldown, words by Edwin Arlington Robinson, music by Lewis M. Isaacs, 1924 (sheet music); Three songs for low voice by Wintter Watts. Song is so old [words by Herman Hagedorn] . . . Miniver Cheevy [words by Edwin Arlington Robinson] . . . Dark hills [words by Edwin Arlington Robinson], 1924 (cover-title; sheet music; 3 vols.); The house on the hill, song, words by Edwin Arlington Robinson, music by Louise Souther, 1932 (cover-title; sheet music); Twilight song, for mixed voices [words by] Edwin Arlington Robinson [music by] Daniel Gregory Mason, 1934 (caption-title; sheet music); Credo, song, words by Edwin Arlington Robinson, music by Louise Souther, 1935 (cover-title; sheet music).

Editor

Selections from the letters of Thomas Sergeant Perry edited with an introduction, 1929.

STUDIES AND ARTICLES

† Beebe, Lucius M. Aspects of the poetry of Edwin Arlington Robinson . . . with a bibliography by Bradley Fisk. 1928

Beebe, Lucius M. Edwin Arlington Robinson and the Arthurian legend. 1927

† Beebe, Lucius M. and Bulkley, Robert J., *comps.* A bibliography of the writings of Edwin Arlington Robinson. 1931

Blankenship

Boynton (H)

Boynton (L)

Boynton (S)

Braithwaite

Braithwaite, William S. The poetic year for 1916, a critical anthology. [c1917]

Brenner

Brown, Rollo W. Next door to a poet. 1937

Bruns

Cestre, Charles. An introduction to Edwin Arlington Robinson. 1930

Coffin, Robert P. New poetry of New England: Frost and Robinson. 1938

† Collamore, Bacon. Edwin Arlington Robinson, 1869–1935, a collection of his works from the library of Bacon Collamore. 1936 (comp. by Bacon Collamore and Lawrance R. Thompson)

Cook

Deutsch

Drinkwater, John. The muse in council being essays on poets and poetry. 1925

Fairclough, Henry R. The classics and our twentieth-century poets, address as president of the American philological association at Harvard university, December 29, 1926. 1927 (pamphlet)

Farrar

Fraser, James E., *comp.* In tribute. 1935

Gorman, Herbert S. The procession of masks. 1923

Green (C)

Hagedorn, Hermann. Edwin Arlington Robinson, a biography. 1938

Hall, James N. The friends. 1939

Halleck

Halperin, Maurice. Le roman de Tristan et Iseut dans la littérature anglo-américaine au XIXe et au XXe siècles. 1931

† Herrmann

Hicks

† Hogan, Charles B. A bibliography of Edwin Arlington Robinson. 1936

Hughes, Merritt Y. Un poeta americano: Edwin Arlington Robinson, traduzione di Benvenuto Cellini. 1930

† Johnson (1929)

† Johnson (1932)

† Johnson (1936)

Jones

Kilmer

Knight, Grant C. American literature and culture. 1932

Kreymborg

Kunitz (L)

Lewisohn (E)

† Lippincott, Lillian. A bibliography of the writings and criticisms of Edwin Arlington Robinson. 1937

Loggins

Lowden

Lowell

Lowell (P)

Lowell (T)

Luhan, Mabel G. Movers and shakers, volume three of Intimate memories. [c1936]

[Macmillan, *firm, publishers, New York.*] Edwin Arlington Robinson. [1927] (pamphlet)

† Manly
Maynard
Monroe
† Morris, Lloyd R. The poetry of Edwin Arlington Robinson, an essay in appreciation . . . with a bibliography by W. Van R. Whitall. [c1923]
Munson (D)
National
Pattee (N)
Phelps
Phelps (AW)
Redman, Ben R. Edwin Arlington Robinson. 1926
Richards, Laura E. E. A. R. 1936
Richards, Laura E. Stepping westward. 1931
Robinson, Edwin A. Collected poems . . . with an introduction by John Drinkwater. [1922]
Rourke
Schelling
† Schwartz (O)
Scott, Winfield T. Elegy for Robinson, a poem. [c1936]
Sessions
Sinclair
Smith
Souther, Louise. The dark hills, song, words by Edwin Arlington Robinson, music by Louise Souther. [c1937] (cover-title; sheet music)
Squire
Tate
† Taylor
Travis, Ralph R. The dark hills, song with piano accompaniment . . . [words by Edwin Arlington Robinson]. [c1936] (cover-title; sheet music)
Untermeyer
Untermeyer (C)
Untermeyer (M)
Untermeyer (N)
Van Doren
Van Doren (A)
Van Doren, Mark. Edwin Arlington Robinson. 1927
Van Doren (R)
Van Doren (T)
Van Doren (W)
Vočadlo
Ward
The Warner library. University edition, The Warner library, in thirty volumes, volume 20. The world's best literature, editors John W. Cunliffe, Ashley H. Thorndike . . . founded by Charles Dudley Warner. 1917
Weirick
Whipple
Wilkinson
Wood
Zabel

Aiken, Conrad. "A letter from America." *Merc.*, June 1922, pp. 196–98; Anonymous. "Edwin Arlington Robinson." *AB.*, Jan. 1923, pp. 565–69; App, Austin J. "Edwin Arlington Robinson's Arthurian poems." *Thought*, Dec. 1935, pp. 468–79; Arns, Karl. "Amerikas grösster lebender dichter im urteil seiner zeitgenossen." *ZFEU.*, Vol. XXVII, 1928, pp. 500–13; Arns. "Edwin Arlington Robinson." *GRM.*, July–Aug. 1924, pp. 224–33; Bates, Robert C. "Edwin Arlington Robinson's 'Three poems.'" *YULG.*, Oct. 1933, pp. 81–82; Beebe, Lucius. "Dignified faun, a portrait of E. A. R." *OI.*, Aug. 27, 1931, pp. 647–50, 677; Blackmur, Richard P. "Verse that is to easie." *P.*, Jan. 1934, pp. 221–25; Bogan, Louise. "Tilbury town and beyond." *P.*, Jan. 1931, pp. 216–21; Bois, Jules. "Le poète américain de la conscience, Edwin Arlington Robinson." *RPL.*, June 16, 1928, pp. 369–74; Boynton, Percy H. "Edwin Arlington Robinson." *EJ.*, Sept. 1922, pp. 383–91; Brown, David. "E. A. Robinson's later poems." *NEQ.*, Sept. 1937, pp. 487–502; Brown. "Some rejected poems of Edwin Arlington Robinson." *AL.*, Jan. 1936, pp. 395–414; Burton, Richard. "Robinson as I saw him." *MTQ.*, Spring 1938, p. 8; Carpenter, Frederic I. "Tristram the transcendent." *NEQ.*, Sept. 1938, pp. 501–23; Cestre, Charles. "Amy Lowell, Robert Frost, and Edwin Arlington Robinson." *JHAM.*, Mar. 1926, pp. 363–88; Cestre. "Avec Edwin Arlington Robinson dans l'"inferno' de l'art." *RAA.*, Apr. 1935, pp. 323–27; Cestre. "Le dernier poème d'E. A. Robinson, 'Cavender's house.'" *RAA.*, Aug. 1929, pp. 489–507; Cestre. "Edwin Arlington Robinson, artiste dans les jeux de l'humour et de la fantaisie." *RAA.*, Feb. 1934, pp. 246–50; Cestre. "Edwin Arlington Robinson, maker of myths." *MTQ.*, Spring 1938, pp. 3–8, 24; Cestre. "L'oeuvre poétique d'Edwin Arlington Robinson." *RAA.*, Apr. 1924, pp. 279–94; Cestre. "Récit, drame et symbole chez Edwin Arlington Robinson." *RAA.*, June 1932, pp. 406–12; Cestre. "Le Tristan d'Edwin Arlington Robinson." *RAA.*, Dec. 1927, pp. 97–110; Cestre. "Le Tristan d'Edwin Arlington Robinson." *RAA.*, Feb. 1928, pp. 219–28; Daly, James. "The inextinguishable god." *P.*, Oct. 1925, pp. 40–44; Daniels, Mabel. "Robinson's interest in music." *MTQ.*, Spring 1938, pp. 15, 24; Deutsch, Babette. "A new light on Lancelot." *P.*, July 1920, pp. 217–19; Drinkwater. "Edwin Arlington Robinson." *YR.*, Apr. 1922, pp. 467–76; Du Bois, Arthur E. "The cosmic humorist." *MTQ.*, Spring 1938, pp. 11–13; Dudley, Dorothy. "Wires and cross-wires." *P.*, May 1924, pp. 96–103; Evans, Nancy. "Edwin Arlington Robinson," *AB.*, Nov. 1932, pp. 675–81; Flint, Frank C. "Matthias at the door." *Symp.*, Apr. 1932, pp. 237–48; Gorman, Herbert S. "Edwin Arlington Robinson." *NR.*, Feb. 8, 1922, pp. 311–13; Gregory, Horace. "The weapon of irony." *P.*, Dec. 1934, pp. 158–61; Hammond, Josephine. "The man against the sky, Edwin Arlington Robinson." *Pers.*, July 1929, pp. 178–84; Henderson, Lawrence J. "Edwin Arlington Robinson (1869–1935)." *PAAAS.*, 1936, pp. 570–73; Hillyer, Robert. "E. A. Robinson and his 'Tristram.'" *Adel.*, Sept. 1928, pp. 90–94; Hogan, Charles B. "A poet at the phonic shrine." *Col.*, Summer 1938, pp. 359–63; † Johnson, Merle D. and Hopkins, Frederick M., *eds.* "American first editions, a series of bibliographic check-lists . . . number 25. Edwin Arlington Robinson, 1869– compiled by H. F. Latham." *PW.*, Mar. 17, 1923, p. 945; Latham, G. W. "Robinson at Harvard." *MTQ.*, Spring 1938, pp. 19–20; Ledoux, Louis V. "Psychologist of New England." *SRL.*, Oct. 19, 1935, pp. 3–4, 16, 18; Le Gallienne, Richard. "Three American poets." *Forum*, Jan. 1911, pp. 80–90; Lowell, Amy. "A bird's-eye view of E. A. Robinson." *D.*, Feb. 1922, pp. 130–42; MacKaye, Percy. "E. A., a milestone for America." *N.Amer.Rev.*, Jan. 1920, pp. 121–27; MacVeagh, Lincoln. "Edwin Arlington Robinson." *NR.*, Apr. 10, 1915, pp. 267–68; Mason, Daniel G., *ed.* "Early letters of Edwin Arlington Robinson." *VQR.*, Jan. 1937, pp. 52–69; Mason, *ed.* "Edwin Arlington Robinson, a group of letters." *YR.*, June 1936, pp. 860–64; Mason, *ed.* "Edwin Arlington Robinson to Daniel Gregory Mason." *VQR.*, Spring 1937, pp. 223–40; Mattiessen, Francis O. "Yeats and four American poets." *YR.*, Spring 1934, pp. 611–17; Maynard, Theodore. "Edwin Arlington Robinson." *CW.*, June 1922, pp. 371–81; Maynard. "Edwin Arlington Robinson." *CW.*, June 1935, pp. 266–75; Monroe, Harriet. "Edwin Arlington Robinson." *P.*, Jan. 1925, pp. 206–17; Monroe. "Mr. Robinson in Camelot." *P.*, July 1917, pp. 211–13; Monroe. "Mr. Robinson's jubilee." *P.*, Feb. 1920, pp. 265–67; Monroe. "On foreign ground." *P.*, Dec. 1927, pp. 160–67; Monroe. "A pioneer." *P.*, Apr. 1916, pp. 46–48; Monroe. "Robinson as man and poet." *P.*, June 1935, pp. 150–57; Monroe. "Robinson's double harvest." *P.*, Aug. 1921, pp. 273–76; Monroe. "Robinson's Matthias." *P.*, Jan. 1932, pp. 212–17; North, Jessica. "A classic of indirection." *P.*, July 1929, pp. 233–36; Peltier, Florence. "Edwin Arlington Robinson, himself." *MTQ.*, Fall 1936, pp. 6, 11–14; Pipkin, Emily. "The Arthur of Edwin Arlington Robinson." *EJ.*, Mar. 1930, pp. 183–95; Preston, John H. "Three American poets, Tristram." *VQR.*, July 1927, pp. 450–62; Robinson, Edwin A. "The first seven years." *Col.*, Part 4, Art. 8, pp. 1–8 (1930); Rosenberg, Harold. "Judgment and passion." *P.*, Dec. 1932, pp. 158–61; Roth, Samuel. "Edwin Arlington Robinson."

AB., Jan. 1920, pp. 507–11; St. Clair, George. "E. A. Robinson and Tilbury town." *NMQ.*, May 1934, pp. 95–107; Schönemann, Friedrich. "Der lyriker der amerikanischen skepsis, Edwin Arlington Robinson." *Die Lit.*, May 1933, pp. 446–48; Scott, Winfield T. "The unaccredited profession." *P.*, June 1937, pp. 150–54; Scott. "Robinson to Robinson." *P.*, May 1939, pp. 92–100; Shepard, Odell. "Poetry in a time of doubt." *YR.*, Spring 1933, pp. 592–95; Sinclair, May. "Three American poets of today." *A.Mo.*, Sept. 1906, pp. 330–33; Stovall, Floyd. "The optimism behind Robinson's tragedies." *AL.*, Mar. 1938, pp. 1–23; Theis, O. F. "Edwin Arlington Robinson." *Forum*, Feb. 1914, pp. 305–12; Tittle, Walter. "Glimpses of interesting Americans, Edwin Arlington Robinson." *Cent.*, June 1925, pp. 189–92; Trent, William P. "A new poetic venture." *SR.*, Apr.–June 1897, pp. 243–46; Van Doorn, Willem. "How it strikes a contemporary." *E.Studies*, Oct. 1926, pp. 129–42; White, Newman I. "Collected poems." *SR.*, July–Sept. 1922, pp. 365–69; Winters, Yvor. "A cool master." *P.*, Feb. 1922, pp. 278–88; Zabel, Morton D. "Edwin Arlington Robinson." *Com.*, Feb. 15, 1933, pp. 436–38; Zabel. "Robinson in America." *P.*, June 1935, pp. 157–62. For references to reviews, see *BRD.*, 1906, 1911, 1914–17, 1920–25, 1927–37.

O(le) E(dvart) Rölvaag, 1876–1931

Born on the Island of Donna, Helgeland, Norway, in a fisherman's hamlet, on April 22, 1876. He came of seafaring folk, and was bred to follow the fishing life. As a boy he read eagerly—his first book was *The Last of the Mohicans*—and went to school a few weeks every year until he was fourteen, when his father withdrew him as not fit for education and placed him in the fisheries, in which the boy spent six years and became a skilled sailor.

At the end of this time, feeling dissatisfied with the future for which he appeared to be groomed and hoping for something better, he refused the offer of the command of a beautiful new boat, borrowed money from an American uncle, and came to the United States, where, in 1896, he began working on his uncle's farm in South Dakota.

He managed by this work to save money and to learn some English, and at twenty-three he began his preparatory study at Augustana (Norwegian Lutheran) College, Canton, South Dakota. He was immensely absorbed in books and learning; and, feeling that at last he had found what he wanted to do, he entered St. Olaf College, Northfield, Minnesota. In 1905, after four years of study and two summers of work as a country salesman, he graduated with honors; and in the same year he borrowed money and returned to Norway for a year of graduate study at the University of Oslo. Upon his return, in 1906, he joined the faculty of St. Olaf College, and he remained there until the year of his death. He was professor of Norwegian, and in 1916 he was made head of the department. In 1908, the year of his marriage, he was naturalized an American citizen.

Even as a small boy he had tried to write, and in his senior year in college he wrote a novel of Norwegian-American life. After his return to this country from Norway he began writing novels in Norwegian. His especial interest was always the position and the life in America of Norwegian immigrants, and he felt that efforts should be made to keep these people from abandoning their native culture. When he read that a Norwegian novelist was planning to write a novel of pioneer life in the Northwest, he took a leave of absence from his classes and spent his time in the Northwest, in London, and in Norway writing such a novel. *Giants in the Earth* (1927) was the result, and an English version, prepared with the help of Lincoln Colcord, brought the author considerable notice in this country.

An admirer of Julia Peterkin and Glenway Wescott in American literature, Rölvaag made Norwegian novelists, Jonas Lie, Knut Hamsun, and Sigrid Undset his models, and attempted to produce scrupulously faithful, realistic work. He read much, and, in addition to his teaching, was from the time of its founding until his death, secretary of the Norwegian-American Historical Association, of which for a time he was president. He belonged also to the Minnesota Educational Association and the Society for the Advancement of Scandinavian Study. In 1926 he was created Knight of the Order of St. Olaf by King Haakon of Norway, and at the Ibsen Centenary, celebrated in 1928, he was a guest of the Norwegian government. On November 5, 1931, less than three months after his resignation of his professorship, he died in Northfield, survived by his wife and two of his four children.

For further comment, see Critical Survey, p. 64.

BIBLIOGRAPHY

Novels

Amerika-breve fra P. A. Smevik til hans far og bror i Norge, samlet ved Paal Mørck [*pseud.*], 1912; Paa glemte veie av Paal Mørck [*pseud.*], 1914; To tullinger et billede fra idag, 1920; Længselens baat, film-billeder, 1921; I de dage—. Fortælling om norske nykommere i Amerika, 1924; I de dage—. Riket grundlægges, 1925 (Sequel to I de dage—. Fortælling om norske nykommere i Amerika); * Giants in the earth, a saga of the prairie by O. E. Rölvaag . . . translated from the Norwegian, 1927 (translated from I de dage; English text by Lincoln Colcord and the author); Peder Seier, 1928; Peder Victorious, a novel by O. E. Rölvaag . . . translated from the Norwegian, English text by Nora O. Solum . . . and the author, 1929 (trans. of Peder Seier, 1928); Pure gold by O. E. Rölvaag, English text by Sivert Erdahl and the author, 1930 (trans. of To tullinger et billede fra idag, 1920); Den signede dag, 1931; Their fathers' God, a novel by O. E. Rölvaag . . . translated from the Norwegian by Trygve M. Ager, 1931 (trans. of Den signede dag, 1931); Rent guld, 1932 (trans. of Pure gold, 1930, which was a rev. English ed. of To tullinger et billede fra idag, 1920); The boat of longing, a novel by O. E. Rölvaag translated from the Norwegian Længselens baat by Nora O. Solum, 1933.

Essays

Omkring fædrearven, 19--.

Textbooks

Haandbok i norsk retskrivning og uttale til skolebruk og selvstudium av P. J. Eikeland og O. E. Rølvaag, 1916; Deklamationsboken samlet og utgit av O. E. Rølvaag, 1918; Norsk læsebok, bind I, for barneskolen og hjemmet av O. E. Rølvaag og P. J. Eikeland, 1919; Norsk læsebok, bind II, for skolen og hjemmet av O. E. Rølvaag og P. J. Eikeland, 1920; Norsk læsebok, bind III, for de høiere skoler og hjemmet, Norge i saga og digtning, av O. E. Rølvaag og P. J. Eikeland, 1925.

STUDIES AND ARTICLES

Dictionary
Job, Thomas. Giants in the earth, a tragedy . . . from the novel by O. E. Rölvaag. 1929.
Jorgenson, Theodore and Solum, Nora O. Ole Edvart Rölvaag, a biography. 1939
Kildal
Kunitz (L)
Norwegian-American historical association. Norwegian-American studies and records, volume VII. 1933
Parrington
Rölvaag, Ole E. Giants in the earth by O. E. Rölvaag, with an introduction by Vernon L. Parrington. [c1929]
White

Anonymous. "Ole Edvart Rölvaag." *ASR.*, Jan. 1932, pp. 7–9; Boynton, Percy H. "O. E. Rölvaag and the conquest of the pioneer." *EJ.*, Sept. 1929, pp. 535–42; Colcord, Lincoln. "Rölvaag the fisherman shook his fist at fate." *A.Mag.*, Mar. 1928, pp. 36–37; Olson, Julius E. "Rölvaag's novels of Norwegian pioneer life in the Dakotas." *SSN.*, Aug. 1926, pp. 45–55. For references to reviews, see *BRD.*, 1927, 1929–31, 1933.

Constance (Mayfield) Rourke, 1885–

Born in Cleveland, November 14, 1885. She graduated at Vassar in 1907 and in that year received a grant from the Borden Fund which enabled her to travel and study abroad. For the next two years she was a student at the Sorbonne and she read diligently in the Bibliothèque Nationale and the library of the British Museum, 1908–10. On her return to this country in 1910 she became an instructor in English at Vassar, and she remained there until 1915. Since then she has engaged independently in "living research" into folk history and customs in America, written books, and contributed to periodicals.

"Whenever possible," she says, describing her methods of study, "I have tried to know the region of which I was writing, and to learn at first hand the traditions from earlier periods which still remain. I have listened extensively to old timers in many parts of the country—old stagecoach drivers, miners, actors, jig dancers, stage-managers, lumberjacks, river-drivers, dulcimer players, ballad-singers, steamboat captains, farmers, plantation owners, and other elderly people who never had a vocation—so extensively that I have sometimes thought that my best vocation was to let members of an older generation pour out their long pent-up autobiographies. Of course I have done this because I like it. I am sure I have wasted a great deal of time in these pursuits. Yet I do feel that this kind of thing is essential if one is to write about American traditions. A good many current theories as to the American character can be upset by this sort of unplotted discussion."

Besides her interest in literature and customs of the people, Miss Rourke confesses to "a lifelong interest in art, with a mounting excitement about American art;" and, as editor, she has directed research and selected material for the *Index of American Design*, the Federal Art Project in which a record is compiled of the arts in American life. "The Index," she declares, "seems to me one of the really momentous cultural enterprises of our period."

She feels very strongly the intimate relation between the folk traditions and national artistic development. Writing in 1935 on the future of American art in the *American Magazine of Art*, Miss Rourke said, "A process of discovery and rediscovery is going on, just now with acceleration, but until the materials of all our culture become known and are easily possessed the creative worker in any of the arts will necessarily be thwarted. . . . Perhaps the American artist cannot now assume those simple and intuitive attitudes which the artist always wants—which most of us want—but he may consciously work toward a discovery of our traditions, attempt to use them, and eventually take his inevitable place."

For further comment, see Critical Survey, pp. 172–73.

BIBLIOGRAPHY

Biography

Trumpets of jubilee: Henry Ward Beecher, Harriet Beecher Stowe, Lyman Beecher, Horace Greeley, P. T. Barnum, 1927; Troupers of the Gold Coast, or, The rise of Lotta Crabtree, 1928; Davy Crockett . . . illustrated by James MacDonald, 1934; * Audubon . . . with 12 colored plates from original Audubon prints, black and white illustrations by James MacDonald, 1936; Charles Sheeler, artist in the American tradition . . . with 48 halftones of paintings, drawings, and photographs by Charles Sheeler, 1938.

Studies

American humor, a study of the national character, 1931.

Editor

The fiftieth anniversary of the opening of Vassar college, October 10 to 13, 1915, a record, 1916 (foreword signed: Constance Mayfield Rourke, chronicler).

ARTICLES

Allen, Gay W. "Humor in America." *SR.*, Jan.–Mar. 1932, pp. 111–13; Kelsey, Vera. "Lotta." *TAM.*, Nov. 1928, pp. 844–45; Weeks, Mangum. "Artist and backwoodsman." *VQR.*, Jan. 1937, pp. 140–43. For references to reviews, see *BRD.*, 1927–29, 1931, 1934, 1936, 1938.

I. S. *See* Isidor Schneider

Carl Sandburg, 1878–

Born in Galesburg, Illinois, the son of Swedish immigrants. His father worked on a railroad construction crew, and the son took odd jobs. He worked on a milk wagon, in a barber shop, in a theater (as sceneshifter), in a brickyard, in hotel kitchens, and in wheat fields, and made his way about the West.

In 1898, when he was a house painter's apprentice in Galesburg, he entered the Spanish-American War and served for eight months in Porto Rico with the Sixth Illinois Infantry. In the army a friend from Lombard College in Galesburg interested him in improving his necessarily limited educational background; and when he returned from war he entered the college. He earned his way by work as tutor, bell ringer, and janitor, and was captain of the basketball team.

In college his ability as a writer found expression in the college paper, of which he was editor-in-chief, and an appreciator in Professor Philip Green

Wright, who organized a Poor Writers' Club for student-writing and criticism and helped Sandburg in the publication of his first book in 1904.

After college and a period of business experience he entered politics and journalism in Milwaukee, where he was an organizer for the Social-Democratic party and from 1910 to 1912 was secretary to the mayor. Moving to Chicago, he became associate editor of the *System Magazine* (1913) and helped N. D. Cochran with an experimental tabloid, the *Daybook*, containing no advertising. It ceased publication in 1917, and Sandburg joined the staff of the *Daily News*. After his trip in 1918 to Norway and Sweden as correspondent for the Newspaper Enterprise Association he was made an editorial writer on the *News*, with relative freedom from administrative interference.

He had continued, in the meantime, to write poetry since his college days. The publication in *Poetry* of a considerable body of his verse in 1914 gave him recognition, and "Chicago" was given the Helen Haire Levinson Prize of two hundred dollars. In 1919 and 1921 he shared the award given by the Poetry Society of America. He traveled about, giving lectures and singing and reading his own work; and he gathered the old ballads and folk songs for *The American Songbag*. In 1933 he left the *News* and retired to his home at Harbert, Michigan, where he lives now on the shore of Lake Michigan and works on his study of Lincoln.

In 1928 he was Phi Beta Kappa poet at Harvard. He holds honorary doctorates from Lombard College, Knox College, and Northwestern University, and is a member of the National Institute of Arts and Letters. He has been also a member of the editorial board of the National Labor Defense Council. In 1939 he was awarded a medal by the Roosevelt Memorial Association for his biography of Abraham Lincoln.

Sandburg has reached a large audience not only through his poetry but also by his singing of folk songs, accompanied on the guitar. Of some of these songs he has made recordings. More than one hundred of the songs in *The American Songbag* had never before seen print, and were acquired by the poet from the lips of pioneers, hoboes, railroad men, and other people.

In an interview published in the New York *Times* at the time of his fifty-ninth birthday, Sandburg said that he regarded modern literature as vastly superior to the literature of his boyhood; and, despite his recognition of the serious problems confronting the present generation, he declared, "I have never seen the time when I had more faith in the human mind and its workings."

For further comment, see Critical Survey, pp. 19, 137, 139–40, 173.

BIBLIOGRAPHY

Poems

Chicago poems, 1916; Cornhuskers, 1918; Smoke and steel, 1920; Slabs of the sunburnt West, 1922; Carl Sandburg, The pamphlet poets, price 25 cents, 1926 (ed. by Hughes Mearns); * Selected poems of Carl Sandburg edited by Rebecca West [*pseud.*], 1926; Good morning, America, 1928; * The people, yes, 1936.

Biography

Abraham Lincoln, the prairie years . . . with 105 illustrations from photographs and many cartoons, sketches, maps, and letters, 1926 (2 vols.); Steichen, the photographer, 1929; Mary Lincoln, wife and widow. Part I by Carl Sandburg. Part II, letters, documents, & appendix by Paul M. Angle, 1932; Abraham Lincoln, the war years . . . with 414 half-tones of photographs, and 249 cuts of cartoons, letters, documents, volume one [–four], 1939.

Children's Books

Rootabaga stories . . . illustrations and decorations by Maud and Miska Petersham, 1922; Rootabaga pigeons . . . illustrations and decorations by Maud and Miska Petersham, 1923; Abe Lincoln grows up . . . reprinted from "Abraham Lincoln: the prairie years," with illustrations by James Daugherty, 1928; Rootabaga country, selections from Rootabaga stories and Rootabaga pigeons . . . with illustrations by Peggy Bacon, 1929; Early moon . . . illustrated by James Daugherty, 1930; Potato face, 1930.

Social Study

The Chicago race riots, July, 1919 . . . with an introductory note by Walter Lippmann, 1919 (pamphlet).

Verses Set to Music

Prairie waters by night . . . [words by] Carl Sandburg [music by] Constance Mills Herreshoff, 1929 (caption-title; sheet music); Under the harvest moon . . . [words by] Carl Sandburg [music by] Constance Mills Herreshoff, 1929 (caption-title; sheet music).

Miscellany

In reckless ecstasy [by] Charles A. Sandburg, 1904 (pamphlet; foreword by Philip G. Wright); Incidentals, 1908? (pamphlet); Abraham Lincoln, the prairie years, a prospectus, 1926 (pamphlet); If Lincoln had lived, addresses by M. Llewellyn Raney, Lloyd Lewis, Carl Sandburg, William E. Dodd, 1935; A Lincoln and Whitman miscellany, 1938.

Editor

The American songbag, 1927.

STUDIES AND ARTICLES

Aiken
Blankenship
Bowdoin
Boynton
Boynton (L)
Boynton (S)
Brenner
Bruns
Combs
Compton, Charles H. Who reads Carl Sandburg? [1929] (pamphlet)
Compton, Charles H. Who reads what? Essays on the readers of Mark Twain, Hardy, Sandburg, Shaw, William James, the Greek classics . . . with an introduction by Dorothy Canfield Fisher. 1934
Cook
Cowley
Dell
Deutsch
† Ford (E)
Frank (O)
Frank (T)
Gard
Graham

Hackett
Halleck
Hansen
Hansen, Harry. Carl Sandburg, the man and his poetry. [c1925] (pamphlet)
Herrmann
† Johnson (1929)
† Johnson (1932)
† Johnson (1936)
Jones
Karsner
Kreymborg
Kreymborg, Alfred. Troubadour, an autobiography. 1925
Kunitz (L)
Lewisohn (E)
Loggins
Lowell
Lowell (P)
Lowell (T)
Lundkvist
† Manly
Markey
Maynard
Monroe
National
Pattee (N)
Phelps
Rascoe
Rosenfeld (P)
Sandburg, Carl. Abe Lincoln grows up, with introduction and notes by Max J. Herzberg. 1931
Schelling
Schyberg
Sherman
Sherman (M)
† Taylor
Tietjens
Untermeyer
Untermeyer (C)
Untermeyer (M)
Untermeyer (N)
Van Doren
Van Doren (A)
† Van Doren (M)
Vočadlo
Ward
Weirick
Whipple
Widdemer
Wood
Zabel

Anonymous. "The poet of American industrialism." *Liv.Age*, Jan. 22, 1921, pp. 231–34; Arvin, Newton. "Carl Sandburg." *NR.*, Sept. 9, 1936, pp. 119–21; Benjamin, Paul L. "A poet of the commonplace." *Survey*, Oct. 2, 1920, pp. 12–13; Boynton, Percy H. "The voice of Chicago, Edgar Lee Masters and Carl Sandburg." *EJ.*, Dec. 1922, pp. 610–20; Carnevali, Emanuel. "Our great Carl Sandburg." *P.*, Feb. 1921, pp. 266–72; Carnevali. "The Sandburg-Sarett recital." *P.*, Feb. 1920, pp. 271–72; Coffin, Robert P. T. "Poets of the people." *VQR.*, Jan. 1937, pp. 126–31; Compton, Charles. "Who reads Carl Sandburg?" *SAQ.*, Apr. 1929, pp. 190–200; Cowley, Malcolm. "Two American poets." *D.*, Nov. 1922, pp. 563–67; Deutsch, Babette. "Poetry for the people." *EJ.*, Apr. 1937, pp. 265–74; Gregory, Horace. "Sandburg's salutation." *P.*, Jan. 1929, pp. 214–18; Hansen, Harry. "Carl Sandburg, poet of the prairie." *Pict.Rev.*, Sept. 1925, pp. 114–18; Holcomb, Esther L. "Whitman and Sandburg." *EJ.*, Sept. 1928, pp. 549–55; † Johnson, Merle D. and Hopkins, Frederick M., *eds.* "American first editions, a series of bibliographic check-lists . . . number 17. Carl Sandburg, 1878, compiled by Frederic G. Melcher." *PW.*, Jan. 20, 1923, p. 149; Jones, Howard M. "Backgrounds of sorrow." *VQR.*, Jan. 1927, pp. 111–23; Jones, Llewellyn. "Carl Sandburg, formalist." *AR.*, July–Aug. 1924, pp. 356–62; Kreymborg, Alfred. "Carl Sandburg's new book." *P.*, Dec. 1918, pp. 155–61; Loeber, William. "The literary tough." *DD.*, Feb. 1922, pp. 105–07; Lunderbergh, Holger. "Carl Sandburg." *ASR.*, Spring 1938, pp. 49–51; Monroe, Harriet. "Carl Sandburg." *P.*, Sept. 1924, pp. 320–26; Monroe. "Chicago granite." *P.*, May 1916, pp. 90–93; Monroe. "His home town." *P.*, Sept. 1922, pp. 332–38; Munson, Gorham B. "The single portent of Carl Sandburg." *DD.*, Oct. 1924, pp. 17–26; Nash, James V. "Carl Sandburg, an American Homer." *OC.*, Oct. 1930, pp. 633–39; Pawlik, Martin. "Smoke and steel." *E.Studien*, Mar. 1928, pp. 415–20; Rascoe, Burton. "Carl Sandburg." *Lit.Rev.*, Sept. 27, 1924, pp. 1–2; Rosenfeld, Paul. "Carl Sandburg." *AB.*, July 1921, pp. 389–96; † Schenk, William P., *comp.* "Carl Sandburg—a bibliography." *BBDI.*, Sept.–Dec. 1936, pp. 4–7; Search-light, *pseud.* *N.Yer.*, Nov. 14, 1925, pp. 13–14; Skinner, Constance L. "Songs that give reason for singing." *N.Amer.Rev.*, Dec. 1926, pp. 695–700; Van Doren, Carl. "Flame and slag, Carl Sandburg, poet with both fists." *Cent.*, Sept. 1923, pp. 786–92; West, Rebecca. "The voice of Chicago." *SRL.*, Sept. 4, 1926, pp. 81–83; Yust, Walter. "Carl Sandburg, human being." *AB.*, Jan. 1921, pp. 285–90; Zabel, Morton D. "Sandburg's testament." *P.*, Oct. 1936, pp. 33–45. For references to reviews, see *BRD.*, 1916, 1918, 1920, 1922–23, 1926–30, 1932, 1936, 1938.

Charles August Sandburg. *See* Carl Sandburg

George Santayana, 1863–

Born in Madrid, December 16, 1863, the son of Spanish parents. His mother had three children by a previous marriage to an American, and had pledged herself to bring them up, in case of their father's death, in Boston, where they had relatives and property. George Santayana, accordingly, was taken to Boston in 1872 and placed in a kindergarten, in which he readily learned English by ear so thoroughly that he was able to speak it without noticeable accent.

He was sent to the Brimmer School, the Boston Latin School, and Harvard. Traditionally affiliated with the Catholic Church, although he has never been a practicing Catholic and refuses to trust completely any religious creed, he found religion more interesting than scholarship or learning, which he regarded as a means and never an end. At Harvard he studied with Josiah Royce, William James, and George Herbert Palmer. Graduating in 1886, he went to Germany for two years of advanced work at Berlin and studied with Paulsen.

He returned to Harvard and began teaching philosophy in 1889. He remained until 1912, becoming one of the most notable men in the university. A year's leave of absence in 1896–97 enabled him to spend time in study at Cambridge; in 1905–06 he was Hyde Lecturer at the Sorbonne, and in 1923 he was Spencer Lecturer at Oxford. Among his students were Conrad Aiken, T. S. Eliot, Felix Frankfurter, and Walter Lippmann.

Although he enjoyed teaching and was a popular lecturer, he disliked the academic tradition of scholarship; and upon receiving an inheritance he resigned his professorship in 1912 and went to Oxford to live. After the war he went to Paris, and later he moved to Rome, where he lives quietly by himself.

In the course of the years he has written poetry, works of aesthetic and religious analysis, and philosophy. His philosophical books have received as much attention for their literary qualities as for their thought. Hugo Münsterberg considered *The Sense of Beauty* the best book on aesthetics ever written in this country, and *The Life of Reason* won praise from William James and many other philosophers. *The Last Puritan*, occupied with moral problems, is the author's only novel. Not only did it receive a great deal of discussion, but it enjoyed a wide sale and was the February, 1936, choice of the Book-of-the-Month Club.

Santayana regards his naturalism as the result, not of academic thought, but of personal experience and self-analysis. Although he has been especially interested in art, he feels that there is no such thing as a separate philosophy of aesthetics or a real distinction between moral and aesthetic values. Beauty springs from the moments when through intuition one perceives a broad synthesis of experience. The attainment of this sort of intuitive experience has been the object of Santayana's philosophy.

For further comment, see Critical Survey, pp. 40, 131.

BIBLIOGRAPHY

Essays and Studies

Platonism in the Italian poets . . . written for the Contemporary club and read at the meeting of February fifth, eighteen hundred and ninety-six, 1896? (pamphlet); * The sense of beauty, being the outlines of æsthetic theory, 1896; Interpretations of poetry and religion, 1900; The life of reason, or, The phases of human progress . . . Introduction and Reason in common sense, 1905 (vol. I); The life of reason, or, The phases of human progress . . . Reason in society, 1905 (vol. II); The life of reason, or, The phases of human progress . . . Reason in religion, 1905 (vol. III); The life of reason, or, The phases of human progress . . . Reason in art, 1905 (vol. IV); The life of reason, or, The phases of human progress . . . Reason in science, 1906 (vol. V); Three philosophical poets: Lucretius, Dante, and Goethe, 1910; Winds of doctrine, studies in contemporary opinion, 1913; Egotism in German philosophy, 1916; The British academy, third annual philosophical lecture, Henriette Hertz trust. Philosophical opinion in America . . . ⟨From the Proceedings of the British Academy, vol. VIII⟩, 1918 (pamphlet); Character & opinion in the United States with reminiscences of William James and Josiah Royce and academic life in America, 1920; Essays in critical realism, a co-operative study of the problem of knowledge by Durant Drake, Arthur O. Lovejoy, James Bissett Pratt, Arthur K. Rogers, George Santayana, Roy Wood Sellars, C. A. Strong, 1920; Little essays drawn from the writings of George Santayana by Logan Pearsall Smith with the collaboration of the author, 1920; Soliloquies in England and later soliloquies, 1922; * Scepticism and animal faith, introduction to a system of philosophy, 1923; The unknowable, the Herbert Spencer lecture delivered at Oxford, 24 October 1923, 1923 (pamphlet); Dialogues in limbo, 1925; Platonism and the spiritual life, 1927; The realm of essence. Book first of Realms of being, 1927; The realm of matter. Book second of Realms of being, 1930; The genteel tradition at bay, 1931; Some turns of thought in modern philosophy, five essays . . . published under the auspices of the Royal society of literature, 1933; Boston Latin school, 1635: 1935, 1935 (leaflet); Obiter scripta, lectures, essays, and reviews by George Santayana edited by Justus Buchler and Benjamin Schwartz, 1936; The philosophy of Santayana, selections from the works of George Santayana, edited with an introductory essay by Irwin Edman, 1936; The realm of truth. Book third of Realms of being, 1937.

Poems

Lines on leaving the Bedford st. schoolhouse, 1880 (caption-title; leaflet); Sonnets and other verses, 1894; A hermit of Carmel and other poems, 1901; Poems . . . selected by the author and revised, 1922.

Novel

* The last Puritan, a memoir in the form of a novel, 1935.

Play in Verse

Lucifer, a theological tragedy, 1899 (rev. ed., Lucifer, or, The heavenly truce, a theological tragedy, 1924).

Verses Set to Music

Ode to the Mediterranean [by] George Santayana [music by] Reginald C. Robbins, 1924 (caption-title; sheet music); The ploughman [by] George Santayana [music by] Reginald C. Robbins, 1924 (caption-title; sheet music).

Translations

The complete writings of Alfred de Musset: Rolla, Novels in verse, Silvia, Stories in verse, The nights, Simone, done into English by George Santayana, Emily Shaw Forman, Marie Agathe Clarke, illustrations by M. Bida, Henri Pille. Volume two. Revised edition, 1907.

Collected Works

The works of George Santayana. Triton edition . . ., 1936–37 (half-title; 14 vols.).

STUDIES AND ARTICLES

American (C)
Ames, Van Meter. Proust and Santayana, the aesthetic way of life. 1937
Archer, William. Poets of the younger generation . . . with thirty-three full-page portraits from woodcuts by Robert Bryden. 1902
Bookman
Brande
Bridges, Robert S. Collected essays, papers &c. of Robert Bridges, XVI The Bible, XVII Bunyan's Pilgrim's progress, XVIII Sir Thomas Browne, XIX George Santayana, XX The glamour of grammar. 1934
Cambridge
Clemens, Cyril. George Santayana: an American philosopher in exile . . . with a foreword by Joseph F. Thorning, S. J. 1937 (pamphlet)
Durant
Durant (S)
Howgate, George W. George Santayana. 1938
† Johnson (1936)
Kunitz (L)
Lewisohn
Lewisohn (E)
MacCarthy
Macy
Mais (W)
† Manly
Morley, Christopher D. The powder of sympathy. 1923
Mueller
Munson (S)
National
Phelps (AW)
Priestley, John B. Figures in modern literature. 1924
Ransom
Rittenhouse (Y)
Rogers
Russell (J)
† Santayana, George. Obiter scripta, lectures, essays, and reviews . . . edited by Justus Buchler and Benjamin Schwartz. 1936
Schelling
[Scribner, *firm, publishers, New York.*] The Triton edition of the complete works of George San-

tayana is strictly limited to nine hundred and forty copies. Twenty copies are for presentation. The edition will be numbered and the first volume of each copy will be signed by Mr. Santayana. [1936] (pamphlet; prospectus)

Sherwood, Margaret P. Undercurrents of influence in English romantic poetry. 1934

Smith (P)

Ten Hoor, Marten. George Santayana's theory of knowledge. [1923] (cover-title; pamphlet)

Untermeyer

Van Doren

Van Doren (A)

† Van Doren (M)

Voegelin, Erich. Ueber die form des amerikanischen geistes. 1928

Watkin, Edward I. Men and tendencies. 1937

Wickham, Harvey. The unrealists, James, Bergson, Santayana, Einstein, Bertrand Russell, John Dewey, Alexander, and Whitehead. 1930

Aaron, Daniel. "A postscript to The last puritan." *NEQ.*, Dec. 1936, pp. 683–86; Anonymous. "Professor Miller and Mr. Santayana." *HGM.*, Sept. 1921, pp. 32–36; Buchler, Justus. "First novels by two poets, George Santayana's 'The last puritan.'" *NEQ.*, June 1936, pp. 281–85; Canby, Henry S. "The American Santayana." *SRL.*, Apr. 17, 1937, pp. 3–4, 14; Clyne, Anthony. "George Santayana." *Bookm.*, Apr. 1926, pp. 11–13; Cohen, Morris R. "On American philosophy, George Santayana." *NR.*, July 21, 1920, pp. 221–23; Cory, Daniel M. "The later philosophy of Mr. Santayana." *Crit.*, Apr. 1936, pp. 379–92; Cory. "A study of Santayana, with some remarks on critical realism." *J.Phil.S.*, July 1927, pp. 349–64; Costello, Harry T. "Philosophy as literature." *YR.*, Oct. 1926, pp. 174–76; De Ruggero, Guido. "Note, sulla piu recente filosofia europea e americana." *Critica*, July 1932, pp. 261–71; Dunbar, Olivia H. "Some critics of the English mind." *YR.*, Oct. 1923, pp. 176–80; Fehr, Bernard. "Zwei angelsächsische ideenromane." *N.S.Rund.*, Mar. 1937, pp. 671–75; Fischer, Walther. "Der letzte puritaner ein philosophischer roman von George Santayana." *Ang.*, May 1938, pp. 437–52; Gilbert, Katherine. "Santayana's doctrine of aesthetic expression." *Phil.Rev.*, May 1926, pp. 221–35; Guérard, Albert, Jr. "The pattern of puritanism." *VQR.*, Apr. 1936, pp. 278–82; Harap, Louis. "A note on moralities in the philosophy of Santayana." *Phil.Rev.*, Nov. 1935, pp. 577–81; Howgate, George W. "Santayana and humanism." *SR.*, Jan.–Mar. 1935, pp. 49–57; Joad, Cyril E. M. "A criticism of critical realism." *Monist*, Oct. 1922, pp. 520–29; Kallen, Horace M. "America and the life of reason." *J.Phil.*, Sept. 29, 1921, pp. 533–51; Kallen. "America and the life of reason." *J.Phil.*, Oct. 13, 1921, pp. 568–75; Knickerbocker, William S. "Asides and soliloquies." *SR.*, Apr.–June 1936, pp. 129–34; Lamprecht, Sterling P. "Naturalism and agnosticism in Santayana." *J.Phil.*, Oct. 12, 1933, pp. 561–74; Lamprecht. "Santayana then and now." *J.Phil.*, Sept. 27, 1928, pp. 533–50; Lane, James W. "The dichotomy of George Santayana." *CW.*, Oct. 1934, pp. 20–28; Larrabee, Harold A. "George Santayana, American philosopher?" *SR.*, Apr.–June 1931, pp. 209–21; Larrabee. "George Santayana, philosopher for America?" *SR.*, July–Sept. 1931, pp. 325–39; Larrabee. "Robert Bridges and George Santayana." *A.Schol.*, Mar. 1932, pp. 167–82; Leavis, Queenie D. "The critical writings of George Santayana, an introductory note." *Scrut.*, Dec. 1935, pp. 278–95; Le Boutillier, Cornelia G. "Spiritual life, Santayana's approach to essence." *Philos.*, Oct. 1936, pp. 433–44; Lee, Muna. "Bronze of Syracuse." *P.*, Mar. 1924, pp. 338–41; MacCampbell, Donald. "Santayana's debt to New England." *NEQ.*, June 1935, pp. 203–14; McDowall, Arthur. "Three philosopher-prophets, Dean Inge, Bertrand Russell, George Santayana." *Liv.Age*, July 23, 1921, pp. 200–08; MacLeish, Archibald. "Santayana, the poet." *AB.*, Oct. 1925, pp. 187–89; Miller, Dickinson S. "Mr. Santayana and William James." *HGM.*, Mar. 1921, pp. 348–64; Mumford, Lewis. "Mr. Santayana's philosophy." *Freeman*, May 23, 1923, pp. 258–60; Münsterberg, Margaret. "Santayana and his pilgrim's progress." *AM.*, May 1936, pp. 115–20; Münsterberg. "Santayana at Cambridge." *AM.*, Jan. 1924, pp. 69–74; Murry, John M. "Mr. Santayana on the United States." *Liv.Age*, Jan. 29, 1921, pp. 300–03; Noxon, Frank W. "College professors who are men of letters." *Critic*, Feb. 1903, pp. 129–31; O'Neill, George. "Poetry, religion and Professor Santayana." *Studies*, Sept. 1921, pp. 451–63; Randall, John H., Jr. "The latent idealism of a materialist." *J.Phil.*, Nov. 19, 1931, pp. 645–60; Ransom, John C. "Art and Mr. Santayana." *VQR.*, Summer 1937, pp. 420–36; Ratner, Joseph. "George Santayana, a philosophy of piety." *Monist*, Apr. 1924, pp. 236–59; Ratner. "George Santayana's theory of religion." *J.Relig.*, Sept. 1923, pp. 458–75; Saglio, Hugo T. "Implications of the life of reason." *J.Phil.*, Sept. 24, 1931, pp. 533–44; Smith, Herbert W. "George Santayana." *AR.*, Mar.–Apr. 1923, pp. 190–204; Ten Hoor, Marten. "George Santayana's theory of knowledge." *J.Phil.*, Apr. 12, 1923, pp. 197–211; Trueblood, Charles K. "A rhetoric of intuition." *D.*, May 1928, pp. 401–04; Van Doren, Carl. "The tower of irony, George Santayana, ambassador to the barbarians." *Cent.*, Oct. 1923, pp. 950–56; Watkin, Edward I. "The philosophy of George Santayana." *Dub.Rev.*, Jan.–June 1928, pp. 32–45; Wecter, Dixon. "The Harvard exiles." *VQR.*, Apr. 1934, pp. 244–57. For references to reviews, see *BRD.*, 1906–07, 1910, 1913, 1916–17, 1920, 1922–23, 1925, 1927–28, 1930–31, 1933, 1936, 1938.

Lew (R.) Sarett, 1888–

Born in Chicago, May 16, 1888, of mixed European parentage. When he was eight or nine, the family moved to Marquette, Michigan, on Lake Superior, where his father took a foreman's job in the State prison and the little boy made his first acquaintance with nature; but when he was twelve he was brought back to the city and, because of the absence of his father, obliged to help support his mother, with whom he lived in a tenement. He worked in department stores, sold newspapers, and ran errands for a factory. Upon the return of his father and improvement in the family financial position he was taken, at about fourteen, to Benton Harbor, Michigan, where he did farm work and attended high school.

At eighteen, having saved a drowning person in Michigan, he was made a lifeguard in a Chicago park; and he worked in a summer camp in Wisconsin and for several seasons guided sportsmen through the Chippewa country. He has also been a government ranger in the Rocky Mountains and national parks.

Thus he earned money for college. After a year at the University of Michigan he accepted a position as assistant physical director at Beloit College and graduated in 1911. He proceeded to the Harvard Law School, where, during the next year, he supported himself by teaching English in a settlement house, coaching club athletics, and teaching business law. In the fall of 1912 he went to the University of Illinois as an instructor in English and public speaking. In 1916, the year when he took his law degree, he was made head of the division of public speaking, and in 1918 became associate in English.

Feeling that teaching afforded more freedom than the legal profession, he made no effort to enter the law but accepted an associate professorship of oratory at Northwestern University in 1920, leaving Illinois in spite of the petition of three or four thousand students asking him to remain. Since 1921 he has been professor of argumentation and persuasion in the Northwestern University School of Speech. From 1926 until 1930 he lived at Laona, Wisconsin, in order to write, and commuted some six hundred miles every week to teach in Evanston during the three months of his duties there. Since 1930 he has been teaching full-time and living in Ravinia.

Sarett has been writing poetry since 1912, when his feeling for nature prompted him to begin. He has enjoyed the encouragement of Stuart P. Sherman, Harriet Monroe, and Carl Sandburg; and he is an admirer of their work and that of the Benéts, Edna St. Vincent Millay, and Louis Untermeyer. In 1921 he was awarded the Helen Haire Levinson Prize, given by *Poetry*, for "The Box of God," and *Slow Smoke* received the award of the Poetry Society of America for 1925. Since 1921 he has been advisory editor of *Poetry*. For many years he has given lectures, not only on literature, but on the North, Indians, wild life, and similar subjects. In 1924 he delivered a commemoration ode on the occasion of the dedication of the War Memorial Stadium at the University of Illinois; and in 1926 he was given an honorary doctorate in letters by Baylor University.

A fine athlete, Sarett is an expert canoeist, and in 1919 he was adopted by the Chippewa Indians in a tribal ceremony and given a name meaning "Lone Caribou." He attributes his fearlessness to his conscious efforts at conquering fear and his consequent mastery over himself. Although he enjoys writing, teaching, and giving lectures, he remains loyal to the outdoors and the Indians and other people of the North woods; and these interests are reflected in his writings.

"The only thing worth remembering in life," writes Sarett, "is the poetry in it. A layman might be disposed to question that statement. He will not doubt it if he understands what poetry is, or means. The essential ingredient of poetry is beauty, fresh beauty. Poetry is a record of the beauty and the implications which sensitive, observant men have salvaged from life. . . . Take out of life the poetry—the beauty—of nature, of her varied seasons and their freight of loveliness; take out of life the beauty of man's struggle to understand and to control nature, her lightning and floods, her tremendous forces for good or for evil; take out of life the beauty of man's bitter but heroic struggle for survival, with bugs and blights, with hardships and obstacles; take out of life the beauty of man's cries in that struggle for survival, of his prayers and weeping, of his laughter and ecstasy and triumphant shouting, recorded in the lyrics of our literature; take out of life the homely beauty of his daily routine, of his gardens and books, of his home and his children and his friends; take out of life the beauty of his aspirations, of the religions and philosophies that sustain him in his conflict, that give meaning and order to this bewildering life and bewildering universe; take out of life these aspects of poetry, and a hundred others which I could mention—then what is there left worth living for, remembering, or fighting for?"

For further comment, see Critical Survey, p. 140.

BIBLIOGRAPHY

Poems

Many many moons, a book of wilderness poems . . . with an introduction by Carl Sandburg, 1920; The box of God, 1922; Slow smoke, 1925; Fir of the Yule, 1931 (pamphlet; repr. from Wings against the moon); Wings against the moon, 1931.

Textbooks

Basic principles of speech by Lew Sarett . . . and William Trufant Foster, 1936 (also pub. as Personal power through speech, 1937); Modern speeches on basic issues compiled and edited by Lew Sarett . . . and William Trufant Foster, 1939.

STUDIES AND ARTICLES

Hansen
[Holt, Henry, and company, *firm.*]
Wings against the moon by Lew Sarett. [1931] (cover-title; leaflet)
Kunitz
Monroe
National
Zeitlin

Frink, Maurice. "Out a'fishing with Lew Sarett." *Nature*, Aug. 1930, pp. 113–16; Henderson, Alice C. "Tall timber and a loon." *P.*, Dec. 1920, pp. 158–61; McCole, Camille J. "Lew Sarett." *W.*, May 1929, pp. 120–23; Monroe, Harriet. "Beasts and humans." *P.*, Dec. 1931, pp. 155–57; Monroe. "A contrast." *P.*, Mar. 1923, pp. 325–30; Monroe. "Lew Sarett and our aboriginal inheritance." *P.*, Nov. 1925, pp. 88–95. For references to reviews, see *BRD.*, 1920, 1922, 1925, 1931, 1937.

William Saroyan, 1908–

Born in Fresno, California, August 31, 1908, the son of an Armenian immigrant who had been a teacher and writer in his own country, and who died when William Saroyan was still young. The boy attended public schools until he was fifteen. At eight he began selling papers; at thirteen he became a telegraph boy and worked every day from afternoon until midnight. When he was sixteen he joined the Japanese and Mexicans pruning grapevines in his uncle's vineyard.

In the meantime he had been reading widely in public libraries and learning to use the typewriter; he began writing at about nine. "I mean I began to write. I didn't think of writing, I did it." "A few years later," he writes, "I began to read writers who were said to be great. I found them sometimes great, but very often quite the contrary. This was so, I reasoned, because they hadn't had daring enough to do (a) what they needed to do, and (b) what they felt like doing. They had done what they had been directly or indirectly instructed to do by the world. I decided not to make this error. In order to write the way the world wanted me to write I would have to work twice and three times as hard as I would have to work writing the way I wished to write, so I decided to write the way I wished to write. So far this is the only way I have written. Of course it took me a long time to get myself recognized."

In 1933 a short story was published in an Armenian newspaper; and in 1934 *Story* began publishing his work. Since then he has written some three hundred short stories, of which more than one hundred have appeared in American magazines and in books. "Offhand," he declares, "my performance would seem to be the consequence of great industry. The contrary, however, is true."

The success of *The Daring Young Man on the Flying Trapeze* enabled him to spend the summer of 1935 traveling in Russia and Armenia. Now he lives on his uncle's grape farm in the San Joaquin valley, California. "I spend most of my time loafing, walking to the ocean or around town, shooting rotation pool, drinking, playing poker, betting on the horses, and so on. I seldom read. The stuff bores me."

"In my opinion," Saroyan writes, "I am what is known as a natural-born writer. That is to say, although strictly speaking I don't know anything about anything, let alone literature, I can write and do, sometimes greatly, and in my opinion never utterly ungreatly. . . . My personal theory about literature and everything else is this: that the only thing that matters is the man himself. In my opinion he ought to be one who knows as much as the next man about everything, which is so little it amounts to nothing, and at the same time be able to smile, if not laugh. I was born with a very loud laugh." "I am not a hard worker. The mere thought of working irritates me. I have no regular hours. I do not follow a program. I write only when I feel like writing and when I feel like writing I write swiftly, easily and without any of the agony which is supposed to accompany the activity of writing. I write each of my short stories in from one to three hours. Once in a while I spend four or five hours on a story, but not often. I write directly on the typewriter and write a story only once. If a story isn't right I throw it in the closet and write another. I have enough notes and ideas to keep me reasonably busy for the rest of my life, if I live to be one hundred and seventeen years of age. In addition to these notes and ideas, new notes and new ideas come up every day. If I feel like writing I can write anywhere. . . . I never use a dictionary. . . . I know nothing about formal grammar and punctuation. I have a system of grammar and punctuation of my own. The basis of this system is to be lucid and to put down one idea at a time. . . . I never talk about writing. I speak the same language any other loafer speaks. I don't enjoy the company of writers or any other kind of people who fancy they are special, although I know quite a few writers who would no more think of talking about writing than I would."

For further comment, see Critical Survey, pp. 96–97.

BIBLIOGRAPHY

Short Stories

* The daring young man on the flying trapeze and other stories, 1934; Inhale & exhale, 1936; Three times three, 1936; The gay and melancholy flux, 1937; Little children, 1937; Love, here is my hat, 1938; A native American . . . illustrated by 'hans,' 1938; The trouble with tigers, 1938; Peace, it's wonderful, 1939.

Plays

My heart's in the highlands, a play, 1939 (pref. by Harold Clurman); The time of your life, 1939.

Pamphlets

A Christmas psalm, 1935, 1935; Those who write them and those who collect them, 1936.

STUDIES AND ARTICLES

McCole

Fadiman, Clifton. "71 varieties." *N.Yer.*, Feb. 22, 1936, pp. 67–69; Hatcher, Harlan. "William Saroyan." *EJ.*, Mar. 1939, pp. 169–77. For references to reviews, see *BRD.*, 1934, 1936–39.

Isidor Schneider, 1896–

Born August 25, 1896, in Horodenko (Poland), then a part of Austria-Hungary. In 1902 he was brought to this country, and his family settled on the East Side in New York. He was a gifted boy and in early childhood showed artistic talent.

He attended public schools and the College of the City of New York. In 1918 he left college and entered the publishing business. Since then he has written poetry, fiction, and criticism, and has become an informed student of Chinese culture. He has contributed to the *Nation*, the *New Republic*, *Poetry*, the *Dial*, and other magazines. He has also done work in pencil and water color. In 1934 he was given a Guggenheim fellowship.

In reaction against the simplicity that has been the fashion in recent years he thinks that complexity and detail in writing can contribute toward clarity of thought, and he believes that there will be a revival of interest in rhetoric and the mechanisms of style.

BIBLIOGRAPHY

Poems

The temptation of Anthony, a novel in verse and other poems, 1928; Comrade: mister, poems by Isidor Schneider, two pen drawings by Gyula Zilzer, 1934.

Novels

Doctor Transit by I. S., 1925; From the kingdom of necessity, 1935.

Editor

Proletarian literature in the United States, an anthology edited by Granville Hicks, Joseph North, Michael Gold, Paul Peters, Isidor Schneider, Alan Calmer, with a critical introduction by Joseph Freeman, 1935.

STUDIES

Kreymborg Kunitz (L)

For references to reviews, see *BRD.*, 1928, 1934–35.

Evelyn (D.) Scott, 1893–

Born in Clarksville, Tennessee, January 17, 1893. She spent her youth in New Orleans, and was educated at the H. Sophie Newcomb Memorial College of Tulane University, to which she was the youngest student to have been admitted; she studied art. Some of her stories were published when she was fourteen.

In 1913, when she was twenty, she left the United States and lived for three hard years in "exile" in Brazil with Cyril Kay Scott, whom she married. After her return she worked at her writing. She has lived in Bermuda, Canada, and Europe. In 1928 she married John Metcalfe, an English author. She was awarded a Guggenheim fellowship in 1932.

"During twenty-four years," she wrote in 1937, "I have spent some five years in the U.S.A.; and conclude, after this experience, that expatriatism does not, in any true sense, exist. Such absences, though they preclude regional enthusiasms, make one recognize one's self more, not less, American. There is, however, with the gain in perspective, a loss in contentment. . . . Once America was overmodest in an unexamining acceptance of European culture; but the present 'healthier' insistence on indigenous products, while it will doubtless lead to better things, hasn't, it seems to me, elevated the standard for art or an intellectual out-put. At present, all the fallacies of Democracy (though I continue to dislike dictators with all my heart) are re-emerging as art. . . . I think we incline to distrust and misunderstand what is represented in intellectual attainment as much now as ever.

"I am a confirmed 'escapist' in that I prefer remote places to those over-inhabited; and that I am 'maladjusted' is demonstrated continually by a passion for animals which exceeds any interest I have in my own kind. If circumstances will permit, when I am sixty, I expect to retire to some semi-tropical spot and assemble a zoo. Naturally, with such a temperament, I find the machine age highly uncongenial.

"All my life I have been politically a 'left-winger,' until the present art-propaganda controversy was inaugurated; when I suddenly discovered that a society conducted under the auspices of minds capable of an exclusively propaganda view of art would not be, for me, one worth living in. So I am now in the anomalous category of 'liberals.' Personally I am convinced 'liberalism' implies an outlook, in the long run, far more realistic than either Communism or Fascism; but in the 'short run,' when problems to be solved require action that is both practical and immediate, it does not. Such immediate, practical acts are not art's first concern; but are the concern of the large public, and I often wonder if the artist, in what I regard as his true sense, is not under threat of being wiped out. However, a Utopia for artists has probably been as remote in one era as in another—even further off than it seems for most people. I think the material of a vital art is 'realistic' in its sources (whatever the individual interpretation), and in all significant creative expression there is some reflection from the creator's own times. But 'inspiration' is a quality of personality, and all art utterance—even in the name of a majority—is 'conditioned' in a very individual sense. The logical representation of pure machine culture would be at once formal and characterless."

For further comment, see Critical Survey, pp. 33, 60–61, 179.

BIBLIOGRAPHY

Novels

The narrow house, 1921; Narcissus, 1922 (English ed., Bewilderment, 1922); The golden door, 1925; Migrations, an arabesque in histories, 1927; * The wave, 1929; Blue rum [by] Ernest Souza [*pseud.*], 1930; A calendar of sin, American melodramas, 1931 (2 vols.); Eva Gay, a romantic novel, 1933; Breathe upon these slain, 1934; Bread and a sword, 1937.

Short Stories

Ideals, a book of farce & comedy, 1927.

Poems

Precipitations, 1920; The winter alone, 1930.

Autobiography

Escapade, 1923; Background in Tennessee, 1937.

Children's Books

In the endless sands, a Christmas book for boys and girls by Evelyn and C. Kay Scott, 1925; Witch Perkins, a story of the Kentucky hills, 1929; Billy, the maverick, 1934.

Criticism

On William Faulkner's The sound and the fury, 1929 (pamphlet).

STUDIES AND ARTICLES

Beach (T)
Kunitz (L)
Morley (P)
National
Overton (WW)
Van Doren (R)

Fitts, Dudley. "The verse of Evelyn Scott." *P.*, Sept. 1930, pp. 338–43; Lovett, Robert M. "The evolution of Evelyn Scott." *AB.*, Oct. 1929, pp. 153–56; Radford, Manson. "Bread and a sword." *So.R.*, Spring 1938, pp. 824–28; Ridge, Lola. "Evelyn Scott." *P.*, Mar. 1921, pp. 334–37; Salpeter, Harry. "Portrait of a disciplined artist." *AB.*, Nov. 1931, pp. 281–86. For references to reviews, see *BRD.*, 1921–23, 1925, 1927, 1929–31, 1933–34, 1937.

Search-light, *pseud.* *See* **Waldo Frank**

Anne Douglas Sedgwick, 1873–1935

Born in Englewood, New Jersey, March 28, 1873. When she was nine she was taken to England, and from that time until her death, except for two visits to the United States, she lived in England and France.

She was educated at home by a governess and went to Paris for five years of art study. Her portrait of her sister was hung in the Champs de Mars salon. In 1898 a story of hers was published, and she turned her attention to literature.

She married, in 1908, Basil de Sélincourt, an English writer. They lived in Oxfordshire, in the Cotswolds. Mrs. de Sélincourt worked hard and regularly on her writing and rewriting and sang in the village chorus conducted by her husband. In addition to her novels, she wrote much for magazines. She was a very great admirer of Tolstoy's *War and Peace.* She and her husband both felt the beauty and charm of France, and during the war she served as nurse in a French hospital.

She died July 21, 1935, in Hampstead.

For further comment, see Critical Survey, pp. 25, 66.

BIBLIOGRAPHY

Novels

The dull Miss Archinard, 1898; The confounding of Camelia, 1899; The rescue, 1902; Paths of judgement, 1904; The shadow of life, 1906; A fountain sealed, 1907 (English ed., Valerie Upton, 1907); Amabel Channice, 1908; Franklin Winslow Kane, 1910 (English ed., Franklin Kane, 1910); * Tante, 1911; The encounter, 1914; The third window, 1920; Adrienne Toner, 1921; * The little French girl, 1924; The old countess, 1927; Dark Hester, 1929; Philippa, 1930.

Short Stories

The nest, 1912 (American eds., The nest, The white pagoda, The suicide, A forsaken temple, Miss Jones and the masterpiece, 1913; The nest and other stories, 1926); Christmas roses and other stories, 1920 (English ed., Autumn crocuses, 1920).

Letters

Anne Douglas Sedgwick, a portrait in letters chosen and edited by Basil de Sélincourt, 1936.

Biographical Sketches

A childhood in Brittany eighty years ago . . . with illustrations by Paul de Leslie, 1919.

STUDIES AND ARTICLES

Beach (T)
Forbes, Esther L. Anne Douglas Sedgwick, an interview . . . and appreciations by William Lyon Phelps, Dorothy Canfield, Hugh Walpole, and others. [1928] (pamphlet)
Kunitz (L)
† Manly
National
Overton (H)
Overton (WW)
Phelps (A)
Quinn
Sedgwick

Forbes, Esther. "Anne Douglas Sedgwick and her novels." *AB.*, Aug. 1929, pp. 568–74; Overton, Grant. "The security of Anne Douglas Sedgwick." *AB.*, Apr. 1927, pp. 125–32; Phelps, William L. "Anne Sedgwick, American novelist." *Forum*, Oct. 1924, pp. 515–19; Sélincourt, Basil de, *ed.* "Anne Douglas Sedgwick's letters." *Forum*, Sept. 1936, pp. 111–15. For references to reviews, see *BRD.*, 1906–08, 1910, 1912–14, 1919–22, 1924–25, 1927, 1929–30, 1936.

Mrs. Basil de Sélincourt. *See* **Anne Douglas Sedgwick**

(James) Vincent Sheean, 1899–

Born December 5, 1899, in Christian County, Illinois. He was reared in Pana, Illinois, and his parents, comfortably prosperous, gave him a good education. He read widely in French as well as English and attended the University of Chicago at a time when Elizabeth Madox Roberts and Glenway Wescott were students.

Upon the death of his mother he was compelled to leave the university, after three years and a half of college; and he found a job as reporter on the Chicago *Daily News*. Later he reported for the New York *Daily News*, and in 1922 he went to Paris to serve as European correspondent for the Chicago *Tribune*.

In the three years he spent in this position he reported wars, invasions, conferences, and crises, including the march of the Fascists on Rome, the Lausanne Conference, and Primo de Rivera's becoming dictator in Spain. In the war between Spain and the Riff tribes he interviewed Abd-el-Krim and presented to Rivera the former's demands. When war broke out between France and the Riffs, he went to Er Rif to report for the North American Newspaper Alliance.

The next year he spent in Russia and Persia, and in a time of dissension and trouble he traveled through China. He saw the Hankow massacres and the overthrow of the Hankow government in 1927. After lecturing in the United States in 1927–28 on Morocco and China, he went abroad again and reported the Arab-Jewish riots in Palestine in 1929. In 1930 Sheean was associated with Plymouth World Tours and radio programs broadcast from European capitals.

In more recent years Sheean has spent most of his time on literary work. His autobiography, *Personal History*, the selection of the Literary Guild for February, 1935, was a best-seller and was the book of the month chosen by the London *Evening Standard* for May. It received, by unanimous decision, the non-fiction prize of the Foundation for Literature of the Friends of American Writers, in Chicago. The historical novel *Sanfelice* was the choice of the Literary Guild for July, 1936.

Sheean, who is a gifted linguist and an appreciative lover of music, likes to do his writing in French and Italian villages; his leisure he often enjoys in Paris, where he has many friends. In 1935 he married Diana Forbes-Robertson, daughter of the English actor Sir Johnston Forbes-Robertson. He sympathized warmly with the cause of the Spanish Loyalists, and wrote the narrative commentary for the film, *Crisis*, a documentary of the Nazi march into Czechoslovakia.

For further comment, see Critical Survey, pp. 67, 73, 175.

BIBLIOGRAPHY

Novels

The anatomy of virtue, a novel, 1927 (English ed., The little duchess, 1928); Gog and Magog, a novel, 1930; The tide, a novel, 1933; Sanfelice, a novel, 1936; A day of battle, a novel, 1938.

Short Stories

The pieces of a fan, 1937.

Autobiography

* Personal history, 1935 (English ed., In search of history, 1935).

Travel and Sociological Observation

An American among the Riffi, 1926 (English ed., Adventures among the Riffi, 1926); The new Persia, 1927; Not peace but a sword, 1939 (English ed., The eleventh hour, 1939).

Opera

The Blackfriars, the University of Chicago, present Barbara, behave! Sixteenth annual college comic opera. Producer—E. Mortimer Shuter. Musical direction—Frank E. Barry. Mandel hall, May 21, 22, 28, and 29, 1920, 1920 (written by James V. Sheean and Harold E. Stansbury).

Translations

Medicine man in China by A. Gervais translated from the French, 1934 (English ed., A surgeon's China, 1934); Madame Curie, a biography by Eve Curie, 1937.

For references to reviews, see *BRD.*, 1926–28, 1930, 1933, 1935–38.

Edward (Brewster) Sheldon, 1886–

Born in Chicago, February 4, 1886. He was educated at Harvard, where he took bachelor's (1907) and master's (1908) degrees and studied in Professor Baker's playwriting course.

His knowledge of dramatic technique, derived from study and reading, was so successful that the Harrison Grey Fiskes bought his play *Salvation Nell* when he was fresh from college, even though alterations, cuts, and revisions were necessary before actual production in 1908 with Mrs. Fiske. Later (1931) the play was filmed. *Romance* (1913), played for years by Doris Keane in England and America, was a notable box-office success and was filmed in 1930 with Greta Garbo. *The Jest*, an adaptation from Sam Benelli's *La Cena delle Beffe*, was performed by a cast including both John and Lionel Barrymore; and Katharine Cornell acted in *Dishonored Lady*, in which Sheldon collaborated with Mrs. Margaret Ayer Barnes. In 1936 the authors obtained a court decision against the Metro-Goldwyn Pictures Corporation declaring the motion picture *Letty Lynton* (1932) to be a plagiarism of *Dishonored Lady*.

Sheldon has collaborated also with his nephew Charles MacArthur and with Sidney Howard, and he has made stage adaptations. His writing has been limited by the restrictions imposed by years of illness.

For further comment, see Critical Survey, pp. 100, 123.

BIBLIOGRAPHY

Plays

Salvation Nell, a play in three acts, 1908; The nigger, 1909 (cover-title; anonymous); Egypt, a play in four acts, 1912 (cover-title); The high road, a play in five acts, 1912 (cover-title); * Romance, a play in three acts with a prologue and an epilogue, 1913 (cover-title); "The garden of paradise," a play in nine scenes . . . based on a story of Hans Andersen, 1914; The song of songs, a love story . . . (based upon the novel by Hermann Sudermann), 1914; The boss, 1916.

Novel

The boss by J. W. McConaughy . . . & Edward Sheldon, 1911.

STUDIES AND ARTICLES

Burton
Clark (B)
Davies, Acton. Romance, a novel . . . from the drama by Edward Sheldon with pictures from the play. 1913
Dickinson (P)
Eaton
Eaton, Walter P. Plays and players, leaves from a critic's scrapbook. 1916
Mayorga (S)
Moses (A)
Nathan, George J. Another book on the theatre. 1915
Nathan, George J. Comedians all. 1919
† Quinn (H)
Quinn (R)
"Sheldon et al. v. Metro-Goldwyn pictures corporation et al. Circuit court of appeals, Second circuit, Jan. 17, 1936." *Federal reporter*, second series, 1936, vol. 81, pp. 49–56

Stuart P(ratt) Sherman, 1881–1926

Born in Anita, Iowa, October 1, 1881, of old New England stock. He spent his early childhood on a farm near Rolfe, Iowa, where the family moved in 1882. In 1887, because of his father's tuberculosis, he was taken to Los Angeles. At about this time the boy spent eight months with a gold-prospecting expedition in Arizona; and when he was thirteen, having already had verse published in the Los Angeles *Times* when he was seven, he wrote his autobiography.

After his father's death in 1892 he was brought to Dorset, Vermont. He spent a year in the village school, then proceeded to the Troy Conference Academy at Poultney, Vermont, and high school in Williamstown, Massachusetts. He won recognition as actor, singer, and athlete, as well as in his studies, took a prize in Greek, and in his senior year taught Latin and English. At Williams College, where he took prizes in languages, he was on the staff of the *Williams Literary Monthly* and, in his senior year, editor. He graduated in 1903, salutatorian and "brightest" and "most versatile" man of his class.

For graduate work he went, on a three-year fellowship, to Harvard, where he came under the influence of Irving Babbitt and Humanism. He took the master's degree in English in 1904 and the doctorate in 1906. For his dissertation, which was regarded as the best ever completed in the department at Harvard, he wrote on John Ford's plays.

In the fall of the same year he went to Northwestern University as instructor in English, and in that winter he was married. He proceeded to the University of Illinois in 1907 and after several promotions became head of the English department in 1914. In 1908 he wrote a letter to the *Nation* criticizing methods of graduate study at Harvard. It was widely discussed, and its vigor and force led the editor, Paul Elmer More, to accept essays and verse from Sherman. During the war the author was an enthusiastic supporter of the national policy, and wrote his pamphlet, *American and Allied Ideals*, for the Committee on Public Information.

After almost twenty years of teaching, he left the University of Illinois to become literary editor, in April, 1924, of the New York *Herald Tribune*. In this capacity he became a critical figure of great importance, and his sudden death August 21, 1926, near his summer cottage in Michigan, from heart attack and drowning, removed a powerful personality from contemporary letters.

Sherman was a disciple of Matthew Arnold and the chief critical upholder, as scholar, lecturer, writer, and critic, of the Puritan tradition in the years during and after the war. Although in later years he modified his early view, which had been the result of the influence of Irving Babbitt and Paul Elmer More, and stood champion for Sherwood Anderson and D. H. Lawrence, he is remembered principally for his conservative stand in literature and politics, and his interest in ethical and moral questions in literature.

For further comment, see Critical Survey, pp. 186, 190–91.

BIBLIOGRAPHY

Critical Essays

English and the Latin question, a paper read at the Illinois high school conference, Nov. 24, 1911, 1912 (pamphlet); * On contemporary literature, 1917; Americans, 1922; The significance of Sinclair Lewis, 1922 (cover-title; pamphlet); The genius of America, studies in behalf of the younger generation, 1923; Criticism in America, its function and status, essays by Irving Babbitt, Van Wyck Brooks, W. C. Brownell, Ernest Boyd, T. S. Eliot, H. L. Mencken, Stuart P. Sherman, J. E. Spingarn, and George E. Woodberry, 1924; Men of letters of the British Isles, portrait medallions from the life by Theodore Spicer-Simson, with critical essays by Stuart P. Sherman and a preface by G. F. Hill, 1924; My dear Cornelia, 1924; Points of view, 1924; Critical woodcuts . . . illustrated with portraits engraved on wood by Bertrand Zadig, 1926; The main stream, 1927; Shaping men and women, essays on literature and life . . . edited by Jacob Zeitlin, 1928; Ellen Glasgow, critical essays, 1929 (pamphlet; with Sara Haardt and Emily Clark); The emotional discovery of America and other essays, 1932.

Criticism and Biography

Matthew Arnold, how to know him, 1917.

Novel

Letters to a lady in the country, together with her replies, by Paul and Caroline, with an introduction by Stuart Sherman, 1925 (by Stuart P. Sherman and Garreta Busey).

Letters

Life and letters of Stuart P. Sherman by Jacob Zeitlin and Homer Woodbridge, 1929 (2 vols.).

Miscellany

Porro unum est necessarium, or, The gaiety of Socrates, 1915; American and allied ideals, an appeal to those who are neither hot nor cold . . . Issued by the Committee on public information, Washington, D.C., 1918 (pamphlet).

Editor

Stevenson's Treasure Island, 1911; The tragedy of Coriolanus [by William Shakespeare], 1912; A book of short stories selected and edited, 1914; 'Tis pity she's a whore and The broken heart by John Ford, 1915; The Cambridge history of American literature edited by William Peterfield Trent . . . John Erskine . . . Stuart P. Sherman . . . Carl Van Doren . . ., 1917–21 (4 vols.; English ed., A history of American literature); A short history of American literature based upon the Cambridge history of American literature edited by William Peterfield Trent, John Erskine, Stuart P. Sherman, and Carl Van Doren, 1922; The poetical works of Joaquin Miller edited with an introduction and notes, 1923.

STUDIES AND ARTICLES

American academy of arts and letters. Commemorative tributes to: Metcalf by Royal Cortissoz, Bartlett by Royal Cortissoz, Sherman by Hamlin Garland. Prepared for the American academy of arts and letters, 1927. 1927 (pamphlet)
American (C)
Ashley
Beach
Boynton (C)
Boynton (L)
Calverton (N)
Cleaton
Crockett
De Mille, George E. Literary criticism in America, a preliminary survey. [c1931]
Dictionary
Farrar
Foerster
Foerster (T)
Garland
Green (C)
Hackett
Hough
Kunitz
Lawrence
† Manly
Markey
Munson
National
New York herald tribune Books, Sept. 26, 1926 (In memoriam Stuart Sherman, pp. 13–20)
Rascoe
Saturday
Stahl, John M. Growing with the West, the story of a busy, quiet life. 1930
Stearns
† Van Doren (M)
Van Doren (T)
† Zeitlin, Jacob and Woodbridge, Homer E. Life and letters of Stuart P. Sherman. [c1929] (2 vols.)

Anonymous. "The life and times of Stuart Sherman." *AB.*, Nov. 1929, pp. 289–305; Anonymous. "Professor Sherman's tradition." *Freeman*, Oct. 27, 1920, pp. 151–53; Anonymous. "Stuart P. Sherman." *AB.*, June 1922, pp. 354–58; Anonymous. "Whose flag is it?" *NR.*, Feb. 9, 1921, pp. 304–06; Arvin, Newton. "Stuart Sherman." *HH.*, Apr.–June 1930, pp. 304–13; Burgum, Edwin B. "Stuart Sherman." *EJ.* Col. Ed., Feb. 1930, pp. 137–51; Canby, Henry S. "Stuart P. Sherman, the American scholar." *SRL.*, Oct. 5, 1929, pp. 201–02, 205–06; Carson, Gerald. "Mr. Stuart Sherman discovers Aphrodite pandemos." *AB.*, June 1926, pp. 389–96; De Mille, George E. "Stuart P. Sherman, the Illinois Arnold." *SR.*, Jan.–Mar. 1927, pp. 78–93; Elliott, George R. "Stuart Sherman and the war age." *AB.*, Apr. 1930, pp. 173–81; Foerster, Norman. "The literary historians." *AB.*, July 1930, pp. 365–74; Heaton, Charles. "A philosophical litterateur." *Monist*, Oct. 1918, pp. 608–12; Perry, Bliss. "Stuart Sherman." *YR.*, Dec. 1929, pp. 386–89; Van Doren,

Carl. "The great and good tradition, Stuart P. Sherman, scourge of sophomores." *Cent.*, Aug. 1923, pp. 631–36; Warren, Austin. "Humanist into journalist, Stuart Sherman." *SR.*, July–Sept. 1931, pp. 357–65; Zeitlin, Jacob, *ed.* "Stuart P. Sherman and Paul Elmer More, correspondence." *AB.*, Sept. 1929, pp. 43–53. For references to reviews, see *BRD.*, 1917, 1922–28, 1932.

Robert Emmet Sherwood, 1896–

Born in New Rochelle, New York, April 4, 1896. A precocious child, descending from a family of artistic and political prominence, he edited, at seven, a children's magazine, the *Children's Life;* and, a year later, he abandoned it for the task of rewriting *A Tale of Two Cities*, with a view to improving the dénouement.

He graduated in 1914 from Milton Academy, in Massachusetts, and proceeded to Harvard. He took his degree in 1918 and during the war served at the front in the "Black Watch," the Forty-second Brigade of Royal Highlanders of Canada. He was gassed at Arras and wounded at Amiens, and after his discharge in 1919 he entered upon his editorial career.

The *Vanity Fair* number of the Harvard *Lampoon*, which he had edited, had attracted the attention of the editors of *Vanity Fair*, and in 1919 Mr. Sherwood was given a job as motion-picture critic. At this time Robert Benchley and Dorothy Parker were the dramatic writers on the magazine; and when Mrs. Parker was discharged in 1920 both Benchley and Sherwood resigned their jobs. Mr. Sherwood transferred his column to *Life*, for which he wrote reviews and of which he became an associate editor and later the chief editor. For a time he wrote film criticism for the New York *Herald*.

The success of his play *The Road to Rome* (1927), which was performed all over the country, led him to give up journalism for dramatic work. He has explained the play as a development of his admiration, in childhood, of the character of Hannibal. *Reunion in Vienna*, played by Alfred Lunt and Lynne Fontanne, was a sensational success of the season 1931–32, and received the Megrue Prize for Comedy in 1932. *Idiot's Delight*, an anti-war play, took the Pulitzer Prize for 1935–36, as well as the award of the Drama Study Club, and *Abe Lincoln in Illinois* won the 1938 Pulitzer Prize. With Maxwell Anderson, Samuel Behrman, Sidney Howard, and Elmer Rice he founded, in 1938, the Playwrights' Producing Company, an attempt to finance production of the dramatists' plays without the assistance of the commercial manager. His plays have made successful films, and in 1936 Sherwood spent five months in England writing (with Aben Kandel) and helping film *Thunder in the City*. In 1932, after the success of *Reunion in Vienna*, he traveled in Europe and spent some time writing in Normandy. He has the reputation of thinking out his materials at great length and doing the actual writing in a very short time. He believes that emotion and idealism are necessary and proper in a dramatist.

For further comment, see Critical Survey, p. 115.

BIBLIOGRAPHY

Plays

The road to Rome, 1927 (also pub. as The acting edition of The road to Rome, a play in three acts, 1929); The queen's husband, 1928; Waterloo bridge, a play in two acts, 1930; This is New York, a play in three acts, 1931; * Reunion in Vienna, a play in three acts, 1932; The petrified forest, 1935; * Idiot's delight, 1936; Abe Lincoln in Illinois, a play in twelve scenes . . . with a foreword by Carl Sandburg, 1939.

Novel

The virtuous knight, 1931 (English ed., Unending crusade, 1932).

Moving-Picture Scripts

"The Glourie ghost" [i.e. The ghost goes west], 1936 (mimeographed); How to write and sell film stories by Frances Marion with a complete shooting script for Marco Polo by Robert E. Sherwood, 1937.

Adaptation

Tovarich by Jacques Deval adapted by Robert E. Sherwood, 1937.

Essay

E. V. Lucas, appreciations by John Farrar, R. E. Sherwood, Grant Overton, Llwellyn [!] Jones, with brief notes on his books taken from the press, 1925? (pamphlet).

Editor

The best moving pictures of 1922–23, also Who's who in the movies and the Yearbook of the American screen, 1923.

STUDIES AND ARTICLES

Agate (F)
Brown
Flexner
[Kenyon, Charles and Daves, Delmer L.] "The petrified forest" . . . [screen play by Charles Kenyon and Delmer Daves from the play by R. E. Sherwood]. 1935 (mimeographed)
Kunitz
Lawson
Mantle
Mantle (C)
Moses (A)
Nathan (TM)
Waugh

Isaacs, Edith J. R. "Robert Sherwood, man of the hours." *TAM.*, Jan. 1939, pp. 31–34, 37–40. For references to reviews, see *BRD.*, 1926–27, 1929–32, 1935–36, 1939.

Upton (Beall) Sinclair, 1878–

Born in Baltimore, September 20, 1878, of southern parentage. His ancestors had been British and American naval officers, and his grandfather, two granduncles, three uncles, and his father had all served in the Confederate navy. His mother belonged to a well-to-do family of Maryland.

He was reared in a home of post-war poverty. In 1888 the family moved to New York, and the ten-year-old boy first attended school on the East Side. A lover of books, he was an apt student and finished grammar school, after two years, at twelve. In 1892, after repeating the final year of school because he was too young to enter upon the combined high-school and college course, he enrolled at the College of the City of New York and, refusing an offer of an appointment to the United States Naval Academy, studied to be a lawyer.

A story he wrote while he was in college, however, was accepted for publication by *Argosy* at twenty-five dollars; and from the age of fifteen he supported himself with his pen. Upon graduation (1897) he secured work writing for a popular magazine. He wrote about fifty stories of West Point life for Street and Smith's "Starry Flag Library" and a considerable number of tales of life at Annapolis for the same publishers' "True Blue Library." This hack-writing supported him while he read, practiced the violin, and sampled courses at Columbia, including two given by Edward MacDowell.

In 1900 he retired to the country and wrote a novel. *Springtime and Harvest*, privately published, failed to sell, even when reissued by Funk and Wagnalls as *King Midas;* and, by this time married, the author was forced to support himself by writing potboilers. Borrowing money from a Socialist friend, in 1903, with his wife and child, he moved to the country near Princeton, where he spent three years and a half, much of the time living in a cabin he had helped build, while writing *Manassas* and *The Jungle.* In this same period, having allied himself with the Socialists in 1902, he founded (1905) the Intercollegiate Socialist Society, now the League for Industrial Democracy.

The Jungle, written for a Socialist paper, the *Appeal to Reason*, and based upon seven weeks' observations in Chicago in 1904 of stockyard conditions, was published in book form by the author, who in a month or two took in four thousand dollars, and also by Doubleday, Page and Company. The tremendous interest aroused by this exposé resulted in an investigation instituted by President Theodore Roosevelt, the Pure Food and Drug Act of 1906, and an offer to make Sinclair head of a packing company. The book was a best-seller in both America and England for six months and was translated into seventeen languages.

With the proceeds Sinclair organized a Socialist colony in New Jersey, Helicon Home, in 1906. Among the members was Sinclair Lewis; and John Dewey and William James were visitors. The building was destroyed by fire early in 1907, and Sinclair himself discharged all the debts. Subsequently he was a member of single-tax communities in Alabama and Delaware.

In 1912 he made a trip to Europe. In the Netherlands he secured a divorce from his wife, and he visited Socialists in England and Germany. After his return in 1913 he married Mary Craig Kimbrough. In 1913–14 he called national attention to conditions in the strike in the coal mines of Colorado. *The Brass Check* tells of the author's difficulties in his efforts to secure publicity for the strikers. In 1915 he settled in Pasadena, California, which is still his home.

During the war he resigned from the Socialist party to protest against the anti-war position taken by its leaders in 1917; and in 1918–19 he published *Upton Sinclair's*, a magazine supporting "a clean peace and the internation." Assuming the good faith of the Allied governments, he consistently supported the Wilson administration. He remained, however, an ardent Socialist, and it was the anti-Soviet stand of the American government that disillusioned him. *Jimmie Higgins*, begun as a novel to educate Socialists to the necessity of throwing their support to the Allies, ended with a section designed to convert the readers to a view more sympathetic to the new Russian state.

In 1923, when, in the course of a harbor strike, the right of free speech was denied by Los Angeles police to members of the Industrial Workers of the World, Sinclair was arrested for publicly reading aloud to his associates three sentences from the Constitution guaranteeing freedom of speech. An active member of the Socialist party, Sinclair was a candidate for Congress for New Jersey in 1906; and in California, where he founded the American Civil Liberties Union, he was a candidate for Congress in 1920, for the Senate in 1922, and for governor in 1926 and 1930. In 1934, on the platform of a public-works program of "production for use," designed to "end poverty in California" ("E.P.I.C."), he secured the Democratic nomination for governor of the state. In the election he was defeated.

Sinclair has attributed the vitality of his idealism, which has led him to sacrifice money, health, and position to his causes, to his early realization, as a poor member of a wealthy family, of the evils of inequality and to the influence of the Christian religion nominally professed by his relatives. His interests reach out to matters of health and inquiries concerning mental and spiritualistic phenomena. His stanch advocacy of prohibition he ascribes to his early memories of his father's being a slave to the drinking habit. He has published many of his own books and sold them at low cost or given them away. He was influential in the establishment of the Vanguard Press, dedicated to the publishing of significant books at low prices. He has never deviated from his purpose of exposing the social evils of modern life, and he remains one of the American authors most widely read in Europe.

For further comment, see Critical Survey, pp. 5, 40, 47, 77, 156–57, 196.

BIBLIOGRAPHY

Novels

Springtime and harvest, a romance by Upton B. Sinclair, jr., 1901 (also pub. as King Midas, a romance . . . illustrations by C. M. Relyea, 1901); The journal of Arthur Stirling ("The valley of the shadow") revised and condensed with an introductory sketch, 1903 (anonymous); Prince Hagen, a phantasy, 1903; Manassas, a novel of the war, 1904; A captain of industry, being the story of a civilized man, 1906; * The jungle, 1906; The Metropolis, 1908; The moneychangers, 1908; Samuel the seeker, 1910; Love's pilgrimage, a novel, 1911; Damaged goods, the great play "Les avariés" of Brieux novelized with the approval of the author, 1913; Sylvia, a novel, 1913; Sylvia's marriage, a novel, 1914; King Coal, a novel . . . with an introduction by Dr. Georg Brandes, 1917; Jimmie Higgins, a story, 1919; 100%, the story of a patriot, 1920 (English ed., The spy, 1921); They call me Carpenter, a tale of the second coming, 1922; Little blue book no. 590, edited by E. Haldeman-Julius. The millennium, a comedy of the year 2000, volume I, 1924 (pamphlet); Little blue book no. 591, edited by E. Haldeman-Julius. The millennium, a comedy of the year 2000, volume II, 1924 (pamphlet); Little blue book no. 592, edited by E. Haldeman-Julius. The millennium, a comedy of the year 2000, volume III, 1924 (pamphlet); Oil! A novel, 1927; * Boston, a novel, 1928 (2 vols.); Mountain City, 1930; Roman holiday, 1931; The wet parade, 1931; Co-op, a novel of living together, 1936; The flivver king, a story of Ford-America, 1937 (pamphlet); No pasaran! (They shall not pass) A story of the battle of Madrid, 1937 (pamphlet; cover-title); Little steel, 1938; Our lady, 1938.

Plays

Prince Hagen, a drama in four acts, 1909?; Plays of protest: The naturewoman, The machine, The second-story man, Prince Hagen, 1912; Hell, a verse drama and photo-play, 1923; Little blue book no. 589, edited by E. Haldeman-Julius. The pot boiler, a comedy in four acts, 1924 (pamphlet); Little blue book no. 631, edited by E. Haldeman-Julius. The naturewoman, 1924? (pamphlet); Singing jailbirds, a drama in four acts, 1924; Bill Porter, a drama of O. Henry in prison, 1925; Oil! A play in four acts . . . (from the novel by the author), 1929; Depression island, 1935; Wally for queen! The private life of royalty, 1936 (cover-title; pamphlet); Marie Antoinette, a play, 1939.

Political and Social Studies

Our bourgeois literature: the reason and the remedy, 1905 (pamphlet); The industrial republic, a study of the America of ten years hence, 1907; Sinclair-Astor letters, famous correspondence between socialist and millionaire, also The parable of the water tank by Edward Bellamy, 1914 (pamphlet); The social problem as seen from the view point of trade unionism, capital, and socialism, 1914 (cover-title; pamphlet; with Vincent Astor and others); The price I paid, 1917 (pamphlet); The profits of religion, an essay in economic interpretation, 1918; The brass check, a study of American journalism, 1919; The Associated press and labor, being seven chapters from The brass check, a study of American journalism . . . I now, over my own signature and as a deliberate challenge, charge that the Associated press has poisoned the news of the Colorado situation at its source. Will the owners and managers of the Associated press take up this challenge and make an attempt to send me to prison? I am waiting, gentlemen, for your answer, 1921? (cover-title; pamphlet); The crimes of the "Times," a test of newspaper decency, 1921 (pamphlet); Little blue book no. 234, edited by E. Haldeman-Julius. McNeal-Sinclair debate on socialism, 1921 (pamphlet); The goose-step, a study of American education, 1923; To the chief of police of Los Angeles, 1923 (pamphlet); The goslings, a study of the American schools, 1924; * Mammonart, an essay in economic interpretation, 1925; Letters to Judd, an American workingman, 1926 (pamphlet); The spokesman's secretary, being the letters of Mame to mom, 1926; Upton Sinclair, candidate for governor, 1926 (broadside); Money writes! 1927; Little blue book no. 1690, edited by E. Haldeman-Julius. What is socialism and culture? 1931 (pamphlet); I, governor of California and how I ended poverty, a true story of the future, 1933; Upton Sinclair presents William Fox, 1933; The way out: what lies ahead for America, 1933; EPIC answers, how to end poverty in California, 1934 (cover-title; pamphlet); The EPIC plan for California, 1934 (I, governor of California; EPIC answers; The lie factory starts; Immediate EPIC); Immediate EPIC, the final statement of the plan, 1934 (cover-title; pamphlet); The lie factory starts, 1934 (cover-title; pamphlet); I, candidate for governor: and how I got licked, 1935; We, people of America, and how we ended poverty, a true story of the future, 1935 (cover-title; pamphlet); Terror in Russia? Two views [by] Upton Sinclair [and] Eugene Lyons, 1938; Upton Sinclair on the Soviet union, 1938 (cover-title; pamphlet); What can be done about America's economic troubles? 1939 (pamphlet); Your million dollars . . ., 1939 (cover-title; pamphlet).

Studies in Health

Good health and how we won it with an account of the new hygiene by Upton Sinclair and Michael Williams with sixteen full-page illustrations from photographs, 1909 (English ed., The art of health, a primer of the new hygiene, 1909); Health and strength, 1910 (with Michael Williams; repr. from Good health and how we won it); The fasting cure, 1911; My life and diet, 1924 (pamphlet).

Studies in the Conduct of Life

The book of life, mind, and body, 1921; The book of life . . . Volume two: Love and society, 1922; The book of love, 1934.

Studies in Religion

What God means to me, an attempt at a working religion, 1936.

Studies in Telepathy

Mental radio . . . introduction by William McDougall, 1930.

Short Stories

The overman, 1907; Peter Gudge becomes a secret agent, 1930 (pamphlet; from 100%).

Autobiography

What life means to me, 1906 (cover-title; pamphlet); American outpost, a book of reminiscences, 1932 (English ed., Candid reminiscences, my first thirty years, 1932).

Boys' Books

Courtmartialed by Ensign Clarke Fitch, U.S.N. [*pseud.*], 1898; Saved by the enemy, 1898 (by Clarke Fitch, *pseud.*); A soldier monk by Ensign Clarke Fitch, U.S.N. [*pseud.*], 1899; Clif, the naval cadet, or, Exciting days at Annapolis by Ensign Clarke Fitch [*pseud.*], 1903; The cruise of the training ship, or, Clif Faraday's pluck by Ensign Clarke Fitch [*pseud.*], 1903; Off for West Point, or, Mark Mallory's struggle by Lieut. Frederick Garrison [*pseud.*], 1903.

Children's Book

The gnomobile, a gnice gnew gnarrative with gnonsense, but gnothing gnaughty . . . illustrated by John O'Hara Cosgrave, II, 1936.

Attributed Works

The fighting squadron, 1898 (by Clarke Fitch, *pseud.*); A prisoner of Morro, 1898 (by Clarke Fitch, *pseud.*); A gauntlet of fire, 1899 (by Clarke Fitch, *pseud.*); Holding the fort, 1899 (by Clarke Fitch, *pseud.*); A soldier's pledge, 1899 (by Clarke Fitch, *pseud.*); Wolves of the navy, or, Clif Faraday's search for a traitor, 1899 (by Clarke Fitch, *pseud.*); A cadet's honor, or, Mark Mallory's heroism by Lieut. Frederick Garrison [*pseud.*], 1903; From port to port, or, Clif Faraday in many waters by Ensign Clarke Fitch [*pseud.*], 1903; On guard, or, Mark Mallory's celebration by Lieut. Frederick Garrison [*pseud.*], 1903; A strange cruise, or, Clif Faraday's yacht chase by Ensign Clarke Fitch [*pseud.*], 1903; The West Point rivals, or, Mark Mallory's stratagem by Lieut. Frederick Garrison [*pseud.*], 1903; A West Point treasure, or, Mark Mallory's strange find by Lieut. Frederick Garrison [*pseud.*], 1903; The Helicon home colony, Englewood, N. J. Constitution, 1906? (broadside); Helicon home colony, 1907 (cover-title; pamphlet).

Miscellany

A home colony, a prospectus, 1906 (pamphlet); The Helicon home colony, a confidential statement, 1907 (caption-title; leaflet); From Upton Sinclair, a statement to the readers of his books, 1920 (caption-title; leaflet); What's the use of books, 1926 (cover-title; pamphlet); Books of Upton Sinclair in translations and foreign editions, a bibliography of 525 titles in 34 countries. August 1930, 1930 (cover-title; pamphlet); Upton Sinclair, Station A, Pasadena, California, February, 1930. Dear friend: 1930 (caption-title; leaflet); Books of Upton Sinclair in Russia, proceedings of literary groups and workers' clubs of the metal workers of Leningrad, 1931 (pamphlet); Upton Sinclair, Los Angeles, West branch, California, August 21, 1933. Dear friend: 1933 (broadside on the moving picture Thunder over Mexico).

Editor

The cry for justice, an anthology of the literature of social protest, the writings of philosophers, poets, novelists, social reformers, and others who have voiced the struggle against social injustice, selected from twenty-five languages covering a period of five thousand years edited by Upton Sinclair . . . with an introduction by Jack London . . . illustrated with reproductions of social protest in art, 1915.

Selected Works

An Upton Sinclair anthology with a preface by Upton Sinclair, compiled by I. O. Evans, 1934.

STUDIES AND ARTICLES

American messiahs by the Unofficial observer. 1935
Baldwin
Baldwin (M)
Blankenship
Brooks
Brooks, Van Wyck. Emerson and others. [c1927]
Bruns
Chamberlain
[Committee for the candidacy of Upton Sinclair for the Nobel prize for literature.] The candidacy of Upton Sinclair for the Nobel prize for literature. [1932] (cover-title; pamphlet)
Cowley
Dell, Floyd. Upton Sinclair, a study in social protest. [c1927]
Evans, Idrisyn O. Upton Sinclair. [1931] (pamphlet)
Freeman

† Gaer, Joseph, *ed.* Upton Sinclair, bibliography and biographical data. [1935] (mimeographed)

Harris, Frank. Contemporary portraits (third series). [c1920]

† Harte, James L. This is Upton Sinclair. [c1938]

Hartwick

Hatcher

Herrmann

Hicks

Higbee, Roscoe B. An independent's survey of Vincent Astor's fling at socialism. [c1914] (pamphlet)

† Johnson (1936)

Karsner

Kunitz (L)

Levinson

Lewisohn (E)

Llona

Loggins

Lovett, Robert M. Preface to fiction, a discussion of great modern novels. 1931

Luccock

† Manly

Maxfield, Mina R. and Eggleston, Lena. The wet parade, dramatized . . . from the novel by Upton Sinclair. [c1932] (pamphlet)

Mencken (P)

Michaud (M)

Michaud (P)

National

Pattee (N)

Pickerill, Thomas E. I, assemblyman from Orange county and how I supported Upton Sinclair (74th Assembly district). A measurement of the qualifications of the candidate for the state Legislature and the story of the campaign. It must not be assumed that the author is the candidate. The things presented are assumed in order to form a basis of reasoning and investigation. [c1934] (cover-title; pamphlet)

Quinn

Schreiber

Schyberg

Scott-James, Rolfe A. Modernism and romance. 1908

Sinclair, Upton B. Books by Upton Sinclair. [1937] (caption-title; leaflet)

Sinclair, Upton B. Books of Upton Sinclair in Russia, proceedings of literary groups and workers' clubs of the metal workers of Leningrad. 1931 (pamphlet)

† Sinclair, Upton B. Books of Upton Sinclair in translations and foreign editions, a bibliography of 525 titles in 34 countries. August, 1930. [1930] (cover-title; pamphlet)

† Sinclair, Upton B. Books of Upton Sinclair in translations and foreign editions, a bibliography of 772 titles in 47 languages, 39 countries. Second edition, August, 1938. [1938] (cover-title; pamphlet)

† Sinclair, Upton B. An Upton Sinclair anthology with a preface by Upton Sinclair, compiled by I. O. Evans. [1934]

Upton Sinclair, biographical and critical opinions from: England, France, Germany, Belgium, Holland, Denmark, Sweden, Switzerland, Austria, Hungary, Russia, Spain, Egypt, India, China, Japan, Australia, South Africa, Argentine, and the U.S.A., including: Henri Barbusse, Robert Blatchford, Georg Brandes, Luther Burbank, Floyd Dell, Max Eastman, Frank Harris, Robert Herrick, George D. Herron, V. Blasco Ibañez, W. L. George, Ellen Key, Richard Le Gallienne, Sinclair Lewis, Jack London, H. L. Mencken, David Graham Phillips, Eden Phillpotts, Romain Rolland, Bertrand Russell, May Sinclair, Carl Van Doren, Frederick van Eeden, H. G. Wells, Clement Wood, and others. 1923? (cover-title; pamphlet)

Upton Sinclair's, a monthly magazine: for a clean peace and the internation. Vol. 1 (nos. 1–10) Apr. 1918–Feb. 1919

Upton Sinclair's national EPIC *news.* Vol. 1–date, Dec. 26 [1933]–date

Van Doren (A)
Van Doren (C)
Whiteman, Luther and Lewis, Samuel L. Glory roads, the psychological state of California. [c1936]

Cantwell, Robert. "Upton Sinclair." *NR.*, Feb. 24, 1937, pp. 69–71; Dell, Floyd. "The artist in revolt." *AB.*, May 1927, pp. 316–22; Dell. "Upton Sinclair in America." *N.Masses*, Nov. 1928, pp. 6–7; Gans, Jacques. "La campagne électorale d'Upton Sinclair." *EN.*, May 4, 1935, pp. 428–30; Garlin, Sender. "Upton Sinclair, reactionary utopian." *N.Masses*, May 22, 1934, pp. 10–12; Grattan, Clinton H. "Upton Sinclair on current literature, summary of a conversation." *AB.*, Apr. 1932, pp. 61–64; Harris, Mrs. Lundy H. "Upton Sinclair and Helicon hall." *Ind.*, Mar. 28, 1907, pp. 711–13; Hitchcock, Curtice N. "The brass check, by U. Sinclair." *JPE.*, Apr. 1921, pp. 336–48; Kauffmann, Kurt. "Upton Sinclair, The brass check." *E.Studien*, Jan. 1922, pp. 162–65; Lippmann, Walter. "Upton Sinclair." *SRL.*, Mar. 3, 1928, pp. 641–43; Lovett, Robert M. "Upton Sinclair." *EJ.*, Nov. 1928, pp. 706–14; Morris, Lawrence S. "Upton Sinclair, the way of the reformer." *NR.*, Mar. 7, 1928, pp. 90–93; Talbert, Ernest L. "A comment on 'The goose step.'" *SS.*, Oct. 27, 1923, pp. 491–97; Van Doren, Carl. "Upton Sinclair." *Nation*, Sept. 28, 1921, pp. 347–48; Whyte, J. H. "Upton Sinclair, puritan and socialist." *Mod. Scot*, Aug. 1932, pp. 149–55; Wilson, Edmund. "Lincoln Steffens and Upton Sinclair." *NR.*, Sept. 28, 1932, pp. 173–75. For references to reviews, see *BRD.*, 1906–15, 1917, 1919–20, 1922–38.

Tess Slesinger, 1905–

Born in New York, July 16, 1905. She was educated at the Ethical Culture School and spent two years at Swarthmore and two at the School of Journalism of Columbia University, from which she graduated in 1927.

In 1926 she became assistant fashion editor for the New York *Herald Tribune*, and later transferred to the *Literary Review*, published by the *Evening Post*. Her first story was published in 1928 in the *Menorah Journal*, and her work has appeared also in the *American Mercury*, *Forum*, and other magazines. She held several miscellaneous jobs and traveled extensively in Europe, although she felt New York to be her home. In 1933–34 she taught creative writing at Briarcliff Manor, Briarcliff, New York. More recently she has written scenarios for Metro-Goldwyn-Mayer. In 1936 she married Frank Davis, a motion-picture producer, with whom she lives in Santa Monica.

Miss Slesinger has said that she is very much aware of class differences, and that she feels especially powerfully the isolated position, in the modern world, of intellectual groups, whose equipment makes them more keenly conscious than others of many contemporary issues.

For further comment, see Critical Survey, p. 96.

BIBLIOGRAPHY

Novel

The unpossessed, 1934.

Short Stories

Time: the present, a book of short stories, 1935.

For references to reviews, see *BRD.*, 1934–35.

(Lloyd) Logan Pearsall Smith, 1865–

Born in Millville, New Jersey, October 18, 1865; of Quaker descent. His parents were both evangelists of note, and his father, Robert Pearsall Smith, was influential and much respected in England and in Continental Europe, where wealth, aristocracy, and even royalty listened to his teachings. A sect founded by him in Germany has persisted to this day.

Logan Pearsall Smith's conversion at four by a six-year-old sister was made the subject of a religious tract widely distributed and unusually efficacious among Indians in the West. His handsome father's unusual success as a preacher in his European trip (1872), however, led to gossip and scandal; and he retired, as opportunity made it possible, from the work of conducting revivals and applied himself to the family business of running a glass factory. The son, a pious boy who distributed tracts in streetcars, developed into a normal American schoolboy, more interested in outdoor sports than in books. He gave up the early plan, born of his childish porings over old books, of holding a hereditary family librarianship in the Philadelphia Library, and looked forward to a career in the glass factory. He spent a sheltered, comfortable youth in Germantown, with summer vacations at Newport.

He was educated at the Penn Charter School in Philadelphia and proceeded at sixteen to Haverford College. He showed no unusual intellectual interest at first, but his early love of reading reasserted itself, and desire to emulate his ambitious sister made him read Ruskin, Carlyle, and Emerson. A close family friendship with Walt Whitman began in 1882, and *Leaves of Grass* opened to the young man a new source of joy in life and people and nature.

In 1884 he went to Harvard for a year, where his money and participation in good social groups made him feel too snobbish to have a true appreciation of the intellects so near him. His courses were too miscellaneous to give him a solid education, but the family friendship with William James supplied a stimulating guide, and about this time he fell under the spell of the teachings of Matthew Arnold.

After leaving Harvard he went abroad with his family and returned in 1886, expecting to enter the prosperous family business. A short, even though successful, experience in the office of the New York branch, and the promptings of an energetic cousin operated to make him feel a desire for culture and especially European culture. A groping desire to write resulted in his getting published in the New York *Evening Post* a narrative of a sailing trip; and, with a new, rather crude story finished and ready to present as evidence, and the support of his mother and sister, he asked his father for freedom from the business and an allowance for European study.

After some protest his father offered him the choice between a good allowance and the capital sum of twenty-five thousand dollars. Mr. Smith chose the capital sum, which was invested so carefully that it supported him in England and on the Continent for some thirty years and made it unnecessary for him to earn his living while writing.

Going to England in 1888, he entered Balliol College at Oxford, where he was an intimate student of the classical scholar Benjamin Jowett. The Oxford "greats," which he described in 1938 as "to my mature judgment the best scheme of education that I have ever heard of," and the earnest attention of his tutors helped to correct the deficiencies in his educational background. He interested himself in Liberal politics and in charity and reform movements, and felt the attraction of the writings of Pater. He took bachelor's and master's degrees in 1893 and 1906.

Since his college career Smith has lived in England and in Europe and returned to the United States only for visits. His lifelong hobby has been hunting valuable old manuscripts. He has made for himself a reputation as one of the greatest prose stylists of his language and period. So faultless, from the British point of view, has his pronunciation of English become that in 1926 he was named on a committee to teach pronunciation to announcers of the British Broadcasting Company. A literary craftsman and a great admirer of Flaubert, Smith feels that contemporary writers are led astray by their requirement of money, and he thinks that his solution, living modestly and independently in the environment best suited to writing, is the answer to their problem.

For further comment, see Critical Survey, p. 155.

BIBLIOGRAPHY

Essays and Aphorisms

Trivia, printed from the papers of Anthony Woodhouse, esq., 1902; Trivia, 1917; More trivia, 1921; Afterthoughts, 1931; * All trivia: Trivia, More trivia, Afterthoughts, Last words, 1933; Reperusals and re-collections, 1936.

Poems

Sonnets, 1908 (pamphlet); Songs and sonnets, 1909 (pamphlet).

Autobiography

Unforgotten years, 1938.

Writings on the English Language

The English language, 1912; S.P.E. Tract no. III. A few practical suggestions by Logan Pearsall Smith: editorial, co-operation of members, etc., report to Easter, 1920, 1920 (pamphlet); S.P.E. Tract no. XII. English idioms, 1923 (pamphlet); S.P.E. Tract no. XVII. Four words: romantic, originality, creative, genius, 1924 (pamphlet); Words and idioms, studies in the English language, 1925; S.P.E. Tract no. XXXI. Needed words by Logan Pearsall Smith. Words wanted in connexion with arts by Roger Fry. Jeremy Bentham and word-creation by Professor Graham Wallas, 1928 (pamphlet).

Literary Studies

The prospects of literature, 1927 (pamphlet); On reading Shakespeare, 1933; S.P.E. Tract no. XLVI. Fine writing, 1936 (pamphlet).

Short Stories

The youth of Parnassus and other stories, 1895.

Bible Stories

Stories from the Old Testament retold, 1920 (pamphlet).

Biography

The life and letters of Sir Henry Wotton . . . in two volumes, 1907; S.P.E. Tract no. xxxv. Robert Bridges. Recollections by Logan Pearsall Smith, His work on the English language by Elizabeth Daryush, 1931 (pamphlet).

Editor

Donne's sermons, selected passages with an essay, 1919; A treasury of English prose, 1919; Little essays drawn from the writings of George Santayana . . . with the collaboration of the author, 1920; A treasury of English aphorisms edited with an introduction, 1928; The Golden grove, selected passages from the sermons and writings of Jeremy Taylor, edited by Logan Pearsall Smith with a bibliography of the works of Jeremy Taylor by Robert Gathorne-Hardy, 1930; Robert Pearsall Smith, How little Logan was brought to Jesus, edited with a preface by Logan Pearsall Smith, 1934.

STUDIES AND ARTICLES

Bridges, Robert S. On receiving Trivia from the author. 1930
Mais, Stuart P. Books and their writers. 1920
Mais (W)
[Morley, Christopher D.] In re Logan Pearsall Smith. [1921?] (leaflet)
Morley, Christopher D. The youth of Parnassus. [1921?] (pamphlet)
Morley (L)
Whitall

Edman, Irwin. "Man of letters." *SRL.*, Dec. 31, 1938, p. 5; Wilson, Edmund. "The ghost of an anglophile." *NR.*, Jan. 25, 1939, pp. 347–48. For references to reviews, see *BRD.*, 1920–21, 1925, 1929, 1931, 1933, 1934, 1937, 1939.

S. S. Smith. *See* Thames Williamson

(Charles) Wilbert Snow, 1884–

Born on White Head Island, St. George, a lighthouse station at the entrance to Penobscot Bay, in Maine, April 6, 1884. He attended school in the fishing village of Spruce Head, to which the family moved from the island; and at fourteen he left school for sailing, deep-sea fishing, lobster-catching, and seining. He entered, at seventeen, the high school at Thomaston, finished in two years, and graduated in 1907 from Bowdoin. Two years of graduate study at Columbia followed, and he took his master's degree in 1910.

His career as a teacher of English began at New York University. He taught at Bowdoin and Williams colleges and then spent a year on the Seward Peninsula in Alaska as Eskimo teacher and reindeer agent. In the following summer he was in Utah and Arizona as a member of a group from the Smithsonian Institute, and when he resumed college teaching it was at the University of Utah, from which he was eventually dismissed for making political speeches opposing Reed Smoot.

In 1915 he left Indiana University to take part in the Plattsburg Naval Cruise, and during the war he was second and first lieutenant of field artillery.

He taught at Reed College in Oregon and at Indiana after the war and in 1921, the year of his marriage, went to Wesleyan University, where he has been a full professor since 1929. In 1937, he, his wife, and their five sons toured the United States in a trailer. He has contributed to *Century*, *Forum*, *Scribner's*, the *Nation*, and *Poetry*, and other periodicals.

Of his taste in poetry, he writes, "As a boy at Spruce Head I enjoyed Longfellow, Whittier, and Poe. I discovered them one day in the attic between the covers of an old Swinton's *Sixth Reader*. At High School in Thomaston Milton's minor poems led me into the realms of magic, and their spell is upon me still. The other Milton poems were 'acquired' tastes. Wordsworth spoke to me in college, and I wrote my commencement part for graduation day on the subject, 'The Message of Wordsworth.' I think of Wordsworth today as an excellent nature poet who *thought* he was a philosopher. Tennyson impressed me more than Browning, and you can put this fact down as a revelation of my limitations, if you so wish. (But, damn it, Tennyson is a greater artist.) In the so-called modern field Frost's *North of Boston* made the deepest dent. Its subject matter struck me as terribly true, and its tone struck me as exactly right for the subject matter. As for Lindsay and Sandburg there is just enough of the folk element in them both to arouse my interest and admiration. Robinson's *Captain Craig* I discovered as an undergraduate at Bowdoin when Robinson was entirely unknown. I remember staying up all night with Bill Norton over the volume. In the ultra-modern field Wallace Stevens and T. S. Eliot have given me the most pleasure. I must say that in later years few books of verse give me the old-time thrill I knew as a young man. Stevens's *The Man with the Blue Guitar* is an exception to this dictum. All in all I prefer folk music in poetry to chamber music in poetry—at least nine days out of ten. On the tenth day I like to go completely off the reservation. Sidney's definition of poetry as something which 'tells a story so sweetly that it will draw the old men from the chimney corner and the children from their play' is still my own definition, although I realize it is having tough sledding in this sophisticated age."

For further comment, see Critical Survey, p. 136.

BIBLIOGRAPHY

Poems

Songs of the Neukluk [by] Ewen MacLennan and Charles Wilbert Snow, 1913; Maine coast, 1923; The inner harbor, more Maine coast poems, 1926; Down east, poems, 1932; The selected poems of Wilbert Snow, 1936; Before the wind . . . with illustrations by Gordon Grant, 1938.

STUDIES AND ARTICLES

Gotham house, *firm, publishers, New York*. Critics write of Wilbert Snow. [1938] (broadside)

Monroe, Harriet. "Maine again." *P.*, June 1927, pp. 170–71; Monroe. "Sea country." *P.*, Oct. 1923, pp. 45–48. For references to reviews, see *BRD.*, 1923, 1926, 1932, 1936, 1939.

Ernest Souza, *pseud. See* **Evelyn Scott**

Gordon Stairs, *pseud.* *See* **Mary (Hunter) Austin**

Laurence Stallings, 1894–

Born in Macon, Georgia, November 25, 1894. In 1915, after graduating from Wake Forest College, he began reporting for the Atlanta *Journal.* Two years later, when he was asked to write an article on the campaign conducted by the marines for recruits, he did so but first signed up himself for five years of service. During the war he was a second lieutenant and a first lieutenant in the Fifth United States Marines, and finally captain of the Forty-seventh Company, Third Battalion, Second Division. He was in command of a company at Belleau Wood. As a result of serious injury he spent almost a year in hospitals in France and the United States, and his life was saved by the amputation of a leg.

After his return and his recovery he re-entered newspaper work, this time on the Washington *Times*, and studied at Georgetown University, from which he took the master's degree in 1922. In that year he went to New York and joined the staff of the *World*, as copy-reader. He worked up rapidly into theatrical reporting, the writing of book reviews, and the conducting of a literary column, "The Feature Reader," which he gave up in 1926 to return to Georgia and live on a farm. In 1930 he went back to New York as writer of a book column on the *Sun.*

With Maxwell Anderson, then an editorial writer on the *World*, Stallings collaborated in *What Price Glory?* in 1924, which, as an early war play, made a tremendous success. War experiences served him for material also in the novel *Plumes*, the scenario for the motion picture, *The Big Parade*, and the book of war photographs he edited in 1933, *The First World War*, which was a best-seller. In 1935 he accompanied Ethiopian troops as reporter for the North American Newspaper Alliance, the New York *Times*, and Fox Movietone News.

His dramatization (1930) of Hemingway's *A Farewell to Arms* was unsuccessful. He has written the libretti for the musical entertainments *Rainbow* and (with Owen Davis) *Virginia*, and has done a great deal of writing for the films. With Maxwell Anderson he collaborated on *The Cock-Eyed World* (1929), and he helped in the screen adaptation of Stark Young's *So Red the Rose.* In 1937 he signed a contract as script-writer for Metro-Goldwyn-Mayer.

For further comment, see Critical Survey, pp. 107, 123.

BIBLIOGRAPHY

Plays

Three American plays by Maxwell Anderson and Laurence Stallings, 1926 (What price glory; First flight; The buccaneer).

Novel

Plumes, 1924.

Verses set to Music

Vocal gems. Arthur Hopkins presents "Deep River," a native opera with jazz, music by Frank Harling, book and lyrics by Laurence Stallings, staged by Mr. Hopkins . . . Contents, "Ashes and fire," "Soft in de moonlight,"

"Dis is de day," "De old clay road," "Serenade Creole," "Po' lil' black chile," "Cherokee rose," "Love lasts a day," "Two little stars," 1926 (cover-title; sheet music).

Editor

The first world war, a photographic history edited with captions and an introduction, 1933; The world war in photographs uncensored, a pictorial review with the lid off, the world war in a startling array of uncensored photographs taken on the fields of battle, in the air, and on the high seas, 1934 (from The first world war).

STUDIES

American (M)
Clark
Fort
Kunitz
Littell
Mantle
Moses (A)
Simon and Schuster, *publishers, New York*. The first world war, a photographic history edited by Laurence Stallings. Notes on the photographs . . . [1933] (cover-title; pamphlet)

For references to reviews, see *BRD.*, 1924, 1933.

Wilbur Daniel Steele, 1886–

Born March 17, 1886, in Greensboro, North Carolina. His grandfather was a Greek scholar, and his father, at this time, was principal of Bennett Seminary at Greensboro. At a very tender age, when his father went to Berlin for graduate study, the little boy was sent to a German kindergarten supervised by the niece of Froebel. He continued his education in Denver when his father went there in 1892 to be professor of Biblical science at the university, and proceeded through grammar school, preparatory school, and the university. In his free time at night and during the summer he attended an art school.

Graduating in 1907, he went to the Museum of Fine Arts in Boston, where he studied in the life class of Philip Hale, and then spent a year abroad studying painting at the Académie Julian in Paris and etching in Florence and Venice, and another year at the Art Students' League in New York. When abroad he had begun writing short stories; and, despite his securing a number of art prizes, he decided, encouraged by his friend Mary Heaton Vorse, to make writing, rather than painting or etching, his career.

By 1915 he was known as a writer, and in 1919 he was awarded second prize by the O. Henry Memorial Award Committee for his story "They Know Not What They Do." In 1921 he was given by the same committee a special award for greatest sustained excellence in the three-year period preceding, and in 1925 he tied with Julian Street for first prize. First prizes followed in 1926 and 1931, and he won also a short-story contest conducted by *Harper's*. In 1932 he received an honorary doctorate in letters from the University of Denver.

He had in the meantime been traveling in the West Indies, Bermuda, northern Africa, France, and England; and during the war, as naval correspondent, he had visited the North Sea, Dunkirk, Brest, and northern Ireland. In the United

States he lived in Provincetown and Nantucket in Massachusetts, where he secured much New England material, and Charleston, South Carolina. Now he lives in Connecticut.

"My short-story career seems to be about finished," he writes. "Whether temporarily or permanently, my peculiar type of story appears to have gone out of style. Luckily, I have had enough sense to see and accept this rather quickly, and take up apprenticeship in another trade, hopefully setting out, by the old-fashioned method of writing 'em, to learn to write plays. I do feel, however, that this shift is a natural one, given the type of stories I have always done."

For further comment, see Critical Survey, p. 91.

BIBLIOGRAPHY

Novels

Storm, 1914; Isles of the blest, 1924; Taboo, 1925; Meat, a novel, 1928 (English ed., The third generation, 1929); Sound of rowlocks, 1938.

Short Stories

Land's end and other stories, 1918; The shame dance and other stories, 1923; * Urkey Island, 1926; The man who saw through heaven and other stories, 1927; Tower of sand & other stories, 1929; Diamond wedding, with analysis and notes by Frances A. Harris, 1931.

Plays

The giants' stair, a play in one act, 1924; The terrible woman and other one act plays . . . introduction by Frank Shay, 1925 (The terrible woman; The giants' stair; Not smart; Ropes); Post road, a comedy in two acts and four scenes by Wilbur Daniel Steele and Norma Mitchell, 1935.

STUDIES AND ARTICLES

Kunitz (L)
O'Brien
Undertow, a thrilling romantic tale of love and sacrifice based on the motion picture story by Wilbur Daniel Steele, a Universal pictures production. [c1930]
Williams

Elser, Frank B. "Oh, yes . . . Wilbur Daniel Steele." *AB.*, Feb. 1926, pp. 691–94. For references to reviews, see *BRD.*, 1918, 1923–29, 1938.

Gertrude Stein, 1874–

Born February 3, 1874, in Allegheny, Pennsylvania. Her German-Jewish family, comfortably wealthy, took her to Vienna and Paris when she was a baby and brought her back when she was a very little girl to live in California.

She grew up in Oakland and San Francisco, attended school, and read enormously. Entering Radcliffe in 1893, she studied with William James, who greatly admired her ability. Her scientific interest led her to undertake advanced work in brain anatomy at Johns Hopkins in 1897, but after several years of work she left without a degree.

She had become ambitious to be a writer and had been encouraged by the interest of William Vaughn Moody. Going to London in 1902, she spent a year studying English literature, and in 1903 she took up her residence in Paris.

For some thirty years she lived a quiet, regular life, interrupted by the war, in which she drove an ambulance, and enlivened by her acquaintance with a significant group of artists and writers. Picasso and Matisse were both her close friends, and she was influential in the development of Ernest Hemingway. She published her first book, *Three Lives*, at her own expense, in 1909, and *The Making of Americans*, though completed early in her career, was not published until 1926.

In 1933 appeared *The Autobiography of Alice B. Toklas.* Much more conventionally intelligible than her earlier and more experimental books, it leaped to popular success, was selected by the Literary Guild, and became a best-seller. In the following season *Four Saints in Three Acts*, an opera set to music by Virgil Thomson and performed by a cast of Negroes, was a *succès d'estime* in New York; subsequently it went on tour. Miss Stein was famous and, after more than thirty years abroad, revisited her own country as a popular author and lecturer. She has made recordings of some of her experimental prose.

Although she enjoyed her trip to the United States and refuses to regard herself as an expatriate, she returned to Paris, where she can live in the midst of the hospitable but unobtrusive French. In 1938 she moved from the Montparnasse salon she had had for years to a seventeenth-century Latin Quarter apartment once occupied by Queen Christina of Sweden. Her own valuable collection of more than one hundred paintings includes portraits of her by Cézanne and Picasso. She has selected the Yale Library as the place of safekeeping for the manuscripts of her writings.

In recognition of her services during the war the French government has decorated Miss Stein with the Medal of French Recognition.

For further comment, see Critical Survey, pp. 19, 66, 94–95, 179.

BIBLIOGRAPHY

Experimental Writing

Have they attacked Mary. He giggled. (A political caricature), 19— (pamphlet); Portrait of Mabel Dodge at the Villa Curonia, 19— (pamphlet); Tender buttons, objects, food, rooms, 1914; Geography and plays, 1922 (contains The work of Gertrude Stein by Sherwood Anderson); The making of Americans, being a history of a family's progress written by Gertrude Stein 1906–1908, 1925; A book concluding with As a wife has a cow, a love story, orné de lithographies par Juan Gris, 1926; Composition as explanation, 1926; An elucidation . . . printed in transition, April, 1927, 1927 (cover-title; pamphlet); . . . Useful knowledge Useful knowledge Useful knowledge . . ., 1928; A village, are you ready yet not yet, a play in four acts, illustré de lithographies par Elie Lascaux, 1928; An acquaintance with description, 1929; Dix portraits, texte anglais accompagné de la traduction de G. Hugnet et de V. Thomson, préface de Pierre de Massot, 1930; A novel of romantic beauty and nature and which looks like an engraving: Lucy Church amiably. And with a nod she turned her head toward the falling water. Amiably. First edition, 1930; Before the flowers of friendship faded friendship faded, written on a poem by

Georges Hugnet, 1931 (pamphlet); How to write . . . First edition, 1931; Operas and plays, 1932; Matisse, Picasso, and Gertrude Stein, with two shorter stories, 1933; Four saints in three acts, an opera to be sung, introduction by Carl Van Vechten, 1934; Portraits and prayers, 1934; Lectures in America, 1935; Narration, four lectures . . . with an introduction by Thornton Wilder, 1935; The geographical history of America, or, The relation of human nature to the human mind, 1936 (intro. by Thornton Wilder); Everybody's autobiography, 1937.

Autobiography

* The autobiography of Alice B. Toklas, illustrated, 1933.

Short Stories

* Three lives, stories of the good Anna, Melanctha, and the gentle Lena, 1909.

Art Criticism

[Henri Matisse. Pablo Picasso], 1912 (IN *Camera work, a photographic quarterly.* Special number, August 1912); Picasso, 1938 (French ed., Picasso . . . 63 reproductions dont 8 en couleurs, 1938).

Children's book

The world . . . is round, pictures by Clement Hurd, 1939.

Verses Set to Music

Pigeons on the grass alas, recitation and air for barytone, from the opera, Four saints in three acts, text by Gertrude Stein, music by Virgil Thomson, as sung by Edward Mathews, 1935 (cover-title; sheet music).

STUDIES AND ARTICLES

Anderson
Anderson (S)
Burnett
Canby
Chesterton
Cleaton
[Grieve, Christopher M.] At the sign of the thistle, a collection of essays by Hugh MacDiarmid [*pseud.*]. [1934]
Imbs, Bravig. confessions of another young man. [c1936]
Kunitz (L)
Lewis (T)
Llona
Loggins
Luhan, Mabel G. European experiences, volume two of Intimate memories. [c1935]
MacCarthy
Munson (S)
Nathan (P)
National
Riding
Riding, Laura. Contemporaries and snobs. [1928]
Rosenfeld
Sherman (P)
Sitwell
Stein, Gertrude. The making of Americans, the Hersland family, preface by Bernard Faÿ. [c1934]
Stein, Gertrude. Three lives . . . introduction by Carl Van Vechten. [c1933]
transition. Testimony against Gertrude Stein [by] Georges Braque, Eugene Jolas, Maria Jolas, Henri Matisse, André Salmon, Tristan Tzara. 1935 (cover-title; pamphlet)
[United States. Works progress

administration.] American stuff, an anthology of prose & verse by members of the Federal writers' project, with sixteen prints by the Federal art project. 1937

Walter, Erich A., *ed.* 1935 Essay annual . . . 1935 Wilson

Aldington, Richard. "The disciples of Gertrude Stein." *P.*, Oct. 1920, pp. 35–40; Anderson, Sherwood. "Four American impressions." *NR.*, Oct. 11, 1922, pp. 171–73; Anderson. "The work of Gertrude Stein." *Little Rev.*, Spring 1922, pp. 29–32; Eagleson, Harvey. "Gertrude Stein, method in madness." *SR.*, Apr.–June 1936, pp. 164–77; Fadiman, Clifton. "Genius self-revealed." *N.Yer.*, Dec. 4, 1937, pp. 115–16, 118; Faÿ, Bernard. "Gertrude Stein, poète de l'Amérique." *R.d.P.*, Nov. 15, 1935, pp. 294–312; Knickerbocker, William S. "Stunning Stein." *SR.*, Oct.–Dec. 1933, pp. 498–99; Preston, John H. "A conversation." *A.Mo.*, Aug. 1935, pp. 187–94; Riding, Laura. "The new barbarian and Gertrude Stein." *trans.*, June 1927, pp. 153–68; Skinner, Burrhus F. "Has Gertrude Stein a secret?" *A.Mo.*, Jan. 1934, pp. 50–57; † Stein, Gertrude. "Bibliography." *trans.*, Feb. 1929, pp. 47–55; Stein, Gertrude. "The war and Gertrude Stein, Autobiography of Alice B. Toklas." *A.Mo.*, July 1933, pp. 56–69. For references to reviews, see *BRD.*, 1910, 1923, 1929, 1933–37, 1939.

John (Ernst) Steinbeck, 1902–

Born February 27, 1902, in Salinas, California, of German and Irish extraction. He attended local schools, and during his high-school course he did odd jobs on farms and in the laboratory of a sugar refinery. In 1919 he entered Stanford as a special student, and in 1925, after an interrupted career, he left without a degree.

By this time he had decided upon writing as a profession, and he went to New York on a freight boat, in the hope of securing work. He had a job as reporter, and he laid bricks for the Madison Square Garden building. He returned to California, took a job as winter watchman for a house in the Sierras, then worked in a trout hatchery, and wrote *Cup of Gold.* Though it was published, it made no money, and his next two books were also financial failures.

Tortilla Flat, however, turned the scale so successfully that it was bought by film producers, although it was not produced. *In Dubious Battle* won the author the annual medal of the Commonwealth Club of California for the best novel of the year by a California writer, and *Of Mice and Men*, written as an experiment (in that the author tried to see how nearly he could make a short novel approach a play), was a best-seller and enabled Steinbeck and his wife to take a trip to the Scandinavian countries in 1937. The play adapted by Steinbeck from the book received the award of the New York Drama Critics Circle in April, 1938, for the best American play of the season 1937–38. In 1939 he was elected to membership in the National Institute of Arts and Letters.

In addition to his fiction and drama Mr. Steinbeck has written articles on California labor camps for the San Francisco *News.* He lives on a farm in central California, where he keeps regular hours in his writing. He has said that all characters in his work represent people he has known.

For further comment, see Critical Survey, p. 50.

BIBLIOGRAPHY

Novels

Cup of gold, a life of Henry Morgan, buccaneer, with occasional reference to history, 1929; The Pastures of heaven, 1932; To a god unknown, 1933; * Tortilla flat . . . illustrated by Ruth Gannett, 1935; In dubious battle, 1936; * Of mice and men, 1937; The grapes of wrath, 1939.

Short Stories

Nothing so monstrous, a story, 1936 (from The Pastures of heaven); Saint Katy the Virgin, 1936; The red pony. I. The gift, II. The great mountains, III. The promise, 1937; The long valley, 1938.

Play

Of mice and men, a play in three acts, 1937.

Social Study

"Their blood is strong," 1938.

STUDIES AND ARTICLES

Brown
Mantle (C)
† Moore, Harry T. The novels of John Steinbeck, a first critical study. 1939
† Schwartz, Harry W., *book shop, Milwaukee.* 10th anniversary catalog. Modern first editions with a check list of John Steinbeck. [1937] (cover-title; pamphlet)
Steinbeck, John. Cup of gold, a life of Sir Henry Morgan, buccaneer, with occasional reference to history. [c1936] (pref. by Lewis Gannett)
Steinbeck, John. Of mice and men . . . with an introduction by Joseph Henry Jackson. [1938]

Abramson, Ben. "John Steinbeck." *RC.*, Dec. 1936, pp. 4–5, 18; † Blanck, Jacob, *ed.* "American first editions." *PW.*, Apr. 17, 1937, p. 1701 (checklist by Lawrence C. Powell); Davis, Elmer. "The Steinbeck country." *SRL.*, Sept. 24, 1938, p. 11; Jackson, Joseph H. "John Steinbeck, a portrait." *SRL.*, Sept. 25, 1937, pp. 11–12, 18; Powell, Lawrence C. "Toward a bibliography of John Steinbeck." *Col.*, Autumn 1938, pp. 558–68; Rascoe, Burton. "John Steinbeck." *EJ.*, Mar. 1938, pp. 205–16; Richards, Edmund C. "The challenge of John Steinbeck." *N.Amer.Rev.*, Summer 1937, pp. 406–13; Shedd, Margaret. "Of mice and men." *TAM.*, Oct. 1937, pp. 774–80; Whipple, Thomas K. "Steinbeck through a glass, though brightly." *NR.*, Oct. 12, 1938, pp. 274–75. For references to reviews, see *BRD.*, 1929, 1932–33, 1935–39.

Mabel Dodge Sterne. *See* Mabel Dodge Luhan

Wallace Stevens, 1879–

Born in Reading, Pennsylvania. He was educated at Harvard and entered the law. He joined the staff of the Hartford Accident and Indemnity Company, with which he has been associated for many years.

Four poems were published in the "war number" of *Poetry* in 1914, but the author was reluctant to rush into print, and his first book was issued years later. He was awarded the Helen Haire Levinson Prize in 1920. His retirement and infrequent publication have made Stevens almost a myth to other poets. In 1936 he won the *Nation's* poetry prize with "The Men That Are Falling."

For further comment, see Critical Survey, p. 146.

BIBLIOGRAPHY

Poems

Harmonium, 1923; Ideas of order, 1935; Owl's clover, 1936; The man with the blue guitar & other poems, 1937.

STUDIES AND ARTICLES

Blackmur
Kreymborg
Monroe
Rosenfeld (M)
Taupin
Untermeyer
Zabel

Baker, Howard. "Wallace Stevens and other poets." *So.R.*, Autumn 1935, pp. 373–89; Blackmur, Richard P. "Examples of Wallace Stevens." *HH.*, Jan.–Mar. 1932, pp. 223–55; Blake, Howard. "Thoughts on modern poetry." *SR.*, Apr.–June 1935, pp. 187–96; Fitzgerald, Robert. "Thoughts revolved." *P.*, Dec. 1937, pp. 153–57; Hays, Hoffman R. "Laforgue and Wallace Stevens." *Rom.Rev.*, July 1934, pp. 242–48; Monroe, Harriet. "A cavalier of beauty." *P.*, Mar. 1924, pp. 322–27; Monroe. "He plays the present." *P.*, Dec. 1935, pp. 153–57; Moore, Marianne. "Unanimity and fortitude." *P.*, Feb. 1937, pp. 268–72; Munson, Gorham. "The dandyism of Wallace Stevens." *D.*, Nov. 1925, pp. 413–17; Powys, Lewellyn. "The thirteenth way." *D.*, July 1924, pp. 45–50; Seiffert, Marjorie A. "The intellectual tropics." *P.*, Dec. 1923, pp. 154–60; Zabel, Morton D. "The harmonium of Wallace Stevens." *P.*, Dec. 1931, pp. 148–54. For references to reviews, see *BRD.*, 1923, 1931, 1935–37.

Arthur Stirling, *pseud. See* **Upton Sinclair**

Grace Zaring Stone, 1896–

Born Grace Zaring, January 9, 1896, in New York. She is a descendant of the reformer Robert Owen. She was sent to school at the Sacred Heart Convent in New York and given private tutors. Later she studied music and dancing in Paris.

In 1913 she made a trip around the world and returned to Paris to study music. During the war she joined the British Red Cross, and in 1917 she married Ellis S. Stone of the United States navy. With him she has lived in Europe, the West Indies, and China. Now they live in Washington, D.C.

Mrs. Stone is still much interested in dancing and music. "After I have spent a morning writing and re-writing and re-writing," she confesses, "I wish savagely I had gone on with theory and counter-point and were writing fugues." She has contributed fiction to the magazines and has a reputation for brilliant conversation.

BIBLIOGRAPHY

Novels

Letters to a djinn, 1922; The heaven and earth of Doña Elena, 1929; The bitter tea of General Yen . . . illustrated by Barbara Macfarlane, 1930 (English ed., Bitter tea, 1930); The almond tree, 1931 (English ed., All the daughters of music, 1932); The cold journey, 1934.

STUDIES

Kunitz (L)

For references to reviews, see *BRD.*, 1922, 1929–31, 1934.

Phil(ip Duffield) Stong, 1899–

Born in Keosauqua, Iowa, January 27, 1899. He attended Drake University in Des Moines and graduated in 1919. Until 1923 he taught and served as athletic director in high schools, and in 1920–21 he did graduate work at Columbia. Later (1923–24) he studied at the University of Kansas and became an instructor in debate and journalism in Drake University. He wrote editorials for the Des Moines *Register* until 1925, and in the following year became wire editor for the Associated Press in New York and copy editor in the North American Newspaper Alliance. In 1928 he joined the staff of *Liberty*, and from 1929 to 1931 he was on the New York *World*.

After he had written about a dozen unsuccessful novels, *State Fair* made a phenomenal sale and brought the author some forty thousand dollars. The book was filmed with Will Rogers, and Stong assisted in preparing the scenario. In 1932 he went to Hollywood and wrote scenarios for Metro-Goldwyn-Mayer and other firms. In 1939 he received a Litt. D. from Parsons College, and was awarded a Herald Tribune juvenile literature prize for *The Hired Man's Elephant*.

Stong, who lives on the farm he owns in Connecticut and enjoys piano-playing, photography, and working with his microscope, says that he writes instead of doing these other things because he can do it better. "The purpose is essentially anyone's purpose at any occupation, to show myself in my best colors." Feeling that character, more than plot or setting, is the backbone of any piece of writing, he regrets the necessities that have made some of the greatest European writers turn to political themes of pure propaganda and admires Willa Cather and Sinclair Lewis in this country because of their work dealing with permanent social values. "I am a Socialist," he declares, "in so far as I believe that a society should be responsible to its individuals for basic necessities; also, I think that the opportunities for the accumulation of great personal wealth have been grossly abused in this country . . ."

"There are so many kinds of writing that please or delight me," he says, "that it would be much easier to mention some things that I don't like—the pallid, the affected and the defeatist. . . . I suppose that my special preference is for writing that is virile, truthful and good-humored; Sterne, Fielding, Dickens, Thackeray, Mark Twain, Irving, Holmes, Balzac, Cervantes, Chekov and so on. I am largely in agreement with Mr. Cabell's theory of alcoves and I think that a writer's principal job is to take his audience from the confusion of the streets and into the theater before he tries to explain, concisely and quietly, the meanings of the chaos outside."

BIBLIOGRAPHY

Novels

* State fair, 1932; Stranger's return, 1933 (English ed., The stranger's return, 1933); Village tale, 1934; The farmer in the dell, 1935; Week-end, 1935; Career, 1936; Buckskin breeches, 1937; The rebellion of Lennie Barlow, 1937; The long lane . . . decorated by F. E. Warren, 1939.

Children's Books

Farm boy, a hunt for Indian treasure, story by Phil Stong, pictures by Kurt Wiese, 1934; Honk: the moose, story by Phil Stong, pictures by Kurt Wiese, 1935; No-Sitch: the hound, story by Phil Stong, pictures by Kurt Wiese, 1936; High water, story by Phil Stong, pictures by Kurt Wiese, 1937; Edgar: the 7:58 . . . illustrated by Lois Lenski, 1938; Young settler, story by Phil Strong, pictures by Kurt Wiese, 1938; The hired man's elephant . . . illustrated by Doris Lee, 1939.

Miscellany

Shake 'em up! A practical handbook of polite drinking by Virginia Elliott and Phil D. Stong, 1930; County fair, photographs by Josephine von Miklos and others, 1938.

STUDIES

[Farrar & Rinehart, inc., *firm, publishers, New York.*] Buckskin breeches by Phil Stong, a selection of the Discoverers. [1937] (pamphlet)

For references to reviews, see *BRD.*, 1932–39.

T(homas) S(igismund) Stribling, 1881–

Born in Clifton, Tennessee, March 4, 1881. His father ran a country newspaper, and early in his youth the boy was ambitious to write. A clerk in his father's village store, he began writing fiction on wrapping-paper. He passed his summers with an aunt in Alabama, and the settings of *The Forge* and *The Store* are the result of what he had seen on these visits.

He went to public schools in Clifton and studied at the normal school in Florence, Alabama. As he was too unsuccessful a disciplinarian to be a good teacher, he withdrew from that career and studied law at the University of Alabama, where he took his degree in 1905. He practiced law in Florence for a few months, but gave it up to take a job in the office of the *Taylor-Trotwood Magazine* in Nashville.

His desire to write, however, which had made him neglect his studies, continued to assert itself, and he wrote stories when he should have been working. He began sending stories to Sunday-school magazines, and for some ten years was successful in selling them. He financed in this way a trip to Cuba, and, after he had worked up a syndicate for children's stories, he went to Europe and to South America, where he spent a year in Caracas. During the war he worked on the Chattanooga *News* and as a stenographer in the aviation bureau in Washington.

Abandoning children's stories and pulpwood serials, he returned home to Clifton and began working seriously on novels. *Birthright* secured the respect of publishers, and *Teeftallow* was a best-seller and the first selection of the Book-of-the-Month Club. *The Forge* was the first American book to be selected by the English Book League; *The Store*, *Unfinished Cathedral*, and *The Sound Wagon* were all selections of the Literary Guild; and *The Store* was the Pulitzer Prize Novel of 1932.

Stribling, who feels that small villages offer the novelist the best opportunity for insight into life and character, still lives at least part of every year in Clifton. He believes that good novels should be built on skeletons of philosophic thought. "It seems to me," he writes, "that literature, including in the term books, movies and the stage, is one of the greatest moulding forces in human life. From this source more than any other women and adolescents draw their ideas of morals and manners. In fact literature has been left almost predominant in this field since the decline of religious leadership. . . . The very spirit of literary creativeness is a complete freedom to use the material of life to embody its inner urge. If that urge itself be not fundamentally moral, no morality or ethical content can be applied from the outside. Moreover if the urge be too obvious even from the inside the result is a tract and not literature unless the writer be a very great artist indeed. I am therefore drawing around to the conclusion that whereas literature is certainly one of the moulds of life, life unavoidably moulds and reproduces its own image in literature. So letters act as a sort of cathartic, a purifier of life, not in the sense of making it better or more moral, but in the sense of making it more unified, possessing a uniform ethical content, of whatever kind it may be, all the way through. In short literature is society's circulatory system."

For further comment, see Critical Survey, pp. 43–44.

BIBLIOGRAPHY

Novels

The cruise of the dry dock . . . illustrated by Herbert Morton Stoops, 1917; Birthright, a novel . . . illustrated by F. Luis Mora, 1922; Fombombo, 1923; Red sand, 1924; Teeftallow, 1926; Bright metal, 1928; East is East, 1928; Strange moon, 1929; Backwater, 1930; * The forge, 1931; The store, 1932; Unfinished cathedral, 1934; The sound wagon, 1935; These bars of flesh, 1938.

Detective Stories

Clues of the Caribbees, being certain criminal investigations of Henry Poggioli, Ph.D., 1929.

Literary Criticism

America's town meeting of the air, December 26, 1935, number 9. Literature and life [by] Christopher Morley, Fannie Hurst, Audrey Wurdemann, T. S. Stribling, Francis Talbot, S. J., 1935 (cover-title; pamphlet; ed. by Lyman Bryson).

STUDIES AND ARTICLES

Baldwin (M)
Hatcher
Kunitz (L)
Luccock
Schreiber
Smith
Zabel

Bates, Ernest S. "Thomas Sigismund Stribling." *EJ.*, Feb. 1935, pp. 91–100; † Blanck, Jacob, *ed.* "American first editions." *PW.*, Aug. 21, 1937, p. 592 (checklist by Frank Stone); Dickens, Byron. "T. S. Stribling and the south." *SR.*, July–Sept. 1934, pp. 341–49; Lebreton, Maurice. "L'évolution sociale dans les états du sud, d'après T. S. Stribling." *EA.*, Jan. 1937, pp. 36–52; Wade, John D. "Two souths." *VQR.*, Oct. 1934, pp. 616–19; Warren, Robert P. "T. S. Stribling, a paragraph in the history of critical realism." *AR.*, Feb. 1934, pp. 463–86; Wilson, James S. "Poor-white and negro." *VQR.*, Oct. 1932, pp. 621–24. For references to reviews, see *BRD.*, 1922–24, 1926, 1928–32, 1934–36, 1938.

Ruth Suckow, 1892–

Born August 6, 1892, in Hawarden, Iowa, the daughter of a Congregational minister. As a girl she moved about from parish to parish with her family and secured acquaintance with the lives of many people at the time when she was beginning to write. In 1910 she entered Grinnell College; later she attended the School of Expression in Boston, and she graduated in 1917 from the University of Denver. For a time she taught at the University of Denver. For six years she owned and managed the Orchard Apiary at Earlville, Iowa, and her profits in the summer enabled her to write in the winter in independence of public taste. Her reputation came when H. L. Mencken published her work in the *Smart Set* and the *American Mercury*. The result was that she began to write for many other magazines, and soon she was able to support herself by her novels and stories. In 1929 she married Ferner Nuhn. They live in Cedar Rapids, Iowa.

"I neither hold, nor hold with, hard-and-fast theories concerning literature," she writes. ". . . I think every piece of literature holds some aspect of reality, presented through a concrete instance, but possessing wider implications and applications; that until a writer has dropped personal feelings and aims for impersonality, no matter how brilliant his talent, he is not really ready to write; that style should fit content; and the whole give delight as a work of art."

For further comment, see Critical Survey, pp. 47, 92.

BIBLIOGRAPHY

Novels

Country people, 1924; The Odyssey of a nice girl, 1925; The Bonney family, 1928; Cora, 1929; The Kramer girls, 1930; * The folks . . . drawings by Robert Ward Johnson, 1934.

Short Stories

* Iowa interiors, 1926 (English ed., People and houses, 1927); Children and older people, 1931.

Omnibus Volume

Carry-over . . . containing: "Country people," "The Bonney family," and sixteen short stories, 1936.

Social Study

The folk idea in American life, 1934 (pamphlet).

STUDIES AND ARTICLES

Brigham	Knopf (B)
Hatcher	Kunitz (L)
Herrmann	Maillard

Frederick, John T. "Ruth Suckow and the middle western literary movement." *EJ.*, Jan. 1931, pp. 1–8. For references to reviews, see *BRD.*, 1924–26, 1928–31, 1934, 1936.

Genevieve Taggard, 1894–

Born in Waitsburg, Washington, November 28, 1894. When she was two her parents moved to Hawaii, settling at Kalili, near Honolulu, where they built a school and a mission, and remained for eighteen years. In 1914 Miss Taggard came back to the United States to college.

She had studied at the Punahou Academy and Oahu College, and she graduated in 1919 from the University of California. She moved east to New York and became one of the group associated at the outset with the *Measure*, a magazine of poetry, of which she was an editor until 1926. She wrote also for the *Masses* and other periodicals.

After a year in France, she began her teaching career in 1929 as instructor in English at Mount Holyoke, where she remained until 1931. In that year the award of a Guggenheim fellowship made it possible for her to go to Mallorca for a year of writing, and on her return in 1932 she taught literature at Bennington College. Since 1935 she has taught at Sarah Lawrence College. "As a teacher," she wrote in 1937, ". . . I am deeply interested in relating poetry to the lives of children in public schools. . . . At present I teach a class chiefly composed of workers under the auspices of the League of American Writers." She has been fascinated by the possibilities in the use of radio, film, and phonograph as means for increasing the influence of poetry.

She has traveled in the Soviet Union, and her poems have been translated into both Ukrainian and Russian. "I am romantic in spite of a great love for writers in both categories," she declares. "I am a radical—that is I believe in the future of American life; I hope to live to see it achieve economic democracy and by this means lay a foundation for a great culture."

For further comment, see Critical Survey, p. 151.

BIBLIOGRAPHY

Poems

For eager lovers, 1922; Hawaiian hilltop, 1923; Words for the chisel, 1926; Travelling standing still, poems 1918–1928, 1928; Monologue for mothers (aside), 1929 (pamphlet); Remembering Vaughan in New England . . . woodcuts by J. J. Lankes, 1933; Not mine to finish, poems 1928–1934, 1934; Calling Western union, 1936; * Collected poems 1918–1938, 1938.

Biography
The life and mind of Emily Dickinson, 1930.

Editor
Continent's end, an anthology of contemporary California poets edited with introductions by George Sterling, Genevieve Taggard, & James Rorty, 1925; May days, an anthology of verse from Masses-Liberator chosen and edited by Genevieve Taggard with woodcuts by J. J. Lankes, 1925; The unspoken and other poems by Anne Bremer, 1927; Circumference, varieties of metaphysical verse, 1456–1928, 1929; Ten introductions, a collection of modern verse edited by Genevieve Taggard and Dudley Fitts, 1934.

STUDIES AND ARTICLES

Herrmann
Jones
Kreymborg
Kunitz (L)

Field, Sara B. "Chiseled lines." *P.*, July 1926, pp. 221–24; Knister, Raymond. "Hawaiian flights." *P.*, May 1925, pp. 108–09; North, Jessica N. "The edge of the sword." *P.*, Dec. 1934, pp. 168–70; Wilson, Edmund. "A poet of the pacific." *NR.*, Dec. 12, 1928, pp. 99–100; Wilson, Ted C. "Protest and hope." *P.*, May 1937, pp. 106–08; Zabel, Morton D. "An early retrospect." *P.*, Dec. 1928, pp. 154–56; Zaturensky, Marya. "Enameled poems." *P.*, Apr. 1923, pp. 43–45. For references to reviews, see *BRD.*, 1923, 1926, 1928, 1930, 1934, 1936, 1938–39.

(Newton) Booth Tarkington, 1869–

Born in Indianapolis, July 29, 1869, in a family of New England origin. Before he could write he dictated stories to his sister; he attended local schools and came to be a warm friend of his neighbor, James Whitcomb Riley. He continued his education at Phillips Exeter, Purdue, and Princeton, and graduated in 1893, after a career noteworthy for social prominence and leadership in writing, drawing, singing, and composing. A musical comedy in which he had collaborated with George Post Wheeler was presented by the Triangle Club.

After graduation he returned to Indianapolis and lived as man about town while he worked out his future. He hoped to be an illustrator, but succeeded in selling only one drawing and turned instead to literature. Waiting brought him only $22.50 for his first five years of work; with the publication, however, of *Monsieur Beaucaire* in *McClure's*, his position became secure. Dramatized by the author and E. G. Sutherland, it was played by Richard Mansfield; subsequently it was filmed with Valentino. He is the only novelist to have taken two Pulitzer Prizes (1919, *The Magnificent Ambersons;* 1922, *Alice Adams*), and in 1933 he was awarded the Gold Medal of the National Institute of Arts and Letters for distinguished work in fiction. In 1935 he was awarded the Silver Buffalo, the highest honor conferred by the Boy Scouts for distinguished service to boyhood. He is a member of the American Academy of Arts and Letters and holds several honorary degrees.

For a year (1902–03) he was a member of the Indiana House of Representatives. Otherwise he has led an independent life, with foreign travel and summers in Maine. His sight, completely lost by 1930, was partially restored by operations in 1931. A semi-invalid, he divides his time between Indianapolis and Kennebunkport (in "the House That Penrod Built"), with short visits in Philadelphia. "My principal interests," he says, "seem to be old portraits, the art of painting in general, and motor-boating."

In literature he has shown a marked preference for French authors and especially enjoys French autobiography. In English literature he is an admirer of Hardy and Meredith, and Wells and Bennett, and he thinks that Riley, Mark Twain, and especially Howells have made important contributions to American letters. He regards plot as of secondary importance and character as the proper origin of plot, and, although he disapproves of some features of many realistic novels, feels that the function of the novelist is to reveal life as vividly as possible in its color, sound, and sensation.

For further comment, see Critical Survey, pp. 28–29, 45–46, 71.

BIBLIOGRAPHY

Novels

* The gentleman from Indiana, 1899; Monsieur Beaucaire . . . illustrated by C. D. Williams, 1900; The two Vanrevels . . . illustrations by Henry Hutt, 1902; Cherry, 1903; The beautiful lady, 1905; The conquest of Canaan, a novel . . . illustrations by Lucius W. Hitchcock, 1905; His own people . . . illustrated by Lawrence Mazzanovich and F. R. Gruger, decorated by Wm. St. John Harper, 1907; The guest of Quesnay . . . illustrations by W. J. Duncan, 1908; Beasley's Christmas party . . . illustrated by Ruth Sypherd Clements, 1909; Beauty and the Jacobin, an interlude of the French revolution . . . with illustrations by C. D. Williams, 1912; The flirt . . . illustrations by Clarence F. Underwood, 1913; * Penrod . . . illustrated by Gordon Grant, 1914; The turmoil, a novel . . . illustrated by C. E. Chambers, 1915; Penrod and Sam . . . illustrated by Worth Brehm, 1916; Seventeen, a tale of youth, and summer time, and the Baxter family, especially William, 1916; The magnificent Ambersons . . . illustrated by Arthur William Brown, 1918; Ramsey Milholland . . . illustrated by Gordon Grant, 1919; * Alice Adams . . . illustrated by Arthur William Brown, 1921; Harlequin and Columbine . . . frontispiece by E. Stetson Crawford, 1921; Gentle Julia . . . illustrated by C. Allan Gilbert and Worth Brehm, 1922; The midlander, 1923; Women, 1925; Growth, 1927 (The magnificent Ambersons; The turmoil; National avenue); The plutocrat, a novel, 1927; Claire Ambler, 1928; The new Penrod book, Penrod Jashber . . . illustrations by Gordon Grant, 1929; Young Mrs. Greeley, 1929; Mirthful Haven, 1930; Penrod, his complete story: Penrod, Penrod and Sam, Penrod Jashber . . . illustrated by Gordon Grant, 1931; Mary's Neck . . . frontispiece by Wallace Morgan, 1932; Wanton Mally . . . with drawings by Joseph Simont, 1932; Presenting Lily Mars, 1933; Little Orvie . . . illustrated by George Brehm, 1934; The Lorenzo bunch, 1936; Rumbin galleries, illustrated by Ritchie Cooper, 1937.

Plays

The kisses of Marjorie, a play, 190–? (cover-title; hectographed); The guardian, a play in four acts by Booth Tarkington and Harry Leon Wilson, 1907 (also pub. as The man from home by Booth Tarkington and Harry Leon Wilson with illustrations from scenes in the play, 1908); The Ohio lady by N. Booth Tarkington and Julian Street, 1916 (cover-title; also pub. as The country cousin, a comedy in four acts by Booth Tarkington and Julian Street, 1921); The Gibson upright by Booth Tarkington and Harry Leon Wilson, 1919; Clarence, a comedy in four acts, 1921; The intimate strangers, a comedy in three acts, 1921; The ghost story, a one-act play for persons of no great age, 1922; The wren, a comedy in three acts, 1922; The trysting place, a farce in one act, 1923; Tweedles, a comedy by Booth Tarkington and Harry Leon Wilson, 1924; Bimbo, the pirate, a comedy, 1926 (pamphlet); Station YYYY, 1927 (pamphlet); The travelers, 1927 (pamphlet); How's your health? A comedy in three acts by N. Booth Tarkington and Harry Leon Wilson . . . rewritten and revised (1930) by N. Booth Tarkington and Harry Leon Wilson, 1930; The Help each other club, 1934 (pamphlet); Mister Antonio, a play in four acts, 1935.

Short Stories

In the arena, stories of political life . . . illustrated by A. I. Keller, Power O'Malley, and J. J. Gould, 1905; An overwhelming Saturday, a Penrod story, 1913 (pamphlet); The spring concert, 1916 (pamphlet); The works of Booth Tarkington. Harlequin and Columbine and other stories, volume VIII, 1918; The fascinating stranger and other stories, 1923; Marriage, short stories of married life by American writers, Tarkington, Cutting, Hergesheimer, Miller, Street, Delano, Norris, Gale, Harrison, Kelland, Hopper, Adams, Butler, Foster, Hughes, Dreiser, Cooper, Turner, Webster, Lincoln, 1923; Anthony, the joker by George Barr McCutcheon, A great man's wife by Booth Tarkington, The unpresentable appearance of Col. Crane by G. K. Chesterton, 1924; Mr. White, The red barn, Hell, and Bridewater, 1935.

Reminiscences

The world does move, 1928.

Essays

Looking forward and others, 1926; Commemorative tributes to: Beveridge by Booth Tarkington, Mead by Royal Cortissoz, Brownell by Bliss Perry, Sloane by Henry Van Dyke. Prepared for the American academy of arts and letters. 1928, 1929 (pamphlet).

Literary Criticism

Samuel Brohl and company translated from the French of Victor Cherbuliez with a critical introduction by Booth Tarkington, 1902; The name of Old glory, poems of patriotism by James Whitcomb Riley, with an appreciation of the poet by Booth Tarkington, frontispiece by Howard Chandler Christy, 1917.

Humor

The collector's whatnot, a compendium, manual, and syllabus of information and advice on all subjects appertaining to the collection of antiques, both ancient and not so ancient. Compiled by Cornelius Obenchain Van Loot [*pseud.* of Booth Tarkington] Milton Kilgallen [*pseud.* of Kenneth Roberts] and Murgatroyd Elphinstone [*pseud.* of Hugh MacNair Kahler], 1923.

Radio Plays

Maud and Cousin Bill, 1932–33 (caption-title; caption-titles vary; mimeographed; 77 [i.e. 75] parts).

Verses Set to Music

Love and the moon, words by Booth Tarkington, music by Jerome Kern. Sung by Billie Burke in Florenz Ziegfeld jr's production of Booth Tarkington's latest comedy "Rose Briar," 1922 (cover-title; sheet music).

Miscellany

The great German bluff about America, 1918 (cover-title; pamphlet); "Stay me with flagons," the story of the passing of a Lotos club motto as told by a committee of its members with illustrations by James Montgomery Flagg. Members contributing: George Ade, Irvin S. Cobb, John Elderkin, James Montgomery Flagg, J. Hartley Manners, Charles W. Price, Booth Tarkington, 1922 (cover-title; pamphlet).

Illustrator

Character sketches. The boss girl, a Christmas story and other sketches by James Whitcomb Riley, 1886 (cover design by Booth Tarkington); Poe's run and other poems, being the true and authentic narration of certain notable games wherein are set forth many marvelous good deeds wrought by the Princeton team, all done into verse in the vulgar tongue: to which is appended The book of the chronicles of the Elis, by M'Cready Sykes, with many pictures by Booth Tarkington, William B. Pell, and Harold Imbrie, 1904; Antiquamania edited by Kenneth L. Roberts, the collected papers of Professor Milton Kilgallen [*pseud.*] F. R. S., of Ugsworth college, elucidating the difficulties in the path of the antique dealer and collector and presenting various methods of meeting and overcoming them. With further illustrations, elucidations, and wood-cuts done on feather-edged boards by Booth Tarkington, 1928.

Selections

Strack selections from Booth Tarkington's stories arranged by Lilian Holmes Strack, 1926.

Collected Works

The works of Booth Tarkington . . . , 1918–28 (Autograph ed.; 21 vols.); The works of Booth Tarkington . . . , 1922–1932 (Seawood ed.; 27 vols.).

STUDIES AND ARTICLES

Baldwin (M)
Boynton (S)
Burgess
Chamberlain
Clark (B)
Cohen
Cohen, Helen L., *ed.* One-act plays by modern authors. 1921
Cooper (F)
† Currie, Barton W. Booth Tarkington, a bibliography. 1932
† Dickinson, Asa D. Booth Tarking-

ton, a gentleman from Indiana, the man—his work—his opinions. [1914] (caption-title; pamphlet; enl. ed., Booth Tarkington, a sketch. 1926)
Doubleday
Eaton
Egan
Farrar
Frank (S)
Freeman, Ethel H. A dramatization of Monsieur Beaucaire . . . made from Booth Tarkington's popular novel. 1916
Hamilton
Harkins (L)
Holliday, Robert C. Booth Tarkington. 1918
Holliday, Robert C. Broome street straws. [c1919]
Holliday, Robert C. Men, and books, and cities. [c1920]
† Johnson (1929)
† Johnson (1932)
† Johnson (1936)
Karsner
Kilmer
Kunitz (J)
Kunitz (L)
Loggins
Maillard
† Manly
Mantle
Marble
Markey
Mayorga (S)
Messager, André C. Monsieur Beaucaire, a romantic opera in three acts. (Founded on Booth Tarkington's story.) Book by Frederick Lonsdale. Lyrics by Adrian Ross [*pseud.*]. Music by André Messager. 1919
National
Overton
Overton (A)
Overton (H)
Pattee (N)
Phelps (A)
Quinn
† Quinn (H)
Rose, Edward E. Penrod, a comedy in four acts adapted for the stage from Booth Tarkington's Penrod stories. c1921
Sherman (P)
Stange, Hugh S. Booth Tarkington's Seventeen, a play of youth, and love, and summertime in four acts by Hugh Stanislaus Stange and Stannard Mears in collaboration with Stuart Walker. c1924
Tarkington, Booth. Penrod . . . illustrated by Gordon Grant. 1915 (contains Booth Tarkington, a gentleman from Indiana . . . by Asa Don Dickinson)
Van Doren
Van Doren (C)
Williams
Wilson, Harry L. The man from home, a novel . . . founded upon the play by N. Booth Tarkington and Harry Leon Wilson, illustrated by C. H. Taffs. 1915
Woolf
Woollcott, Alexander. Enchanted aisles. 1924
Yost, Dorothy and Offner, Mortimer. Alice Adams by Booth Tarkington, revised script by Dorothy Yost & Mortimer Offner, revised final script. 1935 (cover-title; mimeographed)

Anonymous. "The personal Tarkington." *AB.*, Jan. 1916, pp. 505–10; Barrett, Charles H. "Booth Tarkington." *Outl.*, Dec. 6, 1902, pp. 817–19; Boynton, Percy H. "Booth Tarkington." *EJ.*, Feb. 1923, pp. 117–25; Collins, Joseph. "The new Mr. Tarkington." *AB.*, Mar. 1927, pp. 12–21; Corbett, Elizabeth F. "Tarkington and the veiled lady." *AR.*, Sept. 1925, pp. 601–05; Currie, Barton. "Hints to Tarkingtonians." *Col.*, Part 9, Art. 4, pp. 1–16 (1932); Dennis, Alfred P. "Getting Booth Tarkington educated." *WW.*, Jan. 1930, pp. 57–60; Doubleday, Russell. "Booth Tarkington of the midlands." *LDIBR.*, Feb. 1924, pp. 224–25; Hélys, Marc. "Un romancier regionaliste américain, Booth Tarkington." *Corres.*, Aug. 25, 1923, pp. 644–62; Holliday, Robert C. "Tarkingtonapolis, from mule-car to flivver." *AB.*, Sept. 1918, pp. 84–92; Maurice, Arthur B. "The history of their books, Booth Tarkington, a preliminary paper." *AB.*, Dec. 1928, pp. 445–48; Maurice. "Newton Booth Tarkington." *AB.*, Feb. 1907, pp. 605–16; Roberts, Richard E. "Mr. Booth Tarkington through British eyes." *Liv.Age*, Mar. 1, 1919, pp. 541–45; Wyatt, Edith F. "Booth Tarkington, the seven ages of man." *N.Amer.Rev.*, Oct. 1922, pp. 499–512. For references to reviews, see *BRD.*, 1906–09, 1912–16, 1918–19, 1921–37.

(John Orley) Allen Tate, 1899–

Born November 19, 1899, in Winchester, Clark County, in the Blue Grass region of Kentucky. He is descended from Scotch-Irish pioneers and Virginia and Maryland tidewater stock. Taught at home in his early years, he attended private and public schools in Louisville, Nashville, and Washington, and, after studying at Georgetown University and the University of Virginia, took his bachelor's degree, *magna cum laude*, at Vanderbilt University in 1922.

A founder of the *Fugitive*, a journal of southern letters, and one of the editors (1922–25), he became a free-lance reviewer and critic in New York (1924–28), a contributor to many magazines, and southern editor of the *Hound and Horn* (1931–34). From 1928 to 1930 he held a Guggenheim fellowship for creative writing abroad, and lived in France. In 1936 he was a member of the staff of the Olivet Writers' Conference and delivered a Phi Beta Kappa address at the University of Virginia. He has lectured on English literature at Southwestern College, Memphis (1934–36), and on modern poetry at Columbia (1936). For his poetry he has been awarded the Caroline Sinkler Prize of the Poetry Society of South Carolina (1928, 1932), and the Midland Authors Prize (1933).

"Apart from poetry and criticism . . . ," he writes, "I am greatly interested in American history of the period preceding the War between the States, and as an amateur have written two books in that field." He feels that the significant values of life for the purposes of literature are the points at which individual emotional and instinctive experience are met and worked upon by the force of reason in time, as revealed in traditions. "Poetry does not dispense with tradition; it probes the deficiencies of a tradition," he declared in 1932 in the *Symposium.* ". . . The prior conditions for great poetry, given a great talent, are two: the thoroughness of the poet's discipline in a great objective system of 'truths,' and his lack of consciousness of such a discipline." The poet's background, thoroughly assimilated but almost unknown to him, shapes everything he writes and restrains his personal expression by serving as a point of reference. The traditions which have most influenced Tate have been those common to Americans and Western Europeans, and, more specifically, those of the Confederacy and his own family.

He has been described, because of this poetic philosophy and because of his imagery and poetic oppositions, as a "metaphysical" poet. "I suppose I belong," he writes, "to what is at present known, and I think improperly known, as the modern metaphysical school of poetry. I have never felt any of the influence of Whitman, who stands back of the Middle Western revival (Sandburg, Lindsay), nor of Robinson and Frost, who come directly from the nineteenth century. I should imagine that our best contemporary instance is the work of Yeats, with plenty of room for Eliot and Pound in the immediate background, and going back, in this country, to Dickinson and Poe. More remotely but no less powerfully the seventeenth-century metaphysicals would stand as the historical justification of this contemporary school. I think this fact largely explains the so-called obscurity of this sort of modern verse."

For further comment, see Critical Survey, p. 147.

BIBLIOGRAPHY

Poems

Mr. Pope and other poems, 1928; Three poems, 1930; Poems: 1928–1931, 1932; Robert E. Lee, 1932; The Mediterranean and other poems, 1936; * Selected poems, 1937.

Novel

The fathers, 1938.

Biography

Stonewall Jackson, the good soldier, a narrative, 1928; Jefferson Davis: his rise and fall, a biographical narrative, 1929.

Essays

I'll take my stand, the South and the agrarian tradition by twelve southerners, 1930; Reactionary essays on poetry and ideas, 1936.

Editor

Who owns America? A new declaration of independence edited by Herbert Agar & Allen Tate, 1936; America through the essay, an anthology for English courses edited by A. Theodore Johnson . . . and Allen Tate, 1938.

STUDIES AND ARTICLES

Kunitz (L) Riding

Burke, Kenneth. "Tentative proposal." *P.*, May 1937, pp. 96–100; Flint, Frank C. "Poems, 1928–1931." *Symp.*, July 1932, pp. 407–14; Glicksberg, Charles I. "Allen Tate and mother earth." *SR.*, July–Sept. 1937, pp. 284–95; Knickerbocker, William S. "The return of the native." *SR.*, Oct.–Dec. 1930, pp. 479–83; Morse, Samuel F. "Second reading." *P.*, Feb. 1938, pp. 262–66; Shafer, Robert. "Humanism and impudence, discussion of 'The fallacy of humanism.'" *AB.*, Jan. 1930, pp. 489–98; Zabel, Morton D. "The creed of Memory." *P.*, Apr. 1932, pp. 34–39; Zabel. "A critic's poetry." *P.*, Feb. 1929, pp. 281–84. For references to reviews, see *BRD.*, 1928–29, 1932, 1936–38.

Sara Teasdale, 1884–1933

Born August 8, 1884, in St. Louis, of colonial ancestry. She was the youngest of several children, and frail, and received her earliest education at home. She later attended a private school, from which she graduated in 1903.

She had begun early to write, and in school had made translations of German classics. With several friends she published a monthly manuscript magazine, with original illustrations, the *Potter's Wheel.* She had read widely also, and she traveled much and spent several winters in California and Arizona. From 1905 until 1907 she lived in Europe and the Near East, writing verse. When she returned, "Guenevere" was published in *Reedy's Mirror*, and in the same year appeared *Sonnets to Duse and Other Poems*. She wrote for *Century*, *Harper's*, *Scribner's*, and other magazines, and *Helen of Troy and Other Poems* brought her much favorable attention. "Vignettes Overseas" (in *Rivers to the Sea*) are the result of a summer visit in 1912 to Italy and Switzerland.

In 1914 she married Ernst B. Filsinger, an exporter, and in 1916 they settled in New York. Despite delicate health Miss Teasdale continued to write, and *Love Songs* won a prize awarded by Columbia University and the Poetry Society of America for work published in 1917. She went to England in 1923, and she wrote "Pictures in Autumn" (in *Dark of the Moon*) in France.

In the summer of 1932, in search of material for a biography of Christina Rossetti, she contracted pneumonia in London and returned in September to the United States. At first her health slowly improved, but she had a nervous breakdown from which she never recovered, and on January 29, 1933, she was found dead in her apartment in New York.

Miss Teasdale was never an ardent partisan in literary movements of her time. "I try to say what moves me," she once declared of her own work. "I never care to surprise my reader." A lyricist, she regarded her poems subjectively, not as the mere product of careful workmanship, but as an expression of her own feeling and a release for her own emotions.

For further comment, see Critical Survey, p. 132.

BIBLIOGRAPHY

Poems

Sonnets to Duse and other poems, 1907; Helen of Troy and other poems, 1911; Rivers to the sea, 1915; Love songs, 1917; Flame and shadow, 1920; Dark of the moon, 1926; Stars to-night, verses new and old for boys and girls . . . illustrated by Dorothy P. Lathrop, 1930; A country house . . . with drawings by Herbert F. Roese, 1932 (cover-title; pamphlet); Strange victory . . . with portrait and a poem in facsimile, 1933; * The collected poems of Sara Teasdale, 1937.

Verses Set to Music

Wings of night, a song by Wintter Watts [words by Sara Teasdale], 1917 (cover-title; sheet music); Pastoral (The look) [words by] Sara Teasdale [music by] Dagmar de Corval Rybner, 1918 (caption-title; sheet music); Swans, words by Sara Teasdale, music by Dagmar de C. Rybner, 1918 (cover-title; sheet music); A cycle of nine songs for high voice. Vignettes of Italy, text by Sara Teasdale, music by Wintter Watts, 1919 (sheet music); The kiss, song for medium voice, words by Sara Teasdale, music by Agide Jacchia, 1920 (cover-title; sheet music); Joy, a song by Wintter Watts, high voice [words by Sara Teasdale], 1922 (cover-title; sheet music); Two songs by Sara Teasdale set to music by Wintter Watts. I. Only a cry, medium voice. II. Let it be forgotten, high voice, 1923 (cover-title; sheet music; 2 vols.); At the evening's end [words by] Sara Teasdale [music by] A. Walter Kramer, 1931 (caption-title; sheet music); April song, for three-part chorus of women's voices, poem by Sara Teasdale, set to music by Harry B. Harelson, 1933 (cover-title; sheet music); Deep in the night, song, high voice—F# minor, low voice—D minor [by] Iris Brussels, words by Sara Teasdale, 1933 (cover-title; sheet music); Like barley bending, for male voices [words by] Sara Teasdale [music by] Leo Rich Lewis, 1933 (caption-title; sheet music); Stars [words by] Sara Teasdale [music by] William Berwald, 1934 (caption-title; sheet music); Sung by Oscar Davis. I shall not care, song, after a poem by Sara Teasdale, music by McNair Ilgenfritz, 1934 (cover-title; sheet music); Swans [words by] Sara Teasdale . . . [music by] A. Walter Kramer, 1934 (caption-title; sheet music); Elegy, words by Sara Teasdale, music by George Crandall, 1936 (cover-title; sheet music); Peace, song, with piano accompaniment by May Sabeston Walker, lyric by Sara Teasdale, 1936 (cover-title; sheet music).

Compiler

The answering voice, one hundred love lyrics by women selected by Sara Teasdale, 1917; Rainbow gold, poems old and new selected for boys and girls . . . with illustrations by Dugald Walker, 1922; The answering voice, love lyrics by women selected by Sara Teasdale. New edition with fifty recent poems added, 1928.

STUDIES AND ARTICLES

Cook
Dictionary
† Johnson (1929)
† Johnson (1932)
† Johnson (1936)
Kunitz (L)
Lowell
Lucas
[Macmillan, *firm, publishers, New York.*] Sara Teasdale. [1927?] (cover-title; pamphlet)
[Macmillan, *firm, publishers, New York.*] Sara Teasdale. [1937] (pamphlet)
The Mentor. Makers of modern American poetry—women, Sara Teasdale, two. c1920 (broadside)
Monroe
Rittenhouse
Tietjens
Untermeyer
Untermeyer (N)
Vočadlo
Ward
Wilkinson

Aiken, Conrad. "It is in truth a pretty toy." *D.*, Feb. 1925, pp. 107–14; Colum, Padraic. "Sara Teasdale's poems." *NR.*, June 22, 1918, pp. 239, 241; Deutsch, Babette. "The solitary ironist." *P.*, Dec. 1937, pp. 148–53; Fisher, Irene. "Strange victory, one woman's life." *NMQ.*, May 1934, pp. 123–26; Monroe, Harriet. "A farewell." *P.*, Nov. 1933, pp. 96–98; Monroe. "New lyrics by Sara Teasdale." *P.*, Dec. 1926, pp. 157–60; Monroe. "Sara Teasdale." *P.*, Feb. 1925, pp. 262–68; Monroe. "Sara Teasdale." *P.*, Apr. 1933, pp. 30–33; Monroe. "Sara Teasdale's prize." *P.*, Aug. 1918, pp. 264–69; Rittenhouse, Jessie B. "Sara Teasdale." *AB.*, May 1927, pp. 290–94; Skinner, Constance L. "Songs that give reason for singing." *N.Amer.Rev.*, Dec. 1926, pp. 695–700; † Smith, Mildred C. "American first editions, a series of bibliographic check-lists edited by Merle Johnson and Frederick M. Hopkins, number 32. Sara Teasdale (Mrs. Ernst B. Filsinger) 1884–." *PW.*, May 5, 1923, p. 1380; Tietjens, Eunice. "A singer." *P.*, Feb. 1921, pp. 272–75; Wilkinson, Marguerite. "Sara Teasdale's poems." *Forum*, Feb. 1921, pp. 229–35. For references to reviews, see *BRD.*, 1907, 1911, 1915, 1917, 1920, 1922, 1926, 1928, 1930, 1933, 1937.

James (Grover) Thurber, 1894–

Born December 8, 1894, in Columbus, Ohio, the son of a politician. He was educated in Columbus and attended Ohio State University. In 1918 he became a code clerk in the State Department, serving in the Paris Embassy until 1920. Since 1920 he has been engaged in journalism. He was a reporter on the Columbus *Dispatch* in 1920–24, and on the Paris edition of the Chicago *Tribune*, 1924–25; in 1925 he joined the staff of the New York *Evening Post* and in less than a year proceeded to the *New Yorker*. At present he is not a staff member, but he contributes frequently, and his work has appeared also in other magazines. His sketches and illustrations, noteworthy especially for the shapeless and spineless droopiness of the human figures, are familiar to readers of the *New Yorker*.

"My theories and views of literature," he writes, "vary with the lateness of the hour, the quality of my companions, and the quantity of liquor. I have a great affection for the works of Henry James and lug the 35 volumes of the definitive edition around with me wherever I go. I am interested in the writings of George Milburn, William March, Robert M. Coates, John O'Hara, Conrad Aiken, Hemingway, Fitzgerald, Edmund Wilson. I am opposed to every restriction, mould, pattern, and commandment for literature that is set up by the Marxist literary critics. A few of my special favorites in fiction are *The Great Gatsby*, *Lady into Fox*, Cather's *My Ântonia*, *My Mortal Enemy* and *A Lost Lady*, which will indicate that I like the perfectly done, the well-ordered, as against the sprawling chunk of life. . . . I owe a great debt to the late Prof. Joseph Russell Taylor of Ohio State University, whose rich understanding of literature and life gave my urge to write a push and a direction. I also owe a debt to E. B. White . . . whose perfect clarity of expression is it seems to me equalled by very few and surpassed by simply nobody. . . . I came to the *New Yorker* a writer of journalese and it was my study of White's writing, I think, that helped me to straighten out my prose so that people could see what it meant."

For further comment, see Critical Survey, p. 162.

BIBLIOGRAPHY

Humorous Sketches and Drawings

Is sex necessary? or, Why you feel the way you do by James Thurber and E. B. White, 1929; * The owl in the attic and other perplexities . . . with many drawings by the author, 1931 (intro. by E. B. White); My life and hard times, 1933; The middle-aged man on the flying trapeze, a collection of short pieces with drawings by the author, 1935; Let your mind alone! And other more or less inspirational pieces . . . with drawings by the author, 1937.

Drawings

The seal in the bedroom & other predicaments . . . with an introduction by Dorothy Parker, 1932; The last flower, a parable in pictures, 1939.

Illustrator

Her foot is on the brass rail by Don Marquis, 1935; How to raise a dog: in the city, in the suburbs, by James R. Kinney . . . with Ann Honeycutt, illustrated by James Thurber, 1938; In a word by Margaret S. Ernst, drawings by James Thurber, 1939.

STUDIES AND ARTICLES

Birchman

Bacon, Leonard. "Humors and careers." *SRL.*, Apr. 29, 1939, pp. 3–4, 22. For references to reviews, see *BRD.*, 1929, 1931, 1933, 1935, 1937.

Dan Totheroh, 1895–

Born in San Francisco. When he finished high school, he decided against further education and immediately entered the theatrical profession. As a member of the Alcazar Stock Company he played various roles in the years (1915–17) immediately preceding the entry of the United States into the World War. In the war, during which he was working in an engineering group, he wrote military notes for the San Francisco *Bulletin*, and stories for *Argosy* and other magazines.

Upon his return to San Francisco he directed the Players' Club, a little-theater group playing in regular seasons in the spring and fall. In his own vaudeville sketch *Her Kid Brother* he toured the Coast and the Middle West for six months. When he reached Hollywood, he joined the cast of *The Pilgrimage Play*, an outdoor spectacle.

Observations made on his travels in Nebraska were the foundation for *Wild Birds*. The author submitted the play in a contest held by the University of California for a work by a California dramatist to be presented at the Greek Theatre of the University at Berkeley. Of the more than eighty plays submitted to the jury, which consisted of Susan Glaspell, George Jean Nathan, and Eugene O'Neill, Totheroh's was the choice; and it was produced in Wheeler Hall at the University in March, 1922. After two weeks in Berkeley it ran for two more in San Francisco, acted by the Players' Club, and returned to Berkeley for a third fortnight.

Although he won another honor with *In the Darkness*, a one-act play that took the prize of $150 offered by the United Neighborhood Playhouses of New York, Totheroh spent most of this period directing; and he earned a considerable reputation by producing outdoor pageants like his own *Tamalpa*, performed at Mount Talampais, near San Francisco, and *Ersa of the Red Trees*, given in the Redwood National Forest. In 1924 the little theater of the artists' colony at Carmel presented his *The Princess Salome*, and in the fall he became director of the Greek Theatre of the University of California.

To secure a New York production of a play, he went to New York in the same year. Thanks to the efforts of Charles and Kathleen Norris, *Wild Birds* was produced at Cherry Lane Playhouse in April, 1925.

BIBLIOGRAPHY

Plays

Wild birds, a play in three acts by Dan Totheroh, first produced in Wheeler hall, University of California, March 25, 1922, under the direction of Irving

Pichel. Editorial board: Charles Mills Gayley, Max Radin, Stephen C. Pepper, 1922; The Kelly kid, a comedy in one act by Kathleen Norris and Dan Totheroh, 1926; The breaking of the calm, a play in one act, 1928; The lost princess, fantasy in one act (a sequel to "The stolen prince"), 193–; Pearls, play in one act, 193–; The stolen prince, fantasy in one act, 193–; One-act plays for everyone, 1931 (The stolen prince; The lost princess; Good vintage; In the darkness; The breaking of the calm; Pearls; The great dark; While the mushrooms bubble; The widdy's mite; A tune of a tune; Mirthful marionettes); * Distant drums, a play in three acts, 1932; The great dark, a play in one act by Dan Totheroh revised by Harold Brighouse, 1934; Moor born, a play, 1934.

Novels

Wild orchard, 1927; Burlesque, from the play by Arthur Hopkins and George Manker Watters novelized by Dan Totheroh, 1928 (also pub. as: The dance of life, 1929); Men call me fool, 1929.

Juvenile Literature

David Hotfoot . . . illustrated by Maurice Day, 1926; The last dragon . . . illustrated by Eleanor Osborn Eadie, 1927.

Moving-Picture Script

"The count of Monte Cristo" [scenario by Phillip Dunne, Dan Totheroh, and Rowland W. Lee, adapted from the novel by Alexander Dumas]. 1934 (caption-title; mimeographed).

STUDIES

Cohen (M)

For references to reviews, see *BRD.*, 1925, 1927, 1929, 1934.

Gregory Trent, *pseud.* *See* Thames Williamson

Louis Untermeyer, 1885–

Born in New York, October 1, 1885. He was educated in New York City and attended De Witt Clinton High School, from which he never graduated. Although he was ambitious for a career as composer and was a pianist of skill, he entered, at seventeen, his father's jewelry-manufacturing firm in Newark, in which, as designer, factory manager, and vice-president, he spent some twenty years.

In 1923, having already published many volumes of prose and verse, he retired from business for two years of study abroad, and since then his only profession has been literature. In 1928 he moved from New York City to a farm in the Adirondacks. "My days," he writes, "are fairly well divided, like Caesar's Gaul, into three parts: farming, writing, and lecturing. . . . I was the Honnold Lecturer at Knox during its centenary year, in 1937, and I became Poetry Editor of the *American Mercury* in 1935."

His lectures cover a range of topics in modern literature, and he has contributed articles to the *Encyclopaedia Britannica* on modern American poetry.

He has been actively associated with the *Masses*, the *Liberator*, and the *Seven Arts*, and he has been a frequent lecturer at colleges and universities. *The Donkey of God* won the Enit Prize for the best book to be written about Italy by someone not an Italian.

"My general attitude," he says, "seems to be 'centrist.' While I appreciate the value of tradition, I applaud the validity of experiment. Since I refuse to ally myself with any particular group, I naturally receive pot-shots and counterblasts from both camps. If I had to choose either—a choice which, thank God, has not yet been forced upon me—I would go over unhesitatingly to the radicals and experimenters, even though I am by nature a son of Libra, and hence a hesitating Liberal."

For further comment, see Critical Survey, pp. 168, 189, 204.

BIBLIOGRAPHY

Poems

First love, a lyric sequence, 1911; Challenge, 1914; These times, 1917; The new Adam, 1920; Roast Leviathan, 1923; By Richard Starr Untermeyer, 1927 (contains collaborations by Richard and Louis Untermeyer); Burning bush, 1928; Adirondack cycle, 1929 (pamphlet); Food and drink . . . with drawings by George Plank, 1932; First words before spring . . . with designs by George Plank, 1933 (cover-title; pamphlet).

Parodies

The younger quire, 1910; "—and other poets" . . . with frontispiece by George Wolfe Plank, 1916; Including Horace, 1919; Heavens . . . with a cover design and frontispiece by C. Bertram Hartman, 1922; Collected parodies, 1926.

Novel

Moses, a novel, 1928.

Autobiography

From another world, the autobiography of Louis Untermeyer, 1939.

Books on Poetry

The new era in American poetry, 1919; American poetry since 1900, 1923 (Based on The new era in American poetry); The forms of poetry, a pocket dictionary of verse, 1926; Poetry, its appreciation and enjoyment by Louis Untermeyer . . . and Carter Davidson, 1934; Merrill Moore, 1935 (pamphlet); Doorways to poetry by Louis Untermeyer in consultation with Bertha Evans Ward . . . and Ruth M. Stauffer, 1938; Play in poetry . . . The Henry Ward Beecher lectures delivered at Amherst college, October, 1937, 1938.

Biography

* Heinrich Heine, paradox and poet . . . The life, 1937.

Children's Books

The donkey of God . . . illustrated by James MacDonald, 1932; Chip: my life and times as overheard by Louis Untermeyer, illustrated by Vera Neville and the author, 1933; The last pirate, tales from the Gilbert and Sullivan operas . . . illustrated by Reginald Birch, 1934.

Travel

Blue Rhine, Black Forest, a hand- and day-book, 1930.

Verses Set to Music

Prayer, song, words by Louis Untermeyer, music by Maurice Baron, 1934 (cover-title; sheet music); Only of thee and me, song, the words by Louis Untermeyer, the music by James Spencer, 1937 (cover-title; sheet music).

Selected Work

Selected poems and parodies of Louis Untermeyer, 1935.

Editor

Modern American poetry, an introduction, 1919 (rev. eds., 1921, 1925, 1930, 1936); Modern British poetry, 1920 (rev. eds., 1925, 1930, 1936); Modern American and British poetry, 1922 (rev. ed., 1928); This singing world, an anthology of modern poetry for young people collected and edited . . . illustrations by Florence Wyman Ivins, 1923 (rev. eds., This singing world [Junior edition] A collection of modern poetry for young people collected and edited . . . illustrations by Decie Merwin, 1926; This singing world for younger children, modern poems selected, 1926); Walt Whitman, The pamphlet poets, price 25 cents, 1926 (cover-title); Yesterday and today, a comparative anthology, 1926 (also pub. as Yesterday and today, a collection of verse [mostly modern] designed for the average person of nine to nineteen and possibly higher, arranged and selected by L. Untermeyer . . . with many delectable drawings as well as linoleum blocks by Edna Reindel, 1927); Conrad Aiken, The pamphlet poets, price 25 cents, 1927 (cover-title); Emily Dickinson, The pamphlet poets, price 25 cents, 1927 (cover-title); New songs for new voices edited by Louis Untermeyer and Clara and David Mannes with pen drawings by Peggy Bacon, 1928; A critical anthology: Modern American poetry, Modern British poetry, combined edition, 1930 (rev. ed., 1936); American poetry from the beginning to Whitman, 1931; The book of living verse, English and American poetry from the thirteenth century to the present day, 1932 (English ed., The Albatross book of living verse, English and American poetry from the thirteenth century to the present day, 1933); The Albatross book of modern living verse, English and American poetry of the later nineteenth and of the twentieth centuries, 1933 (also pub. as The Albatross book of recent living verse, English and American poetry of the twentieth century, 1933; repr. from The Albatross book of living verse); Rainbow in the sky collected and edited . . . illustrated by Reginald Birch, 1935; The new modern American & British poetry edited with suggestions for study and appreciation, 1939.

Compiler

A miscellany of American poetry 1920, 1920; American poetry 1922, a miscellany, 1922; American poetry 1925, a miscellany, 1925; American poetry 1927, a miscellany, 1927.

Translations

Poems of Heinrich Heine, three hundred and twenty-five poems selected and translated, 1917; Man and the masses (Masse mensch) a play of the social revolution in seven scenes by Ernst Toller. . . . The Theatre guild version with six illustrations from photographs of the Theatre guild production, 1924; The fat of the cat and other stories [by Gottfried Keller] freely adapted . . . illustrated by Albert Sallak, 1925; Heinrich Heine, paradox and poet . . . The poems, 1937.

STUDIES AND ARTICLES

Aiken
Farrar
Hart, Olive E. Enjoyment of modern poetry, a pamphlet for teachers. [c1924] (cover-title; pamphlet)
Kreymborg
Kunitz (L)
Lowell
† Manly
Markey
Mersand
National
Phelps
Smith
Untermeyer (M)
Wier, Albert E., *comp.* Songs to sing to children selected with additions by Albert E. Wier from New songs for new voices edited by Louis Untermeyer and Clara and David Mannes. [c1935]

Anonymous. "Louis Untermeyer." *AB.*, Oct. 1921, pp. 124–27; Deutsch, Babette. "Louis Untermeyer's buch der liebe." *AB.*, Nov. 1925, pp. 323–26; Fuller, Henry B. "A parodist." *P.*, Sept. 1916, pp. 321–22; Henderson, Alice C. "The old Adam." *P.*, Jan. 1921, pp. 212–16; Henderson. "On 'the movement.'" *P.*, June 1919, pp. 159–67; Lowell, Amy. "A poet of the present." *P.*, Dec. 1917, pp. 157–64; Monroe, Harriet. "Challenge." *P.*, Aug. 1914, pp. 203–05; Pawlik, Martin. "Amerikanische literatur." *E.Studien*, Feb. 1925, pp. 137–48; Peckham, Harry H. "The poetry of Louis Untermeyer." *SAQ.*, Jan. 1918, pp. 58–64; Sale, William M., jr. "Another exile." *P.*, Apr. 1938, pp. 46–51. For references to reviews, see *BRD.*, 1914, 1916–17, 1919–20, 1922–23, 1927–38.

Carl (Clinton) Van Doren, 1885–

Born September 10, 1885, in Hope, Illinois, the eldest of the five sons of a country doctor. His parents were prosperous and better educated than most of the neighbors, and the children had the advantages of books and schools. After five years in the village the family moved to a farm, and until he was fifteen Van Doren lived in this environment and attended a local school.

In Urbana, to which they subsequently moved, he finished high school in three years, with social and athletic, as well as scholastic, distinctions, and in this period he began writing. At the University of Illinois he discovered Marlowe and became an eager reader of poetry. When he graduated in 1907, it was with honors in all fields of student activity: he had been class poet, editor of the literary magazine, and president of the honorary senior society. He remained for another year as a graduate student and assistant in rhetoric. He has said that he was self-taught under the generous provisions made by the university; when he finished, he had a broad background in classical, European, and English literature, and had even written Anglo-Saxon verse.

The most potent influence on him at Illinois had been Stuart Sherman, and, encouraged by Sherman's erudition and scholarly enthusiasm, he went to New York in 1908 to study for the Ph.D. at Columbia. In the course of his work on Thomas Love Peacock, the subject of his dissertation, he went to Europe with Sherman in the summer of 1910. He returned, after visiting England, Scotland, Holland, Germany, and Paris, early in 1911 and took his degree at Columbia in that year.

He accepted an instructorship at Columbia in the same year, which enabled him to live in New York and to spend his summers writing. Working closely with Professor W. P. Trent, he was managing editor of *The Cambridge History of American Literature*, and with Trent he conducted a seminar in which both Mark Van Doren and Joseph Wood Krutch were students.

In 1916 he resigned his assistant professorship at Columbia, keeping only his graduate class in American literature, and became headmaster at the Brearley School in New York, a secondary school for girls. His disliked his duties; and, resigning them in 1919, he accepted, at the invitation of the editor, Oswald Garrison Villard, whose daughter was a student in the school, a post as literary editor of the *Nation*. In this capacity he was free to outline and present the critical position of the magazine and to select reviewers of fresh and unhackneyed views. His associates included Mark Van Doren, Joseph Wood Krutch, Ludwig Lewisohn, and H. L. Mencken, and in this period there was a critical and literary revival that he has compared to that in Boston in the middle of the nineteenth century.

In 1922 he left the *Nation* for the *Century*, and in 1926, having resigned his post with the *Century*, he founded, with Glenn Frank, Zona Gale, and Joseph Wood Krutch, the Literary Guild, from which he retired in 1934. In the same year he was made a member of the managing committee of *The Dictionary of American Biography*. In recent years he has conducted a weekly book column for the Boston *Herald*. In 1932 he made a transcontinental lecture tour; since 1935, however, he has given up all other activities for writing. He has many literary and artistic friends. He was elected in 1924 to membership in the National Institute of Arts and Letters, but declined. His *Benjamin Franklin* was awarded the Pulitzer Prize for biography in 1939. He gave the German rights to the book to an exiled German publisher in Holland.

Van Doren is interested in literature as a revelation of human experience, and he studies the differences in individuals and the changes brought about in them by the "three worlds" in which he has lived. He has remained aloof from the narrower literary controversies, trying to find intrinsic qualities of excellence, rather than a pronounced tendency, in a work under criticism. In politics he has retained his faith in the democratic ideal and in the ability of Americans to make effective use of the powers and forces in their possession.

For further comment, see Critical Survey, pp. 168, 180, 200–01, 202.

BIBLIOGRAPHY

Novel

The ninth wave, 1926.

Short Stories

Other provinces, 1925.

Autobiography

* Three worlds, 1936.

Biography

The life of Thomas Love Peacock . . . with three photogravure plates, 1911; Swift, 1930; * Benjamin Franklin, 1938 (3 vols.; also pub. in 1 vol. ed.).

Literary Criticism

The American novel, 1921; Contemporary American novelists, 1900–1920, 1922; Contemporary fiction and the high school teacher of English, 1923 (pamphlet); The roving critic, 1923; Many minds, 1924; American and British literature since 1890 by Carl Van Doren and Mark Van Doren, 1925; James Branch Cabell, 1925; Edna St. Vincent Millay. Youth and wings, Edna St. Vincent Millay, singer, 1927? (pamphlet); American literature, an introduction, 1933 (also pub. as What is American literature? 1935); Sinclair Lewis, a biographical sketch . . . with a bibliography by Harvey Taylor, 1933.

Miscellany

A map of Sinclair Lewis' United States as it appears in his novels [by George Anand] with notes by Carl Van Doren, 1934 (broadside).

Editor

The Cambridge history of American literature edited by William Peterfield Trent . . . John Erskine . . . Stuart P. Sherman . . . Carl Van Doren . . ., 1917–21 (4 vols.; English ed., A history of American literature); Tales by Washington Irving, selected and edited with an introduction, 1918; Benjamin Franklin and Jonathan Edwards, selections from their writings edited with an introduction, 1920; Seven stories by Nathaniel Hawthorne edited with an introduction, 1920; Tales by Nathaniel Hawthorne, selected and edited with an introduction, 1921; Selections from the writings of Thomas Paine edited with an introduction, 1922; A short history of American literature based upon the Cambridge history of American literature edited by William Peterfield Trent, John Erskine, Stuart P. Sherman, and Carl Van Doren, 1922; The London omnibus, with an introduction, 1932; An American omnibus, with an introduction, 1933; Modern American prose, 1934; An anthology of world prose edited by Carl Van Doren with translations by William Caxton, John Dryden, Percy Bysshe Shelley, Dante Gabriel Rossetti, Walter Pater, Sir Richard F. Burton, Andrew Lang, Havelock Ellis, Thorstein Veblen, Arthur Waley, D. H. Lawrence, Pearl S. Buck, and many others, 1935; The world wide illustrated encyclopedia prepared under the editorship of C. Ralph Taylor, associate editor Carl Van Doren, with special articles and departmental supervision by 462 leading editors, educators, and specialists in the United States and Europe. Complete in two volumes, 1935 (also pub. in 6 vol. ed.); The Borzoi reader edited with an introduction and notes, 1936.

STUDIES AND ARTICLES

Herrmann
Kunitz (L)
National
Saturday
Schreiber
† Van Doren (M)
Zeitlin

Glicksberg, Charles I. "Carl Van Doren, scholar and skeptic." *SR.*, Apr.–June 1938, pp. 223–34; Jones, William P. "The American novel." *SR.*, Oct.–Dec. 1921, pp. 497–99. For references to reviews, see *BRD.*, 1912, 1921–26, 1930, 1933–36, 1938.

Mark (Albert) Van Doren, 1894–

Born in Hope, Illinois, June 13, 1894. The eldest of his four brothers is Carl Van Doren, who has described him as "the most gifted and charming of us all." He was educated in Urbana and graduated in 1914, with a brilliant record, at the University of Illinois. Taking his master's degree under Stuart Sherman in the following year, he proceeded to Columbia for advanced work.

Ready in 1917 for his Ph.D., with his dissertation on Dryden almost finished, he was drafted and served in the infantry during the war. Subsequently, with his friend Joseph Wood Krutch, he traveled in England and France on a fellowship from Columbia. After his return he took his doctor's degree and began his academic career at Columbia, where he has been a popular teacher. He has lectured also for the New School of Social Research.

After his return from Europe he joined the staff of the *Nation*, and with his brother he wrote reviews of poetry. His own poems began to appear in magazines, and from 1924 to 1928 he was literary editor of the *Nation*. More recently, his wife, Dorothy Van Doren, has been an associate editor. They live in New York and spend their leisure time on their farm in Connecticut.

Van Doren is interested in criticism and enjoys reviewing as a means of keeping up with contemporary writing, but he is more absorbed in making his own contributions to literature. His main interest is writing poetry.

For further comment, see Critical Survey, pp. 200–01.

BIBLIOGRAPHY

Poems

Spring thunder and other poems, 1924; 7 P.M. & other poems, 1926; Now the sky & other poems, 1928; Jonathan Gentry . . . illustrated by H. R. Bishop, 1931; A winter diary and other poems, 1935; The last look and other poems, 1937; Collected poems, 1922–1938, 1939.

Novel

The transients, 1935.

Children's Books

Dick and Tom, tales of two ponies . . . illustrated by George M. Richards: endpapers by Margaret Van Doren, 1931; Dick and Tom in town . . . illustrated by George Richards, 1932.

Literary Criticism

Henry David Thoreau, a critical study, 1916; The poetry of John Dryden, 1920 (also issued as The poetry of John Dryden . . . submitted in partial fulfilment of the requirements for the degree of doctor of philosophy in the Faculty of philosophy, Columbia university, 1920); American and British literature since 1890 by Carl Van Doren and Mark Van Doren, 1925; Edwin

Arlington Robinson, 1927; Shakespeare, 1939; Studies in metaphysical poetry [by] Theodore Spencer and Mark Van Doren, two essays and a bibliography, 1939.

Editor

A history of the life and death, virtues & exploits of General George Washington by Mason Weems, 1927; Samuel Sewall's diary, 1927; An anthology of world poetry . . . in English translations by Chaucer, Swinburne, Dowson, Symons, Rossetti, Waley, Herrick, Pope, Francis Thompson, E. A. Robinson, and others, 1928; A journey to the land of Eden and other papers by William Byrd, 1928; Nick of the woods, or, The Jibbenainosay, a tale of Kentucky by Robert Montgomery Bird, 1928; The travels of William Bartram, 1928; An autobiography of America, 1929; Correspondence of Aaron Burr and his daughter Theodosia, edited with a preface, 1929; A junior anthology of world poetry edited by Mark Van Doren . . . and Garibaldi M. Lapolla, 1929; The life of Sir William Phips by Cotton Mather, edited with a preface, 1929; American poets, 1630–1930, 1932 (also pub. as Masterpieces of American poets . . . de luxe edition, 1936); The Oxford book of American prose, chosen & edited, 1932; The world's best poems edited by Mark Van Doren . . . and Garibaldi M. Lapolla, 1932; An anthology of English and American poetry edited with an introduction . . . being the English, Irish, and American sections of An anthology of world poetry, 1936 (also pub. as An anthology of the finest English and American poetry, edited with an introduction, 1938).

STUDIES AND ARTICLES

Herrmann
Kreymborg
Kunitz (L)

Baker, Howard. "A note on the poetry of Mark Van Doren." *So.R.*, Winter 1936, pp. 601–08; Gilmore, William. "A few ghosts." *P.*, Dec. 1937, pp. 164–67; Kunitz, Stanley J. "A house in the country." *P.*, Oct. 1935, pp. 46–49; Monroe, Harriet. "Slants and whimsies." *P.*, Oct. 1927, pp. 47–50; Moore, Marianne. "Victorious defeats." *P.*, July 1932, pp. 222–24; Strobel, Marion. "Mellowness." *P.*, Feb. 1925, pp. 279–81; Zabel, Morton D. "But still of earth." *P.*, Apr. 1930, pp. 50–51. For references to reviews see *BRD.*, 1916, 1920, 1924, 1927–32, 1935–37, 1939.

Hendrik Willem van Loon, 1882–

Born in Rotterdam, January 14, 1882, into a well-to-do Dutch family. He was reared in Europe and attended Dutch private schools, but came to this country when he was twenty-one. He graduated in 1905 at Cornell, did graduate work at Harvard, and took his Ph.D. at Munich in 1911.

During the Russian Revolution of 1906 he was correspondent for the Associated Press in various European cities. Until the beginning of the World War he taught history in American universities, and in 1915 he returned from Europe to lecture on modern history at Cornell. During the war he served as correspondent in many countries, and was interested especially in the situation of the neutral countries.

After serious injury in a boat explosion he returned to the United States and supported himself by writing advertising. With the publication of *Ancient Man* and the great popularity of *The Story of Mankind*, which, rejected at first by publishers, was translated into more than a dozen languages, and won the Newberry Medal, he was made independent. In 1922–23 he was professor of history at Antioch College, and in the next year he was associate editor of the Baltimore *Sun*. His later works have enjoyed a wide sale in this country and elsewhere, and he received a decoration in 1937 from Queen Wilhelmina of the Netherlands. He has been a radio commentator for the National Broadcasting Company, and he wrote the commentary for *The Fight for Peace*, a documentary anti-war film.

Equipped with a knowledge of many languages and gifted with an accurate memory, he immerses himself completely in any historical period of which he intends to write, and he writes and rewrites many times. He has practiced most of the arts and feels more concerned with them than with politics. "While appreciating the comforts and luxuries of our own time," he writes, "I am convinced . . . that in the basic principles we are completely wrong. But I can not change it. So all I can do is to try and make people wonder and worry whether this is the best of all possible forms of civilization." He declares himself to be hopelessly in the middle of the road and distressed by the fanaticism of religious or political partisanship, and he describes himself as preferring, with Erasmus, "the Popish way of living with the Lutheran way of thinking."

BIBLIOGRAPHY

Historical Studies

The fall of the Dutch republic, 1913 (new ed., with illus. by the author, 1924); The rise of the Dutch kingdom, 1795–1813, a short account of the early development of the modern kingdom of the Netherlands, 1915 (illus. by the author); The golden book of the Dutch navigators . . . illustrated with seventy reproductions of old prints, 1916 (rev. ed., illus. by the author, 1938); Tolerance, 1925 (English ed., The liberation of mankind, the story of man's struggle for the right to think, 1926); America, 1927 (illus. by the author; also pub. as The story of America, 1934); Life and times of Pieter Stuyvesant, 1928 (illus. by the author); Ships & how they sailed the seven seas (5000 B.C.–A.D. 1935), 1935 (illus. by the author); Our battle . . . being one man's answer to My battle by Adolf Hitler, 1938.

Juvenile Literature

History with a match, being an account of the earliest navigators and the discovery of America, written and drawn and done into color, 1917 (illustrated title, mounted on cover: A short history of discovery from the earliest times to the founding of colonies on the American continent. At two in the morning of the 12th of October of the year 1492, America was discovered; also pub. as The romance of discovery, being an account of the earliest navigators and the discovery of America, written and drawn and done into color, 1936); Ancient man, the beginning of civilizations, written and drawn and done into color, 1920; * The story of mankind, 1921 (illus. by the author); The story of the Bible, written and drawn, 1923; Episodes from The story of mankind, 1927; Man, the miracle maker, 1928 (illus. by the author; also pub. as The story of inventions, man, the miracle maker, 1934; English ed., Multiplex man, or, The story of survival through invention, 1928); How to do it, a book for children with introduction and pen and ink sketches by Hendrik Willem van Loon, compiled from articles in the Encyclopaedia britannica, 1933; Around the world with the alphabet and Hendrik Willem van Loon. To teach little children their letters and at the same time give their papas and mamas something to think about, 1935 (illus. by the author).

Biography

Adriaen Block, skipper, trader, explorer . . . illustrations by the author, 1928; * R.v.R., being an account of the last years and the death of one Rembrandt Harmenszoon van Rijn, a painter and etcher of some renown who lived and worked (which in his case was the same) in the town of Amsterdam (which is in Holland) and died of general neglect and diverse other unfortunate circumstances on the fourth of October of the year of grace 1669 (God have mercy upon his soul) and who was attended in his afflictions by one Joannis van Loon, doctor medicinae and chirurgeon in extraordinary to a vast number of humble citizens whose enduring gratitude has erected him a monument less perishable than granite and more enduring than porphyry and who during a most busy life yet found time to write down these personal recollections of the greatest of his fellow-citizens and which are now for the first time presented (provided with as few notes, emendations, and critical observations as possible) by his great-great-grandson, nine times removed, Hendrik Willem van Loon, in the year of grace 1930, and in the town of Veere which is in Zeeland, and printed by Horace Liveright in the town of Nieuw Amsterdam which is in America, 1930 (illus. lining-papers by the author; also pub. with The literary guild imprint, 1930; also pub. as Life and times of Rembrandt, R.v.R., originally published as "R.v.R., the life and times of Rembrandt van Rijn," 1932); The last of the troubadours, Carl Michael Bellman, 1740–1795, his life and his music by Hendrik Willem van Loon and Grace Castagnetta, 1939 (illus. by Hendrik van Loon).

Essays

To have or to be—take your choice . . . with decorations by the author, 1932 (pamphlet); Air-storming, a collection of 40 radio talks delivered . . . over the stations of the National broadcasting company, 1935 (illus. by the author; English ed., Van Loon on the air, broadcasts from the studio of the National broadcasting co., New York, 1936); A world divided is a world lost, 1935 (illus. by the author); Observations on the mystery of print and the work of Johann Gutenberg, 1937 (illus. by the author).

History of Art

* The arts, written and illustrated, 1937 (English ed., The arts of mankind, 1938).

Geography and History

Van Loon's geography, the story of the world we live in, written and illustrated, 1932 (English ed., The home of mankind, the story of the world we live in, 1933).

Travel

An indiscreet itinerary, or, How the unconventional traveler should see Holland by one who was actually born there and whose name is Hendrik Willem van Loon, 1933 (illus. by the author).

Satire

The story of Wilbur the hat, being a true account of the strange things which sometimes happen in a part of the world which does not exist. Written and drawn for the fun of it, 1925; N⁰ 432198. P. RX. Secret and confidential. Re: An elephant up a tree. This is the true story of Sir John, or, Why the elephants decided to remain elephants as told by one of them (in the strictest confidence however and therefore you must not repeat this to a soul) to Hendrik Willem van Loon in the year 29,395,721 after the birth of the first of the pachyderms which we human beings call anno Domini 1933, 1933 (illus. by the author).

Pictorial Map

A graphic history of the evolution of silk, 1922 (broadside).

Game

Hendrik Van Loon's Wide world game, 1933 (game board and box with playing pieces; illus. by Hendrik van Loon).

Anthologies

The songs we sing, 1936 (cover-title; illus. by Hendrik van Loon; music arranged by Grace Castagnetta); Christmas carols, illustrated and done into simple music by Grace Castagnetta and Hendrik Willem Van Loon, 1937; Folk songs of many lands by Grace Castagnetta and Hendrik Willem van Loon, 1938 (illus. by Hendrik van Loon).

Illustrator

This changing world, as I see its trend and purpose, by Samuel S. Fels, drawings by Hendrik Willem van Loon, 1933; Here and now story book by Lucy Mitchell illustrated by Hendrik Willem Van Loon, 1936; The wonder book of travellers' tales by H. C. Adams with an introduction and illustrations by Hendrik Willem Van Loon, additional decorations by William Siegel, 1936; Why social security? [by Mary Ross], 1938 (cover-title; pamphlet).

STUDIES AND ARTICLES

Frank (T)
† Johnson (1936)
Karsner
Kunitz (J)
Kunitz (L)
Markey
National
Schreiber
[Simon and Schuster, inc., *publishers*.] A few of the author's drawings from Van Loon's geography. [1932] (cover-title; pamphlet)
West (S)

Search-light. "Poor little rich boy." *N.Yer.*, June 19, 1926, pp. 19–20;
Snider, Charles L. "Tolerance, two social studies." *VQR.*, Oct. 1926, pp. 623–

30; Wahlen, Francis J. "Hendrik Van Loon and his Dutch critics." *CW.*, July 1925, pp. 499–502. For references to reviews, see *BRD.*, 1913, 1915, 1920–21, 1923, 1925, 1927–30, 1932–33, 1935–38.

Cornelius Obenchain Van Loot, *pseud.* *See* Booth Tarkington

Carl Van Vechten, 1880–

Born in Cedar Rapids, Iowa, June 17, 1880, into an old New York State family of Dutch origin. His father was an insurance agent and a bank director. He attended high school in Cedar Rapids and graduated from the University of Chicago in 1903; for a time he reported for the Chicago *American*. In 1906 he joined the staff of the New York *Times* as assistant music critic under Richard Aldrich, and he remained until 1913, except for the interruption of a year in Paris as correspondent for the *Times* in 1908–09. He edited program notes for the Symphony Society of New York for the season 1910–11, contributed musical biographies to the revision (1911) of the *Century Dictionary*, and conducted two departments in the *New Music Review*. In 1913–14 he was dramatic critic for the New York *Press*.

Since 1914, the year of his marriage to the Russian actress Fania Marinoff, he has held no staff positions on newspapers but has written independently. At first a contributor to literary and musical publications, he abandoned criticism when he was about forty and turned to the novel. *Peter Whiffle* was a best-seller, and succeeding volumes maintained this record.

Van Vechten is a composer and a collector of books, manuscripts, clippings, post cards, paintings, and book jackets, and a connoisseur of cats. His intimate knowledge of such matters has contributed to his essays and novels and resulted in his bringing to public attention a number of authors, including M. P. Shiel, Edgar Saltus, Arthur Machen, and Baron Corvo. He was also a leader in the revival of enthusiasm for Melville. ". . . For the past five years," he writes, "I have devoted myself exclusively to photography."

For further comment, see Critical Survey, p. 35.

BIBLIOGRAPHY

Novels

* Peter Whiffle, his life and works, 1922; The blind bow-boy . . . with a decoration by Robert E. Locher, 1923; The tattooed countess, a romantic novel with a happy ending, 1924; Firecrackers, a realistic novel, 1925; Nigger heaven, 1926; Spider boy, a scenario for a moving picture, 1928; Parties, scenes from contemporary New York life, 1930.

Books on Music

Music after the great war and other studies, 1915; Music and bad manners, 1916; Interpreters and interpretations, 1917; The merry-go-round, 1918; The music of Spain, 1918 (What the critics say about Mr. Van Vechten's work, pp. [211]–223); In the garret, 1920; Interpreters . . . a new edition, revised, with sixteen illustrations, and an epilogue, 1920 (repr. from Interpreters and interpretations); Red, papers on musical subjects, 1925; Excavations, a book of advocacies, 1926.

Essays

Sacred and profane memories, 1932.

Books on Cats

The tiger in the house, 1920; Lords of the housetops, thirteen cat tales [collected] with a preface by Carl Van Vechten, 1921; Feathers, 1930 (pamphlet).

Program Notes

Symphony society bulletin, vol. IV, no. I, October 24, 1910 . . . program notes by Carl Van Vechten, 1910 (caption-title; leaflet); Symphony society bulletin, vol. IV, no. II, November 7, 1910 . . . program notes by Carl Van Vechten, 1910 (caption-title; leaflet); Symphony society bulletin, vol. IV, no. III, November 21, 1910 . . . program notes by Carl Van Vechten, 1910 (caption-title; leaflet); Symphony society bulletin, vol. IV, no. IV, December 5, 1910 . . . program notes by Carl Van Vechten, 1910 (caption-title; leaflet); Symphony society bulletin, vol. IV, no. V, January 2, 1911 . . . program notes by Carl Van Vechten, 1911 (caption-title; leaflet); Symphony society bulletin, vol. IV, no. VI, January 30, 1911 . . . program notes by Carl Van Vechten, 1911 (caption-title; leaflet); Symphony society bulletin, vol. IV, no. VII, February 14, 1911 . . . program notes by Carl Van Vechten, 1911 (caption-title; leaflet); Symphony society bulletin, vol. IV, no. VIII, March 8, 1911 . . . program notes by Carl Van Vechten, 1911 (caption-title; leaflet).

Miscellany

Why and what, 1914 (cover-title; leaflet; signed: Atlas); A letter written in 1837 by Morgan Lewis Fitch with a postscript by Amanda Roberts Fitch together with a foreword by Charles Lewis Fitch, and an introductory note by Carl Van Vechten, 1919; Reprinted from the Musical courier, issue of April 22, 1920. Marguerite D'Alvarez, a remarkable tribute to a remarkable artist, contralto, 1920 (caption-title; leaflet).

Music

Five old English ditties with music by Carl Van Vechten. Pious Selinda ----- William Congreve, Apelle's song ----- John Lyly, Sabina wakes ----- William Congreve, A lenten ditty ----- F. C., The petition ----- William Congreve, 1904 (sheet music).

Editor

Nikolay Andreyevich Rimsky-Korsakoff. My musical life translated from the revised second Russian edition by Judah A. Joffe edited with an introduction by Carl Van Vechten, 1923.

STUDIES AND ARTICLES

Ashley
Baldwin (M)
Beach
Clark (E)
† Cunningham, Scott. A bibliography of the writings of Carl Van Vechten . . . with an overture in the form of a funeral march by Carl Van Vechten. 1924
Gard
† Herrmann
† Johnson (1929)

† Johnson (1932)
† Johnson (1936)
Knopf
Knopf (B)
Kunitz (L)
Markey
McKay
† Manly
National
† Schwartz (O)
Schyberg
Sinclair
Stein, Gertrude. Geography and plays. [c1922]
Van Vechten, Carl. The music of Spain . . . with preface and notes by Pedro G. Morales. 1920
† Van Vechten, Carl. Parties, scenes from contemporary New York life. 1930
† Van Vechten, Carl. Sacred and profane memories. 1932

Beach, Joseph W. "The peacock's tail." *AS.*, Nov. 1925, pp. 65–73; Van Vechten, Carl. "Notes for an autobiography." *Col.*, Part 3, Art. 3, pp. 1–4 (1930). For references to reviews, see *BRD.*, 1915, 1917–18, 1920–26, 1928, 1930, 1932.

Dexter Wallace, *pseud.* *See* Edgar Lee Masters

Robert Penn Warren, 1905–

Born in Guthrie, Kentucky, April 24, 1905. He was educated in public schools and at Vanderbilt University, where he was one of the group contributing to the *Fugitive*, a magazine devoted to southern poetry. He graduated in 1925 and subsequently held fellowships at the University of California, where he took the master's degree in 1927, and at Yale. He was a Rhodes Scholar and in 1930 was awarded the degree of bachelor of letters at Oxford.

He has taught English at Southwestern College and Vanderbilt University, and at present he is on the faculty at Louisiana State University, and a managing editor of the *Southern Review*, of which he was a founder. He has contributed much to periodicals and conducted writing conferences at the Universities of Montana and Colorado. In 1936 he was awarded the Caroline Sinkler Prize of the Poetry Society of South Carolina for "Love's Parable," the Helen Haire Levinson Prize of *Poetry* for "The Garden," and a Houghton Mifflin literary fellowship for writing *Night Rider* (1939). He was awarded a Guggenheim fellowship for creative writing in 1939.

In his critical writing Warren has pointed out what he considers to be imperfections in "propaganda" literature and stated his feeling that a work of art, to the extent that it is related to external emotional points of reference and made merely a document for a thesis, without integrity and independent coherence of structure, falls short of its highest potentialities.

For further comment, see Critical Survey, p. 147.

BIBLIOGRAPHY

Biography

John Brown, the making of a martyr, 1929.

Poems

Thirty-six poems, 1935.

Novel

Night rider, 1939 (title on facing papers).

Social Study

I'll take my stand, the South and the agrarian tradition by twelve southerners, 1930.

Editor

An approach to literature, a collection of prose and verse with analyses and discussions by Cleanth Brooks, jr., John Thibaut Purser, Robert Penn Warren, 1936; A southern harvest, short stories by southern writers, 1937; Understanding poetry, an anthology for college students by Cleanth Brooks, jr., and Robert Penn Warren, 1938.

ARTICLES

Zabel, Morton D. "Problems of knowledge." *P.*, Apr. 1936, pp. 37–41. For references to reviews, see *BRD.*, 1929–30, 1936–37, 1939.

Winifred Welles, 1893–

Born January 26, 1893, in Norwich Town, Connecticut. She was educated in her native town. Her verse began to appear in the magazines in the years before the entry of the United States into the war, and her first volume, *The Hesitant Heart*, was published in 1919. The author was one of the editors of the *Measure*, and she worked for a time in the offices of a motion-picture company. Since her marriage to Harold Shearer she has lived in New York and in Connecticut. In 1929 she received a prize from the Friends of American Writers in Chicago.

Her own fanciful lyrics Miss Welles modestly describes as "verse . . . of the simplest personal variety written in the traditional forms without any novelties."

For further comment, see Critical Survey, pp. 133, 136.

BIBLIOGRAPHY

Poems

The hesitant heart, 1919; This delicate love, 1929; Blossoming antlers, 1933; A spectacle for scholars, 1935.

Children's Poems

Skipping along alone . . . illustrated by Marguerite Davis, 1931.

ARTICLES

Bogan, Louise. "A true flight." *P.*, June 1934, pp. 159–62; Flanner, Hildegarde. "American eccentrics." *P.*, Aug. 1936, pp. 285–87; Monroe, Harriet. "Delicate indeed." *P.*, Jan. 1930, pp. 217–19. For references to reviews, see *BRD.*, 1920, 1930–31, 1933, 1935.

M(orris) R(obert) Werner, 1897–

Born in New York, March 6, 1897. He was reared in New York and attended public schools. In his boyhood be became thoroughly familiar with the New

York Public Library, which he regards as the most powerful influence in his education, and for two years and a half he studied at the School of Journalism at Columbia University. Two biographical sketches, of Paganini and Rossini, appeared in *Etude.*

He left in 1917 to go to France with Base Hospital No. 2 of the United States Medical Corps, and from May, 1917, until February, 1919, he was stationed at Étretat, in Normandy.

Back in New York, he took a job as obituary editor on the New York *Tribune.* Finding this distasteful, he left in 1920 to join his brother in business in Japan and China and sent special articles to the *Tribune.* Upon his return later in the same year, he worked in a moving-picture studio; then he began to write.

His first biography, of P. T. Barnum, was conceived almost accidentally when he was trying to write short stories. He wrote it from materials in the New York Public Library, the Harvard Theatre Collection, and private sources; and in the course of his research he found material that led to his choosing Brigham Young for similar treatment. *Tammany Hall* was written at the suggestion of Doubleday, Doran and Company, and his biography of Bryan was written for *Liberty. Orderly!*, inspired by Remarque's *All Quiet on the Western Front*, is based upon the author's own war experiences.

In 1930 Werner visited Russia and, after leaving the country, wrote, with the aid of a Russian friend, *To Whom It May Concern.* His interest in government and business found expression in his studies of the Bank of United States and Senate investigations. In 1935–36 he did research for the Works Progress Administration, and accepted an invitation by members of the Rosenwald family to write a biography of Julius Rosenwald.

Werner believes that he is able to write good biography only when the subject appeals to him, and he abandons any subject that proves to be unsympathetic. Although he necessarily makes his studies, by the selection of materials, expressions of his own point of view, he tries to include everything essential to a fair treatment and to let the materials, as far as possible, speak for themselves.

For further comment, see Critical Survey, pp. 170–71.

BIBLIOGRAPHY

Biography

* Barnum, 1923 (English ed., P. T. Barnum, 1923); Brigham Young, 1925; Bryan, 1929; To whom it may concern, the story of Victor Ilyitch Seroff, 1931; Julius Rosenwald, the life of a practical humanitarian, 1939.

Political Studies

Tammany hall, 1928; Privileged characters, 1935.

War Experiences

"Orderly!" 1930.

Journalism

Little Napoleons and dummy directors, being the narrative of the Bank of United States, 1933.

For references to reviews, see *BRD.*, 1923, 1925, 1928–31, 1933, 1935.

Glenway Wescott, 1901–

Born in Kewaskum, Wisconsin, April 11, 1901. He was educated in public high schools in West Bend and Waukesha, Wisconsin, and attended the University of Chicago in 1917–19, leaving without a degree. His family had planned for him to be a minister, and he himself had hoped to become a musician.

At Chicago, however, he was a member, and later president, of the Poetry Club, to which influence he ascribes his new desire to follow literature as a career. The club he has described as "a snobbish, impassionated, and clever group of young poets." Some of his verse appeared in *Poetry*.

After an illness and a year in New Mexico he wrote the first part of *The Apple of the Eye* in Massachusetts, went to England, and spent a year in Germany. Since then he has lived much in France, usually in Villefranche, a fishing village in the south, where distractions are few. He finds it impossible to break away from his middle western background, dreadful as he thinks it, and, although unable to accept Wisconsin, he cannot escape it. He feels that literary treatment of Americans, whom he professes to like until they reach about the senior year in college, must be analytical and diagnostic. He dislikes living in Paris or New York.

The Grandmothers was the Harper Prize Novel for 1927–28.

For further comment, see Critical Survey, p. 47.

BIBLIOGRAPHY

Novels

The apple of the eye, 1924; * The grandmothers, a family portrait, 1927 (English ed., A family portrait, 1927).

Short Stories

Like a lover, 1926; Good-bye, Wisconsin, 1928; The babe's bed, 1930.

Poems

The bitterns, a book of twelve poems . . . the pattern upon the cover was made by Fredrik Nyquist, 1920; Natives of rock: xx poems: 1921–1922, with decorations by Pamela Bianco, 1925 [1926].

Essays

Elizabeth Madox Roberts, a personal note by Glenway Wescott, with criticisms by Robert Morss Lovett, Edward Garnett, Mary Ross, Allan Nevins, Carl Van Doren, Louis Untermeyer, 1930 (pamphlet); Fear and trembling, 1932; Julien Levy gallery, Feb. 23, Mar. 15. Paintings, Tonny, drawings. Biography and impression by Glenway Wescott, 1937 (caption-title; leaflet).

Belles Lettres

A calendar of saints for unbelievers, the text by Glenway Wescott, the signs of the zodiac by Pavel Tchelitchew, 1932; The deadly friend, 1933.

STUDIES AND ARTICLES

Boynton (L)
Hicks
† Johnson (1932)
† Johnson (1936)
Kunitz (L)
Llona

Kohler, Dayton. "Glenway Wescott, legend-maker." *AB.*, Apr. 1931, pp. 142–45; Monroe, Harriet. "Youth and the desert." *P.*, Sept. 1921, pp. 339–43. For references to reviews, see *BRD.*, 1924, 1927–28, 1931–33.

John Wexley, 1907–

Born in New York City, September 14, 1907. His uncle was Maurice Schwartz, actor and producer of plays in Yiddish; and the boy was ambitious to be an actor, a director, and a playwright. He attended New York University and took different sorts of laboring jobs that prepared him for writing labor plays. He helped his father in the roofing trade, and he waited on tables, installed engines, stoked fires on ships, and worked as bellboy, floorwalker, and salesman, and as social director in summer camps. He acted with his uncle's company, the Yiddish Art Theatre, and with Eva Le Gallienne's Civic Repertory Theatre company, and in a rivival (1930) by Leo Bulgakor of *At the Bottom*, by Maxim Gorky; and he wrote one-act plays for the Washington Square Players.

After some personal investigation into actual prison conditions and visits to state penitentiaries in Illinois and New York, Wexley took one of these short plays, *Rules*, and enlarged it to *The Last Mile*, which was produced in 1930. It ran for three hundred performances and was made into a motion picture. *Steel*, written after the author had made trips to Europe and to Hollywood, appeared in 1931, and was subsequently thoroughly revised. "It was again produced under the same title by Labor Stage on Broadway at the old Princess Theatre (now Labor Stage) and ran from Jan. 17th to June 5th 1937," he writes. "It was an unusual offering in that it was sponsored and produced by Labor Stage, a cultural adjunct of the C.I.O. and it was acted by members of the International Garment Workers Union. The play therefore aside from merits and deficiencies represents two important steps in the history of the American Theatre. It was the very first labor play produced on Broadway (November 18, 1931) and again in January, 1937 it was the first play produced by a labor union with worker-actors, in a workers' theatre on Broadway." *They Shall Not Die*, a presentation of the plight of the defendants in the Scottsboro trial, was produced in New York by the Theatre Guild in 1934. From 1930 to 1936 Wexley wrote scenarios for several motion-picture producers, and his short story "Southern Highway 51" was included in the volume of O. Henry Memorial Award prize stories for 1934.

"My interests," declares the author, "have remained constant: they center chiefly on the world theatre and on the struggle of social forces throughout the world. In my personal life they center about a farm on which I live now permanently in Pennsylvania and on handicrafts and some oil-painting. My views of literature (in the dramatic field) are pessimistic. I believe the American theatre, although it has made notable strides forward in many ways, is still lacking in all too many instances. It is at present once more an unadulterated commercial theatre: it is more of a business than ever, it has too close an eye on Hollywood; its standards are lamentably low (the recent Pulitzer Prize awards the past few years); spurious and specious writing is lauded; there are very few advances made in the ways of direction, scene design and dramaturgy. Efforts by talented men to achieve new goals, pave new approaches, more mature thought and technique are discouraged and unwelcomed. In my own opinion there is but one solution and that is the creation of a National Theatre, subsidized in all large cities by the Federal government on a large scale and with the highest standards (not on the relief-roll standards of the present W.P.A. theatres). The only other solution seems to be in the slow plodding trial and error progress being made by the various worker theatres throughout the country.

"I believe the novel is greatly in advance of the drama: we are seeing tremendous progress each year in this field. I also feel hopeful about the present trend of the general reader toward the field of non-fiction books on social, political and economic subjects. If our theatre could forget its absurd worship of the contemporary smart-crack, caricature, quick repartee plays containing childish content and trite, stale themes and plots and move toward the rapidly developing and maturer audience that is alive today, the theatre would progress with leaps and bounds."

For further comment, see Critical Survey, pp. 124–25.

BIBLIOGRAPHY

Plays

The last mile, a play in three acts by John Wexley, preface by Lewis E. Lawes, 1930; The last mile, drama in one act . . . being the first act of the long play of the same title, arranged for performance as an independent work, 1931; They shall not die, a play, 1934.

For references to reviews, see *BRD.*, 1934.

Edith (Newbold Jones) Wharton, 1862–1937

Born in New York, January 24, 1862, the descendant of almost three centuries of colonial ancestors, including Schermerhorns and Rhinelanders, a line of merchant ship-owners. Her father, George Frederick Jones, had an independent income and was free to travel. Her earliest years she passed in New York and Newport, but at four she was taken abroad to Italy, Spain, and France. She read and made up stories even as a little girl, and she acquired foreign languages as the family moved from Paris to the Black Forest and then to Florence in an effort to keep down, by living in Europe, the losses resulting from the currency depreciation in the United States.

Upon her return to New York she was placed in the care of governesses, and, while heavy study was considered too strenuous, she was given a good background in English, modern languages, poetry, and manners, although Latin and Greek were denied her. Good English was her natural heritage. The society in which she grew up was a leisure class made independent by land-value increases and oblivious of the fluctuations of trade. An omnivorous reader, she rapidly learned to know the classics of English literature and, in French, Hugo, Corneille, and Racine. At eleven she tried to write a novel, and some of her juvenile poetry appeared in the New York *World* and (thanks to the influence of Longfellow) the *Atlantic Monthly*. She produced another novel at fifteen.

She was regarded as too much interested in books, and her parents had her "come out" when she was seventeen. Somewhat shy, she became a member of a "set" engaged in luncheons, parties, calling, and drives. This situation was changed by the necessity of returning to Europe, because of her father's health, and the family lived on the Riviera, until her father's death in the following spring.

After her return to New York and her resumption of social life she was married in 1885 to Edward Wharton, a Boston banker of a Virginia family, with whom she settled at Newport, spending a part of every year in foreign travel. In 1888 they took a yacht cruise on the Mediterranean. At this time her literary friendships began to be formed. With her husband she settled at Newport, and then moved to a house near Lenox, Massachusetts, her happiest home.

With the publication of poetry and short stories in magazines, and the wide sale of *The House of Mirth*, a best-seller, her literary career was under way. As her own circle in society either disapproved of her work or cared nothing for it, she was forced to seek understanding among writers and artists, and she spent much of the rest of her life in their company.

In 1903 she went to Italy to study villas for a volume to be illustrated by Maxfield Parrish. Her life became more settled and regular as the need grew for leisure for work; and she came to divide her time between Lenox and New York. Among her friends were Howells, Henry James, Charles Eliot Norton, and Clyde Fitch. In her travels abroad she met Alice Meynell, Thomas Hardy, Sir George Trevelyan, Mrs. Humphry Ward, John Singer Sargent, and George Meredith.

From 1907 she passed most of her time in France, having moved there to spare her husband the rigors of New York winters. Meeting brilliant and fashionable society, she found the Parisians more sympathetic to her ambitions than her own group in New York. She entertained Theodore Roosevelt on his world tour of 1909–10. Her summers were passed in Massachusetts, but with the breakdown of her husband's health they made trips to Italy and Spain, Germany, Sicily, and northern Africa.

The outbreak of the war found her in Paris, and she threw herself into Red Cross work, organizing an American committee, raising funds, and helping provide care for the sick and the homeless. She also organized a workroom for seamstresses and women garment workers. "Edith Wharton" committees appeared in Boston, New York, Washington, Philadelphia, and Providence; and she issued *The Book of the Homeless*, translating much of the material into English, in order to raise funds. To stimulate American contributions she made six trips to the lines and wrote up the hospital needs; and the Queen of the Belgians interviewed her on the subject of refugee children. By the end of the war her forces were caring for five thousand refugees, four large colonies for children and old people, and four large sanatoria for tubercular women and children. At the invitation of the French government she made a three-week tour of the French colony in Morocco; she was awarded (1915) the Cross of the Legion of Honor; and Belgium made her Chevalier of the Order of Leopold.

After the war her circle of friends was depleted, and her old world had gone. She wrote, as an escape, *The Age of Innocence*, which took the Pulitzer Prize for 1920, produced her war novel, *A Son at the Front*, and settled down to reading, gardening, and travel. She divided her time between her villa near St.

Brice, bought after the war, and her property at Hyères, in Provence. In 1926 she made another yacht trip in the Mediterranean. For the rest of her life she remained in France.

Mrs. Wharton's social background and her literary ambitions and inclinations were so at variance that she was obliged to lead virtually two lives. Her family and their friends regarded her writing with indifference or actual disapproval, and refrained, as if it had been a disgrace, from speaking of her work. Even literary men and the literary public were disturbed by her mention, in her novels, of such a subject as illicit passion, and one indignant reader wrote to ask her if she had ever known a respectable woman.

She found, however, no lack of subjects, and was keenly interested in the technique of fiction, which she discussed with Henry James and Paul Bourget. She was much influenced by Goethe, Thackeray, Balzac, Meredith, and Flaubert. She found that characters came to her with their names already chosen, unusual names that were hard to change. The characters sometimes, especially in the novels, presented themselves before she had in mind an appropriate situation; at other times, as in some of the short stories, the situation appeared first. The dialogue—heightened speech, used sparingly—dictated itself to her, and the doom of the characters, fixed and unchangeable, was hit upon at the very outset. "My last page is always latent in my first," she wrote in her autobiography. She felt that a novelist should deal with material within his reach and with subjects in which he can see values, but she resented the efforts made to identify characters with real persons. To her they were real persons in their own right, and as real as any of her friends. As she grew older, storytelling absorbed her more and more completely. She described *Ethan Frome* as "the book to the making of which I brought the greatest joy and the fullest ease."

She died at her residence near St. Brice sous Forêt, August 11, 1937, and was buried in the Protestant cemetery at Versailles. She left her villa, with its fine garden, to be sold for funds to maintain her post-war benefactions in St. Brice. A collection of Mrs. Wharton's manuscripts and papers, including letters, has been presented to the Yale Collection of American Literature in the Yale University Library by her literary executor, Gaillard Lapsley. The letters are not open to inspection until 1968.

She was the first woman to be given (1923) an honorary doctorate in letters at Yale, and (1924) the Gold Medal of the National Institute of Arts and Letters; in 1930 she was made a member of the National Institute of Arts and Letters, and in 1934 she was the second woman to be elected to membership in the American Academy of Arts and Sciences. France made her officer of the Legion of Honor in 1924, and the French Academy awarded her a Montyon prize.

For further comment, see Critical Survey, pp. 24–25, 39, 66, 71, 86–87, 178.

BIBLIOGRAPHY

Novels

The touchstone, 1900 (English ed., A gift from the grave, 1900); The valley of decision, a novel, 1902 (2 vols.); Sanctuary . . . with illustrations by

Walter Appleton Clark, 1903; * The house of mirth . . . with illustrations by A. B. Wenzell, 1905; The fruit of the tree . . . with illustrations by Alonzo Kimball, 1907; Madame de Treymes, 1907; * Ethan Frome, 1911; The reef, a novel, 1912; The custom of the country, 1913; Summer, a novel, 1917; The Marne, 1918; * The age of innocence, 1920; The glimpses of the moon, 1922; A son at the front, 1923; Old New York. False dawn (The 'forties) . . . decorations by E. C. Caswell, 1924; Old New York. New Year's day (The 'seventies) . . . decorations by E. C. Caswell, 1924; Old New York. The old maid (The 'fifties) . . . decorations by E. C. Caswell, 1924; Old New York. The spark (The 'sixties) . . . decorations by E. C. Caswell, 1924; The mother's recompense, 1925; Twilight sleep, 1927; The children, 1928 (photoplay ed., The marriage playground, 1930); Hudson River bracketed, 1929; The gods arrive, 1932; The buccaneers, 1938.

Short Stories

The greater inclination, 1899; Crucial instances, 1901; The descent of man and other stories, 1904; The hermit and the wild woman and other stories, 1908; Tales of men and ghosts, 1910; * Xingu and other stories, 1916; Here and beyond . . . decorations by E. C. Caswell, 1926; Certain people, 1930; Human nature, 1933; The world over, 1936; Ghosts, 1937.

Poems

Artemis to Actæon and other verse, 1909; Twelve poems, 1926.

Autobiography

A backward glance, 1934.

Literary Criticism

The writing of fiction, 1925.

Travel

Italian backgrounds . . . illustrated by E. C. Peixotto, 1905; A motor-flight through France, 1908; In Morocco, 1920.

Social Study

French ways and their meaning, 1919.

Miscellany

The decoration of houses by Edith Wharton and Ogden Codman, jr., 1897; Italian villas and their gardens . . . illustrated with pictures by Maxfield Parrish and by photographs, 1904; Fighting France from Dunkerque to Belfort, 1915; Edith Wharton's war charities in France, Mrs. Wharton's general report from 1914–1918 and report of the New York committee from November 1st, 1916, to December 31st, 1917, 1918 (cover-title; pamphlet).

Editor

The book of the homeless (Le livre des sans-foyer) edited by Edith Wharton, original articles in verse and prose, illustrations reproduced from original paintings & drawings. The book is sold for the benefit of the American hostels for refugees (with the Foyer franco-belge) and of the Children of Flanders rescue committee, 1916.

Compiler

Eternal passion in English poetry selected by Edith Wharton and Robert Norton with the collaboration of Gaillard Lapsley, 1939.

Translations

The joy of living (Es lebe das leben) A play in five acts by Hermann Sudermann translated from the German, 1902.

STUDIES AND ARTICLES

Akins, Zoë. The old maid dramatized . . . from the novel by Edith Wharton. 1935
Appleton, D., & company. On one day (May 16) Appleton will publish four remarkably fine books, all new stories of Old New York by America's foremost novelist—Edith Wharton. [1924] (caption-title; leaflet)
Beach (T)
Björkman
Blankenship
Boas
Boynton (H)
Boynton (S)
† Brown, Edward K. Edith Wharton, étude critique. 1935
Bruns
Canby (D)
Chanler, Margaret T. Autumn in the valley by Mrs. Winthrop Chanler. 1936
Collins (T)
Cooper (F)
† Davis, Lavinia R. A bibliography of the writings of Edith Wharton. 1933
Davis, Owen and Davis, Donald. Ethan Frome, a dramatization of Edith Wharton's novel . . . suggested by a dramatization by Lowell Barrington. 1936
Dickinson
† Edgar
Edith Wharton's war charities in France. Sanatoria for tuberculous women and children. [n.d.] (leaflet)
Follett
Garland
Gerould, Katharine F. Edith Wharton, a critical study. [192–?] (cover-title; pamphlet)
Green (C)
Hackett
Halsey
Hartwick
Hatcher
Hicks
Hind
† Johnson (1929)
† Johnson (1932)
† Johnson (1936)
Kaltenbacher
Klooster, Jantina H. van. Moderne amerikaansche letterkunde, Edith Wharton. [1924]
Knight
Kunitz (L)
Lawrence (S)
Lawrence (W)
Lewisohn (E)
Loggins
† Lovett, Robert M. Edith Wharton. 1925
† Manly
Marble
† Melish, Lawson M. A bibliography of the collected writings of Edith Wharton. 1927
Michaud
Michaud (M)
Morley, Christopher D. Streamlines. 1936
National
O'Brien
Overton

Overton (A)
Overton, Grant M. Cargoes for Crusoes. [c1924]
Overton (H)
Overton (W)
Overton (WW)
Parrington
Pattee (N)
Phelps (A)
Quinn
Schyberg
Sedgwick
Sherman (M)
Smith
Squire
Stewart
† Taylor
Underwood
Van Doren
Van Doren (A)
Van Doren (C)
Vočadlo
Ward
Ward (T)
Wharton, Edith N. The age of innocence, edited by Orton Lowe. [c1932]
Wharton, Edith N. Ethan Frome . . . with an introduction by Bernard DeVoto. 1938
Williams

Boynton, Percy H. "Edith Wharton." *EJ.*, Jan. 1923, pp. 24–32; Brown, Edward K. "A bibliography of the writings of Edith Wharton." *AL.*, Nov. 1933, pp. 288–90; Brown. "Edith Wharton." *EA.*, Jan.–Mar. 1938, pp. 12–26; Burdett, Osbert. "Edith Wharton." *Merc.*, Nov. 1925, pp. 13, 52–61; Canby, Henry S. "Edith Wharton." *SRL.*, Aug. 21, 1937, pp. 6–7; Coolidge, Bertha. "Mrs. Wharton's works." *SRL.*, July 8, 1933, p. 694; Cross, Wilbur L. "Edith Wharton." *AB.*, Aug. 1926, pp. 641–46; Dwight, Harry G. "Edith Wharton." *Putnam's*, Feb. 1908, pp. 590–96; Flanner, Janet. "Dearest Edith." *N.Yer.*, Mar. 2, 1929, pp. 26–28; Gilbertson, Catherine. "Mrs. Wharton, an agate lamp within thy hand." *Cent.*, Autumn 1929, pp. 112–19; Herrick, Robert. "Mrs. Wharton's world." *NR.*, Feb. 13, 1915, pp. 40–42; Huneker, James. "Three disagreeable girls, Undine." *Forum*, Nov. 1914, pp. 765–75; † Johnson, Merle D. and Hopkins, Frederick M., *eds.* "American first editions, a series of bibliographic check-lists . . . number 24, Edith Wharton, 1862– ." *PW.*, March 10, 1923, p. 796; Leavis, Queenie D. "Henry James's heiress, the importance of Edith Wharton." *Scrut.*, Dec. 1938, pp. 261–76; Lubbock, Percy. "The novels of Edith Wharton." *QR.*, Jan. 1915, pp. 182–201; McCole, Camille J. "Some notes on Edith Wharton." *CW.*, Jan. 1938, pp. 425–31; Parrington, Vernon L. "Our literary aristocrat." *Pac.R.*, June 1921, pp. 157–60; Randall, David A. "A bibliography of the writings of Edith Wharton by Lavinia Davis." *PW.*, June 17, 1933, pp. 1975–76; Ransom, John C. "Characters and character, a note on fiction." *AR.*, Jan. 1936, pp. 271–88; Repplier, Agnes. "Edith Wharton." *Com.*, Nov. 25, 1938, pp. 125–26; Roberts, Richard E. "Edith Wharton." *Bookm.*, Sept. 1923, pp. 262–64; Russell, Frances T. "Edith Wharton's use of imagery." *EJ.*, June 1932, pp. 452–61; Russell. "Melodramatic Mrs. Wharton." *SR.*, Oct.–Dec. 1932, pp. 425–37; Sedgwick, Henry D. "The novels of Mrs. Wharton." *A.Mo.*, Aug. 1906, pp. 217–28; Sencourt, Robert. "The poetry of Edith Wharton." *AB.*, July 1931, pp. 478–86; Sencourt. "Edith Wharton." *CM.*, June 1938, pp. 721–36; Sholl, Anna M. "The work of Edith Wharton." *Gunton's*, Nov. 1903, pp. 426–32; Trueblood, Charles K. "Edith Wharton." *D.*, Jan. 1920, pp. 80–91; Waldstein, Charles. "Social ideals." *N.Amer.Rev.*, June 1906, pp. 840–52; Waldstein. "Social ideals." *N.Amer.Rev.*, July, 1906, pp. 125–26; Wharton, Edith. "The writing of Ethan Frome." *Col.*, Part 11, Art. 4, pp. 1–4 (1931); Willcox, Louise C. "Edith Wharton." *Outl.*, Nov. 25, 1905, pp. 719–24; Wilson, Edmund. "Justice to Edith Wharton." *NR.*, June 29, 1938, pp. 209–

13; Winter, Calvin. "Edith Wharton." *AB.*, May 1911, pp. 302–09. For references to reviews, see *BRD.*, 1906–13, 1915–21, 1923–30, 1932–34, 1936–38.

John Hall Wheelock, 1886–

Born in Far Rockaway, Long Island. He was reared in New York City and spent his summers usually at the family country home at Easthampton on Long Island. He wrote verse while he was still in elementary school, and he made metrical translations of his Latin assignments. At Harvard, where he knew Van Wyck Brooks and Alan Seeger, he published, with Van Wyck Brooks, *Verses by Two Undergraduates.*

After graduating in 1908 as class poet he went abroad for two years of study and travel. He was in residence at the University of Göttingen and the University of Berlin, and he made trips through France, Italy, and Dalmatia.

In 1911, the year in which his first book, *The Human Fantasy*, was published, he accepted a position with a prominent New York publisher, with whom, after more than twenty-five years, he is still associated as an adviser. He is a member of the Poetry Society of America. In 1937 *Poems, 1911–1936* took the annual award for 1936 of the New England Poetry Society.

"My poetry has often been defined as 'lyrical metaphysics,'" he writes. "The poems supplement each other, or are intended to. I hope that they build up architecturally into something which represents a definite philosophy of life. Spinoza is my favorite philosopher, and I suppose whatever philosophy I have might be called a form of naturalism. My poetry is addressed to the ear, rather than to the eye: it is orchestral in character and very much out of the present movement."

For further comment, see Critical Survey, pp. 132–33.

BIBLIOGRAPHY

Poems

Verses by two undergraduates [Van Wyck Brooks and John Hall Wheelock], 1905 (cover-title); The human fantasy, 1911; The belovéd adventure, 1912; Love and liberation, the songs of Adsched of Meru and other poems, 1913; Dust and light, 1919; The black panther, a book of poems, 1922; The bright doom, a book of poems, 1927; * Poems, 1911–1936, 1936.

Bibliography

A bibliography of Theodore Roosevelt, 1920.

Verses Set to Music

Song to --- [by] J. H. Wheelock [music by] Charles Seeger, jr., 1911 (caption-title; sheet music).

STUDIES AND ARTICLES

Untermeyer
Untermeyer (N)
Wood

Hubbell, Jay B. "The poetry of John Hall Wheelock." *Sw.R.*, Fall 1926, pp. 60–67; Monroe, Harriet. "A lover of earth." *P.*, Mar. 1920, pp. 343–45;

Scott, Evelyn. "The tone of time." *P.*, May 1937, pp. 100–03; Zabel, Morton D. "Poems stately and grave." *P.*, Feb. 1928, pp. 280–82. For references to reviews, see *BRD.*, 1913–14, 1919, 1921–22, 1927, 1936–37.

Helen C(onstance) White, 1896–

Born in New Haven, November 26, 1896. She was brought up in Boston and educated at Radcliffe, where she took her bachelor's degree in 1916 and her master's degree in 1917. For two years she held an assistant-ship in English at Smith College; then she went to the University of Wisconsin, where she took her doctorate in 1924 and where she is now a professor of English. A Guggenheim fellowship enabled her to spend 1928–29 and the summer of 1930 in Oxford and the British Museum, working on material included in *English Devotional Literature.*

"One of my major teaching interests over a good many years now," she writes, "has been my course in creative writing, English 5, and that has been a source of great pleasure and stimulus to me. I also am teaching Shakespeare and giving some graduate work in the seventeenth century. For a number of years I gave courses in the romantic movement and Victorian literature. . . ." Of her own literary field, historical fiction, she says: " . . . I don't write historical novels as a means of escape. Indeed, I think the historical novel is a valuable instrument for a wider and freer study of some of the persistent problems and interests of human life."

For further comment, see Critical Survey, p. 73.

BIBLIOGRAPHY

Novels

A watch in the night, 1933; Not built with hands, 1935.

Literary Studies

The mysticism of William Blake, 1927; English devotional literature ⟨prose⟩ 1600–1640, 1931; The metaphysical poets, a study in religious experience, 1936.

Editor

Victorian prose, a book of selections edited by Finley M. K. Foster . . . and Helen C. White, 1930.

For references to reviews, see *BRD.*, 1933, 1935–37.

Stewart Edward White, 1873–

Born in Grand Rapids, Michigan, March 12, 1873. As a child he knew the life of a Michigan mill town and lumber camps, and in his early teens he lived in California and learned riding, hunting, and ranch life.

Until he was sixteen he was privately educated, but in 1889 he entered high school in Grand Rapids. He was successful in athletics, president of his class, and an eager student of bird and animal life. A bird pamphlet he wrote was published by the Ornithologists' Union. His earliest literary preferences were for history and historical fiction. He graduated from the University of Michigan in 1895, and, after a period of work in a packing house and a gold-rush excursion to the Black Hills, he went to Columbia to study law.

There he came under the influence of Brander Matthews, who suggested that he submit a class composition to a magazine. It was accepted, and White was able to sell other stories to periodicals. After working for a bookseller in Chicago and spending some time living in the outlands, he wrote *The Blazed Trail.*

An efficient, sure-handed writer, who has his material thought out before it is written, he works steadily, with slight revision, for short periods of time, and has been able to average better than a book a year. Many of his novels have been filmed; no fewer than five pictures were made from *Arizona Nights.* In the frequent intervals when he has not been working, he has traveled to such remote places as Africa and Alaska. He has also done research in California libraries. During the war he served as major in the field artillery.

In recent years he has lived near San Francisco. The trophy room in his house, with its collection of guns, spears, mounted animals, and other treasures, has been a magnet for boy visitors.

He is a member of the National Institute of Arts and Letters and a fellow of the Royal Geographical Society, and holds an honorary degree from the University of Michigan. In 1939 he presented to the University of Michigan the manuscripts of *The Blazed Trail* and *The Riverman.*

For further comment, see Critical Survey, pp. 49, 58, 63, 64.

BIBLIOGRAPHY

Novels

The claim jumpers, a romance, 1901; The westerners, 1901; * The blazed trail . . . illustrated by Thomas Fogarty, 1902; Conjuror's house, a romance of the free forest, 1903 (also pub. with title: The call of the North, being a dramatized version of Conjuror's house, a romance of the free forest, 1914); The silent places . . . illustrated by Philip R. Goodwin, 1904; Arizona nights . . . illustrations by N. C. Wyeth, 1907; The mystery by Stewart Edward White and Samuel Hopkins Adams, illustrations by Will Crawford, 1907; The riverman . . . illustrations by N. C. Wyeth and Clarence F. Underwood, 1908; The rules of the game . . . illustrated by Lejaren A. Hiller, 1910; The sign at six . . . illustrated by M. Leone Bracker, 1912; Gold . . . illustrated by Thomas Fogarty, 1913 (contains: Stewart Edward White who has brought the East, and South, and North to understand the West, a little chat about the man and his books by Eugene F. Saxton); The gray dawn . . . illustrated by Thomas Fogarty, 1915; The Leopard Woman . . . illustrated by W. H. D. Koerner, 1916; The killer, 1919; The rose dawn, 1920; On tiptoe, a romance of the redwoods . . . with a frontispiece by Thomas Fogarty, 1922; The glory hole, 1924; Skookum Chuck, a novel, 1925; Secret harbour, 1926; Back of beyond, 1927; The story of California: Gold, The gray dawn, The rose dawn, 1927; The long rifle, 1932; Ranchero, 1933; Folded hills, 1934; Pole star by Stewart Edward White and Harry DeVighne, 1935.

Short Stories

Blazed trail stories and Stories of the wild life, 1904; Simba, 1918 (English ed., White magic, 1918); The killer, 1920 (The killer issued separately in 1919); The hold-up . . . with a foreword by the author, 1937 (pamphlet).

Dog Stories

Dog days, other times, other dogs, the autobiography of a man and his dog friends through four decades of changing America . . . illustrations by Will Crawford, 1930; The shepper-newfounder . . . illustrated by H. T. Webster, 1931.

Description and Travel

The pass . . . frontispiece in color by Fernand Lungren and many other illustrations from photographs, 1906; The land of footprints . . . illustrated from photographs by the author and two drawings by Philip R. Goodwin, 1912; African camp fires . . . illustrated from photographs, 1913; The rediscovered country . . . illustrated from photographs, 1915; Lions in the path, a book of adventure on the high veldt, 1926.

Outdoor Life

The forest . . . illustrated by Thomas Fogarty, 1903; The mountains . . . illustrated by Fernand Lungren, 1904; Camp and trail . . . frontispiece in color by Fernand Lungren and many other illustrations from photographs, etc., 1907; The cabin . . . illustrated with photographs by the author, 1911; The outdoor omnibus. The mountains, The forest, The cabin, complete and unabridged, 1936?

Biography

Daniel Boone, wilderness scout . . . illustrated by Remington Schuyler, 1922.

History

The forty-niners, a chronicle of the California trail and El Dorado, 1918 (also pub. as The last frontier. Part 1: The forty-niners by Stewart Edward White. Part 2: The passing of the frontier by Emerson Hough, 1926); Old California in picture and story . . . illustrated in color and black and white from contemporary prints, 1937.

Personal Philosophy

Credo, 1925; Why be a mud turtle? 1928.

Juvenile Literature

The magic forest, a modern fairy story, 1903; The adventures of Bobby Orde . . . illustrated by Worth Brehm, 1910; Wild animals, stories . . . drawings by Sydney Joseph. Printed in an edition of 350 copies by the Grabhorn press of San Francisco of which 50 copies have been signed by the author and artist, 1932.

Psychical Research

The Betty book, excursions into the world of other-consciousness made by

Betty [*pseud.*] between 1919 and 1936, now recorded by Stewart Edward White, 1937.

Miscellany

The birds of Mackinac island, 1893 (pamphlet); The ceremony of the cremation of care as presented annually at Bohemian grove, volume I, number IV, containing the production of 1921, pages 57 to 72, 1921 (cover-title; pamphlet; book by Stewart Edward White and Charles K. Field).

STUDIES AND ARTICLES

Baldwin
Baldwin (M)
Burgess
Doubleday
† Johnson (1929)
† Johnson (1932)
† Johnson (1936)
Kunitz
Lieberman
McClure, Phillips & co., *firm, publishers, New York.* Novels by Stewart Edward White. The silent places, just published. The blazed trail, sixteenth edition. The westerners, fifth edition. Conjuror's house, second edition. [1904] (cover-title; leaflet)
[McClure, Phillips & co., *firm, publishers, New York.*] The blazed trail by Stewart Edward White, author of "The westerners," illustrations by Thomas Fogarty. [1902] (broadside)
† Manly
Overton (A)
Overton, Grant M. When winter comes to Main street. [c1922]
Saxton, Eugene F. Stewart Edward White who has brought the East, and South, and North to understand the West, a little chat about the man and his books. [191–?] (caption-title; pamphlet)
Underwood
White, Stewart E. Daniel Boone, wilderness scout . . . edited by Helen E. Hawkins. [c1926]

Clark, Ward. "Stewart Edward White." *AB.*, July 1910, pp. 486–92; Denison, Lindsay. "Stewart Edward White." *AB.*, May 1903, pp. 308–11; Hélys, Marc. "Les romanciers américains contemporains, Stewart Edward White." *Corres.*, Aug. 10, 1921, pp. 444–63; Maurice, Arthur B. "A history of their books, Stewart Edward White." *AB.*, Aug. 1929, pp. 588–89. For references to reviews, see *BRD.*, 1906–08, 1910–13, 1915–16, 1918–20, 1922, 1924–27, 1929–30, 1932–35, 1937.

Thornton (Niven) Wilder, 1897–

Born April 17, 1897, in Madison, Wisconsin, where his father edited the *Wisconsin State Journal.* His mother was the daughter of a Presbyterian minister, and both his parents were of New England stock. In 1906, when his father was made consul general at Hong Kong, he was taken to China. After three years in Hong Kong and five more in Shanghai, he returned to this country in 1914.

Prepared in a high school in Chefoo, China, and in schools in Berkeley and Ojai in California, he entered Oberlin College in 1915 and studied there for two years. During the war he served in the Coast Artillery Corps, stationed at Narragansett Bay; and he finished the work for his bachelor's degree at Yale, where he was conspicuous in literary and musical activities, in 1920.

The year 1920–21 he passed at the American Academy in Rome; then he returned to become housemaster in a preparatory school in Lawrenceville, New Jersey, and in 1926 he took the master's degree at Princeton. His work as teacher of French enabled him to read and write as he pleased, and he made up his mind to write not for profit but for enjoyment.

He became a famous literary figure in 1927 with the appearance of *The Bridge of San Luis Rey*, which made a phenomenal sales record, took the Pulitzer Prize, and was filmed. The next year, having previously refused the requests of editors and publishers for more work, he left teaching to write *The Woman of Andros*, and in the following year he made a lecture tour. From 1930 to 1936 he lectured for a part of the academic year at the University of Chicago. He has lived in the MacDowell colony, in Peterboro, New Hampshire, and is a member of the National Institute of Arts and Letters. Wilder has selected Yale Library as the place of safekeeping for the manuscripts of his writings.

In recent years his attention has turned from fiction to drama; and in 1935 he announced his abandonment of the novel, as unduly influenced by "the editorial presence," and his intention to write for the stage. He has done work for the motion pictures and has written plays all his life; but, although Katharine Cornell had presented his translation of Obey's *Lucrece* in 1932–33 and his new acting version of Ibsen's *A Doll's House* had been performed in 1937–38, *Our Town* (1938) was his first full-length play to be produced on Broadway. It was awarded the Pulitzer Prize. He has acted as the commentator in *Our Town* in New York and in various summer theaters.

Not himself a theater-goer, Wilder is very fond of listening to music and of reading, and he has done a great deal of long-distance cross-country walking in England and on the Continent. He has not linked himself with any literary coterie, as he feels that a writer's duty is to free the actual creative process from any considerations of public, press, or criticism, which are strictly irrelevant to his task. He thinks that only in a "great" period, like that of Shakespeare, in which art is recognized as a supreme value, can the association of artists result in genuine fruitfulness; and he regards literary technique as something acquired through unconscious absorption from the work of admired masters. He recognizes the value and importance of the work of writers struggling for improvement in the advance of civilization, but he feels that the race needs also the less immediate but finally valid affirmations of human dignity to be found in more universal works of art. "The great poet describing an apparently impersonal suffering," he declared in an interview recorded in the *Saturday Review of Literature* in 1938, "is saying something about the dignity of man which ultimately finds its way into legislation and into concrete humanitarian work. A poet is a triumph of common sense, but on a time scale of centuries. A pamphleteer works in decades."

For further comment, see Critical Survey, pp. 67, 72.

BIBLIOGRAPHY

Novels

The cabala, 1926; * The bridge of San Luis Rey, illustrated by Amy Drevenstedt, 1927; The woman of Andros, 1930; The stories of Thornton Wilder: The bridge of San Luis Rey, The cabala, The woman of Andros, 1933; Heaven's my destination, 1934.

Plays

The angel that troubled the waters and other plays, 1928; The long Christmas dinner & other plays in one act, 1931 (The long Christmas dinner; Queens of France; Pullman car Hiawatha; Love, and how to cure it; Such things only happen in books; The happy journey to Trenton and Camden); Love and how to cure it, a play in one act, 1932; The long Christmas dinner, a play in one act, 1933; The happy journey, play in one act . . . Revised edition with full stage directions by Alexander Dean . . . as directed at its first production on any stage in a joint performance by the Yale dramatic association and the Vassar Philaletheis, 1934; * Our town, a play in three acts, 1938; The merchant of Yonkers, a farce in four acts, 1939.

Translations

Lucrece from 'Le viol de Lucrèce' by André Obey, 1933.

STUDIES AND ARTICLES

Benchley
Brown
Hatcher
Henderson
Herrmann
† Johnson (1932)
† Johnson (1936)
Kunitz (L)
Levinson
Linati
Loggins
Mantle (C)
Proletarian
Schyberg
Van Dyke
Vočadlo
Wilder, Thornton N. The cabala . . . introduction by Herbert Gorman. [c1929]

Adcock, St. John. "Thornton Wilder." *Bookm.*, Mar. 1929, pp. 316–19; Anonymous. "The economic interpretation of Wilder." *NR.*, Nov. 26, 1930, pp. 31–32; Bergholz, Harry. "Thornton Wilder, cabala, The bridge of San Luis Rey, The angel that troubled the waters." *E.Studien*, Feb. 1931, pp. 301–06; Brown, Edward K. "A christian humanist, Thornton Wilder." *UTQ.*, Apr. 1935, pp. 356–70; Chambrun, Clara Longworth-. "L'américanisme de Thornton Wilder." *RAA.*, Apr. 1931, pp. 341–44; Fischer, Walther. "Thornton Wilders The bridge of san luis rey und Prosper Mérimées Le carosse du saint sacrement." *Ang.*, Jan. 1936, pp. 234–40; Gold, Michael. "Wilder, prophet of the genteel Christ." *NR.*, Oct. 22, 1930, pp. 266–67; Hazlitt, Henry. "Communist criticism." *Nation*, Nov. 26, 1930, pp. 583–84; Heinrich, Gregor. "Thornton Wilder, ein christlicher dichter amerikas." *DR.*, Jan. 1934, pp. 62–63; Heinrich. "Das werk des amerikanischen dichters Thornton Wilder." *Hochl.*, Nov. 1932, pp. 176–80; Kohler, Dayton. "Thornton Wilder." *EJ.*, Jan. 1939, pp. 1–11; McNamara, Robert. "Phases of American religion in Thornton Wilder and Willa Cather." *CW.*, Sept. 1932, pp. 641–49; Parmenter, Ross. "Novelist and playwright." *SRL.*, June 11, 1938, pp. 10–11; Tritsch, Walther. "Thornton Wilder in Berlin." *Liv.Age*, Sept. 1931, pp. 44–47; Twitchett, Eric G. "Mr. Thornton Wilder." *Merc.*, May 1930, pp. 32–39; Wilson, Edmund. "Thornton Wilder." *NR.*, Aug. 8, 1928, pp. 303–05. For references to reviews, see *BRD.*, 1926–28, 1930, 1932, 1935, 1938.

William Carlos Williams, 1883–

Born September 17, 1883, in Rutherford, New Jersey. His father was of Danish-English stock, and his mother was of French-Spanish extraction.

Until 1897 he attended school in Rutherford. Then he was sent for a year to Chateau de Lancy in Geneva. He finished his preparatory education at the Horace Mann School in New York and entered the University of Pennsylvania. After taking his M.D. degree in 1906 he had two years of interneship in New York and a year of graduate study in pediatrics in Leipzig, and in 1910 he returned to Rutherford, where he has practiced ever since.

Although he had begun writing in college, he was introduced to the public in 1914 as an Imagist, with the publication of some of his work in the *Glebe*. Since then he has written for many small literary magazines. In 1926 he was given the *Dial* Award of two thousand dollars for distinguished service to American literature, and in 1931 he won the Guarantors Prize awarded by *Poetry*.

Williams is profoundly interested in the technical problems of modern verse. He feels that the proper use of the American, rather than the English, language is essential for modern American poetry, and he believes that all art depends for its assurance and firmness upon local and immediate tradition. He takes the objectivist point of view that poems must represent the fusion and transformation of content and form, and that every poem, just as it must be more than an empty verse form, must contain more significance than the mere prose meaning of its statements. It is the task of the modern American poet to discover a form appropriate to America.

For further comment, see Critical Survey, p. 146.

BIBLIOGRAPHY

Poems

Poems, 1909; The tempers, 1913; A book of poems, Al que quiere! 1917; Kora in hell: improvisations, 1920; Sour grapes, a book of poems, 1921; Spring and all, 1922; The cod head, 1932 (pamphlet); Collected poems, 1921–1931, with a preface by Wallace Stevens, 1934; An early martyr and other poems, 1935; Adam & Eve & the city, 1936; * The complete collected poems of William Carlos Williams, 1906–1938, 1938.

Novels

A voyage to Pagany, 1928; White mule, 1937.

Short Stories

The knife of the times and other stories, 1932; Life along the Passaic river, 1938.

Belles Lettres

The great American novel, 1923; A novelette and other prose (1921–1931), 1932.

Essays

In the American grain, 1925.

Translation

Last nights of Paris [by] Philippe Soupault translated from the French, 1929.

STUDIES AND ARTICLES

Aiken
Deutsch
Herrmann
Kunitz (L)
Lawrence
Linati
Michaud
Monroe (P)
Pound, Ezra L. Polite essays. [1937]
Riding
Rosenfeld (P)
Taupin
Untermeyer
Winters

Bartlett, Helen Birch-. "Koral grisaille." *P.*, Mar. 1921, pp. 329–32; Burke, Kenneth. "William Carlos Williams, the methods of." *D.*, Feb. 1927, pp. 94–98; Dudley, Dorothy. "To whom it may concern." *P.*, Apr. 1918, pp. 38–43; Farrell, James T. "White mule." *So.R.*, Winter 1938, pp. 615–18; Fitzgerald, Robert. "Actual and archaic." *P.*, Nov. 1936, pp. 94–96; Moore, Marianne. "Things others never notice." *P.*, May 1934, pp. 103–06; Pound, Ezra. "Dr. Williams' position." *D.*, Nov. 1928, pp. 395–404; Rakosi, Carl. "William Carlos Williams." *Symp.*, Oct. 1933, pp. 439–47; Rosenfeld, Paul. "Williams the stylist." *SRL.*, Feb. 11, 1939, p. 16; Seiffert, Marjorie. "Against the middle-aged mind." *P.*, Apr. 1924, pp. 45–50; Strobel, Marion. "Middle-aged adolescence." *P.*, Nov. 1923, pp. 103–05; Untermeyer, Louis. "Experiment and tradition." *YR.*, Spring 1939, pp. 612–13; Wilson, Ted C. "The example of Dr. Williams." *P.*, May 1936, pp. 105–07; Winters, Yvor. "Carlos Williams' new book." *P.*, July 1922, pp. 216–20. For references to reviews, see *BRD.*, 1926, 1928, 1932, 1934, 1936–38.

Thames (Ross) Williamson, 1894–

Born February 7, 1894, on the Nez Perce Indian reservation near Genesee, Idaho. His father and mother were respectively Welsh-Norwegian and French-Irish.

At fourteen he ran away from home and knocked about as hobo, circus hand, and cabin boy, and had other miscellaneous jobs. He reported for a San Francisco newspaper and he was private secretary to the warden at the Iowa State Prison and an interpreter at Hull-House in Chicago.

He graduated *cum laude* at the University of Iowa in 1917 and accepted a scholarship at Harvard, where, in 1918, he took the master's degree in economics and anthropology. Although he studied for the Ph.D. degree, he never took his examinations. In 1920–21 he taught economics at Simmons College and in the following year he was an assistant professor at Smith. The textbooks he wrote on social sciences made it possible for him to leave teaching and devote himself to literature.

For some time he worked hard writing novels, but, although *Hunky* and *The Woods Colt* were both selections of the Book-of-the-Month Club, he was dissatisfied with his popular reception. ". . . I never seemed to get anywhere as a novelist," he writes; "I began with the firm conviction (I hope it was not mere conceit) that I had something important and different to contribute, but for some reason I failed to make any great mass of people think likewise. When

I try to analyze it I think it was partly that my philosophy of life was hard, ironical, and lone-wolfish, which of course would alienate the hordes of paunchy clubwomen who wield such power over writers' reputations in this country. Added to this, I was stubbornly interested in subjects and types which did not coincide with the interests of the majority of novel readers. Conventional novels, packed with commonplace patter and reeking of personal details of a (to me) trivial nature, have always disgusted me—but there are many more readers wanting this sort of thing than there were persons interested in my stuff. . . .

"Several years ago I decided to abandon novels. I had made no money to speak of, I had lived for my ideals many years, I had a family to support, and I finally could no longer keep up my courage against what I think of as stupid lower-middle-class interests in 'literature.' The combination downed me, and I was and am very sad about it . . . . At present I am leisurely interesting myself in playwriting, but more immediately I am working in moving pictures, chiefly writing and adapting original ideas of my own. . . .

"I might add that I consider myself more playwright than novelist, and in my heart more poet than playwright. When I have stored away a goodly amount of Hollywood gold, and have oriented my professional aims, I think I shall spend the rest of my days—barring a too sudden descent of a lynching mob—to plays and to dramatic poems of the general type of Masefield's longer things."

BIBLIOGRAPHY

Novels

Run, sheep, run, 1925; Gypsy down the lane . . . The American panorama, 1926; The man who cannot die . . . The American panorama, 1926; Stride of man, 1928; * Hunky, 1929; The earth told me, 1930; In Krusack's house, 1931; Sad Indian, a novel about Mexico, 1932; The woods colt, a novel of the Ozark hills . . . illustrated by Raymond Bishop, 1933; D is for Dutch, a last regional novel, 1934; Beginning at dusk, an interlude, 1935; Under the linden tree, an interlude, 1935.

Juvenile Literature

Opening Davy Jones's locker, a boy explores the bottom of the sea . . . with illustrations by Hubert Rogers, 1930; The flood-fighters, a boy's adventures with the raging Mississippi . . . with illustrations by Hubert Rogers, 1931; The glacier mystery, a boy's story of the Tyrolese Alps by S. S. Smith [*pseud.*] illustrated by Clinton Balmer, 1932 (with Sarah Storer Smith); On the reindeer trail . . . with illustrations by Lee Townsend, 1932; Against the jungle . . . with illustrations by Heman Fay, jr., 1933; The feud mystery, a boys' story of wild Sardinia by S. S. Smith [*pseud.*], 1934; The Lapp mystery, a boy's story of Finnish Lapland by S. S. Smith [*pseud.*] . . . illustrated by James Reid, 1934; North after seals . . . illustrated by Paul Quinn, 1934; The cave mystery, a boys' story of the Spanish Pyrenees by S. S. Smith [*pseud.*] . . . illustrated by James Reid, 1935; The lobster war . . . with illustrations by Forrest W. Orr, 1935; The lost caravan, a boys' story of the Sahara desert by Waldo Fleming [*pseud.*], 1935; Beyond the great wall, a boys' story of Manchoukuo by

Edward Dragonet [*pseud.*] with illustrations by W. R. Lohse, 1936; The falcon mystery, a boys' story of the Hungarian plain by S. S. Smith [*pseud.*] illustrated by James Reid, 1936; In the stone age, a boys' story of early paleolithic times by Gregory Trent [*pseud.*] illustrated by Carle M. Boog, 1936; Talking drums, a boys' story of the African Gold coast by Waldo Fleming [*pseud.*] illustrated by Frank Dobias, 1936; Hunters long ago, a boys' story of late paleolithic times by Gregory Trent [*pseud.*] . . . illustrated by Carle M. Boog, 1937; The last of the gauchos, a boys' tale of Argentine adventure . . . illustrated by Frank Hubbard, 1937; Messenger to the pharaoh, a story of ancient Egypt by De Wolfe Morgan [*pseud.*] illustrated by William O'Brian, 1937; A riddle in Fez, a boys' story of Morocco by Waldo Fleming [*pseud.*] illustrated by Frank Dobias, 1937; The spy mystery, a boys' story of Soviet Russia by S. S. Smith [*pseud.*] illustrated by James Reid, 1937; Before Homer, a boys' story of the earliest Greeks by De Wolfe Morgan [*pseud.*], 1938; Saltar the Mongol by Edward Dragonet [*pseud.*] . . . with pictures by Sidney Riesenberg, 1938; A tale of mystery and adventure in the Belgian Congo, The pygmy's arrow by Waldo Fleming [*pseud.*] illustrated by Frank Dobias, 1938; A tamer of beasts, a boys' story of the early neolithic period by Gregory Trent [*pseud.*] illustrated by Carle M. Boog, 1938.

Textbooks

Problems in American democracy, 1922; Readings in American democracy selected and edited by Thames Ross Williamson, 1922; Introduction to economics, 1923; Readings in economics selected and edited by Thames Ross Williamson, 1923; Introduction to sociology with practical applications, 1926; Civics at work, a textbook in social and vocational citizenship, 1928 (also pub. as: Civics at work, a textbook in elementary civics by Thames Ross Williamson, revised by William A. Hamm, 1934); Principles of social science, a survey of problems in American democracy by Thames Ross Williamson . . . and Edgar Bruce Wesley, 1932.

STUDIES

Kunitz

Wesley, Edgar B. Workbook in problems in American democracy by Edgar Bruce Wesley . . . T. M. Stinnett . . . Crawford Greene. [c1933] (basal text Williamson and Wesley's Principles of social science)

For references to reviews, see *BRD.*, 1923, 1925–27, 1929–38.

Edmund Wilson, 1895–

Born May 8, 1895, in Red Bank, New Jersey. His father was prominent in the State as a lawyer and politician. After preparation (1909–12) at the Hill School, he entered Princeton, where he became a friend of F. Scott Fitzgerald and John Peale Bishop. Both in school and in college he wrote and edited material for magazines; and in Princeton he collaborated with F. Scott Fitzgerald on a libretto for a production by the Triangle Club.

Upon graduation (1916) he took a job as reporter on the New York *Evening Sun.* In the next year he entered the army, and for two years he served in the war, in a hospital unit in France and in the Intelligence Corps, remaining in service until the summer of 1919. After his return he joined the staff of *Vanity Fair*, of which he became managing editor. Subsequently (1926) he became an associate editor of the *New Republic* and held this position until 1931. In 1935 he was awarded a Guggenheim fellowship. In recent years he has done much critical writing, much of it for the *New Republic*. With the critic Mary McCarthy, whom he married early in 1938, he lives in Stamford, Connecticut. In 1939 he was awarded another Guggenheim fellowship, to complete a book entitled "To the Finland Station: A Study of the Writing and Acting of History."

As a critic Wilson has been much interested in contemporary views on literature. Writing in the *Atlantic Monthly* in December, 1937, he questioned current assumptions concerning Marxist literary theory, pointed out that Marxists, like Humanists, had failed to find any works of art that would satisfy their standards, indicated the difference between the literary views of Marx and Engels and those of their present-day followers, and suggested that the function of Marxism is not to pass literary judgments but rather to clear up matters of origins and social significance. And, in a literary essay appearing in the *Nation* early in 1938, he said, of contemporary critical practice: "The young . . . are today not enthusiastic . . . about books: they merely approve when the book suits their politics. . . . I think it is a pity that they do not learn to read for pleasure. They may presently find that an acquaintance with the great works of art and thought is their only real insurance against the increasing barbarism of the time."

For further comment, see Critical Survey, pp. 197–98.

BIBLIOGRAPHY

Poems

Poets, farewell! 1929.

Novel

I thought of Daisy, 1929.

Plays and Dialogues

Discordant encounters, plays and dialogues, 1926; This room and this gin and these sandwiches, three plays . . . The crime in the Whistler room, A winter in Beech street, Beppo and Beth, 1937.

Literary Criticism

* Axel's castle, a study in the imaginative literature of 1870–1930, 1931; The triple thinkers, ten essays on literature, 1938.

Articles on Social and Economic Conditions

The American jitters, a year of the slump, 1932 (English ed., Devil take the hindmost, a year of the slump, 1932).

Sketches and Travel

Travels in two democracies, 1936.

Belles Lettres

The undertaker's garland [by] John Peale Bishop [and] Edmund Wilson, jr., decorations by Boris Artzybasheff, 1922.

Musical Comedy

The evil eye, a musical comedy in two acts, presented by the Princeton university Triangle club, 1915–1916. Book by E. Wilson, jr., '16, Lyrics by F. Scott Fitzgerald, '17, 1915 (cover-title).

STUDIES AND ARTICLES

Cowley (E)
Kunitz (L)
Markey
Shafer

Boyd, Ernest. "Edmund Wilson's essays." *SRL.*, Mar. 26, 1938, p. 10; Clark, John A. "The sad case of Edmund Wilson." *Com.*, July 8, 1938, pp. 292–95; Freeman, Joseph. "Edmund Wilson's globe of glass." *N.Masses, Lit.Sec.*, Apr. 12, 1938, pp. 73–79; Glicksberg, Charles I. "Edmund Wilson, radicalism at the crossroads." *SAQ.*, Oct. 1937, pp. 466–77; Jerome, V. J. "Edmund Wilson, to the Munich station." *N.Masses*, Apr. 4, 1939, pp. 23–26; McCarty, Norma. "Edmund Wilson." *N.Amer.Rev.*, Autumn 1938, pp. 192–97; Wilson, Ted C. "The muse and Edmund Wilson." *P.*, June 1938, pp. 144–52; Zabel, Morton D. "Marginalia of a critic." *P.*, Jan. 1930, pp. 222–26. For references to reviews, see *BRD.*, 1927, 1929, 1931–32, 1936–38.

(Arthur) Yvor Winters, 1900–

Born in Chicago. He passed his early childhood in southern California and in Seattle, and returned to the Middle West when he was ready for high school. After preparation in high schools in Evanston and Chicago he entered the University of Chicago in 1917. At the University he knew Elizabeth Madox Roberts and Glenway Wescott and met Vincent Sheean and Donald Culross Peattie. He left the university in 1919 because of tuberculosis and spent almost three years in a sanitarium in Santa Fe.

After two years of schoolteaching in coal camps near Santa Fe he resumed his studies in 1923 at the University of Colorado. In 1925 he took bachelor's and master's degrees in Romance languages.

Since 1925 he has taught French and Spanish at the University of Idaho and English at Stanford, where he went in 1927 for further graduate study. From 1932 until 1934 he was western editor of the *Hound & Horn.* In 1934 he took his Ph.D. in English, and at present he is teaching elementary composition, American literature, English lyric poetry, and the writing of poetry.

For further comment, see Critical Survey, p. 187.

BIBLIOGRAPHY

Poems

The immobile wind, 1921; The bare hills, a book of poems, 1927; The proof, 1930; The journey and other poems, 1931; Before disaster, 1934.

Criticism

Notes on the mechanics of the poetic image, The testament of a stone . . .

[by] Ivor Winters, 1925 (cover-title; pamphlet); * Primitivism and decadence, a study of American experimental poetry, 1937; Maule's curse, seven studies in the history of American obscurantism, Hawthorne—Cooper—Melville, Poe—Emerson—Jones Very, Emily Dickinson—Henry James, 1938.

Miscellany

The case of David Lamson, a summary prepared by Frances Theresa Russell . . . and by Yvor Winters . . . introduction by Peter B. Kyne. This summary follows for the greater part the briefs for the appeal by Edwin V. MacKenzie, though some additional material and analysis are introduced, 1934.

Editor

Twelve poets of the Pacific, 1937.

STUDIES AND ARTICLES

Horton

Andelson, Pearl. "One poet speaks for himself." *P.*, Sept. 1922, pp. 342–44; Cunningham, J. V. "Obscurity and dust." *P.*, June 1932, pp. 163–65; Donahue, Charles. "Philosophy vs. literature." *Com.*, Feb. 10, 1939, p. 442; Fitzgerald, Robert. "Against the grain." *P.*, June 1937, pp. 173–77; Flint, Frank C. "A critique of experimental poetry." *VQR.*, Summer 1937, pp. 453–57; Freer, Agnes L. "A poet-philosopher." *P.*, Apr. 1928, pp. 41–47; Horton, Philip. "The California classicism." *P.*, Oct. 1937, pp. 48–52; Humphries, Rolfe. "Foreword, with poems." *P.*, Feb. 1935, pp. 288–91; Monroe, Harriet. "Youth and the desert." *P.*, Sept. 1921, pp. 339–43; Schwartz, Delmore. "Primitivism and decadence." *So.R.*, Autumn 1938, pp. 597–614; Zabel, Morton D. "A poetry of ideas." *P.*, Jan. 1931, pp. 225–30. For references to reviews, see *BRD.*, 1928, 1930, 1937–38.

Owen Wister, 1860–1938

Born in Philadelphia, July 14, 1860, into a family of literary traditions. His mother was a daughter of Pierce Butler and Frances Anne ("Fanny") Kemble, and Mrs. Siddons was his great-grandaunt. Reared in Germantown, the boy soon became a reader and indulged in the usual outdoor games. In his boyhood he was taken abroad and spent some time in schools in Switzerland and England. In 1873 he entered St. Paul's School in Concord, New Hampshire. Here he took part in sports, wrote for the school paper, and profited by splendid instruction in English and the classics. In 1878 he proceeded to Harvard and graduated in 1882 *summa cum laude*, after a career notable for contributions to university publications, editorship in them, and an opera bouffe written for the Hasty Pudding Club. In his senior year the interest in music that had come with his early education in Switzerland became dominant; and in 1882, after graduating with highest honors in music, he went to Paris to study composition.

After two years in Europe, during which he studied with Guiraud and received the encouragement of Liszt, he was forced by ill health to return to the United States. He took a clerical job in a New York bank. When, in 1885, his health became precarious, he spent the summer in Wyoming on the advice of the physician-novelist, S. Weir Mitchell; and in the fall, having decided to give up composing as a career, he entered the Harvard Law School, from which he graduated in 1888. In the next year he was admitted to the bar in Pennsylvania and began practicing in Philadelphia.

In the meantime he had been spending summers in the West and writing for the *Atlantic* and *Lippincott's*. In 1891 he wrote two western sketches and sent them to *Harper's*. They were enthusiastically accepted, and subsequent success made a literary, rather than a legal, career certain. Wister devoted himself to the problem of catching the flavor of the old West and presenting it faithfully and vividly for new generations. *The Virginian*, dramatized and three times filmed, was a best-seller for months. In his literary work he was influenced by Stevenson, Kipling, and Mérimée, and was thrown into contact with Theodore Roosevelt, whom he had known at Harvard, William D. Howells, and Henry James, who assisted him with suggestions and advice. Roosevelt, when president, was so much interested in *Lady Baltimore*, a novel of old Charleston, of which he did not entirely approve, that he wrote the author a letter of more than five thousand words concerning it.

Besides these stories of American life and background Wister wrote political and social volumes on Anglo-American relations. His influence was recognized in England as bringing about closer relationships between the two countries. "Before the war was very old," commented the London *Graphic*, reviewing *A Straight Deal*, "Mr. Wister wrote a little volume, *The Pentecost of Calamity*, which did much to bring America into it. . . . Now there comes along . . . another book which he who runs in England or America would be wise to read. . . . Why doesn't some President send Owen Wister to England as American Ambassador?"

He once ran for the Philadelphia City Council as a protest against the political boss who dominated the city. He lost, but got more votes than he expected. In 1930 the first issue of his *Roosevelt—The Story of a Friendship* was recalled in order to expunge some remarks concerning a southern hostess of Theodore Roosevelt. He became the honorary chairman of *Defenders, Inc.*, and was arrested for his activities in the arrangement of a meeting to oppose F. D. Roosevelt's reorganization of the Supreme Court. The charges were dropped.

Wister, who was an Honorary Fellow of the Royal Society of Literature, received honorary degrees and other recognition, including membership in the American Academy of Arts and Letters. He was a corresponding member of the French Société des gens de lettres. In 1912–18 and 1919–25 he served as an Overseer at Harvard and helped to change the character of the instruction in freshman English. He retained his interest in education and his early love for music, especially that of the seventeenth and eighteenth centuries; and in his travels he was most impressed by the beauty of French cathedrals and the excellence of French wines.

"Horace is my personally favorite poet," Wister wrote in 1937. "I think he has uttered more truth in fewer words than any other known to me." Of American literature he said: "I hold that our historians have done better than our novelists and poets; that Henry James is our most important novelist, but that he wrote no individual work to rank with *Uncle Tom's Cabin*, *The Scarlet Letter*, *Moby Dick*, or *Huckleberry Finn*. I think the greatest novels have not been written in our language, but in Russian. If all Walt Whitman's pages were on a level with 'When lilacs last in the door-yard bloomed,' I should count him by far our greatest poet."

Wister died on July 21, 1938, at his summer home, "Crowfield," at North Kingstown, R.I. In 1939 a peak in Grand Teton National Park, Wyoming, was named for him.

For further comment, see Critical Survey, p. 63.

BIBLIOGRAPHY

Novels

The dragon of Wantley, his rise, his voracity, & his downfall, a romance . . . illustrations by John Stewardson, 1892; * The Virginian, a horseman of the plains . . . with illustrations by Arthur I. Keller, 1902; Lady Baltimore . . . with illustrations by Vernon Howe Bailey and Lester Ralph, 1906.

Short Stories

Red men and white . . . illustrated by Frederic Remington, 1896 [1895]; Lin McLean, 1898 [1897]; The Jimmyjohn boss and other stories, 1900; Philosophy 4, a story of Harvard university, 1903 (contains: Owen Wister . . . [a biographical sketch]); A journey in search of Christmas . . . illustrated by Frederic Remington, 1904 (from Lin McLean); Mother . . . illustrations & decorations by John Rae, 1907; Members of the family . . . with illustrations by H. T. Dunn, 1911; Padre Ignacio, or, The song of temptation, 1911; When West was west, 1928.

Poems

Done in the open, drawings by Frederic Remington with an introduction and verses by Owen Wister, 1902; Christmas at the Tavern club, 1919, 1919 (leaflet; signed: O. W.).

Humor and Satire

The new Swiss family Robinson, a tale for children of all ages . . . illustrated by F. Nichols, 1882; How doth the simple spelling bee . . . with illustrations by F. R. Gruger, 1907; Indispensable information for infants, or, Easy entrance to education earnestly compiled by Owen Wister . . . with careful charts by George Howe, 1921; Watch your thirst, a dry opera in three acts . . . with a preface by Samuel Johnson, illustrations by George Howe, 1923.

Biography

Ulysses S. Grant, 1900; The seven ages of Washington, a biography, 1907; Horace Howard Furness, a short memoir . . . reprinted from the Harvard graduates' magazine, December, 1912, 1912 (cover-title); * Roosevelt, the story of a friendship, 1880–1919, 1930 (English ed., Theodore Roosevelt, the story of a friendship, 1880–1919, 1930); Two appreciations of John Jay Chapman, 1934 (pamphlet).

Nature Studies

Musk-ox, bison, sheep, and goat by Caspar Whitney, George Bird Grinnell, and Owen Wister, 1904.

War Books

The Pentecost of calamity, 1915; A straight deal, or, The ancient grudge, 1920; Neighbors henceforth, 1922.

Miscellany

The ancient grudge, 1918? (caption-title; pamphlet); E. J. W., 1922 (broadside); Animal heroes of the great war by Ernest Harold Baynes with an account of the writer "The man and his enemies" by Owen Wister, 1925; Henry Winchester Cunningham, March 26, 1860–Oct. 27, 1930, 1931 (broadside; signed: O. W.).

Collected Works

The writings of Owen Wister of the American academy of arts and letters, membre correspondant de la Société des gens de lettres, honorary fellow of the Royal society of literature . . ., 1928 (11 vols.; new uniform ed. rev. and reset).

STUDIES AND ARTICLES

Baldwin
Baldwin (M)
Cooper (F)
Droste, Christian L. Germany's Golgotha, a reply to Owen Wister's Pentecost of calamity . . . with introduction by Professor Yandell Henderson. 1917
Harkins (L)
† Johnson (1929)
† Johnson (1932)
† Johnson (1936)
Kunitz (L)
† Manly
Marble
National
O'Connell, Daniel T. Owen Wister, advocate of racial hatred, an unpatriotic American who seeks to destroy American traditions. 1920 (cover-title; pamphlet)
Stearns
Wister, Owen. The Virginian, a horseman of the plains . . . edited by James Fleming Hosic. 1917
Woollcott (W)

Angell, James R. "The university and free speech." *U.Chi.Mag.*, Mar. 1916, pp. 207–08; Boynton, Henry W. "A word on the genteel critic." *D.*, Oct. 14, 1915, pp. 303–06; Hubbell, Jay B. "Owen Wister's work." *SAQ.*, Oct. 1930, pp. 440–43; Marsh, Edward C. "Owen Wister." *AB.*, July 1908, pp. 458–66; Ritchie, Robert W. "Some scenes of 'The Virginian.'" *AB.*, Jan. 1917, pp. 460–63; Van der Essen, Leon. "The university and free speech." *U.Chi.Mag.*, Mar. 1916, pp. 207–08; Woollcott, Alexander. "Wisteria." *N.Yer.*, Aug. 30, 1930, p. 30. For references to reviews, see *BRD.*, 1906–08, 1911, 1915, 1920, 1922, 1928, 1930–31.

Thomas (Clayton) Wolfe, 1900–1938

Born in Asheville, North Carolina, October 3, 1900. His father (a stonecutter), his mother, and his brothers and sisters resembled the Gant family of *Look Homeward, Angel.* His childhood was misunderstood and unhappy. He ran errands, helped about the house, read widely, and attended school, where his fellow students thought him peculiar.

At the University of North Carolina, where he studied from 1916 until 1920, he edited the college paper and magazine, studied playwriting, and wrote three plays. He was a member of the first playwriting group there, and acted in his first play, *The Return of Buck Gavin* (1919), and in his *The Third Night* (1919). The former play, his first published work, was printed in *Carolina Folk-Plays, Second Series* (1924). The latter was first published in *The Carolina Play-Book* for September, 1938. At Harvard, where he took his master's degree in 1922, he attended Professor Baker's playwriting class and continued his dramatic writing.

After traveling abroad for a time he went to New York and in 1924 became an instructor in English at Washington Square College of New York University. He remained in this position until early 1930, when he resigned to write, and to travel and study abroad on a Guggenheim fellowship (1930–31).

In the meantime, having begun scribbling at fourteen, he had been writing voluminously. His first long novel, refused elsewhere, was brought to Scribner's and the promise made that every word would be read. After Wolfe's return from Europe the task of cutting its length for publication was carried out, and it was brought out in 1929 as *Look Homeward, Angel.* Although sales in the first year were not startling, the figure was doubled in the next, and the book, reissued in the Modern Library, has enjoyed a fine sale.

Returning from a year on the Continent and in England in the spring of 1931, Wolfe brought with him three or four hundred thousand words of material; and late in the year he began writing industriously on a new book. In 1933 Maxwell Perkins, editor in Scribner's, persuaded him to stop writing and begin the organization of his material for publication. *The October Fair*, which was twelve times the size of the average novel, and *The Hills Beyond Pentland* required all of 1934 for revision; and in 1935 they were published as *Of Time and the River*, a week after the author had left for Paris.

"Since the publication of 'Of Time and the River' two years ago," Wolfe wrote in 1937, "my history, briefly, has been as follows: I went abroad just before the publication of the book and stayed four or five months, chiefly in Germany, where my books have been translated, and have been fortunate enough to enjoy a good deal of success. On my return I went out west for two or three months, returned to New York in the autumn and got busy on a new book. I went abroad again last summer and spent the time chiefly in Germany and Austria; then I returned to New York and have been pretty steadily at work ever since. I am now enjoying the experience of being back home again in my native hills of western North Carolina, for the first time in more than seven years since the publication of 'Look Homeward, Angel.' That book . . . aroused, to my great regret, a great deal of feeling and controversy among the people of my native town. But, I am happy to say, all that seems to be forgotten now, and I know it is very good to be home again."

Mr. Wolfe's experiences as a writer, as set forth in *The Story of a Novel*, suggest the activity of some outside power or force working through him. His writings were all achieved through furious and copious production, almost forced from the author, and subsequent revision and tremendous condensation. Mr. Perkins at one sitting cut out fifty thousand words from *Of Time and the River*. Chapters of fifty thousand words had to be reduced to ten or fifteen; and the author, in filling up gaps, again overwrote. The wealth of material and the necessity for condensation explain also the impossibility of final polishing.

The richness of material was due, not only to a memory retentive of all kinds of sense impressions (he never forgot a picture he had seen, and could describe most famous masterpieces in European galleries), but also to Wolfe's habit of recording and collecting facts. He spent long nights prowling about New York streets, and one of his strange hobbies was reading the *World Almanac.* Once before departing for Europe he left with his publisher four crates of manuscript notebooks. These big ledgers contained facts and miscellaneous information on numbers of unrelated subjects: lists of towns; descriptive notes about a railroad coach; statistics; and similar details calculated to satisfy his thirst for experience and to assist him to plumb his possibilities as a writer.

That much of the material in *Look Homeward, Angel* and *Of Time and the River* was derived from his own experiences Wolfe freely admitted; and in *The Story of a Novel* he stated his belief that, although it is impossible for a truly original writer to record his own experience without altering facts in accord with his personality and genius, all serious literary creation of substantial value is fundamentally autobiographical.

He fell ill of pneumonia in July, 1938, but was recovering in Seattle when an infection developed and spread to his kidneys and heart. He underwent two operations at Johns Hopkins Hospital (Baltimore, Md.) after his arrival Saturday, September 10, 1938, and died September 15, 1938.

In 1939 the manuscript of *Look Homeward, Angel* was bought by Gabriel Wells for $1,700 at a sale for the benefit of German refugees and presented to the Harvard College Library.

For further comment, see Critical Survey, pp. 34, 44, 67.

BIBLIOGRAPHY

Novels

* Look homeward, angel, a story of the buried life, 1929; Of time and the river, a legend of man's hunger in his youth, 1935; The web and the rock, 1939.

Short Stories and Sketches

From death to morning, 1935.

Autobiographical Sketch

The story of a novel, 1936.

Selections

The face of a nation, poetical passages from the writings of Thomas Wolfe, decorations by Edward Shenton, 1939 (intro. by John Hall Wheelock).

STUDIES AND ARTICLES

Canby (S)
Cowley
DeVoto
Dodd, Martha. Through embassy eyes. [c1939]
Hatcher
† Johnson (1936)
Kildal
Kunitz (L)
Loggins
Lundkvist
McCole
Muller
Saturday
Schreiber
Zabel

Barr, Stringfellow. "The Dandridges and the Gants." *VQR.*, Apr. 1930, pp. 310–13; Basso, Hamilton. "Thomas Wolfe, a portrait." *NR.*, June 24, 1936, pp. 199–202; Bates, Ernest S. "Thomas Wolfe." *EJ.*, Sept. 1937, pp. 519–27; Bishop, John Peale. "The Sorrows of Thomas Wolfe." *Kenyon Review*, Winter, 1939, pp. 7–17; Bridgers, Ann. P. "Thomas Wolfe, legends of a man's hunger in his youth." *SRL.*, Apr. 6, 1935, pp. 599, 609; Daniels, Jonathan. "Thomas Wolfe." *SRL.*, Sept. 24, 1938, p. 8; Fadiman, Clifton. "Thomas Wolfe." *N.Yer.*, Mar. 9, 1935, pp. 68–70; Koch, Frederick H. "Thomas Wolfe, playmaker of the first playwriting group, 1918–1920." *The Carolina Playbook*, Sept. 1938, pp. 65–69; MaCauley, Thurston. "Thomas Wolfe, a writer's problems." *PW.*, Dec. 24, 1938, pp. 2150–52; McCole, Camille J. "Thomas Wolfe embraces life." *CW.*, Apr. 1936, pp. 42–48; Stevens, George. "Always Looking Homeward." *SRL.*, June 24, 1939, pp. 5–6; Volkening, Henry T. "Tom Wolfe, penance no more." *VQR.*, Apr. 1939, pp. 196–215; Wade, John D. "Prodigal." *So.R.*, July 1935, pp. 192–98; Warren, Robert P. "A note on the Hamlet of Thomas Wolfe." *AR.*, May 1935, pp. 191–208. For references to reviews, see *BRD.*, 1929, 1935–36.

Alexander (Humphreys) Woollcott, 1887–

Born January 19, 1887, in Phalanx, New Jersey, where the family lived in an old house that had been the headquarters of a socialistic community of which his grandfather had been president. He passed his childhood in Kansas City, in Phalanx, and in Philadelphia, where he attended the Central High School and supported himself by writing reviews and other material for the *Evening Telegraph* and the *Record.* Finishing his preparatory schooling in 1905, he entered Hamilton College, where he was a brilliant student, editor of the monthly magazine, and founder and director of the dramatic club. In high school he had won a gold medal for essay-writing; in college he won a prize for a short story that was published in the *Black Cat.*

He graduated in 1909 and went to New York, where at first he worked as a bank clerk. Soon, however, he began reporting for the *Times;* and in 1914 he was made dramatic critic, a position he held until 1922, when he accepted a similar one on the *Herald.* In the meantime he had been overseas and spent six months as private and sergeant in the Medical Corps in a base hospital in Savenay, Loire-Inférieure, and a considerably longer period on the staff of the *Stars and Stripes*, the weekly newspaper of the American Expeditionary Force. When the New York *Herald* was sold to the *Tribune,* Woollcott transferred his connection to the *Sun*, then, in 1925, succeeded Heywood Broun as drama critic on the *World.* He resigned in 1928 and abandoned newspaper writing.

Having already begun to write magazine articles of a personal nature, he turned to radio broadcasting in 1929, as a book reviewer and as the "Town Crier." When he resumed broadcasting in 1933, after an absence of two years, he was enormously popular, received more "high-class" "fan mail" than any other single performer on the network of the Columbia Broadcasting System, and enjoyed great freedom in the expression of his own interests and enthusiasms. His column "Shouts and Murmurs," which he abandoned in 1935, was one of the most popular features of the *New Yorker.*

In addition to the plays *The Channel Road* (1931) (adapted from Maupassant) and *The Dark Tower* (1933), both written in collaboration with George S. Kaufman, Woollcott has to his credit performances as an actor in two plays by

S. N. Behrman, *Brief Moment* (1931) and *Wine of Choice* (1938), and he also played with Noel Coward in the motion picture *The Scoundrel* (1935). *While Rome Burns* sold some 290,000 copies, and the two Woollcott "readers" have made handsome sums for the compiler. As a critic he has been active in turning public attention from the more ambitious and pretentious productions of the day to little-known and inconspicuous works, and he prefers to use his influence to promote causes, literary and humanitarian, of his own discovery. He has made recordings of some of his favorite stories and essays under the title *The Woollcott Hearer* for the American Foundation for the Blind. Although he has recently been characterized as "one of the most sentimental men alive," he has been a central figure in the most sophisticated literary society of New York.

For further comment, see Critical Survey, p. 161.

BIBLIOGRAPHY

Essays and Sketches

Nonsenseorship by Heywood Broun, George S. Chappell, Ruth Hale, Ben Hecht, Wallace Irwin, Robert Keable, Helen Bullitt Lowry, Frederick O'Brien, Dorothy Parker, Frank Swinnerton, H. M. Tomlinson, Charles Hanson Towne, John V. A. Weaver, Alexander Woollcott, and the author of "The mirrors of Washington," edited by G. P. P. Sundry observations concerning prohibitions, inhibitions, and illegalities, illustrated by Ralph Barton, 1922; Shouts and murmurs, echoes of a thousand and one first nights, 1922; Enchanted aisles, 1924; Going to pieces, 1928; * While Rome burns, 1934; The good companions, 1936.

Stories

The command is forward, tales of the A.E.F. battlefields as they appeared in the Stars and stripes by Sergeant Alexander Woollcott illustrated by drawings by Pvt. C. Le Roy Baldridge, A.E.F., 1919; Two gentlemen and a lady by Alexander Woollcott, illustrations by Edwina, 1928 (also pub. as Verdun Belle, 1934).

Plays

The dark tower, a melodrama by Alexander Woollcott and George S. Kaufman, 1934.

Biography

The story of Irving Berlin . . . with 16 illustrations, portrait by Neysa McMein, 1925.

Miscellany

Mrs. Fiske, her views on actors, acting, and the problems of production recorded by Alexander Woolcott [!] with photographs, 1917; Château-Thierry by Sergeant Alexander Woollcott with sketches by Private C. Le Roy Baldridge, a friendly guide for American pilgrims to the shrines between the Marne and the Vesle, 1919.

Editor

Mr. Dickens goes to the play, 1922; Fifteen years old being letters, notes, & manuscripts left behind by William Duncan Saunders and picked up by his friends G. C. R. and A. W., 1923; The Woollcott reader, bypaths in the realms of gold, 1935; Woollcott's second reader, 1937.

STUDIES AND ARTICLES

Brown (U)
† Ford (E)
Markey

Gibbs, Wolcott. "Big nemo." *N.Yer.*, Mar. 18, 1939, pp. 24–29; Gibbs. "Big nemo." *N.Yer.*, Mar. 25, 1939, pp. 24–29; Gibbs. "Big nemo." *N.Yer.*, Apr. 1, 1939, pp. 22–27; Morris, Don. "Bird thou never wert." *University of Chicago Magazine*, June 1939, pp. 8–10. For references to reviews, see *BRD.*, 1919, 1922, 1924–25, 1928–29, 1934–35, 1937–38.

Audrey Wurdemann, 1911–

Born in Seattle, January 1, 1911. She is a descendant of Shelley and Harriet Westbrook.

As a little girl she was educated at home. When she was eleven she entered the St. Nicholas School for Girls, in Seattle. Her literary gifts soon brought her attention, and when she was in her early teens some of her poems, published in the *Step-Ladder*, the organ of the Bookfellows of Chicago, caught the eye of the California poet George Sterling. Through his influence her first book of verse, *The House of Silk*, was published before she entered college.

After graduating from the University of Washington with a distinguished record she traveled in the United States and the Orient. Returning in 1932, she went to New York, where she met Joseph Auslander, poet and lecturer at Columbia University. They were married in 1933, and they live in New York.

In 1935 Miss Wurdemann, the youngest writer to have received this honor, was awarded the Pulitzer Prize for *Bright Ambush*, her second volume of poetry.

BIBLIOGRAPHY

Poems

The house of silk, 1927; Bright ambush, poems, 1934; The seven sins, 1935; Splendour in the grass, 1936; Testament of love, a sonnet sequence, 1938.

Literary Criticism

America's town meeting of the air, December 26, 1935, number 9. Literature and life [by] Christopher Morley, Fannie Hurst, Audrey Wurdemann, T. S. Stribling, Francis Talbot, S. J., 1935 (cover-title; pamphlet; ed. by Lyman Bryson).

STUDIES AND ARTICLES

Wurdemann, Audrey. Bright ambush, poems. [1935] (foreword by William Rose Benét)

Crawford, Nelson A. "Promise, not genius." *P.*, Jan. 1928, pp. 226–28; Scott, Winfield T. "Unselected poems." *P.*, Mar. 1937, pp. 340–42; Zaturenska, Marya. "The proud of spirit." *P.*, Jan. 1935, pp. 220–23. For references to reviews, see *BRD.*, 1934–36, 1939.

Elinor (Hoyt) Wylie, 1885–1928

Born Elinor Hoyt, September 7, 1885, at Somerville, New Jersey, of a distinguished Pennsylvania family. Her great-grandfather had been a mayor of Philadelphia, her grandfather had been governor of Pennsylvania, and her father was Solicitor General of the United States under President Theodore Roosevelt. Her brother, Henry Martin Hoyt, became a noted painter, and her sister, Nancy, a novelist.

She passed her childhood and youth in a suburb of Philadelphia and in Washington, and she was educated at Miss Baldwin's School, Bryn Mawr, and the Holton Arms School in Washington. When she was eighteen, she was a member of a life class in the Corcoran School of Art in Washington.

After a début in Washington society and an unhappy romance, she married (1905) Philip Hichborn, by whom she had a son. The marriage proved unfortunate; and, unable to secure a divorce, she eloped with Horace Wylie in December, 1910, and spent several years with him in England. After the death of her husband and the securing of a divorce by Mr. Wylie, they were married. The war forced them to return to this country, and they lived in Boston, at Mount Desert, Maine, and in Georgia.

In the meantime she had been writing. Torn between painting and literary work, she had secretly written poems in her youth, and in England she issued *Incidental Numbers* privately in 1912. Back in America, she wrote for magazines, and settled in Washington, where her husband had taken a government post in 1919 and where she became a member of a group including William Rose Benét. In 1921, the year when she removed to New York, she issued *Nets to Catch the Wind*, which brought her the Julia Ellsworth Ford Prize awarded by the Poetry Society of America.

In 1923 she married Mr. Benét, with whom she established herself in New York as a literary figure of importance. For the rest of her life she devoted herself to slow, careful writing of poetry and novels, the latter involving considerable research, and collected a fine library, noteworthy particularly for the Shelley items, including two letters for which Mrs. Wylie paid $2,400. *The Orphan Angel* was a selection of the Book-of-the-Month Club. She was awarded the Helen Haire Levinson Prize in 1928. She spent her summers in England and visited the places associated intimately with Shelley. Her friend Carl Van Doren described her as having "as sure and strong an intelligence as I have ever known," and said, "No formal scholar, she had a scholar's instinct for exactness." Her writing, because of the careful preparation, required almost no revision. At the time of her sudden death from a paralytic stroke December 16, 1928, she was arranging for printing the poems issued as *Angels and Earthly Creatures* in 1929.

Mrs. Wylie is said to have suggested some of the traits of the characters of Mrs. Ventress in William Rose Benét's *The First Person Singular* (1922), Christabel Caine in Anne Parrish's *All Kneeling* (1928), the American girl in

Nancy Hoyt's *Bright Intervals* (1929), Eva Litchfield in Isa Glenn's *East of Eden* (1932), and Victoria Rising in Kathleen Coyle's *Immortal Ease* (1939).

For further comment, see Critical Survey, pp. 72, 146.

BIBLIOGRAPHY

Poems

Incidental numbers, 1912 (anonymous); Nets to catch the wind, 1921; Black armour, a book of poems, 1923; Elinor Wylie, The pamphlet poets, price 25 cents, 1926 (ed. by Laurence Jordan); Angels and earthly creatures, a sequence of sonnets, 1928 (51 copies privately printed); Trivial breath, 1928; Angels and earthly creatures, 1929; Birthday sonnet, 1929 (pamphlet); Rondeau. A windy day, 1935? (cover-title; leaflet); Nadir, 1937 (caption-title; leaflet).

Novels

Jennifer Lorn: a sedate extravaganza . . . Complete herein in three books. Illuminating episodes in the lives of the Hon. Gerald Poynyard and his bride, 1923; The Venetian glass nephew, 1925; The orphan angel, 1926 (English ed., Mortal image, 1927); Mr. Hodge & Mr. Hazard, 1928.

Verses Set to Music

On a singing girl [words by] Elinor Wiley [!], [music by] Constance Herreshoff, 1928 (caption-title; sheet music).

Collected Works

* Collected poems of Elinor Wylie, 1932 (ed. by William Rose Benét); Collected prose of Elinor Wylie, 1933 (prefaces by Carl Van Vechten, Carl Van Doren, Stephen Vincent Benét, Isabel Paterson, William Rose Benét; contents: Jennifer Lorn, The Venetian glass nephew, The orphan angel, Mr. Hodge and Mr. Hazard, Fugitive prose); The novels of Elinor Wylie, 1934.

STUDIES AND ARTICLES

Ashley
Auslander
Benét, William R. The prose and poetry of Elinor Wylie. 1934
Cabell
Clark (E)
Deutsch
Dictionary
Hatcher
Hoyt, Nancy. Elinor Wylie, the portrait of an unknown lady. [c1935]
† Johnson (1932)
† Johnson (1936)
Jones
Kreymborg
Kunitz
Loggins
Moore, Virginia. Distinguished women writers. [c1934]
National
Overton (WW)
Saturday
Sergeant
Tietjens
Untermeyer
Untermeyer (C)
Untermeyer (M)
Van Doren (B)
Van Doren (T)
Vočadlo
Ward
Wood

Burdett, Osbert. "The novels of Elinor Wylie." *Eng.Rev.*, Oct. 1934, pp. 488–90, 492; Cabell, James B. "Sanctuary in porcelain, a note as to Elinor Wylie." *VQR.*, July 1930, pp. 335–41; Collamore, H. Bacon. "Some notes on modern first editions." *Col.*, Summer 1938, pp. 356–58; Colum, Mary M. "In memory of Elinor Wylie." *NR.*, Feb. 6, 1929, pp. 317–19; Deutsch, Babette. "Proud lady." *VQR.*, Oct. 1932, pp. 618–20; Dillon, George. "A light never upon land or sea." *P.*, July 1929, pp. 230–33; Gorman, Herbert S. "Daughter of Donne." *N.Amer.Rev.*, May 1924, pp. 679–86; Johnson, Merle. "American first editions, Elinor Hoyt Wylie." *PW.*, Dec. 21, 1929, pp. 2845–46; Kohler, Dayton. "Elinor Wylie, heroic mask." *SAQ.*, Apr. 1937, pp. 218–28; Ludeke, H. "Venetian glass: the poetry and prose of Elinor Wylie." *E.Studies*, Dec. 1938, pp. 241–50; MacLeish, Archibald. "Black armour." *NR.*, Dec. 5, 1923, Suppl. pp. 16–18; Monroe, Harriet. "Elinor Wylie." *P.*, Feb. 1929, pp. 266–72; Monroe. "Mrs. Wylie's poems." *P.*, Jan. 1922, pp. 220–22; North, Jessica. "Poems and cloisonné." *P.*, Nov. 1928, pp. 96–99; Sergeant, Elizabeth S. "Elinor Wylie, intricate and crystal." *NR.*, Dec. 1, 1926, pp. 36–39; Tietjens, Eunice. "Armor of the spirit." *P.*, Feb. 1924, pp. 276–79; Van Doren, Carl. "Elinor Wylie, a portrait from memory." *Harper's*, Sept. 1936, pp. 358–67; Walbridge, Earle E. "Incense and praise, and whim, and glory, real people in poetry." *Col.*, Part 16, Art. 3, pp. 1–8 (1934); Wilson, Edmund. "In memory of Elinor Wylie." *NR.*, Feb. 6, 1929, pp. 316–17; Wylie, Elinor. "Portrait in black paint, with a very sparing use of whitewash." *N.Yer.*, Mar. 19, 1927, p. 24; Zabel, Morton D. "The pattern of the atmosphere." *P.*, Aug. 1932, pp. 273–82. For references to reviews, see *BRD.*, 1921, 1923, 1925–26, 1928–29, 1932–33.

Stark Young, 1881–

Born in Como, Mississippi, October 11, 1881. He attended a private preparatory school until a typhoid epidemic closed it and deprived him of the usual diet of English and American literature; and at a tender age he entered the state university. There he was trained by impoverished gentlemen of the ante-bellum school and graduated in 1901. He proceeded to graduate work at Columbia in the same year and took the master's degree in English in 1902.

After six months in the mountains of North Carolina, where he lived in a cabin, wrote verse, and studied Dante and Catullus, he taught in a military school in Mississippi and later (1904) joined the faculty of the University of Mississippi. In 1907 he went to the University of Texas to teach literature, and from 1915 to 1921, at the invitation of Alexander Meiklejohn, he was professor of English at Amherst.

Since 1921, except for the season 1924–25, which he spent as dramatic critic on the New York *Times*, he has been an editor of the *New Republic* and *Theatre Arts Monthly*. In 1923 he directed Lenormand's *The Failures*, produced by the Theatre Guild, and in 1924 he directed the Selwyn production of *Welded*, by Eugene O'Neill. He lectured in Italy in 1931 on the George Westinghouse Foundation.

Young, who lives in New York and amuses himself by painting, is an original playwright as well as a critic. His plays have been produced by the Stage Society of London and the Provincetown Players, and his translation of *The Sea Gull* of Chekhov was used in the production of that play by the Theatre Guild, with Lynn Fontanne and Alfred Lunt, in 1937–38.

For further comment, see Critical Survey, p. 58.

BIBLIOGRAPHY

Novels

Heaven trees, 1926; The torches flare, 1928; River house, 1929; * So red the rose, 1934.

Short Stories

The street of the islands . . . woodcuts by Ilse Bischoff, 1930; Feliciana, 1935.

Plays

Guenevere, a play in five acts, 1906; Addio, Madretta, and other plays, 1912 (Addio; Madretta; The star in the trees; The twilight saint; The dead poet; The seven kings and the wind; The Queen of Sheba); Three one-act plays: Madretta, At the shrine, Addio, 1921; The twilight saint, 1921 (pamphlet; also issued with title: The twilight saint, play in one act, 1925); The Queen of Sheba, 1922; The colonnade, 1924; The saint, a play in four acts, 1925.

Children's Plays

Sweet times and The blue policeman . . . with decorations by Edwin Avery Park, 1925.

Poems

The blind man at the window and other poems, 1906.

Books about the Theater

The flower in drama, a book of papers on the theatre, 1923; Glamour, essays on the art of the theatre, 1925; Theatre practice, 1926; The theater, 1927.

Essays and Sketches

Encaustics, 1926; I'll take my stand, the South and the agrarian tradition by twelve southerners, 1930.

Travel

The three fountains, 1924.

Textbooks

The English humorists of the eighteenth century by William Makepeace Thackeray edited by Stark Young, 1911; Treasury of life and literature . . . by Rollo L. Lyman, Nelle E. Moore, Howard C. Hill, Stark Young . . . Reading and living, 1937 (4 vols.).

Translations

Le legataire universel (The sole heir) by Jean Francois Regnard translated for the Curtain club . . . with a brief introduction, 1912 (Bulletin of the University of Texas, no. 259, general series no. 29); Mandragola by Niccolo Machiavelli, 1927; Anton Chekhov. The sea gull, 1939.

Editor

Southern treasury of life and literature, selected, 1937.

STUDIES AND ARTICLES

Brown (U)
† Johnson (1936)
Kunitz (L)
Library
† Manly

Barr, Stringfellow. "The Dandridges and the Gants." *VQR.*, Apr. 1930, pp. 310–13; Brown, John M. "The flower in criticism." *TAM.*, June 1925, pp. 417–18; Clark, Emily. "Stark Young's south." *VQR.*, Oct. 1935, pp. 626–28; Gilder, Rosamond. "Theatre practice." *TAM.*, Sept. 1926, pp. 647–48; Martin, Abbott. "Stark Young and the Ransomists." *SR.*, Jan.–Mar. 1930, pp. 114–15; Payne, Leonidas W., Jr. "A new southern poet, Stark Young of Mississippi." *SAQ.*, Oct. 1909, pp. 316–27; Wade, John D. "Two souths." *VQR.*, Oct. 1934, pp. 616–19. For references to reviews, see *BRD.*, 1921, 1923–30, 1934–35, 1937.

Leane Zugsmith, 1903–

Born in Louisville, Kentucky, January 18, 1903. Her early childhood was spent in Philadelphia and Atlantic City, and she was educated in high schools in Louisville and Atlantic City and at Goucher College, the University of Pennsylvania, and Columbia University. She held jobs as copy editor and reader for *Western Story Magazine* and *Detective Story Magazine*, and edited copy later on a similar publication. After a year in Europe, mainly in Paris, she left copy-editing for advertising and publicity work for Putnam's and subsequently Liveright.

Her first book, *Bits of Fairyland*, was printed privately when she was five, and she wrote for high-school magazines in Louisville and Atlantic City. Her first story appeared in *Scribner's*. Her work is careful and often requires study and reworking. "For certain books," she writes, "I had to spend as much time in research as in the actual writing. Some of my characters have been based in part on real persons. I always have a notebook in my handbag and have made use of many of the observations noted there. Some books I have written fairly rapidly (all of them on the typewriter) and rewritten entirely three or four times."

"As to my preferences in literature," she declares, "I am an admirer of Balzac, Stendhal, Tolstoi, Dostoievsky, Chekov, Thomas Mann, André Malraux, Jane Austen. This list is misleading because it is composed only of the favorites in my library; but my library, like my reading, is far from complete, and there are, I am certain, many books I might have included, had I been introduced to them. My interest in poetry has declined to such an extent that I really cannot name any one who still gives me pleasure. Aristophanes, Shakespeare and Chekov are the dramatists to my taste. I like Brahms and Beethoven; I'm not touched by Bach; and I don't care for modern music. I prefer the piano to the violin because the latter is too much like the human voice and too well adapted to sentimental compositions. The symphony and chamber music give me genuine satisfaction. My tastes in sculpture and painting are an unreliable index to what they might be, if I were as interested in those forms as I was ten years ago. But Epstein and Maillol are still enthusiasms of mine. In oils, my likes are a hodge podge; there's no use giving a stream of names. I don't like the rococo in early Italian work or the surrealist now or any of the candy pieces of any age and I've never seen anything by an Englishman to which I wanted to return. I do not see many motion pictures and almost none of American manufacture that are worth watching. Russian, French, and pre-Hitler German films have given me the most pleasure.

"My sympathies are with the working-class. Although I have no political affiliations, I am strongly opposed to Fascism, not only in its overt forms, as in Italy and Germany, but in its disguised forms as it exists in other parts of the world, including some parts of our own country. It seems to me shameful that in a country with resources as abundant as ours, decent lives cannot be provided for every one. The writing men and women who are concerned about such contradictions are, in my estimation, creating a renascence in American writing. With the exception of novelists like Dos Passos (whom I admire) most of these writers are young, in the writing sense, and some of them are still immature and uncertain as artists. But in them lies the great hope of American letters and from them, already, a few first-rate works have reached us. The average English novelist employs the English language with much more grace and precision than the average American novelist; but I think we have more to say and are saying it. To France we must still look, not only for distinguished prose but for content; and the same applies to that band of exiled writers whose books are burned in the Germany they once helped to ennoble.

"I dislike using the name 'proletarian novels' for the books I have in mind. The term is loose and inaccurate. I don't know what such literature should be called, but it should be composed of works that add to our knowledge of human beings and the society they live in. Great works do not come from writers who regard themselves only as entertainers. I want my books to be interesting to all kinds of readers but I want them also to serve as penetrating analyses of human beings in relation to one another; from that an understanding of the society in which they live and which has moulded them naturally follows. I do not believe that such books should be disguised economic treatises or polemics."

BIBLIOGRAPHY

Novels

All victories are alike, 1929; Goodbye and tomorrow, 1931; Never enough, a novel, 1932; The reckoning, 1934; A time to remember, 1936; The summer soldier, 1938.

Short Stories

* Home is where you hang your childhood and other stories, 1937.

Glossary

L is for labor, a glossary of labor terms, 1938 (cover-title; pamphlet).

For references to reviews, see *BRD.*, 1929, 1931–32, 1934, 1936–38.

SELECT BIBLIOGRAPHIES

CONTEMPORARY SOCIAL, POLITICAL, AND LITERARY HISTORY

I. POLITICAL AND SOCIAL HISTORY[1]

Allen, Frederick L. Only yesterday, an informal history of the nineteen-twenties. 1933
Bassett, John S. Expansion and reform, 1889–1926. "Epochs of American history, vol. IV." 1926
Bassett, John S. Makers of a new nation. "The pageant of America, a pictorial history of the United States, vol. 9." 1928
Beard, Charles A. and Beard, Mary R. America in midpassage. 1939
Beard, Charles A. and Beard, Mary R. The rise of American civilization. Rev. and enl. ed. 1933
Burlingame, Roger. March of the iron men, a social history of union through invention. 1938
Coad, Oral S. and Mims, Edwin, Jr. The American stage. "The pageant of America, a pictorial history of the United States, vol. 14." 1929
Couch, William T., *ed.* Culture in the south. 1934
Daniels, Jonathan. A southerner discovers the south. 1938
Faulkner, Harold U. American political and social history. 1937
Faulkner, Harold U. The quest for social justice, 1898–1914. "A history of American life, vol. XI." 1931
Federal Writers Project. These are our lives. As told by the people and written by members of the Federal Writers Project in North Carolina, Tennessee and Georgia. 1939
Gabriel, Ralph H. Toilers of land and sea. "The pageant of America, a pictorial history of the United States, vol. 3." 1926
Gruening, Ernest H., *ed.* These United States, a symposium. 1923–26
Hacker, Louis M. and Kendrick, Benjamin B. The United States since 1865. 1939
Keir, Malcolm. The epic of industry. "The pageant of America, a pictorial history of the United States, vol. 5." 1926
Keir, Malcolm. The march of commerce. "The pageant of America, a pictorial history of the United States, vol. 4." 1927
Keppel, Frederick P. and Duffus, Robert L. The arts in American life. 1933
Lynd, Robert S. and Lynd, Helen M. Middletown, a study in American culture. 1937
Morison, Samuel E. and Commager, Henry S. The growth of the American republic. Rev. ed. 1937. Two volumes
Murrell, William. A history of American graphic humor, 1865–1938. 1938
Nichols, Jeannette P. and Nichols, Roy F. The growth of American democracy. 1939
Odum, Howard W. and Moore, Harry Estill. American regionalism. 1938
Paxson, Frederic L. Recent history of the United States, 1865 to the present. Rev. and enl. ed. 1937

[1] In this section of the select bibliography, the dates are those of the latest and not of the first editions.

Recent social trends in the United States, report of the president's research committee on social trends, with a foreword by Herbert Hoover. 1933

Rogers, Agnes, *comp.* and Allen, Frederick L. The American procession, American life since 1860 in photographs. 1933

Shippee, Lester B. Recent American history. Rev. ed. 1930

Siegfried, André. America comes of age, a French analysis. 1930

Slosson, Preston W. The great crusade and after, 1914–1928. "A history of American life, vol. XII." 1930

Stearns, Harold E. America now, an inquiry into civilization in the United States by 36 Americans. 1938

Stearns, Harold E., *ed.* Civilization in the United States, an inquiry by thirty Americans. 1922

Stephenson, George M. American history since 1865. 1939

Sullivan, Mark. Our times, the United States, 1900–1925. I. The turn of the century, 1900–1904. 1926; II. America finding herself. 1927; III. Pre-war America. 1930; IV. The war begins, 1909–1914. 1932; V. Over here, 1914–1918. 1933; VI. The twenties. 1935

Williams, Stanley T. The American spirit in letters. "The pageant of America, a pictorial history of the United States, vol. 11." 1926

Wood, William C. H. and Gabriel, Ralph H. In defense of liberty. "The pageant of America, a pictorial history of the United States, vol. 7." 1928

II. LITERARY HISTORY: GENERAL

Blankenship, Russell. American literature as an expression of the national mind. 1931

Boynton, Percy H. Literature and American life, for students of American literature. 1936

Brawley, Benjamin. The Negro in literature and art in the United States. 1918

Dickinson, Thomas H. The making of American literature, being a near view of the procession of American writings and writing men from the earliest settlements up to our own times, with some consideration of the way men and women lived, their vocations, opinions, and amusements. 1932

Hubbell, Jay B., *ed.* American life in literature. 1936

Knight, Grant C. American literature and culture. 1932

Leisy, Ernest E. American literature, an interpretive survey. 1929

Lewisohn, Ludwig. Expression in America. 1932

Loggins, Vernon. The Negro author, his development in America. 1931

Long, William J. American literature, a study of the men and the books that in the earlier and later times reflect the American spirit. Rev. ed. 1923

Michaud, Régis. Panorama de la littérature américaine contemporaine. 1928

Miller, James M. An outline of American literature. 1934

Parrington, Vernon L. Main currents in American thought, an interpretation of American literature from the beginnings to 1920. I. The colonial mind, 1620–1800, 1927; II. The romantic revolution in America, 1800–1860, 1927; III. The beginnings of critical realism in America, 1860–1920, 1930

Taylor, Walter F. A history of American letters, with bibliographies by Harry Hartwick. "American literature series." 1936

III. LITERARY HISTORY: CONTEMPORARY

Anderson, Margaret C. My thirty years' war. 1930

Cargill, Oscar, *ed.* The social revolt, American literature from 1888 to 1914. "American literature, a period anthology." 1933

Cleaton, Irene and Cleaton, Allen. Books and battles, American literature, 1920–1930. 1937
Cowley, Malcolm. Exile's return, a narrative of ideas. 1934
Haight, Anne L. Banned books, informal notes on some books banned for various reasons at various times and in various places. 1935
Hicks, Granville. The great tradition, an interpretation of American literature since the civil war. Rev. ed. 1935
Loggins, Vernon. I hear America, literature in the United States since 1900. 1937
Manly, John M. and Rickert, Edith M. Contemporary American literature. 1922
Manly, John M. and Rickert, Edith M. Contemporary American literature, bibliographies and study outlines. Introduction and revision by Fred B. Millett. 1929
Mersand, Joseph. Traditions in American literature, a study of Jewish characters and authors. 1939
Nelson, John H., *ed.* Contemporary trends, American literature since 1914. "American literature, a period anthology." 1933
Pattee, Fred L. The new American literature, 1890–1930. 1930
Schyberg, Frederik. Modern Amerikansk litteratur, 1900–1930. 1930
Van Doren, Carl and Van Doren, Mark. American and British literature since 1890. 1925
Vočadlo, Otakar. Současná literatura Spojených Států, od zuoleni presidenta Wilsona po velkou haspodářskou krist. 1934
Ward, Alfred C. American literature, 1880–1930. 1932

IV. HISTORY OF THE NOVEL AND SHORT STORY

Beach, Joseph W. The twentieth century novel, studies in technique. 1932
Brodin, Pierre. Le roman régionaliste Américain, esquisse d'une géographie morale et pittoresque des Etats-Unis. 1937
Cooper, Frederic T. Some American story tellers. 1911
Follett, Helen T. and Follett, Wilson. Some modern novelists, appreciations and estimates. 1918
Ford, Nick A. The contemporary Negro novel, a study in race relations. 1936
Hartwick, Harry. The foreground of American fiction. 1934
Hatcher, Harlan H. Creating the modern American novel. 1935
Marble, Annie R. A study of the modern novel, British and American, since 1900. 1928
Michaud, Régis. The American novel today, a social and psychological study. 1928
Mohrmann, Hermann. Kultur- und gesellschaftsprobleme des Amerikanischen romanes der nachkriegszeit, 1920–27. 1934
Novel of tomorrow and the scope of fiction. 1922
O'Brien, Edward J. The advance of the American short story. Rev. ed. 1931
O'Brien, Edward J., *ed.* The best short stories of 1915, and yearbook of American short story. 1915. Published annually.
Pattee, Fred L. The development of the American short story, an historical survey. 1923
Quinn, Arthur Hobson. American fiction, an historical and critical survey. 1936
Van Doren, Carl. Contemporary American novelists, 1900–1920. 1922
Widenmann, Helene. Neuengland in der erzählenden literatur Amerikas. 1935
Williams, Blanche C. Our short story writers. "Modern American writers." 1920

V. HISTORY OF THE DRAMA AND THEATER

Andrews, Charlton. The drama today. 1913
Arvold, Alfred G. The little country theater. 1922
Bricker, Herschel L., *ed.* Our theatre today, a composite handbook on the art, craft, and management of the contemporary theatre. 1936
Carter, Jean and Ogden, Jess. Everyman's drama, a study of the non-commercial theatre in the United States. 1938
Clark, Barrett H. The British and American drama of today, outlines for their study. Rev. ed. 1921
Deutsch, Helen and Hanau, Stella. The Provincetown, a story of the theatre. 1931
Dickinson, Thomas H. The case of American drama. 1915
Dickinson, Thomas H. Playwrights of the new American theater. 1925
Eaton, Walter P. The theatre guild, the first ten years. 1929
Hornblow, Arthur. A history of the theatre in America from its beginnings to the present time. 1919
McCleery, Albert and Glick, Carl. Curtains going up. 1939
MacGowan, Kenneth. Footlights across America, towards a national theater. 1929
MacGowan, Kenneth. The theatre of tomorrow. 1921
Mackay, Constance D. The little theatre in the United States. 1917
Mantle, Burns. American playwrights of today. 1929
Mantle, Burns. Contemporary American playwrights. 1938
Mantle, Burns and Sherwood, Garrison P., *eds.* The best plays of 1909–1919, and the yearbook of the drama in America. 1933
Mantle, Burns, *ed.* The best plays of 1920, and the yearbook of the drama in America. 1920. Published annually
Mersand, Joseph. A decade of biographical plays, 1928–1938. 1939
Mersand, Joseph. When ladies write plays. 1937
Moderwell, Hiram K. The theatre of today. 1927
Moses, Montrose J. The American dramatist. Rev. ed. 1925
Plessow, Gustav L. Das Amerikanische kurzschauspiel zwischen 1910 und 1930. 1933
Quinn, Arthur H. A history of the American drama, from the civil war to the present day. 1936
Sayler, Oliver M. Our American theatre. 1923
Skinner, Richard D. Our changing theatre. 1931
Villard, Léonie. Le théâtre Américain. 1929
Waugh, Jennie. Das theater als spiegel der Amerikanischen demokratie. 1936
Whitman, Willson. Bread and circuses, a study of federal theatre. 1937

VI. HISTORY OF POETRY

Bruns, Friedrich. Die amerikanische dichtung der gegenwart. 1930
Cook, Howard W. Our poets of today. Rev. ed. 1923
Deutsch, Babette. This modern poetry. 1935
Hughes, Glenn. Imagism and the imagists, a study in modern poetry. 1931
Kreymborg, Alfred. A history of American poetry, our singing strength. 1934
Lowell, Amy. Tendencies in modern American poetry. 1917
Untermeyer, Louis. The new era in American poetry. 1919
Untermeyer, Louis. American poetry since 1900. 1923
Vordtriede, Fränze. Der imagismus, sein wesen und seine bedeutung. 1935
Weirick, Bruce. From Whitman to Sandburg in American poetry, a critical survey. 1924

VII. HISTORY OF BIOGRAPHY

Longaker, Mark. Contemporary biography. 1934
Merrill, Dana K. The development of American biography. 1932
O'Neill, Edward H. A history of American biography, 1800–1935. 1935

VIII. HISTORY OF CRITICISM

Babbitt, Irving and others. Criticism in America, its functions and status, essays. 1924
Boynton, Percy H. The challenge of modern criticism, tradition, criticism, humanism, a series of lectures. 1931
DeMille, George E. Literary criticism in America, a preliminary survey. 1931
Farrell, James T. A note on literary criticism. 1936
Foerster, Norman. American criticism, a study in literary theory from Poe to the present. 1928
Foerster, Norman, *ed.* American critical essays, XIXth and XXth centuries. 1930
Foerster, Norman, *ed.* Humanism and America, essays on the outlook of modern civilization. 1930
Foerster, Norman. Toward standards, a study of the present critical movement in American letters. 1930
Grattan, Clinton H., *ed.* The critique of humanism, a symposium. 1930
Hackett, Francis, *ed.* On American books, a symposium by five American critics as printed in the London Nation. 1920
Hazlitt, Henry. The anatomy of criticism, a trialogue. 1933
Smith, Bernard. Forces in American criticism, a study in the history of American literary thought. 1939
Zabel, Morton D. The condition of American criticism, 1939. 1939
Zabel, Morton D., *ed.* Literary opinion in America, essays illustrating the status, methods, and problems of criticism in the United States since the war. 1937

RECOMMENDED BOOKS BY CONTEMPORARY AMERICAN AUTHORS

AUTOBIOGRAPHY

Adamic, Louis. The native's return. 1934
Austin, Mary. Earth horizon. 1932
Canby, Henry Seidel. The age of confidence. 1934
Cowley, Malcolm. Exile's return. 1934
Dreiser, Theodore. A history of myself, Dawn. 1931
Kent, Rockwell. N by E. 1930
Kent, Rockwell. Salamina. 1935
Kreymborg, Alfred. Troubadour. 1925
Leonard, William Ellery. The locomotive-god. 1927
Lewisohn, Ludwig. Up stream. 1922
Lindsay, Vachel. Adventures while preaching the gospel of beauty. 1914
Luhan, Mabel Dodge. Movers and shakers. 1936
Sheean, Vincent. Personal history. 1935
Stein, Gertrude. The autobiography of Alice B. Toklas. 1933
Van Doren, Carl. Three worlds. 1936

BIOGRAPHY

Allen, Hervey. Israfel. 1926
Bradford, Gamaliel. Damaged souls. 1923
Bradford, Gamaliel. Portraits and personalities. 1933
Brooks, Van Wyck. The pilgrimage of Henry James. 1925
Garland, Hamlin. A son of the middle border. 1917
Lowell, Amy. John Keats. 1925
MacKaye, Percy. Epoch. 1927
Masters, Edgar Lee. Vachel Lindsay. 1935
Peattie, Donald Culross. Green laurels. 1936
Rourke, Constance. Audubon. 1936
Untermeyer, Louis. Heinrich Heine. 1937
Van Doren, Carl. Benjamin Franklin. 1938
Van Loon, Hendrik Willem. R. v. R. 1930
Werner, W. R. Barnum. 1923
Wister, Owen. Roosevelt. 1930

CRITICISM

Babbitt, Irving. The new Laokoon. 1910
Babbitt, Irving. Rousseau and romanticism. 1919
Brooks, Van Wyck. America's coming-of-age. 1915
Brooks, Van Wyck. The flowering of New England. 1936
Burke, Kenneth. Counter-statement. 1931
DeVoto, Bernard. Mark Twain's America. 1932
Eastman, Max. Artists in uniform. 1934

Eastman, Max. Enjoyment of poetry. 1913
Foerster, Norman. Towards standards. 1930
Hicks, Granville. The great tradition. 1933
Lewisohn, Ludwig. Expression in America. 1932
Nathan, George Jean. Since Ibsen. 1933
Sherman, Stuart P. On contemporary literature. 1917
Sinclair, Upton. Mammonart. 1925
Wilson, Edmund. Axel's castle. 1931
Winters, Yvor. Primitivism and decadence. 1937

DRAMAS

Akins, Zoë. Déclassée. 1923
Anderson, Maxwell. Elizabeth the queen. 1930
Anderson, Maxwell. High Tor. 1937
Anderson, Maxwell. Winterset. 1935
Anderson, Maxwell and Stallings, Laurence. What price glory. 1926
Barry, Philip. Holiday. 1929
Barry, Philip. Hotel Universe. 1930
Behrman, S. N. Biography. 1933
Behrman, S. N. The second man. 1927
Connelly, Marc. The green pastures. 1929
Crothers, Rachel. Let us be gay. 1929
Crothers, Rachel. Susan and God. 1938
Ferber, Edna and Kaufman, George S. Dinner at eight. 1932
Glaspell, Susan. Inheritors. 1921
Green, Paul. The house of Connelly. 1931
Green, Paul. In Abraham's bosom. 1926
Hecht, Ben and MacArthur, Charles. The front page. 1928
Howard, Sidney. The silver cord. 1927
Howard, Sidney. They knew what they wanted. 1925
Kaufman, George S. and Connelly, Marc. Dulcy. 1921
Kaufman, George S. and Ferber, Edna. The royal family. 1928
Kaufman, George S. and Ferber, Edna. Stage door. 1936
Kaufman, George S. and Hart, Moss. You can't take it with you. 1936
Kelly, George. Craig's wife. 1926
Kelly, George. The show-off. 1924
Kingsley, Sidney. Dead end. 1936
Kreymborg, Alfred. Puppet plays. 1923
Kummer, Clare. Rollo's wild oat. 1922
Lawson, John Howard. Processional. 1925
MacKaye, Percy. Kentucky mountain fantasies. 1928
MacKaye, Percy. The scarecrow. 1908
Odets, Clifford. Golden boy. 1937
O'Neill, Eugene. Desire under the elms. 1925
O'Neill, Eugene. The Emperor Jones. 1921
O'Neill, Eugene. Mourning becomes Electra. 1931
Rice, Elmer. The adding machine. 1923
Rice, Elmer. Street scene. 1929
Riggs, Lynn. Green grow the lilacs. 1931
Sheldon, Edward. Romance. 1913
Sherwood, Robert Emmet. Idiot's delight. 1936
Sherwood, Robert Emmet. Reunion in Vienna. 1932
Totheroh, Dan. Distant drums. 1932
Wilder, Thornton. Our town. 1938

ESSAYS

Austin, Mary. The land of little rain. 1903
Beebe, William. Beneath tropic seas. 1928
Beebe, William. Edge of the jungle. 1921
Beebe, William. Jungle peace. 1918
Broun, Heywood. It seems to me. 1935
Cabell, James Branch. Straws and prayer-books. 1924
Chase, Stuart. Mexico. 1931 (in collaboration with Marian Tyler)
Chase, Stuart. A new deal. 1932
Chase, Stuart. Rich land, poor land. 1936
Dewey, John. Art as experience. 1934
Dewey, John. Experience and nature. 1925
Dewey, John. Human nature and conduct. 1922
Frank, Waldo. The re-discovery of America. 1929
Krutch, Joseph Wood. The modern temper. 1929
Lippmann, Walter. A preface to morals. 1929
Lippmann, Walter. A preface to politics. 1913
Mencken, H. L. Selected prejudices. 1927
More, Paul Elmer. The drift of romanticism. 1913
More, Paul Elmer. Selected Shelburne essays. 1935
Morley, Christopher. Essays. 1928
Mumford, Lewis. Technics and civilization. 1934
Peattie, Donald Culross. An almanac for moderns. 1935
Repplier, Agnes. Eight decades. 1937
Santayana, George. Scepticism and animal faith. 1923
Santayana, George. The sense of beauty. 1896
Smith, Logan Pearsall. All trivia. 1933

HISTORY

Adams, James Truslow. The epic of America. 1931
Beard, Charles A. An economic interpretation of the Constitution of the United States. 1913
Beard, Charles A. and Beard, Mary R. The rise of American civilization. Vol. I, The agricultural era. 1927
Beard, Charles A. and Beard, Mary R. The rise of American civilization. Vol. II, The industrial era. 1927
Josephson, Matthew. The robber barons. 1934
Van Loon, Hendrik Willem. The arts. 1937
Van Loon, Hendrik Willem. The story of mankind. 1921

HUMOR

Adams, Franklin P. The melancholy lute. 1936
Benchley, Robert. Of all things. 1921
Benchley, Robert. The treasurer's report and other aspects of community singing. 1930
Day, Clarence. Life with father. 1935
Marquis, Don. archy and mehitabel. 1927
Marquis, Don. Hermione. 1916
Nash, Ogden. I'm a stranger here myself. 1938
Thurber, James. The owl in the attic. 1931
Woollcott, Alexander. While Rome burns. 1934

NOVELS

Allen, Hervey. Anthony Adverse. 1933
Anderson, Sherwood. Poor white. 1920
Atherton, Gertrude. Black oxen. 1923
Atherton, Gertrude. The conqueror. 1902
Barnes, Margaret Ayer. Years of grace. 1930
Boyd, James. Drums. 1925
Boyle, Kay. Plagued by the nightingale. 1931
Bromfield, Louis. The farm. 1933
Bromfield, Louis. The green bay tree. 1924
Buck, Pearl. The good earth. 1931
Burnett, W. R. Little Caesar. 1929
Cabell, James Branch. Figures of earth. 1921
Cabell, James Branch. Jurgen. 1919
Caldwell, Erskine. Tobacco road. 1932
Canfield, Dorothy. The bent twig. 1915
Canfield, Dorothy. The brimming cup. 1921
Cather, Willa. Death comes for the archbishop. 1927
Cather, Willa. A lost lady. 1923
Cather, Willa. My Ántonia. 1918
Churchill, Winston. The crisis. 1901
Churchill, Winston. The inside of the cup. 1913
Cummings, E. E. The enormous room. 1922
Dell, Floyd. Moon-calf. 1920
Dos Passos, John. Manhattan transfer. 1925
Dos Passos, John. U. S. A. 1937
Dreiser, Theodore. An American tragedy. 1925
Dreiser, Theodore. Sister Carrie. 1900
Edmonds, Walter D. Drums along the Mohawk. 1936
Erskine, John. The private life of Helen of Troy. 1925
Farrell, James T. Studs Lonigan. 1935
Faulkner, William. The sound and the fury. 1929
Ferber, Edna. Show boat. 1926
Ferber, Edna. So big. 1924
Field, Rachel. All this, and heaven too. 1938
Fisher, Vardis. In tragic life. 1932
Fitzgerald, F. Scott. This side of paradise. 1920
Frank, Waldo. City block. 1922
Gale, Zona. Miss Lulu Bett. 1920
Glasgow, Ellen. Barren ground. 1925
Halper, Albert. Union square. 1933
Hecht, Ben. Erik Dorn. 1921
Hemingway, Ernest. A farewell to arms. 1929
Herbst, Josephine. Pity is not enough. 1933
Hergesheimer, Joseph. Java head. 1919
Herrick, Robert. Clark's field. 1914
Herrick, Robert. The memoirs of an American citizen. 1905
Heyward, DuBose. Porgy. 1925
Hurst, Fannie. Lummox. 1923
Kantor, Mackinlay. Long remember. 1934
La Farge, Oliver. Laughing boy. 1929
Lewis, Sinclair. Arrowsmith. 1925
Lewis, Sinclair. Babbitt. 1922

Lewis, Sinclair. Main street. 1920
McFee, William. Casuals of the sea. 1916
Morley, Christopher. The haunted bookshop. 1919
Morley, Christopher. Where the blue begins. 1922
Nathan, Robert. The Barly fields. 1938
Peterkin, Julia. Scarlet sister Mary. 1928
Poole, Ernest. The harbor. 1915
Roberts, Elizabeth Madox. The time of man. 1926
Roberts, Kenneth. Northwest passage. 1937
Rölvaag, O. E. Giants in the earth. 1927
Santayana, George. The last Puritan. 1935
Scott, Evelyn. The wave. 1929
Sedgwick, Anne Douglas. The little French girl. 1924
Sedgwick, Anne Douglas. Tante. 1911
Sinclair, Upton. Boston. 1928
Sinclair, Upton. The jungle. 1906
Steinbeck, John. Of mice and men. 1937
Steinbeck, John. Tortilla flat. 1935
Stong, Phil. State fair. 1932
Stribling, T. S. The forge. 1931
Suckow, Ruth. The folks. 1934
Tarkington, Booth. Alice Adams. 1921
Tarkington, Booth. The gentleman from Indiana. 1899
Tarkington, Booth. Penrod. 1914
Van Vechten, Carl. Peter Whiffle. 1922
Wescott, Glenway. The grandmothers. 1927
Wharton, Edith. The age of innocence. 1920
Wharton, Edith. Ethan Frome. 1911
Wharton, Edith. The house of mirth. 1905
White, Stewart Edward. The blazed trail. 1902
Wilder, Thornton. The bridge of San Luis Rey. 1927
Williamson, Thames. Hunky. 1929
Wister, Owen. The Virginian. 1902
Wolfe, Thomas. Look homeward, angel. 1929
Young, Stark. So red the rose. 1934

POETRY

Aiken, Conrad. Selected poems. 1929
Benét, Stephen Vincent. John Brown's body. 1928
Benét, William Rose. Man possessed. 1927
Bogan, Louise. The sleeping fury. 1937
Bynner, Witter. Selected poems. 1936
Coffin, Robert P. Tristram. Strange holiness. 1935
Crane, Hart. The collected poems of Hart Crane. 1933
Cummings, E. E. Collected poems. 1938
Davidson, Donald. The tall men. 1927
Dillon, George. The flowering stone. 1931
H. D. Collected poems of H. D. 1925
Fletcher, John Gould. Selected poems. 1938
Frost, Robert. Collected poems. 1939
Gregory, Horace. Chorus for survival. 1935
Hillyer, Robert. The collected verse of Robert Hillyer. 1933
Hughes, Langston. The weary blues. 1926

Jeffers, Robinson. Selected poetry. 1938
Johnson, James Weldon. God's trombones. 1927
Leonard, William Ellery. Two lives. 1923
Lindsay, Vachel. Selected poems. 1931
Lowell, Amy. Selected poems. 1928
McKay, Claude. Harlem shadows. 1922
MacLeish, Archibald. Poems, 1924–1933. 1933
Masters, Edgar Lee. Spoon River anthology. 1915
Millay, Edna St. Vincent. Fatal interview. 1931
Millay, Edna St. Vincent. The harp-weaver. 1923
Moore, Marianne. Selected poems. 1935
Neihardt, John G. Collected poems of John G. Neihardt. Vol. I. 1926
Pound, Ezra. A draft of xxx cantos. 1930
Pound, Ezra. Selected poems. 1928
Ransom, John Crowe. Chills and fever. 1924
Reese, Lizette Woodworth. The selected poems of Lizette Woodworth Reese. 1926
Ridge, Lola. The Ghetto and other poems. 1918
Robinson, Edwin Arlington. Collected poems. 1937
Sandburg, Carl. The people, yes. 1936
Sandburg, Carl. Selected poems. 1926
Taggard, Genevieve. Collected poems 1918–1938. 1938
Tate, Allen. Selected poems. 1937
Teasdale, Sara. The collected poems of Sara Teasdale. 1937
Wheelock, John Hall. Poems, 1911–1936. 1936
Williams, William Carlos. The complete collected poems of William Carlos Williams, 1906–1938. 1938
Wylie, Elinor. Collected poems. 1932

SHORT STORIES

Anderson, Sherwood. Winesburg, Ohio. 1919
Benét, Stephen Vincent. Thirteen o'clock. 1937
Boyle, Kay. The first lover. 1933
Burt, Struthers. Chance encounters. 1921
Caldwell, Erskine. Kneel to the rising sun. 1935
Garland, Hamlin. Main-travelled roads. 1891
Gerould, Katharine Fullerton. Vain oblations. 1914
Hemingway, Ernest. Men without women. 1927
Lardner, Ring W. The love nest. 1926
Porter, Katherine Anne. Flowering Judas. 1930
Saroyan, William. The daring young man on the flying trapeze. 1934
Steele, Wilbur Daniel. Urkey Island. 1926
Stein, Gertrude. Three lives. 1909
Suckow, Ruth. Iowa interiors. 1926
Wharton, Edith. Xingu. 1916
Zugsmith, Leane. Home is where you hang your childhood. 1937

CLASSIFIED INDEXES

INDEXES OF AUTHORS BY TYPES

AUTOBIOGRAPHERS

Louis Adamic
Sherwood Anderson
Gertrude Atherton
Mary Austin
Struthers Burt
Henry Seidel Canby
Mary Ellen Chase
Robert P. Tristram Coffin
Malcolm Cowley
Floyd Dell
Theodore Dreiser
John Gould Fletcher
Zona Gale
Joseph Hergesheimer
James Weldon Johnson
Alfred Kreymborg
William Ellery Leonard
Ludwig Lewisohn
Vachel Lindsay
Mabel Dodge Luhan
William McFee
Claude McKay
Percy MacKaye
Edgar Lee Masters
Paul Elmer More
Lizette Woodworth Reese
Agnes Repplier
Evelyn Scott
Vincent Sheean
Upton Sinclair
Logan Pearsall Smith
Gertrude Stein
Carl Van Doren
M. R. Werner
Edith Wharton
Thomas Wolfe

BIOGRAPHERS

James Truslow Adams
Hervey Allen
Thomas Boyd
Gamaliel Bradford
Van Wyck Brooks
Heywood Broun
Pearl S. Buck
Robert P. Tristram Coffin
Clarence Day
Floyd Dell
Max Eastman
Rachel Field
John Gould Fletcher
Waldo Frank
Zona Gale
Hamlin Garland
Susan Glaspell
Joseph Hergesheimer
Granville Hicks
Matthew Josephson
Amy Lowell
Mable Dodge Luhan
William McFee
Percy MacKaye
Edgar Lee Masters
Paul Elmer More
Lewis Mumford
Donald Culross Peattie
Ezra Pound
Agnes Repplier
Constance Rourke
Carl Sandburg
Anne Douglas Sedgwick
Stuart P. Sherman
Logan Pearsall Smith
Genevieve Taggard
Allen Tate
Louis Untermeyer
Carl Van Doren
Hendrik Willem Van Loon
Robert Penn Warren
M. R. Werner
Stewart Edward White
Owen Wister
Alexander Woollcott

CRITICS

DRAMATISTS

Thornton Wilder
Edmund Wilson
Alexander Woollcott
Stark Young

ESSAYISTS

Sherwood Anderson
Gertrude Atherton
Mary Austin
Irving Babbitt
Charles A. Beard
William Rose Benét
Van Wyck Brooks
Heywood Broun
Struthers Burt
Witter Bynner
James Branch Cabell
Henry Seidel Canby
Dorothy Canfield
Willa Cather
Mary Ellen Chase
Stuart Chase
Robert P. Tristram Coffin
Donald Davidson
Clarence Day
Floyd Dell
Bernard DeVoto
John Dewey
Theodore Dreiser
Max Eastman
John Erskine
Vardis Fisher
John Gould Fletcher
Norman Foerster
Waldo Frank
Robert Frost
Zona Gale
Hamlin Garland
Katharine Fullerton Gerould
Robert Hillyer
Fannie Hurst
James Weldon Johnson
Joseph Wood Krutch
John Howard Lawson
William Ellery Leonard
Walter Lippmann
William McFee
Percy MacKaye
Edgar Lee Masters
H. L. Mencken
Paul Elmer More
Christopher Morley
Lewis Mumford
George Jean Nathan
Donald Culross Peattie
Julia Peterkin
Ernest Poole
Ezra Pound
Agnes Repplier
Laura Riding
Kenneth Roberts
Ole Rölvaag
Constance Rourke
George Santayana
Upton Sinclair
Logan Pearsall Smith
Booth Tarkington
Hendrik Willem van Loon
Carl Van Vechten
Glenway Wescott
William Carlos Williams
Alexander Woollcott
Stark Young

HISTORIANS

James Truslow Adams
Charles A. Beard
Gamaliel Bradford
Struthers Burt
Waldo Frank
Hamlin Garland
Joseph Hergesheimer
Matthew Josephson
Edgar Lee Masters
John G. Neihardt
Donald Culross Peattie
Agnes Repplier
Hendrik Willem van Loon
Stewart Edward White

HUMORISTS

Franklin P. Adams
Robert Benchley
E. E. Cummings
Robert Frost

Clare Kummer
Ring W. Lardner
Don Marquis
Edna St. Vincent Millay
Christopher Morley
Ogden Nash
Dorothy Parker
Kenneth Roberts
Booth Tarkington
James Thurber
Owen Wister

NOVELISTS

Louis Adamic
Conrad Aiken
Zoë Akins
Hervey Allen
Sherwood Anderson
Gertrude Atherton
Mary Austin
Margaret Ayer Barnes
Philip Barry
Stephen Vincent Benét
William Rose Benét
Alvah C. Bessie
John Peale Bishop
James Boyd
Thomas Boyd
Kay Boyle
Gamaliel Bradford
Louis Bromfield
Heywood Broun
Pearl S. Buck
Kenneth Burke
W. R. Burnett
Struthers Burt
James Branch Cabell
Erskine Caldwell
Henry Seidel Canby
Dorothy Canfield
Robert Cantwell
Helen Grace Carlisle
Willa Cather
Mary Ellen Chase
Winston Churchill
Robert P. Tristram Coffin
James Gould Cozzens
Countee Cullen
E. E. Cummings
Floyd Dell
Bernard DeVoto
John Dos Passos
Theodore Dreiser
Max Eastman
Walter D. Edmonds
John Erskine
James T. Farrell
William Faulkner
Edna Ferber
Rachel Field
Vardis Fisher
F. Scott Fitzgerald
Waldo Frank
Zona Gale
Hamlin Garland
Katharine Fullerton Gerould
Ellen Glasgow
Susan Glaspell
Anne Green
Paul Green
Albert Halper
Ben Hecht
Ernest Hemingway
Joseph Hergesheimer
Josephine Herbst
Robert Herrick
DuBose Heyward
Robert Hillyer
Langston Hughes
Fannie Hurst
James Weldon Johnson
Josephine Johnson
Mackinlay Kantor
Alfred Kreymborg
Oliver La Farge
Ring W. Lardner
Sinclair Lewis
Ludwig Lewisohn
Grace Lumpkin
William McFee
Claude McKay
William March
Don Marquis
Edgar Lee Masters
George Milburn
Paul Elmer More
Christopher Morley
Robert Nathan
John G. Neihardt
John O'Hara
Donald Culross Peattie
Julia Peterkin
Ernest Poole

Frederic Prokosch
Lizette Woodworth Reese
Elmer Rice
Laura Riding
Elizabeth Madox Roberts
Kenneth Roberts
Ole Rölvaag
George Santayana
Isidor Schneider
Evelyn Scott
Anne Douglas Sedgwick
Vincent Sheean
Edward Sheldon
Stuart P. Sherman
Robert Emmet Sherwood
Upton Sinclair
Tess Slesinger
Laurence Stallings
Wilbur Daniel Steele
Gertrude Stein
John Steinbeck
Grace Zaring Stone
Phil Stong
T. S. Stribling
Ruth Suckow
Booth Tarkington
Allen Tate
Dan Totheroh
Louis Untermeyer
Carl Van Doren
Mark Van Doren
Carl Van Vechten
Glenway Wescott
Edith Wharton
Helen C. White
Stewart Edward White
Thornton Wilder
William Carlos Williams
Thames Williamson
Edmund Wilson
Owen Wister
Thomas Wolfe
Elinor Wylie
Stark Young
Leane Zugsmith

PHILOSOPHERS

John Dewey
Ludwig Lewisohn
Paul Elmer More
George Santayana

POETS

Franklin P. Adams
Léonie Adams
Conrad Aiken
Zoë Akins
Hervey Allen
Maxwell Anderson
Sherwood Anderson
Mary Austin
Stephen Vincent Benét
William Rose Benét
John Peale Bishop
Louise Bogan
Kay Boyle
Gamaliel Bradford
Van Wyck Brooks
Struthers Burt
Witter Bynner
James Branch Cabell
Willa Cather
Robert P. Tristram Coffin
Malcolm Cowley
Hart Crane
Countee Cullen
E. E. Cummings
Donald Davidson
George Dillon
H. D.
John Dos Passos
Theodore Dreiser
Max Eastman
Paul Engle
John Erskine
William Faulkner
Kenneth Fearing
Rachel Field
Vardis Fisher
John Gould Fletcher
Robert Frost
Zona Gale
Hamlin Garland
Ellen Glasgow
Horace Gregory
DuBose Heyward
Granville Hicks
Robert Hillyer
Langston Hughes

Robinson Jeffers
James Weldon Johnson
Josephine Johnson
Matthew Josephon
Mackinlay Kantor
Alfred Kreymborg
William Ellery Leonard
Vachel Lindsay
Amy Lowell
William McFee
Claude McKay
Percy MacKaye
Archibald MacLeish
Don Marquis
Edgar Lee Masters
H. L. Mencken
Edna St. Vincent Millay
Marianne Moore
Merrill Moore
Paul Elmer More
Christopher Morley
Robert Nathan
John G. Neihardt
Eugene O'Neill
Dorothy Parker
Ezra Pound
Frederic Prokosch
Phelps Putnam
John Crowe Ransom
Lizette Woodworth Reese
Lola Ridge
Laura Riding
Lynn Riggs
Elizabeth Madox Roberts
Edwin Arlington Robinson
Carl Sandburg
George Santayana
Lew Sarett
Isidor Schneider
Evelyn Scott
Logan Pearsall Smith
Wilbert Snow
Wallace Stevens
Genevieve Taggard
Allen Tate
Sara Teasdale
Louis Untermeyer
Mark Van Doren
Robert Penn Warren
Winifred Welles
Glenway Wescott
Edith Wharton
John Hall Wheelock
William Carlos Williams
Edmund Wilson
Yvor Winters
Owen Wister
Audrey Wurdemann
Elinor Wylie
Stark Young

SHORT-STORY WRITERS

Louis Adamic
Conrad Aiken
Sherwood Anderson
Gertrude Atherton
Mary Austin
Margaret Ayer Barnes
Stephen Vincent Benét
John Peale Bishop
Thomas Boyd
Kay Boyle
Louis Bromfield
Heywood Broun
Pearl S. Buck
Kenneth Burke
Struthers Burt
James Branch Cabell
Erskine Caldwell
Dorothy Canfield
Willa Cather
Winston Churchill
Floyd Dell
H. D.
Theodore Dreiser
Walter D. Edmonds
John Erskine
James T. Farrell
William Faulkner
Edna Ferber
Vardis Fisher
F. Scott Fitzgerald
Zona Gale
Hamlin Garland
Katharine Fullerton Gerould
Ellen Glasgow
Susan Glaspell
Paul Green
Albert Halper
Ben Hecht
Ernest Hemingway
Joseph Hergesheimer
Robert Herrick
DuBose Heyward

Sidney Howard
Langston Hughes
Fannie Hurst
Josephine Johnson
Mackinlay Kantor
Alfred Kreymborg
Oliver La Farge
Ring W. Lardner
Sinclair Lewis
Ludwig Lewisohn
William McFee
Claude McKay
William March
Don Marquis
George Milburn
Christopher Morley
John G. Neihardt
John O'Hara
Dorothy Parker
Julia Peterkin
Ernest Poole
Katherine Anne Porter
Laura Riding
Elizabeth Madox Roberts
William Saroyan
Evelyn Scott
Anne Douglas Sedgwick
Vincent Sheean
Upton Sinclair
Tess Slesinger
Logan Pearsall Smith
Wilbur Daniel Steele
John Steinbeck
Ruth Suckow
Booth Tarkington
Carl Van Doren
Glenway Wescott
Edith Wharton
Stewart Edward White
William Carlos Williams
Owen Wister
Thomas Wolfe
Alexander Woollcott
Stark Young
Leane Zugsmith

TRAVELERS

Louis Adamic
John Dewey
John Dos Passos
Theodore Dreiser
Waldo Frank
Hamlin Garland
Katharine Fullerton Gerould
Ernest Hemingway
Joseph Hergesheimer
Rockwell Kent
William McFee
H. L. Mencken
Christopher Morley
John G. Neihardt
Donald Culross Peattie
Kenneth Roberts
Vincent Sheean
Louis Untermeyer
Hendrik Willem van Loon
Edith Wharton
Stewart Edward White
Edmund Wilson
Stark Young

WRITERS OF CHILDREN'S BOOKS

Laura Adams Armer
Mary Austin
William Rose Benét
Dorothy Canfield
Mary Ellen Chase
Rachel Field
Langston Hughes
Sinclair Lewis
Christopher Morley
Ogden Nash
Donald Culross Peattie
Carl Sandburg
Evelyn Scott
Upton Sinclair
Phil Stong
Dan Totheroh
Louis Untermeyer
Mark Van Doren
Hendrik Willem van Loon
Winifred Welles
Stewart Edward White
Thames Williamson
Stark Young

ABBREVIATIONS OF BOOKS CONTAINING STUDIES

Adamic—Adamic, Louis. My America, 1928–1938. 1938

Adcock—Adcock, Arthur St. John. The glory that was Grub street, impressions of contemporary authors . . . with thirty-two camera studies by E. O. Hoppé. [1928]

Agate—Agate, James E. The contemporary theatre, 1924 . . . with an introduction by Noël Coward. 1925

Agate (F)—Agate, James E. First nights. 1934

Agate (M)—Agate, James E. More first nights. 1937

Aiken—Aiken, Conrad P. Scepticisms, notes on contemporary poetry. 1919

American—The American academy of arts and letters. Commemorative tributes to Hastings, French, Hill, Bradford, Melchers, John Van Dyke, Henry Van Dyke, Babbitt, Platt, Shorey, Gilbbert [!], Whitlock, Thomas, Baker, and Loeffler . . . Academy publication no. 88. 1936

American (C)—American criticism, 1926, edited by William A. Drake. [c1926]

American (M)—American mercury. Readings from the American mercury edited by Grant C. Knight. 1926

Anderson—Anderson, Margaret C. My thirty years' war, an autobiography. 1930

Anderson (S)—Anderson, Sherwood. No swank. 1934

Ashley—Ashley, Schuyler. Essay reviews by Schuyler Ashley, born 1897, died 1927, introduction by Rose Adelaide Witham. 1929

Auslander—Auslander, Joseph. Letters to women . . . frontispiece woodcut and decorations by Clare Leighton. 1929

Baldwin—[Baldwin, Charles C.] The men who make our novels by George Gordon [*pseud.*]. 1919

Baldwin (M)—Baldwin, Charles C. The men who make our novels . . . revised edition. 1924

Beach—Beach, Joseph W. The outlook for American prose. [c1926]

Beach (T)—Beach, Joseph W. The twentieth century novel, studies in technique. [c1932]

Benchley—Benchley, Robert C. 20,000 leagues under the sea, or, David Copperfield . . . with illustrations by Gluyas Williams. [c1928]

Berg—Berg, Ruben G. Moderna amerikaner. [1925]

Best—The Best plays of 1909–1919 and the year book of the drama in America edited by Burns Mantle and Garrison P. Sherwood, with illustrations. 1933

Birchman—Birchman, Willis. Faces & facts by and about 26 contemporary artists, with an introduction by James Montgomery Flagg & biographies by Willis Birchman. 1937

Björkman—Björkman, Edwin A. Voices of to-morrow: critical studies of the new spirit in literature. 1913

Blackmur—Blackmur, Richard P. The double agent, essays in craft and elucidation. [c1935]

Blankenship—Blankenship, Russell. American literature as an expression of the national mind. [c1931]

Block—Block, Anita. The changing world in plays and theatre. 1939

Canby—Canby, Henry S. American estimates. [c1929]
Canby (D)—Canby, Henry S. Definitions, essays in contemporary criticism. [c1922]
Canby (S)—Canby, Henry S. Seven years' harvest, notes on contemporary literature. [c1936]
Canby (2d ser.)—Canby, Henry S. Definitions, essays in contemporary criticism (Second series). [c1924]
Cappon—Cappon, Lester J. Bibliography of Virginia history since 1865 by Lester Jesse Cappon . . . under the direction of Dumas Malone. 1930
Carnegie—Carnegie, Dale. Five minute biographies. [c1937]
Chamberlain—Chamberlain, John. Farewell to reform, being a history of the rise, life, and decay of the progressive mind in America. [c1932]
Chesterton—Chesterton, Gilbert K. All I survey, a book of essays. 1933
Clark—Clark, Barrett H. An hour of American drama. [c1930]
Clark (B)—Clark, Barrett H. A study of the modern drama, a handbook for the study and appreciation of typical plays, European, English, and American of the last three-quarters of a century . . . revised edition. 1938
Clark (E)—Clark, Emily. Innocence abroad. 1931
Cleaton—Cleaton, Irene and Cleaton, Allen. Books & battles, American literature, 1920–1930. 1937
Cohen—Cohen, Helen L., *ed.* Longer plays by modern authors (American). [c1922]
Cohen (M)—Cohen, Helen L., *ed.* More one-act plays by modern authors . . . designs by art classes of Washington Irving high school. [c1927]
Collins—Collins, Joseph. The doctor looks at biography, psychological studies of life and letters. [c1925]
Collins (T)—Collins, Joseph. Taking the literary pulse, psychological studies of life and letters. [c1924]
Combs—Combs, George H. These amazing moderns. [c1933]
Cook—Cook, Howard W. Our poets of today. 1923
Cooper—Cooper, Anice P. Authors and others. 1927
Cooper (F)—Cooper, Frederic T. Some American story tellers. 1911
Cowley—Cowley, Malcolm, *ed.* After the genteel tradition, American writers since 1910. [c1937]
Cowley (E)—Cowley, Malcolm. Exile's return, a narrative of ideas. [c1934]
Crockett—Crockett, Walter H., *ed.* Vermonters, a book of biographies. [c1931]
DeCasseres—DeCasseres, Benjamin. The elect and the damned. [c1936]
Dell—Dell, Floyd. Looking at life. 1924
Deutsch—Deutsch, Babette. This modern poetry. 1935
DeVoto—DeVoto, Bernard A. Forays and rebuttals. 1936
Dickinson—Dickinson, Thomas H. The making of American literature . . . [c1932]
Dickinson (P)—Dickinson, Thomas H. Playwrights of the new American theater. 1925
Dictionary—Dictionary of American biography, under the auspices of the American council of learned societies . . . 1928–36
Dondore—Dondore, Dorothy A. The prairie and the making of middle America: four centuries of description. 1926
Doubleday—Doubleday, Page & company. The Country life press, Garden City, New York. 1919
Dukes—Dukes, Ashley. The youngest drama, studies of fifty dramatists. 1923
Durant—Durant, William J. Contemporary American philosophers, Santayana, James, and Dewey. [c1925]

New York ⟨1926⟩ by Julius Caesar, Aristotle, and a third individual of less importance. 1926

Freeman—The Freeman. The Freeman book, typical editorials, essays, critiques, and other selections from the eight volumes of the Freeman, 1920–1924. 1924

Freeman (J)—Freeman, Joseph. An American testament, a narrative of rebels and romantics. [c1936]

Gard—Gard, Wayne. Book reviewing. 1927

Garland—Garland, Hamlin. Afternoon neighbors, further excerpts from a literary log. 1934

Garnett—Garnett, Edward. Friday nights, literary criticisms and appreciations ⟨First series⟩. 1922

Gillis—Gillis, Adolph and Ketchum, Roland. Our America, a survey of contemporary America as exemplified in the lives and achievements of twenty-four men and women drawn from representative fields. 1936

Goldberg—Goldberg, Isaac. The drama of transition, native and exotic playcraft. [c1922]

Goldberg (T)—Goldberg, Isaac. The theatre of George Jean Nathan, chapters and documents toward a history of the new American drama. 1926

Graham—Graham, Stephen. The death of yesterday. [c1930]

Grattan—Grattan, Clinton H., *ed.* The critique of humanism, a symposium. 1930

Green—Green, Elizabeth L. The Negro in contemporary American literature . . . an outline for individual and group study. 1928

Green (C)—Green, Paul and Green, Elizabeth L. Contemporary American literature, a study of fourteen outstanding American writers by Paul Green . . . and Elizabeth Lay Green . . . A program for women's clubs issued by the Bureau of public discussion. [c1925]

Haas—Haas, Jakob. Versuch einer darstellung der heimatliteratur in den Vereinigten Staaten von Nordamerika. (Einige typische heimatschriftsteller aus verschiedenen gegenden der Vereinigten Staaten) 1935

Hackett—Hackett, Francis. Horizons, a book of criticism. 1918

Halleck—Halleck, Reuben P. The romance of American literature . . . illustrated by John Ushler. [c1934]

Halline—Halline, Allan G., *ed.* American plays, selected and edited with critical introductions and bibliographies. [c1935]

Halsey—Halsey, Francis W. Women authors of our day in their homes, personal descriptions & interviews edited with additions by Francis Whiting Halsey, with many full-page illustrations. 1903

Hamilton—Hamilton, Clayton M. Seen on the stage. 1920

Hamilton (C)—Hamilton, Cosmo. People worth talking about . . . with caricatures by Conrado Massaguer. 1933

Hammond—Hammond, Percy. But—is it art? 1927

Hansen—Hansen, Harry. Midwest portraits, a book of memories and friendships. [c1923]

Harkins—Harkins, Edward F. Little pilgrimages among the men who have written famous books. 1902

Harkins (L)—Harkins, Edward F. Little pilgrimages among the men who have written famous books. Second series. 1903

Harkins (LP)—Harkins, Edward F. and Johnston, Charles H. Little pilgrimages among the women who have written famous books. 1902

Hartwick—Hartwick, Harry. The foreground of American fiction. [c1934]

Hatcher—Hatcher, Harlan H. Creating the modern American novel. [c1935]

Hazard—Hazard, Lucy L. The frontier in American literature. [c1927]

Heath—Heath, Oscar M. Pulitzer prize winners, the drama. 1930
Henderson—Henderson, Philip. The novel today, studies in contemporary attitudes. [1936]
Herrmann—Herrmann, Eva. On parade, caricatures by Eva Herrmann, edited by Erich Posselt, contributions by prominent authors. 1929
Hicks—Hicks, Granville. The great tradition, an interpretation of American literature since the civil war. 1933
Hind—Hind, Charles L. Authors and I. 1921
Hind (M)—Hind, Charles L. More authors and I. 1922
Horton—Horton, Philip. Hart Crane, the life of an American poet. [c1937]
Hough—Hough, Lynn H. The lion in his den, a series of discussions of books and life. 1925
Huddleston—Huddleston, Sisley. Paris salons, cafés, studios . . . being social, artistic, and literary memories. 1928
Hughes—Hughes, Glenn. Imagism & the imagists, a study in modern poetry. 1931
Johnson—Johnson, James W. Black Manhattan. 1930
Johnson (1929)—Johnson, Merle D., *ed.* American first editions, bibliographic check lists of the works of one hundred and five American authors. 1929
Johnson (1932)—Johnson, Merle D., *ed.* American first editions, bibliographic check lists of the works of 146 American authors, revised and enlarged. 1932
Johnson (1936)—Johnson, Merle D., *ed.* Merle Johnson's American first editions, bibliographic check lists of the works of 199 American authors. Third edition. 1936 (rev. by Jacob Blanck)
Jones—Jones, Llewellyn. First impressions, essays on poetry, criticism, and prosody. 1925
Kallen—Kallen, Horace M. Indecency and the seven arts and other adventures of a pragmatist in aesthetics. 1930
Kaltenbacher—Kaltenbacher, Therese. Frauenfragen im amerikanischen frauenroman. 1936
Karsner—Karsner, David. Sixteen authors to one . . . intimate sketches of leading American story tellers, illustrations by Esther M. Mattsson. 1928
Keiser—Keiser, Albert. The Indian in American literature. 1933
Kerlin—Kerlin, Robert T. Negro poets and their poems. [c1923]
Kildal—Kildal, Arne. Amerikas stemme fra amerikansk litteratur og kulturliv. [c1935]
Kilmer—Kilmer, Joyce, *comp.* Literature in the making by some of its makers presented by Joyce Kilmer. [c1917]
Kirkland—Kirkland, Winifred M. and Kirkland, Frances. Girls who became writers. 1933
Knight—Knight, Grant C. The novel in English. 1931
Knopf—Knopf, *firm, publishers, New York.* The Borzoi 1920, being a sort of record of five years' publishing. 1920
Knopf (B)—Knopf, *firm, publishers, New York.* The Borzoi 1925, being a sort of record of ten years of publishing. [c1925]
Kreymborg—Kreymborg, Alfred. Our singing strength, an outline of American poetry (1620–1930). 1929
Kunitz—Kunitz, Stanley J. and others, *eds.* Authors today and yesterday, a companion volume to Living authors, edited by Stanley J. Kunitz, Howard Haycraft . . . Wilbur C. Hadden . . . illustrated with 320 photographs and drawings. 1933
Kunitz (J)—Kunitz, Stanley J. and others, *eds.* The junior book of authors, an introduction to the lives of writers and illustrators for younger readers from

Lewis Carroll and Louisa Alcott to the present day edited by Stanley J. Kunitz and Howard Haycraft, assisted by Wilbur C. Hadden [and] Julia E. Johnsen, illustrated with 260 photographs and drawings, with an introduction by Effie L. Power. 1934

Kunitz (L)—[Kunitz, Stanley J., *ed.*] Living authors, a book of biographies edited by Dilly Tante [*pseud.*] and illustrated with 371 photographs and drawings. 1931

Lawrence—Lawrence, David H. Phoenix, the posthumous papers of D. H. Lawrence edited and with an introduction by Edward D. McDonald. 1936

Lawrence (S)—Lawrence, Margaret. The school of femininity, a book for and about women as they are interpreted through feminine writers of yesterday and today. 1936

Lawrence (W)—Lawrence, Margaret. We write as women. [1937]

Lawson—Lawson, John H. Theory and technique of playwriting. [c1936]

Levinson—Levinson, Andreĭ Y. Figures américaines, dix-huit études sur des écrivains de ce temps. 1929

Lewis—Lewis, Wyndham. Men without art. [1934]

Lewis (P)—Lewis, Wyndham. Paleface, the philosophy of the "melting-pot." 1929

Lewis (T)—Lewis, Wyndham. Time and western man. 1927

Lewisohn—Lewisohn, Ludwig. Cities and men. 1927

Lewisohn (E)—Lewisohn, Ludwig. Expression in America. 1932 (also pub. with title The story of American literature. [1937])

Library—Library of southern literature compiled under the direct supervision of southern men of letters. Edwin Anderson Alderman, Joel Chandler Harris, editors in chief; Charles William Kent, literary editor. [c1908–23]

Lieberman—Lieberman, Elias. The American short story, a study of the influence of locality in its development. 1912

Linati—Linati, Carlo. Scrittori anglo americani d'oggi. [1932]

Linn—Linn, James W. and Taylor, Houghton W. A foreword to fiction. [c1935]

Lippmann—Lippmann, Walter. Men of destiny . . . drawings by Rollin Kirby. 1927

Littell—Littell, Robert. Read America first. 1926

Llona—Llona, Victor, *ed.* Les romanciers américains, nouvelles de S. Anderson, L. Bromfield, J.-B. Cabell, John Dos Passos, Th. Dreiser, E. Hemingway, Sinclair Levis [!], L. Lewisohn, J. London, Upton Sinclair, G. Stein, G. Wescott. Textes choisis par V. Llona. Préfaces et traductions de Victor Llona, Bernard Fay, Régis Michaud, L. Savitzky, A. Maurois, M.-E. Coindreau, Luc Durtain, Salemson, M.-J. Arnaud, Gruyer et Postif, M. Rémcn, Delgove et Raimbault, etc. [1931]

Loggins—Loggins, Vernon. I hear America . . . literature in the United States since 1900. [c1937]

Lowden—Lowden, Samuel M. Understanding great poems. [c1927]

Lowell—[Lowell, Amy.] Dear sir (or dear madam) who happen to glance at this title-page, printed you'll see to enhance its æsthetic attraction, pray buy, if you're able, this excellent bargain: A critical fable . . . by a poker of fun . . . 1922

Lowell (P)—Lowell, Amy. Poetry and poets, essays. 1930

Lowell (T)—Lowell, Amy. Tendencies in modern American poetry. 1917

Lucas—Lucas, Frank L. Authors dead & living. 1926

Luccock—Luccock, Halford E. Contemporary American literature and religion. 1934

Lundkvist—Lundkvist, Artur. Atlantvind. [1932]

MacCarthy—MacCarthy, Desmond. Criticism. [1932]
McCole—McCole, C. J. Lucifer at large. 1937
MacCollough—MacCollough, Martin. Letters on contemporary American authors. 1921
McKay—McKay, Claude. A long way from home. [c1937]
MacLean—MacLean, Malcolm S. and Holmes, Elisabeth K., *comps.* Men & books. 1930
Macy—Macy, John A., *ed.* American writers on American literature, by thirty-seven contemporary writers. [c1931]
Maillard—Maillard, Denyse. L'enfant américain dans le roman du middle-west, thèse pour le doctorat d'université présentée à la Faculté des lettres de l'Université de Paris. 1935
Mais—Mais, Stuart P. Some modern authors. 1923
Mais (W)—Mais, Stuart P. Why we should read—. 1921
Mallory—Mallory, Herbert S., *ed.* Backgrounds of book reviewing. 1923
Manly—Manly, John M. Contemporary American literature, bibliographies and study outlines by John Matthews Manly and Edith Rickert, introduction and revision by Fred B. Millett. [c1929]
Mantle—Mantle, Robert B. American playwrights of today. 1929
Mantle (C)—Mantle, Robert B. Contemporary American playwrights. 1938
Marble—Marble, Annie R. A study of the modern novel, British and American since 1900. 1928
Markey—Markey, Gene. Literary lights, a book of caricatures. 1923 (contains caricatures and captions only)
Masson—Masson, Thomas L. Our American humorists. 1922
Maynard—Maynard, Theodore. Our best poets, English and American. 1922
Mayorga—Mayorga, Margaret G., *ed.* Representative one-act plays by American authors, selected, with biographical notes . . . revised edition. 1937
Mayorga (S)—Mayorga, Margaret G., *ed.* A short history of the American drama, commentaries on plays prior to 1920 . . . with illustrations and bibliographies. 1932
Meade—Meade, Julian R. I live in Virginia. 1935
Mencken—Mencken, Henry L. Prejudices, first series. [1919]
Mencken (P)—Mencken, Henry L. Prejudices, fifth series. [c1926]
Mercier—Mercier, Louis J. The challenge of humanism, an essay in comparative criticism. 1933
Mercier (M)—Mercier, Louis J. Le mouvement humaniste aux États-Unis, W. C. Brownell, Irving Babbitt, Paul Elmer More. 1928
Mersand—Mersand, Joseph. Traditions in American literature, a study of Jewish characters and authors. 1939
Michaud—Michaud, Régis. Le roman américain d'aujourd'hui, critique d'une civilisation. [c1926] (Am. ed., The American novel to-day, a social and psychological study. 1928)
Michaud (M)—Michaud, Régis. Mystiques et réalistes anglo-saxons d'Emerson à Bernard Shaw. 1918
Michaud (P)—Michaud, Régis. Panorama de la littérature américaine contemporaine. [1928]
Mims—Mims, Edwin. The advancing South, stories of progress and reaction. 1926
Monro—Monro, Harold. Some contemporary poets (1920). [1920]
Monroe—Monroe, Harriet. Poets & their art. 1926
Monroe (P)—Monroe, Harriet. A poet's life, seventy years in a changing world. 1938

More—More, Paul E. The demon of the absolute . . . New Shelburne essays, volume I. 1928
More (O)—More, Paul E. On being human . . . New Shelburne essays, volume III. 1936
Morley—Morley, Christopher D. Essays. 1928
Morley (L)—Morley, Christopher D. Letters of askance. [c1939]
Morley (P)—Morley, Christopher D. Plum pudding, of divers ingredients, discreetly blended & seasoned . . . and merrily embellished by Walter Jack Duncan. 1921
Morley (S)—Morley, Christopher D. Shandygaff, a number of most agreeable inquirendoes upon life and letters, interspersed with short stories and skitts, the whole most diverting to the reader, accompanied also by some notes for teachers whereby the booke may be made usefull in class-room or for private improvement. 1918
Moses—Moses, Montrose J. The American dramatist. 1925
Moses (A)—Moses, Montrose J. and Brown, John M., *eds.* The American theatre as seen by its critics, 1752–1934. [c1934]
Moses (R)—Moses, Montrose J., *ed.* Representative American dramas, national and local, edited with introductions . . . Students' edition. 1933
Mueller—Mueller, Gustav E. Amerikanische philosophie. 1936
Muller—Muller, Herbert J. Modern fiction, a study of values. 1937
Mumford—Mumford, Lewis. The golden day, a study in American experience and culture. 1926
Munson—Munson, Gorham B. The dilemma of the liberated, an interpretation of twentieth century humanism. 1930
Munson (D)—Munson, Gorham B. Destinations, a canvass of American literature since 1900. [c1928]
Munson (S)—Munson, Gorham B. Style and form in American prose. 1929
Nathan—Nathan, George J. Art of the night. 1928
Nathan (H)—Nathan, George J. The house of Satan. 1926
Nathan (I)—Nathan, George J. The intimate notebooks of George Jean Nathan. 1932
Nathan (M)—Nathan, George J. The morning after the first night. 1938
Nathan (P)—Nathan, George J. Passing judgments. 1935
Nathan (T)—Nathan, George J. Testament of a critic. 1931
Nathan (TD)—Nathan, George J. The theatre, the drama, the girls. 1921
Nathan (TM)—Nathan, George J. The theatre of the moment, a journalistic commentary. 1936
National—The National cyclopædia of American biography, being the history of the United States as illustrated in the lives of the founders, builders, and defenders of the republic, and of the men and women who are doing the work and moulding the thought of the present time, edited by distinguished biographers, selected from each state, revised and approved by the most eminent historians, scholars, and statesmen of the day . . . 1893–1938; Current vols., A–D, 1926–34
New—The New republic. The New republic anthology, 1915:1935, edited by Groff Conklin, introduction by Bruce Bliven. [c1936]
O'Brien—O'Brien, Edward J. The advance of the American short story, revised edition. 1931
Overton—Overton, Grant M. American nights entertainment. 1923
Overton (A)—Overton, Grant M. Authors of the day . . . studies in contemporary literature. [c1924]
Overton (H)—Overton, Grant M. An hour of the American novel. 1929
Overton (W)—Overton, Grant M. The women who make our novels. 1918

Overton (WW)—Overton, Grant M. The women who make our novels . . . New and completely revised edition. 1928

Ovington—Ovington, Mary W. Portraits in color. 1927

Parrington—Parrington, Vernon L. The beginnings of critical realism in America, 1860–1920, completed to 1900 only. [c1930] (*His* Main currents in American thought . . . vol. III)

Pattee—Pattee, Fred L. A history of American literature since 1870. 1915

Pattee (N)—Pattee, Fred L. The new American literature, 1890–1930. [c1930]

Pellizzi—Pellizzi, Camillo. English drama, the last great phase (Il teatro inglese) . . . translated by Rowan Williams with a foreword by Orlo Williams. 1935

Phelps—Phelps, William L. The advance of English poetry in the twentieth century. 1918

Phelps (A)—Phelps, William L. The advance of the English novel. 1916

Phelps (AW)—Phelps, William L. Autobiography with letters. 1939

Phillips—Phillips, Marie T. More truth than poetry, essays and critical articles on poetry and prose practice, sketches, and book reviews. [c1934]

Pollard—Pollard, Percival. Their day in court. 1909

Proletarian—Proletarian literature in the United States, an anthology edited by Granville Hicks, Joseph North, Michael Gold, Paul Peters, Isidor Schneider, Alan Calmer, with a critical introduction by Joseph Freeman. [c1935]

Quinn—Quinn, Arthur H. American fiction, an historical and critical survey. [c1936]

Quinn (H)—Quinn, Arthur H. A history of the American drama from the civil war to the present day. 1936

Quinn (R)—Quinn, Arthur H., *ed.* Representative American plays from 1767 to the present day edited with introductions and notes . . . Sixth edition, revised and enlarged. 1938

Raines—Raines, Lester C., *comp.* Writers and writings of New Mexico. 1934 (mimeographed)

Ransom—Ransom, John C. The world's body. 1938

Rascoe—Rascoe, Burton. Before I forget. 1937

Rascoe (B)—Rascoe, Burton. A bookman's daybook . . . edited with an introduction by C. Hartley Grattan. 1929

Rascoe (P)—Rascoe, Burton. Prometheans, ancient and modern. 1933

Riding—Riding, Laura and Graves, Robert. A survey of modernist poetry. 1927

Rittenhouse—Rittenhouse, Jessie B. My house of life, an autobiography. 1934

Rittenhouse (Y)—Rittenhouse, Jessie B. The younger American poets. 1904

Roberts—Roberts, Carl E. The literary renaissance in America by C. E. Bechhofer. [1923]

Rogers—Rogers, Arthur K. English and American philosophy since 1800, a critical survey. 1922

Rosenfeld—Rosenfeld, Paul. By way of art, criticisms of music, literature, painting, sculpture, and the dance. 1928

Rosenfeld (M)—Rosenfeld, Paul. Men seen, twenty-four modern authors. 1925

Rosenfeld (P)—Rosenfeld, Paul. Port of New York, essays on fourteen American moderns . . . with camera portraits by Alfred Stieglitz, Alice Boughton, Paul Strand, and Dana Desboro. [c1924]

Rourke—Rourke, Constance M. American humor, a study of the national character. [c1931]

Russell—Russell, Caro M. Modern plays and playwrights . . . with some notes on the theater and the screen by Paul Green. 1936 (University of North Carolina. Library. Extension publication, vol. II, July 1936, no. 6)

Russell (J)—Russell, Charles E. Julia Marlowe, her life and art. 1926

Salzman—Salzman, Maurice. Plagiarism, the "art" of stealing literary material. [c1931]

Saturday—The Saturday review of literature. Designed for reading, an anthology drawn from the Saturday review of literature, 1924–1934, by the editors of the Saturday review of literature: Henry Seidel Canby . . . Amy Loveman . . . William Rose Benét . . . Christopher Morley . . . May Lamberton Becker. 1934

Sayler—Sayler, Oliver M. Our American theatre . . . with twenty-five illustrations from drawings by Lucie R. Sayler. [c1923]

Schelling—Schelling, Felix E. Appraisements and asperities as to some contemporary writers. 1922

Schreiber—Schreiber, Georges. Portraits and self-portraits collected and illustrated. 1936

Schwartz—Schwartz, Harry W. Checklists of twentieth century authors, first series, H. E. Bates, Rhys Davies, Liam O'Flaherty, Siegfried Sassoon, William Faulkner, Ernest Hemingway. 1931 (cover-title; comp. by H. Warren Schwartz and Paul Romaine)

Schwartz (O)—Schwartz, Jacob. 1100 obscure points, the bibliographies of 25 English and 21 American authors . . . [1931]

Schyberg—Schyberg, Frederik. Moderne amerikansk litteratur, 1900–1930. 1930

Sedgwick—Sedgwick, Henry D. The new American type and other essays. 1908

Sergeant—Sergeant, Elizabeth S. Fire under the Andes, a group of North American portraits . . . with camera portraits by E. O. Hoppé. 1927

Sessions—Sessions, Ina B. A study of the dramatic monologue in American and continental literature. 1933

Shafer—Shafer, Robert. Paul Elmer More and American criticism. 1935

Shaw—Shaw, Charles G. The low-down. [c1928]

Sherman—Sherman, Stuart P. Americans. 1922

Sherman (C)—Sherman, Stuart P. Critical woodcuts . . . illustrated with portraits engraved on wood by Bertrand Zadig. 1926

Sherman (M)—Sherman, Stuart P. The main stream. 1927

Sherman (P)—Sherman, Stuart P. Points of view. 1924

Sinclair—Sinclair, Upton B. Money writes! 1927

Sitwell—Sitwell, Edith. Aspects of modern poetry. [1934]

Skinner—Skinner, Richard D. Our changing theatre. 1931

Skolsky—Skolsky, Sidney. Times square tintypes, being typewriter caricatures of those who made their names along the not so straight and very narrow path of Broadway . . . illustrated by Gard. 1930

Smart—The Smart set. The Smart set anthology edited by Burton Rascoe and Groff Conklin. [c1934]

Smith—Smith, Lewis W., *ed.* Current reviews. [c1926]

Smith (P)—Smith, Thomas V. The philosophic way of life. [c1929]

Sparrow—Sparrow, John H. Sense and poetry, essays on the place of meaning in contemporary verse. 1934

Squire—Squire, Sir John C. and others. Contemporary American authors by J. C. Squire and associated critics of the London mercury with an introduction by Henry Seidel Canby. [c1928]

Stearns—Stearns, Harold E. America and the young intellectual. [c1921]

Stedman—Stedman, Edmund C. Life and letters of Edmund Clarence Stedman by Laura Stedman and George M. Gould . . . Volume two. 1910

Stewart—Stewart, Donald O. A parody outline of history wherein may be found a curiously irreverent treatment of American historical events imagining them as they would be narrated by America's most charac-

White—White, George L. Scandinavian themes in American fiction. 1937

Whitman—Whitman, Charles H., *ed.* Representative modern dramas. 1936

Wickham—Wickham, Harvey. The impuritans, a glimpse of that new world whose Pilgrim fathers are Otto Weininger, Havelock Ellis, James Branch Cabell, Marcel Proust, James Joyce, H. L. Mencken, D. H. Lawrence, Sherwood Anderson, et id genus omne. 1929

Widdemer—Widdemer, Margaret. A tree with a bird in it, a symposium of contemporary American poets on being shown a pear-tree on which sat a grackle . . . with illustrations by William Saphier. [c1922]

Wilkinson—Wilkinson, Marguerite O. New voices, an introduction to contemporary poetry . . . New edition revised and enlarged. 1928

Williams—Williams, Blanche C. Our short story writers. 1926

Williams-Ellis—Williams-Ellis, Amabel. An anatomy of poetry. [c1922]

West—West, Rebecca, *pseud.* Ending in earnest, a literary log. 1931

West (S)—West, Rebecca, *pseud.* The strange necessity, essays. 1928

Wilson—Wilson, Edmund. Axel's castle, a study in the imaginative literature of 1870–1930. 1931

Wilson (D)—Wilson, Edmund. Discordant encounters, plays and dialogues. 1926

Winters—Winters, Yvor. Primitivism and decadence, a study of American experimental poetry. [c1937]

Wood—Wood, Clement. Poets of America. [c1925]

Woolf—Woolf, Samuel J. Drawn from life. [c1932]

Woollcott—Woollcott, Alexander. Going to pieces. 1928

Woollcott (S)—Woollcott, Alexander. Shouts and murmurs, echoes of a thousand and one first nights. 1922

Woollcott (W)—Woollcott, Alexander. While Rome burns. 1934

Zabel—Zabel, Morton D., *ed.* Literary opinion in America, essays illustrating the status, methods, and problems of criticism in the United States since the war, edited with an introduction. 1937

Zeitlin—Zeitlin, Jacob and Woodbridge, Homer E. Life and letters of Stuart P. Sherman. [c1929] (2 vols.)

INDEX OF ABBREVIATIONS OF PERIODICALS CONTAINING ARTICLES

AB.	American Bookman
AC.	American Collector
Adel.	New Adelphi
AL.	American Literature
AM.	American Mercury
A.Mag.	American Magazine
Am.Fed.	American Federationist
Am.J.Phil.	American Journal of Philology
Am.J.Psych.	American Journal of Psychology
Am.J.Soc.	American Journal of Sociology
A.Mo.	Atlantic Monthly
Ang.	Anglia
AP.	American Parade
Apollon	Apollon
AR.	American Review
Arena	Arena
Arts & Dec.	Arts and Decoration
AS.	American Speech
A.Schol.	American Scholar
A.Spect.	American Spectator
ASR.	American Scandinavian Review
BBDI.	Bulletin of Bibliography and Dramatic Index
BCQ.	Book Collector's Quarterly
BJ.	The Bookman's Journal
BLM.	Bonnier's Litterära Magasin
BNM.	Book News Monthly
Bookm.	The Bookman (London)
BRD.	Book Review Digest
Broom	Broom
CB.	Canadian Bookman
CE.	Correct English
Cent.	Century
CF.	Canadian Forum
CH.	Current History
CJ.	Classical Journal
CL.	Country Life
Cl.Q.	Classical Quarterly
Cl.R.	Classical Review
CM.	Cornhill Magazine
Col.	Colophon
Collier's	Collier's
Com.	Commonweal
Commercial Appeal.	Commercial Appeal (Memphis, Tenn.)

JEM. . . . . Journal of Educational Method
JHAM. . . . . Johns Hopkins Alumni Magazine
JHE. . . . . Journal of Higher Education
JP. . . . . Journal of Political Economy
J.Phil. . . . . Journal of Philosophy
J.Phil.S. . . . . Journal of Philosophical Studies
J.Relig. . . . . Journal of Religion
JSF. . . . . Journal of Social Forces

L. . . . . Letters
Lang. . . . . Language
Lat.Q. . . . . Latin Quarterly
LDIBR. . . . . Literary Digest International Book Review
Letras . . . . Letras
Lit.Echo . . . . Literary Echo
Lit.Rev. . . . . Literary Review
Little Rev. . . . . Little Review
Liv.Age.. . . . . Living Age
LL. . . . . Life and Letters
LQR. . . . . London Quarterly Review

Meas. . . . . The Measure
Men.J. . . . . Menorah Journal
Mentor . . . . Mentor
Merc. . . . . London Mercury
Meth.R. . . . . Methodist Review
MF. . . . . Mercure de France
Mid. . . . . Midland
M.Lang. . . . . Modern Languages
MLN. . . . . Modern Language Notes
MLR.. . . . . Modern Language Review
Mod.Lib. . . . . Modern Librarian
Mod.M. . . . . Modern Monthly
Mod.Scot. . . . . Modern Scot
Monist. . . . . Monist
MP. . . . . Modern Philology
MQ. . . . . Modern Quarterly
MT. . . . . Modern Thinker
MTQ.. . . . . Mark Twain Quarterly

N.Amer.Rev. . . . . . . North American Review
Nation . . . . Nation
Nat.Rev. . . . . National Review
Nature. . . . . Nature
N.Cent. . . . . Nineteenth Century
NEQ. . . . . New England Quarterly
NGH.. . . . . Nachrichten d. Giesener Hochschulgesellschaft
NH. . . . . New Humanist
NHJ. . . . . Neue Heidelberger Jahrbücher
NJWJ. . . . . Neue Jahrbücher f. Wiss. u. Jugendbildung
NL. . . . . Nouvelles Littéraires
N.Masses. . . . . New Masses
NMQ. . . . . New Mexico Quarterly
N.Mon. . . . . Neuphilologische Monatsschrift

NQ.	Notes and Queries
NR.	New Republic
NRF.	Nouvelle Revue Française
N.Rund.	Die Neue Rundschau
NS.	Die Neueren Sprachen
NS.Rund.	Die Neue Schweizer Rundschau
N.St.	New Statesman
Nuova Ant.	Nuova Antologia
NWM.	New World Monthly
N.Yer.	New Yorker
NYHTB.	New York Herald Tribune Books
NYTBR.	New York Times Book Review
OC.	Open Court
OI.	Outlook and Independent
Outl.	Outlook
Overland M.	Overland Monthly
P.	Poetry
PAAAS.	Proceedings of the American Academy of Arts and Sciences
Pac.R.	Pacific Review
Pal.	Palimpsest
Pan M.	Pan (Milano)
Pers.	Personalist
Philos.	Philosophy
Phil.Rev.	Philosophical Review
Pict.Rev.	Pictorial Review
P.Jb.	Preussische Jahrbücher
P.Lore	Poet Lore
PMLA.	Publications of the Modern Language Association of America
PP.	Poetry and the Play
PQ.	Philological Quarterly
Putnam's	Putnam's
PW.	Publishers' Weekly
QJS.	Quarterly Journal of Speech
QJUND.	Quarterly Journal of the University of North Dakota
QR.	Quarterly Review
R.	Reviewer
RAA.	Revue Anglo-Americaine
RC.	Reading and Collecting
RDM.	Revue des Deux Mondes
R.d.P.	Revue de Paris
R.d.UB.	Revue de l'Universitaire de Bruxelles
Reflex.	Reflex
RES.	Review of English Studies
RH.	Revue Hebdomadaire
RLC.	Revue de Littérature Comparée
Rom.Rev.	Romanic Review
RPL.	Revue Politique et Littéraire
RR.	Review of Reviews
R.Sci.	Revue Scientifique

SAB.	Shakespeare Association Bulletin
SAQ.	South Atlantic Quarterly
Sat.Rev.	Saturday Review
Scrib.	Scribner's
Scrut.	Scrutiny
SEP.	Saturday Evening Post
Sev.Arts.	The Seven Arts
So.R.	Southern Review
Spect.	Spectator
SR.	Sewanee Review
SRL.	Saturday Review of Literature
S.Rund.	Schweizerisches Rundschau
SS.	School and Society
SSN.	Scandinavian Studies and Notes
S.Soc.	Science and Society
SSR.	Sociology and Social Research
Stand.	Standard
Studies	Studies (Irish Quarterly Review)
Survey	Survey
Sw.Bul.	Southwestern Bulletin
Sw.R.	Southwest Review
Symp.	Symposium
TAM.	Theater Arts Monthly
TCR.	Teachers College Record
Thought	Thought
Touchstone	Touchstone
trans.	transition
UCC.	University of California Chronicle
U.Chi.Mag.	University of Chicago Magazine
Univ.(Mex.)	Universidad (Mexico)
Unpop.Rev.	Unpopular Review
UTQ.	University of Toronto Quarterly
VQR.	Virginia Quarterly Review
W.	The Writer
World Today	World Today
WRUB.	Western Reserve University Bulletin
WT.	World Tomorrow
WU.	World Unity
WW.	World's Work
YR.	Yale Review
YULG.	Yale University Library Gazette
ZFEU.	Zeitschrift für französische u. englische Unterricht

INDEX OF AUTHORS

The authors whose names appear in this Index are the American and British authors treated in *Contemporary American Authors* and *Contemporary British Literature.* The British authors are included for the convenience of readers who may be unsure of the nationality of minor authors. An asterisk marks the names of those authors treated in *this volume,* and the pages noted refer to *this volume, only.*

Symbols:
CAA—Millett, Fred B., *Contemporary American Authors,* 1940
CBL—Millett, Fred B., Manly, John M., and Rickert, Edith, *Contemporary British Literature,* 1935